Beginning Java 7

Jeff Friesen

Apress®

Beginning Java 7

Copyright © 2011 by Jeff Friesen

ISBN-13 (pbk): 978-1-4302-3909-3

ISBN-13 (electronic): 978-1-4302-3910-9

President and Publisher: Paul Manning
Lead Editor: Tom Welsh
Technical Reviewer: Chád Darby
Editorial Board: Steve Anglin, Mark Beckner, Ewan Buckingham, Gary Cornell, Morgan Ertel, Jonathan Gennick, Jonathan Hassell, Michelle Lowman, James Markham, Matthew Moodie, Jeff Olson, Jeffrey Pepper, Douglas Pundick, Ben Renow-Clarke, Dominic Shakeshaft, Gwenan Spearing, Matt Wade, Tom Welsh
Coordinating Editor: Corbin Collins
Copy Editor: Linda Seifert
Compositor: Bytheway Publishing Services
Indexer: BMI Indexing & Proofreading Services
Artist: SPI Global
Cover Designer: Anna Ishchenko

Distributed to the book trade worldwide by Springer Science+Business Media New York, LLC., 233 Spring Street, 6th Floor, New York, NY 10013. Phone 1-800-SPRINGER, fax (201) 348-4505, e-mail orders-ny@springer-sbm.com, or visit www.springeronline.com.

For information on translations, please e-mail rights@apress.com, or visit www.apress.com.

Apress and friends of ED books may be purchased in bulk for academic, corporate, or promotional use. eBook versions and licenses are also available for most titles. For more information, reference our Special Bulk Sales–eBook Licensing web page at www.apress.com/bulk-sales.

The source code for this book is available to readers at www.apress.com. You will need to answer questions pertaining to this book in order to successfully download the code.

Contents at a Glance

About the Author xiv

About the Technical Reviewer xv

Acknowledgments xvii

Introduction xix

Chapter 1: Getting Started with Java 1

Chapter 2: Discovering Classes and Objects 51

Chapter 3: Exploring Advanced Language Features 131

Chapter 4: Touring Language APIs 227

Chapter 5: Collecting Objects 319

Chapter 6: Touring Additional Utility APIs 401

Chapter 7: Creating and Enriching Graphical User Interfaces 435

Chapter 8: Interacting with Filesystems 511

Chapter 9: Interacting with Networks and Databases 585

Chapter 10: Parsing, Creating, and Transforming XML Documents 663

Chapter 11: Working with Web Services 751

Chapter 12: Java 7 Meets Android 831

Index 873

Contents

■ About the Author.. xiv

■ About the Technical Reviewer xv

■ Acknowledgments xvi

■ Preface... xvii

■ Chapter 1: Getting Started with Java... 1

What Is Java? 1

Java Is a Language... 1

Java Is a Platform... 3

Installing and Working with JDK 7... 4

Installing JDK 7... 4

Working with JDK 7 5

Installing and Working with NetBeans 7.. 7

Installing NetBeans 7.. 8

Working with NetBeans 7 9

Java Language Fundamentals 12

Comments 12

Identifiers 16

Types... 16

Variables.. 19

Expressions 20

Statements 36

Summary 49

■ Chapter 2: Discovering Classes and Objects 51

Declaring Classes and Creating Objects 52

Declaring Classes 52

Creating Objects with the new Operator and a Constructor 52

Specifying Constructor Parameters and Local Variables 53

Creating Arrays with the new Operator 57

Encapsulating State and Behaviors 59

Representing State via Fields 60

Representing Behaviors via Methods 65

Hiding Information 74

Initializing Classes and Objects 78

Inheriting State and Behaviors 84

Extending Classes 85

The Ultimate Superclass 91

Composition 100

The Trouble with Implementation Inheritance 100

Changing Form 104

Upcasting and Late Binding 105

Abstract Classes and Abstract Methods 109

Downcasting and Runtime Type Identification 111

Covariant Return Types 113

Formalizing Class Interfaces 115

Declaring Interfaces 115

Implementing Interfaces 117

Extending Interfaces 120

Why Use Interfaces? 122

Collecting Garbage 124

Summary 129

Chapter 3: Exploring Advanced Language Features 131

Nested Types 131

Static Member Classes 131

Nonstatic Member Classes 135

Anonymous Classes 138

Local Classes 140

Interfaces Within Classes 143

Packages 144

What Are Packages? 144

The Package Statement 145

The Import Statement 146

Searching for Packages and Types 147

Playing with Packages 148

Packages and JAR Files 153

Static Imports 153

Exceptions 155

What Are Exceptions? 155

Representing Exceptions in Source Code 155

Throwing Exceptions 161

Handling Exceptions 163

Performing Cleanup 170

Assertions 175

Declaring Assertions 176

Using Assertions 177

Avoiding Assertions 183

Enabling and Disabling Assertions 183

Annotations 184

Discovering Annotations 185

Declaring Annotation Types and Annotating Source Code 188

Processing Annotations 192

Generics 194

Collections and the Need for Type Safety 195

Generic Types 197

Generic Methods 206

Arrays and Generics 208

Varargs and Generics 211

Enums 212

The Trouble with Traditional Enumerated Types 213

The Enum Alternative 214

The Enum Class 218

Summary 222

Chapter 4: Touring Language APIs 227

Math and StrictMath 227

Package 235

Primitive Type Wrapper Class 240

Boolean 240

Character 242

Float and Double 243

Integer, Long, Short, and Byte 247

Number 249

Reference 249

Basic Terminology 250

Reference and ReferenceQueue 251

SoftReference 252

WeakReference 254

PhantomReference 255

Reflection 257

String 272

StringBuffer and StringBuilder 276

System 279

Threading 282

    Runnable and Thread 282

    Thread Synchronization 291

BigDecimal 306

BigInteger 312

Summary 317

Chapter 5: Collecting Objects 319

The Collections Framework 319

    Architecture Overview 319

    Iterable and Collection 322

    List 329

    Set 335

    SortedSet 344

    NavigableSet 351

    Queue 355

    Deque 359

    Map 364

    SortedMap 380

    NavigableMap 383

    Utilities 388

Legacy Collections APIs 391

Creating Your Own Collections 395

Summary 400

■ **Chapter 6: Touring Additional Utility APIs** **401**

Concurrency Utilities..**401**

Executors.. 401

Synchronizers 410

Concurrent Collections 413

Locks 416

Atomic Variables.. 419

Additional Concurrency Utilities 419

Objects...**426**

Random **430**

Summary **434**

■ **Chapter 7: Creating and Enriching Graphical User Interfaces** **435**

Abstract Window Toolkit..**435**

Toolkits 436

Components, Containers, Layout Managers, and Events 436

Images.. 456

Data Transfer 461

Swing...**463**

An Extended Architecture 464

Sampling Swing Components.. 470

Java 2D..**477**

GraphicsEnvironment, GraphicsDevice, and GraphicsConfiguration 477

Graphics2D 481

Shapes.. 493

Buffered Images 498

Summary **509**

Chapter 8: Interacting with Filesystems 511

File 511

RandomAccessFile 525

Streams 536

Stream Classes Overview 537

OutputStream and InputStream 539

FileOutputStream and FileInputStream 542

FilterOutputStream and FilterInputStream 545

BufferedOutputStream and BufferedInputStream 551

DataOutputStream and DataInputStream 552

Object Serialization and Deserialization 554

PrintStream 566

Writers and Readers 567

Writer and Reader Classes Overview 568

Writer and Reader 570

OutputStreamWriter and InputStreamReader 570

FileWriter and FileReader 572

Summary 583

Chapter 9: Interacting with Networks and Databases 585

Interacting with Networks 585

Communicating via Sockets 585

Communicating via URLs 609

Authentication 620

Cookie Management 626

Interacting with Databases 628

Java DB 629

JDBC 636

Summary 660

Chapter 10: Parsing, Creating, and Transforming XML Documents 663

What Is XML? 663

XML Declaration 665

Elements and Attributes 666

Character References and CDATA Sections 668

Namespaces 669

Comments and Processing Instructions 672

Well-Formed Documents 673

Valid Documents 673

Parsing XML Documents with SAX 683

Exploring the SAX API 683

Demonstrating the SAX API 690

Creating a Custom Entity Resolver 697

Parsing and Creating XML Documents with DOM 700

A Tree of Nodes 701

Exploring the DOM API 703

Parsing and Creating XML Documents with StAX 712

Parsing XML Documents 714

Creating XML Documents 720

Selecting XML Document Nodes with XPath 727

XPath Language Primer 727

XPath and DOM 731

Advanced XPath 736

Transforming XML Documents with XSLT 742

Exploring the XSLT API 742

Demonstrating the XSLT API 745

Summary 750

Chapter 11: Working with Web Services 751

What Are Web Services? 751

SOAP-Based Web Services.. 753

RESTful Web Services 756

Java and Web Services.. 758

Web Service APIs.. 759

Web Service Annotations 759

Web Service Tools 760

Lightweight HTTP Server 761

Working with SOAP-Based Web Services.. 764

Creating and Accessing a Temperature-Conversion Web Service 764

Accessing the Image Cutout Web Service.. 776

Working with RESTful Web Services 780

Creating and Accessing a Library Web Service 781

Accessing Google's Charts Web Service 795

Advanced Web Service Topics.. 798

Working with SAAJ... 799

Logging SOAP Messages with a JAX-WS Handler.. 815

Authentication and a Customized Lightweight HTTP Server 820

RESTful Web Services and Attachments 822

Providers and Dispatch Clients... 825

Summary 830

Chapter 12: Java 7 Meets Android 831

Exploring Android and Android App Architectures.. 831

Android Architecture.. 832

App Architecture... 836

Installing the Android SDK and an Android Platform 850

Accessing System Requirements 850

Installing the Android SDK...851

Installing an Android Platform 852

Creating and Starting an AVD 856

Creating an AVD...856

Starting the AVD 858

Creating, Installing, and Running an App 861

Introducing Java7MeetsAndroid..861

Creating Java7MeetsAndroid 866

Installing and Running Java7MeetsAndroid 868

Summary 871

About the Author

Jeff Friesen is a freelance tutor and software developer with an emphasis on Java (and now Android). Besides writing this book, Jeff has authored Apress's *Learn Java for Android Development* (ISBN13: 978-1-4302-3156-1), has coauthored Apress's *Android Recipes* (ISBN13: 978-1-4302-3413-5) with Dave Smith, and has written numerous articles on Java and other technologies for Java.net (www.java.net), JavaWorld (www.javaworld.com), InformIT (www.informit.com), and DevSource (www.devsource.com). Jeff can be contacted via his TutorTutor website at tutortutor.ca.

About the Technical Reviewer

Chád Darby is an author, instructor, and speaker in the Java development world. As a recognized authority on Java applications and architectures, he has presented technical sessions at software development conferences worldwide. In his 15 years as a professional software architect, he's had the opportunity to work for Blue Cross/Blue Shield, Merck, Boeing, Northrop Grumman, and various IT companies.

Chád is a contributing author to several Java books, including *Professional Java E-Commerce* (Wrox Press), *Beginning Java Networking* (Wrox Press), and *XML and Web Services Unleashed* (Sams Publishing). He is also the author of numerous magazine articles for the Java Developer's Journal (Sys-Con Publishing).

Chád has Java certifications from Sun Microsystems and IBM. He holds a B.S. in Computer Science from Carnegie Mellon University. In his free time, Chád enjoys running half-marathons..

Acknowledgments

Beginning Java 7 wouldn't have been possible without the wonderful folks at Apress. I thank Steve Anglin for giving me the opportunity to write this book, Corbin Collins for guiding me through the various aspects of the book-writing process, Tom Welsh for helping me with the development of my chapters and appendixes, and Chad Darby for his diligence in catching various flaws. I couldn't ask for better editors and a better technical reviewer. Thanks guys.

Introduction

Java 7 is Oracle's latest release of the popular Java language and platform. *Beginning Java 7* guides you through this language and a huge assortment of platform APIs via its 12 chapters and 4 appendixes.

▧ **Note** Java was created by Sun Microsystems, which was later bought out by Oracle.

Chapter 1 (Getting Started with Java) introduces you to Java and begins to cover the Java language by focusing on fundamental concepts such as comments, identifiers, variables, expressions, and statements.

Chapter 2 (Discovering Classes and Objects) continues to explore this language by presenting all of its features for working with classes and objects. You learn about features related to class declaration and object creation, encapsulation, information hiding, inheritance, polymorphism, interfaces, and garbage collection.

Chapter 3 (Exploring Advanced Language Features) focuses on the more advanced language features related to nested classes, packages, static imports, exceptions, assertions, annotations, generics, and enums. Subsequent chapters introduce you to the few features not covered in Chapters 1 through 3.

Chapter 4 (Touring Language APIs) largely moves away from covering language features (although it does introduce class literals and strictfp) while focusing on language-oriented APIs. You learn about Math, StrictMath, Package, Primitive Type Wrapper Classes, Reference, Reflection, String, StringBuffer and StringBuilder, Threading, BigDecimal, and BigInteger in this chapter.

Chapter 5 (Collecting Objects) begins to explore Java's utility APIs by focusing largely on the Collections Framework. However, it also discusses legacy collection-oriented APIs and how to create your own collections.

Chapter 6 (Touring Additional Utility APIs) continues to focus on utility APIs by presenting the concurrency utilities along with the Objects and Random classes.

Chapter 7 (Creating and Enriching Graphical User Interfaces) moves you away from the command-line user interfaces that appear in previous chapters and toward graphical user interfaces. You first learn about the Abstract Window Toolkit foundation and then explore the Java Foundation Classes in terms of Swing and Java 2D. (Appendix C introduces you to Accessibility and Drag and Drop.)

Chapter 8 (Interacting with Filesystems) explores filesystem-oriented I/O in terms of the File, RandomAccessFile, stream, and writer/reader classes. (New I/O is covered in Appendix C.)

Chapter 9 (Interacting with Networks and Databases) introduces you to Java's network APIs (e.g., sockets). It also introduces you to the JDBC API for interacting with databases.

Chapter 10 (Parsing, Creating, and Transforming XML Documents) dives into Java's XML support by first presenting an introduction to XML (including DTDs and schemas). It next explores the SAX, DOM, StAX, XPath, and XSLT APIs; and even briefly touches on the Validation API. While exploring XPath, you encounter namespace contexts, extension functions and function resolvers, and variables and variable resolvers.

Chapter 11 (Working with Web Services) introduces you to Java's support for SOAP-based and RESTful web services. Besides providing you with the basics of these web service categories, Chapter 11 presents some advanced topics, such as working with the SAAJ API to communicate with a SOAP-based web service without having to rely on JAX-WS. You'll appreciate having learned about XML in Chapter 10 before diving into this chapter.

Chapter 12 (Java 7 Meets Android) helps you put to use some of the knowledge you've gathered in previous chapters by showing you how to use Java to write an Android app's source code. This chapter introduces you to Android, discusses its architecture, shows you how to install necessary tools, and develops a simple app.

As well as creating these twelve chapters, I've created four appendices:

Appendix A (Solutions to Exercises) presents the solutions to the programming exercises that appear near the end of Chapters 1 through 12.

Appendix B (Scripting API and Dynamically Typed Language Support) introduces you to Java's Scripting API along with the support for dynamically typed languages that's new in Java 7.

Appendix C (Odds and Ends) introduces you to additional APIs and architecture topics: Accessibility, ByteArrayOutputStream and ByteArrayInputStream, classloaders, Console, Desktop, Drag and Drop, Dynamic Layout, Extension Mechanism and ServiceLoader, File Partition-Space, File Permissions, Formatter, Image I/O, Internationalization, Java Native Interface, NetworkInterface and InterfaceAddress, New I/O (including NIO.2), PipedOutputStream and PipedInputStream, Preferences, Scanner, Security, Smart Card, Splash Screen, StreamTokenizer, StringTokenizer, SwingWorker, System Tray, Timer and TimerTask, Tools and the Compiler API, Translucent and Shaped Windows, and XML Digital Signature.

Appendix D (Applications Gallery) presents a gallery of significant applications that demonstrate various aspects of Java and gives you an opportunity to have more fun with this technology.

Unfortunately, there are limits to how much knowledge can be crammed into a print book. For this reason, Appendixes A, B, C, and D are not included in this book's pages–adding these appendixes would have exceeded the Print-On-Demand (http://en.wikipedia.org/wiki/Print_on_demand) limit of 1,000 pages cover to cover. Instead, these appendixes are freely distributed as PDF files. Appendixes A and B are bundled with the book's associated code file at the Apress website (http://www.apress.com/9781430239093). Appendixes C and D are bundled with their respective code files on my TutorTutor website (http://tutortutor.ca/cgi-bin/makepage.cgi?/books/bj7).

Appendixes C and D are "living documents" in that I'll occasionally add new material to them. When I first encountered Java, I fell in love with this technology and dreamed about writing a book that explored the entire language and all standard edition APIs. Perhaps I would be the first person to do so.

There are various obstacles to achieving this goal. For one thing, it's not easy to organize a vast amount of content, and Java keeps getting bigger with each new release, so there's always more to write about.

Another obstacle is that it's not possible to adequately cover everything within the limits of a 1,000-page book. And then there are the time constraints, which make it impossible to complete everything in just a few months.

Proper organization is essential to creating a book that satisfies both Java beginners and more seasoned Java developers. Regrettably, lack of proper organization in my former *Learn Java for Android Development* book resulted in something that isn't beginner friendly (this has been pointed out on numerous occasions). For example, the second chapter mixes coverage of basic features (e.g., expressions and statements) with objects and classes, and this approach is too confusing for the novice. *Beginning Java 7*'s coverage of the Java language is better organized.

It's not possible to cover everything within 1,000 pages, which is the upper limit for a Print-On-Demand book. For this reason, I've designed Appendixes C and D to be "living" extensions to the book. They make it possible for me to complete my coverage of the entire Java 7 Standard Edition. I might even cover Java 8's new features in a separate area of Appendix C.

I spent nearly six months writing *Beginning Java 7*. Given the vast scope of this project, that's a very small amount of time. It will take me many more months to complete my tour of Java 7 Standard Edition; I'll occasionally post updated Appendixes C and D on my website that take you even deeper into this technology.

If you've previously purchased a copy of *Learn Java for Android Development*, you'll probably be shocked to discover that I've plagiarized much of my own content. I did so to speed *Beginning Java 7*'s development, which contains much material beyond what appeared in my former book (e.g., Swing and web services). *Beginning Java 7* would have taken many more months to complete if I didn't leverage its predecessor. (If I thought that *Learn Java for Android Development* was crap, and I don't, I never would have used it as the basis for this new book.)

Don't get the idea that *Beginning Java 7* is a rehash of *Learn Java for Android Development*–it's not. In those portions of *Beginning Java 7* where I've stolen heavily from its predecessor, there typically are numerous changes and additions. For example, I've rewritten parts of the exceptions and generics content that appear in Chapter 3; I did so to introduce new Java 7 features and to provide better coverage of difficult topics. Also, Chapter 5 introduces navigable sets and navigable maps, which is something that I couldn't discuss in *Learn Java for Android Development* because these features were introduced in Java 6. (I wrote *Learn Java for Android Development* to teach the Java language and APIs to prepare the reader for Android–Android apps are written in Java. However, Android doesn't support language features and APIs beyond Java 5.)

Beginning Java 7 goes far beyond *Learn Java for Android Development* in that it also discusses user interface APIs (e.g., Abstract Window Toolkit, Swing, and Java 2D) and web services (JAX-WS and RESTful). As well as new content, you'll also find many new examples (e.g., a chat server) and new exercises (e.g., create a networked Blackjack game with a graphical user interface).

At the end of Chapter 10 in *Learn Java for Android Development*, I rashly promised to write the following free chapters:

Chapter 11: Performing I/O Redux

Chapter 12: Parsing and Creating XML Documents

Chapter 13: Accessing Networks

Chapter 14: Accessing Databases

Chapter 15: Working with Security

Chapter 16: Odds and Ends

I originally intended to write these chapters and add them to *Learn Java for Android Development*. However, I ran out of time and would probably have also run into the Print-On-Demand limit that I previously mentioned.

Given beginner-oriented organizational difficulties with *Learn Java for Android Development*, I decided to not write these chapters in that book's context. Instead, I pursued *Beginning Java 7* in a new (and hopefully better organized) attempt to cover all of Java, and to attempt to create a book that broadly appeals to Java beginners and veterans alike.

Although I won't write the aforementioned six free chapters as described in *Learn Java for Android Development* (I can't keep the entire promise anyway because I've integrated Chapters 12, 13, and 14 into *Beginning Java 7* as Chapters 9 and 10), the other three chapters (11, 15, and 16) are merged into Appendix C, which is free. As time passes, additional chapters will appear in that appendix; and so I will finally keep my promise, but in a different way.

Note I don't discuss code conventions for writing source code in this book. Instead, I've adopted my own conventions, and try to apply them consistently throughout the book. If you're interested in what Oracle has to say about Java code conventions, check out the "Code Conventions for the Java Programming Language" document at http://www.oracle.com/technetwork/java/codeconv-138413.html.

CHAPTER 1

Getting Started with Java

Welcome to Java. This chapter launches you on a tour of this technology by focusing on fundamentals. First, you receive an answer to the "What is Java?" question. If you have not previously encountered Java, the answer might surprise you. Next, you are introduced to some basic tools that will help you start developing Java programs, and to the NetBeans integrated development environment, which simplifies the development of these programs. Finally, you explore fundamental language features.

What Is Java?

Java is a language for describing programs, and Java is a platform on which to run programs written in Java and other languages (e.g., Groovy, Jython, and JRuby). This section introduces you to Java the language and Java the platform.

■ **Note** To discover Java's history, check out Wikipedia's "Java (programming language)" (http://en.wikipedia.org/wiki/Java_(programming_language)#History) and "Java (software platform)" (http://en.wikipedia.org/wiki/Java_(software_platform)#History) entries.

Java Is a Language

Java is a general-purpose, class-based, and object-oriented language patterned after C and C++ to make it easier for existing C/C++ developers to migrate to this language. Not surprisingly, Java borrows elements from these languages. The following list identifies some of these elements:

- Java supports the same single-line and multiline comment styles as found in C/C++ for documenting source code.

- Java provides the if, switch, while, for, and other reserved words as found in the C and C++ languages. Java also provides the try, catch, class, private, and other reserved words that are found in C++ but not in C.

- As with C and C++, Java supports character, integer, and other primitive types. Furthermore, Java shares the same reserved words for naming these types; for example, char (for character) and int (for integer).

- Java supports many of the same operators as C/C++: the arithmetic operators (+, -, *, /, and %) and conditional operator (?:) are examples.

- Java also supports the use of brace characters { and } to delimit blocks of statements.

Although Java is similar to C and C++, it also differs in many respects. The following list itemizes some of these differences:

- Java supports an additional comment style known as Javadoc.

- Java provides transient, synchronized, strictfp, and other reserved words not found in C or C++.

- Java's character type has a larger size than the version of this type found in C and C++, Java's integer types do not include unsigned variants of these types (Java has no equivalent of the C/C++ unsigned long integer type, for example), and Java's primitive types have guaranteed sizes, whereas no guarantees are made for the equivalent C/C++ types.

- Java doesn't support all of the C/C++ operators. For example, there is no sizeof operator. Also, Java provides some operators not found in C/C++. For example, >>> (unsigned right shift) and instanceof are exclusive to Java.

- Java provides labeled break and continue statements. These variants of the C/C++ break and continue statements provide a safer alternative to C/C++'s goto statement, which Java doesn't support.

Note Comments, reserved words, types, operators, and statements are examples of fundamental language features, which are discussed later in this chapter.

A Java program starts out as source code that conforms to Java *syntax*, rules for combining symbols into meaningful entities. The Java compiler translates the source code stored in files that have the ".java" file extension into equivalent executable code, known as *bytecode*, which it stores in files that have the ".class" file extension.

Note The files that store compiled Java code are known as *classfiles* because they often store the runtime representation of Java classes, a language feature discussed in Chapter 2.

The Java language was designed with portability in mind. Ideally, Java developers write a Java program's source code once, compile this source code into bytecode once, and run the bytecode on any platform (e.g., Windows, Linux, and Mac OS X) where Java is supported, without ever having to change the source code and recompile. Portability is achieved in part by ensuring that primitive types have the same sizes across platforms. For example, the size of Java's integer type is always 32 bits.

The Java language was also designed with robustness in mind. Java programs should be less vulnerable to crashes than their C/C++ counterparts. Java achieves robustness in part by not implementing certain C/C++ features that can make programs less robust. For example, *pointers* (variables that store the addresses of other variables) increase the likelihood of program crashes, which is why Java doesn't support this C/C++ feature.

Java Is a Platform

Java is a platform that executes Java-based programs. Unlike platforms with physical processors (e.g., an Intel processor) and operating systems (e.g., Windows 7), the Java platform consists of a virtual machine and execution environment.

A *virtual machine* is a software-based processor with its own set of instructions. The Java Virtual Machine (JVM)'s associated *execution environment* consists of a huge library of prebuilt functionality, commonly known as the *standard class library*, that Java programs can use to perform routine tasks (e.g., open a file and read its contents). The execution environment also consists of "glue" code that connects the JVM to the underlying operating system.

■ **Note** The "glue" code consists of platform-specific libraries for accessing the operating system's windowing, networking, and other subsystems. It also consists of code that uses the Java Native Interface (JNI) to bridge between Java and the operating system. I discuss the JNI in Appendix C. You might also want to check out Wikipedia's "Java Native Interface" entry (http://en.wikipedia.org/wiki/Java_Native_Interface) to learn about the JNI.

When a Java program launcher starts the Java platform, the JVM is launched and told to load a Java program's starting classfile into memory, via a component known as a *classloader*. After the classfile has loaded, the following tasks are performed:

- The classfile's bytecode instruction sequences are verified to ensure that they don't compromise the security of the JVM and underlying environment. Verification ensures that a sequence of instructions doesn't find a way to exploit the JVM to corrupt the environment and possibly steal sensitive information. The component that handles this task is known as the *bytecode verifier*.

- The classfile's main sequence of bytecode instructions is executed. The component that handles this task is known as the *interpreter* because instructions are *interpreted* (identified and used to select appropriate sequences of native processor instructions to carry out the equivalent of what the bytecode instructions mean). When the interpreter discovers that a bytecode instruction sequence is executed repeatedly, it informs the *Just-In-Time (JIT) compiler* component to compile this sequence into an equivalent sequence of native instructions. The JIT helps the Java program achieve faster execution than would be possible through interpretation alone. Note that the JIT and the Java compiler that compiles source code into bytecode are two separate compilers with two different goals.

During execution, a classfile might refer to another classfile. In this situation, a classloader is used to load the referenced classfile, the bytecode verifier then verifies the classfile's bytecodes, and the interpreter/JIT executes the appropriate bytecode sequence in this other classfile.

The Java platform was designed with portability in mind. By providing an abstraction over the underlying operating system, bytecode instruction sequences should execute consistently across Java platforms. However, this isn't always borne out in practice. For example, many Java platforms rely on the underlying operating system to schedule threads (discussed in Chapter 4), and the thread scheduling implementation varies from operating system to operating system. As a result, you must be careful to ensure that the program is designed to adapt to these vagaries.

The Java platform was also designed with security in mind. As well as the bytecode verifier, the platform provides a security framework to help ensure that malicious programs don't corrupt the underlying environment on which the program is running. Appendix C discusses Java's security framework.

Installing and Working with JDK 7

Three software development kits (SDKs) exist for developing different kinds of Java programs:

- The Java SE (Standard Edition) Software Development Kit (known as the JDK) is used to create desktop-oriented *standalone applications* and web browser-embedded applications known as *applets*. You are introduced to standalone applications later in this section. I don't discuss applets because they aren't as popular as they once were.

- The Java ME (Mobile Edition) SDK is used to create applications known as MIDlets and Xlets. *MIDlets* target mobile devices, which have small graphical displays, simple numeric keypad interfaces, and limited HTTP-based network access. *Xlets* typically target television-oriented devices such as Blu-ray Disc players. The Java ME SDK requires that the JDK also be installed. I don't discuss MIDlets or Xlets.

- The Java EE (Enterprise Edition) SDK is used to create component-based enterprise applications. Components include *servlets*, which can be thought of as the server equivalent of applets, and servlet-based Java Server Pages (JSPs). The Java EE SDK requires that the JDK also be installed. I don't discuss servlets.

This section introduces you to JDK 7 (also referred to as *Java 7*, a term used in later chapters) by first showing you how to install this latest major Java SE release. It then shows you how to use JDK 7 tools to develop a simple standalone application—I'll use the shorter *application* term from now on.

Installing JDK 7

Point your browser to http://www.oracle.com/technetwork/java/javase/downloads/index-jsp-138363.html and follow the instructions on the resulting web page to download the appropriate JDK 7 installation exe or gzip tarball file for your Windows, Solaris, or Linux platform.

Following the download, run the Windows executable or unarchive the Solaris/Linux gzip tarball, and modify your PATH environment variable to include the resulting home directory's bin subdirectory so that you can run JDK 7 tools from anywhere in your filesystem. For example, you might include the C:\Program Files\Java\jdk1.7.0 home directory in the PATH on a Windows platform. You should also update your JAVA_HOME environment variable to point to JDK 7's home directory, to ensure that any Java-dependent software can find this directory.

JDK 7's home directory contains several files (e.g., README.html and LICENSE) and subdirectories. The most important subdirectory from this book's perspective is bin, which contains various tools that we'll use throughout this book. The following list identifies some of these tools:

- jar: a tool for packaging classfiles and resource files into special ZIP files with ".jar" file extensions

- java: a tool for running applications

- javac: a tool that launches the Java compiler to compile one or more source files

- javadoc: a tool that generates special HTML-based documentation from Javadoc comments

The JDK's tools are run in a command-line environment. You establish this by launching a command window (Windows) or shell (Linux/Solaris), which presents to you a sequence of prompts for entering *commands* (program names and their arguments). For example, a command window (on Windows platforms) prompts you to enter a command by presenting a drive letter and path combination (e.g., C:\).

You respond to the prompt by typing the command, and then press the Return/Enter key to tell the operating system to execute the command. For example, javac x.java followed by a Return/Enter key press causes the operating system to launch the javac tool, and to pass the name of the source file being compiled (x.java) to this tool as its command-line argument. If you specified the asterisk (*) wildcard character, as in javac *.java, javac would compile all source files in the current directory. To learn more about working at the command line, check out Wikipedia's "Command-line interface" entry (http://en.wikipedia.org/wiki/Command-line_interface).

Another important subdirectory is jre, which stores the JDK's private copy of the Java Runtime Environment (JRE). The JRE implements the Java platform, making it possible to run Java programs. Users interested in running (but not developing) Java programs would download the public JRE. Because the JDK contains its own copy of the JRE, developers do not need to download and install the public JRE.

■ **Note** JDK 7 comes with external documentation that includes an extensive reference to Java's many *APIs* (see http://en.wikipedia.org/wiki/Application_programming_interface to learn about this term). You can download the documentation archive from http://www.oracle.com/technetwork/java/javase/downloads/index-jsp-138363.html so that you can view this documentation offline. However, because the archive is fairly large, you might prefer to view the documentation online at http://download.oracle.com/javase/7/docs/index.html.

Working with JDK 7

An application consists of a class with an entry-point method named main. Although a proper discussion of classes and methods must wait until Chapter 2, it suffices for now to just think of a class as a factory for creating objects (also discussed in Chapter 2), and to think of a method as a named sequence of instructions that are executed when the method is called. Listing 1-1 introduces you to your first application.

Listing 1-1. Greetings from Java

```
class HelloWorld
{
   public static void main(String[] args)
   {
      System.out.println("Hello, world!");
   }
}
```

Listing 1-1 declares a class named HelloWorld that provides a framework for this simple application. It also declares a method named main within this class. When you run this application, and you will learn how to do so shortly, it is this entry-point method that is called and its instructions that are executed.

The main() method includes a header that identifies this method and a block of code located between an open brace character ({) and a close brace character (}). As well as naming this method, the header provides the following information:

- public: This reserved word makes main() visible to the startup code that calls this method. If public wasn't present, the compiler would output an error message stating that it could not find a main() method.

- static: This reserved word causes this method to associate with the class instead of associating with any objects created from this class. Because the startup code that calls main() doesn't create an object from the class in order to call this method, it requires that the method be declared static. Although the compiler will not report an error if static is missing, it will not be possible to run HelloWorld, which will not be an application if the proper main() method doesn't exist.

- void: This reserved word indicates that the method doesn't return a value. If you change void to a type's reserved word (e.g., int) and then insert a statement that returns a value of this type (e.g., return 0;), the compiler will not report an error. However, you won't be able to run HelloWorld because the proper main() method would not exist.

- (String[] args): This parameter list consists of a single parameter named args of type String[]. Startup code passes a sequence of command-line arguments to args, which makes these arguments available to the code that executes within main(). You'll learn about parameters and arguments in Chapter 2.

The block of code consists of a single System.out.println("Hello, world!"); method call. From left to write, System identifies a standard class of system utilities, out identifies an object variable located in System whose methods let you output values of various types optionally followed by a newline character to the standard output device, println identifies a method that prints its argument followed by a newline character to standard output, and "Hello, world!" is a *string* (a sequence of characters delimited by double quote " characters and treated as a unit) that is passed as the argument to println and written to standard output (the starting " and ending " double quote characters are not written; these characters delimit but are not part of the string).

■ **Note** All desktop Java/nonJava applications can be run at the command line. Before graphical user interfaces with their controls for inputting and outputting values (e.g., textfields), these applications obtained their input and generated their output with the help of *Standard I/O*, an input/output mechanism that originated with the Unix operating system, and which consists of standard input, standard output, and standard error devices.

The user would input data via the standard input device (typically the keyboard, but a file could be specified instead—Unix treats everything as files). The application's output would appear on the standard output device (typically a computer screen, but optionally a file or printer). Output messages denoting errors would be output to the standard error device (screen, file, or printer) so that these messages could be handled separately.

Now that you understand how Listing 1-1 works, you'll want to create this application. Complete the following steps to accomplish this task:

1. Copy Listing 1-1 to a file named HelloWorld.java.

2. Execute javac HelloWorld.java to compile this source file. javac will complain if you do not specify the ".java" file extension.

If all goes well, you should see a HelloWorld.class file in the current directory. Now execute java HelloWorld to run this classfile's main() method. Don't specify the ".class" file extension or java will complain. You should observe the following output:

```
Hello, world!
```

Congratulations! You have run your first Java-based application. You'll have an opportunity to run more applications throughout this book.

Installing and Working with NetBeans 7

For small projects, it's no big deal to work at the command line with JDK tools. Because you'll probably find this scenario tedious (and even unworkable) for larger projects, you should consider obtaining an Integrated Development Environment (IDE) tool.

Three popular IDEs for Java development are Eclipse (http://www.eclipse.org/), IntelliJ IDEA (http://www.jetbrains.com/idea/), which is free to try but must be purchased if you want to continue to use it, and NetBeans (http://netbeans.org/). I focus on the NetBeans 7 IDE in this section because of its JDK 7 support. (IntelliJ IDEA 10.5 also supports JDK 7.)

■ **Note** For a list of NetBeans 7 IDE enhancements that are specific to JDK 7, check out the page at http://wiki.netbeans.org/NewAndNoteworthyNB70#JDK7_support.

This section shows you how to install the NetBeans 7 IDE. It then introduces you to this IDE while developing HelloWorld.

■ **Note** NetBeans is more than an IDE. It's also a platform framework that lets developers create applications much faster by leveraging the modular NetBeans architecture.

Installing NetBeans 7

Point your browser to http://netbeans.org/downloads/ and perform the following tasks:

1. Select an appropriate IDE language (English is the default).

2. Select an appropriate platform (Windows is the default).

3. Click the Download button underneath the next-to-leftmost (Java EE) column to initiate the download process for the appropriate installer file. I chose to download the English Java EE installer for the Windows platform, which is a file named netbeans-7.x-ml-javaee-windows.exe. (Because I don't explore Java EE in Beginning Java 7, it might seem pointless to install the Java EE version of NetBeans. However, you might as well install this software now in case you decide to explore Java EE after reading this book.)

Run the installer. After configuring itself, the installer presents a Welcome dialog that gives you the option of choosing which application servers you want to install with the IDE. Ensure that both the GlassFish Server and Apache Tomcat checkboxes remain checked (you might want to play with both application servers when exploring Java EE), and click the Next button.

On the resulting License Agreement dialog, read the agreement, indicate its acceptance by checking the checkbox, and click Next. Repeat this process on the subsequent JUnit License Agreement dialog.

The resulting NetBeans IDE 7.0 Installation dialog presents the default location where NetBeans will be installed (C:\Program Files\NetBeans 7.0 on my platform) and the JDK 7 home directory location (C:\Program Files\Java\jdk1.7.0 on my platform). Change these locations if necessary and click Next.

The resulting GlassFish 3.1 Installation dialog box presents the default location where the GlassFish application server will be installed (C:\Program Files\glassfish-3.1 on my platform). Change this location if necessary and click Next.

The resulting Apache Tomcat 7.0.11 Installation dialog presents the default location where the Apache Tomcat application server will be installed (C:\Program Files\Apache Software Foundation\Apache Tomcat 7.0.11 on my platform). Change this location if necessary and click Next.

The resulting Summary dialog presents your chosen options as well as the combined installation size for all software being installed. After reviewing this information, click the Install button to begin installation.

Installation takes a few minutes and culminates in a Setup Complete dialog. After reviewing this dialog's information, click the Finish button to complete installation.

Assuming a successful installation, start this IDE. NetBeans first presents a splash screen while it performs various initialization tasks, and then presents a main window similar to that shown in Figure 1-1.

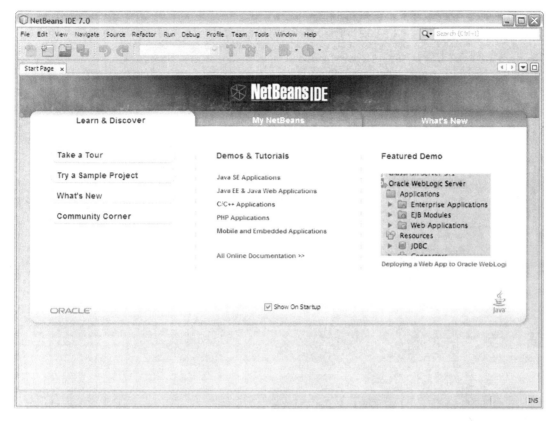

Figure 1-1. *The NetBeans 7 IDE's main window initially presents a Start Page tab.*

If you've worked with previous versions of the NetBeans IDE, you might want to click the Take a Tour button to learn how version 7 differs from its predecessors. You are taken to a web page that provides video tours of the IDE, such as NetBeans IDE 7.0 Overview.

Working with NetBeans 7

NetBeans presents a user interface whose main window is divided into a menu bar, a toolbar, a workspace, and a status bar. The workspace presents a Start Page tab for learning about NetBeans, accessing your NetBeans projects, and more.

To help you get comfortable with this IDE, I'll show you how to create a HelloWorld project that reuses Listing 1-1's source code. I'll also show you how to compile and run the HelloWorld application. Complete the following steps to create the HelloWorld project:

1. Select New Project from the File menu.

2. Make sure that Java is the selected category and Java Application is the selected Project in their respective Categories and Projects lists on the resulting New Project dialog box's Choose Project pane. Click Next.

9

3. On the resulting Name and Location pane, enter **HelloWorld** into the Project Name textfield. Notice that helloworld.HelloWorld appears in the textfield to the right of the Create Main Class checkbox (which must be checked). The helloworld portion of this string refers to a package that stores the HelloWorld class portion of this string. (Packages are discussed in Chapter 3.) Click Finish.

NetBeans spends a few moments creating the HelloWorld project. Once it finishes, NetBeans presents the workspace shown in Figure 1-2.

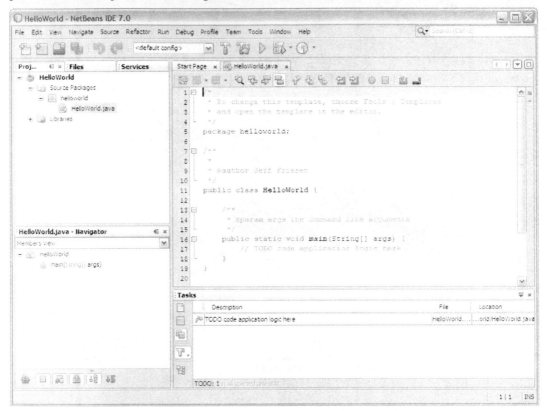

Figure 1-2. The workspace is organized into multiple work areas.

After creating HelloWorld, NetBeans organizes the workspace into projects, editor, navigator, and tasks work areas. The projects area helps you manage your projects and is organized into the following tabs:

- The Projects tab is the main entry point to your project's source and resource files. It presents a logical view of important project contents.

- The Files tab presents a directory-based view of your projects. This view includes any files and folders not shown on the Projects tab.

- The Services tab presents a logical view of resources registered with the IDE, for example, servers, databases, and web services.

The editor area helps you edit a project's source files. Each file is associated with its own tab, which is labeled with the filename. For example, Figure 1-2 reveals a HelloWorld.java tab that provides a skeletal version of this source file's contents.

The navigator area presents the Navigator tab, which offers a compact view of the currently selected file, and which simplifies navigation between various parts of the file (e.g., class and method headers).

Finally, the task area presents a Tasks tab that reveals a to-do list of items that need to be resolved for the project's various files. Each item consists of a description, a filename, and the location within the file where resolution must take place.

Replace the HelloWorld.java tab's contents with Listing 1-1, keeping the package helloworld; statement at the top of the file to prevent NetBeans from complaining about an incorrect package. Continuing, select Run Main Project from the Run menu to compile and run this application. Figure 1-3's Output tab shows HelloWorld's greeting.

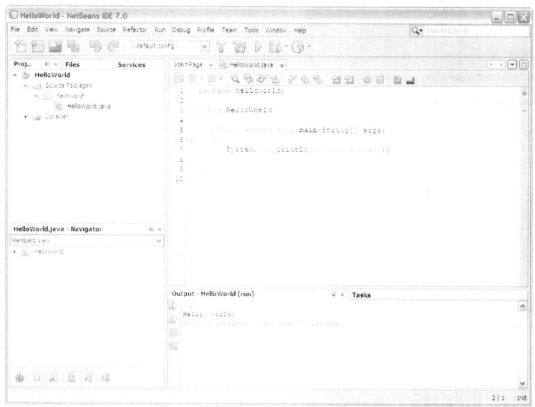

Figure 1-3. An Output tab appears to the left of Tasks and shows HelloWorld's greeting.

■ **Tip** To pass command-line arguments to an application, first select Project Properties from the File menu. On the resulting Project Properties dialog box, select Run in the Categories tree, and enter the arguments (separated by spaces; for example, **first second third**) in the Arguments textfield on the resulting pane.

For more information on the NetBeans 7 IDE, study the tutorials via the Start Page tab, access IDE help via the Help menu, and explore the NetBeans knowledge base at http://netbeans.org/kb/.

Java Language Fundamentals

Most computer languages support comments, identifiers, types, variables, expressions, and statements. Java is no exception, and this section introduces you to these fundamental language features from Java's perspective.

Comments

A program's source code needs to be documented so that you (and any others who have to maintain it) can understand it, now and later. Source code should be documented while being written and whenever it is modified. If these modifications impact existing documentation, the documentation must be updated so that it accurately explains the code.

Java provides the *comment* feature for embedding documentation in source code. When the source code is compiled, the Java compiler ignores all comments—no bytecodes are generated. Single-line, multiline, and Javadoc comments are supported.

Single-Line Comments

A *single-line comment* occupies all or part of a single line of source code. This comment begins with the // character sequence and continues with explanatory text. The compiler ignores everything from // to the end of the line in which // appears. The following example presents a single-line comment:

```
int x = (int) (Math.random()*100); // Obtain a random x coordinate from 0 through 99.
```

Single-line comments are useful for inserting short but meaningful explanations of source code into this code. Don't use them to insert unhelpful information. For example, when declaring a variable, don't insert a meaningless comment such as // this variable is an integer.

Multiline Comments

A *multiline comment* occupies one or more lines of source code. This comment begins with the /* character sequence, continues with explanatory text, and ends with the */ character sequence. Everything from /* through */ is ignored by the compiler. The following example demonstrates a multiline comment:

```
static boolean isLeapYear(int year)
{
    /*
```

```
   A year is a leap year if it is divisible by 400, or divisible by 4 but
   not also divisible by 100.
*/
if (year%400 == 0)
   return true;
else
if (year%100 == 0)
   return false;
else
if (year%4 == 0)
   return true;
else
   return false;
}
```

This example introduces a method for determining whether or not a year is a leap year. The important part of this code to understand is the multiline comment, which clarifies the expression that determines whether year's value does or doesn't represent a leap year.

■ **Caution** You cannot place one multiline comment inside another. For example, /*/* Nesting multiline comments is illegal! */*/ is not a valid multiline comment.

Javadoc Comments

A *Javadoc comment* (also known as a *documentation comment*) occupies one or more lines of source code. This comment begins with the /** character sequence, continues with explanatory text, and ends with the */ character sequence. Everything from /** through */ is ignored by the compiler. The following example demonstrates a Javadoc comment:

```
/**
 * Application entry point
 *
 * @param args array of command-line arguments passed to this method
 */
public static void main(String[] args)
{
   // TODO code application logic here
}
```

This example begins with a Javadoc comment that describes the main() method. Sandwiched between /** and */ is a description of the method, which could (but doesn't) include HTML tags (such as <p> and <code>/</code>), and the @param *Javadoc tag* (an @-prefixed instruction).

The following list identifies several commonly used tags:

- @author identifies the source code's author.

- @deprecated identifies a source code entity (e.g., a method) that should no longer be used.

- @param identifies one of a method's parameters.

- @see provides a see-also reference.

- @since identifies the software release where the entity first originated.

- @return identifies the kind of value that the method returns.

Listing 1-2 presents our HelloWorld application with documentation comments that describe the HelloWorld class and its main() method.

Listing 1-2. Greetings from Java with documentation comments

```
/**
    A simple class for introducing a Java application.

    @author Jeff Friesen
*/
class HelloWorld
{
    /**
       Application entry point

       @param args array of command-line arguments passed to this method
    */
    public static void main(String[] args)
    {
        System.out.println("Hello, world!");
    }
}
```

We can extract these documentation comments into a set of HTML files by using the JDK's javadoc tool, as follows:

```
javadoc -private HelloWorld.java
```

javadoc defaults to generating HTML-based documentation for public classes and public/protected members of these classes—you'll learn about these concepts in Chapter 2. Because HelloWorld is not public, specifying javadoc HelloWorld.java causes javadoc to complain that no public or protected classes were found to document. The remedy is to specify javadoc's -private command-line option.

javadoc responds by outputting the following messages:

```
Loading source file HelloWorld.java...
Constructing Javadoc information...
Standard Doclet version 1.7.0
Building tree for all the packages and classes...
Generating \HelloWorld.html...
Generating \package-frame.html...
Generating \package-summary.html...
Generating \package-tree.html...
Generating \constant-values.html...
Building index for all the packages and classes...
Generating \overview-tree.html...
```

```
Generating \index-all.html...
Generating \deprecated-list.html...
Building index for all classes...
Generating \allclasses-frame.html...
Generating \allclasses-noframe.html...
Generating \index.html...
Generating \help-doc.html...
```

It also generates several files, including the index.html entry-point file. Point your browser to this file and you should see a page similar to that shown in Figure 1-4.

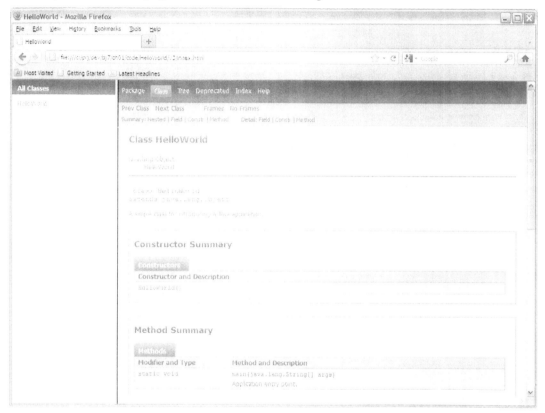

Figure 1-4. The entry-point page into HelloWorld's javadoc provides easy access to the documentation.

Note JDK 7's external documentation has a similar appearance and organization to Figure 1-4 because this documentation was also generated by javadoc.

Identifiers

Source code entities such as classes and methods need to be named so that they can be referenced from elsewhere in the code. Java provides the identifiers feature for this purpose.

An *identifier* consists of letters (A-Z, a-z, or equivalent uppercase/lowercase letters in other human alphabets), digits (0-9 or equivalent digits in other human alphabets), connecting punctuation characters (e.g., the underscore), and currency symbols (e.g., the dollar sign $). This name must begin with a letter, a currency symbol, or a connecting punctuation character; and its length cannot exceed the line in which it appears.

Examples of valid identifiers include i, counter, loop10, border$color and _char. Examples of invalid identifiers include 50y (starts with a digit) and first#name (# is not a valid identifier symbol).

■ **Note** Java is a *case-sensitive language*, which means that identifiers differing only in case are considered separate identifiers. For example, salary and Salary are separate identifiers.

Almost any valid identifier can be chosen to name a class, method, or other source code entity. However, some identifiers are reserved for special purposes; they are known as *reserved words*. Java reserves the following identifiers: abstract, assert, boolean, break, byte, case, catch, char, class, const, continue, default, do, double, enum, else, extends, false, final, finally, float, for, goto, if, implements, import, instanceof, int, interface, long, native, new, null, package, private, protected, public, return, short, static, strictfp, super, switch, synchronized, this, throw, throws, transient, true, try, void, volatile, and while. The compiler outputs an error message if you attempt to use any of these reserved words outside of their usage contexts.

■ **Note** Most of Java's reserved words are also known as *keywords*. The three exceptions are false, null, and true, which are examples of *literals* (values specified verbatim).

Types

Programs process different types of values such as integers, floating-point values, characters, and strings. A *type* identifies a set of values (and their representation in memory) and a set of operations that transform these values into other values of that set. For example, the integer type identifies numeric values with no fractional parts and integer-oriented math operations, such as adding two integers to yield another integer.

■ **Note** Java is a strongly typed language, which means that every expression, variable, and so on has a type known to the compiler. This capability helps the compiler detect type-related errors at compile time rather than having these errors manifest themselves at runtime. Expressions and variables are discussed later in this chapter.

Java classifies types as primitive types, user-defined types, and array types.

Primitive Types

A *primitive type* is a type that is defined by the language and whose values are not objects. Java supports the Boolean, character, byte integer, short integer, integer, long integer, floating-point, and double precision floating-point primitive types. They are described in Table 1-1.

Table 1-1. Primitive Types

Primitive Type	Reserved Word	Size	Min Value	Max Value
Boolean	boolean	--	--	--
Character	char	16-bit	Unicode 0	Unicode 2^{16}- 1
Byte integer	byte	8-bit	-128	+127
Short integer	short	16-bit	-2^{15}	$+2^{15}$- 1
Integer	int	32-bit	-2^{31}	$+2^{31}$- 1
Long integer	long	64-bit	-2^{63}	$+2^{63}$- 1
Floating-point	float	32-bit	IEEE 754	IEEE 754
Double precision floating-point	double	64-bit	IEEE 754	IEEE 754

Table 1-1 describes each primitive type in terms of its reserved word, size, minimum value, and maximum value. A "--" entry indicates that the column in which it appears is not applicable to the primitive type described in that entry's row.

The size column identifies the size of each primitive type in terms of the number of *bits* (binary digits—each digit is either 0 or 1) that a value of that type occupies in memory. Except for Boolean (whose size is implementation dependent—one Java implementation might store a Boolean value in a single bit, whereas another implementation might require an eight-bit *byte* for performance efficiency), each primitive type's implementation has a specific size.

The minimum value and maximum value columns identify the smallest and largest values that can be represented by each type. Except for Boolean (whose only values are true and false), each primitive type has a minimum value and a maximum value.

The minimum and maximum values of the character type refer to *Unicode*, which is a standard for the consistent encoding, representation, and handling of text expressed in most of the world's writing systems. Unicode was developed in conjunction with the *Universal Character Set*, a standard for encoding the various symbols making up the world's written languages. **Unicode 0** is shorthand for "the first Unicode code point"—a *code point* is an integer that represents a symbol (e.g., A) or a control character (e.g., newline or tab), or that combines with other code points to form a symbol. Check out Wikipedia's "Unicode" entry (http://en.wikipedia.org/wiki/Unicode) to learn more about this standard, and Wikipedia's "Universal Character Set" entry (http://en.wikipedia.org/wiki/Universal_Character_Set) to learn more about this standard.

■ **Note** The character type's limits imply that this type is unsigned (all character values are positive). In contrast, each numeric type is signed (it supports positive and negative values).

The minimum and maximum values of the byte integer, short integer, integer, and long integer types reveal that there is one more negative value than positive value (0 is typically not regarded as a positive value). The reason for this imbalance has to do with how integers are represented.

Java represents an integer value as a combination of a *sign bit* (the leftmost bit—0 for a positive value and 1 for a negative value) and *magnitude bits* (all remaining bits to the right of the sign bit). If the sign bit is 0, the magnitude is stored directly. However, if the sign bit is 1, the magnitude is stored using *twos-complement* representation in which all 1s are flipped to 0s, all 0s are flipped to 1s, and 1 is added to the result. Twos-complement is used so that negative integers can naturally coexist with positive integers. For example, adding the representation of -1 to +1 yields 0. Figure 1-5 illustrates byte integer 2's direct representation and byte integer -2's twos-complement representation.

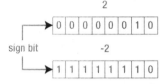

Figure 1-5. The binary representation of two byte integer values begins with a sign bit.

The minimum and maximum values of the floating-point and double precision floating-point types refer to *IEEE 754*, which is a standard for representing floating-point values in memory. Check out Wikipedia's "IEEE 754-2008" entry (http://en.wikipedia.org/wiki/IEEE_754) to learn more about this standard.

■ **Note** Developers who argue that Java should only support objects are not happy about the inclusion of primitive types in the language. However, Java was designed to include primitive types to overcome the speed and memory limitations of early 1990s-era devices, to which Java was originally targeted.

User-Defined Types

A *user-defined type* is a type that is defined by the developer using a class, an interface, an enum, or an annotation type; and whose values are objects. For example, Java's String class defines the string user-defined type; its values describe strings of characters, and its methods perform various string operations such as concatenating two strings together. Chapter 2 discusses classes, interfaces, and methods. Chapter 3 discusses enums and annotation types.

User-defined types are also known as *reference types* because a variable of that type stores a *reference* (a memory address or some other identifier) to a region of memory that stores an object of that type. In contrast, variables of primitive types store the values directly; they don't store references to these values.

Array Types

An *array type* is a special reference type that signifies an *array*, a region of memory that stores values in equal-size and contiguous slots, which are commonly referred to as *elements*.

This type consists of the element type (a primitive type or a user-defined type) and one or more pairs of square brackets that indicate the number of *dimensions* (extents). A single pair of brackets signifies a one-dimensional array (a vector), two pairs of brackets signify a two-dimensional array (a table), three pairs of brackets signify a one-dimensional array of two-dimensional arrays (a vector of tables), and so on. For example, int[] signifies a one-dimensional array (with int as the element type), and double[][] signifies a two-dimensional array (with double as the element type).

Variables

Programs manipulate values that are stored in memory, which is symbolically represented in source code through the use of the variables feature. A *variable* is a named memory location that stores some type of value. Variables that store references are often referred to as *reference variables*.

Variables must be declared before they are used. A declaration minimally consists of a type name, optionally followed by a sequence of square bracket pairs, followed by a name, optionally followed by a sequence of square bracket pairs, and terminated with a semicolon character (;). Consider the following examples:

```
int counter;
double temperature;
String firstName;
int[] ages;
char gradeLetters[];
float[][] matrix;
```

The first example declares an integer variable named counter, the second example declares a double precision floating-point variable named temperature, the third example declares a string variable named firstName, the fourth example declares a one-dimensional integer array variable named ages, the fifth example declares a one-dimensional character array variable named gradeLetters, and the sixth example declares a two-dimensional floating-point array variable named matrix. No string is yet associated with firstName, and no arrays are yet associated with ages, gradeLetters, and matrix.

Caution Square brackets can appear after the type name or after the variable name, but not in both places. For example, the compiler reports an error when it encounters int[] x[];. It is common practice to place the square brackets after the type name (as in int[] ages;) instead of after the variable name (as in char gradeLetters[];).

You can declare multiple variables on one line by separating each variable from its predecessor with a comma, as demonstrated by the following example:

```
int x, y[], z;
```

This example declares three variables named x, y, and z. Each variable shares the same type, which happens to be integer. Unlike x and z, which store single integer values, y[] signifies a one-dimensional array whose element type is integer – each element stores an integer value. No array is yet associated with y.

The square brackets must appear after the variable name when the array is declared on the same line as the other variables. If you place the square brackets before the variable name, as in int x, []y, z;, the compiler reports an error. If you place the square brackets after the type name, as in int[] x, y, z;, all three variables signify one-dimensional arrays of integers.

Expressions

The previously declared variables were not explicitly initialized to any values. As a result, they are either initialized to default values (e.g., 0 for int and 0.0 for double) or remain uninitialized, depending upon the contexts in which they appear (declared within classes or declared within methods). Chapter 2 discusses variable contexts in terms of fields, local variables, and parameters.

Java provides the expressions feature for initializing variables and for other purposes. An *expression* is a combination of literals, variable names, method calls, and operators. At runtime, it evaluates to a value whose type is referred to as the expression's type. If the expression is being assigned to a variable, the expression's type must agree with the variable's type; otherwise, the compiler reports an error.

Java classifies expressions as simple expressions and compound expressions.

Simple Expressions

A *simple expression* is a *literal* (a value expressed verbatim), a variable name (containing a value), or a method call (returning a value). Java supports several kinds of literals: string, Boolean true and false, character, integer, floating-point, and null.

■ **Note** A method call that doesn't return a value—the called method is known as a *void method*—is a special kind of simple expression; for example, System.out.println("Hello, World!");. This standalone expression cannot be assigned to a variable. Attempting to do so (as in int i = System.out.println("X");) causes the compiler to report an error.

A *string literal* consists of a sequence of Unicode characters surrounded by a pair of double quotes; for example, "The quick brown fox jumps over the lazy dog." It might also contain *escape sequences*, which are special syntax for representing certain printable and nonprintable characters that otherwise cannot appear in the literal. For example, "The quick brown \"fox\" jumps over the lazy dog." uses the \" escape sequence to surround fox with double quotes.

Table 1-2 describes all supported escape sequences.

Table 1-2. Escape Sequences

Escape Syntax	Description
\\	Backslash
\"	Double quote
\'	Single quote
\b	Backspace
\f	Form feed
\n	Newline (also referred to as line feed)
\r	Carriage return
\t	Horizontal tab

Finally, a string literal might contain *Unicode escape sequences*, which are special syntax for representing Unicode characters. A Unicode escape sequence begins with \u and continues with four hexadecimal digits (0-9, A-F, a-f) with no intervening space. For example, \u0041 represents capital letter A, and \u20ac represents the European Union's euro currency symbol.

A *Boolean literal* consists of reserved word true or reserved word false.

A *character literal* consists of a single Unicode character surrounded by a pair of single quotes ('A' is an example). You can also represent, as a character literal, an escape sequence ('\'', for example) or a Unicode escape sequence (e.g., '\u0041').

An *integer literal* consists of a sequence of digits. If the literal is to represent a long integer value, it must be suffixed with an uppercase L or lowercase l (L is easier to read). If there is no suffix, the literal represents a 32-bit integer (an int).

Integer literals can be specified in the decimal, hexadecimal, octal, and binary formats:

- The decimal format is the default format; for example, 127.

- The hexadecimal format requires that the literal begin with 0x or 0X and continue with hexadecimal digits (0-9, A-F, a-f); for example, 0x7F.

- The octal format requires that the literal be prefixed with 0 and continue with octal digits (0-7); for example, 0177.

- The binary format requires that the literal be prefixed with 0b or 0B and continue with 0s and 1s; for example, 0b01111111.

To improve readability, you can insert underscores between digits; for example, 204_555_1212. Although you can insert multiple successive underscores between digits (as in 0b1111__0000), you cannot specify a leading underscore (as in _123) because the compiler would treat the literal as an identifier. Also, you cannot specify a trailing underscore (as in 123_). A *floating-point literal* consists of an integer part, a decimal point (represented by the period character [.]), a fractional part, an exponent (starting with letter E or e), and a type suffix (letter D, d, F, or f). Most parts are optional, but enough information must be present to differentiate the floating-point literal from an integer literal. Examples include 0.1 (double precision floating-point), 89F (floating-point), 600D (double precision floating-point), and 13.08E+23 (double precision floating-point). As with integer literals, you can make floating-point literals easier to read by placing underscores between digits (3.141_592_654, for example).

Finally, the null literal is assigned to a reference variable to indicate that the variable does not refer to an object.

The following examples use literals to initialize the previously presented variables:

```
int counter = 10;
double temperature = 98.6; // Assume Fahrenheit scale.
String firstName = "Mark";
int[] ages = { 52, 28, 93, 16 };
char gradeLetters[] = { 'A', 'B', 'C', 'D', 'F' };
float[][] matrix = { { 1.0F, 2.0F, 3.0F }, { 4.0F, 5.0F, 6.0F }};
int x = 1, y[] = { 1, 2, 3 }, z = 3;
```

The last four examples use array initializers to initialize the ages, gradeletters, matrix, and y arrays. An *array initializer* consists of a brace-and-comma-delimited list of expressions, which (as the matrix example shows) may themselves be array initializers. The matrix example results in a table that looks like the following:

```
1.0F 2.0F 3.0F
4.0F 5.0F 6.0F
```

ORGANIZING VARIABLES IN MEMORY

Perhaps you're curious about how variables are organized in memory. Figure 1-6 presents one possible high-level organization for the counter, ages, and matrix variables, along with the arrays assigned to ages and matrix.

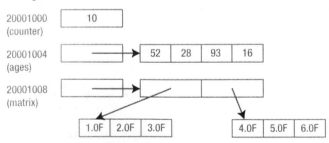

Figure 1-6. The counter *variable stores a four-byte integer value, whereas* ages *and* matrix *store four-byte references to their respective arrays.*

Figure 1-6 reveals that each of counter, ages, and matrix is stored at a memory address (starting at a fictitious 20001000 value in this example) and divisible by four (each variable stores a four-byte value), that counter's four-byte value is stored at this address, and that each of the ages and matrix four-byte memory locations stores the 32-bit address of its respective array (64-bit addresses would most likely be used on 64-bit JVMs). Also, a one-dimensional array is stored as a list of values, whereas a two-dimensional array is stored as a one-dimensional row array of addresses, where each address identifies a one-dimensional column array of values for that row.

Although Figure 1-6 implies that array addresses are stored in ages and matrix, which equates references with addresses, a Java implementation might equate references with *handles* (integer values that identify slots in a list). This alternative is presented in Figure 1-7 for ages and its referenced array.

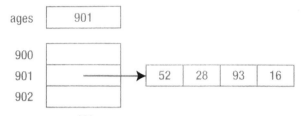

Figure 1-7. *A handle is stored in ages, and the list entry identified by this handle stores the address of the associated array.*

Handles make it easy to move around regions of memory during garbage collection (discussed in Chapter 2). If multiple variables referenced the same array via the same address, each variable's address value would have to be updated when the array was moved. However, if multiple variables referenced the array via the same handle, only the handle's list entry would need to be updated. A downside to using handles is that accessing memory via these handles can be slower than directly accessing this memory via an address. Regardless of how references are implemented, this implementation detail is hidden from the Java developer in order to promote portability.

The following example shows a simple expression where one variable is assigned the value of another variable:

```
int counter1 = 1;
int counter2 = counter1;
```

Finally, the following example shows a simple expression that assigns the result of a method call to a variable named isLeap:

```
boolean isLeap = isLeapYear(2011);
```

The previous examples have assumed that only those expressions whose types are the same as the types of the variables that they are initializing can be assigned to those variables. However, under certain circumstances, it's possible to assign an expression having a different type. For example, Java permits you to assign certain integer literals to short integer variables, as in short s = 20;, and assign a short integer expression to an integer variable, as in int i = s;.

Java permits the former assignment because 20 can be represented as a short integer (no information is lost). In contrast, Java would complain about short s = 40000; because integer literal 40000 cannot be represented as a short integer (32767 is the maximum positive integer that can be stored in a short integer variable). Java permits the latter assignment because no information is lost when Java converts from a type with a smaller set of values to a type with a wider set of values.

Java supports the following primitive type conversions via widening conversion rules:

- Byte integer to short integer, integer, long integer, floating-point, or double precision floating-point

- Short integer to integer, long integer, floating-point, or double precision floating-point

- Character to integer, long integer, floating-point, or double precision floating-point

- Integer to long integer, floating-point, or double precision floating-point

- Long integer to floating-point or double precision floating-point

- Floating-point to double precision floating-point

■ **Note** When converting from a smaller integer to a larger integer, Java copies the smaller integer's sign bit into the extra bits of the larger integer.

Chapter 2 discusses the widening conversion rules for performing type conversions in the context of user-defined and array types.

Compound Expressions

A *compound expression* is a sequence of simple expressions and operators, where an *operator* (a sequence of instructions symbolically represented in source code) transforms its *operand* expression value(s) into another value. For example, -6 is a compound expression consisting of operator - and integer literal 6 as its operand. This expression transforms 6 into its negative equivalent. Similarly, x+5 is a compound expression consisting of variable name x, integer literal 5, and operator + sandwiched between these operands. Variable x's value is fetched and added to 5 when this expression is evaluated. The sum becomes the value of the expression.

■ **Note** If x's type is byte integer or short integer, this variable's value is widened to an integer. However, if x's type is long integer, floating-point, or double precision floating-point, 5 is widened to the appropriate type. The addition operation is performed after the widening conversion takes place.

Java supplies a wide variety of operators that are classified by the number of operands they take. A *unary operator* takes only one operand (unary minus [-] is an example), a *binary operator* takes two operands (addition [+] is an example), and Java's single *ternary operator* (conditional [?:]) takes three operands.

Operators are also classified as prefix, postfix, and infix. A *prefix operator* is a unary operator that precedes its operand (as in -6), a *postfix operator* is a unary operator that trails its operand (as in x++), and an *infix operator* is a binary or ternary operator that is sandwiched between the binary operator's two or the ternary operator's three operands (as in x+5). Table 1-3 presents all supported operators in terms of their symbols, descriptions, and precedence levels—the concept of precedence is discussed at the end of this section. Various operator descriptions refer to "integer type," which is shorthand for specifying any of byte integer, short integer, integer, or long integer unless "integer type" is qualified as a 32-bit integer. Also, "numeric type" refers to any of these integer types along with floating-point and double precision floating-point.

Table 1-3. Operators

Operator	Symbol	Description	Precedence
Addition	+	Given *operand1* + *operand2*, where each operand must be o f character or numeric type, add *operand2* to *operand1* and return the sum.	10
Array index	[]	Given *variable*[*index*], where *index* must be of integer type, rea d value from or s tore value into *variable*'s storage element at location *index*.	13
Assignment	=	Given *variable* = *operand*, which must be assignment-compatible (their types must agree), store *operand* in *variable*.	0
Bitwise AND	&	Given *operand1* & *operand2*, where each operand must be of character or in teger type, bitwise AND their correspo nding bits and return the result. A result bit is set to 1 if each o perand's corresponding bit is 1. Otherwise, the result bit is set to 0.	6
Bitwise complement	~	Given ~*operand*, where *operand* must be of character or integer type, flip *operand*'s bits (1s to 0s and 0s to 1s) and return the result.	12
Bitwise exclusive OR	^	Given *operand1* ^ *operand2*, where each operand must be of character or in teger type, bitwise exclusive OR their corresp onding bits and return the result. A result bit is set to 1 if one operand's corresponding bit is 1 and t he other oper and's corresponding bit is 0. Otherwise, the result bit is set to 0.	5
Bitwise inclusive OR	|	Given *operand1* | *operand2*, which must be of character or integer type, bitwis e inclusive OR their corresponding bits and return the res ult. A result bit is set to 1 if eith er (or both) of the	4

operands' corresponding bits is 1. Otherwise, the
result bit is set to 0.

Cast	*(type)*	Given *(type) operand*, convert *operand* to an equivalent value that can be represented by *type*. For example, you could use this operator to convert a floating-point value to a 32-bit integer value.	12
Compound assignment	+=, -=, *=, /=, %=, &=, |=, ^=, <<=, >>=, >>>=	Given *variable operator operand*, where *operator* is one of the listed compound operator symbols, and where *operand* is assignment-compatible with *variable*, perform the indicated operation using *variable*'s value as *operator*'s left operand value, and store the resulting value in *variable*.	0
Conditional	?:	Given *operand1* ? *operand2* : *operand3*, where *operand1* must be of Boolean type, re turn *operand2* if *operand1* is true or *operand3* if *operand1* is false. The types of *operand2* and *operand3* must agree.	1
Conditional AND	&&	Given *operand1* && *operand2*, where each operand must be of Boolean type, return true if both operands are true. Ot herwise, return false. If *operand1* is false, *operand2* is not examined. This is known as *short-circuiting*.	3
Conditional OR	||	Given *operand1* || *operand2*, where each operand must be of Boolean type, return true if at least one operand is true. Otherwise, return false. If *operand1* is true, *operand2* is not examined. This is known as *short-circuiting*.	2
Division	/	Given *operand1* / *operand2*, where each operand must be o f character or numeric type, divide *operand1* by *operand2* and return the quotient.	11
Equality	==	Given *operand1* == *operand2*, where both operands must be co mparable (you cannot compare an integer with a string li teral, for example), compare both operands for equality. Return true if thes e operands are equa l. Otherwise, return false.	7
Inequality	!=	Given *operand1* != *operand2*, where both operands must be co mparable (you cannot compare an integer with a string li teral, for	7

example), compare both operands for inequality. Return true if these operands are not equal. Otherwise, return false.

Left shift	<<	Given *operand1* << *operand2*, where each operand must be of character or integer type, shift *operand1*'s binary representation left by the number of bits that *operand2* specifies. For each shift, a 0 is shifted into the rightmost bit and the leftmost bit is discarded. Only the five low-order bits of *operand2* are used when shifting a 32-bit integer (to prevent shifting more than the number of bits in a 32-bit integer). Only the six low-order bits of *operand2* are used when shifting a 64-bit integer (to prevent shifting more than the number of bits in a 64-bit integer). The shift preserves negative values. Furthermore, it is equivalent to (but faster than) multiplying by a multiple of 2.	9
Logical AND	&	Given *operand1* & *operand2*, where each operand must be of Boolean type, return true if both operands are true. Otherwise, return false. In contrast to conditional AND, logical AND does not perform short-circuiting.	6
Logical complement	!	Given !*operand*, where *operand* must be of Boolean type, flip *operand*'s value (true to false or false to true) and return the result.	12
Logical exclusive OR	^	Given *operand1* ^ *operand2*, where each operand must be of Boolean type, return true if one operand is true and the other operand is false. Otherwise, return false.	5
Logical inclusive OR			Given *operand1*	*operand2*, where each operand must be of Boolean type, return true if at least one operand is true. Otherwise, return false. In contrast to conditional OR, logical inclusive OR does not perform short-circuiting.	4
Member access	.	Given *identifier1*.*identifier2*, access the *identifier2* member of *identifier1*.	13
Method call	()	Given *identifier*(*argument list*), call the method identified by *identifier* and matching parameter list.	13

Multiplication	*	Given *operand1* * *operand2*, where each operand must be of character or numeric type, multiply *operand1* by *operand2* and return the product.	11
Object creation	new	Given new *identifier(argument list)*, allocate memory for object and call constructor (discussed in Chapter 2) specified as *identifier(argument list)*. Given new *identifier[integer size]*, allocate a one-dimensional array of values.	12
Postdecrement	--	Given *variable*--, where *variable* must be of character or numeric type, subtract 1 from *variable*'s value (storing the result in *variable*) and return the original value.	13
Postincrement	++	Given *variable*++, where *variable* must be of character or numeric type, add 1 to *variable*'s value (storing the result in *variable*) and return the original value.	13
Predecrement	--	Given --*variable*, where *variable* must be of character or numeric type, subtract 1 from its value, store the result in *variable*, and return this value.	12
Preincrement	++	Given ++*variable*, where *variable* must be of character or numeric type, add 1 to its value, store the result in *variable*, and return this value.	12
Relational greater than	>	Given *operand1* > *operand2*, where each operand must be of character or numeric type, return true if *operand1* is greater than *operand2*. Otherwise, return false.	8
Relational greater than or equal to	>=	Given *operand1* >= *operand2*, where each operand must be of character or numeric type, return true if *operand1* is greater than or equal to *operand2*. Otherwise, return false.	8
Relational less than	<	Given *operand1* < *operand2*, where each operand must be of character or numeric type, return true if *operand1* is less than *operand2*. Otherwise, return false.	8
Relational less than or equal to	<=	Given *operand1* <= *operand2*, where each operand must be of character or numeric type,	8

		return true if *operand1* is less than or equal to *operand2*. Otherwise, return false.	
Relational type checking	instanceof	Given *operand1* instanceof *operand2*, where *operand1* is an object and *operand2* is a class (o r other user-defined type), return true if *operand1* is an instance of *operand2*. Otherwise, return false.	8
Remainder	%	Given *operand1* % *operand2*, where each operand must be o f character or numeric type, divide *operand1* by *operand2* and return the remainder.	11
Signed right shift	>>	Given *operand1* >> *operand2*, where each operand must be o f character or integer type, shift *operand1*'s binary repre sentation right by the number of bits that *operand2* specifies. For each shift, a copy of the sign bit (the leftmost bit) is shifted to t he right a nd the rightmost bit is discarded. Only the fi ve low-order b its of *operand2* are used when shifting a 32-bit integer (to prevent s hifting more than the num ber of bits in a 32-bit integer). Only the s ix low-order bits of *operand2* are used wh en shifting a 64-bit integer (to prevent shifting more than the number of bi ts in a 64-bit integer). The shift preserves negative values. Furthermore, it is equivalent to (but fast er than) dividing by a multiple of 2.	9
String concatenation	+	Given *operand1* + *operand2*, where at least one operand is of String type, append *operand2*'s string representation to *operand1*'s string representation and return the concatenated result.	10
Subtraction	-	Given *operand1* - *operand2*, where each operand must be o f character or numeric type, subtract *operand2* from *operand1* and return the difference.	10
Unary minus	-	Given -*operand*, where *operand* must be of character or numeric type, return *operand*'s arithmetic negative.	12
Unary plus	+	Like its predecessor, but return *operand*. Rarely used.	12

| Unsigned right shift | >>> | Given *operand1* >>> *operand2*, where each operand must be o f character or integer type, shift *operand1*'s binary repre sentation right by the number of bits that *operand2* specifies. For each shift, a zero is shifted into the leftm ost bit and the rightm ost bit is discarded. Only the five low-order bits of *operand2* are used when shifting a 32-bit integer (to prevent shifting more than the number of bits in a 32-bit integer). Only the six low-order bits of *operand2* are used when shifting a 64-bit integer (to prevent shifting more than the number of bits in a 64-bit integer). The shift does not pres erve negative values. Furthermore, it is equivalent to (but faster than) dividing by a multiple of 2. | 9 |

Table 1-3's operators can be classified as additive, array index, assignment, bitwise, cast, conditional, equality, logical, member access, method call, multiplicative, object creation, relational, shift, and unary minus/plus.

Additive Operators

The additive operators consist of addition (+), subtraction (-), postdecrement (--), postincrement (++), predecrement (--), preincrement (++), and string concatenation (+). Addition returns the sum of its operands (e.g., 6+4 returns 10), subtraction returns the difference between its operands (e.g., 6-4 returns 2 and 4-6 returns 2), postdecrement subtracts one from its variable operand and returns the variable's prior value (e.g., x--), postincrement adds one to its variable operand and returns the variable's prior value (e.g., x++), predecrement subtracts one from its variable operand and returns the variable's new value (e.g., --x), preincrement adds one to its variable operand and returns the variable's new value (e.g., ++x), and string concatenation merges its string operands and returns the merged string (e.g., "A"+"B" returns "AB").

The addition, subtraction, postdecrement, postincrement, predecrement, and preincrement operators can yield values that overflow or underflow the limits of the resulting value's type. For example, adding two large positive 32-bit integer values can produce a value that cannot be represented as a 32-bit integer value. The result is said to overflow. Java does not detect overflows and underflows.

Java provides a special widening conversion rule for use with string operands and the string concatenation operator. If either operand is not a string, the operand is first converted to a string prior to string concatenation. For example, when presented with "A"+5, the compiler generates code that first converts 5 to "5" and then performs the string concatenation operation, resulting in "A5".

Array Index Operator

The array index operator ([]) accesses an array element by presenting the location of that element as an integer *index*. This operator is specified after an array variable's name; for example, ages[0].

Indexes are relative to 0, which implies that ages[0] accesses the first element, whereas ages[6] accesses the seventh element. The index must be greater than or equal to 0 and less than the length of the array; otherwise, the JVM throws ArrayIndexOutOfBoundsException (consult Chapter 3 to learn about exceptions).

An array's length is returned by appending ".length" to the array variable. For example, ages.length returns the length of (the number of elements in) the array that ages references. Similarly, matrix.length returns the number of row elements in the matrix two-dimensional array, whereas matrix[0].length returns the number of column elements assigned to the first row element of this array.

Assignment Operators

The assignment operator (=) assigns an expression's result to a variable (as in int x = 4;). The types of the variable and expression must agree; otherwise, the compiler reports an error.

Java also supports several compound assignment operators that perform a specific operation and assign its result to a variable. For example, the += operator evaluates the numeric expression on its right and adds the result to the contents of the variable on its left. The other compound assignment operators behave in a similar way.

Bitwise Operators

The bitwise operators consist of bitwise AND (&), bitwise complement (~), bitwise exclusive OR (^), and bitwise inclusive OR (|). These operators are designed to work on the binary representations of their character or integral operands. Because this concept can be hard to understand if you haven't previously worked with these operators in another language, the following example demonstrates these operators:

```
~0B00000000000000000000000010110101 results in 11111111111111111111111101001010
0B00011010&0B10110111 results in 00000000000000000000000000010010
0B00011010^0B10110111 results in 00000000000000000000000010101101
0B00011010|0B10110111 results in 00000000000000000000000010111111
```

The &, ^, and | operators in the last three lines first convert their byte integer operands to 32-bit integer values (through *sign bit extension*, copying the sign bit's value into the extra bits) before performing their operations.

Cast Operator

The cast operator—(*type*)—attempts to convert the type of its operand to *type*. This operator exists because the compiler will not allow you to convert a value from one type to another in which information will be lost without specifying your intention do so (via the cast operator). For example, when presented with short s = 1.65+3;, the compiler reports an error because attempting to convert a double precision floating-point value to a short integer results in the loss of the fraction .65—s would contain 4 instead of 4.65.

Recognizing that information loss might not always be a problem, Java permits you to explicitly state your intention by casting to the target type. For example, short s = (short) 1.65+3; tells the compiler that you want 1.65+3 to be converted to a short integer, and that you realize that the fraction will disappear.

The following example provides another demonstration of the need for a cast operator:

```
char c = 'A';
byte b = c;
```

The compiler reports an error about loss of precision when it encounters byte b = c;. The reason is that c can represent any unsigned integer value from 0 through 65535, whereas b can only represent a signed integer value from -128 through +127. Even though 'A' equates to +65, which can fit within b's range, c could just have easily been initialized to '\u0323', which would not fit.

The solution to this problem is to introduce a (byte) cast, as follows, which causes the compiler to generate code to cast c's character type to byte integer:

```
byte b = (byte) c;
```

Java supports the following primitive type conversions via cast operators:

- Byte integer to character

- Short integer to byte integer or character

- Character to byte integer or short integer

- Integer to byte integer, short integer, or character

- Long integer to byte integer, short integer, character, or integer

- Floating-point to byte integer, short integer, character, integer, or long integer

- Double precision floating-point to byte integer, short integer, character, integer, long integer, or floating-point

A cast operator is not always required when converting from more to fewer bits, and where no data loss occurs. For example, when it encounters byte b = 100;, the compiler generates code that assigns integer 100 to byte integer variable b because 100 can easily fit into the 8-bit storage location assigned to this variable.

Conditional Operators

The conditional operators consist of conditional AND (&&), conditional OR (||), and conditional (?:). The first two operators always evaluate their left operand (a Boolean expression that evaluates to true or false) and conditionally evaluate their right operand (another Boolean expression). The third operator evaluates one of two operands based upon a third Boolean operand.

Conditional AND always evaluates its left operand and evaluates its right operand only when its left operand evaluates to true. For example, age > 64 && stillWorking first evaluates age > 64. If this subexpression is true, stillWorking is evaluated, and its true or false value (stillWorking is a Boolean variable) serves as the value of the overall expression. If age > 64 is false, stillWorking is not evaluated.

Conditional OR always evaluates its left operand and evaluates its right operand only when its left operand evaluates to false. For example, value < 20 || value > 40 first evaluates value < 20. If this subexpression is false, value > 40 is evaluated, and its true or false value serves as the overall expression's value. If value < 20 is true, value > 40 is not evaluated.

Conditional AND and conditional OR boost performance by preventing the unnecessary evaluation of subexpressions, which is known as *short-circuiting*. For example, if its left operand is false, there is no way that conditional AND's right operand can change the fact that the overall expression will evaluate to false.

If you aren't careful, short-circuiting can prevent *side effects* (the results of subexpressions that persist after the subexpressions have been evaluated) from executing. For example, age > 64 && ++numEmployees > 5 increments numEmployees for only those employees whose ages are greater than 64. Incrementing numEmployees is an example of a side effect because the value in numEmployees persists after the subexpression ++numEmployees > 5 has evaluated.

The conditional operator is useful for making a decision by evaluating and returning one of two operands based upon the value of a third operand. The following example converts a Boolean value to its integer equivalent (1 for true and 0 for false):

```
boolean b = true;
int i = b ? 1 : 0; // 1 assigns to i
```

Equality Operators

The equality operators consist of equality (==) and inequality (!=). These operators compare their operands to determine whether they are equal or unequal. The former operator returns true when equal; the latter operator returns true when unequal. For example, each of 2 == 2 and 2 != 3 evaluates to true, whereas each of 2 == 4 and 4 != 4 evaluates to false.

When it comes to object operands (discussed in Chapter 2), these operators do not compare their contents. For example, "abc" == "xyz" does not compare a with x. Instead, because string literals are really String objects stored in memory (Chapter 4 discusses this concept further), == compares the references to these objects.

Logical Operators

The logical operators consist of logical AND (&), logical complement (!), logical exclusive OR (^), and logical inclusive OR (|). Although these operators are similar to their bitwise counterparts, whose operands must be integer/character, the operands passed to the logical operators must be Boolean. For example, !false returns true. Also, when confronted with age > 64 & stillWorking, logical AND evaluates both subexpressions. This same pattern holds for logical exclusive OR and logical inclusive OR.

Member Access Operator

The member access operator (.) is used to access a class's members or an object's members. For example, String s = "Hello"; int len = s.length(); returns the length of the string assigned to variable s. It does so by calling the length() method member of the String class. Chapter 2 discusses this topic in more detail.

Arrays are special objects that have a single length member. When you specify an array variable followed by the member access operator, followed by length, the resulting expression returns the number of elements in the array as a 32-bit integer. For example, ages.length returns the length of (the number of elements in) the array that ages references.

Method Call Operator

The method call operator—()—is used to signify that a method (discussed in Chapter 2) is being called. Furthermore, it identifies the number, order, and types of arguments that are passed to the method, to be picked up by the method's parameters. System.out.println("Hello"); is an example.

Multiplicative Operators

The multiplicative operators consist of multiplication (*), division (/), and remainder (%). Multiplication returns the product of its operands (e.g., 6*4 returns 24), division returns the quotient of dividing its left operand by its right operand (e.g., 6/4 returns 1), and remainder returns the remainder of dividing its left operand by its right operand (e.g., 6%4 returns 2).

The multiplication, division, and remainder operators can yield values that overflow or underflow the limits of the resulting value's type. For example, multiplying two large positive 32-bit integer values can produce a value that cannot be represented as a 32-bit integer value. The result is said to overflow. Java does not detect overflows and underflows.

Dividing a numeric value by 0 (via the division or remainder operator) also results in interesting behavior. Dividing an integer value by integer 0 causes the operator to throw an `ArithmeticException` object (Chapter 3 covers exceptions). Dividing a floating-point/double precision floating-point value by 0 causes the operator to return +infinity or -infinity, depending on whether the dividend is positive or negative. Finally, dividing floating-point 0 by 0 causes the operator to return NaN (Not a Number).

Object Creation Operator

The object creation operator (`new`) creates an object from a class and also creates an array from an initializer. These topics are discussed in Chapter 2.

Relational Operators

The relational operators consist of relational greater than (`>`), relational greater than or equal to (`>=`), relational less than (`<`), relational less than or equal to (`<=`), and relational type checking (`instanceof`). The former four operators compare their operands and return true if the left operand is (respectively) greater than, greater than or equal to, less than, or less than or equal to the right operand. For example, each of `5.0 > 3`, `2 >= 2`, `16.1 < 303.3`, and `54.0 <= 54.0` evaluates to true.

The relational type-checking operator is used to determine whether an object belongs to a specific type. This topic is discussed in Chapter 2.

Shift Operators

The shift operators consist of left shift (`<<`), signed right shift (`>>`), and unsigned right shift (`>>>`). Left shift shifts the binary representation of its left operand leftward by the number of positions specified by its right operand. Each shift is equivalent to multiplying by 2. For example, `2 << 3` shifts 2's binary representation left by 3 positions; the result is equivalent to multiplying 2 by 8.

Each of signed and unsigned right shift shifts the binary representation of its left operand rightward by the number of positions specified by its right operand. Each shift is equivalent to dividing by 2. For example, `16 >> 3` shifts 16's binary representation right by 3 positions; the result is equivalent to dividing 16 by 8.

The difference between signed and unsigned right shift is what happens to the sign bit during the shift. Signed right shift includes the sign bit in the shift, whereas unsigned right shift ignores the sign bit. As a result, signed right shift preserved negative numbers, but unsigned right shift does not. For example, `-4 >> 1` (the equivalent of -4/2) evaluates to -2, whereas `-4 >>> 1` evaluates to 2147483646.

Tip The shift operators are faster than multiplying or dividing by powers of 2.

Unary Minus/Plus Operators

Unary minus (-) and unary plus (+) are the simplest of all operators. Unary minus returns the negative of its operand (such as -5 returns -5 and --5 returns 5), whereas unary plus returns its operand verbatim (such as +5 returns 5 and +-5 returns -5). Unary plus is not commonly used, but is present for completeness.

Precedence and Associativity

When evaluating a compound expression, Java takes each operator's *precedence* (level of importance) into account to ensure that the expression evaluates as expected. For example, when presented with the expression 60+3*6, we expect multiplication to be performed before addition (multiplication has higher precedence than addition), and the final result to be 78. We do not expect addition to occur first, yielding a result of 378.

■ **Note** Table 1-3's rightmost column presents a value that indicates an operator's precedence: the higher the number, the higher the precedence. For example, addition's precedence level is 10 and multiplication's precedence level is 11, which means that multiplication is performed before addition.

Precedence can be circumvented by introducing open and close parentheses, (and), into the expression, where the innermost pair of nested parentheses is evaluated first. For example, 2*((60+3)*6) results in (60+3) being evaluated first, (60+3)*6 being evaluated next, and the overall expression being evaluated last. Similarly, in the expression 60/(3-6), subtraction is performed before division.

During evaluation, operators with the same precedence level (e.g., addition and subtraction, which both have level 10) are processed according to their *associativity* (a property that determines how operators having the same precedence are grouped when parentheses are missing).

For example, expression 9*4/3 is evaluated as if it was (9*4)/3 because * and / are left-to-right associative operators. In contrast, expression x=y=z=100 is evaluated as if it was x=(y=(z=100))—100 is assigned to z, z's new value (100) is assigned to y, and y's new value (100) is assigned to x – because = is a right-to-left associative operator.

Most of Java's operators are left-to-right associative. Right-to-left associative operators include assignment, bitwise complement, cast, compound assignment, conditional, logical complement, object creation, predecrement, preincrement, unary minus, and unary plus.

■ **Note** Unlike languages such as C++, Java doesn't let you overload operators. However, Java overloads the +, ++, and -- operator symbols.

Statements

Statements are the workhorses of a program. They assign values to variables, control a program's flow by making decisions and/or repeatedly executing other statements, and perform other tasks. A *statement* can be expressed as a simple statement or as a compound statement:

- A *simple statement* is a single standalone source code instruction for performing some task; it's terminated with a semicolon.

- A *compound statement* is a (possibly empty) sequence of simple and other compound statements sandwiched between open and close brace delimiters—a *delimiter* is a character that marks the beginning or end of some section. A method body (e.g., the main() method's body) is an example. Compound statements can appear wherever simple statements appear and are alternatively referred to as *blocks*.

This section introduces you to many of Java's statements. Additional statements are covered in later chapters. For example, Chapter 2 discusses the return statement.

Assignment Statements

The *assignment statement* is an expression that assigns a value to a variable. This statement begins with a variable name, continues with the assignment operator (=) or a compound assignment operator (such as +=), and concludes with an expression and a semicolon. Below are three examples:

```
x = 10;
ages[0] = 25;
counter += 10;
```

The first example assigns integer 10 to variable x, which is presumably of type integer as well. The second example assigns integer 25 to the first element of the ages array. The third example adds 10 to the value stored in counter and stores the sum in counter.

■ **Note** Initializing a variable in the variable's declaration (e.g., int counter = 1;) can be thought of as a special form of the assignment statement.

Decision Statements

The previously described conditional operator (?:) is useful for choosing between two expressions to evaluate, and cannot be used to choose between two statements. For this purpose, Java supplies three decision statements: if, if-else, and switch.

If Statement

The if statement evaluates a Boolean expression and executes another statement when this expression evaluates to true. This statement has the following syntax:

```
if (Boolean expression)
    statement
```

If consists of reserved word if, followed by a *Boolean expression* in parentheses, followed by a *statement* to execute when *Boolean expression* evaluates to true.

The following example demonstrates this statement:

```
if (numMonthlySales > 100)
    wage += bonus;
```

If the number of monthly sales exceeds 100, numMonthlySales > 100 evaluates to true and the wage += bonus; assignment statement executes. Otherwise, this assignment statement does not execute.

If-Else Statement

The if-else statement evaluates a Boolean expression and executes one of two statements depending on whether this expression evaluates to true or false. This statement has the following syntax:

```
if (Boolean expression)
    statement1
else
    statement2
```

If-else consists of reserved word if, followed by a *Boolean expression* in parentheses, followed by a *statement1* to execute when *Boolean expression* evaluates to true, followed by a *statement2* to execute when *Boolean expression* evaluates to false.

The following example demonstrates this statement:

```
if ((n&1) == 1)
    System.out.println("odd");
else
    System.out.println("even");
```

This example assumes the existence of an int variable named n that has been initialized to an integer. It then proceeds to determine whether the integer is odd (not divisible by 2) or even (divisible by 2).

The Boolean expression first evaluates n&1, which bitwise ANDs n's value with 1. It then compares the result to 1. If they are equal, a message stating that n's value is odd outputs; otherwise, a message stating that n's value is even outputs.

The parentheses are required because == has higher precedence than &. Without these parentheses, the expression's evaluation order would change to first evaluating 1 == 1 and then trying to bitwise AND the Boolean result with n's integer value. This order results in a compiler error message because of a type mismatch: you cannot bitwise AND an integer with a Boolean value.

You could rewrite this if-else statement example to use the conditional operator, as follows: System.out.println((n&1) == 1 ? "odd" : "even");. However, you cannot do so with the following example:

```
if ((n&1) == 1)
    odd();
else
    even();
```

This example assumes the existence of odd() and even() methods that don't return anything. Because the conditional operator requires that each of its second and third operands evaluates to a value, the compiler reports an error when attempting to compile (n&1) == 1 ? odd() : even().

You can chain multiple if-else statements together, resulting in the following syntax:

```
if (Boolean expression1)
    statement1
else
if (Boolean expression2)
    statement2
else

    ...
else
    statementN
```

If *Boolean expression1* evaluates to true, *statement1* executes. Otherwise, if *Boolean expression2* evaluates to true, *statement2* executes. This pattern continues until one of these expressions evaluates to true and its corresponding statement executes, or the final else is reached and *statementN* (the default statement) executes.

The following example demonstrates this chaining:

```
if (testMark >= 90)
{
    gradeLetter = 'A';
    System.out.println("You aced the test.");
}
else
if (testMark >= 80)
{
    gradeLetter = 'B';
    System.out.println("You did very well on this test.");
}
else
if (testMark >= 70)
{
    gradeLetter = 'C';
    System.out.println("Not bad, but you need to study more for future tests.");
}
else
if (testMark >= 60)
{
    gradeLetter = 'D';
    System.out.println("Your test result suggests that you need a tutor.");
else
{
    gradeLetter = 'F';
    System.out.println("Your test result is pathetic; you need summer school.");
}
```

DANGLING-ELSE PROBLEM

When if and if-else are used together, and the source code is not properly indented, it can be difficult to determine which if associates with the else. For example:

```
if (car.door.isOpen())
   if (car.key.isPresent())
      car.start();
else car.door.open();
```

Did the developer intend for the else to match the inner if, but improperly formatted the code to make it appear otherwise? For example:

```
if (car.door.isOpen())
   if (car.key.isPresent())
      car.start();
   else
      car.door.open();
```

If `car.door.isOpen()` and `car.key.isPresent()` each return true, `car.start()` executes. If `car.door.isOpen()` returns true and `car.key.isPresent()` returns false, `car.door.open();` executes. Attempting to open an open door makes no sense.

The developer must have wanted the else to match the outer if, but forgot that else matches the nearest if. This problem can be fixed by surrounding the inner if with braces, as follows:

```
if (car.door.isOpen())
{
   if (car.key.isPresent())
      car.start();
}
else
   car.door.open();
```

When `car.door.isOpen()` returns true, the compound statement executes. When this method returns false, `car.door.open();` executes, which makes sense.

Forgetting that else matches the nearest if and using poor indentation to obscure this fact is known as the *dangling-else problem*.

Switch Statement

The switch statement lets you choose from among several execution paths in a more efficient manner than with equivalent chained if-else statements. This statement has the following syntax:

```
switch (selector expression)
{
   case value1: statement1 [break;]
   case value2: statement2 [break;]
   ...
   case valueN: statementN [break;]
   [default: statement]
}
```

Switch consists of reserved word switch, followed by a *selector expression* in parentheses, followed by a body of cases. The *selector expression* is any expression that evaluates to an integer, character, or string value. For example, it might evaluate to a 32-bit integer or to a 16-bit character.

Each case begins with reserved word case, continues with a literal value and a colon character (:), continues with a statement to execute, and optionally concludes with a break statement, which causes execution to continue after the switch statement.

After evaluating the *selector expression*, switch compares this value with each case's value until it finds a match. If there is a match, the case's statement is executed. For example, if the *selector expression*'s value matches *value1*, *statement1* executes.

The optional break statement (anything placed in square brackets is optional), which consists of reserved word break followed by a semicolon, prevents the flow of execution from continuing with the next case's statement. Instead, execution continues with the first statement following switch.

■ **Note** You will usually place a break statement after a case's statement. Forgetting to include break can lead to a hard-to-find bug. However, there are situations where you want to group several cases together and have them execute common code. In such a situation, you would omit the break statement from the participating cases.

If none of the cases' values match the *selector expression*'s value, and if a default case (signified by the default reserved word followed by a colon) is present, the default case's statement is executed.

The following example demonstrates this statement:

```
switch (direction)
{
   case 0: System.out.println("You are travelling north."); break;
   case 1: System.out.println("You are travelling east."); break;
   case 2: System.out.println("You are travelling south."); break;
   case 3: System.out.println("You are travelling west."); break;
   default: System.out.println("You are lost.");
}
```

This example assumes that direction stores an integer value. If this value is in the range 0-3, an appropriate direction message is output; otherwise, a message about being lost is output.

■ **Note** This example hardcodes values 0, 1, 2, and 3, which is not a good idea in practice. Instead, constants should be used. Chapter 2 introduces you to constants.

Loop Statements

It's often necessary to repeatedly execute a statement, and this repeated execution is called a *loop*. Java provides three kinds of loop statements: for, while, and do-while. This section first discusses these statements. It then examines the topic of looping over the empty statement. Finally, the section discusses the break, labeled break, continue, and labeled continue statements for prematurely ending all or part of a loop.

For Statement

The for statement lets you loop over a statement a specific number of times, or even indefinitely. This statement has the following syntax:

```
for ([initialize]; [test]; [update])
    statement
```

For consists of reserved word for, followed by a header in parentheses, followed by a statement to execute. The header consists of an optional *initialize* section, followed by an optional *test* section, followed by an optional *update* section. A nonoptional semicolon separates each of the first two sections from the next section.

The *initialize* section consists of a comma-separated list of variable declarations or variable assignments. Some or all of these variables are typically used to control the loop's duration, and are known as *loop-control variables*.

The *test* section consists of a Boolean expression that determines how long the loop executes. Execution continues as long as this expression evaluates to true.

Finally, the *update* section consists of a comma-separated list of expressions that typically modify the loop-control variables.

For is perfect for *iterating* (looping) over an array. Each *iteration* (loop execution) accesses one of the array's elements via an *array[index]* expression, where *array* is the array whose element is being accessed, and *index* is the zero-based location of the element being accessed.

The following example uses the for statement to iterate over the array of command-line arguments that is passed to the main() method:

```java
public static void main(String[] args)
{
   for (int i = 0; i < args.length; i++)
     switch (args[i])
     {
        case "-v":
        case "-V": System.out.println("version 1.0");
                   break;
        default  : showUsage();
     }
}
```

For's initialization section declares variable i for controlling the loop, its test section compares i's current value to the length of the args array to ensure that this value is less than the array's length, and its update section increments i by 1. The loop continues until i's value equals the array's length.

Each iteration accesses one of the array's values via the args[i] expression. This expression returns this array's ith value (which happens to be a String object in this example). The first value is stored in args[0].

The args[i] expression serves as the switch statement's selector expression. If this String object contains -V, the second case is executed, which calls System.out.println() to output a version number message. The subsequent break statement keeps execution from falling into the default case, which calls showUsage() to output usage information when main() is called with unexpected arguments.

If this String object contains -v, the lack of a break statement following the first case causes execution to fall through to the second case, calling System.out.println(). This example demonstrates the occasional need to group cases to execute common code.

Note Although I've named the array containing command-line arguments args, this name isn't mandatory. I could as easily have named it arguments (or even some_other_name).

The following example uses the for statement to output the contents of the previously declared matrix array, which is redeclared here for convenience:

```java
float[][] matrix = { { 1.0F, 2.0F, 3.0F }, { 4.0F, 5.0F, 6.0F }};
for (int row = 0; row < matrix.length; row++)
{
    for (int col = 0; col < matrix[row].length; col++)
        System.out.print(matrix[row][col]+" ");
    System.out.print("\n");
}
```

Expression matrix.length returns the number of rows in this tabular array. For each row, expression matrix[row].length returns the number of columns for that row. This latter expression suggests that each row can have a different number of columns, although each row has the same number of columns in the example.

System.out.print() is closely related to System.out.println(). Unlike the latter method, System.out.print() outputs its argument without a trailing newline.

This example generates the following output:

```
1.0 2.0 3.0
4.0 5.0 6.0
```

While Statement

The while statement repeatedly executes a statement while its Boolean expression evaluates to true. This statement has the following syntax:

```java
while (Boolean expression)
    statement
```

While consists of reserved word while, followed by a parenthesized *Boolean expression* header, followed by a *statement* to repeatedly execute.

The while statement first evaluates the *Boolean expression*. If it is true, while executes the other *statement*. Once again, the *Boolean expression* is evaluated. If it is still true, while re-executes the *statement*. This cyclic pattern continues.

Prompting the user to enter a specific character is one situation where while is useful. For example, suppose that you want to prompt the user to enter a specific uppercase letter or its lowercase equivalent. The following example provides a demonstration:

```
int ch = 0;
while (ch != 'C' && ch != 'c')
{
   System.out.println("Press C or c to continue.");
   ch = System.in.read();
}
```

This example begins by initializing variable ch. This variable must be initialized; otherwise, the compiler will report an uninitialized variable when it tries to read ch's value in the while statement's Boolean expression.

This expression uses the conditional AND operator (&&) to test ch's value. This operator first evaluates its left operand, which happens to be expression ch != 'C'. (The != operator converts 'C' from 16-bit unsigned char type to 32-bit signed int type prior to the comparison.)

If ch does not contain C (it does not at this point—0 was just assigned to ch), this expression evaluates to true.

The && operator next evaluates its right operand, which happens to be expression ch != 'c'. Because this expression also evaluates to true, conditional AND returns true and while executes the compound statement.

The compound statement first outputs, via the System.out.println() method call, a message that prompts the user to press the C key with or without the Shift key. It next reads the entered keystroke via System.in.read(), saving its integer value in ch.

From left to right, System identifies a standard class of system utilities, in identifies an object located in System that provides methods for inputting one or more bytes from the standard input device, and read() returns the next byte (or -1 when there are no more bytes).

Following this assignment, the compound statement ends and while re-evaluates its Boolean expression.

Suppose ch contains C's integer value. Conditional AND evaluates ch != 'C', which evaluates to false. Seeing that the expression is already false, conditional AND short circuits its evaluation by not evaluating its right operand, and returns false. The while statement subsequently detects this value and terminates.

Suppose ch contains c's integer value. Conditional AND evaluates ch != 'C', which evaluates to true. Seeing that the expression is true, conditional AND evaluates ch != 'c', which evaluates to false. Once again, the while statement terminates.

■ **Note** A for statement can be coded as a while statement. For example,

```
for (int i = 0; i < 10; i++)
    System.out.println(i);
```

is equivalent to

```
int i = 0;
while (i < 10)
{
    System.out.println(i);
    i++;
}
```

Do-While Statement

The do-while statement repeatedly executes a statement while its Boolean expression evaluates to true. Unlike the while statement, which evaluates the Boolean expression at the top of the loop, do-while evaluates the Boolean expression at the bottom of the loop. This statement has the following syntax:

```
do
    statement
while(Boolean expression);
```

Do-while consists of the do reserved word, followed by a *statement* to repeatedly execute, followed by the while reserved word, followed by a parenthesized *Boolean expression* header, followed by a semicolon.

The do-while statement first executes the other *statement*. It then evaluates the *Boolean expression*. If it is true, do-while executes the other *statement*. Once again, the *Boolean expression* is evaluated. If it is still true, do-while re-executes the *statement*. This cyclic pattern continues.

The following example demonstrates do-while prompting the user to enter a specific uppercase letter or its lowercase equivalent:

```
int ch;
do
{
    System.out.println("Press C or c to continue.");
    ch = System.in.read();
}
while (ch != 'C' && ch != 'c');
```

This example is similar to its predecessor. Because the compound statement is no longer executed prior to the test, it's no longer necessary to initialize ch – ch is assigned System.in.read()'s return value prior to the Boolean expression's evaluation.

Looping Over the Empty Statement

Java refers to a semicolon character appearing by itself as the *empty statement*. It's sometimes convenient for a loop statement to execute the empty statement repeatedly. The actual work performed by the loop statement takes place in the statement header. Consider the following example:

```
for (String line; (line = readLine()) != null; System.out.println(line));
```

This example uses for to present a programming idiom for copying lines of text that are read from some source, via the fictitious readLine() method in this example, to some destination, via System.out.println() in this example. Copying continues until readLine() returns null. Note the semicolon (empty statement) at the end of the line.

▪ **Caution** Be careful with the empty statement because it can introduce subtle bugs into your code. For example, the following loop is supposed to output the string Hello on ten lines. Instead, only one instance of this string is output, because it is the empty statement and not System.out.println() that's executed ten times:

```
for (int i = 0; i < 10; i++); // this ; represents the empty statement
   System.out.println("Hello");
```

Break and Labeled Break Statements

What do for(;;);, while(true); and do;while(true); have in common? Each of these loop statements presents an extreme example of an *infinite loop* (a loop that never ends). An infinite loop is something that you should avoid because its unending execution causes your application to hang, which is not desirable from the point of view of your application's users.

▪ **Caution** An infinite loop can also arise from a loop header's Boolean expression comparing a floating-point value against a nonzero value via the equality or inequality operator, because many floating-point values have inexact internal representations. For example, the following code fragment never ends because 0.1 does not have an exact internal representation:

```
for (double d = 0.0; d != 1.0; d += 0.1)
   System.out.println(d);
```

However, there are times when it is handy to code a loop as if it were infinite by using one of the aforementioned programming idioms. For example, you might code a while(true) loop that repeatedly prompts for a specific keystroke until the correct key is pressed. When the correct key is pressed, the loop must end. Java provides the break statement for this purpose.

The break statement transfers execution to the first statement following a switch statement (as discussed earlier) or a loop. In either scenario, this statement consists of reserved word break followed by a semicolon.

The following example uses break with an if decision statement to exit a while(true)-based infinite loop when the user presses the C or c key:

```java
int ch;
while (true)
{
   System.out.println("Press C or c to continue.");
   ch = System.in.read();
   if (ch == 'C' || ch == 'c')
      break;
}
```

The break statement is also useful in the context of a finite loop. For example, consider a scenario where an array of values is searched for a specific value, and you want to exit the loop when this value is found. The following example reveals this scenario:

```java
int[] employeeIDs = { 123, 854, 567, 912, 224 };
int employeeSearchID = 912;
boolean found = false;
for (int i = 0; i < employeeIDs.length; i++)
   if (employeeSearchID == employeeIDs[i])
   {
      found = true;
      break;
   }
System.out.println((found) ? "employee "+employeeSearchID+" exists"
                           : "no employee ID matches "+employeeSearchID);
```

The example uses for and if to search an array of employee IDs to determine whether a specific employee ID exists. If this ID is found, if's compound statement assigns true to found. Because there is no point in continuing the search, it then uses break to quit the loop.

The labeled break statement transfers execution to the first statement following the loop that's prefixed by a *label* (an identifier followed by a colon). It consists of reserved word break, followed by an identifier for which the matching label must exist. Furthermore, the label must immediately precede a loop statement.

Labeled break is useful for breaking out of *nested loops* (loops within loops). The following example reveals the labeled break statement transferring execution to the first statement that follows the outer for loop:

```
outer:
for (int i = 0; i < 3; i++)
   for (int j = 0; j < 3; j++)
      if (i == 1 && j == 1)
         break outer;
      else
         System.out.println("i="+i+", j="+j);
System.out.println("Both loops terminated.");
```

When i's value is 1 and j's value is 1, break outer; is executed to terminate both for loops. This statement transfers execution to the first statement after the outer for loop, which happens to be System.out.println("Both loops terminated.");.

The following output is generated:

```
i=0, j=0
i=0, j=1
i=0, j=2
i=1, j=0
Both loops terminated.
```

Continue and Labeled Continue Statements

The continue statement skips the remainder of the current loop iteration, re-evaluates the header's Boolean expression, and performs another iteration (if true) or terminates the loop (if false). Continue consists of reserved word continue followed by a semicolon.

Consider a while loop that reads lines from a source and processes nonblank lines in some manner. Because it should not process blank lines, while skips the current iteration when a blank line is detected, as demonstrated in the following example:

```
String line;
while ((line = readLine()) != null)
{
   if (isBlank(line))
      continue;
   processLine(line);
}
```

This example employs a fictitious isBlank() method to determine whether the currently read line is blank. If this method returns true, if executes the continue statement to skip the rest of the current iteration and read the next line whenever a blank line is detected. Otherwise, the fictitious processLine() method is called to process the line's contents.

Look carefully at this example and you should realize that the continue statement is not needed. Instead, this listing can be shortened via *refactoring* (rewriting source code to improve its readability, organization, or reusability), as demonstrated in the following example:

```
String line;
while ((line = readLine()) != null)
{
   if (!isBlank(line))
      processLine(line);
}
```

This example's refactoring modifies if's Boolean expression to use the logical complement operator (!). Whenever isBlank() returns false, this operator flips this value to true and if executes processLine(). Although continue isn't necessary in this example, you'll find it convenient to use this statement in more complex code where refactoring isn't as easy to perform.

The labeled continue statement skips the remaining iterations of one or more nested loops and transfers execution to the labeled loop. It consists of reserved word continue, followed by an identifier for which a matching label must exist. Furthermore, the label must immediately precede a loop statement.

Labeled continue is useful for breaking out of nested loops while still continuing to execute the labeled loop. The following example reveals the labeled continue statement terminating the inner for loop's iterations:

```
outer:
for (int i = 0; i < 3; i++)
   for (int j = 0; j < 3; j++)
      if (i == 1 && j == 1)
         continue outer;
      else
         System.out.println("i="+i+", j="+j);
System.out.println("Both loops terminated.");
```

When i's value is 1 and j's value is 1, continue outer; is executed to terminate the inner for loop and continue with the outer for loop at its next value of i. Both loops continue until they finish.

The following output is generated:

```
i=0, j=0
i=0, j=1
i=0, j=2
i=1, j=0
i=2, j=0
i=2, j=1
i=2, j=2
Both loops terminated.
```

EXERCISES

The following exercises are designed to test your understanding of applications and language fundamentals:

1. Declare an EchoArgs class whose main() method outputs its command-line arguments, one argument per line. Store this class in a file named EchoArgs.java. Compile this source code (javac EchoArgs.java) and run the application; for example, java EchoArgs A B C. You should see each of A, B, and C appearing on a separate line.

2. Declare a Circle class whose main() method declares a double precision floating-point variable named PI that's initialized to 3.14159, declares a double precision floating-point variable named radius that's initialized to 15, calculates and outputs the circle's circumference (PI times the diameter), and calculates and

outputs the circle's area (PI times the square of the radius). Compile and run this application.

3. Declare an `Input` class whose `main()` method is declared as follows: `public static void main(String[] args) throws java.io.IOException`—don't worry about `throws java.io.IOException`; you'll learn about this language feature in Chapter 3. Continuing, insert the "loop until C or c is input" example from the "Break and Labeled Break Statements" section into the `main()` method. Compile and run this application. When prompted, type a key and press the Enter/Return key. What happens when you type multiple keys (**abc**, for example) and press Enter/Return?

4. Declare a `Triangle` class whose `main()` method uses a pair of nested for statements along with `System.out.print()` to output a 10-row triangle of asterisks, where each row contains an odd number of asterisks (1, 3, 5, 7, and so on), as follows:

```
         *
        ***
       *****
      *******
     *********
    ***********
   *************
  ***************
 *****************
*******************
```

Compile and run this application.

5. Declare an `OutputReversedInt` class whose `main()` method declares an `int` variable named x that's assigned a positive integer. This declaration is followed by a while loop that outputs this integer's digits in reverse. For example, `876432094` outputs as `490234678`.

Summary

Java is a language for describing programs. This general-purpose, class-based, and object-oriented language is patterned after C and C++ to make it easier for existing C/C++ developers to migrate to Java.

Java is also a platform on which to run programs written in Java and other languages (e.g., Groovy, Jython, and JRuby). Unlike platforms with physical processors (e.g., an Intel processor) and operating systems (e.g., Windows 7), the Java platform consists of a virtual machine and execution environment.

Before you can develop Java programs, you need to determine what kind(s) of programs you want to develop and then install the appropriate software. Use the JDK to develop standalone applications and applets, the Java ME SDK to develop MIDlets and Xlets, and the Java EE SDK to develop servlets and JSPs.

For small projects, it's no big deal to work at the command line with JDK tools. Because you'll probably find this scenario tedious (and even unworkable) for larger projects, you should also consider obtaining an IDE such as NetBeans 7, which includes support for those language features introduced by JDK 7.

Most computer languages support comments, identifiers, types, variables, expressions, and statements. Comments let you document your source code; identifiers name things (e.g., classes and methods); types identify sets of values (and their representations in memory) and sets of operations that transform these values into other values of that set; variables store values; expressions combine variables, method calls, literals, and operators; and statements are the workhorses of a program, and include assignment, decision, loop, break and labeled break, and continue and labeled continue.

Now that you possess a basic understanding of Java's fundamental language features, you're ready to learn about Java's language support for classes and objects. Chapter 2 introduces you to this support.

CHAPTER 2

Discovering Classes and Objects

Chapter 1 gently introduced you to the Java language by focusing mainly on fundamental language features ranging from comments to statements. Using only these features, you can create simple applications (such as HelloWorld and the applications mentioned in the chapter's exercises) that are reminiscent of those written in structured programming languages such as C.

Note *Structured programming* is a programming paradigm that enforces a logical structure on programs through *data structures* (named aggregates of data items), *functions* (named blocks of code that return values to the code that calls [passes program execution to] them), and *procedures* (named blocks of code that don't return values to their callers). Structured programs use sequence (one statement follows another statement), selection/choice (if/switch), and repetition/iteration (for/while/do) programming constructs; use of the potentially harmful GOTO statement (see http://en.wikipedia.org/wiki/GOTO) is discouraged.

Structured programs separate data from behaviors. This separation makes it difficult to model real-world entities (such as a bank accounts and employees) and often leads to maintenance headaches when programs become complex. In contrast, classes and objects combine data and behaviors into program entities; programs based on classes and objects are typically easier to understand and maintain.

Chapter 2 takes you deeper into the Java language by focusing on its support for classes and objects. You first learn how to declare classes and create objects from these classes, and then learn how to encapsulate state and behaviors into these program entities through fields and methods. After learning about class and object initialization, you move beyond this *object-based programming* model and dive into *object-oriented programming*, by exploring Java's inheritance- and polymorphism-oriented language features.

At this point, the chapter presents one of Java's more confusing language features: interfaces. You learn what interfaces are, how they relate to classes, and what makes them so useful.

Java programs create objects that occupy memory. To reduce the possibility of running out of memory, the Java Virtual Machine (JVM)'s garbage collector occasionally performs garbage collection by locating objects that are no longer being used and removing this garbage to free up memory. Chapter 2 concludes by introducing you to the garbage collection process.

Declaring Classes and Creating Objects

Structured programs create data structures that organize and store data items, and manipulate the data stored in these data structures via functions and procedures. The fundamental units of a structured program are its data structures and the functions or procedures that manipulate them. Although Java lets you create applications in a similar fashion, this language is really about declaring classes and creating objects from these classes. These program entities are the fundamental units of a Java program.

This section first shows you how to declare a class, and then shows you how to create objects from this class with the help of the new operator and a constructor. The section then shows you how to specify constructor parameters and local variables. Finally, you learn how to create arrays using the same new operator that's used to create an object from a class.

Declaring Classes

A *class* is a template for manufacturing *objects* (named aggregates of code and data), which are also known as *class instances*, or *instances* for short. Classes generalize real-world entities, and objects are specific manifestations of these entities at the program level. You might think of classes as cookie cutters and objects as the cookies that cookie cutters create.

Because you cannot instantiate objects from a class that does not exist, you must first declare the class. The declaration consists of a header followed by a body. At minimum, the header consists of reserved word class followed by a name that identifies the class (so that it can be referred to from elsewhere in the source code). The body starts with an open brace character ({) and ends with a close brace (}). Sandwiched between these delimiters are various kinds of declarations. Consider Listing 2-1.

Listing 2-1. Declaring a skeletal Image class

```
class Image
{
   // various member declarations
}
```

Listing 2-1 declares a class named Image, which presumably describes some kind of image for displaying on the screen. By convention, a class's name begins with an uppercase letter. Furthermore, the first letter of each subsequent word in a multiword class name is capitalized. This is known as *camelcasing*.

Creating Objects with the new Operator and a Constructor

Image is an example of a user-defined type from which objects can be created. You create these objects by using the new operator with a constructor, as follows:

```
Image image = new Image();
```

The new operator allocates memory to store the object whose type is specified by new's solitary operand, which happens to be Image() in this example. The object is stored in a region of memory known as the *heap*.

The parentheses (round brackets) that follow Image signify a *constructor*, which is a block of code for constructing an object by initializing it in some manner. The new operator *invokes* (calls) the constructor immediately after allocating memory to store the object.

When the constructor ends, new returns a *reference* (a memory address or other identifier) to the object so that it can be accessed elsewhere in the program. Regarding the newly created Image object, its reference is stored in a variable named image whose type is specified as Image. (It's common to refer to the variable as an object, as in the image object, although it stores only an object's reference and not the object itself.)

■ **Note** new's returned reference is represented in source code by keyword this. Wherever this appears, it represents the current object. Also, variables that store references are called *reference variables*.

Image does not explicitly declare a constructor. When a class does not declare a constructor, Java implicitly creates a constructor for that class. The created constructor is known as the *default noargument constructor* because no arguments (discussed shortly) appear between its (and) characters when the constructor is invoked.

■ **Note** Java does not create a default noargument constructor when at least one constructor is declared.

Specifying Constructor Parameters and Local Variables

You explicitly declare a constructor within a class's body by specifying the name of the class followed by a *parameter list*, which is a round bracket-delimited and comma-separated list of zero or more parameter declarations. A *parameter* is a constructor or method variable that receives an expression value passed to the constructor or method when it is called. This expression value is known as an *argument*.

Listing 2-2 enhances Listing 2-1's Image class by declaring three constructors with parameter lists that declare zero, one, or two parameters; and a main() method for testing this class.

Listing 2-2. Declaring an Image class with three constructors and a main() method

```
class Image
{
   Image()
   {
      System.out.println("Image() called");
   }
   Image(String filename)
   {
      this(filename, null);
      System.out.println("Image(String filename) called");
   }
   Image(String filename, String imageType)
   {
      System.out.println("Image(String filename, String imageType) called");
      if (filename != null)
      {
         System.out.println("reading "+filename);
```

```
            if (imageType != null)
                System.out.println("interpreting "+filename+" as storing a "+
                                        imageType+" image");
        }
        // Perform other initialization here.
    }
    public static void main(String[] args)
    {
        Image image = new Image();
        System.out.println();
        image = new Image("image.png");
        System.out.println();
        image = new Image("image.png", "PNG");
    }
}
```

Listing 2-2's Image class first declares a noargument constructor for initializing an Image object to default values (whatever they may be). This constructor simulates default initialization by invoking System.out.println() to output a message signifying that it's been called.

Image next declares an Image(String filename) constructor whose parameter list consists of a single parameter declaration—a parameter declaration consists of a variable's type followed by the variable's name. The java.lang.String parameter is named filename, signifying that this constructor obtains image content from a file.

Note Throughout this book's chapters, I typically prefix the first use of a predefined type (such as String) with the package hierarchy in which the type is stored. For example, String is stored in the lang subpackage of the java package. I do so to help you learn where types are stored so that you can more easily specify import statements for importing these types (without having to first search for a type's package) into your source code—you don't have to import types that are stored in the java.lang package, but I still prefix the java.lang package to the type name for completeness. I will have more to say about packages and the import statement in Chapter 3.

Some constructors rely on other constructors to help them initialize their objects. This is done to avoid redundant code, which increases the size of an object, and unnecessarily takes memory away from the heap that could be used for other purposes. For example, Image(String filename) relies on Image(String filename, String imageType) to read the file's image content into memory.

Although it appears otherwise, constructors don't have names (although it is common to refer to a constructor by specifying the class name and parameter list). A constructor calls another constructor by using keyword this and a round bracket-delimited and comma-separated list of arguments. For example, Image(String filename) executes this(filename, null); to execute Image(String filename, String imageType).

Caution You must use this to call another constructor—you cannot use the class's name, as in Image(). The this() constructor call (if present) must be the first code that is executed within the constructor. This rule prevents you from specifying multiple this() constructor calls in the same constructor. Finally, you cannot specify this() in a method—constructors can be called only by other constructors and during object creation. (I will discuss methods later in this chapter.)

When present, the constructor call must be the first code that is specified within a constructor; otherwise, the compiler reports an error. For this reason, a constructor that calls another constructor can only perform additional work after the other constructor has finished. For example, Image(String filename) executes System.out.println("Image(String filename) called"); after the invoked Image(String filename, String imageType) constructor finishes.

The Image(String filename, String imageType) constructor declares an imageType parameter that signifies the kind of image stored in the file—a Portable Network Graphics (PNG) image, for example. Presumably, the constructor uses imageType to speed up processing by not examining the file's contents to learn the image format. When null is passed to imageType, as happens with the Image(String filename) constructor, Image(String filename, String imageType) examines file contents to learn the format. If null was also passed to filename, Image(String filename, String imageType) wouldn't read the file, but would presumably notify the code attempting to create the Image object of an error condition.

After declaring the constructors, Listing 2-2 declares a main() method that lets you create Image objects and view output messages. main() creates three Image objects, calling the first constructor with no arguments, the second constructor with argument "image.png", and the third constructor with arguments "image.png" and "PNG".

Note The number of arguments passed to a constructor or method, or the number of operator operands is known as the constructor's, method's, or operator's *arity*.

Each object's reference is assigned to a reference variable named image, replacing the previously stored reference for the second and third object assignments. (Each occurrence of System.out.println(); outputs a blank line to make the output easier to read.)

The presence of main() changes Image from only a class to an application. You typically place main() in classes that are used to create objects in order to test such classes. When constructing an application for use by others, you usually declare main() in a class where the intent is to run an application and not to create an object from that class—the application is then run from only that class. See Chapter 1's HelloWorld class for an example.

After saving Listing 2-2 to Image.java, compile this file by executing javac Image.java at the command line. Assuming that there are no error messages, execute the application by specifying java Image. You should observe the following output:

```
Image() called

Image(String filename, String imageType) called
```

```
reading image.png
Image(String filename) called

Image(String filename, String imageType) called
reading image.png
interpreting image.png as storing a PNG image
```

The first output line indicates that the noargument constructor has been called. Subsequent output lines indicate that the second and third constructors have been called.

In addition to declaring parameters, a constructor can declare variables within its body to help it perform various tasks. For example, the previously presented Image(String filename, String imageType) constructor might create an object from a (hypothetical) File class that provides the means to read a file's contents. At some point, the constructor instantiates this class and assigns the instance's reference to a variable, as demonstrated in the following:

```
Image(String filename, String imageType)
{
    System.out.println("Image(String filename, String imageType) called");
    if (filename != null)
    {
        System.out.println("reading "+filename);
        File file = new File(filename);
        // Read file contents into object.
        if (imageType != null)
            System.out.println("interpreting "+filename+" as storing a "+
                               imageType+" image");
        else
            // Inspect image contents to learn image type.
            ; // Empty statement is used to make if-else syntactically valid.
    }
    // Perform other initialization here.
}
```

As with the filename and imageType parameters, file is a variable that is local to the constructor, and is known as a *local variable* to distinguish it from a parameter. Although all three variables are local to the constructor, there are two key differences between parameters and local variables:

- The filename and imageType parameters come into existence at the point where the constructor begins to execute and exist until execution leaves the constructor. In contrast, file comes into existence at its point of declaration and continues to exist until the block in which it is declared is terminated (via a closing brace character). This property of a parameter or a local variable is known as *lifetime*.

- The filename and imageType parameters can be accessed from anywhere in the constructor. In contrast, file can be accessed only from its point of declaration to the end of the block in which it is declared. It cannot be accessed before its declaration or after its declaring block, but nested subblocks can access the local variable. This property of a parameter or a local variable is known as *scope*.

■ **Note** The lifetime and scope (also known as visibility) properties also apply to classes, objects, and fields (discussed later). Classes come into existence when loaded into memory and cease to exist when unloaded from memory, typically when an application exits. Also, loaded classes are typically visible to other classes, but this isn't always the case—Appendix C will have more to say about this issue when it presents classloaders.

An object's lifetime ranges from its creation via the new operator until the moment when it is removed from memory by the garbage collector. Its scope depends on various factors, such as when its reference is assigned to a local variable or to a field. I discuss fields later in this chapter.

The lifetime of a field depends upon whether it is an instance field or a class field. If the field belongs to an object, it comes into existence when the object is created and dies when the object disappears from memory. If the field belongs to a class, the field begins its existence when the class is loaded and disappears when the class is removed from memory. As with an object, a field's scope depends upon various factors, such as whether the field is declared to have private access or not—you'll learn about private access later in this chapter.

A local variable cannot have the same name as a parameter because a parameter always has the same scope as the local variable. However, a local variable can have the same name as another local variable provided that both variables are located within different scopes (that is, within different blocks). For example, you could specify int x = 1; within an if-else statement's if block and specify double x = 2.0; within the statement's corresponding else block, and each local variable would be distinct.

■ **Note** The discussion of constructor parameters, arguments, and local variables also applies to method parameters, arguments, and local variables—I discuss methods later in this chapter.

Creating Arrays with the new Operator

The new operator is also used to create an array of objects in the heap, and is an alternative to the array initializer presented in Chapter 1.

■ **Note** An array is implemented as a special Java object whose read-only length field contains the array's size (the number of elements). You'll learn about fields later in this chapter.

When creating the array, specify new followed by a name that identifies the type of values that are stored in the array, followed by one or more pairs of square brackets that signify the number of dimensions occupied by the array. The leftmost pair of square brackets must contain an integral expression that specifies the size of the array (the number of elements), whereas remaining pairs contain integral expressions or are empty.

For example, you can use new to create a one-dimensional array of object references, as demonstrated by the following example, which creates a one-dimensional array that can store ten Image object references:

```
Image[] imArray = new Image[10];
```

When you create a one-dimensional array, new zeros the bits in each array element's storage location, which you interpret at the source code level as literal value false, '\u0000', 0, 0L, 0.0, 0.0F, or null (depending on element type). In the previous example, each of imArray's elements is initialized to null, which represents the *null reference* (a reference to no object).

After creating an array, you need to assign object references to its elements. The following example demonstrates this task by creating Image objects and assigning their references to imArray elements:

```
for (int i = 0; i < imArray.length; i++)
   imArray[i] = new Image("image"+i+".png"); // image0.png, image1.png, and so on
```

The "image"+i+".png" expression uses the string concatenation operator (+) to combine image with the string equivalent of the integer value stored in variable i with .png. The resulting string is passed to Image's Image(String filename) constructor.

Caution Use of the string concatenation operator in a loop context can result in a lot of unnecessary String object creation, depending on the length of the loop. I will discuss this topic in Chapter 4 when I introduce you to the String class.

You can also use new to create arrays of primitive type values (such as integers or double precision floating-point numbers). For example, suppose you want to create a two-dimensional three-row-by-two-column array of double precision floating-point temperature values. The following example accomplishes this task:

```
double[][] temperatures = new double[3][2];
```

After creating a two-dimensional array, you will want to populate its elements with suitable values. The following example initializes each temperatures element, which is accessed as temperatures[row][col], to a randomly generated temperature value via Math.random(), which I'll explain in Chapter 4:

```
for (int row = 0; row < temperatures.length; row++)
   for (int col = 0; col < temperatures[row].length; col++)
     temperatures[row][col] = Math.random()*100;
```

You can subsequently output these values in a tabular format by using a for loop, as demonstrated by the following example—the code makes no attempt to align the temperature values in perfect columns:

```
for (int row = 0; row < temperatures.length; row++)
```

```
{
   for (int col = 0; col < temperatures[row].length; col++)
      System.out.print(temperatures[row][col]+" ");
   System.out.println();
}
```

Java provides an alternative for creating a multidimensional array in which you create each dimension separately. For example, to create a two-dimensional array via new in this manner, first create a one-dimensional row array (the outer array), and then create a one-dimensional column array (the inner array), as demonstrated here:

```
// Create the row array.
double[][] temperatures = new double[3][]; // Note the extra empty pair of brackets.
// Create a column array for each row.
for (int row = 0; row < temperatures.length; row++)
   temperatures[row] = new double[2]; // 2 columns per row
```

This kind of an array is known as a *ragged array* because each row can have a different number of columns; the array is not rectangular, but is ragged.

Note When creating the row array, you must specify an extra pair of empty brackets as part of the expression following new. (For a three-dimensional array—a one-dimensional array of tables, where this array's elements reference row arrays—you must specify two pairs of empty brackets as part of the expression following new.)

You can combine new with Chapter 1's array initialization syntax if desired. For example, Image[] imArray = new Image[] { new Image("image0.png"), new Image("image1.png") }; creates a pair of Image objects and a two-element Image array object initialized to the Image objects' references, and assigns the array's reference to imArray.

When you create an array in this manner, you are not permitted to specify an integral expression between the square brackets. For example, the compiler reports an error when it encounters Image[] imArray = new Image[2] { new Image("image0.png"), new Image("image1.png") };. To correct this error, remove the 2 from between the square brackets.

Encapsulating State and Behaviors

Classes model real-world entities from a template perspective; for example, car and savings account. Objects represent specific entities; for example, John's red Toyota Camry (a car instance) and Cuifen's savings account with a balance of twenty thousand dollars (a savings account instance).

Entities have *attributes*, such as color red, make Toyota, model Camry, and balance twenty thousand dollars. An entity's collection of attributes is referred to as its *state*. Entities also have *behaviors*, such as open car door, drive car, display fuel consumption, deposit, withdraw, and show account balance.

A class and its objects model an entity by combining state with behaviors into a single unit—the class abstracts state whereas its objects provide concrete state values. This bringing together of state and behaviors is known as *encapsulation*. Unlike structured programming, where the developer focuses on modeling behaviors through structured code, and modeling state through data structures that store data items for the structured code to manipulate, the developer working with classes and objects focuses on templating entities by declaring classes that encapsulate state and behaviors, instantiating objects with specific state values from these classes to represent specific entities, and interacting with objects through their behaviors.

This section first introduces you to Java's language features for representing state, and then introduces you to its language features for representing behaviors. Because some state and behaviors support the class's internal architecture, and should not be visible to those wanting to use the class, this section concludes by presenting the important concept of information hiding.

Representing State via Fields

Java lets you represent state via *fields,* which are variables declared within a class's body. Entity attributes are described via *instance fields.* Because Java also supports state that's associated with a class and not with an object, Java provides *class fields* to describe this class state.

You first learn how to declare and access instance fields and then learn how to declare and access class fields. After discovering how to declare read-only instance and class fields, you review the rules for accessing fields from different contexts.

Declaring and Accessing Instance Fields

You can declare an instance field by minimally specifying a type name, followed by an identifier that names the field, followed by a semicolon character (;). Listing 2-3 presents a Car class with three instance field declarations.

Listing 2-3. Declaring a Car class with make, model, and numDoors instance fields

```
class Car
{
   String make;
   String model;
   int numDoors;
}
```

Listing 2-3 declares two String instance fields named make and model. It also declares an int instance field named numDoors. By convention, a field's name begins with a lowercase letter, and the first letter of each subsequent word in a multiword field name is capitalized.

When an object is created, instance fields are initialized to default zero values, which you interpret at the source code level as literal value false, '\u0000', 0, 0L, 0.0, or 0.0F, or null (depending on element type). For example, if you were to execute Car car = new Car();, make and model would be initialized to null and numDoors would be initialized to 0.

You can assign values to or read values from an object's instance fields by using the member access operator (.); the left operand specifies the object's reference and the right operand specifies the instance field to be accessed. Listing 2-4 uses this operator to initialize a Car object's make, model, and numDoors instance fields.

Listing 2-4. Initializing a Car object's instance fields

```
class Car
{
   String make;
   String model;
```

```
   int numDoors;
   public static void main(String[] args)
   {
      Car car = new Car();
      car.make = "Toyota";
      car.model = "Camry";
      car.numDoors = 4;
   }
}
```

Listing 2-4 presents a main() method that instantiates Car. The car instance's make instance field is assigned the "Toyota" string, its model instance field is assigned the "Camry" string, and its numDoors instance field is assigned integer literal 4. (A string's double quotes delimit a string's sequence of characters but are not part of the string.)

You can explicitly initialize an instance field when declaring that field to provide a nonzero default value, which overrides the default zero value. Listing 2-5 demonstrates this point.

Listing 2-5. Initializing Car's numDoors instance field to a default nonzero value

```
class Car
{
   String make;
   String model;
   int numDoors = 4;
   Car()
   {
   }
   public static void main(String[] args)
   {
      Car johnDoeCar = new Car();
      johnDoeCar.make = "Chevrolet";
      johnDoeCar.model = "Volt";
   }
}
```

Listing 2-5 explicitly initializes numDoors to 4 because the developer has assumed that most cars being modeled by this class have four doors. When Car is initialized via the Car() constructor, the developer only needs to initialize the make and model instance fields for those cars that have four doors.

It is usually not a good idea to directly initialize an object's instance fields, and you will learn why when I discuss information hiding (later in this chapter). Instead, you should perform this initialization in the class's constructor(s)—see Listing 2-6.

Listing 2-6. Initializing Car's instance fields via constructors

```
class Car
{
   String make;
   String model;
   int numDoors;
   Car(String make, String model)
   {
      this(make, model, 4);
```

```
   }
   Car(String make, String model, int nDoors)
   {
      this.make = make;
      this.model = model;
      numDoors = nDoors;
   }
   public static void main(String[] args)
   {
      Car myCar = new Car("Toyota", "Camry");
      Car yourCar = new Car("Mazda", "RX-8", 2);
   }
}
```

Listing 2-6's Car class declares Car(String make, String model) and Car(String make, String model, int nDoors) constructors. The first constructor lets you specify the make and model, whereas the second constructor lets you specify values for the three instance fields.

The first constructor executes this(make, model, 4); to pass the values of its make and model parameters, along with a default value of 4 to the second constructor. Doing so demonstrates an alternative to explicitly initializing an instance field, and is preferable from a code maintenance perspective.

The Car(String make, String model, int numDoors) constructor demonstrates another use for keyword this. Specifically, it demonstrates a scenario where constructor parameters have the same names as the class's instance fields. Prefixing a variable name with "this." causes the Java compiler to create bytecode that accesses the instance field. For example, this.make = make; assigns the make parameter's String object reference to this (the current) Car object's make instance field. If make = make; was specified instead, it would accomplish nothing by assigning make's value to itself; a Java compiler might not generate code to perform the unnecessary assignment. In contrast, "this." isn't necessary for the numDoors = nDoors; assignment, which initializes the numDoors field from the nDoors parameter value.

Declaring and Accessing Class Fields

In many situations, instance fields are all that you need. However, you might encounter a situation where you need a single copy of a field no matter how many objects are created.

For example, suppose you want to track the number of Car objects that have been created, and introduce a counter instance field (initialized to 0) into this class. You also place code in the class's constructor that increases counter's value by 1 when an object is created. However, because each object has its own copy of the counter instance field, this field's value never advances past 1. Listing 2-7 solves this problem by declaring counter to be a class field, by prefixing the field declaration with the static keyword.

Listing 2-7. Adding a counter class field to Car

```
class Car
{
   String make;
   String model;
   int numDoors;
   static int counter;
```

```
Car(String make, String model)
{
    this(make, model, 4);
}
Car(String make, String model, int numDoors)
{
    this.make = make;
    this.model = model;
    this.numDoors = numDoors;
    counter++;
}
public static void main(String[] args)
{
    Car myCar = new Car("Toyota", "Camry");
    Car yourCar = new Car("Mazda", "RX-8", 2);
    System.out.println(Car.counter);
}
}
```

Listing 2-7's static prefix implies that there is only one copy of the counter field, not one copy per object. When a class is loaded into memory, class fields are initialized to default zero values. For example, counter is initialized to 0. (As with instance fields, you can alternatively assign a value to a class field in its declaration.) Each time an object is created, counter will increase by 1 thanks to the counter++ expression in the Car(String make, String model, int numDoors) constructor.

Unlike instance fields, class fields are normally accessed directly via the member access operator. Although you could access a class field via an object reference (as in myCar.counter), it is conventional to access a class field by using the class's name, as in Car.counter. (It is also easier to tell that the code is accessing a class field.)

Note Because the main() method is a member of Listing 2-7's Car class, you could access counter directly, as in System.out.println(counter);. To access counter in the context of another class's main() method, however, you would have to specify Car.counter.

If you run Listing 2-7, you will notice that it outputs 2, because two Car objects have been created.

Declaring Read-Only Instance and Class Fields

The previously declared fields can be written to as well as read from. However, you might want to declare a field that is read-only; for example, a field that names a constant value such as pi (3.14159...). Java lets you accomplish this task by providing reserved word final.

Each object receives its own copy of a read-only instance field. This field must be initialized, as part of the field's declaration or in the class's constructor. If initialized in the constructor, the read-only instance field is known as a *blank final* because it does not have a value until one is assigned to it in the constructor. Because a constructor can potentially assign a different value to each object's blank final, these read-only variables are not truly constants.

If you want a true *constant*, which is a single read-only value that is available to all objects, you need to create a read-only class field. You can accomplish this task by including the reserved word static with final in that field's declaration.

Listing 2-8 shows you how to declare a read-only class field.

Listing 2-8. Declaring a true constant in the Employee class

```
class Employee
{
    final static int RETIREMENT_AGE = 65;
}
```

Listing 2-8's RETIREMENT_AGE declaration is an example of a *compile-time constant*. Because there is only one copy of its value (thanks to the static keyword), and because this value will never change (thanks to the final keyword), the compiler is free to optimize the compiled code by inserting the constant value into all calculations where it is used. The code runs faster because it doesn't have to access a read-only class field.

Reviewing Field-Access Rules

The previous examples of field access may seem confusing because you can sometimes specify the field's name directly, whereas you need to prefix a field name with an object reference or a class name and the member access operator at other times. The following rules dispel this confusion by giving you guidance on how to access fields from the various contexts:

- Specify the name of a class field as is from anywhere within the same class as the class field declaration. Example: counter

- Specify the name of a class field's class, followed by the member access operator, followed by the name of the class field from outside the class. Example: Car.counter

- Specify the name of an instance field as is from any instance method, constructor, or instance initializer (discussed later) in the same class as the instance field declaration. Example: numDoors

- Specify an object reference, followed by the member access operator, followed by the name of the instance field from any class method or class initializer (discussed later) within the same class as the instance field declaration, or from outside the class. Example: Car car = new Car(); car.numDoors = 2;

Although the latter rule might seem to imply that you can access an instance field from a class context, this is not the case. Instead, you are accessing the field from an object context.

The previous access rules are not exhaustive because there exist two more field-access scenarios to consider: declaring a local variable (or even a parameter) with the same name as an instance field or as a class field. In either scenario, the local variable/parameter is said to *shadow* (hide or mask) the field.

If you find that you have declared a local variable or a parameter that shadows a field, you can rename the local variable/parameter, or you can use the member access operator with reserved word this (instance field) or class name (class field) to explicitly identify the field. For example, Listing 2-6's Car(String make, String model, int nDoors) constructor demonstrated this latter solution by specifying statements such as this.make = make; to distinguish an instance field from a same-named parameter.

Representing Behaviors via Methods

Java lets you represent behaviors via *methods*, which are named blocks of code declared within a class's body. Entity behaviors are described via *instance methods*. Because Java also supports behaviors that are associated with a class and not with an object, Java provides *class methods* to describe these class behaviors.

You first learn how to declare and invoke instance methods, and then learn how to create instance method call chains. Next, you discover how to declare and invoke class methods, encounter additional details about passing arguments to methods, and explore Java's return statement. After learning how to invoke methods recursively as an alternative to iteration, and how to overload methods, you review the rules for invoking methods from different contexts.

Declaring and Invoking Instance Methods

You can declare an instance method by minimally specifying a return type name, followed by an identifier that names the method, followed by a parameter list, followed by a brace-delimited body. Listing 2-9 presents a Car class with a printDetails() instance method.

Listing 2-9. Declaring a printDetails() instance method in the Car class

```
class Car
{
    String make;
    String model;
    int numDoors;
    Car(String make, String model)
    {
        this(make, model, 4);
    }
    Car(String make, String model, int numDoors)
    {
        this.make = make;
        this.model = model;
        this.numDoors = numDoors;
    }
    void printDetails()
    {
        System.out.println("Make = "+make);
        System.out.println("Model = "+model);
        System.out.println("Number of doors = "+numDoors);
        System.out.println();
    }
    public static void main(String[] args)
    {
        Car myCar = new Car("Toyota", "Camry");
        myCar.printDetails();
        Car yourCar = new Car("Mazda", "RX-8", 2);
        yourCar.printDetails();
    }
}
```

Listing 2-9 declares an instance method named printDetails(). By convention, a method's name begins with a lowercase letter, and the first letter of each subsequent word in a multiword method name is capitalized.

Methods are like constructors in that they have parameter lists. You pass arguments to these parameters when you call the method. Because printDetails() does not take arguments, its parameter list is empty.

■ **Note** A method's name and the number, types, and order of its parameters are known as its *signature*.

When a method is invoked, the code within its body is executed. In the case of printDetails(), this method's body executes a sequence of System.out.println() method calls to output the values of its make, model, and numDoors instance fields.

Unlike constructors, methods are declared to have return types. A return type identifies the kind of values returned by the method (e.g., int count() returns 32-bit integers). If a method does not return a value (and printDetails() does not), its return type is replaced with keyword void, as in void printDetails().

■ **Note** Constructors don't have return types because they cannot return values. If a constructor could return an arbitrary value, how would that value be returned? After all, the new operator returns a reference to an object, and how could new also return a constructor value?

A method is invoked by using the member access operator; the left operand specifies the object's reference and the right operand specifies the method to be called. For example, the myCar.printDetails() and yourCar.printDetails() expressions invoke the printDetails() instance method on the myCar and yourCar objects.

Compile Listing 2-9 (javac Car.java) and run this application (java Car). You should observe the following output, whose different instance field values prove that printDetails() associates with an object:

```
Make = Toyota
Model = Camry
Number of doors = 4

Make = Mazda
Model = RX-8
Number of doors = 2
```

When an instance method is invoked, Java passes a hidden argument to the method (as the leftmost argument in a list of arguments). This argument is the reference to the object on which the method is invoked, and is represented at the source code level via reserved word this. You don't need to prefix an instance field name with "this." from within the method whenever you attempt to access an instance field name that isn't also the name of a parameter because "this." is assumed in this situation.

METHOD-CALL STACK

Method invocations require a *method-call stack* (also known as a *method-invocation stack*) to keep track of the statements to which execution must return. Think of the method-call stack as a simulation of a pile of clean trays in a cafeteria—you *pop* (remove) the clean tray from the top of the pile and the dishwasher will *push* (insert) the next clean tray onto the top of the pile.

When a method is invoked, the JVM pushes its arguments and the address of the first statement to execute following the invoked method onto the method-call stack. The JVM also allocates stack space for the method's local variables. When the method returns, the JVM removes local variable space, pops the address and arguments off the stack, and transfers execution to the statement at this address.

Chaining Together Instance Method Calls

Two or more instance method calls can be chained together via the member access operator, which results in more compact code. To accomplish instance method call chaining, you need to re-architect your instance methods somewhat differently, as Listing 2-10 reveals.

Listing 2-10. Implementing instance methods so that calls to these methods can be chained together

```java
class SavingsAccount
{
    int balance;
    SavingsAccount deposit(int amount)
    {
        balance += amount;
        return this;
    }
    SavingsAccount printBalance()
    {
        System.out.println(balance);
        return this;
    }
    public static void main(String[] args)
    {
        new SavingsAccount().deposit(1000).printBalance();
    }
}
```

Listing 2-10 shows that you must specify the class's name as the instance method's return type. Each of deposit() and printBalance() must specify SavingsAccount as the return type. Also, you must specify return this; (return current object's reference) as the last statement—I discuss the return statement later.

For example, new SavingsAccount().deposit(1000).printBalance(); creates a SavingsAccount object, uses the returned SavingsAccount reference to invoke SavingsAccount's deposit() instance method, to add one thousand dollars to the savings account (I'm ignoring cents for convenience), and finally uses deposit()'s returned SavingsAccount reference (which is the same SavingsAccount instance) to invoke SavingsAccount's printBalance() instance method to output the account balance.

Declaring and Invoking Class Methods

In many situations, instance methods are all that you need. However, you might encounter a situation where you need to describe a behavior that is independent of any object.

For example, suppose you would like to introduce a *utility class* (a class consisting of static [class] methods) whose methods perform various kinds of conversions (such as converting from degrees Celsius to degrees Fahrenheit). You don't want to create an object from this class in order to perform a conversion. Instead, you simply want to call a method and obtain its result. Listing 2-11 addresses this requirement by presenting a Conversions class with a pair of class methods. These methods can be called without having to create a Conversions object.

Listing 2-11. A Conversions utility class with a pair of class methods

```
class Conversions
{
   static double c2f(double degrees)
   {
      return degrees*9.0/5.0+32;
   }
   static double f2c(double degrees)
   {
      return (degrees-32)*5.0/9.0;
   }
}
```

Listing 2-11's Conversions class declares c2f() and f2c() methods for converting from degrees Celsius to degrees Fahrenheit and vice versa, and returning the results of these conversions. Each *method header* (method signature and other information) is prefixed with keyword static to turn the method into a class method.

To execute a class method, you typically prefix its name with the class name. For example, you can execute Conversions.c2f(100.0); to find out the Fahrenheit equivalent of 100 degrees Celsius, and Conversions.f2c(98.6); to discover the Celsius equivalent of the normal body temperature. You don't need to instantiate Conversions and then call these methods via that instance, although you could do so (but that isn't good form).

■ **Note** Every application has at least one class method. Specifically, an application must specify public static void main(String[] args) to serve as the application's entry point. The static reserved word makes this method a class method. (I will explain reserved word public later in this chapter.)

Because class methods are not called with a hidden argument that refers to the current object, c2f(), f2c(), and main() cannot access an object's instance fields or call its instance methods. These class methods can only access class fields and call class methods.

Passing Arguments to Methods

A method call includes a list of (zero or more) arguments being passed to the method. Java passes arguments to methods via a style of argument passing called *pass-by-value*, which the following example demonstrates:

```
Employee emp = new Employee("John ");
int recommendedAnnualSalaryIncrease = 1000;
printReport(emp, recommendAnnualSalaryIncrease);
printReport(new Employee("Cuifen"), 1500);
```

Pass-by-value passes the value of a variable (the reference value stored in emp or the 1000 value stored in recommendedAnnualSalaryIncrease, for example) or the value of some other expression (such as new Employee("Cuifen") or 1500) to the method.

Because of pass-by-value, you cannot assign a different Employee object's reference to emp from inside printReport() via the printReport() parameter for this argument. After all, you have only passed a copy of emp's value to the method.

Many methods (and constructors) require you to pass a fixed number of arguments when they are called. However, Java also can pass a variable number of arguments—such methods/constructors are often referred to as *varargs methods/constructors*. To declare a method (or constructor) that takes a variable number of arguments, specify three consecutive periods after the type name of the method's/constructor's rightmost parameter. The following example presents a sum() method that accepts a variable number of arguments:

```
double sum(double... values)
{
   int total = 0;
   for (int i = 0; i < values.length; i++)
      total += values[i];
   return total;
}
```

sum()'s implementation totals the number of arguments passed to this method; for example, sum(10.0, 20.0) or sum(30.0, 40.0, 50.0). (Behind the scenes, these arguments are stored in a one-dimensional array, as evidenced by values.length and values[i].) After these values have been totaled, this total is returned via the return statement.

Returning from a Method via the Return Statement

The execution of statements within a method that does not return a value (its return type is set to void) flows from the first statement to the last statement. However, Java's return statement lets a method (or a constructor) exit before reaching the last statement. As Listing 2-12 shows, this form of the return statement consists of reserved word return followed by a semicolon.

Listing 2-12. Using the return statement to return prematurely from a method

```
class Employee
{
    String name;
    Employee(String name)
    {
        setName(name);
    }
    void setName(String name)
    {
        if (name == null)
        {
            System.out.println("name cannot be null");
            return;
        }
        else
            this.name = name;
    }
    public static void main(String[] args)
    {
        Employee john = new Employee(null);
    }
}
```

Listing 2-12's `Employee(String name)` constructor invokes the `setName()` instance method to initialize the name instance field. Providing a separate method for this purpose is a good idea because it lets you initialize the instance field at construction time and also at a later time. (Perhaps the employee changes his or her name.)

Note When you invoke a class's instance or class method from a constructor or method within the same class, you specify only the method's name. You don't prefix the method invocation with the member access operator and an object reference or class name.

`setName()` uses an if statement to detect an attempt to assign a null reference to the name field. When such an attempt is detected, it outputs the "`name cannot be null`" error message and returns prematurely from the method so that the null value cannot be assigned (and replace a previously assigned name).

Caution When using the return statement, you might run into a situation where the compiler reports an "unreachable code" error message. It does so when it detects code that will never be executed and occupies memory unnecessarily. One area where you might encounter this problem is the switch statement. For example, suppose you specify `case "-v": printUsageInstructions(); return; break;` as part of this statement. The compiler reports an error when it detects the break statement following the return statement because the break statement is unreachable; it never can be executed.

The previous form of the return statement is not legal in a method that returns a value. For such methods, Java provides an alternate version of return that lets the method return a value (whose type must match the method's return type). The following example demonstrates this version:

```
double divide(double dividend, double divisor)
{
   if (divisor == 0.0)
   {
      System.out.println("cannot divide by zero");
      return 0.0;
   }
   return dividend/divisor;
}
```

`divide()` uses an if statement to detect an attempt to divide its first argument by 0.0, and outputs an error message when this attempt is detected. Furthermore, it returns `0.0` to signify this attempt. If there is no problem, the division is performed and the result is returned.

Caution You cannot use this form of the return statement in a constructor because constructors do not have return types.

Invoking Methods Recursively

A method normally executes statements that may include calls to other methods, such as `printDetails()` invoking `System.out.println()`. However, it is occasionally convenient to have a method call itself. This scenario is known as *recursion*.

For example, suppose you need to write a method that returns a *factorial* (the product of all the positive integers up to and including a specific integer). For example, 3! (the ! is the mathematical symbol for factorial) equals $3 \times 2 \times 1$ or 6.

Your first approach to writing this method might consist of the code presented in the following example:

```
int factorial(int n)
{
   int product = 1;
   for (int i = 2; i <= n; i++)
      product *= i;
   return product;
}
```

Although this code accomplishes its task (via iteration), factorial() could also be written according to the following example's recursive style.

```
int factorial(int n)
{
   if (n == 1)
      return 1; // base problem
   else
      return n*factorial(n-1);
}
```

The recursive approach takes advantage of being able to express a problem in simpler terms of itself. According to this example, the simplest problem, which is also known as the *base problem*, is 1! (1).

When an argument greater than 1 is passed to factorial(), this method breaks the problem into a simpler problem by calling itself with the next smaller argument value. Eventually, the base problem will be reached.

For example, calling factorial(4) results in the following stack of expressions:

```
4*factorial(3)
3*factorial(2)
2*factorial(1)
```

This last expression is at the top of the stack. When factorial(1) returns 1, these expressions are evaluated as the stack begins to unwind:

- 2*factorial(1) now becomes 2*1 (2)

- 3*factorial(2) now becomes 3*2 (6)

- 4*factorial(3) now becomes 4*6 (24)

Recursion provides an elegant way to express many problems. Additional examples include searching tree-based data structures for specific values and, in a hierarchical file system, finding and outputting the names of all files that contain specific text.

■ **Caution** Recursion consumes stack space, so make sure that your recursion eventually ends in a base problem; otherwise, you will run out of stack space and your application will be forced to terminate.

Overloading Methods

Java lets you introduce methods with the same name but different parameter lists into the same class. This feature is known as *method overloading*. When the compiler encounters a method invocation expression, it compares the called method's arguments list with each overloaded method's parameter list as it looks for the correct method to invoke.

Two same-named methods are overloaded when their parameter lists differ in number or order of parameters. For example, Java's String class provides overloaded public int indexOf(int ch) and public int indexOf(int ch, int fromIndex) methods. These methods differ in parameter counts. (I explore String in Chapter 4.)

Two same-named methods are overloaded when at least one parameter differs in type. For example, Java's java.lang.Math class provides overloaded public static double abs(double a) and public static int abs(int a) methods. One method's parameter is a double; the other method's parameter is an int. (I explore Math in Chapter 4.)

You cannot overload a method by changing only the return type. For example, double sum(double... values) and int sum(double... values) are not overloaded. These methods are not overloaded because the compiler does not have enough information to choose which method to call when it encounters sum(1.0, 2.0) in source code.

Reviewing Method-Invocation Rules

The previous examples of method invocation may seem confusing because you can sometimes specify the method's name directly, whereas you need to prefix a method name with an object reference or a class name and the member access operator at other times. The following rules dispel this confusion by giving you guidance on how to invoke methods from the various contexts:

- Specify the name of a class method as is from anywhere within the same class as the class method. Example: c2f(37.0);

- Specify the name of the class method's class, followed by the member access operator, followed by the name of the class method from outside the class. Example: Conversions.c2f(37.0); (You can also invoke a class method via an object instance, but that is considered bad form because it hides from casual observation the fact that a class method is being invoked.)

- Specify the name of an instance method as is from any instance method, constructor, or instance initializer in the same class as the instance method. Example: setName(name);

- Specify an object reference, followed by the member access operator, followed by the name of the instance method from any class method or class initializer within the same class as the instance method, or from outside the class. Example: Car car = new Car("Toyota", "Camry"); car.printDetails();

Although the latter rule might seem to imply that you can call an instance method from a class context, this is not the case. Instead, you call the method from an object context.

Also, don't forget to make sure that the number of arguments passed to a method, along with the order in which these arguments are passed, and the types of these arguments agree with their parameter counterparts in the method being invoked.

▨ **Note** Field access and method call rules are combined in expression System.out.println();, where the leftmost member access operator accesses the out class field (of type java.io.PrintStream) in the java.lang.System class, and where the rightmost member access operator calls this field's println() method. You'll learn about PrintStream in Chapter 8 and System in Chapter 4.

Hiding Information

Every class *X* exposes an *interface* (a protocol consisting of constructors, methods, and [possibly] fields that are made available to objects created from other classes for use in creating and communicating with *X*'s objects).

An interface serves as a one-way contract between a class and its *clients*, which are the external constructors, methods, and other (initialization-oriented) class entities (discussed later in this chapter) that communicate with the class's instances by calling constructors and methods, and by accessing fields (typically `public static final` fields, or constants). The contract is such that the class promises to not change its interface, which would break clients that depend upon the interface.

X also provides an *implementation* (the code within exposed methods along with optional helper methods and optional supporting fields that should not be exposed) that codifies the interface. *Helper methods* are methods that assist exposed methods and should not be exposed.

When designing a class, your goal is to expose a useful interface while hiding details of that interface's implementation. You hide the implementation to prevent developers from accidentally accessing parts of your class that do not belong to the class's interface, so that you are free to change the implementation without breaking client code. Hiding the implementation is often referred to as *information hiding*. Furthermore, many developers consider implementation hiding to be part of encapsulation.

Java supports implementation hiding by providing four levels of access control, where three of these levels are indicated via a reserved word. You can use the following access control levels to control access to fields, methods, and constructors, and two of these levels to control access to classes:

- *Public*: A field, method, or constructor that is declared `public` is accessible from anywhere. Classes can be declared `public` as well.

- *Protected*: A field, method, or constructor that is declared `protected` is accessible from all classes in the same package as the member's class, as well as subclasses of that class regardless of package. (I will discuss packages in Chapter 3.)

- *Private*: A field, method, or constructor that is declared `private` cannot be accessed from beyond the class in which it is declared.

- *Package-private*: In the absence of an access-control reserved word, a field, method, or constructor is only accessible to classes within the same package as the member's class. The same is true for non-public classes. The absence of `public`, `protected`, or `private` implies package-private.

Note A class that is declared `public` must be stored in a file with the same name. For example, a `public Image` class must be stored in `Image.java`. A source file can declare one `public` class only.

You will often declare your class's instance fields to be `private` and provide special `public` instance methods for setting and getting their values. By convention, methods that set field values have names starting with `set` and are known as *setters*. Similarly, methods that get field values have names with `get` (or `is`, for Boolean fields) prefixes and are known as *getters*. Listing 2-13 demonstrates this pattern in the context of an `Employee` class declaration.

Listing 2-13. *Separation of interface from implementation*

```
public class Employee
{
   private String name;
   public Employee(String name)
   {
      setName(name);
   }
   public void setName(String empName)
   {
      name = empName; // Assign the empName argument to the name field.
   }
   public String getName()
   {
      return name;
   }
}
```

Listing 2-13 presents an interface consisting of the public Employee class, its public constructor, and its public setter/getter methods. This class and these members can be accessed from anywhere. The implementation consists of the private name field and constructor/method code, which is only accessible within the Employee class.

It might seem pointless to go to all this bother when you could simply omit private and access the name field directly. However, suppose you are told to introduce a new constructor that takes separate first and last name arguments and new methods that set/get the employee's first and last names into this class. Furthermore, suppose that it has been determined that the first and last names will be accessed more often than the entire name. Listing 2-14 reveals these changes.

Listing 2-14. *Revising implementation without affecting existing interface*

```
public class Employee
{
   private String firstName;
   private String lastName;
   public Employee(String name)
   {
      setName(name);
   }
   public Employee(String firstName, String lastName)
   {
      setName(firstName+" "+lastName);
   }
   public void setName(String name)
   {
      // Assume that the first and last names are separated by a
      // single space character. indexOf() locates a character in a
      // string; substring() returns a portion of a string.
      setFirstName(name.substring(0, name.indexOf(' ')));
      setLastName(name.substring(name.indexOf(' ')+1));
   }
   public String getName()
```

```
    {
        return getFirstName()+" "+getLastName();
    }
    public void setFirstName(String empFirstName)
    {
        firstName = empFirstName;
    }
    public String getFirstName()
    {
        return firstName;
    }
    public void setLastName(String empLastName)
    {
        lastName = empLastName;
    }
    public String getLastName()
    {
        return lastName;
    }
}
```

Listing 2-14 reveals that the name field has been removed in favor of new firstName and lastName fields, which were added to improve performance. Because setFirstName() and setLastName() will be called more frequently than setName(), and because getFirstName() and getLastName() will be called more frequently than getName(), it is more performant (in each case) to have the first two methods set/get firstName's and lastName's values rather than merging either value into/extracting this value from name's value.

Listing 2-14 also reveals setName() calling setFirstName() and setLastName(), and getName() calling getFirstName() and getLastName(), rather than directly accessing the firstName and lastName fields. Although avoiding direct access to these fields is not necessary in this example, imagine another implementation change that adds more code to setFirstName(), setLastName(), getFirstName(), and getLastName(); not calling these methods will result in the new code not executing.

Client code (code that instantiates and uses a class, such as Employee) will not break when Employee's implementation changes from that shown in Listing 2-13 to that shown in Listing 2-14, because the original interface remains intact, although the interface has been extended. This lack of breakage results from hiding Listing 2-13's implementation, especially the name field.

■ **Note** setName() invokes the String class's indexOf() and substring() methods. You'll learn about these and other String methods in Chapter 4.

Java provides a little known information hiding-related language feature that lets one object (or class method/initializer) access another object's private fields or invoke its private methods. Listing 2-15 provides a demonstration.

Listing 2-15. One object accessing another object's private field

```
class PrivateAccess
{
   private int x;
   PrivateAccess(int x)
   {
      this.x = x;
   }
   boolean equalTo(PrivateAccess pa)
   {
      return pa.x == x;
   }
   public static void main(String[] args)
   {
      PrivateAccess pa1 = new PrivateAccess(10);
      PrivateAccess pa2 = new PrivateAccess(20);
      PrivateAccess pa3 = new PrivateAccess(10);
      System.out.println("pa1 equal to pa2: "+pa1.equalTo(pa2));
      System.out.println("pa2 equal to pa3: "+pa2.equalTo(pa3));
      System.out.println("pa1 equal to pa3: "+pa1.equalTo(pa3));
      System.out.println(pa2.x);
   }
}
```

Listing 2-15's PrivateAccess class declares a private int field named x. It also declares an equalTo() method that takes a PrivateAccess argument. The idea is to compare the argument object with the current object to determine if they are equal.

The equality determination is made by using the == operator to compare the value of the argument object's x instance field with the value of the current object's x instance field, returning Boolean true when they are the same. What may seem baffling is that Java lets you specify pa.x to access the argument object's private instance field. Also, main() is able to directly access x, via the pa2 object.

I previously presented Java's four access-control levels and presented the following statement regarding the private access-control level: "A field, method, or constructor that is declared private cannot be accessed from beyond the class in which it is declared." When you carefully consider this statement and examine Listing 2-15, you will realize that x is not being accessed from beyond the PrivateAccess class in which it is declared. Therefore, the private access-control level is not being violated.

The only code that can access this private instance field is code located within the PrivateAccess class. If you attempted to access x via a PrivateAccess object that was created in the context of another class, the compiler would report an error.

Being able to directly access x from within PrivateAccess is a performance enhancement; it is faster to directly access this implementation detail than to call a method that returns its value.

Compile PrivateAccess.java (javac PrivateAccess.java) and run the application (java PrivateAccess). You should observe the following output:

```
pa1 equal to pa2: false
pa2 equal to pa3: false
pa1 equal to pa3: true
20
```

Tip Get into the habit of developing useful interfaces while hiding implementations because it will save you much trouble when maintaining your classes.

Initializing Classes and Objects

Classes and objects need to be properly initialized before they are used. You've already learned that class fields are initialized to default zero values after a class loads, and can be subsequently initialized by assigning values to them in their declarations via *class field initializers*; for example, static int counter = 1;. Similarly, instance fields are initialized to default values when an object's memory is allocated via new, and can be subsequently initialized by assigning values to them in their declarations via *instance field initializers*; for example, int numDoors = 4;.

Another aspect of initialization that's already been discussed is the constructor, which is used to initialize an object, typically by assigning values to various instance fields, but is also capable of executing arbitrary code, such as code that opens a file and reads the file's contents.

Java provides two additional initialization features: class initializers and instance initializers. After introducing you to these features, this section discusses the order in which all of Java's initializers perform their work.

Class Initializers

Constructors perform initialization tasks for objects. Their counterpart from a class initialization perspective is the class initializer.

A *class initializer* is a static-prefixed block that is introduced into a class body. It is used to initialize a loaded class via a sequence of statements. For example, I once used a class initializer to load a custom database driver class. Listing 2-16 shows the loading details.

Listing 2-16. Loading a database driver via a class initializer

```
class JDBCFilterDriver implements Driver
{
    static private Driver d;
    static
    {
        // Attempt to load JDBC-ODBC Bridge Driver and register that
        // driver.
        try
        {
            Class c = Class.forName("sun.jdbc.odbc.JdbcOdbcDriver");
            d = (Driver) c.newInstance();
            DriverManager.registerDriver(new JDBCFilterDriver());
        }
        catch (Exception e)
        {
            System.out.println(e);
        }
    }
```

```
    //...
}
```

Listing 2-16's `JDBCFilterDriver` class uses its class initializer to load and instantiate the class that describes Java's JDBC-ODBC Bridge Driver, and to register a `JDBCFilterDriver` instance with Java's database driver. Although this listing's JDBC-oriented code is probably meaningless to you right now, the listing illustrates the usefulness of class initializers. (I discuss JDBC in Chapter 9.)

A class can declare a mix of class initializers and class field initializers, as demonstrated in Listing 2-17.

Listing 2-17. *Mixing class initializers with class field initializers*

```
class C
{
    static
    {
        System.out.println("class initializer 1");
    }
    static int counter = 1;
    static
    {
        System.out.println("class initializer 2");
        System.out.println("counter = "+counter);
    }
}
```

Listing 2-17 declares a class named `C` that specifies two class initializers and one class field initializer. When the Java compiler compiles into a classfile a class that declares at least one class initializer or class field initializer, it creates a special void `<clinit>()` class method that stores the bytecode equivalent of all class initializers and class field initializers in the order they occur (from top to bottom).

Note `<clinit>` is not a valid Java method name, but is a valid name from the runtime perspective. The angle brackets were chosen as part of the name to prevent a name conflict with any `clinit()` methods that you might declare in the class.

For class `C`, `<clinit>()` would first contain the bytecode equivalent of `System.out.println("class initializer 1");`, it would next contain the bytecode equivalent of `static int counter = 1;`, and it would finally contain the bytecode equivalent of `System.out.println("class initializer 2");` `System.out.println("counter = "+counter);`.

When class `C` is loaded into memory, `<clinit>()` executes immediately and generates the following output:

```
class initializer 1
class initializer 2
counter = 1
```

Instance Initializers

Not all classes can have constructors, as you will discover in Chapter 3 when I present anonymous classes. For these classes, Java supplies the instance initializer to take care of instance initialization tasks.

An *instance initializer* is a block that is introduced into a class body, as opposed to being introduced as the body of a method or a constructor. The instance initializer is used to initialize an object via a sequence of statements, as demonstrated in Listing 2-18.

Listing 2-18. Initializing a pair of arrays via an instance initializer

```
class Graphics
{
   double[] sines;
   double[] cosines;
   {
      sines = new double[360];
      cosines = new double[sines.length];
      for (int i = 0; i < sines.length; i++)
      {
         sines[i] = Math.sin(Math.toRadians(i));
         cosines[i] = Math.cos(Math.toRadians(i));
      }
   }
}
```

Listing 2-18's Graphics class uses an instance initializer to create an object's sines and cosines arrays, and to initialize these arrays' elements to the sines and cosines of angles ranging from 0 through 359 degrees. It does so because it's faster to read array elements than to repeatedly call Math.sin() and Math.cos() elsewhere; performance matters. (Chapter 4 introduces Math.sin() and Math.cos().)

A class can declare a mix of instance initializers and instance field initializers, as shown in Listing 2-19.

Listing 2-19. Mixing instance initializers with instance field initializers

```
class C
{
   {
      System.out.println("instance initializer 1");
   }
   int counter = 1;
   {
      System.out.println("instance initializer 2");
      System.out.println("counter = "+counter);
   }
}
```

Listing 2-19 declares a class named C that specifies two instance initializers and one instance field initializer. When the Java compiler compiles a class into a classfile, it creates a special void <init>() method representing the default noargument constructor when no constructor is explicitly declared; otherwise, it create an <init>() method for each encountered constructor. Furthermore, it stores in each constructor the bytecode equivalent of all instance initializers and instance field initializers in the order they occur (from top to bottom).

> ▒ **Note** `<init>` is not a valid Java method name, but is a valid name from the runtime perspective. The angle brackets were chosen as part of the name to prevent a name conflict with any `init()` methods that you might declare in the class.

For class C, `<init>()` would first contain the bytecode equivalent of `System.out.println("instance initializer 1");`, it would next contain the bytecode equivalent of `int counter = 1;`, and it would finally contain the bytecode equivalent of `System.out.println("instance initializer 2"); System.out.println("counter = "+counter);`.

When `new C()` executes, `<init>()` executes immediately and generates the following output:

```
instance initializer 1
instance initializer 2
counter = 1
```

> ▒ **Note** You should rarely need to use the instance initializer, which is not commonly used in industry.

Initialization Order

A class's body can contain a mixture of class field initializers, class initializers, instance field initializers, instance initializers, and constructors. (You should prefer constructors to instance field initializers, although I am guilty of not doing so consistently, and restrict your use of instance initializers to anonymous classes.) Furthermore, class fields and instance fields initialize to default values. Understanding the order in which all of this initialization occurs is necessary to preventing confusion, so check out Listing 2-20.

Listing 2-20. A complete initialization demo

```
class InitDemo
{
   static double double1;
   double double2;
   static int int1;
   int int2;
   static String string1;
   String string2;
   static
   {
      System.out.println("[class] double1 = "+double1);
      System.out.println("[class] int1 = "+int1);
      System.out.println("[class] string1 = "+string1);
      System.out.println();
   }
   {
```

```java
      System.out.println("[instance] double2 = "+double2);
      System.out.println("[instance] int2 = "+int2);
      System.out.println("[instance] string2 = "+string2);
      System.out.println();
   }
   static
   {
      double1 = 1.0;
      int1 = 1000000000;
      string1 = "abc";
   }
   {
      double2 = 1.0;
      int2 = 1000000000;
      string2 = "abc";
   }
   InitDemo()
   {
      System.out.println("InitDemo() called");
      System.out.println();
   }
   static double double3 = 10.0;
   double double4 = 10.0;
   static
   {
      System.out.println("[class] double3 = "+double3);
      System.out.println();
   }
   {
      System.out.println("[instance] double4 = "+double3);
      System.out.println();
   }
   public static void main(String[] args)
   {
      System.out.println ("main() started");
      System.out.println();
      System.out.println("[class] double1 = "+double1);
      System.out.println("[class] double3 = "+double3);
      System.out.println("[class] int1 = "+int1);
      System.out.println("[class] string1 = "+string1);
      System.out.println();
      for (int i = 0; i < 2; i++)
      {
         System.out.println("About to create InitDemo object");
         System.out.println();
         InitDemo id = new InitDemo();
         System.out.println("id created");
         System.out.println();
         System.out.println("[instance] id.double2 = "+id.double2);
         System.out.println("[instance] id.double4 = "+id.double4);
         System.out.println("[instance] id.int2 = "+id.int2);
         System.out.println("[instance] id.string2 = "+id.string2);
```

```
            System.out.println();
        }
    }
}
```

Listing 2-20's InitDemo class declares two class fields and two instance fields for the double precision floating-point primitive type, one class field and one instance field for the integer primitive type, and one class field and one instance field for the String reference type. It also introduces one explicitly initialized class field, one explicitly initialized instance field, three class initializers, three instance initializers, and one constructor. If you compile and run this code, you will observe the following output:

```
[class] double1 = 0.0
[class] int1 = 0
[class] string1 = null

[class] double3 = 10.0

main() started

[class] double1 = 1.0
[class] double3 = 10.0
[class] int1 = 1000000000
[class] string1 = abc

About to create InitDemo object

[instance] double2 = 0.0
[instance] int2 = 0
[instance] string2 = null

[instance] double4 = 10.0

InitDemo() called

id created

[instance] id.double2 = 1.0
[instance] id.double4 = 10.0
[instance] id.int2 = 1000000000
[instance] id.string2 = abc

About to create InitDemo object

[instance] double2 = 0.0
[instance] int2 = 0
[instance] string2 = null

[instance] double4 = 10.0

InitDemo() called
```

```
id created

[instance] id.double2 = 1.0
[instance] id.double4 = 10.0
[instance] id.int2 = 1000000000
[instance] id.string2 = abc
```

As you study this output in conjunction with the aforementioned discussion of class initializers and instance initializers, you will discover some interesting facts about initialization:

- Class fields initialize to default or explicit values just after a class is loaded. Immediately after a class loads, all class fields are zeroed to default values. Code within the <clinit>() method performs explicit initialization.

- All class initialization occurs prior to the <clinit>() method returning.

- Instance fields initialize to default or explicit values during object creation. When new allocates memory for an object, it zeroes all instance fields to default values. Code within an <init>() method performs explicit initialization.

- All instance initialization occurs prior to the <init>() method returning.

Additionally, because initialization occurs in a top-down manner, attempting to access the contents of a class field before that field is declared, or attempting to access the contents of an instance field before that field is declared causes the compiler to report an *illegal forward reference*.

Inheriting State and Behaviors

We tend to categorize stuff by saying things like "cars are vehicles" or "savings accounts are bank accounts." By making these statements, we really are saying that cars inherit vehicular state (e.g., make and color) and behaviors (e.g., park and display mileage), and that savings accounts inherit bank account state (e.g., balance) and behaviors (e.g., deposit and withdraw). Car, vehicle, savings account, and bank account are examples of real-world entity categories, and *inheritance* is a hierarchical relationship between similar entity categories in which one category inherits state and behaviors from at least one other entity category. Inheriting from a single category is called *single inheritance*, and inheriting from at least two categories is called *multiple inheritance*.

Java supports single inheritance and multiple inheritance to facilitate code reuse—why reinvent the wheel? Java supports single inheritance in a class context, in which a class inherits state and behaviors from another class through class extension. Because classes are involved, Java refers to this kind of inheritance as *implementation inheritance*.

Java supports multiple inheritance only in an interface context, in which a class inherits behavior templates from one or more interfaces through interface implementation, or in which an interface inherits behavior templates from one or more interfaces through interface extension. Because interfaces are involved, Java refers to this kind of inheritance as *interface inheritance*. (I discuss interfaces later in this chapter.)

This section introduces you to Java's support for implementation inheritance by first focusing on class extension. It then introduces you to a special class that sits at the top of Java's class hierarchy. After introducing you to composition, which is an alternative to implementation inheritance for reusing code, this section shows you how composition can be used to overcome problems with implementation inheritance.

Extending Classes

Java provides the reserved word extends for specifying a hierarchical relationship between two classes. For example, suppose you have a Vehicle class and want to introduce Car and Truck classes that extend Vehicle. Listing 2-21 uses extends to cement these relationships.

Listing 2-21. Relating classes via extends

```
class Vehicle
{
    // member declarations
}
class Car extends Vehicle
{
    // member declarations
}
class Truck extends Vehicle
{
    // Member declarations
}
```

Listing 2-21 codifies relationships that are known as "is-a" relationships: a car or a truck is a kind of vehicle. In this relationship, Vehicle is known as the *base class, parent class,* or *superclass*; and each of Car and Truck is known as the *derived class, child class,* or *subclass.*

▓ **Caution** You cannot extend a final class. For example, if you declared Vehicle as final class Vehicle, the compiler would report an error upon encountering class Car extends Vehicle or class Truck extends Vehicle. Developers declare their classes final when they do not want these classes to be extended (for security or other reasons).

As well as being capable of providing its own member declarations, each of Car and Truck is capable of inheriting member declarations from its Vehicle superclass. As Listing 2-22 shows, non-private inherited members become accessible to members of the Car and Truck classes.

Listing 2-22. Inheriting members

```
class Vehicle
{
    private String make;
    private String model;
    private int year;
    Vehicle(String make, String model, int year)
    {
        this.make = make;
        this.model = model;
        this.year = year;
```

```java
    }
    String getMake()
    {
        return make;
    }
    String getModel()
    {
        return model;
    }
    int getYear()
    {
        return year;
    }
}
class Car extends Vehicle
{
    private int numWheels;
    Car(String make, String model, int year, int numWheels)
    {
        super(make, model, year);
        this.numWheels = numWheels;
    }
    public static void main(String[] args)
    {
        Car car = new Car("Toyota", "Camry", 2011, 4);
        System.out.println("Make = "+car.getMake());
        System.out.println("Model = "+car.getModel());
        System.out.println("Year = "+car.getYear());
        System.out.println("Number of wheels = "+car.numWheels);
        System.out.println();
        car = new Car("Aptera Motors", "Aptera 2e/2h", 2012, 3);
        System.out.println("Make = "+car.getMake());
        System.out.println("Model = "+car.getModel());
        System.out.println("Year = "+car.getYear());
        System.out.println("Number of wheels = "+car.numWheels);
    }
}
class Truck extends Vehicle
{
    private boolean isExtendedCab;
    Truck(String make, String model, int year, boolean isExtendedCab)
    {
        super(make, model, year);
        this.isExtendedCab = isExtendedCab;
    }
    public static void main(String[] args)
    {
        Truck truck = new Truck("Chevrolet", "Silverado", 2011, true);
        System.out.println("Make = "+truck.getMake());
        System.out.println("Model = "+truck.getModel());
        System.out.println("Year = "+truck.getYear());
        System.out.println("Extended cab = "+truck.isExtendedCab);
```

```
    }
}
```

Listing 2-22's Vehicle class declares private fields that store a vehicle's make, model, and year; a constructor that initializes these fields to passed arguments; and getter methods that retrieve these fields' values.

The Car subclass provides a private numWheels field, a constructor that initializes a Car object's Vehicle and Car layers, and a main() class method for testing this class. Similarly, the Truck subclass provides a private isExtendedCab field, a constructor that initializes a Truck object's Vehicle and Truck layers, and a main() class method for testing this class.

Car's and Truck's constructors use reserved word super to call Vehicle's constructor with Vehicle-oriented arguments, and then initialize Car's numWheels and Truck's isExtendedCab instance fields, respectively. The super() call is analogous to specifying this() to call another constructor in the same class, but invokes a superclass constructor instead.

Caution The super() call can only appear in a constructor. Furthermore, it must be the first code that is specified in the constructor. If super() is not specified, and if the superclass does not have a noargument constructor, the compiler will report an error because the subclass constructor must call a noargument superclass constructor when super() is not present.

Car's main() method creates two Car objects, initializing each object to a specific make, model, year, and number of wheels. Four System.out.println() method calls subsequently output each object's information. Similarly, Truck's main() method creates a single Truck object, and also initializes this object to a specific make, model, year, and *flag* (Boolean true/false value) indicating that the truck is an extended cab. The first three System.out.println() method calls retrieve their pieces of information by calling a Car or Truck instance's inherited getMake(), getModel(), and getYear() methods.

The final System.out.println() method call directly accesses the instance's numWheels or isExtendedCab instance field. Although it's generally not a good idea to access an instance field directly (because it violates information hiding), each of the Car and Truck class's main() methods, which provides this access, is present only to test these classes and would not exist in a real application that uses these classes.

Assuming that Listing 2-22 is stored in a file named Vehicle.java, execute javac Vehicle.java to compile this source code into Vehicle.class, Car.class, and Truck.class classfiles. Then execute java Car to test the Car class. This execution results in the following output:

```
Make = Toyota
Model = Camry
Year = 2011
Number of wheels = 4

Make = Aptera Motors
Model = Aptera 2e/2h
Year = 2012
Number of wheels = 3
```

Continuing, execute java Truck to test the Truck class. This execution results in the following output:

```
Make = Chevrolet
Model = Silverado
Year = 2011
Extended cab = true
```

■ **Note** A class whose instances cannot be modified is known as an *immutable class*. Vehicle is an example. If Car's and Truck's main() methods, which can directly read/write numWheels or isExtendedCab, were not present, Car and Truck would also be examples of immutable classes. Also, a class cannot inherit constructors, nor can it inherit private fields and methods. For example, Car does not inherit Vehicle's constructor, nor does it inherit Vehicle's private make, model, and year fields.

A subclass can *override* (replace) an inherited method so that the subclass's version of the method is called instead. Listing 2-23 shows you that the overriding method must specify the same name, parameter list, and return type as the method being overridden.

Listing 2-23. Overriding a method

```
class Vehicle
{
   private String make;
   private String model;
   private int year;
   Vehicle(String make, String model, int year)
   {
      this.make = make;
      this.model = model;
      this.year = year;
   }
   void describe()
   {
      System.out.println(year+" "+make+" "+model);
   }
}
class Car extends Vehicle
{
   private int numWheels;
   Car(String make, String model, int year, int numWheels)
   {
      super(make, model, year);
   }
   void describe()
   {
      System.out.print("This car is a "); // Print without newline - see Chapter 1.
      super.describe();
   }
   public static void main(String[] args)
```

```
    {
        Car car = new Car("Ford", "Fiesta", 2009, 4);
        car.describe();
    }
}
```

Listing 2-23's Car class declares a describe() method that overrides Vehicle's describe() method to output a car-oriented description. This method uses reserved word super to call Vehicle's describe() method via super.describe();.

■ **Note** Call a superclass method from the overriding subclass method by prefixing the method's name with reserved word super and the member access operator. If you don't do this, you end up recursively calling the subclass's overriding method. Use super and the member access operator to access non-private superclass fields from subclasses that mask these fields by declaring same-named fields.

If you were to compile Listing 2-23 (javac Vehicle.java) and run the Car application (java Car), you would discover that Car's overriding describe() method executes instead of Vehicle's overridden describe() method, and outputs This car is a 2009 Ford Fiesta.

■ **Caution** You cannot override a final method. For example, if Vehicle's describe() method was declared as final void describe(), the compiler would report an error upon encountering an attempt to override this method in the Car class. Developers declare their methods final when they do not want these methods to be overridden (for security or other reasons). Also, you cannot make an overriding method less accessible than the method it overrides. For example, if Car's describe() method was declared as private void describe(), the compiler would report an error because private access is less accessible than the default package access. However, describe() could be made more accessible by declaring it public, as in public void describe().

Suppose you were to replace Listing 2-23's describe() method with the method shown here:

```
void describe(String owner)
{
    System.out.print("This car, which is owned by "+owner+", is a ");
    super.describe();
}
```

The modified Car class now has two describe() methods, the preceding explicitly declared method and the method inherited from Vehicle. The void describe(String owner) method does not override Vehicle's describe() method. Instead, it overloads this method.

The Java compiler helps you detect an attempt to overload instead of override a method at compile time by letting you prefix a subclass's method header with the @Override annotation, as shown below—I discuss annotations in Chapter 3:

```
@Override
void describe()
{
    System.out.print("This car is a ");
    super.describe();
}
```

Specifying @Override tells the compiler that the method overrides another method. If you overload the method instead, the compiler reports an error. Without this annotation, the compiler would not report an error because method overloading is a valid feature.

■ **Tip** Get into the habit of prefixing overriding methods with the @Override annotation. This habit will help you detect overloading mistakes much sooner.

I previously presented the initialization order of classes and objects, where you learned that class members are always initialized first, and in a top-down order (the same order applies to instance members). Implementation inheritance adds a couple more details:

- A superclass's class initializers always execute before a subclass's class initializers.

- A subclass's constructor always calls the superclass constructor to initialize an object's superclass layer before initializing the subclass layer.

Java's support for implementation inheritance only permits you to extend a single class. You cannot extend multiple classes because doing so can lead to problems. For example, suppose Java supported multiple implementation inheritance, and you decided to model a *flying horse* (from Greek mythology) via the class structure shown in Listing 2-24.

Listing 2-24. A fictional demonstration of multiple implementation inheritance

```
class Horse
{
    void describe()
    {
        // Code that outputs a description of a horse's appearance and behaviors.
    }
}
class Bird
{
    void describe()
    {
        // Code that outputs a description of a bird's appearance and behaviors.
    }
}
class FlyingHorse extends Horse, Bird
{
    public static void main(String[] args)
    {
```

```
        FlyingHorse pegasus = new FlyingHorse();
        pegasus.describe();
    }
}
```

This class structure reveals an ambiguity resulting from each of `Horse` and `Bird` declaring a `describe()` method. Which of these methods does `FlyingHorse` inherit? A related ambiguity arises from same-named fields, possibly of different types. Which field is inherited?

The Ultimate Superclass

A class that does not explicitly extend another class implicitly extends Java's `Object` class (located in the `java.lang` package—I will discuss packages in the next chapter). For example, Listing 2-1's `Image` class extends `Object`, whereas Listing 2-21's `Car` and `Truck` classes extend `Vehicle`, which extends `Object`.

`Object` is Java's ultimate superclass because it serves as the ancestor of every other class, but does not itself extend any other class. `Object` provides a common set of methods that other classes inherit. Table 2-1 describes these methods.

Table 2-1. *Object's Methods*

Method	Description
`Object clone()`	Create and return a copy of the current object.
`boolean equals(Object obj)`	Determine whether the current object is equal to the object identified by `obj`.
`void finalize()`	Finalize the current object.
`Class<?> getClass()`	Return the current object's `Class` object.
`int hashCode()`	Return the current object's hash code.
`void notify()`	Wake up one of the threads that are waiting on the current object's monitor.
`void notifyAll()`	Wake up all threads that are waiting on the current object's monitor.
`String toString()`	Return a string representation of the current object.
`void wait()`	Cause the current thread to wait on the current object's monitor until it is woken up via `notify()` or `notifyAll()`.
`void wait(long timeout)`	Cause the current thread to wait on the current object's monitor until it is woken up via `notify()` or `notifyAll()`, or until the specified `timeout` value (in

milliseconds) has elapsed, whichever comes first.

void wait(long timeout, int nanos)	Cause the current thread to wait on the current object's monitor until it is woken up via notify() or notifyAll(), or until the specified timeout value (in milliseconds) plus nanos value (in nanoseconds) has elapsed, whichever comes first.

I will discuss the clone(), equals(), finalize(), hashCode(), and toString() methods shortly, but defer a discussion of getClass(), notify(), notifyAll(), and the wait() methods to Chapter 4.

■ **Note** Chapter 6 introduces you to the java.util.Objects class, which provides several null-safe or null-tolerant class methods for comparing two objects, computing the hash code of an object, requiring that a reference not be null, and returning a string representation of an object.

Cloning

The clone() method *clones* (duplicates) an object without calling a constructor. It copies each primitive or reference field's value to its counterpart in the clone, a task known as *shallow copying* or *shallow cloning*. Listing 2-25 demonstrates this behavior.

Listing 2-25. Shallowly cloning an Employee object

```
class Employee implements Cloneable
{
   String name;
   int age;
   Employee(String name, int age)
   {
      this.name = name;
      this.age = age;
   }
   public static void main(String[] args) throws CloneNotSupportedException
   {
      Employee e1 = new Employee("John Doe", 46);
      Employee e2 = (Employee) e1.clone();
      System.out.println(e1 == e2); // Output: false
      System.out.println(e1.name == e2.name); // Output: true
   }
}
```

Listing 2-25 declares an Employee class with name and age instance fields, and a constructor for initializing these fields. The main() method uses this constructor to initialize a new Employee object's copies of these fields to John Doe and 46.

> ▨ **Note** A class must implement the `java.lang.Cloneable` interface or its instances cannot be shallowly cloned via `Object`'s `clone()` method—this method performs a runtime check to see if the class implements `Cloneable`. (I will discuss interfaces later in this chapter.) If a class does not implement `Cloneable`, `clone()` throws `java.lang.CloneNotSupportedException`. (Because `CloneNotSupportedException` is a checked exception, it is necessary for Listing 2-25 to satisfy the compiler by appending `throws CloneNotSupportedException` to the `main()` method's header. I will discuss exceptions in the next chapter.) `String` is an example of a class that does not implement `Cloneable`; hence, `String` objects cannot be shallowly cloned.

After assigning the `Employee` object's reference to local variable e1, `main()` calls the `clone()` method on this variable to duplicate the object, and then assigns the resulting reference to variable e2. The `(Employee)` cast is needed because `clone()` returns `Object`.

To prove that the objects whose references were assigned to e1 and e2 are different, `main()` next compares these references via `==` and outputs the Boolean result, which happens to be false. To prove that the `Employee` object was shallowly cloned, `main()` next compares the references in both `Employee` objects' name fields via `==` and outputs the Boolean result, which happens to be true.

> ▨ **Note** `Object`'s `clone()` method was originally specified as a `public` method, which meant that any object could be cloned from anywhere. For security reasons, this access was later changed to `protected`, which means that only code within the same package as the class whose `clone()` method is to be called, or code within a subclass of this class (regardless of package) can call `clone()`.

Shallow cloning is not always desirable because the original object and its clone refer to the same object via their equivalent reference fields. For example, each of Listing 2-25's two `Employee` objects refers to the same `String` object via its name field.

Although not a problem for `String`, whose instances are immutable, changing a mutable object via the clone's reference field causes the original (noncloned) object to see the same change via its reference field. For example, suppose you add a reference field named hireDate to `Employee`. This field is of type Date with year, month, and day instance fields. Because Date is intended to be mutable, you can change the contents of these fields in the Date instance assigned to hireDate.

Now suppose you plan to change the clone's date, but want to preserve the original `Employee` object's date. You cannot do this with shallow cloning because the change is also visible to the original `Employee` object. To solve this problem, you must modify the cloning operation so that it assigns a new Date reference to the `Employee` clone's hireDate field. This task, which is known as *deep copying* or *deep cloning*, is demonstrated in Listing 2-26.

Listing 2-26. Deeply cloning an Employee object

```
class Date
{
   int year, month, day;
```

```
        Date(int year, int month, int day)
        {
            this.year = year;
            this.month = month;
            this.day = day;
        }
    }
    class Employee implements Cloneable
    {
        String name;
        int age;
        Date hireDate;
        Employee(String name, int age, Date hireDate)
        {
            this.name = name;
            this.age = age;
            this.hireDate = hireDate;
        }
        @Override
        protected Object clone() throws CloneNotSupportedException
        {
            Employee emp = (Employee) super.clone();
            if (hireDate != null) // no point cloning a null object (one that does not exist)
                emp.hireDate = new Date(hireDate.year, hireDate.month, hireDate.day);
            return emp;
        }
        public static void main(String[] args) throws CloneNotSupportedException
        {
            Employee e1 = new Employee("John Doe", 46, new Date(2000, 1, 20));
            Employee e2 = (Employee) e1.clone();
            System.out.println(e1 == e2); // Output: false
            System.out.println(e1.name == e2.name); // Output: true
            System.out.println(e1.hireDate == e2.hireDate); // Output: false
            System.out.println(e2.hireDate.year+" "+e2.hireDate.month+" "+
                               e2.hireDate.day); // Output: 2000 1 20
        }
    }
```

Listing 2-26 declares Date and Employee classes. The Date class declares year, month, and day fields and a constructor.

Employee overrides the clone() method to deeply clone the hireDate field. This method first calls Object's clone() method to shallowly clone the current Employee object's instance fields, and then stores the new object's reference in emp. It next assigns a new Date object's reference to emp's hireDate field; this object's fields are initialized to the same values as those in the original Employee object's hireDate instance.

At this point, you have an Employee clone with shallowly cloned name and age fields, and a deeply cloned hireDate field. The clone() method finishes by returning this Employee clone.

⬛ **Note** If you are not calling `Object`'s `clone()` method from an overriding `clone()` method (because you prefer to deeply clone reference fields and do your own shallow copying of nonreference fields), it isn't necessary for the class containing the overriding `clone()` method to implement `Cloneable`, but it should implement this interface for consistency. `String` does not override `clone()`, so `String` objects cannot be deeply cloned.

Equality

The `==` and `!=` operators compare two primitive values (such as integers) for equality (`==`) or inequality (`!=`). These operators also compare two references to see whether they refer to the same object or not. This latter comparison is known as an *identity check*.

You cannot use `==` and `!=` to determine whether two objects are logically the same (or not). For example, two `Truck` objects with the same field values are logically equivalent. However, `==` reports them as unequal because of their different references.

⬛ **Note** Because `==` and `!=` perform the fastest possible comparisons, and because string comparisons need to be performed quickly (especially when sorting a huge number of strings), the `String` class contains special support that allows literal strings and string-valued constant expressions to be compared via `==` and `!=`. (I will discuss this support when I present `String` in Chapter 4.) The following statements demonstrate these comparisons:

```
System.out.println("abc" == "abc"); // Output: true
System.out.println("abc" == "a"+"bc"); // Output: true
System.out.println("abc" == "Abc"); // Output: false
System.out.println("abc" != "def"); // Output: true
System.out.println("abc" == new String("abc")); // Output: false
```

Recognizing the need to support logical equality in addition to reference equality, Java provides an `equals()` method in the `Object` class. Because this method defaults to comparing references, you need to override `equals()` to compare object contents.

Before overriding `equals()`, make sure that this is necessary. For example, Java's `java.lang.StringBuffer` class (discussed in Chapter 4) does not override `equals()`. Perhaps this class's designers did not think it necessary to determine if two `StringBuffer` objects are logically equivalent.

You cannot override `equals()` with arbitrary code. Doing so will probably prove disastrous to your applications. Instead, you need to adhere to the contract that is specified in the Java documentation for this method, and which I present next.

The `equals()` method implements an equivalence relation on nonnull object references:

- *It is reflexive.* For any nonnull reference value x, x`.equals(`x`)` returns true.

- *It is symmetric.* For any nonnull reference values *x* and *y*, *x*.equals(*y*) returns true if and only if *y*.equals(*x*) returns true.

- *It is transitive.* For any nonnull reference values *x*, *y*, and *z*, if *x*.equals(*y*) returns true and *y*.equals(*z*) returns true, then *x*.equals(*z*) returns true.

- *It is consistent.* For any nonnull reference values *x* and *y*, multiple invocations of *x*.equals(*y*) consistently return true or consistently return false, provided no information used in equals() comparisons on the objects is modified.

- For any nonnull reference value *x*, *x*.equals(null) returns false.

Although this contract probably looks somewhat intimidating, it is not that difficult to satisfy. For proof, take a look at the implementation of the equals() method in Listing 2-27's Point class.

Listing 2-27. Logically comparing Point objects

```java
class Point
{
    private int x, y;
    Point(int x, int y)
    {
        this.x = x;
        this.y = y;
    }
    int getX() { return x; }
    int getY() { return y; }
    @Override
    public boolean equals(Object o)
    {
        if (!(o instanceof Point))
            return false;
        Point p = (Point) o;
        return p.x == x && p.y == y;
    }
    public static void main(String[] args)
    {
        Point p1 = new Point(10, 20);
        Point p2 = new Point(20, 30);
        Point p3 = new Point(10, 20);
        // Test reflexivity
        System.out.println(p1.equals(p1)); // Output: true
        // Test symmetry
        System.out.println(p1.equals(p2)); // Output: false
        System.out.println(p2.equals(p1)); // Output: false
        // Test transitivity
        System.out.println(p2.equals(p3)); // Output: false
        System.out.println(p1.equals(p3)); // Output: true
        // Test nullability
        System.out.println(p1.equals(null)); // Output: false
        // Extra test to further prove the instanceof operator's usefulness.
        System.out.println(p1.equals("abc")); // Output: false
    }
```

}

Listing 2-27's overriding equals() method begins with an if statement that uses the instanceof operator to determine whether the argument passed to parameter o is an instance of the Point class. If not, the if statement executes return false;.

The o instanceof Point expression satisfies the last portion of the contract: For any nonnull reference value *x*, *x*.equals(null) returns false. Because the null reference is not an instance of any class, passing this value to equals() causes the expression to evaluate to false.

The o instanceof Point expression also prevents a java.lang.ClassCastException instance from being thrown via expression (Point) o in the event that you pass an object other than a Point object to equals(). (I will discuss exceptions in the next chapter.)

Following the cast, the contract's reflexivity, symmetry, and transitivity requirements are met by only allowing Points to be compared with other Points, via expression p.x == x && p.y == y. The final contract requirement, consistency, is met by making sure that the equals() method is deterministic. In other words, this method does not rely on any field value that could change from method call to method call.

■ **Tip** You can optimize the performance of a time-consuming equals() method by first using == to determine if o's reference identifies the current object. Simply specify if (o == this) return true; as the equals() method's first statement. This optimization is not necessary in Listing 2-27's equals() method, which has satisfactory performance.

It is important to always override the hashCode() method when overriding equals(). I did not do so in Listing 2-27 because I have yet to formally introduce hashCode().

Finalization

Finalization refers to cleanup via the finalize() method, which is known as a *finalizer*. The finalize() method's Java documentation states that finalize() is "called by the garbage collector on an object when garbage collection determines that there are no more references to the object. A subclass overrides the finalize() method to dispose of system resources or to perform other cleanup."

Object's version of finalize() does nothing; you must override this method with any needed cleanup code. Because the JVM might never call finalize() before an application terminates, you should provide an explicit cleanup method, and have finalize() call this method as a safety net in case the method is not otherwise called.

■ **Caution** Never depend on finalize() for releasing limited resources such as graphics contexts or file descriptors. For example, if an application object opens files, expecting that its finalize() method will close them, the application might find itself unable to open additional files when a tardy JVM is slow to call finalize(). What makes this problem worse is that finalize() might be called more frequently on another JVM, resulting in

---

this too-many-open-files problem not revealing itself. The developer might thus falsely believe that the application behaves consistently across different JVMs.

If you decide to override finalize(), your object's subclass layer must give its superclass layer an opportunity to perform finalization. You can accomplish this task by specifying super.finalize(); as the last statement in your method, which the following example demonstrates:

```
@Override
protected void finalize() throws Throwable
{
   try
   {
      // Perform subclass cleanup.
   }
   finally
   {
      super.finalize();
   }
}
```

The example's finalize() declaration appends throws Throwable to the method header because the cleanup code might throw an exception. If an exception is thrown, execution leaves the method and, in the absence of try-finally, super.finalize(); never executes. (I will discuss exceptions and try-finally in Chapter 3.)

To guard against this possibility, the subclass's cleanup code executes in a block that follows reserved word try. If an exception is thrown, Java's exception-handling logic executes the block following the finally reserved word, and super.finalize(); executes the superclass's finalize() method.

The finalize() method has often been used to perform *resurrection* (making an unreferenced object referenced), to implement object pools that recycle the same objects when these objects are expensive (time-wise) to create (database connection objects are an example).

Resurrection occurs when you assign this (a reference to the current object) to a class or instance field (or to another long-lived variable). For example, you might specify r = this; within finalize() to assign the unreferenced object identified as this to a class field named r.

Because of the possibility for resurrection, there is a severe performance penalty imposed on the garbage collection of an object that overrides finalize(). You'll learn about this penalty and a better alternative to overriding finalize() in Chapter 4.

Note A resurrected object's finalizer cannot be called again.

Hash Codes

The hashCode() method returns a 32-bit integer that identifies the current object's *hash code*, a small value that results from applying a mathematical function to a potentially large amount of data. The calculation of this value is known as *hashing*.

You must override hashCode() when overriding equals(), and in accordance with the following contract, which is specified in hashCode()'s Java documentation:

- Whenever it is invoked on the same object more than once during an execution of a Java application, the hashCode() method must consistently return the same integer, provided no information used in equals(Object) comparisons on the object is modified. This integer need not remain consistent from one execution of an application to another execution of the same application.

- If two objects are equal according to the equals(Object) method, then calling the hashCode() method on each of the two objects must produce the same integer result.

- It is not required that if two objects are unequal according to the equals(Object) method, then calling the hashCode() method on each of the two objects must produce distinct integer results. However, the programmer should be aware that producing distinct integer results for unequal objects might improve the performance of hash tables.

Fail to obey this contract and your class's instances will not work properly with Java's hash-based Collections Framework classes, such as java.util.HashMap. (I will discuss HashMap and other Collections Framework classes in Chapter 5.)

If you override equals() but not hashCode(), you most importantly violate the second item in the contract: The hash codes of equal objects must also be equal. This violation can lead to serious consequences, as demonstrated in the following example:

```
java.util.Map<Point, String> map = new java.util.HashMap<>();
map.put(p1, "first point");
System.out.println(map.get(p1)); // Output: first point
System.out.println(map.get(new Point(10, 20))); // Output: null
```

Assume that the example's statements are appended to Listing 2-27's main() method—the java.util. prefix, <Point, String>, and <> have to do with packages and generics, which I discuss in Chapter 3.

After main() creates its Point objects and calls its System.out.println() methods, it executes this example's statements, which perform the following tasks:

- The first statement instantiates HashMap, which is in the java.util package.

- The second statement calls HashMap's put() method to store Listing 2-27's p1 object key and the "first point" value in the hashmap.

- The third statement retrieves the value of the hashmap entry whose Point key is logically equal to p1 via HashMap's get() method.

- The fourth statement is equivalent to the third statement, but returns the null reference instead of "first point".

Although objects p1 and Point(10, 20) are logically equivalent, these objects have different hash codes, resulting in each object referring to a different entry in the hashmap. If an object is not stored (via put()) in that entry, get() returns null.

Correcting this problem requires that hashCode() be overridden to return the same integer value for logically equivalent objects. I'll show you how to accomplish this task when I discuss HashMap in Chapter 5.

String Representation

The toString() method returns a string-based representation of the current object. This representation defaults to the object's class name, followed by the @ symbol, followed by a hexadecimal representation of the object's hash code.

For example, if you were to execute System.out.println(p1); to output Listing 2-27's p1 object, you would see a line of output similar to Point@3e25a5. (System.out.println() calls p1's inherited toString() method behind the scenes.)

You should strive to override toString() so that it returns a concise but meaningful description of the object. For example, you might declare, in Listing 2-27's Point class, a toString() method that is similar to the following:

```
@Override
public String toString()
{
    return "("+x+", "+y+")";
}
```

This time, executing System.out.println(p1); results in more meaningful output, such as (10, 20).

Composition

Implementation inheritance and composition offer two different approaches to reusing code. As you have learned, implementation inheritance is concerned with extending a class with a new class, which is based upon an "is-a" relationship between them: a Car is a Vehicle, for example.

On the other hand, *composition* is concerned with composing classes out of other classes, which is based upon a "has-a" relationship between them. For example, a Car has an Engine, Wheels, and a SteeringWheel.

You have already seen examples of composition in this chapter. For example, Listing 2-3's Car class includes String make and String model fields. Listing 2-28's Car class provides another example of composition.

Listing 2-28. A Car class whose instances are composed of other objects

```
class Car extends Vehicle
{
    private Engine engine;
    private Wheel[] wheels;
    private SteeringWheel steeringWheel;
}
```

Listing 2-28 demonstrates that composition and implementation inheritance are not mutually exclusive. Although not shown, Car inherits various members from its Vehicle superclass, in addition to providing its own engine, wheels, and steeringwheel instance fields.

The Trouble with Implementation Inheritance

Implementation inheritance is potentially dangerous, especially when the developer does not have complete control over the superclass, or when the superclass is not designed and documented with extension in mind.

The problem is that implementation inheritance breaks encapsulation. The subclass relies on implementation details in the superclass. If these details change in a new version of the superclass, the subclass might break, even if the subclass is not touched.

For example, suppose you have purchased a library of Java classes, and one of these classes describes an appointment calendar. Although you do not have access to this class's source code, assume that Listing 2-29 describes part of its code.

Listing 2-29. An appointment calendar class

```java
public class ApptCalendar
{
    private final static int MAX_APPT = 1000;
    private Appt[] appts;
    private int size;
    public ApptCalendar()
    {
        appts = new Appt[MAX_APPT];
        size = 0; // redundant because field automatically initialized to 0
                  // adds clarity, however
    }
    public void addAppt(Appt appt)
    {
        if (size == appts.length)
            return; // array is full
        appts[size++] = appt;
    }
    public void addAppts(Appt[] appts)
    {
        for (int i = 0; i < appts.length; i++)
            addAppt(appts[i]);
    }
}
```

Listing 2-29's ApptCalendar class stores an array of appointments, with each appointment described by an Appt instance. For this discussion, Appt's details are irrelevant—it could be as trivial as class Appt {}.

Suppose you want to log each appointment in a file. Because a logging capability is not provided, you extend ApptCalendar with Listing 2-30's LoggingApptCalendar class, which adds logging behavior in overriding addAppt() and addAppts() methods.

Listing 2-30. Extending the appointment calendar class

```
public class LoggingApptCalendar extends ApptCalendar
{
   // A constructor is not necessary because the Java compiler will add a
   // noargument constructor that calls the superclass's noargument
   // constructor by default.
   @Override
   public void addAppt(Appt appt)
   {
      Logger.log(appt.toString());
      super.addAppt(appt);
   }
   @Override
   public void addAppts(Appt[] appts)
   {
      for (int i = 0; i < appts.length; i++)
         Logger.log(appts[i].toString());
      super.addAppts(appts);
   }
}
```

Listing 2-30's LoggingApptCalendar class relies on a Logger class whose void log(String msg) class method logs a string to a file (the details are unimportant). Notice the use of toString() to convert an Appt object to a String object, which is then passed to log().

Although this class looks okay, it does not work as you might expect. Suppose you instantiate this class and add a few Appt instances to this instance via addAppts(), in the following manner:

```
LoggingApptCalendar lapptc = new LoggingApptCalendar();
lapptc.addAppts(new Appt[] {new Appt(), new Appt(), new Appt()});
```

If you also add a System.out.println(msg); method call to Logger's log(String msg) method, to output this method's argument to standard output, you will discover that log() outputs a total of six messages; each of the expected three messages (one per Appt object) is duplicated.

When LoggingApptCalendar's addAppts() method is called, it first calls Logger.log() for each Appt instance in the appts array that is passed to addAppts(). This method then calls ApptCalendar's addAppts() method via super.addAppts(appts);.

ApptCalendar's addAppts() method calls LoggingApptCalendar's overriding addAppt() method for each Appt instance in its appts array argument. addAppt() executes Logger.log(appt.toString()); to log its appt argument's string representation, and you end up with three additional logged messages.

If you did not override the addAppts() method, this problem would go away. However, the subclass would be tied to an implementation detail: ApptCalendar's addAppts() method calls addAppt().

It is not a good idea to rely on an implementation detail when the detail is not documented. (I previously stated that you do not have access to ApptCalendar's source code.) When a detail is not documented, it can change in a new version of the class.

Because a base class change can break a subclass, this problem is known as the *fragile base class problem*. A related cause of fragility that also has to do with overriding methods occurs when new methods are added to a superclass in a subsequent release.

For example, suppose a new version of the library introduces a new public void addAppt(Appt appt, boolean unique) method into the ApptCalendar class. This method adds the appt instance to the calendar when unique is false, and, when unique is true, it adds the appt instance only if it has not previously been added.

Because this method has been added after the LoggingApptCalendar class was created, LoggingApptCalendar does not override the new addAppt() method with a call to Logger.log(). As a result, Appt instances passed to the new addAppt() method are not logged.

Here is another problem: You introduce a method into the subclass that is not also in the superclass. A new version of the superclass presents a new method that matches the subclass method signature and return type. Your subclass method now overrides the superclass method, and probably does not fulfill the superclass method's contract.

There is a way to make these problems disappear. Instead of extending the superclass, create a private field in a new class, and have this field reference an instance of the "superclass." This task demonstrates composition because you are forming a "has-a" relationship between the new class and the "superclass."

Additionally, have each of the new class's instance methods call the corresponding "superclass" method via the "superclass" instance that was saved in the private field, and also return the called method's return value. This task is known as *forwarding*, and the new methods are known as *forwarding methods*.

Listing 2-31 presents an improved LoggingApptCalendar class that uses composition and forwarding to forever eliminate the fragile base class problem and the additional problem of the unanticipated method overriding.

Listing 2-31. *A composed logging appointment calendar class*

```
public class LoggingApptCalendar
{
    private ApptCalendar apptCal;
    public LoggingApptCalendar(ApptCalendar apptCal)
    {
        this.apptCal = apptCal;
    }
    public void addAppt(Appt appt)
    {
        Logger.log(appt.toString());
        apptCal.addAppt(appt);
    }
    public void addAppts(Appt[] appts)
    {
        for (int i = 0; i < appts.length; i++)
            Logger.log(appts[i].toString());
        apptCal.addAppts(appts);
    }
}
```

Listing 2-31's LoggingApptCalendar class does not depend upon implementation details of the ApptCalendar class. You can add new methods to ApptCalendar and they will not break LoggingApptCalendar.

■ **Note** Listing 2-31's `LoggingApptCalendar` class is an example of a *wrapper class*, a class whose instances wrap other instances. Each `LoggingApptCalendar` instance wraps an `ApptCalendar` instance. `LoggingApptCalendar` is also an example of the *Decorator design pattern*, which is presented on page 175 of *Design Patterns: Elements of Reusable Object-Oriented Software* by Erich Gamma, Richard Helm, Ralph Johnson, and John Vlissides (Addison-Wesley, 1995; ISBN: 0201633612).

When should you extend a class and when should you use a wrapper class? Extend a class when an "is-a" relationship exists between the superclass and the subclass, and either you have control over the superclass or the superclass has been designed and documented for class extension. Otherwise, use a wrapper class.

What does "design and document for class extension" mean? Design means provide protected methods that hook into the class's inner workings (to support writing efficient subclasses), and ensure that constructors and the `clone()` method never call overridable methods. Document means clearly state the impact of overriding methods.

■ **Caution** Wrapper classes should not be used in a *callback framework*, an object framework in which an object passes its own reference to another object (via `this`) so that the latter object can call the former object's methods at a later time. This "calling back to the former object's method" is known as a *callback*. Because the wrapped object does not know of its wrapper class, it passes only its reference (via `this`), and resulting callbacks do not involve the wrapper class's methods.

Changing Form

Some real-world entities can change their forms. For example, water (on Earth as opposed to interstellar space) is naturally a liquid, but it changes to a solid when frozen, and it changes to a gas when heated to its boiling point. Insects such as butterflies that undergo metamorphosis are another example.

The ability to change form is known as *polymorphism*, and is useful to model in a programming language. For example, code that draws arbitrary shapes can be expressed more concisely by introducing a single Shape class and its draw() method, and by invoking that method for each Circle instance, Rectangle instance, and other Shape instance stored in an array. When Shape's draw() method is called for an array instance, it is the Circle's, Rectangle's or other Shape instance's draw() method that gets called. We say that there are many forms of Shape's draw() method, or that this method is polymorphic.

Java supports four kinds of polymorphism:

- *Coercion*: An operation serves multiple types through implicit type conversion. For example, division lets you divide an integer by another integer, or divide a floating-point value by another floating-point value. If one operand is an integer and the other operand is a floating-point value, the compiler *coerces* (implicitly converts) the integer to a floating-point value, to prevent a type error. (There is no division operation that supports an integer operand and a floating-point operand.) Passing a subclass object reference to a method's superclass parameter is another example of coercion polymorphism. The compiler coerces the subclass type to the superclass type, to restrict operations to those of the superclass.

- *Overloading*: The same operator symbol or method name can be used in different contexts. For example, + can be used to perform integer addition, floating-point addition, or string concatenation, depending on the types of its operands. Also, multiple methods having the same name can appear in a class (through declaration and/or inheritance).

- *Parametric*: Within a class declaration, a field name can associate with different types and a method name can associate with different parameter and return types. The field and method can then take on different types in each class instance. For example, a field might be of type java.lang.Integer and a method might return an Integer reference in one class instance, and the same field might be of type String and the same method might return a String reference in another class instance. Java supports parametric polymorphism via generics, which I will discuss in Chapter 3.

- *Subtype*: A type can serve as another type's subtype. When a subtype instance appears in a supertype context, executing a supertype operation on the subtype instance results in the subtype's version of that operation executing. For example, suppose that Circle is a subclass of Point, and that both classes contain a draw() method. Assigning a Circle instance to a variable of type Point, and then calling the draw() method via this variable, results in Circle's draw() method being called. Subtype polymorphism partners with implementation inheritance.

Many developers do not regard coercion and overloading as valid kinds of polymorphism. They see coercion and overloading as nothing more than type conversions and *syntactic sugar* (syntax that simplifies a language, making it "sweeter" to use). In contrast, parametric and subtype are regarded as valid kinds of polymorphism.

This section introduces you to subtype polymorphism through upcasting and late binding. We then move on to abstract classes and abstract methods, downcasting and runtime type identification, and covariant return types.

Upcasting and Late Binding

Listing 2-27's Point class represents a point as an x-y pair. Because a circle (in this example) is an x-y pair denoting its center, and has a radius denoting its extent, you can extend Point with a Circle class that introduces a radius field. Check out Listing 2-32.

Listing 2-32. A Circle class extending the Point class

```
class Circle extends Point
{
   private int radius;
```

```
    Circle(int x, int y, int radius)
    {
        super(x, y);
        this.radius = radius;
    }
    int getRadius()
    {
        return radius;
    }
}
```

Listing 2-32's Circle class describes a Circle as a Point with a radius, which implies that you can treat a Circle instance as if it was a Point instance. Accomplish this task by assigning the Circle instance to a Point variable, as demonstrated here:

```
Circle c = new Circle(10, 20, 30);
Point p = c;
```

The cast operator is not needed to convert from Circle to Point because access to a Circle instance via Point's interface is legal. After all, a Circle is at least a Point. This assignment is known as *upcasting* because you are implicitly casting up the type hierarchy (from the Circle subclass to the Point superclass). It is also an example of *covariance* in that a type with a wider range of values (Circle) is being converted to a type with a narrower range of values (Point).

After upcasting Circle to Point, you cannot call Circle's getRadius() method because this method is not part of Point's interface. Losing access to subtype features after narrowing it to a superclass seems useless, but is necessary for achieving subtype polymorphism.

In addition to upcasting the subclass instance to a variable of the superclass type, subtype polymorphism involves declaring a method in the superclass and overriding this method in the subclass. For example, suppose Point and Circle are to be part of a graphics application, and you need to introduce a draw() method into each class to draw a point and a circle, respectively. You end with the class structure shown in Listing 2-33.

Listing 2-33. Declaring a graphics application's Point and Circle classes

```
class Point
{
    private int x, y;
    Point(int x, int y)
    {
        this.x = x;
        this.y = y;
    }
    int getX()
    {
        return x;
    }
    int getY()
    {
        return y;
    }
    @Override
    public String toString()
```

```
    {
        return "("+x+", "+y+")";
    }
    void draw()
    {
        System.out.println("Point drawn at "+toString ());
    }
}
class Circle extends Point
{
    private int radius;
    Circle(int x, int y, int radius)
    {
        super(x, y);
        this.radius = radius;
    }
    int getRadius()
    {
        return radius;
    }
    @Override
    public String toString()
    {
        return ""+radius;
    }
    @Override
    void draw()
    {
        System.out.println("Circle drawn at "+super.toString()+
                            " with radius "+toString());
    }
}
```

Listing 2-33's draw() methods will ultimately draw graphics shapes, but simulating their behaviors via System.out.println() method calls is sufficient during the early testing phase of the graphics application.

Now that you have temporarily finished with Point and Circle, you want to test their draw() methods in a simulated version of the graphics application. To achieve this objective, you write Listing 2-34's Graphics class.

Listing 2-34. *A Graphics class for testing Point's and Circle's draw() methods*

```
class Graphics
{
    public static void main(String[] args)
    {
        Point[] points = new Point[] { new Point(10, 20),
                                       new Circle(10, 20, 30) };
        for (int i = 0; i < points.length; i++)
            points[i].draw();
    }
}
```

107

Listing 2-34's main() method first declares an array of Points. Upcasting is demonstrated by first having the array's initializer instantiate the Circle class, and then by assigning this instance's reference to the second element in the points array.

Moving on, main() uses a for loop to call each Point element's draw() method. Because the first iteration calls Point's draw() method, whereas the second iteration calls Circle's draw() method, you observe the following output:

```
Point drawn at (10, 20)
Circle drawn at (10, 20) with radius 30
```

How does Java "know" that it must call Circle's draw() method on the second loop iteration? Should it not call Point's draw() method because Circle is being treated as a Point thanks to the upcast?

At compile time, the compiler does not know which method to call. All it can do is verify that a method exists in the superclass, and verify that the method call's arguments list and return type match the superclass's method declaration.

In lieu of knowing which method to call, the compiler inserts an instruction into the compiled code that, at runtime, fetches and uses whatever reference is in points[1] to call the correct draw() method. This task is known as *late binding*.

Late binding is used for calls to non-final instance methods. For all other method calls, the compiler knows which method to call, and inserts an instruction into the compiled code that calls the method associated with the variable's type (not its value). This task is known as *early binding*.

You can also upcast from one array to another provided that the array being upcast is a subtype of the other array. Consider Listing 2-35.

Listing 2-35. *Demonstrating array upcasting*

```
class Point
{
   private int x, y;
   Point(int x, int y)
   {
      this.x = x;
      this.y = y;
   }
   int getX() { return x; }
   int getY() { return y; }
}
class ColoredPoint extends Point
{
   private int color;
   ColoredPoint(int x, int y, int color)
   {
      super(x, y);
      this.color = color;
   }
   int getColor() { return color; }
}
class UpcastArrayDemo
{
   public static void main(String[] args)
   {
      ColoredPoint[] cptArray = new ColoredPoint[1];
```

```
        cptArray[0] = new ColoredPoint(10, 20, 5);
        Point[] ptArray = cptArray;
        System.out.println(ptArray[0].getX()); // Output: 10
        System.out.println(ptArray[0].getY()); // Output: 20
//      System.out.println(ptArray[0].getColor()); // Illegal
    }
}
```

Listing 2-35's main() method first creates a ColoredPoint array consisting of one element. It then instantiates this class and assigns the object's reference to this element. Because ColoredPoint[] is a subtype of Point[], main() is able to upcast cptArray's ColoredPoint[] type to Point[] and assign its reference to ptArray. main() then invokes the ColoredPoint instance's getX() and getY() methods via ptArray[0]. It cannot invoke getColor() because ptArray has narrower scope than cptArray. In other words, getColor() is not part of Point's interface.

Abstract Classes and Abstract Methods

Suppose new requirements dictate that your graphics application must include a Rectangle class. Also, this class must include a draw() method, and this method must be tested in a manner similar to that shown in Listing 2-34's Graphics class.

In contrast to Circle, which is a Point with a radius, it does not make sense to think of a Rectangle as a being a Point with a width and height. Rather, a Rectangle instance would probably be composed of a Point indicating its origin and a Point indicating its width and height extents.

Because circles, points, and rectangles are examples of shapes, it makes more sense to declare a Shape class with its own draw() method than to specify class Rectangle extends Point. Listing 2-36 presents Shape's declaration.

Listing 2-36. *Declaring a Shape class*

```
class Shape
{
    void draw()
    {
    }
}
```

Listing 2-36's Shape class declares an empty draw() method that only exists to be overridden and to demonstrate subtype polymorphism.

You can now refactor Listing 2-33's Point class to extend Listing 2-36's Shape class, leave Circle as is, and introduce a Rectangle class that extends Shape. You can then refactor Listing 2-34's Graphics class's main() method to take Shape into account. Check out the following main() method:

```
public static void main(String[] args)
{
    Shape[] shapes = new Shape[] { new Point(10, 20), new Circle(10, 20, 30),
                                   new Rectangle(20, 30, 15, 25) };
    for (int i = 0; i < shapes.length; i++)
        shapes[i].draw();
}
```

Because Point and Rectangle directly extend Shape, and because Circle indirectly extends Shape by extending Point, main() responds to shapes[i].draw(); by calling the correct subclass's draw() method.

Although Shape makes the code more flexible, there is a problem. What is to stop someone from instantiating Shape and adding this meaningless instance to the shapes array, as follows?

```
Shape[] shapes = new Shape[] { new Point(10, 20), new Circle(10, 20, 30),
                               new Rectangle(20, 30, 15, 25), new Shape() };
```

What does it mean to instantiate Shape? Because this class describes an abstract concept, what does it mean to draw a generic shape? Fortunately, Java provides a solution to this problem, which is demonstrated in Listing 2-37.

Listing 2-37. Abstracting the Shape class

```
abstract class Shape
{
    abstract void draw(); // semicolon is required
}
```

Listing 2-37 uses Java's abstract reserved word to declare a class that cannot be instantiated. The compiler reports an error should you try to instantiate this class.

Tip Get into the habit of declaring classes that describe generic categories (e.g., shape, animal, vehicle, and account) abstract. This way, you will not inadvertently instantiate them.

The abstract reserved word is also used to declare a method without a body—the compiler reports an error when you supply a body or omit the semicolon. The draw() method does not need a body because it cannot draw an abstract shape.

Caution The compiler reports an error when you attempt to declare a class that is both abstract and final. For example, abstract final class Shape is an error because an abstract class cannot be instantiated and a final class cannot be extended. The compiler also reports an error when you declare a method to be abstract but do not declare its class to be abstract. For example, removing abstract from the Shape class's header in Listing 2-37 results in an error. This removal is an error because a non-abstract (concrete) class cannot be instantiated when it contains an abstract method. Finally, when you extend an abstract class, the extending class must override all the abstract class's abstract methods, or else the extending class must itself be declared to be abstract; otherwise, the compiler will report an error.

An abstract class can contain non-abstract methods in addition to or instead of abstract methods. For example, Listing 2-22's Vehicle class could have been declared abstract. The constructor would still be present, to initialize private fields, even though you could not instantiate the resulting class.

Downcasting and Runtime Type Identification

Moving up the type hierarchy via upcasting causes loss of access to subtype features. For example, assigning a Circle instance to Point variable p means that you cannot use p to call Circle's getRadius() method.

However, it is possible to once again access the Circle instance's getRadius() method by performing an explicit cast operation; for example, Circle c = (Circle) p;. This assignment is known as *downcasting* because you are explicitly moving down the type hierarchy (from the Point superclass to the Circle subclass). It is also an example of *contravariance* in that a type with a narrower range of values (Point) is being converted to a type with a wider range of values (Circle).

Although an upcast is always safe (the superclass's interface is a subset of the subclass's interface), the same cannot be said of a downcast. Listing 2-38 shows you what kind of trouble you can get into when downcasting is used incorrectly.

Listing 2-38. The trouble with downcasting

```
class A
{
}
class B extends A
{
   void m() {}
}
class DowncastDemo
{
   public static void main(String[] args)
   {
      A a = new A();
      B b = (B) a;
      b.m();
   }
}
```

Listing 2-38 presents a class hierarchy consisting of a superclass named A and a subclass named B. Although A does not declare any members, B declares a single m() method.

A third class named DowncastDemo provides a main() method that first instantiates A, and then tries to downcast this instance to B and assign the result to variable b. The compiler will not complain because downcasting from a superclass to a subclass in the same type hierarchy is legal.

However, if the assignment is allowed, the application will undoubtedly crash when it tries to execute b.m();. The crash happens because the JVM will attempt to call a method that does not exist— class A does not have an m() method.

Fortunately, this scenario will never happen because the JVM verifies that the cast is legal. Because it detects that A does not have an m() method, it does not permit the cast by throwing an instance of the ClassCastException class.

The JVM's cast verification illustrates *runtime type identification* (or RTTI, for short). Cast verification performs RTTI by examining the type of the cast operator's operand to see whether the cast should be allowed. Clearly, the cast should not be allowed.

A second form of RTTI involves the instanceof operator. This operator checks the left operand to see whether it is an instance of the right operand, and returns true if this is the case. The following example introduces instanceof to Listing 2-38 to prevent the ClassCastException:

```
if (a instanceof B)
```

```
{
   B b = (B) a;
   b.m();
}
```

The instanceof operator detects that variable a's instance was not created from B and returns false to indicate this fact. As a result, the code that performs the illegal cast will not execute. (Overuse of instanceof probably indicates poor software design.)

Because a subtype is a kind of supertype, instanceof will return true when its left operand is a subtype instance or a supertype instance of its right operand supertype. The following example demonstrates:

```
A a = new A();
B b = new B();
System.out.println(b instanceof A); // Output: true
System.out.println(a instanceof A); // Output: true
```

This example assumes the class structure shown in Listing 2-38 and instantiates superclass A and subclass B. The first System.out.println() method call outputs true because b's reference identifies an instance of a subclass of A; the second System.out.println() method call outputs true because a's reference identifies an instance of superclass A.

You can also downcast from one array to another provided that the array being downcast is a supertype of the other array, and whose elements types are those of the subtype. Consider Listing 2-39.

Listing 2-39. Demonstrating array downcasting

```
class Point
{
   private int x, y;
   Point(int x, int y)
   {
      this.x = x;
      this.y = y;
   }
   int getX() { return x; }
   int getY() { return y; }
}
class ColoredPoint extends Point
{
   private int color;
   ColoredPoint(int x, int y, int color)
   {
      super(x, y);
      this.color = color;
   }
   int getColor() { return color; }
}
class DowncastArrayDemo
{
   public static void main(String[] args)
   {
      ColoredPoint[] cptArray = new ColoredPoint[1];
      cptArray[0] = new ColoredPoint(10, 20, 5);
```

```
          Point[] ptArray = cptArray;
          System.out.println(ptArray[0].getX()); // Output: 10
          System.out.println(ptArray[0].getY()); // Output: 20
//           System.out.println(ptArray[0].getColor()); // Illegal
          if (ptArray instanceof ColoredPoint[])
          {
             ColoredPoint cp = (ColoredPoint) ptArray[0];
             System.out.println(cp.getColor());
          }
      }
}
```

Listing 2-39 is similar to Listing 2-35 except that it also demonstrates downcasting. Notice its use of instanceof to verify that ptArray's referenced object is of type ColoredPoint[]. If this operator returns true, it is safe to downcast ptArray[0] from Point to ColoredPoint and assign the reference to ColoredPoint.

So far, you have encountered two forms of RTTI. Java also supports a third form that is known as reflection. I will introduce you to this form of RTTI when I cover reflection in Chapter 4.

Covariant Return Types

A *covariant return type* is a method return type that, in the superclass's method declaration, is the supertype of the return type in the subclass's overriding method declaration. Listing 2-40 demonstrates this feature.

Listing 2-40. A demonstration of covariant return types

```
class SuperReturnType
{
    @Override
    public String toString()
    {
        return "superclass return type";
    }
}
class SubReturnType extends SuperReturnType
{
    @Override
    public String toString()
    {
        return "subclass return type";
    }
}
class Superclass
{
    SuperReturnType createReturnType()
    {
        return new SuperReturnType();
    }
}
class Subclass extends Superclass
{
```

```
    @Override
    SubReturnType createReturnType()
    {
        return new SubReturnType();
    }
}
class CovarDemo
{
    public static void main(String[] args)
    {
        SuperReturnType suprt = new Superclass().createReturnType();
        System.out.println(suprt); // Output: superclass return type
        SubReturnType subrt = new Subclass().createReturnType();
        System.out.println(subrt); // Output: subclass return type
    }
}
```

Listing 2-40 declares SuperReturnType and Superclass superclasses, and SubReturnType and Subclass subclasses; each of Superclass and Subclass declares a createReturnType() method. Superclass's method has its return type set to SuperReturnType, whereas Subclass's overriding method has its return type set to SubReturnType, a subclass of SuperReturnType.

Covariant return types minimize upcasting and downcasting. For example, Subclass's createReturnType() method does not need to upcast its SubReturnType instance to its SubReturnType return type. Furthermore, this instance does not need to be downcast to SubReturnType when assigning to variable subrt.

In the absence of covariant return types, you would end up with Listing 2-41.

Listing 2-41. Upcasting and downcasting in the absence of covariant return types

```
class SuperReturnType
{
    @Override
    public String toString()
    {
        return "superclass return type";
    }
}
class SubReturnType extends SuperReturnType
{
    @Override
    public String toString()
    {
        return "subclass return type";
    }
}
class Superclass
{
    SuperReturnType createReturnType()
    {
        return new SuperReturnType();
    }
}
```

```
class Subclass extends Superclass
{
   @Override
   SuperReturnType createReturnType()
   {
      return new SubReturnType();
   }
}
class CovarDemo
{
   public static void main(String[] args)
   {
      SuperReturnType suprt = new Superclass().createReturnType();
      System.out.println(suprt); // Output: superclass return type
      SubReturnType subrt = (SubReturnType) new Subclass().createReturnType();
      System.out.println(subrt); // Output: subclass return type
   }
}
```

In Listing 2-41, the first bolded code reveals an upcast from SubReturnType to SuperReturnType, and the second bolded code uses the required (SubReturnType) cast operator to downcast from SuperReturnType to SubReturnType, prior to the assignment to subrt.

Formalizing Class Interfaces

In my introduction to information hiding, I stated that every class *X* exposes an *interface* (a protocol consisting of constructors, methods, and [possibly] fields that are made available to objects created from other classes for use in creating and communicating with *X*'s objects).

Java formalizes the interface concept by providing reserved word interface, which is used to introduce a type without implementation. Java also provides language features to declare, implement, and extend interfaces. After looking at interface declaration, implementation, and extension, this section explains the rationale for using interfaces.

Declaring Interfaces

An interface declaration consists of a header followed by a body. At minimum, the header consists of reserved word interface followed by a name that identifies the interface. The body starts with an open brace character and ends with a close brace. Sandwiched between these delimiters are constant and method header declarations. Consider Listing 2-42.

Listing 2-42. *Declaring a Drawable interface*

```
interface Drawable
{
   int RED = 1;   // For simplicity, integer constants are used. These
   int GREEN = 2; // constants are not that descriptive, as you will see.
   int BLUE = 3;
   int BLACK = 4;
   void draw(int color);
}
```

Listing 2-42 declares an interface named Drawable. By convention, an interface's name begins with an uppercase letter. Also, the first letter of each subsequent word in a multiword interface name is capitalized.

■ **Note** Many interface names end with the able suffix. For example, Java's standard class library includes interfaces named Adjustable, Callable, Comparable, Cloneable, Iterable, Runnable, and Serializable. It's not mandatory to use this suffix; the standard class library also provides interfaces named CharSequence, Collection, Composite, Executor, Future, Iterator, List, Map, and Set.

Drawable declares four fields that identify color constants. Drawable also declares a draw() method that must be called with one of these constants to specify the color used to draw something.

■ **Note** You can precede interface with public, to make your interface accessible to code outside of its package. (I will discuss packages in Chapter 3.) Otherwise, the interface is only accessible to other types in its package. You can also precede interface with abstract, to emphasize that an interface is abstract. Because an interface is already abstract, it is redundant to specify abstract in the interface's declaration. An interface's fields are implicitly declared public, static, and final. It is therefore redundant to declare them with these reserved words. Because these fields are constants, they must be explicitly initialized; otherwise, the compiler reports an error. Finally, an interface's methods are implicitly declared public and abstract. Therefore, it is redundant to declare them with these reserved words. Because these methods must be instance methods, do not declare them static or the compiler will report errors.

Drawable identifies a type that specifies what to do (draw something) but not how to do it. It leaves implementation details to classes that implement this interface. Instances of such classes are known as *drawables* because they know how to draw themselves.

■ **Note** An interface that declares no members is known as a *marker interface* or a *tagging interface*. It associates metadata with a class. For example, the Cloneable marker/tagging interface states that instances of its implementing class can be shallowly cloned. RTTI is used to detect that an object's class implements a marker/tagging interface. For example, when Object's clone() method detects, via RTTI, that the calling instance's class implements Cloneable, it shallowly clones the object.

Implementing Interfaces

By itself, an interface is useless. To be of any benefit to an application, the interface needs to be implemented by a class. Java provides the implements reserved word for this task. Listing 2-43 demonstrates using implements to implement the aforementioned Drawable interface.

Listing 2-43. Implementing the Drawable interface

```
class Point implements Drawable
{
   private int x, y;
   Point(int x, int y)
   {
      this.x = x;
      this.y = y;
   }
   int getX()
   {
      return x;
   }
   int getY()
   {
      return y;
   }
   @Override
   public String toString()
   {
      return "("+x+", "+y+")";
   }
   @Override
   public void draw(int color)
   {
      System.out.println("Point drawn at "+toString()+" in color "+color);
   }
}
class Circle extends Point implements Drawable
{
   private int radius;
   Circle(int x, int y, int radius)
   {
      super(x, y);
      this.radius = radius;
   }
   int getRadius()
   {
      return radius;
   }
   @Override
   public String toString()
   {
      return ""+radius;
   }
}
```

117

```
@Override
public void draw(int color)
{
    System.out.println("Circle drawn at "+super.toString()+
                       " with radius "+toString()+" in color "+color);
}
}
```

Listing 2-43 retrofits Listing 2-33's class hierarchy to take advantage of Listing 2-42's Drawable interface. You will notice that each of classes Point and Circle implements this interface by attaching the implements Drawable clause to its class header.

To implement an interface, the class must specify, for each interface method header, a method whose header has the same signature and return type as that in the interface's method header, and a code body to go with the method header.

Caution When implementing a method, do not forget that the interface's methods are implicitly declared public. If you forget to include public in the implemented method's declaration, the compiler will report an error because you are attempting to assign weaker access to the implemented method.

When a class implements an interface, the class inherits the interface's constants and method headers, and overrides the method headers by providing implementations (hence the @Override annotation). This is known as *interface inheritance*.

It turns out that Circle's header does not need the implements Drawable clause. If this clause is not present, Circle inherits Point's draw() method, and is still considered to be a Drawable, whether or not it overrides this method.

An interface specifies a type whose data values are the objects whose classes implement the interface, and whose behaviors are those specified by the interface. This fact implies that you can assign an object's reference to a variable of the interface type, provided that the object's class implements the interface. The following example provides a demonstration:

```
public static void main(String[] args)
{
    Drawable[] drawables = new Drawable[] { new Point(10, 20),
                                            new Circle(10, 20, 30) };
    for (int i = 0; i < drawables.length; i++)
        drawables[i].draw(Drawable.RED);
}
```

Because Point and Circle instances are drawables by virtue of these classes implementing the Drawable interface, it is legal to assign Point and Circle instance references to variables (including array elements) of type Drawable.

When you run this method, it generates the following output:

```
Point drawn at (10, 20) in color 1
Circle drawn at (10, 20) with radius 30 in color 1
```

Listing 2-42's Drawable interface is useful for drawing a shape's outline. Suppose you also need to fill a shape's interior. You might attempt to satisfy this requirement by declaring Listing 2-44's Fillable interface.

Listing 2-44. Declaring a Fillable interface

```
interface Fillable
{
   int RED = 1;
   int GREEN = 2;
   int BLUE = 3;
   int BLACK = 4;
   void fill(int color);
}
```

Given Listings 2-42 and 2-44, you can declare that the Point and Circle classes implement both interfaces by specifying class Point implements Drawable, Fillable and class Circle implements Drawable, Fillable. You can then modify the main() method to also treat the drawables as *fillables* so that you can fill these shapes, as follows:

```
public static void main(String[] args)
{
   Drawable[] drawables = new Drawable[] { new Point(10, 20),
                                           new Circle(10, 20, 30) };
   for (int i = 0; i < drawables.length; i++)
      drawables[i].draw(Drawable.RED);
   Fillable[] fillables = new Fillable[drawables.length];
   for (int i = 0; i < drawables.length; i++)
   {
      fillables[i] = (Fillable) drawables[i];
      fillables[i].fill(Fillable.GREEN);
   }
}
```

After invoking each drawable's draw() method, main() creates a Fillable array of the same length as the Drawable array. It then proceeds to copy each Drawable array element to a Fillable array element, and then invoke the fillable's fill() method. The (Fillable) cast is necessary because a drawable is not a fillable. This cast operation will succeed because the Point and Circle instances being copied implement Fillable as well as Drawable.

Tip You can list as many interfaces as you need to implement by specifying a comma-separated list of interface names after implements.

Implementing multiple interfaces can lead to name collisions, and the compiler will report errors. For example, suppose that you attempt to compile Listing 2-45's interface and class declarations.

Listing 2-45. Colliding interfaces

```
interface A
{
   int X = 1;
   void foo();
}
interface B
{
   int X = 1;
   int foo();
}
class Collision implements A, B
{
   @Override
   public void foo();
   @Override
   public int foo() { return X; }
}
```

Each of Listing 2-45's A and B interfaces declares a constant named X. Despite each constant having the same type and value, the compiler will report an error when it encounters X in Collision's second foo() method because it does not know which X is being inherited.

Speaking of foo(), the compiler reports an error when it encounters Collision's second foo() declaration because foo() has already been declared. You cannot overload a method by changing only its return type.

The compiler will probably report additional errors. For example, the Java 7 compiler has this to say when told to compile Listing 2-45:

```
Collision.java:16: error: foo() is already defined in Collision
   public int foo() { return X; }
            ^
Collision.java:11: error: Collision is not abstract and does not override abstract↵ method
foo() in B
class Collision implements A, B
^
Collision.java:14: error: foo() in Collision cannot implement foo() in B
   public void foo();
            ^
  return type void is not compatible with int
Collision.java:16: error: reference to X is ambiguous, both variable X in A and↵ variable X
in B match
   public int foo() { return X; }
                           ^
4 errors
```

Extending Interfaces

Just as a subclass can extend a superclass via reserved word extends, you can use this reserved word to have a *subinterface* extend a *superinterface*. This, too, is known as *interface inheritance*.

For example, the duplicate color constants in Drawable and Fillable lead to name collisions when you specify their names by themselves in an implementing class. To avoid these name collisions, prefix a name with its interface name and the member access operator, or place these constants in their own interface, and have Drawable and Fillable extend this interface, as demonstrated in Listing 2-46.

Listing 2-46. *Extending the Colors interface*

```
interface Colors
{
   int RED = 1;
   int GREEN = 2;
   int BLUE = 3;
   int BLACK = 4;
}
interface Drawable extends Colors
{
   void draw(int color);
}
interface Fillable extends Colors
{
   void fill(int color);
}
```

The fact that Drawable and Fillable each inherit constants from Colors is not a problem for the compiler. There is only a single copy of these constants (in Colors) and no possibility of a name collision, and so the compiler is satisfied.

If a class can implement multiple interfaces by declaring a comma-separated list of interface names after implements, it seems that an interface should be able to extend multiple interfaces in a similar way. This feature is demonstrated in Listing 2-47.

Listing 2-47. *Extending a pair of interfaces*

```
interface A
{
   int X = 1;
}
interface B
{
   double X = 2.0;
}
interface C extends A, B
{
}
```

Listing 2-47 will compile even though C inherits two same-named constants X with different return types and initializers. However, if you implement C and then try to access X, as in Listing 2-48, you will run into a name collision.

Listing 2-48. Discovering a name collision

```
class Collision implements C
{
   public void output()
   {
      System.out.println(X); // Which X is accessed?
   }
}
```

Suppose you introduce a void foo(); method header declaration into interface A, and an int foo(); method header declaration into interface B. This time, the compiler will report an error when you attempt to compile the modified Listing 2-47.

Why Use Interfaces?

Now that the mechanics of declaring, implementing, and extending interfaces are out of the way, we can focus on the rationale for using them. Unfortunately, newcomers to Java's interfaces feature are often told that this feature was created as a workaround to Java's lack of support for multiple implementation inheritance. While interfaces are useful in this capacity, this is not their reason for existence. Instead, *Java's interfaces feature was created to give developers the utmost flexibility in designing their applications, by decoupling interface from implementation. You should always code to the interface.*

Those who are adherents to *agile software development* (a group of software development methodologies based on iterative development that emphasizes keeping code simple, testing frequently, and delivering functional pieces of the application as soon as they are deliverable) know the importance of flexible coding. They cannot afford to tie their code to a specific implementation because a change in requirements for the next iteration could result in a new implementation, and they might find themselves rewriting significant amounts of code, which wastes time and slows development.

Interfaces help you achieve flexibility by decoupling interface from implementation. For example, the main() method following Listing 2-36 creates an array of objects from classes that subclass the Shape class, and then iterates over these objects, calling each object's draw() method. The only objects that can be drawn are those that subclass Shape.

Suppose you also have a hierarchy of classes that model resistors, transistors, and other electronic components. Each component has its own symbol that allows the component to be shown in a schematic diagram of an electronic circuit. Perhaps you want to add a drawing capability to each class that draws that component's symbol.

You might consider specifying Shape as the superclass of the electronic component class hierarchy. However, electronic components are not shapes (although they have shapes) so it makes no sense to place these classes in a class hierarchy rooted in Shape.

However, you can make each component class implement the Drawable interface, which lets you add expressions that instantiate these classes to the drawables array in the main() method appearing prior to Listing 2-44 (so you can draw their symbols). This is legal because these instances are drawables.

Wherever possible, you should strive to specify interfaces instead of classes in your code, to keep your code adaptable to change. This is especially true when working with Java's Collections Framework, which I will discuss at length in Chapter 5.

For now, consider a simple example that consists of the Collections Framework's java.util.List interface, and its java.util.ArrayList and java.util.LinkedList implementation classes. The following example presents inflexible code based on the ArrayList class:

```
ArrayList<String> arrayList = new ArrayList<String>();
```

```
void dump(ArrayList<String> arrayList)
{
    // suitable code to dump out the arrayList
}
```

This example uses the generics-based parameterized type language feature (which I will discuss in Chapter 3) to identify the kind of objects stored in an ArrayList instance. In this example, String objects are stored.

The example is inflexible because it hardwires the ArrayList class into multiple locations. This hardwiring focuses the developer into thinking specifically about array lists instead of generically about lists.

Lack of focus is problematic when a requirements change, or perhaps a performance issue brought about by *profiling* (analyzing a running application to check its performance), suggests that the developer should have used LinkedList.

The example only requires a minimal number of changes to satisfy the new requirement. In contrast, a larger code base might need many more changes. Although you only need to change ArrayList to LinkedList, to satisfy the compiler, consider changing arrayList to linkedList, to keep *semantics* (meaning) clear—you might have to change multiple occurrences of names that refer to an ArrayList instance throughout the source code.

The developer is bound to lose time while refactoring the code to adapt to LinkedList. Instead, the developer could have saved time by writing this example to use the equivalent of constants. In other words, the example could have been written to rely on interfaces, and to only specify ArrayList in one place. The following example shows you what the resulting code would look like:

```
List<String> list = new ArrayList<String>();
void dump(List<String> list)
{
    // suitable code to dump out the list
}
```

This example is much more flexible than the previous example. If a requirements or profiling change suggests that LinkedList should be used instead of ArrayList, simply replace Array with Linked and you are done. You do not even have to change the parameter name.

INTERFACES VERSUS ABSTRACT CLASSES

Java provides interfaces and abstract classes for describing *abstract types* (types that cannot be instantiated). Abstract types represent abstract concepts (drawable and shape, for example), and instances of such types would be meaningless.

Interfaces promote flexibility through lack of implementation—Drawable and List illustrate this flexibility. They are not tied to any single class hierarchy, but can be implemented by any class in any hierarchy.

Abstract classes support implementation, but can be genuinely abstract (Listing 2-37's abstract Shape class, for example). However, they are limited to appearing in the upper levels of class hierarchies.

Interfaces and abstract classes can be used together. For example, the Collections Framework's java.util package provides List, Map, and Set interfaces; and AbstractList, AbstractMap, and AbstractSet abstract classes that provide skeletal implementations of these interfaces.

The skeletal implementations make it easy for you to create your own interface implementations, to address your unique requirements. If they do not meet your needs, you can optionally have your class directly implement the appropriate interface.

Collecting Garbage

Objects are created via reserved word new, but how are they destroyed? Without some way to destroy objects, they will eventually fill up the heap's available space and the application will not be able to continue. Java does not provide the developer with the ability to remove them from memory. Instead, Java handles this task by providing a *garbage collector*, which is code that runs in the background and occasionally checks for unreferenced objects. When the garbage collector discovers an unreferenced object (or multiple objects that reference each other, and where there are no other references to each other—only A references B and only B references A, for example), it removes the object from the heap, making more heap space available.

An *unreferenced object* is an object that cannot be accessed from anywhere within an application. For example, new Employee("John", "Doe"); is an unreferenced object because the Employee reference returned by new is thrown away. In contrast, a *referenced object* is an object where the application stores at least one reference. For example, Employee emp = new Employee("John", "Doe"); is a referenced object because variable emp contains a reference to the Employee object.

A referenced object becomes unreferenced when the application removes its last stored reference. For example, if emp is a local variable that contains the only reference to an Employee object, this object becomes unreferenced when the method in which emp is declared returns. An application can also remove a stored reference by assigning null to its reference variable. For example, emp = null; removes the reference to the Employee object that was previously stored in emp.

Java's garbage collector eliminates a form of memory leakage in C++ implementations that do not rely on a garbage collector. In these C++ implementations, the developer must destroy dynamically created objects before they go out of scope. If they vanish before destruction, they remain in the heap. Eventually, the heap fills and the application halts.

Although this form of memory leakage is not a problem in Java, a related form of leakage is problematic: continually creating objects and forgetting to remove even one reference to each object causes the heap to fill up and the application to eventually come to a halt. This form of memory leakage typically occurs in the context of *collections* (object-based data structures that store objects), and is a major problem for applications that run for lengthy periods of time—a web server is one example. For shorter-lived applications, you will normally not notice this form of memory leakage.

Consider Listing 2-49.

Listing 2-49. A memory-leaking stack

```
public class Stack
{
   private Object[] elements;
   private int top;
   public Stack(int size)
   {
      elements = new Object[size];
      top = -1; // indicate that stack is empty
   }
   public void push(Object o)
   {
```

```
        if (top+1 == elements.length)
        {
            System.out.println("stack is full");
            return;
        }
      elements[++top] = o;
   }
   public Object pop()
   {
        if (top == -1)
        {
            System.out.println("stack is empty");
            return null;
        }
        Object element = elements[top--];
//        elements[top+1] = null;
        return element;
   }
   public static void main(String[] args)
   {
        Stack stack = new Stack(2);
        stack.push("A");
        stack.push("B");
        stack.push("C");
        System.out.println(stack.pop());
        System.out.println(stack.pop());
        System.out.println(stack.pop());
   }
}
```

Listing 2-49 describes a collection known as a *stack*, a data structure that stores elements in last-in, first-out order. Stacks are useful for remembering things, such as the instruction to return to when a method stops executing and must return to its caller.

Stack provides a push() method for pushing arbitrary objects onto the *top* of the stack, and a pop() method for popping objects off the stack's top in the reverse order to which they were pushed.

After creating a Stack object that can store a maximum of two objects, main() invokes push() three times, to push three String objects onto the stack. Because the stack's internal array can store two objects only, push() outputs an error message when main() tries to push "C".

At this point, main() attempts to pop three Objects off of the stack, outputting each object to the standard output device. The first two pop() method calls succeed, but the final method call fails and outputs an error message because the stack is empty when it is called.

When you run this application, it generates the following output:

```
stack is full
B
A
stack is empty
null
```

There is a problem with the Stack class: it leaks memory. When you push an object onto the stack, its reference is stored in the internal elements array. When you pop an object off the stack, the object's reference is obtained and top is decremented, but the reference remains in the array (until you invoke push()).

Imagine a scenario where the Stack object's reference is assigned to a class field, which means that the Stack object hangs around for the life of the application. Furthermore, suppose that you have pushed three 50-megabyte Image objects onto the stack, and then subsequently popped them off the stack. After using these objects, you assign null to their reference variables, thinking that they will be garbage collected the next time the garbage collector runs. However, this won't happen because the Stack object still maintains its references to these objects, and so 150 megabytes of heap space will not be available to the application, and maybe the application will run out of memory.

The solution to this problem is for pop() to explicitly assign null to the elements entry prior to returning the reference. Simply uncomment the elements[top+1] = null; line in Listing 2-49 to make this happen.

You might think that you should always assign null to reference variables when their referenced objects are no longer required. However, doing so often does not improve performance or free up significant amounts of heap space, and can lead to thrown instances of the java.lang.NullPointerException class when you're not careful. (I discuss NullPointerException in the context of Chapter 3's coverage of Java's exceptions-oriented language features). You typically nullify reference variables in classes that manage their own memory, such as the aforementioned Stack class.

Note Garbage collection is a complex process and has resulted in various garbage collectors being developed for the JVM. If you want to learn more about garbage collection, I recommend that you start by reading the "Memory Management in the Java HotSpot Virtual Machine" whitepaper at http://www.oracle.com/technetwork/java/javase/tech/memorymanagement-whitepaper-1-150020.pdf. Next, you will want to learn about the Garbage-First collector, which is new in Java 7. Check out "The Garbage-First Garbage Collector" whitepaper (http://www.oracle.com/technetwork/java/javase/tech/g1-intro-jsp-135488.html) to learn about this garbage collector. For additional information on Java's garbage collection process, you can explore the other whitepapers that are accessible from Oracle's "Java HotSpot Garbage Collection" page at http://www.oracle.com/technetwork/java/javase/tech/index-jsp-140228.html.

Chapter 4 pursues garbage collection further by introducing you to Java's Reference API, which lets your application receive notifications when objects are about to be finalized or have been finalized.

Note Throughout this book, I often refer to *API* in both broad and narrow contexts. On the one hand, I refer to Reference as an API, but I also refer to the individual classes of Reference as APIs themselves.

EXERCISES

The following exercises are designed to test your understanding of classes and objects:

1. Listing 2-2 presents an `Image` class with three constructors and a `main()` method for testing this class. Expand `Image` by introducing private `int` fields named `width` and `height`, and a private one-dimensional byte array field named `image`. Refactor the `Image()` constructor to invoke the `Image(String filename)` constructor via `this(null)`. Refactor the `Image(String filename, String imageType)` constructor such that, when the `filename` reference is not null, it creates a byte array of arbitrary size, perhaps with the help of an expression such as `(int) (Math.random()*100000)` (return a randomly generated integer between 0 and 99999 inclusive), and assigns this array's reference to the `image` field. Similarly, it assigns an arbitrary width to the `width` field and an arbitrary height to the `height` field. If `filename` contains null, it assigns -1 to each of `width` and `height`. Continuing, introduce `getWidth()`, `getHeight()`, and `getImage()` methods that return the values of their respective fields, and introduce a `getSize()` method that returns the length of the array assigned to the `image` field (or 0 if `image` contains the null reference). Finally, refactor the `main()` method such that, for each constructor, the following sequence of method calls occurs:
    ```
    System.out.println("Image = "+image.getImage());
    System.out.println("Size = "+image.getSize());
    System.out.println("Width = "+image.getWidth());
    System.out.println("Height = "+image.getHeight());.
    ```

2. Model part of an animal hierarchy by declaring `Animal`, `Bird`, `Fish`, `AmericanRobin`, `DomesticCanary`, `RainbowTrout`, and `SockeyeSalmon` classes:

    *   `Animal` is public and abstract, declares private `String`-based `kind` and `appearance` fields, declares a public constructor that initializes these fields to passed-in arguments, declares public and abstract `eat()` and `move()` methods that take no arguments and whose return type is `void`, and overrides the `toString()` method to output the contents of `kind` and `appearance`.

    *   `Bird` is public and abstract, extends `Animal`, declares a public constructor that passes its `kind` and `appearance` parameter values to its superclass constructor, overrides its `eat()` method to output `eats seeds and insects` (via `System.out.println()`), and overrides the `move()` method to output `flies through the air`.

    *   `Fish` is public and abstract, extends `Animal`, declares a public constructor that passes its `kind` and `appearance` parameter values to its superclass constructor, overrides its `eat()` method to output `eats krill, algae, and insects`, and overrides its `move()` method to output `swims through the water`.

- `AmericanRobin` is `public`, extends `Bird`, and declares a `public` noargument constructor that passes `"americanrobin"` and `"red breast"` to its superclass constructor.

- `DomesticCanary` is `public`, extends `Bird`, and declares a `public` noargument constructor that passes `"domesticcanary"` and `"yellow, orange, black, brown, white, red"` to its superclass constructor.

- `RainbowTrout` is `public`, extends `Fish`, and declares a `public` noargument constructor that passes `"rainbowtrout"` and `"bands of brilliant speckled multicolored stripes running nearly the whole length of its body"` to its superclass constructor.

- `SockeyeSalmon` is `public`, extends `Fish`, and declares a `public` noargument constructor that passes `"sockeyesalmon"` and `"bright red with a green head"` to its superclass constructor.

  For brevity, I have omitted from the `Animal` hierarchy abstract `Robin`, `Canary`, `Trout`, and `Salmon` classes that generalize robins, canaries, trout, and salmon. Perhaps you might want to include these classes in the hierarchy.

  Although this exercise illustrates the accurate modeling of a natural scenario using inheritance, it also reveals the potential for *class explosion*—too many classes may be introduced to model a scenario, and it might be difficult to maintain all these classes. Keep this in mind when modeling with inheritance.

3. Continuing from the previous exercise, declare an `Animals` class with a `main()` method. This method first declares an `animals` array that is initialized to `AmericanRobin`, `RainbowTrout`, `DomesticCanary`, and `SockeyeSalmon` objects. The method then iterates over this array, first outputting `animals[i]` (which causes `toString()` to be called), and then calling each object's `eat()` and `move()` methods (demonstrating subtype polymorphism).

4. Continuing from the previous exercise, declare a `public Countable` interface with a `String getID()` method. Modify `Animal` to implement `Countable` and have this method return `kind`'s value. Modify `Animals` to initialize the `animals` array to `AmericanRobin`, `RainbowTrout`, `DomesticCanary`, `SockeyeSalmon`, `RainbowTrout`, and `AmericanRobin` objects. Also, introduce code that computes a census of each kind of animal. This code will use the `Census` class that is declared in Listing 2-50.

    Listing 2-50. The Census class stores census data on four kinds of animals

```
public class Census
{
    public final static int SIZE = 4;
    private String[] IDs;
    private int[] counts;
    public Census()
```

```java
   {
      IDs = new String[SIZE];
      counts = new int[SIZE];
   }
   public String get(int index)
   {
      return IDs[index]+" "+counts[index];
   }
   public void update(String ID)
   {
      for (int i = 0; i < IDs.length; i++)
      {
         // If ID not already stored in the IDs array (which is indicated by
         // the first null entry that is found), store ID in this array, and
         // also assign 1 to the associated element in the counts array, to
         // initialize the census for that ID.
         if (IDs[i] == null)
         {
            IDs[i] = ID;
            counts[i] = 1;
            return;
         }

         // If a matching ID is found, increment the associated element in
         // the counts array to update the census for that ID.
         if (IDs[i].equals(ID))
         {
            counts[i]++;
            return;
         }
      }
   }
}
```

Summary

Structured programs create data structures that organize and store data items, and manipulate the data stored in these data structures via functions and procedures. The fundamental units of a structured program are its data structures and the functions or procedures that manipulate them. Although Java lets you create applications in a similar fashion, this language is really about declaring classes and creating objects from these classes.

A class is a template for manufacturing objects (named aggregates of code and data), which are also known as class instances, or instances for short. Classes generalize real-world entities, and objects are specific manifestations of these entities at the program level.

Classes model real-world entities from a template perspective. Objects represent specific entities. Entities have attributes. An entity's collection of attributes is referred to as its state. Entities also have behaviors.

A class and its objects model an entity by combining state with behaviors into a single unit—the class abstracts state whereas its objects provide concrete state values. This bringing together of state and behaviors is known as encapsulation. Unlike structured programming, where the developer focuses on modeling behaviors through structured code, and modeling state through data structures that store data items for the structured code to manipulate, the developer working with classes and objects focuses on templating entities by declaring classes that encapsulate state and behaviors expressed as fields and methods, instantiating objects with specific field values from these classes to represent specific entities, and interacting with objects by invoking their methods.

We tend to categorize stuff by saying things like "cars are vehicles" or "savings accounts are bank accounts." By making these statements, we really are saying that cars inherit vehicular state (such as make and color) and behaviors (such as park and display mileage), and similarly are saying that savings accounts inherit bank account state (such as balance) and behaviors (such as deposit and withdraw). Car, vehicle, savings account, and bank account are examples of real-world entity categories, and inheritance is a hierarchical relationship between similar entity categories in which one category inherits state and behaviors from at least one other entity category. Inheriting from a single category is called single inheritance, and inheriting from at least two categories is called multiple inheritance.

Java supports single inheritance and multiple inheritance to facilitate code reuse—why reinvent the wheel? Java supports single inheritance in a class context, in which a class inherits fields and methods from another class through class extension. Because classes are involved, Java refers to this kind of inheritance as implementation inheritance.

Java supports multiple inheritance only in an interface context, in which a class inherits method templates from one or more interfaces through interface implementation, or in which an interface inherits method templates from one or more interfaces through interface extension. Because interfaces are involved, Java refers to this kind of inheritance as interface inheritance.

Some real-world entities can change their forms. For example, water is naturally a liquid, but it changes to a solid when frozen, and it changes to a gas when heated to its boiling point. Insects such as butterflies that undergo metamorphosis are another example.

The ability to change form is known as polymorphism, and is useful to model in a programming language. For example, code that draws arbitrary shapes can be expressed more concisely by introducing a single Shape class and its draw() method, and by invoking that method for each Circle instance, Rectangle instance, and other Shape instance stored in an array. When Shape's draw() method is called for an array instance, it is the Circle's, Rectangle's or other Shape instance's draw() method that gets called. We say that there are many forms of Shape's draw() method, or that this method is polymorphic.

Every class X exposes an interface (a protocol consisting of constructors, methods, and [possibly] fields that are made available to objects created from other classes for use in creating and communicating with X's objects). Java formalizes the interface concept by providing reserved word interface, which is used to introduce a type without implementation. Although many believe that this language feature was created as a workaround to Java's lack of support for multiple implementation inheritance, this is not the real reason for its existence. Instead, Java's interfaces feature was created to give developers the utmost flexibility in designing their applications, by decoupling interface from implementation.

Objects are created via reserved word new, but how are they destroyed? Without some way to destroy objects, they will eventually fill up the heap's available space and the application will not be able to continue. Java does not provide the developer with the ability to remove them from memory. Instead, Java handles this task by providing a garbage collector, which is code that runs in the background and occasionally checks for unreferenced objects. When the garbage collector discovers an unreferenced object (or multiple objects that reference each other, and where there are no other references to each other—only A references B and only B references A, for example), it removes the object from the heap, making more heap space available.

Now that you understand Java's support for classes and objects, you're ready to explore this language's support for more advanced features such as packages and generics. Chapter 3 introduces you to Java's support for these and other advanced language features.

CHAPTER 3

Exploring Advanced Language Features

Chapters 1 and 2 introduced you to Java's fundamental language features along with its support for classes and objects. Chapter 3 builds onto this foundation by introducing you to Java's advanced language features, specifically those features related to nested types, packages, static imports, exceptions, assertions, annotations, generics, and enums.

Nested Types

Classes that are declared outside of any class are known as *top-level classes*. Java also supports *nested classes*, which are classes declared as members of other classes or scopes. Nested classes help you implement top-level class architecture.

There are four kinds of nested classes: static member classes, nonstatic member classes, anonymous classes, and local classes. The latter three categories are known as *inner classes*.

This section introduces you to static member classes and inner classes. For each kind of nested class, I provide you with a brief introduction, an abstract example, and a more practical example. The section then briefly examines the topic of nesting interfaces within classes.

Static Member Classes

A *static member class* is a static member of an enclosing class. Although enclosed, it does not have an enclosing instance of that class, and cannot access the enclosing class's instance fields and invoke its instance methods. However, it can access the enclosing class's static fields and invoke its static methods, even those members that are declared private. Listing 3-1 presents a static member class declaration.

Listing 3-1. *Declaring a static member class*

```
class EnclosingClass
{
   private static int i;
   private static void m1()
   {
      System.out.println(i);
   }
   static void m2()
```

```
    {
        EnclosedClass.accessEnclosingClass();
    }
    static class EnclosedClass
    {
        static void accessEnclosingClass()
        {
            i = 1;
            m1();
        }
        void accessEnclosingClass2()
        {
            m2();
        }
    }
}
```

Listing 3-1 declares a top-level class named EnclosingClass with class field i, class methods m1() and m2(), and static member class EnclosedClass. Also, EnclosedClass declares class method accessEnclosingClass() and instance method accessEnclosingClass2().

Because accessEnclosingClass() is declared static, m2() must prefix this method's name with EnclosedClass and the member access operator to invoke this method.

Listing 3-2 presents the source code to an application that demonstrates how to invoke EnclosedClass's accessEnclosingClass() class method, and instantiate EnclosedClass and invoke its accessEnclosingClass2() instance method.

Listing 3-2. *Invoking a static member class's class and instance methods*

```
class SMCDemo
{
    public static void main(String[] args)
    {
        EnclosingClass.EnclosedClass.accessEnclosingClass(); // Output: 1
        EnclosingClass.EnclosedClass ec = new EnclosingClass.EnclosedClass();
        ec.accessEnclosingClass2(); // Output: 1
    }
}
```

Listing 3-2's main() method reveals that you must prefix the name of an enclosed class with the name of its enclosing class to invoke a class method; for example, EnclosingClass.EnclosedClass.accessEnclosingClass();.

This listing also reveals that you must prefix the name of the enclosed class with the name of its enclosing class when instantiating the enclosed class; for example, EnclosingClass.EnclosedClass ec = new EnclosingClass.EnclosedClass();. You can then invoke the instance method in the normal manner; for example, ec.accessEnclosingClass2();.

Static member classes have their uses. For example, Listing 3-3's Double and Float static member classes provide different implementations of their enclosing Rectangle class. The Float version occupies less memory because of its 32-bit float fields, and the Double version provides greater accuracy because of its 64-bit double fields.

Listing 3-3. Using static member classes to declare multiple implementations of their enclosing class

```
abstract class Rectangle
{
   abstract double getX();
   abstract double getY();
   abstract double getWidth();
   abstract double getHeight();
   static class Double extends Rectangle
   {
      private double x, y, width, height;
      Double(double x, double y, double width, double height)
      {
         this.x = x;
         this.y = y;
         this.width = width;
         this.height = height;
      }
      double getX() { return x; }
      double getY() { return y; }
      double getWidth() { return width; }
      double getHeight() { return height; }
   }
   static class Float extends Rectangle
   {
      private float x, y, width, height;
      Float(float x, float y, float width, float height)
      {
         this.x = x;
         this.y = y;
         this.width = width;
         this.height = height;
      }
      double getX() { return x; }
      double getY() { return y; }
      double getWidth() { return width; }
      double getHeight() { return height; }
   }
   // Prevent subclassing. Use the type-specific Double and Float
   // implementation subclass classes to instantiate.
   private Rectangle() {}
   boolean contains(double x, double y)
   {
      return (x >= getX() && x < getX()+getWidth()) &&
             (y >= getY() && y < getY()+getHeight());
   }
}
```

Listing 3-3's Rectangle class demonstrates nested subclasses. Each of the Double and Float static member classes subclass the abstract Rectangle class, providing private floating-point or double precision floating-point fields, and overriding Rectangle's abstract methods to return these fields' values as doubles.

Rectangle is abstract because it makes no sense to instantiate this class. Because it also makes no sense to directly extend Rectangle with new implementations (the Double and Float nested subclasses should be sufficient), its default constructor is declared private. Instead, you must instantiate Rectangle.Float (to save memory) or Rectangle.Double (when accuracy is required), as demonstrated by Listing 3-4.

Listing 3-4. *Instantiating nested subclasses*

```
class SMCDemo
{
   public static void main(String[] args)
   {
      Rectangle r = new Rectangle.Double(10.0, 10.0, 20.0, 30.0);
      System.out.println("x = "+r.getX());
      System.out.println("y = "+r.getY());
      System.out.println("width = "+r.getWidth());
      System.out.println("height = "+r.getHeight());
      System.out.println("contains(15.0, 15.0) = "+r.contains(15.0, 15.0));
      System.out.println("contains(0.0, 0.0) = "+r.contains(0.0, 0.0));
      System.out.println();
      r = new Rectangle.Float(10.0f, 10.0f, 20.0f, 30.0f);
      System.out.println("x = "+r.getX());
      System.out.println("y = "+r.getY());
      System.out.println("width = "+r.getWidth());
      System.out.println("height = "+r.getHeight());
      System.out.println("contains(15.0, 15.0) = "+r.contains(15.0, 15.0));
      System.out.println("contains(0.0, 0.0) = "+r.contains(0.0, 0.0));
   }
}
```

Listing 3-4 first instantiates Rectangle's Double subclass via new Rectangle.Double(10.0, 10.0, 20.0, 30.0) and then invokes its various methods. Continuing, Listing 3-4 instantiates Rectangle's Float subclass via new Rectangle.Float(10.0f, 10.0f, 20.0f, 30.0f) before invoking Rectangle methods on this instance.

Compile both listings (javac SMCDemo.java or javac *.java) and run the application (java SMCDemo). You will then observe the following output:

```
x = 10.0
y = 10.0
width = 20.0
height = 30.0
contains(15.0, 15.0) = true
contains(0.0, 0.0) = false

x = 10.0
y = 10.0
width = 20.0
height = 30.0
contains(15.0, 15.0) = true
contains(0.0, 0.0) = false
```

Java's class library contains many static member classes. For example, the `java.lang.Character` class encloses a static member class named Subset whose instances represent subsets of the Unicode character set. `java.util.AbstractMap.SimpleEntry`, `java.io.ObjectInputStream.GetField`, and `java.security.KeyStore.PrivateKeyEntry` are other examples.

Note When you compile an enclosing class that contains a static member class, the compiler creates a classfile for the static member class whose name consists of its enclosing class's name, a dollar-sign character, and the static member class's name. For example, compile Listing 3-1 and you will discover `EnclosingClass$EnclosedClass.class` as well as `EnclosingClass.class`. This format also applies to nonstatic member classes.

Nonstatic Member Classes

A *nonstatic member class* is a non-static member of an enclosing class. Each instance of the nonstatic member class implicitly associates with an instance of the enclosing class. The nonstatic member class's instance methods can call instance methods in the enclosing class and access the enclosing class instance's nonstatic fields. Listing 3-5 presents a nonstatic member class declaration.

Listing 3-5. *Declaring a nonstatic member class*

```
class EnclosingClass
{
   private int i;
   private void m()
   {
      System.out.println(i);
   }
   class EnclosedClass
   {
      void accessEnclosingClass()
      {
         i = 1;
         m();
      }
   }
}
```

Listing 3-5 declares a top-level class named EnclosingClass with instance field i, instance method m(), and nonstatic member class EnclosedClass. Furthermore, EnclosedClass declares instance method accessEnclosingClass().

Because accessEnclosingClass() is nonstatic, EnclosedClass must be instantiated before this method can be called. This instantiation must take place via an instance of EnclosingClass. Listing 3-6 accomplishes these tasks.

Listing 3-6. Calling a nonstatic member class's instance method

```
class NSMCDemo
{
   public static void main(String[] args)
   {
      EnclosingClass ec = new EnclosingClass();
      ec.new EnclosedClass().accessEnclosingClass(); // Output: 1
   }
}
```

Listing 3-6's `main()` method first instantiates `EnclosingClass` and saves its reference in local variable `ec`. Then, `main()` uses this reference as a prefix to the `new` operator, to instantiate `EnclosedClass`, whose reference is then used to call `accessEnclosingClass()`, which outputs 1.

■ **Note** Prefixing `new` with a reference to the enclosing class is rare. Instead, you will typically call an enclosed class's constructor from within a constructor or an instance method of its enclosing class.

Suppose you need to maintain a to-do list of items, where each item consists of a name and a description. After some thought, you create Listing 3-7's ToDo class to implement these items.

Listing 3-7. Implementing to-do items as name-description pairs

```
class ToDo
{
   private String name;
   private String desc;
   ToDo(String name, String desc)
   {
      this.name = name;
      this.desc = desc;
   }
   String getName()
   {
      return name;
   }
   String getDesc()
   {
      return desc;
   }
   @Override
   public String toString()
   {
      return "Name = "+getName()+", Desc = "+getDesc();
   }
}
```

You next create a ToDoList class to store ToDo instances. ToDoList uses its ToDoArray nonstatic member class to store ToDo instances in a growable array – you do not know how many instances will be stored, and Java arrays have fixed lengths. See Listing 3-8.

Listing 3-8. Storing a maximum of two ToDo instances in a ToDoArray instance

```
class ToDoList
{
    private ToDoArray toDoArray;
    private int index = 0;
    ToDoList()
    {
        toDoArray = new ToDoArray(2);
    }
    boolean hasMoreElements()
    {
        return index < toDoArray.size();
    }
    ToDo nextElement()
    {
        return toDoArray.get(index++);
    }
    void add(ToDo item)
    {
        toDoArray.add(item);
    }
    private class ToDoArray
    {
        private ToDo[] toDoArray;
        private int index = 0;
        ToDoArray(int initSize)
        {
            toDoArray = new ToDo[initSize];
        }
        void add(ToDo item)
        {
            if (index >= toDoArray.length)
            {
                ToDo[] temp = new ToDo[toDoArray.length*2];
                for (int i = 0; i < toDoArray.length; i++)
                    temp[i] = toDoArray[i];
                toDoArray = temp;
            }
            toDoArray[index++] = item;
        }
        ToDo get(int i)
        {
            return toDoArray[i];
        }
        int size()
        {
            return index;
```

```
        }
      }
}
```

As well as providing an add() method to store ToDo instances in the ToDoArray instance, ToDoList provides hasMoreElements() and nextElement() methods to iterate over and return the stored instances. Listing 3-9 demonstrates these methods.

Listing 3-9. Creating and iterating over a ToDoList of ToDo instances

```
class NSMCDemo
{
   public static void main(String[] args)
   {
      ToDoList toDoList = new ToDoList();
      toDoList.add(new ToDo("#1", "Do laundry."));
      toDoList.add(new ToDo("#2", "Buy groceries."));
      toDoList.add(new ToDo("#3", "Vacuum apartment."));
      toDoList.add(new ToDo("#4", "Write report."));
      toDoList.add(new ToDo("#5", "Wash car."));
      while (toDoList.hasMoreElements())
         System.out.println(toDoList.nextElement());
   }
}
```

Compile all three listings (javac NSMCDemo.java or javac *.java) and run the application (java NSMCDemo). You will then observe the following output:

```
Name = #1, Desc = Do laundry.
Name = #2, Desc = Buy groceries.
Name = #3, Desc = Vacuum apartment.
Name = #4, Desc = Write report.
Name = #5, Desc = Wash car.
```

Java's class library presents many examples of nonstatic member classes. For example, the java.util package's HashMap class declares private HashIterator, ValueIterator, KeyIterator, and EntryIterator classes for iterating over a hashmap's values, keys, and entries. (I will discuss HashMap in Chapter 5.)

■ **Note** Code within an enclosed class can obtain a reference to its enclosing class instance by qualifying reserved word this with the enclosing class's name and the member access operator. For example, if code within accessEnclosingClass() needed to obtain a reference to its EnclosingClass instance, it would specify EnclosingClass.this.

Anonymous Classes

An *anonymous class* is a class without a name. Furthermore, it is not a member of its enclosing class. Instead, an anonymous class is simultaneously declared (as an anonymous extension of a class or as an anonymous implementation of an interface) and instantiated any place where it is legal to specify an expression. Listing 3-10 demonstrates an anonymous class declaration and instantiation.

Listing 3-10. Declaring and instantiating an anonymous class that extends a class

```
abstract class Speaker
{
   abstract void speak();
}
class ACDemo
{
   public static void main(final String[] args)
   {
      new Speaker()
      {
         String msg = (args.length == 1) ? args[0] : "nothing to say";
         @Override
         void speak()
         {
            System.out.println(msg);
         }
      }
      .speak();
   }
}
```

Listing 3-10 introduces an abstract class named Speaker and a concrete class named ACDemo. The latter class's main() method declares an anonymous class that extends Speaker and overrides its speak() method. When this method is called, it outputs main()'s first command-line argument or a default message if there are no arguments; for example, java ACDemo Hello outputs Hello.

An anonymous class does not have a constructor (because the anonymous class does not have a name). However, its classfile does contain an <init>() method that performs instance initialization. This method calls the superclass's noargument constructor (prior to any other initialization), which is the reason for specifying Speaker() after new.

Anonymous class instances should be able to access the surrounding scope's local variables and parameters. However, an instance might outlive the method in which it was conceived (as a result of storing the instance's reference in a field), and try to access local variables and parameters that no longer exist after the method returns.

Because Java cannot allow this illegal access, which would most likely crash the Java Virtual Machine (JVM), it lets an anonymous class instance only access local variables and parameters that are declared final. Upon encountering a final local variable/parameter name in an anonymous class instance, the compiler does one of two things:

- If the variable's type is primitive (int or double, for example), the compiler replaces its name with the variable's read-only value.

- If the variable's type is reference (java.lang.String, for example), the compiler introduces, into the classfile, a *synthetic variable* (a manufactured variable) and code that stores the local variable's/parameter's reference in the synthetic variable.

Listing 3-11 demonstrates an alternative anonymous class declaration and instantiation.

Listing 3-11. Declaring and instantiating an anonymous class that implements an interface

```
interface Speakable
{
   void speak();
}
class ACDemo
{
   public static void main(final String[] args)
   {
      new Speakable()
      {
         String msg = (args.length == 1) ? args[0] : "nothing to say";
         @Override
         public void speak()
         {
            System.out.println(msg);
         }
      }
      .speak();
   }
}
```

Listing 3-11 is very similar to Listing 3-10. However, instead of subclassing a Speaker class, this listing's anonymous class implements an interface named Speakable. Apart from the <init>() method calling java.lang.Object() (interfaces have no constructors), Listing 3-11 behaves like Listing 3-10.

Although an anonymous class does not have a constructor, you can provide an instance initializer to handle complex initialization. For example, new Office() {{addEmployee(new Employee("John Doe"));}}; instantiates an anonymous subclass of Office and adds one Employee object to this instance by calling Office's addEmployee() method.

You will often find yourself creating and instantiating anonymous classes for their convenience. For example, suppose you need to return a list of all filenames having the ".java" suffix. The following example shows you how an anonymous class simplifies using the java.io package's File and FilenameFilter classes to achieve this objective:

```
String[] list = new File(directory).list(new FilenameFilter()
            {
                @Override
                public boolean accept(File f, String s)
                {
                    return s.endsWith(".java");
                }
            });
```

Local Classes

A *local class* is a class that is declared anywhere that a local variable is declared. Furthermore, it has the same scope as a local variable. Unlike an anonymous class, a local class has a name and can be reused. Like anonymous classes, local classes only have enclosing instances when used in nonstatic contexts.

A local class instance can access the surrounding scope's local variables and parameters. However, the local variables and parameters that are accessed must be declared final. For example, Listing 3-12's local class declaration accesses a final parameter and a final local variable.

Listing 3-12. Declaring a local class

```
class EnclosingClass
{
   void m(final int x)
   {
      final int y = x*2;
      class LocalClass
      {
         int a = x;
         int b = y;
      }
      LocalClass lc = new LocalClass();
      System.out.println(lc.a);
      System.out.println(lc.b);
   }
}
```

Listing 3-12 declares EnclosingClass with its instance method m() declaring a local class named LocalClass. This local class declares a pair of instance fields (a and b) that are initialized to the values of final parameter x and final local variable y when LocalClass is instantiated: new EnclosingClass().m(10);, for example.

Listing 3-13 demonstrates this local class.

Listing 3-13. Demonstrating a local class

```
class LCDemo
{
   public static void main(String[] args)
   {
      EnclosingClass ec = new EnclosingClass();
      ec.m(10);
   }
}
```

After instantiating EnclosingClass, Listing 3-13's main() method invokes m(10). The called m() method multiplies this argument by 2, instantiates LocalClass, whose <init>() method assigns the argument and the doubled value to its pair of instance fields (in lieu of using a constructor to perform this task), and outputs the LocalClass instance fields. The following output results:

```
10
20
```

Local classes help improve code clarity because they can be moved closer to where they are needed. For example, Listing 3-14 declares an Iterator interface and a refactored ToDoList class whose iterator() method returns an instance of its local Iter class as an Iterator instance (because Iter implements Iterator).

Listing 3-14. The Iterator interface and the refactored ToDoList class

```
interface Iterator
{
   boolean hasMoreElements();
   Object nextElement();
}
class ToDoList
{
   private ToDo[] toDoList;
   private int index = 0;
   ToDoList(int size)
   {
      toDoList = new ToDo[size];
   }
   Iterator iterator()
   {
      class Iter implements Iterator
      {
         int index = 0;
         @Override
         public boolean hasMoreElements()
         {
            return index < toDoList.length;
         }
         @Override
         public Object nextElement()
         {
            return toDoList[index++];
         }
      }
      return new Iter();
   }
   void add(ToDo item)
   {
      toDoList[index++] = item;
   }
}
```

Listing 3-15 demonstrates Iterator, the refactored ToDoList class, and Listing 3-7's ToDo class.

Listing 3-15. Creating and iterating over a ToDoList of ToDo instances with a reusable iterator

```
class LCDemo
{
   public static void main(String[] args)
   {
      ToDoList toDoList = new ToDoList(5);
      toDoList.add(new ToDo("#1", "Do laundry."));
      toDoList.add(new ToDo("#2", "Buy groceries."));
      toDoList.add(new ToDo("#3", "Vacuum apartment."));
```

```
        toDoList.add(new ToDo("#4", "Write report."));
        toDoList.add(new ToDo("#5", "Wash car."));
        Iterator iter = toDoList.iterator();
        while (iter.hasMoreElements())
            System.out.println(iter.nextElement());
    }
}
```

The Iterator instance that is returned from iterator() returns ToDo items in the same order as when they were added to the list. Although you can only use the returned Iterator object once, you can call iterator() whenever you need a new Iterator object. This capability is a big improvement over the one-shot iterator presented in Listing 3-9.

Interfaces Within Classes

Interfaces can be nested within classes. Once declared, an interface is considered to be static, even if it is not declared static. For example, Listing 3-16 declares an enclosing class named X along with two nested static interfaces named A and B.

Listing 3-16. *Declaring a pair of interfaces within a class*

```
class X
{
    interface A
    {
    }
    static interface B
    {
    }
}
```

You would access Listing 3-16's interfaces in the same way. For example, you would specify class C implements X.A {} or class D implements X.B {}.

As with nested classes, nested interfaces help to implement top-level class architecture by being implemented via nested classes. Collectively, these types are nested because they cannot (as in Listing 3-14's Iter local class) or need not appear at the same level as a top-level class and pollute its package namespace.

■ **Note** Chapter 2's introduction to interfaces showed you how to declare constants and method headers in the body of an interface. You can also declare interfaces and classes in an interface's body. Because there are few good reasons to do this (java.util.Map.Entry, which is discussed in Chapter 5, is one exception), it is probably best to avoid nesting interfaces and/or classes within interfaces.

Packages

Hierarchical structures organize items in terms of hierarchical relationships that exist between those items. For example, a filesystem might contain a taxes directory with multiple year subdirectories, where each subdirectory contains tax information pertinent to that year. Also, an enclosing class might contain multiple nested classes that only make sense in the context of the enclosing class.

Hierarchical structures also help to avoid name conflicts. For example, two files cannot have the same name in a nonhierarchical filesystem (which consists of a single directory). In contrast, a hierarchical filesystem lets same-named files exist in different directories. Similarly, two enclosing classes can contain same-named nested classes. Name conflicts do not exist because items are partitioned into different *namespaces*.

Java also supports the partitioning of top-level user-defined types into multiple namespaces, to better organize these types and to also prevent name conflicts. Java uses packages to accomplish these tasks.

This section introduces you to packages. After defining this term and explaining why package names must be unique, the section presents the package and import statements. It next explains how the JVM searches for packages and types, and then presents an example that shows you how to work with packages. This section closes by showing you how to encapsulate a package of classfiles into JAR files.

■ **Tip** Except for the most trivial of top-level types and (typically) those classes that serve as application entry points, you should consider storing your types (especially if they are reusable) in packages.

What Are Packages?

A *package* is a unique namespace that can contain a combination of top-level classes, other top-level types, and subpackages. Only types that are declared public can be accessed from outside the package. Furthermore, the constants, constructors, methods, and nested types that describe a class's interface must be declared public to be accessible from beyond the package.

■ **Note** Throughout this book, I typically don't declare top-level types and their accessible members public, unless I'm creating a package.

Every package has a name, which must be a nonreserved identifier. The member access operator separates a package name from a subpackage name, and separates a package or subpackage name from a type name. For example, the two member access operators in graphics.shapes.Circle separate package name graphics from the shapes subpackage name, and separate subpackage name shapes from the Circle type name.

▪ **Note** The standard class library organizes its many classes and other top-level types into multiple packages. Many of these packages are subpackages of the standard `java` package. Examples include `java.io` (types related to input/output operations), `java.lang` (language-oriented types), `java.lang.reflect` (reflection-oriented language types), `java.net` (network-oriented types), and `java.util` (utility types).

Package Names Must Be Unique

Suppose you have two different `graphics.shapes` packages, and suppose that each `shapes` subpackage contains a `Circle` class with a different interface. When the compiler encounters `System.out.println(new Circle(10.0, 20.0, 30.0).area());` in the source code, it needs to verify that the `area()` method exists.

The compiler will search all accessible packages until it finds a `graphics.shapes` package that contains a `Circle` class. If the found package contains the appropriate `Circle` class with an `area()` method, everything is fine; otherwise, if the `Circle` class does not have an `area()` method, the compiler will report an error.

This scenario illustrates the importance of choosing unique package names. Specifically, the top-level package name must be unique. The convention in choosing this name is to take your Internet domain name and reverse it. For example, I would choose `ca.tutortutor` as my top-level package name because `tutortutor.ca` is my domain name. I would then specify `ca.tutortutor.graphics.shapes.Circle` to access `Circle`.

▪ **Note** Reversed Internet domain names are not always valid package names. One or more of its component names might start with a digit (`6.com`), contain a hyphen (-) or other illegal character (`aq-x.com`), or be one of Java's reserved words (`int.com`). Convention dictates that you prefix the digit with an underscore (`com._6`), replace the illegal character with an underscore (`com.aq_x`), and suffix the reserved word with an underscore (`com.int_`).

The Package Statement

The package statement identifies the package in which a source file's types are located. This statement consists of reserved word `package`, followed by a member access operator-separated list of package and subpackage names, followed by a semicolon.

For example, `package graphics;` specifies that the source file's types locate in a package named `graphics`, and `package graphics.shapes;` specifies that the source file's types locate in the `graphics` package's `shapes` subpackage.

By convention, a package name is expressed in lowercase. If the name consists of multiple words, each word except for the first word is capitalized.

Only one package statement can appear in a source file. When it is present, nothing apart from comments must precede this statement.

Caution Specifying multiple package statements in a source file or placing anything apart from comments above a package statement causes the compiler to report an error.

Java implementations map package and subpackage names to same-named directories. For example, an implementation would map graphics to a directory named graphics, and would map graphics.shapes to a shapes subdirectory of graphics. The Java compiler stores the classfiles that implement the package's types in the corresponding directory.

Note If a source file does not contain a package statement, the source file's types are said to belong to the *unnamed package*. This package corresponds to the current directory.

The Import Statement

Imagine having to repeatedly specify ca.tutortutor.graphics.shapes.Circle or some other lengthy package-qualified type name for each occurrence of that type in source code. Java provides an alternative that lets you avoid having to specify package details. This alternative is the import statement.

The import statement imports types from a package by telling the compiler where to look for unqualified type names during compilation. This statement consists of reserved word import, followed by a member access operator-separated list of package and subpackage names, followed by a type name or * (asterisk), followed by a semicolon.

The * symbol is a wildcard that represents all unqualified type names. It tells the compiler to look for such names in the import statement's specified package, unless the type name is found in a previously searched package. (Using the wildcard does not have a performance penalty or lead to code bloat, but can lead to name conflicts, as you will see.)

For example, import ca.tutortutor.graphics.shapes.Circle; tells the compiler that an unqualified Circle class exists in the ca.tutortutor.graphics.shapes package. Similarly, import ca.tutortutor.graphics.shapes.*; tells the compiler to look in this package if it encounters a Rectangle class, a Triangle class, or even an Employee class (if Employee has not already been found).

Tip You should avoid using the * wildcard so that other developers can easily see which types are used in source code.

Because Java is case sensitive, package and subpackage names specified in an import statement must be expressed in the same case as that used in the package statement.

When import statements are present in source code, only a package statement and comments can precede them.

■ **Caution** Placing anything other than a package statement, import statements, static import statements (discussed shortly), and comments above an import statement causes the compiler to report an error.

You can run into name conflicts when using the wildcard version of the import statement because any unqualified type name matches the wildcard. For example, you have graphics.shapes and geometry packages that each contain a Circle class, the source code begins with import geometry.*; and import graphics.shape.*; statements, and it also contains an unqualified occurrence of Circle. Because the compiler does not know if Circle refers to geometry's Circle class or graphics.shape's Circle class, it reports an error. You can fix this problem by qualifying Circle with the correct package name.

■ **Note** The compiler automatically imports the String class and other types from the java.lang package, which is why it is not necessary to qualify String with java.lang.

Searching for Packages and Types

Newcomers to Java who first start to work with packages often become frustrated by "no class definition found" and other errors. This frustration can be partly avoided by understanding how the JVM searches for packages and types.

This section explains how the search process works. To understand this process, you need to realize that the compiler is a special Java application that runs under the control of the JVM. Furthermore, there are two different forms of search.

Compile-Time Search

When the compiler encounters a type expression (such as a method call) in source code, it must locate that type's declaration to verify that the expression is legal (a method exists in the type's class whose parameter types match the types of the arguments passed in the method call, for example).

The compiler first searches the Java platform packages (which contain class library types). It then searches extension packages (for extension types). If the -sourcepath command-line option was specified when starting the JVM (via javac), the compiler searches the indicated path's source files.

■ **Note** Java platform packages are stored in rt.jar and a few other important JAR files. Extension packages are stored in a special extensions directory named ext.

Otherwise, the compiler searches the user classpath (in left-to-right order) for the first user classfile or source file containing the type. If no user classpath is present, the current directory is searched. If no package matches or the type still cannot be found, the compiler reports an error. Otherwise, the compiler records the package information in the classfile.

■ **Note** The user classpath is specified via the -classpath option used to start the JVM or, if not present, the CLASSPATH environment variable.

Runtime Search

When the compiler or any other Java application runs, the JVM will encounter types and must load their associated classfiles via special code known as a *classloader* (discussed in Appendix C). The JVM will use the previously stored package information that is associated with the encountered type in a search for that type's classfile.

The JVM searches the Java platform packages, followed by extension packages, followed by the user classpath (in left-to-right order) for the first classfile that contains the type. If no user classpath is present, the current directory is searched. If no package matches or the type cannot be found, a "no class definition found" error is reported. Otherwise, the classfile is loaded into memory.

■ **Note** Whether you use the -classpath option or the CLASSPATH environment variable to specify a user classpath, there is a specific format that must be followed. Under Windows, this format is expressed as path1;path2;..., where path1, path2, and so on are the locations of package directories. Under Unix and Linux, this format changes to path1:path2:....

Playing with Packages

Suppose your application needs to log messages to the console, to a file, or to another destination. It can accomplish this task with the help of a logging library. My implementation of this library consists of an interface named Logger, an abstract class named LoggerFactory, and a pair of package-private classes named Console and File.

■ **Note** The logging library that I present is an example of the *Abstract Factory design pattern*, which is presented on page 87 of *Design Patterns: Elements of Reusable Object-Oriented Software* by Erich Gamma, Richard Helm, Ralph Johnson, and John Vlissides (Addison-Wesley, 1995; ISBN: 0201633612).

Listing 3-17 presents the Logger interface, which describes objects that log messages.

Listing 3-17. Describing objects that log messages via the Logger interface

```
package logging;

public interface Logger
{
   boolean connect();
   boolean disconnect();
   boolean log(String msg);
}
```

Each of the connect(), disconnect(), and log() methods returns true upon success, and false upon failure. (Later in this chapter, you will discover a better technique for dealing with failure.) These methods are not declared public explicitly because an interface's methods are implicitly public.

Listing 3-18 presents the LoggerFactory abstract class.

Listing 3-18. Obtaining a logger for logging messages to a specific destination

```
package logging;

public abstract class LoggerFactory
{
   public final static int CONSOLE = 0;
   public final static int FILE = 1;
   public static Logger newLogger(int dstType, String... dstName)
   {
      switch (dstType)
      {
         case CONSOLE: return new Console(dstName.length == 0 ? null
                                                              : dstName[0]);
         case FILE   : return new File(dstName.length == 0 ? null
                                                          : dstName[0]);
         default     : return null;
      }
   }
}
```

newLogger() returns a Logger instance for logging messages to an appropriate destination. It uses the variable number of arguments feature (see Chapter 2) to optionally accept an extra String argument for those destination types that require the argument. For example, FILE requires a filename.

Listing 3-19 presents the package-private Console class – this class is not accessible beyond the classes in the logging package because reserved word class is not preceded by reserved word public.

Listing 3-19. Logging messages to the console

```
package logging;

class Console implements Logger
{
   private String dstName;
   Console(String dstName)
```

```
    {
        this.dstName = dstName;
    }
    @Override
    public boolean connect()
    {
        return true;
    }
    @Override
    public boolean disconnect()
    {
        return true;
    }
    @Override
    public boolean log(String msg)
    {
        System.out.println(msg);
        return true;
    }
}
```

Console's package-private constructor saves its argument, which most likely will be null because there is no need for a String argument. Perhaps a future version of Console will use this argument to identify one of multiple console windows.

Listing 3-20 presents the package-private File class.

Listing 3-20. Logging messages to a file (eventually)

```
package logging;

class File implements Logger
{
    private String dstName;
    File(String dstName)
    {
        this.dstName = dstName;
    }
    @Override
    public boolean connect()
    {
        if (dstName == null)
            return false;
        System.out.println("opening file "+dstName);
        return true;
    }
    @Override
    public boolean disconnect()
    {
        if (dstName == null)
            return false;
        System.out.println("closing file "+dstName);
        return true;
```

```
   }
   @Override
   public boolean log(String msg)
   {
      if (dstName == null)
         return false;
      System.out.println("writing "+msg+" to file "+dstName);
      return true;
   }
}
```

Unlike Console, File requires a nonnull argument. Each method first verifies that this argument is not null. If the argument is null, the method returns false to signify failure. (In Chapter 8, I refactor File to incorporate appropriate file-writing code.)

The logging library allows us to introduce portable logging code into an application. Apart from a call to newLogger(), this code will remain the same regardless of the logging destination. Listing 3-21 presents an application that tests this library.

Listing 3-21. Testing the logging library

```
import logging.Logger;
import logging.LoggerFactory;

class TestLogger
{
   public static void main(String[] args)
   {
      Logger logger = LoggerFactory.newLogger(LoggerFactory.CONSOLE);
      if (logger.connect())
      {
         logger.log("test message #1");
         logger.disconnect();
      }
      else
         System.out.println("cannot connect to console-based logger");
      logger = LoggerFactory.newLogger(LoggerFactory.FILE, "x.txt");
      if (logger.connect())
      {
         logger.log("test message #2");
         logger.disconnect();
      }
      else
         System.out.println("cannot connect to file-based logger");
      logger = LoggerFactory.newLogger(LoggerFactory.FILE);
      if (logger.connect())
      {
         logger.log("test message #3");
         logger.disconnect();
      }
      else
         System.out.println("cannot connect to file-based logger");
   }
```

}

Follow these steps (which assume that the JDK has been installed) to create the logging package and TestLogger application, and to run this application:

1. Create a new directory and make this directory current.

2. Create a logging directory in the current directory.

3. Copy Listing 3-17 to a file named Logger.java in the logging directory.

4. Copy Listing 3-18 to a file named LoggerFactory.java in the logging directory.

5. Copy Listing 3-19 to a file named Console.java in the logging directory.

6. Copy Listing 3-20 to a file named File.java in the logging directory.

7. Copy Listing 3-21 to a file named TestLogger.java in the current directory.

8. Execute javac TestLogger.java, which also compiles logger's source files.

9. Execute java TestLogger.

After completing the final step, you should observe the following output from the TestLogger application:

```
test message #1
opening file x.txt
writing test message #2 to file x.txt
closing file x.txt
cannot connect to file-based logger
```

What happens when logging is moved to another location? For example, move logging to the root directory and run TestLogger. You will now observe an error message about the JVM not finding the logging package and its LoggerFactory classfile.

You can solve this problem by specifying -classpath when running the java tool, or by adding the location of the logging package to the CLASSPATH environment variable. You'll probably find it more convenient to use the former option, as demonstrated in the following Windows-specific command line:

```
java -classpath \;. TestLogger
```

The backslash represents the root directory in Windows. (I could have specified a forward slash as an alternative.) Also, the period represents the current directory. If it is missing, the JVM complains about not finding the TestLogger classfile.

■ **Tip** If you discover an error message where the JVM reports that it cannot find an application classfile, try appending a period character to the classpath. Doing so will probably fix the problem.

Packages and JAR Files

Chapter 1 briefly introduced you to the JDK's `jar` tool, which is used to archive classfiles in JAR files, and is also used to extract a JAR file's classfiles. It probably comes as no surprise that you can store packages in JAR files, which greatly simplify the distribution of your package-based class libraries.

To show you how easy it is to store a package in a JAR file, we will create a `logger.jar` file that contains the `logging` package's four classfiles (`Logger.class`, `LoggerFactory.class`, `Console.class`, and `File.class`). Complete the following steps to accomplish this task:

1. Make sure that the current directory contains the previously created `logging` directory with its four classfiles.

2. Execute `jar cf logger.jar logging\*.class`. You could alternatively execute `jar cf logger.jar logging/*.class`. (The `c` option stands for "create new archive" and the `f` option stands for "specify archive filename.")

You should now find a `logger.jar` file in the current directory. To prove to yourself that this file contains the four classfiles, execute `jar tf logger.jar`. (The `t` option stands for "list table of contents.")

You can run `TestLogger.class` by adding `logger.jar` to the classpath. For example, you can run `TestLogger` under Windows via `java -classpath logger.jar;. TestLogger`.

Static Imports

An interface should only be used to declare a type. However, some developers violate this principle by using interfaces to only export constants. Such interfaces are known as *constant interfaces*, and Listing 3-22 presents an example.

Listing 3-22. Declaring a constant interface

```
interface Directions
{
   int NORTH = 0;
   int SOUTH = 1;
   int EAST = 2;
   int WEST = 3;
}
```

Developers who resort to constant interfaces do so to avoid having to prefix a constant's name with the name of its class (as in `Math.PI`, where `PI` is a constant in the `java.lang.Math` class). They do this by implementing the interface—see Listing 3-23.

Listing 3-23. Implementing a constant interface

```
class TrafficFlow implements Directions
{
   public static void main(String[] args)
   {
      showDirection((int)(Math.random()*4));
   }
   static void showDirection(int dir)
   {
      switch (dir)
```

```
    {
        case NORTH: System.out.println("Moving north"); break;
        case SOUTH: System.out.println("Moving south"); break;
        case EAST : System.out.println("Moving east"); break;
        case WEST : System.out.println("Moving west");
    }
  }
}
```

Listing 3-23's `TrafficFlow` class implements `Directions` for the sole purpose of not having to specify `Directions.NORTH`, `Directions.SOUTH`, `Directions.EAST`, and `Directions.WEST`.

This is an appalling misuse of an interface. These constants are nothing more than an implementation detail that should not be allowed to leak into the class's exported *interface*, because they might confuse the class's users (what is the purpose of these constants?). Also, they represent a future commitment: even when the class no longer uses these constants, the interface must remain to ensure binary compatibility.

Java 5 introduced an alternative that satisfies the desire for constant interfaces while avoiding their problems. This static imports feature lets you import a class's `static` members so that you do not have to qualify them with their class names. It is implemented via a small modification to the import statement, as follows:

```
import static packagespec . classname . ( staticmembername | * );
```

The static import statement specifies `static` after `import`. It then specifies a member access operator-separated list of package and subpackage names, which is followed by the member access operator and a class's name. Once again, the member access operator is specified, followed by a single static member name or the asterisk wildcard.

Caution Placing anything apart from a package statement, import/static import statements, and comments above a static import statement causes the compiler to report an error.

You specify a single static member name to import only that name:

```
import static java.lang.Math.PI; // Import the PI static field only.
import static java.lang.Math.cos; // Import the cos() static method only.
```

In contrast, you specify the wildcard to import all static member names:

```
import static java.lang.Math.*;   // Import all static members from Math.
```

You can now refer to the static member(s) without having to specify the class name:

```
System.out.println(cos(PI));
```

Using multiple static import statements can result in name conflicts, which causes the compiler to report errors. For example, suppose your geom package contains a `Circle` class with a static member named PI. Now suppose you specify `import static java.lang.Math.*;` and `import static geom.Circle.*;` at the top of your source file. Finally, suppose you specify `System.out.println(PI);` somewhere in that file's code. The compiler reports an error because it does not know if `PI` belongs to `Math` or `Circle`.

Exceptions

In an ideal world, nothing bad ever happens when an application runs. For example, a file always exists when the application needs to open the file, the application is always able to connect to a remote computer, and the JVM never runs out of memory when the application needs to instantiate objects.

In contrast, real-world applications occasionally attempt to open files that do not exist, attempt to connect to remote computers that are unable to communicate with them, and require more memory than the JVM can provide. Your goal is to write code that properly responds to these and other exceptional situations (exceptions).

This section introduces you to exceptions. After defining this term, the section looks at representing exceptions in source code. It then examines the topics of throwing and handling exceptions, and concludes by discussing how to perform cleanup tasks before a method returns, whether or not an exception has been thrown.

What Are Exceptions?

An *exception* is a divergence from an application's normal behavior. For example, the application attempts to open a nonexistent file for reading. The normal behavior is to successfully open the file and begin reading its contents. However, the file cannot be read if the file does not exist.

This example illustrates an exception that cannot be prevented. However, a workaround is possible. For example, the application can detect that the file does not exist and take an alternate course of action, which might include telling the user about the problem. Unpreventable exceptions where workarounds are possible must not be ignored.

Exceptions can occur because of poorly written code. For example, an application might contain code that accesses each element in an array. Because of careless oversight, the array-access code might attempt to access a nonexistent array element, which leads to an exception. This kind of exception is preventable by writing correct code.

Finally, an exception might occur that cannot be prevented, and for which there is no workaround. For example, the JVM might run out of memory, or perhaps it cannot find a classfile. This kind of exception, known as an *error*, is so serious that it is impossible (or at least inadvisable) to work around; the application must terminate, presenting a message to the user that explains why it is terminating.

Representing Exceptions in Source Code

An exception can be represented via error codes or objects. After discussing each kind of representation and explaining why objects are superior, I introduce you to Java's exception and error class hierarchy, emphasizing the difference between checked and runtime exceptions. I close my discussion on representing exceptions in source code by discussing custom exception classes.

Error Codes Versus Objects

One way to represent exceptions in source code is to use error codes. For example, a method might return true on success and false when an exception occurs. Alternatively, a method might return 0 on success and a nonzero integer value that identifies a specific kind of exception.

Developers traditionally designed methods to return error codes; I demonstrated this tradition in each of the three methods in Listing 3-17's Logger interface. Each method returns true on success, or returns false to represent an exception (unable to connect to the logger, for example).

Although a method's return value must be examined to see if it represents an exception, error codes are all too easy to ignore. For example, a lazy developer might ignore the return code from Logger's connect() method and attempt to call log(). Ignoring error codes is one reason why a new approach to dealing with exceptions has been invented.

This new approach is based on objects. When an exception occurs, an object representing the exception is created by the code that was running when the exception occurred. Details describing the exception's surrounding context are stored in the object. These details are later examined to work around the exception.

The object is then *thrown*, or handed off to the JVM to search for a *handler*, code that can handle the exception. (If the exception is an error, the application should not provide a handler because errors are so serious [e.g., the JVM has run out of memory] that there's practically nothing that can be done about them.) When a handler is located, its code is executed to provide a workaround. Otherwise, the JVM terminates the application.

■ **Caution** Code that handles exceptions can be a source of bugs because it's often not thoroughly tested. Always make sure to test any code that handles exceptions.

Apart from being too easy to ignore, an error code's Boolean or integer value is less meaningful than an object name. For example, fileNotFound is self-explanatory, but what does false mean? Also, an object can contain information about what led to the exception. These details can be helpful to a suitable workaround.

The Throwable Class Hierarchy

Java provides a hierarchy of classes that represent different kinds of exceptions. These classes are rooted in java.lang.Throwable, the ultimate superclass for all *throwables* (exception and error objects—exceptions and errors, for short—that can be thrown). Table 3-1 identifies and describes most of Throwable's constructors and methods.

Table 3-1. Throwable's Constructors and Methods

Method	Description
Throwable()	Create a throwable with a null detail message and cause.
Throwable(String message)	Create a throwable with the specified detail message and a null cause.
Throwable(String message, Throwable cause)	Create a throwable with the specified detail message and cause.
protected Throwable(String message, Throwable cause, boolean enableSuppression, boolean writableStackTrace)	Create a throwable with the specified detail message, cause, suppression enabled or disabled, and writable stack trace enabled or disabled.

`Throwable(Throwable cause)`	Create a throwable whose detail message is the string representation of a nonnull cause, or null.
`void addSuppressed(Throwable exception)`	Append the specified exception to the exceptions that were suppressed in order to deliver this exception.
`Throwable fillInStackTrace()`	Fill in the execution stack trace. This method records information about the current state of the stack frames for the current thread within this throwable. (I discuss threads in Chapter 4.)
`Throwable getCause()`	Return the cause of this throwable. If there is no cause, null is returned.
`String getMessage()`	Return this throwable's detail message, which might be null.
`StackTraceElement[] getStackTrace()`	Provide programmatic access to the stack trace information printed by `printStackTrace()` as an array of stack trace elements, each representing one stack frame.
`Throwable[] getSuppressed()`	Return an array containing all exceptions that were suppressed (typically by the try-with-resources statement, discussed later) in order to deliver this exception.
`Throwable initCause(Throwable cause)`	Initialize the cause of this throwable to the specified value.
`void printStackTrace()`	Print this throwable and its backtrace of stack frames to the standard error stream.
`void setStackTrace(StackTraceElement[] stackTrace)`	Set the stack trace elements that will be returned by `getStackTrace()` and printed by `printStackTrace()` and related methods.

It is not uncommon for a class's public methods to call helper methods that throw various exceptions. A public method will probably not document exceptions thrown from a helper method because they are implementation details that often should not be visible to the public method's caller.

However, because this exception might be helpful in diagnosing the problem, the public method can wrap the lower-level exception in a higher-level exception that is documented in the public method's contract interface. The wrapped exception is known as a *cause* because its existence causes the higher-level exception to be thrown. A cause is created by invoking the `Throwable(Throwable cause)` or `Throwable(String message, Throwable cause)` constructor, which invoke the `initCause()` method to store the cause. If you do not call either constructor, you can alternatively call initCause() directly, but must do so immediately after creating the throwable. Call the getCause() method to return the cause.

When one exception causes another exception, the first exception is usually caught and then the second exception is thrown in response. In other words, there is a causal connection between the two exceptions. In contrast, there are situations where two independent exceptions can be thrown in sibling code blocks; for example, in the try block of a try-with-resources statement (discussed later in this chapter) and the compiler-generated finally that closes the resource. In these situations, only one of the thrown exceptions can be propagated.

In the try-with-resources statement, when there are two such exceptions, the exception originating from the try block is propagated and the exception from the finally block is added (via the addSuppressed() method) to the list of exceptions *suppressed* by the exception from the try block. As an exception unwinds the stack, it can accumulate multiple suppressed exceptions. An array of the suppressed expressions can be retrieved by calling getSuppressed().

When an exception is thrown, it leaves behind a stack of unfinished method calls. Throwable's constructors call fillInStackTrace() to record this *stack trace* information, which is output by calling printStackTrace().

The getStackTrace() method provides programmatic access to the stack trace by returning this information as an array of java.lang.StackTraceElement instances – each instance represents one stack entry. StackTraceElement provides methods to return stack trace information. For example, String getMethodName() returns the name of an unfinished method.

The setStackTrace() method is designed for use by Remote Procedure Call (RPC) frameworks (RPC is briefly discussed in Chapter 11) and other advanced systems, allowing the client to override the default stack trace that is generated by fillInStackTrace() when a throwable is constructed, or deserialized when a throwable is read from a serialization stream. (I will discuss serialization in Chapter 8.)

Except for Throwable(String message, Throwable cause, boolean enableSuppression, boolean writableStackTrace), each Throwable constructor always treats suppression as being enabled, and always calls fillInStackTrace(). In contrast, this constructor lets you disable suppression by passing false to enableSuppression, and prevent fillInStackTrace() from being called by passing false to writableStackTrace. Pass false to writableStackTrace when you plan to override the default stack trace and want to avoid the unnecessary fillInStackTrace() method calls. Similarly, pass false to enableSuppression when repeatedly catching and rethrowing the same exception object (to implement control flow between two subsystems, for example) or in other exceptional circumstances.

You will notice that Throwable(String message, Throwable cause, boolean enableSuppression, boolean writableStackTrace) is signified as a protected constructor. Also, its Java documentation includes the following sentence: "Subclasses of Throwable should document any conditions under which suppression is disabled and document conditions under which the stack trace is not writable." This is an example of "design and document for class extension," which I discuss in Chapter 2.

Moving down the throwable hierarchy, you encounter the java.lang.Exception and java.lang.Error classes, which respectively represent exceptions and errors. Each class offers five constructors that pass their arguments to their Throwable counterparts, but provides no methods apart from those that are inherited from Throwable.

Exception is itself subclassed by java.lang.CloneNotSupportedException (discussed in Chapter 2), java.io.IOException (discussed in Chapter 8), and other classes. Similarly, Error is itself subclassed by java.lang.AssertionError (discussed later in this chapter), java.lang.OutOfMemoryError, and other classes.

Caution Never instantiate `Throwable`, `Exception`, or `Error`. The resulting objects are meaningless because they are too generic.

Checked Exceptions Versus Runtime Exceptions

A *checked exception* is an exception that represents a problem with the possibility of recovery, and for which the developer must provide a workaround. The compiler checks (examines) the code to ensure that the exception is handled in the method where it is thrown, or is explicitly identified as being handled elsewhere.

Exception and all subclasses except for java.lang.RuntimeException (and its subclasses) describe checked exceptions. For example, the CloneNotSupportedException and IOException classes describe checked exceptions. (CloneNotSupportedException should not be checked because there is no runtime workaround for this kind of exception.)

A *runtime exception* is an exception that represents a coding mistake. This kind of exception is also known as an *unchecked exception* because it does not need to be handled or explicitly identified—the mistake must be fixed. Because these exceptions can occur in many places, it would be burdensome to be forced to handle them.

RuntimeException and its subclasses describe unchecked exceptions. For example, java.lang.ArithmeticException describes arithmetic problems such as integer division by zero. Another example is java.lang.ArrayIndexOutOfBoundsException. (In hindsight, RuntimeException should have been named UncheckedException because all exceptions occur at runtime.)

Note Many developers are not happy with checked exceptions because of the work involved in having to handle them. This problem is made worse by libraries providing methods that throw checked exceptions when they should throw unchecked exceptions. As a result, many modern languages support only unchecked exceptions.

Custom Exception Classes

You can declare your own exception classes. Before doing so, ask yourself if an existing exception class in Java's standard class library meets your needs. If you find a suitable class, you should reuse it. (Why reinvent the wheel?) Other developers will already be familiar with the existing class, and this knowledge will make your code easier to learn.

If no existing class meets your needs, think about whether to subclass Exception or RuntimeException. In other words, will your exception class be checked or unchecked? As a rule of thumb, your class should subclass RuntimeException if you think that it will describe a coding mistake.

Tip When you name your class, follow the convention of providing an `Exception` suffix. This suffix clarifies that your class describes an exception.

Suppose you are creating a Media class whose static methods perform various media-oriented utility tasks. For example, one method converts sound files in non-MP3 media formats to MP3 format. This method will be passed source file and destination file arguments, and will convert the source file to the format implied by the destination file's extension.

Before performing the conversion, the method needs to verify that the source file's format agrees with the format implied by its file extension. If there is no agreement, an exception must be thrown. Furthermore, this exception must store the expected and existing media formats so that a handler can identify them when presenting a message to the user.

Because Java's class library does not provide a suitable exception class, you decide to introduce a class named InvalidMediaFormatException. Detecting an invalid media format is not the result of a coding mistake, and so you also decide to extend Exception to indicate that the exception is checked. Listing 3-24 presents this class's declaration.

Listing 3-24. Declaring a custom exception class

```java
package media;

public class InvalidMediaFormatException extends Exception
{
   private String expectedFormat;
   private String existingFormat;
   public InvalidMediaFormatException(String expectedFormat,
                                      String existingFormat)
   {
      super("Expected format: "+expectedFormat+", Existing format: "+
          existingFormat);
      this.expectedFormat = expectedFormat;
      this.existingFormat = existingFormat;
   }
   public String getExpectedFormat()
   {
      return expectedFormat;
   }
   public String getExistingFormat()
   {
      return existingFormat;
   }
}
```

InvalidMediaFormatException provides a constructor that calls Exception's public Exception(String message) constructor with a detail message that includes the expected and existing formats. It is wise to capture such details in the detail message because the problem that led to the exception might be hard to reproduce.

InvalidMediaFormatException also provides getExpectedFormat() and getExistingFormat() methods that return these formats. Perhaps a handler will present this information in a message to the user. Unlike the detail message, this message might be *localized*, expressed in the user's language (French, German, English, and so on).

Throwing Exceptions

Now that you have created an InvalidMediaFormatException class, you can declare the Media class and begin to code its convert() method. The initial version of this method validates its arguments, and then verifies that the source file's media format agrees with the format implied by its file extension. Check out Listing 3-25.

Listing 3-25. Throwing exceptions from the convert() method

```
package media;

import java.io.IOException;

public final class Media
{
    public static void convert(String srcName, String dstName)
        throws InvalidMediaFormatException, IOException
    {
        if (srcName == null)
            throw new NullPointerException(srcName+" is null");
        if (dstName == null)
            throw new NullPointerException(dstName+" is null");
        // Code to access source file and verify that its format matches the
        // format implied by its file extension.
        //
        // Assume that the source file's extension is RM (for Real Media) and
        // that the file's internal signature suggests that its format is
        // Microsoft WAVE.
        String expectedFormat = "RM";
        String existingFormat = "WAVE";
        throw new InvalidMediaFormatException(expectedFormat, existingFormat);
    }
}
```

Listing 3-25 declares the Media class to be final because this class will only consist of class methods and there's no reason to extend it.

Media's convert() method appends throws InvalidMediaFormatException, IOException to its header. A *throws clause* identifies all checked exceptions that are thrown out of the method, and which must be handled by some other method. It consists of reserved word throws followed by a comma-separated list of checked exception class names, and is always appended to a method header. The convert() method's throws clause indicates that this method is capable of throwing an InvalidMediaFormatException or IOException instance to the JVM.

convert() also demonstrates the throw statement, which consists of reserved word throw followed by an instance of Throwable or a subclass. (You typically instantiate an Exception subclass.) This statement throws the instance to the JVM, which then searches for a suitable handler to handle the exception.

The first use of the throw statement is to throw a java.lang.NullPointerException instance when a null reference is passed as the source or destination filename. This unchecked exception is commonly thrown to indicate that a contract has been violated via a passed null reference. (Chapter 6's discussion of the java.util.Objects class presents an alternative approach to dealing with null references passed to parameters.) For example, you cannot pass null filenames to convert().

The second use of the throw statement is to throw a media.InvalidMediaFormatException instance when the expected media format does not match the existing format. In the contrived example, the exception is thrown because the expected format is RM and the existing format is WAVE.

Unlike InvalidMediaFormatException, NullPointerException is not listed in convert()'s throws clause because NullPointerException instances are unchecked. They can occur so frequently that it is too big a burden to force the developer to properly handle these exceptions. Instead, the developer should write code that minimizes their occurrences.

Although not thrown from convert(), IOException is listed in this method's throws clause in preparation for refactoring this method to perform the conversion with the help of file-handling code.

NullPointerException is one kind of exception that is thrown when an argument proves to be invalid. The java.lang.IllegalArgumentException class generalizes the illegal argument scenario to include other kinds of illegal arguments. For example, the following method throws an IllegalArgumentException instance when a numeric argument is negative:

```
public static double sqrt(double x)
{
    if (x < 0)
        throw new IllegalArgumentException(x+" is negative");
    // Calculate the square root of x.
}
```

There are a few additional items to keep in mind when working with throws clauses and throw statements:

- You can append a throws clause to a constructor and throw an exception from the constructor when something goes wrong while the constructor is executing. The resulting object will not be created.

- When an exception is thrown out of an application's main() method, the JVM terminates the application and calls the exception's printStackTrace() method to print, to the console, the sequence of nested method calls that was awaiting completion when the exception was thrown.

- If a superclass method declares a throws clause, the overriding subclass method does not have to declare a throws clause. However, if the subclass method does declare a throws clause, the clause must not include the names of checked exception classes that are not also included in the superclass method's throws clause, unless they are the names of exception subclasses. For example, given superclass method void foo() throws IOException {}, the overriding subclass method could be declared as void foo() {}, void foo() throws IOException {}, or void foo() throws FileNotFoundException—the java.io.FileNotFoundException class subclasses IOException.

- A checked exception class name does not need to appear in a throws clause when the name of its superclass appears.

- The compiler reports an error when a method throws a checked exception and does not also handle the exception or list the exception in its throws clause.

- Do not include the names of unchecked exception classes in a throws clause. These names are not required because such exceptions should never occur. Furthermore, they only clutter source code, and possibly confuse someone who is trying to understand that code.

- You can declare a checked exception class name in a method's throws clause without throwing an instance of this class from the method. (Perhaps the method has yet to be fully coded.) However, Java requires that you provide code to handle this exception, even though it is not thrown.

Handling Exceptions

A method indicates its intention to handle one or more exceptions by specifying a try statement that includes one or more appropriate catch blocks. The try statement consists of reserved word try followed by a brace-delimited body. You place code that throws exceptions into this block.

A catch block consists of reserved word catch, followed by a round bracket-delimited single-parameter list that specifies an exception class name, followed by a brace-delimited body. You place code that handles exceptions whose types match the type of the catch block's parameter list's exception class parameter in this block.

A catch block is specified immediately after a try block. When an exception is thrown, the JVM searches for a handler by first examining the catch block to see whether its parameter type matches or is the superclass type of the exception that has been thrown.

If the catch block is found, its body executes and the exception is handled. Otherwise, the JVM proceeds up the method-call stack, looking for the first method whose try statement contains an appropriate catch block. This process continues unless a catch block is found or execution leaves the main() method.

The following example illustrates try and catch:

```
try
{
   int x = 1/0;
}
catch (ArithmeticException ae)
{
   System.out.println("attempt to divide by zero");
}
```

When execution enters the try block, an attempt is made to divide integer 1 by integer 0. The JVM responds by instantiating ArithmeticException and throwing this exception. It then detects the catch block, which is capable of handling thrown ArithmeticException objects, and transfers execution to this block, which invokes System.out.println() to output a suitable message—the exception is handled.

Because ArithmeticException is an example of an unchecked exception type, and because unchecked exceptions represent coding mistakes that must be fixed, you typically don't catch them, as demonstrated previously. Instead, you would fix the problem that led to the thrown exception.

Tip You might want to name your catch block parameters using the abbreviated style shown in the preceding section. Not only does this convention result in more meaningful exception-oriented parameter names (ae implies that an ArithmeticException object has been thrown), it can help reduce compiler errors. For example, it is common practice to name a catch block's parameter e, for convenience. (Why type a long name?) However, the compiler will report an error when a previously declared local variable or parameter also uses e as its name—multiple same-named local variables and parameters cannot exist in the same scope.

Handling Multiple Exception Types

You can specify multiple catch blocks after a try block. For example, Listing 3-25's convert() method specifies a throws clause indicating that convert() can throw InvalidMediaFormatException, which is currently thrown, and IOException, which will be thrown when convert() is refactored. This refactoring will result in convert() throwing IOException when it cannot read from the source file or write to the destination file, and throwing FileNotFoundException (a subclass of IOException) when it cannot open the source file or create the destination file. All these exceptions must be handled, as demonstrated in Listing 3-26.

Listing 3-26. Handling different kinds of exceptions

```java
import java.io.FileNotFoundException;
import java.io.IOException;

import media.InvalidMediaFormatException;
import media.Media;

class Converter
{
   public static void main(String[] args)
   {
      if (args.length != 2)
      {
         System.err.println("usage: java Converter srcfile dstfile");
         return;
      }
      try
      {
         Media.convert(args[0], args[1]);
      }
      catch (InvalidMediaFormatException imfe)
      {
         System.out.println("Unable to convert "+args[0]+" to "+args[1]);
         System.out.println("Expecting "+args[0]+" to conform to "+
                            imfe.getExpectedFormat()+" format.");
         System.out.println("However, "+args[0]+" conformed to "+
                            imfe.getExistingFormat()+" format.");
      }
      catch (FileNotFoundException fnfe)
      {
      }
      catch (IOException ioe)
      {
      }
   }
}
```

The call to Media's convert() method in Listing 3-26 is placed in a try block because this method is capable of throwing an instance of the checked InvalidMediaFormatException, IOException, or FileNotFoundException class—checked exceptions must be handled or be declared to be thrown via a throws clause that is appended to the method.

The catch (InvalidMediaFormatException imfe) block's statements are designed to provide a descriptive error message to the user. A more sophisticated application would localize these names so that the user could read the message in the user's language. The developer-oriented detail message is not output because it is not necessary in this trivial application.

Note A developer-oriented detail message is typically not localized. Instead, it is expressed in the developer's language. Users should never see detail messages.

Although not thrown, a catch block for IOException is required because this checked exception type appears in convert()'s throws clause. Because the catch (IOException ioe) block can also handle thrown FileNotFoundException instances (because FileNotFoundException subclasses IOException), the catch (FileNotFoundException fnfe) block isn't necessary at this point, but is present to separate out the handling of a situation where a file cannot be opened for reading or created for writing (which will be addressed once convert() is refactored to include file code).

Assuming that the current directory contains Listing 3-26 and a media subdirectory containing InvalidMediaFormatException.java and Media.java, compile this listing (javac Converter.java), which also compiles media's source files, and run the application, as in java Converter A B. Converter responds by presenting the following output:

```
Unable to convert A to B
Expecting A to conform to RM format.
However, A conformed to WAVE format.
```

Listing 3-26's empty FileNotFoundException and IOException catch blocks illustrate the often-seen problem of leaving catch blocks empty because they are inconvenient to code. Unless you have a good reason, do not create an empty catch block. It swallows exceptions and you do not know that the exceptions were thrown. (For brevity, I don't always code catch blocks in this book's examples.)

Caution The compiler reports an error when you specify two or more catch blocks with the same parameter type after a try body. Example: try {} catch (IOException ioe1) {} catch (IOException ioe2) {}. You must merge these catch blocks into one block.

Although you can write catch blocks in any order, the compiler restricts this order when one catch block's parameter is a supertype of another catch block's parameter. The subtype parameter catch block must precede the supertype parameter catch block; otherwise, the subtype parameter catch block will never be executed.

For example, the FileNotFoundException catch block must precede the IOException catch block. If the compiler allowed the IOException catch block to be specified first, the FileNotFoundException catch block would never execute because a FileNotFoundException instance is also an instance of its IOException superclass.

Multicatch

Suppose you have two or more catch blocks whose code is identical or nearly identical. To eliminate this redundancy, you might be tempted to refactor this code into a single catch block with a common superclass exception type (such as catch (Exception e) {}). However, catching overly broad exceptions is not a good idea because doing so masks the purpose for the handler (what exceptions are handled by catch (Exception e) {}, for example). Also, the single catch block might inadvertently handle thrown exceptions that should be handled elsewhere. (Perhaps these exceptions are thrown as a result of refactored code.)

Java provides the *multicatch* language feature to avoid redundancy and also the problems inherent with catching overly broad exceptions. Multicatch lets you specify multiple exception types in a catch block where each successive type is separated from its predecessor by placing a vertical bar (|) between these types. Consider the following example:

```
try
{
   Media.convert(args[0], args[1]);
}
catch (InvalidMediaFormatException | UnsupportedMediaFormatException imfeumfe)
{
   // common code to respond to these similar exceptions
}
```

This example assumes that convert() is also capable of throwing media.UnsupportedMediaFormatException when it detects a media format that it cannot handle (such as a video format). When convert() throws either InvalidMediaFormatException or UnsupportedMediaFormatException, the catch block will handle either exception.

When multiple exception types are listed in a catch block's single parameter list, the parameter is implicitly regarded as final. As a result, you cannot change the parameter's value. For example, you cannot change the reference stored in the example's imfeumfe parameter.

Multicatch is not always necessary. For example, you do not need to specify catch (FileNotFoundException | IOException fnfeioe) { /* suitable common code */ } to handle FileNotFoundException and IOException because catch (IOException ioe) accomplishes the same task, by catching FileNotFoundException as well as IOException. For this reason, the compiler reports an error when it detects a catch block whose parameter list exception types include a supertype and a subtype.

■ **Note** The bytecode resulting from compiling a catch block that handles multiple exception types will be smaller than compiling several catch blocks that each handle only one of the listed exception types. A catch block that handles multiple exception types contributes no duplicate bytecode during compilation. In other words, the bytecode doesn't contain replicated exception handlers.

Rethrowing Exceptions

While discussing the Throwable class, I discussed wrapping lower-level exceptions in higher-level exceptions. This activity will typically take place in a catch block, and is illustrated in the following example:

```
catch (IOException ioe)
{
    throw new ReportCreationException(ioe);
}
```

This example assumes that a helper method has just thrown a generic IOException instance as the result of trying to create a report. The public method's contract states that ReportCreationException is thrown in this case. To satisfy the contract, the latter exception is thrown. To satisfy the developer who is responsible for debugging a faulty application, the IOException instance is wrapped inside the ReportCreationException instance that is thrown to the public method's caller.

Sometimes, a catch block might not be able to fully handle an exception. Perhaps it needs access to information provided by some ancestor method in the method-call stack. However, the catch block might be able to partly handle the exception. In this case, it should partly handle the exception, and then rethrow the exception so that a handler in the ancestor method can finish handling the exception. This scenario is demonstrated in the following example:

```
catch (FileNotFoundException fnfe)
{
    // Provide code to partially handle the exception here.
    throw fnfe; // Rethrow the exception here.
}
```

Final Rethrow

Java 7's compiler analyzes rethrown exceptions more precisely than its predecessors, but only when no assignments are made to the rethrown exception's catch block parameter (the parameter is effectively final). When an exception originates from the preceding try block and is a supertype/subtype of the parameter's type, the compiler throws the actual type of the caught exception instead of throwing the type of the parameter (as is done in previous Java versions).

The purpose of this *final rethrow* feature is to facilitate adding a try statement around a block of code to intercept, process, and rethrow an exception without affecting the statically determined set of exceptions thrown from the code. Also, this feature lets you provide a common exception handler to partly handle the exception close to where it's thrown, and provide more precise handlers elsewhere that handle the rethrown exception. Consider Listing 3-27.

Listing 3-27. A pressure simulation

```
class PressureException extends Exception
{
    PressureException(String msg)
    {
        super(msg);
    }
}
class TemperatureException extends Exception
{
    TemperatureException(String msg)
    {
        super(msg);
    }
}
```

```java
class MonitorEngine
{
   public static void main(String[] args)
   {
      try
      {
         monitor();
      }
      catch (Exception e)
      {
         if (e instanceof PressureException)
            System.out.println("correcting pressure problem");
         else
            System.out.println("correcting temperature problem");
      }
   }
   static void monitor() throws Exception
   {
      try
      {
         if (Math.random() < 0.1)
            throw new PressureException("pressure too high");
         else
         if (Math.random() > 0.9)
            throw new TemperatureException("temperature too high");
         else
            System.out.println("all is well");
      }
      catch (Exception e)
      {
         System.out.println(e.getMessage());
         throw e;
      }
   }
}
```

Listing 3-27 simulates the testing of an experimental rocket engine to see if the engine's pressure or temperature exceeds a safety threshold. It performs this testing via the monitor() helper method.

monitor()'s try block throws PressureException when it detects a pressure extreme, and throws TemperatureException when it detects a temperature extreme. (Because this is only a simulation, random numbers are used. I'll have more to say about random numbers in Chapter 4.) The try block is followed by a catch block, which is designed to partly handle the exception by outputting a warning message. This exception is then rethrown so that monitor()'s calling method can finish handling the exception.

Before Java 7, you couldn't specify PressureException and TemperatureException in monitor()'s throws clause because the catch block's e parameter is of type Exception and rethrowing an exception was treated as throwing the parameter's type. Starting with Java 7, you can specify these exception types in the throws clause because the compiler determines that the exception thrown by throw e came from the try block, and only PressureException and TemperatureException can be thrown from this block.

Because you can now specify static void monitor() throws PressureException, TemperatureException, you can provide more precise handlers where monitor() is called, as the following example demonstrates:

```
try
{
   monitor();
}
catch (PressureException pe)
{
   System.out.println("correcting pressure problem");
}
catch (TemperatureException te)
{
   System.out.println("correcting temperature problem");
}
```

Because of the improved type checking offered by final rethrow, source code that compiled under previous versions of Java might fail to compile under Java 7. For example, consider Listing 3-28.

Listing 3-28. Demonstrating code breakage as a result of final rethrow

```
class SuperException extends Exception
{
}
class SubException1 extends SuperException
{
}
class SubException2 extends SuperException
{
}
class BreakageDemo
{
   public static void main(String[] args) throws SuperException
   {
      try
      {
         throw new SubException1();
      }
      catch (SuperException se)
      {
         try
         {
            throw se;
         }
         catch (SubException2 se2)
         {
         }
      }
   }
}
```

Listing 3-28 compiles under Java 6 and earlier. However, it fails to compile under Java 7, whose compiler detects and reports the fact that SubException2 is never thrown in the body of the corresponding try statement.

Although unlikely to occur, it's possible to run into this problem. Instead of grumbling about the breakage, consider the value in having the compiler detect a source of redundant code whose removal results in cleaner source code and a smaller classfile.

Performing Cleanup

In some situations, you might want to prevent an exception from being thrown out of a method before the method's cleanup code is executed. For example, you might want to close a file that was opened, but could not be written, possibly because of insufficient disk space. Java provides the finally block for this situation.

The finally block consists of reserved word finally followed by a body, which provides the cleanup code. A finally block follows either a catch block or a try block. In the former case, the exception is handled (and possibly rethrown) before finally executes. In the latter case, finally executes before the exception is thrown and handled.

Listing 3-29 demonstrates the finally block in the context of a file-copying application.

Listing 3-29. Cleaning up after handling a thrown exception

```java
import java.io.FileInputStream;
import java.io.FileOutputStream;
import java.io.FileNotFoundException;
import java.io.IOException;

class Copy
{
   public static void main(String[] args)
   {
      if (args.length != 2)
      {
         System.err.println("usage: java Copy srcfile dstfile");
         return;
      }
      FileInputStream fis = null;
      try
      {
         fis = new FileInputStream(args[0]);
         FileOutputStream fos = null;
         try
         {
            fos = new FileOutputStream(args[1]);
            int b; // I chose b instead of byte because byte is a reserved word.
            while ((b = fis.read()) != -1)
               fos.write(b);
         }
         catch (FileNotFoundException fnfe)
         {
            String msg = args[1]+" could not be created, possibly because "+
                         "it might be a directory";
            System.err.println(msg);
         }
         catch (IOException ioe)
```

```
      {
         String msg = args[0]+" could not be read, or "+args[1]+
                      " could not be written";
         System.err.println(msg);
      }
      finally
      {
         if (fos != null)
            try
            {
               fos.close();
            }
            catch (IOException ioe)
            {
               System.err.println("unable to close "+args[1]);
            }
      }
   }
   catch (FileNotFoundException fnfe)
   {
      String msg = args[0]+" could not be found or might be a directory";
      System.err.println(msg);
   }
   finally
   {
      if (fis != null)
         try
         {
            fis.close();
         }
         catch (IOException ioe)
         {
            System.err.println("unable to close "+args[0]);
         }
   }
   }
}
```

■ **Note** Do not be concerned if you find this listing's file-oriented code difficult to grasp; I will formally introduce I/O and the listing's file-oriented types in Chapter 8. I'm presenting this code here because file copying provides a perfect example of the finally block.

Listing 3-29 presents an application that copies bytes from a source file to a destination file via a nested pair of try blocks. The outer try block uses a java.io.FileInputStream object to open the source file for reading; the inner try block uses a java.io.FileOutputStream object to create the destination file for writing, and also contains the file-copying code.

If the fis = new FileInputStream(args[0]); expression throws FileNotFoundException, execution flows into the outer try statement's catch (FileNotFoundException fnfe) block, which outputs a suitable message to the user. Execution then enters the outer try statement's finally block.

The outer try statement's finally block closes an open source file. However, when FileNotFoundException is thrown, the source file is not open—no reference was assigned to fis. The finally block uses if (fis != null) to detect this situation, and does not attempt to close the file.

If fis = new FileInputStream(args[0]); succeeds, execution flows into the inner try block, which executes fos = new FileOutputStream(args[1]);. If this expression throws FileNotFoundException, execution moves into the inner try's catch (FileNotFoundException fnfe) block, which outputs a suitable message to the user.

This time, execution continues with the inner try statement's finally block. Because the destination file was not created, no attempt is made to close this file. In contrast, the open source file must be closed, and this is accomplished when execution moves from the inner finally block to the outer finally block.

FileInputStream's and FileOutputStream's close() methods throw IOException when a file is not open. Because IOException is checked, these exceptions must be handled; otherwise, it would be necessary to append a throws IOException clause to the main() method header.

You can specify a try statement with only a finally block. You would do so when you are not prepared to handle an exception in the enclosing method (or enclosing try statement, if present), but need to perform cleanup before the thrown exception causes execution to leave the method. Listing 3-30 provides a demonstration.

Listing 3-30. Cleaning up before handling a thrown exception

```java
import java.io.FileInputStream;
import java.io.FileOutputStream;
import java.io.FileNotFoundException;
import java.io.IOException;

class Copy
{
   public static void main(String[] args)
   {
      if (args.length != 2)
      {
         System.err.println("usage: java Copy srcfile dstfile");
         return;
      }
      try
      {
         copy(args[0], args[1]);
      }
      catch (FileNotFoundException fnfe)
      {
         String msg = args[0]+" could not be found or might be a directory,"+
                      " or "+args[1]+" could not be created, "+
                      "possibly because "+args[1]+" is a directory";
         System.err.println(msg);
      }
      catch (IOException ioe)
      {
```

```
                String msg = args[0]+" could not be read, or "+args[1]+
                             " could not be written";
                System.err.println(msg);
        }
    }
    static void copy(String srcFile, String dstFile) throws IOException
    {
        FileInputStream fis = new FileInputStream(srcFile);
        try
        {
            FileOutputStream fos = new FileOutputStream(dstFile);
            try
            {
                int b;
                while ((b = fis.read()) != -1)
                    fos.write(b);
            }
            finally
            {
                try
                {
                    fos.close();
                }
                catch (IOException ioe)
                {
                    System.err.println("unable to close "+dstFile);
                }
            }
        }
        finally
        {
            try
            {
                fis.close();
            }
            catch (IOException ioe)
            {
                System.err.println("unable to close "+srcFile);
            }
        }
    }
}
```

Listing 3-30 provides an alternative to Listing 3-29 that attempts to be more readable. It accomplishes this task by introducing a copy() method that uses a nested pair of try-finally constructs to perform the file-copy operation, and also close each open file whether an exception is or is not thrown. If the FileInputStream fis = new FileInputStream(srcFile); expression results in a thrown FileNotFoundException, execution leaves copy() without entering the outer try statement. This statement is only entered after the FileInputStream object has been created, indicating that the source file was opened.

If the FileOutputStream fos = new FileOutputStream(dstFile); expression results in a thrown FileNotFoundException, execution leaves copy() without entering the inner try statement. However, execution leaves copy() only after entering the finally block that is mated with the outer try block. This finally block closes the open source file.

If the read() or write() method in the inner try statement's body throws an IOException object, the finally block associated with the inner try block is executed. This finally block closes the open destination file. Execution then flows into the outer finally block, which closes the open source file, and continues on out of copy().

■ **Caution** If the body of a try statement throws an exception, and if the finally block results in another exception being thrown, this new exception replaces the previous exception, which is lost.

Despite Listing 3-30 being somewhat more readable than Listing 3-29, there is still a lot of boilerplate thanks to each finally block requiring a try statement to close a file. This boilerplate is necessary; its removal results in a new IOException possibly being thrown from the catch block, which would mask a previously thrown IOException.

Automatic Resource Management

Listings 3-29 and 3-30 are hideous because of the amount of code that's necessary to ensure that each file is closed. However, you don't have to code this way. Instead, you can use Java's try-with-resources statement to automatically close *resources* (objects that must be closed when they are no longer needed) on your behalf.

The try-with-resources statement minimally consists of a try block that features the following syntax:

```
try ([resource declaration; ...] resource declaration)
{
   // code to execute
}
```

Reserved word try is followed by a round bracket-delimited and semicolon-separated list of resource declarations. Each of the declared resources is to be closed when execution leaves the try block, either normally or via a thrown exception. The following example uses try-with-resources to shorten Listing 3-30's copy() method considerably:

```
static void copy(String srcFile, String dstFile) throws IOException
{
   try (FileInputStream fis = new FileInputStream(srcFile);
        FileOutputStream fos = new FileOutputStream(dstFile))
   {
      int b;
      while ((b = fis.read()) != -1)
         fos.write(b);
   }
}
```

The example's try-with-resources statement declares two file resources that must be closed; the resource declarations are separated with a mandatory semicolon. When the copy() method ends (normally or via a thrown exception), fis's and fos's close() methods are called, but in the opposite order to which these resources were created (fis was created before fos). Hence, fos.close() is called before fis.close().

Suppose that fos.write(buffer, 0, n) throws an IOException instance. Now suppose that the behind-the-scenes fos.close() method call results in a thrown IOException instance. This latter exception is suppressed, and the exception thrown by fos.write(buffer, 0, n) is the exception thrown out of the copy() method. The suppressed exception can be retrieved by calling Throwable's Throwable[] getSuppressed() method, which I previously presented.

Note A try-with-resources statement can include catch and finally. These blocks are executed after all declared resources have been closed.

To take advantage of try-with-resources with your own classes, keep in mind that a resource class must implement the java.lang.AutoCloseable interface or its java.lang.Closeable subinterface. Each interface provides a close() method that performs the close operation.

Unlike Closeable's close() method, which is declared to throw only IOException (or a subtype), AutoCloseable's close() method is declared to throw Exception. As a result, classes that implement AutoCloseable, Closeable, or a subinterface can declare their close() methods to throw any kind of exception. The close() method should be declared to throw a more specific exception, or (as with java.util.Scanner's close() method) to not throw an exception if the method cannot fail.

Note Implementations of Closeable's close() method are *idempotent*; subsequent calls to close() have no effect on the resource. In contrast, implementations of AutoCloseable's close() method are not required to be idempotent, but making them idempotent is recommended.

Assertions

Writing source code is not an easy task. All too often, *bugs* (defects) are introduced into the code. When a bug is not discovered before compiling the source code, it makes it into runtime code, which will probably fail unexpectedly. At this point, the cause of failure can be very difficult to determine.

Developers often make assumptions about application correctness, and some developers think that specifying comments that state their beliefs about what they think is true at the comment locations is sufficient for determining correctness. However, comments are useless for preventing bugs because the compiler ignores them.

Many languages address this problem by providing a language feature called assertions that lets the developer codify assumptions about application correctness. When the application runs, and if an assertion fails, the application terminates with a message that helps the developer diagnose the failure's cause.

This section introduces you to Java's assertions language feature. After defining this term, showing you how to declare assertions, and providing examples, the section looks at using and avoiding assertions. Finally, you learn how to selectively enable and disable assertions via the `javac` compiler tool's command-line arguments.

Declaring Assertions

An *assertion* is a statement that lets you express an assumption of program correctness via a Boolean expression. If this expression evaluates to true, execution continues with the next statement. Otherwise, an error that identifies the cause of failure is thrown.

There are two forms of the assertion statement, each of which begins with reserved word `assert`:

```
assert expression1 ;
assert expression1 : expression2 ;
```

In both forms of this statement, *expression1* is the Boolean expression. In the second form, *expression2* is any expression that returns a value. It cannot be a call to a method whose return type is void.

When *expression1* evaluates to false, this statement instantiates the `AssertionError` class. The first statement form calls this class's noargument constructor, which does not associate a message identifying failure details with the `AssertionError` instance.

The second form calls an `AssertionError` constructor whose type matches the type of *expression2*'s value. This value is passed to the constructor and its string representation is used as the error's detail message.

When the error is thrown, the name of the source file and the number of the line from where the error was thrown are output to the console as part of the thrown error's stack trace. In many situations, this information is sufficient for identifying what led to the failure, and the first form of the assertion statement should be used.

Listing 3-31 demonstrates the first form of the assertion statement.

Listing 3-31. Throwing an assertion error without a detail message

```
class AssertionDemo
{
   public static void main(String[] args)
   {
      int x = 1;
      assert x == 0;
   }
}
```

When assertions are enabled (I discuss this task later), running the previous application results in the following output:

```
Exception in thread "main" java.lang.AssertionError
        at AssertionDemo.main(AssertionDemo.java:6)
```

In other situations, more information is needed to help diagnose the cause of failure. For example, suppose *expression1* compares variables x and y, and throws an error when x's value exceeds y's value. Because this should never happen, you would probably use the second statement form to output these values so you could diagnose the problem.

Listing 3-32 demonstrates the second form of the assertion statement.

Listing 3-32. Throwing an assertion error with a detail message

```
class AssertionDemo
{
   public static void main(String[] args)
   {
      int x = 1;
      assert x == 0: x;
   }
}
```

Once again, it is assumed that assertions are enabled. Running the previous application results in the following output:

```
Exception in thread "main" java.lang.AssertionError: 1
        at AssertionDemo.main(AssertionDemo.java:6)
```

The value in x is appended to the end of the first output line, which is somewhat cryptic. To make this output more meaningful, you might want to specify an expression that also includes the variable's name: assert x == 0: "x = "+x;, for example.

Using Assertions

There are many situations where assertions should be used. These situations organize into internal invariant, control-flow invariant, and design-by-contract categories. An *invariant* is something that does not change.

Internal Invariants

An *internal invariant* is expression-oriented behavior that is not expected to change. For example, Listing 3-33 introduces an internal invariant by way of chained if-else statements that output the state of water based on its temperature.

Listing 3-33. Discovering that an internal invariant can vary

```
class IIDemo
{
   public static void main(String[] args)
   {
      double temperature = 50.0; // Celsius
      if (temperature < 0.0)
         System.out.println("water has solidified");
      else
      if (temperature >= 100.0)
         System.out.println("water is boiling into a gas");
      else
      {
         // temperature > 0.0 and temperature < 100.0
         assert(temperature > 0.0 && temperature < 100.0): temperature;
         System.out.println("water is remaining in its liquid state");
```

```
        }
    }
}
```

A developer might specify only a comment stating an assumption as to what expression causes the final else to be reached. Because the comment might not be enough to detect the lurking < 0.0 expression bug, an assertion statement is necessary.

Another example of an internal invariant concerns a switch statement with no default case. The default case is avoided because the developer believes that all paths have been covered. However, this is not always true, as Listing 3-34 demonstrates.

Listing 3-34. *Another buggy internal invariant*

```
class IIDemo
{
    final static int NORTH = 0;
    final static int SOUTH = 1;
    final static int EAST = 2;
    final static int WEST = 3;
    public static void main(String[] args)
    {
        int direction = (int) (Math.random()*5);
        switch (direction)
        {
            case NORTH: System.out.println("travelling north"); break;
            case SOUTH: System.out.println("travelling south"); break;
            case EAST : System.out.println("travelling east"); break;
            case WEST : System.out.println("travelling west"); break;
            default   : assert false;
        }
    }
}
```

Listing 3-34 assumes that the expression tested by switch will only evaluate to one of four integer constants. However, (int) (Math.random()*5) can also return 4, causing the default case to execute assert false;, which always throws AssertionError. (You might have to run this application a few times to see the assertion error, but first you need to learn how to enable assertions, which I discuss later in this chapter.)

Tip When assertions are disabled, assert false; does not execute and the bug goes undetected. To always detect this bug, replace assert false; with throw new AssertionError(direction);.

Control-Flow Invariants

A *control-flow invariant* is a flow of control that is not expected to change. For example, Listing 3-34 uses an assertion to test an assumption that switch's default case will not execute. Listing 3-35, which fixes Listing 3-34's bug, provides another example.

Listing 3-35. A buggy control-flow invariant

```java
class CFDemo
{
   final static int NORTH = 0;
   final static int SOUTH = 1;
   final static int EAST = 2;
   final static int WEST = 3;
   public static void main(String[] args)
   {
      int direction = (int)(Math.random()*4);
      switch (direction)
      {
         case NORTH: System.out.println("travelling north"); break;
         case SOUTH: System.out.println("travelling south"); break;
         case EAST : System.out.println("travelling east"); break;
         case WEST : System.out.println("travelling west");
         default   : assert false;
      }
   }
}
```

Because the original bug has been fixed, the default case should never be reached. However, the omission of a break statement that terminates case WEST causes execution to reach the default case. This control-flow invariant has been broken. (Again, you might have to run this application a few times to see the assertion error, but first you need to learn how to enable assertions, which I discuss later in this chapter.)

■ **Caution** Be careful when using an assertion statement to detect code that should never be executed. If the assertion statement cannot be reached according to the rules set forth in *The Java Language Specification, Third Edition,* by James Gosling, Bill Joy, Guy Steele, and Gilad Bracha (Addison-Wesley, 2005; ISBN: 0321246780) (also available at (http://java.sun.com/docs/books/jls/third_edition/html/j3TOC.html), the compiler will report an error. For example, for(;;); assert false; causes the compiler to report an error because the infinite for loop prevents the assertion statement from executing.

Design-by-Contract

Design-by-Contract (see http://en.wikipedia.org/wiki/Design_by_contract) is a way to design software based on preconditions, postconditions, and invariants (internal, control-flow, and class). Assertion statements support an informal design-by-contract style of development.

Preconditions

A *precondition* is something that must be true when a method is called. Assertion statements are often used to satisfy a helper method's preconditions by checking that its arguments are legal. Listing 3-36 provides an example.

Listing 3-36. Verifying a precondition

```
class Lotto649
{
   public static void main(String[] args)
   {
      // Lotto 649 requires that six unique numbers be chosen.
      int[] selectedNumbers = new int[6];
      // Assign a unique random number from 1 to 49 (inclusive) to each slot
      // in the selectedNumbers array.
      for (int slot = 0; slot < selectedNumbers.length; slot++)
      {
         int num;
         // Obtain a random number from 1 to 49. That number becomes the
         // selected number if it has not previously been chosen.
         try_again:
         do
         {
            num = rnd(49)+1;
            for (int i = 0; i < slot; i++)
               if (selectedNumbers[i] == num)
                  continue try_again;
            break;
         }
         while (true);
         // Assign selected number to appropriate slot.
         selectedNumbers[slot] = num;
      }
      // Sort all selected numbers into ascending order and then print these
      // numbers.
      sort(selectedNumbers);
      for (int i = 0; i < selectedNumbers.length; i++)
         System.out.print(selectedNumbers[i]+" ");
   }
   static int rnd(int limit)
   {
      // This method returns a random number (actually, a pseudorandom number)
      // ranging from 0 through limit-1 (inclusive).
      assert limit > 1: "limit = "+limit;
      return (int) (Math.random()*limit);
   }
   static void sort(int[] x)
   {
      // This method sorts the integers in the passed array into ascending
      // order.
      for (int pass = 0; pass < x.length-1; pass++)
```

```
        for (int i = x.length-1; i > pass; i--)
            if (x[i] < x[pass])
            {
                int temp = x[i];
                x[i] = x[pass];
                x[pass] = temp;
            }
    }
}
```

Listing 3-36's application simulates Lotto 6/49, one of Canada's national lottery games. The rnd() helper method returns a randomly chosen integer between 0 and limit-1. An assertion statement verifies the precondition that limit's value must be 2 or higher.

▪ **Note** The sort() helper method *sorts* (orders) the selectedNumbers array's integers into ascending order by implementing an *algorithm* (a recipe for accomplishing some task) called *Bubble Sort*.

Bubble Sort works by making multiple passes over the array. During each pass, various comparisons and swaps ensure that the next smallest element value "bubbles" toward the top of the array, which would be the element at index 0.

Bubble Sort is not efficient, but is more than adequate for sorting a six-element array. Although I could have used one of the efficient sort() methods located in the java.util package's Arrays class (for example, Arrays.sort(selectedNumbers); accomplishes the same objective as Listing 3-36's sort(selectedNumbers); method call, but does so more efficiently), I chose to use Bubble Sort because I prefer to wait until Chapter 5 before getting into the Arrays class.

Postconditions

A *postcondition* is something that must be true after a method successfully completes. Assertion statements are often used to satisfy a helper method's postconditions by checking that its result is legal. Listing 3-37 provides an example.

Listing 3-37. Verifying a postcondition as well as preconditions

```
class MergeArrays
{
    public static void main(String[] args)
    {
        int[] x = { 1, 2, 3, 4, 5 };
        int[] y = { 1, 2, 7, 9 };
        int[] result = merge(x, y);
        for (int i = 0; i < result.length; i++)
```

```java
            System.out.println(result[i]);
    }
    static int[] merge(int[] a, int[] b)
    {
        if (a == null)
            throw new NullPointerException("a is null");
        if (b == null)
            throw new NullPointerException("b is null");
        int[] result = new int[a.length+b.length];
        // Precondition
        assert result.length == a.length+b.length: "length mismatch";
        for (int i = 0; i < a.length; i++)
            result[i] = a[i];
        for (int i = 0; i < b.length; i++)
            result[a.length+i-1] = b[i];
        // Postcondition
        assert containsAll(result, a, b): "value missing from array";
        return result;
    }
    static boolean containsAll(int[] result, int[] a, int[] b)
    {
        for (int i = 0; i < a.length; i++)
            if (!contains(result, a[i]))
                return false;
        for (int i = 0; i < b.length; i++)
            if (!contains(result, b[i]))
                return false;
        return true;
    }
    static boolean contains(int[] a, int val)
    {
        for (int i = 0; i < a.length; i++)
            if (a[i] == val)
                return true;
        return false;
    }
}
```

Listing 3-37 uses an assertion statement to verify the postcondition that all the values in the two arrays being merged are present in the merged array. The postcondition is not satisfied, however, because this listing contains a bug.

Listing 3-37 also shows preconditions and postconditions being used together. The solitary precondition verifies that the merged array length equals the lengths of the arrays being merged prior to the merge logic.

Class Invariants

A *class invariant* is a kind of internal invariant that applies to every instance of a class at all times, except when an instance is transitioning from one consistent state to another.

For example, suppose instances of a class contain arrays whose values are sorted in ascending order. You might want to include an isSorted() method in the class that returns true if the array is still sorted, and verify that each constructor and method that modifies the array specifies `assert isSorted();` prior to exit, to satisfy the assumption that the array is still sorted when the constructor/method exists.

Avoiding Assertions

Although there are many situations where assertions should be used, there also are situations where they should be avoided. For example, you should not use assertions to check the arguments that are passed to public methods, for the following reasons:

- Checking a public method's arguments is part of the contract that exists between the method and its caller. If you use assertions to check these arguments, and if assertions are disabled, this contract is violated because the arguments will not be checked.

- Assertions also prevent appropriate exceptions from being thrown. For example, when an illegal argument is passed to a public method, it is common to throw `IllegalArgumentException` or `NullPointerException`. However, `AssertionError` is thrown instead.

You should also avoid using assertions to perform work required by the application to function correctly. This work is often performed as a side effect of the assertion's Boolean expression. When assertions are disabled, the work is not performed.

For example, suppose you have a list of `Employee` objects and a few null references that are also stored in this list, and you want to remove all the null references. It would not be correct to remove these references via the following assertion statement:

```
assert employees.removeAll(null);
```

Although the assertion statement will not throw `AssertionError` because there is at least one null reference in the `employees` list, the application that depends upon this statement executing will fail when assertions are disabled.

Instead of depending on the former code to remove the null references, you would be better off using code similar to the following:

```
boolean allNullsRemoved = employees.removeAll(null);
assert allNullsRemoved;
```

This time, all null references are removed regardless of whether assertions are enabled or disabled, and you can still specify an assertion to verify that nulls were removed.

Enabling and Disabling Assertions

The compiler records assertions in the classfile. However, assertions are disabled at runtime because they can affect performance. An assertion might call a method that takes awhile to complete, and this would impact the running application's performance.

You must enable the classfile's assertions before you can test assumptions about the behaviors of your classes. Accomplish this task by specifying the -enableassertions or -ea command-line option when running the java application launcher tool.

The -enableassertions and -ea command-line options let you enable assertions at various granularities based upon one of the following arguments (except for the noargument scenario, you must use a colon to separate the option from its argument):

- *No argument*: Assertions are enabled in all classes except system classes.

- *PackageName*...: Assertions are enabled in the specified package and its subpackages by specifying the package name followed by ....

- ...: Assertions are enabled in the unnamed package, which happens to be whatever directory is current.

- *ClassName*: Assertions are enabled in the named class by specifying the class name.

For example, you can enable all assertions except system assertions when running the MergeArrays application via java -ea MergeArrays. Also, you could enable any assertions in this chapter's logging package by specifying java -ea:logging TestLogger.

Assertions can be disabled, and also at various granularities, by specifying either of the -disableassertions or -da command-line options. These options take the same arguments as -enableassertions and -ea.

For example, java -ea -da:*loneclass mainclass* enables all assertions except for those in *loneclass*. (*loneclass* and *mainclass* are placeholders for the actual classes that you specify.)

The previous options apply to all classloaders (discussed in Appendix C). Except when taking no arguments, they also apply to system classes. This exception simplifies the enabling of assertion statements in all classes except for system classes, which is often desirable.

To enable system assertions, specify either -enablesystemassertions or -esa; for example, java -esa -ea:logging TestLogger. Specify either -disablesystemassertions or -dsa to disable system assertions.

Annotations

While developing a Java application, you might want to *annotate* various application elements, or associate *metadata* (data that describes other data) with them. For example, you might want to identify methods that are not fully implemented so that you will not forget to implement them. Java's annotations language feature lets you accomplish this task.

This section introduces you to annotations. After defining this term and presenting three kinds of compiler-supported annotations as examples, the section shows you how to declare your own annotation types and use these types to annotate source code. Finally, you discover how to process your own annotations to accomplish useful tasks.

▪ **Note** Java has always supported ad hoc annotation mechanisms. For example, the java.lang.Cloneable interface identifies classes whose instances can be shallowly cloned via Object's clone() method, the transient reserved word marks fields that are to be ignored during serialization (discussed in Chapter 8), and the @deprecated javadoc tag documents methods that are no longer supported. Java 6 formalized the need for annotations by introducing the annotations language feature.

Discovering Annotations

An *annotation* is an instance of an annotation type and associates metadata with an application element. It is expressed in source code by prefixing the type name with the @ symbol. For example, @Readonly is an annotation and Readonly is its type.

Note You can use annotations to associate metadata with constructors, fields, local variables, methods, packages, parameters, and types (annotation, class, enum, and interface).

The compiler supports the Override, Deprecated, SuppressWarnings, and SafeVarargs annotation types. These types are located in the java.lang package.

@Override annotations are useful for expressing that a subclass method overrides a method in the superclass, and does not overload that method instead. The following example reveals this annotation being used to prefix the overriding method:

```
@Override
public void draw(int color)
{
    // drawing code
}
```

@Deprecated annotations are useful for indicating that the marked application element is *deprecated* (phased out) and should no longer be used. The compiler warns you when a deprecated application element is accessed by nondeprecated code.

In contrast, the @deprecated javadoc tag and associated text warns you against using the deprecated item, and tells you what to use instead. The following example demonstrates that @Deprecated and @deprecated can be used together:

```
/**
 * Allocates a <code>Date</code> object and initializes it so that
 * it represents midnight, local time, at the beginning of the day
 * specified by the <code>year</code>, <code>month</code>, and
 * <code>date</code> arguments.
 *
 * @param   year    the year minus 1900.
 * @param   month   the month between 0-11.
 * @param   date    the day of the month between 1-31.
 * @see     java.util.Calendar
 * @deprecated As of JDK version 1.1,
 * replaced by <code>Calendar.set(year + 1900, month, date)</code>
 * or <code>GregorianCalendar(year + 1900, month, date)</code>.
 */
@Deprecated
public Date(int year, int month, int date)
{
    this(year, month, date, 0, 0, 0);
}
```

This example excerpts one of the constructors in Java's Date class (located in the java.util package). Its Javadoc comment reveals that Date(int year, int month, int date) has been deprecated in favor of using the set() method in the Calendar class (also located in the java.util package). (I explore Date and Calendar in Appendix C.)

The compiler suppresses warnings when a compilation unit (typically a class or interface) refers to a deprecated class, method, or field. This feature lets you modify legacy APIs without generating deprecation warnings, and is demonstrated in Listing 3-38.

Listing 3-38. Referencing a deprecated field from within the same class declaration

```
class Employee
{
   /**
    * Employee's name
    * @deprecated New version uses firstName and lastName fields.
    */
   @Deprecated
   String name;
   String firstName;
   String lastName;
   public static void main(String[] args)
   {
      Employee emp = new Employee();
      emp.name = "John Doe";
   }
}
```

Listing 3-38 declares an Employee class with a name field that has been deprecated. Although Employee's main() method refers to name, the compiler will suppress a deprecation warning because the deprecation and reference occur in the same class.

Suppose you refactor this listing by introducing a new UseEmployee class and moving Employee's main() method to this class. Listing 3-39 presents the resulting class structure.

Listing 3-39. Referencing a deprecated field from within another class declaration

```
class Employee
{
   /**
    * Employee's name
    * @deprecated New version uses firstName and lastName fields.
    */
   @Deprecated
   String name;
   String firstName;
   String lastName;
}
class UseEmployee
{
   public static void main(String[] args)
   {
      Employee emp = new Employee();
      emp.name = "John Doe";
```

```
    }
}
```

If you attempt to compile this source code via the javac compiler tool, you will discover the following messages:

```
Note: Employee.java uses or overrides a deprecated API.
Note: Recompile with -Xlint:deprecation for details.
```

You will need to specify -Xlint:deprecation as one of javac's command-line arguments (as in javac -Xlint:deprecation Employee.java) to discover the deprecated item and the code that refers to this item:

```
Employee.java:17: warning: [deprecation] name in Employee has been deprecated
    emp.name = "John Doe";
       ^
1 warning
```

@SuppressWarnings annotations are useful for suppressing deprecation or unchecked warnings via a "deprecation" or "unchecked" argument. (Unchecked warnings occur when mixing code that uses generics with pre-generics legacy code. I discuss generics and unchecked warnings later in this chapter.)

For example, Listing 3-40 uses @SuppressWarnings with a "deprecation" argument to suppress the compiler's deprecation warnings when code within the UseEmployee class's main() method accesses the Employee class's name field.

Listing 3-40. *Suppressing the previous deprecation warning*

```
class Employee
{
    /**
     * Employee's name
     * @deprecated New version uses firstName and lastName fields.
     */
    @Deprecated
    String name;
    String firstName;
    String lastName;
}
class UseEmployee
{
    @SuppressWarnings("deprecation")
    public static void main(String[] args)
    {
        Employee emp = new Employee();
        emp.name = "John Doe";
    }
}
```

■ **Note** As a matter of style, you should always specify `@SuppressWarnings` on the most deeply nested element where it is effective. For example, if you want to suppress a warning in a particular method, you should annotate that method rather than its class.

Finally, `@SafeVarargs` annotations are useful for asserting that the body of the annotated method or constructor does not perform potentially unsafe operations on its variable number of arguments parameter. I'll have more to say about this annotation when I present generics later in this chapter.

Declaring Annotation Types and Annotating Source Code

Before you can annotate source code, you need annotation types that can be instantiated. Java supplies many annotation types as well as `Override`, `Deprecated`, `SuppressWarnings`, and `SafeVarargs`. Java also lets you declare your own types.

You declare an annotation type by specifying the `@` symbol, immediately followed by reserved word `interface`, followed by the type's name, followed by a body. For example, Listing 3-41 uses `@interface` to declare an annotation type named Stub.

Listing 3-41. Declaring the Stub annotation type

```java
public @interface Stub
{
}
```

Instances of annotation types that supply no data apart from a name – their bodies are empty – are known as *marker annotations* because they mark application elements for some purpose. As Listing 3-42 reveals, `@Stub` is used to mark empty methods (stubs).

Listing 3-42. Annotating a stubbed-out method

```java
public class Deck // Describes a deck of cards.
{
    @Stub
    public void shuffle()
    {
        // This method is empty and will presumably be filled in with appropriate
        // code at some later date.
    }
}
```

Listing 3-42's Deck class declares an empty `shuffle()` method. This fact is indicated by instantiating Stub and prefixing `shuffle()`'s method header with the resulting `@Stub` annotation.

■ **Note** Although marker interfaces (introduced in Chapter 2) appear to have been replaced by marker annotations, this is not the case, because marker interfaces have advantages over marker annotations. One advantage is that a marker interface specifies a type that is implemented by a marked class, which lets you catch problems at compile time. For example, if a class does not implement the Cloneable interface, its instances cannot be shallowly cloned via Object's clone() method. If Cloneable had been implemented as a marker annotation, this problem would not be detected until runtime.

Although marker annotations are useful (@Override and @Deprecated are good examples), you will typically want to enhance an annotation type so that you can store metadata via its instances. You accomplish this task by adding elements to the type.

An *element* is a method header that appears in the annotation type's body. It cannot have parameters or a throws clause, and its return type must be a primitive type (such as int), String, Class, an enum, an annotation type, or an array of the preceding types. However, it can have a default value.

Listing 3-43 adds three elements to Stub.

Listing 3-43. Adding three elements to the Stub annotation type

```
public @interface Stub
{
   int id(); // A semicolon must terminate an element declaration.
   String dueDate();
   String developer() default "unassigned";
}
```

The id() element specifies a 32-bit integer that identifies the stub. The dueDate() element specifies a String-based date that identifies when the method stub is to be implemented. Finally, developer() specifies the String-based name of the developer responsible for coding the method stub.

Unlike id() and dueDate(), developer() is declared with a default value, "unassigned". When you instantiate Stub and do not assign a value to developer() in that instance, as is the case with Listing 3-44, this default value is assigned to developer().

Listing 3-44. Initializing a Stub instance's elements

```
public class Deck
{
   @Stub
   (
      id = 1,
      dueDate = "12/21/2012"
   )
   public void shuffle()
   {
   }
}
```

Listing 3-44 reveals one @Stub annotation that initializes its id() element to 1 and its dueDate() element to "12/21/2012". Each element name does not have a trailing (), and the comma-separated list of two element initializers appears between (and).

Suppose you decide to replace Stub's id(), dueDate(), and developer() elements with a single String value() element whose string specifies comma-separated ID, due date, and developer name values. Listing 3-45 shows you two ways to initialize value.

Listing 3-45. Initializing each Stub instance's value() element

```
public class Deck
{
    @Stub(value = "1,12/21/2012,unassigned")
    public void shuffle()
    {
    }
    @Stub("2,12/21/2012,unassigned")
    public Card[] deal(int ncards)
    {
        return null;
    }
}
```

Listing 3-45 reveals special treatment for the value() element. When it is an annotation type's only element, you can omit value()'s name and = from the initializer. I used this fact to specify @SuppressWarnings("deprecation") in Listing 3-40.

Using Meta-Annotations in Annotation Type Declarations

Each of the Override, Deprecated, and SuppressWarnings annotation types is itself annotated with *meta-annotations* (annotations that annotate annotation types). For example, Listing 3-46 shows you that the SuppressWarnings annotation type is annotated with two meta-annotations.

Listing 3-46. The annotated SuppressWarnings type declaration

```
@Target({TYPE, FIELD, METHOD, PARAMETER, CONSTRUCTOR, LOCAL_VARIABLE})
@Retention(RetentionPolicy.SOURCE)
public @interface SuppressWarnings
```

The Target annotation type, which is located in the java.lang.annotation package, identifies the kinds of application elements to which an annotation type applies. @Target indicates that @SuppressWarnings annotations can be used to annotate types, fields, methods, parameters, constructors, and local variables.

Each of TYPE, FIELD, METHOD, PARAMETER, CONSTRUCTOR, and LOCAL_VARIABLE is a member of the ElementType enum, which is also located in the java.lang.annotation package.

The { and } characters surrounding the comma-separated list of values assigned to Target's value() element signify an array—value()'s return type is String[]. Although these braces are necessary (unless the array consists of one item), value= could be omitted when initializing @Target because Target declares only a value() element.

The Retention annotation type, which is located in the java.lang.annotation package, identifies the retention (also known as lifetime) of an annotation type's annotations. @Retention indicates that @SuppressWarnings annotations have a lifetime that is limited to source code—they do not exist after compilation.

SOURCE is one of the members of the RetentionPolicy enum (located in the java.lang.annotation package). The other members are CLASS and RUNTIME. These three members specify the following retention policies:

- CLASS: The compiler records annotations in the classfile, but the JVM does not retain them (to save memory space). This policy is the default.

- RUNTIME: The compiler records annotations in the classfile, and the JVM retains them so that they can be read via the Reflection API (discussed in Chapter 4) at runtime.

- SOURCE: The compiler discards annotations after using them.

There are two problems with the Stub annotation types shown in Listings 3-41 and 3-43. First, the lack of an @Target meta-annotation means that you can annotate any application element @Stub. However, this annotation only makes sense when applied to methods and constructors. Check out Listing 3-47.

Listing 3-47. *Annotating undesirable application elements*

```
@Stub("1,12/21/2012,unassigned")
public class Deck
{
   @Stub("2,12/21/2012,unassigned")
   private Card[] cardsRemaining = new Card[52];
   @Stub("3,12/21/2012,unassigned")
   public Deck()
   {
   }
   @Stub("4,12/21/2012,unassigned")
   public void shuffle()
   {
   }
   @Stub("5,12/21/2012,unassigned")
   public Card[] deal(@Stub("5,12/21/2012,unassigned") int ncards)
   {
      return null;
   }
}
```

Listing 3-47 uses @Stub to annotate the Deck class, the cardsRemaining field, and the ncards parameter as well as annotating the constructor and the two methods. The first three application elements are inappropriate to annotate because they are not stubs.

You can fix this problem by prefixing the Stub annotation type declaration with @Target({ElementType.METHOD, ElementType.CONSTRUCTOR}) so that Stub only applies to methods and constructors. After doing this, the javac compiler tool will output the following error messages when you attempt to compile Listing 3-47:

```
Deck.java:1: error: annotation type not applicable to this kind of declaration
@Stub("1,12/21/2012,unassigned")
^
Deck.java:4: error: annotation type not applicable to this kind of declaration
   @Stub("2,12/21/2012,unassigned")
   ^
Deck.java:15: error: annotation type not applicable to this kind of declaration
   public Card[] deal(@Stub("5,12/21/2012,unassigned") int ncards)
                      ^
3 errors
```

The second problem is that the default CLASS retention policy makes it impossible to process @Stub annotations at runtime. You can fix this problem by prefixing the Stub type declaration with @Retention(RetentionPolicy.RUNTIME).

Listing 3-48 presents the Stub annotation type with the desired @Target and @Retention meta-annotations.

Listing 3-48. A revamped Stub annotation type

```
import java.lang.annotation.ElementType;
import java.lang.annotation.Retention;
import java.lang.annotation.RetentionPolicy;
import java.lang.annotation.Target;

@Target({ElementType.METHOD, ElementType.CONSTRUCTOR})
@Retention(RetentionPolicy.RUNTIME)
public @interface Stub
{
   String value();
}
```

■ **Note** Java also provides Documented and Inherited meta-annotation types in the java.lang.annotation package. Instances of @Documented-annotated annotation types are to be documented by javadoc and similar tools, whereas instances of @Inherited-annotated annotation types are automatically inherited. According to Inherited's Java documentation, if "the user queries the annotation type on a class declaration, and the class declaration has no annotation for this type, then the class's superclass will automatically be queried for the annotation type. This process will be repeated until an annotation for this type is found, or the top of the class hierarchy (Object) is reached. If no superclass has an annotation for this type, then the query will indicate that the class in question has no such annotation."

Processing Annotations

It is not enough to declare an annotation type and use that type to annotate source code. Unless you do something specific with those annotations, they remain dormant. One way to accomplish something specific is to write an application that processes the annotations. Listing 3-49's StubFinder application does just that.

Listing 3-49. The StubFinder application

```
import java.lang.reflect.Method;

class StubFinder
{
   public static void main(String[] args) throws Exception
   {
```

```
if (args.length != 1)
{
    System.err.println("usage: java StubFinder classfile");
    return;
}
Method[] methods = Class.forName(args[0]).getMethods();
for (int i = 0; i < methods.length; i++)
    if (methods[i].isAnnotationPresent(Stub.class))
    {
        Stub stub = methods[i].getAnnotation(Stub.class);
        String[] components = stub.value().split(",");
        System.out.println("Stub ID = "+components[0]);
        System.out.println("Stub Date = "+components[1]);
        System.out.println("Stub Developer = "+components[2]);
        System.out.println();
    }
}
}
```

StubFinder loads a classfile whose name is specified as a command-line argument, and outputs the metadata associated with each @Stub annotation that precedes each public method header. These annotations are instances of Listing 3-48's Stub annotation type.

StubFinder next uses a special class named Class (in the java.lang package) and its forName() class method to load a classfile. Class also provides a getMethods() method that returns an array of Method objects describing the loaded class's public methods.

For each loop iteration, a Method object's isAnnotationPresent() method is called to determine if the method is annotated with the annotation described by the Stub class (referred to as Stub.class).

If isAnnotationPresent() returns true, Method's getAnnotation() method is called to return the annotation Stub instance. This instance's value() method is called to retrieve the string stored in the annotation.

Next, String's split() method is called to split the string's comma-separated list of ID, date, and developer values into an array of String objects. Each object is then output along with descriptive text.

Class's forName() method is capable of throwing various exceptions that must be handled or explicitly declared as part of a method's header. For simplicity, I chose to append a throws Exception clause to the main() method's header.

■ **Caution** There are two problems with throws Exception. First, it is better to handle the exception and present a suitable error message than to "pass the buck" by throwing it out of main(). Second, Exception is generic—it hides the names of the kinds of exceptions that are thrown. However, it is convenient to specify throws Exception in a throwaway utility.

Do not be concerned if you do not understand Class, forName(), getMethods(), Method, isAnnotationPresent(), .class, getAnnotation(), and split(). You will learn about these items in Chapter 4.

After compiling StubFinder (javac StubFinder.java), Stub (javac Stub.java), and Listing 3-45's Deck class (javac Deck.java), run StubFinder with Deck as its single command-line argument (java StubFinder Deck). You will observe the following output:

```
Stub ID = 2
Stub Date = 12/21/2012
Stub Developer = unassigned

Stub ID = 1
Stub Date = 12/21/2012
Stub Developer = unassigned
```

If you expected the output to reflect the order of appearance of @Stub annotations in Deck.java, you are probably surprised by the output's unsorted order. This lack of order is caused by getMethods(). According to this method's Java documentation, "the elements in the array returned are not sorted and are not in any particular order."

Note Java 5 introduced an apt tool for processing annotations. This tool's functionality has been integrated into the compiler beginning with Java 6 – apt is being phased out. My "Java Tools Annotation Processors" tutorial (http://tutortutor.ca/cgi-bin/makepage.cgi?/tutorials/ct/jtap) provides a tutorial on using the Java compiler to process annotations.

Generics

Java 5 introduced *generics*, language features for declaring and using type-agnostic classes and interfaces. When working with Java's Collections Framework (which I introduce in Chapter 5), these features help you avoid thrown instances of the java.lang.ClassCastException class.

Note Although the main use for generics is the Collections Framework, Java's class library also contains *generified* (retrofitted to make use of generics) classes that have nothing to do with this framework: java.lang.Class, java.lang.ThreadLocal, and java.lang.ref.WeakReference are three examples.

This section introduces you to generics. You first learn how generics promote type safety in the context of the Collections Framework classes, and then you explore generics in the contexts of generic types and generic methods. After learning about generics in the context of arrays, you learn how to use the SafeVarargs annotation type.

Collections and the Need for Type Safety

Java's Collections Framework makes it possible to store objects in various kinds of object containers (known as collections) and later retrieve those objects. For example, you can store objects in a list, a set, or a map. You can then retrieve a single object, or iterate over the collection and retrieve all objects.

Before Java 5 overhauled the Collections Framework to take advantage of generics, there was no way to prevent a collection from containing objects of mixed types. The compiler did not check an object's type to see if it was suitable before it was added to a collection, and this lack of static type checking led to ClassCastExceptions.

Listing 3-50 demonstrates how easy it is to generate a ClassCastException.

Listing 3-50. Lack of type safety leading to a ClassCastException at runtime

```java
import java.util.ArrayList;
import java.util.Iterator;
import java.util.List;

class Employee
{
    private String name;
    Employee(String name)
    {
        this.name = name;
    }
    String getName()
    {
        return name;
    }
}
class TypeSafety
{
    public static void main(String[] args)
    {
        List employees = new ArrayList();
        employees.add(new Employee("John Doe"));
        employees.add(new Employee("Jane Smith"));
        employees.add("Jack Frost");
        Iterator iter = employees.iterator();
        while (iter.hasNext())
        {
            Employee emp = (Employee) iter.next();
            System.out.println(emp.getName());
        }
    }
}
```

Listing 3-50's main() method first instantiates java.util.ArrayList, and then uses this list collection object's reference to add a pair of Employee objects to the list. It then adds a String object, which violates the implied contract that ArrayList is supposed to store only Employee objects.

Moving on, main() obtains a java.util.Iterator instance for iterating over the list of Employees. As long as Iterator's hasNext() method returns true, its next() method is called to return an object stored in the array list.

The Object that next() returns must be downcast to Employee so that the Employee object's getName() method can be called to return the employee's name. The string that this method returns is then output to the standard output device via System.out.println().

The (Employee) cast checks the type of each object returned by next() to make sure that it is Employee. Although this is true of the first two objects, it is not true of the third object. Attempting to cast "Jack Frost" to Employee results in a ClassCastException.

The ClassCastException occurs because of an assumption that a list is *homogenous*. In other words, a list stores only objects of a single type or a family of related types. In reality, the list is *heterogeneous* in that it can store any Object.

Listing 3-51's generics-based homogenous list avoids ClassCastException.

Listing 3-51. *Lack of type safety leading to a compiler error*

```
import java.util.ArrayList;
import java.util.Iterator;
import java.util.List;

class Employee
{
    private String name;
    Employee(String name)
    {
        this.name = name;
    }
    String getName()
    {
        return name;
    }
}
class TypeSafety
{
    public static void main(String[] args)
    {
        List<Employee> employees = new ArrayList<Employee>();
        employees.add(new Employee("John Doe"));
        employees.add(new Employee("Jane Smith"));
        employees.add("Jack Frost");
        Iterator<Employee> iter = employees.iterator();
        while (iter.hasNext())
        {
            Employee emp = iter.next();
            System.out.println(emp.getName());
        }
    }
}
```

Listing 3-51's refactored main() method illustrates the central feature of generics, which is the *parameterized type* (a class or interface name followed by an angle bracket-delimited type list identifying what kinds of objects are legal in that context).

For example, List<Employee> indicates only Employee objects can be stored in the List. As shown, the <Employee> designation can be repeated with ArrayList, as in Arraylist<Employee>, which is the collection implementation that stores the Employees. Because the compiler can figure out this type argument from the context, you can omit the redundant `Employee` type name from between `ArrayList`'s `<` and `>` characters, resulting in `List<Employee> employees = new ArrayList<>();`.

Note Because of its appearance, many developers refer to the `<>` character sequence as the *diamond operator*. I don't regard `<>` as a true operator, which is why I don't include it in Table 1-3's list of Java operators.

Also, `Iterator<Employee>`—you cannot use the diamond operator in this context—indicates that `iterator()` returns an `Iterator` whose `next()` method returns only `Employee` objects. It is not necessary to cast `iter.next()`'s returned value to `Employee` because the compiler inserts the cast on your behalf.

If you attempt to compile this listing, the compiler will report an error when it encounters `employees.add("Jack Frost");`. The error message will tell you that the compiler cannot find an `add(java.lang.String)` method in the `java.util.List<Employee>` interface.

Unlike in the pre-generics `List` interface, which declares an `add(Object)` method, the generified `List` interface's `add()` method parameter reflects the interface's parameterized type name. For example, `List<Employee>` implies `add(Employee)`.

Listing 3-50 revealed that the unsafe code causing the `ClassCastException` (`employees.add("Jack Frost");`) and the code that triggers the exception (`(Employee) iter.next()`) are quite close. However, they are often farther apart in larger applications.

Rather than having to deal with angry clients while hunting down the unsafe code that ultimately led to the `ClassCastException`, you can rely on the compiler saving you this frustration and effort by reporting an error when it detects this code during compilation. Detecting type safety violations at compile time is the benefit of using generics.

Generic Types

A *generic type* is a class or interface that introduces a family of parameterized types by declaring a *formal type parameter list* (a comma-separated list of *type parameter* names between angle brackets). This syntax is expressed as follows:

```
class identifier<formal_type_parameter_list> {}
interface identifier<formal_type_parameter_list> {}
```

For example, `List<E>` is a generic type, where `List` is an interface and type parameter `E` identifies the list's element type. Similarly, `Map<K, V>` is a generic type, where `Map` is an interface and type parameters `K` and `V` identify the map's key and value types.

Note When declaring a generic type, it is conventional to specify single uppercase letters as type parameter names. Furthermore, these names should be meaningful. For example, `E` indicates element, `T` indicates type, `K` indicates key, and `V` indicates value. If possible, you should avoid choosing a type parameter name that is meaningless where it is used. For example, `List<E>` means list of elements, but what does `List<S>` mean?

Parameterized types instantiate generic types. Each parameterized type replaces the generic type's type parameters with type names. For example, List<Employee> (List of Employee) and List<String> (List of String) are examples of parameterized types based on List<E>. Similarly, Map<String, Employee> is an example of a parameterized type based on Map<K, V>.

The type name that replaces a type parameter is known as an *actual type argument*. Generics supports five kinds of actual type arguments:

- *Concrete type*: The name of a class or interface is passed to the type parameter. For example, List<Employee> employees; specifies that the list elements are Employee instances.

- *Concrete parameterized type*: The name of a parameterized type is passed to the type parameter. For example, List<List<String>> nameLists; specifies that the list elements are lists of strings.

- *Array type*: An array is passed to the type parameter. For example, List<String[]> countries; specifies that the list elements are arrays of Strings, possibly city names.

- *Type parameter*: A type parameter is passed to the type parameter. For example, given class declaration class X<E> { List<E> queue; }, X's type parameter E is passed to List's type parameter E.

- *Wildcard*: The ? is passed to the type parameter, indicating an unknown actual type argument. For example, List<?> list; specifies that the list elements are unknown. You will learn about wildcards later in the chapter.

A generic type also identifies a *raw type*, which is a generic type without its type parameters. For example, List<Employee>'s raw type is List. Raw types are nongeneric and can hold any Object.

Note Java allows raw types to be intermixed with generic types to support the vast amount of legacy code that was written prior to the arrival of generics. However, the compiler outputs a warning message whenever it encounters a raw type in source code.

Declaring and Using Your Own Generic Types

It is not difficult to declare your own generic types. In addition to specifying a formal type parameter list, your generic type specifies its type parameter(s) throughout its implementation. For example, Listing 3-52 declares a Queue<E> generic type.

Listing 3-52. Declaring and using a Queue<E> generic type

```
class Queue<E>
{
    private E[] elements;
    private int head, tail;
    @SuppressWarnings("unchecked")
    Queue(int size)
```

```java
{
   if (size < 2)
      throw new IllegalArgumentException(""+size);
   elements = (E[]) new Object[size];
   head = 0;
   tail = 0;
}
void insert(E element) throws QueueFullException
{
   if (isFull())
      throw new QueueFullException();
   elements[tail] = element;
   tail = (tail+1)%elements.length;
}
E remove() throws QueueEmptyException
{
   if (isEmpty())
      throw new QueueEmptyException();
   E element = elements[head];
   head = (head+1)%elements.length;
   return element;
}
boolean isEmpty()
{
   return head == tail;
}
boolean isFull()
{
   return (tail+1)%elements.length == head;
}
public static void main(String[] args)
   throws QueueFullException, QueueEmptyException
{
   Queue<String> queue = new Queue<>(6);
   System.out.println("Empty: "+queue.isEmpty());
   System.out.println("Full: "+queue.isFull());
   System.out.println("Adding A");
   queue.insert("A");
   System.out.println("Adding B");
   queue.insert("B");
   System.out.println("Adding C");
   queue.insert("C");
   System.out.println("Adding D");
   queue.insert("D");
   System.out.println("Adding E");
   queue.insert("E");
   System.out.println("Empty: "+queue.isEmpty());
   System.out.println("Full: "+queue.isFull());
   System.out.println("Removing "+queue.remove());
   System.out.println("Empty: "+queue.isEmpty());
   System.out.println("Full: "+queue.isFull());
   System.out.println("Adding F");
```

```
        queue.insert("F");
        while (!queue.isEmpty())
            System.out.println("Removing "+queue.remove());
        System.out.println("Empty: "+queue.isEmpty());
        System.out.println("Full: "+queue.isFull());
    }
}
class QueueEmptyException extends Exception
{
}
class QueueFullException extends Exception
{
}
```

Listing 3-52 declares Queue, QueueEmptyException, and QueueFullException classes. The latter two classes describe checked exceptions that are thrown from methods of the former class.

Queue implements a *queue*, a data structure that stores elements in first-in, first-out order. An element is inserted at the *tail* and removed at the *head*. The queue is empty when the head equals the tail, and full when the tail is one less than the head. As a result, a queue of size n can store a maximum of n-1 elements.

Notice that Queue<E>'s E type parameter appears throughout the source code. For example, E appears in the elements array declaration to denote the array's element type. E is also specified as the type of insert()'s parameter and as remove()'s return type.

E also appears in elements = (E[]) new Object[size];. (I will explain later why I specified this expression instead of specifying the more compact elements = new E[size]; expression.)

The E[] cast results in the compiler warning about this cast being unchecked. The compiler is concerned that downcasting from Object[] to E[] might result in a violation of type safety because any kind of object can be stored in Object[].

The compiler's concern is not justified in this example. There is no way that a non-E object can appear in the E[] array. Because the warning is meaningless in this context, it is suppressed by prefixing the constructor with @SuppressWarnings("unchecked").

■ **Caution** Be careful when suppressing an unchecked warning. You must first prove that a ClassCastException cannot occur, and then you can suppress the warning.

When you run this application, it generates the following output:

```
Empty: true
Full: false
Adding A
Adding B
Adding C
Adding D
Adding E
Empty: false
Full: true
Removing A
Empty: false
```

```
Full: false
Adding F
Removing B
Removing C
Removing D
Removing E
Removing F
Empty: true
Full: false
```

Type Parameter Bounds

List<E>'s E type parameter and Map<K, V>'s K and V type parameters are examples of *unbounded type parameters*. You can pass any actual type argument to an unbounded type parameter.

It is sometimes necessary to restrict the kinds of actual type arguments that can be passed to a type parameter. For example, you might want to declare a class whose instances can only store instances of classes that subclass an abstract Shape class (such as Circle and Rectangle).

To restrict actual type arguments, you can specify an *upper bound*, a type that serves as an upper limit on the types that can be chosen as actual type arguments. The upper bound is specified via reserved word extends followed by a type name.

For example, ShapesList<E extends Shape> identifies Shape as an upper bound. You can specify ShapesList<Circle>, ShapesList<Rectangle>, and even ShapesList<Shape>, but not ShapesList<String> because String is not a subclass of Shape.

You can assign more than one upper bound to a type parameter, where the first bound is a class or interface, and where each additional upper bound is an interface, by using the ampersand character (&) to separate bound names. Consider Listing 3-53.

Listing 3-53. Assigning multiple upper bounds to a type parameter

```
abstract class Shape
{
}
class Circle extends Shape implements Comparable<Circle>
{
   private double x, y, radius;
   Circle(double x, double y, double radius)
   {
      this.x = x;
      this.y = y;
      this.radius = radius;
   }
   @Override
   public int compareTo(Circle circle)
   {
      if (radius < circle.radius)
         return -1;
      else
      if (radius > circle.radius)
         return 1;
      else
```

```java
            return 0;
        }
        @Override
        public String toString()
        {
            return "("+x+", "+y+", "+radius+")";
        }
    }
    class SortedShapesList<S extends Shape&Comparable<S>>
    {
        @SuppressWarnings("unchecked")
        private S[] shapes = (S[]) new Shape[2];
        private int index = 0;
        void add(S shape)
        {
            shapes[index++] = shape;
            if (index < 2)
                return;
            System.out.println("Before sort: "+this);
            sort();
            System.out.println("After sort: "+this);
        }
        private void sort()
        {
            if (index == 1)
                return;
            if (shapes[0].compareTo(shapes[1]) > 0)
            {
                S shape = (S) shapes[0];
                shapes[0] = shapes[1];
                shapes[1] = shape;
            }
        }
        @Override
        public String toString()
        {
            return shapes[0].toString()+" "+shapes[1].toString();
        }
    }
    class SortedShapesListDemo
    {
        public static void main(String[] args)
        {
            SortedShapesList<Circle> ssl = new SortedShapesList<>();
            ssl.add(new Circle(100, 200, 300));
            ssl.add(new Circle(10, 20, 30));
        }
    }
```

Listing 3-53's Circle class extends Shape and implements the java.lang.Comparable interface, which is used to specify the *natural ordering* of Circle objects. The interface's compareTo() method implements this ordering by returning a value to reflect the order:

- A negative value is returned if the current object should precede the object passed to compareTo() in some fashion.

- A zero value is returned if the current and argument objects are the same.

- A positive value is returned if the current object should succeed the argument object.

Circle's overriding compareTo() method compares two Circle objects based on their radii. This method orders a Circle instance with the smaller radius before a Circle instance with a larger radius.

The SortedShapesList class specifies <S extends Shape&Comparable<S>> as its parameter list. The actual type argument passed to the S parameter must subclass Shape, and it must also implement the Comparable interface.

Note A type parameter bound that includes the type parameter is known as a *recursive type bound*. For example, Comparable<S> in S extends Shape&Comparable<S> is a recursive type bound. Recursive type bounds are rare and typically show up in conjunction with the Comparable interface, for specifying a type's natural ordering.

Circle satisfies both criteria: it subclasses Shape and implements Comparable. As a result, the compiler does not report an error when it encounters the main() method's SortedShapesList<Circle> ssl = new SortedShapesList<>(); statement.

An upper bound offers extra static type checking that guarantees that a parameterized type adheres to its bounds. This assurance means that the upper bound's methods can be called safely. For example, sort() can call Comparable's compareTo() method.

If you run this application, you will discover the following output, which shows that the two Circle objects are sorted in ascending order of radius:

```
Before sort: (100.0, 200.0, 300.0) (10.0, 20.0, 30.0)
After sort: (10.0, 20.0, 30.0) (100.0, 200.0, 300.0)
```

Note Type parameters cannot have lower bounds. Angelika Langer explains the rationale for this restriction in her "Java Generics FAQs" (see

http://www.angelikalanger.com/GenericsFAQ/FAQSections/TypeParameters.html#FAQ107).

Type Parameter Scope

A type parameter's *scope* (visibility) is its generic type except where *masked* (hidden). This scope includes the formal type parameter list of which the type parameter is a member. For example, the scope of S in SortedShapesList<S extends Shape&Comparable<S>> is all of SortedShapesList and the formal type parameter list.

It is possible to mask a type parameter by declaring a same-named type parameter in a nested type's formal type parameter list. For example, Listing 3-54 masks an enclosing class's T type parameter.

Listing 3-54. Masking a type variable

```
class EnclosingClass<T>
{
   static class EnclosedClass<T extends Comparable<T>>
   {
   }
}
```

EnclosingClass's T type parameter is masked by EnclosedClass's T type parameter, which specifies an upper bound where only those types that implement the Comparable interface can be passed to EnclosedClass. Referencing T from within EnclosedClass refers to the bounded T and not the unbounded T passed to EnclosingClass.

If masking is undesirable, it is best to choose a different name for the type parameter. For example, you might specify EnclosedClass<U extends Comparable<U>>. Although U is not as meaningful a name as T, this situation justifies this choice.

The Need for Wildcards

Suppose that you have created a List of String and want to output this list. Because you might create a List of Employee and other kinds of lists, you want this method to output an arbitrary List of Object. You end up creating Listing 3-55.

Listing 3-55. Attempting to output a List of Object

```
import java.util.ArrayList;
import java.util.List;

class OutputList
{
   public static void main(String[] args)
   {
      List<String> ls = new ArrayList<>();
      ls.add("first");
      ls.add("second");
      ls.add("third");
      outputList(ls);
   }
   static void outputList(List<Object> list)
   {
      for (int i = 0; i < list.size(); i++)
         System.out.println(list.get(i));
   }
}
```

Now that you've accomplished your objective (or so you think), you compile Listing 3-55 via javac OutputList.java. Much to your surprise, you receive the following error message:

```
OutputList.java:12: error: method outputList in class OutputList cannot be applied to given
types;
      outputList(ls);
      ^
  required: List<Object>
  found: List<String>
  reason: actual argument List<String> cannot be converted to List<Object> by method
invocation conversion
1 error
```

This error message results from being unaware of the fundamental rule of generic types: **for a given subtype x of type y, and given G as a raw type declaration, $G<x>$ is not a subtype of $G<y>$.**

To understand this rule, you must refresh your understanding of subtype polymorphism (see Chapter 2). Basically, a subtype is a specialized kind of supertype. For example, Circle is a specialized kind of Shape and String is a specialized kind of Object. This polymorphic behavior also applies to related parameterized types with the same type parameters (e.g., List<Object> is a specialized kind of java.util.Collection<Object>).

However, this polymorphic behavior does not apply to multiple parameterized types that differ only in regard to one type parameter being a subtype of another type parameter. For example, List<String> is not a specialized kind of List<Object>. The following example reveals why parameterized types differing only in type parameters are not polymorphic:

```
List<String> ls = new ArrayList<>();
List<Object> lo = ls;
lo.add(new Employee());
String s = ls.get(0);
```

This example will not compile because it violates type safety. If it compiled, a ClassCastException would be thrown at runtime because of the implicit cast to String on the final line.

The first line instantiates a List of String and the second line upcasts its reference to a List of Object. The third line adds a new Employee object to the List of Object. The fourth line obtains the Employee object via get() and attempts to assign it to the List of String reference variable. However, ClassCastException is thrown because of the implicit cast to String—an Employee is not a String.

Note Although you cannot upcast List<String> to List<Object>, you can upcast List<String> to the raw type List in order to interoperate with legacy code.

The aforementioned error message reveals that List of String is not also List of Object. To call Listing 3-55's outputList() method without violating type safety, you can only pass an argument of List<Object> type, which limits the usefulness of this method.

However, generics offer a solution: the wildcard argument (?), which stands for any type. By changing outputList()'s parameter type from List<Object> to List<?>, you can call outputList() with a List of String, a List of Employee, and so on.

Generic Methods

Suppose you need a method to copy a List of any kind of object to another List. Although you might consider coding a void copyList(List<Object> src, List<Object> dest) method, this method would have limited usefulness because it could only copy lists whose element type is Object. You couldn't copy a List<Employee>, for example.

If you want to pass source and destination lists whose elements are of arbitrary type (but their element types agree), you need to specify the wildcard character as a placeholder for that type. For example, you might consider writing the following copyList() class method that accepts collections of arbitrary-typed objects as its arguments:

```
static void copyList(List<?> src, List<?> dest)
{
   for (int i = 0; i < src.size(); i++)
      dest.add(src.get(i));
}
```

This method's parameter list is correct, but there is another problem: the compiler outputs the following error message when it encounters dest.add(src.get(i));:

```
CopyList.java:18: error: no suitable method found for add(Object)
        dest.add(src.get(i));
            ^
    method List.add(int,CAP#1) is not applicable
      (actual and formal argument lists differ in length)
    method List.add(CAP#1) is not applicable
      (actual argument Object cannot be converted to CAP#1 by method invocation conversion)
  where CAP#1 is a fresh type-variable:
    CAP#1 extends Object from capture of ?
1 error
```

This error message assumes that copyList() is part of a class named CopyList. Although it appears to be incomprehensible, the message basically means that the dest.add(src.get(i)) method call violates type safety. Because ? implies that any type of object can serve as a list's element type, it's possible that the destination list's element type is incompatible with the source list's element type.

For example, suppose you create a List of String as the source list and a List of Employee as the destination list. Attempting to add the source list's String elements to the destination list, which expects Employees, violates type safety. If this copy operation were allowed, a ClassCastException instance would be thrown when trying to obtain the destination list's elements.

You could avoid this problem by specifying void copyList(List<String> src, List<String> dest), but this method header limits you to copying only lists of String objects. Alternatively, you might restrict the wildcard argument, which is demonstrated here:

```
static void copyList(List<? extends String> src,
                     List<? super String> dest)
{
   for (int i = 0; i < src.size(); i++)
      dest.add(src.get(i));
}
```

This method demonstrates a feature of the wildcard argument: You can supply an upper bound or (unlike with a type parameter) a lower bound to limit the types that can be passed as actual type arguments to the generic type. Specify an upper bound via extends followed by the upper bound type after the ?, and a lower bound via super followed by the lower bound type after the ?.

You interpret ? extends String to mean that any actual type argument that is String or a subclass can be passed, and you interpret ? super String to imply that any actual type argument that is String or a superclass can be passed. Because String cannot be subclassed, this means that you can only pass source lists of String and destination lists of String or Object.

The problem of copying lists of arbitrary element types to other lists can be solved through the use of a *generic method* (a class or instance method with a type-generalized implementation). Generic methods are syntactically expressed as follows:

<formal_type_parameter_list> return_type identifier(parameter_list)

The *formal_type_parameter_list* is the same as when specifying a generic type: it consists of type parameters with optional bounds. A type parameter can appear as the method's *return_type*, and type parameters can appear in the *parameter_list*. The compiler infers the actual type arguments from the context in which the method is invoked.

You'll discover many examples of generic methods in the Collections Framework. For example, its java.util.Collections class provides a public static <T extends Object & Comparable<? super T>> T min(Collection<? extends T> coll) method for returning the minimum element in the given Collection according to the ordering specified by the supplied java.util.Comparator instance.

You can easily convert copyList() into a generic method by prefixing the return type with <T> and replacing each wildcard with T. The resulting method header is <T> void copyList(List<T> src, List<T> dest), and Listing 3-56 presents its source code as part of an application that copies a List of Circle to another List of Circle.

Listing 3-56. Declaring and using a copyList() generic method

```java
import java.util.ArrayList;
import java.util.List;

class Circle
{
   private double x, y, radius;
   Circle(double x, double y, double radius)
   {
      this.x = x;
      this.y = y;
      this.radius = radius;
   }
   @Override
   public String toString()
   {
      return "("+x+", "+y+", "+radius+")";
   }
}
class CopyList
{
   public static void main(String[] args)
   {
      List<String> ls = new ArrayList<String>();
      ls.add("A");
      ls.add("B");
```

```
        ls.add("C");
        outputList(ls);
        List<String> lsCopy = new ArrayList<String>();
        copyList(ls, lsCopy);
        outputList(lsCopy);
        List<Circle> lc = new ArrayList<Circle>();
        lc.add(new Circle(10.0, 20.0, 30.0));
        lc.add(new Circle (5.0, 4.0, 16.0));
        outputList(lc);
        List<Circle> lcCopy = new ArrayList<Circle>();
        copyList(lc, lcCopy);
        outputList(lcCopy);
    }
    static <T> void copyList(List<T> src, List<T> dest)
    {
        for (int i = 0; i < src.size(); i++)
            dest.add(src.get(i));
    }
    static void outputList(List<?> list)
    {
        for (int i = 0; i < list.size(); i++)
            System.out.println(list.get(i));
        System.out.println();
    }
}
```

The generic method's type parameters are inferred from the context in which the method was invoked. For example, the compiler determines that copyList(ls, lsCopy); copies a List of String to another List of String. Similarly, it determines that copyList(lc, lcCopy); copies a List of Circle to another List of Circle.

When you run this application, it generates the following output:

```
A
B
C

A
B
C

(10.0, 20.0, 30.0)
(5.0, 4.0, 16.0)

(10.0, 20.0, 30.0)
(5.0, 4.0, 16.0)
```

Arrays and Generics

After presenting Listing 3-52's Queue<E> generic type, I mentioned that I would explain why I specified elements = (E[]) new Object[size]; instead of the more compact elements = new E[size]; expression. Because of Java's generics implementation, it isn't possible to specify array-creation expressions that involve type parameters (e.g., new E[size] or new List<E>[50]) or actual type arguments (e.g., new Queue<String>[15]). If you attempt to do so, the compiler will report a generic array creation error message.

Before I present an example that demonstrates why allowing array-creation expressions that involve type parameters or actual type arguments is dangerous, you need to understand reification and covariance in the context of arrays, and erasure, which is at the heart of how generics are implemented.

Reification is representing the abstract as if it was concrete —for example, making a memory address available for direct manipulation by other language constructs. Java arrays are reified in that they're aware of their element types (an element type is stored internally) and can enforce these types at runtime. Attempting to store an invalid element in an array causes the JVM to throw an instance of the java.lang.ArrayStoreException class.

Listing 3-57 teaches you how array manipulation can lead to an ArrayStoreException:

Listing 3-57. How an ArrayStoreException arises

```
class Point
{
    int x, y;
}
class ColoredPoint extends Point
{
    int color;
}
class ReificationDemo
{
    public static void main(String[] args)
    {
        ColoredPoint[] cptArray = new ColoredPoint[1];
        Point[] ptArray = cptArray;
        ptArray[0] = new Point();
    }
}
```

Listing 3-57's main() method first instantiates a ColoredPoint array that can store one element. In contrast to this legal assignment (the types are compatible), specifying ColoredPoint[] cptArray = new Point[1]; is illegal (and won't compile) because it would result in a ClassCastException at runtime—the array knows that the assignment is illegal.

■ **Note** If it's not obvious, ColoredPoint[] cptArray = new Point[1]; is illegal because Point instances have fewer members (only x and y) than ColoredPoint instances (x, y, and color). Attempting to access a Point instance's nonexistent color field from its entry in the ColoredPoint array would result in a memory violation (because no memory has been assigned to color) and ultimately crash the JVM.

The second line (Point[] ptArray = cptArray;) is legal because of *covariance* (an array of supertype references is a supertype of an array of subtype references). In this case, an array of Point references is a supertype of an array of ColoredPoint references. The nonarray analogy is that a subtype is also a supertype. For example, a Throwable instance is a kind of Object instance.

Covariance is dangerous when abused. For example, the third line (ptArray[0] = new Point();) results in ArrayStoreException at runtime because a Point instance is not a ColoredPoint instance. Without this exception, an attempt to access the nonexistent member color crashes the JVM.

Unlike with arrays, a generic type's type parameters are not reified. They're not available at runtime because they're thrown away after the source code is compiled. This "throwing away of type parameters" is a result of *erasure*, which also involves inserting casts to appropriate types when the code isn't type correct, and replacing type parameters by their upper bounds (such as Object).

Note The compiler performs erasure to let generic code interoperate with legacy (nongeneric) code. It transforms generic source code into nongeneric runtime code. One consequence of erasure is that you cannot use the instanceof operator with parameterized types apart from unbounded wildcard types. For example, it's illegal to specify List<Employee> le = null; if (le instanceof ArrayList<Employee>) {}. Instead, you must change the instanceof expression to le instanceof ArrayList<?> (unbounded wildcard) or le instanceof ArrayList (raw type, which is the preferred use).

Suppose you could specify an array-creation expression involving a type parameter or an actual type argument. Why would this be bad? For an answer, consider the following example, which should generate an ArrayStoreException instead of a ClassCastException but doesn't do so:

```
List<Employee>[] empListArray = new List<Employee>[1];
List<String> strList = new ArrayList<>();
strList.add("string");
Object[] objArray = empListArray;
objArray[0] = strList;
Employee e = empListArray[0].get(0);
```

Let's assume that the first line, which creates a one-element array where this element stores a List of Employee, is legal. The second line creates a List of String, and the third line stores a single String object in this list.

The fourth line assigns empListArray to objArray. This assignment is legal because arrays are covariant and erasure converts List<Employee>[] to the List runtime type, and List subtypes Object.

Because of erasure, the JVM doesn't throw ArrayStoreException when it encounters objArray[0] = strList;. After all, we're assigning a List reference to a List[] array at runtime. However, this exception would be thrown if generic types were reified because we'd then be assigning a List<String> reference to a List<Employee>[] array.

However, there is a problem. A List<String> instance has been stored in an array that can only hold List<Employee> instances. When the compiler-inserted cast operator attempts to cast empListArray[0].get(0)'s return value ("string") to Employee, the cast operator throws a ClassCastException object.

Perhaps a future version of Java will reify type parameters, making it possible to specify array-creation expressions that involve type parameters or actual type arguments.

Varargs and Generics

When you invoke a *varargs* (variable number of arguments) method whose parameter is declared to be a parameterized type (as in List<String>), the compiler emits a warning message at the point of call. This message can be confusing and tends to discourage the use of varargs in third-party APIs.

The warning message is related to *heap pollution*, which occurs when a variable of a parameterized type refers to an object that is not of that parameterized type. Heap pollution can only occur when an application performs an operation that would give rise to an unchecked warning at compile time. (*The Java Language Specification, Third Edition* discusses the concept of heap pollution [http://java.sun.com/docs/books/jls/third_edition/html/typesValues.html#4.12.2.1]).

Unchecked warnings occur in calls to varargs methods whose parameter types are not reifiable. In other words, the parameter's type information cannot be completely expressed at runtime because of erasure.

Varargs are implemented via arrays and arrays are reified. In other words, an array's element type is stored internally and used when required for various runtime type checks. However, this stored type information cannot include information required to represent a parameterized type that is nonreifiable.

This mismatch between a reified array passing nonreified (and nonreifiable) parameterized types to a method is at the heart of the unchecked warning when the method is called.

In Java 5, calling one of these methods causes a compile-time warning; declaring such a method doesn't result in a similar warning. Although the existence of such a varargs method doesn't cause heap pollution, its existence contributes to heap pollution by offering an easy way to cause heap pollution to occur. Furthermore, it influences heap pollution by offering the method to be called. For this reason, method declarations that contribute to heap pollution deserve a compiler warning, just as this warning is already present for method calls that cause heap pollution.

The Java 7 compiler outputs warnings in both locations, and Listing 3-58 presents a scenario that leads to these warnings.

Listing 3-58. Merging a variable number of Lists of Strings

```java
import java.util.ArrayList;
import java.util.List;

class SafeVarargsDemo
{
   public static void main(String[] args)
   {
      List<String> list1 = new ArrayList<>();
      list1.add("A");
      list1.add("B");
      List<String> list2 = new ArrayList<>();
      list2.add("C");
      list2.add("D");
      list2.add("E");
      System.out.println(merge(list1, list2)); // Output: [A, B, C, D, E]
   }
   //@SafeVarargs
   static List<String> merge(List<String>... lists)
   {
      List<String> mergedLists = new ArrayList<>();
      for (int i = 0; i < lists.length; i++)
         mergedLists.addAll(lists[i]);
```

```
        return mergedLists;
    }
}
```

Listing 3-58 declares a merge() method whose purpose is to merge a variable number of List of String arguments into a single List of String that this method returns. Because erasure converts the method's List<String> parameter type to List, there is a potential for this array parameter to refer to a List that doesn't store String objects, which is an example of heap pollution. For this reason, the compiler emits the following warnings when you compile Listing 3-58 via javac -Xlint:unchecked SafeVarargsDemo.java:

```
SafeVarargsDemo.java:15: warning: [unchecked] unchecked generic array creation for↵ varargs
parameter of type List<String>[]
        System.out.println(merge(list1, list2)); // Output: [A, B, C, D, E]
                                 ^
SafeVarargsDemo.java:18: warning: [unchecked] Possible heap pollution from parameterized↵
vararg type List<String>
    static List<String> merge(List<String>... lists)
                                           ^
2 warnings
```

The merge() method does nothing that can lead to a ClassCastException. Therefore, these warning messages are spurious and can be ignored by annotating merge() with @SafeVarargs to assert that the body of the merge() method does not perform potentially unsafe operations on its varargs parameter.

Uncomment //@SafeVarargs in Listing 3-58 and recompile. You'll discover that these warning messages disappear.

Note Various standard class library methods, such as the Arrays class's public static <T> List<T> asList(T... a) method, are annotated @SafeVarargs because they don't throw ClassCastExceptions when their varargs array arguments are created by the compiler using proper type inference.

Enums

An *enumerated type* is a type that specifies a named sequence of related constants as its legal values. The months in a calendar, the coins in a currency, and the days of the week are examples of enumerated types.

Java developers have traditionally used sets of named integer constants to represent enumerated types. Because this form of representation has proven to be problematic, Java 5 introduced the enum alternative.

This section introduces you to enums. After discussing the problems with traditional enumerated types, the section presents the enum alternative. It then introduces you to the Enum class, from which enums originate.

The Trouble with Traditional Enumerated Types

Listing 3-59 declares a Coin enumerated type whose set of constants identifies different kinds of coins in a currency.

Listing 3-59. An enumerated type identifying coins

```
class Coin
{
   final static int PENNY = 0;
   final static int NICKEL = 1;
   final static int DIME = 2;
   final static int QUARTER = 3;
}
```

Listing 3-60 declares a Weekday enumerated type whose set of constants identifies the days of the week.

Listing 3-60. An enumerated type identifying weekdays

```
class Weekday
{
   final static int SUNDAY = 0;
   final static int MONDAY = 1;
   final static int TUESDAY = 2;
   final static int WEDNESDAY = 3;
   final static int THURSDAY = 4;
   final static int FRIDAY = 5;
   final static int SATURDAY = 6;
}
```

Listing 3-59's and 3-60's approach to representing an enumerated type is problematic, where the biggest problem is the lack of compile-time type safety. For example, you can pass a coin to a method that requires a weekday and the compiler will not complain.

You can also compare coins to weekdays, as in Coin.NICKEL == Weekday.MONDAY, and specify even more meaningless expressions, such as Coin.DIME+Weekday.FRIDAY-1/Coin.QUARTER. The compiler does not complain because it only sees ints.

Applications that depend upon enumerated types are brittle. Because the type's constants are compiled into an application's classfiles, changing a constant's int value requires you to recompile dependent applications or risk them behaving erratically.

Another problem with enumerated types is that int constants cannot be translated into meaningful string descriptions. For example, what does 4 mean when debugging a faulty application? Being able to see THURSDAY instead of 4 would be more helpful.

■ **Note** You could circumvent the previous problem by using String constants. For example, you might specify final static String THURSDAY = "THURSDAY";. Although the constant value is more meaningful, String-based constants can impact performance because you cannot use == to efficiently compare just any old strings (as you will discover in Chapter 4). Other problems related to String-based constants include hard-coding the constant's value ("THURSDAY") instead of the constant's name (THURSDAY) into source code, which makes it difficult to change the constant's value at a later time; and misspelling a hard-coded constant ("THURZDAY"), which compiles correctly but is problematic at runtime.

The Enum Alternative

Java 5 introduced enums as a better alternative to traditional enumerated types. An *enum* is an enumerated type that is expressed via reserved word enum. The following example uses enum to declare Listing 3-59's and 3-60's enumerated types:

```
enum Coin { PENNY, NICKEL, DIME, QUARTER }
enum Weekday { SUNDAY, MONDAY, TUESDAY, WEDNESDAY, THURSDAY, FRIDAY, SATURDAY }
```

Despite their similarity to the int-based enumerated types found in C++ and other languages, this example's enums are classes. Each constant is a public static final field that represents an instance of its enum class.

Because constants are final, and because you cannot call an enum's constructors to create more constants, you can use == to compare constants efficiently and (unlike string constant comparisons) safely. For example, you can specify c == Coin.NICKEL.

Enums promote compile-time type safety by preventing you from comparing constants in different enums. For example, the compiler will report an error when it encounters Coin.PENNY == Weekday.SUNDAY.

The compiler also frowns upon passing a constant of the wrong enum kind to a method. For example, you cannot pass Weekday.FRIDAY to a method whose parameter type is Coin.

Applications depending upon enums are not brittle because the enum's constants are not compiled into an application's classfiles. Also, the enum provides a toString() method for returning a more useful description of a constant's value.

Because enums are so useful, Java 5 enhanced the switch statement to support them. Listing 3-61 demonstrates this statement switching on one of the constants in the previous example's Coin enum.

Listing 3-61. Using the switch statement with an enum

```
class EnhancedSwitch
{
   enum Coin { PENNY, NICKEL, DIME, QUARTER }
   public static void main(String[] args)
   {
      Coin coin = Coin.NICKEL;
      switch (coin)
      {
         case PENNY  : System.out.println("1 cent"); break;
         case NICKEL : System.out.println("5 cents"); break;
         case DIME   : System.out.println("10 cents"); break;
         case QUARTER: System.out.println("25 cents"); break;
         default     : assert false;
      }
   }
}
```

}

Listing 3-61 demonstrates switching on an enum's constants. This enhanced statement only allows you to specify the name of a constant as a case label. If you prefix the name with the enum, as in case Coin.DIME, the compiler reports an error.

Enhancing an Enum

You can add fields, constructors, and methods to an enum – you can even have the enum implement interfaces. For example, Listing 3-62 adds a field, a constructor, and two methods to Coin to associate a denomination value with a Coin constant (such as 1 for penny and 5 for nickel) and convert pennies to the denomination.

Listing 3-62. Enhancing the Coin enum

```
enum Coin
{
   PENNY(1),
   NICKEL(5),
   DIME(10),
   QUARTER(25);

   private final int denomValue;
   Coin(int denomValue)
   {
      this.denomValue = denomValue;
   }
   int denomValue()
   {
      return denomValue;
   }
   int toDenomination(int numPennies)
   {
      return numPennies/denomValue;
   }
}
```

Listing 3-62's constructor accepts a denomination value, which it assigns to a private blank final field named denomValue—all fields should be declared final because constants are immutable. Notice that this value is passed to each constant during its creation (PENNY(1), for example).

■ **Caution** When the comma-separated list of constants is followed by anything other than an enum's closing brace, you must terminate the list with a semicolon or the compiler will report an error.

Furthermore, this listing's denomValue() method returns denomValue, and its toDenomination() method returns the number of coins of that denomination that are contained within the number of pennies passed to this method as its argument. For example, 3 nickels are contained in 16 pennies.

Listing 3-63 shows you how to use the enhanced Coin enum.

Listing 3-63. *Exercising the enhanced Coin enum*

```
class Coins
{
   public static void main(String[] args)
   {
      if (args.length == 1)
      {
         int numPennies = Integer.parseInt(args[0]);
         System.out.println(numPennies+" pennies is equivalent to:");
         int numQuarters = Coin.QUARTER.toDenomination(numPennies);
         System.out.println(numQuarters+" "+Coin.QUARTER.toString()+
                            (numQuarters != 1 ? "s," : ","));
         numPennies -= numQuarters*Coin.QUARTER.denomValue();
         int numDimes = Coin.DIME.toDenomination(numPennies);
         System.out.println(numDimes+" "+Coin.DIME.toString()+
                            (numDimes != 1 ? "s, " : ","));
         numPennies -= numDimes*Coin.DIME.denomValue();
         int numNickels = Coin.NICKEL.toDenomination(numPennies);
         System.out.println(numNickels+" "+Coin.NICKEL.toString()+
                            (numNickels != 1 ? "s, " : ", and"));
         numPennies -= numNickels*Coin.NICKEL.denomValue();
         System.out.println(numPennies+" "+Coin.PENNY.toString()+
                            (numPennies != 1 ? "s" : ""));
      }
      System.out.println();
      System.out.println("Denomination values:");
      for (int i = 0; i < Coin.values().length; i++)
         System.out.println(Coin.values()[i].denomValue());
   }
}
```

Listing 3-63 describes an application that converts its solitary "pennies" command-line argument to an equivalent amount expressed in quarters, dimes, nickels, and pennies. In addition to calling a Coin constant's denomValue() and toDenomValue() methods, the application calls toString() to output a string representation of the coin.

Another called enum method is values(). This method returns an array of all Coin constants that are declared in the Coin enum (value()'s return type, in this example, is Coin[]). This array is useful when you need to iterate over these constants. For example, Listing 3-63 calls this method to output each coin's denomination.

When you run this application with 119 as its command-line argument (java Coins 119), it generates the following output:

```
119 pennies is equivalent to:
4 QUARTERs,
1 DIME,
1 NICKEL, and
4 PENNYs

Denomination values:
```

```
1
5
10
25
```

The output shows that toString() returns a constant's name. It is sometimes useful to override this method to return a more meaningful value. For example, a method that extracts *tokens* (named character sequences) from a string might use a Token enum to list token names and, via an overriding toString() method, values – see Listing 3-64.

Listing 3-64. Overriding toString() to return a Token constant's value

```
enum Token
{
    IDENTIFIER("ID"),
    INTEGER("INT"),
    LPAREN("("),
    RPAREN(")"),
    COMMA(",");
    private final String tokValue;
    Token(String tokValue)
    {
        this.tokValue = tokValue;
    }
    @Override
    public String toString()
    {
        return tokValue;
    }
    public static void main(String[] args)
    {
        System.out.println("Token values:");
        for (int i = 0; i < Token.values().length; i++)
            System.out.println(Token.values()[i].name()+" = "+
                                Token.values()[i]);
    }
}
```

Listing 3-64's main() method calls values() to return the array of Token constants. For each constant, it calls the constant's name() method to return the constant's name, and implicitly calls toString() to return the constant's value. If you were to run this application, you would observe the following output:

```
Token values:
IDENTIFIER = ID
INTEGER = INT
LPAREN = (
RPAREN = )
COMMA = ,
```

Another way to enhance an enum is to assign a different behavior to each constant. You can accomplish this task by introducing an abstract method into the enum and overriding this method in an anonymous subclass of the constant. Listing 3-65's TempConversion enum demonstrates this technique.

Listing 3-65. Using anonymous subclasses to vary the behaviors of enum constants

```java
enum TempConversion
{
    C2F("Celsius to Fahrenheit")
    {
        @Override
        double convert(double value)
        {
            return value*9.0/5.0+32.0;
        }
    },
    F2C("Fahrenheit to Celsius")
    {
        @Override
        double convert(double value)
        {
            return (value-32.0)*5.0/9.0;
        }
    };
    TempConversion(String desc)
    {
        this.desc = desc;
    }
    private String desc;
    @Override
    public String toString()
    {
        return desc;
    }
    abstract double convert(double value);
    public static void main(String[] args)
    {
        System.out.println(C2F+" for 100.0 degrees = "+C2F.convert(100.0));
        System.out.println(F2C+" for 98.6 degrees = "+F2C.convert(98.6));
    }
}
```

When you run this application, it generates the following output:

```
Celsius to Fahrenheit for 100.0 degrees = 212.0
Fahrenheit to Celsius for 98.6 degrees = 37.0
```

The Enum Class

The compiler regards enum as syntactic sugar. When it encounters an enum type declaration (enum Coin {}), it generates a class whose name (Coin) is specified by the declaration, and which also subclasses the abstract Enum class (in the java.lang package), the common base class of all Java-based enumeration types.

If you examine Enum's Java documentation, you will discover that it overrides Object's clone(), equals(), finalize(), hashCode(), and toString() methods:

- `clone()` is overridden to prevent constants from being cloned so that there is never more than one copy of a constant; otherwise, constants could not be compared via ==.

- `equals()` is overridden to compare constants via their references—constants with the same identities (==) must have the same contents (`equals()`), and different identities imply different contents.

- `finalize()` is overridden to ensure that constants cannot be finalized.

- `hashCode()` is overridden because `equals()` is overridden.

- `toString()` is overridden to return the constant's name.

Except for `toString()`, all of the overriding methods are declared `final` so that they cannot be overridden in a subclass.

Enum also provides its own methods. These methods include the `final compareTo()`, (Enum implements `Comparable`), `getDeclaringClass()`, `name()`, and `ordinal()` methods:

- `compareTo()` compares the current constant with the constant passed as an argument to see which constant precedes the other constant in the enum, and returns a value indicating their order. This method makes it possible to sort an array of unsorted constants.

- `getDeclaringClass()` returns the `Class` object corresponding to the current constant's enum. For example, the `Class` object for `Coin` is returned when calling `Coin.PENNY.getDeclaringClass()` for enum `Coin { PENNY, NICKEL, DIME, QUARTER }`. Also, `TempConversion` is returned when calling `TempConversion.C2F.getDeclaringClass()` for Listing 3-65's `TempConversion` enum. The `compareTo()` method uses `Class`'s `getClass()` method and `Enum`'s `getDeclaringClass()` method to ensure that only constants belonging to the same enum are compared. Otherwise, a `ClassCastException` is thrown. (I will discuss `Class` in Chapter 4.)

- `name()` returns the constant's name. Unless overridden to return something more descriptive, `toString()` also returns the constant's name.

- `ordinal()` returns a zero-based *ordinal*, an integer that identifies the position of the constant within the enum type. `compareTo()` compares ordinals.

Enum also provides the `public static <T extends Enum<T>> T valueOf(Class<T> enumType, String name)` method for returning the enum constant from the specified enum with the specified name:

- `enumType` identifies the `Class` object of the enum from which to return a constant.

- `name` identifies the name of the constant to return.

For example, `Coin penny = Enum.valueOf(Coin.class, "PENNY");` assigns the `Coin` constant whose name is `PENNY` to penny.

You will not discover a `values()` method in Enum's Java documentation because the compiler *synthesizes* (manufactures) this method while generating the class.

Extending the Enum Class

Enum's generic type is Enum<E extends Enum<E>>. Although the formal type parameter list looks ghastly, it is not that hard to understand. But first, take a look at Listing 3-66.

Listing 3-66. The Coin class as it appears from the perspective of its classfile

```
final class Coin extends Enum<Coin>
{
   public static final Coin PENNY = new Coin("PENNY", 0);
   public static final Coin NICKEL = new Coin("NICKEL", 1);
   public static final Coin DIME = new Coin("DIME", 2);
   public static final Coin QUARTER = new Coin("QUARTER", 3);
   private static final Coin[] $VALUES = { PENNY, NICKEL, DIME, QUARTER };
   public static Coin[] values()
   {
      return Coin.$VALUES.clone();
   }
   public static Coin valueOf(String name)
   {
      return Enum.valueOf(Coin.class, "Coin");
   }
   private Coin(String name, int ordinal)
   {
      super(name, ordinal);
   }
}
```

Behind the scenes, the compiler converts enum Coin { PENNY, NICKEL, DIME, QUARTER } into a class declaration that is similar to Listing 3-66.

The following rules show you how to interpret Enum<E extends Enum<E>> in the context of Coin extends Enum<Coin>:

- Any subclass of Enum must supply an actual type argument to Enum. For example, Coin's header specifies Enum<Coin>.

- The actual type argument must be a subclass of Enum. For example, Coin is a subclass of Enum.

- A subclass of Enum (such as Coin) must follow the idiom that it supplies its own name (Coin) as an actual type argument.

The third rule allows Enum to declare methods—compareTo(), getDeclaringClass(), and valueOf()—whose parameter and/or return types are specified in terms of the subclass (Coin), and not in terms of Enum. The rationale for doing this is to avoid having to specify casts. For example, you do not need to cast valueOf()'s return value to Coin in Coin penny = Enum.valueOf(Coin.class, "PENNY");.

■ **Note** You cannot compile Listing 3-66 because the compiler will not compile any class that extends Enum. It will also complain about super(name, ordinal);.

EXERCISES

The following exercises are designed to test your understanding of nested types, packages, static imports, exceptions, assertions, annotations, generics, and enums:

1. A 2D graphics package supports two-dimensional drawing and transformations (rotation, scaling, translation, and so on). These transformations require a 3-by-3 matrix (a table). Declare a G2D class that encloses a `private` `Matrix` nonstatic member class. In addition to declaring a `Matrix(int nrows, int ncols)` constructor, `Matrix` declares a `void dump()` method that outputs the matrix values to standard output in a tabular format. Instantiate `Matrix` within G2D's noargument constructor, and initialize the `Matrix` instance to the *identity matrix* (a matrix where all entries are 0 except for those on the upper-left to lower-right diagonal, which are 1. Then invoke this instance's `dump()` method from the constructor. Include a `main()` method to test G2D.

2. Extend the `logging` package to support a null device in which messages are thrown away.

3. Continuing from Exercise 1, introduce the following matrix-multiplication method into `Matrix`:

```
Matrix multiply(Matrix m)
{
   Matrix result = new Matrix(matrix.length, matrix[0].length);
   for (int i = 0; i < matrix.length; i++)
      for (int j = 0; j < m.matrix[0].length; j++)
         for (int k = 0; k < m.matrix.length; k++)
            result.matrix[i][j] = result.matrix[i][j]+
                                  matrix[i][k]*m.matrix[k][j];
   return result;
}
```

Next, declare a `void rotate(double angle)` method in G2D. This method's first task is to negate its `angle` argument (to ensure counterclockwise rotation), which specifies a rotation angle in degrees. It then creates a 3-by-3 rotation `Matrix` and initializes the following (row, column) entries: (0, 0) to the cosine of the angle, (1, 0) to the sine of the angle, (0, 1) to the negative of the angle's sine, (1, 1) to the cosine of the angle, and (2, 2) to 1.0. Statically import all necessary `Math` class methods. Finally, `rotate()` multiplies the identity matrix created in G2D's constructor by this rotation matrix, and invokes `dump()` to dump the result. Test `rotate()` from the `main()` method by executing G2D g2d = new G2D(); g2d.rotate(45);. You should observe the following output:

```
1.0 0.0 0.0
0.0 1.0 0.0
0.0 0.0 1.0

0.7071067811865476 0.7071067811865475 0.0
```

```
-0.7071067811865475 0.7071067811865476 0.0
0.0 0.0 1.0
```

4. Modify the `logging` package so that `Logger`'s `connect()` method throws `CannotConnectException` when it cannot connect to its logging destination, and the other two methods each throw `NotConnectedException` when `connect()` was not called or when it threw `CannotConnectException`. Modify `TestLogger` to respond appropriately to thrown `CannotConnectException` and `NotConnectedException` objects.

5. Continuing from Exercise 3, use an assertion to verify the class invariant that the transformation matrix is initialized to the identity matrix before `G2D`'s constructor ends.

6. Declare a `ToDo` marker annotation type that annotates only type elements, and that also uses the default retention policy.

7. Rewrite the `StubFinder` application to work with Listing 3-43's `Stub` annotation type (with appropriate `@Target` and `@Retention` annotations) and Listing 3-44's `Deck` class.

8. Implement a `Stack<E>` generic type in a manner that is similar to Listing 3-52's `Queue` class. `Stack` must declare `push()`, `pop()`, and `isEmpty()` methods (it could also declare an `isFull()` method but that method is not necessary in this exercise), `push()` must throw a `StackFullException` instance when the stack is full, and `pop()` must throw a `StackEmptyException` instance when the stack is empty. (You must create your own `StackFullException` and `StackEmptyException` helper classes because they are not provided for you in Java's standard class library.) Declare a similar `main()` method, and insert two assertions into this method that validate your assumptions about the stack being empty immediately after being created and immediately after popping the last element.

9. Declare a `Compass` enum with `NORTH`, `SOUTH`, `EAST`, and `WEST` members. Declare a `UseCompass` class whose `main()` method randomly selects one of these constants and then switches on that constant. Each of the switch statement's cases should output a message such as `heading north`.

Summary

Java supports advanced language features related to nested types, packages, static imports, exceptions, assertions, annotations, generics, and enums.

Classes that are declared outside of any class are known as top-level classes. Java also supports nested classes, which are classes declared as members of other classes or scopes, and which help you implement top-level class architecture.

There are four kinds of nested classes: static member classes, nonstatic member classes, anonymous classes, and local classes. The latter three categories are known as inner classes.

Java supports the partitioning of top-level types into multiple namespaces, to better organize these types and to also prevent name conflicts. Java uses packages to accomplish these tasks.

The package statement identifies the package in which a source file's types are located. The import statement imports types from a package by telling the compiler where to look for unqualified type names during compilation.

An exception is a divergence from an application's normal behavior. Although it can be represented by an error code or object, Java uses objects because error codes are meaningless and cannot contain information about what led to the exception.

Java provides a hierarchy of classes that represent different kinds of exceptions. These classes are rooted in Throwable. Moving down the throwable hierarchy, you encounter the Exception and Error classes, which represent nonerror exceptions and errors.

Exception and its subclasses, except for RuntimeException (and its subclasses), describe checked exceptions. They are checked because the compiler checks the code to ensure that an exception is handled where thrown or identified as being handled elsewhere.

RuntimeException and its subclasses describe unchecked exceptions. You do not have to handle these exceptions because they represent coding mistakes (fix the mistakes). Although the names of their classes can appear in throws clauses, doing so adds clutter.

The throw statement throws an exception to the JVM, which searches for an appropriate handler. If the exception is checked, its name must appear in the method's throws clause, unless the name of the exception's superclass is listed in this clause.

A method handles one or more exceptions by specifying a try statement and appropriate catch blocks. A finally block can be included to execute cleanup code whether or not an exception is thrown, and before a thrown exception leaves the method.

An assertion is a statement that lets you express an assumption of application correctness via a Boolean expression. If this expression evaluates to true, execution continues with the next statement; otherwise, an error that identifies the cause of failure is thrown.

There are many situations where assertions should be used. These situations organize into internal invariant, control-flow invariant, and design-by-contract categories. An invariant is something that does not change.

Although there are many situations where assertions should be used, there also are situations where they should be avoided. For example, you should not use assertions to check the arguments that are passed to public methods.

The compiler records assertions in the classfile. However, assertions are disabled at runtime because they can affect performance. You must enable the classfile's assertions before you can test assumptions about the behaviors of your classes.

Annotations are instances of annotation types and associate metadata with application elements. They are expressed in source code by prefixing their type names with @ symbols. For example, @Readonly is an annotation and Readonly is its type.

Java supplies a wide variety of annotation types, including the compiler-oriented Override, Deprecated, SuppressWarnings, and SafeVarargs types. However, you can also declare your own annotation types by using the @interface syntax.

Annotation types can be annotated with meta-annotations that identify the application elements they can target (such as constructors, methods, or fields), their retention policies, and other characteristics.

Annotations whose types are assigned a runtime retention policy via @Retention annotations can be processed at runtime using custom applications or Java's apt tool, whose functionality has been integrated into the compiler starting with Java 6.

Java 5 introduced generics, language features for declaring and using type-agnostic classes and interfaces. When working with Java's Collections Framework, these features help you avoid ClassCastExceptions.

A generic type is a class or interface that introduces a family of parameterized types by declaring a formal type parameter list. The type name that replaces a type parameter is known as an actual type argument.

There are five kinds of actual type arguments: concrete type, concrete parameterized type, array type, type parameter, and wildcard. Furthermore, a generic type also identifies a raw type, which is a generic type without its type parameters.

Many type parameters are unbounded in that they can accept any actual type argument. To restrict actual type arguments, you can specify an upper bound, a type that serves as an upper limit on the types that can be chosen as actual type arguments. The upper bound is specified via reserved word extends followed by a type name. However, lower bounds are not supported.

A type parameter's scope is its generic type except where masked. This scope includes the formal type parameter list of which the type parameter is a member.

To preserve type safety, you are not allowed to violate the fundamental rule of generic types: **for a given subtype x of type y, and given G as a raw type declaration, $G<x>$ is not a subtype of $G<y>$.** In other words, multiple parameterized types that differ only in regard to one type parameter being a subtype of another type parameter are not polymorphic. For example, List<String> is not a specialized kind of List<Object>.

This restriction can be ameliorated without violating type safety by using wildcards. For example, where a void output(List<Object> list) method can only output a List that contains Objects (to adhere to the aforementioned rule), a void output(List<?> list) method can output a List of arbitrary objects.

Wildcards alone cannot solve the problem where you want to copy one List to another. The solution is to use a generic method, a static or non-static method with a type-generalized implementation. For example, a <T> void copyList(List<T> src, List<T> dest) method can copy a source List of arbitrary objects (whose type is specified by T) to another List of arbitrary objects (having the same type). The compiler infers the actual type arguments from the context in which the method is invoked.

Reification is representing the abstract as if it was concrete -- for example, making a memory address available for direct manipulation by other language constructs. Java arrays are reified in that they're aware of their element types (an element type is stored internally) and can enforce these types at runtime. Attempting to store an invalid element in an array causes the JVM to throw an instance of the ArrayStoreException class.

Unlike with arrays, a generic type's type parameters are not reified. They're not available at runtime because they're thrown away after the source code is compiled. This "throwing away of type parameters" is a result of erasure, which also involves inserting casts to appropriate types when the code isn't type correct, and replacing type parameters by their upper bounds (such as Object).

When you invoke a varargs method whose parameter is declared to be a parameterized type (as in List<String>), the compiler emits a warning message at the point of call. This message can be confusing and tends to discourage the use of varargs in third-party APIs.

The warning message is related to heap pollution, which occurs when a variable of a parameterized type refers to an object that is not of that parameterized type.

If a varargs method is declared such that this warning message occurs, and if the varargs method doesn't perform a potentially unsafe operation on its varargs parameter, you can annotate the method @SafeVarargs, and eliminate the warning message.

An enumerated type is a type that specifies a named sequence of related constants as its legal values. Java developers have traditionally used sets of named integer constants to represent enumerated types.

Because sets of named integer constants have proven to be problematic, Java 5 introduced the enum alternative. An enum is an enumerated type that is expressed via reserved word enum.

You can add fields, constructors, and methods to an enum—you can even have the enum implement interfaces. Also, you can override `toString()` to provide a more useful description of a constant's value, and subclass constants to assign different behaviors.

The compiler regards `enum` as syntactic sugar for a class that subclasses `Enum`. This abstract class overrides various `Object` methods to provide default behaviors (usually for safety reasons), and provides additional methods for various purposes.

This chapter largely completes our tour of the Java language. However, there are a few more advanced language features to explore. You will encounter a couple of these minor features in Chapter 4, which begins a multichapter exploration of additional types that are located in Java's standard class library.

CHAPTER 4

Touring Language APIs

Java's standard class library provides various language-oriented APIs. Most of these APIs reside in the java.lang package and its subpackages, although a few APIs reside in java.math. Chapter 4 first introduces you to the java.lang/subpackage Math and StrictMath, Package, Primitive Type Wrapper Class, Reference, Reflection, String, StringBuffer and StringBuilder, System, and Threading APIs. This chapter then introduces you to java.math's BigDecimal and BigInteger APIs.

Math and StrictMath

The java.lang.Math class declares double constants E and PI that represent the natural logarithm base value (2.71828...) and the ratio of a circle's circumference to its diameter (3.14159...). E is initialized to 2.718281828459045 and PI is initialized to 3.141592653589793. Math also declares assorted class methods to perform various math operations. Table 4-1 describes many of these methods.

Table 4-1. Math Methods

Method	Description
double abs(double d)	Return the absolute value of d. There are four special cases: abs(-0.0) = +0.0, abs(+infinity) = +infinity, abs(-infinity) = +infinity, and abs(NaN) = NaN.
float abs(float f)	Return the absolute value of f. There are four special cases: abs(-0.0) = +0.0, abs(+infinity) = +infinity, abs(-infinity) = +infinity, and abs(NaN) = NaN.
int abs(int i)	Return the absolute value of i. There is one special case: the absolute value of Integer.MIN_VALUE is Integer.MIN_VALUE.
long abs(long l)	Return the absolute value of l. There is one special case: the absolute value of Long.MIN_VALUE is Long.MIN_VALUE.
double acos(double d)	Return angle d's arc cosine within the range 0 through PI. There are three special cases: acos(anything > 1) = NaN, acos(anything < -1) = NaN, and acos(NaN) = NaN.

`double asin(double d)`	Return angle d's arc sine within the range -PI/2 through PI/2. There are three special cases: `asin(anything > 1)` = `NaN`, `asin(anything < -1)` = `NaN`, and `asin(NaN)` = `NaN`.
`double atan(double d)`	Return angle d's arc tangent within the range -PI/2 through PI/2. There are five special cases: `atan(+0.0)` = `+0.0`, `atan(-0.0)` = `-0.0`, `atan(+infinity)` = `+PI/2`, `atan(-infinity)` = `-PI/2`, and `atan(NaN)` = `NaN`.
`double ceil(double d)`	Return the smallest value (closest to negative infinity) that is not less than d and is equal to an integer. There are six special cases: `ceil(+0.0)` = `+0.0`, `ceil(-0.0)` = `-0.0`, `ceil(anything > -1.0 and < 0.0)` = `-0.0`, `ceil(+infinity)` = `+infinity`, `ceil(-infinity)` = `-infinity`, and `ceil(NaN)` = `NaN`.
`double cos(double d)`	Return the cosine of angle d (expressed in radians). There are three special cases: `cos(+infinity)` = `NaN`, `cos(-infinity)` = `NaN`, and `cos(NaN)` = `NaN`.
`double exp(double d)`	Return Euler's number e to the power d. There are three special cases: `exp(+infinity)` = `+infinity`, `exp(-infinity)` = `+0.0`, and `exp(NaN)` = `NaN`.
`double floor(double d)`	Return the largest value (closest to positive infinity) that is not greater than d and is equal to an integer. There are five special cases: `floor(+0.0)` = `+0.0`, `floor(-0.0)` = `-0.0`, `floor(+infinity)` = `+infinity`, `floor(-infinity)` = `-infinity`, and `floor(NaN)` = `NaN`.
`double log(double d)`	Return the natural logarithm (base e) of d. There are six special cases: `log(+0.0)` = `-infinity`, `log(-0.0)` = `-infinity`, `log(anything < 0)` = `NaN`, `log(+infinity)` = `+infinity`, `log(-infinity)` = `NaN`, and `log(NaN)` = `NaN`.
`double log10(double d)`	Return the base 10 logarithm of d. There are six special cases: `log10(+0.0)` = `-infinity`, `log10(-0.0)` = `-infinity`, `log10(anything < 0)` = `NaN`, `log10(+infinity)` = `+infinity`, `log10(-infinity)` = `NaN`, and `log10(NaN)` = `NaN`.
`double max(double d1, double d2)`	Return the most positive (closest to positive infinity) of d1 and d2. There are four special cases: `max(NaN, anything)` = `NaN`, `max(anything, NaN)` = `NaN`, `max(+0.0, -0.0)` = `+0.0`, and `max(-0.0, +0.0)` = `+0.0`.
`float max(float f1, float f2)`	Return the most positive (closest to positive infinity) of f1 and f2. There are four special cases: `max(NaN, anything)` = `NaN`, `max(anything, NaN)` = `NaN`, `max(+0.0, -0.0)` = `+0.0`,

	and max(-0.0, +0.0) = +0.0.
int max(int i1, int i2)	Return the most positive (closest to positive infinity) of i1 and i2.
long max(long l1, long l2)	Return the most positive (closest to positive infinity) of l1 and l2.
double min(double d1, double d2)	Return the most negative (closest to negative infinity) of d1 and d2. There are four special cases: min(NaN, anything) = NaN, min(anything, NaN) = NaN, min(+0.0, -0.0) = -0.0, and min(-0.0, +0.0) = -0.0.
float min(float f1, float f2)	Return the most negative (closest to negative infinity) of f1 and f2. There are four special cases: min(NaN, anything) = NaN, min(anything, NaN) = NaN, min(+0.0, -0.0) = -0.0, and min(-0.0, +0.0) = -0.0.
int min(int i1, int i2)	Return the most negative (closest to negative infinity) of i1 and i2.
long min(long l1, long l2)	Return the most negative (closest to negative infinity) of l1 and l2.
double random()	Return a pseudorandom number between 0.0 (inclusive) and 1.0 (exclusive).
long round(double d)	Return the result of rounding d to a long integer. The result is equivalent to (long) Math.floor(d+0.5). There are seven special cases: round(+0.0) = +0.0, round(-0.0) = +0.0, round(anything > Long.MAX_VALUE) = Long.MAX_VALUE, round(anything < Long.MIN_VALUE) = Long.MIN_VALUE, round(+infinity) = Long.MAX_VALUE, round(-infinity) = Long.MIN_VALUE, and round(NaN) = +0.0.
int round(float f)	Return the result of rounding f to an integer. The result is equivalent to (int) Math.floor(f+0.5). There are seven special cases: round(+0.0) = +0.0, round(-0.0) = +0.0, round(anything > Integer.MAX_VALUE) = Integer.MAX_VALUE, round(anything < Integer.MIN_VALUE) = Integer.MIN_VALUE, round(+infinity) = Integer.MAX_VALUE, round(-infinity) = Integer.MIN_VALUE, and round(NaN) = +0.0.
double signum(double d)	Return the sign of d as -1.0 (d less than 0.0), 0.0 (d equals 0.0), and 1.0 (d greater than 0.0). There are five special cases: signum(+0.0) = +0.0, signum(-0.0) = -0.0, signum(+infinity) = +1.0, signum(-infinity) = -1.0, and

	signum(NaN) = NaN.
float signum(float f)	Return the sign of f as -1.0 (f less than 0.0), 0.0 (f equals 0.0), and 1.0 (f greater than 0.0). There are five special cases: signum(+0.0) = +0.0, signum(-0.0) = -0.0, signum(+infinity) = +1.0, signum(-infinity) = -1.0, and signum(NaN) = NaN.
double sin(double d)	Return the sine of angle d (expressed in radians). There are five special cases: sin(+0.0) = +0.0, sin(-0.0) = -0.0, sin(+infinity) = NaN, sin(-infinity) = NaN, and sin(NaN) = NaN.
double sqrt(double d)	Return the square root of d. There are five special cases: sqrt(+0.0) = +0.0, sqrt(-0.0) = -0.0, sqrt(anything < 0) = NaN, sqrt(+infinity) = +infinity, and sqrt(NaN) = NaN.
double tan(double d)	Return the tangent of angle d (expressed in radians). There are five special cases: tan(+0.0) = +0.0, tan(-0.0) = -0.0, tan(+infinity) = NaN, tan(-infinity) = NaN, and tan(NaN) = NaN.
double toDegrees(double angrad)	Convert angle angrad from radians to degrees via expression angrad*180/PI. There are five special cases: toDegrees(+0.0) = +0.0, toDegrees(-0.0) = -0.0, toDegrees(+infinity) = +infinity, toDegrees(-infinity) = -infinity, and toDegrees(NaN) = NaN.
double toRadians(angdeg)	Convert angle angdeg from degrees to radians via expression angdeg/180*PI. There are five special cases: toRadians(+0.0) = +0.0, toRadians(-0.0) = -0.0, toRadians(+infinity) = +infinity, toRadians(-infinity) = -infinity, and toRadians(NaN) = NaN.

Table 4-1 reveals a wide variety of useful math-oriented methods. For example, each abs() method returns its argument's *absolute value* (number without regard for sign).

abs(double) and abs(float) are useful for comparing double precision floating-point and floating-point values safely. For example, 0.3 == 0.1+0.1+0.1 evaluates to false because 0.1 has no exact representation. However, you can compare these expressions with abs() and a tolerance value, which indicates an acceptable range of error. For example, Math.abs(0.3-(0.1+0.1+0.1)) < 0.1 returns true because the absolute difference between 0.3 and 0.1+0.1+0.1 is less than a 0.1 tolerance value.

Previous chapters demonstrated other Math methods. For example, Chapter 2 demonstrated Math's random(), sin(), cos(), and toRadians() methods.

As Chapter 3's Lotto649 application revealed, random() (which returns a number that appears to be randomly chosen but is actually chosen by a predictable math calculation, and hence is *pseudorandom*) is useful in simulations (as well as in games and wherever an element of chance is needed). However, its double precision floating-point range of 0.0 through (almost) 1.0 isn't practical. To make random() more useful, its return value must be transformed into a more useful range, perhaps integer values 0 through

49, or maybe -100 through 100. You will find the following rnd() method useful for making these transformations:

```java
static int rnd(int limit)
{
   return (int) (Math.random()*limit);
}
```

rnd() transforms random()'s 0.0 to (almost) 1.0 double precision floating-point range to a 0 through limit-1 integer range. For example, rnd(50) returns an integer ranging from 0 through 49. Also, -100+rnd(201) transforms 0.0 to (almost) 1.0 into -100 through 100 by adding a suitable offset and passing an appropriate limit value.

Caution Do not specify (int) Math.random()*limit because this expression always evaluates to 0. The expression first casts random()'s double precision floating-point fractional value (0.0 through 0.99999. . .) to integer 0 by truncating the fractional part, and then multiplies 0 by limit, resulting in 0.

The sin() and cos() methods implement the sine and cosine trigonometric functions—see http://en.wikipedia.org/wiki/Trigonometric_functions. These functions have uses ranging from the study of triangles to modeling periodic phenomena (such as simple harmonic motion—see http://en.wikipedia.org/wiki/Simple_harmonic_motion).

We can use sin() and cos() to generate and display sine and cosine waves. Listing 4-1 presents the source code to an application that does just this.

Listing 4-1. Graphing sine and cosine waves

```java
class Graph
{
   final static int ROWS = 11; // Must be odd
   final static int COLS= 23;
   public static void main(String[] args)
   {
      char[][] screen = new char[ROWS][];
      for (int row = 0; row < ROWS; row++)
         screen[row] = new char[COLS];
      double scaleX = COLS/360.0;
      for (int degree = 0; degree < 360; degree++)
      {
         int row = ROWS/2+
                   (int) Math.round(ROWS/2*Math.sin(Math.toRadians(degree)));
         int col = (int) (degree*scaleX);
         screen[row][col] = 'S';
         row = ROWS/2+
               (int) Math.round(ROWS/2*Math.cos(Math.toRadians(degree)));
         screen[row][col] = (screen[row][col] == 'S') ? '*' : 'C';
      }
      for (int row = ROWS-1; row >= 0; row--)
```

```
            {
                for (int col = 0; col < COLS; col++)
                    System.out.print(screen[row][col]);
                System.out.println();
            }
        }
    }
}
```

Listing 4-1 introduces a Graph class that first declares a pair of constants: NROWS and NCOLS. These constants specify the dimensions of an array on which the graphs are generated. NROWS must be assigned an odd integer; otherwise, an instance of the java.lang.ArrayIndexOutOfBoundsException class is thrown.

Tip It's a good idea to use constants wherever possible. The source code is easier to maintain because you only need to change the constant's value in one place instead of having to change each corresponding value throughout the source code.

Graph next declares its main() method, which first creates a two-dimensional screen array of characters. This array is used to simulate an old-style character-based screen for viewing the graphs.

main() next calculates a horizontal scale value for scaling each graph horizontally so that 360 horizontal (degree) positions fit into the number of columns specified by NCOLS.

Continuing, main() enters a for loop that, for each of the sine and cosine graphs, creates (row, column) coordinates for each degree value, and assigns a character to the screen array at those coordinates. The character is S for the sine graph, C for the cosine graph, and * when the cosine graph intersects the sine graph.

The row calculation invokes toRadians() to convert its degree argument to radians, which is required by the sin() and cos() methods. The value returned from sin() or cos() (-1 to 1) is then multiplied by ROWS/2 to scale this value to half the number of rows in the screen array. After rounding the result to the nearest long integer via the long round(double d) method, a cast is used to convert from long integer to integer, and this integer is added to ROW/2 to offset the row coordinate so that it's relative to the array's middle row. The column calculation is simpler, multiplying the degree value by the horizontal scale factor.

The screen array is dumped to the standard output device via a pair of nested for loops. The outer for loop inverts the screen so that it appears right side up—row number 0 should output last.

Compile Listing 4-1 (javac Graph.java) and run the application (java Graph). You observe the following output:

```
CC  SSSS            CC
 CSSS  SS           CC
 S*C   SS          CC
 S CC   SS        CC
SS CC    SS      CC
S   CC    S    CC    S
     C    SS  C    SS
     CC   SS CC    S
      CC    SCC   SS
       CC   CSS  SSS
        CCCCC SSSS
```

▓ **Note** When I created the `screen` array, I took advantage of the fact that every element is initialized to 0, which is interpreted as the null character. When a `System.out.print()` or `System.out.println()` method detects this character, it outputs a space character instead.

Table 4-1 also reveals a few curiosities starting with +infinity, -infinity, +0.0, -0.0, and NaN (Not a Number).

Java's floating-point calculations are capable of returning +infinity, -infinity, +0.0, -0.0, and NaN because Java largely conforms to IEEE 754 (`http://en.wikipedia.org/wiki/IEEE_754`), a standard for floating-point calculations. The following are the circumstances under which these special values arise:

- +infinity returns from attempting to divide a positive number by 0.0. For example, `System.out.println(1.0/0.0);` outputs `Infinity`.

- -infinity returns from attempting to divide a negative number by 0.0. For example, `System.out.println(-1.0/0.0);` outputs `-Infinity`.

- NaN returns from attempting to divide 0.0 by 0.0, attempting to calculate the square root of a negative number, and attempting other strange operations. For example, `System.out.println(0.0/0.0);` and `System.out.println(Math.sqrt(-1.0));` each output `NaN`.

- +0.0 results from attempting to divide a positive number by +infinity. For example, `System.out.println(1.0/(1.0/0.0));` outputs `+0.0`.

- -0.0 results from attempting to divide a negative number by +infinity. For example, `System.out.println(-1.0/(1.0/0.0));` outputs `-0.0`.

Once an operation yields +infinity, -infinity, or NaN, the rest of the expression usually equals that special value. For example, `System.out.println(1.0/0.0*20.0);` outputs `Infinity`. Also, an expression that first yields +infinity or -infinity might devolve into NaN. For example, `1.0/0.0*0.0` yields +infinity (`1.0/0.0`) and then NaN (+infinity*0.0).

Another curiosity is `Integer.MAX_VALUE`, `Integer.MIN_VALUE`, `Long.MAX_VALUE`, and `Long.MIN_VALUE`. Each of these items is a primitive type wrapper class constant that identifies the maximum or minimum value that can be represented by the class's associated primitive type. (I discuss primitive type wrapper classes later in this chapter.)

Finally, you might wonder why the abs(), max(), and min() overloaded methods do not include byte and short versions, as in byte abs(byte b) and short abs(short s). There is no need for these methods because the limited ranges of bytes and short integers make them unsuitable in calculations. If you need such a method, check out Listing 4-2.

Listing 4-2. Obtaining absolute values for byte integers and short integers

```
class AbsByteShort
{
   static byte abs(byte b)
   {
      return (b < 0) ? (byte) -b : b;
   }
   static short abs(short s)
   {
      return (s < 0) ? (short) -s : s;
   }
   public static void main(String[] args)
   {
      byte b = -2;
      System.out.println(abs(b)); // Output: 2
      short s = -3;
      System.out.println(abs(s)); // Output: 3
   }
}
```

Listing 4-2's (byte) and (short) casts are necessary because -b converts b's value from a byte to an int, and -s converts s's value from a short to an int. In contrast, these casts are not needed with (b < 0) and (s < 0), which automatically cast b's and s's values to an int before comparing them with int-based 0.

Tip Their absence from Math suggests that byte and short are not very useful in method declarations. However, these types are useful when declaring arrays whose elements store small values (such as a binary file's byte values). If you declared an array of int or long to store such values, you would end up wasting heap space (and might even run out of memory).

While searching through the Java documentation for the java.lang package, you will probably encounter a class named StrictMath. Apart from a longer name, this class appears to be identical to Math. The differences between these classes can be summed up as follows:

- StrictMath's methods return exactly the same results on all platforms. In contrast, some of Math's methods might return values that vary ever so slightly from platform to platform.

- Because StrictMath cannot utilize platform-specific features such as an extended-precision math coprocessor, an implementation of StrictMath might be less efficient than an implementation of Math.

For the most part, Math's methods call their StrictMath counterparts. Two exceptions are toDegrees() and toRadians(). Although these methods have identical code bodies in both classes, StrictMath's implementations include reserved word strictfp in the method headers:

```
public static strictfp double toDegrees(double angrad)
public static strictfp double toRadians(double angdeg)
```

Wikipedia's "strictfp" entry (http://en.wikipedia.org/wiki/Strictfp) mentions that strictfp restricts floating-point calculations to ensure portability. This reserved word accomplishes portability in the context of intermediate floating-point representations and overflows/underflows (generating a value too large or small to fit a representation).

■ **Note** The previously cited "strictfp" article states that Math contains public static strictfp double abs(double); and other strictfp methods. If you check out this class's source code under Java 7, you will not find strictfp anywhere in the source code. However, many Math methods (such as sin()) call their StrictMath counterparts, which are implemented in a platform-specific library, and the library's method implementations are strict.

Without strictfp, an intermediate calculation is not limited to the IEEE 754 32-bit and 64-bit floating-point representations that Java supports. Instead, the calculation can take advantage of a larger representation (perhaps 128 bits) on a platform that supports this representation.

An intermediate calculation that overflows/underflows when its value is represented in 32/64 bits might not overflow/underflow when its value is represented in more bits. Because of this discrepancy, portability is compromised. strictfp levels the playing field by requiring all platforms to use 32/64 bits for intermediate calculations.

When applied to a method, strictfp ensures that all floating-point calculations performed in that method are in strict compliance. However, strictfp can be used in a class header declaration (as in public strictfp class FourierTransform) to ensure that all floating-point calculations performed in that class are strict.

■ **Note** Math and StrictMath are declared final so that they cannot be extended. Also, they declare private empty noargument constructors so that they cannot be instantiated. Finally, Math and StrictMath are examples of utility classes because they exist as placeholders for static methods.

Package

The java.lang.Package class provides access to information about a package (see Chapter 3 for an introduction to packages). This information includes version details about the implementation and specification of a Java package, the name of the package, and an indication of whether or not the package has been *sealed* (all classes that are part of a package are archived in the same JAR file).

Table 4-2 describes some of Package's methods.

Table 4-2. Package Methods

Method	Description
String getImplementationTitle()	Return the title of this package's implementation, which might be null. The format of the title is unspecified.
String getImplementationVendor()	Return the name of the vendor or organization that provides this package's implementation. This name might be null. The format of the name is unspecified.
String getImplementationVersion()	Return the version number of this package's implementation, which might be null. This version string must be a sequence of positive decimal integers separated by periods and might have leading zeros.
String getName()	Return the name of this package in standard dot notation; for example, java.lang.
static Package getPackage(String packageName)	Return the Package object that is associated with the package identified as packageName, or null when the package identified as packageName cannot be found. This method throws java.lang.NullPointerException when packageName is null.
static Package[] getPackages()	Return an array of all Package objects that are accessible to this method's caller.
String getSpecificationTitle()	Return the title of this package's specification, which might be null. The format of the title is unspecified.
String getSpecificationVendor()	Return the name of the vendor or organization that provides the specification that is implemented by this package. This name might be null. The format of the name is unspecified.
String getSpecificationVersion()	Return the version number of the specification of this package's implementation, which might be null. This version string must be a sequence of positive decimal integers separated by periods, and might have leading zeros.
boolean isCompatibleWith(String desired)	Check this package to determine if it is compatible with the specified version string, by comparing this package's specification version with the desired version. Return true when this package's specification version number is greater than or equal to the desired version number (this package is compatible); otherwise, return false. This method throws NullPointerException when desired is null, and java.lang.NumberFormatException when this package's version

number or the desired version number is not in dotted form.

boolean isSealed()   Return true when this package has been sealed; otherwise, return false.

I have created a PackageInfo application that demonstrates most of Table 4-2's Package methods. Listing 4-3 presents this application's source code.

Listing 4-3. *Obtaining information about a package*

```
class PackageInfo
{
   public static void main(String[] args)
   {
      if (args.length == 0)
      {
         System.err.println("usage: java PackageInfo packageName [version]");
         return;
      }
      Package pkg = Package.getPackage(args[0]);
      if (pkg == null)
      {
         System.err.println(args[0]+" not found");
         return;
      }
      System.out.println("Name: "+pkg.getName());
      System.out.println("Implementation title: "+
                         pkg.getImplementationTitle());
      System.out.println("Implementation vendor: "+
                         pkg.getImplementationVendor());
      System.out.println("Implementation version: "+
                         pkg.getImplementationVersion());
      System.out.println("Specification title: "+
                         pkg.getSpecificationTitle());
      System.out.println("Specification vendor: "+
                         pkg.getSpecificationVendor());
      System.out.println("Specification version: "+
                         pkg.getSpecificationVersion());
      System.out.println("Sealed: "+pkg.isSealed());
      if (args.length > 1)
         System.out.println("Compatible with "+args[1]+": "+
                            pkg.isCompatibleWith(args[1]));
   }
}
```

After compiling Listing 4-3 (javac PackageInfo.java), specify at least a package name on the command line when you run this application. For example, java PackageInfo java.lang returns the following output under Java 7:

```
Name: java.lang
Implementation title: Java Runtime Environment
```

```
Implementation vendor: Oracle Corporation
Implementation version: 1.7.0
Specification title: Java Platform API Specification
Specification vendor: Oracle Corporation
Specification version: 1.7
Sealed: false
```

PackageInfo also lets you determine if the package's specification is compatible with a specific version number. A package is compatible with its predecessors.

For example, java PackageInfo java.lang 1.7 outputs Compatible with 1.7: true, whereas java PackageInfo java.lang 1.8 outputs Compatible with 1.8: false.

You can also use PackageInfo with your own packages, which you learned to create in Chapter 3. For example, that chapter presented a logging package.

Copy PackageInfo.class into the directory containing the logging package directory (which contains the compiled classfiles), and execute java PackageInfo logging.

PackageInfo responds by displaying the following output:

```
logging not found
```

This error message is presented because getPackage() requires at least one classfile to be loaded from the package before it returns a Package object describing that package.

The only way to eliminate the previous error message is to load a class from the package. Accomplish this task by merging the following code fragment into Listing 4-3.

```
if (args.length == 3)
try
{
    Class.forName(args[2]);
}
catch (ClassNotFoundException cnfe)
{
    System.err.println("cannot load "+args[2]);
    return;
}
```

This code fragment, which must precede Package pkg = Package.getPackage(args[0]);, loads the classfile named by the revised PackageInfo application's third command-line argument. (I'll discuss Class.forName() later in this chapter.)

Run the new PackageInfo application via java PackageInfo logging 1.5 logging.File and you will observe the following output—this command line identifies logging's File class as the class to load:

```
Name: logging
Implementation title: null
Implementation vendor: null
Implementation version: null
Specification title: null
Specification vendor: null
Specification version: null
Sealed: false
Exception in thread "main" java.lang.NumberFormatException: Empty version string
        at java.lang.Package.isCompatibleWith(Package.java:228)
        at PackageInfo.main(PackageInfo.java:42)
```

It is not surprising to see all of these null values because no package information has been added to the logging package. Also, NumberFormatException is thrown from isCompatibleWith() because the logging package does not contain a specification version number in dotted form (it is null).

Perhaps the simplest way to place package information into the logging package is to create a logging.jar file in a similar manner to the example shown in Chapter 3. But first, you must create a small text file that contains the package information. You can choose any name for the file. Listing 4-4 reveals my choice of manifest.mf.

Listing 4-4. manifest.mf containing the package information

```
Implementation-Title: Logging Implementation
Implementation-Vendor: Jeff Friesen
Implementation-Version: 1.0a
Specification-Title: Logging Specification
Specification-Vendor: Jeff Friesen
Specification-Version: 1.0
Sealed: true
```

Note Make sure to press the Return/Enter key at the end of the final line (Sealed: true). Otherwise, you will probably observe Sealed: false in the output because this entry will not be stored in the logging package by the JDK's jar tool—jar is a bit quirky.

Execute the following command line to create a JAR file that includes logging and its files, and whose *manifest*, a special file named MANIFEST.MF that stores information about the contents of a JAR file, contains the contents of Listing 4-4:

```
jar cfm logging.jar manifest.mf logging/*.class
```

This command line creates a JAR file named logging.jar (via the c [create] and f [file] options). It also merges the contents of manifest.mf (via the m [manifest] option) into MANIFEST.MF, which is stored in the package's META-INF directory.

Note To learn more about a JAR file's manifest, read the "JAR Manifest" section of the JDK documentation's "JAR File Specification" page (http://download.oracle.com/javase/7/docs/technotes/guides/jar/jar.html#JAR Manifest).

Assuming that the jar tool presents no error messages, execute the following Windows-oriented command line (or a command line suitable for your platform) to run PackageInfo and extract the package information from the logging package:

```
java -cp logging.jar;. PackageInfo logging 1.0 logging.File
```

This time, you should see the following output:

```
Name: logging
Implementation title: Logging Implementation
Implementation vendor: Jeff Friesen
Implementation version: 1.0a
Specification title: Logging Specification
Specification vendor: Jeff Friesen
Specification version: 1.0
Sealed: true
Compatible with 1.0: true
```

Primitive Type Wrapper Class

The java.lang package includes Boolean, Byte, Character, Double, Float, Integer, Long, and Short. These classes are known as *primitive type wrapper classes* because their instances wrap themselves around values of primitive types.

■ **Note** The primitive type wrapper classes are also known as *value classes*.

Java provides these eight primitive type wrapper classes for two reasons:

- The Collections Framework (discussed in Chapter 5) provides lists, sets, and maps that can only store objects; they cannot store primitive values. You store a primitive value in a primitive type wrapper class instance and store the instance in the collection.

- These classes provide a good place to associate useful constants (such as MAX_VALUE and MIN_VALUE) and class methods (such as Integer's parseInt() methods and Character's isDigit(), isLetter(), and toUpperCase() methods) with the primitive types.

This section introduces you to each of these primitive type wrapper classes and a java.lang class named Number.

Boolean

Boolean is the smallest of the primitive type wrapper classes. This class declares three constants, including TRUE and FALSE, which denote precreated Boolean objects. It also declares a pair of constructors for initializing a Boolean object:

- Boolean(boolean value) initializes the Boolean object to value.

- Boolean(String s) converts s's text to a true or false value and stores this value in the Boolean object.

The second constructor compares s's value with true. Because the comparison is case-insensitive, any uppercase/lowercase combination of these four letters (such as true, TRUE, or tRue) results in true being stored in the object. Otherwise, the constructor stores false in the object.

■ **Note** Boolean's constructors are complemented by `boolean booleanValue()`, which returns the wrapped Boolean value.

Boolean also declares or overrides the following methods:

- `int compareTo(Boolean b)` compares the current Boolean object with b to determine their relative order. The method returns 0 when the current object contains the same Boolean value as b, a positive value when the current object contains true and b contains false, and a negative value when the current object contains false and b contains true.

- `boolean equals(Object o)` compares the current Boolean object with o and returns true when o is not null, o is of type Boolean, and both objects contain the same Boolean value.

- `static boolean getBoolean(String name)` returns true when a system property (discussed later in this chapter) identified by name exists and is equal to true.

- `int hashCode()` returns a suitable hash code that allows Boolean objects to be used with hash-based collections (discussed in Chapter 5).

- `static boolean parseBoolean(String s)` parses s, returning true if s equals "true", "TRUE", "True", or any other uppercase/lowercase combination. Otherwise, this method returns false. (*Parsing* breaks a sequence of characters into meaningful components, known as *tokens*.)

- `String toString()` returns "true" when the current Boolean instance contains true; otherwise, this method returns "false".

- `static String toString(boolean b)` returns "true" when b contains true; otherwise, this method returns "false".

- `static Boolean valueOf(boolean b)` returns TRUE when b contains true or FALSE when b contains false.

- `static Boolean valueOf(String s)` returns TRUE when s equals "true", "TRUE", "True", or any other uppercase/lowercase combination of these letters. Otherwise, this method returns FALSE.

■ **Caution** Newcomers to the Boolean class often think that `getBoolean()` returns a Boolean object's true/false value. However, `getBoolean()` returns the value of a Boolean-based system property—I discuss system properties later in this chapter. If you need to return a Boolean object's true/false value, use the `booleanValue()` method instead.

It is often better to use TRUE and FALSE than to create Boolean objects. For example, suppose you need a method that returns a Boolean object containing true when the method's double argument is negative, or false when this argument is zero or positive. You might declare your method like the following isNegative() method:

```
Boolean isNegative(double d)
{
   return new Boolean(d < 0);
}
```

Although this method is concise, it unnecessarily creates a Boolean object. When the method is called frequently, many Boolean objects are created that consume heap space. When heap space runs low, the garbage collector runs and slows down the application, which impacts performance.

The following example reveals a better way to code isNegative():

```
Boolean isNegative(double d)
{
   return (d < 0) ? Boolean.TRUE : Boolean.FALSE;
}
```

This method avoids creating Boolean objects by returning either the precreated TRUE or FALSE object.

Tip You should strive to create as few objects as possible. Not only will your applications have smaller memory footprints, they'll perform better because the garbage collector will not run as often.

Character

Character is the largest of the primitive type wrapper classes, containing many constants, a constructor, many methods, and a trio of nested classes (Subset, UnicodeBlock, and UnicodeScript).

Note Character's complexity derives from Java's support for Unicode (http://en.wikipedia.org/wiki/Unicode). For brevity, I ignore much of Character's Unicode-related complexity, which is beyond the scope of this chapter.

Character declares a single Character(char value) constructor, which you use to initialize a Character object to value. This constructor is complemented by char charValue(), which returns the wrapped character value.

When you start writing applications, you might codify expressions such as ch >= '0' && ch <= '9' (test ch to see if it contains a digit) and ch >= 'A' && ch <= 'Z' (test ch to see if it contains an uppercase letter). You should avoid doing so for three reasons:

- It is too easy to introduce a bug into the expression. For example, ch > '0' && ch <= '9' introduces a subtle bug that does not include '0' in the comparison.

- The expressions are not very descriptive of what they are testing.

- The expressions are biased toward Latin digits (0-9) and letters (A-Z and a-z). They do not take into account digits and letters that are valid in other languages. For example, '\u0beb' is a character literal representing one of the digits in the Tamil language.

Character declares several comparison and conversion class methods that address these concerns. These methods include the following:

- `static boolean isDigit(char ch)` returns true when ch contains a digit (typically 0 through 9, but also digits in other alphabets).

- `static boolean isLetter(char ch)` returns true when ch contains a letter (typically A-Z or a-z, but also letters in other alphabets).

- `static boolean isLetterOrDigit(char ch)` returns true when ch contains a letter or digit (typically A-Z, a-z, or 0-9; but also letters or digits in other alphabets).

- `static boolean isLowerCase(char ch)` returns true when ch contains a lowercase letter.

- `static boolean isUpperCase(char ch)` returns true when ch contains an uppercase letter.

- `static boolean isWhitespace(char ch)` returns true when ch contains a whitespace character (typically a space, a horizontal tab, a carriage return, or a line feed).

- `static char toLowerCase(char ch)` returns the lowercase equivalent of ch's uppercase letter; otherwise, this method returns ch's value.

- `static char toUpperCase(char ch)` returns the uppercase equivalent of ch's lowercase letter; otherwise, this method returns ch's value.

For example, `isDigit(ch)` is preferable to `ch >= '0' && ch <= '9'` because it avoids a source of bugs, is more readable, and returns true for non-Latin digits (e.g., '\u0beb') as well as Latin digits.

Float and Double

Float and Double store floating-point and double precision floating-point values in Float and Double objects, respectively. These classes declare the following constants:

- `MAX_VALUE` identifies the maximum value that can be represented as a float or double.

- `MIN_VALUE` identifies the minimum value that can be represented as a float or double.

- `NaN` represents 0.0F/0.0F as a float and 0.0/0.0 as a double.

- `NEGATIVE_INFINITY` represents -infinity as a float or double.

- `POSITIVE_INFINITY` represents +infinity as a float or double.

Float and Double also declare the following constructors for initializing their objects:

- Float(float value) initializes the Float object to value.

- Float(double value) initializes the Float object to the float equivalent of value.

- Float(String s) converts s's text to a floating-point value and stores this value in the Float object.

- Double(double value) initializes the Double object to value.

- Double(String s) converts s's text to a double precision floating-point value and stores this value in the Double object.

Float's constructors are complemented by float floatValue(), which returns the wrapped floating-point value. Similarly, Double's constructors are complemented by double doubleValue(), which returns the wrapped double precision floating-point value.

Float declares several utility methods as well as floatValue(). These methods include the following:

- static int floatToIntBits(float value) converts value to a 32-bit integer.

- static boolean isInfinite(float f) returns true when f's value is +infinity or -infinity. A related boolean isInfinite() method returns true when the current Float object's value is +infinity or -infinity.

- static boolean isNaN(float f) returns true when f's value is NaN. A related boolean isNaN() method returns true when the current Float object's value is NaN.

- static float parseFloat(String s) parses s, returning the floating-point equivalent of s's textual representation of a floating-point value, or throwing NumberFormatException when this representation is invalid (contains letters, for example).

Double declares several utility methods as well as doubleValue(). These methods include the following:

- static long doubleToLongBits(double value) converts value to a long integer.

- static boolean isInfinite(double d) returns true when d's value is +infinity or -infinity. A related boolean isInfinite() method returns true when the current Double object's value is +infinity or -infinity.

- static boolean isNaN(double d) returns true when d's value is NaN. A related boolean isNaN() method returns true when the current Double object's value is NaN.

- static double parseDouble(String s) parses s, returning the double precision floating-point equivalent of s's textual representation of a double precision floating-point value, or throwing NumberFormatException when this representation is invalid.

The floatToIntBits() and doubleToIntBits() methods are used in implementations of the equals() and hashCode() methods that must take float and double fields into account. floatToIntBits() and doubleToIntBits() allow equals() and hashCode() to respond properly to the following situations:

- equals() must return true when f1 and f2 contain Float.NaN (or d1 and d2 contain Double.NaN). If equals() was implemented in a manner similar to f1.floatValue() == f2.floatValue() (or d1.doubleValue() == d2.doubleValue()), this method would return false because NaN is not equal to anything, including itself.

- equals() must return false when f1 contains +0.0 and f2 contains -0.0 (or vice-versa), or d1 contains +0.0 and d2 contains -0.0 (or vice-versa). If equals() was implemented in a manner similar to f1.floatValue() == f2.floatValue() (or d1.doubleValue() == d2.doubleValue()), this method would return true because +0.0 == -0.0 returns true.

These requirements are needed for hash-based collections (discussed in Chapter 5) to work properly. Listing 4-5 shows how they impact Float's and Double's equals() methods:

Listing 4-5. Demonstrating Float's equals() method in a NaN context and Double's equals() method in a +/-0.0 context

```
class FloatDoubleDemo
{
   public static void main(String[] args)
   {
      Float f1 = new Float(Float.NaN);
      System.out.println(f1.floatValue());
      Float f2 = new Float(Float.NaN);
      System.out.println(f2.floatValue());
      System.out.println(f1.equals(f2));
      System.out.println(Float.NaN == Float.NaN);
      System.out.println();
      Double d1 = new Double(+0.0);
      System.out.println(d1.doubleValue());
      Double d2 = new Double(-0.0);
      System.out.println(d2.doubleValue());
      System.out.println(d1.equals(d2));
      System.out.println(+0.0 == -0.0);
   }
}
```

Compile Listing 4-5 (javac FloatDoubleDemo.java) and run this application (java FloatDoubleDemo). The following output proves that Float's equals() method properly handles NaN and Double's equals() method properly handles +/-0.0:

```
NaN
NaN
true
false

0.0
-0.0
false
true
```

Tip If you want to test a float or double value for equality with +infinity or -infinity (but not both), do not use isInfinite(). Instead, compare the value with NEGATIVE_INFINITY or POSITIVE_INFINITY via ==. For example, f == Float.NEGATIVE_INFINITY.

You will find parseFloat() and parseDouble() useful in many contexts. For example, Listing 4-6 uses parseDouble() to parse command-line arguments into doubles.

Listing 4-6. Parsing command-line arguments into double precision floating-point values

```java
class Calc
{
   public static void main(String[] args)
   {
      if (args.length != 3)
      {
         System.err.println("usage: java Calc value1 op value2");
         System.err.println("op is one of +, -, *, or /");
         return;
      }
      try
      {
         double value1 = Double.parseDouble(args[0]);
         double value2 = Double.parseDouble(args[2]);
         if (args[1].equals("+"))
            System.out.println(value1+value2);
         else
         if (args[1].equals("-"))
            System.out.println(value1-value2);
         else
         if (args[1].equals("*"))
            System.out.println(value1*value2);
         else
         if (args[1].equals("/"))
            System.out.println(value1/value2);
         else
            System.err.println("invalid operator: "+args[1]);
      }
      catch (NumberFormatException nfe)
      {
         System.err.println("Bad number format: "+nfe.getMessage());
      }
   }
}
```

Specify java Calc 10E+3 + 66.0 to try out the Calc application. This application responds by outputting 10066.0. If you specified java Calc 10E+3 + A instead, you would observe Bad number format: For input string: "A" as the output, which is in response to the second parseDouble() method call's throwing of a NumberFormatException object.

Although NumberFormatException describes an unchecked exception, and although unchecked exceptions are often not handled because they represent coding mistakes, NumberFormatException does not fit this pattern in this example. The exception does not arise from a coding mistake; it arises from someone passing an illegal numeric argument to the application, which cannot be avoided through proper coding. Perhaps NumberFormatException should have been implemented as a checked exception type.

Integer, Long, Short, and Byte

Integer, Long, Short, and Byte store 32-bit, 64-bit, 16-bit, and 8-bit integer values in Integer, Long, Short, and Byte objects, respectively.

Each class declares MAX_VALUE and MIN_VALUE constants that identify the maximum and minimum values that can be represented by its associated primitive type. These classes also declare the following constructors for initializing their objects:

- Integer(int value) initializes the Integer object to value.

- Integer(String s) converts s's text to a 32-bit integer value and stores this value in the Integer object.

- Long(long value) initializes the Long object to value.

- Long(String s) converts s's text to a 64-bit integer value and stores this value in the Long object.

- Short(short value) initializes the Short object to value.

- Short(String s) converts s's text to a 16-bit integer value and stores this value in the Short object.

- Byte(byte value) initializes the Byte object to value.

- Byte(String s) converts s's text to an 8-bit integer value and stores this value in the Byte object.

Integer's constructors are complemented by int intValue(), Long's constructors are complemented by long longValue(), Short's constructors are complemented by short shortValue(), and Byte's constructors are complemented by byte byteValue(). These methods return wrapped integers.

These classes declare various useful integer-oriented methods. For example, Integer declares the following utility methods for converting a 32-bit integer to a java.lang.String instance according to a specific representation (binary, hexadecimal, octal, and decimal):

- static String toBinaryString(int i) returns a String object containing i's binary representation. For example, Integer.toBinaryString(255) returns a String object containing 11111111.

- static String toHexString(int i) returns a String object containing i's hexadecimal representation. For example, Integer.toHexString(255) returns a String object containing ff.

- static String toOctalString(int i) returns a String object containing i's octal representation. For example, toOctalString(64) returns a String object containing 100.

- static String toString(int i) returns a String object containing i's decimal representation. For example, toString(255) returns a String object containing 255.

It is often convenient to prepend zeros to a binary string so that you can align multiple binary strings in columns. For example, you might want to create an application that displays the following aligned output:

```
11110001
+
00000111
--------
11111000
```

Unfortunately, toBinaryString() does not let you accomplish this task. For example, Integer.toBinaryString(7) returns a String object containing 111 instead of 00000111. Listing 4-7's toAlignedBinaryString() method addresses this oversight.

Listing 4-7. Aligning binary strings

```java
class AlignBinary
{
   public static void main(String[] args)
   {
      System.out.println(toAlignedBinaryString(7, 8));
      System.out.println(toAlignedBinaryString(255, 16));
      System.out.println(toAlignedBinaryString(255, 7));
   }
   static String toAlignedBinaryString(int i, int numBits)
   {
      String result = Integer.toBinaryString(i);
      if (result.length() > numBits)
         return null; // cannot fit result into numBits columns
      int numLeadingZeros = numBits-result.length();
      String zerosPrefix = "";
      for (int j = 0; j < numLeadingZeros; j++)
         zerosPrefix += "0";
      return zerosPrefix+result;
   }
}
```

The toAlignedBinaryString() method takes two arguments: the first argument specifies the 32-bit integer that is to be converted into a binary string, and the second argument specifies the number of bit columns in which to fit the string.

After calling toBinaryString() to return i's equivalent binary string without leading zeros, toAlignedBinaryString() verifies that the string's digits can fit into the number of bit columns specified by numBits. If they do not fit, this method returns null. (You will learn about length() and other String methods later in this chapter.)

Moving on, toAlignedBinaryString() calculates the number of leading "0"s to prepend to result, and then uses a for loop to create a string of leading zeros. This method ends by returning the leading zeros string prepended to the result string.

Although using the compound string concatenation with assignment operator (+=) in a loop to build a string looks okay, it is very inefficient because intermediate String objects are created and thrown away. However, I employed this inefficient code so that I can contrast it with the more efficient code that I present later in this chapter.

When you run this application, it generates the following output:

```
00000111
0000000011111111
null
```

Number

Each of Float, Double, Integer, Long, Short, and Byte provides the other classes' *x*Value() methods as well as its own *x*Value() method. For example, Float provides doubleValue(), intValue(), longValue(), shortValue(), and byteValue() as well as floatValue().

All six methods are members of Number, which is the abstract superclass of Float, Double, Integer, Long, Short, and Byte—Number's floatValue(), doubleValue(), intValue(), and longValue() methods are abstract. Number is also the superclass of java.math.BigDecimal and java.math.BigInteger (discussed later in this chapter), and a pair of concurrency-related classes (one of these classes is presented in Chapter 6).

Number exists to simplify iterating over a collection of Number subclass objects. For example, you can declare a variable of java.util.List<Number> type and initialize it to an instance of java.util.ArrayList<Number> (or ArrayList<>, for short). You can then store a mixture of Number subclass objects in the collection, and iterate over this collection by calling a subclass method polymorphically.

Reference

Chapter 2 introduced you to garbage collection, where you learned that the garbage collector removes an object from the heap when there are no more references to the object. This statement isn't completely true, as you will shortly discover.

Chapter 2 also introduced you to java.lang.Object's finalize() method, where you learned that the garbage collector calls this method before removing an object from the heap. The finalize() method gives the object an opportunity to perform cleanup.

This section continues from where Chapter 2 left off by introducing you to Java's Reference API. After acquainting you with some basic terminology, it introduces you to the API's Reference and ReferenceQueue classes, followed by the API's SoftReference, WeakReference, and PhantomReference classes. These classes let applications interact with the garbage collector in limited ways.

■ **Note** As well as this section, you will find Brian Goetz's "Java theory and practice: Plugging memory leaks with soft references" (http://www.ibm.com/developerworks/java/library/j-jtp01246/index.html) and "Java theory and practice: Plugging memory leaks with weak references" (http://www.ibm.com/developerworks/java/library/j-jtp11225/index.html) tutorials to be helpful in understanding the Reference API.

Basic Terminology

When an application runs, its execution reveals a *root set of references*, a collection of local variables, parameters, class fields, and instance fields that currently exist and that contain (possibly null) references to objects. This root set changes over time as the application runs. For example, parameters disappear after a method returns.

Many garbage collectors identify this root set when they run. They use the root set to determine if an object is *reachable* (referenced, also known as *live*) or *unreachable* (not referenced). The garbage collector cannot collect reachable objects. Instead, it can only collect objects that, starting from the root set of references, cannot be reached.

Note Reachable objects include objects that are indirectly reachable from root-set variables, which means objects that are reachable through live objects that are directly reachable from those variables. An object that is unreachable by any path from any root-set variable is eligible for garbage collection.

Beginning with Java 1.2, reachable objects are classified as strongly reachable, softly reachable, weakly reachable, and phantom reachable. Unlike strongly reachable objects, softly, weakly, and phantom reachable objects can be garbage collected.

Going from strongest to weakest, the different levels of reachability reflect the life cycle of an object. They are defined as follows:

- An object is *strongly reachable* if it can be reached from some thread without traversing any Reference objects. A newly created object (such as the object referenced by d in Double d = new Double(1.0);) is strongly reachable by the thread that created it. (I will discuss threads later in this chapter.)

- An object is *softly reachable* if it is not strongly reachable but can be reached by traversing a *soft reference* (a reference to the object where the reference is stored in a SoftReference object). The strongest reference to this object is a soft reference. When the soft references to a softly reachable object are cleared, the object becomes eligible for finalization (discussed in Chapter 2).

- An object is *weakly reachable* if it is neither strongly reachable nor softly reachable, but can be reached by traversing a *weak reference* (a reference to the object where the reference is stored in a WeakReference object). The strongest reference to this object is a weak reference. When the weak references to a weakly reachable object are cleared, the object becomes eligible for finalization. (Apart from the garbage collector being more eager to clean up the weakly reachable object, a weak reference is exactly like a soft reference.)

- An object is *phantom reachable* if it is neither strongly, softly, nor weakly reachable, it has been finalized, and it is referred to by some *phantom reference* (a reference to the object where the reference is stored in a PhantomReference object). The strongest reference to this object is a phantom reference.

- Finally, an object is unreachable, and therefore eligible for removal from memory during the next garbage collection cycle, when it is not reachable in any of the above ways.

The object whose reference is stored in a SoftReference, WeakReference, or PhantomReference object is known as a *referent*.

Reference and ReferenceQueue

The Reference API consists of five classes located in the java.lang.ref package. Central to this package are Reference and ReferenceQueue.

Reference is the abstract superclass of this package's concrete SoftReference, WeakReference, and PhantomReference subclasses.

ReferenceQueue is a concrete class whose instances describe queue data structures. When you associate a ReferenceQueue instance with a Reference subclass object (Reference object, for short), the Reference object is added to the queue when the referent to which its encapsulated reference refers becomes garbage.

Note You associate a ReferenceQueue object with a Reference object by passing the ReferenceQueue object to an appropriate Reference subclass constructor.

Reference is declared as generic type Reference<T>, where T identifies the referent's type. This class provides the following methods:

- void clear() assigns null to the stored reference; the Reference object on which this method is called is not *enqueued* (inserted) into its associated reference queue (if there is an associated reference queue). (The garbage collector clears references directly; it does not call clear(). Instead, this method is called by applications.)

- boolean enqueue() adds the Reference object on which this method is called to the associated reference queue. This method returns true when this Reference object has become enqueued; otherwise, this method returns false—this Reference object was already enqueued or was not associated with a queue when created. (The garbage collector enqueues Reference objects directly; it does not call enqueue(). Instead, this method is called by applications.)

- T get() returns this Reference object's stored reference. The return value is null when the stored reference has been cleared, either by the application or by the garbage collector.

- boolean isEnqueued() returns true when this Reference object has been enqueued, either by the application or by the garbage collector. Otherwise, this method returns false—this Reference object was not associated with a queue when created.

251

■ **Note** Reference also declares constructors. Because these constructors are package-private, only classes in the java.lang.ref package can subclass Reference. This restriction is necessary because instances of Reference's subclasses must work closely with the garbage collector.

ReferenceQueue is declared as generic type ReferenceQueue<T>, where T identifies the referent's type. This class declares the following constructor and methods:

- ReferenceQueue() initializes a new ReferenceQueue instance.

- Reference<? extends T> poll() polls this queue to check for an available Reference object. If one is available, the object is removed from the queue and returned. Otherwise, this method returns immediately with a null value.

- Reference<? extends T> remove() removes the next Reference object from the queue and returns this object. This method waits indefinitely for a Reference object to become available, and throws java.lang.InterruptedException when this wait is interrupted.

- Reference<? extends T> remove(long timeout) removes the next Reference object from the queue and returns this object. This method waits until a Reference object becomes available or until timeout milliseconds have elapsed—passing 0 to timeout causes the method to wait indefinitely. If timeout's value expires, the method returns null. This method throws java.lang.IllegalArgumentException when timeout's value is negative, or InterruptedException when this wait is interrupted.

SoftReference

The SoftReference class describes a Reference object whose referent is softly reachable. As well as inheriting Reference's methods and overriding get(), this generic class provides the following constructors for initializing a SoftReference object:

- SoftReference(T r) encapsulates r's reference. The SoftReference object behaves as a soft reference to r. No ReferenceQueue object is associated with this SoftReference object.

- SoftReference(T r, ReferenceQueue<? super T> q) encapsulates r's reference. The SoftReference object behaves as a soft reference to r. The ReferenceQueue object identified by q is associated with this SoftReference object. Passing null to q indicates a soft reference without a queue.

SoftReference is useful for implementing caches of objects that are expensive timewise to create (e.g., a database connection) and/or occupy significant amounts of heap space, such as large images. An image cache keeps images in memory (because it takes time to load them from disk) and ensures that duplicate (and possibly very large) images are not stored in memory.

The image cache contains references to image objects that are already in memory. If these references were strong, the images would remain in memory. You would then need to figure out which images are no longer needed and remove them from memory so that they can be garbage collected.

Having to manually remove images duplicates the work of a garbage collector. However, if you wrap the references to the image objects in SoftReference objects, the garbage collector will determine when to remove these objects (typically when heap memory runs low) and perform the removal on your behalf.

Listing 4-8 shows how you could use SoftReference to cache an image.

Listing 4-8. Caching an image

```
import java.lang.ref.SoftReference;

class Image
{
   private byte[] image;
   private Image(String name)
   {
      image = new byte[1024*1024*100];
   }
   static Image getImage(String name)
   {
      return new Image(name);
   }
}
class ImageCache
{
   public static void main(String[] args)
   {
      Image image = Image.getImage("large.png");
      System.out.println("caching image");
      SoftReference<Image> cache = new SoftReference<>(image);
      image = null;
      byte[] b = new byte[1024];
      while (cache.get() != null)
      {
         System.out.println("image is still cached");
         b = new byte[b.length*10];
      }
      System.out.println("image is no longer cached");
      b = null;
      System.out.println("reloading and recaching image");
      cache = new SoftReference<>(Image.getImage("large.png"));
      int counter = 0;
      while (cache.get() != null && ++counter != 7)
         System.out.println("image is still cached");
   }
}
```

Listing 4-8 declares an Image class that simulates loading a large image, and an ImageCache class that demonstrates the SoftReference-based caching of an Image object.

The main() method first creates an Image instance by calling the getImage() class method; the instance's private image array occupies 100MB of memory.

main() next creates a SoftReference object that is initialized to an Image object's reference, and clears the strong reference to the Image object by assigning null to image. If this strong reference is not removed, the Image object will be cached always and the application will most likely run out of memory.

After creating a byte array that's used to demonstrate SoftReference, main() enters the application's main loop, which keeps looping as long as cache.get() returns a nonnull reference (the Image object is still in the cache). For each loop iteration, main() outputs a message stating that the Image object is still cached, and doubles the size of the byte array.

At some point, the array doubling will exhaust the heap space. However, before it throws an instance of the java.lang.OutOfMemoryError class, the Java Virtual Machine (JVM) will attempt to obtain sufficient memory by clearing the SoftReference object's Image reference, and removing the Image object from the heap.

The next loop iteration will detect this situation by discovering that get() returns null. The loop ends and main() outputs a suitable message confirming that the Image object is no longer cached.

main() now assigns null to b to ensure that there will be sufficient memory to reload the large image (via getImage()) and once again store it in a SoftReference-based cache.

Finally, main() enters a finite loop to demonstrate that the reloaded Image object is still in the cache.

Compile Listing 4-8 (javac ImageCache.java) and run the application (java ImageCache). You should discover output that's similar to that shown here:

```
caching image
image is still cached
image is still cached
image is still cached
image is still cached
image is still cached
image is no longer cached
reloading and recaching image
image is still cached
image is still cached
image is still cached
image is still cached
image is still cached
image is still cached
```

WeakReference

The WeakReference class describes a Reference object whose referent is weakly reachable. As well as inheriting Reference's methods, this generic class provides the following constructors for initializing a WeakReference object:

- WeakReference(T r) encapsulates r's reference. The WeakReference object behaves as a weak reference to r. No ReferenceQueue object is associated with this WeakReference object.

- WeakReference(T r, ReferenceQueue<? super T> q) encapsulates r's reference. The WeakReference object behaves as a weak reference to r. The ReferenceQueue object identified by q is associated with this WeakReference object. Passing null to q indicates a weak reference without a queue.

WeakReference is useful for preventing memory leaks related to hashmaps. A memory leak occurs when you keep adding objects to a hashmap and never remove them. The objects remain in memory because the hashmap stores strong references to them.

Ideally, the objects should only remain in memory when they are strongly referenced from elsewhere in the application. When an object's last strong reference (apart from hashmap strong references) disappears, the object should be garbage collected.

This situation can be remedied by storing weak references to hashmap entries so they are discarded when no strong references to their keys exist. Java's java.util.WeakHashMap class (discussed in Chapter 5), whose private Entry static member class extends WeakReference, accomplishes this task.

■ **Note** Reference queues are more useful with WeakReference than they are with SoftReference. In the context of WeakHashMap, these queues provide notification of weakly referenced keys that have been removed. Code within WeakHashMap uses the information provided by the queue to remove all hashmap entries that no longer have valid keys so that the value objects associated with these invalid keys can be garbage collected. However, a queue associated with SoftReference can alert the application that heap space is beginning to run low.

PhantomReference

The PhantomReference class describes a Reference object whose referent is phantom reachable. As well as inheriting Reference's methods and overriding get(), this generic class provides a single constructor for initializing a PhantomReference object:

- PhantomReference(T r, ReferenceQueue<? super T> q) encapsulates r's reference. The PhantomReference object behaves as a phantom reference to r. The ReferenceQueue object identified by q is associated with this PhantomReference object. Passing null to q makes no sense because get() is overridden to return null and the PhantomReference object will never be enqueued.

Although you cannot access a PhantomReference object's referent (its get() method returns null), this class is useful because enqueuing the PhantomReference object signals that the referent has been finalized but its memory space has not yet been reclaimed. This signal lets you perform cleanup without using the finalize() method.

The finalize() method is problematic because the garbage collector requires at least two garbage collection cycles to determine if an object that overrides finalize() can be garbage collected. When the first cycle detects that the object is eligible for garbage collection, it calls finalize(). Because this method might perform resurrection (see Chapter 2), which makes the unreachable object reachable, a second garbage collection cycle is needed to determine if resurrection has happened. This extra cycle slows down garbage collection.

If finalize() is not overridden, the garbage collector does not need to call that method, and considers the object to be finalized. Hence, the garbage collector requires only one cycle.

Although you cannot perform cleanup via finalize(), you can still perform cleanup via PhantomReference. Because there is no way to access the referent (get() returns null), resurrection cannot happen.

Listing 4-9 shows how you might use PhantomReference to detect the finalization of a large object.

Listing 4-9. Detecting a large object's finalization

```
import java.lang.ref.PhantomReference;
import java.lang.ref.ReferenceQueue;
```

```
class LargeObject
{
    private byte[] memory = new byte[1024*1024*50]; // 50 megabytes
}
class LargeObjectDemo
{
    public static void main(String[] args)
    {
        ReferenceQueue<LargeObject> rq;
        rq = new ReferenceQueue<LargeObject>();
        PhantomReference<LargeObject> pr;
        pr = new PhantomReference<LargeObject>(new LargeObject(), rq);
        byte[] b = new byte[1024];
        while (rq.poll() == null)
        {
            System.out.println("waiting for large object to be finalized");
            b = new byte[b.length*10];
        }
        System.out.println("large object finalized");
        System.out.println("pr.get() returns "+pr.get());
    }
}
```

Listing 4-9 declares a LargeObject class whose private memory array occupies 50MB. If your JVM throws OutOfMemoryError when you run LargeObject, you might need to reduce the array's size.

The main() method first creates a ReferenceQueue object describing a queue onto which a PhantomReference object that initially contains a LargeObject reference will be enqueued.

main() next creates the PhantomReference object, passing a reference to a newly created LargeObject object and a reference to the previously created ReferenceQueue object to the constructor.

After creating a byte array that's used to demonstrate PhantomReference, main() enters a polling loop.

The polling loop begins by calling poll() to detect the finalization of the LargeObject object. As long as this method returns null, meaning that the LargeObject object is still unfinalized, the loop outputs a message and doubles the size of the byte array.

At some point, heap space will exhaust and the garbage collector will attempt to obtain sufficient memory, by first clearing the PhantomReference object's LargeObject reference and finalizing the LargeObject object prior to its removal from the heap. The PhantomReference object is then enqueued onto the rq-referenced ReferenceQueue; poll() returns the PhantomReference object.

main() now exits the loop, outputs a message confirming the large object's finalization, and outputs pr.get()'s return value, which is null proving that you cannot access a PhantomReference object's referent. At this point, any additional cleanup operations related to the finalized object (such as closing a file that was opened in the file's constructor but not otherwise closed) could be performed.

Compile Listing 4-9 and run the application. You should see output that's similar to that shown here:

```
waiting for large object to be finalized
waiting for large object to be finalized
waiting for large object to be finalized
waiting for large object to be finalized
waiting for large object to be finalized
large object finalized
```

```
pr.get() returns null
```

■ **Note** For a more useful example of `PhantomReference`, check out Keith D Gregory's "Java Reference Objects" blog post (`http://www.kdgregory.com/index.php?page=java.refobj`).

Reflection

Chapter 2 referred to *reflection* (also known as *introspection*) as a third form of runtime type identification (RTTI). Java's Reflection API lets applications learn about loaded classes, interfaces, enums (a kind of class), and annotation types (a kind of interface). It also lets applications load classes dynamically, instantiate them, find a class's fields and methods, access fields, call methods, and perform other tasks reflectively.

Chapter 3 presented a `StubFinder` application that used part of the Reflection API to load a class and identify all the loaded class's public methods that are annotated with `@Stub` annotations. This tool is one example where using reflection is beneficial. Another example is the *class browser*, a tool that enumerates the members of a class.

■ **Caution** Reflection should not be used indiscriminately. Application performance suffers because it takes longer to perform operations with reflection than without reflection. Also, reflection-oriented code can be harder to read, and the absence of compile-time type checking can result in runtime failures.

The `java.lang` package's `Class` class is the entry point into the Reflection API, whose types are mainly stored in the `java.lang.reflect` package. `Class` is generically declared as `Class<T>`, where `T` identifies the class, interface, enum, or annotation type that is being modeled by the `Class` object. `T` can be replaced by `?` (as in `Class<?>`) when the type being modeled is unknown.

Table 4-3 describes some of `Class`'s methods.

Table 4-3. Class Methods

Method	Description
`static Class<?>` `forName(String typename)`	Return the `Class` object that is associated with `typename`, which must include the type's qualified package name when the type is part of a package (`java.lang.String`, for example). If the class or interface type has not been loaded into memory, this method takes care of *loading* (reading the classfile's contents into memory), *linking* (taking these contents and combining them into the runtime state of the JVM so that they can be executed), and *initializing* (setting class fields to default values, running class initializers, and performing other class initialization) prior to returning the `Class` object. This method

throws java.lang.ClassNotFoundException when the type cannot be found, java.lang.LinkageError when an error occurs during linkage, and java.lang.ExceptionInInitializerError when an exception occurs during a class's static initialization.

Annotation[] getAnnotations()	Return an array (that's possibly empty) containing all annotations that are declared for the class represented by this Class object.
Class<?>[] getClasses()	Return an array containing Class objects representing all public classes and interfaces that are members of the class represented by this Class object. This includes public class and interface members inherited from superclasses, and public class and interface members declared by the class. This method returns a zero-length array when this Class object has no public member classes or interfaces. This method also returns a zero-length array when this Class object represents a primitive type, an array class, or void.
Constructor[] getConstructors()	Return an array containing java.lang.reflect.Constructor objects representing all public constructors of the class represented by this Class object. A zero-length array is returned when the represented class has no public constructors, this Class object represents an array class, or this Class object represents a primitive type or void.
Annotation[] getDeclaredAnnotations()	Return an array containing all annotations that are directly declared on the class represented by this Class object—inherited annotations are not included. The returned array might be empty.
Class<?>[] getDeclaredClasses()	Return an array of Class objects representing all classes and interfaces declared as members of the class represented by this Class object. This includes public, protected, default (package) access, and private classes and interfaces declared by the class, but excludes inherited classes and interfaces. This method returns a zero-length array when the class declares no classes or interfaces as members, or when this Class object represents a primitive type, an array class, or void.
Constructor[] getDeclaredConstructors()	Return an array of Constructor objects representing all constructors declared by the class represented by this Class object. These are public, protected, default (package) access, and private constructors. The returned array's elements are not sorted and are not in any order. If the class has a default constructor, it is included in the returned array. This method returns a zero-length array when this Class object represents an interface, a primitive type, an array class, or void.

`Field[] getDeclaredFields()`	Return an array of `java.lang.reflect.Field` objects representing all fields declared by the class or interface represented by this `Class` object. This array includes public, protected, default (package) access, and private fields, but excludes inherited fields. The returned array's elements are not sorted and are not in any order. This method returns a zero-length array when the class/interface declares no fields, or when this `Class` object represents a primitive type, an array class, or void.
`Method[] getDeclaredMethods()`	Return an array of `java.lang.reflect.Method` objects representing all methods declared by the class or interface represented by this `Class` object. This array includes public, protected, default (package) access, and private methods, but excludes inherited methods. The elements in the returned array are not sorted and are not in any order. This method returns a zero-length array when the class or interface declares no methods, or when this `Class` object represents a primitive type, an array class, or void.
`Field[] getFields()`	Return an array containing `Field` objects representing all public fields of the class or interface represented by this `Class` object, including those public fields inherited from superclasses and superinterfaces. The elements in the returned array are not sorted and are not in any order. This method returns a zero-length array when this `Class` object represents a class or interface with no accessible public fields, or when this `Class` object represents an array class, a primitive type, or void.
`Method[] getMethods()`	Return an array containing `Method` objects representing all public methods of the class or interface represented by this `Class` object, including those public methods inherited from superclasses and superinterfaces. Array classes return all the public member methods inherited from the `Object` class. The elements in the returned array are not sorted and are not in any order. This method returns a zero-length array when this `Class` object represents a class or interface that has no public methods, or when this `Class` object represents a primitive type or void. The class initialization method `<clinit>` (see Chapter 2) is not included in the returned array.
`int getModifiers()`	Returns the Java language modifiers for this class or interface, encoded in an integer. The modifiers consist of the JVM's constants for `public`, `protected`, `private`, `final`, `static`, `abstract` and `interface`; they should be decoded using the methods of class `java.lang.reflect.Modifier`. If the underlying class is an array class, then its `public`, `private` and `protected` modifiers are the same as those of its

	component type. If this Class object represents a primitive type or void, its public modifier is always true, and its protected and private modifiers are always false. If this Class object represents an array class, a primitive type or void, then its final modifier is always true and its interface modifier is always false. The values of its other modifiers are not determined by this specification.
String getName()	Return the name of the class represented by this Class object.
Package getPackage()	Return a Package object—I presented Package earlier in this chapter—that describes the package in which the class represented by this Class object is located, or null when the class is a member of the unnamed package.
Class<? super T> getSuperclass()	Return the Class object representing the superclass of the entity (class, interface, primitive type, or void) represented by this Class object. When the Class object on which this method is called represents the Object class, an interface, a primitive type, or void, null is returned. When this object represents an array class, the Class object representing the Object class is returned.
boolean isAnnotation()	Return true when this Class object represents an annotation type. If this method returns true, isInterface() also returns true because all annotation types are also interfaces.
boolean isEnum()	Return true if and only if this class was declared as an enum in the source code.
boolean isInterface()	Return true when this Class object represents an interface.
T newInstance()	Create and return a new instance of the class represented by this Class object. The class is instantiated as if by a new expression with an empty argument list. The class is initialized when it has not already been initialized. This method throws java.lang.IllegalAccessException when the class or its noargument constructor is not accessible; java.lang.InstantiationException when this Class object represents an abstract class, an interface, an array class, a primitive type, or void, or when the class does not have a noargument constructor (or when instantiation fails for some other reason); and ExceptionInInitializerError when initialization fails because the object threw an exception during initialization.

Table 4-3's description of the forName() method reveals one way to obtain a Class object. This method loads, links, and initializes a class or interface that is not in memory, and returns a Class object that represents the class or interface. Listing 4-10 demonstrates forName() and additional methods described in this table.

Listing 4-10. Using reflection to decompile a type

```
import java.lang.reflect.Constructor;
import java.lang.reflect.Field;
import java.lang.reflect.Method;
import java.lang.reflect.Modifier;

class Decompiler
{
   public static void main(String[] args)
   {
      if (args.length != 1)
      {
         System.err.println("usage: java Decompiler classname");
         return;
      }
      try
      {
         decompileClass(Class.forName(args[0]), 0);
      }
      catch (ClassNotFoundException cnfe)
      {
         System.err.println("could not locate "+args[0]);
      }
   }
   static void decompileClass(Class<?> clazz, int indentLevel)
   {
      indent(indentLevel*3);
      System.out.print(Modifier.toString(clazz.getModifiers())+" ");
      if (clazz.isEnum())
         System.out.println("enum "+clazz.getName());
      else
      if (clazz.isInterface())
      {
         if (clazz.isAnnotation())
            System.out.print("@");
         System.out.println(clazz.getName());
      }
      else
         System.out.println(clazz);
      indent(indentLevel*3);
      System.out.println("{");
      Field[] fields = clazz.getDeclaredFields();
      for (int i = 0; i < fields.length; i++)
      {
         indent(indentLevel*3);
         System.out.println("   "+fields[i]);
      }
      Constructor[] constructors = clazz.getDeclaredConstructors();
```

```java
      if (constructors.length != 0 && fields.length != 0)
         System.out.println();
      for (int i = 0; i < constructors.length; i++)
      {
         indent(indentLevel*3);
         System.out.println("   "+constructors[i]);
      }
      Method[] methods = clazz.getDeclaredMethods();
      if (methods.length != 0 &&
         (fields.length != 0 || constructors.length != 0))
         System.out.println();
      for (int i = 0; i < methods.length; i++)
      {
         indent(indentLevel*3);
         System.out.println("   "+methods[i]);
      }
      Method[] methodsAll = clazz.getMethods();
      if (methodsAll.length != 0 &&
         (fields.length != 0 || constructors.length != 0 ||
          methods.length != 0))
         System.out.println();
      if (methodsAll.length != 0)
      {
         indent(indentLevel*3);
         System.out.println("   ALL PUBLIC METHODS");
         System.out.println();
      }
      for (int i = 0; i < methodsAll.length; i++)
      {
         indent(indentLevel*3);
         System.out.println("   "+methodsAll[i]);
      }
      Class<?>[] members = clazz.getDeclaredClasses();
      if (members.length != 0 && (fields.length != 0 ||
          constructors.length != 0 || methods.length != 0 ||
          methodsAll.length != 0))
         System.out.println();
      for (int i = 0; i < members.length; i++)
         if (clazz != members[i])
         {
            decompileClass(members[i], indentLevel+1);
            if (i != members.length-1)
               System.out.println();
         }
      indent(indentLevel*3);
      System.out.println("}");
   }
   static void indent(int numSpaces)
   {
      for (int i = 0; i < numSpaces; i++)
         System.out.print(' ');
   }
```

}

Listing 4-10 presents the source code to a decompiler tool that uses reflection to obtain information about this tool's solitary command-line argument, which must be a Java reference type (such as a class). The decompiler lets you output the type and name information for a class's fields, constructors, methods, and nested types; it also lets you output the members of interfaces, enums, and annotation types.

After verifying that one command-line argument has been passed to this application, main() calls forName() to try to return a Class object representing the class or interface identified by this argument. If successful, the returned object's reference is passed to decompileClass(), which decompiles the type.

forName() throws an instance of the checked ClassNotFoundException class when it cannot locate the class's classfile (perhaps the classfile was erased prior to executing the application). It also throws LinkageError when a class's classfile is malformed, and ExceptionInInitializerError when a class's static initialization fails.

Note ExceptionInInitializerError is often thrown as the result of a class initializer throwing an unchecked exception. For example, the class initializer in the following FailedInitialization class results in ExceptionInInitializerError because someMethod() throws NullPointerException:

```
class FailedInitialization
{
   static
   {
      someMethod(null);
   }
   static void someMethod(String s)
   {
      int len = s.length(); // s contains null
      System.out.println(s+"'s length is "+len+" characters");
   }
   public static void main(String[] args)
   {
   }
}
```

Much of the printing code is concerned with making the output look nice. For example, this code manages indentation, and only allows a newline character to be output to separate one section from another; a newline character is not output unless content appears before and after the newline.

Listing 4-10 is recursive in that it invokes decompileClass() for every encountered nested type.

Compile Listing 4-10 (javac Decompiler.java) and run this application with java.lang.Boolean as its solitary command line argument (java Decompiler java.lang.Boolean). You will observe the following output:

```
public final class java.lang.Boolean
{
   public static final java.lang.Boolean java.lang.Boolean.TRUE
   public static final java.lang.Boolean java.lang.Boolean.FALSE
   public static final java.lang.Class java.lang.Boolean.TYPE
   private final boolean java.lang.Boolean.value
   private static final long java.lang.Boolean.serialVersionUID

   public java.lang.Boolean(java.lang.String)
   public java.lang.Boolean(boolean)

   public int java.lang.Boolean.hashCode()
   public boolean java.lang.Boolean.equals(java.lang.Object)
   public java.lang.String java.lang.Boolean.toString()
   public static java.lang.String java.lang.Boolean.toString(boolean)
   public static int java.lang.Boolean.compare(boolean,boolean)
   public int java.lang.Boolean.compareTo(java.lang.Object)
   public int java.lang.Boolean.compareTo(java.lang.Boolean)
   public static java.lang.Boolean java.lang.Boolean.valueOf(boolean)
   public static java.lang.Boolean java.lang.Boolean.valueOf(java.lang.String)
   public boolean java.lang.Boolean.booleanValue()
   public static boolean java.lang.Boolean.getBoolean(java.lang.String)
   public static boolean java.lang.Boolean.parseBoolean(java.lang.String)
   private static boolean java.lang.Boolean.toBoolean(java.lang.String)

ALL PUBLIC METHODS

   public int java.lang.Boolean.hashCode()
   public boolean java.lang.Boolean.equals(java.lang.Object)
   public java.lang.String java.lang.Boolean.toString()
   public static java.lang.String java.lang.Boolean.toString(boolean)
   public static int java.lang.Boolean.compare(boolean,boolean)
   public int java.lang.Boolean.compareTo(java.lang.Object)
   public int java.lang.Boolean.compareTo(java.lang.Boolean)
   public static java.lang.Boolean java.lang.Boolean.valueOf(boolean)
   public static java.lang.Boolean java.lang.Boolean.valueOf(java.lang.String)
   public boolean java.lang.Boolean.booleanValue()
   public static boolean java.lang.Boolean.getBoolean(java.lang.String)
   public static boolean java.lang.Boolean.parseBoolean(java.lang.String)
   public final native java.lang.Class java.lang.Object.getClass()
   public final native void java.lang.Object.notify()
   public final native void java.lang.Object.notifyAll()
   public final void java.lang.Object.wait(long,int) throws↵ java.lang.InterruptedException
   public final void java.lang.Object.wait() throws java.lang.InterruptedException
   public final native void java.lang.Object.wait(long) throws↵
java.lang.InterruptedException
}
```

The output reveals the difference between calling getDeclaredMethods() and getMethods(). For example, the output associated with getDeclaredMethods() includes the private toBoolean() method. Also, the output associated with getMethods() includes Object methods that are not overridden by Boolean; getClass() is an example.

One of Table 4-3's methods not demonstrated in Listing 4-10 is newInstance(), which is useful for instantiating a dynamically loaded class, provided that the class has a noargument constructor.

Suppose you plan to create a viewer application that lets the user view different kinds of files. For example, the viewer can view the instruction sequence of a disassembled Windows EXE file, the graphical contents of a PNG file, or the contents of some other file. Furthermore, the user can choose to view this content in its normal state (disassembly versus graphical image, for example), in an informational manner (descriptive labels and content; for example, EXE HEADER: MZ), or as a table of hexadecimal values.

The viewer application will start out with a few viewers, but you plan to add more viewers over time. You don't want to integrate the viewer source code with the application source code because you would have to recompile the application and all of its viewers every time you added a new viewer (for example, a viewer that lets you view the contents of a Java classfile).

Instead, you create these viewers in a separate project, and distribute their classfiles only. Also, you design the application to enumerate its currently accessible viewers when the application starts running (perhaps the viewers are stored in a JAR file), and present this list to the user. When the user selects a specific viewer from this list, the application loads the viewer's classfile and instantiates this class via its Class object. The application can then invoke the object's methods.

Listing 4-11 presents the Viewer superclass that all viewer classes must extend.

Listing 4-11. Abstracting a viewer

```
abstract class Viewer
{
   enum ViewMode { NORMAL, INFO, HEX };
   abstract void view(byte[] content, ViewMode vm);
}
```

Viewer declares an enum to describe the three viewing modes. It also declares a view() method that displays the content of its byte array argument according to the viewer mode specified by its vm argument.

Listing 4-12 presents a Viewer subclass for viewing an EXE file's contents.

Listing 4-12. A viewer for viewing EXE content

```
class ViewerEXE extends Viewer
{
   @Override
   void view(byte[] content, ViewMode vm)
   {
      switch (vm)
      {
         case NORMAL:
            System.out.println("outputting EXE content normally");
            break;
         case INFO:
            System.out.println("outputting EXE content informationally");
            break;
```

```
        case HEX:
            System.out.println("outputting EXE content in hexadecimal");
      }
   }
}
```

ViewerEXE's view() method demonstrates using the switch statement to switch on an enum constant. For brevity, I've limited this method to printing messages to standard output. Also, I don't present the corresponding ViewPNG class, which has a similar structure.

Listing 4-13 presents an application that dynamically loads ViewerEXE or ViewerPNG, instantiates the loaded class via newInstance(), and invokes the view() method.

Listing 4-13. Loading, instantiating, and using Viewer subclasses

```
class ViewerDemo
{
   public static void main(String[] args)
   {
      if (args.length != 1)
      {
         System.err.println("usage  : java ViewerDemo filetype");
         System.err.println("example: java ViewerDemo EXE");
         return;
      }
      try
      {
         Class<?> clazz = Class.forName("Viewer"+args[0]);
         Viewer viewer = (Viewer) clazz.newInstance();
         viewer.view(null, Viewer.ViewMode.HEX);
      }
      catch (ClassNotFoundException cnfe)
      {
         System.err.println("Class not found: "+cnfe.getMessage());
      }
      catch (IllegalAccessException iae)
      {
         System.err.println("Illegal access: "+iae.getMessage());
      }
      catch (InstantiationException ie)
      {
         System.err.println("Unable to instantiate loaded class");
      }
   }
}
```

Assuming that you've compiled all source files (javac *.java, for example), execute java ViewerDemo EXE. You should observe the following output:

```
outputting EXE content in hexadecimal
```

If you were to execute java ViewerDemo PNG, you should see similar output.

Suppose you attempted to load and instantiate the abstract `Viewer` class via `java ViewerDemo ""`. Although this class would load, `newInstance()` would throw an instance of the `InstantiationException` class, and you would see the following output:

```
Unable to instantiate loaded class
```

Table 4-3's descriptions of the `getAnnotations()` and `getDeclaredAnnotations()` methods reveal that each method returns an array of `Annotation`, an interface that is located in the `java.lang.annotation` package. `Annotation` is the superinterface of `Override`, `SuppressWarnings`, and all other annotation types.

Table 4-3's method descriptions also refer to `Constructor`, `Field`, and `Method`. Instances of these classes represent a class's constructors and a class's or an interface's fields and methods.

`Constructor` represents a constructor and is generically declared as `Constructor<T>`, where `T` identifies the class in which the constructor represented by `Constructor` is declared. `Constructor` declares various methods, including the following methods:

- `Annotation[] getDeclaredAnnotations()` returns an array of all annotations declared on the constructor. The returned array has zero length when there are no annotations.

- `Class<T> getDeclaringClass()` returns a `Class` object that represents the class in which the constructor is declared.

- `Class[]<?> getExceptionTypes()` returns an array of `Class` objects representing the types of exceptions listed in the constructor's throws clause. The returned array has zero length when there is no throws clause.

- `String getName()` returns the constructor's name.

- `Class[]<?> getParameterTypes()` returns an array of `Class` objects representing the constructor's parameters. The returned array has zero length when the constructor does not declare parameters.

Tip If you want to instantiate a class via a constructor that takes arguments, you cannot use `Class`'s `newInstance()` method. Instead, you must use `Constructor`'s `T newInstance(Object... initargs)` method to perform this task. Unlike `Class`'s `newInstance()` method, which bypasses the compile-time exception checking that would otherwise be performed by the compiler, `Constructor`'s `newInstance()` method avoids this problem by wrapping any exception thrown by the constructor in an instance of the `java.lang.reflect.InvocationTargetException` class.

`Field` represents a field and declares various methods, including the following getter methods:

- `Object get(Object object)` returns the value of the field for the specified object.

- `boolean getBoolean(Object object)` returns the value of the Boolean field for the specified object.

- `byte getByte(Object object)` returns the value of the byte integer field for the specified object.

- `char getChar(Object object)` returns the value of the character field for the specified object.

- `double getDouble(Object object)` returns the value of the double precision floating-point field for the specified object.

- `float getFloat(Object object)` returns the value of the floating-point field for the specified object.

- `int getInt(Object object)` returns the value of the integer field for the specified object.

- `long getLong(Object object)` returns the value of the long integer field for the specified object.

- `short getShort(Object object)` returns the value of the short integer field for the specified object.

`get()` returns the value of any type of field. In contrast, the other listed methods return the values of specific types of fields. These methods throw `NullPointerException` when object is null and the field is an instance field, `IllegalArgumentException` when object is not an instance of the class or interface declaring the underlying field (or not an instance of a subclass or interface implementor), and `IllegalAccessException` when the underlying field cannot be accessed (it is private, for example).

Listing 4-14 demonstrates `Field`'s `getInt(Object)` method along with its void `setInt(Object obj, int i)` counterpart.

Listing 4-14. Reflectively getting and setting the values of instance and class fields

```
import java.lang.reflect.Field;

class X
{
   public int i = 10;
   public static final double PI = 3.14;
}
class FieldAccessDemo
{
   public static void main(String[] args)
   {
      try
      {
         Class<?> clazz = Class.forName("X");
         X x = (X) clazz.newInstance();
         Field f = clazz.getField("i");
         System.out.println(f.getInt(x)); // Output: 10
         f.setInt(x, 20);
         System.out.println(f.getInt(x)); // Output: 20
         f = clazz.getField("PI");
         System.out.println(f.getDouble(null)); // Output: 3.14
         f.setDouble(x, 20);
         System.out.println(f.getDouble(null)); // Never executed
      }
      catch (Exception e)
```

```
      {
         System.err.println(e);
      }
   }
}
```

Listing 4-14 declares classes X and FieldAccessDemo. I've included X's source code with FieldAccessDemo's source code for convenience. However, you can imagine this source code being stored in a separate source file.

FieldAccessDemo's main() method first attempts to load X, and then tries to instantiate this class via newInstance(). If successful, the instance is assigned to reference variable x.

main() next invokes Class's Field getField(String name) method to return a Field instance that represents the public field identified by name, which happens to be i (in the first case) and PI (in the second case). This method throws java.lang.NoSuchFieldException when the named field doesn't exist.

Continuing, main() invokes Field's getInt() and setInt() methods (with an object reference) to get the instance field's initial value, change this value to another value, and get the new value. The initial and new values are output.

At this point, main() demonstrates class field access in a similar manner. However, it passes null to getInt() and setInt() because an object reference isn't required to access a class field. Because PI is declared final, the call to setInt() results in a thrown instance of the IllegalAccessException class.

▩ **Note** I've specified catch (Exception e) to avoid having to specify multiple catch blocks. You could also use multicatch (see Chapter 3) where appropriate.

Method represents a method and declares various methods, including the following methods:

- int getModifiers() returns a 32-bit integer whose bit fields identify the method's reserved word modifiers (such as public, abstract, or static). These bit fields must be interpreted via the Modifier class. For example, you might specify (method.getModifiers()&Modifier.ABSTRACT) == Modifier.ABSTRACT to find out if the method (represented by the Method object whose reference is stored in method) is abstract—this expression evaluates to true when the method is abstract.

- Class<?> getReturnType() returns a Class object that represents the method's return type.

- Object invoke(Object receiver, Object... args) calls the method on the object identified by receiver (which is ignored when the method is a class method), passing the variable number of arguments identified by args to the called method. The invoke() method throws NullPointerException when receiver is null and the method being called is an instance method, IllegalAccessException when the method is not accessible (it is private, for example), IllegalArgumentException when an incorrect number of arguments are passed to the method (and other reasons), and InvocationTargetException when an exception is thrown from the called method.

- boolean isVarArgs() returns true when the method is declared to receive a variable number of arguments.

Listing 4-15 demonstrates Method's invoke(Object, Object...) method.

Listing 4-15. Reflectively invoking instance and class methods

```java
import java.lang.reflect.Method;

class X
{
   public void objectMethod(String arg)
   {
      System.out.println("Instance method: "+arg);
   }
   public static void classMethod()
   {
      System.out.println("Class method");
   }
}
class MethodInvocationDemo
{
   public static void main(String[] args)
   {
      try
      {
         Class<?> clazz = Class.forName("X");
         X x = (X) clazz.newInstance();
         Class[] argTypes = { String.class };
         Method method = clazz.getMethod("objectMethod", argTypes);
         Object[] data = { "Hello" };
         method.invoke(x, data); // Output: Instance method: Hello
         method = clazz.getMethod("classMethod", (Class<?>[]) null);
         method.invoke(null, (Object[]) null); // Output: Class method
      }
      catch (Exception e)
      {
         System.err.println(e);
      }
   }
}
```

Listing 4-15 declares classes X and MethodInvocationDemo. MethodInvocationDemo's main() method first attempts to load X, and then tries to instantiate this class via newInstance(). If successful, the instance is assigned to reference variable x.

main() next creates a one-element Class array that describes the types of objectMethod()'s parameter list. This array is used in the subsequent call to Class's Method getMethod(String name, Class<?>... parameterTypes) method to return a Method object for invoking a public method named objectMethod with this parameter list. This method throws java.lang.NoSuchMethodException when the named method doesn't exist.

Continuing, main() creates an Object array that specifies the data to be passed to the method's parameters; in this case, the array consists of a single String argument. It then reflectively invokes objectMethod() by passing this array along with the object reference stored in x to the invoke() method.

At this point, main() shows you how to reflectively invoke a class method. The (Class<?>[]) and (Object[]) casts are used to suppress warning messages that have to do with variable numbers of arguments and null references. Notice that the first argument passed to invoke() is null when invoking a class method.

The java.lang.reflect.AccessibleObject class is the superclass of Constructor, Field, and Method. This superclass provides methods for reporting a constructor's, field's, or method's accessibility (is it private?) and making an inaccessible constructor, field, or method accessible. AccessibleObject's methods include the following:

- T getAnnotation(Class<T> annotationType) returns the constructor's, field's, or method's annotation of the specified type when such an annotation is present; otherwise, null returns.

- boolean isAccessible() returns true when the constructor, field, or method is accessible.

- boolean isAnnotationPresent(Class<? extends Annotation> annotationType) returns true when an annotation of the type specified by annotationType has been declared on the constructor, field, or method. This method takes inherited annotations into account.

- void setAccessible(boolean flag) attempts to make an inaccessible constructor, field, or method accessible when flag is true.

Note The java.lang.reflect package also includes an Array class whose class methods make it possible to reflectively create and access Java arrays.

I previously showed you how to obtain a Class object via Class's forName() method. Another way to obtain a Class object is to call Object's getClass() method on an object reference; for example, Employee e = new Employee(); Class<? extends Employee> clazz = e.getClass();. The getClass() method does not throw an exception because the class from which the object was created is already present in memory.

There is one more way to obtain a Class object, and that is to employ a *class literal*, which is an expression consisting of a class name, followed by a period separator, followed by reserved word class. Examples of class literals include Class<Employee> clazz = Employee.class; and Class<String> clazz = String.class.

Perhaps you are wondering about how to choose between forName(), getClass(), and a class literal. To help you make your choice, the following list compares each competitor:

- forName() is very flexible in that you can dynamically specify any reference type by its package-qualified name. If the type is not in memory, it is loaded, linked, and initialized. However, lack of compile-time type safety can lead to runtime failures.

- getClass() returns a Class object describing the type of its referenced object. If called on a superclass variable containing a subclass instance, a Class object representing the subclass type is returned. Because the class is in memory, type safety is assured.

- A class literal returns a Class object representing its specified class. Class literals are compact and the compiler enforces type safety by refusing to compile the source code when it cannot locate the literal's specified class.

■ **Note** You can use class literals with primitive types, including void. Examples include int.class, double.class, and void.class. The returned Class object represents the class identified by a primitive type wrapper class's TYPE field or java.lang.Void.TYPE. For example, each of int.class == Integer.TYPE and void.class == Void.TYPE evaluates to true.

You can also use class literals with primitive type-based arrays. Examples include int[].class and double[].class. For these examples, the returned Class objects represent Class<int[]> and Class<double[]>.

String

String is the first predefined reference type presented in this book (in Chapter 1). Instances of this type represent sequences of characters, or *strings*.

Unlike other reference types, the Java language treats the String class specially, by providing syntactic sugar that simplifies working with strings. For example, Java recognizes String favLanguage = "Java"; as the assignment of string literal "Java" to String variable favLanguage. Without this sugar, you would have to specify String favLanguage = new String("Java");. The Java language also overloads the + and += operators to perform string concatenation.

Table 4-4 describes some of String's constructors and methods for initializing String objects and working with strings.

Table 4-4. String Constructors and Methods

Method	Description
String(char[] data)	Initialize this String object to the data array's characters. Modifying data after initializing this String object has no effect on the object.
String(String s)	Initialize this String object to s's string.
char charAt(int index)	Return the character located at the zero-based index in this String object's string. This method throws java.lang.StringIndexOutOfBoundsException when index is less than 0 or greater than or equal to the length of the string.
String concat(String s)	Return a new String object containing this String object's string followed by the s argument's string.

`boolean endsWith(String suffix)`	Return true when this `String` object's string ends with the characters in the `suffix` argument, when `suffix` is empty (contains no characters), or when `suffix` contains the same character sequence as this `String` object's string. This method performs a case-sensitive comparison (a is not equal to A, for example), and throws `NullPointerException` when `suffix` is null.
`boolean equals(Object object)`	Return true when `object` is of type `String` and this argument's string contains the same characters (and in the same order) as this `String` object's string.
`boolean equalsIgnoreCase(String s)`	Return true when s and this `String` object contain the same characters (ignoring case). This method returns false when the character sequences differ or when null is passed to s.
`int indexOf(int c)`	Return the zero-based index of the first occurrence (from the start of the string to the end of the string) of the character represented by c in this `String` object's string. Return -1 when this character is not present.
`int indexOf(String s)`	Return the zero-based index of the first occurrence (from the start of the string to the end of the string) of s's character sequence in this `String` object's string. Return -1 when s is not present. This method throws `NullPointerException` when s is null.
`String intern()`	Search an internal table of `String` objects for an object whose string is equal to this `String` object's string. This `String` object's string is added to the table when not present. Return the object contained in the table whose string is equal to this `String` object's string. The same `String` object is always returned for strings that are equal.
`int lastIndexOf(int c)`	Return the zero-based index of the last occurrence (from the start of the string to the end of the string) of the character represented by c in this `String` object's string. Return -1 when this character is not present.
`int lastIndexOf(String s)`	Return the zero-based index of the last occurrence (from the start of the string to the end of the string) of s's character sequence in this `String` object's string. Return -1 when s is not present. This method throws `NullPointerException` when s is null.
`int length()`	Return the number of characters in this `String` object's string.
`String replace(char oldChar,`	Return a new `String` object whose string matches this `String`

`char newChar)`	object's string except that all occurrences of `oldChar` have been replaced by `newChar`.
`String[] split(String expr)`	Split this `String` object's string into an array of `String` objects using the *regular expression* (a string whose *pattern* [template] is used to search a string for substrings that match the pattern) specified by `expr` as the basis for the split. This method throws `NullPointerException` when `expr` is null and `java.util.regex.PatternSyntaxException` when `expr`'s syntax is invalid.
`boolean startsWith(String prefix)`	Return true when this `String` object's string starts with the characters in the `prefix` argument, when `prefix` is empty (contains no characters), or when `prefix` contains the same character sequence as this `String` object's string. This method performs a case-sensitive comparison (a is not equal to A, for example), and throws `NullPointerException` when `prefix` is null.
`String substring(int start)`	Return a new `String` object whose string contains this `String` object's characters beginning with the character located at `start`. This method throws `StringIndexOutOfBoundsException` when `start` is negative or greater than the length of this `String` object's string.
`char[] toCharArray()`	Return a character array that contains the characters in this `String` object's string.
`String toLowerCase()`	Return a new `String` object whose string contains this `String` object's characters where uppercase letters have been converted to lowercase. This `String` object is returned when it contains no uppercase letters to convert.
`String toUpperCase()`	Return a new `String` object whose string contains this `String` object's characters where lowercase letters have been converted to uppercase. This `String` object is returned when it contains no lowercase letters to convert.
`String trim()`	Return a new `String` object that contains this `String` object's string with *whitespace characters* (characters whose Unicode values are 32 or less) removed from the start and end of the string, or this `String` object if there is no leading/trailing whitespace.

Table 4-4 reveals a couple of interesting items about `String`. First, this class's `String(String s)` constructor does not initialize a `String` object to a string literal. Instead, it behaves similarly to the C++ copy constructor by initializing the `String` object to the contents of another `String` object. This behavior suggests that a string literal is more than what it appears to be.

In reality, a string literal is a `String` object. You can prove this to yourself by executing `System.out.println("abc".length());` and `System.out.println("abc" instanceof String);`. The first method call outputs 3, which is the length of the "abc" `String` object's string, and the second method call outputs true ("abc" is a `String` object).

Note String literals are stored in a classfile data structure known as the *constant pool*. When a class is loaded, a `String` object is created for each literal and is stored in an internal table of `String` objects.

The second interesting item is the `intern()` method, which *interns* (stores a unique copy of) a `String` object in an internal table of `String` objects. `intern()` makes it possible to compare strings via their references and == or !=. These operators are the fastest way to compare strings, which is especially valuable when sorting a huge number of strings.

By default, `String` objects denoted by literal strings ("abc") and string-valued constant expressions ("a"+"bc") are interned in this table, which is why `System.out.println("abc" == "a"+"bc");` outputs true. However, `String` objects created via `String` constructors are not interned, which is why `System.out.println("abc" == new String("abc"));` outputs false. In contrast, `System.out.println("abc" == new String("abc").intern());` outputs true.

Caution Be careful with this string comparison technique (which only compares references) because you can easily introduce a bug when one of the strings being compared has not been interned. When in doubt, use the `equals()` or `equalsIgnoreCase()` method.

Table 4-4 also reveals the `charAt()` and `length()` methods, which are useful for iterating over a string's characters. For example, `String s = "abc"; for (int i = 0; i < s.length(); i++) System.out.println(s.charAt(i));` returns each of s's a, b, and c characters and outputs each character on a separate line.

Finally, Table 4-4 presents `split()`, a method that I employed in Chapter 3's `StubFinder` application to split a string's comma-separated list of values into an array of `String` objects. This method uses a regular expression that identifies a sequence of characters around which the string is split. (I discuss regular expressions in Appendix C.)

Note `StringIndexOutOfBoundsException` and `ArrayIndexOutOfBoundsException` are sibling classes that share a common `java.lang.IndexOutOfBoundsException` superclass.

StringBuffer and StringBuilder

String objects are immutable: you cannot modify a String object's string. The various String methods that appear to modify the String object actually return a new String object with modified string content instead. Because returning new String objects is often wasteful, Java provides the java.lang.StringBuffer and java.lang.StringBuilder classes as a workaround. These classes are identical apart from the fact that StringBuffer can be used in the context of multiple threads (discussed later in this chapter), and that StringBuilder is faster than StringBuffer but cannot be used in the context of multiple threads without explicit synchronization (also discussed later in this chapter).

Table 4-5 describes some of StringBuffer's constructors and methods for initializing StringBuffer objects and working with string buffers. StringBuilder's constructors and methods are identical.

Table 4-5. StringBuffer Constructors and Methods

Method	Description
StringBuffer()	Initialize this StringBuffer object to an empty array with an initial capacity of 16 characters.
StringBuffer(int capacity)	Initialize this StringBuffer object to an empty array with an initial capacity of capacity characters. This constructor throws java.lang.NegativeArraySizeException when capacity is negative.
StringBuffer(String s)	Initialize this StringBuffer object to an array containing s's characters. This object's initial capacity is 16 plus the length of s. This constructor throws NullPointerException when s is null.
StringBuffer append(boolean b)	Append "true" to this StringBuffer object's array when b is true and "false" to the array when b is false, and return this StringBuffer object.
StringBuffer append(char ch)	Append ch's character to this StringBuffer object's array, and return this StringBuffer object.
StringBuffer append(char[] chars)	Append the characters in the chars array to this StringBuffer object's array, and return this StringBuffer object. This method throws NullPointerException when chars is null.
StringBuffer append(double d)	Append the string representation of d's double precision floating-point value to this StringBuffer object's array, and return this StringBuffer object.
StringBuffer append(float f)	Append the string representation of f's floating-point value to this StringBuffer object's array, and return this StringBuffer object.

`StringBuffer append(int i)`	Append the string representation of i's integer value to this `StringBuffer` object's array, and return this `StringBuffer` object.
`StringBuffer append(long l)`	Append the string representation of l's long integer value to this `StringBuffer` object's array, and return this `StringBuffer` object.
`StringBuffer append(Object obj)`	Call obj's `toString()` method and append the returned string's characters to this `StringBuffer` object's array. Append "null" to the array when `null` is passed to obj. Return this `StringBuffer` object.
`StringBuffer append(String s)`	Append s's string to this `StringBuffer` object's array. Append "null" to the array when `null` is passed to s. Return this `StringBuffer` object.
`int capacity()`	Return the current capacity of this `StringBuffer` object's array.
`char charAt(int index)`	Return the character located at index in this `StringBuffer` object's array. This method throws `StringIndexOutOfBoundsException` when index is negative or greater than or equal to this `StringBuffer` object's length.
`void ensureCapacity(int min)`	Ensure that this `StringBuffer` object's capacity is at least that specified by min. If the current capacity is less than min, a new internal array is created with greater capacity. The new capacity is set to the larger of min and the current capacity multiplied by 2, with 2 added to the result. No action is taken when min is negative or zero.
`int length()`	Return the number of characters stored in this `StringBuffer` object's array.
`StringBuffer reverse()`	Return this `StringBuffer` object with its array contents reversed.
`void setCharAt(int index, char ch)`	Replace the character at index with ch. This method throws `StringIndexOutOfBoundsException` when index is negative or greater than or equal to the length of this `StringBuffer` object's array.
`void setLength(int length)`	Set the length of this `StringBuffer` object's array to length. If the length argument is less than the current length, the array's contents are truncated. If the length argument is greater than or equal to the current length, sufficient null characters (`'\u0000'`) are appended to the array. This method throws

	StringIndexOutOfBoundsException when length is negative.
String substring(int start)	Return a new String object that contains all characters in this StringBuffer object's array starting with the character located at start. This method throws StringIndexOutOfBoundsException when start is less than 0 or greater than or equal to the length of this StringBuffer object's array.
String toString()	Return a new String object whose string equals the contents of this StringBuffer object's array.

A StringBuffer or StringBuilder object's internal array is associated with the concepts of capacity and length. *Capacity* refers to the maximum number of characters that can be stored in the array before the array grows to accommodate additional characters. *Length* refers to the number of characters that are already stored in the array.

The toAlignedBinaryString() method presented earlier in this chapter included the following inefficient loop in its implementation:

```
int numLeadingZeros = numBits-result.length();
String zerosPrefix = "";
for (int j = 0; j < numLeadingZeros; j++)
   zerosPrefix += "0";
```

This loop is inefficient because each of the iterations creates a StringBuilder object and a String object. The compiler transforms this code fragment into the following fragment:

```
int numLeadingZeros = 3;
String zerosPrefix = "";
for (int j = 0; j < numLeadingZeros; j++)
   zerosPrefix = new StringBuilder().append(zerosPrefix).append("0").toString();
```

A more efficient way to code the previous loop involves creating a StringBuffer/StringBuilder object prior to entering the loop, calling the appropriate append() method in the loop, and calling toString() after the loop. The following code fragment demonstrates this more efficient scenario:

```
int numLeadingZeros = 3;
StringBuilder sb = new StringBuilder();
for (int j = 0; j < numLeadingZeros; j++)
    sb.append("0");
String zerosPrefix = sb.toString();
```

Caution Avoid using the string concatenation operator in a lengthy loop because it results in the creation of many unnecessary StringBuilder and String objects.

System

The java.lang.System class provides access to system-oriented resources, including standard input, standard output, and standard error.

System declares in, out, and err class fields that support standard input, standard output, and standard error, respectively. The first field is of type java.io.InputStream, and the last two fields are of type java.io.PrintStream. (I will formally introduce these classes in Chapter 8.)

System also declares various static methods, including those methods that are described in Table 4-6.

Table 4-6. System Methods

Method	Description
void arraycopy(Object src, int srcPos, Object dest, int destPos, int length)	Copy the number of elements specified by length from the src array starting at zero-based offset srcPos into the dest array starting at zero-based offset destPos. This method throws NullPointerException when src or dest is null, ArrayIndexOutOfBoundsException when copying causes access to data outside array bounds, and java.lang.ArrayStoreException when an element in the src array could not be stored into the dest array because of a type mismatch.
long currentTimeMillis()	Return the current system time in milliseconds since January 1, 1970 00:00:00 UTC.
void gc()	Inform the JVM that now would be a good time to run the garbage collector. This is only a hint; there is no guarantee that the garbage collector will run.
String getProperty(String prop)	Return the value of the *system property* (platform-specific attribute, such as a version number) identified by prop or null when no such property exists.
void runFinalization()	Inform the JVM that now would be a good time to perform any outstanding object finalizations. This is only a hint; there is no guarantee that outstanding object finalizations will be performed.
void setErr(PrintStream err)	Reassign the standard error stream to err. This is equivalent to specifying, for example, java Application 2>errlog on Windows XP.
void setIn(InputStream in)	Reassign the standard input stream to in. This is equivalent to specifying, for example, java Application <input on Windows XP.

void setOut(PrintStream out)	Reassign the standard output stream to out. This is equivalent to specifying, for example, java Application >output on Windows XP.

Listing 4-16 demonstrates the arraycopy(), currentTimeMillis(), and getProperty() methods.

Listing 4-16. Experimenting with System methods

```
class SystemTasks
{
   public static void main(String[] args)
   {
      int[] grades = { 86, 92, 78, 65, 52, 43, 72, 98, 81 };
      int[] gradesBackup = new int[grades.length];
      System.arraycopy(grades, 0, gradesBackup, 0, grades.length);
      for (int i = 0; i < gradesBackup.length; i++)
         System.out.println(gradesBackup[i]);
      System.out.println("Current time: "+System.currentTimeMillis());
      String[] propNames =
      {
         "java.vendor.url",
         "java.class.path",
         "user.home",
         "java.class.version",
         "os.version",
         "java.vendor",
         "user.dir",
         "user.timezone",
         "path.separator",
         "os.name",
         "os.arch",
         "line.separator",
         "file.separator",
         "user.name",
         "java.version",
         "java.home"
      };
      for (int i = 0; i < propNames.length; i++)
         System.out.println(propNames[i]+": "+
                            System.getProperty(propNames[i]));
   }
}
```

Listing 4-16's main() method begins by demonstrating arraycopy(). It uses this method to copy the contents of a grades array to a gradesBackup array.

■ **Tip** The arraycopy() method is the fastest portable way to copy one array to another. Also, when you write a class whose methods return a reference to an internal array, you should use arraycopy() to create a copy of the array, and then return the copy's reference. That way, you prevent clients from directly manipulating (and possibly screwing up) the internal array.

---

main() next calls currentTimeMillis() to return the current time as a milliseconds value. Because this value is not human-readable, you might want to use the java.util.Date class (discussed in Appendix C). The Date() constructor calls currentTimeMillis() and its toString() method converts this value to a readable date and time.

main() concludes by demonstrating getProperty() in a for loop. This loop iterates over all of Table 4-6's property names, outputting each name and value.

When I run this application on my platform, it generates the following output:

```
86
92
78
65
52
43
72
98
81
Current time: 1312236551718
java.vendor.url: http://java.oracle.com/
java.class.path: .
user.home: C:\Documents and Settings\Jeff Friesen
java.class.version: 51.0
os.version: 5.1
java.vendor: Oracle Corporation
user.dir: C:\prj\dev\bj7\ch04\code\SystemTasks
user.timezone:
path.separator: ;
os.name: Windows XP
os.arch: x86
line.separator:

file.separator: \
user.name: Jeff Friesen
java.version: 1.7.0
java.home: C:\Program Files\Java\jdk1.7.0\jre
```

■ **Note** line.separator stores the actual line separator character/characters, not its/their representation (such as \r\n), which is why a blank line appears after line.separator:.

Threading

Applications execute via *threads*, which are independent paths of execution through an application's code. When multiple threads are executing, each thread's path can differ from other thread paths. For example, a thread might execute one of a switch statement's cases, and another thread might execute another of this statement's cases.

■ **Note** Applications use threads to improve performance. Some applications can get by with only the default main thread to carry out their tasks, but other applications need additional threads to perform time-intensive tasks in the background, so that they remain responsive to their users.

The JVM gives each thread its own method-call stack to prevent threads from interfering with each other. Separate stacks let threads keep track of their next instructions to execute, which can differ from thread to thread. The stack also provides a thread with its own copy of method parameters, local variables, and return value.

Java supports threads via its Threading API. This API consists of one interface (Runnable) and four classes (Thread, ThreadGroup, ThreadLocal, and InheritableThreadLocal) in the java.lang package. After exploring Runnable and Thread (and mentioning ThreadGroup during this exploration), this section explores thread synchronization, ThreadLocal, and InheritableThreadLocal.

■ **Note** Java 5 introduced the java.util.concurrent package as a high-level alternative to the low-level Threading API. (I will discuss this package in Chapter 6.) Although java.util.concurrent is the preferred API for working with threads, you should also be somewhat familiar with Threading because it is helpful in simple threading scenarios. Also, you might have to analyze someone else's source code that depends on Threading.

Runnable and Thread

Java provides the Runnable interface to identify those objects that supply code for threads to execute via this interface's solitary void run() method—a thread receives no arguments and returns no value. Classes implement Runnable to supply this code, and one of these classes is Thread.

Thread provides a consistent interface to the underlying operating system's threading architecture. (The operating system is typically responsible for creating and managing threads.) Thread makes it possible to associate code with threads, as well as start and manage those threads. Each Thread instance associates with a single thread.

Thread declares several constructors for initializing Thread objects. Some of these constructors take Runnable arguments: you can supply code to run without having to extend Thread. Other constructors do not take Runnable arguments: you must extend Thread and override its run() method to supply the code to run.

For example, Thread(Runnable runnable) initializes a new Thread object to the specified runnable whose code is to be executed. In contrast, Thread() does not initialize Thread to a Runnable argument.

Instead, your Thread subclass provides a constructor that calls Thread(), and the subclass also overrides Thread's run() method.

In the absence of an explicit name argument, each constructor assigns a unique default name (starting with Thread-) to the Thread object. Names make it possible to differentiate threads. In contrast to the previous two constructors, which choose default names, Thread(String threadName) lets you specify your own thread name.

Thread also declares methods for starting and managing threads. Table 4-7 describes many of the more useful methods.

Table 4-7. Thread Methods

Method	Description
static Thread currentThread()	Return the Thread object associated with the thread that calls this method.
String getName()	Return the name associated with this Thread object.
Thread.State getState()	Return the state of the thread associated with this Thread object. The state is identified by the Thread.State enum as one of BLOCKED (waiting to acquire a lock, discussed later), NEW (created but not started), RUNNABLE (executing), TERMINATED (the thread has died), TIMED_WAITING (waiting for a specified amount of time to elapse), or WAITING (waiting indefinitely).
void interrupt()	Set the interrupt status flag in this Thread object. If the associated thread is blocked or waiting, clear this flag and wake up the thread by throwing an instance of the InterruptedException class.
static boolean interrupted()	Return true when the thread associated with this Thread object has a pending interrupt request. Clear the interrupt status flag.
boolean isAlive()	Return true to indicate that this Thread object's associated thread is alive and not dead. A thread's lifespan ranges from just before it is actually started within the start() method to just after it leaves the run() method, at which point it dies.
boolean isDaemon()	Return true when the thread associated with this Thread object is a *daemon thread*, a thread that acts as a helper to a *user thread* (nondaemon thread) and dies automatically when the application's last nondaemon thread dies so the application can exit.
boolean isInterrupted()	Return true when the thread associated with this Thread object has a pending interrupt request.
void join()	The thread that calls this method on this Thread object waits for the thread associated with this object to die. This method

	throws InterruptedException when this Thread object's interrupt() method is called.
void join(long millis)	The thread that calls this method on this Thread object waits for the thread associated with this object to die, or until millis milliseconds have elapsed, whichever happens first. This method throws InterruptedException when this Thread object's interrupt() method is called.
void setDaemon(boolean isDaemon)	Mark this Thread object's associated thread as a daemon thread when isDaemon is true. This method throws java.lang.IllegalThreadStateException when the thread has not yet been created and started.
void setName(String threadName)	Assign threadName's value to this Thread object as the name of its associated thread.
static void sleep(long time)	Pause the thread associated with this Thread object for time milliseconds. This method throws InterruptedException when this Thread object's interrupt() method is called while the thread is sleeping.
void start()	Create and start this Thread object's associated thread. This method throws IllegalThreadStateException when the thread was previously started and is running or has died.

Listing 4-17 introduces you to the Threading API via a main() method that demonstrates Runnable, Thread(Runnable runnable), currentThread(), getName(), and start().

Listing 4-17. A pair of counting threads

```
class CountingThreads
{
   public static void main(String[] args)
   {
      Runnable r = new Runnable()
                   {
                      @Override
                      public void run()
                      {
                         String name = Thread.currentThread().getName();
                         int count = 0;
                         while (true)
                            System.out.println(name+": "+count++);
                      }
                   };
      Thread thdA = new Thread(r);
      Thread thdB = new Thread(r);
      thdA.start();
```

```
        thdB.start();
    }
}
```

According to Listing 4-17, the default main thread that executes main() first instantiates an anonymous class that implements Runnable. It then creates two Thread objects, initializing each object to the runnable, and calls Thread's start() method to create and start both threads. After completing these tasks, the main thread exits main() and dies.

Each of the two started threads executes the runnable's run() method. It calls Thread's currentThread() method to obtain its associated Thread instance, uses this instance to call Thread's getName() method to return its name, initializes count to 0, and enters an infinite loop where it outputs name and count, and increments count on each iteration.

■ **Tip** To stop an application that does not end, press the Ctrl and C keys simultaneously (at least on Windows platforms).

I observe both threads alternating in their execution when I run this application on the Windows XP platform. Partial output from one run appears here:

```
Thread-0: 0
Thread-0: 1
Thread-0: 2
Thread-0: 3
Thread-0: 4
Thread-0: 5
Thread-0: 6
Thread-0: 7
Thread-1: 0
Thread-1: 1
Thread-1: 2
Thread-1: 3
```

The operating system assigns a separate thread to each processor or core so the threads execute *concurrently* (at the same time). When a computer does not have enough processors and/or cores, a thread must wait its turn to use the shared processor/core.

The operating system uses a *scheduler* (http://en.wikipedia.org/wiki/Scheduling_(computing)) to determine when a waiting thread executes. The following list identifies three different schedulers:

- Linux 2.6 through 2.6.22 uses the O(1) scheduler (http://en.wikipedia.org/wiki/O(1)_scheduler).

- Linux 2.6.23 uses the Completely Fair Scheduler (http://en.wikipedia.org/wiki/Completely_Fair_Scheduler).

- Windows NT-based operating systems (e.g., NT, 2000, XP, Vista, and 7) use a multilevel feedback queue scheduler (http://en.wikipedia.org/wiki/Multilevel_feedback_queue).

The previous output from the counting threads application resulted from running this application via Windows XP's *multilevel feedback queue* scheduler. Because of this scheduler, both threads take turns executing.

Caution Although this output indicates that the first thread starts executing, never assume that the thread associated with the Thread object whose start() method is called first is the first thread to execute. While this might be true of some schedulers, it might not be true of others.

A multilevel feedback queue and many other thread schedulers take the concept of *priority* (thread relative importance) into account. They often combine *preemptive scheduling* (higher priority threads *preempt*—interrupt and run instead of—lower priority threads) with *round robin scheduling* (equal priority threads are given equal slices of time, which are known as *time slices*, and take turns executing).

Thread supports priority via its void setPriority(int priority) method (set the priority of this Thread object's thread to priority, which ranges from Thread.MIN_PRIORITY to Thread.MAX_PRIORITY— Thread.NORMAL_PRIORITY identifies the default priority) and int getPriority() method (return the current priority).

Caution Using the setPriority() method can impact an application's portability across platforms because different schedulers can handle a priority change in different ways. For example, one platform's scheduler might delay lower priority threads from executing until higher priority threads finish. This delaying can lead to *indefinite postponement* or *starvation* because lower priority threads "starve" while waiting indefinitely for their turn to execute, and this can seriously hurt the application's performance. Another platform's scheduler might not indefinitely delay lower priority threads, improving application performance.

Listing 4-18 refactors Listing 4-17's main() method to give each thread a nondefault name, and to put each thread to sleep after outputting name and count.

Listing 4-18. A pair of counting threads revisited

```
class CountingThreads
{
   public static void main(String[] args)
   {
      Runnable r = new Runnable()
                   {
                       @Override
                       public void run()
                       {
                           String name = Thread.currentThread().getName();
                           int count = 0;
```

```
                            while (true)
                            {
                                System.out.println(name+": "+count++);
                                try
                                {
                                    Thread.sleep(100);
                                }
                                catch (InterruptedException ie)
                                {
                                }
                            }
                        }
                    };
        Thread thdA = new Thread(r);
        thdA.setName("A");
        Thread thdB = new Thread(r);
        thdB.setName("B");
        thdA.start();
        thdB.start();
    }
}
```

Listing 4-18 reveals that Threads A and B execute `Thread.sleep(100);` to sleep for 100 milliseconds. This sleep results in each thread executing more frequently, as the following partial output reveals:

```
A: 0
B: 0
A: 1
B: 1
A: 2
B: 2
A: 3
B: 3
```

A thread will occasionally start another thread to perform a lengthy calculation, download a large file, or perform some other time-consuming activity. After finishing its other tasks, the thread that started the worker thread is ready to process the results of the worker thread and waits for the worker thread to finish and die.

It is possible to wait for the worker thread to die by using a while loop that repeatedly calls Thread's `isAlive()` method on the worker thread's Thread object and sleeps for a certain length of time when this method returns true. However, Listing 4-19 demonstrates a less verbose alternative: the `join()` method.

Listing 4-19. *Joining the default main thread with a background thread*

```
class JoinDemo
{
    public static void main(String[] args)
    {
        Runnable r = new Runnable()
                    {
                        @Override
                        public void run()
                        {
```

```
                        System.out.println("Worker thread is simulating "+
                                            "work by sleeping for 5 seconds.");
                        try
                        {
                            Thread.sleep(5000);
                        }
                        catch (InterruptedException ie)
                        {
                        }
                        System.out.println("Worker thread is dying");
                    }
                };
        Thread thd = new Thread(r);
        thd.start();
        System.out.println("Default main thread is doing work.");
        try
        {
            Thread.sleep(2000);
        }
        catch (InterruptedException ie)
        {
        }
        System.out.println("Default main thread has finished its work.");
        System.out.println("Default main thread is waiting for worker thread "+
                           "to die.");
        try
        {
            thd.join();
        }
        catch (InterruptedException ie)
        {
        }
        System.out.println("Main thread is dying");
    }
}
```

Listing 4-19 demonstrates the default main thread starting a worker thread, performing some work, and then waiting for the worker thread to die by calling join() via the worker thread's thd object. When you run this application, you will discover output similar to the following (message order might differ somewhat):

```
Default main thread is doing work.
Worker thread is simulating work by sleeping for 5 seconds.
Default main thread has finished its work.
Default main thread is waiting for worker thread to die.
Worker thread is dying
Main thread is dying
```

Every Thread object belongs to some ThreadGroup object; Thread declares a ThreadGroup getThreadGroup() method that returns this object. You should ignore thread groups because they are not that useful. If you need to logically group Thread objects, you should use an array or collection instead.

Caution Various ThreadGroup methods are flawed. For example, int enumerate(Thread[] threads) will not include all active threads in its enumeration when its threads array argument is too small to store their Thread objects. Although you might think that you could use the return value from the int activeCount() method to properly size this array, there is no guarantee that the array will be large enough because activeCount()'s return value fluctuates with the creation and death of threads.

However, you should still know about ThreadGroup because of its contribution in handling exceptions that are thrown while a thread is executing. Listing 4-20 sets the stage for learning about exception handling by presenting a run() method that attempts to divide an integer by 0, which results in a thrown java.lang.ArithmeticException instance.

Listing 4-20. Throwing an exception from the run() method

```
class ExceptionThread
{
    public static void main(String[] args)
    {
        Runnable r = new Runnable()
                     {
                         @Override
                         public void run()
                         {
                             int x = 1/0;
                         }
                     };
        Thread thd = new Thread(r);
        thd.start();
    }
}
```

Run this application and you will see an exception trace that identifies the thrown ArithmeticException:

```
Exception in thread "Thread-0" java.lang.ArithmeticException: / by zero
        at ExceptionThread$1.run(ExceptionThread.java:10)
        at java.lang.Thread.run(Thread.java:722)
```

When an exception is thrown out of the run() method, the thread terminates and the following activities take place:

- The JVM looks for an instance of Thread.UncaughtExceptionHandler installed via Thread's void setUncaughtExceptionHandler(Thread.UncaughtExceptionHandler eh) method. When this handler is found, it passes execution to the instance's void uncaughtException(Thread t, Throwable e) method, where t identifies the Thread object of the thread that threw the exception, and e identifies the thrown exception or error—perhaps an OutOfMemoryError instance was thrown. If this method throws an exception/error, the exception/error is ignored by the JVM.

- Assuming that setUncaughtExceptionHandler() was not called to install a handler, the JVM passes control to the associated ThreadGroup object's uncaughtException(Thread t, Throwable e) method. Assuming that ThreadGroup was not extended, and that its uncaughtException() method was not overridden to handle the exception, uncaughtException() passes control to the parent ThreadGroup object's uncaughtException() method when a parent ThreadGroup is present. Otherwise, it checks to see if a default uncaught exception handler has been installed (via Thread's static void setDefaultUncaughtExceptionHandler(Thread.UncaughtExceptionHandler handler) method.) If a default uncaught exception handler has been installed, its uncaughtException() method is called with the same two arguments. Otherwise, uncaughtException() checks its Throwable argument to determine if it is an instance of java.lang.ThreadDeath. If so, nothing special is done. Otherwise, as Listing 4-20's exception message shows, a message containing the thread's name, as returned from the thread's getName() method, and a stack backtrace, using the Throwable argument's printStackTrace() method, is printed to the standard error stream.

Listing 4-21 demonstrates Thread's setUncaughtExceptionHandler() and setDefaultUncaughtExceptionHandler() methods.

Listing 4-21. Demonstrating uncaught exception handlers

```
class ExceptionThread
{
   public static void main(String[] args)
   {
      Runnable r = new Runnable()
                   {
                      @Override
                      public void run()
                      {
                         int x = 1/0;
                      }
                   };
      Thread thd = new Thread(r);
      Thread.UncaughtExceptionHandler uceh;
      uceh = new Thread.UncaughtExceptionHandler()
             {
                public void uncaughtException(Thread t, Throwable e)
                {
                   System.out.println("Caught throwable "+e+" for thread "+t);
                }
             };
      thd.setUncaughtExceptionHandler(uceh);
      uceh = new Thread.UncaughtExceptionHandler()
             {
                public void uncaughtException(Thread t, Throwable e)
                {
                   System.out.println("Default uncaught exception handler");
                   System.out.println("Caught throwable "+e+" for thread "+t);
                }
```

```
      };
   thd.setDefaultUncaughtExceptionHandler(uceh);
   thd.start();
   }
}
```

When you run this application, you will observe the following output:

```
Caught throwable java.lang.ArithmeticException: / by zero for thread Thread[Thread-↩0,5,main]
```

You also will not see the default uncaught exception handler's output because the default handler is not called. To see that output, you must comment out thd.setUncaughtExceptionHandler(uceh);. If you also comment out thd.setDefaultUncaughtExceptionHandler(uceh);, you will see Listing 4-20's output.

Caution Thread declares several deprecated methods, including stop() (stop an executing thread). These methods have been deprecated because they are unsafe. Do *not* use these deprecated methods. (I will show you how to safely stop a thread later in this chapter.) Also, you should avoid the static void yield() method, which is intended to switch execution from the current thread to another thread, because it can affect portability and hurt application performance. Although yield() might switch to another thread on some platforms (which can improve performance), yield() might only return to the current thread on other platforms (which hurts performance because the yield() call has only wasted time).

Thread Synchronization

Throughout its execution, each thread is isolated from other threads because it has been given its own method-call stack. However, threads can still interfere with each other when they access and manipulate shared data. This interference can corrupt the shared data, and this corruption can cause an application to fail.

For example, consider a checking account in which a husband and wife have joint access. Suppose that the husband and wife decide to empty this account at the same time without knowing that the other is doing the same thing. Listing 4-22 demonstrates this scenario.

Listing 4-22. A problematic checking account

```
class CheckingAccount
{
   private int balance;
   CheckingAccount(int initialBalance)
   {
      balance = initialBalance;
   }
   boolean withdraw(int amount)
   {
      if (amount <= balance)
      {
         try
```

```
            {
                Thread.sleep((int)(Math.random()*200));
            }
            catch (InterruptedException ie)
            {
            }
            balance -= amount;
            return true;
        }
        return false;
    }
    public static void main(String[] args)
    {
        final CheckingAccount ca = new CheckingAccount(100);
        Runnable r = new Runnable()
                     {
                         public void run()
                         {
                             String name = Thread.currentThread().getName();
                             for (int i = 0; i < 10; i++)
                                 System.out.println (name+" withdraws $10: "+
                                                     ca.withdraw(10));
                         }
                     };
        Thread thdHusband = new Thread(r);
        thdHusband.setName("Husband");
        Thread thdWife = new Thread(r);
        thdWife.setName("Wife");
        thdHusband.start();
        thdWife.start();
    }
}
```

This application lets more money be withdrawn than is available in the account. For example, the following output reveals $110 being withdrawn when only $100 is available:

```
Wife withdraws $10: true
Wife withdraws $10: true
Husband withdraws $10: true
Wife withdraws $10: true
Husband withdraws $10: true
Wife withdraws $10: true
Husband withdraws $10: true
Husband withdraws $10: true
Husband withdraws $10: true
Husband withdraws $10: true
Husband withdraws $10: false
Husband withdraws $10: false
Husband withdraws $10: false
Husband withdraws $10: false
Wife withdraws $10: true
Wife withdraws $10: false
Wife withdraws $10: false
```

```
Wife withdraws $10: false
Wife withdraws $10: false
Wife withdraws $10: false
```

The reason why more money is withdrawn than is available for withdrawal is that a race condition exists between the husband and wife threads.

■ **Note** A *race condition* is a scenario in which multiple threads update the same object at the same time or nearly at the same time. Part of the object stores values written to it by one thread, and another part of the object stores values written to it by another thread.

The race condition exists because the actions of checking the amount for withdrawal to ensure that it is less than what appears in the balance and deducting the amount from the balance are not *atomic* (indivisible) operations. (Although atoms are divisible, *atomic* is commonly used to refer to something being indivisible.)

■ **Note** The Thread.sleep() method call that sleeps for a variable amount of time (up to a maximum of 199 milliseconds) is present so that you can observe more money being withdrawn than is available for withdrawal. Without this method call, you might have to execute the application hundreds of times (or more) to witness this problem, because the scheduler might rarely pause a thread between the amount <= balance expression and the balance -= amount; expression statement—the code executes rapidly.

Consider the following scenario:

- The Husband thread executes withdraw()'s amount <= balance expression, which returns true. The scheduler pauses the Husband thread and lets the Wife thread execute.

- The Wife thread executes withdraw()'s amount <= balance expression, which returns true.

- The Wife thread performs the withdrawal. The scheduler pauses the Wife thread and lets the Husband thread execute.

- The Husband thread performs the withdrawal.

This problem can be corrected by synchronizing access to withdraw() so that only one thread at a time can execute inside this method. You synchronize access at the method level by adding reserved word synchronized to the method header prior to the method's return type; for example, synchronized boolean withdraw(int amount).

As I demonstrate later, you can also synchronize access to a block of statements by specifying synchronized(*object*) { /* synchronized statements */ }, where *object* is an arbitrary object reference. No thread can enter a synchronized method or block until execution leaves the method/block; this is known as *mutual exclusion.*

Synchronization is implemented in terms of monitors and locks. A *monitor* is a concurrency construct for controlling access to a *critical section,* a region of code that must execute atomically. It is identified at the source code level as a synchronized method or a synchronized block.

A *lock* is a token that a thread must acquire before a monitor allows that thread to execute inside a monitor's critical section. The token is released automatically when the thread exits the monitor, to give another thread an opportunity to acquire the token and enter the monitor.

Note A thread that has acquired a lock does not release this lock when it calls one of Thread's sleep() methods.

A thread entering a synchronized instance method acquires the lock associated with the object on which the method is called. A thread entering a synchronized class method acquires the lock associated with the class's Class object. Finally, a thread entering a synchronized block acquires the lock associated with the block's controlling object.

Tip Thread declares a static boolean holdsLock(Object o) method that returns true when the calling thread holds the monitor lock on object o. You will find this method handy in assertion statements, such as assert Thread.holdsLock(o);.

The need for synchronization is often subtle. For example, Listing 4-23's ID utility class declares a getNextID() method that returns a unique long-based ID, perhaps to be used when generating unique filenames. Although you might not think so, this method can cause data corruption and return duplicate values.

Listing 4-23. A utility class for returning unique IDs

```
class ID
{
   private static long nextID = 0;
   static long getNextID()
   {
      return nextID++;
   }
}
```

There are two lack-of-synchronization problems with getNextID(). Because 32-bit JVM implementations require two steps to update a 64-bit long integer, adding 1 to nextID is not atomic: the scheduler could interrupt a thread that has only updated half of nextID, which corrupts the contents of this variable.

Note Variables of type `long` and `double` are subject to corruption when being written to in an unsynchronized context on 32-bit JVMs. This problem does not occur with variables of type `boolean`, `byte`, `char`, `float`, `int`, or `short`; each type occupies 32 bits or less.

Assume that multiple threads call getNextID(). Because postincrement (++) reads and writes the nextID field in two steps, multiple threads might retrieve the same value. For example, thread A executes ++, reading nextID but not incrementing its value before being interrupted by the scheduler. Thread B now executes and reads the same value.

Both problems can be corrected by synchronizing access to nextID so that only one thread can execute this method's code. All that is required is to add synchronized to the method header prior to the method's return type; for example, static synchronized int getNextID().

Synchronization is also used to communicate between threads. For example, you might design your own mechanism for stopping a thread (because you cannot use Thread's unsafe stop() methods for this task). Listing 4-24 shows how you might accomplish this task.

Listing 4-24. Attempting to stop a thread

```java
class ThreadStopping
{
   public static void main(String[] args)
   {
      class StoppableThread extends Thread
      {
         private boolean stopped = false;
         @Override
         public void run()
         {
            while(!stopped)
               System.out.println("running");
         }
         void stopThread()
         {
            stopped = true;
         }
      }
      StoppableThread thd = new StoppableThread();
      thd.start();
      try
      {
         Thread.sleep(1000); // sleep for 1 second
      }
      catch (InterruptedException ie)
      {
      }
      thd.stopThread();
   }
}
```

295

Listing 4-24 introduces a main() method with a local class named StoppableThread that subclasses Thread. StoppableThread declares a stopped field initialized to false, a stopThread() method that sets this field to true, and a run() method whose infinite loop checks stopped on each loop iteration to see if its value has changed to true.

After instantiating StoppableThread, the default main thread starts the thread associated with this Thread object. It then sleeps for one second and calls StoppableThread's stop() method before dying. When you run this application on a single-processor/single-core machine, you will probably observe the application stopping.

You might not see this stoppage when the application runs on a multiprocessor machine or a uniprocessor machine with multiple cores. For performance reasons, each processor or core probably has its own cache with its own copy of stopped. When one thread modifies its copy of this field, the other thread's copy of stopped is not changed.

Listing 4-25 refactors Listing 4-24 to guarantee that the application will run correctly on all kinds of machines.

Listing 4-25. Guaranteed stoppage on a multiprocessor/multicore machine

```java
class ThreadStopping
{
    public static void main(String[] args)
    {
        class StoppableThread extends Thread
        {
            private boolean stopped = false;
            @Override
            public void run()
            {
                while(!isStopped())
                    System.out.println("running");
            }
            synchronized void stopThread()
            {
                stopped = true;
            }
            private synchronized boolean isStopped()
            {
                return stopped;
            }
        }
        StoppableThread thd = new StoppableThread();
        thd.start();
        try
        {
            Thread.sleep(1000); // sleep for 1 second
        }
        catch (InterruptedException ie)
        {
        }
        thd.stopThread();
    }
}
```

Listing 4-25's stopThread() and isStopped() methods are synchronized to support thread communication (between the default main thread that calls stopThread() and the started thread that executes inside run()). When a thread enters one of these methods, it is guaranteed to access a single shared copy of the stopped field (not a cached copy).

Synchronization is necessary to support mutual exclusion or mutual exclusion combined with thread communication. However, there is an alternative to synchronization when the only purpose is to communicate between threads. This alternative is reserved word volatile, which Listing 4-26 demonstrates.

Listing 4-26. *The* volatile *alternative to synchronization for thread communication*

```
class ThreadStopping
{
   public static void main(String[] args)
   {
      class StoppableThread extends Thread
      {
         private volatile boolean stopped = false;
         @Override
         public void run()
         {
            while(!stopped)
               System.out.println("running");
         }
         void stopThread()
         {
            stopped = true;
         }
      }
      StoppableThread thd = new StoppableThread();
      thd.start();
      try
      {
         Thread.sleep(1000); // sleep for 1 second
      }
      catch (InterruptedException ie)
      {
      }
      thd.stopThread();
   }
}
```

Listing 4-26 declares stopped to be volatile; threads that access this field will always access a single shared copy (not cached copies on multiprocessor/multicore machines). As well as generating code that is less verbose, volatile might offer improved performance over synchronization.

When a field is declared volatile, it cannot also be declared final. If you're depending on the *semantics* (meaning) of volatility, you still get those from a final field. In his "Java theory and practice: Fixing the Java Memory Model, Part 2" article (http://www.ibm.com/developerworks/library/j-jtp03304/), Brian Goetz has this to say about this issue: "The new JMM [Java Memory Model] also seeks to provide a new guarantee of initialization safety—that as long as an object is properly constructed (meaning that a reference to the object is not published before the constructor has completed), then all threads will see the values for its final fields that were set in its constructor, regardless of whether or not synchronization is used to pass the reference from one thread to another. Further, any variables that can be reached through a final field of a properly constructed object, such as fields of an object referenced by a final field, are also guaranteed to be visible to other threads as well. This means that if a final field contains a reference to, say, a LinkedList, in addition to the correct value of the reference being visible to other threads, also the contents of that LinkedList at construction time would be visible to other threads without synchronization. The result is a significant strengthening of the meaning of final—that final fields can be safely accessed without synchronization, and that compilers can assume that final fields will not change and can therefore optimize away multiple fetches."

Caution You should only use volatile in the context of thread communication. Also, you can only use this reserved word in the context of field declarations. Although you can declare double and long fields volatile, you should avoid doing so on 32-bit JVMs because it takes two operations to access a double or long variable's value, and mutual exclusion via synchronization is required to access their values safely.

Object's wait(), notify(), and notifyAll() methods support a form of thread communication where a thread voluntarily waits for some *condition* (a prerequisite for continued execution) to arise, at which time another thread notifies the waiting thread that it can continue. wait() causes its calling thread to wait on an object's monitor, and notify() and notifyAll() wake up one or all threads waiting on the monitor.

Caution Because the wait(), notify(), and notifyAll() methods depend on a lock, they cannot be called from outside of a synchronized method or synchronized block. If you fail to heed this warning, you will encounter a thrown instance of the java.lang.IllegalMonitorStateException class. Also, a thread that has acquired a lock releases this lock when it calls one of Object's wait() methods.

A classic example of thread communication involving conditions is the relationship between a producer thread and a consumer thread. The producer thread produces data items to be consumed by the consumer thread. Each produced data item is stored in a shared variable.

Imagine that the threads are not communicating and are running at different speeds. The producer might produce a new data item and record it in the shared variable before the consumer retrieves the previous data item for processing. Also, the consumer might retrieve the contents of the shared variable before a new data item is produced.

To overcome those problems, the producer thread must wait until it is notified that the previously produced data item has been consumed, and the consumer thread must wait until it is notified that a new data item has been produced. Listing 4-27 shows you how to accomplish this task via wait() and notify().

Listing 4-27. The producer-consumer relationship

```
class PC
```

```
{
   public static void main(String[] args)
   {
      Shared s = new Shared();
      new Producer(s).start();
      new Consumer(s).start();
   }
}
class Shared
{
   private char c = '\u0000';
   private boolean writeable = true;
   synchronized void setSharedChar(char c)
   {
      while (!writeable)
         try
         {
            wait();
         }
         catch (InterruptedException e) {}
      this.c = c;
      writeable = false;
      notify();
   }
   synchronized char getSharedChar()
   {
      while (writeable)
         try
         {
            wait();
         }
         catch (InterruptedException e) {}
      writeable = true;
      notify();
      return c;
   }
}
class Producer extends Thread
{
   private Shared s;
   Producer(Shared s)
   {
      this.s = s;
   }
   @Override
   public void run()
   {
      for (char ch = 'A'; ch <= 'Z'; ch++)
      {
         synchronized(s)
         {
            s.setSharedChar(ch);
```

```
                    System.out.println(ch+" produced by producer.");
                }
            }
        }
    }
}
class Consumer extends Thread
{
    private Shared s;
    Consumer(Shared s)
    {
        this.s = s;
    }
    @Override
    public void run()
    {
        char ch;
        do
        {
            synchronized(s)
            {
                ch = s.getSharedChar();
                System.out.println(ch+" consumed by consumer.");
            }
        }
        while (ch != 'Z');
    }
}
```

The application creates a Shared object and two threads that get a copy of the object's reference. The producer calls the object's setSharedChar() method to save each of 26 uppercase letters; the consumer calls the object's getSharedChar() method to acquire each letter.

The writeable instance field tracks two conditions: the producer waiting on the consumer to consume a data item, and the consumer waiting on the producer to produce a new data item. It helps coordinate execution of the producer and consumer. The following scenario, where the consumer executes first, illustrates this coordination:

1. The consumer executes s.getSharedChar() to retrieve a letter.

2. Inside of that synchronized method, the consumer calls wait() because writeable contains true. The consumer now waits until it receives notification from the producer.

3. The producer eventually executes s.setSharedChar(ch);.

4. When the producer enters that synchronized method (which is possible because the consumer released the lock inside of the wait() method prior to waiting), the producer discovers writeable's value to be true and does not call wait().

5. The producer saves the character, sets writeable to false (which will cause the producer to wait on the next setSharedChar() call when the consumer has not consumed the character by that time), and calls notify() to awaken the consumer (assuming the consumer is waiting).

6. The producer exits setSharedChar(char c).

7. The consumer wakes up (and reacquires the lock), sets writeable to true (which will cause the consumer to wait on the next getSharedChar() call when the producer has not produced a character by that time), notifies the producer to awaken that thread (assuming the producer is waiting), and returns the shared character.

Although the synchronization works correctly, you might observe output (on some platforms) that shows multiple producing messages before a consuming message. For example, you might see A produced by producer., followed by B produced by producer., followed by A consumed by consumer., at the beginning of the application's output.

This strange output order is caused by the call to setSharedChar() followed by its companion System.out.println() method call not being atomic, and by the call to getSharedChar() followed by its companion System.out.println() method call not being atomic. The output order is corrected by wrapping each of these method call pairs in a synchronized block that synchronizes on the s-referenced Shared object.

When you run this application, its output should always appear in the same alternating order, as shown next (only the first few lines are shown for brevity):

```
A produced by producer.
A consumed by consumer.
B produced by producer.
B consumed by consumer.
C produced by producer.
C consumed by consumer.
D produced by producer.
D consumed by consumer.
```

Caution Never call wait() outside of a loop. The loop tests the condition (!writeable or writeable in the previous example) before and after the wait() call. Testing the condition before calling wait() ensures *liveness*. If this test was not present, and if the condition held and notify() had been called prior to wait() being called, it is unlikely that the waiting thread would ever wake up. Retesting the condition after calling wait() ensures *safety*. If retesting did not occur, and if the condition did not hold after the thread had awakened from the wait() call (perhaps another thread called notify() accidentally when the condition did not hold), the thread would proceed to destroy the lock's protected invariants.

Too much synchronization can be problematic. If you are not careful, you might encounter a situation where locks are acquired by multiple threads, neither thread holds its own lock but holds the lock needed by some other thread, and neither thread can enter and later exit its critical section to release its held lock because some other thread holds the lock to that critical section. Listing 4-28's atypical example demonstrates this scenario, which is known as *deadlock*.

Listing 4-28. A pathological case of deadlock

```
class Deadlock
```

```
{
    private Object lock1 = new Object();
    private Object lock2 = new Object();
    void instanceMethod1()
    {
        synchronized(lock1)
        {
            synchronized(lock2)
            {
                System.out.println("first thread in instanceMethod1");
                // critical section guarded first by
                // lock1 and then by lock2
            }
        }
    }
    void instanceMethod2()
    {
        synchronized(lock2)
        {
            synchronized(lock1)
            {
                System.out.println("second thread in instanceMethod2");
                // critical section guarded first by
                // lock2 and then by lock1
            }
        }
    }
    public static void main(String[] args)
    {
        final Deadlock dl = new Deadlock();
        Runnable r1 = new Runnable()
                    {
                        @Override
                        public void run()
                        {
                            while(true)
                                dl.instanceMethod1();
                        }
                    };
        Thread thdA = new Thread(r1);
        Runnable r2 = new Runnable()
                    {
                        @Override
                        public void run()
                        {
                            while(true)
                                dl.instanceMethod2();
                        }
                    };
        Thread thdB = new Thread(r2);
        thdA.start();
        thdB.start();
```

```
    }
}
```

Listing 4-28's thread A and thread B call instanceMethod1() and instanceMethod2(), respectively, at different times. Consider the following execution sequence:

1. Thread A calls instanceMethod1(), obtains the lock assigned to the lock1-referenced object, and enters its outer critical section (but has not yet acquired the lock assigned to the lock2-referenced object).

2. Thread B calls instanceMethod2(), obtains the lock assigned to the lock2-referenced object, and enters its outer critical section (but has not yet acquired the lock assigned to the lock1-referenced object).

3. Thread A attempts to acquire the lock associated with lock2. The JVM forces the thread to wait outside of the inner critical section because thread B holds that lock.

4. Thread B attempts to acquire the lock associated with lock1. The JVM forces the thread to wait outside of the inner critical section because thread A holds that lock.

5. Neither thread can proceed because the other thread holds the needed lock. We have a deadlock situation and the program (at least in the context of the two threads) freezes up.

Although the previous example clearly identifies a deadlock state, it is often not that easy to detect deadlock. For example, your code might contain the following circular relationship among various classes (in several source files):

- Class A's synchronized method calls class B's synchronized method.

- Class B's synchronized method calls class C's synchronized method.

- Class C's synchronized method calls class A's synchronized method.

If thread A calls class A's synchronized method and thread B calls class C's synchronized method, thread B will block when it attempts to call class A's synchronized method and thread A is still inside of that method. Thread A will continue to execute until it calls class C's synchronized method, and then block. Deadlock results.

Note Neither the Java language nor the JVM provides a way to prevent deadlock, and so the burden falls on you. The simplest way to prevent deadlock from happening is to avoid having either a synchronized method or a synchronized block call another synchronized method/block. Although this advice prevents deadlock from happening, it is impractical because one of your synchronized methods/blocks might need to call a synchronized method in a Java API, and the advice is overkill because the synchronized method/block being called might not call any other synchronized method/block, so deadlock would not occur.

You will sometimes want to associate per-thread data (such a user ID) with a thread. Although you can accomplish this task with a local variable, you can only do so while the local variable exists. You could use an instance field to keep this data around longer, but then you would have to deal with synchronization. Thankfully, Java supplies ThreadLocal as a simple (and very handy) alternative.

Each instance of the ThreadLocal class describes a *thread-local variable*, which is a variable that provides a separate storage slot to each thread that accesses the variable. You can think of a thread-local variable as a multi-slot variable in which each thread can store a different value in the same variable. Each thread sees only its value and is unaware of other threads having their own values in this variable.

ThreadLocal is generically declared as ThreadLocal<T>, where T identifies the type of value that is stored in the variable. This class declares the following constructor and methods:

- ThreadLocal() creates a new thread-local variable.

- T get() returns the value in the calling thread's storage slot. If an entry does not exist when the thread calls this method, get() calls initialValue().

- T initialValue() creates the calling thread's storage slot and stores an initial (default) value in this slot. The initial value defaults to null. You must subclass ThreadLocal and override this protected method to provide a more suitable initial value.

- void remove() removes the calling thread's storage slot. If this method is followed by get() with no intervening set(), get() calls initialValue().

- void set(T value) sets the value of the calling thread's storage slot to value.

Listing 4-29 shows you how to use ThreadLocal to associate a different user ID with each of two threads.

Listing 4-29. Different user IDs for different threads

```java
class ThreadLocalDemo
{
   private static volatile ThreadLocal<String> userID =
      new ThreadLocal<String>();
   public static void main(String[] args)
   {
      Runnable r = new Runnable()
                   {
                      @Override
                      public void run()
                      {
                         String name = Thread.currentThread().getName();
                         if (name.equals("A"))
                            userID.set("foxtrot");
                         else
                            userID.set("charlie");
                         System.out.println(name+" "+userID.get());
                      }
                   };
      Thread thdA = new Thread(r);
      thdA.setName("A");
      Thread thdB = new Thread(r);
```

```
        thdB.setName("B");
        thdA.start();
        thdB.start();
    }
}
```

After instantiating ThreadLocal and assigning the reference to a volatile class field named userID (the field is volatile because it is accessed by different threads, which might execute on a multiprocessor/multicore machine), the default main thread creates two more threads that store different String objects in userID and output their objects.

When you run this application, you will observe the following output (possibly not in this order):

```
A foxtrot
B charlie
```

Values stored in thread-local variables are not related. When a new thread is created, it gets a new storage slot containing initialValue()'s value. Perhaps you would prefer to pass a value from a parent thread, a thread that creates another thread, to a *child thread*, the created thread. You accomplish this task with InheritableThreadLocal.

InheritableThreadLocal is a subclass of ThreadLocal. As well as declaring an InheritableThreadLocal() constructor, this class declares the following protected method:

- T childValue(T parentValue) calculates the child's initial value as a function of the parent's value at the time the child thread is created. This method is called from the parent thread before the child thread is started. The method returns the argument passed to parentValue and should be overridden when another value is desired.

Listing 4-30 shows you how to use InheritableThreadLocal to pass a parent thread's Integer object to a child thread.

Listing 4-30. Different user IDs for different threads

```
class InheritableThreadLocalDemo
{
    private static volatile InheritableThreadLocal<Integer> intVal =
        new InheritableThreadLocal<Integer>();
    public static void main(String[] args)
    {
        Runnable rP = new Runnable()
                      {
                          @Override
                          public void run()
                          {
                              intVal.set(new Integer(10));
                              Runnable rC = new Runnable()
                                            {
                                                public void run()
                                                {
                                                    Thread thd;
                                                    thd = Thread.currentThread();
                                                    String name = thd.getName();
                                                    System.out.println(name+" "+
```

```
                                                        intVal.get());
                              }
                          };
                  Thread thdChild = new Thread(rC);
                  thdChild.setName("Child");
                  thdChild.start();
              }
          };
      new Thread(rP).start();
   }
}
```

After instantiating `InheritableThreadLocal` and assigning it to a `volatile` class field named `intVal`, the default main thread creates a parent thread, which stores an `Integer` object containing 10 in `intVal`. The parent thread creates a child thread, which accesses `intVal` and retrieves its parent thread's `Integer` object.

When you run this application, you will observe the following output:

```
Child 10
```

BigDecimal

Chapter 2 introduced you to a `SavingsAccount` class with a `balance` field. I declared this field to be of type `int`, and mentioned that `balance` represents the number of dollars that can be withdrawn. Alternatively, I could have stated that `balance` represents the number of pennies that can be withdrawn.

Perhaps you are wondering why I did not declare `balance` to be of type `double` or `float`. That way, `balance` could store values such as 18.26 (18 dollars in the whole number part and 26 pennies in the fraction part). I did not declare `balance` to be a `double` or `float` for the following reasons:

- Not all floating-point values that can represent monetary amounts (dollars and cents) can be stored exactly in memory. For example, 0.1 (which you might use to represent 10 cents) has no exact storage representation. If you executed `double total = 0.1; for (int i = 0; i < 50; i++) total += 0.1; System.out.println(total);`, you would observe `5.099999999999998` instead of the correct `5.1` as the output.

- The result of each floating-point calculation needs to be rounded to the nearest cent. Failure to do so introduces tiny errors that can cause the final result to differ from the correct result. Although `Math` supplies a pair of `round()` methods that you might consider using to round a calculation to the nearest cent, these methods round to the nearest integer (dollar).

Listing 4-31's `InvoiceCalc` application demonstrates both problems. However, the first problem is not serious because it contributes very little to the inaccuracy. The more serious problem occurs from failing to round to the nearest cent after performing a calculation.

Listing 4-31. Floating-point-based invoice calculations leading to confusing results

```
import java.text.NumberFormat;

class InvoiceCalc
{
```

```
final static double DISCOUNT_PERCENT = 0.1; // 10%
final static double TAX_PERCENT = 0.05; // 5%
public static void main(String[] args)
{
   double invoiceSubtotal = 285.36;
   double discount = invoiceSubtotal*DISCOUNT_PERCENT;
   double subtotalBeforeTax = invoiceSubtotal-discount;
   double salesTax = subtotalBeforeTax*TAX_PERCENT;
   double invoiceTotal = subtotalBeforeTax+salesTax;
   NumberFormat currencyFormat = NumberFormat.getCurrencyInstance();
   System.out.println("Subtotal: "+currencyFormat.format(invoiceSubtotal));
   System.out.println("Discount: "+currencyFormat.format(discount));
   System.out.println("SubTotal after discount: "+
                   currencyFormat.format(subtotalBeforeTax));
   System.out.println("Sales Tax: "+currencyFormat.format(salesTax));
   System.out.println("Total: "+currencyFormat.format(invoiceTotal));
}
}
```

Listing 4-31 relies on the NumberFormat class (located in the java.text package) and its format() method to format a double precision floating-point value into a currency—I discuss NumberFormat in the Internationalization section of Appendix C. When you run InvoiceCalc, you will discover the following output:

```
Subtotal: $285.36
Discount: $28.54
SubTotal after discount: $256.82
Sales Tax: $12.84
Total: $269.67
```

This output reveals the correct subtotal, discount, subtotal after discount, and sales tax. In contrast, it incorrectly reveals 269.67 instead of 269.66 as the final total. The customer will not appreciate paying an extra penny, even though 269.67 is the correct value according to the floating-point calculations:

```
Subtotal: 285.36
Discount: 28.536
SubTotal after discount: 256.824
Sales Tax: 12.8412
Total: 269.6652
```

The problem arises from not rounding the result of each calculation to the nearest cent before performing the next calculation. As a result, the 0.024 in 256.824 and 0.0012 in 12.84 contribute to the final value, causing NumberFormat's format() method to round this value to 269.67.

Caution Never using float or double to represent monetary values.

Java provides a solution to both problems in the form of a BigDecimal class. This immutable class (a BigDecimal instance cannot be modified) represents a signed decimal number (such as 23.653) of arbitrary *precision* (number of digits) with an associated *scale* (an integer that specifies the number of digits after the decimal point).

BigDecimal declares three convenience constants: ONE, TEN, and ZERO. Each constant is the BigDecimal equivalent of 1, 10, and 0 with a zero scale.

■ **Caution** BigDecimal declares several ROUND_-prefixed constants. These constants are largely obsolete and should be avoided, along with the BigDecimal divide(BigDecimal divisor, int scale, int roundingMode) and BigDecimal setScale(int newScale, int roundingMode) methods, which are still present so that dependent legacy code continues to compile.

BigDecimal also declares a variety of useful constructors and methods. A few of these constructors and methods are described in Table 4-8.

Table 4-8. BigDecimal Constructors and Methods

Method	Description
BigDecimal(int val)	Initialize the BigDecimal instance to val's digits. Set the scale to 0.
BigDecimal(String val)	Initialize the BigDecimal instance to the decimal equivalent of val. Set the scale to the number of digits after the decimal point, or 0 if no decimal point is specified. This constructor throws NullPointerException when val is null, and NumberFormatException when val's string representation is invalid (contains letters, for example).
BigDecimal abs()	Return a new BigDecimal instance that contains the absolute value of the current instance's value. The resulting scale is the same as the current instance's scale.
BigDecimal add(BigDecimal augend)	Return a new BigDecimal instance that contains the sum of the current value and the argument value. The resulting scale is the maximum of the current and argument scales. This method throws NullPointerException when augend is null.
BigDecimal divide(BigDecimal divisor)	Return a new BigDecimal instance that contains the quotient of the current value divided by the argument value. The resulting scale is the difference of the current and argument scales. It might be adjusted when the result requires more digits. This method throws NullPointerException when divisor is null, or ArithmeticException when divisor represents 0 or the result cannot be represented exactly.

`BigDecimal max(BigDecimal val)`	Return either this or `val`, whichever `BigDecimal` instance contains the larger value. This method throws `NullPointerException` when `val` is null.
`BigDecimal min(BigDecimal val)`	Return either this or `val`, whichever `BigDecimal` instance contains the smaller value. This method throws `NullPointerException` when `val` is null.
`BigDecimal multiply(BigDecimal multiplicand)`	Return a new `BigDecimal` instance that contains the product of the current value and the argument value. The resulting scale is the sum of the current and argument scales. This method throws `NullPointerException` when `multiplicand` is null.
`BigDecimal negate()`	Return a new `BigDecimal` instance that contains the negative of the current value. The resulting scale is the same as the current scale.
`int precision()`	Return the precision of the current `BigDecimal` instance.
`BigDecimal remainder(BigDecimal divisor)`	Return a new `BigDecimal` instance that contains the remainder of the current value divided by the argument value. The resulting scale is the difference of the current scale and the argument scale. It might be adjusted when the result requires more digits. This method throws `NullPointerException` when `divisor` is null, or `ArithmeticException` when `divisor` represents 0.
`int scale()`	Return the scale of the current `BigDecimal` instance.
`BigDecimal setScale(int newScale, RoundingMode roundingMode)`	Return a new `BigDecimal` instance with the specified scale and rounding mode. If the new scale is greater than the old scale, additional zeros are added to the unscaled value. In this case no rounding is necessary. If the new scale is smaller than the old scale, trailing digits are removed. If these trailing digits are not zero, the remaining unscaled value has to be rounded. For this rounding operation, the specified rounding mode is used. This method throws `NullPointerException` when `roundingMode` is null, and `ArithmeticException` when `roundingMode` is set to `RoundingMode.ROUND_UNNECESSARY` but rounding is necessary based on the current scale.
`BigDecimal subtract(BigDecimal subtrahend)`	Return a new `BigDecimal` instance that contains the current value minus the argument value. The resulting scale is the maximum of the current and argument scales. This method throws `NullPointerException` when `subtrahend` is null.

`String toString()`	Return a string representation of this `BigDecimal` instance. Scientific notation is used when necessary.

Table 4-8 refers to `java.math.RoundingMode`, which is an enum containing various rounding mode constants. These constants are described in Table 4-9.

Table 4-9. RoundingMode Constants

Constant	Description
`CEILING`	Round toward positive infinity.
`DOWN`	Round toward zero.
`FLOOR`	Round toward negative infinity.
`HALF_DOWN`	Round toward the "nearest neighbor" unless both neighbors are equidistant, in which case round down.
`HALF_EVEN`	Round toward the "nearest neighbor" unless both neighbors are equidistant, in which case, round toward the even neighbor.
`HALF_UP`	Round toward "nearest neighbor" unless both neighbors are equidistant, in which case round up. (This is the rounding mode commonly taught at school.)
`UNNECESSARY`	Rounding is not necessary because the requested operation produces the exact result.
`UP`	Positive values are rounded toward positive infinity and negative values are rounded toward negative infinity.

The best way to get comfortable with `BigDecimal` is to try it out. Listing 4-32 uses this class to correctly perform the invoice calculations that were presented in Listing 4-31.

Listing 4-32. BigDecimal-based invoice calculations not leading to confusing results

```
import java.math.BigDecimal;
import java.math.RoundingMode;

class InvoiceCalc
{
   public static void main(String[] args)
   {
      BigDecimal invoiceSubtotal = new BigDecimal("285.36");
      BigDecimal discountPercent = new BigDecimal("0.10");
      BigDecimal discount = invoiceSubtotal.multiply(discountPercent);
```

```
        discount = discount.setScale(2, RoundingMode.HALF_UP);
        BigDecimal subtotalBeforeTax = invoiceSubtotal.subtract(discount);
        subtotalBeforeTax = subtotalBeforeTax.setScale(2, RoundingMode.HALF_UP);
        BigDecimal salesTaxPercent = new BigDecimal("0.05");
        BigDecimal salesTax = subtotalBeforeTax.multiply(salesTaxPercent);
        salesTax = salesTax.setScale(2, RoundingMode.HALF_UP);
        BigDecimal invoiceTotal = subtotalBeforeTax.add(salesTax);
        invoiceTotal = invoiceTotal.setScale(2, RoundingMode.HALF_UP);
        System.out.println("Subtotal: "+invoiceSubtotal);
        System.out.println("Discount: "+discount);
        System.out.println("SubTotal after discount: "+subtotalBeforeTax);
        System.out.println("Sales Tax: "+salesTax);
        System.out.println("Total: "+invoiceTotal);
    }
}
```

Listing 4-32's main() method first creates BigDecimal objects invoiceSubtotal and discountPercent that are initialized to 285.36 and 0.10, respectively. It then multiplies invoiceSubtotal by discountPercent and assigns the BigDecimal result to discount.

At this point, discount contains 28.5360. Apart from the trailing zero, this value is the same as that generated by invoiceSubtotal*DISCOUNT_PERCENT in Listing 4-31. The value that should be stored in discount is 28.54. To correct this problem before performing another calculation, main() calls discount's setScale() method with these arguments:

- 2: Two digits after the decimal point

- RoundingMode.HALF_UP: The conventional approach to rounding

After setting the scale and proper rounding mode, main() subtracts discount from invoiceSubtotal, and assigns the resulting BigDecimal instance to subtotalBeforeTax. main() calls setScale() on subtotalBeforeTax to properly round its value before moving on to the next calculation.

main() next creates a BigDecimal object named salesTaxPercent that is initialized to 0.05. It then multiplies subtotalBeforeTax by salesTaxPercent, assigning the result to salesTax, and calls setScale() on this BigDecimal object to properly round its value.

Moving on, main() adds salesTax to subtotalBeforeTax, saving the result in invoiceTotal, and rounds the result via setScale(). The values in these objects are sent to the standard output device via System.out.println(), which calls their toString() methods to return string representations of the BigDecimal values.

When you run this new version of InvoiceCalc, you will discover the following output:

```
Subtotal: 285.36
Discount: 28.54
SubTotal after discount: 256.82
Sales Tax: 12.84
Total: 269.66
```

Caution BigDecimal declares a BigDecimal(double val) constructor that you should avoid using if at all possible. This constructor initializes the BigDecimal instance to the value stored in val, making it possible for this instance to reflect an invalid representation when the double value cannot be stored exactly. For example,

BigDecimal(0.1) results in 0.1000000000000000055511151231257827021181583404541015625 being stored in the instance. In contrast, BigDecimal("0.1") stores 0.1 exactly.

BigInteger

BigDecimal stores a signed decimal number as an unscaled value with a 32-bit integer scale. The unscaled value is stored in an instance of the BigInteger class.

BigInteger is an immutable class that represents a signed integer of arbitrary precision. It stores its value in *two's complement format* (all bits are flipped—1s to 0s and 0s to 1s—and 1 is added to the result to be compatible with the two's complement format used by Java's byte integer, short integer, integer, and long integer types).

■ **Note** Check out Wikipedia's "Two's complement" entry (http://en.wikipedia.org/wiki/Two's_complement) to learn more about two's complement.

BigInteger declares three convenience constants: ONE, TEN, and ZERO. Each constant is the BigInteger equivalent of 1, 10, and 0.

BigInteger also declares a variety of useful constructors and methods. A few of these constructors and methods are described in Table 4-10.

Table 4-10. BigInteger Constructors and Methods

Method	Description
BigInteger(byte[] val)	Initialize the BigInteger instance to the integer that is stored in the val array, with val[0] storing the integer's most significant (leftmost) eight bits. This constructor throws NullPointerException when val is null, and NumberFormatException when val.length equals 0.
BigInteger(String val)	Initialize the BigInteger instance to the integer equivalent of val. This constructor throws NullPointerException when val is null, and NumberFormatException when val's string representation is invalid (contains letters, for example).
BigInteger abs()	Return a new BigInteger instance that contains the absolute value of the current instance's value.
BigInteger add(BigInteger augend)	Return a new BigInteger instance that contains the sum of the current value and the argument value. This method throws NullPointerException when augend is null.

`BigInteger divide(BigInteger divisor)`	Return a new `BigInteger` instance that contains the quotient of the current value divided by the argument value. This method throws `NullPointerException` when `divisor` is `null`, and `ArithmeticException` when `divisor` represents 0 or the result cannot be represented exactly.
`BigInteger max(BigInteger val)`	Return either this or `val`, whichever `BigInteger` instance contains the larger value. This method throws `NullPointerException` when `val` is `null`.
`BigInteger min(BigInteger val)`	Return either this or `val`, whichever `BigInteger` instance contains the smaller value. This method throws `NullPointerException` when `val` is `null`.
`BigInteger multiply(BigInteger multiplicand)`	Return a new `BigInteger` instance that contains the product of the current value and the argument value. This method throws `NullPointerException` when `multiplicand` is `null`.
`BigInteger negate()`	Return a new `BigInteger` instance that contains the negative of the current value.
`BigInteger remainder(BigInteger divisor)`	Return a new `BigInteger` instance that contains the remainder of the current value divided by the argument value. This method throws `NullPointerException` when `divisor` is `null`, and `ArithmeticException` when `divisor` represents 0.
`BigInteger subtract(BigInteger subtrahend)`	Return a new `BigInteger` instance that contains the current value minus the argument value. This method throws `NullPointerException` when `subtrahend` is `null`.
`String toString()`	Return a string representation of this `BigInteger`.

■ **Note** `BigInteger` also declares several bit-oriented methods, such as `BigInteger and (BigInteger val)`, `BigInteger flipBit(int n)`, and `BigInteger shiftLeft(int n)`. These methods are useful for when you need to perform low-level bit manipulation.

The best way to get comfortable with `BigInteger` is to try it out. Listing 4-33 uses this class in a factorial() method comparison context.

Listing 4-33. Comparing factorial() methods

```
import java.math.BigInteger;
```

```
class FactComp
{
   public static void main(String[] args)
   {
      System.out.println(factorial(12));
      System.out.println();
      System.out.println(factorial(20L));
      System.out.println();
      System.out.println(factorial(170.0));
      System.out.println();
      System.out.println(factorial(new BigInteger("170")));
      System.out.println();
      System.out.println(factorial(25.0));
      System.out.println();
      System.out.println(factorial(new BigInteger("25")));
   }
   static int factorial(int n)
   {
      if (n == 0)
         return 1;
      else
         return n*factorial(n-1);
   }
   static long factorial(long n)
   {
      if (n == 0)
         return 1;
      else
         return n*factorial(n-1);
   }
   static double factorial(double n)
   {
      if (n == 1.0)
         return 1.0;
      else
         return n*factorial(n-1);
   }
   static BigInteger factorial(BigInteger n)
   {
      if (n.equals(BigInteger.ZERO))
         return BigInteger.ONE;
      else
         return n.multiply(factorial(n.subtract(BigInteger.ONE)));
   }
}
```

Listing 4-33 compares four versions of the recursive factorial() method. This comparison reveals the largest argument that can be passed to each of the first three methods before the returned factorial value becomes meaningless, because of limits on the range of values that can be accurately represented by the numeric type.

The first version is based on int and has a useful argument range of 0 through 12. Passing any argument greater than 12 results in a factorial that cannot be represented accurately as an int.

You can increase the useful range of factorial(), but not by much, by changing the parameter and return types to long. After making these changes, you will discover that the upper limit of the useful range is 20.

To further increase the useful range, you might create a version of factorial() whose parameter and return types are double. This is possible because whole numbers can be represented exactly as doubles. However, the largest useful argument that can be passed is 170.0. Anything higher than this value results in factorial() returning +infinity.

It is possible that you might need to calculate a higher factorial value, perhaps in the context of calculating a statistics problem involving combinations or permutations. The only way to accurately calculate this value is to use a version of factorial() based on BigInteger.

When you run this application, as in java FactComp, it generates the following output:

```
479001600

2432902008176640000

7.257415615307994E306

725741561530799896739672821112926311471699168129645137654357779890056184340170615785235074924
261745951149099123783852077666602256544275302532890077320751090240043028005829560396661259965
8257104398558294257568966313439612262571094946806711205568880457193340212661452800000000000000000
000000000000000000000000000

1.5511210043330986E25

1551121004333098598400000
```

The first three values represent the highest factorials that can be returned by the int-based, long-based, and double-based factorial() methods. The fourth value represents the BigInteger equivalent of the highest double factorial.

Notice that the double method fails to accurately represent 170! (! is the math symbol for factorial). Its precision is simply too small. Although the method attempts to round the smallest digit, rounding does not always work—the number ends in 7994 instead of 7998. Rounding is only accurate up to argument 25.0, as the last two output lines reveal.

Note RSA encryption, BigDecimal, and factorial are practical examples of BigInteger's usefulness. However, you can also use BigInteger in unusual ways. For example, my February 2006 *JavaWorld* article titled "Travel Through Time with Java" (http://www.javaworld.com/javaworld/jw-02-2006/jw-0213-funandgames.html), a part of my Java Fun and Games series, used BigInteger to store an image as a very large integer. The idea was to experiment with BigInteger methods to look for images (possibly by discovering mathematical patterns) of people and places that existed in the past, will exist in the future, or might never exist. If this craziness appeals to you, check out my article.

EXERCISES

The following exercises are designed to test your understanding of Java's language APIs:

1. A *prime number* is a positive integer greater than 1 that is evenly divisible by 1 and itself. Create a PrimeNumberTest application that determines if its solitary integer argument is prime or not prime, and outputs a suitable message. For example, java PrimeNumberTest 289 should output the message 289 is not prime. A simple way to check for primality is to loop from 2 through the square root of the integer argument, and use the remainder operator in the loop to determine if the argument is divided evenly by the loop index. For example, because 6/2 yields a remainder of 0 (2 divides evenly into 6), integer 6 is not a prime number.

2. Reflection is useful in a device driver context, where an application needs to interact with different versions of a driver. If an older version is detected, the application invokes its methods. If a newer version is detected, the application can invoke the older methods or invoke newer versions of those methods. Create two versions of a Driver class. The first version declares a String getCapabilities() method that returns "basic capabilities", and the second version declares this method along with a String getCapabilitiesEx() method that returns "extended capabilities". Create a DriverDemo class that uses reflection to determine if the current Driver.class classfile supports getCapabilitiesEx(), and invoke that method if it does. If the method does not exist, use reflection to determine if it supports getCapabilities(), and invoke that method if that is the case. Otherwise, output an error message.

3. Java arrays have fixed lengths. Create a growable array class, GArray<E>, whose instances store objects of the type specified by the actual type argument passed to E. This class declares a GArray(int initCapacity) constructor that creates an internal array with the number of elements specified by initCapacity. Also, this class declares E get(int index) and void set(int index, E value) methods that respectively return the object at the index position within the internal array, and store the specified value in the array at the index position. The get() method must throw ArrayIndexOutOfBoundsException when the argument passed to index is out of range (negative or greater than/equal to the array's length). The set() method must throw the same exception when the argument passed to index is negative. However, when the argument is positive, it must create a new internal array whose size is twice that of the old array, copy elements from the old array to the new array via System.arraycopy(), and store the new value at the index position. This class also declares an int size() method that returns the array's size. Test this class with the GArrayDemo application described in Listing 4-34.

Listing 4-34. Demonstrating a growable array

```java
import ca.tutortutor.collections.GArray;

class GArrayDemo
{
    public static void main(String[] args)
    {
        GArray<String> ga = new GArray<>(10);
        System.out.println("Size = "+ga.size());
        ga.set(3, "ABC");
        System.out.println("Size = "+ga.size());
        ga.set(22, "XYZ");
        System.out.println("Size = "+ga.size());
        System.out.println(ga.get(3));
        System.out.println(ga.get(22));
        System.out.println(ga.get(20));
        ga.set(20, "PQR");
        System.out.println(ga.get(20));
        System.out.println("Size = "+ga.size());
    }
}
```

When you run this application, it should generate the following output:

```
Size = 0
Size = 4
Size = 23
ABC
XYZ
null
PQR
Size = 23
```

4. Modify Listing 4-17's `CountingThreads` application by marking the two counting threads as daemon threads. What happens when you run the resulting application?

5. Modify Listing 4-17's `CountingThreads` application by adding logic to stop both counting threads when the user presses the Enter key. The default main thread should call `System.in.read()` prior to terminating, and assign `true` to a variable named `stopped` after this method call returns. Each counting thread should test this variable to see if it contains true at the start of each loop iteration, and only continue the loop when the variable contains false.

Summary

Java's standard class library provides various language-oriented APIs via the java.lang and java.math packages. These APIs include Math and StrictMath, Package, Primitive Type Wrapper Class, Reference, Reflection, String, StringBuffer and StringBuilder, System, Threading, BigDecimal, and BigInteger.

The Math and StrictMath classes offer a wide variety of useful math-oriented methods for calculating trigonometric values, generating pseudorandom numbers, and so on. StrictMath differs from Math by ensuring that all of these mathematical operations yield the same results on all platforms.

The Package class provides access to package information. This information includes version details about the implementation and specification of a Java package, the package's name, and an indication of whether the package is sealed or not.

Instances of the Boolean, Byte, Character, Double, Float, Integer, Long, and Short primitive type wrapper classes wrap themselves around values of primitive types. These classes are useful for storing primitive values in collections, and for providing a good place to associate useful constants (such as MAX_VALUE and MIN_VALUE) and class methods (such as Integer's parseInt() methods and Character's isDigit(), isLetter(), and toUpperCase() methods) with the primitive types.

The Reference API makes it possible for an application to interact with the garbage collector in limited ways. This API consists of classes Reference, ReferenceQueue, SoftReference, WeakReference, and PhantomReference.

SoftReference is useful for implementing image caches, WeakReference is useful for preventing memory leaks related to hashmaps, and PhantomReference is useful for learning when an object has been finalized so that its resources can be cleaned up.

The Reflection API lets applications learn about loaded classes, interfaces, enums (a kind of class), and annotation types (a kind of interface). It also lets applications load classes dynamically, instantiate them, find a class's fields and methods, access fields, call methods, and perform other tasks reflectively.

The entry point into the Reflection API is a special class named Class. Additional classes include Constructor, Field, Method, AccessibleObject, and Array.

The String class represents a string as a sequence of characters. Because instances of this class are immutable, Java provides StringBuffer and StringBuilder for building a string more efficiently. The former class can be used in a multithreaded context, whereas the latter class is more performant.

The System class provides access to standard input, standard output, standard error, and other system-oriented resources. For example, System provides the arraycopy() method as the fastest portable way to copy one array to another.

Java supports threads via its low-level Threading API. This API consists of one interface (Runnable) and four classes (Thread, ThreadGroup, ThreadLocal, and InheritableThreadLocal).

Throughout its execution, each thread is isolated from other threads because it has been given its own method-call stack. However, threads can still interfere with each other when they access and manipulate shared data. This interference can corrupt the shared data, and this corruption can cause an application to fail. Java provides a thread-synchronization mechanism to prevent this interference.

Money must never be represented by floating-point and double precision floating-point variables because not all monetary values can be represented exactly. In contrast, the BigDecimal class lets you accurately represent and manipulate these values.

BigDecimal relies on the BigInteger class for representing its unscaled value. A BigInteger instance describes an integer value that can be of arbitrary length (subject to the limits of the JVM's memory).

This chapter briefly referred to the Collections Framework while introducing the Primitive Type Wrapper Class API. Chapter 5 introduces you to this broad utility API for collecting objects.

CHAPTER 5

Collecting Objects

Applications often must manage collections of objects. Although you can use arrays for this purpose, they are not always a good choice. For example, arrays have fixed sizes, making it tricky to determine an optimal size when you need to store a variable number of objects. Also, arrays can be indexed by integers only, which make them unsuitable for mapping arbitrary objects to other objects.

Java's standard class library provides the Collections Framework and legacy APIs to manage collections on behalf of applications. Chapter 5 first presents this framework, and then introduces you to these legacy APIs (in case you encounter them in legacy code). Because the framework and legacy APIs may not satisfy specific needs, this chapter lastly focuses on creating special-purpose collections APIs.

Note Java's concurrency utilities (discussed in Chapter 6) extend the Collections Framework.

The Collections Framework

The *Collections Framework* is a standard architecture for representing and manipulating *collections*, which are groups of objects stored in instances of classes designed for this purpose. After presenting an overview of this framework's architecture, this section introduces you to the various types (mainly located in the java.util package) that contribute to this architecture.

Architecture Overview

The Collection Framework's architecture is divided into three sections:

- *Core interfaces*: The framework provides core interfaces for manipulating collections independently of their implementations.

- *Implementation classes*: The framework provides classes that provide different core interface implementations to address performance and other requirements.

- *Utility classes*: The framework provides utility classes whose methods let you sort arrays, obtain synchronized collections, and perform other operations.

The core interfaces include java.lang.Iterable, Collection, List, Set, SortedSet, NavigableSet, Queue, Deque, Map, SortedMap, and NavigableMap. Collection extends Iterable; List, Set, and Queue each extend Collection; SortedSet extends Set; NavigableSet extends SortedSet; Deque extends Queue; SortedMap extends Map; and NavigableMap extends SortedMap.

Figure 5-1 illustrates the core interfaces hierarchy (arrows point to parent interfaces).

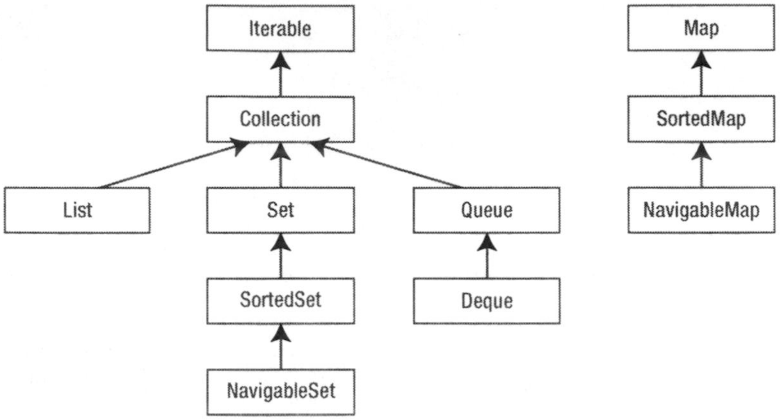

Figure 5-1. *The Collections Framework is based on a hierarchy of core interfaces.*

The framework's implementation classes include ArrayList, LinkedList, TreeSet, HashSet, LinkedHashSet, EnumSet, PriorityQueue, ArrayDeque, TreeMap, HashMap, LinkedHashMap, IdentityHashMap, WeakHashMap, and EnumMap. The name of each concrete class ends in a core interface name, identifying the core interface on which it is based.

■ **Note** Additional implementation classes are part of the concurrency utilities.

The framework's implementation classes also include the abstract AbstractCollection, AbstractList, AbstractSequentialList, AbstractSet, AbstractQueue, and AbstractMap classes. These classes offer skeletal implementations of the core interfaces to facilitate the creation of concrete implementation classes.

Finally, the framework provides two utility classes: Arrays and Collections.

Comparable Versus Comparator

A collection implementation stores its elements in some *order* (arrangement). This order may be unsorted, or it may be sorted according to some criterion (such as alphabetical, numerical, or chronological).

A sorted collection implementation defaults to storing its elements according to their *natural ordering*. For example, the natural ordering of String objects is *lexicographic* or *dictionary* (also known as alphabetical) order.

A collection cannot rely on equals() to dictate natural ordering because this method can only determine if two elements are equivalent. Instead, element classes must implement the java.lang.Comparable<T> interface and its int compareTo(T o) method.

■ **Note** According to `Comparable`'s Java documentation, this interface is considered to be part of the Collections Framework, even though it is a member of the `java.lang` package.

A sorted collection uses `compareTo()` to determine the natural ordering of this method's element argument o in a collection. `compareTo()` compares argument o with the current element (which is the element on which `compareTo()` was called) and does the following:

- It returns a negative value when the current element should precede o.

- It returns a zero value when the current element and o are the same.

- It returns a positive value when the current element should succeed o.

When you need to implement `Comparable`'s `compareTo()` method, there are some rules that you must follow. These rules, listed next, are similar to those shown in Chapter 2 for implementing the `equals()` method:

- *compareTo() must be reflexive.* For any nonnull reference value x, x.`compareTo`(x) must return 0.

- *compareTo() must be symmetric.* For any nonnull reference values x and y, x.`compareTo`(y) `==` -y.`compareTo`(x) must hold.

- *compareTo() must be transitive.* For any nonnull reference values x, y, and z, if x.`compareTo`(y) `>` 0 is true, and if y.`compareTo`(z) `>` 0 is true, then x.`compareTo`(z) `>` 0 must also be true.

Also, `compareTo()` should throw `NullPointerException` when the null reference is passed to this method. However, you do not need to check for null because this method throws `NullPointerException` when it attempts to access a null reference's members.

■ **Note** Before Java 5 and its introduction of generics, `compareTo()`'s argument was of type `java.lang.Object` and had to be cast to the appropriate type before the comparison could be made. The cast operator would throw a `java.lang.ClassCastException` instance when the argument's type was not compatible with the cast.

You might occasionally need to store in a collection objects that are sorted in some order that differs from their natural ordering. In this case, you would supply a comparator to provide that ordering.

A *comparator* is an object whose class implements the `Comparator` interface. This interface, whose generic type is `Comparator<T>`, provides the following pair of methods:

- `int compare(T o1, T o2)` compares both arguments for order. This method returns 0 when o1 equals o2, a negative value when o1 is less than o2, and a positive value when o1 is greater than o2.

- boolean equals(Object o) returns true when o "equals" this Comparator in that o is also a Comparator and imposes the same ordering. Otherwise, this method returns false.

Note Comparator declares equals() because this interface places an extra condition on this method's contract. *Additionally, this method can return true only if the specified object is also a comparator and it imposes the same ordering as this comparator.* You do not have to override Object's equals() method, but doing so *may improve performance by allowing programs to determine that two distinct comparators impose the same order.*

Chapter 3 provided an example that illustrated implementing Comparable, and you will discover another example later in this chapter. Also, this chapter will present examples of implementing Comparator.

Iterable and Collection

Most of the core interfaces are rooted in Iterable and its Collection subinterface. Their generic types are Iterable<T> and Collection<E>.

Iterable describes any object that can return its contained objects in some sequence. This interface declares an Iterator<T> iterator() method that returns an Iterator instance for iterating over all the contained objects.

Collection represents a collection of objects that are known as *elements*. This interface provides methods that are common to the Collection subinterfaces on which many collections are based. Table 5-1 describes these methods.

Table 5-1. Collection Methods

Method	Description
boolean add(E e)	Add element e to this collection. Return true if this collection was modified as a result; otherwise, return false. (Attempting to add e to a collection that does not permit duplicates and already contains a same-valued element results in e not being added.) This method throws java.lang.UnsupportedOperationException when add() is not supported, ClassCastException when e's class is not appropriate for this collection, java.lang.IllegalArgumentException when some property of e prevents it from being added to this collection, java.lang.NullPointerException when e contains the null reference and this collection does not support null elements, and java.lang.IllegalStateException when the element cannot be added at this time because of insertion restrictions.
	IllegalStateException signals that a method has been

invoked at an illegal or inappropriate time. In other words, the Java environment or Java application is not in an appropriate state for the requested operation. It is often thrown when you try to add an element to a bounded queue (a queue with a maximum length) and the queue is full.

`boolean addAll(Collection<? extends E> c)`	Add all elements of collection c to this collection. Return true if this collection was modified as the result; otherwise, return false. This method throws `UnsupportedOperationException` when this collection does not support `addAll()`, `ClassCastException` when the class of one of c's elements is inappropriate for this collection, `IllegalArgumentException` when some property of an element prevents it from being added to this collection, `NullPointerException` when c contains the null reference or when one of its elements is null and this collection does not support null elements, and `IllegalStateException` when not all the elements can be added at this time because of insertion restrictions.
`void clear()`	Remove all elements from this collection. This method throws `UnsupportedOperationException` when this collection does not support `clear()`.
`boolean contains(Object o)`	Return true when this collection contains o; otherwise, return false. This method throws `ClassCastException` when the class of o is inappropriate for this collection, and `NullPointerException` when o contains the null reference and this collection does not support null elements.
`boolean containsAll(Collection<?> c)`	Return true when this collection contains all the elements that are contained in the collection specified by c; otherwise, return false. This method throws `ClassCastException` when the class of one of c's elements is inappropriate for this collection, and `NullPointerException` when c contains the null reference or when one of its elements is null and this collection does not support null elements.
`boolean equals(Object o)`	Compare o with this collection and return true when o equals this collection; otherwise, return false.
`int hashCode()`	Return this collection's hash code. Equal collections have equal hash codes.
`boolean isEmpty()`	Return true when this collection contains no elements; otherwise, return false.
`Iterator<E> iterator()`	Return an `Iterator` instance for iterating over all of the elements contained in this collection. There are no

guarantees concerning the order in which the elements are returned (unless this collection is an instance of some class that provides a guarantee). This Iterable method is redeclared in Collection for convenience.

boolean remove(Object o)

Remove the element identified as o from this collection. Return true when the element is removed; otherwise, return false. This method throws UnsupportedOperationException when this collection does not support remove(), ClassCastException when the class of o is inappropriate for this collection, and NullPointerException when o contains the null reference and this collection does not support null elements.

boolean removeAll(Collection<?> c)

Remove all the elements from this collection that are also contained in collection c. Return true when this collection is modified by this operation; otherwise, return false. This method throws UnsupportedOperationException when this collection does not support removeAll(), ClassCastException when the class of one of c's elements is inappropriate for this collection, and NullPointerException when c contains the null reference or when one of its elements is null and this collection does not support null elements.

boolean retainAll(Collection<?> c)

Retain all the elements in this collection that are also contained in collection c. Return true when this collection is modified by this operation; otherwise, return false. This method throws UnsupportedOperationException when this collection does not support retainAll(), ClassCastException when the class of one of c's elements is inappropriate for this collection, and NullPointerException when c contains the null reference or when one of its elements is null and this collection does not support null elements.

int size()

Return the number of elements contained in this collection, or java.lang.Integer.MAX_VALUE when there are more than Integer.MAX_VALUE elements contained in the collection.

Object[] toArray()

Return an array containing all the elements stored in this collection. If this collection makes any guarantees as to what order its elements are returned in by its iterator, this method returns the elements in the same order.

The returned array is "safe" in that no references to it are maintained by this collection. (In other words, this method allocates a new array even when this collection is backed by an array.) The caller can safely modify the returned array.

`<T> T[] toArray(T[] a)`	Return an array containing all the elements in this collection; the runtime type of the returned array is that of the specified array. If the collection fits in the specified array, it is returned in the array. Otherwise, a new array is allocated with the runtime type of the specified array and the size of this collection. This method throws `NullPointerException` when `null` is passed to a, and `java.lang.ArrayStoreException` when a's runtime type is not a supertype of the runtime type of every element in this collection.

Table 5-1 reveals three exceptional things about various `Collection` methods. First, some methods can throw instances of the `UnsupportedOperationException` class. For example, `add()` throws `UnsupportedOperationException` when you attempt to add an object to an *immutable* (unmodifiable) collection (discussed later in this chapter).

Second, some of `Collection`'s methods can throw instances of the `ClassCastException` class. For example, `remove()` throws `ClassCastException` when you attempt to remove an entry (also known as mapping) from a tree-based map whose keys are `Strings`, but specify a non-`String` key instead.

Finally, `Collection`'s `add()` and `addAll()` methods throw `IllegalArgumentException` instances when some *property* (attribute) of the element to be added prevents it from being added to this collection. For example, a third-party collection class's `add()` and `addAll()` methods might throw this exception when they detect negative `Integer` values.

■ **Note** Perhaps you are wondering why `remove()` is declared to accept any `Object` argument instead of accepting only objects whose types are those of the collection. In other words, why is `remove()` not declared as `boolean remove(E e)`? Also, why are `containsAll()`, `removeAll()`, and `retainAll()` not declared with an argument of type `Collection<? extends E>`, to ensure that the collection argument only contains elements of the same type as the collection on which these methods are called? The answer to these questions is the need to maintain backward compatibility. The Collections Framework was introduced before Java 5 and its introduction of generics. To let legacy code written before version 5 continue to compile, these four methods were declared with weaker type constraints.

Iterator and the Enhanced For Statement

By extending `Iterable`, `Collection` inherits that interface's `iterator()` method, which makes it possible to iterate over a collection. `iterator()` returns an instance of a class that implements the `Iterator` interface, whose generic type is expressed as `Iterator<E>` and which declares the following three methods:

- `boolean hasNext()` returns true when this `Iterator` instance has more elements to return; otherwise, this method returns false.

- E next() returns the next element from the collection associated with this Iterator instance, or throws java.util.NoSuchElementException when there are no more elements to return.

- void remove() removes the last element returned by next() from the collection associated with this Iterator instance. This method can be called only once per next() call. The behavior of an Iterator instance is unspecified when the underlying collection is modified while iteration is in progress in any way other than by calling remove(). This method throws UnsupportedOperationException when it is not supported by this Iterator, and IllegalStateException when remove() has been called without a previous call to next() or when multiple remove() calls occur with no intervening next() calls.

The following example shows you how to iterate over a collection after calling iterator() to return an Iterator instance:

```
Collection<String> col = ... // This code does not compile because of the "...".
// Add elements to col.
Iterator iter = col.iterator();
while (iter.hasNext())
   System.out.println(iter.next());
```

The while loop repeatedly calls the iterator's hasNext() method to determine whether or not iteration should continue, and (if it should continue) the next() method to return the next element from the associated collection.

Because this idiom is commonly used, Java 5 introduced syntactic sugar to the for statement to simplify iteration in terms of the idiom. This sugar makes this statement appear like the foreach statement found in languages such as Perl, and is revealed in the following simplified equivalent of the previous example:

```
Collection<String> col = ... // This code does not compile because of the "...".
// Add elements to col.
for (String s: col)
   System.out.println(s);
```

This sugar hides col.iterator(), a method call that returns an Iterator instance for iterating over col's elements. It also hides calls to Iterator's hasNext() and next() methods on this instance. You interpret this sugar to read as follows: "for each String object in col, assign this object to s at the start of the loop iteration."

Note The enhanced for statement is also useful in an arrays context, in which it hides the array index variable. Consider the following example:

```
String[] verbs = { "run", "walk", "jump" };
for (String verb: verbs)
   System.out.println(verb);
```

This example, which reads as "for each String object in the verbs array, assign that object to verb at the start of the loop iteration," is equivalent to the following example:

```
String[] verbs = { "run", "walk", "jump" };
for (int i = 0; i < verbs.length; i++)
    System.out.println(verbs[i]);
```

The enhanced for statement is limited in that you cannot use this statement where access to the iterator is required to remove an element from a collection. Also, it is not usable where you must replace elements in a collection/array during a traversal, and it cannot be used where you must iterate over multiple collections or arrays in parallel.

■ **Tip** To have your classes support the enhanced for statement, design these classes to implement the java.lang.Iterable interface.

Autoboxing and Unboxing

Developers who believe that Java should support only reference types have complained about Java's support for primitive types. One area where the dichotomy of Java's type system is clearly seen is the Collections Framework: you can store objects but not primitive type-based values in collections.

Although you cannot directly store a primitive type-based value in a collection, you can indirectly store this value by first wrapping it in an object created from a primitive type wrapper class (see Chapter 4) such as Integer, and then storing this primitive type wrapper class instance in the collection—see the following example:

```
Collection<Integer> col = ...; // This code does not compile because of the "...".
int x = 27;
col.add(new Integer(x)); // Indirectly store int value 27 via an Integer object.
```

The reverse situation is also tedious. When you want to retrieve the int from col, you must invoke Integer's intValue() method (which, if you recall, is inherited from Integer's java.lang.Number superclass). Continuing on from this example, you would specify int y = col.iterator().next().intValue(); to assign the stored 32-bit integer to y.

To alleviate this tedium, Java 5 introduced autoboxing and unboxing, which are a pair of complementary syntactic sugar-based language features that make primitive values appear more like objects. (This "sleight of hand" is not complete because you cannot specify expressions such as 27.doubleValue().)

Autoboxing automatically *boxes* (wraps) a primitive value in an object of the appropriate primitive type wrapper class whenever a primitive type is specified but a reference is required. For example, you could change the example's third line to col.add(x); and have the compiler box x into an Integer object.

Unboxing automatically *unboxes* (unwraps) a primitive value from its wrapper object whenever a reference is specified but a primitive type is required. For example, you could specify int y = col.iterator().next(); and have the compiler unbox the returned Integer object to int value 27 prior to the assignment.

Although autoboxing and unboxing were introduced to simplify working with primitive values in a collections context, these language features can be used in other contexts, and this arbitrary use can lead to a problem that is difficult to understand without knowledge of what is happening behind the scenes. Consider the following example:

```
Integer i1 = 127;
Integer i2 = 127;
System.out.println(i1 == i2); // Output: true
System.out.println(i1 < i2); // Output: false
System.out.println(i1 > i2); // Output: false
System.out.println(i1+i2); // Output: 254
i1 = 30000;
i2 = 30000;
System.out.println(i1 == i2); // Output: false
System.out.println(i1 < i2); // Output: false
System.out.println(i1 > i2); // Output: false
i2 = 30001;
System.out.println(i1 < i2); // Output: true
System.out.println(i1+i2); // Output: 60001
```

With one exception, this example's output is as expected. The exception is the i1 == i2 comparison where each of i1 and i2 contains 30000. Instead of returning true, as is the case where each of i1 and i2 contains 127, i1 == i2 returns false. What is causing this problem?

Examine the generated code and you will discover that Integer i1 = 127; is converted to Integer i1 = Integer.valueOf(127); and Integer i2 = 127; is converted to Integer i2 = Integer.valueOf(127);. According to valueOf()'s Java documentation, this method takes advantage of caching to improve performance.

■ **Note** valueOf() is also used when adding a primitive value to a collection. For example, col.add(27) is converted to col.add(Integer.valueOf(27)).

Integer maintains an internal cache of unique Integer objects over a small range of values. The low bound of this range is -128, and the high bound defaults to 127. However, you can change the high bound by assigning a different value to system property java.lang.Integer.IntegerCache.high (via the java.lang.System class's String setProperty(String prop, String value) method—I demonstrated this method's getProperty() counterpart in Chapter 4).

■ **Note** Each of Byte, Long, and Short also maintains an internal cache of unique Byte, Long, and Short objects, respectively.

Because of the cache, each Integer.valueOf(127) call returns the same Integer object reference, which is why i1 == i2 (which compares references) evaluates to true. Because 30000 lies outside of the default range, each Integer.valueOf(30000) call returns a reference to a new Integer object, which is why i1 == i2 evaluates to false.

In contrast to == and !=, which do not unbox the boxed values prior to the comparison, operators such as <, >, and + unbox these values before performing their operations. As a result, i1 < i2 is converted to i1.intValue() < i2.intValue() and i1+i2 is converted to i1.intValue()+i2.intValue().

■ **Caution** Don't assume that autoboxing and unboxing are used in the context of the == and != operators.

List

A *list* is an ordered collection, which is also known as a *sequence*. Elements can be stored in and accessed from specific locations via integer indexes. Some of these elements may be duplicates or null (when the list's implementation allows null elements). Lists are described by the List interface, whose generic type is List<E>.

List extends Collection and redeclares its inherited methods, partly for convenience. It also redeclares iterator(), add(), remove(), equals(), and hashCode() to place extra conditions on their contracts. For example, List's contract for add() specifies that it appends an element to the end of the list, rather than adding the element to the collection.

List also declares Table 5-2's list-specific methods.

Table 5-2. List-specific Methods

Method	Description
void add(int index, E e)	Insert element e into this list at position index. Shift the element currently at this position (if any) and any subsequent elements to the right. This method throws UnsupportedOperationException when this list does not support add(), ClassCastException when e's class is inappropriate for this list, IllegalArgumentException when some property of e prevents it from being added to this list, NullPointerException when e contains the null reference and this list doesn't support null elements, and java.lang.IndexOutOfBoundsException when index is less than 0 or index is greater than size().
boolean addAll(int index, Collection<? extends E> c)	Insert all c's elements into this list starting at position index and in the order that they are returned by c's iterator. Shift the element currently at this position (if any) and any subsequent elements to the right. This method throws UnsupportedOperationException when this list does not support addAll(), ClassCastException when the class of one of c's elements is inappropriate for this list, IllegalArgumentException when some property of an

	element prevents it from being added to this list, NullPointerException when c contains the null reference or when one of its elements is null and this list does not support null elements, and IndexOutOfBoundsException when index is less than 0 or index is greater than size().
E get(int index)	Return the element stored in this list at position index. This method throws IndexOutOfBoundsException when index is less than 0 or index is greater than or equal to size().
int indexOf(Object o)	Return the index of the first occurrence of element o in this list, or -1 when this list does not contain the element. This method throws ClassCastException when o's class is inappropriate for this list, and NullPointerException when o contains the null reference and this list does not support null elements.
int lastIndexOf(Object o)	Return the index of the last occurrence of element o in this list, or -1 when this list does not contain the element. This method throws ClassCastException when o's class is inappropriate for this list, and NullPointerException when o contains the null reference and this list does not support null elements.
ListIterator<E> listIterator()	Return a list iterator over the elements in this list. The elements are returned in the same order as they appear in the list.
ListIterator<E> listIterator(int index)	Return a list iterator over this list's elements starting with the element at index. Elements are returned in the same order as they appear in the list. IndexOutOfBoundsException is thrown when index is less than 0 or index is greater than size().
E remove(int index)	Remove the element at position index from this list, shift any subsequent elements to the left, and return this element. UnsupportedOperationException is thrown when this list does not support remove(); IndexOutOfBoundsException is thrown when index is less than 0, or greater than or equal to size().
E set(int index, E e)	Replace the element at position index in this list with element e and return the element previously stored at this position. This method throws UnsupportedOperationException when this list does not support set(), ClassCastException when e's class is inappropriate for this list, IllegalArgumentException when some property of e prevents it from being added to this list, NullPointerException when e contains the null reference and this list does not support null elements, and

	IndexOutOfBoundsException when index is less than 0 or index is greater than or equal to size().
List<E> subList(int fromIndex, int toIndex)	Return a view (discussed later) of the portion of this list between fromIndex (inclusive) and toIndex (exclusive). (If fromIndex and toIndex are equal, the returned list is empty.) The returned list is backed by this list, so nonstructural changes in the returned list are reflected in this list and vice-versa. The returned list supports all the optional list methods (those methods that can throw UnsupportedOperationException) supported by this list. This method throws IndexOutOfBoundsException when fromIndex is less than 0, toIndex is greater than size(), or fromIndex is greater than toIndex.

Table 5-2 refers to the ListIterator interface, which is more flexible than its Iterator superinterface in that ListIterator provides methods for iterating over a list in either direction, modifying the list during iteration, and obtaining the iterator's current position in the list.

Note The Iterator and ListIterator instances that are returned by the iterator() and listIterator() methods in the ArrayList and LinkedList List implementation classes are *fail-fast*: when a list is structurally modified (by calling the implementation's add() method to add a new element, for example) after the iterator is created, in any way except through the iterator's own add() or remove() methods, the iterator throws ConcurrentModificationException. Therefore, in the face of concurrent modification, the iterator fails quickly and cleanly, rather than risking arbitrary, nondeterministic behavior at some time in the future.

ListIterator declares the following methods:

- void add(E e) inserts e into the list being iterated over. This element is inserted immediately before the next element that would be returned by next(), if any, and after the next element that would be returned by previous(), if any. This method throws UnsupportedOperationException when this list iterator does not support add(), ClassCastException when e's class is inappropriate for this list, and IllegalArgumentException when some property of e prevents it from being added to this list.

- boolean hasNext() returns true when this list iterator has more elements when traversing the list in the forward direction.

- boolean hasPrevious() returns true when this list iterator has more elements when traversing the list in the reverse direction.

- E next() returns the next element in this list and advances the cursor position. This method throws NoSuchElementException when there is no next element.

- int nextIndex() returns the index of the element that would be returned by a subsequent call to next(), or the size of the list when at the end of the list.

- E previous() returns the previous element in this list and moves the cursor position backwards. This method throws NoSuchElementException when there is no previous element.

- int previousIndex() returns the index of the element that would be returned by a subsequent call to previous(), or -1 when at the beginning of the list.

- void remove() removes from the list the last element that was returned by next() or previous(). This call can be made only once per call to next() or previous(). Furthermore, it can be made only when add() has not been called after the last call to next() or previous(). This method throws UnsupportedOperationException when this list iterator does not support remove(), and IllegalStateException when neither next() nor previous() has been called, or remove() or add() has already been called after the last call to next() or previous().

- void set(E e) replaces the last element returned by next() or previous() with element e. This call can be made only when neither remove() nor add() has been called after the last call to next() or previous(). This method throws UnsupportedOperationException when this list iterator does not support set(), ClassCastException when e's class is inappropriate for this list, IllegalArgumentException when some property of e prevents it from being added to this list, and IllegalStateException when neither next() nor previous() has been called, or remove() or add() has already been called after the last call to next() or previous().

A ListIterator instance does not have the concept of a current element. Instead, it has the concept of a *cursor* for navigating through a list. The nextIndex() and previousIndex() methods return the *cursor position*, which always lies between the element that would be returned by a call to previous() and the element that would be returned by a call to next(). A list iterator for a list of length *n* has *n*+1 possible cursor positions, as illustrated by each caret (^) as shown here:

```
                  Element(0)   Element(1)   Element(2)   ... Element(n-1)
cursor positions:  ^           ^            ^            ^                ^
```

The remove() and set() methods are not defined in terms of the cursor position; they are defined to operate on the last element returned by a call to next() or previous().

Note You can mix calls to next() and previous() as long as you are careful. Keep in mind that the first call to previous() returns the same element as the last call to next(). Furthermore, the first call to next() following a sequence of calls to previous() returns the same element as the last call to previous().

Table 5-2's description of the subList() method refers to the concept of a *view*, which is a list that is backed by another list. Changes that are made to the view are reflected in this backing list. The view can cover the entire list or, as subList()'s name implies, only part of the list.

The subList() method is useful for performing *range-view* operations over a list in a compact manner. For example, list.subList(fromIndex, toIndex).clear(); removes a range of elements from list where the first element is located at fromIndex and the last element is located at toIndex-1.

■ **Caution** A view's meaning becomes undefined when changes are made to the backing list. Therefore, you should only use subList() temporarily, whenever you need to perform a sequence of range operations on the backing list.

ArrayList

The ArrayList class provides a list implementation that is based on an internal array (see Chapters 1 and 2). As a result, access to the list's elements is fast. However, because elements must be moved to open a space for insertion or to close a space after deletion, insertions and deletions of elements is slow.

ArrayList supplies three constructors:

- ArrayList() creates an empty array list with an initial *capacity* (storage space) of ten elements. Once this capacity is reached, a larger array is created, elements from the current array are copied into the larger array, and the larger array becomes the new current array. This process repeats as more elements are added to the array list.

- ArrayList(Collection<? extends E> c) creates an array list containing c's elements in the order in which they are returned by c's iterator. NullPointerException is thrown when c contains the null reference.

- ArrayList(int initialCapacity) creates an empty array list with an initial capacity of initialCapacity elements. IllegalArgumentException is thrown when initialCapacity is negative.

Listing 5-1 demonstrates an array list.

Listing 5-1. A demonstration of an array-based list

```
import java.util.ArrayList;
import java.util.List;

class ArrayListDemo
{
   public static void main(String[] args)
   {
      List<String> ls = new ArrayList<>();
      String[] weekDays = {"Sun", "Mon", "Tue", "Wed", "Thu", "Fri", "Sat"};
      for (String weekDay: weekDays)
         ls.add(weekDay);
      dump("ls:", ls);
      ls.set(ls.indexOf("Wed"), "Wednesday");
      dump("ls:", ls);
```

```
        ls.remove(ls.lastIndexOf("Fri"));
        dump("ls:", ls);
    }
    static void dump(String title, List<String> ls)
    {
        System.out.print(title+" ");
        for (String s: ls)
            System.out.print(s+" ");
        System.out.println();
    }
}
```

The List<String> ls = new ArrayList<>(); assignment reveals a couple of items to note:

- I've declared variable ls to be of List<String> interface type, and have assigned to this variable a reference to an instance of the ArrayList class that implements this interface. When working with the Collections Framework, it is common practice to declare variables to be of interface type. Doing so eliminates extensive code changes when you need to work with a different implementation class; for example, List<String> ls = new LinkedList<>();. Check out Chapter 2's "Why Use Interfaces?" section for more information about this practice.

- The *diamond operator* <> (which is new in Java 7) reduces verbosity by forcing the compiler to infer actual type arguments for the constructors of generic classes. Without this operator, I would need to specify String as the actual type argument passed to ArrayList<E>, resulting in the more verbose List<String> ls = new ArrayList<String>(); instead of the shorter List<String> ls = new ArrayList<>();. (I don't regard the diamond operator as a true operator, which is why I don't include it in Chapter 1's table of operators—Table 1-3.)

The dump() method's enhanced for statement uses iterator(), hasNext(), and next() behind the scenes.

When you run this application, it generates the following output:

```
ls: Sun Mon Tue Wed Thu Fri Sat
ls: Sun Mon Tue Wednesday Thu Fri Sat
ls: Sun Mon Tue Wednesday Thu Sat
```

LinkedList

The LinkedList class provides a list implementation that is based on linked nodes. Because links must be traversed, access to the list's elements is slow. However, because only node references need to be changed, insertions and deletions of elements is fast. (I will introduce you to nodes later in this chapter.)

LinkedList supplies two constructors:

- LinkedList() creates an empty linked list.

- LinkedList(Collection<? extends E> c) creates a linked list containing c's elements in the order in which they are returned by c's iterator. NullPointerException is thrown when c contains the null reference.

Listing 5-2 demonstrates a linked list.

Listing 5-2. A demonstration of a linked list of nodes

```java
import java.util.LinkedList;
import java.util.List;
import java.util.ListIterator;

class LinkedListDemo
{
   public static void main(String[] args)
   {
      List<String> ls = new LinkedList<>();
      String[] weekDays = {"Sun", "Mon", "Tue", "Wed", "Thu", "Fri", "Sat"};
      for (String weekDay: weekDays)
         ls.add(weekDay);
      dump("ls:", ls);
      ls.add(1, "Sunday");
      ls.add(3, "Monday");
      ls.add(5, "Tuesday");
      ls.add(7, "Wednesday");
      ls.add(9, "Thursday");
      ls.add(11, "Friday");
      ls.add(13, "Saturday");
      dump("ls:", ls);
      ListIterator<String> li = ls.listIterator(ls.size());
      while (li.hasPrevious())
         System.out.print(li.previous()+" ");
      System.out.println();
   }
   static void dump(String title, List<String> ls)
   {
      System.out.print(title+" ");
      for (String s: ls)
         System.out.print(s+" ");
      System.out.println();
   }
}
```

This application demonstrates that each successive add() method call must increase its index by 2 to account for the previously added element when adding longer weekday names to the list. It also shows you how to output a list in reverse order: return a list iterator with its cursor initialized past the end of the list and repeatedly call previous().

When you run this application, it generates the following output:

```
ls: Sun Mon Tue Wed Thu Fri Sat
ls: Sun Sunday Mon Monday Tue Tuesday Wed Wednesday Thu Thursday Fri Friday Sat Saturday
Saturday Sat Friday Fri Thursday Thu Wednesday Wed Tuesday Tue Monday Mon Sunday Sun
```

Set

A *set* is a collection that contains no duplicate elements. In other words, a set contains no pair of elements e1 and e2 such that e1.equals(e2) returns true. Furthermore, a set can contain at most one null element. Sets are described by the Set interface, whose generic type is Set<E>.

Set extends Collection and redeclares its inherited methods, for convenience and also to add stipulations to the contracts for add(), equals(), and hashCode(), to address how they behave in a set context. Also, Set's documentation states that all constructors of implementation classes must create sets that contain no duplicate elements.

Set does not introduce new methods.

TreeSet

The TreeSet class provides a set implementation that is based on a tree data structure. As a result, elements are stored in sorted order. However, accessing these elements is somewhat slower than with the other Set implementations (which are not sorted) because links must be traversed.

■ **Note** Check out Wikipedia's "Tree (data structure)" entry

(http://en.wikipedia.org/wiki/Tree_(data_structure)) to learn about trees.

TreeSet supplies four constructors:

- TreeSet() creates a new, empty tree set that is sorted according to the natural ordering of its elements. All elements inserted into the set must implement the Comparable interface.

- TreeSet(Collection<? extends E> c) creates a new tree set containing c's elements, sorted according to the natural ordering of its elements. All elements inserted into the new set must implement the Comparable interface. This constructor throws ClassCastException when c's elements do not implement Comparable or are not mutually comparable, and NullPointerException when c contains the null reference.

- TreeSet(Comparator<? super E> comparator) creates a new, empty tree set that is sorted according to the specified comparator. Passing null to comparator implies that natural ordering will be used.

- TreeSet(SortedSet<E> s) creates a new tree set containing the same elements and using the same ordering as s. (I discuss sorted sets later in this chapter.) This constructor throws NullPointerException when s contains the null reference.

Listing 5-3 demonstrates a tree set.

Listing 5-3. A demonstration of a tree set with String elements sorted according to their natural ordering

```
import java.util.Set;
import java.util.TreeSet;

class TreeSetDemo
{
   public static void main(String[] args)
   {
```

```
        Set<String> ss = new TreeSet<>();
        String[] fruits = {"apples", "pears", "grapes", "bananas", "kiwis"};
        for (String fruit: fruits)
            ss.add(fruit);
        dump("ss:", ss);
    }
    static void dump(String title, Set<String> ss)
    {
        System.out.print(title+" ");
        for (String s: ss)
            System.out.print(s+" ");
        System.out.println();
    }
}
```

Because String implements Comparable, it is legal for this application to use the TreeSet() constructor to insert the contents of the fruits array into the set.

When you run this application, it generates the following output:

```
ss: apples bananas grapes kiwis pears
```

HashSet

The HashSet class provides a set implementation that is backed by a hashtable data structure (implemented as a HashMap instance, discussed later, which provides a quick way to determine if an element has already been stored in this structure). Although this class provides no ordering guarantees for its elements, HashSet is much faster than TreeSet. Furthermore, HashSet permits the null reference to be stored in its instances.

■ **Note** Check out Wikipedia's "Hash table" entry (http://en.wikipedia.org/wiki/Hash_table) to learn about hashtables.

HashSet supplies four constructors:

- HashSet() creates a new, empty hashset where the backing HashMap instance has an initial capacity of 16 and a load factor of 0.75. You will learn what these items mean when I discuss HashMap later in this chapter.

- HashSet(Collection<? extends E> c) creates a new hashset containing c's elements. The backing HashMap has an initial capacity sufficient to contain c's elements and a load factor of 0.75. This constructor throws NullPointerException when c contains the null reference.

- HashSet(int initialCapacity) creates a new, empty hashset where the backing HashMap instance has the capacity specified by initialCapacity and a load factor of 0.75. This constructor throws IllegalArgumentException when initialCapacity's value is less than 0.

- HashSet(int initialCapacity, float loadFactor) creates a new, empty hashset where the backing HashMap instance has the capacity specified by initialCapacity and the load factor specified by loadFactor. This constructor throws IllegalArgumentException when initialCapacity is less than 0 or when loadFactor is less than or equal to 0.

Listing 5-4 demonstrates a hashset.

Listing 5-4. A demonstration of a hashset with String elements unordered

```java
import java.util.HashSet;
import java.util.Set;

class HashSetDemo
{
   public static void main(String[] args)
   {
      Set<String> ss = new HashSet<>();
      String[] fruits = {"apples", "pears", "grapes", "bananas", "kiwis",
                          "pears", null};
      for (String fruit: fruits)
         ss.add(fruit);
      dump("ss:", ss);
   }
   static void dump(String title, Set<String> ss)
   {
      System.out.print(title+" ");
      for (String s: ss)
         System.out.print(s+" ");
      System.out.println();
   }
}
```

In Listing 5-3's TreeSetDemo application, I did not add null to the fruits array because TreeSet throws NullPointerException when it detects an attempt to add this element. In contrast, HashSet permits null to be added, which is why Listing 5-4 includes null in HashSetDemo's fruits array.

When you run this application, it generates unordered output such as the following:

```
ss: null grapes bananas kiwis pears apples
```

Suppose you want to add instances of your classes to a hashset. As with String, your classes must override equals() and hashCode(); otherwise, duplicate class instances can be stored in the hashset. For example, Listing 5-5 presents the source code to an application whose Planet class overrides equals() but fails to also override hashCode().

Listing 5-5. A custom Planet class not overriding hashCode()

```java
import java.util.HashSet;
import java.util.Set;

class CustomClassAndHashSet
{
   public static void main(String[] args)
```

```
    {
        Set<Planet> sp = new HashSet<>();
        sp.add(new Planet("Mercury"));
        sp.add(new Planet("Venus"));
        sp.add(new Planet("Earth"));
        sp.add(new Planet("Mars"));
        sp.add(new Planet("Jupiter"));
        sp.add(new Planet("Saturn"));
        sp.add(new Planet("Uranus"));
        sp.add(new Planet("Neptune"));
        sp.add(new Planet("Fomalhaut b"));
        Planet p1 = new Planet("51 Pegasi b");
        sp.add(p1);
        Planet p2 = new Planet("51 Pegasi b");
        sp.add(p2);
        System.out.println(p1.equals(p2));
        System.out.println(sp);
    }
}
class Planet
{
    private String name;
    Planet(String name)
    {
        this.name = name;
    }
    @Override
    public boolean equals(Object o)
    {
        if (!(o instanceof Planet))
            return false;
        Planet p = (Planet) o;
        return p.name.equals(name);
    }
    String getName()
    {
        return name;
    }
    @Override
    public String toString()
    {
        return name;
    }
}
```

Listing 5-5's Planet class declares a single name field of type String. Although it might seem pointless to declare Planet with a single String field because I could refactor this listing to remove Planet and work with String, I might want to introduce additional fields to Planet (perhaps to store a planet's mass and other characteristics) in the future.

When you run this application, it generates unordered output such as the following:

```
true
```

[Venus, Fomalhaut b, Uranus, Mars, Neptune, Jupiter, Earth, Mercury, Saturn, 51 Pegasi↵ b, 51 Pegasi b]

This output reveals two 51 Pegasi b elements in the hashset. Although these elements are equal from the perspective of the overriding equals() method (the first output line, true, proves this point), overriding equals() is not enough to avoid duplicate elements being stored in a hashset: you must also override hashCode().

The easiest way to override hashCode() in Listing 5-5's Planet class is to have the overriding method call the name field's hashCode() method and return its value. (This technique only works with a class whose single reference field's class provides a valid hashCode() method.) Listing 5-6 presents this overriding hashCode() method.

Listing 5-6. A custom Planet class overriding hashCode()

```java
import java.util.HashSet;
import java.util.Set;

class CustomClassAndHashSet
{
   public static void main(String[] args)
   {
      Set<Planet> sp = new HashSet<>();
      sp.add(new Planet("Mercury"));
      sp.add(new Planet("Venus"));
      sp.add(new Planet("Earth"));
      sp.add(new Planet("Mars"));
      sp.add(new Planet("Jupiter"));
      sp.add(new Planet("Saturn"));
      sp.add(new Planet("Uranus"));
      sp.add(new Planet("Neptune"));
      sp.add(new Planet("Fomalhaut b"));
      Planet p1 = new Planet("51 Pegasi b");
      sp.add(p1);
      Planet p2 = new Planet("51 Pegasi b");
      sp.add(p2);
      System.out.println(p1.equals(p2));
      System.out.println(sp);
   }
}
class Planet
{
   private String name;
   Planet(String name)
   {
      this.name = name;
   }
   @Override
   public boolean equals(Object o)
   {
      if (!(o instanceof Planet))
         return false;
      Planet p = (Planet) o;
```

CHAPTER 5 ■ COLLECTING OBJECTS

```
        return p.name.equals(name);
    }
    String getName()
    {
        return name;
    }
    @Override
    public int hashCode()
    {
        return name.hashCode();
    }
    @Override
    public String toString()
    {
        return name;
    }
}
```

Compile Listing 5-6 (javac CustomClassAndHashSet.java) and run the application (java CustomClassAndHashSet). You will observe output (similar to that shown below) that reveals no duplicate elements:

```
true
[Saturn, Earth, Uranus, Fomalhaut b, 51 Pegasi b, Venus, Jupiter, Mercury, Mars,↵ Neptune]
```

■ **Note** LinkedHashSet is a subclass of HashSet that uses a linked list to store its elements. As a result, LinkedHashSet's iterator returns elements in the order in which they were inserted. For example, if Listing 5-4 had specified Set<String> ss = new LinkedHashSet<>();, the application's output would have been ss: apples pears grapes bananas kiwis null. Also, LinkedHashSet offers slower performance than HashSet and faster performance than TreeSet.

EnumSet

Chapter 3 introduced you to traditional enumerated types and their enum replacement. (An *enum* is an enumerated type that is expressed via reserved word enum.) The following example demonstrates the traditional enumerated type:

```
static final int SUNDAY = 1;
static final int MONDAY = 2;
static final int TUESDAY = 4;
static final int WEDNESDAY = 8;
static final int THURSDAY = 16;
static final int FRIDAY = 32;
static final int SATURDAY = 64;
```

Although the enum has many advantages over the traditional enumerated type, the traditional enumerated type is less awkward to use when combining constants into a set; for example, `static final int DAYS_OFF = SUNDAY | MONDAY;`.

DAYS_OFF is an example of an integer-based, fixed-length *bitset*, which is a set of bits where each bit indicates that its associated member belongs to the set when the bit is set to 1, and is absent from the set when the bit is set to 0.

Note An `int`-based bitset cannot contain more than 32 members because `int` has a size of 32 bits. Similarly, a `long`-based bitset cannot contain more than 64 members because `long` has a size of 64 bits.

This bitset is formed by bitwise inclusive ORing the traditional enumerated type's integer constants together via the bitwise inclusive OR operator (|): you could also use +. Each constant must be a unique power of two (starting with one) because otherwise it is impossible to distinguish between the members of this bitset.

To determine if a constant belongs to the bitset, create an expression that involves the bitwise AND operator (&). For example, ((DAYS_OFF&MONDAY) == MONDAY) bitwise ANDs DAYS_OFF (3) with MONDAY (2), which results in 2. This value is compared via == with MONDAY (2), and the result of the expression is true: MONDAY is a member of the DAYS_OFF bitset.

You can accomplish the same task with an enum by instantiating an appropriate Set implementation class and calling the add() method multiple times to store the constants in the set. Listing 5-7 illustrates this more awkward alternative.

Listing 5-7. Creating the Set equivalent of DAYS_OFF

```
import java.util.Set;
import java.util.TreeSet;

enum Weekday
{
   SUNDAY, MONDAY, TUESDAY, WEDNESDAY, THURSDAY, FRIDAY, SATURDAY
}
class DaysOff
{
   public static void main(String[] args)
   {
      Set<Weekday> daysOff = new TreeSet<>();
      daysOff.add(Weekday.SUNDAY);
      daysOff.add(Weekday.MONDAY);
      System.out.println(daysOff);
   }
}
```

When you run this application, it generates the following output:

```
[SUNDAY, MONDAY]
```

As well as being more awkward to use (and verbose) than the bitset, the Set alternative requires more memory to store each constant and is not as fast. Because of these problems, EnumSet was introduced.

The EnumSet class provides a Set implementation that is based on a bitset. Its elements are constants that must come from the same enum, which is specified when the enum set is created. Null elements are not permitted; any attempt to store a null element results in a thrown NullPointerException.

Listing 5-8 demonstrates EnumSet.

Listing 5-8. *Creating the EnumSet equivalent of DAYS_OFF*

```java
import java.util.EnumSet;
import java.util.Iterator;
import java.util.Set;

enum Weekday
{
    SUNDAY, MONDAY, TUESDAY, WEDNESDAY, THURSDAY, FRIDAY, SATURDAY
}
class EnumSetDemo
{
    public static void main(String[] args)
    {
        Set<Weekday> daysOff = EnumSet.of(Weekday.SUNDAY, Weekday.MONDAY);
        Iterator<Weekday> iter = daysOff.iterator();
        while (iter.hasNext())
            System.out.println(iter.next());
    }
}
```

EnumSet, whose generic type is EnumSet<E extends Enum<E>>, provides various class methods for conveniently constructing enum sets. For example, <E extends Enum<E>> EnumSet<E> of(E e1, E e2) returns an EnumSet instance consisting of elements e1 and e2. In this example, those elements are Weekday.SUNDAY and Weekday.MONDAY.

When you run this application, it generates the following output:

```
SUNDAY
MONDAY
```

```
Set<Weekday> allWeekDays = EnumSet.allOf(Weekday.class);
```

Similarly, `range()` returns an `EnumSet` instance containing a range of an enum's elements (with the range's limits as specified by this method's two arguments):

```
for (WeekDay wd : EnumSet.range(WeekDay.MONDAY, WeekDay.FRIDAY))
    System.out.println(wd);
```

SortedSet

`TreeSet` is an example of a *sorted set*, which is a set that maintains its elements in ascending order, sorted according to their natural ordering or according to a comparator that is supplied when the sorted set is created. Sorted sets are described by the `SortedSet` interface.

`SortedSet`, whose generic type is `SortedSet<E>`, extends `Set`. With two exceptions, the methods it inherits from `Set` behave identically on sorted sets as on other sets:

- The `Iterator` instance returned from `iterator()` traverses the sorted set in ascending element order.

- The array returned by `toArray()` contains the sorted set's elements in order.

■ **Note** Although not guaranteed, the `toString()` methods of `SortedSet` implementations in the Collections Framework (such as `TreeSet`) return a string containing all the sorted set's elements in order.

SortedSet's documentation requires that an implementation must provide the four standard constructors that I presented in my discussion of `TreeSet`. Furthermore, implementations of this interface must implement the methods that are described in Table 5-3.

Table 5-3. SortedSet-specific Methods

Method	Description
Comparator<? super E> comparator()	Return the comparator used to order the elements in this set, or null when this set uses the natural ordering of its elements.
E first()	Return the first (lowest) element currently in this set, or throw a NoSuchElementException instance when this set is empty.

SortedSet<E> headSet(E toElement)	Return a view of that portion of this set whose elements are strictly less than toElement. The returned set is backed by this set, so changes in the returned set are reflected in this set and vice versa. The returned set supports all optional set operations that this set supports. This method throws ClassCastException when toElement is not compatible with this set's comparator (or, when the set has no comparator, when toElement does not implement Comparable), NullPointerException when toElement is null and this set does not permit null elements, and IllegalArgumentException when this set has a restricted range and toElement lies outside of this range's bounds.
E last()	Return the last (highest) element currently in this set, or throw a NoSuchElementException instance when this set is empty.
SortedSet<E> subSet(E fromElement, E toElement)	Return a view of the portion of this set whose elements range from fromElement, inclusive, to toElement, exclusive. (When fromElement and toElement are equal, the returned set is empty.) The returned set is backed by this set, so changes in the returned set are reflected in this set and vice versa. The returned set supports all optional set operations that this set supports. This method throws ClassCastException when fromElement and toElement cannot be compared to one another using this set's comparator (or, when the set has no comparator, using natural ordering), NullPointerException when fromElement or toElement is null and this set does not permit null elements, and IllegalArgumentException when fromElement is greater than toElement or when this set has a restricted range and fromElement or toElement lies outside of this range's bounds.
SortedSet<E> tailSet(E fromElement)	Return a view of that portion of this set whose elements are greater than or equal to fromElement. The returned set is backed by this set, so changes in the returned set are reflected in this set and vice versa. The returned set supports all optional set operations that this set supports. This method throws ClassCastException when fromElement is not compatible with this set's comparator (or, when the set has no comparator, when fromElement does not implement Comparable), NullPointerException when fromElement is null and this set does not permit null elements, and IllegalArgumentException when this set has a restricted range and fromElement lies outside of the range's bounds.

The set-based range views returned from headSet(), subSet(), and tailSet() are analogous to the list-based range view returned from List's subList() method except that a set-based range view remains valid even when the backing sorted set is modified. As a result, a set-based range view can be used for a lengthy period of time.

■ **Note** Unlike a list-based range view whose endpoints are elements in the backing list, the endpoints of a set-based range view are absolute points in element space, allowing a set-based range view to serve as a window onto a portion of the set's element space. Any changes made to the set-based range view are written back to the backing sorted set and vice versa.

Each range view returned by headSet(), subSet(), or tailSet() is *half open* because it does not include its high endpoint (headSet() and subSet()) or its low endpoint (tailSet()). For the first two methods, the high endpoint is specified by argument toElement; for the last method, the low endpoint is specified by argument fromElement.

■ **Note** You could also regard the returned range view as being *half closed* because it includes only one of its endpoints.

Listing 5-9 demonstrates a sorted set based on a tree set.

Listing 5-9. A sorted set of fruit and vegetable names

```java
import java.util.SortedSet;
import java.util.TreeSet;

class SortedSetDemo
{
    public static void main(String[] args)
    {
        SortedSet<String> sss = new TreeSet<>();
        String[] fruitAndVeg =
        {
            "apple", "potato", "turnip", "banana", "corn", "carrot", "cherry",
            "pear", "mango", "strawberry", "cucumber", "grape", "banana",
            "kiwi", "radish", "blueberry", "tomato", "onion", "raspberry",
            "lemon", "pepper", "squash", "melon", "zucchini", "peach", "plum",
            "turnip", "onion", "nectarine"
        };
        System.out.println("Array size = "+fruitAndVeg.length);
        for (String fruitVeg: fruitAndVeg)
            sss.add(fruitVeg);
        dump("sss:", sss);
        System.out.println("Sorted set size = "+sss.size());
        System.out.println("First element = "+sss.first());
```

```
            System.out.println("Last element = "+sss.last());
            System.out.println("Comparator = "+sss.comparator());
            dump("hs:", sss.headSet("n"));
            dump("ts:", sss.tailSet("n"));
            System.out.println("Count of p-named fruits & vegetables = "+
                              sss.subSet("p", "q").size());
            System.out.println("Incorrect count of c-named fruits & vegetables = "+
                              sss.subSet("carrot", "cucumber").size());
            System.out.println("Correct count of c-named fruits & vegetables = "+
                              sss.subSet("carrot", "cucumber\0").size());
      }
      static void dump(String title, SortedSet<String> sss)
      {
            System.out.print(title+" ");
            for (String s: sss)
                System.out.print(s+" ");
            System.out.println();
      }
}
```

When you run this application, it generates the following output:

```
Array size = 29
sss: apple banana blueberry carrot cherry corn cucumber grape kiwi lemon mango melon⏎
nectarine onion peach pear pepper plum potato radish raspberry squash strawberry⏎ tomato
turnip zucchini
Sorted set size = 26
First element = apple
Last element = zucchini
Comparator = null
hs: apple banana blueberry carrot cherry corn cucumber grape kiwi lemon mango melon⏎
ts: nectarine onion peach pear pepper plum potato radish raspberry squash strawberry⏎ tomato
turnip zucchini
Count of p-named fruits & vegetables = 5
Incorrect count of c-named fruits & vegetables = 3
Correct count of c-named fruits & vegetables = 4
```

This output reveals that the sorted set's size is less than the array's size because a set cannot contain duplicate elements: the duplicate banana, turnip, and onion elements are not stored in the sorted set.

The comparator() method returns null because the sorted set was not created with a comparator. Instead, the sorted set relies on the natural ordering of String elements to store them in sorted order.

The headSet() and tailSet() methods are called with argument "n" to return, respectively, a set of elements whose names begin with a letter that is strictly less than n, and a letter that is greater than or equal to n.

Finally, the output shows you that you must be careful when passing an upper limit to subSet(). As you can see, ss.subSet("carrot", "cucumber") does not include cucumber in the returned range view because cucumber is subSet()'s high endpoint.

To include cucumber in the range view, you need to form a *closed range* or *closed interval* (both endpoints are included). With String objects, you accomplish this task by appending \0 to the string. For example, ss.subSet("carrot", "cucumber\0") includes cucumber because it is less than cucumber\0.

This same technique can be applied wherever you need to form an *open range* or *open interval* (neither endpoint is included). For example, ss.subSet("carrot\0", "cucumber") does not include carrot because it is less than carrot\0. Furthermore, it does not include high endpoint cucumber.

■ **Note** When you want to create closed and open ranges for elements created from your own classes, you need to provide some form of predecessor() and successor() methods that return an element's predecessor and successor.

You need to be careful when designing classes that work with sorted sets. For example, the class must implement Comparable when you plan to store the class's instances in a sorted set where these elements are sorted according to their natural ordering. Consider Listing 5-10.

Listing 5-10. A custom Employee class not implementing Comparable

```
import java.util.SortedSet;
import java.util.TreeSet;

class CustomClassAndSortedSet
{
    public static void main(String[] args)
    {
        SortedSet<Employee> sse = new TreeSet<>();
        sse.add(new Employee("Sally Doe"));
        sse.add(new Employee("Bob Doe")); // ClassCastException thrown here
        sse.add(new Employee("John Doe"));
        System.out.println(sse);
    }
}
class Employee
{
    private String name;
    Employee(String name)
    {
        this.name = name;
    }
    @Override
    public String toString()
    {
        return name;
    }
}
```

When you run this application, it generates the following output:

```
Exception in thread "main" java.lang.ClassCastException: Employee cannot be cast to↵
java.lang.Comparable
        at java.util.TreeMap.compare(TreeMap.java:1188)
```

```
        at java.util.TreeMap.put(TreeMap.java:531)
        at java.util.TreeSet.add(TreeSet.java:255)
        at CustomClassAndSortedSet.main(CustomClassAndSortedSet.java:9)
```

The ClassCastException instance is thrown during the second add() method call because the sorted set implementation, an instance of TreeSet, is unable to call the second Employee element's compareTo() method, because Employee does not implement Comparable.

The solution to this problem is to have the class implement Comparable, which is exactly what is revealed in Listing 5-11.

Listing 5-11. Making Employee elements comparable

```java
import java.util.SortedSet;
import java.util.TreeSet;

class CustomClassAndSortedSet
{
    public static void main(String[] args)
    {
        SortedSet<Employee> sse = new TreeSet<>();
        sse.add(new Employee("Sally Doe"));
        sse.add(new Employee("Bob Doe"));
        Employee e1 = new Employee("John Doe");
        Employee e2 = new Employee("John Doe");
        sse.add(e1);
        sse.add(e2);
        System.out.println(sse);
        System.out.println(e1.equals(e2));
    }
}
class Employee implements Comparable<Employee>
{
    private String name;
    Employee(String name)
    {
        this.name = name;
    }
    @Override
    public int compareTo(Employee e)
    {
        return name.compareTo(e.name);
    }
    @Override
    public String toString()
    {
        return name;
    }
}
```

Listing 5-11's main() method differs from Listing 5-10 in that it also creates two Employee objects initialized to "John Doe", adds these objects to the sorted set, and compares these objects for equality via equals(). Furthermore, Listing 5-11 declares Employee to implement Comparable, introducing a compareTo() method into Employee.

When you run this application, it generates the following output:

```
[Bob Doe, John Doe, Sally Doe]
false
```

This output shows that only one "John Doe" Employee object is stored in the sorted set. After all, a set cannot contain duplicate elements. However, the false value (resulting from the equals() comparison) also shows that the sorted set's natural ordering is inconsistent with equals(), which violates SortedSet's contract:

The ordering maintained by a sorted set (whether or not an explicit comparator is provided) must be consistent with equals() if the sorted set is to correctly implement the Set interface. This is so because the Set interface is defined in terms of the equals() operation, but a sorted set performs all element comparisons using its compareTo() (or compare()) method, so two elements that are deemed equal by this method are, from the standpoint of the sorted set, equal.

Because the application works correctly, why should SortedSet's contract matter? Although the contract does not appear to matter with respect to the TreeSet implementation of SortedSet, perhaps it will matter in the context of a third-party class that implements this interface.

Listing 5-12 shows you how to correct this problem and make Employee instances work with any implementation of a sorted set.

Listing 5-12. A contract-compliant Employee class

```java
import java.util.SortedSet;
import java.util.TreeSet;

class CustomClassAndSortedSet
{
    public static void main(String[] args)
    {
        SortedSet<Employee> sse = new TreeSet<>();
        sse.add(new Employee("Sally Doe"));
        sse.add(new Employee("Bob Doe"));
        Employee e1 = new Employee("John Doe");
        Employee e2 = new Employee("John Doe");
        sse.add(e1);
        sse.add(e2);
        System.out.println(sse);
        System.out.println(e1.equals(e2));
    }
}
class Employee implements Comparable<Employee>
{
    private String name;
    Employee(String name)
    {
        this.name = name;
    }
    @Override
    public int compareTo(Employee e)
    {
```

```
        return name.compareTo(e.name);
    }
    @Override
    public boolean equals(Object o)
    {
        if (!(o instanceof Employee))
            return false;
        Employee e = (Employee) o;
        return e.name.equals(name);
    }
    @Override
    public String toString()
    {
        return name;
    }
}
```

Listing 5-12 corrects the SortedSet contract violation by overriding equals(). Run the resulting application and you will observe [Bob Doe, John Doe, Sally Doe] as the first line of output and true as the second line: the sorted set's natural ordering is now consistent with equals().

Note Although it is important to override hashCode() whenever you override equals(), I did not override hashCode() (although I overrode equals()) in Listing 5-12's Employee class to emphasize that tree-based sorted sets ignore hashCode().

NavigableSet

TreeSet is an example of a *navigable set*, which is a sorted set that can be iterated over in descending order as well as ascending order, and which can report closest matches for given search targets. Navigable sets are described by the NavigableSet interface, whose generic type is NavigableSet<E>, which extends SortedSet, and which is described in Table 5-4.

Table 5-4. NavigableSet-specific Methods

Method	Description
E ceiling(E e)	Return the least element in this set greater than or equal to e, or null when there is no such element. This method throws ClassCastException when e cannot be compared with the elements currently in the set, and NullPointerException when e is null and this set does not permit null elements.
Iterator<E> descendingIterator()	Return an iterator over the elements in this set, in descending order. Equivalent in effect to descendingSet().iterator().

NavigableSet<E> descendingSet()	Return a reverse order view of the elements contained in this set. The descending set is backed by this set, so changes to the set are reflected in the descending set and vice versa. If either set is modified (except through the iterator's own remove() operation) while iterating over the set, the results of the iteration are undefined.
E floor(E e)	Return the greatest element in this set less than or equal to e, or null when there is no such element. This method throws ClassCastException when e cannot be compared with the elements currently in the set, and NullPointerException when e is null and this set does not permit null elements.
NavigableSet<E> headSet(E toElement, boolean inclusive)	Return a view of the portion of this set whose elements are less than (or equal to, when inclusive is true) toElement. The returned set is backed by this set, so changes in the returned set are reflected in this set and vice versa. The returned set supports all optional set operations that this set supports. This method throws ClassCastException when toElement is not compatible with this set's comparator (or, when the set has no comparator, when toElement does not implement Comparable), NullPointerException when toElement is null and this set does not permit null elements, and IllegalArgumentException when this set has a restricted range and toElement lies outside of this range's bounds.
E higher(E e)	Return the least element in this set strictly greater than the given element, or null when there is no such element. This method throws ClassCastException when e cannot be compared with the elements currently in the set, and NullPointerException when e is null and this set does not permit null elements.
E lower(E e)	Return the greatest element in this set strictly less than the given element, or null when there is no such element. This method throws ClassCastException when e cannot be compared with the elements currently in the set, and NullPointerException when e is null and this set does not permit null elements.
E pollFirst()	Return and remove the first (lowest) element from this set, or return null when this set is empty.
E pollLast()	Return and remove the last (highest) element from this set, or return null when this set is empty.
NavigableSet<E> subSet(E fromElement, boolean fromInclusive, E toElement,	Return a view of the portion of this set whose elements range from fromElement to toElement. (When fromElement and toElement are equal, the returned set is empty unless

boolean toInclusive)	fromInclusive and toInclusive are both true.) The returned set is backed by this set, so changes in the returned set are reflected in this set and vice versa. The returned set supports all optional set operations that this set supports. This method throws ClassCastException when fromElement and toElement cannot be compared to one another using this set's comparator (or, when the set has no comparator, using natural ordering), NullPointerException when fromElement or toElement is null and this set does not permit null elements, and IllegalArgumentException when fromElement is greater than toElement or when this set has a restricted range and fromElement or toElement lies outside of this range's bounds.
NavigableSet<E> tailSet(E fromElement, boolean inclusive)	Return a view of the portion of this set whose elements are greater than (or equal to, when inclusive is true) fromElement. The returned set is backed by this set, so changes in the returned set are reflected in this set and vice versa. The returned set supports all optional set operations that this set supports. This method throws ClassCastException when fromElement is not compatible with this set's comparator (or, when the set has no comparator, when fromElement does not implement Comparable), NullPointerException when fromElement is null and this set does not permit null elements, and IllegalArgumentException when this set has a restricted range and fromElement lies outside of this range's bounds.

Listing 5-13 demonstrates a navigable set based on a tree set.

Listing 5-13. Navigating a set of integers

```java
import java.util.Iterator;
import java.util.NavigableSet;
import java.util.TreeSet;

class NavigableSetDemo
{
   public static void main(String[] args)
   {
      NavigableSet<Integer> ns = new TreeSet<>();
      int[] ints = { 82, -13, 4, 0, 11, -6, 9 };
      for (int i: ints)
         ns.add(i);
      System.out.print("Ascending order: ");
      Iterator iter = ns.iterator();
      while (iter.hasNext())
         System.out.print(iter.next()+" ");
      System.out.println();
      System.out.print("Descending order: ");
```

```
        iter = ns.descendingIterator();
        while (iter.hasNext())
            System.out.print(iter.next()+" ");
        System.out.println("\n");
        outputClosestMatches(ns, 4);
        outputClosestMatches(ns.descendingSet(), 12);
    }
    static void outputClosestMatches(NavigableSet<Integer> ns, int i)
    {
        System.out.println("Element < "+i+" is "+ns.lower(i));
        System.out.println("Element <= "+i+" is "+ns.floor(i));
        System.out.println("Element > "+i+" is "+ns.higher(i));
        System.out.println("Element >= "+i+" is "+ns.ceiling(i));
        System.out.println();
    }
}
```

Listing 5-13 creates a navigable set of Integer elements. It takes advantage of autoboxing to ensure that ints are converted to Integers.

When you run this application, it generates the following output:

```
Ascending order: -13 -6 0 4 9 11 82
Descending order: 82 11 9 4 0 -6 -13

Element < 4 is 0
Element <= 4 is 4
Element > 4 is 9
Element >= 4 is 4

Element < 12 is 82
Element <= 12 is 82
Element > 12 is 11
Element >= 12 is 11
```

The first four output lines beginning with Element pertain to an ascending-order set where the element being matched (4) is a member of the set. The second four Element-prefixed lines pertain to a descending-order set where the element being matched (12) is not a member.

As well as letting you conveniently locate set elements via its closest-match methods (ceiling(), floor(), higher(), and lower()), NavigableSet lets you return set views containing all elements within certain ranges, as demonstrated by the following examples:

- ns.subSet(-13, true, 9, true): Return all elements from -13 through 9.

- ns.tailSet(-6, false): Return all elements greater than -6.

- ns.headSet(4, true): Return all elements less than or equal to 4.

Finally, you can return and remove from the set the first (lowest) element by calling pollFirst() and the last (highest) element by calling pollLast(). For example, ns.pollFirst() removes and returns -13, and ns.pollLast() removes and returns -82.

Queue

A *queue* is a collection in which elements are stored and retrieved in a specific order. Most queues are categorized as one of the following:

- *First-in, first-out (FIFO) queue:* Elements are inserted at the queue's *tail* and removed at the queue's *head*.

- *Last-in, first-out (LIFO) queue:* Elements are inserted and removed at one end of the queue such that the last element inserted is the first element retrieved. This kind of queue behaves as a *stack*.

- *Priority queue:* Elements are inserted according to their natural ordering, or according to a comparator that is supplied to the queue implementation.

Queue, whose generic type is Queue<E>, extends Collection, redeclaring add() to adjust its contract (insert the specified element into this queue if it is possible to do so immediately without violating capacity restrictions), and inheriting the other methods from Collection. Table 5-5 describes add() and the other Queue-specific methods.

Table 5-5. Queue-specific Methods

Method	Description
boolean add(E e)	Insert element e into this queue if it is possible to do so immediately without violating capacity restrictions. Return true on success; otherwise, throw IllegalStateException when the element cannot be added at this time because no space is currently available. This method also throws ClassCastException when e's class prevents e from being added to this queue, NullPointerException when e contains the null reference and this queue does not permit null elements to be added, and IllegalArgumentException when some property of e prevents it from being added to this queue.
E element()	Return but do not also remove the element at the head of this queue. This method throws NoSuchElementException when this queue is empty.
boolean offer(E e)	Insert element e into this queue if it is possible to do so immediately without violating capacity restrictions. Return true on success; otherwise, return false when the element cannot be added at this time because no space is currently available. This method throws ClassCastException when e's class prevents e from being added to this queue, NullPointerException when e contains the null reference and this queue does not permit null elements to be added, and IllegalArgumentException when some property of e prevents it from being added to this queue.

E peek()	Return but do not also remove the element at the head of this queue. This method returns null when this queue is empty.
E poll()	Return and also remove the element at the head of this queue. This method returns null when this queue is empty.
E remove()	Return and also remove the element at the head of this queue. This method throws NoSuchElementException when this queue is empty. This is the only difference between remove() and poll().

Table 5-5 reveals two sets of methods: in one set, a method (such as add()) throws an exception when an operation fails; in the other set, a method (such as offer()) returns a special value (false or null) in the presence of failure. The methods that return a special value are useful in the context of capacity-restricted Queue implementations where failure is a normal occurrence.

■ **Note** The offer() method is generally preferable to add() when using a capacity-restricted queue because offer() does not throw IllegalStateException.

Java supplies many Queue implementation classes, where most of these classes are members of the java.util.concurrent package: LinkedBlockingQueue, LinkedTransferQueue, and SynchronousQueue are examples. In contrast, the java.util package provides LinkedList and PriorityQueue as its Queue implementation classes.

■ **Caution** Many Queue implementation classes do not allow null elements to be added. However, some classes (such as LinkedList) permit null elements. You should avoid adding a null element because null is used as a special return value by the peek() and poll() methods to indicate that a queue is empty.

PriorityQueue

The PriorityQueue class provides an implementation of a *priority queue*, which is a queue that orders its elements according to their natural ordering or by a comparator provided when the queue is instantiated. Priority queues do not permit null elements, and do not permit insertion of non-Comparable objects when relying on natural ordering.

The element at the head of the priority queue is the least element with respect to the specified ordering. If multiple elements are tied for least element, one of those elements is arbitrarily chosen as the least element. Similarly, the element at the tail of the priority queue is the greatest element, which is arbitrarily chosen when there is a tie.

Priority queues are unbounded, but have a capacity that governs the size of the internal array that is used to store the priority queue's elements. The capacity value is at least as large as the queue's length, and grows automatically as elements are added to the priority queue.

PriorityQueue (whose generic type is PriorityQueue<E>) supplies six constructors:

- PriorityQueue() creates a PriorityQueue instance with an initial capacity of 11 elements, and which orders its elements according to their natural ordering.

- PriorityQueue(Collection<? extends E> c) creates a PriorityQueue instance containing c's elements. If c is a SortedSet or PriorityQueue instance, this priority queue will be ordered according to the same ordering. Otherwise, this priority queue will be ordered according to the natural ordering of its elements. This constructor throws ClassCastException when c's elements cannot be compared to one another according to the priority queue's ordering, and NullPointerException when c or any of its elements contain the null reference.

- PriorityQueue(int initialCapacity) creates a PriorityQueue instance with the specified initialCapacity, and which orders its elements according to their natural ordering. This constructor throws IllegalArgumentException when initialCapacity is less than 1.

- PriorityQueue(int initialCapacity, Comparator<? super E> comparator) creates a PriorityQueue instance with the specified initialCapacity, and which orders its elements according to the specified comparator. Natural ordering is used when comparator contains the null reference. This constructor throws IllegalArgumentException when initialCapacity is less than 1.

- PriorityQueue(PriorityQueue<? extends E> pq) creates a PriorityQueue instance containing pq's elements. This priority queue will be ordered according to the same ordering as pq. This constructor throws ClassCastException when pq's elements cannot be compared to one another according to pq's ordering, and NullPointerException when pq or any of its elements contains the null reference.

- PriorityQueue(SortedSet<? extends E> ss) creates a PriorityQueue instance containing ss's elements. This priority queue will be ordered according to the same ordering as ss. This constructor throws ClassCastException when sortedSet's elements cannot be compared to one another according to ss's ordering, and NullPointerException when sortedSet or any of its elements contains the null reference.

Listing 5-14 demonstrates a priority queue.

Listing 5-14. Adding randomly generated integers to a priority queue

```
import java.util.PriorityQueue;
import java.util.Queue;

class PriorityQueueDemo
{
   public static void main(String[] args)
   {
      Queue<Integer> qi = new PriorityQueue<>();
      for (int i = 0; i < 15; i++)
```

```
            qi.add((int) (Math.random()*100));
        while (!qi.isEmpty())
            System.out.print(qi.poll()+" ");
        System.out.println();
    }
}
```

After creating a priority queue, the main thread adds 15 randomly generated integers (ranging from 0 through 99) to this queue. It then enters a while loop that repeatedly polls the priority queue for the next element and outputs that element until the queue is empty.

When you run this application, it outputs a line of 15 integers in ascending numerical order from left to right. For example, I observed the following output from one run:

11 21 29 35 40 53 66 70 72 75 80 83 87 88 89

Because poll() returns null when there are no more elements, I could have coded this loop as follows:

```
Integer i;
while ((i = qi.poll()) != null)
    System.out.print(i+" ");
```

Suppose you want to reverse the order of the previous application's output so that the largest element appears on the left and the smallest element appears on the right. As Listing 5-15 demonstrates, you can achieve this task by passing a comparator to the appropriate PriorityQueue constructor.

Listing 5-15. Using a comparator with a priority queue

```
import java.util.Comparator;
import java.util.PriorityQueue;
import java.util.Queue;

class PriorityQueueDemo
{
    final static int NELEM = 15;
    public static void main(String[] args)
    {
        Comparator<Integer> cmp;
        cmp = new Comparator<Integer>()
                {
                    public int compare(Integer e1, Integer e2)
                    {
                        return e2-e1;
                    }
                };
        Queue<Integer> qi = new PriorityQueue<>(NELEM, cmp);
        for (int i = 0; i < NELEM; i++)
            qi.add((int) (Math.random()*100));
        while (!qi.isEmpty())
            System.out.print(qi.poll()+" ");
        System.out.println();
    }
}
```

Listing 5-15 is similar to Listing 5-14, but there are some differences. First, I have declared an NELEM constant so that I can easily change both the priority queue's initial capacity and the number of elements inserted into the priority queue by specifying the new value in one place.

Second, Listing 5-15 declares and instantiates an anonymous class that implements Comparator. Its compareTo() method subtracts element e2 from element e1 to achieve descending numerical order. The compiler handles the task of unboxing e2 and e1 by converting e2-e1 to e2.intValue()-e1.intValue().

Finally, Listing 5-15 passes an initial capacity of NELEM elements and the instantiated comparator to the PriorityQueue(int initialCapacity, Comparator<? super E> comparator) constructor. The priority queue will use this comparator to order these elements.

Run this application and you will now see a single output line of 15 integers shown in descending numerical order from left to right. For example, I observed this output line:

```
90 86 78 74 65 53 45 44 30 28 18 9 9 7 5
```

Deque

A *deque* (pronounced deck) is a double-ended queue in which element insertion or removal occurs at its *head* or *tail*. Deques can be used as queues or stacks.

Deque, whose generic type is Deque<E>, extends Queue, in which the inherited add(E e) method inserts e at the deque's tail. Table 5-6 describes Deque-specific methods.

Table 5-6. Deque-specific Methods

Method	Description
void addFirst(E e)	Insert e at the head of this deque if it is possible to do so immediately without violating capacity restrictions. When using a capacity-restricted deque, it is generally preferable to use method offerFirst(). This method throws IllegalStateException when e cannot be added at this time because of capacity restrictions, ClassCastException when e's class prevents e from being added to this deque, NullPointerException when e contains the null reference and this deque does not permit null elements to be added, and IllegalArgumentException when some property of e prevents it from being added to this deque.
void addLast(E e)	Insert e at the tail of this deque if it is possible to do so immediately without violating capacity restrictions. When using a capacity-restricted deque, it is generally preferable to use method offerLast(). This method throws IllegalStateException when e cannot be added at this time because of capacity restrictions, ClassCastException when e's class prevents e from being added to this deque, NullPointerException when e contains the null reference and this deque does not permit null elements to be added, and IllegalArgumentException when some property of e prevents it from being added to this deque.
Iterator<E>	Return an iterator over the elements in this deque in reverse

descendingIterator()	sequential order. The elements will be returned in order from last (tail) to first (head). The inherited Iterator<E> iterator() method returns elements from the head to the tail.
E element()	Retrieve but do not remove the first element of this deque (at the head). This method differs from peek() only in that it throws NoSuchElementException when this deque is empty. This method is equivalent to getFirst().
E getFirst()	Retrieve but do not remove the first element of this deque. This method differs from peekFirst() only in that it throws NoSuchElementException when this deque is empty.
E getLast()	Retrieve but do not remove the last element of this deque. This method differs from peekLast() only in that it throws NoSuchElementException when this deque is empty.
boolean offer(E e)	Insert e at the tail of this deque if it is possible to do so immediately without violating capacity restrictions, returning true upon success and false when no space is currently available. When using a capacity-restricted deque, this method is generally preferable to the add() method, which can fail to insert an element only by throwing an exception. This method throws ClassCastException when e's class prevents e from being added to this deque, NullPointerException when e contains the null reference and this deque does not permit null elements to be added, and IllegalArgumentException when some property of e prevents it from being added to this deque. This method is equivalent to offerLast().
boolean offerFirst(E e)	Insert the specified element at the head of this deque unless it would violate capacity restrictions. When using a capacity-restricted deque, this method is generally preferable to the addFirst() method, which can fail to insert an element only by throwing an exception. This method throws ClassCastException when e's class prevents e from being added to this deque, NullPointerException when e contains the null reference and this deque does not permit null elements to be added, and IllegalArgumentException when some property of e prevents it from being added to this deque.
boolean offerLast(E e)	Insert e at the tail of this deque unless it would violate capacity restrictions. When using a capacity-restricted deque, this method is generally preferable to the addLast() method, which can fail to insert an element only by throwing an exception. This method throws ClassCastException when

e's class prevents e from being added to this deque, `NullPointerException` when e contains the null reference and this deque does not permit null elements to be added, and `IllegalArgumentException` when some property of e prevents it from being added to this deque.

`E peek()`	Retrieve but do not remove the first element of this deque (at the head), or return null when this deque is empty. This method is equivalent to `peekFirst()`.
`E peekFirst()`	Retrieve but do not remove the first element of this deque (at the head), or return null when this deque is empty.
`E peekLast()`	Retrieve but do not remove the last element of this deque (at the tail), or return null when this deque is empty.
`E poll()`	Retrieve and remove the first element of this deque (at the head), or return null when this deque is empty. This method is equivalent to `pollFirst()`.
`E pollFirst()`	Retrieve and remove the first element of this deque (at the head), or return null when this deque is empty.
`E pollLast()`	Retrieve and remove the last element of this deque (at the tail), or return null when this deque is empty.
`E pop()`	Pop an element from the stack represented by this deque. In other words, remove and return the first element of this deque. This method is equivalent to `removeFirst()`.
`void push(E e)`	Push e onto the stack represented by this deque (in other words, at the head of this deque) if it is possible to do so immediately without violating capacity restrictions, returning true upon success and throwing `IllegalStateException` when no space is currently available. This method also throws `ClassCastException` when e's class prevents e from being added to this deque, `NullPointerException` when e contains the null reference and this deque does not permit null elements to be added, and `IllegalArgumentException` when some property of e prevents it from being added to this deque. This method is equivalent to `addFirst()`.
`E remove()`	Retrieve and remove the first element of this deque (at the head). This method differs from `poll()` only in that it throws `NoSuchElementException` when this deque is empty. This method is equivalent to `removeFirst()`.

`E removeFirst()`	Retrieve and remove the first element of this deque. This method differs from `pollFirst()` only in that it throws `NoSuchElementException` when this deque is empty.
`boolean removeFirstOccurrence(Object o)`	Remove the first occurrence of o from this deque. If the deque does not contain o, it is unchanged. Return true when this deque contained o (or equivalently, when this deque changed as a result of the call). This method throws `ClassCastException` when o's class prevents o from being added to this deque, and `NullPointerException` when o contains the null reference and this deque does not permit null elements to be added. The inherited `boolean remove(Object o)` method is equivalent to this method.
`E removeLast()`	Retrieve and remove the last element of this deque. This method differs from `pollLast()` only in that it throws `NoSuchElementException` when this deque is empty.
`boolean removeLastOccurrence(Object o)`	Remove the last occurrence of o from this deque. If the deque does not contain o, it is unchanged. Return true when this deque contained o (or equivalently, when this deque changed as a result of the call). This method throws `ClassCastException` when o's class prevents o from being added to this deque, and `NullPointerException` when o contains the null reference and this deque does not permit null elements to be added.

As Table 5-6 reveals, Deque declares methods to access elements at both ends of the deque. Methods are provided to insert, remove, and examine the element. Each of these methods exists in two forms: one throws an exception when the operation fails, the other returns a special value (either null or false, depending on the operation). The latter form of the insert operation is designed specifically for use with capacity-restricted Deque implementations; in most implementations, insert operations cannot fail.

Figure 5-2 reveals a table from Deque's Java documentation that nicely summarizes both forms of the insert, remove, and examine methods for both the head and the tail.

	First Element (Head)		Last Element (Tail)	
	Throws exception	*Special value*	*Throws exception*	*Special value*
Insert	addFirst(e)	offerFirst(e)	addLast(e)	offerLast(e)
Remove	removeFirst()	pollFirst()	removeLast()	pollLast()
Examine	getFirst()	peekFirst()	getLast()	peekLast()

Figure 5-2. Deque declares twelve methods for inserting, removing, and examining elements at the head or tail of a deque.

When a deque is used as a queue, FIFO (First-In-First-Out) behavior results. Elements are added at the end of the deque and removed from the beginning. The methods inherited from the Queue interface are precisely equivalent to the Deque methods as indicated in Table 5-7.

Table 5-7. Queue and equivalent Deque Methods

Queue Method	Equivalent Deque Method
add(e)	addLast(e)
offer(e)	offerLast(e)
remove()	removeFirst()
poll()	pollFirst()
element()	getFirst()
peek()	peekFirst()

Finally, deques can also be used as LIFO (Last-In-First-Out) stacks. When a deque is used as a stack, elements are pushed and popped from the beginning of the deque. Because a stack's push(e) method would be equivalent to Deque's addFirst(e) method, its pop() method would be equivalent to Deque's removeFirst() method, and its peek() method would be equivalent to Deque's peekFirst() method, Deque declares the E peek(), E pop(), and void push(E e) stack-oriented convenience methods.

ArrayDeque

The ArrayDeque class provides a resizable-array implementation of the Deque interface. It prohibits null elements from being added to a deque, and its iterator() method returns fail-fast iterators.

ArrayDeque supplies three constructors:

- ArrayDeque() creates an empty array list with an initial capacity of 16 elements.

- ArrayDeque(Collection<? extends E> c) creates an array deque containing c's elements in the order in which they are returned by c's iterator. (The first element returned by c's iterator becomes the first element, or front of the deque.) NullPointerException is thrown when c contains the null reference.

- ArrayDeque(int numElements) creates an empty array deque with an initial capacity sufficient to hold numElements elements. No exception is thrown when the argument passed to numElements is less than or equal to zero.

Listing 5-16 demonstrates an array deque.

Listing 5-16. Using an array deque as a stack

```
import java.util.ArrayDeque;
import java.util.Deque;

class ArrayDequeDemo
{
   public static void main(String[] args)
   {
      Deque<String> stack = new ArrayDeque<>();
      String[] weekdays = { "Sunday", "Monday", "Tuesday", "Wednesday",
                            "Thursday", "Friday", "Saturday" };
      for (String weekday: weekdays)
         stack.push(weekday);
      while (stack.peek() != null)
         System.out.println(stack.pop());
   }
}
```

When you run this application, it generates the following output:

```
Saturday
Friday
Thursday
Wednesday
Tuesday
Monday
Sunday
```

Map

A *map* is a group of key/value pairs (also known as *entries*). Because the *key* identifies an entry, a map cannot contain duplicate keys. Furthermore, each key can map to at most one value. Maps are described by the Map interface, which has no parent interface, and whose generic type is Map<K,V> (K is the key's type; V is the value's type).

Table 5-8 describes Map's methods.

Table 5-8. Map-specific Methods

Method	Description
`void clear()`	Remove all elements from this map, leaving it empty. This method throws `UnsupportedOperationException` when `clear()` is not supported.
`boolean containsKey(Object key)`	Return true when this map contains an entry for the specified key; otherwise, return false. This method throws `ClassCastException` when key is of an inappropriate type for this map, and `NullPointerException` when key contains the null reference and this map does not permit null keys.
`boolean containsValue(Object value)`	Return true when this map maps one or more keys to value. This method throws `ClassCastException` when value is of an inappropriate type for this map, and `NullPointerException` when value contains the null reference and this map does not permit null values.
`Set<Map.Entry<K,V>> entrySet()`	Return a Set view of the entries contained in this map. Because this map backs the view, changes that are made to the map are reflected in the set and vice versa.
`boolean equals(Object o)`	Compare o with this map for equality. Return true when o is also a map and the two maps represent the same entries; otherwise, return false.
`V get(Object key)`	Return the value to which key is mapped, or null when this map contains no entry for key. If this map permits null values, then a return value of null does not necessarily indicate that the map contains no entry for key; it is also possible that the map explicitly maps key to the null reference. The `containsKey()` method may be used to distinguish between these two cases. This method throws `ClassCastException` when key is of an inappropriate type for this map, and `NullPointerException` when key contains the null reference and this map does not permit null keys.
`int hashCode()`	Return the hash code for this map. A map's hash code is defined to be the sum of the hash codes for the entries in the map's `entrySet()` view.
`boolean isEmpty()`	Return true when this map contains no entries; otherwise, return false.
`Set<K> keySet()`	Return a Set view of the keys contained in this map. Because this map backs the view, changes that are made to the map

are reflected in the set and vice versa.

V put(K key,V value)

Associate value with key in this map. If the map previously contained an entry for key, the old value is replaced by value. This method returns the previous value associated with key, or null when there was no entry for key. (The null return value can also indicate that the map previously associated the null reference with key, if the implementation supports null values.) This method throws UnsupportedOperationException when put() is not supported, ClassCastException when key's or value's class is not appropriate for this map, IllegalArgumentException when some property of key or value prevents it from being stored in this map, and NullPointerException when key or value contains the null reference and this map does not permit null keys or values.

void putAll(Map<? extends K,? extends V> m)

Copy all the entries from map m to this map. The effect of this call is equivalent to that of calling put(k, v) on this map once for each mapping from key k to value v in map m. This method throws UnsupportedOperationException when putAll() is not supported, ClassCastException when the class of a key or value in map m is not appropriate for this map, IllegalArgumentException when some property of a key or value in map m prevents it from being stored in this map, and NullPointerException when m contains the null reference or when m contains null keys or values and this map does not permit null keys or values.

V remove(Object key)

Remove key's entry from this map if it is present. This method returns the value to which this map previously associated with key, or null when the map contained no entry for key. If this map permits null values, then a return value of null does not necessarily indicate that the map contained no entry for key; it is also possible that the map explicitly mapped key to null. This map will not contain an entry for key once the call returns. This method throws UnsupportedOperationException when remove() is not supported, ClassCastException when the class of key is not appropriate for this map, and NullPointerException when key contains the null reference and this map does not permit null keys.

int size()

Return the number of key/value entries in this map. If the map contains more than Integer.MAX_VALUE entries, this method returns Integer.MAX_VALUE.

Collection<V> values()	Return a Collection view of the values contained in this map. Because this map backs the view, changes that are made to the map are reflected in the collection and vice versa.

Unlike List, Set, and Queue, Map does not extend Collection. However, it is possible to view a map as a Collection instance by calling Map's keySet(), values(), and entrySet() methods, which respectively return a Set of keys, a Collection of values, and a Set of key/value pair entries.

Note The values() method returns Collection instead of Set because multiple keys can map to the same value, and values() would then return multiple copies of the same value.

The Collection views returned by these methods (recall that a Set is a Collection because Set extends Collection) provide the only means to iterate over a Map. For example, suppose you declare Listing 5-17's Color enum with its three Color constants, RED, GREEN, and BLUE.

Listing 5-17. A colorful enum

```
enum Color
{
   RED(255, 0, 0),
   GREEN(0, 255, 0),
   BLUE(0, 0, 255);
   private int r, g, b;
   private Color(int r, int g, int b)
   {
      this.r = r;
      this.g = g;
      this.b = b;
   }
   @Override
   public String toString()
   {
      return "r = "+r+", g = "+g+", b = "+b;
   }
}
```

The following example declares a map of String keys and Color values, adds several entries to the map, and iterates over the keys and values:

```
Map<String, Color> colorMap = ...; // ... represents creation of a Map implementation
colorMap.put("red", Color.RED);
colorMap.put("blue", Color.BLUE);
colorMap.put("green", Color.GREEN);
colorMap.put("RED", Color.RED);
for (String colorKey: colorMap.keySet())
```

```
    System.out.println(colorKey);
Collection<Color> colorValues = colorMap.values();
for (Iterator<Color> it = colorValues.iterator(); it.hasNext();)
    System.out.println(it.next());
```

When running this example against a hashmap implementation (discussed later) of colorMap, you should observe output similar to the following:

```
red
blue
green
RED
r = 255, g = 0, b = 0
r = 0, g = 0, b = 255
r = 0, g = 255, b = 0
r = 255, g = 0, b = 0
```

The first four output lines identify the map's keys; the second four output lines identify the map's values.

The entrySet() method returns a Set of Map.Entry objects. Each of these objects describes a single entry as a key/value pair and is an instance of a class that implements the Map.Entry interface, where Entry is a nested interface of Map. Table 5-9 describes Map.Entry's methods.

Table 5-9. Map.Entry Methods

Method	Description
boolean equals(Object o)	Compare o with this entry for equality. Return true when o is also a map entry and the two entries have the same key and value.
K getKey()	Return this entry's key. This method optionally throws IllegalStateException when this entry has previously been removed from the backing map.
V getValue()	Return this entry's value. This method optionally throws IllegalStateException when this entry has previously been removed from the backing map.
int hashCode()	Return this entry's hash code.
V setValue(V value)	Replace this entry's value with value. The backing map is updated with the new value. This method throws UnsupportedOperationException when setValue() is not supported, ClassCastException when value's class prevents it from being stored in the backing map, NullPointerException when value contains the null reference and the backing map does not permit null, IllegalArgumentException when some property of value prevents it from being stored in the backing map, and (optionally) IllegalStateException when this entry has previously been removed from the backing map.

The following example shows you how you might iterate over the previous example's map entries:

```
for (Map.Entry<String, Color> colorEntry: colorMap.entrySet())
    System.out.println(colorEntry.getKey()+": "+colorEntry.getValue());
```

When running this example against the previously mentioned hashmap implementation, you would observe the following output:

```
red: r = 255, g = 0, b = 0
blue: r = 0, g = 0, b = 255
green: r = 0, g = 255, b = 0
RED: r = 255, g = 0, b = 0
```

TreeMap

The TreeMap class provides a map implementation that is based on a red-black tree. As a result, entries are stored in sorted order of their keys. However, accessing these entries is somewhat slower than with the other Map implementations (which are not sorted) because links must be traversed.

Note Check out Wikipedia's "Red-black tree" entry (http://en.wikipedia.org/wiki/Red-black_tree) to learn about red-black trees.

TreeMap supplies four constructors:

- TreeMap() creates a new, empty tree map that is sorted according to the natural ordering of its keys. All keys inserted into the map must implement the Comparable interface.

- TreeMap(Comparator<? super K> comparator) creates a new, empty tree map that is sorted according to the specified comparator. Passing null to comparator implies that natural ordering will be used.

- TreeMap(Map<? extends K, ? extends V> m) creates a new tree map containing m's entries, sorted according to the natural ordering of its keys. All keys inserted into the new map must implement the Comparable interface. This constructor throws ClassCastException when m's keys do not implement Comparable or are not mutually comparable, and NullPointerException when m contains the null reference.

- TreeMap(SortedMap<K, ? extends V> sm) creates a new tree map containing the same entries and using the same ordering as sm. (I discuss sorted maps later in this chapter.) This constructor throws NullPointerException when sm contains the null reference.

Listing 5-18 demonstrates a tree map.

Listing 5-18. Sorting a map's entries according to the natural ordering of their String-based keys

```
import java.util.Map;
import java.util.TreeMap;

class TreeMapDemo
{
    public static void main(String[] args)
    {
        Map<String, Integer> msi = new TreeMap<>();
        String[] fruits = {"apples", "pears", "grapes", "bananas", "kiwis"};
        int[] quantities = {10, 15, 8, 17, 30};
        for (int i = 0; i < fruits.length; i++)
            msi.put(fruits[i], quantities[i]);
        for (Map.Entry<String, Integer> entry: msi.entrySet())
            System.out.println(entry.getKey()+": "+entry.getValue());
    }
}
```

When you run this application, it generates the following output:

```
apples: 10
bananas: 17
grapes: 8
kiwis: 30
pears: 15
```

HashMap

The HashMap class provides a map implementation that is based on a hashtable data structure. This implementation supports all Map operations, and permits null keys and null values. It makes no guarantees on the order in which entries are stored.

A hashtable maps keys to integer values with the help of a *hash function*. Java provides this function in the form of Object's hashCode() method, which classes override to provide appropriate hash codes.

A *hash code* identifies one of the hashtable's array elements, which is known as a *bucket* or *slot*. For some hashtables, the bucket may store the value that is associated with the key. Figure 5-3 illustrates this kind of hashtable.

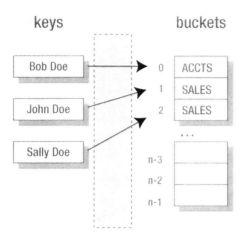

keys

buckets

hash function

Figure 5-3. *A simple hashtable maps keys to buckets that store values associates with those keys.*

The hash function hashes Bob Doe to 0, which identifies the first bucket. This bucket contains ACCTS, which is Bob Doe's employee type. The hash function also hashes John Doe and Sally Doe to 1 and 2 (respectively) whose buckets contain SALES.

A perfect hash function hashes each key to a unique integer value. However, this ideal is very difficult to meet. In practice, some keys will hash to the same integer value. This nonunique mapping is referred to as a *collision.*

To address collisions, most hashtables associate a linked list of entries with a bucket. Instead of containing a value, the bucket contains the address of the first node in the linked list, and each node contains one of the colliding entries. See Figure 5-4.

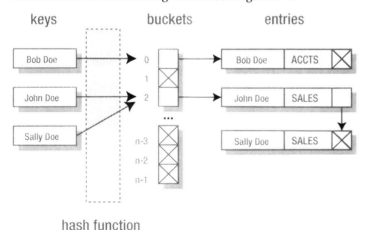

keys

buckets

entries

hash function

Figure 5-4. *A complex hashtable maps keys to buckets that store references to linked lists whose node values are hashed from the same keys.*

When storing a value in a hashtable, the hashtable uses the hash function to hash the key to its hash code, and then searches the appropriate linked list to see if an entry with a matching key exists. If there is an entry, its value is updated with the new value. Otherwise, a new node is created, populated with the key and value, and appended to the list.

When retrieving a value from a hashtable, the hashtable uses the hash function to hash the key to its hash code, and then searches the appropriate linked list to see if an entry with a matching key exists. If there is an entry, its value is returned. Otherwise, the hashtable may return a special value to indicate that there is no entry, or it might throw an exception.

The number of buckets is known as the hashtable's *capacity*. The ratio of the number of stored entries divided by the number of buckets is known as the hashtable's *load factor*. Choosing the right load factor is important for balancing performance with memory use:

- As the load factor approaches 1, the probability of collisions and the cost of handling them (by searching lengthy linked lists) increase.

- As the load factor approaches 0, the hashtable's size in terms of number of buckets increases with little improvement in search cost.

- For many hashtables, a load factor of 0.75 is close to optimal. This value is the default for HashMap's hashtable implementation.

HashMap supplies four constructors:

- HashMap() creates a new, empty hashmap with an initial capacity of 16 and a load factor of 0.75.

- HashMap(int initialCapacity) creates a new, empty hashmap with a capacity specified by initialCapacity and a load factor of 0.75. This constructor throws IllegalArgumentException when initialCapacity's value is less than 0.

- HashMap(int initialCapacity, float loadFactor) creates a new, empty hashmap with a capacity specified by initialCapacity and a load factor specified by loadFactor. This constructor throws IllegalArgumentException when initialCapacity is less than 0 or when loadFactor is less than or equal to 0.

- HashMap(Map<? extends K, ? extends V> m) creates a new hashmap containing m's entries. This constructor throws NullPointerException when m contains the null reference.

Listing 5-19 demonstrates a hashmap.

Listing 5-19. Using a hashmap to count command-line arguments

```
import java.util.HashMap;
import java.util.Map;

class HashMapDemo
{
   public static void main(String[] args)
   {
      Map<String, Integer> argMap = new HashMap<>();
      for (String arg: args)
      {
         Integer count = argMap.get(arg);
```

```
            argMap.put(arg, (count == null) ? 1 : count+1);
        }
        System.out.println(argMap);
        System.out.println("Number of distinct arguments = "+argMap.size());
    }
}
```

HashMapDemo creates a hashmap of String keys and Integer values. Each key is one of the command-line arguments passed to this application, and its value is the number of occurrences of that argument on the command line.

For example, java HashMapDemo how much wood could a woodchuck chuck if a woodchuck could chuck wood generates the following output:

```
{wood=2, could=2, how=1, if=1, chuck=2, a=2, woodchuck=2, much=1}
Number of distinct arguments = 8
```

Because the String class overrides equals() and hashCode(), Listing 5-19 can use String objects as keys in a hashmap. When you create a class whose instances are to be used as keys, you must ensure that you override both methods.

Listing 5-6 showed you that a class's overriding hashCode() method can call a reference field's hashCode() method and return its value, provided that the class declares a single reference field (and no primitive type fields).

More commonly, classes declare multiple fields, and a better implementation of the hashCode() method is required. The implementation should try to generate hash codes that minimize collisions.

There is no rule on how to best implement hashCode(), and various *algorithms* (recipes for accomplishing tasks) have been created. My favorite algorithm appears in *Effective Java Second Edition*, by Joshua Bloch (Addison-Wesley, 2008; ISBN: 0321356683).

The following algorithm, which assumes the existence of an arbitrary class that is referred to as *X*, closely follows Bloch's algorithm, but is not identical:

1. Initialize int variable hashCode (the name is arbitrary) to an arbitrary nonzero integer value, such as 19. This variable is initialized to a nonzero value to ensure that it takes into account any initial fields whose hash codes are zeros. If you initialize hashCode to 0, the final hash code will be unaffected by such fields and you run the risk of increased collisions.

2. For each field f that is also used in *X*'s equals() method, calculate f's hash code and assign it to int variable hc as follows:

    a. If f is of Boolean type, calculate hc = f?1:0.

    b. If f is of byte integer, character, integer, or short integer type, calculate hc = (int) f. The integer value is the hash code.

    c. If f is of long integer type, calculate hc = (int) (f^(f>>>32)). This expression exclusive ORs the long integer's least significant 32 bits with its most significant 32 bits.

    d. If f is of type floating-point, calculate hc = Float.floatToIntBits(f). This method takes +infinity, -infinity, and NaN into account.

    e. If f is of type double precision floating-point, calculate long l = Double.doubleToLongBits(f); hc = (int) (l^(l>>>32)).

    f. If f is a reference field with a null reference, calculate hc = 0.

g.   If f is a reference field with a nonnull reference, and if X's equals() method compares the field by recursively calling equals() (as in Listing 5-12's Employee class), calculate hc = f.hashCode(). However, if equals() employs a more complex comparison, create a *canonical* (simplest possible) representation of the field and call hashCode() on this representation.

h.   If f is an array, treat each element as a separate field by applying this algorithm recursively and combining the hc values as shown in the next step.

3.   Combine hc with hashCode as follows: hashCode = hashCode*31+hc. Multiplying hashCode by 31 makes the resulting hash value dependent on the order in which fields appear in the class, which improves the hash value when a class contains multiple fields that are similar (several ints, for example). I chose 31 to be consistent with the String class's hashCode() method.

4.   Return hashCode from hashCode().

Tip Instead of using this or another algorithm to create a hash code, you might find it easier to work with the HashCodeBuilder class (see http://commons.apache.org/lang/api-2.4/org/apache/commons/lang/builder/HashCodeBuilder.html for an explanation of this class). This class, which follows Bloch's rules, is part of the Apache Commons Lang component, which you can download from http://commons.apache.org/lang/.

In Chapter 2, Listing 2-27's Point class overrides equals() but does not override hashCode(). I later presented a small code fragment that must be appended to Point's main() method to demonstrate the problem of not overriding hashCode(). I restate this problem here:

Although objects p1 and Point(10, 20) are logically equivalent, these objects have different hash codes, resulting in each object referring to a different entry in the hashmap. If an object is not stored (via put()) in that entry, get() returns null.

Listing 5-20 modifies Listing 2-27's Point class by declaring a hashCode() method. This method uses the aforementioned algorithm to ensure that logically equivalent Point objects hash to the same entry.

Listing 5-20. Using a hashmap to count command-line arguments

```java
import java.util.HashMap;
import java.util.Map;

class Point
{
   private int x, y;
   Point(int x, int y)
   {
      this.x = x;
      this.y = y;
   }
   int getX()
```

```
{
    return x;
}
int getY()
{
    return y;
}
@Override
public boolean equals(Object o)
{
    if (!(o instanceof Point))
        return false;
    Point p = (Point) o;
    return p.x == x && p.y == y;
}
@Override
public int hashCode()
{
    int hashCode = 19;
    int hc = x;
    hashCode = hashCode*31+hc;
    hc = y;
    hashCode = hashCode*31+hc;
    return hc;
}
public static void main(String[] args)
{
    Point p1 = new Point(10, 20);
    Point p2 = new Point(20, 30);
    Point p3 = new Point(10, 20);
    // Test reflexivity
    System.out.println(p1.equals(p1)); // Output: true
    // Test symmetry
    System.out.println(p1.equals(p2)); // Output: false
    System.out.println(p2.equals(p1)); // Output: false
    // Test transitivity
    System.out.println(p2.equals(p3)); // Output: false
    System.out.println(p1.equals(p3)); // Output: true
    // Test nullability
    System.out.println(p1.equals(null)); // Output: false
    // Extra test to further prove the instanceof operator's usefulness.
    System.out.println(p1.equals("abc")); // Output: false
    Map<Point, String> map = new HashMap<Point, String>();
    map.put(p1, "first point");
    System.out.println(map.get(p1)); // Output: first point
    System.out.println(map.get(new Point(10, 20))); // Output: null
}
}
```

Listing 5-20's hashCode() method is a little verbose in that it assigns each of x and y to local variable hc, rather than directly using these fields in the hash code calculation. However, I decided to follow this approach to more closely mirror the hash code algorithm.

When you run this application, its last two lines of output are of the most interest. Instead of presenting first point followed by null on two separate lines, the application now correctly presents first point followed by first point on these lines.

■ **Note** LinkedHashMap is a subclass of HashMap that uses a linked list to store its entries. As a result, LinkedHashMap's iterator returns entries in the order in which they were inserted. For example, if Listing 5-19 had specified Map<String, Integer> argMap = new LinkedHashMap<>();, the application's output for java HashMapDemo how much wood could a woodchuck chuck if a woodchuck could chuck wood would have been {how=1, much=1, wood=2, could=2, a=2, woodchuck=2, chuck=2, if=1} followed by Number of distinct arguments = 8.

IdentityHashMap

The IdentityHashMap class provides a Map implementation that uses reference equality (==) instead of object equality (equals()) when comparing keys and values. This is an intentional violation of Map's general contract, which mandates the use of equals() when comparing elements.

IdentityHashMap obtains hash codes via System's static int identityHashCode(Object x) method instead of via each key's hashCode() method. identityHashCode() returns the same hash code for x as returned by Object's hashCode() method, whether or not x's class overrides hashCode(). The hash code for the null reference is zero.

These characteristics give IdentityHashMap a performance advantage over other Map implementations. Also, IdentityHashMap supports *mutable keys* (objects used as keys and whose hash codes change when their field values change while in the map). Listing 5-21 contrasts IdentityHashMap with HashMap where mutable keys are concerned.

Listing 5-21. Contrasting IdentityHashMap with HashMap in a mutable key context

```
import java.util.IdentityHashMap;
import java.util.HashMap;
import java.util.Map;

class IdentityHashMapDemo
{
   public static void main(String[] args)
   {
      Map<Employee, String> map1 = new IdentityHashMap<>();
      Map<Employee, String> map2 = new HashMap<>();
      Employee e1 = new Employee("John Doe", 28);
      map1.put(e1, "SALES");
      System.out.println(map1);
      Employee e2 = new Employee("Jane Doe", 26);
      map2.put(e2, "MGMT");
      System.out.println(map2);
      System.out.println("map1 contains key e1 = "+map1.containsKey(e1));
      System.out.println("map2 contains key e2 = "+map2.containsKey(e2));
```

```
            e1.setAge(29);
            e2.setAge(27);
            System.out.println(map1);
            System.out.println(map2);
            System.out.println("map1 contains key e1 = "+map1.containsKey(e1));
            System.out.println("map2 contains key e2 = "+map2.containsKey(e2));
        }
}
class Employee
{
        private String name;
        private int age;
        Employee(String name, int age)
        {
            this.name = name;
            this.age = age;
        }
        @Override
        public boolean equals(Object o)
        {
            if (!(o instanceof Employee))
                return false;
            Employee e = (Employee) o;
            return e.name.equals(name) && e.age == age;
        }
        @Override
        public int hashCode()
        {
            int hashCode = 19;
            hashCode = hashCode*31+name.hashCode();
            hashCode = hashCode*31+age;
            return hashCode;
        }
        void setAge(int age)
        {
            this.age = age;
        }
        void setName(String name)
        {
            this.name = name;
        }
        @Override
        public String toString()
        {
            return name+" "+age;
        }
}
```

Listing 5-21's main() method creates IdentityHashMap and HashMap instances that each store an entry consisting of an Employee key and a String value. Because Employee instances are mutable (because of setAge() and setName()), main() changes their ages while these keys are stored in their maps. These changes result in the following output:

```
{John Doe 28=SALES}
{Jane Doe 26=MGMT}
map1 contains key e1 = true
map2 contains key e2 = true
{John Doe 29=SALES}
{Jane Doe 27=MGMT}
map1 contains key e1 = true
map2 contains key e2 = false
```

The last four lines show that the changed entries remain in their maps. However, map2's containsKey() method reports that its HashMap instance no longer contains its Employee key (which should be Jane Doe 27), whereas map1's containsKey() method reports that its IdentityHashMap instance still contains its Employee key, which is now John Doe 29.

Note IdentityHashMap's documentation states that "a typical use of this class is topology-preserving object graph transformations, such as serialization or deep copying." (I discuss serialization in Chapter 8.) It also states the following: "another typical use of this class is to maintain proxy objects." Also, developers responding to stackoverflow's "Use Cases for Identity HashMap" topic (http://stackoverflow.com/questions/838528/use-cases-for-identity-hashmap) mention that it is much faster to use IdentityHashMap than HashMap when the keys are Class objects.

WeakHashMap

The WeakHashMap class provides a Map implementation that is based on weakly reachable keys. Because each key object is stored indirectly as the referent of a weak reference, the key is automatically removed from the map only after the garbage collector clears all weak references to the key (inside and outside of the map).

Note Check out Chapter 4's "Reference API" section to learn about weakly reachable and weak references.

In contrast, value objects are stored via strong references (and should not strongly refer to their own keys, either directly or indirectly, because doing so prevents their associated keys from being discarded). When a key is removed from a map, its associated value object is also removed.

Listing 5-22 provides a simple demonstration of the WeakHashMap class.

Listing 5-22. Detecting a weak hashmap entry's removal

```
import java.util.Map;
import java.util.WeakHashMap;

class LargeObject
```

```
{
    private byte[] memory = new byte[1024*1024*50]; // 50 megabytes
}
class WeakHashMapDemo
{
    public static void main(String[] args)
    {
        Map<LargeObject, String> map = new WeakHashMap<>();
        LargeObject lo = new LargeObject();
        map.put(lo, "Large Object");
        System.out.println(map);
        lo = null;
        while (!map.isEmpty())
        {
            System.gc();
            new LargeObject();
        }
        System.out.println(map);
    }
}
```

Listing 5-22's main() method stores a 50MB LargeObject key and a String value in the weak hashmap, and then removes the key's strong reference by assigning null to lo. main() next enters a while loop that executes until the map is empty (map.isEmpty() returns true).

Each loop iteration begins with a System.gc() method call, which may or may not cause a garbage collection to take place (depending upon platform). To encourage a garbage collection, the iteration then creates a LargeObject object and throws away its reference. This activity should eventually cause the garbage collector to run and remove the map's solitary entry.

When I run this application on my Windows XP platform, I observe the following output—you might need to modify the code if you find that the application is in an infinite loop:

```
{LargeObject@5224ee=Large Object}
{}
```

Note WeakHashMap is useful for avoiding memory leaks, as explained in Brian Goetz's article "Java Theory and Practice: Plugging Memory Leaks with Weak References"

(http://www.ibm.com/developerworks/java/library/j-jtp11225/).

EnumMap

The EnumMap class provides a Map implementation whose keys are the members of the same enum. Null keys are not permitted; any attempt to store a null key results in a thrown NullPointerException. Because an enum map is represented internally as an array, an enum map approaches an array in terms of performance.

EnumMap supplies the following constructors:

- EnumMap(Class<K> keyType) creates an empty enum map with the specified keyType. This constructor throws NullPointerException when keyType contains the null reference.

- EnumMap(EnumMap<K,? extends V> m) creates an enum map with the same key type as m, and with m's entries. This constructor throws NullPointerException when m contains the null reference.

- EnumMap(Map<K,? extends V> m) creates an enum map initialized with m's entries. If m is an EnumMap instance, this constructor behaves like the previous constructor. Otherwise, m must contain at least one entry in order to determine the new enum map's key type. This constructor throws NullPointerException when m contains the null reference, and IllegalArgumentException when m is not an EnumMap instance and is empty.

Listing 5-23 demonstrates EnumMap.

Listing 5-23. An enum map of Coin constants

```
import java.util.EnumMap;
import java.util.Map;

enum Coin
{
   PENNY, NICKEL, DIME, QUARTER
}
class EnumMapDemo
{
   public static void main(String[] args)
   {
      Map<Coin, Integer> map = new EnumMap<>(Coin.class);
      map.put(Coin.PENNY, 1);
      map.put(Coin.NICKEL, 5);
      map.put(Coin.DIME, 10);
      map.put(Coin.QUARTER, 25);
      System.out.println(map);
      Map<Coin,Integer> mapCopy = new EnumMap<>(map);
      System.out.println(mapCopy);
   }
}
```

When you run this application, it generates the following output:

```
{PENNY=1, NICKEL=5, DIME=10, QUARTER=25}
{PENNY=1, NICKEL=5, DIME=10, QUARTER=25}
```

SortedMap

TreeMap is an example of a *sorted map*, which is a map that maintains its entries in ascending order, sorted according to the keys' natural ordering or according to a comparator that is supplied when the sorted map is created. Sorted maps are described by the SortedMap interface.

SortedMap, whose generic type is SortedMap<K,V>, extends Map. With two exceptions, the methods it inherits from Map behave identically on sorted maps as on other maps:

- The Iterator instance returned by the iterator() method on any of the sorted map's Collection views traverses the collections in order.

- The arrays returned by the Collection views' toArray() methods contain the keys, values, or entries in order.

Note Although not guaranteed, the toString() methods of the Collection views of SortedSet implementations in the Collections Framework (such as TreeMap) return a string containing all of the view's elements in order.

SortedMap's documentation requires that an implementation must provide the four standard constructors that I presented in my discussion of TreeMap. Furthermore, implementations of this interface must implement the methods that are described in Table 5-10.

Table 5-10. SortedMap-specific Methods

Method	Description
Comparator<? super K> comparator()	Return the comparator used to order the keys in this map, or null when this map uses the natural ordering of its keys.
Set<Map.Entry<K,V>> entrySet()	Return a Set view of the mappings contained in this map. The set's iterator returns these entries in ascending key order. Because this map backs the view, changes that are made to the map are reflected in the set and vice versa.
K firstKey()	Return the first (lowest) key currently in this map, or throw a NoSuchElementException instance when this map is empty.
SortedMap<K,V> headMap(K toKey)	Return a view of that portion of this map whose keys are strictly less than toKey. Because this map backs the returned map, changes in the returned map are reflected in this map and vice versa. The returned map supports all optional map operations that this map supports. This method throws ClassCastException when toKey is not compatible with this map's comparator (or, when the map has no comparator, when toKey does not implement Comparable), NullPointerException when toKey is null and this map does not permit null keys, and IllegalArgumentException when this map has a restricted range and toKey lies outside of this range's bounds.

`Set<K> keySet()`	Return a Set view of the keys contained in this map. The set's iterator returns the keys in ascending order. Because the map backs the view, changes that are made to the map are reflected in the set and vice versa.
`K lastKey()`	Return the last (highest) key currently in this map, or throw a `NoSuchElementException` instance when this map is empty.
`SortedMap<K,V> subMap(K fromKey, K toKey)`	Return a view of the portion of this map whose keys range from `fromKey`, inclusive, to `toKey`, exclusive. (When `fromKey` and `toKey` are equal, the returned map is empty.) Because this map backs the returned map, changes in the returned map are reflected in this map and vice versa. The returned map supports all optional map operations that this map supports. This method throws `ClassCastException` when `fromKey` and `toKey` cannot be compared to one another using this map's comparator (or, when the map has no comparator, using natural ordering), `NullPointerException` when `fromKey` or `toKey` is null and this map does not permit null keys, and `IllegalArgumentException` when `fromKey` is greater than `toKey` or when this map has a restricted range and `fromKey` or `toKey` lies outside its bounds.
`SortedMap<K,V> tailMap(K fromKey)`	Return a view of that portion of this map whose keys are greater than or equal to `fromKey`. Because this map backs the returned map, changes in the returned map are reflected in this map and vice versa. The returned map supports all optional map operations that this map supports. This method throws `ClassCastException` when `fromKey` is not compatible with this map's comparator (or, when the map has no comparator, when `fromKey` does not implement `Comparable`), `NullPointerException` when `fromKey` is null and this map does not permit null keys, and `IllegalArgumentException` when this map has a restricted range and `fromKey` lies outside of the range's bounds.
`Collection<V> values()`	Return a `Collection` view of the values contained in this map. The collection's iterator returns the values in ascending order of the corresponding keys. Because the map backs the collection, changes that are made to the map are reflected in the collection and vice versa.

Listing 5-24 demonstrates a sorted map based on a tree map.

Listing 5-24. A sorted map of office supply names and quantities

```
import java.util.Comparator;
import java.util.SortedMap;
import java.util.TreeMap;
```

```
class SortedMapDemo
{
    public static void main(String[] args)
    {
        SortedMap<String, Integer> smsi = new TreeMap<>();
        String[] officeSupplies =
        {
            "pen", "pencil", "legal pad", "CD", "paper"
        };
        int[] quantities =
        {
            20, 30, 5, 10, 20
        };
        for (int i = 0; i < officeSupplies.length; i++)
            smsi.put(officeSupplies[i], quantities[i]);
        System.out.println(smsi);
        System.out.println(smsi.headMap("pencil"));
        System.out.println(smsi.headMap("paper"));
        SortedMap<String, Integer> smsiCopy;
        Comparator<String> cmp;
        cmp = new Comparator<String>()
                {
                    public int compare(String key1, String key2)
                    {
                        return key2.compareTo(key1); // descending order
                    }
                };
        smsiCopy = new TreeMap<String, Integer>(cmp);
        smsiCopy.putAll(smsi);
        System.out.println(smsiCopy);
    }
}
```

When you run this application (java SortedMapDemo), it generates the following output:

```
{CD=10, legal pad=5, paper=20, pen=20, pencil=30}
{CD=10, legal pad=5, paper=20, pen=20}
{CD=10, legal pad=5}
{pencil=30, pen=20, paper=20, legal pad=5, CD=10}
```

NavigableMap

TreeMap is an example of a *navigable map*, which is a sorted map that can be iterated over in descending order as well as ascending order, and which can report closest matches for given search targets. Navigable maps are described by the NavigableMap interface, whose generic type is NavigableMap<K,V>, which extends SortedMap, and which is described in Table 5-11.

Table 5-11. NavigableMap-specific Methods

Method	Description
`Map.Entry<K,V> ceilingEntry(K key)`	Return the key-value mapping associated with the least key greater than or equal to key, or null when there is no such key. This method throws ClassCastException when key cannot be compared with the keys currently in the map, and NullPointerException when key is null and this map does not permit null keys.
`K ceilingKey(K key)`	Return the least key greater than or equal to key, or null when there is no such key. This method throws ClassCastException when key cannot be compared with the keys currently in the map, and NullPointerException when key is null and this map does not permit null keys.
`NavigableSet<K> descendingKeySet()`	Return a reverse order navigable set-based view of the keys contained in this map. The set's iterator returns the keys in descending order. This map backs the set, so changes to the map are reflected in the set and vice versa. If the map is modified (except through the iterator's own remove() operation) while iterating over the set, the results of the iteration are undefined.
`NavigableMap<K,V> descendingMap()`	Return a reverse order view of the mappings contained in this map. This map backs the descending map, so changes to the map are reflected in the descending map and vice versa. If either map is modified while iterating over a collection view of either map (except through the iterator's own remove() operation), the results of the iteration are undefined.
`Map.Entry<K,V> firstEntry()`	Return a key-value mapping associated with the least key in this map, or null when the map is empty.
`Map.Entry<K,V> floorEntry(K key)`	Return a key-value mapping associated with the greatest key less than or equal to key, or null when there is no such key. This method throws ClassCastException when key cannot be compared with the keys currently in the map, and NullPointerException when key is null and this map does not permit null keys.
`K floorKey(K key)`	Return the greatest key less than or equal to key, or null when there is no such key. This method throws ClassCastException when key cannot be compared with the keys currently in the map, and NullPointerException when key is null and this map does not permit null keys.

`NavigableMap<K,V> headMap(K toKey, boolean inclusive)`	Return a view of the portion of this map whose keys are less than (or equal to, when `inclusive` is `true`) toKey. This map backs the returned map, so changes in the returned map are reflected in this map and vice versa. The returned map supports all optional map operations that this map supports. This method throws `ClassCastException` when toKey is not compatible with this map's comparator (or, when the map has no comparator, when toMap does not implement `Comparable`), `NullPointerException` when toMap is `null` and this map does not permit null keys, and `IllegalArgumentException` when this map has a restricted range and toKey lies outside of this range's bounds.
`Map.Entry<K,V> higherEntry(K key)`	Return a key-value mapping associated with the least key strictly greater than key, or null when there is no such key. This method throws `ClassCastException` when key cannot be compared with the keys currently in the map, and `NullPointerException` when key is `null` and this map does not permit null keys.
`K higherKey(K key)`	Return the least key strictly greater than key, or null when there is no such key. This method throws `ClassCastException` when key cannot be compared with the keys currently in the map, and `NullPointerException` when key is `null` and this map does not permit null keys.
`Map.Entry<K,V> lastEntry()`	Return a key-value mapping associated with the greatest key in this map, or null when the map is empty.
`Map.Entry<K,V> lowerEntry(K key)`	Return a key-value mapping associated with the greatest key strictly less than key, or null when there is no such key. This method throws `ClassCastException` when key cannot be compared with the keys currently in the map, and `NullPointerException` when key is `null` and this map does not permit null keys.
`K lowerKey(K key)`	Return the greatest key strictly less than key, or null when there is no such key. This method throws `ClassCastException` when key cannot be compared with the keys currently in the map, and `NullPointerException` when key is `null` and this map does not permit null keys.
`NavigableSet<K> navigableKeySet()`	Return a navigable set-based view of the keys contained in this map. The set's iterator returns the keys in ascending order. This map backs the set, so changes to the map are reflected in the set and vice versa. If the map is modified while iterating over the set (except through the iterator's own remove( ) operation), the results of the iteration are

	undefined.
`Map.Entry<K,V>` `pollFirstEntry()`	Remove and return a key-value mapping associated with the least key in this map, or null when the map is empty.
`Map.Entry<K,V>` `pollLastEntry()`	Remove and return a key-value mapping associated with the greatest key in this map, or null when the map is empty.

`NavigableMap<K,V> subMap(K`
`fromKey, boolean`
`fromInclusive, K toKey,`
`boolean toInclusive)`
	Return a view of the portion of this map whose keys range from fromKey to toKey. (When fromKey and toKey are equal, the returned map is empty unless fromInclusive and toInclusive are both true.) This map backs the returned map, so changes in the returned map are reflected in this map and vice versa. The returned map supports all optional map operations that this map supports. This method throws ClassCastException when fromKey and toKey cannot be compared to one another using this map's comparator (or, when the map has no comparator, using natural ordering), NullPointerException when fromKey or toKey is null and this map does not permit null elements, and IllegalArgumentException when fromKey is greater than toKey or when this map has a restricted range and fromKey or toMap lies outside of this range's bounds.

`NavigableMap<K,V> tailMap(K` `fromKey, boolean inclusive)`	Return a view of the portion of this map whose keys are greater than (or equal to, when inclusive is true) fromKey. This map backs the returned map, so changes in the returned map are reflected in this map and vice versa. The returned map supports all optional map operations that this map supports. This method throws ClassCastException when fromKey is not compatible with this map's comparator (or, when the map has no comparator, when fromKey does not implement Comparable), NullPointerException when fromKey is null and this map does not permit null keys, and IllegalArgumentException when this map has a restricted range and fromKey lies outside of this range's bounds.

Table 5-11's methods describe the NavigableMap equivalents of the NavigableSet methods presented in Table 5-4, and even return NavigableSet instances in two instances.

Listing 5-25 demonstrates a navigable map based on a tree map.

Listing 5-25. Navigating a map of (bird, count within a small acreage) entries

```
import java.util.Iterator;
import java.util.NavigableMap;
import java.util.NavigableSet;
import java.util.TreeMap;

class NavigableMapDemo
```

```
{
    public static void main(String[] args)
    {
        NavigableMap<String,Integer> nm = new TreeMap<>();
        String[] birds = { "sparrow", "bluejay", "robin" };
        int[] ints = { 83, 12, 19 };
        for (int i = 0; i < birds.length; i++)
            nm.put(birds[i], ints[i]);
        System.out.println("Map = "+nm);
        System.out.print("Ascending order of keys: ");
        NavigableSet<String> ns = nm.navigableKeySet();
        Iterator iter = ns.iterator();
        while (iter.hasNext())
            System.out.print(iter.next()+" ");
        System.out.println();
        System.out.print("Descending order of keys: ");
        ns = nm.descendingKeySet();
        iter = ns.iterator();
        while (iter.hasNext())
            System.out.print(iter.next()+" ");
        System.out.println();
        System.out.println("First entry = "+nm.firstEntry());
        System.out.println("Last entry = "+nm.lastEntry());
        System.out.println("Entry < ostrich is "+nm.lowerEntry("ostrich"));
        System.out.println("Entry > crow is "+nm.higherEntry("crow"));
        System.out.println("Poll first entry: "+nm.pollFirstEntry());
        System.out.println("Map = "+nm);
        System.out.println("Poll last entry: "+nm.pollLastEntry());
        System.out.println("Map = "+nm);
    }
}
```

Listing 5-25's System.out.println("Map = "+nm); method calls rely on TreeMap's toString() method to obtain the contents of a navigable map.

When you run this application, you observe the following output:

```
Map = {bluejay=12, robin=19, sparrow=83}
Ascending order of keys: bluejay robin sparrow
Descending order of keys: sparrow robin bluejay
First entry = bluejay=12
Last entry = sparrow=83
Entry < ostrich is bluejay=12
Entry > crow is robin=19
Poll first entry: bluejay=12
Map = {robin=19, sparrow=83}
Poll last entry: sparrow=83
Map = {robin=19}
```

Utilities

The Collections Framework would not be complete without its Arrays and Collections utility classes. Each class supplies various class methods that implement useful algorithms in the contexts of arrays and collections.

Following is a sampling of the Arrays class's array-oriented utility methods:

- static <T> List<T> asList(T... a) returns a fixed-size list backed by array a. (Changes to the returned list "write through" to the array.) For example, List<String> birds = Arrays.asList("Robin", "Oriole", "Bluejay"); converts the three-element array of Strings (recall that a variable sequence of arguments is implemented as an array) to a List whose reference is assigned to birds.

- static int binarySearch(int[] a, int key) searches array a for entry key using the binary search algorithm (explained following this list). The array must be sorted before calling this method; otherwise, the results are undefined. This method returns the index of the search key, if it is contained in the array; otherwise, (-(insertion point)-1) is returned. The insertion point is the point at which key would be inserted into the array (the index of the first element greater than key, or a.length if all elements in the array are less than key) and guarantees that the return value will be greater than or equal to 0 if and only if key is found. For example, Arrays.binarySearch(new String[] {"Robin", "Oriole", "Bluejay"}, "Oriole") returns 1, "Oriole"'s index.

- static void fill(char[] a, char ch) stores ch in each element of the specified character array. For example, Arrays.fill(screen[i], ' '); fills the ith row of a 2D screen array with spaces.

- static void sort(long[] a) sorts the elements in long integer array a into ascending numerical order; for example, long lArray = new long[] { 20000L, 89L, 66L, 33L}; Arrays.sort(lArray);.

- static <T> void sort(T[] a, Comparator<? super T> c) sorts the elements in array a using comparator c to order them. For example, when given Comparator<String> cmp = new Comparator<String>() { public int compare(String e1, String e2) { return e2.compareTo(e1); } }; String[] innerPlanets = { "Mercury", "Venus", "Earth", "Mars" };, Arrays.sort(innerPlanets, cmp); uses cmp to help in sorting innerPlanets into descending order of its elements: Venus, Mercury, Mars, Earth is the result.

There are two common algorithms for searching an array for a specific element. *Linear search* searches the array element by element from index 0 to the index of the searched-for element or the end of the array. On average, half of the elements must be searched; larger arrays take longer to search. However, the arrays do not need to be sorted.

In contrast, *binary search* searches ordered array *a*'s *n* items for element *e* in a much faster amount of time. It works by recursively performing the following steps:

1. Set low index to 0.

2. Set high index to n-1.

3. If low index > high index, then Print "Unable to find " e. End.

4. Set middle index to (low index+high index)/2.

5. If e > a[middle index], then set low index to middle index+1. Go to 3.

6. If e < a[middle index], then set high index to middle index-1. Go to 3.

7. Print "Found " e " at index " middle index.

The algorithm is similar to optimally looking for a name in a phone book. Start by opening the book to the exact middle. If the name is not on that page, proceed to open the book to the exact middle of the first half or the second half, depending on in which half the name occurs. Repeat until you find the name (or not).

Applying a linear search to 4,000,000,000 elements results in approximately 2,000,000,000 comparisons (on average), which takes time. In contrast, applying a binary search to 4,000,000,000 elements results in a maximum of 32 comparisons. This is why Arrays contains binarySearch() methods and not also linearSearch() methods.

Following is a sampling of the Collections class's collection-oriented class methods:

- static <T extends Object&Comparable<? super T>> T min(Collection<? extends T> c) returns the minimum element of collection c according to the natural ordering of its elements. For example, System.out.println(Collections.min(Arrays.asList(10, 3, 18, 25))); outputs 3. All of c's elements must implement the Comparable interface. Furthermore, all elements must be mutually comparable. This method throws NoSuchElementException when c is empty.

- static void reverse(List<?> l) reverses the order of list l's elements. For example, List<String> birds = Arrays.asList("Robin", "Oriole", "Bluejay"); Collections.reverse(birds); System.out.println(birds); results in [Bluejay, Oriole, Robin] as the output.

- static <T> List<T> singletonList(T o) returns an immutable list containing only object o. For example, list.removeAll(Collections.singletonList(null)); removes all null elements from list.

- static <T> Set<T> synchronizedSet(Set<T> s) returns a synchronized (thread-safe) set backed by set s; for example, Set<String> ss = Collections.synchronizedSet(new HashSet<String>());. In order to guarantee serial access, it is critical that all access to the backing set is accomplished through the returned set.

- static <K,V> Map<K,V> unmodifiableMap(Map<? extends K,? extends V> m) returns an unmodifiable view of map m; for example, Map<String, Integer> msi = Collections.synchronizedMap(new HashMap<String, Integer>());. Query operations on the returned map "read through" to the specified map, and attempts to modify the returned map, whether direct or via its collection views, result in an UnsupportedOperationException.

■ **Note** For performance reasons, collections implementations are unsynchronized—unsynchronized collections have better performance than synchronized collections. To use a collection in a multithreaded context, however, you need to obtain a synchronized version of that collection. You obtain that version by calling a method such as synchronizedSet().

You might be wondering about the purpose for the various "empty" class methods in the Collections class. For example, static final <T> List<T> emptyList() returns an immutable empty list, as in List<String> ls = Collections.emptyList();. These methods are present because they offer a useful alternative to returning null (and avoiding potential NullPointerExceptions) in certain contexts. Consider Listing 5-26.

Listing 5-26. Empty and nonempty Lists of Birds

```java
import java.util.ArrayList;
import java.util.Collections;
import java.util.Iterator;
import java.util.List;

class Birds
{
    private List<String> birds;
    Birds()
    {
        birds = Collections.emptyList();
    }
    Birds(String... birdNames)
    {
        birds = new ArrayList<String>();
        for (String birdName: birdNames)
            birds.add(birdName);
    }
    @Override
    public String toString()
    {
        return birds.toString();
    }
}

class EmptyListDemo
{
    public static void main(String[] args)
    {
        Birds birds = new Birds();
        System.out.println(birds);
        birds = new Birds("Swallow", "Robin", "Bluejay", "Oriole");
        System.out.println(birds);
    }
}
```

Listing 5-26 declares a `Birds` class that stores the names of various birds in a list. This class provides two constructors, a noargument constructor and a constructor that takes a variable number of `String` arguments identifying various birds.

The noargument constructor invokes `emptyList()` to initialize its private `birds` field to an empty `List` of `String`—`emptyList()` is a generic method and the compiler infers its return type from its context.

If you're wondering about the need for `emptyList()`, look at the `toString()` method. Notice that this method evaluates `birds.toString()`. If we did not assign a reference to an empty `List<String>` to `birds`, `birds` would contain `null` (the default value for this instance field when the object is created), and a `NullPointerException` instance would be thrown when attempting to evaluate `birds.toString()`.

When you run this application (java `EmptyListDemo`), it generates the following output:

```
[]
[Swallow, Robin, Bluejay, Oriole]
```

The `emptyList()` method is implemented as follows: `return (List<T>) EMPTY_LIST;`. This statement returns the single `List` instance assigned to the `EMPTY_LIST` class field in the `Collections` class.

You might want to work with `EMPTY_LIST` directly, but you'll run into an unchecked warning message if you do, because `EMPTY_LIST` is declared to be of the raw type `List`, and mixing raw types with generic types leads to such messages. Although you could suppress the warning, you're better off using the `emptyList()` method.

Suppose you add a `void setBirds(List<String> birds)` method to `Birds`, and pass an empty list to this method, as in `birds.setBirds(Collections.emptyList());`. The compiler will respond with an error message stating that it requires the argument to be of type `List<String>`, but instead the argument is of type `List<Object>`. It does so because the compiler cannot figure out the proper type from this context, and so it chooses `List<Object>`.

There is a way to solve this problem, which will probably look very strange. Specify `birds.setBirds(Collections.<String>emptyList());`, where the formal type parameter list and its actual type argument appear after the member access operator and before the method name. The compiler will now know that the proper type argument is `String`, and that `emptyList()` is to return `List<String>`.

Legacy Collections APIs

Java 1.2 introduced the Collections Framework. Prior to the framework's inclusion in Java, developers had two choices where collections were concerned: create their own frameworks, or use the `Vector`, `Enumeration`, `Stack`, `Dictionary`, `Hashtable`, `Properties`, and `BitSet` types, which were introduced by Java 1.0.

`Vector` is a concrete class that describes a growable array, much like `ArrayList`. Unlike an `ArrayList` instance, a `Vector` instance is synchronized. `Vector` has been generified and also retrofitted to support the Collections Framework, which makes statements such as `List<String> list = new Vector<String>();` legal.

The Collections Framework provides `Iterator` for iterating over a collection's elements. In contrast, `Vector`'s `elements()` method returns an instance of a class that implements the `Enumeration` interface for *enumerating* (iterating over and returning) a `Vector` instance's elements via `Enumeration`'s `hasMoreElements()` and `nextElement()` methods.

`Vector` is subclassed by the concrete `Stack` class, which represents a LIFO data structure. `Stack` provides an `E push(E item)` method for pushing an object onto the stack, an `E pop()` method for popping an item off the top of the stack, and a few other methods, such as `boolean empty()` for determining whether or not the stack is empty.

`Stack` is a good example of bad API design. By inheriting from `Vector`, it is possible to call `Vector`'s `void add(int index, E element)` method to add an element anywhere you wish, and violate a `Stack` instance's integrity. In hindsight, Stack should have used composition in its design: use a Vector instance to store a Stack instance's elements.

Dictionary is an abstract superclass for subclasses that map keys to values. The concrete Hashtable class is Dictionary's only subclass. As with Vector, HashTable instances are synchronized, HashTable has been generified, and HashTable has been retrofitted to support the Collections Framework.

Hashtable is subclassed by Properties, a concrete class representing a persistent set of *properties* (String-based key/value pairs that identify application settings). Properties provides Object setProperty(String key, String value) for storing a property, and public String getProperty(String key) for returning a property's value.

■ **Note** Application's use properties for various purposes. For example, if your application has a graphical user interface, you might persist its main window's screen location and size to a file via a Properties object so that the application can restore the window's location and size when it next runs.

Properties is another good example of bad API design. By inheriting from Hashtable, you can call Hashtable's V put(K key, V value) method to store an entry with a non-String key and/or a non-String value. In hindsight, Properties should have leveraged composition: store a Properties instance's elements in a Hashtable instance.

■ **Note** Chapter 2 discusses wrapper classes, which is how Stack and Properties should have been implemented.

Finally, BitSet is a concrete class that describes a variable-length set of bits. This class's ability to represent bitsets of arbitrary length contrasts with the previously described integer-based, fixed-length bitset that is limited to a maximum number of members: 32 members for an int-based bitset, or 64 members for a long-based bitset.

BitSet provides a pair of constructors for initializing a BitSet instance: BitSet() initializes the instance to initially store an implementation-dependent number of bits, whereas BitSet(int nbits) initializes the instance to initially store nbits bits. BitSet also provides various methods, including the following:

- void and(BitSet bs) bitwise ANDs this bitset with bs. This bitset is modified such that a bit is set to 1 when it and the bit at the same position in bs are 1.

- void andNot(BitSet bs) sets all the bits in this bitset to 0 whose corresponding bits are set to 1 in bs.

- void clear() sets all the bits in this bitset to 0.

- Object clone() clones this bitset to produce a new bitset. The clone has exactly the same bits set to one as this bitset.

- boolean get(int bitIndex) returns the value of this bitset's bit, as a Boolean true/false value (true for 1, false for 0) at the zero-based bitIndex. This method throws IndexOutOfBoundsException when bitIndex is less than 0.

- int length() returns the "logical size" of this bitset, which is the index of the highest 1 bit plus 1, or 0 when this bitset contains no 1 bits.

- void or(BitSet bs) bitwise inclusive ORs this bitset with bs. This bitset is modified such that a bit is set to 1 when it or the bit at the same position in bs is 1, or when both bits are 1.

- void set(int bitIndex, boolean value) sets the bit at the zero-based bitIndex to value (true is converted to 1; false is converted to 0). This method throws IndexOutOfBoundsException when bitIndex is less than 0.

- int size() returns the number of bits that are being used by this bitset to represent bit values.

- String toString() returns a string representation of this bitset in terms of the positions of bits that are 1; for example, {4, 5, 9, 10}.

- void xor(BitSet set) bitwise exclusive ORs this bitset with bs. This bitset is modified such that a bit is set to 1 when either it or the bit at the same position in bs (but not both) is 1.

Listing 5-27 presents an application that demonstrates some of these methods, and gives you more insight into how the bitwise AND (&), bitwise inclusive OR (|), and bitwise exclusive OR (^) operators work.

Listing 5-27. Working with variable-length bitsets

```
import java.util.BitSet;

class BitSetDemo
{
   public static void main(String[] args)
   {
      BitSet bs1 = new BitSet();
      bs1.set(4, true);
      bs1.set(5, true);
      bs1.set(9, true);
      bs1.set(10, true);
      BitSet bsTemp = (BitSet) bs1.clone();
      dumpBitset("          ", bs1);
      BitSet bs2 = new BitSet();
      bs2.set(4, true);
      bs2.set(6, true);
      bs2.set(7, true);
      bs2.set(9, true);
      dumpBitset("          ", bs2);
      bs1.and(bs2);
      dumpSeparator(Math.min(bs1.size(), 16));
      dumpBitset("AND (&) ", bs1);
```

```
        System.out.println();
        bs1 = bsTemp;
        dumpBitset("           ", bs1);
        dumpBitset("           ", bs2);
        bsTemp = (BitSet) bs1.clone();
        bs1.or(bs2);
        dumpSeparator(Math.min(bs1.size(), 16));
        dumpBitset("OR (|)  ", bs1);
        System.out.println();
        bs1 = bsTemp;
        dumpBitset("           ", bs1);
        dumpBitset("           ", bs2);
        bsTemp = (BitSet) bs1.clone();
        bs1.xor(bs2);
        dumpSeparator(Math.min(bs1.size(), 16));
        dumpBitset("XOR (^) ", bs1);
    }
    static void dumpBitset(String preamble, BitSet bs)
    {
        System.out.print(preamble);
        int size = Math.min(bs.size(), 16);
        for (int i = 0; i < size; i++)
            System.out.print(bs.get(i) ? "1" : "0");
        System.out.print("  size("+bs.size()+"), length("+bs.length()+")");
        System.out.println();
    }
    static void dumpSeparator(int len)
    {
        System.out.print("           ");
        for (int i = 0; i < len; i++)
            System.out.print("-");
        System.out.println();
    }
}
```

Why did I specify Math.min(bs.size(), 16) in dumpBitset(), and pass a similar expression to dumpSeparator()? I wanted to display exactly 16 bits and 16 dashes (for aesthetics), and needed to account for a bitset's size being less than 16. Although this does not happen with the JDK's BitSet class, it might happen with a non-JDK variant.

When you run this application, it generates the following output:

```
          0000110001100000  size(64), length(11)
          0000101101000000  size(64), length(10)
          ----------------
AND (&)   0000100001000000  size(64), length(10)

          0000110001100000  size(64), length(11)
          0000101101000000  size(64), length(10)
          ----------------
OR (|)    0000111101100000  size(64), length(11)

          0000110001100000  size(64), length(11)
```

```
     0000101101000000  size(64), length(10)
     ----------------
XOR (^) 0000011100100000  size(64), length(11)
```

■ **Caution** Unlike Vector and Hashtable, BitSet is not synchronized. You must externally synchronize access to this class when using BitSet in a multithreaded context.

The Collections Framework has made Vector, Stack, Dictionary, and Hashtable obsolete. These types continue to be part of the standard class library to support legacy code.

The framework's Iterator interface has largely obsoleted the Enumeration interface. However, because the java.util.StringTokenizer class (which is somewhat useful, and which is briefly discussed in Chapter 6) uses Enumeration, this interface still has some credibility.

The Preferences API (see Appendix C) has made Properties largely obsolete. However, the standard class library still uses Properties in various places (such as in the context of XSLT, discussed in Chapter 10). You'll probably have a few uses for this class as well.

Because BitSet is still relevant, this class continues to be improved. For example, Java 7 introduces new valueOf() class methods (such as static BitSet valueOf(byte[] bytes)) and instance methods (such as int previousSetBit(int fromIndex)) into this class.

■ **Note** It is not surprising that BitSet is still being improved (as recently as Java 7 at time of writing) when you realize the usefulness of variable-length bitsets. Because of their compactness and other advantages, variable-length bitsets are often used to implement an operating system's priority queues and facilitate memory page allocation. Unix-oriented file systems also use bitsets to facilitate the allocation of *inodes* (information nodes) and disk sectors. And bitsets are useful in *Huffman coding*, a data-compression algorithm for achieving lossless data compression.

Creating Your Own Collections

Arrays, the Collections Framework, and legacy classes such as BitSet are suitable for organizing groups of objects (or, in the case of BitSet, sets of bits that are interpreted as Boolean true/false values), and you should use them wherever possible before creating your own collection APIs. After all, why "reinvent the wheel?"

The Collections Framework supports lists, sets, queues, deques, and maps. If your collection requirement can fit into one of these categories, then go with this framework. Keep in mind that you can also take advantage of trees in TreeSet and TreeMap implementation contexts, and stacks in deque contexts.

Perhaps you need a different implementation of one of the Collections Framework core interfaces. If so, you can extend this framework by implementing the interface, or by subclassing one of the more convenient "Abstract" classes, such as AbstractQueue. For example, author Cay Horstmann demonstrates extending this class to implement a circular array queue (see

http://www.java2s.com/Code/Java/Collections-Data-
Structure/Howtoextendthecollectionsframework.htm).

OBEYING CONTRACTS

When you implement a core interface or extend one of the Abstract classes, you should ensure that your implementation class doesn't deviate from the various contracts described in the Java documentation for these interfaces. For example, List places the following stipulation on the hashCode() method that it inherits from Collection:

The hash code of a list is defined to be the result of the following calculation:

```
int hashCode = 1;
for (E e: list)
    hashCode = 31*hashCode+(e==null ? 0 : e.hashCode());
```

This calculation ensures that list1.equals(list2) implies that list1.hashCode() == list2.hashCode() for any two lists, list1 and list2, as required by the general contract of Object.hashCode().

The AbstractList class, which partially implements List, has this to say about hashCode():*This implementation uses exactly the code that is used to define the list hash function in the documentation for the List.hashCode() method.*

When it comes to lists, you should also be aware of the RandomAccess interface:

ArrayList implements the RandomAccess interface, which is a marker interface used by List implementation classes to indicate that they support fast (generally constant time) random access. The primary purpose of this interface is to allow generic algorithms to alter their behavior to provide good performance when applied to either random or sequential access lists.

The best algorithms for manipulating random access List implementations (such as ArrayList) can produce quadratic behavior when applied to sequential access List implementations (such as LinkedList). Generic list algorithms are encouraged to check whether the given list is an instance of this interface (via instanceof) before applying an algorithm that would provide poor performance if it were applied to a sequential access list, and to alter their behavior if necessary to guarantee acceptable performance.

The distinction between random and sequential access is often fuzzy. For example, some List implementations provide asymptotically linear (a line whose distance to a given curve tends to zero) access times if they get huge, but constant access times in practice. Such a List implementation class should generally implement this interface. As a rule of thumb, a List implementation class should implement this interface if, for typical instances of the class, the following loop:

```
for (int i=0, n=list.size(); i < n; i++) list.get(i);
```

runs faster than the following loop:

```
for (Iterator i=list.iterator(); i.hasNext();) i.next();
```

Keep these advices in mind and you should find it easier to extend the Collections Framework.

You might require a collection that isn't supported by the Collections Framework (or perhaps you only think it isn't supported). For example, you might want to model a *sparse matrix*, a table where many or most of its elements are zeros (see http://en.wikipedia.org/wiki/Sparse_matrix). A sparse matrix is a good data structure for implementing a spreadsheet, for example.

If the elements represent bits, you could use BitSet to represent the matrix. If the elements are objects, you might use an array. The problem with either approach is scalability and the limits of heap space. For example, suppose you need a table with 100,000 rows and 100,000 columns, yielding a maximum of 10 billion elements.

You can forget about using BitSet (assuming that each entry occupies a single bit) because 10,000,000,000 is too large to pass to the BitSet(int nbits) constructor; some information will be lost when you cast this long integer to an integer. You can also forget about using an array because you'll exhaust the JVM's memory and obtain a java.lang.OutOfMemoryError at runtime.

Because you're dealing with a sparse matrix, assume that no more than 25,000 table entries are nonzero at any one time. After all, a sparse matrix has a sparse number of nonzero entries. This is a lot more manageable.

You won't use BitSet to represent this matrix because you'll assume that each matrix entry is an object. You can't use a two-dimensional array to store these objects because the array would need 100,000 rows by 100,000 columns to properly index the sparse matrix, and you would exhaust memory by being extremely wasteful in storing zero (or null, in the case of object) values.

There is another way to represent this matrix, and that is to create a linked list of nodes.

A *node* is an object consisting of value and link fields. Unlike an array, where each element stores a single value of the same primitive type or reference supertype, a node can store multiple values of different types. It can also store *links* (references to other nodes).

Consider Listing 5-28's Node class:

Listing 5-28. *A node consists of value fields and link fields*

```
class Node
{
   // value field
   String name;
   // link field
   Node next;
}
```

Node describes simple nodes where each node consists of a single name value field and a single next link field. Notice that next is of the same type as the class in which it is declared. This arrangement lets a node instance store a reference to another node instance (which is the next node) in this field. The resulting nodes are *linked* together.

Listing 5-29 presents a Nodes class that demonstrates connecting Nodes together into a *linked list*, and then iterating over this list to output the values of the name fields.

Listing 5-29. *Creating and iterating over a linked list of nodes*

```
class Nodes
{
   public static void main(String[] args)
   {
      Node top = new Node();
```

```
            top.name = "node 1";
            top.next = new Node();
            top.next.name = "node 2";
            top.next.next = new Node();
            top.next.next.name = "node 3";
            top.next.next.next = null;
            Node temp = top;
            while (temp != null)
            {
                System.out.println(temp.name);
                temp = temp.next;
            }
        }
    }
```

Listing 5-29 demonstrates the creation of a *singly linked list* (a list where each node consists of a single link field). The first Node instance is pointed to by reference variable top, which identifies the top of the list. Each subsequent node in this linked list is referenced from its predecessor's next field. The final next field is set to null to signify the end of the linked list. (This explicit initialization is unnecessary because the field defaults to the null reference during instance initialization, but is present for clarity).

Figure 5-5 reveals this three-node linked list.

Figure 5-5. Reference variable top points to the first node in this three-node linked list.

Listing 5-29 also shows you how to traverse this singly linked list by following each Node object's next field. Prior to the traversal, top's reference is assigned to variable temp, to preserve the start of this linked list so that further manipulations (node insertions, removals, updates) and searches can be performed.

The while loop iterates until temp contains the null reference, outputting each node's name field and assigning the reference in the current node's next field to temp.

When you run this application, it generates the following output:

```
node 1
node 2
node 3
```

You might declare the following Cell class to represent a sparse matrix node for a spreadsheet, which is known as a *cell*:

```
class Cell
{
    int row;
    int col;
    Object value;
    Node next;
}
```

When called upon to update the spreadsheet on the screen, your spreadsheet application's rendering code traverses its linked list of Cell nodes. For each cell, it first examines (row, col) to learn if the cell is visible and should be rendered. If the cell is visible, the instanceof operator is used to determine value's type, and value is then displayed. As soon as null is encountered, the rendering code knows that there are no more spreadsheet elements to render.

Before creating your own linked list class to store Cell instances, you should realize that doing so isn't necessary. Instead, you can leverage the Collection Framework's LinkedList class to store Cell instances (without the unnecessary next fields). Although you might occasionally need to create your own node-based collections, the moral of this exercise is that you should always think about using arrays, the Collections Framework, or a legacy class such as BitSet before inventing your own API to collect objects.

EXERCISES

The following exercises are designed to test your understanding of collections:

1. As an example of array list usefulness, create a JavaQuiz application that presents a multiple-choice-based quiz on Java features. The JavaQuiz class's main() method first populates the array list with the entries in a QuizEntry array (e.g., new QuizEntry("What was Java's original name?", new String[] { "Oak", "Duke", "J", "None of the above" },'A')). Each entry consists of a question, four possible answers, and the letter (A, B, C, or D) of the correct answer. main() then uses the array list's iterator() method to return an Iterator instance, and this instance's hasNext() and next() methods to iterate over the list. Each of the iterations outputs the question and four possible answers, and then prompts the user to enter the correct choice. After the user enters A, B, C, or D (via System.in.read()), main() outputs a message stating whether or not the user made the correct choice.

2. Create a word-counting application (WC) that reads words from the standard input (via System.in.read()) and stores them in a map along with their frequency counts. For this exercise, a word consists of letters only; use the java.lang.Character class's isLetter() method to make this determination. Also, use Map's get() and put() methods and take advantage of autoboxing to record a new entry or update an existing entry's count—the first time a word is seen, its count is set to 1. Use Map's entrySet() method to return a Set of entries, and iterate over these entries, outputting each entry to the standard output.

3. Collections provides the static int frequency(Collection<?> c, Object o) method to return the number of collection c elements that are equal to o. Create a FrequencyDemo application that reads its command-line arguments and stores all arguments except for the last argument in a list, and then calls frequency() with the list and last command-line argument as this method's arguments. It then outputs this method's return value (the number of occurrences of the last command-line argument in the previous command-line arguments). For example, java FrequencyDemo should output Number of occurrences of null = 0, and java FrequencyDemo how much wood could a woodchuck chuck if a woodchuck could chuck wood wood should output Number of occurrences of wood = 2.

399

Summary

The Collections Framework is a standard architecture for representing and manipulating collections, which are groups of objects stored in instances of classes designed for this purpose. This framework largely consists of core interfaces, implementation classes, and utility classes.

The core interfaces make it possible to manipulate collections independently of their implementations. They include Iterable, Collection, List, Set, SortedSet, NavigableSet, Queue, Deque, Map, SortedMap, and NavigableMap. Collection extends Iterable; List, Set, and Queue each extend Collection; SortedSet extends Set; NavigableSet extends SortedSet; Deque extends Queue; SortedMap extends Map; and NavigableMap extends SortedMap.

The framework's implementation classes include ArrayList, LinkedList, TreeSet, HashSet, LinkedHashSet, EnumSet, PriorityQueue, ArrayDeque, TreeMap, HashMap, LinkedHashMap, IdentityHashMap, WeakHashMap, and EnumMap. The name of each concrete class ends in a core interface name, identifying the core interface on which it is based.

The framework's implementation classes also include the abstract AbstractCollection, AbstractList, AbstractSequentialList, AbstractSet, AbstractQueue, and AbstractMap classes. These classes offer skeletal implementations of the core interfaces to facilitate the creation of concrete implementation classes.

The Collections Framework would not be complete without its Arrays and Collections utility classes. Each class supplies various class methods that implement useful algorithms in the contexts of arrays and collections.

Before Java 1.2's introduction of the Collections Framework, developers had two choices where collections were concerned: create their own frameworks, or use the Vector, Enumeration, Stack, Dictionary, Hashtable, Properties, and BitSet types, which were introduced by Java 1.0.

The Collections Framework has made Vector, Stack, Dictionary, and Hashtable obsolete. The framework's Iterator interface has largely obsoleted the Enumeration interface. The Preferences API has made Properties largely obsolete. Because BitSet is still relevant, this class continues to be improved.

Arrays, the Collections Framework, and legacy classes such as BitSet are suitable for organizing groups of objects (or, in the case of BitSet, sets of bits that are interpreted as Boolean true/false values), and you should use them wherever possible before creating your own collection APIs.

However, you might need a different implementation of one of the Collections Framework core interfaces. If so, you can extend this framework by implementing the interface, or by subclassing one of the more convenient "Abstract" classes, such as AbstractQueue.

You might require a collection that isn't supported by the Collections Framework (or perhaps you only think it isn't supported). For example, you might want to model a sparse matrix, a table where many or most of its elements are zeros. A sparse matrix is a good data structure for implementing a spreadsheet, for example.

To model a spreadsheet or other sparse matrix, you can work with nodes, which are objects consisting of value and link fields. Unlike an array, where each element stores a single value of the same primitive type or reference supertype, a node can store multiple values of different types. It can also store references to other nodes, which are known as links.

You can connect nodes together into linked lists, but (at least for singly linked lists) there is no need to do so because you can take advantage of the Collections Framework's LinkedList class for this task. After all, you should not "reinvent the wheel."

Broadly speaking, the Collections Framework is an example of a utility API. Chapter 6 continues to focus on utility APIs by introducing you to Java's concurrency utilities, which extend the Collections Framework, the java.util.Objects class, and more.

CHAPTER 6

Touring Additional Utility APIs

Chapter 5 introduced you to the Collections Framework, which is a collection of utility APIs. Chapter 6 introduces you to additional utility APIs, specifically the concurrency utilities, `Objects`, and `Random`.

Concurrency Utilities

Java 5 introduced the *concurrency utilities*, which are classes and interfaces that simplify the development of *concurrent* (multithreaded) applications. These types are located in the `java.util.concurrent` package and in its `java.util.concurrent.atomic` and `java.util.concurrent.locks` subpackages.

The concurrency utilities leverage the low-level Threading API (see Chapter 4) in their implementations and provide higher-level building blocks to simplify creating multithreaded applications. They are organized into executor, synchronizer, concurrent collection, lock, atomic variable, and additional utility categories.

Executors

Chapter 4 introduced the Threading API, which lets you execute runnable tasks via expressions such as `new Thread(new RunnableTask()).start();`. These expressions tightly couple task submission with the task's execution mechanics (run on the current thread, a new thread, or a thread arbitrarily chosen from a *pool* [group] of threads).

Note A *task* is an object whose class implements the `java.lang.Runnable` interface (a runnable task) or the `java.util.concurrent.Callable` interface (a callable task).

The concurrency utilities provide executors as a high-level alternative to low-level Threading API expressions for executing runnable tasks. An *executor* is an object whose class directly or indirectly implements the `java.util.concurrent.Executor` interface, which decouples task submission from task-execution mechanics.

> **Note** The executor framework's use of interfaces to decouple task submission from task-execution mechanics is analogous to the Collections Framework's use of core interfaces to decouple lists, sets, queues, deques, and maps from their implementations. Decoupling results in flexible code that is easier to maintain.

Executor declares a solitary void execute(Runnable runnable) method that executes the runnable task named runnable at some point in the future. execute() throws java.lang.NullPointerException when runnable is null, and java.util.concurrent.RejectedExecutionException when it cannot execute runnable.

> **Note** RejectedExecutionException can be thrown when an executor is shutting down and does not want to accept new tasks. Also, this exception can be thrown when the executor does not have enough room to store the task (perhaps the executor uses a bounded blocking queue to store tasks and the queue is full—I discuss blocking queues later in this chapter).

The following example presents the Executor equivalent of the aforementioned new Thread(new RunnableTask()).start(); expression:

```
Executor executor = ...; //  ... represents some executor creation
executor.execute(new RunnableTask());
```

Although Executor is easy to use, this interface is limited in various ways:

- Executor focuses exclusively on Runnable. Because Runnable's run() method does not return a value, there is no convenient way for a runnable task to return a value to its caller.

- Executor does not provide a way to track the progress of executing runnable tasks, cancel an executing runnable task, or determine when the runnable task finishes execution.

- Executor cannot execute a collection of runnable tasks.

- Executor does not provide a way for an application to shut down an executor (much less to properly shut down an executor).

These limitations are addressed by the java.util.concurrent.ExecutorService interface, which extends Executor, and whose implementation is typically a *thread pool* (a group of reusable threads). Table 6-1 describes ExecutorService's methods.

Table 6-1. ExecutorService Methods

Method	Description
`boolean awaitTermination(long timeout, TimeUnit unit)`	Block (wait) until all tasks have finished after a shutdown request, the `timeout` (measured in `unit` time units) expires, or the current thread is interrupted, whichever happens first. Return true when this executor has terminated, and false when the `timeout` elapses before termination. This method throws `java.lang.InterruptedException` when interrupted.
`<T> List<Future<T>> invokeAll(Collection<? extends Callable<T>> tasks)`	Execute each callable task in the `tasks` collection, and return a `java.util.List` of `java.util.concurrent.Future` instances that hold task statuses and results when all tasks complete—a task completes through normal termination or by throwing an exception. The `List` of `Futures` is in the same sequential order as the sequence of tasks returned by `tasks`' iterator. This method throws `InterruptedException` when it is interrupted while waiting, in which case unfinished tasks are canceled, `NullPointerException` when `tasks` or any of its elements is `null`, and `RejectedExecutionException` when any one of `tasks`' tasks cannot be scheduled for execution.
`<T> List<Future<T>> invokeAll(Collection<? extends Callable<T>> tasks, long timeout, TimeUnit unit)`	Execute each callable task in the `tasks` collection, and return a `List` of `Future` instances that hold task statuses and results when all tasks complete—a task completes through normal termination or by throwing an exception—or the `timeout` (measured in `unit` time units) expires. Tasks that are not completed at expiry are canceled. The `List` of `Futures` is in the same sequential order as the sequence of tasks returned by `tasks`' iterator. This method throws `InterruptedException` when it is interrupted while waiting, in which case unfinished tasks are canceled. It also throws `NullPointerException` when `tasks`, any of its elements, or `unit` is `null`; and throws `RejectedExecutionException` when any one of `tasks`' tasks cannot be scheduled for execution.
`<T> T invokeAny(Collection<? extends Callable<T>> tasks)`	Execute the given tasks, returning the result of an arbitrary task that has completed successfully (i.e., without throwing an exception), if any does. Upon normal or exceptional return, tasks that have not completed are canceled. This method throws `InterruptedException` when it is interrupted while waiting, `NullPointerException` when `tasks` or any of its elements is `null`, `java.lang.IllegalArgumentException` when `tasks` is empty, `java.util.concurrent.ExecutionException` when no task completes successfully, and `RejectedExecutionException` when none of the tasks can be scheduled for execution.

`<T> T invokeAny(Collection<? extends Callable<T>> tasks, long timeout, TimeUnit unit)`	Execute the given tasks, returning the result of an arbitrary task that has completed successfully (i.e., without throwing an exception), if any does before the timeout (measured in unit time units) expires—tasks that are not completed at expiry are canceled. Upon normal or exceptional return, tasks that have not completed are canceled. This method throws InterruptedException when it is interrupted while waiting, NullPointerException when tasks, any of its elements, or unit is null, IllegalArgumentException when tasks is empty, java.util.concurrent.TimeoutException when the timeout elapses before any task successfully completes, ExecutionException when no task completes successfully, and RejectedExecutionException when none of the tasks can be scheduled for execution.
`boolean isShutdown()`	Return true when this executor has been shut down; otherwise, return false.
`boolean isTerminated()`	Return true when all tasks have completed following shutdown; otherwise, return false. This method will never return true prior to shutdown() or shutdownNow() being called.
`void shutdown()`	Initiate an orderly shutdown in which previously submitted tasks are executed, but no new tasks will be accepted. Calling this method has no effect after the executor has shut down. This method does not wait for previously submitted tasks to complete execution. Use awaitTermination() if waiting is necessary.
`List<Runnable> shutdownNow()`	Attempt to stop all actively executing tasks, halt the processing of waiting tasks, and return a list of the tasks that were awaiting execution. There are no guarantees beyond best-effort attempts to stop processing actively executing tasks. For example, typical implementations will cancel via Thread.interrupt(), so any task that fails to respond to interrupts may never terminate. This method does not wait for actively executing tasks to terminate. Use awaitTermination() if waiting is necessary.
`<T> Future<T> submit(Callable<T> task)`	Submit a callable task for execution and return a Future instance representing task's pending results. The Future instance's get() method returns task's result upon successful completion. This method throws RejectedExecutionException when task cannot be scheduled for execution, and NullPointerException when task is null. If you would like to immediately block while waiting for a task to complete, you can use constructions of

the form result = exec.submit(aCallable).get();.

Future<?> submit(Runnable task)	Submit a runnable task for execution and return a Future instance representing task's pending results. The Future instance's get() method returns task's result upon successful completion. This method throws RejectedExecutionException when task cannot be scheduled for execution, and NullPointerException when task is null.
<T> Future<T> submit(Runnable task, T result)	Submit a runnable task for execution and return a Future instance whose get() method returns result upon successful completion. This method throws RejectedExecutionException when task cannot be scheduled for execution, and NullPointerException when task is null.

Table 6-1 refers to java.util.concurrent.TimeUnit, an enum that represents time durations at given units of granularity: DAYS, HOURS, MICROSECONDS, MILLISECONDS, MINUTES, NANOSECONDS, and SECONDS. Furthermore, TimeUnit declares methods for converting across units (e.g., long toHours(long duration)), and for performing timing and delay operations (e.g., void sleep(long timeout)) in these units.

Table 6-1 also refers to callable tasks, which are analogous to runnable tasks. Unlike Runnable, whose void run() method cannot throw checked exceptions, Callable<V> declares a V call() method that returns a value, and which can throw checked exceptions because call() is declared with a throws Exception clause.

Finally, Table 6-1 refers to the Future interface, which represents the result of an asynchronous computation. Future, whose generic type is Future<V>, provides methods for canceling a task, for returning a task's value, and for determining whether or not the task has finished. Table 6-2 describes Future's methods.

Table 6-2. Future Methods

Method	Description
boolean cancel(boolean mayInterruptIfRunning)	Attempt to cancel execution of this task, and return true when the task was canceled; otherwise, return false (perhaps the task completed normally before this method was called).
	The cancellation attempt fails when the task has completed, has already been canceled, or could not be canceled for some other reason. If successful and this task had not started when cancel() was called, the task should never run. If the task has already started, then mayInterruptIfRunning determines whether (true) or not (false) the thread executing this task should be interrupted in an attempt to stop the task. After this method returns, subsequent calls to isDone() always return true. Subsequent calls to isCancelled() always return true when cancel() returns true.

V get()	Wait if necessary for the task to complete and return the result. This method throws java.util.concurrent.CancellationException when the task was canceled prior to this method being called, ExecutionException when the task threw an exception, and InterruptedException when the current thread was interrupted while waiting.
V get(long timeout, TimeUnit unit)	Wait at most timeout units (as specified by unit) for the task to complete and then return the result (if available). This method throws CancellationException when the task was canceled prior to this method being called, ExecutionException when the task threw an exception, InterruptedException when the current thread was interrupted while waiting, and TimeoutException when this method's timeout value expires (the wait times out).
boolean isCancelled()	Return true when this task was canceled before it completed normally; otherwise, return false.
boolean isDone()	Return true when this task completed; otherwise, return false. Completion may be due to normal termination, an exception, or cancellation—this method returns true in all these cases.

Suppose you intend to write an application whose graphical user interface (GUI) lets the user enter a word. After the user enters the word, the application presents this word to several online dictionaries and obtains each dictionary's entry. These entries are subsequently displayed to the user.

Because online access can be slow, and because the user interface should remain responsive (perhaps the user might want to end the application), you offload the "obtain word entries" task to an executor that runs this task on a separate thread. The following example employs ExecutorService, Callable, and Future to accomplish this objective:

```
ExecutorService executor = ...; //  ... represents some executor creation
Future<String[]> taskFuture = executor.submit(new Callable<String[]>()
                                    {
                                        public String[] call()
                                        {
                                            String[] entries = ...;
                                            // Access online dictionaries
                                            // with search word and populate
                                            // entries with their resulting
                                            // entries.
                                            return entries;
                                        }
                                    });
// Do stuff.
String entries = taskFuture.get();
```

After obtaining an executor in some manner (you will learn how shortly), the example's main thread submits a callable task to the executor. The submit() method immediately returns with a reference to a Future object for controlling task execution and accessing results. The main thread ultimately calls this object's get() method to get these results.

Note The java.util.concurrent.ScheduledExecutorService interface extends ExecutorService and describes an executor that lets you schedule tasks to run once or to execute periodically after a given delay.

Although you could create your own Executor, ExecutorService, and ScheduledExecutorService implementations (such as class DirectExecutor implements Executor { public void execute(Runnable r) { r.run(); } }—run executor directly on the calling thread), the concurrency utilities offer a simpler alternative: java.util.concurrent.Executors.

Tip If you intend to create your own ExecutorService implementations, you will find it helpful to work with the java.util.concurrent.AbstractExecutorService and java.util.concurrent.FutureTask classes.

The Executors utility class declares several class methods that return instances of various ExecutorService and ScheduledExecutorService implementations (and other kinds of instances). This class's static methods accomplish the following tasks:

- Create and return an ExecutorService instance that is configured with commonly used configuration settings.

- Create and return a ScheduledExecutorService instance that is configured with commonly used configuration settings.

- Create and return a "wrapped" ExecutorService or ScheduledExecutorService instance that disables reconfiguration of the executor service by making implementation-specific methods inaccessible.

- Create and return a java.util.concurrent.ThreadFactory instance for creating new threads.

- Create and return a Callable instance out of other closure-like forms so that it can be used in execution methods requiring Callable arguments (e.g., ExecutorService's submit(Callable) method). (Check out Wikipedia's "Closure (computer science)" entry [http://en.wikipedia.org/wiki/Closure_(computer_science)] to learn about closures.)

For example, static ExecutorService newFixedThreadPool(int nThreads) creates a thread pool that reuses a fixed number of threads operating off a shared unbounded queue. At most, nThreads threads are actively processing tasks. If additional tasks are submitted when all threads are active, they wait in the queue for an available thread.

If any thread terminates because of a failure during execution before the executor shuts down, a new thread will take its place when needed to execute subsequent tasks. The threads in the pool will exist until the executor is explicitly shut down. This method throws IllegalArgumentException when you pass zero or a negative value to nThreads.

■ **Note** Threads pools are used to eliminate the overhead from having to create a new thread for each submitted task. Thread creation is not cheap, and having to create many threads could severely impact an application's performance.

You would commonly use executors, runnables, callables, and futures in an input/output context. (I discuss Java's support for filesystem input/output in Chapter 8.) Performing a lengthy calculation offers another scenario where you could use these types. For example, Listing 6-1 uses an executor, a callable, and a future in a calculation context of Euler's number e (2.71828...).

Listing 6-1. Calculating Euler's number e

```java
import java.math.BigDecimal;
import java.math.MathContext;
import java.math.RoundingMode;

import java.util.concurrent.Callable;
import java.util.concurrent.ExecutionException;
import java.util.concurrent.ExecutorService;
import java.util.concurrent.Executors;
import java.util.concurrent.Future;

class CalculateE
{
    final static int LASTITER = 17;
    public static void main(String[] args)
    {
        ExecutorService executor = Executors.newFixedThreadPool(1);
        Callable<BigDecimal> callable;
        callable = new Callable<BigDecimal>()
                {
                    public BigDecimal call()
                    {
                        MathContext mc = new MathContext(100,
                                                    RoundingMode.HALF_UP);
                        BigDecimal result = BigDecimal.ZERO;
                        for (int i = 0; i <= LASTITER; i++)
                        {
                            BigDecimal factorial = factorial(new BigDecimal(i));
                            BigDecimal res = BigDecimal.ONE.divide(factorial, mc);
                            result = result.add(res);
                        }
                        return result;
```

```
                     }
                     public BigDecimal factorial(BigDecimal n)
                     {
                         if (n.equals(BigDecimal.ZERO))
                             return BigDecimal.ONE;
                         else
                             return n.multiply(factorial(n.subtract(BigDecimal.ONE)));
                     }
                 };
      Future<BigDecimal> taskFuture = executor.submit(callable);
      try
      {
         while (!taskFuture.isDone())
             System.out.println("waiting");
         System.out.println(taskFuture.get());
      }
      catch(ExecutionException ee)
      {
         System.err.println("task threw an exception");
         System.err.println(ee);
      }
      catch(InterruptedException ie)
      {
         System.err.println("interrupted while waiting");
      }
      executor.shutdownNow();
   }
}
```

The main thread that executes Listing 6-1's main() method first obtains an executor by calling Executors' newFixedThreadPool() method. It then instantiates an anonymous class that implements Callable and submits this task to the executor, receiving a Future instance in response.

After submitting a task, a thread typically does some other work until it needs to obtain the task's result. I have chosen to simulate this work by having the main thread repeatedly output a waiting message until the Future instance's isDone() method returns true. (In a realistic application, I would avoid this looping.) At this point, the main thread calls the instance's get() method to obtain the result, which is then output.

▪ **Caution** It is important to shut down the executor after it completes; otherwise, the application might not end. The application accomplishes this task by calling shutdownNow().

The callable's call() method calculates e by evaluating the mathematical power series e = $1/0!+1/1!+1/2!+\dots$. This series can be evaluated by summing $1/n!$, where n ranges from 0 to infinity.

call() first instantiates java.math.MathContext to encapsulate a *precision* (number of digits) and a rounding mode. I chose 100 as an upper limit on e's precision and HALF_UP as the rounding mode.

Tip Increase the precision as well as LASTITER's value to converge the series to a lengthier and more accurate approximation of e.

---

call() next initializes a java.math.BigDecimal local variable named result to BigDecimal.ZERO. It then enters a loop that calculates a factorial, divides BigDecimal.ONE by the factorial, and adds the division result to result.

The divide() method takes the MathContext instance as its second argument to ensure that the division does not result in a *nonterminating decimal expansion* (the quotient result of the division cannot be represented exactly—0.3333333..., for example), which throws java.lang.ArithmeticException (to alert the caller to the fact that the quotient cannot be represented exactly), which the executor rethrows as ExecutionException.

When you run this application, you should observe output similar to the following:

```
waiting
waiting
waiting
waiting
2.7182818284590450705160477958486050611789796352510326989007350040652250425048433140558879743
42457417300394540627711
```

Synchronizers

The Threading API offers synchronization primitives for synchronizing thread access to critical sections. Because it can be difficult to correctly write synchronized code that is based on these primitives, the concurrency utilities include *synchronizers*, classes that facilitate common forms of synchronization.

Five commonly used synchronizers are countdown latches, cyclic barriers, exchangers, phasers, and semaphores:

- A *countdown latch* lets one or more threads wait at a "gate" until another thread opens this gate, at which point these other threads can continue. The java.util.concurrent.CountDownLatch class implements this synchronizer.

- A *cyclic barrier* lets a group of threads wait for each other to reach a common *barrier point*. The java.util.concurrent.CyclicBarrier class implements this synchronizer, and makes use of the java.util.concurrent.BrokenBarrierException class. CyclicBarrier instances are useful in applications involving fixed sized parties of threads that must occasionally wait for each other. CyclicBarrier supports an optional Runnable, known as a *barrier action*, which runs once per barrier point after the last thread in the party arrives but before any threads are released. This barrier action is useful for updating shared state before any of the parties continue.

- An *exchanger* lets a pair of threads exchange objects at a synchronization point. The java.util.concurrent.Exchanger class implements this synchronizer. Each thread presents some object on entry to Exchanger's exchange() method, matches with a partner thread, and receives its partner's object on return. Exchangers may be useful in applications such as *genetic algorithms* (see http://en.wikipedia.org/wiki/Genetic_algorithm) and pipeline designs.

- A *phaser* is a reusable synchronization barrier that is similar in functionality to CyclicBarrier and CountDownLatch, but offers more flexibility. For example, unlike with other barriers, the number of threads that register to synchronize on a phaser may vary over time. The java.util.concurrent.Phaser class implements this synchronizer. Phaser may be used instead of a CountDownLatch to control a one-shot action that serves a variable number of parties. It may also be used by tasks executing in the context of the Fork/Join Framework, discussed later in this chapter.

- A *semaphore* maintains a set of permits for restricting the number of threads that can access a limited resource. The java.util.concurrent.Semaphore class implements this synchronizer. Each call to one of Semaphore's acquire() methods blocks if necessary until a permit is available, and then takes it. Each call to release() adds a permit, potentially releasing a blocking acquirer. However, no actual permit objects are used; the Semaphore instance only keeps a count of the number of available permits and acts accordingly. Semaphores are often used to restrict the number of threads than can access some (physical or logical) resource.

Consider the CountDownLatch class. Each of its instances is initialized to a nonzero count. A thread calls one of CountDownLatch's await() methods to block until the count reaches zero. Another thread calls CountDownLatch's countDown() method to decrement the count. Once the count reaches zero, the waiting threads are allowed to continue.

Note After waiting threads are released, subsequent calls to await() return immediately. Also, because the count cannot be reset, a CountDownLatch instance can be used only once. When repeated use is a requirement, use the CyclicBarrier class instead.

We can use CountDownLatch to ensure that worker threads start working at approximately the same time. For example, check out Listing 6-2.

Listing 6-2. Using a countdown latch to trigger a coordinated start

```
import java.util.concurrent.CountDownLatch;
import java.util.concurrent.ExecutorService;
import java.util.concurrent.Executors;

class CountDownLatchDemo
{
    final static int NTHREADS = 3;
    public static void main(String[] args)
    {
        final CountDownLatch startSignal = new CountDownLatch(1);
        final CountDownLatch doneSignal = new CountDownLatch(NTHREADS);
        Runnable r = new Runnable()
                    {
                        public void run()
                        {
```

```
                    try
                    {
                        report("entered run()");
                        startSignal.await(); // wait until told to proceed
                        report("doing work");
                        Thread.sleep((int)(Math.random()*1000));
                        doneSignal.countDown(); // reduce count on which
                                                // main thread is waiting
                    }
                    catch (InterruptedException ie)
                    {
                        System.err.println(ie);
                    }
                }
                void report(String s)
                {
                    System.out.println(System.currentTimeMillis()+": "+
                                       Thread.currentThread()+": "+s);
                }
            };
    ExecutorService executor = Executors.newFixedThreadPool(NTHREADS);
    for (int i = 0; i < NTHREADS; i++)
        executor.execute(r);
    try
    {
        System.out.println("main thread doing something");
        Thread.sleep(1000);      // sleep for 1 second
        startSignal.countDown(); // let all threads proceed
        System.out.println("main thread doing something else");
        doneSignal.await();      // wait for all threads to finish
        executor.shutdownNow();
    }
    catch (InterruptedException ie)
    {
        System.err.println(ie);
    }
    }
}
}
```

Listing 6-2's main thread first creates a pair of countdown latches. The startSignal countdown latch prevents any worker thread from proceeding until the main thread is ready for them to proceed. The doneSignal countdown latch causes the main thread to wait until all worker threads have finished.

The main thread next creates a runnable whose run() method is executed by subsequently created worker threads.

The run() method first outputs an initial message and then calls startSignal's await() method to wait for this countdown latch's count to read zero before it can proceed. Once this happens, run() outputs a message that indicates work is being done, and sleeps for a random period of time (0 through 999 milliseconds) to simulate this work.

At this point, run() invokes doneSignal's countDown() method to decrement this latch's count. Once this count reaches zero, the main thread waiting on this signal will continue, shutting down the executor and terminating the application.

After creating the runnable, the main thread obtains an executor that's based on a thread pool of NTHREADS threads, and then calls the executor's execute() method NTHREADS times, passing the runnable to each of the NTHREADS pool-based threads. This action starts the worker threads, which enter run().

Next, the main thread outputs a message and sleeps for one second to simulate doing additional work (giving all the worker threads a chance to have entered run() and invoke startSignal.await()), invokes startSignal's countdown() method to cause the worker threads to start running, outputs a message to indicate that it is doing something else, and invokes doneSignal's await() method to wait for this countdown latch's count to reach zero before it can proceed.

When you run this application, you will observe output similar to the following:

```
main thread doing something
1312936533890: Thread[pool-1-thread-1,5,main]: entered run()
1312936533890: Thread[pool-1-thread-2,5,main]: entered run()
1312936533890: Thread[pool-1-thread-3,5,main]: entered run()
1312936534890: Thread[pool-1-thread-1,5,main]: doing work
1312936534890: Thread[pool-1-thread-2,5,main]: doing work
1312936534890: Thread[pool-1-thread-3,5,main]: doing work
main thread doing something else
```

You might observe the main thread doing something else message appearing between the last "entered run()" message and the first "doing work" message.

■ **Note** For brevity, I have avoided examples that demonstrate CyclicBarrier, Exchanger, Phaser, and Semaphore. Instead, I refer you to the Java documentation for these classes. Each class's documentation provides an example that shows you how to use the class.

Concurrent Collections

The java.util.concurrent package includes several interfaces and classes that are concurrency-oriented extensions to the Collections Framework (see Chapter 5):

- BlockingDeque is a subinterface of BlockingQueue and java.util.Deque that also supports blocking operations that wait for the deque to become nonempty before retrieving an element, and wait for space to become available in the deque before storing an element. The LinkedBlockingDeque class implements this interface.

- BlockingQueue is a subinterface of java.util.Queue that also supports blocking operations that wait for the queue to become nonempty before retrieving an element, and wait for space to become available in the queue before storing an element. Each of the ArrayBlockingQueue, DelayQueue, LinkedBlockingDeque, LinkedBlockingQueue, LinkedTransferQueue, PriorityBlockingQueue, and SynchronousQueue classes implements this interface.

- ConcurrentMap is a subinterface of java.util.Map that declares additional atomic putIfAbsent(), remove(), and replace() methods. The ConcurrentHashMap class (the concurrent equivalent of java.util.HashMap) and the ConcurrentSkipListMap class implement this interface.

- ConcurrentNavigableMap is a subinterface of ConcurrentMap and java.util.NavigableMap. The ConcurrentSkipListMap class implements this interface.

- TransferQueue is a subinterface of BlockingQueue and describes a blocking queue in which producers may wait for consumers to receive elements. The LinkedTransferQueue class implements this interface.

- ConcurrentLinkedDeque is an unbounded concurrent deque based on linked nodes.

- ConcurrentLinkedQueue is an unbounded thread-safe FIFO implementation of the Queue interface.

- ConcurrentSkipListSet is a scalable concurrent NavigableSet implementation.

- CopyOnWriteArrayList is a thread-safe variant of java.util.ArrayList in which all *mutative* (nonimmutable) operations (add, set, and so on) are implemented by making a fresh copy of the underlying array.

- CopyOnWriteArraySet is a java.util.Set implementation that uses an internal CopyOnWriteArrayList instance for all its operations.

Listing 6-3 uses BlockingQueue and ArrayBlockingQueue in an alternative to Listing 4-27's producer-consumer application (PC).

Listing 6-3. The blocking queue equivalent of Listing 4-27's PC application

```
import java.util.concurrent.ArrayBlockingQueue;
import java.util.concurrent.BlockingQueue;
import java.util.concurrent.ExecutorService;
import java.util.concurrent.Executors;

class PC
{
   public static void main(String[] args)
   {
      final BlockingQueue<Character> bq;
      bq = new ArrayBlockingQueue<Character>(26);
      final ExecutorService executor = Executors.newFixedThreadPool(2);
      Runnable producer;
      producer = new Runnable()
                 {
                    public void run()
                    {
                       for (char ch = 'A'; ch <= 'Z'; ch++)
                       {
                          try
                          {
                             bq.put(ch);
                             System.out.println(ch+" produced by producer.");
                          }
                          catch (InterruptedException ie)
```

```
                          {
                              assert false;
                          }
                      }
                  }
              };
      executor.execute(producer);
      Runnable consumer;
      consumer = new Runnable()
                  {
                      public void run()
                      {
                          char ch = '\0';
                          do
                          {
                              try
                              {
                                  ch = bq.take();
                                  System.out.println(ch+" consumed by consumer.");
                              }
                              catch (InterruptedException ie)
                              {
                                  assert false;
                              }
                          }
                          while (ch != 'Z');
                          executor.shutdownNow();
                      }
                  };
      executor.execute(consumer);
   }
}
```

Listing 6-3 uses BlockingQueue's put() and take() methods, respectively, to put an object on the blocking queue and to remove an object from the blocking queue. put() blocks when there is no room to put an object; take() blocks when the queue is empty.

Although BlockingQueue ensures that a character is never consumed before it is produced, this application's output may indicate otherwise. For example, here is a portion of the output from one run:

```
Y consumed by consumer.
Y produced by producer.
Z consumed by consumer.
Z produced by producer.
```

Chapter 4's PC application overcame this incorrect output order by introducing an extra layer of synchronization around setSharedChar()/System.out.println() and an extra layer of synchronization around getSharedChar()/System.out.println(). The next section shows you an alternative in the form of locks.

Locks

The java.util.concurrent.locks package provides interfaces and classes for locking and waiting for conditions in a manner that is distinct from built-in synchronization and monitors.

This package's most basic lock interface is Lock, which provides more extensive locking operations than can be achieved via the synchronized reserved word. Lock also supports a wait/notification mechanism through associated Condition objects.

■ **Note** The biggest advantage of Lock objects over the implicit locks that are obtained when threads enter critical sections (controlled via the synchronized reserved word) is their ability to back out of an attempt to acquire a lock. For example, the tryLock() method backs out when the lock is not available immediately or when a timeout expires (if specified). Also, the lockInterruptibly() method backs out when another thread sends an interrupt before the lock is acquired.

ReentrantLock implements Lock, describing a reentrant mutual exclusion Lock implementation with the same basic behavior and semantics as the implicit monitor lock accessed via synchronized, but with extended capabilities.

Listing 6-4 demonstrates Lock and ReentrantLock in a version of Listing 6-3 that ensures that the output is never shown in incorrect order (a consumed message appearing before a produced message).

Listing 6-4. Achieving synchronization in terms of locks

```java
import java.util.concurrent.ArrayBlockingQueue;
import java.util.concurrent.BlockingQueue;
import java.util.concurrent.ExecutorService;
import java.util.concurrent.Executors;

import java.util.concurrent.locks.Lock;
import java.util.concurrent.locks.ReentrantLock;

class PC
{
   public static void main(String[] args)
   {
      final Lock lock = new ReentrantLock();
      final BlockingQueue<Character> bq;
      bq = new ArrayBlockingQueue<Character>(26);
      final ExecutorService executor = Executors.newFixedThreadPool(2);
      Runnable producer;
      producer = new Runnable()
               {
                  public void run()
                  {
                     for (char ch = 'A'; ch <= 'Z'; ch++)
                     {
                        try
```

```
                        {
                           lock.lock();
                           try
                           {
                              while (!bq.offer(ch))
                              {
                                 lock.unlock();
                                 Thread.sleep(50);
                                 lock.lock();
                              }
                              System.out.println(ch+" produced by producer.");
                           }
                           catch (InterruptedException ie)
                           {
                              assert false;
                           }
                        }
                        finally
                        {
                           lock.unlock();
                        }
                     }
                  }
               };
            executor.execute(producer);
            Runnable consumer;
            consumer = new Runnable()
                        {
                           public void run()
                           {
                              char ch = '\0';
                              do
                              {
                                 try
                                 {
                                    lock.lock();
                                    try
                                    {
                                       Character c;
                                       while ((c = bq.poll()) == null)
                                       {
                                          lock.unlock();
                                          Thread.sleep(50);
                                          lock.lock();
                                       }
                                       ch = c; // unboxing behind the scenes
                                       System.out.println(ch+" consumed by consumer.");
                                    }
                                    catch (InterruptedException ie)
                                    {
                                       assert false;
                                    }
```

```
                              }
                              finally
                              {
                                  lock.unlock();
                              }
                          }
                          while (ch != 'Z');
                          executor.shutdownNow();
                      }
                  };
          executor.execute(consumer);
      }
}
```

Listing 6-4 uses Lock's lock() and unlock() methods to obtain and release a lock. When a thread calls lock() and the lock is unavailable, the thread is disabled (and cannot be scheduled) until the lock becomes available.

This listing also uses BlockingQueue's offer() method instead of put() to store an object in the blocking queue, and its poll() method instead of take() to retrieve an object from the queue. These alternative methods are used because they do not block.

If I had used put() and take(), this application would have deadlocked in the following scenario:

1.   The consumer thread acquires the lock via its lock.lock() call.

2.   The producer thread attempts to acquire the lock via its lock.lock() call and is disabled because the consumer thread has already acquired the lock.

3.   The consumer thread calls take() to obtain the next java.lang.Character object from the queue.

4.   Because the queue is empty, the consumer thread must wait.

5.   The consumer thread does not give up the lock that the producer thread requires before waiting, so the producer thread also continues to wait.

Note If I had access to the private lock used by BlockingQueue implementations, I would have used put() and take(), and also would have called Lock's lock() and unlock() methods on that lock. The resulting application would then have been identical (from a lock perspective) to Listing 4-27's PC application, which used synchronized twice for each of the producer and consumer threads.

Run this application and you will discover that it generates the same output as Listing 4-27's PC application.

Atomic Variables

The java.util.concurrent.atomic package provides Atomic-prefixed classes (e.g., AtomicLong) that support lock-free, thread-safe operations on single variables. Each class declares methods such as get() and set() to read and write this variable without the need for external synchronization.

Listing 4-23 declared a small utility class named ID for returning unique long integer identifiers via ID's getNextID() method. Because this method was not synchronized, multiple threads could obtain the same identifier. Listing 6-5 fixes this problem by including reserved word synchronized in the method header.

Listing 6-5. *Returning unique identifiers in a thread-safe manner via* synchronized

```
class ID
{
   private static long nextID = 0;
   static synchronized long getNextID()
   {
      return nextID++;
   }
}
```

Although synchronized is appropriate for this class, excessive use of this reserved word in more complex classes can lead to deadlock, starvation, or other problems. Listing 6-6 shows you how to avoid these assaults on a concurrent application's *liveness* (the ability to execute in a timely manner) by replacing synchronized with an atomic variable.

Listing 6-6. *Returning unique IDs in a thread-safe manner via* AtomicLong

```
import java.util.concurrent.atomic.AtomicLong;

class ID
{
   private static AtomicLong nextID = new AtomicLong(0);
   static long getNextID()
   {
      return nextID.getAndIncrement();
   }
}
```

In Listing 6-6, I have converted nextID from a long to an AtomicLong instance, initializing this object to 0. I have also refactored the getNextID() method to call AtomicLong's getAndIncrement() method, which increments the AtomicLong instance's internal long integer variable by 1 and returns the previous value in one indivisible step.

Additional Concurrency Utilities

As well as supporting the Java 5-introduced concurrency utilities, Java 7 introduces a pair of concurrency utilities that improve performance, which is achieved in part by taking full advantage of multiple processors/cores. These utilities consist of the java.util.concurrent.ThreadLocalRandom class and the Fork/Join Framework.

ThreadLocalRandom

The ThreadLocalRandom class describes a random number generator that is isolated to the current thread. In other words, it can be accessed from the current thread only.

As with the global random number generator used by the java.lang.Math class (and which I discuss later in this chapter), a ThreadLocalRandom instance is initialized with an internally generated *seed* (starting value) that may not otherwise be modified. When applicable, use of ThreadLocalRandom rather than calls to Math.random() in concurrent programs will typically result in much less overhead and contention.

To use this class, first invoke ThreadLocalRandom's static ThreadLocalRandom current() method to return the current thread's ThreadLocalRandom instance. Continue by invoking one of ThreadLocalRandom's "next" methods, such as double nextDouble(double n), which returns a pseudorandom, uniformly distributed double value between 0 (inclusive) and the specified value n (exclusive). The argument passed to n is the upper bound on the random number to be returned and must be positive; otherwise, IllegalArgumentException is thrown.

The following example provides a demonstration via another "next" method:

```
int r = ThreadLocalRandom.current().nextInt(20, 40);
```

This example invokes ThreadLocalRandom's int nextInt(int least, int bound) method to return a pseudorandom, uniformly distributed value between the given least value (inclusive) and bound (exclusive). In this example, least is 20, which is the smallest value that can be returned, and bound is 40, which is one integer greater than the highest value (39) that can be returned.

■ **Note** ThreadLocalRandom leverages thread-local variables, which I discussed in Chapter 4's coverage of Java's Threading API.

Fork/Join Framework

There is always a need for code to execute faster. Historically, this need was addressed by increasing microprocessor speeds and/or by supporting multiple processors. However, somewhere around 2003, microprocessor speeds stopped increasing because of natural limits. To compensate, processor manufacturers started to add multiple processing cores to their processors, to increase speed through massive parallelism.

■ **Note** *Parallelism* refers to running threads/tasks simultaneously through some combination of multiple processors and cores. In contrast, *concurrency* is a more generalized form of parallelism in which threads run simultaneously or appear to run simultaneously through task switching, also known as *virtual parallelism*. Some people further characterize concurrency as a property of a program or operating system and parallelism as the run-time behavior of executing multiple tasks simultaneously.

Java supports concurrency via the Threading API and concurrency utilities such as thread pools. The problem with concurrency is that it doesn't maximize the use of available processor/core resources. For example, suppose you have created a sorting algorithm that divides an array into two halves, assigns two threads to sort each half, and merges the results after both threads finish.

Let's assume that each thread runs on a different processor. Because different amounts of element reordering may occur in each half of the array, it's possible that one thread will finish before the other thread and must wait before the merge can happen. In this case, a processor resource is wasted.

This problem (and the related problems of the code being verbose and harder to read) can be solved by recursively breaking a task into subtasks and combining results. These subtasks run in parallel and complete approximately at the same time (if not at the same moment), where their results are merged and passed up the stack to the previous layer of subtasks. Hardly any processor time is wasted through waiting, and the recursive code is less verbose and (usually) easier to understand. Java provides the Fork/Join Framework to implement this scenario.

Fork/Join consists of a special executor service and thread pool. The executor service makes a task available to the framework, and this task is broken down into smaller tasks that are *forked* (executed by different threads) from the pool. A task waits until *joined* (its subtasks finish).

Fork/Join uses *work stealing* to minimize thread contention and overhead. Each worker thread from a pool of worker threads has its own double-ended work queue and pushes new tasks to this queue. It reads the task from the head of the queue. If the queue is empty, the worker thread tries to get a task from the tail of another queue. Stealing is infrequent because worker threads put tasks into their queues in a last-in, first-out (LIFO) order, and the size of work items gets smaller as a problem is divided into subproblems. You start by giving the tasks to a central worker and it keeps dividing them into smaller tasks. Eventually all the workers have something to do with minimal synchronization.

Fork/Join largely consists of the `java.util.concurrent` package's `ForkJoinPool`, `ForkJoinTask`, `ForkJoinWorkerThread`, `RecursiveAction`, and `RecursiveTask` classes:

- `ForkJoinPool` is an `ExecutorService` implementation for running `ForkJoinTask`s. A `ForkJoinPool` instance provides the entry point for submissions from non-`ForkJoinTask` clients, as well as providing management and monitoring operations.

- `ForkJoinTask` is the abstract base class for tasks that run within a `ForkJoinPool` context. A `ForkJoinTask` instance is a thread-like entity that is much lighter weight than a normal thread. Huge numbers of tasks and subtasks may be hosted by a small number of actual threads in a `ForkJoinPool`, at the price of some usage limitations.

- `ForkJoinWorkerThread` describes a thread managed by a `ForkJoinPool` instance, which executes `ForkJoinTask`s.

- `RecursiveAction` describes a recursive resultless `ForkJoinTask`.

- `RecursiveTask` describes a recursive result-bearing `ForkJoinTask`.

The Java documentation provides examples of `RecursiveAction`-based tasks (such as sorting) and `RecursiveTask`-based tasks (such as computing Fibonacci numbers). You can also use `RecursiveAction` to accomplish matrix multiplication (see `http://en.wikipedia.org/wiki/Matrix_multiplication`).

For example, suppose that you've created Listing 6-7's `Matrix` class to represent a matrix consisting of a specific number of rows and columns.

Listing 6-7. A class for representing a two-dimensional table

```
class Matrix
{
   private double[][] matrix;
   Matrix(int nrows, int ncols)
   {
      matrix = new double[nrows][ncols];
   }
   int getCols()
   {
      return matrix[0].length;
   }
   int getRows()
   {
      return matrix.length;
   }
   double getValue(int row, int col)
   {
      return matrix[row][col];
   }
   void setValue(int row, int col, double value)
   {
      matrix[row][col] = value;
   }
}
```

Listing 6-8 demonstrates the single-threaded approach to multiplying two Matrix instances:

Listing 6-8. Multiplying two Matrix instances via the standard matrix-multiplication algorithm

```
class MatMult
{
   public static void main(String[] args)
   {
      Matrix a = new Matrix(1, 3);
      a.setValue(0, 0, 1); // | 1 2 3 |
      a.setValue(0, 1, 2);
      a.setValue(0, 2, 3);
      dump(a);
      Matrix b = new Matrix(3, 2);
      b.setValue(0, 0, 4); // | 4 7 |
      b.setValue(1, 0, 5); // | 5 8 |
      b.setValue(2, 0, 6); // | 6 9 |
      b.setValue(0, 1, 7);
      b.setValue(1, 1, 8);
      b.setValue(2, 1, 9);
      dump(b);
      dump(multiply(a, b));
   }
   static void dump(Matrix m)
```

```
{
    for (int i = 0; i < m.getRows(); i++)
    {
        for (int j = 0; j < m.getCols(); j++)
            System.out.print(m.getValue(i, j)+" ");
        System.out.println();
    }
    System.out.println();
}
static Matrix multiply(Matrix a, Matrix b)
{
    if (a.getCols() != b.getRows())
        throw new IllegalArgumentException("rows/columns mismatch");
    Matrix result = new Matrix(a.getRows(), b.getCols());
    for (int i = 0; i < a.getRows(); i++)
        for (int j = 0; j < b.getCols(); j++)
            for (int k = 0; k < a.getCols(); k++)
                result.setValue(i, j, result.getValue(i, j)+a.getValue(i, k)*
                                      b.getValue(k, j));
    return result;
}
}
```

Listing 6-8's MatMult class declares a multiply() method that demonstrates matrix multiplication. After verifying that the number of columns in the first Matrix (a) equals the number of rows in the second Matrix (b), which is essential to the algorithm, multiply() creates a Matrix named result and enters a sequence of nested loops to perform the multiplication.

The essence of these loops is as follows: For each row in a, multiply each of that row's column values by the corresponding column's row values in b. Add together the results of the multiplications, and store the overall total in result at the location specified via the row index (i) in a and the column index (j) in b.

When you run this application, it generates the following output, which indicates that a 1-row-by-3-column matrix multiplied by a 3-row-by-2 column matrix results in a 1-row-by-2-column matrix:

```
1.0 2.0 3.0

4.0 7.0
5.0 8.0
6.0 9.0

32.0 50.0
```

Computer scientists classify this algorithm as $O(n^3)$, which is read "big-oh of n-cubed" or "approximately n-cubed." This notation is an abstract way of classifying the algorithm's performance (without being bogged down in specific details such as microprocessor speed). A $O(n^3)$ classification indicates very poor performance, and this performance worsens as the sizes of the matrixes being multiplied increase.

The performance can be improved (on multiprocessor and/or multicore platforms) by assigning each row-by-column multiplication task to a separate thread-like entity. Listing 6-9 shows you how to accomplish this scenario in the context of the Fork/Join Framework.

Listing 6-9. Multiplying two matrixes via the Fork/Join Framework

```java
import java.util.ArrayList;
import java.util.List;

import java.util.concurrent.ForkJoinPool;
import java.util.concurrent.RecursiveAction;

class MatMult extends RecursiveAction
{
   private Matrix a, b, c;
   private int row;
   MatMult(Matrix a, Matrix b, Matrix c)
   {
      this(a, b, c, -1);
   }
   MatMult(Matrix a, Matrix b, Matrix c, int row)
   {
      if (a.getCols() != b.getRows())
         throw new IllegalArgumentException("rows/columns mismatch");
      this.a = a;
      this.b = b;
      this.c = c;
      this.row = row;
   }
   @Override
   public void compute()
   {
      if (row == -1)
      {
         List<MatMult> tasks = new ArrayList<>();
         for (int row = 0; row < a.getRows(); row++)
            tasks.add(new MatMult(a, b, c, row));
         invokeAll(tasks);
      }
      else
         multiplyRowByColumn(a, b, c, row);
   }
   static void multiplyRowByColumn(Matrix a, Matrix b, Matrix c, int row)
   {
      for (int j = 0; j < b.getCols(); j++)
         for (int k = 0; k < a.getCols(); k++)
            c.setValue(row, j, c.getValue(row, j)+a.getValue(row, k)*
                     b.getValue(k, j));
   }
   static void dump(Matrix m)
   {
      for (int i = 0; i < m.getRows(); i++)
      {
         for (int j = 0; j < m.getCols(); j++)
            System.out.print(m.getValue(i, j)+" ");
```

```
            System.out.println();
         }
         System.out.println();
      }
      public static void main(String[] args)
      {
         Matrix a = new Matrix(2, 3);
         a.setValue(0, 0, 1); // | 1 2 3 |
         a.setValue(0, 1, 2); // | 4 5 6 |
         a.setValue(0, 2, 3);
         a.setValue(1, 0, 4);
         a.setValue(1, 1, 5);
         a.setValue(1, 2, 6);
         dump(a);
         Matrix b = new Matrix(3, 2);
         b.setValue(0, 0, 7); // | 7 1 |
         b.setValue(1, 0, 8); // | 8 2 |
         b.setValue(2, 0, 9); // | 9 3 |
         b.setValue(0, 1, 1);
         b.setValue(1, 1, 2);
         b.setValue(2, 1, 3);
         dump(b);
         Matrix c = new Matrix(2, 2);
         ForkJoinPool pool = new ForkJoinPool();
         pool.invoke(new MatMult(a, b, c));
         dump(c);
      }
   }
}
```

Listing 6-9 presents a MatMult class that extends RecursiveAction. To accomplish meaningful work, RecursiveAction's void compute() method is overridden.

■ **Note** Although compute() is normally used to subdivide a task into subtasks recursively, I've chosen to handle the multiplication task somewhat differently (for brevity and simplicity).

After creating Matrixes a and b, Listing 6-9's main() method creates Matrix c and instantiates ForkJoinPool. It then instantiates MatMult, passing these three Matrix instances as arguments to the MatMult(Matrix a, Matrix b, Matrix c) constructor, and calls ForkJoinPool's T invoke(ForkJoinTask<T> task) method to start running this initial task. This method does not return until the initial task and all of its subtasks complete.

The MatMult(Matrix a, Matrix b, Matrix c) constructor invokes the MatMult(Matrix a, Matrix b, Matrix c, int row) constructor, specifying -1 as row's value. This value is used by compute(), which is invoked as a result of the aforementioned invoke() method call, to distinguish between the initial task and subtasks.

When compute() is initially called (row equals -1), it creates a List of MatMult tasks and passes this List to RecursiveAction's Collection<T> invokeAll(Collection<T> tasks) method (inherited from ForkJoinTask). This method forks all the List collection's tasks, which will start to execute. It then waits until the invokeAll() method returns (which also joins to all these tasks), which happens when the boolean isDone() method (also inherited from ForkJoinTask) returns true for each task.

Notice the tasks.add(new MatMult(a, b, c, row)); method call. This call assigns a specific row value to a MatMult instance. When invokeAll() is called, each task's compute() method is called and detects a different value (other than -1) assigned to row. It then executes multiplyRowByColumn(a, b, c, row); for its specific row.

When you run this application (java MatMult), it generates the following output:

```
1.0 2.0 3.0
4.0 5.0 6.0

7.0 1.0
8.0 2.0
9.0 3.0

50.0 14.0
122.0 32.0
```

Objects

Java 7's new java.util.Objects class consists of class methods for operating on objects. These utilities include null-safe or null-tolerant methods for comparing two objects, computing the hash code of an object, requiring that a reference not be null, and returning a string for an object.

Table 6-3 describes Objects' class methods.

Table 6-3. Objects Methods

Method	Description
`<T> int compare(T a, T b, Comparator<? super T> c)`	Return 0 when the first two arguments are identical (including the case where both arguments are the null reference), and the result of invoking c.compare(a, b) otherwise. An instance of the NullPointerException class may or may not be thrown depending on the java.util.Comparator argument's ordering policy for null references (if there is such a policy). (I discussed Comparator in Chapter 5.)
`boolean deepEquals(Object a, Object b)`	Return true when the passed arguments are deeply equal (discussed later). Otherwise, this method returns false. Two null references are considered to be deeply equal. If both arguments are arrays, the algorithm followed by Arrays.deepEquals() is used to determine equality. Otherwise, equality is determined by calling the first argument's equals() method. (I introduced java.util.Arrays in Chapter 5.)
`boolean equals(Object a, Object b)`	Return true when the passed arguments are equal to each other (including the scenario where both arguments are null). Otherwise, this method returns false (including

	scenarios where only one argument is null). If neither argument is null, equality is determined by calling the first argument's equals() method.
`int hash(Object... values)`	Generate a hash code for a sequence of object arguments. The hash code is generated as if all arguments were put into an array and that array was hashed by calling `Arrays.hashCode(Object[])`.When a single object is passed to values, hash()'s returned value does not equal the hash code of that object. To obtain a single object's hash code, call hashCode(Object).
`int hashCode(Object o)`	Return the hash code of a nonnull argument and 0 for the null argument.
`<T> T requireNonNull(T obj)`	Test the passed object reference for nullness. It either returns the nonnull reference stored in obj or throws NullPointerException when obj contains the null reference.
`<T> T requireNonNull(T obj, String message)`	Test the passed object reference for nullness. It either returns the nonnull reference stored in obj or throws NullPointerException when obj contains the null reference. The thrown NullPointerException instance contains the message provided by message.
`String toString(Object o)`	Return the result of calling toString() for a nonnull argument and "null" for a null argument.
`String toString(Object o, String nullDefault)`	Return the result of calling toString() on the first argument (passed to o) when that argument is not null; otherwise, this method returns the second argument (passed to nullDefault).

Objects implements the null-tolerant compare() method to first compare its arguments for object identity by using == before calling the provided Comparator.

The equals() and deepEquals() methods define equivalence relations over object references. Unlike Object.equals(Object o), Objects.equals(Object a, Object b) handles null values, returning true when both arguments are null, or when the first argument is nonnull and a.equals(b) returns true.

The deepEquals() method is used in the context of arrays (including nested arrays) to determine if two arrays are *deeply equal* (they are both null or they contain the same number of elements and all corresponding pairs of elements in the two arrays are deeply equal).

This method's two (possibly null) arguments, denoted by e1 and e2 below, are deeply equal when any of the following conditions hold:

- e1 and e2 are arrays of object reference types, and Arrays.deepEquals(e1, e2) would return true

- e1 and e2 are arrays of the same primitive type, and the appropriate overloading of Arrays.equals(e1, e2) would return true.

- e1 == e2

- e1.equals(e2) would return true.

Equality implies deep equality, but the converse isn't necessarily true. In the following example, x and y are deeply equal but are not equal:

```
Object common = "string";
Object[] x = {"string"};
Object[] y = {"string"};
System.out.println("x == y: "+(x == y)); // false (two different references)
System.out.println("Objects.equals(x, y): "+Objects.equals(x, y)); // false
System.out.println("Objects.deepEquals(x, y): "+Objects.deepEquals(x, y)); // true
```

Arrays x and y are not equal because they contain two different references and Objects.equals() is using reference equality (comparing their references) in this context. (Object equality, or comparing object contents, occurs when a class overrides Object's equals() method.) However, these arrays are deeply equal because x and y are both arrays of object reference types and Arrays.deepEquals(x, y) would return true.

■ **Note** Unlike the java.lang.Object class, which is automatically imported because of its java.lang prefix, you must explicitly import Objects into your source code (import java.util.Objects;) when you want to avoid having to specify the java.util prefix.

The Java documentation for the requireNonNull() methods states that they are designed primarily for doing parameter validation in methods and constructors. The idea is to check a method's or a constructor's parameter values for null references before attempting to use these references later in the method or constructor, and avoid potential NullPointerExceptions. Listing 6-10 provides a demonstration.

Listing 6-10. Testing constructor parameters for null reference arguments

```
import java.util.Objects;

class Employee
{
   private String firstName, lastName;
   Employee(String firstName, String lastName)
   {
      try
      {
         firstName = Objects.requireNonNull(firstName);
         lastName = Objects.requireNonNull(lastName,
                                       "lastName shouldn't be null");
         lastName = Character.toUpperCase(lastName.charAt(0))+
                     lastName.substring(1);
         this.firstName = firstName;
         this.lastName = lastName;
```

```
      }
      catch (NullPointerException npe)
      {
          // In lieu of a more sophisticated logging mechanism, and also for
          // brevity, I output the exception's message to standard output.
          System.out.println(npe.getMessage());
      }
   }
   String getName()
   {
      return firstName+" "+lastName;
   }
   public static void main(String[] args)
   {
      Employee e1 = new Employee(null, "Doe");
      Employee e2 = new Employee("John", null);
      Employee e3 = new Employee("John", "doe");
      System.out.println(e3.getName());
   }
}
```

Listing 6-10's Employee constructor first invokes Objects.requireNonNull() on each argument value passed to its firstName and lastName parameters. If either argument value is the null reference, NullPointerException is instantiated and thrown; otherwise, the requireNonNull() method returns the argument value, which is guaranteed to be nonnull.

It is now safe to invoke lastName.charAt(), which returns the first character from the string on which this method is called. This character is passed to Character's toUpperCase() utility method, which returns the character when it does not represent a lowercase letter, or the uppercase equivalent of the lowercase letter. After toUpperCase() returns, the (potentially uppercased) letter is prepended to the rest of the string, resulting in a last name starting with an uppercase letter. (Assume that the name consists of letters only.)

Listing 6-10's Objects.requireNonNull() method calls offer a more compact alternative to the following example, which demonstrates how requireNonNull(T obj, String message)'s message parameter is used:

```
if (firstName == null)
   throw new NullPointerException();
if (lastName == null)
   throw new NullPointerException("lastName shouldn't be null");
```

Compile Listing 6-10 (javac Employee.java) and run the resulting application (java Employee). You should observe the following output:

```
null
lastName shouldn't be null
John Doe
```

As Listing 6-10 reveals, the Objects class's methods were introduced to promote null safety by reducing the likelihood of a NullPointerException being thrown unintentionally. As another example, Employee e = null; String s = e.toString(); results in a thrown NullPointerException instance because you cannot invoke toString() on the null reference stored in e. In contrast, Employee e = null; String s = Objects.toString(e); doesn't result in a thrown NullPointerException instance because Objects.toString() returns "null" when it detects that e contains the null reference. Rather than having to explicitly test a reference for null, as in if (e != null) { String s = e.toString(); /* other code here */ }, you can offload the null-checking to the Objects class's various methods.

These methods were also introduced to avoid the "reinventing the wheel" syndrome. Many developers have repeatedly written methods that perform similar operations, but do so in a null-safe manner. The inclusion of Objects in Java's standard class library standardizes this common functionality.

Random

Chapter 4 introduced you to the Math class's random() method. If you were to investigate this method's source code, you would discover the following implementation:

```
private static Random randomNumberGenerator;
private static synchronized Random initRNG()
{
    Random rnd = randomNumberGenerator;
    return (rnd == null) ? (randomNumberGenerator = new Random()) : rnd;
}
public static double random()
{
    Random rnd = randomNumberGenerator;
    if (rnd == null) rnd = intRNG();
    return rnd.nextDouble();
}
```

This implementation, which demonstrates *lazy initialization* (not initializing something until it is first needed, in order to improve performance), shows you that Math's random() method is implemented in terms of a class named Random, which is located in the java.util package. Random instances generate sequences of random numbers and are known as *random number generators*.

Note These numbers are not truly random because they are generated from a mathematical algorithm. As a result, they are often referred to as pseudorandom numbers. However, it is often convenient to drop the "pseudo" prefix and refer to them as random numbers.

Random generates its sequence of random numbers by starting with a special 48-bit value that is known as a *seed*. This value is subsequently modified by a mathematical algorithm, which is known as a *linear congruential generator*.

Note Check out Wikipedia's "Linear congruential generator" entry (http://en.wikipedia.org/wiki/Linear_congruential_generator) to learn about this algorithm for generating random numbers.

Random declares a pair of constructors:

- Random() creates a new random number generator. This constructor sets the seed of the random number generator to a value that is very likely to be distinct from any other call to this constructor.

- Random(long seed) creates a new random number generator using its seed argument. This argument is the initial value of the random number generator's internal state, which the protected int next(int bits) method maintains.

Note The next() method, which is used by the other methods, is protected so that subclasses can change the generator implementation from that shown below

```
protected int next(int bits) {
    long oldseed, nextseed;
    AtomicLong seed = this.seed;
    do {
        oldseed = seed.get();
        nextseed = (oldseed*multiplier+addend)&mask;
    } while (!seed.compareAndSet(oldseed, nextseed));
    return (int) (nextseed >>> (48-bits));
}
```

to something different. For a subclassing example, check out "Subclassing java.util.Random" (http://www.javamex.com/tutorials/random_numbers/java_util_random_subclassing.shtml).

Because Random() does not take a seed argument, the resulting random number generator always generates a different sequence of random numbers. This explains why Math.random() generates a different sequence each time an application starts running.

Tip Random(long seed) gives you the opportunity to reuse the same seed value, allowing the same sequence of random numbers to be generated. You will find this capability useful when debugging a faulty application that involves random numbers.

Random(long seed) calls the void setSeed(long seed) method to set the seed to the specified value. If you call setSeed() after instantiating Random, the random number generator is reset to the state that it was in immediately after calling Random(long seed).

The previous code fragment demonstrates Random's double nextDouble() method, which returns the next pseudorandom, uniformly distributed double precision floating-point value between 0.0 and 1.0 in this random number generator's sequence.

Random also declares the following methods for returning other kinds of values:

- boolean nextBoolean() returns the next pseudorandom, uniformly distributed Boolean value in this random number generator's sequence. Values true and false are generated with (approximately) equal probability.

- void nextBytes(byte[] bytes) generates pseudorandom byte integer values and stores them in the bytes array. The number of generated bytes is equal to the length of the bytes array.

- float nextFloat() returns the next pseudorandom, uniformly distributed floating-point value between 0.0 and 1.0 in this random number generator's sequence.

- double nextGaussian() returns the next pseudorandom, Gaussian ("normally") distributed double precision floating-point value with mean 0.0 and standard deviation 1.0 in this random number generator's sequence.

- int nextInt() returns the next pseudorandom, uniformly distributed integer value in this random number generator's sequence. All 2^{32} possible integer values are generated with (approximately) equal probability.

- int nextInt(int n) returns a pseudorandom, uniformly distributed integer value between 0 (inclusive) and the specified value (exclusive), drawn from this random number generator's sequence. All n possible integer values are generated with (approximately) equal probability.

- long nextLong() returns the next pseudorandom, uniformly distributed long integer value in this random number generator's sequence. Because Random uses a seed with only 48 bits, this method will not return all possible 64-bit long integer values.

The java.util.Collections class declares a pair of shuffle() methods for shuffling the contents of a list. In contrast, the Arrays class does not declare a shuffle() method for shuffling the contents of an array. Listing 6-11 addresses this omission.

Listing 6-11. Shuffling an array of integers

```
import java.util.Random;

class Shuffler
{
    public static void main(String[] args)
    {
        Random r = new Random();
        int[] array = { 0, 1, 2, 3, 4, 5, 6, 7, 8, 9 };
        for (int i = 0; i < array.length; i++)
        {
            int n = r.nextInt(array.length);
            // swap array[i] with array[n]
            int temp = array[i];
            array[i] = array[n];
            array[n] = temp;
```

```
    }
    for (int i = 0; i < array.length; i++)
        System.out.print(array[i]+" ");
    System.out.println();
    }
}
```

Listing 6-11 presents a simple recipe for shuffling an array of integers—this recipe could be generalized. For each array entry from the start of the array to the end of the array, this entry is swapped with another entry whose index is chosen by int nextInt(int n).

When you run this application, you will observe a shuffled sequence of integers that is similar to the following sequence that I observed:

7 1 5 2 9 8 6 4 3 0

EXERCISES

The following exercises are designed to test your understanding of the concurrency utilities, Objects, and Random:

1. The Java documentation for the Semaphore class presents a Pool class that demonstrates how a semaphore can control access to a pool of items. Because Pool is incomplete, introduce a single resource (replace protected Object[] items = ... with an array containing this resource in its single entry) and then demonstrate Pool's getItem() and putItem() methods in the context of a pair of threads launched from the main() method of a SemaphoreDemo class.

2. Create an EqualsDemo application to play with Objects' deepEquals() method. As well as an EqualsDemo class, this application declares Car and Wheel classes. A Car instance contains (typically four) Wheel instances, and a Wheel instance contains a brand name. Each of Car and Wheel must override Object's equals() method but does not have to override hashCode() in this example. Your main() method should contain the following code and generate the output shown in the comments:

```
Car[] cars1 = { new Car(4, "Goodyear"), new Car(4, "Goodyear") };
Car[] cars2 = { new Car(4, "Goodyear"), new Car(4, "Goodyear") };
Car[] cars3 = { new Car(4, "Michelin"), new Car(4, "Goodyear") };
Car[] cars4 = { new Car(3, "Goodyear"), new Car(4, "Goodyear") };
Car[] cars5 = { new Car(4, "Goodyear"), new Car(4, "Goodyear"),
                new Car(3, "Michelin") };
System.out.println(Objects.deepEquals(cars1, cars2)); // Output: true
System.out.println(Objects.deepEquals(cars1, cars3)); // Output: false
System.out.println(Objects.deepEquals(cars1, cars4)); // Output: false
System.out.println(Objects.deepEquals(cars1, cars5)); // Output: false
```

The comments reveal that two arrays are deeply equal when they contain the same number of equal elements.

3. Create a Die application that uses Random to simulate the role of a *die* (a single dice). Output the value.

Summary

Java 5 introduced the concurrency utilities to simplify the development of concurrent applications. The concurrency utilities are organized into executor, synchronizer, concurrent collection, lock, atomic variable, and additional utilities categories, and leverage the low-level Threading API in their implementations.

An executor decouples task submission from task-execution mechanics and is described by the Executor, ExecutorService, and ScheduledExecutorService interfaces. A synchronizer facilitates common forms of synchronization: countdown latches, cyclic barriers, exchangers, phasers, and semaphores are commonly used synchronizers.

A concurrent collection is an extension to the Collections Framework. A lock supports high-level locking and can associate with conditions in a manner that is distinct from built-in synchronization and monitors. An atomic variable encapsulates a single variable, and supports lock-free, thread-safe operations on that variable.

Java 7's new ThreadLocalRandom class describes a random number generator that is isolated to the current thread, and its new Fork/Join Framework lets you recursively break a task into subtasks and combine results to make maximum use out of multiple processors and/or processor cores.

The new Objects class consists of class methods for operating on objects. These utilities include null-safe or null-tolerant methods for comparing two objects, computing the hash code of an object, requiring that a reference not be null, and returning a string for an object.

The Math class's random() method is implemented in terms of the Random class, whose instances are known as random number generators. Random generates a sequence of random numbers by starting with a special 48-bit seed. This value is subsequently modified via a mathematical algorithm that is known as a linear congruential generator.

The examples in this chapter and its predecessors have leveraged the underlying platform's Standard I/O facility to create character-based user interfaces. However, Java also lets you create GUIs to achieve more compelling user interfaces. Chapter 7 introduces you to Java's APIs for creating and enriching GUIs.

CHAPTER 7

Creating and Enriching Graphical User Interfaces

The applications presented in previous chapters featured Standard I/O-based user interfaces. Although these simple character-oriented user interfaces are convenient for demonstrating Java features or for interacting with small utility applications (e.g., Chapter 3's StubFinder application), they are inadequate for more sophisticated needs, such as filling out forms or viewing HTML pages. However, Java also provides APIs that let you create and enrich more sophisticated graphical user interfaces (GUIs).

Abstract Window Toolkit (AWT) is Java's original GUI-oriented API. After introducing AWT to Java, Sun Microsystems introduced Java Foundation Classes (JFC) as an AWT superset with many new capabilities. JFC's main APIs are Swing (for creating more sophisticated GUIs), Accessibility (for supporting assistive technologies), Java 2D (for creating high-quality graphics), and Drag and Drop (for dragging and dropping AWT/Swing GUI components, such as buttons or textfields).

Chapter 7 continues to explore the standard class library by introducing you to AWT, Swing, and Java 2D. Appendix C introduces you to Accessibility and Drag and Drop.

Abstract Window Toolkit

Abstract Window Toolkit (AWT) is Java's original windowing system-independent API for creating GUIs that are based on components, containers, layout managers, and events. AWT also supports graphics, colors, fonts, images, data transfer, and more.

The standard class library organizes AWT's many types into the java.awt package and subpackages. However, not all java.awt types and subpackages belong to AWT. For example, java.awt.Graphics2D and java.awt.geom belong to Java 2D. This arrangement exists because the java.awt-based package structure provides a natural fit for various non-AWT types. (AWT is often viewed as part of JFC nowadays.)

This section introduces you to AWT by first presenting toolkits. It then explores components, containers, layout managers, and events. After exploring graphics, colors, and fonts, the section focuses on images. It closes by discussing AWT's support for data transfer.

AWT HISTORY

Before JDK 1.0's release (on January 23, 1996), developers at Sun Microsystems were tasked with abstracting the various windowing systems of the day and their attendant *widgets* (GUI controls, such as buttons—Java refers to GUI controls as *components*) into a portable windowing system that Java applications could target. AWT was born and was included in JDK 1.0. (Legend has it [see http://www.cs.jhu.edu/~scott/oos/java/doc/TIJ3/html/TIJ316.htm, for example] that the first AWT version had to be designed and implemented in one month.)

The JDK 1.0.1 and 1.0.2 releases corrected various AWT bugs, and JDK 1.1 offered an improved event-handling model that greatly simplified how applications respond to GUI events (such as button clicks and key presses). Subsequent JDK releases brought about additional improvements. For example, JDK 1.2 introduced JFC, JDK 6 introduced the Desktop, Splash Screen, and System Tray APIs, and JDK 7 standardized the support for translucent and shaped windows first introduced in JDK 6 update 10 (build 12).

Appendix C covers Desktop, Splash Screen, System Tray, and translucent/shaped windows.

Toolkits

AWT uses toolkits to abstract over windowing systems. A *toolkit* is a concrete implementation of AWT's abstract java.awt.Toolkit class. AWT provides a separate toolkit for each windowing system used by the Windows, Solaris, Linux, and Mac OS platforms.

Toolkit declares various methods that AWT calls to obtain information about the platform's windowing system, and to perform various windowing system-specific tasks. For example, void beep() emits an audio beep.

Most applications should not call any of Toolkit's methods directly; they are intended for use by AWT. However, you might occasionally find it helpful to call some of these methods.

For example, you might want your application to sound one or more beeps when a long-running task finishes, to alert the user who might not be looking at the screen. You can accomplish this task by specifying code that's similar to the following:

```
Toolkit toolkit = Toolkit.getDefaultToolkit();
for (int i = 0 ; i < 5; i++)
{
   toolkit.beep();
   try { Thread.sleep(200); } catch (InterruptedException ie) {}
}
```

This example reveals that you must obtain a Toolkit instance before you can call a Toolkit method, and that you do so by calling Toolkit's Toolkit getDefaultToolkit() class method. It also reveals that you might want to place a small delay between successive beeps to ensure that each beep is distinct.

Components, Containers, Layout Managers, and Events

AWT lets you create GUIs that are based on components, containers, layout managers, and events.

A *component* is a graphical widget that appears in a window on the screen; a label, a button, or a textfield is an example. A window is represented by a special component known as a *container*.

A *layout manager* is an object that organizes components and containers within a container. It is used to create useful GUIs (e.g., a form consisting of labels, textfields, and buttons).

An *event* is an object describing a button click or other GUI interaction. Applications register *event listener* objects with components to listen for specific events so that application code can respond to them.

Components Overview

AWT provides a wide variety of component classes in the `java.awt` package. Figure 7-1 presents the class hierarchy for AWT's nonmenu component classes.

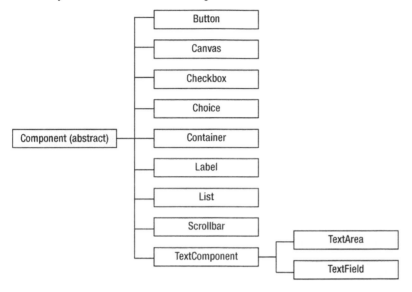

Figure 7-1. AWT's nonmenu component class hierarchy is rooted in `java.awt.Component`.

AWT's abstract `Component` class is the root class for all AWT nonmenu components (and Swing components). Directly beneath `Component` are `Button`, `Canvas`, `Checkbox`, `Choice`, `Container`, `Label`, `List`, `Scrollbar`, and `TextComponent`:

- `Button` describes a clickable label.

- `Canvas` describes a blank rectangular area. You would subclass `Canvas` to introduce your own AWT components.

- `Checkbox` describes a true/false choice. You can use `Checkbox` with `java.awt.CheckboxGroup` to create a set of mutually exclusive radio buttons.

- `Choice` describes a drop-down list (also known as a pop-up menu) of strings.

- `Container` describes a component that stores other components. This nesting capability lets you create GUIs of arbitrary complexity and is very powerful. (Being able to represent containers as components is an example of the *Composite design pattern*, which is presented on page 163 of *Design Patterns: Elements of Reusable Object-Oriented Software* by Erich Gamma, Richard Helm, Ralph Johnson, and John Vlissides [Addison-Wesley, 1995; ISBN: 0201633612].)

- `Label` describes a single line of static text as a visual aid to the user.

- `List` describes a non-drop-down list of strings.

- `Scrollbar` describes a range of values.

- `TextComponent` describes any component that inputs text. Its `TextArea` subclass describes a text component for inputting multiple lines of text, whereas its `TextField` subclass describes a text component for inputting a single line of text.

Figure 7-2 presents the class hierarchy for menu component classes.

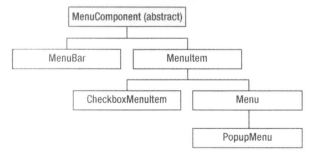

Figure 7-2. *AWT's menu component class hierarchy is rooted in* `java.awt.MenuComponent`.

AWT's abstract `MenuComponent` class (which doesn't extend `Component`) is the root class for all AWT menu components. Directly beneath `MenuComponent` are `MenuBar` and `MenuItem`:

- `MenuBar` encapsulates the windowing system concept of a menubar bound to a frame window. It contains a sequence of `Menu` components, where each `Menu` component contains a sequence of `MenuItem` components.

- `MenuItem` describes a single menuitem. Its `CheckboxMenuItem` subclass describes a menuitem that's implemented via a checkbox. Its `Menu` subclass describes a pull-down menu component that's deployed from a menu bar. (`Menu` extends `MenuItem` to create arbitrarily complex menus.) `Menu` is subclassed by `PopupMenu` to describe a menu that can be dynamically popped up at a specified position within a component.

`Component` declares many nonmenu component-oriented methods. For example, `Component` declares the following methods to inform the caller about the component's displayable, visible, and showing status:

- `boolean isDisplayable()` returns true when a component is in the *displayable state* (the component is connected to a native screen resource [defined shortly], typically by being added to a container).

- `boolean isVisible()` returns true when a component is in the *visible state* (the component appears on the screen). The companion `void setVisible(boolean b)` method lets you show (b is `true`) or hide (b is `false`) a component.

- `boolean isShowing()` returns true when a component is in the *showing state* (the component is visible and is contained in a container that is also visible and showing). This method is useful for determining whether or not a component has been obscured by another component. It returns false when obscured, whereas `isVisible()` would continue to return true.

MenuComponent's repertoire of methods is much shorter. However, it shares some commonality with Component. For example, both classes declare a method for specifying the component's font.

Some of Component's and MenuComponent's methods have been deprecated and should not be used. For example, Component declares java.awt.peer.ComponentPeer getPeer() and MenuComponent declares java.awt.peer.MenuComponentPeer getPeer(). Both deprecated methods hint at how AWT implements its predefined components.

AWT leverages the platform's windowing system to create various components. When you add a component to a container, AWT creates a peer object whose class implements a ComponentPeer or MenuComponentPeer subinterface. For example, AWT creates a java.awt.peer.ButtonPeer instance when you add a Button component class instance to a container.

Note Each AWT toolkit implementation includes its own set of peer interface implementations.

Behind the scenes, the component object communicates with the peer object, which communicates with native code in a JDK library. This code communicates with the platform's windowing system, which manages the *native screen resource* (a native window) that appears on the screen.

For example, when you add a Button instance to a container, AWT calls Component's void addNotify() method, which obtains the current toolkit and calls its ButtonPeer createButton(Button target) method to create this toolkit's Button peer.

Ultimately, the windowing system is asked to create a button native screen resource. For example, on a 32-bit Windows operating system, the native screen resource could be obtained via a call to the CreateWindow() or CreateWindowEx() Win32 API function.

AWT components except for those created from nonpredefined classes that directly extend Component or Container are known as *heavyweight components* because of their corresponding peer interfaces and native screen resources. Components created from custom Component and Container subclasses are known as *lightweight components* because they do not have peer interfaces and native screen resources (they reuse their closest ancestor's peer, which is how Swing works). You can call Component's boolean isLightweight() method to determine if a component is lightweight.

Note Heavyweight and lightweight components can be mixed in a single component hierarchy provided that the entire hierarchy is *valid* (noncontainer components are correctly sized; container components have their contained components laid out). When the hierarchy is *invalidated* (e.g., after changing *component bounds* [width, height, and location relative to the component's parent container], such as when changing a button's text, or after adding/removing components to/from containers), AWT *validates* it by invoking Container's void validate() method on the top-most invalid container of the hierarchy.

As you explore the JDK documentation for the various component classes, you'll discover many useful constructors and methods. For example, Button declares a Button(String label) constructor for initializing a button to the specified label text. Alternatively, you could call the Button() constructor to create a Button with no label. Regardless of which constructor you use, you can always call Button's void setLabel(String label) and String getLabel() methods to specify and retrieve the label text that is displayed on the button. (Changing a button's displayed text invalidates the button; AWT then performs validation, which causes the component hierarchy to be re-laid out.)

Components are easy to create, as demonstrated by the following example, which creates a Yes button:

```
Button btnYes = new Button("Yes");
```

■ **Note** I like to prefix a component variable to indicate its kind. For example, I prefix buttons with btn.

Containers Overview

Buttons, labels, textfields, and other components cannot be placed directly on the screen; they need to be placed in a container window that is placed directly on the screen.

AWT provides several container classes in the java.awt package. Figure 7-3 presents their hierarchy.

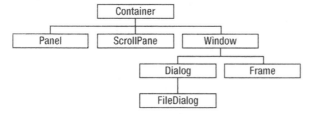

Figure 7-3. AWT's container class hierarchy is rooted in Container.

AWT's Container class is the root class for all AWT containers. Directly beneath Container are Panel, ScrollPane, and Window:

- Panel is the simplest container. It provides space in which an application can attach any other component, including other panels.

- ScrollPane implements automatic horizontal and/or vertical scrolling for a single *child* (contained) component. A container that contains a component is referred to as that component's *parent*.

- Window is a top-level window with no borders. Its Dialog subclass describes a *dialog box* (a window for soliciting input from the user) and its Frame subclass describes a *frame window* (a top-level window with borders, including a titlebar). Dialog's FileDialog subclass describes a dialog box for selecting a file.

Container declares many container-oriented methods. For example, Component add(Component comp) appends component comp to the container, Component[] getComponents() returns an array of the container's components, and int getComponentCount() returns the number of components in the container.

Window declares a void pack() method for making a top-level window just large enough to display all its components at their *preferred* (natural) sizes. Also, pack() makes the window (and any owner of the window—dialog boxes are typically owned by other windows) displayable when not already displayable.

Window also declares a void setSize(int width, int height) method that lets you size a window to a specific size (in pixels).

Continuing from the previous example, suppose you want to add the Yes button to a panel (which might also contain a No button). The following example shows you how to accomplish this task:

```
Panel pnl = new Panel();
pnl.add(btnYes);
```

Layout Managers Overview

Containers can contain components but cannot lay them out on the screen (e.g., in rows, in a grid, or in some other arrangement). Layout managers handle this task. A layout manager is typically associated with a container to lay out the container's components.

■ **Note** Layout managers provide a screen size-independent way to display a GUI. Without them, an application would have to obtain the current screen size and adapt container/component sizes to account for the screen size. Doing so could involve writing hundreds of lines of code, a tedious proposition at best.

AWT provides several layout managers in the java.awt package: BorderLayout (lay out no more than five components in a container's north, south, east, west, and center areas), CardLayout (treat each contained component as a card; only one card is visible at a time, and the container acts as a stack of cards), FlowLayout (arrange components in a horizontal row), GridBagLayout (lay out components vertically, horizontally, or along their *baseline* [line serving as an origin for the purpose of layout] without requiring that the components be of the same size), and GridLayout (lay out the components in a rectangular grid).

Layout manager classes implement the java.awt.LayoutManager interface, which declares methods that AWT calls when a container's components need to be laid out. You don't need to be aware of these methods unless you're planning to create your own layout manager. If so, you'll also want to be aware of java.awt.LayoutManager2, a LayoutManager subinterface.

Layout managers learn about a component's/container's preferred, maximum, and minimum sizes by calling Component's Dimension getPreferredSize(), Dimension getMaximumSize(), and Dimension getMinimumSize() methods. (The aforementioned layout manager classes don't take maximum size into account because these classes were introduced in JDK 1.0, and support for maximum size was not introduced [via LayoutManager2] until JDK 1.1.)

■ **Note** The java.awt.Dimension class declares public width and height fields (of type int) that contain the component's width and height. Although directly accessing these fields violates information hiding, the designers of this class probably felt that it was more performant to access these fields directly. Furthermore, Dimension is one class that will probably never change.

Each container has a default layout manager. For example, Frame's default layout manager is BorderLayout, whereas Panel's default layout manager is FlowLayout. You can replace this default by calling Container's void setLayout(LayoutManager mgr) method to install your own layout manager, as demonstrated here:

```
Panel pnl = new Panel();
pnl.setLayout(new GridLayout(3, 2));
```

The first line creates a Panel that defaults to FlowLayout. The second line replaces this layout manager with a GridLayout that lays out a maximum of six components in a three-row-by-two-column grid.

Events Overview

Users press keys, click buttons, move the mouse, select menuitems, and perform other GUI interactions. Each interaction is known as an *event*, and is described by a concrete java.awt.event subclass of the abstract java.awt.AWTEvent class.

AWTEvent is subclassed by several event classes: ActionEvent, AdjustmentEvent, AncestorEvent, ComponentEvent, HierarchyEvent, InputMethodEvent, InternalFrameEvent, InvocationEvent, ItemEvent, and TextEvent.

ComponentEvent is the superclass for ContainerEvent, FocusEvent, InputEvent, PaintEvent, and WindowEvent. InputEvent is the abstract superclass for KeyEvent, which is subclassed by MenuKeyEvent, and MouseEvent, which is subclassed by MenuDragMouseEvent and MouseWheelEvent.

Note Not all these events are used by AWT. For example, MenuDragMouseEvent is Swing-specific. Also, events can be classified as high-level or low-level. A *high-level event* results from a low-level interaction with the GUI. For example, an action event originates from a keypress or a mouse click. In contrast, keyboard-oriented and mouse-oriented events are *low-level events*.

Components that generate events are known as *event sources*. As events occur, AWTEvent subclass instances are created to describe them. Each instance is posted to an *event queue* and subsequently *dispatched* (sent) to the appropriate event listeners that were previously registered with the event source. Event listeners respond to these events in some way, which typically involves updating the GUI.

An event listener is registered with a component by calling the component class's appropriate add*x*Listener() method on the component instance, where *x* is replaced with an event class name without the Event suffix. For example, you would register an action listener with a button by calling Button's void addActionListener(ActionListener al) method.

ActionListener is an interface in the java.awt.event package. AWT calls its void actionPerformed(ActionEvent ae) method with the ActionEvent object when an action event occurs.

The following example registers an action listener with the previously created Yes button:

```
btnYes.addActionListener(new ActionListener()
                        {
                            public void actionPerformed(ActionEvent ae)
                            {
                                System.out.println("Yes was clicked");
```

```
                                }
                        });
```

When the user clicks the Yes button, AWT calls actionPerformed() with an ActionEvent object as this method's argument. The listener responds by outputting a message on the standard output device.

Button also declares a void removeActionListener(ActionListener al) method for unregistering the previously registered action listener identified as al. Other component classes also declare their own removexListener(xListener) methods.

ActionListener declares a single method, but some listeners declare multiple methods. For example, WindowListener declares seven methods. Because it can be tedious to override each method wherever you need to implement the interface, AWT also provides the concept of an *adapter*, which is a convenience class that implements a multimethod interface by providing an empty version of each method. For example, the java.awt.event package includes a WindowAdapter class, which you'll see demonstrated shortly.

Demonstrating Components, Containers, Layout Managers, and Events

Now that you've learned some basics of components, containers, layout managers, and events (and event listeners), let's find out how to combine them into a useful AWT-based GUI. I've created a simple temperature-conversion application that presents a GUI for obtaining degree input, displaying degree output, and triggering conversions to degrees Celsius/Fahrenheit. Listing 7-1 presents the source code.

Listing 7-1. A simple GUI consisting of two labels, two textfields, and two buttons

```java
import java.awt.Button;
import java.awt.EventQueue;
import java.awt.Frame;
import java.awt.GridLayout;
import java.awt.Label;
import java.awt.Panel;
import java.awt.TextField;
import java.awt.Window;

import java.awt.event.ActionEvent;
import java.awt.event.ActionListener;
import java.awt.event.WindowAdapter;
import java.awt.event.WindowEvent;

class TempVerter extends Frame
{
   TempVerter()
   {
      super("TempVerter");
      addWindowListener(new WindowAdapter()
                        {
                           @Override
                           public void windowClosing(WindowEvent we)
                           {
                              System.out.println("window closing");
                              dispose();
                           }
```

```
                    @Override
                    public void windowClosed(WindowEvent we)
                    {
                        System.out.println("window closed");
                    }
                });
    Panel pnlLayout = new Panel();
    pnlLayout.setLayout(new GridLayout(3, 2));
    pnlLayout.add(new Label("Degrees"));
    final TextField txtDegrees = new TextField(10);
    pnlLayout.add(txtDegrees);
    pnlLayout.add(new Label("Result"));
    final TextField txtResult = new TextField(30);
    pnlLayout.add(txtResult);
    ActionListener al;
    al = new ActionListener()
        {
            @Override
            public void actionPerformed(ActionEvent ae)
            {
                try
                {
                    double value = Double.parseDouble(txtDegrees.getText());
                    double result = (value-32.0)*5.0/9.0;
                    txtResult.setText("Celsius = "+result);
                }
                catch (NumberFormatException nfe)
                {
                    System.err.println("bad input");
                }
            }
        };
    Button btnConvertToCelsius = new Button("Convert to Celsius");
    btnConvertToCelsius.addActionListener(al);
    pnlLayout.add(btnConvertToCelsius);
    al = new ActionListener()
        {
            @Override
            public void actionPerformed(ActionEvent ae)
            {
                try
                {
                    double value = Double.parseDouble(txtDegrees.getText());
                    double result = value*9.0/5.0+32.0;
                    txtResult.setText("Fahrenheit = "+result);
                }
                catch (NumberFormatException nfe)
                {
                    System.err.println("bad input");
                }
            }
        };
```

```
        Button btnConvertToFahrenheit = new Button("Convert to Fahrenheit");
        btnConvertToFahrenheit.addActionListener(al);
        pnlLayout.add(btnConvertToFahrenheit);
        add(pnlLayout);
        pack();
        setResizable(false);
        setVisible(true);
    }
    public static void main(String[] args)
    {
        Runnable r = new Runnable()
                     {
                         @Override
                         public void run()
                         {
                             new TempVerter();
                         }
                     };
        EventQueue.invokeLater(r);
    }
}
```

Following several import statements, Listing 7-1 presents the temperature-conversion application's TempVerter class, which extends the Frame class to describe a frame window that displays the GUI.

TempVerter declares a noargument constructor for constructing the GUI. Its main() method instantiates TempVerter and invokes its noargument constructor to create the GUI.

main() does not directly execute new TempVerter();. Doing so would construct the GUI on the main thread. Instead, main() defers GUI creation to a special AWT thread known as the *event-dispatch thread (EDT)*. It does so by creating a java.lang.Runnable instance whose run() method executes new TempVerter();, and by passing this runnable to the java.awt.EventQueue class's void invokeLater(Runnable runnable) class method, which executes the runnable on the EDT.

main() defers GUI creation to the EDT to avoid potential thread-synchronization problems. Because it's beyond this chapter's scope to discuss these problems, check out *The Java Tutorial* (http://download.oracle.com/javase/tutorial/uiswing/concurrency/dispatch.html) and the "Swing threading and the event-dispatch thread" article (http://www.javaworld.com/javaworld/jw-08-2007/jw-08-swingthreading.html) for more information. (Although these sources discuss this topic in a Swing context, other sources also include AWT. Therefore, you should create AWT-based as well as Swing-based GUIs on the EDT.)

TempVerter() first invokes the Frame(String title) constructor via super("TempVerter"); so that TempVerter will appear on the frame window's titlebar. It then registers a window listener with the frame window so that this window will close (and the application will end) when the user closes the window (by clicking the X button on the window's titlebar, for example).

The listener is an instance of a WindowAdapter anonymous subclass, which overrides WindowListener's void windowClosing(WindowEvent we) and void windowClosed(WindowEvent we) methods. Clicking X or selecting Close from the window's system menu triggers a call to windowClosing(). You would typically override this method to save changes (e.g., a text editor's unsaved edits).

To properly terminate the application, windowClosing() must invoke Window's void dispose() method, which releases all the native screen resources used by the window and posts a window-closed event to the application's event queue. AWT subsequently dispatches this event by invoking windowClosed() to signify that the window has closed. Any final cleanup can be performed in this method.

Note Some people prefer to invoke the java.lang.System class's void exit(int status) method to terminate the application. For more information, check out Oracle's "AWT Threading Issues" page at http://download.oracle.com/javase/7/docs/api/java/awt/doc-files/AWTThreadIssues.html.

Continuing, the constructor instantiates Panel to contain the GUI's components. It then assigns a three-row-by-two-column GridLayout layout manager to this container to manage its components.

Each of the first two grid rows presents Label and TextField instances. The label tells the user what to enter or indicates that the textfield is displaying a result. The textfield solicits input or presents output. The value passed to each TextField constructor specifies the textfield's width in terms of displayable columns, where a *column* is defined as an approximate average character width (and is platform-dependent).

The final grid row presents a pair of Button instances for performing conversions. Each instance is assigned an action listener that responds to a button click by obtaining the top textfield's text (via TextField's String getText() method, which is inherited from TextField's TextComponent superclass), converting it to a number, and assigning it to the bottom textfield by calling TextField's overriding void setText(String t) method.

After populating the panel, the constructor adds the panel to the frame window. It then invokes pack() to ensure that the frame window is made large enough to display its components at their preferred sizes, invokes Frame's void setResizable(boolean resizable) method with a false argument to prevent the user from resizing the frame window (and making it look ugly), and invokes setVisible() with a true argument to display the frame and its components.

After the constructor returns to main(), this class method exits. However, the frame window remains on the screen because it's connected to a native screen resource and because the running EDT is a nondaemon thread (discussed in Chapter 4).

Compile Listing 7-1 (javac TempVerter.java) and run this application (java TempVerter). Figure 7-4 shows the resulting GUI on the Windows XP platform.

Figure 7-4. *Click the X button to close this window and terminate the application.*

When you enter nonnumeric text or leave the Degrees textfield empty, TempVerter outputs a "bad input" message to the standard output device. Also, when you close the window, this application outputs "window closing" followed by "window closed" messages on separate lines.

Note You can move forward to the next component by pressing the Tab key, and move backward to the previous component by pressing Shift-Tab. The component that you tab to has the *focus* when it can obtain input—the only TempVerter components capable of receiving focus are the two textfields and the two buttons. When you disable an input component, by invoking Component's void setEnabled(boolean b) method with a false argument on the component instance, it no longer has the focus.

Figure 7-4 reveals that all components have the same size, which results from GridLayout ignoring a component's preferred size. The resulting GUI doesn't look professional, but we can improve the GUI's appearance with a little bit of effort, as demonstrated in Listing 7-2.

Listing 7-2. Improving TempVerter's GUI

```
import java.awt.Button;
import java.awt.EventQueue;
import java.awt.Frame;
import java.awt.GridLayout;
import java.awt.Label;
import java.awt.Panel;
import java.awt.TextField;

import java.awt.event.ActionEvent;
import java.awt.event.ActionListener;
import java.awt.event.WindowAdapter;
import java.awt.event.WindowEvent;

class TempVerter
{
    static Panel createGUI()
    {
        Panel pnlLayout = new Panel();
        pnlLayout.setLayout(new GridLayout(3, 1));
        Panel pnlTemp = new Panel();
        pnlTemp.add(new Label("Degrees"));
```

```java
final TextField txtDegrees = new TextField(10);
pnlTemp.add(txtDegrees);
pnlLayout.add(pnlTemp);
pnlTemp = new Panel();
pnlTemp.add(new Label("Result"));
final TextField txtResult = new TextField(30);
pnlTemp.add(txtResult);
pnlLayout.add(pnlTemp);
pnlTemp = new Panel();
ActionListener al;
al = new ActionListener()
    {
        @Override
        public void actionPerformed(ActionEvent ae)
        {
            try
            {
                double value = Double.parseDouble(txtDegrees.getText());
                double result = (value-32.0)*5.0/9.0;
                txtResult.setText("Celsius = "+result);
            }
            catch (NumberFormatException nfe)
            {
                System.err.println("bad input");
            }
        }
    };
Button btnConvertToCelsius = new Button("Convert to Celsius");
btnConvertToCelsius.addActionListener(al);
pnlTemp.add(btnConvertToCelsius);
al = new ActionListener()
    {
        @Override
        public void actionPerformed(ActionEvent ae)
        {
            try
            {
                double value = Double.parseDouble(txtDegrees.getText());
                double result = value*9.0/5.0+32.0;
                txtResult.setText("Fahrenheit = "+result);
            }
            catch (NumberFormatException nfe)
            {
                System.err.println("bad input");
            }
        }
    };
Button btnConvertToFahrenheit = new Button("Convert to Fahrenheit");
btnConvertToFahrenheit.addActionListener(al);
pnlTemp.add(btnConvertToFahrenheit);
pnlLayout.add(pnlTemp);
return pnlLayout;
```

```
    }
    public static void main(String[] args)
    {
       Runnable r = new Runnable()
                    {
                        @Override
                        public void run()
                        {
                            final Frame f = new Frame("TempVerter");
                            f.addWindowListener(new WindowAdapter()
                            {
                                @Override
                                public void windowClosing(WindowEvent we)
                                {
                                    f.dispose();
                                }
                            });
                            f.add(createGUI());
                            f.pack();
                            f.setResizable(false);
                            f.setVisible(true);
                        }
                    };
       EventQueue.invokeLater(r);
    }
}
```

Listing 7-2 presents an alternative architecture for creating a GUI. Instead of subclassing Frame, this class is instantiated directly and various methods are called to configure and display the frame window. (It's convenient to create a class method such as createGUI() that returns a Panel object containing the entire GUI. The returned Panel instance is passed to Frame's add() method to install the GUI.)

Figure 7-5 reveals the improved GUI.

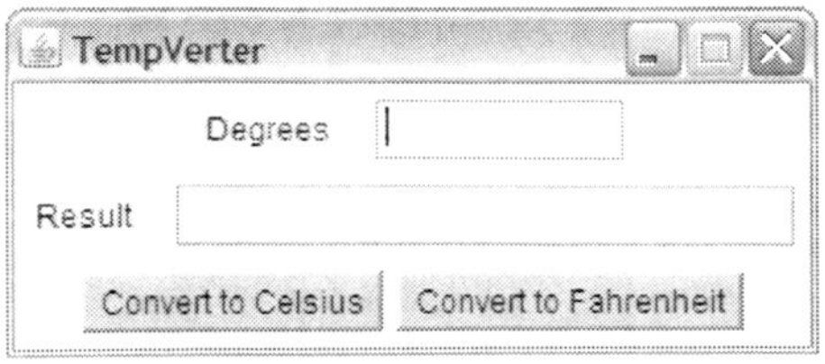

Figure 7-5. *A nicer looking GUI is achieved by wrapping components in nested panels.*

Notice that the components are displayed at their preferred sizes. This is caused by adding a label and a textfield, or by adding the two buttons to a nested panel (whose layout manager is flow), and then adding this panel to the main layout panel. (A flow layout lets each component assume its natural [preferred] size.)

Although Figure 7-5's GUI looks nicer than the GUI shown in Figure 7-4, there's room for improvement. For example, we could left-align the Degrees and Result labels and the textfields. We could also ensure that each button has the same size. Figure 7-6 shows you what the resulting GUI would look like.

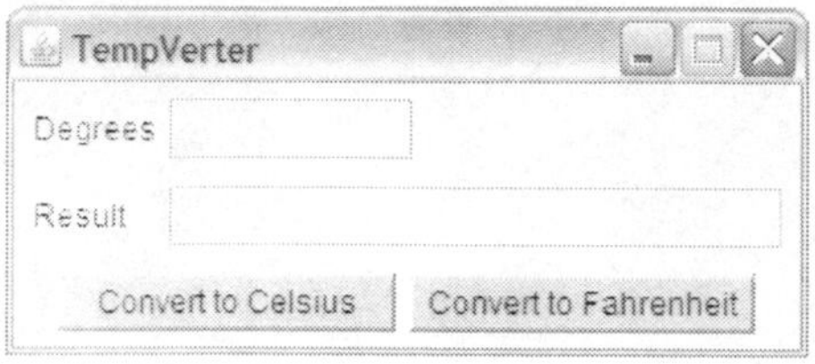

Figure 7-6. An even nicer looking GUI is achieved by aligning and resizing components.

The labels are left-aligned by executing ((FlowLayout) pnlTemp.getLayout()).setAlignment(FlowLayout.LEFT); on each of the two pnlTemp variables that stores a label and a textfield. This method call obtains pnlTemp's default flow layout manager and calls FlowLayout's void setAlignment(int alignment) method on this instance to align the panel's components to the left edge of the container (thanks to FlowLayout's LEFT constant)—FlowLayout leaves a default 5-pixel gap on each side of the panel that serves as a margin.

However, the textfields are not left aligned. To align them, we need to set the preferred size of the wider Degrees label to the preferred size of the narrower Result label. Similarly, we need to set the preferred size of the Convert to Celsius button to the preferred size of the Convert to Fahrenheit button so that they have equal widths.

These tasks can be accomplished in part by introducing the following void fixGUI(Frame) class method into the TempVerter class:

```
static void fixGUI(Frame f)
{
    Panel pnl = (Panel) f.getComponents()[0]; // 1
    Panel pnlRow = (Panel) pnl.getComponents()[0]; // 2
    Label l1 = (Label) pnlRow.getComponents()[0]; // 3
    pnlRow = (Panel) pnl.getComponents()[1]; // 4
    Label l2 = (Label) pnlRow.getComponents()[0]; // 5
    l1.setPreferredSize(l2.getPreferredSize()); // 6
    pnlRow = (Panel) pnl.getComponents()[2]; // 7
    Button btnToC = (Button) pnlRow.getComponents()[0]; // 8
    Button btnToF = (Button) pnlRow.getComponents()[1]; // 9
    btnToC.setPreferredSize(btnToF.getPreferredSize()); // 10
}
```

fixGUI(Frame) is invoked with a reference to the TempVerter frame window (TempVerter.this provides that reference). It first invokes f.getComponents()[0] to obtain the panel that was added to the frame window. (Listing 7-2 identifies this panel as pnlLayout.)

pnl/pnlLayout contains three Panel instances (recall pnlTemp). The second line fetches the first of these instances and assigns its reference to pnlRow. The third line extracts the Degrees label component, which is the first component (at position 0) within this panel.

The fourth line fetches the second Panel instance that contains the Result label and its associated textfield. The fifth line extracts this label.

The sixth line invokes getPreferredSize() on the Result label, and then invokes Component's void setPreferredSize(Dimension preferredSize) method with this preferred size to shrink the width of the Degrees label so that both textfields are left-aligned.

The seventh line fetches the third Panel instance, which contains the two buttons, the eighth and ninth lines extract these buttons, and the tenth line sets the preferred size of the Convert to Celsius button to that of the wider Convert to Fahrenheit button.

Introducing `fixGUI(Frame)` into `TempVerter` is only part of the solution. We must also call this method, and the appropriate place to do so is between the frame window's `pack()` and `setVisible()` method calls.

`fixGUI()` must be called after `pack()` because the preferred sizes are not known until after `pack()` has been called. This method must be called before `setVisible()` because it changes preferred sizes. `setVisible()` can accommodate these changes when they are made before this method is called. However, when they are made after calling `setVisible()`, `pack()` will have to be called a second time.

Note Although `fixGUI()` is convenient for trivial applications, you won't need to use it after learning more about layout management (which unfortunately is beyond the scope of this chapter). `fixGUI()` can be tedious to code, and you need to revise it whenever you change the GUI.Graphics, Colors, and Fonts

---

The `Component` class declares a `void paint(Graphics g)` method to paint a component. Painting occurs when a component is first shown or when it has been damaged (by being partly or completely obscured by another component) and is being reshown.

The argument passed to this method describes a *graphics context*, an object created from a concrete subclass of the abstract `java.awt.Graphics` class. This object describes a *drawing surface* on which pixels are drawn (e.g., a monitor screen, a printer page, or an image buffer).

The drawing surface has a two-dimensional coordinate system with its (0, 0) origin in the upper-left corner, its horizontal (X) axis positively increasing from left to right, and its vertical (Y) axis positively increasing from top to bottom. Figure 7-7 illustrates this coordinate system.

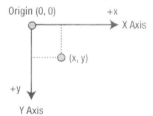

Figure 7-7. A drawing surface's coordinate system is anchored in an origin at its upper-left corner.

`Graphics` declares various methods for drawing on the surface and setting context state. Its drawing methods include the following:

- `void drawLine(int x1, int y1, int x2, int y2)` draws a line in the current color from (x1, y1) to (x2, y2).

- `void drawOval(int x, int y, int width, int height)` draws the outline of an oval in the current color such that the oval fits within the *bounding box* (smallest enclosing rectangle) whose upper-left corner is at (x, y) and whose extents are (width, height). The oval covers an area that is width+1 pixels wide and height+1 pixels tall.

- void drawRect(int x, int y, int width, int height) draws the outline of a rectangle in the current color whose upper-left corner is at (x, y) and whose extents are (width, height), such that the right edge is located at x+width and the bottom edge is located at y+height.

- void drawString(String str, int x, int y) draws the characters specified by str in the current color and using the current font. The baseline of the leftmost character is at (x, y).

- void fillOval(int x, int y, int width, int height) draws a filled oval in the current color such that the oval fits within the bounding box whose upper-left corner is at (x, y) and whose extents are (width, height).

- void fillRect(int x, int y, int width, int height) draws a filled rectangle in the current color whose upper-left corner is at (x, y) and whose extents are (width, height), such that the right edge is located at x+width-1 and the bottom edge is located at y+height-1.

State methods include the following:

- void setColor(Color c) sets the current color to the java.awt.Color instance passed to c. Color declares several uppercase/lowercase Color constants for common colors (e.g., RED/red, GREEN/green, and BLUE/blue) and constructors for describing arbitrary colors—it's conventional to use the uppercase color constants. A companion Color getColor() method returns the current color.

- void setFont(Font f) sets the current font to the java.awt.Font instance passed to f. A companion Font getFont() method returns the current font.

The following example demonstrates various drawing and state methods:

```
public void paint(Graphics g)
{
    g.setColor(Color.RED);
    g.drawLine(10, 10, 20, 20);
    g.setFont(new Font("Arial", Font.BOLD, 10));
    g.drawString("Hello", 35, 35);
}
```

The first statement sets the current color to Color.RED and the second statement draws a line in this color from starting point (10, 10) to ending point (20, 20). (When you don't specify a color before drawing, the color defaults to the component's background color, which is returned from Component's Color getBackground() method.)

The third statement calls Font's Font(String name, int style, int size) constructor to create a Font object that describes a font named Arial with style BOLD and point size 10—a *point* is a typographic measurement that's approximately 1/72 of an inch. (Other supported styles are PLAIN, ITALIC, and ITALIC combined with BOLD.) This object is then installed as the current font.

The font name can be a *font family name* (such as Arial) or a *font face name* (a font family name combined with style information, such as Arial Bold). When a font family name is specified, the style argument is used to select the most appropriate face from the family. When a font face name is specified, the face's style and the style argument are merged to locate the best matching font from the same family. For example, when face name "Arial Bold" is specified with style Font.ITALIC, AWT looks for a face in the "Arial" family that is bold and italic, and may associate the font instance with the physical font face "Arial Bold Italic". The style argument is merged with the specified face's style, not added or subtracted. This means, specifying a bold face and a bold style does not double-embolden the font, and specifying a bold face and a plain style does not lighten the font.

Java supports logical fonts and physical fonts. A *logical font* is a font that's guaranteed to be supported on all platforms; pass one of Font's predefined DIALOG, DIALOG_INPUT, MONOSPACED, SANS_SERIF, and SERIF String constants to Font() to select a logical font. A *physical font* is a nonlogical font that may or may not be supported on all platforms. Arial is an example of a widely supported physical font—it's probably available on all the platforms where Java runs.

■ **Caution** Be careful when specifying a font name because not all fonts are available on all platforms. I'll show you later in this chapter how you can identify all supported font family names.

Finally, the fourth statement draws Hello in the current color and font with baseline at (35, 35).

I previously defined *baseline* as the line serving as an origin for the purpose of layout. This term is also defined as the line separating a font's ascent from its descent, as Figure 7-8 illustrates.

Figure 7-8. A font's ascent and descent are relative to its baseline.

Every font is associated with various measurements. The *ascent* is that portion of the font's characters above the baseline; the *descent* is that portion of these characters below the baseline. Extra space added between lines of text is known as *leading*. When added together, ascent, descent, and leading form the font's *height*. Lastly, the *advance* roughly specifies the baseline location where the next character should appear.

AWT's java.awt.FontMetrics class encapsulates this measurement information. You can obtain an instance of this class by calling the Graphics class's FontMetrics getFontMetrics() method, which returns the font metrics for the current font. Among its various methods, you will find the int stringWidth(String str) method (which returns the total advance width for showing str's characters in the current font) useful for centering a string horizontally.

Although you can paint on any component (including a container) by subclassing the component class and overriding paint(), you should try to avoid doing so, to avoid confusing the user or someone who's reviewing your code. Instead, you should take advantage of AWT's Canvas class, which is intended for this purpose.

To use Canvas, you must extend this class and override paint(). You also need to specify its preferred size so that you can view the canvas on the screen. Accomplish this task by overriding getPreferredSize() to return a Dimension object containing the canvas's extents, or by invoking setPreferredSize() with a Dimension object containing the preferred size (as demonstrated in fixGUI()).

I've created a Geometria application that demonstrates Canvas. (Although Geometria is just a skeleton that presents a Canvas-based splash-screen component, it could be turned into a full-blown application for teaching basic geometry.) Listing 7-3 excerpts this application's SplashCanvas class.

Listing 7-3. Creating a splash screen

```
class SplashCanvas extends Canvas
{
   private Dimension d;
   private Font f;
   private String title;
   private boolean invert; // defaults to false (no invert)
   SplashCanvas()
   {
      d = new Dimension(250, 250);
      f = new Font("Arial", Font.BOLD, 50);
      title = "Geometria";
      addMouseListener(new MouseAdapter()
                      {
                         @Override
                         public void mouseClicked(MouseEvent me)
                         {
                            invert = !invert;
                            repaint();
                         }
                      });
   }
   @Override
   public Dimension getPreferredSize()
   {
      return d;
   }
   @Override
   public void paint(Graphics g)
   {
      int width = getWidth();
      int height = getHeight();
      g.setColor(invert ? Color.BLACK : Color.WHITE);
      g.fillRect(0, 0, width, height);
      g.setColor(invert ? Color.WHITE : Color.BLACK);
      for (int y = 0; y < height; y += 5)
         for (int x = 0; x < width; x += 5)
            g.drawLine(x, y, width-x, height-y);
      g.setColor(Color.YELLOW);
      g.setFont(f);
      FontMetrics fm = g.getFontMetrics();
      int strwid = fm.stringWidth(title);
      g.drawString(title, (width-strwid)/2, height/2);
      g.setColor(Color.RED);
      strwid = fm.stringWidth(title);
      g.drawString(title, (width-strwid)/2+3, height/2+3);
      g.setColor(Color.GREEN);
```

```
        g.fillOval(10, 10, 50, 50);
        g.setColor(Color.BLUE);
        g.fillRect(width-60, height-60, 50, 50);
    }
}
```

Listing 7-3's SplashCanvas class simulates a *splash screen*, a window that appears before a GUI is presented. Splash screens are often presented to users to occupy their attentions while applications initialize. (I'll have more to say about splash screens in Appendix C.)

There are several points of interest:

- I precreate Dimension, Font, and String objects to avoid unneeded object creation.

- I declare a Boolean variable named invert that (when true) results in the background portion of the splash canvas being inverted.

- I declare a constructor that registers a mouse listener with the canvas. Whenever the user clicks a mouse button while the mouse cursor is over this component, the mouse listener's void mouseClicked(MouseEvent me) method is invoked. This method toggles invert and invokes Component's void repaint() method, which tells AWT to invoke paint() as soon as possible.

- I invoke Component's int getWidth() and int getHeight() methods to obtain the canvas's width and height (in pixels).

- I invoke fillRect() to paint all the canvas's pixels using the current color (black or white).

- I use a pair of nested loops to draw lines. You should avoid using lengthy loops in the paint() method because they can make the user interface less performant. Shorter loops are not a problem.

- I center the bottom string horizontally by subtracting the total advance width (returned from stringWidth()) from the canvas's width and dividing the result by 2. I center the string's baseline vertically by dividing the canvas's height by 2.

- I achieve a drop-shadow effect by first drawing the bottom string in yellow (the shadow color) and then drawing the same string in red, but offset three pixels horizontally and three pixels vertically.

Figure 7-9 presents the noninverted canvas with red on yellow text, a green oval, and a blue rectangle.

Figure 7-9. A canvas can be used to paint an application's splash screen.

There's more that I could say about painting but lack of space prevents me from doing so. For example, Component also declares a void update(Graphics g) method for updating a heavyweight component in response to a repaint() method call. You can learn about this method and more by reading "Painting in AWT and Swing" (http://java.sun.com/products/jfc/tsc/articles/painting/index.html) and browsing the JDK documentation for the Component and Container classes.

Images

AWT supports GIF, JPEG, and PNG images via java.awt.Image, Toolkit, and other classes. Because Java 2D largely obviates the need to work with these classes, I won't discuss AWT's support for images in great detail. However, you should know something about this support because various JFC classes (such as javax.swing.ImageIcon) work with Image, and even provide constructors and/or methods that take Image arguments and (in regard to methods) return Image instances.

The Toolkit class declares several createImage() methods for creating and returning Image objects from various sources. For example, Image createImage(String filename) returns an Image object that represents the image defined in the file identified by filename.

Toolkit also declares two getImage() methods that create and return Image objects. Unlike their createImage() counterparts, the getImage() methods cache Image objects and can return the same object to different callers. This sharing mechanism helps AWT save heap space, especially when large images are loaded. In contrast, the createImage() methods always return new Image objects that are not shared among callers.

Image objects represent images but do not contain them: a loaded image is associated with an Image object. This dichotomy exists because Java was originally used mainly in a web browser context.

At that time, computers and network connections were much slower than they are today, and loading large images over the wire was a time-consuming process. Rather than force an *applet* (a browser-based application) to wait until an image had completely loaded (and annoy the user), it was decided that methods for loading images would load them asynchronously via background threads while occupying the user's attention elsewhere.

When you invoke a createImage() or getImage() method, a background thread is started to load the image, and createImage()/getImage() returns immediately with an Image object.

Because the image may not be fully loaded until sometime after the method returns, you cannot immediately obtain the image's width and height, or even draw the entire image. For this reason, Java provides the java.awt.image.ImageObserver interface to provide the current image-loading status.

Note ImageObserver lets you obtain information about a loaded image as soon as it's available while the image is being constructed, by providing a boolean imageUpdate(Image img, int infoflags, int x, int y, int width, int height) method that's called at various times during the loading process. infoflags consists of various ImageObserver constants (such as SOMEBITS and ERROR) that have been combined via the bitwise inclusive OR operator. The other arguments depend upon infoflags. For example, when infoflags is set to SOMEBITS, they define a bounding box for the newly loaded pixels.

Various Image and Graphics methods are declared with ImageObserver parameters. For example, Image's int getWidth(ImageObserver observer) and int getHeight(ImageObserver observer) methods are called with an image observer that helps these methods determine that the image has been loaded to the point where they can return its width or height, or that the width/height is still not available, in which case they return -1.

Similarly, the Graphics class's boolean drawImage(Image img, int x, int y, ImageObserver observer) method is called with an image observer that helps it determine what part of the image to draw—the image's upper-left corner is located at (x, y). When an image is not completely loaded, the image observer calls one of Component's repaint() methods, to reinvoke paint() so that a subsequent call can be made to drawImage() to draw the newly-loaded pixels.

Note You do not need to implement ImageObserver (unless there is a special reason to do so) because Component already implements this interface on your behalf.

I've created an ImageViewer application that shows you how to load and display an image. This application consists of ImageViewer and ImageCanvas classes, and Listing 7-4 presents ImageViewer.

Listing 7-4. A general-purpose image viewer

```
import java.awt.Dimension;
import java.awt.EventQueue;
import java.awt.FileDialog;
import java.awt.Frame;
import java.awt.Menu;
import java.awt.MenuBar;
import java.awt.MenuItem;
import java.awt.Panel;
import java.awt.ScrollPane;
import java.awt.Toolkit;
```

```java
import java.awt.event.ActionEvent;
import java.awt.event.ActionListener;
import java.awt.event.WindowAdapter;
import java.awt.event.WindowEvent;

class ImageViewer
{
    static ImageCanvas ic;
    static ScrollPane sp;
    static Toolkit tk = Toolkit.getDefaultToolkit();
    static ImageCanvas createGUI(final Frame f)
    {
        MenuBar mb = new MenuBar();
        Menu mFile = new Menu("File");
        MenuItem miOpen = new MenuItem("Open...");
        ActionListener al;
        al = new ActionListener()
            {
                @Override
                public void actionPerformed(ActionEvent ae)
                {
                    FileDialog fd = new FileDialog(f, "Open file");
                    fd.setVisible(true);
                    String curFile = fd.getFile();
                    if (curFile != null)
                    {
                        ic.setImage(tk.getImage(fd.getDirectory()+curFile));
                        sp.doLayout();
                    }
                }
            };
        miOpen.addActionListener(al);
        mFile.add(miOpen);
        MenuItem miExit = new MenuItem("Exit");
        miExit.addActionListener(new ActionListener()
                                {
                                    @Override
                                    public void actionPerformed(ActionEvent ae)
                                    {
                                        f.dispose();
                                    }
                                });
        mFile.add(miExit);
        mb.add(mFile);
        f.setMenuBar(mb);
        return new ImageCanvas();
    }
    public static void main(String[] args)
    {
        Runnable r = new Runnable()
                    {
                        @Override
```

```
                    public void run()
                    {
                        final Frame f = new Frame("ImageViewer");
                        WindowAdapter wa;
                        wa = new WindowAdapter()
                            {
                                @Override
                                public void windowClosing(WindowEvent we)
                                {
                                    f.dispose();
                                }
                            };
                        f.addWindowListener(wa);
                        sp = new ScrollPane();
                        sp.setPreferredSize(new Dimension(300, 300));
                        sp.add(ic = createGUI(f));
                        f.add(sp);
                        f.pack();
                        f.setVisible(true);
                    }
                };
        EventQueue.invokeLater(r);
    }
}
```

ImageViewer declares an ImageCanvas class field that references the image canvas used to display the image. It also declares a ScrollPane class field whose scrollpane contains the image canvas, so that you can scroll horizontally and vertically over images that are too large to be displayed in their entirety at the current screen resolution, and a Toolkit instance whose getImage() method is used to start the image-loading process for the user-selected image.

The ImageCanvas createGUI(final Frame f) method creates a GUI consisting of a menubar with a single File menu and an image canvas. File consists of Open and Exit menuitems.

Open's action listener is invoked when the user selects Open... (... indicates that a dialog box will be displayed). This listener first instantiates FileDialog and displays it; the user sees a platform-specific dialog box for selecting a file.

When the user closes this dialog box, FileDialog's String curFile() method is called to return the name of the selected file; this method returns null when a file has not been selected.

If null is not returned, FileDialog's String getDirectory() method is called to return the directory name, which is prepended to the filename so that the selected file can be located. The resulting pathname is passed to Toolkit's getImage() method, and the returned Image instance is passed to ImageCanvas's setImage() method to load and display the image. ScrollPane's void doLayout() method lays out this container by resizing its child (the image canvas) to its preferred size.

Exit's action listener is invoked when the user selects Exit. It invokes dispose() on the frame window to dispose of this window's (and the contained components') native screen resources. Furthermore, a window closing event is triggered and the frame window's window listener's windowClosing() method is invoked.

The main() method creates the GUI on the EDT. It instantiates a scrollpane, and sets its preferred size to an arbitrary value that serves as the frame window's default size (following a pack() method call).

The createGUI() method call installs the menubar on its Frame argument, and returns the image canvas, which is saved in the ImageCanvas class field so that it can be accessed from the Open menuitem listener. The image canvas is also added to the scrollpane, and the scrollpane is added to the frame window.

Listing 7-5 presents ImageCanvas.

Listing 7-5. Displaying a user-selected image

```java
import java.awt.Canvas;
import java.awt.Dimension;
import java.awt.Graphics;
import java.awt.Image;
import java.awt.MediaTracker;

class ImageCanvas extends Canvas
{
   private Image image;
   @Override
   public void paint(Graphics g)
   {
      // drawImage() does nothing when image contains the null reference.
      g.drawImage(image, 0, 0, null);
   }
   void setImage(Image image)
   {
      MediaTracker mt = new MediaTracker(this);
      mt.addImage(image, 1);
      try
      {
         mt.waitForID(1);
      }
      catch (InterruptedException ie)
      {
         assert false;
      }
      setPreferredSize(new Dimension(image.getWidth(null),
                                     image.getHeight(null)));
      this.image = image;
   }
}
```

ImageCanvas declares an Image field that stores a reference to the image to be displayed. It also overrides the paint() method to invoke drawImage(). This method does nothing when the Image argument is the null reference; this is the case when paint() is called before the user selects an image. null is passed as the ImageObserver argument because the image is completely loaded at this point, as you will discover.

The setImage() method is called to load the image, set its preferred size to influence Listing 7-4's sp.doLayout(); method call, and save the Image argument in the Image field so that it can be referenced from a subsequent paint() call, which happens in response to doLayout().

Image loading is accomplished by using the java.awt.MediaTracker class. MediaTracker declares a void addImage(Image image, int id) method that adds an Image object to a list of Image objects being tracked. The associated id value is later used by MediaTracker's void waitForID(int id) method to start loading the identified Image objects, and wait until all these images have finished loading.

After `waitForID()` returns, the image is completely loaded and its width and height are available. This information is obtained in subsequent `getWidth()` and `getHeight()` calls. Although these calls require an image observer, which could be specified by passing `this` as an argument (because `Component` implements `ImageObserver`), doing so isn't necessary because the image is loaded.

The width and height are subsequently used to construct a `Dimension` object that's passed to `setPreferredSize()`. This preferred size will be taken into account by `sp.doLayout();`, which is executed following the call to `ImageCanvas`'s `setImage()` method—see Listing 7-4.

Figure 7-10 presents ImageViewer's GUI with a loaded image.

Figure 7-10. *Is it true that a rose by any other name would smell as sweet?*

▩ **Note** AWT also supports image processing. For example, you can grayscale a colored image, blur an image, and so on. Because Java 2D simplifies image processing, and because I introduce you to Java 2D's image processing support later in this chapter, I don't discuss AWT-based image processing.

Data Transfer

GUI-based applications often need to transfer data between or within themselves. For example, a text editor's user may want to cut selected text to the system clipboard and subsequently paste the clipboard's text to another location within the document being edited.

AWT supports transferring arbitrary objects between applications via the *system clipboard*, and transferring objects within an application via a *private clipboard*. This support consists of the `java.awt.datatransfer` package with its `ClipboardOwner`, `FlavorListener`, `FlavorMap`, `FlavorTable`, and `Transferable` interfaces; and `Clipboard`, `DataFlavor`, `FlavorEvent`, `StringSelection`, `SystemFlavorMap`, `MimeTypeParseException`, and `UnsupportedFlavorException` classes.

`Clipboard` provides a mechanism for transferring data to a clipboard by using cut/copy/paste operations. You can obtain a *singleton* (single instance) `Clipboard` object that provides access to the native clipboard facilities offered by the platform's windowing system by calling `Toolkit`'s `Clipboard getSystemClipboard()` method; for example, `Clipboard clipboard =`

Toolkit.getDefaultToolkit.getSystemClipboard();. Alternatively, you can obtain a private clipboard by instantiating Clipboard.

Clipboard declares a void setContents(Transferable contents, ClipboardOwner owner) method that sets the current contents of the clipboard to the specified transferable object and registers the specified clipboard owner as the owner of the new contents. This method throws java.lang.IllegalStateException when the clipboard is currently unavailable.

The transferable object that's passed to contents is created from a class that implements the Transferable interface in terms of the following three methods:

- Object getTransferData(DataFlavor flavor) returns an object containing the data being transferred. The DataFlavor argument identifies the *flavor* (format) of this data (e.g., a string or a JPEG image) by encapsulating the data's Multipurpose Internet Mail Extensions (MIME) type—http://en.wikipedia.org/wiki/MIME and http://en.wikipedia.org/wiki/Internet_media_type discuss MIME—and a human-presentable name describing this data format. This method throws java.io.IOException when the data is no longer available in the requested flavor, and UnsupportedFlavorException when the requested data flavor isn't supported.

- DataFlavor[] getTransferDataFlavors() returns an array of DataFlavor objects that indicate the flavors of the data that this transferable object can provide.

- boolean isDataFlavorSupported(DataFlavor flavor) indicates whether or not the specified flavor is supported; true returns when flavor is supported.

Each time that you invoke setContents(), the object passed to owner is the owner of the clipboard content. If you call this method with a different owner, AWT notifies the previous owner that it's no longer the owner (some other content is on the clipboard) by calling ClipboardOwner's void lostOwnership(Clipboard clipboard, Transferable contents) method.

Because users typically want to copy, cut, and paste text, java.awt.datatransfer provides StringSelection as an implementation of Transferable and ClipboardOwner (lostOwnership() is left empty; you must subclass StringSelection and override lostOwnership() when you need this notification). You would use StringSelection to transfer strings to and from a clipboard.

The following example presents copy(), cut(), and paste() methods that show you how to perform copy, cut, and paste operations in the context of the TextArea class. The example specifies a ta variable that references a TextArea instance, and a clipboard variable that references a Clipboard instance:

```
void copy()
{
   StringSelection ss = new StringSelection(ta.getSelectedText());
   clipboard.setContents(ss, ss);
}
void cut()
{
   copy();
   ta.replaceRange("", ta.getSelectionStart(), ta.getSelectionEnd());
}
void paste()
{
   Transferable clipData = clipboard.getContents(this);
   if (clipData != null)
      try
      {
```

```
        if (clipData.isDataFlavorSupported(DataFlavor.stringFlavor))
        {
            String text = (String) clipData.getTransferData(DataFlavor.stringFlavor);
            ta.replaceRange(text, ta.getSelectionStart(),
                            ta.getSelectionEnd());
        }
    }
    catch (UnsupportedFlavorException ufe)
    {
        ta.setText("Flavor not supported");
    }
    catch (IOException ioe)
    {
        ta.setText("No data to paste");
    }
}
```

copy()'s first task is to extract the selected text from the textarea by calling TextComponent's String getSelectedText() method. It then passes this text to the StringSelection(String data) constructor to create a transferable object that contains this text.

Continuing, copy() passes this object to the clipboard by invoking clipboard.setContents(ss, ss). The same StringSelection object (ss) is passed as the transferable object and the clipboard owner because StringSelection implements Transferable and ClipboardOwner.

cut() is much simpler. This method first invokes copy() to copy the selected text to the clipboard. It then invokes TextArea's void replaceRange(String str, int start, int end) method to remove the selected text (delimited by the integer values returned from TextComponent's int getSelectionStart() and int getSelectionEnd() methods) by replacing it with the empty string.

paste() is the most complex of the three methods. It first invokes Clipboard's Transferable getContents(Object requestor) method to return a transferable object representing the current contents of the clipboard (or null when the clipboard is empty). The requestor parameter is currently not used; it may be implemented in a future release of the java.awt.datatransfer package.

If the returned transferable isn't null, paste() invokes isDataFlavorSupported() on this object with DataFlavor.stringFlavor as the argument. This method returns true when the requested flavor is supported. In other words, isDataFlavorSupported() returns true when the clipboard contains text; it would return false when the clipboard contained an image (for example).

If isDataFlavorSupported() returns true, paste() calls getTransferData() to return the string and then replaces the selected string with this content.

TextArea contains built-in support for performing copy, cut, and paste operations by pressing the Ctrl-C, Ctrl-X, and Ctrl-V key combinations. However, neither TextArea nor its TextComponent superclass provides methods for performing these tasks. As a result, you would have to supply your own copy(), cut(), and paste() methods (such as those shown previously) when you wanted to programmatically perform these operations (perhaps in response to the user selecting Copy, Cut, or Paste from an Edit menu).

I've created a CopyCutAndPaste application that demonstrates copy, cut, and paste on a textarea via the previous copy(), cut(), and paste() methods. Consult this book's code file for CopyCutAndPaste's source code. (This book's introduction presents instructions on obtaining the code file.)

Swing

Swing is a windowing system-independent API for creating GUIs that are based on components, containers, layout managers, and events. Although Swing extends AWT (you can use AWT layout managers and events in your Swing GUIs), this API differs from its predecessor in several ways, including the following:

- AWT-based GUIs adopt the looks and feels (behaviors) of the windowing systems on which they run because they leverage windowing system native screen resources. For example, a button looks and feels like a Windows button on Windows and a Motif button on X Window-Motif. In contrast, a Swing GUI can look and feel the same when run on any windowing system or (at the developer's discretion) adopt the look and feel of the windowing system on which it's running.

- To be windowing-system independent, AWT components adopt the lowest common denominator of component features. For example, if buttons on one windowing system can display images with text whereas buttons on another windowing system display text only, AWT cannot provide a button feature for optionally displaying an image. In contrast, Swing's noncontainer components and a few of its containers are completely managed by Java so that they can have whatever features are necessary (e.g., tooltips); these features are available regardless of the windowing system. For the same reason, Swing can offer components that might not be available on every windowing system; for example, tables and trees.

The standard class library organizes Swing's many types into the javax.swing package and various subpackages. For example, the javax.swing.table subpackage stores types that support Swing's table component.

This section introduces you to Swing by presenting its architecture and sampling Swing components.

An Extended Architecture

By extending AWT, Swing shares AWT's architecture. However, Swing goes beyond what AWT has to offer by providing an extended architecture. This architecture is largely based on new heavyweight containers, new lightweight components and containers, UI delegates, and pluggable look and feels.

New Heavyweight Containers

The javax.swing package includes JDialog, JFrame, and JWindow container classes that extend their java.awt.Dialog, java.awt.Frame, and java.awt.Window counterparts. These heavyweight containers manage their contained lightweight components (such as javax.swing.JButton) and containers (such as javax.swing.JPanel).

JDialog, JFrame, JWindow, and two other Swing containers use *panes* (special-purpose containers) to organize their contained components/containers. Swing supports root, layered, content, and glass panes:

- The *root pane* contains the layered pane and the glass pane. It's implemented via the javax.swing.JRootPane class.

- The *layered pane* contains the application's menubar and the content pane. It's implemented via the javax.swing.JLayeredPane class.

- The *content pane* is a Container subclass instance that stores the GUI's nonmenu content.

- The *glass pane* is a transparent Component instance that covers the layered pane.

Figure 7-11 reveals a container's pane-based architecture.

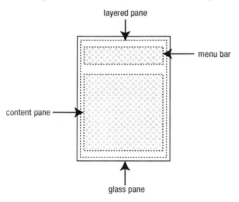

Figure 7-11. Using panes to architect a GUI.

Container classes that support panes store a single JRootPane instance. This instance stores a JLayeredPane instance and a Component instance that serves as the glass pane. The JLayeredPane instance stores a javax.swing.JMenuBar instance and a Container subclass instance that serves as the content pane.

The following example demonstrates how you might create a frame window with a single button:

```
JFrame f = new JFrame();
JRootPane rp = f.getRootPane();
Container cp = rp.getContentPane();
cp.add(new JButton("Ok")); // Add the button to the frame's content pane.
f.pack();
f.setVisible(true);
```

Container classes that support panes implement the javax.swing.RootPaneContainer interface, which provides convenience methods for accessing the root pane and setting/getting the content, glass, and layered panes. For example, RootPaneContainer's Container getContentPane() method behaves as if you called getRootPane().getContentPane(). It lets you shorten the previous example to the following:

```
JFrame f = new JFrame();
getContentPane().add(new JButton("Ok")); // Add the button to the frame's content pane.
f.pack();
f.setVisible(true);
```

RootPaneContainer complements getContentPane() with a void setContentPane(Container content) method that you'll find helpful when you want to replace the current content pane with a new content pane. The following example demonstrates setContentPane() by creating a new panel, populating the panel (as described by the comment), and using setContentPane() to replace the existing content pane with this panel:

```
JFrame f = new JFrame();
JPanel pnl = new JPanel();
// Populate the panel.
f.setContentPane(pnl);
```

> **Tip** Because the glass pane is painted last, you can draw over the GUI. Also, because events are first sent to the glass pane, you can use this pane to block mouse and other events from reaching the GUI.

JFrame declares a void setDefaultCloseOperation(int operation) method for specifying the operation that occurs by default when the user chooses to close this window. The argument passed to operation is one of the following constants (declared in the javax.swing.WindowConstants interface, which JFrame and JDialog implement):

- DO_NOTHING_ON_CLOSE: Don't do anything; require the program to handle the operation in the windowClosing() method of a registered WindowListener object. This operation is equivalent to what you would do in AWT as discussed earlier.

- HIDE_ON_CLOSE: Automatically hide the frame window after invoking any registered WindowListener objects. This is the default operation.

- DISPOSE_ON_CLOSE: Automatically hide and dispose of the frame window after invoking any registered WindowListener objects.

- EXIT_ON_CLOSE (also declared in JFrame): Exit the application via System.exit().

> **Note** EXIT_ON_CLOSE was introduced into the JFrame class in Java 1.3, and subsequently added to WindowsConstants in Java 1.4 (for completeness).

New Lightweight Components and Containers

Swing's lightweight components and containers are implemented by subclasses of the abstract javax.swing.JComponent class, which extends Container. (I previously mentioned that components and containers created from custom Component and Container subclasses are known as lightweight components and containers.) They do not have peers but reuse the peers of their closest heavyweight ancestors. After all, Swing must eventually ensure that the platform's windowing system can display them.

JComponent introduces several new features, including tooltips, borders, and the option of creating nonrectangular components:

- A *tooltip* is a small (typically rectangular) window appearing over a component with a small amount of help text. JComponent declares a void setToolTipText(String text) method for specifying the component's tooltip text.

- A *border* is an object that sits between a Swing component's edges and that of its container. JComponent declares a void setBorder(Border border) method for setting the border to border, which is an instance of a class that implements the javax.swing.border.Border interface. The javax.swing.BorderFactory class declares several class methods for returning different kinds of borders. For example, Border createEtchedBorder(int type) creates an etched border by instantiating the javax.swing.border.EtchedBorder class. The argument passed to type must be one of EtchedBorder.RAISED or EtchedBorder.LOWERED.

- Predefined AWT components (such as buttons) are rectangular because their native screen resources are rectangular. When you create your own components (by subclassing JComponent), you can make them nonrectangular by passing false to JComponent's void setOpaque(boolean isOpaque) method, which indicates that not every pixel is painted (so background pixels can show through). Passing true to this method indicates that the component paints every pixel. (The default value is false.)

I'll demonstrate tooltips and borders later in this chapter.

Note AWT provides the java.awt.Insets class to specify the amount of space that a container leaves empty at its edges. For example, Frame has a top inset that corresponds to the height of the frame window's titlebar. Borders extend the insets concept by letting you select an object that draws over this empty space. Borders leverage insets. For example, Border declares Insets getBorderInsets(Component c) to return the insets for the specified container component.

UI Delegates

In the late 1970s, Xerox PARC invented the Model-View-Controller (MVC) architecture as an architectural pattern for separating application logic from the user interface, to simplify GUI creation. MVC consists of the following entities:

- The *model* maintains a component's state, such as a button's press information or the characters that appear in a textfield.

- The *view* presents a visual representation of the model, giving a component its *look*. For example, a button view would typically display a button as pressed or unpressed according to its model's pressed state.

- The *controller* determines how (and even if) a component responds to input events that originate from input devices (such as mice and keyboards), giving the component its *feel*. For example, when the user presses a button, the controller notifies the model to update its pressed state and the view to repaint the button.

Experience has shown that it's easier to manage an integrated view and controller than to deal with them separately. The integrated result is known as a *User Interface (UI) delegate*.

Swing components are based on models and UI delegates, where the UI delegate makes it possible for a component to look the same no matter what windowing system underlies the GUI. Models and UI delegates are separate and communicate via events, making it possible for a UI delegate to associate with multiple models and for a model to associate with multiple UI delegates.

A Swing component consists of a main class whose name starts with J, a current model, and a current UI delegate. The main class connects the model to the UI delegate and is used to create the component.

For example, the JButton class describes a button component. It's associated with a model that's described by the javax.swing.ButtonModel interface. The model is attached to the component by invoking void setModel(ButtonModel model), which JButton inherits from its javax.swing.AbstractButton superclass.

JButton is associated with a UI delegate that's described by the abstract javax.swing.plaf.ButtonUI class, which extends the abstract javax.swing.plaf.ComponentUI class. Swing attaches the UI delegate to the component by invoking void setUI(ButtonUI ui), which JButton inherits from AbstractButton.

Pluggable Look and Feels

A *look and feel* is a set of UI delegates with one UI delegate per component. For example, Swing provides a look and feel for making a Swing GUI look like a Windows XP GUI. It also provides look and feels that make the GUI look and feel the same regardless of the underlying windowing system.

Swing also provides a mechanism for selecting a specific look and feel. Because this mechanism is used to plug the look and feel into the GUI before the GUI is displayed (or even after it is displayed), a look and feel is also known as a *pluggable look and feel (PLAF)*.

The following PLAFs are supported:

- *Basic* is an abstract PLAF that serves as the foundation on which the other PLAFs are based. It's located in the javax.swing.plaf.basic package and its main class is BasicLookAndFeel.

- *Metal* is a cross-platform PLAF and is also the default. It's located in the javax.swing.plaf.metal package and its main class is MetalLookAndFeel.

- *Multi* is a multiplexing PLAF that combines PLAFs. It's located in the javax.swing.plaf.multi package and its main class is MultiLookAndFeel. (Each multiplexing UI delegate manages its child UI delegates. Multi was created primarily for use with the Accessibility API.)

- *Nimbus* is a polished cross-platform PLAF that uses Java 2D-based vector graphics to draw the GUI so that it looks crisp at any resolution. Nimbus is located in the javax.swing.plaf.nimbus package; its main class is NimbusLookAndFeel.

- *Synth* is a skinnable PLAF that's based on an XML file. It's located in the javax.swing.plaf.synth package and its main class is SynthLookAndFeel.

- *GTK* is a PLAF that implements the look and feel of the X Window-oriented GTK widget toolkit. It's located in the com.sun.java.swing.plaf.gtk package and its main class is GTKLookAndFeel.

- *Motif* is a PLAF that implements the look and feel of the X Window-oriented Motif widget toolkit. It's located in the com.sun.java.swing.plaf.motif package and its main class is MotifLookAndFeel.

- *Windows* is a PLAF that implements the look and feel of the current Windows platform (e.g., classic Windows, Windows XP, or Windows Vista). It's located in the `com.sun.java.swing.plaf.windows` package and its main class is `WindowsLookAndFeel`.

The main PLAF classes ultimately extend the abstract `javax.swing.LookAndFeel` class. Also, for licensing reasons, Swing lets you use the GTK PLAF only on X Window-based platforms, and lets you use the Windows PLAF only on a Windows platform.

The `javax.swing.UIManager` class provides the `void setLookAndFeel(String className)` class method for installing a look and feel prior to displaying the GUI. This method throws one of `java.lang.ClassNotFoundException` when the `LookAndFeel` subclass named by `className` cannot be found, `java.lang.InstantiationException` when a new instance of the class could not be created reflectively, `java.lang.IllegalAccessException` when the class or initializer isn't accessible, `javax.swing.UnsupportedLookAndFeelException` when the PLAF won't run on the current platform, and `java.lang.ClassCastException` when `className` identifies a class that doesn't extend `LookAndFeel`.

The following example attempts to install Nimbus as the current look and feel before creating the GUI:

```
try
{
   UIManager.setLookAndFeel("javax.swing.plaf.nimbus.NimbusLookAndFeel");
   new GUI();
}
catch (Exception e)
{
}
```

Suppose your application provides a menu that lets the user choose the GUI's look and feel. After selecting the menuitem, the visible GUI must be updated to reflect the choice. Swing lets you accomplish this task from the menuitem's action listener (or from somewhere else on the EDT) as follows:

```
try
{
   UIManager.setLookAndFeel("javax.swing.plaf.nimbus.NimbusLookAndFeel");
   SwingUtilities.updateComponentTreeUI(frame); frame.pack();
}
catch (Exception e)
{
}
```

The `javax.swing.SwingUtilities` class declares a `void updateComponentTreeUI(Component c)` class method that changes the look and feel by invoking the `void updateUI()` method of each component located in the tree of components rooted in `c`, which typically references a frame window. `updateUI()` invokes `UIManager`'s `ComponentUI getUI(JComponent target)` method to return the new look and feel's UI delegate, and passes this delegate to the component's `setUI()` method. For example, `JButton`'s `updateUI()` method is implemented as follows:

```
public void updateUI()
{
   setUI((ButtonUI) UIManager.getUI(this));
}
```

frame.pack(); resizes components to their preferred sizes because these sizes will probably change under the new look and feel.

■ **Note** For more information on PLAFs, check out The Java Tutorial's "Modifying the Look and Feel" lesson (http://download.oracle.com/javase/tutorial/uiswing/lookandfeel/index.html).

Sampling Swing Components

Swing provides a wide variety of components that you can explore by running the SwingSet2 demo application, which you probably installed with the other demos when installing JDK 7 (see Chapter 1 for installation instructions). If you didn't install the demos, rerun the JDK 7 installer and make sure that it's configured to install them.

To run SwingSet2, change to the JDK 7 home directory's demo\jfc\SwingSet2 directory and execute java -jar SwingSet2.jar. Figure 7-12 reveals that this application presents a GUI consisting of a menu, a toolbar, and a tabbed workspace that lets you switch between interacting with various component demos and viewing the current demo's source code.

Figure 7-12. SwingSet2 lets you view and interact with Swing components in diverse look and feel contexts.

When SwingSet2 starts running, it presents its GUI based on the default Metal (also known as Java) Look and Feel. However, you can change to another look and feel by selecting from the Look & Feel menu. For example, Figure 7-12 reveals SwingSet2's GUI after the look and feel has been changed to Nimbus.

Note Unfortunately, the need for brevity restrains me from fully covering Swing components in this chapter. You'll find additional component coverage in subsequent chapters and Appendix C.

Revisiting TempVerter

I previously presented a TempVerter application that demonstrates AWT containers, components, layout managers, and events. Listing 7-6 presents a Swing version of this application, to help you compare and contrast Swing GUI code with its AWT counterpart.

Listing 7-6. Refactoring TempVerter for Swing

```
import java.awt.Container;
import java.awt.EventQueue;
import java.awt.FlowLayout;
import java.awt.GridLayout;

import java.awt.event.ActionEvent;
import java.awt.event.ActionListener;

import javax.swing.BorderFactory;
import javax.swing.ImageIcon;
import javax.swing.JButton;
import javax.swing.JFrame;
import javax.swing.JLabel;
import javax.swing.JPanel;
import javax.swing.JTextField;

import javax.swing.border.Border;
import javax.swing.border.EtchedBorder;

class TempVerter
{
    static JPanel createGUI()
    {
        JPanel pnlLayout = new JPanel();
        pnlLayout.setLayout(new GridLayout(3, 1));
        JPanel pnlTemp = new JPanel();
        ((FlowLayout) pnlTemp.getLayout()).setAlignment(FlowLayout.LEFT);
        pnlTemp.add(new JLabel("Degrees"));
        final JTextField txtDegrees = new JTextField(10);
        txtDegrees.setToolTipText("Enter a numeric value in this field.");
        pnlTemp.add(txtDegrees);
        pnlLayout.add(pnlTemp);
        pnlTemp = new JPanel();
```

```java
((FlowLayout) pnlTemp.getLayout()).setAlignment(FlowLayout.LEFT);
pnlTemp.add(new JLabel("Result"));
final JTextField txtResult = new JTextField(30);
txtResult.setToolTipText("Don't enter anything in this field.");
pnlTemp.add(txtResult);
pnlLayout.add(pnlTemp);
pnlTemp = new JPanel();
ImageIcon ii = new ImageIcon("thermometer.gif");
ActionListener al;
al = new ActionListener()
    {
        @Override
        public void actionPerformed(ActionEvent ae)
        {
            try
            {
                double value = Double.parseDouble(txtDegrees.getText());
                double result = (value-32.0)*5.0/9.0;
                txtResult.setText("Celsius = "+result);
            }
            catch (NumberFormatException nfe)
            {
                System.err.println("bad input");
            }
        }
    };
JButton btnConvertToCelsius = new JButton("Convert to Celsius", ii);
btnConvertToCelsius.addActionListener(al);
pnlTemp.add(btnConvertToCelsius);
al = new ActionListener()
    {
        @Override
        public void actionPerformed(ActionEvent ae)
        {
            try
            {
                double value = Double.parseDouble(txtDegrees.getText());
                double result = value*9.0/5.0+32.0;
                txtResult.setText("Fahrenheit = "+result);
            }
            catch (NumberFormatException nfe)
            {
                System.err.println("bad input");
            }
        }
    };
JButton btnConvertToFahrenheit = new JButton("Convert to Fahrenheit", ii);
btnConvertToFahrenheit.addActionListener(al);
pnlTemp.add(btnConvertToFahrenheit);
Border border = BorderFactory.createEtchedBorder(EtchedBorder.LOWERED);
pnlTemp.setBorder(border);
pnlLayout.add(pnlTemp);
```

```
        return pnlLayout;
    }
    static void fixGUI(Container c)
    {
        JPanel pnlRow = (JPanel) c.getComponents()[0];
        JLabel l1 = (JLabel) pnlRow.getComponents()[0];
        pnlRow = (JPanel) c.getComponents()[1];
        JLabel l2 = (JLabel) pnlRow.getComponents()[0];
        l2.setPreferredSize(l1.getPreferredSize());
        pnlRow = (JPanel) c.getComponents()[2];
        JButton btnToC = (JButton) pnlRow.getComponents()[0];
        JButton btnToF = (JButton) pnlRow.getComponents()[1];
        btnToC.setPreferredSize(btnToF.getPreferredSize());
    }
    public static void main(String[] args)
    {
        Runnable r = new Runnable()
                    {
                        @Override
                        public void run()
                        {
                            final JFrame f = new JFrame("TempVerter");
                            f.setDefaultCloseOperation(JFrame.DISPOSE_ON_CLOSE);
                            Border b = BorderFactory.createEmptyBorder(5, 5, 5, 5);
                            f.getRootPane().setBorder(b);
                            f.setContentPane(createGUI());
                            fixGUI(f.getContentPane());
                            f.pack();
                            f.setResizable(false);
                            f.setVisible(true);
                        }
                    };
        EventQueue.invokeLater(r);
    }
}
```

Listing 7-6 presents a similar architecture to that shown in Listing 7-2. However, it also demonstrates various Swing features, including Swing components/containers, ImageIcon, tooltips, borders, and setDefaultCloseOperation().

Because Swing component classes have similar APIs to their AWT counterparts, you can often just prefix an AWT class name with J to refer to the equivalent Swing class—don't forget to change the import statement. For example, prefix Label with J to change from AWT's Label class to javax.swing.JLabel.

ImageIcon is instantiated to load a thermometer icon image—behind the scenes MediaTracker is used to ensure that the image is completely loaded. The ImageIcon instance is then passed to the constructor of each JButton instance so that the button will display this icon along with its label.

Tooltips are handy for presenting small help messages that assist the user in interacting with the GUI. Listing 7-6 demonstrates this feature by invoking setToolTipText() on each of the txtDegrees and txtResult textfields. When the user moves the mouse over a textfield, a tooltip will appear to reveal its help message.

Listing 7-6 attaches an etched border to the panel surrounding the pair of buttons, to set them apart from the other components. Because this border butts up against the frame window, an empty border is created and assigned to the frame's root pane to leave some space around this window's edges.

The setDefaultCloseOperation() method and its DISPOSE_ON_CLOSE argument reduces verbosity by disposing of a window (in response to a user close request) without having to install a window listener.

You may have noticed that I've placed the void fixGUI(Container c) class method before the pack() method call, instead of placing it after pack() as I discussed following Listing 7-2. I previously recommended placing fixGUI() after pack() because (in AWT) preferred sizes are not available until after the pack() method call, and fixGUI() needs to access preferred sizes. In Swing, preferred sizes are available prior to calling pack(), and changing them after calling pack() would require another call to pack() to ensure that the GUI is properly sized.

Compile Listing 7-6 and run this application. Figure 7-13 shows the resulting GUI.

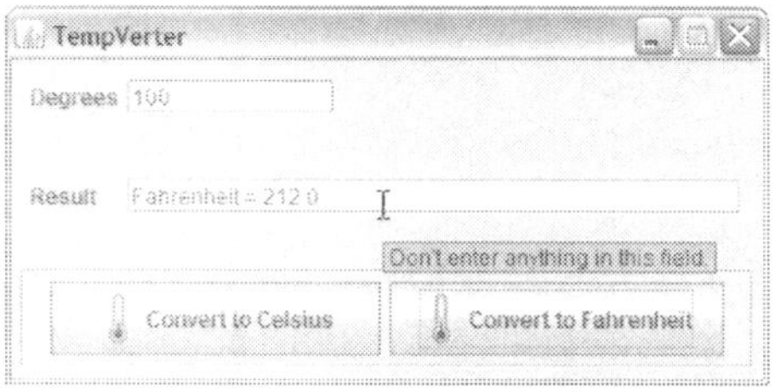

Figure 7-13. A tooltip appears when you move the mouse cursor over a textfield.

Note TempVerter demonstrates some of Swing's many components, which are located in the javax.swing package. Other components that you'll find useful include JScrollPane (Swing's version of ScrollPane), JTextArea (Swing's version of TextArea), and JOptionPane (a class that makes it easy to pop up a standard dialog box that prompts users for a value or informs them of something). JOptionPane declares showConfirmDialog(), showInputDialog(), showMessageDialog(), and showOptionDialog() class methods to ask confirming questions (yes/no/cancel), prompt for input, tell the user about something that has happened, and combine confirmation with input and message display.

TempVerter Meets JLayer

Suppose you plan to distribute your Swing application as shareware (see http://en.wikipedia.org/wiki/Shareware) and want to display a translucent UNREGISTERED message over the GUI until the user registers their copy. You could accomplish this task by working with the glass pane directly, or you could work with the javax.swing.JLayer class, which is new in Java 7.

JLayer's Javadoc describes this class as "a universal decorator for Swing components, which enables you to implement various advanced painting effects as well as receive notifications of all AWTEvents generated within its borders." JLayer works with a glass pane on your behalf.

To use JLayer, first extend the javax.swing.plaf.LayerUI class, overriding various methods to customize painting and event handling. Continuing, pass an instance of this class along with the component being decorated to the JLayer(V view, LayerUI<V> ui) constructor (JLayer's generic type is JLayer<V extends Component>; LayerUI's generic type is LayerUI<V extends Component>.)

The first argument passed to this constructor is the component that you want to decorate, which is known as a *view*. The second argument identifies the *decorator* object.

The following excerpt from a revised version of Listing 7-6 shows you how to use JLayer to add a translucent UNREGISTERED message over the center of TempVerter's GUI:

```
public static void main(String[] args)
{
   Runnable r = new Runnable()
                {
                   @Override
                   public void run()
                   {
                      final JFrame f = new JFrame("TempVerter");
                      f.setDefaultCloseOperation(JFrame.DISPOSE_ON_CLOSE);
                      Border b = BorderFactory.createEmptyBorder(5, 5, 5, 5);
                      f.getRootPane().setBorder(b);
                      LayerUI<JPanel> layerUI;
                      layerUI = new LayerUI<JPanel>()
                      {
                         final Color PALE_BLUE = new Color(0.0f, 0.0f,
                                                           1.0f, 0.1f);
                         final Font FONT = new Font("Arial", Font.BOLD, 30);
                         final String MSG = "UNREGISTERED";
                         @Override
                         public void paint(Graphics g, JComponent c)
                         {
                            super.paint(g, c); // Paint the view.
                            g.setColor(PALE_BLUE);
                            g.setFont(FONT);
                            int w = g.getFontMetrics().stringWidth(MSG);
                            int h = g.getFontMetrics().getHeight();
                            g.drawString(MSG, (c.getWidth()-w)/2,
                                         c.getHeight()/2+h/4);
                         }
                      };
                      JLayer<JPanel> layer;
                      layer = new JLayer<JPanel>(createGUI(), layerUI);
                      f.setContentPane(layer);
                      fixGUI(f.getContentPane());
                      f.pack();
                      f.setResizable(false);
                      f.setVisible(true);
                   }
                };
   EventQueue.invokeLater(r);
}
```

To create a decorator, you minimally override LayerUI's void paint(Graphics g, JComponent c) method. The component passed to c is the view.

The first painting step is to paint the view via the super.paint(g, c); method call. Anything painted in subsequent code appears over the view.

Continuing, a pale blue color is installed via setColor(). This color is created via Color(0.0f, 0.0f, 1.0f, 0.1f)—the first three arguments represent red, green, and blue percentages (between 0.0f and 1.0f), and the last argument represents opacity (from 0.0f, transparent, to 1.0f, opaque).

A font is then installed to ensure that the message being painted is large enough to be seen.

At this point, all that's left to do is obtain the message's width and height, and use these values to determine the location of the first message character and the baseline, and then draw the text.

After creating this decorator, it and the view (returned from createGUI()) are passed to a new JLayer instance, which is installed as the content pane.

Figure 7-14 shows the resulting GUI with the centered and translucent UNREGISTERED message.

Figure 7-14. *The UNREGISTERED message is centered within the frame window's borders.*

SwingCanvas

AWT provides the Canvas class whose paint() method can be overridden to paint graphics or an image over its surface. You can introduce your own Swing-based canvas class by subclassing JComponent and overriding its paint() method, as follows:

```
class SwingCanvas extends JComponent
{
   private Dimension d;
   SwingCanvas()
   {
      d = new Dimension(300, 300); // Create object here to avoid unnecessary
                                   // object creation should getPreferredSize()
                                   // be called more than once.
      // perform other initialization (such as registering a mouse listener) here
   }
   @Override
   public Dimension getPreferredSize()
   {
      return d;
   }
   @Override
   public void paint(Graphics g)
   {
      // perform painting here
   }
}
```

It is often not a good idea to override paint() in the context of Swing because JComponent overrides this method to delegate the work of painting to three protected methods: paintComponent(), paintBorder(), and paintChildren(). These methods are called in this order to ensure that children appear on top of the component.

Generally speaking, the component and its children should not paint in the insets area allocated to the border.

Although, subclasses can override this method, a subclass that only wants to specialize the UI delegate's paint() method should just override paintComponent().

If you're not concerned about UI delegates, borders, and children, the previous SwingCanvas class should meet your needs. For more information, check out The Java Tutorial's "Performing Custom Painting" lesson (http://download.oracle.com/javase/tutorial/uiswing/painting/index.html).

Java 2D

Java 2D is a collection of AWT extensions that provide advanced two-dimensional graphical, textual, and imaging capabilities. This API offers a flexible framework for developing richer GUIs through line art (also known as vector graphics—see http://en.wikipedia.org/wiki/Vector_graphics), text, and images.

Java 2D is implemented by various types located in the java.awt and java.awt.image packages, and by the Java 2D-specific java.awt.color, java.awt.font, java.awt.geom, java.awt.image.renderable, and java.awt.print packages.

This section introduces Java 2D by first presenting the java.awt package's GraphicsEnvironment, GraphicsDevice, and GraphicsConfiguration classes. It then explores the Graphics2D class followed by Java 2D's support for shapes and buffered images. (I don't explore text or printing, for brevity.)

GraphicsEnvironment, GraphicsDevice, and GraphicsConfiguration

Java 2D provides a GraphicsEnvironment class that applications can use to learn about their graphics environments (e.g., available font family names and graphics devices) and perform specialized tasks (e.g., register a font or create a Graphics2D instance for drawing into a buffered image).

Before you can use GraphicsEnvironment, you need to obtain an instance of this class. Accomplish this task by invoking GraphicsEnvironment's GraphicsEnvironment getLocalGraphicsEnvironment() class method to return the platform's GraphicsEnvironment instance, as follows:

```
GraphicsEnvironment ge = GraphicsEnvironment.getLocalGraphicsEnvironment();
```

GraphicsEnvironment's Java documentation states that the returned GraphicsEnvironment instance's resources might be local or located on a remote machine. For example, Linux platforms let users use Secure Shell (see http://en.wikipedia.org/wiki/Secure_Shell) to run GUI applications on another machine and view the GUI on the local machine. (If you're interested in learning more about this, check out "X Over SSH2 - A Tutorial" [http://www.vanemery.com/Linux/XoverSSH/X-over-SSH2.html].)

Once an application has a GraphicsEnvironment instance, it can call GraphicsEnvironment's String[] getAvailableFontFamilyNames() method to enumerate font family names (such as Arial), as Listing 7-7 demonstrates.

Listing 7-7. Enumerating font family names

```
import java.awt.EventQueue;
import java.awt.GraphicsEnvironment;

class EnumFontFamilyNames
{
```

```
public static void main(String[] args)
{
   Runnable r = new Runnable()
                {
                    @Override
                    public void run()
                    {
                        enumerate();
                    }
                };
   EventQueue.invokeLater(r);
}
static void enumerate()
{
   GraphicsEnvironment ge;
   ge = GraphicsEnvironment.getLocalGraphicsEnvironment();
   String[] ffns = ge.getAvailableFontFamilyNames();
   for (String ffn: ffns)
      System.out.println(ffn);
}
}
```

An application might need to enumerate font family names and present this list to the user. For example, a custom font chooser dialog box would probably let the user choose a font based on a list of font family names, styles, and sizes.

GraphicsEnvironment also declares a GraphicsDevice[] getScreenDevices() method that returns an array of GraphicsDevice instances. Each instance describes an image buffer, printer, or *raster screen* (a screen of pixels) that's available to the application. (Because image buffers and printers are not screens, it would have been less confusing to have named this method getGraphicsDevices().)

Assuming that ge references a GraphicsEnvironment instance, execute the following line to obtain this array:

```
GraphicsDevice[] gd = ge.getScreenDevices();
```

You can find out what kind of graphics device is represented by a particular GraphicsDevice instance, by calling GraphicsDevice's int getType() method and comparing the result to one of GraphicsDevice's TYPE_IMAGE_BUFFER, TYPE_PRINTER, and TYPE_RASTER_SCREEN constants.

Note You can access the default graphics device by invoking GraphicsEnvironment's GraphicsDevice getDefaultScreenDevice() method. If there's only one supported device, getDefaultScreenDevice() is equivalent to getScreenDevices()[0].

---

getScreenDevices() throws java.awt.HeadlessException when called on a *headless platform* (a platform that doesn't support a keyboard, mouse, or monitor). For example, the platform may be part of a *server farm* (see http://en.wikipedia.org/wiki/Server_farm). If you're concerned about this possibility, you can have your application first call GraphicsEnvironment's boolean isHeadless() class method, which returns true when the platform is headless.

Once you have a graphics device, you can obtain all supported *configurations* (color models, *bounds* [origin and extents in device coordinates], and so on) by calling GraphicsDevice's GraphicsConfiguration[] getConfigurations() method.

Assuming that gd references a GraphicsDevice instance, execute the following line to obtain this array:

```
GraphicsConfiguration[] gc = gd.getConfigurations();
```

After you have a GraphicsConfiguration instance, you can learn about its color model by invoking ColorModel getColorModel(), its bounds by invoking Rectangle getBounds(), and so on.

Note You can access the default configuration by invoking GraphicsDevice's GraphicsConfiguration getDefaultConfiguration() method. If there's only one supported configuration, getDefaultConfiguration() is equivalent to getConfigurations()[0].

After obtaining an array of GraphicsConfigurations, an application can determine whether it's running in a single-screen environment or in a multiscreen environment.

MULTISCREEN ENVIRONMENTS

A *multiscreen environment* consists of two or more independent screens, two or more screens where one screen is the default and the other screens display copies of what appears on the default screen, or two or more screens that form a *virtual desktop*, which is also called a *virtual device*. Figure 7-15 reveals a multiscreen environment.

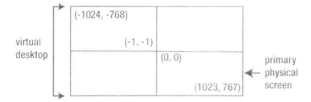

Figure 7-15. Each screen in this example has a resolution of 1024x768 pixels.

When two or more screens are combined into a virtual desktop, Java 2D establishes a *virtual coordinate system*. This coordinate system exists outside of any screen's bounds and is used to identify pixel coordinates within the virtual desktop.

One of the screens is known as the default screen and its upper-left corner is located at (0, 0). If the default screen is not positioned in the upper-left corner of a grid of screens, Java 2D may require you to use negative coordinates, as illustrated in Figure 7-15.

The application accomplishes this task by calling Rectangle getBounds() on each GraphicsConfiguration returned by getConfigurations(), and then checking to see if the origin is something other than (0, 0). GraphicsConfiguration's getBounds() method returns a java.awt.Rectangle instance whose x, y, width, and height fields (of type int) reflect the virtual coordinate system. If any (x, y) origin isn't (0, 0), the environment is a virtual device environment.

I've created an IsVDE application that determines if its environment is a virtual device environment. Listing 7-8 presents this application's source code.

Listing 7-8. Detecting a virtual device environment

```java
import java.awt.EventQueue;
import java.awt.GraphicsConfiguration;
import java.awt.GraphicsDevice;
import java.awt.GraphicsEnvironment;
import java.awt.Rectangle;

class IsVDE
{
   public static void main(String[] args)
   {
      Runnable r = new Runnable()
                   {
                       public void run()
                       {
                           test();
                       }
                   };
      EventQueue.invokeLater(r);
   }
   static void test()
   {
      GraphicsEnvironment ge;
      ge = GraphicsEnvironment.getLocalGraphicsEnvironment();
      GraphicsDevice[] gds = ge.getScreenDevices();
      for (GraphicsDevice gd: gds)
      {
         GraphicsConfiguration[] gcs = gd.getConfigurations();
         for (GraphicsConfiguration gc: gcs)
         {
            Rectangle rect = gc.getBounds();
            if (rect.x != 0 || rect.y != 0)
            {
               System.out.println("virtual device environment detected");
               return;
            }
         }
         System.out.println("no virtual device environment detected");
      }
   }
}
```

Assuming that the environment is a virtual device environment, you can create Frame, javax.swing.JFrame, Window, or javax.swing.JWindow container windows that refer to different graphics devices by calling appropriate constructors, such as Frame(GraphicsConfiguration gc).

In a multiscreen environment in which the desktop area could span multiple physical screen devices, the bounds of GraphicsConfiguration objects are relative to the virtual coordinate system. When setting the location of a component in this coordinate system, use getBounds() to get the bounds of the desired GraphicsConfiguration and offset the location with these coordinates, as the following example illustrates:

```
Frame f = new Frame(gc); // Assume gc is a GraphicsConfiguration instance.
Rectangle bounds = gc.getBounds();
f.setLocation(10+bounds.x, 10+bounds.y);
```

Graphics2D

Java 2D's abstract Graphics2D class (a Graphics subclass) describes a *logical drawing surface* on which *graphics primitives* (2D shapes [such as rectangles and ellipses], text, and images) are drawn.

The logical drawing surface is associated with *user space*, which is a 2D Cartesian (x/y) plane whose pixels are known as *logical pixels*, and which have floating-point coordinates. As a result, various Graphics2D methods accept floating-point coordinate values; for example, void drawString(String str, float x, float y).

While discussing AWT graphics, I previously mentioned that a Graphics subclass instance is passed to a component's paint() method. Prior to Java 1.2, this was always the case. Starting with Java 1.2, a Graphics2D subclass instance is passed to paint(). You can work with this instance as a Graphics instance or (after casting Graphics to Graphics2D) as a Graphics2D instance.

The Graphics2D subclass instance that's passed to a component's paint() method identifies an *output device* (e.g., monitor or printer) with a *physical drawing surface* (e.g., raster screen or printer page). This surface is associated with *device space*, which is a 2D Cartesian plane whose pixels are known as *physical pixels*, and which have integer coordinates.

Typically, the output device is the default monitor, or is the monitor associated with the GraphicsConfiguration that was passed to the Frame, JFrame, Window, or JWindow constructor that contains the component.

At some point, Graphics2D must map logical pixels to physical pixels. It accomplishes this task via an *affine transformation* (a mathematical transformation that transforms straight lines into straight lines and parallel lines into parallel lines).

By default, Java 2D specifies an affine transformation that aligns user space with device space so that you end up with the coordinate system shown in Figure 7-7. Furthermore, it maps 72 user space coordinates to one physical inch. (Some scaling may be performed behind the scenes to ensure that this relationship holds on a particular output device.)

You typically don't need to be concerned with device space and this mapping process. Just keep in mind the default 72 user space coordinates to one inch mapping and Java 2D will make sure that your Java 2D creations appear at the proper sizes on various output devices.

Rendering Pipeline

Graphics2D is also a *rendering pipeline* that *renders* (processes) shapes, text, and images into device-specific pixel colors. This rendering pipeline maintains an internal state that consists of the following attributes:

- *Paint*: A solid color, *gradient* (transition between two solid colors), or *texture* (replicated image) applied to shape interiors and to a shape's outline shape.

- *Stroke*: An object that creates a shape to specify another shape's outline. The resulting *outline shape*, which is also known as a *stroked outline*, is filled with the paint attribute. Outline shapes don't have outlines.

- *Font*: Java 2D renders text by creating shapes that represent the text's characters. The font attribute selects the shapes that are created for these characters. These shapes are then filled.

- *Transformation*: Before being stroked and filled, graphics primitives are geometrically transformed. They may be rotated, *translated* (moved), *scaled* (stretched), or otherwise manipulated. The transformation attribute converts graphics primitives from user space to device space; the default transformation maps 72 user space coordinates to one inch on the output device.

- *Composite rule*: Graphics2D combines graphics primitive colors with the drawing surface's existing colors by using a composite rule, which determines the manner in which the combining occurs.

- *Clipping shape*: Graphics2D restricts its rendering operations to the interior of a clipping shape; pixels outside of this shape are not affected. The clipping shape defaults to the entire drawing surface.

- *Rendering hints*: Graphics2D recognizes various rendering hints that can be specified to control rendering. For example, you can specify *antialiasing* to remove the jagged edges that often surround shapes (e.g., lines) and text.

Graphics primitives enter this pipeline via various Graphics methods (e.g., drawLine() and fillOval()) and the following Graphics2D methods:

- void fill(Shape s) fills a shape's interior with the current paint. Shapes implement the Shape interface.

- void draw(Shape s) draws a shape's outline with the current paint.

- The drawstring() methods draw text via character shapes with the current paint.

- The drawImage() methods draw images.

Note Although you can call Graphics methods to draw shapes, these methods are limited in that they only accept integer coordinates. Furthermore, these shapes (apart from polygon-based shapes) are not reusable. Regarding polygonal shapes, they can only consist of straight line-segments. In contrast, Java 2D's Shape classes, which I briefly introduce later in this chapter don't have these limitations.

Figure 7-16 conceptualizes the rendering pipeline into separate operations. Operations could be combined in a particular implementation.

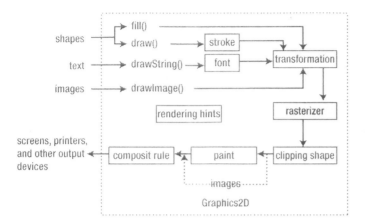

Figure 7-16. *The rendering process reveals that stroke, font, and paint attributes don't apply to images.*

Graphics primitives are presented to the rendering pipeline via various method calls that determine how the rendering proceeds:

- Shapes passed to fill() are not stroked. Instead, they are first transformed and eventually painted (filled).

- Shapes passed to draw() are first stroked and the resulting outline shapes are transformed.

- Text characters are first converted to the shapes specified by the current font. These character shapes are then transformed.

- Image outlines are first transformed.

As Figure 7-16 shows, Graphics2D only fills shapes and draws images. Drawing outline shapes and character shapes are variants of the shape-filling operation.

Rasterizing follows the transformation step. The *rasterizer* converts vector-based shapes to *alpha* (coverage) values that determine how much of each destination pixel underlying the shape is covered by the shape. Regarding images, only image outlines are rasterized. The rasterizer takes any specified rendering hints into account.

The rasterized results are clipped via the current clipping shape. Those portions of filled shapes not thrown away by clipping are colorized via the current paint. Images are not colorized because their pixels provide the colors.

Finally, Graphics2D combines the colored pixels (source pixels) with existing destination pixels to form new pixels according to its current composite rule.

Rasterizing and Compositing

The rasterizer creates a rectangular image that contains only alpha values. There are no colors at this point. An alpha value ranges from 0 (no coverage) to 255 (full coverage), and the image's collection of alpha values is known as its *alpha channel*. (Alpha values also can be expressed as floating-point values ranging from 0.0 through 1.0.)

The rasterizer defaults to choosing alpha values of 255 or 0. Because the resulting source pixel will either fully cover the existing destination pixel or will not cover this pixel, lines, text, and other geometric primitives will tend to have jagged edges. This is known as *aliasing.*

When you specify antialiasing as a rendering hint, the rasterizer slows down somewhat (it has more work to do), but chooses a wider range of alpha values so that graphics primitives look smoother. This smoothness derives from combining percentages of source and current destination pixel red, green, and blue color components (whose values each range from 0 [darkest] through 255 [brightest]) so that parts of the current destination pixels show through when the new destination pixels are drawn.

The final step in the rendering process involves combining source pixels with destination pixels. This step is carried out according to the current composite rule, which determines how this combining takes place.

The composite rule takes alpha value percentages into account. For example, the "source over" rule (which is the most intuitive) combines 100 percent of the source pixel's color (depending on its alpha) with a percentage of the destination pixel's color, which happens to be (255-source pixel's alpha value)/255*100.

Consider a source pixel with an alpha of 255 (it contributes 100 percent to the final color). According to the equation, the destination pixel would have an alpha of 0 (it contributes 0 percent), which means that the destination pixel is completely covered. If the source pixel has an alpha of 0 (it contributes nothing), the destination pixel would have an alpha of 255 (it contributes everything), which means that the source pixel is invisible. Intermediate alpha values combine different percentages of source and destination pixels.

Rendering Attributes

Now that you've grasped the basics of the Graphics2D rendering pipeline, you're ready to further explore its rendering attributes. To help you with this exploration, I've created a Swing-based Graphics2DAttribDemo application. Figure 7-17 shows you this menu-driven application's initial screen.

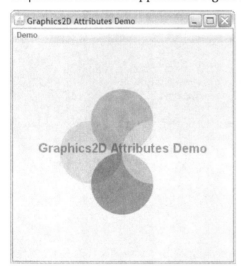

Figure 7-17. Select a menuitem from the Demo menu to view a demonstration of the associated attribute.

Paint

Graphics2D declares void setPaint(Paint paint) for setting the paint attribute. Pass any object whose class implements the java.awt.Paint interface to paint. Call Paint getPaint() to return the current paint.

Several classes implement Paint, including the java.awt package's Color, GradientPaint, and TexturePaint classes. Instances of these classes can be passed to setPaint() or returned from getPaint().

▪ **Note** The Graphics class's setColor() method is equivalent to calling setPaint().

Color lets you create a solid color. Among its various constructors are Color(int r, int g, int b) for creating an opaque solid color and Color(int r, int g, int b, int a) for creating a solid color with an alpha value.

You aren't restricted to specifying integer-based component values that range from 0 through 255. If you prefer values ranging from 0.0 through 1.0, you can call constructors such as Color(float r, float g, float b) and Color(float r, float g, float b, float a).

For your convenience, Color declares several precreated Color constants: BLACK, BLUE, CYAN, DARK_GRAY, GRAY, GREEN, LIGHT_GRAY, MAGENTA, ORANGE, PINK, RED, WHITE, and YELLOW. Although all-lowercase variants are available, you should avoid using them—constants should be uppercased.

GradientPaint lets you create a gradient. It declares several constructors, including GradientPaint(float x1, float y1, Color color1, float x2, float y2, Color color2), which describes a gradient that transitions from upper-left corner (x1, y1) to lower-left corner (x2, y2) in user space. The color at (x1, y1) is color1 and the color at (x2, y2) is color2.

▪ **Note** Java 6 introduced an abstract java.awt.MultipleGradientPaint class and concrete java.awt.LinearGradientPaint and java.awt.RadialGradientPaint subclasses to create different kinds of gradients that are based on multiple (typically more than two) colors. I explore these classes and present demos in my "Java 2D MultiColor Gradient Paints" tutorial (http://tutortutor.ca/cgi-bin/makepage.cgi?/tutorials/ct/j2dmcgp).

TexturePaint lets you create a texture. It declares a TexturePaint(BufferedImage txtr, Rectangle2D anchor) constructor for creating the texture from a combination of a buffered image (which specifies the image on which the texture is based) and a rectangular anchor (which identifies a rectangular portion of the image to be replicated).

Figure 7-18 demonstrates solid color (upper-left corner), gradient (upper-right corner), and texture (bottom) paints.

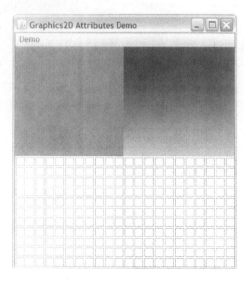

Figure 7-18. *Select Paint from the Demo menu to view the paint demonstration.*

Stroke

Graphics2D declares void setStroke(Stroke stroke) for setting the stroke attribute. Pass any object whose class implements the java.awt.Stroke interface to stroke. Call Stroke getStroke() to return the current stroke.

HOW STROKING WORKS

Stroking is the act of drawing a shape's outline. The first step is to call setStroke() to specify how you want the outline to be drawn (e.g., its width and whether it is solid or consists of a mixtures of dashes and spaces). The next step is to call setPaint() to specify how you want the outline to be painted (e.g., using solid colors, gradients, or textures). The final step is to draw the outline via Graphics2D's draw() method.

When draw() is called, Graphics2D uses the object passed to setStroke() to figure out what the outline looks like and uses the object passed to setPaint() to paint the outline's pixels.

The only class that implements this interface is java.awt.BasicStroke, which lets you define a shape outline in terms of a pen width (measured perpendicularly to the pen's trajectory), end caps, join styles, miter limit, and dash attributes.

A shape's outline is infinitely thin and is drawn with a pen that has a certain width, which is expressed as a floating-point value. The resulting outline shape extends beyond this outline and into the shape's interior.

Line segments can be drawn with or without decorations at both ends. These decorations are known as *end caps*. BasicStroke declares CAP_BUTT, CAP_ROUND, and CAP_SQUARE constants to indicate that no end caps are present, that a semicircle with a radius equal to half of the pen width appears at both ends, or that a rectangle with a length equal to half of the pen width appears at both ends.

When two line segments meet, Graphics2D uses a *join style* to join them together so that they don't present a ragged edge. BasicStroke declares JOIN_BEVEL, JOIN_MITER, and JOIN_ROUND constants to indicate *beveled* (squared off), *mitered* (sharpened to triangular points), or rounded joins. When the miter exceeds a specified miter limit, the join is beveled.

Finally, BasicStroke lets you specify dashed lines by providing a dash array and a dash phase value. The *dash array* contains floating-point values representing the user space lengths of visible and invisible sections of line segments. Even-indexed array elements determine lengths of visible sections; odd-indexed array elements determine lengths of invisible sections.

For example, consider a dash array of [8.0, 6.0]. This array's first (even) element indicates that visible line segments are 8.0 units long, and its second (odd) element indicates that invisible line segments are 6.0 units long. You end up with a pattern of 8 visible units, 6 invisible units, 8 visible units, 6 invisible units, and so on.

The *dash phase* is a floating-point offset into the dash pattern specified by the dash array; it is not an offset into the array. When the dash phase is 0, the line segment is stroked as indicated in the previous example. However, when a nonzero dash phase is specified, the first line segment begins dash phase units from the value provided by the first array entry.

For example, given the previous array, suppose you specified a dash phase of 3.0. This value indicates that the first visible line segment is 8-3 or 5 units long, and is followed by 6 invisible units, 8 visible units, 6 invisible units, and so on.

BasicStroke declares several constructors including BasicStroke(float width, int cap, int join, float miterlimit, float[] dash, float dash_phase), which gives you complete control over a stroke's characteristics, and the shorter BasicStroke(float width, int cap, int join) constructor, which strokes a solid line.

Graphics2DAttribDemo demonstrates both constructors along with pen width, end caps, join styles, miter limit, and dash attributes. These characteristics are shown in Figure 7-19.

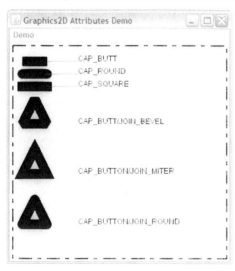

Figure 7-19. Select Stroke from the Demo menu to view the stroke demonstration.

Font

Graphics2D inherits (from Graphics) void setFont(Font font) for setting the font attribute to the specified Font object. Call Font getFont() (also inherited from Graphics) to return the current font.

Figure 7-20 shows the Arial font's plain, bold, italic, and bold plus italic styles.

Figure 7-20. Select Font from the Demo menu to view the font demonstration.

Transformation

Graphics2D contains an internal transformation matrix (transform) for geometrically reorienting graphics primitives during rendering. Primitives can be *translated* (moved), *scaled* (resized), rotated, *sheared* (laterally shifted), or transformed in some other developer-specified fashion.

The internal transformation matrix is an instance of the java.awt.geom.AffineTransform class, which ensures that straight lines map to straight lines and parallel lines map to parallel lines. The initial affine transform represents the *identity transformation* in which nothing changes (e.g., no rotations are performed).

You can modify this matrix in several ways. For example, you can invoke Graphics2D's void setTransform(AffineTransform Tx) method to replace the current transformation matrix with the affine transform passed to Tx. Alternatively, you can invoke Graphics2D's void transform(AffineTransform Tx) method to concatenate Tx to the existing transformation matrix.

■ **Tip** It's a good idea to use transform() instead of setTransform() because the Graphics2D instance passed to a component's paint() method is set up with a default transformation that gives you the coordinate system shown in Figure 7-7. Invoking setTransform() may change this organization and lead to confusing results unless you know what you're doing.

For common transformations, `Graphics2D` declares methods such as `void rotate(double theta)`, `void scale(double sx, double sy)`, and `void translate(double tx, double ty)`. These methods offer a convenient alternative to instantiating `AffineTransform` and passing this instance to `transform()`.

■ **Caution** `Graphics2D` declares a `void translate(int x, int y)` method for translating the origin of the `Graphics2D` context to the point (x, y) in the current coordinate system. This method is invoked instead of `translate(double, double)` when you pass integer arguments, so be careful when passing arguments or you might end up with unexpected results.

Figure 7-21 shows untransformed (blue), rotated (gradient green to red), and sheared (gradient green to red with almost no green) rectangles.

Figure 7-21. *Select Transformation from the Demo menu to view the transformation demonstration.*

Composite Rule

`Graphics2D` declares `void setComposite(Composite comp)` for setting the composite rule attribute. Pass any object whose class implements the `java.awt.Composite` interface to comp. Call `Composite getComposite()` to return the current composite rule.

The only class that implements this interface is `java.awt.AlphaComposite`, which implements basic alpha composite rules for combining source and destination colors to achieve blending and transparency effects with graphics and images. The specific rules implemented by this class are the basic set of 12 rules described in T. Porter's and T. Duff's "Compositing Digital Images" paper (SIGGRAPH 1984, pages 253–259).

`AlphaComposite` declares `CLEAR`, `DST`, `DST_ATOP`, `DST_IN`, `DST_OUT`, `DST_OVER`, `SRC`, `SRC_ATOP`, `SRC_IN`, `SRC_OUT`, `SRC_OVER`, and `XOR` integer constants that describe these rules—`SRC_OVER` is the default. It also declares precreated AlphaComposite instance constants named Clear, Dst, DstAtop, DstIn, DstOut, DstOver, Src, SrcAtop, SrcIn, SrcOut, SrcOver, and Xor.

The difference between these two sets of constants has to do with alpha values. The precreated AlphaComposite instances are wired to an alpha value of 1.0 (opaque). The integer constants and specific floating-point alpha values can be passed to AlphaComposite's AlphaComposite getInstance(int rule, float alpha) class method. This alpha value is used to modify the opacity or coverage of every source pixel before it's used in the blending equations described in AlphaComposite's Java documentation.

Figure 7-22 shows the results of applying these rules.

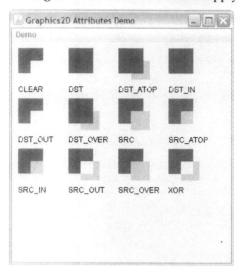

Figure 7-22. *Select Composite Rule from the Demo menu to view the composite rule demonstration.*

Figure 7-22 shows you the rules with an alpha value of 1.0. However, you can also vary the alpha value by using getInstance(int rule, float alpha). I demonstrated the result of doing so in Figure 7-17. If I had not done so, you would have seen the window shown in Figure 7-23.

490

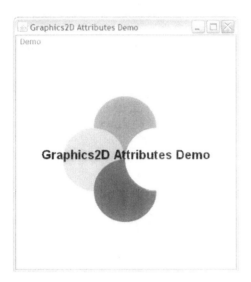

Figure 7-23. *Applying the default SRC_OVER rule with an alpha value of 1.0 .*

Clipping Shape

Graphics2D declares void clip(Shape clipShape) and inherits void setClip(Shape clipShape) from Graphics for setting the clipping shape attribute. Call clip() to make the overall clipping shape smaller; call setClip() to make the overall clipping shape larger. Pass any object whose class implements the java.awt.Shape interface to clipShape. Call Shape getClip() (inherited from Graphics) to return the current clipping shape; null returns when the clipping shape is the entire drawing surface.

Java 2D provides a collection of Shape implementation classes. Also, the java.awt.Polygon class that predates Java 2D has been retrofitted to implement this interface. The following example demonstrates how to create and install a Polygon-based rectangular clip:

```
Polygon polygon = new Polygon();
polygon.addPoint(30, 30);
polygon.addPoint(60, 30);
polygon.addPoint(60, 60);
polygon.addPoint(30, 60);
g.clip(polygon);
```

Figure 7-24 shows the result of trying to paint the entire drawing surface green after a clip has been installed.

Figure 7-24. Select Clipping Shape from the Demo menu to view the clipping shape demonstration.

Rendering Hints

Graphics2D declares void setRenderingHint(RenderingHints.Key hintKey, Object hintValue) for setting one of the rendering hints used by the rasterizer. Call its companion Object getRenderingHint(RenderingHints.Key hintKey) method to return the current value of the specified rendering hint.

The value passed to hintKey is a java.awt.RenderingHints.Key constant declared in the RenderingHints class (e.g., KEY_ANTIALIASING). The value is one of the value constants declared in this class (e.g., VALUE_ANTIALIAS_ON).

The following example shows you how to activate antialiasing:

```
g.setRenderingHint(RenderingHints.KEY_ANTIALIASING,
                   RenderingHints.VALUE_ANTIALIAS_ON);
```

Figure 7-25 reveals the difference between aliased and antialiased text.

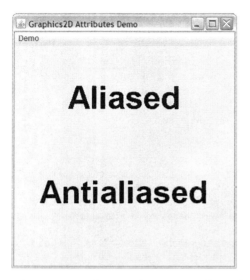

Figure 7-25. *Select Rendering Hints from the Demo menu to view the rendering hints demonstration.*

▪ **Note** Graphics2D also declares void setRenderingHints(Map<?,?> hints) for discarding all rendering hints and installing only those rendering hints in the specified map.

Shapes

The Shape interface represents a vector-based geometric shape, such as a rectangle or an ellipse. It declares getBounds(), contains(), intersects(), and getPathIterator() methods:

- The getBounds() methods return rectangles that enclose the shape's boundaries; these rectangles serve as bounding boxes.

- Shapes have interiors and exteriors. The contains() methods tell you if a point or a rectangle lies inside a shape.

- The intersects() methods tell you if any part of a rectangle intersects the shape's interior.

- The getPathIterator() methods return shape outlines.

The first three method categories are useful in a wide range of tasks, such as game-based *collision detection* (are two shapes occupying the same space?) and graphics application-based *hit testing* (was the mouse cursor over a specific shape when the mouse button was pressed?)—perhaps the graphics application lets the user drag a selected shape. The latter method helps the rendering pipeline obtain a shape outline.

One of the contains() methods takes a java.awt.geom.Point2D argument. Instances of this class specify points in user space. (Point2D instances aren't shapes because Point2D doesn't implement Shape.)

Point2D reveals a pattern that's followed by the shape classes. This abstract class contains a pair of nested Double and Float concrete subclasses, which override its abstract methods. Instantiate Double to increase accuracy and instantiate Float to increase performance.

The following example shows you how to instantiate Point2D, to specify points in user space:

```
Point2D pt1 = new Point2D.Double(10.0, 20.0);
Point2D pt2 = new Point2D.Float(20.0f, 30.0f);
```

The java.awt.geom package contains various geometric classes that implement Shape: Arc2D, Area, CubicCurve2D, Ellipse2D, GeneralPath, Line2D, Path2D, QuadCurve2D, Rectangle2D, RectangularShape, and RoundRectangle2D. RectangularShape is the abstract superclass of Arc2D, Ellipse2D, Rectangle2D, and RoundRectangle2D. Also, the java.awt.Rectangle class that I introduced earlier in this chapter has been retrofitted to extend Rectangle2D. Finally, GeneralPath is a legacy final class (you cannot extend it) that extends Path2D.Float.

RoundRectangle2D describes a rectangle with rounded corners of a specific radius. Its nested Double and Float subclasses declare noargument constructors for constructing a new RoundRectangle2D instance that's initialized to location (0.0, 0.0), size (0.0, 0.0), and corner arcs with radius 0.0. They also declare constructors for specifying location, size, and corner arcs.

If you call the noargument constructors, you can subsequently call Double's or Float's setRoundRect() methods to specify location, size, and rounded corner radius. However, if all you have is a RoundRectangle2D reference (not a RoundRectangle2D.Double or RoundRectangle2D.Float reference), you can call RoundRectangle2D's void setRoundRect(double x, double y, double w, double h, double arcWidth, double arcHeight) method. (You'll find this constructor/set pattern repeated in other shape classes.)

I've created a DragRect application that demonstrates RoundRectangle2D and Shape's boolean contains(double x, double y) method. DragRect shows you how to drag this round rectangle over its drawing surface, and Listing 7-9 presents its source code.

Listing 7-9. Dragging a round rectangle

```
import java.awt.Color;
import java.awt.Dimension;
import java.awt.EventQueue;
import java.awt.Graphics;
import java.awt.Graphics2D;
import java.awt.RenderingHints;

import java.awt.event.MouseEvent;
import java.awt.event.MouseAdapter;
import java.awt.event.MouseMotionAdapter;

import java.awt.geom.RoundRectangle2D;

import javax.swing.JComponent;
import javax.swing.JFrame;

class DragRect
{
    public static void main(String[] args)
```

```
{
    Runnable r = new Runnable()
                {
                    @Override
                    public void run()
                    {
                        JFrame f = new JFrame("Drag Rectangle");
                        f.setDefaultCloseOperation(JFrame.EXIT_ON_CLOSE);
                        f.setContentPane(new DragRectPane());
                        f.pack();
                        f.setVisible(true);
                    }
                };
    EventQueue.invokeLater(r);
    }
}
final class DragRectPane extends JComponent
{
    private boolean dragging;
    private double dragX, dragY;
    private Dimension d;
    private RoundRectangle2D rect;
    DragRectPane()
    {
        d = new Dimension(200, 200);
        rect = new RoundRectangle2D.Double(0.0, 0.0, 30.0, 30.0, 10.0, 10.0);
        addMouseListener(new MouseAdapter()
                    {
                        @Override
                        public void mousePressed(MouseEvent me)
                        {
                            if (!rect.contains(me.getX(), me.getY()))
                                return;
                            dragX = me.getX();
                            dragY = me.getY();
                            dragging = true;
                        }
                        @Override
                        public void mouseReleased(MouseEvent me)
                        {
                            dragging = false;
                        }
                    });
        addMouseMotionListener(new MouseMotionAdapter()
                    {
                        @Override
                        public void mouseDragged(MouseEvent me)
                        {
                            if (!dragging)
                                return;
                            double x = rect.getX()+me.getX()-dragX;
                            double y = rect.getY()+me.getY()-dragY;
```

```
                                   rect.setRoundRect(x, y, rect.getWidth(),
                                                     rect.getHeight(),
                                                     rect.getArcWidth(),
                                                     rect.getArcHeight());
                               repaint();
                               dragX = me.getX();
                               dragY = me.getY();
                           }
                       });
   }
   @Override
   public Dimension getPreferredSize()
   {
      return d;
   }
   @Override
   public void paint(Graphics g)
   {
      Graphics2D g2d = (Graphics2D) g;
      g2d.setRenderingHint(RenderingHints.KEY_ANTIALIASING,
                           RenderingHints.VALUE_ANTIALIAS_ON);
      g2d.setColor(Color.RED);
      g2d.fill(rect);
   }
}
```

Listing 7-9's DragRectPane class subclasses JComponent, presents a noargument constructor, and overrides getPreferredSize() and paint().

The constructor first instantiates Dimension and RoundRectangle2D.Double, and then registers mouse and motion listeners with this component.

When the user presses a mouse button to initiate a drag operation (the mouse button is held down while the mouse cursor is moved), the mouse listener's void mousePressed(MouseEvent me) method is called. This method first invokes the int getX() and int getY() methods on its MouseEvent argument to obtain the component-relative location of the mouse cursor when the mouse button was pressed.

These mouse coordinates are passed to the round rectangle's contains() method to determine whether or not the mouse cursor was over this shape when the button press occurred. If the mouse cursor was not over the round rectangle, this method returns.

Otherwise, the mouse coordinates are saved in dragX and dragY variables to record the origin of the drag operation, and the dragging Boolean variable is assigned true so that the shape is dragged only when the mouse cursor is over the shape when the drag operation begins.

During a drag operation, the mouse motion listener's void mouseDragged(MouseEvent me) method is invoked. Its first task is to test dragging to see if the mouse cursor was over the shape. If this variable contains false, this method returns. (Without this test, pressing the mouse button while the mouse cursor was not on the round rectangle, and then starting to drag the mouse cursor, would result in the shape snapping to the location of the drag and subsequently being dragged.)

If dragging contains true, mouseDragged() next calculates a new upper-left corner origin for the round rectangle by offsetting its current origin with the difference between the current mouse coordinates and the coordinates saved in dragX and dragY. It then passes the new origin along with the current size and arc radius to the round rectangle via a setRoundRect() method call.

Continuing, a call to repaint() causes the round rectangle to be repainted at the new location, and a pair of assignment statements update dragX and dragY to the current mouse coordinates so that the next call to `mouseDragged()` calculates the new round rectangle origin relative to the origin that was just calculated.

When the mouse button is released, the mouse listener's `void mouseReleased(MouseEvent me)` method is called. This method assigns `false` to `dragging` so that the shape isn't dragged when a drag operation is subsequently started but the mouse cursor isn't over the shape when that operation begins.

Compile this source code (`javac DragRect.java`) and run the application (`java DragRect`). Figure 7-26 shows the resulting GUI with a drag operation in progress.

Figure 7-26. *Press the mouse pointer over the round rectangle to begin dragging this shape.*

Constructive Area Geometry

Constructive Area Geometry (CAG) is the creation of a new shape by performing a Boolean operation on two existing shapes. The operations are Boolean OR (create a new shape that combines the existing shapes' pixels), Boolean NOT (create a new shape that contains only the pixels in one shape that are not also in the other shape), Boolean AND (create a new shape that contains only overlapping pixels), and Boolean XOR (create a new shape that contains only nonoverlapping pixels). Boolean OR is also known as union, Boolean NOT is also known as subtraction, and Boolean AND is also known as intersection.

Java 2D provides the `java.awt.geom.Area` class for performing Boolean operations via its `void add(Area rhs)` [union], `void subtract(Area rhs)`, `void intersect(Area rhs)`, and `void exclusiveOr(Area rhs)` methods. Each method performs the specified Boolean operation on the current Area object and its Area object argument, and stores the result in the current Area object.

To use Area, first pass a Shape object to its `Area(Shape s)` constructor and then invoke one of the aforementioned methods on this Area object to perform the operation. Because Area also implements Shape, you can pass the Area object with the Boolean result to Graphics2D's `draw()` and `fill()` methods.

The following example demonstrates the union operation on a pair of ellipses:

```
Ellipse2D ell1 = new Ellipse2D.Double(10.0, 10.0, 40.0, 40.0);
Ellipse2D ell2 = new Ellipse2D.Double(30.0, 10.0, 40.0, 40.0);
Area area1 = new Area(ell1);
Area area2 = new Area(ell2);
area1.add(area2);
```

After creating two ellipse shapes, the example creates two Area objects, where each object contains one ellipse. It then invokes add() on the first Area object to create a union of pixels in the area ranging from upper-left corner (10.0, 10.0) to lower-right corner (70.0, 50.0). The result is stored in the first Area object.

I've created a CAG application that demonstrates these Boolean operations—the application's source code is available in this book's accompanying code file. This application's output appears in Figure 7-27.

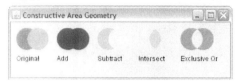

Figure 7-27. *Press the mouse pointer over the round rectangle to begin dragging this shape.*

Buffered Images

AWT's Image class associates with a rectangular array of colored pixels. Although you can draw these pixels (via drawImage()), you need to work with AWT's somewhat tedious producer/consumer model (which I don't discuss for brevity) to access them. In contrast, Java 2D's java.awt.image.BufferedImage class, which extends Image, makes these pixels available to applications and is easier to use.

For example, you can call BufferedImage's int getWidth() and int getHeight() methods to obtain an image's width and height without having to deal with image observers. (Because BufferedImage extends Image, the image observer-oriented width and height getter methods are also available.)

BufferedImage declares three constructors, with BufferedImage(int width, int height, int imageType) being the simplest. The arguments passed to this constructor identify a buffered image's width (in pixels), height (in pixels), and type (the format used to store pixels).

Although BufferedImage declares several type constants, TYPE_INT_RGB (each pixel has red, green, and blue color components but no alpha component), TYPE_INT_ARGB (each pixel has alpha, red, green, and blue components), and TYPE_INT_ARGB_PRE (same as TYPE_INT_ARGB except that each pixel's color component values are premultiplied with its alpha value) are commonly used.

Note The compositing portion of the rendering pipeline normally has to multiply each pixel's color component by its alpha value. Because this takes time, BufferedImage lets you optimize this process by premultiplying each pixel's color components and storing the results as new color component values.

The following example instantiates BufferedImage to describe a 100-column-by-50-row buffered image that stores pixels of RGB type:

```
BufferedImage bi = new BufferedImage(100, 50, BufferedImage.TYPE_INT_RGB);
```

BufferedImage zeros each pixel's color components so that the image is initially empty. If the buffered image is of TYPE_INT_RGB, these pixels are black. If the buffered image is of TYPE_INT_ARGB, these pixels are transparent. Drawing a transparent buffered image over a destination results in only the destination pixels appearing.

One way to populate a buffered image is to invoke its `void setRGB(int x, int y, int rgb)` method. `setRGB()` sets the pixel at (x, y) to the 32-bit `rgb` value. If you specify an alpha component (as the most significant 8 bits), the alpha component is ignored when the type is `TYPE_INT_RGB`. However, the alpha component is stored with the red, green, and blue color components when the type is `TYPE_INT_ARGB`.

The following example sets one of the previously created buffered image's pixels to a specific value:

```
bi.setRGB(10, 10, 0x80ff0000);
```

This example sets the pixel at (10, 10) to `0x80ff0000`. You interpret this 32-bit hexadecimal value (from left to right) as 50% translucency, bright red, no green, and no blue. Because the buffered image was created as `TYPE_INT_RGB`, the alpha component is ignored.

You can access a pixel's value by invoking `int getRGB(int x, int y)`. The following example returns the value stored at location (10, 10):

```
int rgb = bi.getRGB(10, 10);
```

Note Regardless of the buffered image's type, the `setRGB()` and `getRGB()` methods always access the buffered image as if it was created in RGB/ARGB format. `setRGB()` and `getRGB()` translate to or from the underlying format.

Another way to populate a buffered image is to create an `Image` instance and draw its associated image onto the buffered image after the image has fully loaded. You can accomplish this task as follows:

```
Image image = Toolkit.getDefaultToolkit().getImage("image.png");
MediaTracker mt = new MediaTracker(this); // this represents current component
mt.addImage(image, 1);
try { mt.waitForID(1); } catch (InterruptedException ie) { assert false; }
BufferedImage bi = new BufferedImage(image.getWidth(null), image.getHeight(null),
                                     BufferedImage.TYPE_INT_ARGB);
Graphics2D bg = bi.createGraphics();
bg.drawImage(image, 0, 0, null);
bg.dispose(); // Always dispose of a created Graphics2D context.
```

I specified `TYPE_INT_ARGB` as the buffered image's type because PNG images are associated with an alpha channel. Also, I passed `null` to `getWidth()`, `getHeight()`, and `drawImage()` because an image observer isn't required after the image is fully loaded.

`BufferedImage` declares a `Graphics2D createGraphics()` method that returns a `Graphics2D` instance for use in drawing images or graphics on the buffered image. After you finish drawing, you must dispose of this context.

The previous example is verbose because it uses `MediaTracker` to load the image before drawing. You can eliminate the image-loading verbosity by using Swing's `ImageIcon` class, as demonstrated here:

```
ImageIcon ii = new ImageIcon("image.png");
BufferedImage bi = new BufferedImage(ii.getIconWidth(), ii.getIconHeight(),
                                     BufferedImage.TYPE_INT_ARGB);
Graphics2D bg = bi.createGraphics();
bg.drawImage(ii.getImage(), 0, 0, null);
bg.dispose();
```

Buffered Image Architecture

You now have enough knowledge to do a lot with buffered images. (I also show you how to save buffered images to files in Appendix C.) However, because you might want to improve the performance of application code that works with buffered images (or for some other reason), you should also understand buffered image architecture. Consider Figure 7-28.

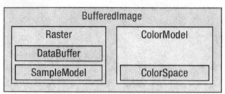

Figure 7-28. A buffered image contains a raster and a color model.

Figure 7-28 reveals that a buffered image encapsulates a raster and a color model. The *raster* stores each pixel in terms of *sample values* that provide color lookup information. For an RGB image, three samples are stored for each pixel, whereas four samples are stored for an ARGB image.

Samples are stored in a *data buffer*, which consists of one or more arrays of primitive type values (such as bytes or short integers). For an RGB image, all red samples would be stored in one array, all green samples would be stored in a second array, and all blue samples would be stored in a third array. Each array of samples is referred to as a *band* or *channel*.

Associated with the data buffer is a *sample model* that communicates with the data buffer to store sample values and retrieve sample values on behalf of the raster.

Finally, the *color model* interprets a pixel's samples as a color according to a specific *color space* (see http://en.wikipedia.org/wiki/Color_space).

When you invoke getRGB() to obtain a pixel's red, green, blue, and (possibly) alpha components (depending on the buffer's type), this method tells the raster to obtain pixel samples, the raster tells the sample model to find the samples, the sample model fetches the samples from the data buffer and passes them to the raster, which passes them to getRGB(). At this point, getRGB() tells the color model to convert the samples to color information. The color model uses the color space to help it perform this conversion.

When you invoke setRGB() to set a pixel's color components, this method tells the color model to obtain sample values corresponding to the color components, and then tells the raster to store these samples. The raster tells the sample model to store the pixel's samples, and the sample model stores these samples in the data buffer.

■ **Note** The raster and color model need to be compatible. In other words, the number of samples (per pixel) must equal the number of color model components.

The java.awt.image package contains a concrete Raster class for describing read-only rasters, an abstract DataBuffer class for describing data buffers, an abstract SampleModel class for describing sample models, and an abstract ColorModel class for describing color models. The java.awt.color package contains an abstract ColorSpace class for describing color spaces. Consult the Java documentation to learn more about these classes and their subclasses (e.g., Raster's WritableRaster subclass).

Buffered Image Processing

Image processing is a form of signal processing (http://en.wikipedia.org/wiki/Signal_processing) where mathematical transformations convert digital images into other digital images. Transformations exist to blur, sharpen, colorize, emboss, sepia tone, and apply other kinds of operations to images.

Java 2D lets you process buffered images or their rasters by providing the java.awt.image.BufferedImageOp and java.awt.image.RasterOp interfaces. Although these interfaces are similar (e.g., each interface declares five methods that perform equivalent tasks), they differ in that BufferedImageOp can access the buffered image's color model, whereas RasterOp cannot access the color model. Also, RasterOp is somewhat more performant than BufferedImageOp, but is a bit more involved to work with.

■ **Note** BufferedImageOp and/or RasterOp implementations are known as *image operators*. They are also known as *filters* because each interface declares a filter() method—filters are used in photography.

The central method of the BufferedImageOp interface is BufferedImage filter(BufferedImage src, BufferedImage dest), which *filters* (transforms) the contents of a source BufferedImage instance into results that are stored in a destination BufferedImage instance. If the color models of both buffered images don't match, a color conversion into the destination buffered image's color model is performed. If you pass null to dest, a BufferedImage instance with an appropriate ColorModel instance is created. This method throws java.lang.IllegalArgumentException when the source and/or destination buffered images are not compatible with the types of images allowed by the class implementing this interface.

The central method of the RasterOp interface is WritableRaster filter(Raster src, WritableRaster dest), which filters the contents of a source Raster instance into results that are stored in a destination WritableRaster instance. If you pass null to dest, a WritableRaster instance is created. This method may throw IllegalArgumentException when the source and/or destination rasters are incompatible with the types of rasters allowed by the class implementing this interface.

■ **Note** Depending on the implementing class, BufferedImageOp's and/or RasterOp's filter() methods may allow *in-place filtering* where the source and destination buffered images/rasters are the same.

Java 2D provides five java.awt.image classes that implement both interfaces: AffineTransformOp, ColorConvertOp, ConvolveOp, LookupOp, and RescaleOp. Furthermore, this package provides the BandCombineOp class, which only implements RasterOp:

- AffineTransformOp geometrically transforms (e.g., rotates) buffered image colors or raster samples.

- BandCombineOp combines raster sample arrays according to a set of coefficient values. You can use this class to invert the sample equivalent of color component bands and perform other operations efficiently.

- ColorConvertOp converts buffered image colors/raster samples from one color space to another.

- ConvolveOp lets you perform *spatial convolutions* (combining source pixel and neighbor pixel colors/samples) such as blurring and sharpening.

- LookupOp lets you modify pixel component values through lookup tables.

- RescaleOp multiplies pixel component values by a scale factor and then adds an offset to the result. This class is useful for brightening and darkening images (although lookup tables can be used for this purpose as well).

Caution LookupOp's Java documentation for its WritableRaster filter(Raster src, WritableRaster dst) method states that a new raster is created when you pass null to dst. However, passing null to dst causes java.lang.NullPointerException to be thrown instead.

Convolving Images

ConvolveOp combines fractions of a source pixel's alpha (when present) and color components with fractions of its immediate neighbor pixels' components to produce a destination pixel. The percentage of each pixel's component values to combine is obtained from a table of floating-point values, which is known as a *kernel*. A component's values are multiplied by the corresponding kernel value and the results are summed. Each sum is clamped to a 0/0.0 (darkest/transparent) minimum and a 255/1.0 (brightest/opaque) maximum.

ConvolveOp moves the kernel across the image to convolve each pixel. The kernel's center value (or the value nearest the center) applies to the source pixel being convolved, whereas the other values apply to the neighboring pixels.

The *identity kernel* has all values set to 0.0 except for the center value, which is set to 1.0. This special kernel doesn't change the image because multiplying the source pixel's component values by 1.0 doesn't change these components, and multiplying neighbor pixel component values by 0.0 results in 0.0 values, which contribute nothing when added to the multiplication results.

Kernels are represented by instances of the java.awt.image.Kernel class. To create a kernel, first create an array of floating-point percentage values, and then pass this array along with the table's width (number of columns) and height (number of rows) to the Kernel(int width, int height, float[] data) constructor.

The following example shows you how to create an identity-based kernel:

```
float[] identityKernel =
{
   0.0f, 0.0f, 0.0f,
   0.0f, 1.0f, 0.0f,
   0.0f, 0.0f, 0.0f
};
Kernel kernel = new Kernel(3, 3, identityKernel);
```

This kernel describes a 3-by-3 table of values that's applied to each source pixel and its eight immediate neighbors. To involve more neighbors, increase the size of the floating-point array and the number of rows and columns. For example, you could create a 5-by-5 kernel that involves the source pixel and its 24 immediate neighbors.

Note Although Kernel doesn't require odd-numbered width and height arguments, you might find kernels with an odd number of columns and an odd number of rows easier to understand.

After creating a kernel, you need to consider what happens when the kernel is positioned over pixels at the edges of an image. Some kernel elements will have no corresponding image pixels. For example, when a 3-by-3 kernel is positioned with its center row over the top image row, the kernel's top row of neighbor values has no corresponding row of image pixels.

ConvolveOp addresses this situation by declaring EDGE_ZERO_FILL and EDGE_NO_OP constants. Specifying EDGE_ZERO_FILL causes ConvolveOp to set edge destination pixels to zero, which is interpreted as black (RGB) or transparent (ARGB). EDGE_NO_OP causes ConvolveOp to copy source edge pixels to the destination unchanged.

To perform a convolution using this kernel, first instantiate ConvolveOp, as follows:

```
BufferedImageOp identityOp = new ConvolveOp(kernel);
RasterOp identityOp = new ConvolveOp(kernel);
```

The ConvolveOp(Kernel kernel) constructor sets the edge behavior to EDGE_ZERO_FILL.

Tip Use the ConvolveOp(Kernel kernel, int edgeCondition, RenderingHints hints) constructor to select the edge behavior and the rendering hints for controlling the rasterizer.

Continue by invoking a filter() method, as follows:

```
BufferedImage biResult = identityOp.filter(bi, null);
WriteableRaster wrResult = identityOp.filter(bi.getRaster(), null);
```

The first filter() method call is passed an existing BufferedImage instance named bi as its first argument. Its second argument is null, which tells filter() to create a new BufferedImage instance as the destination. You cannot pass the same BufferedImage instance as the second argument because ConvolveOp doesn't support in-place filtering for buffered images.

The second filter() method call is passed the buffered image's raster (obtained by invoking BufferedImage's WritableRaster getRaster() method) as its first argument. It is also passed null as its second argument because ConvolveOp doesn't support in-place filtering for rasters.

Note For convenience, I focus on buffered image-based processing. Also, I demonstrate various filters/image operators in the context of a BIP application that's included with this book's code.

You can create a blur kernel that blurs an image by combining equal amounts of source and neighbor pixel component values. The resulting kernel appears here:

```
float ninth = 1.0f/9.0f;
float[] blurKernel =
{
   ninth, ninth, ninth,
   ninth, ninth, ninth,
   ninth, ninth, ninth
};
Kernel kernel = new Kernel(3, 3, blurKernel);
```

Figure 7-29 shows the blur kernel's results—compare with Figure 7-10.

Figure 7-29. *Select Blur from the Process menu to blur the image.*

If you were to apply the blur kernel to an ARGB image, where all alpha component values are 255 (or 1.0) to indicate an opaque image, the destination image's alpha values would be the same as the source image's alpha values. The reason is that the blur kernel divides each of the source and neighbor alpha values by nine and then adds the results together, resulting in the source pixel's original alpha value.

You can create an edge kernel that emphasizes an image's edges by subtracting neighbor pixel components from source pixel components. The resulting kernel appears here:

```
float[] edgeKernel =
{
    0.0f, -1.0f,  0.0f,
   -1.0f,  4.0f, -1.0f,
    0.0f, -1.0f,  0.0f
};
Kernel kernel = new Kernel(3, 3, edgeKernel);
```

Figure 7-30 shows the edge kernel's results.

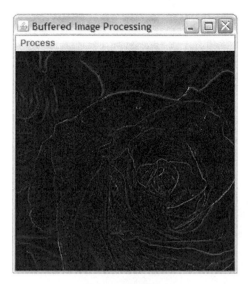

Figure 7-30. *Select Edge from the Process menu to generate an image that reveals edges only.*

If you were to apply the edge kernel to an ARGB image, where all alpha component values are 255/1.0, the destination image would be transparent because each alpha value would be set to 0 (transparent) by the edge kernel.

Finally, you can create a sharpen kernel by adding the identity kernel to the edge kernel. The resulting kernel is as follows:

```
float[] sharpenKernel =
{
    0.0f, -1.0f,  0.0f,
   -1.0f,  5.0f, -1.0f,
    0.0f, -1.0f,  0.0f
};
Kernel kernel = new Kernel(3, 3, sharpenKernel);
```

Figure 7-31 shows the sharpen kernel's results.

Figure 7-31. Select Sharpen from the Process menu to sharpen the image.

If you were to apply the sharpen kernel to an ARGB image, where all alpha component values are 255/1.0, the destination image's alpha values would be the same as the source image's alpha values. The reason is that the sharpen kernel multiplies the source pixel's alpha value by 4 and subtracts four of its neighbor's alpha values from the multiplied result, arriving at the source pixel's original alpha value.

■ **Note** Kernels whose elements sum to 1.0 preserve an image's brightness, as demonstrated in the blur and sharpen kernels. Kernels whose elements sum to less than 1.0 generate darker images, which the edge kernel demonstrates. Kernels whose elements sum to greater than 1.0 generate brighter images.

Using Lookup Tables

LookupOp lets you process a buffered image by using lookup tables, where a lookup table contains one or more arrays of values that are indexed by pixel component values.

Lookup tables are described by concrete subclasses of the abstract java.awt.image.LookupTable class, specifically java.awt.image.ByteLookupTable and java.awt.image.ShortLookupTable, which store byte integers and short integers, respectively. Either subclass can be used, although you'll probably use ShortLookupTable because you can easily represent unsigned byte integers. In contrast, you would have to use negative values to represent byte values ranging from 128 to 255 when choosing ByteLookupTable.

To create a short integer lookup table that applies to all components, first create its underlying array, as follows:

```
short[] invert = new short[256];
for (int i = 0; i < invert.length; i++)
   invert[i] = (short) 255-i;
```

This array is designed to invert a pixel's color (and, when present, alpha) components, and is intended for use with ShortLookupTable.

Continue by instantiating ShortLookupTable, as follows:

```
LookupTable table = new ShortLookupTable(0, invert);
```

The first argument is an offset to subtract from component values prior to indexing into the array. I pass 0 because I don't want to subtract an offset. The second argument is the array itself.

Finally, instantiate LookupOp by calling its LookupOp(LookupTable lookup, RenderingHints hints) constructor, as follows:

```
BufferedImageOp invertOp = new LookupOp(new ShortLookupTable(0, invert), null);
```

I've chosen to not specify rendering hints by passing null as the second argument.

There's a problem with using a single array when dealing with an ARGB image because it can screw up the alpha channel—the lookup table also applies to alpha. To address this situation, you can process the alpha channel separately by providing one array for each component, as demonstrated here:

```
short[] alpha = new short[256];
short[] red = new short[256];
short[] green = new short[256];
short[] blue = new short[256];
for (int i = 0; i < alpha.length; i++)
{
    alpha[i] = 255;
    red[i] = (short) (255-i);
    green[i] = (short) (255-i);
    blue[i] = (short) (255-i);
}
short[][] invert = { red, green, blue, alpha };
BufferedImageOp invertOp = new LookupOp(new ShortLookupTable(0, invert), null);
```

This example first creates a separate array for inverting each component except for alpha—each alpha array entry is assigned 255 to specify opaque. Next, these arrays are passed to a two-dimensional invert array—the alpha array must be passed last. Finally, an alternate ShortLookupTable constructor is called with the two-dimensional invert array and a 0 offset as its arguments. The resulting table along with null (that indicates no rendering hints) are passed to LookupOp's constructor.

Figure 7-32 shows this image operator's results.

Figure 7-32. Select Negative from the Process menu to invert pixel components.

EXERCISES

The following exercises are designed to test your understanding of AWT, Swing, and Java 2D:

1. Create an AWT application named RandomCircles that presents a canvas for displaying filled circular ovals (rendered via fillOval()). A new randomly colored, randomly positioned, and randomly sized (from 5 to 35 pixels for both the width and height—use the same value for each extent) filled circle is displayed by the paint() method at application startup and each time the mouse button is pressed while the mouse pointer appears over the canvas. At startup, you might notice that the canvas first displays one randomly colored/positioned/sized circle and immediately displays another. This has to do with AWT invoking the paint() method at least twice at startup. Because you don't know how many times paint() will be called, never rely on paint() to change the state of the component. Instead, you must only use this method to render the component in response to the current state.

2. Modify Listing 7-6's Swing-based TempVerter application to install the Nimbus Look and Feel before the GUI is created.

3. Swing's AbstractButton class, which JButton extends, declares a void setMnemonic(int mnemonic) method for setting a keyboard *mnemonic* (memory aid), which serves as a keyboard shortcut alternative to clicking a mouse button. The argument passed to mnemonic is one of the virtual key constants declared in the KeyEvent class (e.g., VK_C). When you invoke this method, the first occurrence

of the character (from left to right on the button label) defined by the mnemonic is underlined. When you press this key with the current look and feel's mouseless modifier (typically the Alt key), the button is clicked. Modify Listing 7-6's Swing-based TempVerter application to assign the VK_C mnemonic to the Convert to Celsius button and the VK_F mnemonic to the Fahrenheit button.

4.   The pseudo-splash screen created by Listing 7-3's SplashCanvas class suffers from aliasing that makes the text and graphics look jagged. You can fix this problem by installing the antialiasing rendering hint before rendering graphics. Create a new version of SplashCanvas that takes advantage of antialiasing.

5.   Adding the previous exercise's support for antialiasing slows down rendering. As a result, you may notice that it takes time to redraw the pseudo-splash screen and that the GUI's response to mouse clicks becomes sluggish. You can solve this problem for nonresizable components by precreating the noninverted and inverted images with the help of the BufferedImage class. Create a new version of SplashCanvas that accomplishes this task.

6.   Because you might find Figure 7-29's blurred image hard to distinguish from Figure 7-10, modify BIP by adding a Blur More menuitem. The associated listener will create a 5-by-5-element kernel with each element set to 1.0f/25.0f. Involving more neighbor pixels results in more blurring. Compare the Blur More and Blur results to see this for yourself.

7.   The ColorSpace and ColorConvertOp classes can be used to create a grayscale version of a colored image. Introduce a Grayscale menuitem to BIP and have its associated listener use these classes to generate a grayscale version of the rose.

Summary

Abstract Window Toolkit is Java's original windowing system-independent API for creating GUIs that are based on components, containers, layout managers, and events. AWT also supports graphics, colors, fonts, images, data transfer, and more.

Swing is a windowing system-independent API for creating GUIs that are based on components, containers, layout managers, and events. Although Swing extends AWT (you can use AWT layout managers and events in your Swing GUIs), this API differs from its predecessor in that Swing GUIs can look and feel the same when run on any windowing system or (at the developer's discretion) adopt the look and feel of the windowing system on which it's running. Furthermore, Swing's noncontainer components and a few of its containers are completely managed by Java so that they can have whatever features are necessary (such as tooltips); these features are available regardless of the windowing system. Also, Swing can offer components that might not be available on every windowing system; for example, tables and trees.

Finally, Java 2D is a collection of AWT extensions that provide advanced two-dimensional graphical, textual, and imaging capabilities. This API offers a flexible framework for developing richer GUIs through line art, text, and images.

Applications often interact with the filesystem to output data to and/or input data from files. Chapter 8 introduces you to the standard class library's classic I/O APIs for accomplishing these tasks.

CHAPTER 8

Interacting with Filesystems

Applications often interact with the filesystem to output data to and/or input data from files. Java's standard class library supports filesystem access via its classic File, RandomAccessFile, stream, and writer/reader APIs. Chapter 8 introduces you to File, RandomAccessFile, and various stream and writer/reader APIs.

Note Although it's preferred to access filesystems via Java's New I/O APIs, I don't discuss New I/O in this chapter because aspects of New I/O involve networking, which I don't discuss until Chapter 9. Also, you should know about this chapter's classic I/O APIs because you'll encounter them while modifying legacy code that uses classic I/O. I discuss New I/O in Appendix C.

File

Applications often interact with a *filesystem*, which is usually expressed as a hierarchy of files and directories starting from a *root directory*.

Windows and other platforms on which a Java Virtual Machine (JVM) runs typically support at least one filesystem. For example, a Unix or Linux platform combines all *mounted* (attached and prepared) disks into one virtual filesystem. In contrast, Windows associates a separate filesystem with each active disk drive.

Java offers access to the platform's available filesystem(s) via its concrete java.io.File class. File declares the File[] listRoots() class method to return the root directories (roots) of available filesystems as an array of File objects.

Note The set of available filesystem roots is affected by various platform-level operations, such as inserting or ejecting removable media, and disconnecting or unmounting physical or virtual disk drives.

Listing 8-1 presents a DumpRoots application that uses listRoots() to obtain an array of available filesystem roots and then outputs the array's contents.

Listing 8-1. Dumping available filesystem roots to the standard output device

```java
import java.io.File;

class DumpRoots
{
    public static void main(String[] args)
    {
        File[] roots = File.listRoots();
        for (File root: roots)
            System.out.println(root);
    }
}
```

When I run this application on my Windows XP platform, I receive the following output, which reveals four available roots:

```
A:\
C:\
D:\
E:\
```

If I ran DumpRoots on a Unix or Linux platform, I would receive one output line consisting of the virtual filesystem root (/).

Apart from using listRoots(), you can obtain a File instance by calling a File constructor such as File(String pathname), which creates a File instance that stores the pathname string. The following assignment statements demonstrate this constructor:

```java
File file1 = new File("/x/y");
File file2 = new File("C:\\temp\\x.dat");
```

The first statement assumes a Unix or Linux platform, starts the pathname with root directory symbol /, and continues with directory name x, separator character /, and file or directory name y. (It also works on Windows, which assumes this path begins at the root directory on the current drive.)

■ **Note** A *path* is a hierarchy of directories that must be traversed to locate a file or a directory. A *pathname* is a string representation of a path; a platform-dependent *separator character* (such as the Windows backslash [\] character) appears between consecutive names.

The second statement assumes a Windows platform, starts the pathname with drive specifier C:, and continues with root directory symbol \, directory name temp, separator character \, and filename x.dat (although x.dat might refer to a directory).

■ **Caution** Always double backslash characters that appear in a string literal, especially when specifying a pathname; otherwise, you run the risk of bugs or compiler error messages. For example, I doubled the backslash characters in the second statement to denote a backslash and not a tab (\t), and to avoid a compiler error message (\x is illegal).

Each statement's pathname is an *absolute pathname*, which is a pathname that starts with the root directory symbol; no other information is required to locate the file/directory that it denotes. In contrast, a *relative pathname* doesn't start with the root directory symbol; it's interpreted via information taken from some other pathname.

■ **Note** The java.io package's classes default to resolving relative pathnames against the current user (also known as working) directory, which is identified by system property user.dir, and which is typically the directory in which the JVM was launched. (Chapter 4 shows you how to read system properties via the java.lang.System class's getProperty() method.)

File instances contain abstract representations of file and directory pathnames (these files or directories may or may not exist in their filesystems) by storing *abstract pathnames*, which offer platform-independent views of hierarchical pathnames. In contrast, user interfaces and operating systems use platform-dependent *pathname strings* to name files and directories.

An abstract pathname consists of an optional platform-dependent prefix string, such as a disk-drive specifier, "/" for the Unix root directory, or "\\" for a Windows Universal Naming Convention (UNC) pathname; and a sequence of zero or more string names. The first name in an abstract pathname may be a directory name or, in the case of Windows UNC pathnames, a hostname. Each subsequent name denotes a directory; the last name may denote a directory or a file. The *empty abstract pathname* has no prefix and an empty name sequence.

The conversion of a pathname string to or from an abstract pathname is inherently platform-dependent. When a pathname string is converted to an abstract pathname, the names within it are separated by the default name-separator character or by any other name-separator character that is supported by the underlying platform. For example, File(String pathname) converts pathname string /x/y to abstract pathname /x/y on a Unix or Linux platform, and this same pathname string to abstract pathname \x\y on a Windows platform.

■ **Note** The *default name-separator character* is obtainable from system property file.separator, and is also stored in File's separator and separatorChar class fields. The first field stores the character in a java.lang.String instance and the second field stores it as a char value. Neither name of these final fields follows the convention of appearing entirely in uppercase.

When an abstract pathname is converted into a pathname string, each name is separated from the next by a single copy of the default name-separator character.

File offers additional constructors for instantiating this class. For example, the following constructors merge parent and child pathnames into combined pathnames that are stored in File objects:

- File(String parent, String child) creates a new File instance from a parent pathname string and a child pathname string.

- File(File parent, String child) creates a new File instance from a parent pathname File instance and a child pathname string.

Each constructor's parent parameter is passed a *parent pathname*, a string that consists of all pathname components except for the last name, which is specified by child. The following statement demonstrates this concept via File(String, String):

```
File file3 = new File("prj/books/", "bj7");
```

The constructor merges relative parent pathname prj/books/ with child pathname bj7 into relative pathname prj/books/bj7. (If I had specified prj/books as the parent pathname, the constructor would have added the separator character after books.)

Tip Because File(String pathname), File(String parent, String child), and File(File parent, String child) don't detect invalid pathname arguments (apart from throwing java.lang.NullPointerException when pathname or child is null), you must be careful when specifying pathnames. You should strive to only specify pathnames that are valid for all platforms on which the application will run. For example, instead of hard-coding a drive specifier (such as C:) in a pathname, use the roots that are returned from listRoots(). Even better, keep your pathnames relative to the current user/working directory (returned from the user.dir system property).

After obtaining a File object, you can interrogate it to learn about its stored abstract pathname by calling the methods that are described in Table 8-1.

Table 8-1. File Methods for Learning About a Stored Abstract Pathname

Method	Description
File getAbsoluteFile()	Return the absolute form of this File object's abstract pathname. This method is equivalent to new File(this.getAbsolutePath()).
String getAbsolutePath()	Return the absolute pathname string of this File object's abstract pathname. If it's already absolute, the pathname string is returned as if by calling getPath(). If it's the empty abstract pathname, the pathname string of the current user directory (identified via user.dir) is returned. Otherwise, the

abstract pathname is resolved in a platform-dependent manner. On Unix platforms, a relative pathname is made absolute by resolving it against the current user directory. On Windows platforms, the pathname is made absolute by resolving it against the current directory of the drive named by the pathname, or the current user directory when there's no drive.

`File getCanonicalFile()`	Return the *canonical* (simplest possible, absolute and unique) form of this `File` object's abstract pathname. This method throws `java.io.IOException` when an I/O error occurs (creating the canonical pathname may require filesystem queries); it equates to new `File(this.getCanonicalPath())`.
`String getCanonicalPath()`	Return the canonical pathname string of this `File` object's abstract pathname. This method first converts this pathname to absolute form when necessary, as if by invoking `getAbsolutePath()`, and then maps it to its unique form in a platform-dependent way. Doing so typically involves removing redundant names such as "." and ".." from the pathname, resolving symbolic links (on Unix platforms), and converting drive letters to a standard case (on Windows platforms). This method throws `IOException` when an I/O error occurs (creating the canonical pathname may require filesystem queries).
`String getName()`	Return the filename or directory name denoted by this `File` object's abstract pathname. This name is the last in a pathname's name sequence. The empty string is returned when the pathname's name sequence is empty.
`String getParent()`	Return the parent pathname string of this `File` object's abstract pathname, or return null when this pathname doesn't name a parent directory.
`File getParentFile()`	Return a `File` object storing this `File` object's abstract pathname's parent abstract pathname; return null when the parent pathname isn't a directory.
`String getPath()`	Convert this `File` object's abstract pathname into a pathname string where the names in the sequence are separated by the character stored in `File`'s `separator` field. Return the resulting pathname string.
`boolean isAbsolute()`	Return true when this `File` object's abstract pathname is absolute; otherwise, return false when it's relative. The definition of absolute pathname is system dependent. On Unix platforms, a pathname is absolute when its prefix is "/".

On Windows platforms, a pathname is absolute when its prefix is a drive specifier followed by "\", or when its prefix is "\\".

String toString()   A synonym for getPath().

___

Table 8-1 refers to IOException, which is the common exception superclass for those exception classes that describe various kinds of I/O errors, such as java.io.FileNotFoundException.

Listing 8-2 instantiates File with its pathname command-line argument, and calls some of the File methods described in Table 8-1 to learn about this pathname.

Listing 8-2. Obtaining abstract pathname information

```java
import java.io.File;
import java.io.IOException;

class PathnameInfo
{
   public static void main(String[] args) throws IOException
   {
      if (args.length != 1)
      {
         System.err.println("usage: java PathnameInfo pathname");
         return;
      }
      File file = new File(args[0]);
      System.out.println("Absolute path = "+file.getAbsolutePath());
      System.out.println("Canonical path = "+file.getCanonicalPath());
      System.out.println("Name = "+file.getName());
      System.out.println("Parent = "+file.getParent());
      System.out.println("Path = "+file.getPath());
      System.out.println("Is absolute = "+file.isAbsolute());
   }
}
```

For example, when I specify java PathnameInfo . (the period represents the current directory on my XP platform), I observe the following output:

```
Absolute path = C:\prj\dev\bj7\ch08\code\PathnameInfo\.
Canonical path = C:\prj\dev\bj7\ch08\code\PathnameInfo
Name = .
Parent = null
Path = .
Is absolute = false
```

This output reveals that the canonical pathname doesn't include the period. It also shows that there's no parent pathname and that the pathname is relative.

Continuing, I now specify java PathnameInfo c:\reports\2011\..\2010\February. This time, I observe the following output:

```
Absolute path = c:\reports\2011\..\2010\February
Canonical path = C:\reports\2010\February
```

```
Name = February
Parent = c:\reports\2011\..\2010
Path = c:\reports\2011\..\2010\February
Is absolute = true
```

This output reveals that the canonical pathname doesn't include 2011. It also shows that the pathname is absolute.

For my final example, suppose I specify java PathnameInfo "" to obtain information for the empty pathname. In response, this application generates the following output:

```
Absolute path = C:\prj\dev\bj7\ch08\code\PathnameInfo
Canonical path = C:\prj\dev\bj7\ch08\code\PathnameInfo
Name =
Parent = null
Path =
Is absolute = false
```

The output reveals that getName() and getPath() return the empty string ("") because the empty pathname is empty.

You can interrogate the filesystem to learn about the file or directory represented by a File object's abstract pathname by calling the methods that are described in Table 8-2.

Table 8-2. File Methods for Learning About a File or Directory

Method	Description
boolean canExecute()	Return true when this File object's abstract pathname represents an existing file that the application is allowed to execute.
boolean canRead()	Return true when this File object's abstract pathname represents an existing readable file.
boolean canWrite()	Return true when this File object's abstract pathname represents an existing file that can be modified.
boolean exists()	Return true if and only if the file or directory that's denoted by this File object's abstract pathname exists.
boolean isDirectory()	Return true when this File object's abstract pathname refers to an existing directory.
boolean isFile()	Return true when this File object's abstract pathname refers to an existing normal file. A file is *normal* when it's not a directory and satisfies other platform-dependent criteria: it's not a symbolic link or a named pipe, for example. Any nondirectory file created by a Java application is guaranteed to be a normal file.

boolean isHidden()	Return true when the file denoted by this File object's abstract pathname is hidden. The exact definition of *hidden* is platform dependent. On Unix/Linux platforms, a file is hidden when its name begins with a period character. On Windows platforms, a file is hidden when it has been marked as such in the filesystem.
long lastModified()	Return the time that the file denoted by this File object's abstract pathname was last modified, or 0 when the file doesn't exist or an I/O error occurred during this method call. The returned value is measured in milliseconds since the *Unix epoch* (00:00:00 GMT, January 1, 1970).
long length()	Return the length of the file denoted by this File object's abstract pathname. The return value is unspecified when the pathname denotes a directory, and will be 0 when the file doesn't exist.

Listing 8-3 instantiates File with its pathname command-line argument, and calls all the File methods described in Table 8-2 to learn about the pathname's file/directory.

Listing 8-3. Obtaining file/directory information

```java
import java.io.File;
import java.io.IOException;

import java.util.Date;

class FileDirectoryInfo
{
    public static void main(final String[] args) throws IOException
    {
        if (args.length != 1)
        {
            System.err.println("usage: java FileDirectoryInfo pathname");
            return;
        }
        File file = new File(args[0]);
        System.out.println("About "+file+":");
        System.out.println("Can execute = "+file.canExecute());
        System.out.println("Can read = "+file.canRead());
        System.out.println("Can write = "+file.canWrite());
        System.out.println("Exists = "+file.exists());
        System.out.println("Is directory = "+file.isDirectory());
        System.out.println("Is file = "+file.isFile());
        System.out.println("Is hidden = "+file.isHidden());
        System.out.println("Last modified = "+new Date(file.lastModified()));
        System.out.println("Length = "+file.length());
    }
}
```

For example, suppose I have a three-byte read-only file named x.dat. When I specify java FileDirectoryInfo x.dat, I observe the following output:

```
About x.dat:
Can execute = true
Can read = true
Can write = true
Exists = true
Is directory = false
Is file = true
Is hidden = false
Last modified = Wed Aug 24 18:45:07 CDT 2011
Length = 3
```

Note Java 6 added long getFreeSpace(), long getTotalSpace(), and long getUsableSpace() methods to File that return disk space information about the *partition* (a platform-specific portion of storage for a filesystem; for example, C:\) described by the File instance's pathname.

File declares five methods that return the names of files and directories located in the directory identified by a File object's abstract pathname. Table 8-3 describes these methods.

Table 8-3. *File Methods for Obtaining Directory Content*

Method	Description
String[] list()	Return a potentially empty array of strings naming the files and directories in the directory denoted by this File object's abstract pathname. If the pathname doesn't denote a directory, or if an I/O error occurs, this method returns null. Otherwise, it returns an array of strings, one string for each file or subdirectory in the directory.
	Names denoting the directory itself and the directory's parent directory are not included in the result. Each string is a filename rather than a complete path. Also, there's no guarantee that the name strings in the resulting array will appear in alphabetical or any other order.
String[] list(FilenameFilter filter)	A convenience method for calling list() and returning only those Strings that satisfy filter.
File[] listFiles()	A convenience method for calling list(), converting its array of Strings to an array of Files, and returning the Files array.

`File[] listFiles(FileFilter filter)`	A convenience method for calling `list()`, converting its array of Strings to an array of Files, but only for those Strings that satisfy filter, and returning the Files array.
`File[] listFiles(FilenameFilter filter)`	A convenience method for calling `list()`, converting its array of Strings to an array of Files, but only for those Strings that satisfy filter, and returning the Files array.

The overloaded `list()` methods return arrays of Strings denoting file and directory names. The second method lets you return only those names of interest (such as only names ending with extension `.txt`) via a `java.io.FilenameFilter`-based filter object.

The `FilenameFilter` interface declares a single boolean `accept(File dir, String name)` method that's called for each file/directory located in the directory identified by the File object's abstract pathname:

- `dir` identifies the parent portion of the pathname (the directory path).

- `name` identifies the final directory name or the filename portion of the pathname.

The `accept()` method uses these arguments to determine whether or not the file or directory satisfies its criteria for what is acceptable. It returns true when the file/directory name should be included in the returned array; otherwise, this method returns false.

Listing 8-4 presents a Dir(ectory) application that uses `list(FilenameFilter)` to obtain only those names that end with a specific extension.

Listing 8-4. Listing specific names

```java
import java.io.File;
import java.io.FilenameFilter;

class Dir
{
    public static void main(final String[] args)
    {
        if (args.length != 2)
        {
            System.err.println("usage: java Dir dirpath ext");
            return;
        }
        File file = new File(args[0]);
        FilenameFilter fnf = new FilenameFilter()
                             {
                                 public boolean accept(File dir, String name)
                                 {
                                     return name.endsWith(args[1]);
                                 }
                             };
        String[] names = file.list(fnf);
        for (String name: names)
```

```
        System.out.println(name);
    }
}
```

When I, for example, specify java Dir c:\windows bmp on my XP platform, Dir outputs only those \windows directory filenames that have the bmp (bitmap) extension:

```
Blue Lace 16.bmp
Coffee Bean.bmp
FeatherTexture.bmp
Gone Fishing.bmp
Greenstone.bmp
Prairie Wind.bmp
Rhododendron.bmp
River Sumida.bmp
Santa Fe Stucco.bmp
Soap Bubbles.bmp
winnt.bmp
winnt256.bmp
Zapotec.bmp
```

The overloaded listFiles() methods return arrays of Files. For the most part, they're symmetrical with their list() counterparts. However, listFiles(FileFilter) introduces an asymmetry.

The java.io.FileFilter interface declares a single boolean accept(String pathname) method that's called for each file/directory located in the directory identified by the File object's abstract pathname. The argument passed to pathname identifies the complete path of the file or directory.

The accept() method uses this argument to determine whether or not the file or directory satisfies its criteria for what is acceptable. It returns true when the file/directory name should be included in the returned array; otherwise, this method returns false.

■ **Tip** Because each interface's accept() method accomplishes the same task, you might be wondering which interface to use. If you prefer a path broken into its directory and name components, use FilenameFilter. However, if you prefer a complete pathname, use FileFilter; you can always call getParent() and getName() to get these components.

File also declares several methods for creating files and manipulating existing files. Table 8-4 describes these methods.

Table 8-4. File Methods for Creating Files and Manipulating Existing Files

Method	Description
boolean createNewFile()	Atomically create a new, empty file named by this File object's abstract pathname if and only if a file with this name does not yet exist. The check for file existence and the creation of the file when it doesn't exist are a single operation that's atomic with respect

	to all other filesystem activities that might affect the file. This method returns true when the named file doesn't exist and was successfully created, and returns false when the named file already exists. It throws IOException when an I/O error occurs.
static File createTempFile(String prefix, String suffix)	Create an empty file in the default temporary file directory using the given prefix and suffix to generate its name. This overloaded class method calls its three-parameter variant, passing prefix, suffix, and null to this other method, and returning this other method's return value.
static File createTempFile(String prefix, String suffix, File directory)	Create an empty file in the specified directory using the given prefix and suffix to generate its name. The name begins with the character sequence specified by prefix and ends with the character sequence specified by suffix; ".tmp" is used as the suffix when suffix is null. This method returns the created file's pathname when successful. It throws java.lang.IllegalArgumentException when prefix contains fewer than three characters, and IOException when the file couldn't be created.
boolean delete()	Delete the file or directory denoted by this File object's abstract pathname. Return true when successful; otherwise, return false. If the pathname denotes a directory, the directory must be empty in order to be deleted.
void deleteOnExit()	Request that the file or directory denoted by this File object's abstract pathname be deleted when the JVM terminates. Reinvoking this method on the same File object has no effect. Once deletion has been requested, it's not possible to cancel the request. Therefore, this method should be used with care.
boolean mkdir()	Create the directory named by this File object's abstract pathname. Return true when successful; otherwise, return false.
boolean mkdirs()	Create the directory and any necessary intermediate directories named by this File object's abstract pathname. Return true when successful; otherwise, return false.
boolean renameTo(File dest)	Rename the file denoted by this File object's abstract pathname to dest. Return true when successful; otherwise, return false. This method throws

NullPointerException when dest is null.

Many aspects of this method's behavior are platform dependent. For example, the rename operation might not be able to move a file from one filesystem to another, the operation might not be atomic, or it might not succeed when a file with the destination pathname already exists. The return value should always be checked to make sure that the rename operation was successful.

boolean setLastModified(long time)	Set the last-modified time of the file or directory named by this File object's abstract pathname. Return true when successful; otherwise, return false. This method throws IllegalArgumentException when time is negative.
	All platforms support file-modification times to the nearest second, but some provide more precision. The time value will be truncated to fit the supported precision. If the operation succeeds and no intervening operations on the file take place, the next call to lastModified() will return the (possibly truncated) time value passed to this method.
boolean setReadOnly()	Mark the file or directory denoted by this File object's abstract pathname so that only read operations are allowed. After calling this method, the file or directory is guaranteed not to change until it's deleted or marked to allow write access. Whether or not a read-only file or directory can be deleted depends upon the filesystem.

Suppose you're designing a text-editor application that a user will use to open a text file and make changes to its content. Until the user explicitly saves these changes to the file, you want the text file to remain unchanged.

Because the user doesn't want to lose these changes when the application crashes or the computer loses power, you design the application to save these changes to a temporary file every few minutes. This way, the user has a backup of the changes.

You can use the overloaded createTempFile() methods to create the temporary file. If you don't specify a directory in which to store this file, it's created in the directory identified by the java.io.tmpdir system property.

You probably want to remove the temporary file after the user tells the application to save or discard the changes. The deleteOnExit() method lets you register a temporary file for deletion; it's deleted when the JVM ends without a crash/power loss.

Listing 8-5 presents a TempFileDemo application that lets you experiment with the createTempFile() and deleteOnExit() methods.

Listing 8-5. *Experimenting with temporary files*

```
import java.io.File;
import java.io.IOException;

class TempFileDemo
{
   public static void main(String[] args) throws IOException
   {
      System.out.println(System.getProperty("java.io.tmpdir"));
      File temp = File.createTempFile("text", ".txt");
      System.out.println(temp);
      temp.deleteOnExit();
   }
}
```

After outputting the location where temporary files are stored, TempFileDemo creates a temporary file whose name begins with text and has extension .txt. TempFileDemo next outputs the temporary file's name and registers the temporary file for deletion upon the successful termination of the application.

I observed the following output during one run of TempFileDemo (and the file disappeared on exit):

```
C:\DOCUME~1\JEFFFR~1\LOCALS~1\Temp\
C:\DOCUME~1\JEFFFR~1\LOCALS~1\Temp\text34365024123228813057.txt
```

■ **Note** Java 6 added to File new boolean setExecutable(boolean executable), boolean setExecutable(boolean executable, boolean ownerOnly), boolean setReadable(boolean readable), boolean setReadable(boolean readable, boolean ownerOnly), boolean setWritable(boolean writable), and boolean setWritable(boolean writable, boolean ownerOnly) methods that let you set the owner's or everybody's execute, read, and write permissions (respectively) for the file identified by the File object's abstract pathname.

Finally, File implements the java.lang.Comparable interface's compareTo() method, and overrides equals() and hashCode(). Table 8-5 describes these miscellaneous methods.

Table 8-5. File's Miscellaneous Methods

Method	Description
int compareTo(File pathname)	Compare two pathnames lexicographically. The ordering defined by this method depends upon the underlying platform. On Unix/Linux platforms, alphabetic case is significant when comparing pathnames; on Windows platforms, alphabetic case is insignificant. Return zero when pathname's abstract pathname equals this File object's abstract pathname, a negative value when this File object's pathname is less than pathname, and a positive value otherwise. To accurately compare two File objects, call getCanonicalFile() on each File object and then compare

	the returned `File` objects.
`boolean equals(Object obj)`	Compare this `File` object with `obj` for equality. Abstract pathname equality depends upon the underlying platform. On Unix/Linux platforms, alphabetic case is significant when comparing pathnames; on Windows platforms, alphabetic case is not significant. Return true if and only if `obj` is not `null` and is a `File` object whose abstract pathname denotes the same file/directory as this `File` object's abstract pathname.
`int hashCode()`	Calculate and return a hash code for this abstract pathname. This calculation depends upon the underlying platform. On Unix/Linux platforms, a pathname's hash code is the exclusive OR of its pathname string's hash code and decimal value 1234321. On Windows platforms, the hash code is the exclusive OR of the lowercased pathname string's hash code and decimal value 1234321. The current locale (discussed in Appendix C) is not taken into account when lowercasing the pathname string.

RandomAccessFile

Files can be created and/or opened for *random access* in which write and read operations can occur until the file is closed. Java supports this random access via its concrete `java.io.RandomAccessFile` class.
   `RandomAccessFile` declares the following constructors:

- `RandomAccessFile(File file, String mode)` creates and opens a new file if it doesn't exist, or opens an existing file. The file is identified by `file`'s abstract pathname and is created and/or opened according to `mode`.

- `RandomAccessFile(String pathname, String mode)` creates and opens a new file if it doesn't exist, or opens an existing file. The file is identified by `pathname` and is created and/or opened according to `mode`.

Either constructor's mode argument must be one of `"r"`, `"rw"`, `"rws"`, or `"rwd"`; otherwise, the constructor throws `IllegalArgumentException`. These string literals have the following meanings:

- `"r"` informs the constructor to open an existing file for reading only. Any attempt to write to the file results in a thrown instance of the `IOException` class.

- `"rw"` informs the constructor to create and open a new file when it doesn't exist for reading and writing, or open an existing file for reading and writing.

- `"rwd"` informs the constructor to create and open a new file when it doesn't exist for reading and writing, or open an existing file for reading and writing. Furthermore, each update to the file's content must be written synchronously to the underlying storage device.

- "rws" informs the constructor to create and open a new file when it doesn't exist for reading and writing, or open an existing file for reading and writing. Furthermore, each update to the file's content or metadata must be written synchronously to the underlying storage device.

Note A file's *metadata* is data about the file and not actual file contents. Examples of metadata include the file's length and the time the file was last modified.

The "rwd" and "rws" modes ensure than any writes to a file located on a local storage device are written to the device, which guarantees that critical data isn't lost when the operating system crashes. No guarantee is made when the file doesn't reside on a local device.

Note Operations on a random access file opened in "rwd" or "rws" mode are slower than these same operations on a random access file opened in "rw" mode.

These constructors throw FileNotFoundException when mode is "r" and the file identified by pathname cannot be opened (it might not exist or it might be a directory), or when mode is "rw" and pathname is read-only or a directory.

The following example demonstrates the second constructor by attempting to open an existing random access file via the "r" mode string:

```
RandomAccessFile raf = new RandomAccessFile("employee.dat", "r");
```

A random access file is associated with a *file pointer*, a cursor that identifies the location of the next byte to write or read. When an existing file is opened, the file pointer is set to its first byte, at offset 0. The file pointer is also set to 0 when the file is created.

Write and read operations start at the file pointer and advance it past the number of bytes written or read. Operations that write past the current end of the file cause the file to be extended. These operations continue until the file is closed.

RandomAccessFile declares a wide variety of methods. I present a representative sample of these methods in Table 8-6.

Table 8-6. RandomAccessFile Methods

Method	Description
void close()	Close the file and release any associated platform resources. Subsequent writes or reads result in IOException. Also, the file cannot be reopened with this RandomAccessFile object. This method throws IOException when an I/O error occurs.
FileDescriptor getFD()	Return the file's associated file descriptor object. This

	method throws IOException when an I/O error occurs.
`long getFilePointer()`	Return the file pointer's current zero-based byte offset into the file. This method throws IOException when an I/O error occurs.
`long length()`	Return the length (measured in bytes) of the file. This method throws IOException when an I/O error occurs.
`int read()`	Read and return (as an int in the range 0 to 255) the next byte from the file, or return -1 when the end of the file is reached. This method blocks when no input is available, and throws IOException when an I/O error occurs.
`int read(byte[] b)`	Read up to b.length bytes of data from the file into byte array b. This method blocks until at least one byte of input is available. It returns the number of bytes read into the array, or returns -1 when the end of the file is reached. It throws NullPointerException when b is null, and IOException when an I/O error occurs.
`char readChar()`	Read and return a character from the file. This method reads two bytes from the file starting at the current file pointer. If the bytes read, in order, are b1 and b2, where $0 <= b1, b2 <= 255$, the result is equal to `(char) ((b1<<8)|b2)`. This method blocks until the two bytes are read, the end of the file is detected, or an exception is thrown. It throws java.io.EOFException (a subclass of IOException) when the end of the file is reached before reading both bytes, and IOException when an I/O error occurs.
`int readInt()`	Read and return a signed 32-bit integer from the file. This method reads four bytes from the file starting at the current file pointer. If the bytes read, in order, are b1, b2, b3, and b4, where $0 <= b1, b2, b3, b4 <= 255$, the result is equal to `(b1<<24)|(b2<<16)+(b3<<8)+b4`. This method blocks until the four bytes are read, the end of the file is detected, or an exception is thrown. It throws EOFException when the end of the file is reached before reading all four bytes, and IOException when an I/O error occurs.
`void seek(long pos)`	Set the file pointer's current offset to pos (which is measured in bytes from the beginning of the file). When the offset is set beyond the end of the file, the file's length doesn't change. The file length will only change by writing after the offset has been set beyond the end of the file. This method throws IOException when the value in pos is negative, or when an I/O error occurs.

void setLength(long newLength)	Set the file's length. If the present length as returned by length() is greater than newLength, the file is truncated. In this case, if the file offset as returned by getFilePointer() is greater than newLength, the offset will be equal to newLength after setLength() returns. If the present length is smaller than newLength, the file is extended. In this case, the contents of the extended portion of the file are not defined. This method throws IOException when an I/O error occurs.
int skipBytes(int n)	Attempt to skip over n bytes. This method skips over a smaller number of bytes (possibly zero) when the end of file is reached before n bytes have been skipped. It doesn't throw EOFException in this situation. When n is negative, no bytes are skipped. The actual number of bytes skipped is returned. This method throws IOException when an I/O error occurs.
void write(byte[] b)	Write b.length bytes from byte array b to the file starting at the current file pointer position. This method throws IOException when an I/O error occurs.
void write(int b)	Write the lower eight bits of b to the file at the current file pointer position. This method throws IOException when an I/O error occurs.
void writeChars(String s)	Write string s to the file as a sequence of characters starting at the current file pointer position. This method throws IOException when an I/O error occurs.
void writeInt(int i)	Write 32-bit integer i to the file starting at the current file pointer position. The four bytes are written with the high byte first. This method throws IOException when an I/O error occurs.

Most of Table 8-6's methods are fairly self-explanatory. However, the getFD() method requires further enlightenment.

░ **Note** RandomAccessFile's read-prefixed methods and skipBytes() originate in the java.io.DataInput interface, which this class implements. Furthermore, RandomAccessFile's write-prefixed methods originate in the java.io.DataOutput interface, which this class also implements.

When a file is opened, the underlying platform creates a platform-dependent structure to represent the file. A handle to this structure is stored in an instance of the java.io.FileDescriptor class, which getFD() returns.

> ▪ **Note** A *handle* is an identifier that Java passes to the underlying platform to identify, in this case, a specific open file when it requires that the underlying platform perform a file operation.

FileDescriptor is a small class that declares three FileDescriptor constants named in, out, and err. These constants let System.in, System.out, and System.err provide access to the standard input, standard output, and standard error streams.

FileDescriptor also declares a pair of methods:

- void sync() tells the underlying platform to *flush* (empty) the contents of the open file's output buffers to their associated local disk device. sync() returns after all modified data and attributes have been written to the relevant device. It throws java.io.SyncFailedException when the buffers cannot be flushed, or because the platform cannot guarantee that all the buffers have been synchronized with physical media.

- boolean valid() determines whether or not this file descriptor object is valid. It returns true when the file descriptor object represents an open file or other active I/O connection; otherwise, it returns false.

Data that is written to an open file ends up being stored in the underlying platform's output buffers. When the buffers fill to capacity, the platform empties them to the disk. Buffers improve performance because disk access is slow.

However, when you write data to a random access file that's been opened via mode "rwd" or "rws", each write operation's data is written straight to the disk. As a result, write operations are slower than when the random access file was opened in "rw" mode.

Suppose you have a situation that combines writing data through the output buffers and writing data directly to the disk. The following example addresses this hybrid scenario by opening the file in mode "rw" and selectively calling FileDescriptor's sync() method:

```
RandomAccessFile raf = new RandomAccessFile("employee.dat", "rw");
FileDescriptor fd = raf.getFD();
// Perform a critical write operation.
raf.write(...);
// Synchronize with underlying disk by flushing platform's output buffers to disk.
fd.sync();
// Perform non-critical write operation where synchronization is not necessary.
raf.write(...);
// Do other work.
// Close file, emptying output buffers to disk.
raf.close();
```

RandomAccessFile is useful for creating a *flat file database*, a single file organized into records and fields. A *record* stores a single entry (e.g., a part in a parts database) and a *field* stores a single attribute of the entry (e.g., a part number).

A flat file database typically organizes its content into a sequence of fixed-length records. Each record is further organized into one or more fixed-length fields. Figure 8-1 illustrates this concept in the context of a parts database.

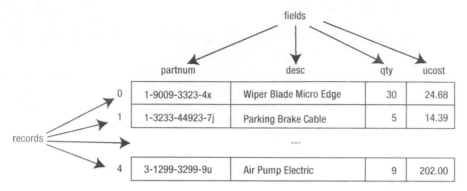

Figure 8-1. This flat file database describes automotive parts.

According to Figure 8-1, each field has a name (partnum, desc, qty, and ucost). Also, each record is assigned a number starting at 0. This example consists of five records, of which only three are shown for brevity.

Note The term *field* is also used to refer to a variable declared within a class. To avoid confusion with this overloaded terminology, think of a field variable as being analogous to a record's field attribute.

To show you how to implement a flat file database in terms of RandomAccessFile, I've created a simple PartsDB class to model Figure 8-1. Check out Listing 8-6.

Listing 8-6. Implementing the parts flat file database

```
import java.io.Closeable;
import java.io.IOException;
import java.io.RandomAccessFile;

class PartsDB implements Closeable
{
   final static int PNUMLEN = 20;
   final static int DESCLEN = 30;
   final static int QUANLEN = 4;
   final static int COSTLEN = 4;
   private final static int RECLEN = 2*PNUMLEN+2*DESCLEN+QUANLEN+COSTLEN;
   private RandomAccessFile raf;
   PartsDB(String pathname) throws IOException
   {
      raf = new RandomAccessFile(pathname, "rw");
   }
   void append(String partnum, String partdesc, int qty, int ucost)
      throws IOException
   {
```

```
      raf.seek(raf.length());
      write(partnum, partdesc, qty, ucost);
   }
   @Override
   public void close() throws IOException
   {
//      throw new IOException("cannot close raf");
      raf.close();
   }
   int numRecs() throws IOException
   {
      return (int) raf.length()/RECLEN;
   }
   Part select(int recno) throws IOException
   {
      if (recno < 0 || recno >= numRecs())
         throw new IllegalArgumentException(recno+" out of range");
      raf.seek(recno*RECLEN);
      return read();
   }
   void update(int recno, String partnum, String partdesc, int qty, int ucost)
      throws IOException
   {
      if (recno < 0 || recno >= numRecs())
         throw new IllegalArgumentException(recno+" out of range");
      raf.seek(recno*RECLEN);
      write(partnum, partdesc, qty, ucost);
   }
   private Part read() throws IOException
   {
      StringBuffer sb = new StringBuffer();
      for (int i = 0; i < PNUMLEN; i++)
         sb.append(raf.readChar());
      String partnum = sb.toString().trim();
      sb.setLength(0);
      for (int i = 0; i < DESCLEN; i++)
         sb.append(raf.readChar());
      String partdesc = sb.toString().trim();
      int qty = raf.readInt();
      int ucost = raf.readInt();
      return new Part(partnum, partdesc, qty, ucost);
   }
   private void write(String partnum, String partdesc, int qty, int ucost)
      throws IOException
   {
      StringBuffer sb = new StringBuffer(partnum);
      if (sb.length() > PNUMLEN)
         sb.setLength(PNUMLEN);
      else
      if (sb.length() < PNUMLEN)
      {
         int len = PNUMLEN-sb.length();
```

```
              for (int i = 0; i < len; i++)
                  sb.append(" ");
          }
          raf.writeChars(sb.toString());
          sb = new StringBuffer(partdesc);
          if (sb.length() > DESCLEN)
              sb.setLength(DESCLEN);
          else
          if (sb.length() < DESCLEN)
          {
              int len = DESCLEN-sb.length();
              for (int i = 0; i < len; i++)
                  sb.append(" ");
          }
          raf.writeChars(sb.toString());
          raf.writeInt(qty);
          raf.writeInt(ucost);
      }
      static class Part
      {
          private String partnum;
          private String desc;
          private int qty;
          private int ucost;
          Part(String partnum, String desc, int qty, int ucost)
          {
              this.partnum = partnum;
              this.desc = desc;
              this.qty = qty;
              this.ucost = ucost;
          }
          String getDesc()
          {
              return desc;
          }
          String getPartnum()
          {
              return partnum;
          }
          int getQty()
          {
              return qty;
          }
          int getUnitCost()
          {
              return ucost;
          }
      }
  }
```

Listing 8-6's PartsDB class implements the java.io.Closeable interface so that it can be used in the context of the try-with-resources statement (see Chapter 3). I could have chosen to implement

Closeable's java.lang.AutoCloseable superinterface, but chose Closeable instead because its close() method is declared to throw IOException.

PartsDB declares constants that identify the lengths of the string and 32-bit integer fields. It then declares a constant that calculates the record length in terms of bytes. The calculation takes into account the fact that a character occupies two bytes in the file.

These constants are followed by a field named raf that's of type RandomAccessFile. This field is assigned an instance of the RandomAccessFile class in the subsequent constructor, which creates/opens a new file or opens an existing file because of "rw".

PartsDB next declares append(), close(), numRecs(), select(), and update(). These methods append a record to the file, close the file, return the number of records in the file, select and return a specific record, and update a specific record:

- The append() method first calls length() and seek(). Doing so ensures that the file pointer is positioned to the end of the file before calling the private write() method to write a record containing this method's arguments.

- The close() method is declared public because it's inherited from Closeable and interface methods are public—you cannot make an overriding method less accessible. This method is also declared to throw IOException because RandomAccessFile's close() method can throw IOException. Because this is a rare occurrence, I've commented out a throw statement that you can use to experiment with suppressed exceptions—I'll show you how to do so when I present UsePartsDB.

- The numRecs() method returns the number of records in the file. These records are numbered starting with 0 and ending with numRecs()-1. Each of the select() and update() methods verifies that its recno argument lies within this range.

- The select() method calls the private read() method to return the record identified by recno as an instance of the Part static member class. Part's constructor initializes a Part object to a record's field values, and its getter methods return these values.

- The update() method is equally simple. As with select(), it first positions the file pointer to the start of the record identified by recno. As with append(), it calls write() to write out its arguments, but replaces a record instead of adding one.

Records are written via the private write() method. Because fields must have exact sizes, write() pads String-based values that are shorter than a field size with spaces on the right, and truncates these values to the field size when needed.

Records are read via the private read() method. read() removes the padding before saving a String-based field value in the Part object.

By itself, PartsDB is useless. We need an application that lets us experiment with this class, and Listing 8-7 fulfills this requirement.

Listing 8-7. Experimenting with the parts flat file database

```
import java.io.IOException;

class UsePartsDB
{
   public static void main(String[] args)
```

```
      {
         try (PartsDB pdb = new PartsDB("parts.db"))
         {
            if (pdb.numRecs() == 0)
            {
               // Populate the database with records.
               pdb.append("1-9009-3323-4x", "Wiper Blade Micro Edge", 30, 2468);
               pdb.append("1-3233-44923-7j", "Parking Brake Cable", 5, 1439);
               pdb.append("2-3399-6693-2m", "Halogen Bulb H4 55/60W", 22, 813);
               pdb.append("2-599-2029-6k", "Turbo Oil Line O-Ring ", 26, 155);
               pdb.append("3-1299-3299-9u", "Air Pump Electric", 9, 20200);
            }
            dumpRecords(pdb);
            pdb.update(1, "1-3233-44923-7j", "Parking Brake Cable", 5, 1995);
            dumpRecords(pdb);
//          throw new IOException("I/O error");
         }
         catch (IOException ioe)
         {
            System.err.println(ioe);
            if (ioe.getSuppressed().length == 1)
               System.err.println("Suppressed = "+ioe.getSuppressed()[0]);
         }
      }
      static void dumpRecords(PartsDB pdb) throws IOException
      {
         for (int i = 0; i < pdb.numRecs(); i++)
         {
            PartsDB.Part part = pdb.select(i);
            System.out.print(format(part.getPartnum(), PartsDB.PNUMLEN, true));
            System.out.print(" | ");
            System.out.print(format(part.getDesc(), PartsDB.DESCLEN, true));
            System.out.print(" | ");
            System.out.print(format(""+part.getQty(), 10, false));
            System.out.print(" | ");
            String s = part.getUnitCost()/100+"."+part.getUnitCost()%100;
            if (s.charAt(s.length()-2) == '.') s += "0";
            System.out.println(format(s, 10, false));
         }
         System.out.println("Number of records = "+pdb.numRecs());
         System.out.println();
      }
      static String format(String value, int maxWidth, boolean leftAlign)
      {
         StringBuffer sb = new StringBuffer();
         int len = value.length();
         if (len > maxWidth)
         {
            len = maxWidth;
            value = value.substring(0, len);
         }
         if (leftAlign)
```

```
    {
        sb.append(value);
        for (int i = 0; i < maxWidth-len; i++)
            sb.append(" ");
    }
    else
    {
        for (int i = 0; i < maxWidth-len; i++)
            sb.append(" ");
        sb.append(value);
    }
    return sb.toString();
    }
}
```

Listing 8-7's main() method first instantiates PartsDB with parts.db as the name of the database file. When this file has no records, numRecs() returns 0 and several records are appended to the file via the append() method.

main() next dumps the five records stored in parts.db to the standard output device, updates the unit cost in the record whose number is 1, once again dumps these records to the standard output device to show this change, and closes the database.

Note I store unit cost values as integer-based penny amounts. For example, I specify literal 1995 to represent 1995 pennies, or $19.95. If I were to use java.math.BigDecimal objects to store currency values, I would have to refactor PartsDB to take advantage of object serialization, and I am not prepared to do that right now. (I discuss object serialization later in this chapter.)

---

main() relies on a dumpRecords() helper method to dump these records, and dumpRecords() relies on a format() helper method to format field values so that they can be presented in properly aligned columns. The following output reveals this alignment:

```
1-9009-3323-4x     | Wiper Blade Micro Edge    |   30 |     24.68
1-3233-44923-7j    | Parking Brake Cable       |    5 |     14.39
2-3399-6693-2m     | Halogen Bulb H4 55/60W     |   22 |      8.13
2-599-2029-6k      | Turbo Oil Line O-Ring     |   26 |      1.55
3-1299-3299-9u     | Air Pump Electric         |    9 |    202.00
Number of records = 5

1-9009-3323-4x     | Wiper Blade Micro Edge    |   30 |     24.68
1-3233-44923-7j    | Parking Brake Cable       |    5 |     19.95
2-3399-6693-2m     | Halogen Bulb H4 55/60W     |   22 |      8.13
2-599-2029-6k      | Turbo Oil Line O-Ring     |   26 |      1.55
3-1299-3299-9u     | Air Pump Electric         |    9 |    202.00
Number of records = 5
```

Listing 8-7 relies on the try-with-resources statement to simplify the code—notice try (PartsDB pdb = new PartsDB("parts.db")). To observe a suppressed exception, uncomment the throw statement in

Listing 8-6's close() method (make sure to comment out raf.close(); in that method or the compiler will complain about unreachable code), and uncomment the throw statement in Listing 8-7's try block. This time, when you run the application, you'll notice the following two lines at the end of the output:

```
java.io.IOException: I/O error
Suppressed = java.io.IOException: cannot close raf
```

And there you have it: a simple flat file database. Despite its lack of support for advanced database features such as transaction management, a flat file database might be all that your application requires.

■ **Note** To learn more about flat file databases, check out Wikipedia's "Flat file database" entry (http://en.wikipedia.org/wiki/Flat_file_database).

Streams

Along with File and RandomAccessFile, Java uses streams to perform I/O operations. A *stream* is an ordered sequence of bytes of arbitrary length. Bytes flow over an *output stream* from an application to a destination, and flow over an *input stream* from a source to an application. Figure 8-2 illustrates these flows.

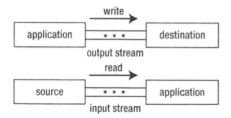

Figure 8-2. Conceptualizing output and input streams as flows.

■ **Note** Java's use of *stream* is analogous to saying "stream of water", "stream of electrons", and so on.

Java recognizes various stream destinations; for example, byte arrays, files, screens, and *sockets* (network endpoints). Java also recognizes various stream sources. Examples include byte arrays, files, keyboards, and sockets. (I discuss sockets in Chapter 9.)

Stream Classes Overview

The java.io package provides several output stream and input stream classes that are descendents of the abstract OutputStream and InputStream classes. Figure 8-3 reveals the hierarchy of output stream classes.

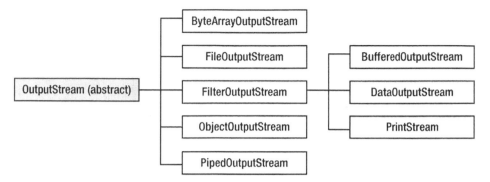

Figure 8-3. All output stream classes except for PrintStream are denoted by their OutputStream suffixes.

Figure 8-4 reveals the hierarchy of input stream classes.

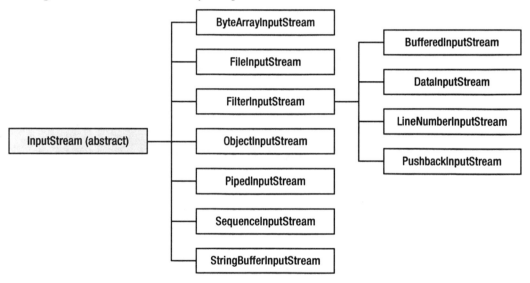

Figure 8-4. LineNumberInputStream and StringBufferInputStream are deprecated.

LineNumberInputStream and StringBufferInputStream have been deprecated because they don't support different character encodings, a topic I discuss later in this chapter. LineNumberReader and StringReader are their replacements. (I discuss readers later in this chapter.)

■ **Note** PrintStream is another class that should be deprecated because it doesn't support different character encodings; PrintWriter is its replacement. However, it's doubtful that Oracle will deprecate this class because

PrintStream is the type of the System class's out and err class fields; too much legacy code depends upon this fact.

Other Java packages provide additional output stream and input stream classes. For example, java.util.zip provides five output stream classes that compress uncompressed data into various formats, and five matching input stream classes that uncompress compressed data from the same formats:

- CheckedOutputStream
- CheckedInputStream
- DeflaterOutputStream
- DeflaterInputStream
- GZIPOutputStream
- GZIPInputStream
- InflaterOutputStream
- InflaterInputStream
- ZipOutputStream
- ZipInputStream

For brevity, I focus only on the OutputStream, InputStream, FileOutputStream, FileInputStream, FilterOutputStream, FilterInputStream, BufferedOutputStream, BufferedInputStream, DataOutputStream, DataInputStream, ObjectOutputStream, ObjectInputStream, and PrintStream classes in this chapter. Appendix C discusses additional stream classes.

OutputStream and InputStream

Java provides the OutputStream and InputStream classes for performing stream I/O. OutputStream is the superclass of all output stream subclasses. Table 8-7 describes OutputStream's methods.

Table 8-7. OutputStream Methods

Method	Description
void close()	Close this output stream and release any system resources associated with the stream. This method throws IOException when an I/O error occurs. (Because OutputStream implements Closeable, you can use output streams with the try-with-resources statement.)
void flush()	Flush this output stream by writing any buffered output bytes to the destination. If the intended destination of this output stream is an abstraction provided by the underlying

	platform (for example, a file), flushing the stream only guarantees that bytes previously written to the stream are passed to the underlying platform for writing; it doesn't guarantee that they're actually written to a physical device such as a disk drive. This method throws IOException when an I/O error occurs.
void write(byte[] b)	Write b.length bytes from byte array b to this output stream. In general, write(b) behaves as if you specified write(b, 0, b.length). This method throws NullPointerException when b is null, and IOException when an I/O error occurs.
void write(byte[] b, int off, int len)	Write len bytes from byte array b starting at offset off to this output stream. This method throws NullPointerException when b is null; java.lang.IndexOutOfBoundsException when off is negative, len is negative, or off+len is greater than b.length; and IOException when an I/O error occurs.
void write(int b)	Write byte b to this output stream. Only the eight low-order bits are written; the 24 high-order bits are ignored. This method throws IOException when an I/O error occurs.

The flush() method is useful in a long-running application where you need to save changes every so often; for example, the previously mentioned text-editor application that saves changes to a temporary file every few minutes. Remember that flush() only flushes bytes to the platform; doing so doesn't necessarily result in the platform flushing these bytes to the disk.

Note The close() method automatically flushes the output stream. When an application ends before close() is called, the output stream is automatically closed and its data is flushed.

InputStream is the superclass of all input stream subclasses. Table 8-8 describes InputStream's methods.

Table 8-8. InputStream Methods

Method	Description
int available()	Return an estimate of the number of bytes that can be read from this input stream via the next read() method call (or skipped over via skip()) without blocking the calling thread. This method throws IOException when an I/O error occurs. It's never correct to use this method's return value to allocate a buffer for holding all the stream's data because a subclass might not return the total size of the stream.

void close()	Close this input stream and release any system resources associated with the stream. This method throws IOException when an I/O error occurs. (Because InputStream implements Closeable, you can use input streams with the try-with-resources statement.)
void mark(int readlimit)	Mark the current position in this input stream. A subsequent call to reset() repositions this stream to the last marked position so that subsequent read operations reread the same bytes. The readlimit argument tells this input stream to allow that many bytes to be read before invalidating this mark (so that the stream cannot be reset to the marked position).
boolean markSupported()	Return true when this input stream supports mark() and reset(); otherwise, return false.
int read()	Read and return (as an int in the range 0 to 255) the next byte from this input stream, or return -1 when the end of the stream is reached. This method blocks until input is available, the end of the stream is detected, or an exception is thrown. It throws IOException when an I/O error occurs.
int read(byte[] b)	Read some number of bytes from this input stream and store them in byte array b. Return the number of bytes actually read (which might be less than b's length but is never more than this length), or return -1 when the end of the stream is reached (no byte is available to read). This method blocks until input is available, the end of the stream is detected, or an exception is thrown. It throws NullPointerException when b is null, and IOException when an I/O error occurs.
int read(byte[] b, int off, int len)	Read no more than len bytes from this input stream and store them in byte array b, starting at the offset specified by off. Return the number of bytes actually read (which might be less than len but is never more than len), or return -1 when the end of the stream is reached (no byte is available to read). This method blocks until input is available, the end of the stream is detected, or an exception is thrown. It throws NullPointerException when b is null; IndexOutOfBoundsException when off is negative, len is negative, or len is greater than b.length-off; and IOException when an I/O error occurs.
void reset()	Reposition this input stream to the position at the time mark() was last called. This method throws IOException when this input stream has not been marked or the mark has been invalidated.

`long skip(long n)`	Skip over and discard n bytes of data from this input stream. This method might skip over some smaller number of bytes (possibly zero); for example, when the end of the file is reached before n bytes have been skipped. The actual number of bytes skipped is returned. When n is negative, no bytes are skipped. This method throws IOException when this input stream doesn't support skipping or when some other I/O error occurs.

InputStream subclasses such as ByteArrayInputStream support marking the current read position in the input stream via the mark() method, and later return to that position via the reset() method.

■ **Caution** Don't forget to call markSupported() to find out if the stream subclass supports mark() and reset().

FileOutputStream and FileInputStream

Files are common stream destinations and sources. The concrete FileOutputStream class lets you write a stream of bytes to a file; the concrete FileInputStream class lets you read a stream of bytes from a file.

FileOutputStream subclasses OutputStream and declares five constructors for creating file output streams. For example, FileOutputStream(String name) creates a file output stream to the existing file identified by name. This constructor throws FileNotFoundException when the file doesn't exist and cannot be created, it is a directory rather than a normal file, or the file cannot be otherwise opened for output.

The following example uses FileOutputStream(String name) to create a file output stream with employee.dat as its destination:

```
FileOutputStream fos = new FileOutputStream("employee.dat");
```

■ **Tip** FileOutputStream(String name) overwrites an existing file. To append data instead of overwriting existing content, call a FileOutputStream constructor that includes a boolean append parameter and pass true to this parameter.

FileInputStream subclasses InputStream and declares three constructors for creating file input streams. For example, FileInputStream(String name) creates a file input stream from the existing file identified by name. This constructor throws FileNotFoundException when the file doesn't exist, it is a directory rather than a normal file, or there is some other reason for why the file cannot be opened for input.

The following example uses FileInputStream(String name) to create a file input stream with employee.dat as its source:

```
FileInputStream fis = new FileInputStream("employee.dat");
```

Listing 8-8 presents the source code to a DumpFileInHex application that uses FileOutputStream and FileInputStream to create a file that contains a hexadecimal representation of another file.

Listing 8-8. Creating a hexadecimal representation of a file

```
import java.io.FileInputStream;
import java.io.FileOutputStream;
import java.io.IOException;

class DumpFileInHex
{
    final static String LINE_SEPARATOR = System.getProperty("line.separator");
    public static void main(String[] args)
    {
        if (args.length != 1)
        {
            System.err.println("usage: java DumpFileInHex pathname");
            return;
        }
        String dest = args[0]+".hex";
        try (FileInputStream fis = new FileInputStream(args[0]);
             FileOutputStream fos = new FileOutputStream(dest))
        {
            StringBuffer sb = new StringBuffer();
            int offset = 0;
            int ch;
            while ((ch = fis.read()) != -1)
            {
                if ((offset%16) == 0)
                {
                    writeStr(fos, toHexStr(offset, 8));
                    fos.write(' ');
                }
                writeStr(fos, toHexStr(ch, 2));
                fos.write(' ');
                if (ch < 32 || ch > 127)
                    sb.append('.');
                else
                    sb.append((char) ch);
                if ((++offset%16) == 0)
                {
                    writeStr(fos, sb.toString()+LINE_SEPARATOR);
                    sb.setLength(0);
                }
            }
            if (sb.length() != 0)
            {
                for (int i = 0; i < 16-sb.length(); i++)
                    writeStr(fos, "   ");
                writeStr(fos, sb.toString()+LINE_SEPARATOR);
            }
        }
```

```
        catch (IOException ioe)
        {
            System.err.println("I/O error: "+ioe.getMessage());
        }
    }
    static String toHexStr(int value, int fieldWidth)
    {
        StringBuffer sb = new StringBuffer(Integer.toHexString(value));
        sb.reverse();
        int len = sb.length();
        for (int i = 0; i < fieldWidth-len; i++)
            sb.append('0');
        sb.reverse();
        return sb.toString();
    }
    static void writeStr(FileOutputStream fos, String s) throws IOException
    {
        for (int i = 0; i < s.length(); i++)
            fos.write(s.charAt(i));
    }
}
```

Listing 8-8's DumpFileInHex class first declares a LINE_SEPARATOR constant that contains the value of the line.separator system property. This constant's value is output to end the current text line and start a new text line. Because different platforms provide different line separators (e.g., newline on Unix/Linux or carriage return followed by newline on Windows), outputting LINE_SEPARATOR ensures maximum portability.

DumpFileInHex next presents its main() method, whose first task is to ensure that only a single command-line argument (identifying the input file) has been specified. Assuming that this is the case, main() next creates the name of the output file by appending .hex to the value of the command-line argument.

Continuing, main() presents a try-with-resources statement that initially opens the input file and creates the output file. The try block then employs a while loop to read each byte from the input file and write that byte's hexadecimal representation and literal value to the output file, with the help of toHexStr() and writeStr() methods:

- toHexStr() ensures that leading zeros are prepended to a hexadecimal value string to fit a field width. For example, if a hexadecimal value must occupy exactly eight field positions, and if its length is less than 8, leading 0s are prepended to the string. (Although Java provides the java.util.Formatter class to handle this task, toHexStr() will have to suffice for now because I don't discuss Formatter until Appendix C.)

- writeStr() writes a string of 8-bit characters to the file output stream. Ordinarily, you would not create such a method because it ignores different character sets (discussed later in this chapter). However, character sets are not an issue with this example.

After compiling this listing (javac DumpFileInHex.java), suppose you want to create a hexadecimal representation of the resulting DumpFileInHex.class file. You can accomplish this task by executing java DumpFileInHex DumpFileInHex.class. If all goes well, this command line creates a DumpFileInHex.class.hex file. The first part of this file is shown below:

```
00000000 ca fe ba be 00 00 00 33 00 88 0a 00 29 00 42 09 .......3....).B.
00000010 00 43 00 44 08 00 45 0a 00 46 00 47 07 00 48 0a .C.D..E..F.G..H.
00000020 00 05 00 42 0a 00 05 00 49 08 00 4a 0a 00 05 00 ...B....I..J....
00000030 4b 07 00 4c 0a 00 0a 00 4d 07 00 4e 0a 00 0c 00 K..L....M..N....
00000040 4d 07 00 4f 0a 00 0e 00 42 0a 00 0a 00 50 0a 00 M..O....B....P..
00000050 28 00 51 0a 00 28 00 52 0a 00 0c 00 53 0a 00 0e (.Q..(.R....S...
00000060 00 54 0a 00 0e 00 4b 09 00 28 00 55 0a 00 0e 00 .T....K..(.U....
00000070 56 0a 00 0e 00 57 08 00 58 0a 00 0c 00 59 07 00 V....W..X....Y..
00000080 5a 0a 00 1b 00 5b 0a 00 0a 00 59 07 00 5c 08 00 Z....[....Y..\..
00000090 5d 0a 00 1e 00 5e 0a 00 5f 00 60 0a 00 0e 00 4d ]....^.._.`....M
000000a0 0a 00 0e 00 61 0a 00 62 00 57 0a 00 62 00 63 08 ....a..b.W..b.c.
000000b0 00 64 0a 00 43 00 65 07 00 66 07 00 67 01 00 0e .d..C.e..f..g...
000000c0 4c 49 4e 45 5f 53 45 50 41 52 41 54 4f 52 01 00 LINE_SEPARATOR..
000000d0 12 4c 6a 61 76 61 2f 6c 61 6e 67 2f 53 74 72 69 .Ljava/lang/Stri
000000e0 6e 67 3b 01 00 06 3c 69 6e 69 74 3e 01 00 03 28 ng;...<init>...(
000000f0 29 56 01 00 04 43 6f 64 65 01 00 0f 4c 69 6e 65 )V...Code...Line
```

FilterOutputStream and FilterInputStream

File streams pass bytes unchanged to their destinations. Java also supports *filter streams* that buffer, compress/uncompress, encrypt/decrypt, or otherwise manipulate an input stream's byte sequence before it reaches its destination.

A *filter output stream* takes the data passed to its write() methods (the input stream), filters it, and writes the filtered data to an underlying output stream, which might be another filter output stream or a destination output stream such as a file output stream.

Filter output streams are created from subclasses of the concrete FilterOutputStream class, an OutputStream subclass. FilterOutputStream declares a single FilterOutputStream(OutputStream out) constructor that creates a filter output stream built on top of out, the underlying output stream.

Listing 8-9 reveals that it's easy to subclass FilterOutputStream. At minimum, declare a constructor that passes its OutputStream argument to FilterOutputStream's constructor and override FilterOutputStream's void write(int b) method.

Listing 8-9. Scrambling a stream of bytes

```java
import java.io.FilterOutputStream;
import java.io.IOException;
import java.io.OutputStream;

class ScrambledOutputStream extends FilterOutputStream
{
    private int[] map;
    ScrambledOutputStream(OutputStream out, int[] map)
    {
        super(out);
        if (map == null)
            throw new NullPointerException("map is null");
        if (map.length != 256)
            throw new IllegalArgumentException("map.length != 256");
        this.map = map;
    }
    @Override
```

```
    public void write(int b) throws IOException
    {
        out.write(map[b]);
    }
}
```

Listing 8-9 presents a ScrambledOutputStream class that performs trivial encryption on its input stream by scrambling the input stream's bytes via a remapping operation. Its constructor takes a pair of arguments:

- out identifies the output stream on which to write the scrambled bytes.

- map identifies an array of 256 byte integer values to which input stream bytes map.

The constructor first passes its out argument to the FilterOutputStream parent via a super(out) call. It then verifies its map argument's integrity (map must be nonnull and have a length of 256—a byte stream offers exactly 256 bytes to map) before saving map.

The write() method is trivial: it calls the underlying output stream's write() method with the byte to which argument b maps. FilterOutputStream declares out to be protected (for performance), which is why I can directly access this field.

▪ **Note** It's only essential to override write(int) because FilterOutputStream's other two write() methods are implemented in terms of this method.

Listing 8-10 presents the source code to a Scramble application for experimenting with scrambling a source file's bytes via ScrambledOutputStream and writing these scrambled bytes to a destination file.

Listing 8-10. Scrambling a file's bytes

```
import java.io.FileInputStream;
import java.io.FileOutputStream;
import java.io.IOException;

import java.util.Random;

class Scramble
{
    public static void main(String[] args)
    {
        if (args.length != 2)
        {
            System.err.println("usage: java Scramble srcpath destpath");
            return;
        }
        try (FileInputStream fis = new FileInputStream(args[0]);
             ScrambledOutputStream sos =
                 new ScrambledOutputStream(new FileOutputStream(args[1]),
                                           makeMap()))
```

```
        {
            int b;
            while ((b = fis.read()) != -1)
                sos.write(b);
        }
        catch (IOException ioe)
        {
            ioe.printStackTrace();
        }
    }
    static int[] makeMap()
    {
        int[] map = new int[256];
        for (int i = 0; i < map.length; i++)
            map[i] = i;
        // Shuffle map.
        Random r = new Random(0);
        for (int i = 0; i < map.length; i++)
        {
            int n = r.nextInt(map.length);
            int temp = map[i];
            map[i] = map[n];
            map[n] = temp;
        }
        return map;
    }
}
```

Scramble's main() method first verifies the number of command-line arguments: the first argument identifies the source path of the file with unscrambled content; the second argument identifies the destination path of the file that stores scrambled content.

Assuming that two command-line arguments have been specified, main() instantiates FileInputStream, creating a file input stream that's connected to the file identified by args[0].

Continuing, main() instantiates FileOutputStream, creating a file output stream that's connected to the file identified by args[1]. It then instantiates ScrambledOutputStream, passing the FileOutputStream instance to ScrambledOutputStream's constructor.

Note When a stream instance is passed to another stream class's constructor, the two streams are *chained together*. For example, the scrambled output stream is chained to the file output stream.

---

main() now enters a loop, reading bytes from the file input stream and writing them to the scrambled output stream by calling ScrambledOutputStream's void write(int b) method. This loop continues until FileInputStream's int read() method returns -1 (end of file).

The try-with-resources statement closes the file input stream and scrambled output stream by calling their close() methods. It doesn't call the file output stream's close() method because FilterOutputStream automatically calls the underlying output stream's close() method.

The makeMap() method is responsible for creating the map array that's passed to ScrambledOutputStream's constructor. The idea is to populate the array with all 256 byte integer values, storing them in random order.

Note I pass 0 as the seed argument when creating the java.util.Random object in order to return a predictable sequence of random numbers. I need to use the same sequence of random numbers when creating the complementary map array in the Unscramble application, which I will present shortly. Unscrambling will not work without the same sequence.

Suppose you have a simple 15-byte file named hello.txt that contains "Hello, World!" (followed by a carriage return and a line feed). When you execute java Scramble hello.txt hello.out on an XP platform, you'll observe Figure 8-5's scrambled output.

Figure 8-5. Different fonts yield different-looking scrambled output.

A *filter input stream* takes the data obtained from its underlying input stream, which might be another filter input stream or a source input stream such as a file input stream, filters it, and makes this data available via its read() methods (the output stream).

Filter input streams are created from subclasses of the concrete FilterInputStream class, an InputStream subclass. FilterInputStream declares a single FilterInputStream(InputStream in) constructor that creates a filter input stream built on top of in, the underlying input stream.

Listing 8-11 shows that it's easy to subclass FilterInputStream. At minimum, declare a constructor that passes its InputStream argument to FilterInputStream's constructor and override FilterInputStream's int read() and int read(byte[] b, int off, int len) methods.

Listing 8-11. Unscrambling a stream of bytes

```
import java.io.FilterInputStream;
import java.io.InputStream;
import java.io.IOException;

class ScrambledInputStream extends FilterInputStream
{
   private int[] map;
   ScrambledInputStream(InputStream in, int[] map)
   {
      super(in);
      if (map == null)
         throw new NullPointerException("map is null");
      if (map.length != 256)
         throw new IllegalArgumentException("map.length != 256");
```

```
        this.map = map;
    }
    @Override
    public int read() throws IOException
    {
        int value = in.read();
        return (value == -1) ? -1 : map[value];
    }
    @Override
    public int read(byte[] b, int off, int len) throws IOException
    {
        int nBytes = in.read(b, off, len);
        if (nBytes <= 0)
            return nBytes;
        for (int i = 0; i < nBytes; i++)
            b[off+i] = (byte) map[off+i];
        return nBytes;
    }
}
```

Listing 8-11 presents a ScrambledInputStream class that performs trivial decryption on its underlying input stream by unscrambling the underlying input stream's scrambled bytes via a remapping operation.

The read() method first reads the scrambled byte from its underlying input stream. If the returned value is -1 (end of file), this value is returned to its caller. Otherwise, the byte is mapped to its unscrambled value, which is returned.

The read(byte[], int, int) method is similar to read(), but stores bytes read from the underlying input stream in a byte array, taking an offset into this array and a length (number of bytes to read) into account.

Once again, -1 might be returned from the underlying read() method call. If so, this value must be returned. Otherwise, each byte in the array is mapped to its unscrambled value, and the number of bytes read is returned.

■ **Note** It's only essential to override read() and read(byte[], int, int) because FilterInputStream's int read(byte[] b) method is implemented via the latter method.

Listing 8-12 presents the source code to an UnScramble application for experimenting with ScrambledInputStream by unscrambling a source file's bytes and writing these unscrambled bytes to a destination file.

Listing 8-12. Unscrambling a file's bytes

```
import java.io.FileInputStream;
import java.io.FileOutputStream;
import java.io.IOException;

import java.util.Random;
```

```
class Unscramble
{
   public static void main(String[] args)
   {
      if (args.length != 2)
      {
         System.err.println("usage: java Unscramble srcpath destpath");
         return;
      }
      try (FileOutputStream fos = new FileOutputStream(args[1]);
           ScrambledInputStream sis =
              new ScrambledInputStream(new FileInputStream(args[0]),
                                       makeMap()))

      {
         int b;
         while ((b = sis.read()) != -1)
            fos.write(b);
      }
      catch (IOException ioe)
      {
         ioe.printStackTrace();
      }
   }
   static int[] makeMap()
   {
      int[] map = new int[256];
      for (int i = 0; i < map.length; i++)
         map[i] = i;
      // Shuffle map.
      Random r = new Random(0);
      for (int i = 0; i < map.length; i++)
      {
         int n = r.nextInt(map.length);
         int temp = map[i];
         map[i] = map[n];
         map[n] = temp;
      }
      int[] temp = new int[256];
      for (int i = 0; i < temp.length; i++)
         temp[map[i]] = i;
      return temp;
   }
}
```

Unscramble's main() method first verifies the number of command-line arguments: the first argument identifies the source path of the file with scrambled content; the second argument identifies the destination path of the file that stores unscrambled content.

Assuming that two command-line arguments have been specified, main() instantiates FileOutputStream, creating a file output stream that's connected to the file identified by args[1].

Continuing, `main()` instantiates `FileInputStream`, creating a file input stream that's connected to the file identified by `args[0]`. It then instantiates `ScrambledInputStream`, passing the `FileInputStream` instance to `ScrambledInputStream`'s constructor.

Note When a stream instance is passed to another stream class's constructor, the two streams are *chained together*. For example, the scrambled input stream is chained to the file input stream.

`main()` now enters a loop, reading bytes from the scrambled input stream and writing them to the file output stream. This loop continues until `ScrambledInputStream`'s `read()` method returns -1 (end of file).

The try-with-resources statement closes the file output stream and scrambled input stream by calling their `close()` methods. It doesn't call the file input stream's `close()` method because `FilterInputStream` automatically calls the underlying input stream's `close()` method.

The `makeMap()` method is responsible for creating the map array that's passed to `ScrambledInputStream`'s constructor. The idea is to duplicate Listing 8-10's map array and then invert it so that unscrambling can be performed.

Continuing from the previous `hello.txt`/`hello.out` example, execute `java Unscramble hello.out hello.bak` and you'll see the same unscrambled content in `hello.bak` that's present in `hello.txt`.

BufferedOutputStream and BufferedInputStream

`FileOutputStream` and `FileInputStream` have a performance problem. Each file output stream `write()` method call and file input stream `read()` method call results in a call to one of the underlying platform's native methods, and these native method calls slow down I/O. (I discuss native methods in Appendix C.)

The concrete `BufferedOutputStream` and `BufferedInputStream` filter stream classes improve performance by minimizing underlying output stream `write()` and underlying input stream `read()` method calls. Instead, calls to `BufferedOutputStream`'s `write()` and `BufferedInputStream`'s `read()` methods take Java buffers into account:

- When a write buffer is full, `write()` calls the underlying output stream `write()` method to empty the buffer. Subsequent calls to `BufferedOutputStream`'s `write()` methods store bytes in this buffer until it's once again full.

- When the read buffer is empty, `read()` calls the underlying input stream `read()` method to fill the buffer. Subsequent calls to `BufferedInputStream`'s `read()` methods return bytes from this buffer until it's once again empty.

`BufferedOutputStream` declares the following constructors:

- `BufferedOutputStream(OutputStream out)` creates a buffered output stream that streams its output to `out`. An internal buffer is created to store bytes written to `out`.

- `BufferedOutputStream(OutputStream out, int size)` creates a buffered output stream that streams its output to `out`. An internal buffer of length `size` is created to store bytes written to `out`.

The following example chains a BufferedOutputStream instance to a FileOutputStream instance. Subsequent write() method calls on the BufferedOutputStream instance buffer bytes and occasionally result in internal write() method calls on the encapsulated FileOutputStream instance:

```
FileOutputStream fos = new FileOutputStream("employee.dat");
BufferedOutputStream bos = new BufferedOutputStream(fos); // Chain bos to fos.
bos.write(0); // Write to employee.dat through the buffer.
// Additional write() method calls.
bos.close(); // This method call internally calls fos's close() method.
```

BufferedInputStream declares the following constructors:

- BufferedInputStream(InputStream in) creates a buffered input stream that streams its input from in. An internal buffer is created to store bytes read from in.

- BufferedInputStream(InputStream in, int size) creates a buffered input stream that streams its input from in. An internal buffer of length size is created to store bytes read from in.

The following example chains a BufferedInputStream instance to a FileInputStream instance. Subsequent read() method calls on the BufferedInputStream instance unbuffer bytes and occasionally result in internal read() method calls on the encapsulated FileInputStream instance:

```
FileInputStream fis = new FileInputStream("employee.dat");
BufferedInputStream bis = new BufferedInputStream(fis); // Chain bis to fis.
int ch = bis.read(); // Read employee.dat through the buffer.
// Additional read() method calls.
bis.close(); // This method call internally calls fis's close() method.
```

DataOutputStream and DataInputStream

FileOutputStream and FileInputStream are useful for writing and reading bytes and arrays of bytes. However, they provide no support for writing and reading primitive type values (such as integers) and strings.

For this reason, Java provides the concrete DataOutputStream and DataInputStream filter stream classes. Each class overcomes this limitation by providing methods to write or read primitive type values and strings in a platform-independent way:

- Integer values are written and read in *big-endian format* (the most significant byte comes first). Check out Wikipedia's "Endianness" entry (http://en.wikipedia.org/wiki/Endianness) to learn about the concept of *endianness*.

- Floating-point and double precision floating-point values are written and read according to the IEEE 754 standard, which specifies four bytes per floating-point value and eight bytes per double precision floating-point value.

- Strings are written and read according to a modified version of *UTF-8*, a variable-length encoding standard for efficiently storing two-byte Unicode characters. Check out Wikipedia's "UTF-8" entry (http://en.wikipedia.org/wiki/Utf-8) to learn more about UTF-8.

DataOutputStream declares a single DataOutputStream(OutputStream out) constructor. Because this class implements the DataOutput interface, DataOutputStream also provides access to the same-named write methods as provided by RandomAccessFile.

DataInputStream declares a single DataInputStream(InputStream in) constructor. Because this class implements the DataInput interface, DataInputStream also provides access to the same-named read methods as provided by RandomAccessFile.

Listing 8-13 presents the source code to a DataStreamsDemo application that uses a DataOutputStream instance to write multibyte values to a FileOutputStream instance, and uses DataInputStream to read multibyte values from a FileInputStream instance.

Listing 8-13. Outputting and then inputting a stream of multibyte values

```java
import java.io.DataInputStream;
import java.io.DataOutputStream;
import java.io.FileInputStream;
import java.io.FileOutputStream;
import java.io.IOException;

class DataStreamsDemo
{
   final static String FILENAME = "values.dat";
   public static void main(String[] args)
   {
      try (DataOutputStream dos =
              new DataOutputStream(new FileOutputStream(FILENAME)))
      {
         dos.writeInt(1995);
         dos.writeUTF("Saving this String in modified UTF-8 format!");
         dos.writeFloat(1.0F);
      }
      catch (IOException ioe)
      {
         System.err.println("I/O error: "+ioe.getMessage());
      }
      try (DataInputStream dis =
              new DataInputStream(new FileInputStream(FILENAME)))
      {
         System.out.println(dis.readInt());
         System.out.println(dis.readUTF());
         System.out.println(dis.readFloat());
      }
      catch (IOException ioe)
      {
         System.err.println("I/O error: "+ioe.getMessage());
      }
   }
}
```

DataStreamsDemo creates a file named values.dat, calls DataOutputStream methods to write an integer, a string, and a floating-point value to this file, and calls DataInputStream methods to read back these values. Unsurprisingly, it generates the following output:

```
1995
Saving this String in modified UTF-8 format!
1.0
```

■ **Caution** When reading a file of values written by a sequence of DataOutputStream method calls, make sure to use the same method-call sequence. Otherwise, you're bound to end up with erroneous data and, in the case of the readUTF() methods, thrown instances of the java.io.UTFDataFormatException class (a subclass of IOException).

Object Serialization and Deserialization

Java provides the DataOutputStream and DataInputStream classes to stream primitive type values and String objects. However, you cannot use these classes to stream non-String objects. Instead, you must use object serialization and deserialization to stream objects of arbitrary types.

Object serialization is a JVM mechanism for *serializing* object state into a stream of bytes. Its *deserialization* counterpart is a JVM mechanism for *deserializing* this state from a byte stream.

■ **Note** An object's state consists of instance fields that store primitive type values and/or references to other objects. When an object is serialized, the objects that are part of this state are also serialized (unless you prevent them from being serialized), their objects are serialized unless prevented, and so on.

Java supports three forms of serialization and deserialization: default serialization and deserialization, custom serialization and deserialization, and externalization.

Default Serialization and Deserialization

Default serialization and deserialization is the easiest form to use but offers little control over how objects are serialized and deserialized. Although Java handles most of the work on your behalf, there are a couple of tasks that you must perform.

Your first task is to have the class of the object that's to be serialized implement the java.io.Serializable interface (directly, or indirectly via the class's superclass). The rationale for implementing Serializable is to avoid unlimited serialization.

■ **Note** Serializable is an empty marker interface (there are no methods to implement) that a class implements to tell the JVM that it's okay to serialize the class's objects. When the serialization mechanism encounters an object whose class doesn't implement `Serializable`, it throws an instance of the `java.io.NotSerializableException` class (an indirect subclass of `IOException`).

Unlimited serialization is the process of serializing an entire *object graph* (all objects that are reachable from a starting object). Java doesn't support unlimited serialization for the following reasons:

- *Security.* If Java automatically serialized an object containing sensitive information (such as a password or a credit card number), it would be easy for a hacker to discover this information and wreak havoc. It's better to give the developer a choice to prevent this from happening.

- *Performance.* Serialization leverages the Reflection API, which I introduced in Chapter 4. In that chapter, you learned that reflection slows down application performance. Unlimited serialization could really hurt an application's performance.

- *Objects not amenable to serialization.* Some objects exist only in the context of a running application and it's meaningless to serialize them. For example, a file stream object that's deserialized no longer represents a connection to a file.

Listing 8-14 declares an `Employee` class that implements the `Serializable` interface to tell the JVM that it's okay to serialize `Employee` objects.

Listing 8-14. Implementing Serializable

```
class Employee implements java.io.Serializable
{
    private String name;
    private int age;
    Employee(String name, int age)
    {
        this.name = name;
        this.age = age;
    }
    String getName() { return name; }
    int getAge() { return age; }
}
```

Because `Employee` implements `Serializable`, the serialization mechanism will not throw `NotSerializableException` when serializing an `Employee` object. Not only does `Employee` implement `Serializable`, the `String` class also implements this interface.

Your second task is to work with the `ObjectOutputStream` class and its void `writeObject(Object obj)` method to serialize an object, and the `OutputInputStream` class and its `Object readObject()` method to deserialize the object.

■ **Note** Although `ObjectOutputStream` extends `OutputStream` instead of `FilterOutputStream`, and although `ObjectInputStream` extends `InputStream` instead of `FilterInputStream`, these classes behave as filter streams.

Java provides the concrete `ObjectOutputStream` class to initiate the serialization of an object's state to an object output stream. This class declares an `ObjectOutputStream(OutputStream out)` constructor that chains the object output stream to the output stream specified by out.

When you pass an output stream reference to out, this constructor attempts to write a serialization header to that output stream. It throws `NullPointerException` when out is null, and `IOException` when an I/O error prevents it from writing this header.

`ObjectOutputStream` serializes an object via its `writeObject()` method. This method attempts to write information about obj's class followed by the values of obj's instance fields to the underlying output stream.

`writeObject()` doesn't serialize the contents of static fields. In contrast, it serializes the contents of all instance fields that are not explicitly prefixed with the `transient` reserved word. For example, consider the following field declaration:

```
public transient char[] password;
```

This declaration specifies `transient` to avoid serializing a password for some hacker to encounter. The JVM's serialization mechanism ignores any instance field that's marked `transient`.

`writeObject()` throws `IOException` or an instance of an `IOException` subclass when something goes wrong. For example, this method throws `NotSerializableException` when it encounters an object whose class doesn't implement `Serializable`.

■ **Note** Because `ObjectOutputStream` implements `DataOutput`, it also declares methods for writing primitive type values and strings to an object output stream.

Java provides the concrete `ObjectInputStream` class to initiate the deserialization of an object's state from an object input stream. This class declares an `ObjectInputStream(InputStream in)` constructor that chains the object input stream to the input stream specified by in.

When you pass an input stream reference to in, this constructor attempts to read a serialization header from that input stream. It throws `NullPointerException` when in is null, `IOException` when an I/O error prevents it from reading this header, and `java.io.StreamCorruptedException` (an indirect subclass of `IOException`) when the stream header is incorrect.

`ObjectInputStream` deserializes an object via its `readObject()` method. This method attempts to read information about obj's class followed by the values of obj's instance fields from the underlying input stream.

`readObject()` throws `java.lang.ClassNotFoundException`, `IOException`, or an instance of an `IOException` subclass when something goes wrong. For example, this method throws `java.io.OptionalDataException` when it encounters primitive values instead of objects.

■ **Note** Because ObjectInputStream implements DataInput, it also declares methods for reading primitive type values and strings from an object input stream.

Listing 8-15 presents an application that uses these classes to serialize and deserialize an instance of Listing 8-14's Employee class to and from an employee.dat file.

Listing 8-15. Serializing and deserializing an Employee object

```java
import java.io.FileInputStream;
import java.io.FileOutputStream;
import java.io.IOException;
import java.io.ObjectInputStream;
import java.io.ObjectOutputStream;

class SerializationDemo
{
   final static String FILENAME = "employee.dat";
   public static void main(String[] args)
   {
      try (ObjectOutputStream oos =
              new ObjectOutputStream(new FileOutputStream(FILENAME)))
      {
         Employee emp = new Employee("John Doe", 36);
         oos.writeObject(emp);
      }
      catch (IOException ioe)
      {
         System.err.println("I/O error: "+ioe.getMessage());
         return;
      }
      try (ObjectInputStream ois =
              new ObjectInputStream(new FileInputStream(FILENAME)))
      {
         Employee emp = (Employee) ois.readObject();
         System.out.println(emp.getName());
         System.out.println(emp.getAge());
      }
      catch (ClassNotFoundException cnfe)
      {
         System.err.println(cnfe.getMessage());
      }
      catch (IOException ioe)
      {
         System.err.println(ioe.getMessage());
      }
   }
}
```

Listing 8-15's `main()` method first instantiates `Employee` and serializes this instance via `writeObject()` to `employee.dat`. It then deserializes this instance from this file via `readObject()` and invokes the instance's `getName()` and `getAge()` methods. Along with `employee.dat`, you'll discover the following output when you run this application:

```
John Doe
36
```

There's no guarantee that the same class will exist when a serialized object is deserialized (perhaps an instance field has been deleted). During deserialization, this mechanism causes `readObject()` to throw an instance of `java.io.InvalidClassException` (an indirect subclass of `IOException`) when it detects a difference between the deserialized object and its class.

Every serialized object has an identifier. The deserialization mechanism compares the identifier of the object being deserialized with the serialized identifier of its class (all serializable classes are automatically given unique identifiers unless they explicitly specify their own identifiers) and causes `InvalidClassException` to be thrown when it detects a mismatch.

Perhaps you've added an instance field to a class, and you want the deserialization mechanism to set the instance field to a default value rather than have `readObject()` throw an `InvalidClassException` instance. (The next time you serialize the object, the new field's value will be written out.)

You can avoid the thrown `InvalidClassException` instance by adding a `static final long serialVersionUID = long integer value;` declaration to the class. The `long integer value` must be unique and is known as a *stream unique identifier (SUID)*.

During deserialization, the JVM will compare the deserialized object's SUID to its class's SUID. If they match, `readObject()` won't throw `InvalidClassException` when it encounters a *compatible class change* (e.g., adding an instance field). However, it will still throw this exception when it encounters an *incompatible class change* (e.g., changing an instance field's name or type).

■ **Note** Whenever you change a class in some way, you must calculate a new SUID and assign it to `serialVersionUID`.

The JDK provides a `serialver` tool for calculating the SUID. For example, to generate an SUID for Listing 8-14's `Employee` class, change to the directory containing `Employee.class` and execute `serialver Employee`. In response, `serialver` generates the following output, which you paste (except for `Employee:`) into `Employee.java`:

```
Employee:    static final long serialVersionUID = -67686341867699132481L;
```

The Windows version of `serialver` also provides a graphical user interface (GUI) that you might find more convenient to use. To access this GUI, specify `serialver -show`. When the GUI appears, enter `Employee` in the Full Class Name textfield and click the Show button, as demonstrated in Figure 8-6.

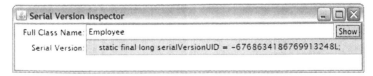

Figure 8-6. The `serialver` GUI reveals `Employee`'s SUID.

Custom Serialization and Deserialization

My previous discussion focused on default serialization and deserialization (with the exception of marking an instance field `transient` to prevent it from being included during serialization). However, situations arise where you need to customize these tasks.

For example, suppose you want to serialize instances of a class that doesn't implement `Serializable`. As a workaround, you subclass this other class, have the subclass implement `Serializable`, and forward subclass constructor calls to the superclass.

Although this workaround lets you serialize subclass objects, you cannot deserialize these serialized objects when the superclass doesn't declare a noargument constructor, which is required by the deserialization mechanism. Listing 8-16 demonstrates this problem.

Listing 8-16. Problematic deserialization

```java
import java.io.FileInputStream;
import java.io.FileOutputStream;
import java.io.ObjectInputStream;
import java.io.ObjectOutputStream;
import java.io.Serializable;

class Employee
{
   private String name;
   Employee(String name) { this.name = name; }
   @Override
   public String toString() { return name; }
}
class SerEmployee extends Employee implements Serializable
{
   SerEmployee(String name) { super(name); }
}
class SerializationDemo
{
   public static void main(String[] args)
   {
      try (ObjectOutputStream oos =
              new ObjectOutputStream(new FileOutputStream("employee.dat")))
      {
         SerEmployee se = new SerEmployee("John Doe");
         System.out.println(se);
         oos.writeObject(se);
         System.out.println("se object written to file");
      }
      catch (Exception e)
      {
         e.printStackTrace();
      }
      try (ObjectInputStream ois =
              new ObjectInputStream(new FileInputStream("employee.dat")))
      {
         Object o = ois.readObject();
```

```
            System.out.println("se object read from byte array");
        }
        catch (Exception e)
        {
            e.printStackTrace();
        }
    }
}
```

Listing 8-16's main() method instantiates SerEmployee with an employee name. This class's SerEmployee(String) constructor passes this argument to its Employee counterpart.

main() next calls Employee's toString() method indirectly via System.out.println(), to obtain this name, which is then output.

Continuing, main() serializes the SerEmployee instance to an employee.dat file via writeObject(). It then attempts to deserialize this object via readObject(), and this is where the trouble occurs as revealed by the following output:

```
John Doe
se object written to file
java.io.InvalidClassException: SerEmployee; SerEmployee; no valid constructor
        at java.io.ObjectStreamClass.checkDeserialize(ObjectStreamClass.java:730)
        at java.io.ObjectInputStream.readOrdinaryObject(ObjectInputStream.java:1751)
        at java.io.ObjectInputStream.readObject0(ObjectInputStream.java:1347)
        at java.io.ObjectInputStream.readObject(ObjectInputStream.java:369)
        at SerializationDemo.main(SerializationDemo.java:37)
Caused by: java.io.InvalidClassException: SerEmployee; no valid constructor
        at java.io.ObjectStreamClass.<init>(ObjectStreamClass.java:488)
        at java.io.ObjectStreamClass.lookup(ObjectStreamClass.java:327)
        at java.io.ObjectOutputStream.writeObject0(ObjectOutputStream.java:1130)
        at java.io.ObjectOutputStream.writeObject(ObjectOutputStream.java:346)
        at SerializationDemo.main(SerializationDemo.java:27)
```

This output reveals a thrown instance of the InvalidClassException class. This exception object was thrown during deserialization because Employee doesn't possess a noargument constructor.

We can overcome this problem by taking advantage of the wrapper class pattern that I presented in Chapter 2. Furthermore, we declare a pair of private methods in the subclass that the serialization and deserialization mechanisms look for and call.

Normally, the serialization mechanism writes out a class's instance fields to the underlying output stream. However, you can prevent this from happening by declaring a private void writeObject(ObjectOutputStream oos) method in that class.

When the serialization mechanism discovers this method, it calls the method instead of automatically outputting instance field values. The only values that are output are those explicitly output via the method.

Conversely, the deserialization mechanism assigns values to a class's instance fields that it reads from the underlying input stream. However, you can prevent this from happening by declaring a private void readObject(ObjectInputStream ois) method.

When the deserialization mechanism discovers this method, it calls the method instead of automatically assigning values to instance fields. The only values that are assigned to instance fields are those explicitly assigned via the method.

Because SerEmployee doesn't introduce any fields, and because Employee doesn't offer access to its internal fields (assume you don't have the source code for this class), what would a serialized SerEmployee object include?

Although we cannot serialize Employee's internal state, we can serialize the argument(s) passed to its constructors, such as the employee name.

Listing 8-17 reveals the refactored SerEmployee and SerializationDemo classes.

Listing 8-17. Solving problematic deserialization

```java
import java.io.FileInputStream;
import java.io.FileOutputStream;
import java.io.IOException;
import java.io.ObjectInputStream;
import java.io.ObjectOutputStream;
import java.io.Serializable;

class Employee
{
    private String name;
    Employee(String name) { this.name = name; }
    @Override
    public String toString() { return name; }
}
class SerEmployee implements Serializable
{
    private Employee emp;
    private String name;
    SerEmployee(String name)
    {
        this.name = name;
        emp = new Employee(name);
    }
    private void writeObject(ObjectOutputStream oos) throws IOException
    {
        oos.writeUTF(name);
    }
    private void readObject(ObjectInputStream ois)
        throws ClassNotFoundException, IOException
    {
        name = ois.readUTF();
        emp = new Employee(name);
    }
    @Override
    public String toString()
    {
        return name;
    }
}
class SerializationDemo
{
    public static void main(String[] args)
    {
        try (ObjectOutputStream oos =
                new ObjectOutputStream(new FileOutputStream("employee.dat")))
        {
```

```
            SerEmployee se = new SerEmployee("John Doe");
            System.out.println(se);
            oos.writeObject(se);
            System.out.println("se object written to file");
        }
        catch (Exception e)
        {
            e.printStackTrace();
        }
        try (ObjectInputStream ois =
                new ObjectInputStream(new FileInputStream("employee.dat")))
        {
            SerEmployee se = (SerEmployee) ois.readObject();
            System.out.println("se object read from file");
            System.out.println(se);
        }
        catch (Exception e)
        {
            e.printStackTrace();
        }
    }
}
```

SerEmployee's writeObject() and readObject() methods rely on DataOutput and DataInput methods: they don't need to call writeObject() and readObject() to perform their tasks.

When you run this application, it generates the following output:

```
John Doe
se object written to file
se object read from file
John Doe
```

The writeObject() and readObject() methods can be used to serialize/deserialize data items beyond the normal state (non-transient instance fields); for example, serializing/deserializing the contents of a static field.

However, before serializing or deserializing the additional data items, you must tell the serialization and deserialization mechanisms to serialize or deserialize the object's normal state. The following methods help you accomplish this task:

- ObjectOutputStream's defaultWriteObject() method outputs the object's normal state. Your writeObject() method first calls this method to output that state, and then outputs additional data items via ObjectOutputStream methods such as writeUTF().

- ObjectInputStream's defaultReadObject() method inputs the object's normal state. Your readObject() method first calls this method to input that state, and then inputs additional data items via ObjectInputStream methods such as readUTF().

Externalization

Along with default serialization/deserialization and custom serialization/deserialization, Java supports externalization. Unlike default/custom serialization/deserialization, *externalization* offers complete control over the serialization and deserialization tasks.

Note Externalization helps you improve the performance of the reflection-based serialization and deserialization mechanisms by giving you complete control over what fields are serialized and deserialized.

Java supports externalization via its java.io.Externalizable interface. This interface declares the following pair of public methods:

- void writeExternal(ObjectOutput out) saves the calling object's contents by calling various methods on the out object. This method throws IOException when an I/O error occurs. (java.io.ObjectOutput is a subinterface of DataOutput and is implemented by ObjectOutputStream.)

- void readExternal(ObjectInput in) restores the calling object's contents by calling various methods on the in object. This method throws IOException when an I/O error occurs, and ClassNotFoundException when the class of the object being restored cannot be found. (java.io.ObjectInput is a subinterface of DataInput and is implemented by ObjectInputStream.)

If a class implements Externalizable, its writeExternal() method is responsible for saving all field values that are to be saved. Also, its readExternal() method is responsible for restoring all saved field values and in the order they were saved.

Listing 8-18 presents a refactored version of Listing 8-14's Employee class to show you how to take advantage of externalization.

Listing 8-18. Refactoring Listing 8-14's Employee class to support externalization

```java
import java.io.Externalizable;
import java.io.IOException;
import java.io.ObjectInput;
import java.io.ObjectOutput;

class Employee implements Externalizable
{
    private String name;
    private int age;
    public Employee()
    {
        System.out.println("Employee() called");
    }
    Employee(String name, int age)
    {
        this.name = name;
```

```
      this.age = age;
   }
   String getName() { return name; }
   int getAge() { return age; }
   @Override
   public void readExternal(ObjectInput in)
      throws IOException, ClassNotFoundException
   {
      System.out.println("readExternal() called");
      name = in.readUTF();
      age = in.readInt();
   }
   @Override
   public void writeExternal(ObjectOutput out) throws IOException
   {
      System.out.println("writeExternal() called");
      out.writeUTF(name);
      out.writeInt(age);
   }
}
```

Employee declares a public Employee() constructor because each class that participates in externalization must declare a public noargument constructor. The deserialization mechanism calls this constructor to instantiate the object.

Caution The deserialization mechanism throws InvalidClassException with a "no valid constructor" message when it doesn't detect a public noargument constructor.

Initiate externalization by instantiating ObjectOutputStream and calling its writeObject() method, or by instantiating ObjectInputStream and calling its readObject() method.

Note When passing an object whose class (directly/indirectly) implements Externalizable to writeObject(), the writeObject()-initiated serialization mechanism writes only the identity of the object's class to the object output stream.

Suppose you compiled Listing 8-15's SerializationDemo.java source code and Listing 8-18's Employee.java source code in the same directory. Now suppose you executed java SerializationDemo. In response, you would observe the following output:

```
writeExternal() called
Employee() called
readExternal() called
John Doe
36
```

Before serializing an object, the serialization mechanism checks the object's class to see if it implements Externalizable. If so, the mechanism calls writeExternal(). Otherwise, it looks for a private writeObject(ObjectOutputStream) method, and calls this method if present. If this method isn't present, the mechanism performs default serialization, which includes only non-transient instance fields.

Before deserializing an object, the deserialization mechanism checks the object's class to see if it implements Externalizable. If so, the mechanism attempts to instantiate the class via the public noargument constructor. Assuming success, it calls readExternal().

If the object's class doesn't implement Externalizable, the deserialization mechanism looks for a private readObject(ObjectInputStream) method. If this method isn't present, the mechanism performs default deserialization, which includes only non-transient instance fields.

PrintStream

Of all the stream classes, PrintStream is an oddball: it should have been named PrintOutputStream for consistency with the naming convention. This filter output stream class writes string representations of input data items to the underlying output stream.

▧ **Note** PrintStream uses the default character encoding to convert a string's characters to bytes. (I'll discuss character encodings when I introduce you to writers and readers in the next section.) Because PrintStream doesn't support different character encodings, you should use the equivalent PrintWriter class instead of PrintStream. However, you need to know about PrintStream when working with System.out and System.err because these class fields are of type PrintStream.

PrintStream instances are print streams whose various print() and println() methods print string representations of integers, floating-point values, and other data items to the underlying output stream. Unlike the print() methods, println() methods append a line terminator to their output.

▧ **Note** The line terminator (also known as line separator) isn't necessarily the newline (also commonly referred to as line feed). Instead, to promote portability, the line separator is the sequence of characters defined by system property line.separator. On Windows platforms, System.getProperty("line.separator") returns the actual carriage return code (13), which is symbolically represented by \r, followed by the actual newline/line feed code (10), which is symbolically represented by \n. In contrast, System.getProperty("line.separator") returns only the actual newline/line feed code on Unix and Linux platforms.

The println() methods call their corresponding print() methods followed by the equivalent of the void println() method, which eventually results in line.separator's value being output. For example, void println(int x) outputs x's string representation and calls this method to output the line separator.

■ **Caution** Never hard-code the \n escape sequence in a literal string that you are going to output via a print() or println() method. Doing so isn't portable. For example, when Java executes System.out.print("first line\n"); followed by System.out.println("second line");, you'll see first line on one line followed by second line on a subsequent line when this output is viewed at the Windows command line. In contrast, you'll see first linesecond line when this output is viewed in the Windows Notepad application (which requires a carriage return/line feed sequence to terminate lines). When you need to output a blank line, the easiest way to do this is to call System.out.println();, which is why you find this method call scattered throughout my book. I confess that I don't always follow my own advice, so you might find instances of \n in literal strings being passed to System.out.print() or System.out.println() elsewhere in this book.

PrintStream offers two other features that you'll find useful:

- Unlike other output streams, a print stream never rethrows an IOException instance thrown from the underlying output stream. Instead, exceptional situations set an internal flag that can be tested by calling PrintStream's boolean checkError() method, which returns true to indicate a problem.

- PrintStream objects can be created to automatically flush their output to the underlying output stream. In other words, the flush() method is automatically called after a byte array is written, one of the println() methods is called, or a newline is written. The PrintStream instances assigned to System.out and System.err automatically flush their output to the underlying output stream.

Writers and Readers

Java's stream classes are good for streaming sequences of bytes, but they're not good for streaming sequences of characters because bytes and characters are two different things: a byte represents an 8-bit data item and a character represents a 16-bit data item. Also, Java's char and String types naturally handle characters instead of bytes.

More importantly, byte streams have no knowledge of *character sets* (sets of mappings between integer values [known as *code points*] and symbols, such as Unicode) and their *character encodings* (mappings between the members of a character set and sequences of bytes that encode these characters for efficiency, such as UTF-8).

If you need to stream characters, you should take advantage of Java's writer and reader classes, which were designed to support character I/O (they work with char instead of byte). Furthermore, the writer and reader classes take character encodings into account.

A BRIEF HISTORY OF CHARACTER SETS AND CHARACTER ENCODINGS

Early computers and programming languages were created mainly by English-speaking programmers in countries where English was the native language. They developed a standard mapping between code points 0 through 127 and the 128 commonly used characters in the English language (e.g., A-Z). The resulting character set/encoding was named *American Standard Code for Information Interchange (ASCII)*.

The problem with ASCII is that it's inadequate for most non-English languages. For example, ASCII doesn't support diacritical marks such as the cedilla used in the French language. Because a byte can represent a maximum of 256 different characters, developers around the world started creating different character sets/encodings that encoded the 128 ASCII characters, but also encoded extra characters to meet the needs of languages such as French, Greek, or Russian. Over the years, many legacy (and still important) files have been created whose bytes represent characters defined by specific character sets/encodings.

The International Organization for Standardization (ISO) and the International Electrotechnical Commission (IEC) have worked to standardize these eight-bit character sets/encodings under a joint umbrella standard called ISO/IEC 8859. The result is a series of substandards named ISO/IEC 8859-1, ISO/IEC 8859-2, and so on. For example, ISO/IEC 8859-1 (also known as Latin-1) defines a character set/encoding that consists of ASCII plus the characters covering most Western European countries. Also, ISO/IEC 8859-2 (also known as Latin-2) defines a similar character set/encoding covering Central and Eastern European countries.

Despite ISO's/IEC's best efforts, a plethora of character sets/encodings is still inadequate. For example, most character sets/encodings only allow you to create documents in a combination of English and one other language (or a small number of other languages). You cannot, for example, use an ISO/IEC character set/encoding to create a document using a combination of English, French, Turkish, Russian, and Greek characters.

This and other problems are being addressed by an international effort that has created and is continuing to develop *Unicode*, a single universal character set. Because Unicode characters are twice as big as ISO/IEC characters, Unicode uses one of several variable-length encoding schemes known as *Unicode Transformation Format (UTF)* to encode Unicode characters for efficiency. For example, UTF-8 encodes every character in the Unicode character set in one to four bytes (and is backward compatible with ASCII).

The terms *character set* and *character encoding* are often used interchangeably. They mean the same thing in the context of ISO/IEC character sets, where a code point is the encoding. However, these terms are different in the context of Unicode, where Unicode is the character set and UTF-8 is one of several possible character encodings for Unicode characters.

Writer and Reader Classes Overview

The java.io package provides several writer and reader classes that are descendents of the abstract Writer and Reader classes. Figure 8-7 reveals the hierarchy of writer classes.

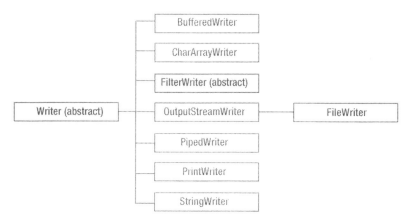

Figure 8-7. *Unlike* `FilterOutputStream`, `FilterWriter` *is abstract.*

Figure 8-8 reveals the hierarchy of reader classes.

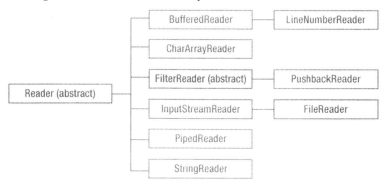

Figure 8-8. *Unlike* `FilterInputStream`, `FilterReader` *is abstract.*

Although the writer and reader class hierarchies are similar to their output stream and input stream counterparts, there are differences. For example, `FilterWriter` and `FilterReader` are abstract, whereas their `FilterOutputStream` and `FilterInputStream` equivalents are not abstract. Also, `BufferedWriter` and `BufferedReader` don't extend `FilterWriter` and `FilterReader`, whereas `BufferedOutputStream` and `BufferedInputStream` extend `FilterOutputStream` and `FilterInputStream`.

The output stream and input stream classes were introduced in JDK 1.0. After their release, design issues emerged. For example, `FilterOutputStream` and `FilterInputStream` should have been abstract. However, it was too late to make these changes because the classes were already being used; making these changes would have resulted in broken code. The designers of JDK 1.1's writer and reader classes took the time to correct these mistakes.

■ **Note** Regarding BufferedWriter and BufferedReader directly subclassing Writer and Reader instead of FilterWriter and FilterReader, I believe that this change has to do with performance. Calls to BufferedOutputStream's write() methods and BufferedInputStream's read() methods result in calls to FilterOutputStream's write() methods and FilterInputStream's read() methods. Because a file I/O activity such as copying one file to another can involve many write()/read() method calls, you want the best performance possible. By not subclassing FileWriter and FileReader, BufferedWriter and BufferedReader achieve better performance.

For brevity, I focus only on the Writer, Reader, OutputStreamWriter, OutputStreamReader, FileWriter, and FileReader classes in this chapter.

Writer and Reader

Java provides the Writer and Reader classes for performing character I/O. Writer is the superclass of all writer subclasses. The following list identifies differences between Writer and OutputStream:

- Writer declares several append() methods for appending characters to this writer. These methods exist because Writer implements the java.lang.Appendable interface, which is used in partnership with the Formatter class (see Appendix C) to output formatted strings.

- Writer declares additional write() methods, including a convenient void write(String str) method for writing a String object's characters to this writer.

Reader is the superclass of all reader subclasses. The following list identifies differences between Reader and InputStream:

- Reader declares read(char[]) and read(char[], int, int) methods instead of read(byte[]) and read(byte[], int, int) methods.

- Reader doesn't declare an available() method.

- Reader declares a boolean ready() method that returns true when the next read() call is guaranteed not to block for input.

- Reader declares an int read(CharBuffer target) method for reading characters from a character buffer. (I discuss CharBuffer in Appendix C.)

OutputStreamWriter and InputStreamReader

The concrete OutputStreamWriter class (a Writer subclass) is a bridge between an incoming sequence of characters and an outgoing stream of bytes. Characters written to this writer are encoded into bytes according to the default or specified character encoding.

■ **Note** The default character encoding is accessible via the `file.encoding` system property.

Each call to an `OutputStreamWriter` `write()` method causes an encoder to be called on the given character(s). The resulting bytes are accumulated in a buffer before being written to the underlying output stream. The characters passed to the `write()` methods are not buffered.

`OutputStreamWriter` declares four constructors, including the following:

- `OutputStreamWriter(OutputStream out)` creates a bridge between an incoming sequence of characters (passed to `OutputStreamWriter` via its `append()` and `write()` methods) and underlying output stream out. The default character encoding is used to encode characters into bytes.

- `OutputStreamWriter(OutputStream out, String charsetName)` creates a bridge between an incoming sequence of characters (passed to `OutputStreamWriter` via its `append()` and `write()` methods) and underlying output stream out. `charsetName` identifies the character encoding used to encode characters into bytes. This constructor throws `java.io.UnsupportedEncodingException` when the named character encoding isn't supported.

■ **Note** `OutputStreamWriter` depends on the abstract `java.nio.charset.Charset` and `java.nio.charset.CharsetEncoder` classes to perform character encoding. (I discuss these classes in Appendix C.)

The following example uses the second constructor to create a bridge to an underlying file output stream so that Polish text can be written to an ISO/IEC 8859-2-encoded file.

```
FileOutputStream fos = new FileOutputStream("polish.txt");
OutputStreamWriter osw = new OutputStreamWriter(fos, "8859_2");
char ch = '\u0323'; // Accented N.
osw.write(ch);
```

The concrete `InputStreamReader` class (a Reader subclass) is a bridge between an incoming stream of bytes and an outgoing sequence of characters. Characters read from this reader are decoded from bytes according to the default or specified character encoding.

Each call to an `InputStreamReader` `read()` method may cause one or more bytes to be read from the underlying input stream. To enable the efficient conversion of bytes to characters, more bytes may be read ahead from the underlying stream than are necessary to satisfy the current read operation.

`InputStreamReader` declares four constructors, including the following:

- `InputStreamReader(InputStream in)` creates a bridge between underlying input stream in and an outgoing sequence of characters (returned from `InputStreamReader` via its `read()` methods). The default character encoding is used to decode bytes into characters.

- InputStreamReader(InputStream in, String charsetName) creates a bridge between underlying input stream in and an outgoing sequence of characters (returned from InputStreamReader via its read() methods). charsetName identifies the character encoding used to decode bytes into characters. This constructor throws UnsupportedEncodingException when the named character encoding isn't supported.

Note InputStreamReader depends on the abstract Charset and java.nio.charset.CharsetDecoder classes to perform character decoding. (I discuss CharsetDecoder in Appendix C.)

The following example uses the second constructor to create a bridge to an underlying file input stream so that Polish text can be read from an ISO/IEC 8859-2-encoded file.

```
FileInputStream fis = new FileInputStream("polish.txt");
InputStreamReader isr = new InputStreamReader(fis, "8859_2");
char ch = isr.read(ch);
```

Note OutputStreamWriter and InputStreamReader declare a String getEncoding() method that returns the name of the character encoding in use. When the encoding has a historical name, that name is returned; otherwise, the encoding's canonical name is returned.

FileWriter and FileReader

FileWriter is a convenience class for writing characters to files. It subclasses OutputStreamWriter, and its constructors call OutputStreamWriter(OutputStream). An instance of this class is equivalent to the following code fragment:

```
FileOutputStream fos = new FileOutputStream(pathname);
OutputStreamWriter osw;
osw = new OutputStreamWriter(fos, System.getProperty("file.encoding"));
```

In Chapter 3, I presented a logging library with a File class (Listing 3-20) that didn't incorporate file-writing code. Listing 8-19 addresses this situation by presenting a revised File class that uses FileWriter to log messages to a file.

Listing 8-19. Logging messages to an actual file

```
package logging;

import java.io.FileWriter;
import java.io.IOException;

class File implements Logger
```

```java
{
    private final static String LINE_SEPARATOR =
        System.getProperty("line.separator");
    private String dstName;
    private FileWriter fw;
    File(String dstName)
    {
        this.dstName = dstName;
    }
    @Override
    public boolean connect()
    {
        if (dstName == null)
            return false;
        try
        {
            fw = new FileWriter(dstName);
        }
        catch (IOException ioe)
        {
            return false;
        }
        return true;
    }
    @Override
    public boolean disconnect()
    {
        if (fw == null)
            return false;
        try
        {
            fw.close();
        }
        catch (IOException ioe)
        {
            return false;
        }
        return true;
    }
    @Override
    public boolean log(String msg)
    {
        if (fw == null)
            return false;
        try
        {
            fw.write(msg+LINE_SEPARATOR);
        }
        catch (IOException ioe)
        {
            return false;
        }
```

```
            return true;
        }
    }
```

Listing 8-19 refactors Listing 3-20 to support FileWriter by making changes to each of the connect(), disconnect(), and log() methods:

- connect() attempts to instantiate FileWriter, whose instance is saved in fw upon success; otherwise, fw continues to store its default null reference.

- disconnect() attempts to close the file by calling FileWriter's close() method, but only when fw doesn't contain its default null reference.

- log() attempts to write its String argument to the file by calling FileWriter's void write(String str) method, but only when fw doesn't contain its default null reference.

connect()'s catch clause specifies IOException instead of FileNotFoundException because FileWriter's constructors throw IOException when they cannot connect to existing normal files; FileOutputStream's constructors throw FileNotFoundException.

log()'s write(String) method appends the line.separator value (which I assigned to a constant for convenience) to the string being output instead of appending \n, which would violate portability.

FileReader is a convenience class for reading characters from files. It subclasses InputStreamReader, and its constructors call InputStreamReader(InputStream). An instance of this class is equivalent to the following code fragment:

```
FileInputStream fis = new FileInputStream(pathname);
InputStreamReader isr;
isr = new InputStreamReader(fis, System.getProperty("file.encoding"));
```

It's often necessary to search text files for occurrences of specific strings. Although regular expressions are ideal for this task, I have yet to discuss them—I discuss regular expressions in the context of New I/O in Appendix C. As a result, Listing 8-20 presents the more verbose alternative to regular expressions.

Listing 8-20. Finding all files that contain content matching a search string

```
import java.io.BufferedReader;
import java.io.File;
import java.io.FileReader;
import java.io.IOException;

class FindAll
{
    public static void main(String[] args)
    {
        if (args.length != 2)
        {
            System.err.println("usage: java FindAll start search-string");
            return;
        }
        if (!findAll(new File(args[0]), args[1]))
            System.err.println("not a directory");
    }
```

```
static boolean findAll(File file, String srchText)
{
   File[] files = file.listFiles();
   if (files == null)
      return false;
   for (int i = 0; i < files.length; i++)
      if (files[i].isDirectory())
         findAll(files[i], srchText);
      else
      if (find(files[i].getPath(), srchText))
         System.out.println(files[i].getPath());
   return true;
}
static boolean find(String filename, String srchText)
{
   try (BufferedReader br = new BufferedReader(new FileReader(filename)))
   {
      int ch;
      outer_loop:
      do
      {
         if ((ch = br.read()) == -1)
            return false;
         if (ch == srchText.charAt(0))
         {
            for (int i = 1; i < srchText.length(); i++)
            {
               if ((ch = br.read()) == -1)
                  return false;
               if (ch != srchText.charAt(i))
                  continue outer_loop;
            }
            return true;
         }
      }
      while (true);
   }
   catch (IOException ioe)
   {
      System.err.println("I/O error: "+ioe.getMessage());
   }
   return false;
}
}
```

Listing 8-20's FindAll class declares main(), findAll(), and find() class methods.

main() validates the number of command-line arguments, which must be two. The first argument identifies the starting location within the filesystem for the search, and is used to construct a File object. The second argument specifies search text. main() then passes the File object and the search text to findAll() to perform a search for all files containing this text.

The recursive findAll() method first invokes listFiles() on the File object passed to this method, to obtain the names of all files in the current directory. If listFiles() returns null, meaning that the File object doesn't refer to an existing directory, findAll() returns false and a suitable error message is output.

For each name in the returned list, findAll() either recursively invokes itself when the name represents a directory, or invokes the find() method to search the file for the text; the file's pathname string is output when the file contains this text.

The find() method first opens the file identified by its first argument via the FileReader class, and then passes the FileReader instance to a BufferedReader instance to improve file-reading performance. It then enters a loop that continues to read characters from the file until the end of the file is reached.

If the currently read character matches the first character in the search text, an inner loop is entered to read subsequent characters from the file and compare them with subsequent characters in the search text. When all characters match, find() returns true. Otherwise, the labeled continue statement is used to skip the remaining iterations of the inner loop and transfer execution to the labeled outer loop. After the last character has been read and there's still no match, find() returns false.

Now that you know how FindAll works, you'll probably want to try it out. The following examples show you how I might use this application on my XP platform:

```
java FindAll \prj\dev OpenGL
```

This example searches the \prj\dev directory on my default drive (C:) for all files that contain the word OpenGL (case is significant) and generates the following output:

```
\prj\dev\bj7\ch13\978-1-4302-3909-3_Friesen_13_Java7Android.doc
\prj\dev\bogl\article.html
\prj\dev\ew32pp\appa\CWinApp.html
\prj\dev\ws\articles\articles.html
\prj\dev\ws\tutorials\ct\air26gsp1\air26gsp1.html
\prj\dev\ws\tutorials\ct\jfx20bgsp1\jfx20bgsp1.html
\prj\dev\ws\tutorials\ct\jfx20bgsp2\jfx20bgsp2.html
```

If I now specify java FindAll \prj\dev opengl, I observe the following abbreviated output:

```
\prj\dev\bogl\article.html
```

FindAll presents a Standard I/O-based user interface, which is appropriate when you only want to run this application from the command line. Because you might prefer a GUI, Listing 8-21 presents a Swing-based version of this application.

Listing 8-21. Refactoring FindAll to support a GUI

```
import java.awt.EventQueue;

import java.awt.event.ActionEvent;
import java.awt.event.ActionListener;

import java.io.BufferedReader;
import java.io.File;
import java.io.FileReader;
import java.io.IOException;

import javax.swing.BoxLayout;
import javax.swing.JButton;
import javax.swing.JFrame;
import javax.swing.JLabel;
import javax.swing.JOptionPane;
```

```java
import javax.swing.JPanel;
import javax.swing.JScrollPane;
import javax.swing.JTextArea;
import javax.swing.JTextField;

class FindAll
{
   final static String LINE_SEPARATOR = System.getProperty("line.separator");
   static JTextArea txtSrchResults;
   static JFrame f;
   static volatile String result;
   static JPanel createGUI()
   {
      JPanel pnl = new JPanel();
      pnl.setLayout(new BoxLayout(pnl, BoxLayout.Y_AXIS));
      JPanel pnlTemp = new JPanel();
      JLabel lblStartDir = new JLabel("Start directory");
      pnlTemp.add(lblStartDir);
      final JTextField txtStartDir = new JTextField(30);
      pnlTemp.add(txtStartDir);
      pnl.add(pnlTemp);
      pnlTemp = new JPanel();
      JLabel lblSrchText = new JLabel("Search text");
      pnlTemp.add(lblSrchText);
      lblSrchText.setPreferredSize(lblStartDir.getPreferredSize());
      final JTextField txtSrchText = new JTextField(30);
      pnlTemp.add(txtSrchText);
      pnl.add(pnlTemp);
      pnlTemp = new JPanel();
      JButton btnSearch = new JButton("Search");
      pnlTemp.add(btnSearch);
      pnl.add(pnlTemp);
      pnlTemp = new JPanel();
      txtSrchResults = new JTextArea(20, 30);
      pnlTemp.add(new JScrollPane(txtSrchResults));
      pnl.add(pnlTemp);
      ActionListener al;
      al = new ActionListener()
            {
               @Override
               public void actionPerformed(ActionEvent ae)
               {
                  final String startDir = txtStartDir.getText();
                  final String srchText = txtSrchText.getText();
                  txtSrchResults.setText("");
                  Runnable r;
                  r = new Runnable()
                        {
                           @Override
                           public void run()
                           {
                              if (!findAll(new File(startDir), srchText))
```

```
                    {
                        Runnable r;
                        r = new Runnable()
                            {
                                @Override
                                public void run()
                                {
                                    String msg = "not a directory";
                                    JOptionPane.showMessageDialog(f, msg);
                                }
                            };
                        EventQueue.invokeLater(r);
                    }
                }
            };
        new Thread(r).start();
        }
    };
    btnSearch.addActionListener(al);
    return pnl;
}
static boolean findAll(File file, String srchText)
{
    File[] files = file.listFiles();
    if (files == null)
        return false;
    for (int i = 0; i < files.length; i++)
        if (files[i].isDirectory())
            findAll(files[i], srchText);
        else
        if (find(files[i].getPath(), srchText))
        {
            result = files[i].getPath();
            Runnable r = new Runnable()
                        {
                            @Override
                            public void run()
                            {
                                txtSrchResults.append(result+LINE_SEPARATOR);
                            }
                        };
            EventQueue.invokeLater(r);
        }
    return true;
}
static boolean find(String filename, String srchText)
{
    try (BufferedReader br = new BufferedReader(new FileReader(filename)))
    {
        int ch;
        outer_loop:
        do
```

```
      {
         if ((ch = br.read()) == -1)
            return false;
         if (ch == srchText.charAt(0))
         {
            for (int i = 1; i < srchText.length(); i++)
            {
               if ((ch = br.read()) == -1)
                  return false;
               if (ch != srchText.charAt(i))
                  continue outer_loop;
            }
            return true;
         }
      }
      while (true);
   }
   catch (IOException ioe)
   {
      System.err.println("I/O error: "+ioe.getMessage());
   }
   return false;
}
public static void main(String[] args)
{
   Runnable r = new Runnable()
               {
                  @Override
                  public void run()
                  {
                     f = new JFrame("FindAll");
                     f.setDefaultCloseOperation(JFrame.EXIT_ON_CLOSE);
                     f.setContentPane(createGUI());
                     f.pack();
                     f.setResizable(false);
                     f.setVisible(true);
                  }
               };
   EventQueue.invokeLater(r);
}
}
```

Listing 8-21's FindAll class declares several class fields along with createGUI(), findAll(), find() and main() class methods. Because much of this content has previously been discussed (in Chapter 7 and earlier in this chapter), I'll focus on only a few items.

FindAll is a multithreaded application. As well as the main thread that executes main(), FindAll's GUI runs on the event-dispatch thread (EDT) and creates a worker thread to execute the findAll() method off of the EDT, to keep the GUI responsive.

At some point, threads must communicate with shared variables and this is where lack-of-synchronization problems can arise. I've eliminated these problems by creating a single volatile result field and using final local variables.

The result field is volatile so that the EDT and worker thread can see result's String reference value on multicore or multiprocessor platforms where each core/processor has a local cached copy of this field. If result wasn't volatile, the EDT might not see the reference to a new String object assigned to result when findAll() finds a match, and would probably append a copy of the previously found match to the textarea. (This isn't a problem on single processor/single core platforms.)

Although this rationale also holds for the startDir and srchText local variables, they're declared final instead of volatile. They need to be declared final so that they can be accessed from the anonymous class that implements java.lang.Runnable in the search button's action listener.

If you recall, Chapter 4 states that final fields can be safely accessed without synchronization. As a result, volatile isn't required for a final field, and you cannot declare a field to be volatile and final at the same time. (A final field can be safely accessed but not necessarily the objects to which final reference fields refer. Because String objects are immutable, there would be no problem if I called String methods on startDir, srchText, and result.)

The search button's action listener declares a runnable within a runnable, and the code probably looks complicated. The following sequence of steps explains how this code works:

1.   When the user clicks the search button, its actionPerformed() method is invoked on the EDT.

2.   actionPerformed() accesses the starting directory and search text textfields, clears the results textarea so that new search results are not appended to previous search results, creates the runnable, and starts a worker thread (that executes this runnable) on the EDT.

3.   Shortly thereafter, the worker thread will start to execute the runnable by invoking its run() method.

4.   run() invokes findAll() to begin the search. If findAll() returns false, a new runnable is created that outputs an error message via a javax.swing.JOptionPane-based dialog box. The worker thread executes java.awt.EventQueue's invokeLater() method to ensure that the dialog box is displayed on the EDT.

Note Appendix C introduces the javax.swing.SwingWorker class, which simplifies communicating between a worker thread and the EDT.

Listing 8-21 reveals the following code:

```
pnl.setLayout(new BoxLayout(pnl, BoxLayout.Y_AXIS));
```

This code uses Swing's javax.swing.BoxLayout class to layout a container's components in a vertical column. Unlike java.awt.GridLayout, BoxLayout doesn't give each component the same size.

Because many search results may be returned, the textarea needs to be scrollable. However, this component isn't scrollable by default, so it must be added to a scrollpane. This task is accomplished with the help of the javax.swing.JScrollPane class.

JScrollPane provides constructors that are called with the component that needs to be made scrollable; for example, JScrollPane(Component view). In contrast, AWT's java.awt.ScrollPane class requires you to pass the component to its add() method.

Figure 8-9 shows `FindAll`'s Swing-based GUI.

Figure 8-9. *Search results are presented in a scrollable textarea.*

Figure 8-10 shows `FindAll`'s GUI with its "not a directory" dialog box.

Figure 8-10. *A dialog box appears when you leave the Start directory textfield empty, or when you enter a path to a filename or a nonexistent directory in this textfield.*

EXERCISES

The following exercises are designed to test your understanding of File and various stream and writer/reader APIs:

1. Create an application named Touch for setting a file's or directory's timestamp to the current or specified time. This application has the following usage syntax: java Touch [-d *timestamp*] *pathname*. If you don't specify [-d *timestamp*], *pathname*'s timestamp is set to the current time; otherwise, it is set to the specified *timestamp* value, which has the format *yyyy-MM-dd HH:mm:ss z* (2010-08-13 02:37:45 UTC and 2006-04-22 12:35:45 EST are examples). Hints: The java.util.Date class (which I formally introduce in Appendix C) has a getTime() method whose return value can be passed to File's setLastModified() method. Also, you'll find Date date = new SimpleDateFormat("yyyy-MM-dd HH:mm:ss z").parse(args[1]); and System.err.println("invalid option: " + args[0]); to be helpful. (Wikipedia's "touch (Unix)" entry [http://en.wikipedia.org/wiki/Touch_(Unix)] introduces you to a standard Unix program named touch. In addition to changing a file's access and modification timestamps, touch is used to create a new empty file.)

2. Create an application named Split for splitting a large file into a number of smaller part*x* files (where *x* starts at 0 and increments; for example, part0, part1, part2, and so on). Each part*x* file (except possibly the last part*x* file, which holds the remaining bytes) will have the same size. This application has the following usage syntax: java Split *pathname*. Furthermore, your implementation must use the BufferedInputStream, BufferedOutputStream, File, FileInputStream, and FileOutputStream classes. (I find Split helpful for storing huge files that don't fit onto a single CD/DVD across multiple CDs/DVDs, and also for emailing huge files to friends. To recombine the part files on a Windows platform, I use the copy command and its /B binary option. When recombining the part files, recombine them in order: part0, part1 ... part9, part10, and so on.)

3. It's often convenient to read lines of text from standard input, and the InputStreamReader and BufferedReader classes make this task possible. Create an application named CircleInfo that, after obtaining a BufferedReader instance that's chained to standard input, enters a loop that prompts the user to enter a radius, parses the entered radius into a double value, and outputs a pair of messages that report the circle's circumference and area based on this radius.

4. FindAll is problematic in that you can start a new search operation while an ongoing search is in progress. Also, there's no way to stop an ongoing search except by starting a new search or closing the window. Modify FindAll by disabling its Search button when a search is in progress. Also, add a Stop button that's initially disabled, and that lets you stop an existing search (and also reenables Search).

Summary

Applications often interact with the filesystem to output data to and/or input data from files. Java's standard class library supports filesystem access via its classic `File`, `RandomAccessFile`, stream, and writer/reader APIs.

Java offers access to the underlying platform's available filesystem(s) via its concrete `File` class. `File` instances contain the abstract pathnames of files and directories that may or may not exist in their filesystems.

Files can be opened for random access in which a mixture of write and read operations can occur until the file is closed. Java supports this random access by providing the concrete `RandomAccessFile` class.

Java uses streams to perform I/O operations. A stream is an ordered sequence of bytes of arbitrary length. Bytes flow over an output stream from an application to a destination, and flow over an input stream from a source to an application.

The `java.io` package provides several output stream and input stream classes that are descendents of the abstract `OutputStream` and `InputStream` classes. Examples of subclasses include `FileOutputStream` and `BufferedInputStream`.

Java's stream classes are good for streaming sequences of bytes, but are not good for streaming sequences of characters because bytes and characters are two different things, and because byte streams have no knowledge of character sets and encodings.

If you need to stream characters, you should take advantage of Java's writer and reader classes, which were designed to support character I/O (they work with `char` instead of `byte`). Furthermore, the writer and reader classes take character encodings into account.

The `java.io` package provides several writer and reader classes that are descendents of the abstract `Writer` and `Reader` classes. Examples of subclasses include `OutputStreamWriter`, `FileWriter`, `InputStreamReader`, `FileReader`, and `BufferedReader`.

As well as filesystems, applications often must interact with networks and databases. Chapter 9 provides an introduction to the standard class library's network-oriented and database-oriented APIs.

CHAPTER 9

Interacting with Networks and Databases

You have three targets for accessing data that's external to an application: filesystem, network, and database. Chapter 8 introduced you to filesystem-oriented data access, whereas this chapter introduces you to data access via networks and databases.

Interacting with Networks

A *network* is a collection of interconnected *nodes* (computers and peripherals [e.g., printers]) that can share hardware and software among users. An *intranet* is a network within an organization and an *internet* is a network that links organizations together. The *Internet* is the global network of networks.

Note Intranets and internets typically use Transmission Control Protocol (TCP), User Datagram Protocol (UDP), and Internet Protocol (IP) to communicate between nodes. TCP is a two-way communication protocol, UDP is a one-way communication protocol, and IP is the fundamental communication protocol over which TCP and UDP perform their communication tasks. TCP, UDP, and IP are combined with other protocols into a model known as TCP/IP (see http://en.wikipedia.org/wiki/TCP/IP_model).

The java.net package supplies assorted classes that support TCP/IP communication between *processes* (executing applications) that are running on the same or different *hosts* (computer-based TCP/IP nodes). After introducing you to each of these classes, this section presents authentication and cookie management.

Communicating via Sockets

A *socket* is an endpoint in a communications link between two processes. The endpoint consists of an *IP address*, which identifies a host, and a *port number*, which identifies a process running on that network node.

One process writes a *message* (sequence of bytes) to a socket, which breaks this message into a series of *packets* (addressable message chunks, which are commonly known as *IP datagrams*) and forwards these packets to the other process's socket, which recombines them into the original message for that process's consumption. Figure 9-1 shows this scenario.

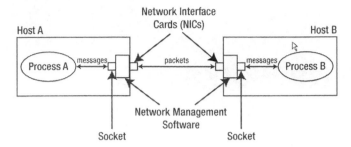

Figure 9-1. *Two processes use sockets to communicate.*

According to Figure 9-1, Process A on Host A sends a message to a socket. Host A's network management software, which is often referred to as a *protocol stack*, breaks this message into a series of packets (each packet includes the destination host's IP address and port number), and sends these packets through Host A's Network Interface Card (NIC) to the destination host, which is Host B in the figure. Host B's protocol stack receives packets through the NIC and reassembles them into the original message, which it then makes available to Process B. This situation reverses when Process B communicates with Process A.

IP ADDRESSES AND PORT NUMBERS

IP addresses are 32-bit or 128-bit unsigned integers that uniquely identify network hosts and other nodes. A 32-bit IP address is commonly specified as four 8-bit integer components in period-separated decimal notation, where each component is a decimal integer ranging from 0 through 255 and is separated from the next component via a period (e.g., 127.0.0.1). In contrast, a 128-bit IP address is commonly specified as eight 16-bit integer components in colon-separated hexadecimal notation, where each component is a hexadecimal integer ranging from 0 through FFFF and is separated from the next component via a colon (e.g., 1080:0:0:0:8:800:200C:417A). A 32-bit IP address is often referred to as an Internet Protocol Version 4 (IPv4) address (see http://en.wikipedia.org/wiki/IPv4). Similarly, a 128-bit IP address is often referred to as an Internet Protocol Version 6 (IPv6) address (see http://en.wikipedia.org/wiki/IPv6).

Port numbers are 16-bit unsigned integers that uniquely identify processes, which are the sources or recipients of messages. Port numbers less than 1024 are reserved for standard processes. For example, port number 25 has traditionally identified the Simple Mail Transfer Protocol (SMTP) process for sending email, although port number 587 is commonly being used these days (see http://en.wikipedia.org/wiki/Smtp).

TCP is used to create an ongoing conversation between two hosts by sending messages back and forth. Before this conversation can occur, a connection must be established between these hosts. After this connection has been established, TCP enters a pattern of sending a message packet and waiting for a reply that the packet arrived correctly (or for a timeout to expire when the reply doesn't arrive because of a network problem). This send/reply cycle guarantees a reliable connection.

Because it can take time to establish a connection, and because it also takes time to send packets because of the need to receive reply acknowledgments (or timeouts), TCP is fairly slow. UDP, which doesn't require connections and packet acknowledgement, is much faster than TCP. However, UDP isn't as reliable (there's no guarantee that a packet will arrive correctly or even arrive) as TCP because there's no acknowledgment. Furthermore, UDP is limited to single-packet one-way conversations.

The java.net package provides Socket and ServerSocket classes for performing TCP-based communications. It also provides DatagramSocket, DatagramPacket, and MulticastSocket classes for performing UDP communications. MulticastSocket is a subclass of DatagramSocket.

Socket Addresses

Instances of the Socket-suffixed classes are associated with *socket addresses* that are comprised of IP addresses and port numbers.

The Socket class relies on the java.net.InetAddress class to represent the IPv4 or IPv6 address portion of the socket address. It represents the port number separately. (The other Socket-suffixed classes also take advantage of InetAddress.)

■ **Note** InetAddress relies on its java.net.Inet4Address subclass to represent an IPv4 address and on its java.net.Inet6Address subclass to represent an IPv6 address.

InetAddress declares several class methods for obtaining an InetAddress instance. These methods include the following:

- InetAddress[] getAllByName(String host) returns an array of InetAddresses that store the IP addresses associated with host. You can pass either a domain name (e.g., "tutortutor.ca") or an IP address (e.g., "70.33.247.10") argument to this parameter. (Check out Wikipedia's "Domain name" entry [http://en.wikipedia.org/wiki/Domain_name] to learn about domain names.) Passing null results in an InetAddress instance that stores the IP address of the loopback interface (defined shortly). This method throws java.net.UnknownHostException when no IP address for the specified host can be found, or when a scope identifier is specified for a global IPv6 address.

- InetAddress getByAddress(byte[] addr) returns an InetAddress object for the given raw IP address. The argument passed to addr is in *network byte order* (most significant byte first) where the highest order byte is in addr[0]. The length of the addr array must be four bytes long for an IPv4 address and sixteen bytes long for an IPv6 address. This method throws UnknownHostException when the array's length is neither 4 nor 16.

- InetAddress getByAddress(String host, byte[] addr) returns an InetAddress instance based on the provided host name and IP address. This method throws UnknownHostException when the array's length is neither 4 nor 16.

- InetAddress getByName(String host) is equivalent to specifying getAllByName(host)[0].

- InetAddress getLocalHost() returns the address of the *local host* (the current host), which is represented by hostname localhost or by an IP address that is typically 127.0.0.1 [IPv4] or ::1 [IPv6)]. This method throws UnknownHostException when localhost couldn't be resolved into an address.

- InetAddress getLoopbackAddress() returns the *loopback address* (a special IP address that allows network-management software to treat outgoing messages as incoming messages). The returned InetAddress instance represents the IPv4 loopback address, 127.0.0.1, or the IPv6 loopback address, ::1. The IPv4 loopback address returned is only one of many in the form 127.*.*.*, where * is a wildcard that ranges from 0 through 255.

Once you have an InetAddress instance, you can interrogate it by invoking instance methods such as byte[] getAddress() (return the raw IP address [in network byte order] of this InetAddress object) and boolean isLoopbackAddress() (determine whether or not this InetAddress instance represents a loopback address).

Java 1.4 introduced the abstract java.net.SocketAddress class to represent a socket address "with no protocol attachment." Perhaps this class's creator anticipated that Java would eventually support low-level communication protocols other than the widely popular Internet Protocol.

SocketAddress is subclassed by the concrete java.net.InetSocketAddress class, which represents a socket address as an IP address and a port number. It can also represent a hostname and a port number, and will make an attempt to resolve the hostname.

InetSocketAddress instances are created by invoking constructors such as InetSocketAddress(InetAddress addr, int port). After an instance has been created, you can call methods such as InetAddress getAddress() and int getPort() to return socket address components.

Socket Options

As well as sharing the concept of socket addresses, the various Socket-suffixed classes share the concept of socket options. A *socket option* is a parameter for configuring socket behavior. The following C language constants identify socket options that the Socket-suffixed classes support via various methods:

- TCP_NODELAY: Disable Nagle's algorithm (http://en.wikipedia.org/wiki/Nagle's_algorithm). This option is valid for Socket.

- SO_LINGER: Specify a linger-on-close timeout. This option is valid for Socket.

- SO_TIMEOUT: Specify a timeout on blocking socket operations. (Don't block forever!) This option is valid for Socket, ServerSocket, and DatagramSocket.

- SO_BINDADDR: Fetch the socket's local address binding. This option is valid for Socket, ServerSocket, and DatagramSocket.

- SO_REUSEADDR: Enable a socket's reuse address. This option is valid for Socket, ServerSocket, and DatagramSocket.

- SO_BROADCAST: Enable a socket to send broadcast messages. This option is valid for DatagramSocket.

- SO_SNDBUF: Set or get the maximum socket send buffer in bytes. This option is valid for Socket, ServerSocket, and DatagramSocket.

- SO_RCVBUF: Set or get the maximum socket receive buffer in bytes. This option is valid for Socket, ServerSocket, and DatagramSocket.

- SO_KEEPALIVE: Turn on socket keepalive. This option is valid for Socket.

- SO_OOBINLINE: Enable inline reception of TCP urgent data. This option is valid for Socket.

- IP_MULTICAST_IF: Specify the outgoing interface for multicast packets (on *multihomed* [e.g., multiple NIC] hosts). This option is valid for MulticastSocket only.

- IP_MULTICAST_LOOP: Enable or disable local loopback of multicast datagrams. This option is valid for MulticastSocket only.

- IP_TOS: Set the type-of-service or traffic class field in the IP header for a TCP or UDP socket. This option is valid for Socket and DatagramSocket.

The Socket-suffixed classes provide setter and getter methods for setting/getting these options. For example, Socket declares void setKeepAlive(boolean on) for setting the SO_KEEPALIVE option and MulticastSocket declares void setLoopbackMode(boolean disable) for setting the IP_MULTICAST_LOOP option. Check out the JDK documentation on java.net's Socket-suffixed classes to learn about these and other socket option methods, to learn more about the various socket options.

Note Socket options that apply to DatagramSocket also apply to its MulticastSocket subclass.

Socket and ServerSocket

The Socket and ServerSocket classes let you perform TCP-based communications between client processes (e.g., an application running on your desktop) and server processes (e.g., an application running on one of your Internet Service Provider's computers that provides access to the World Wide Web). Because Socket is associated with the java.io.InputStream and java.io.OutputStream classes, sockets based on the Socket class are often referred to as *stream sockets*.

Socket is used to create a socket on the client side. It declares several constructors, including the following pair:

- Socket(InetAddress address, int port) creates a stream socket and connects it to the specified port number at the specified IP address. This constructor throws java.io.IOException when an I/O error occurs while creating the socket, java.lang.IllegalArgumentException when the argument passed to port is outside the valid range of port values, which is 0 through 65535, and java.lang.NullPointerException when address is null.

- Socket(String host, int port) creates a stream socket and connects it to the specified port number on the named host. When host is null, this constructor is equivalent to invoking Socket(InetAddress.getByName(null), port). It throws the same IOException and IllegalArgumentException instances as the previous constructor. However, instead of throwing NullPointerException, it throws UnknownHostException when the host's IP address couldn't be determined.

When a Socket instance is created via these constructors, it binds to an arbitrary local host socket address before connecting to the remote host socket address. *Binding* makes a client socket address available to a server socket so that a server process can communicate with the client process via the server socket.

Socket offers additional constructors to give you flexibility. For example, Socket() and Socket(Proxy proxy) create unbound and unconnected sockets. Before you can use these sockets, you need to bind them to local socket addresses by calling void bind(SocketAddress bindpoint), and then make connections by calling Socket's connect() methods, such as void connect(SocketAddress endpoint).

■ **Note** A *proxy* is a computer that sits between an intranet and the Internet for security purposes. Proxy settings are represented by instances of the java.net.Proxy class and help sockets communicate through proxies.

Another constructor is Socket(InetAddress address, int port, InetAddress localAddr, int localPort), which lets you specify your own local host socket address via localAddr and localPort. This constructor automatically binds to the local socket address and then attempts a connection to the remote address.

After creating a Socket instance, and possibly invoking bind() and connect() on that instance, an application typically invokes Socket's InputStream getInputStream() and OutputStream getOutputStream() methods to obtain an input stream for reading bytes from the socket and an output stream for writing bytes to the socket. Also, the application typically calls Socket's void close() method to close the socket once it no longer needs to perform input or output operations.

The following example demonstrates how to create a socket that's bound to port number 1500 on the local host and then access its input and output streams—exceptions are ignored for brevity:

```
Socket socket = new Socket("localhost", 1500);
InputStream is = socket.getInputStream();
OutputStream os = socket.getOutputStream();
```

I've created a GetTime application that demonstrates the Socket class by creating a socket to connect to an American National Institute of Standards & Technology (NIST) timeserver to retrieve and output the current time. Listing 9-1 presents this application's source code.

Listing 9-1. Getting and outputting the current time according to NIST's implementation of the Daytime Protocol

```
import java.io.InputStream;
import java.io.IOException;

import java.net.Socket;
import java.net.UnknownHostException;

class GetTime
{
   public static void main(String[] args)
   {
      if (args.length != 1)
      {
```

```
            System.err.println("usage  : java GetTime server");
            System.err.println("example: java GetTime time.nist.gov");
            return;
        }
        try (Socket socket = new Socket(args[0], 13))
        {
            InputStream is = socket.getInputStream();
            int ch;
            while ((ch = is.read()) != -1)
                System.out.print((char) ch);
        }
        catch (UnknownHostException uhe)
        {
            System.err.println("unknown host: "+uhe.getMessage());
        }
        catch (IOException ioe)
        {
            System.err.println("I/O error: "+ioe.getMessage());
        }
    }
}
```

Listing 9-1 describes an application that creates a Socket instance connected to a remote server on port 13, which is reserved for the Internet's Daytime Protocol. According to this protocol, a client socket connects to a server process on port 13 and the process implementing Daytime immediately returns an ASCII (http://en.wikipedia.org/wiki/Ascii) character string containing the current date and time to the client socket.

■ **Note** The Internet Engineering Task Force publishes memoranda that describe methods, behaviors, research, or innovations applicable to the working of the Internet and Internet-connected systems. These memoranda are collectively known as *Request For Comment (RFC)* documents. RFC 867 describes the Daytime Internet protocol (http://tools.ietf.org/html/rfc867) and doesn't mandate a specific syntax for the ASCII string (its implementers are free to use their own syntax).

Various timeservers implement Daytime (e.g., the server running on the computer associated with Internet domain name time.nist.gov). Recognizing this fact, GetTime requires you to specify the timeserver domain name as a command-line argument. For example, when you specify java GetTime time.nist.gov, you'll receive output similar to that shown here:

```
55811 11-09-07 22:03:15 50 0 0 816.1 UTC(NIST) *
```

This output conforms to the following NIST syntax for the Daytime protocol:

```
JJJJJ YR-MO-DA HH:MM:SS TT L H msADV UTC(NIST) OTM
```

These fields have the following meanings:

- JJJJJ specifies the Julian date.

- YR-MO-DA specifies the date in year/month/day format.

- HH:MM:SS specifies the time in hour/minute/second format. This time is expressed in Coordinated Universal Time (UTC)—see http://en.wikipedia.org/wiki/UTC.

- TT indicates whether the timer server is on Standard Time (ST) or Daylight Saving Time (DST), where 00 indicates Standard Time and 50 indicates DST.

- L indicates how to deal with a leap second at the end of the month; it's one of 0 (no leap second), +1 (add one leap second), or -1 (subtract one leap second).

- H indicates the health of the timeserver. It's one of 0 (healthy) or a positive integer (not healthy).

- msADV indicates the number of milliseconds that the time has been advanced to compensate for network delays.

- UTC(NIST) identifies the originator of the msADV value.

- OTM indicates an ontime marker.

Check out the web page at http://www.nist.gov/pml/div688/grp40/its.cfm to learn more about this syntax.

Although you can read bytes from or write bytes to the socket via the InputStream and OutputStream references, you'll typically use these references as the basis for more convenient character I/O streams by wrapping them in instances of the java.io.BufferedReader and java.io.PrintWriter classes, as demonstrated as follows:

```
InputStreamReader isr = new InputStreamReader(is);
BufferedReader br = new BufferedReader(isr);
PrintWriter pw = new PrintWriter(os);
```

The first line creates a reader that bridges an incoming stream of bytes to an outgoing stream of characters that are decoded from the bytes according to the default character encoding (see Chapter 8). The returned reader is then passed to BufferedReader to improve performance and to obtain access to BufferedReader's String readLine() method, which conveniently lets you read a string of characters terminated by any one of a line feed ('\n'), a carriage return ('\r'), or a carriage return followed immediately by a linefeed.

The third line uses the PrintWriter(OutputStream out) constructor to create a PrintWriter instance for writing a string of characters to the output stream, and converting these characters to a stream of bytes via an internally created output stream writer instance set to the default character encoding.

When you call this constructor, it doesn't automatically flush bytes to the output stream when you invoke a println() method. To ensure that bytes are output, you'll need to invoke the flush() method after println(). However, you can ensure that flushing takes place by using the PrintWriter(OutputStream out, boolean autoFlush) constructor and passing true to autoFlush.

ServerSocket is used to create the server end of a TCP connection. A server socket waits for requests to come in over the network. It performs some operation based on that request, and then possibly returns a result to the requester.

While the server socket is processing a request, additional requests might arrive. These requests are stored in a queue for subsequent processing.

ServerSocket declares four constructors:

- `ServerSocket()` creates an unbound server socket. You can bind this socket to a specific socket address (to which client sockets communicate) by invoking either of ServerSocket's two `bind()` methods. *Binding* makes the server socket address available to a client socket so that a client process can communicate with the server process via the client socket. This constructor throws `IOException` when an I/O error occurs while attempting to open the socket.

- `ServerSocket(int port)` creates a server socket bound to the specified `port` value and an IP address associated with one of the host's NICs. When you pass 0 to `port`, an arbitrary port number is chosen. The port number can be retrieved by calling `int getLocalPort()`. The maximum queue length for incoming *connection indications* (connection requests from clients) is set to 50. If a connection indication arrives when the queue is full, the connection is refused. This constructor throws `IOException` when an I/O error occurs while attempting to open the socket, and `IllegalArgumentException` when `port`'s value lies outside the specified range of valid port values, which is between 0 and 65535, inclusive.

- `ServerSocket(int port, int backlog)` is equivalent to the previous constructor, but it also lets you specify the maximum queue length by passing a positive integer to `backlog`.

- `ServerSocket(int port, int backlog, InetAddress bindAddr)` is equivalent to the previous constructor, but it also lets you specify a different IP address to which the server socket binds. This constructor is useful for machines that have multiple NICs and you want to listen for connection indications on a specific NIC.

After creating a server socket, a server application enters a loop where it first invokes ServerSocket's `Socket accept()` method to listen for a connection indication and return a `Socket` instance that lets it communicate with the associated client socket. It then communicates with the client socket to perform some kind of processing. When processing finishes, the server socket calls the client socket's `close()` method to terminate its connection with the client.

Note ServerSocket declares a `void close()` method for closing a server socket before terminating the server application.

The following example demonstrates how to create a server socket that's bound to port 1500 on the current host, listen for incoming connection indications, return their sockets, perform work on those sockets, and close the sockets—exceptions are ignored for brevity:

```
ServerSocket ss = new ServerSocket(1500);
while (true)
{
   Socket socket = ss.accept();
   // obtain socket input/output streams and communicate with socket
   socket.close();
}
```

The accept() method call blocks until a connection indication is available, and then returns a Socket object so that the server application can communicate with its associated client. The socket is closed after this communication takes place.

This example assumes that socket communication takes place on the server application's main thread, which is a problem when processing takes time to perform because server response time to incoming connection indications decreases. To speed up this response time, it's often necessary to communicate with the socket on a worker thread, as demonstrated in the following example:

```
ServerSocket ss = new ServerSocket(1500);
while (true)
{
   final Socket s = ss.accept();
   new Thread(new Runnable()
              {
                 private volatile Socket socket = s;
                 @Override
                 public void run()
                 {
                    // obtain socket input/output streams and communicate with socket
                    try { socket.close(); } catch (IOException ioe) {}
                 }
              }).start();
}
```

Each time a connection indication arrives, accept() returns a Socket instance, and then a java.lang.Thread object is created whose runnable accesses that socket for communicating with the socket on a worker thread.

Because the socket assignment (socket = s) takes place on the server application's main thread, and because socket is also accessed on the worker thread, socket must be declared volatile to address situations where the main and worker threads run on different processors or cores and have their own cached copies of the socket reference variable.

■ **Tip** Although this example uses the Thread class, you could use an executor (see Chapter 6) instead.

To demonstrate ServerSocket and Socket, I've created ChatServer and ChatClient applications that let multiple users communicate. Listing 9-2 presents ChatServer's source code.

Listing 9-2. Letting multiple users communicate

```
import java.io.BufferedReader;
import java.io.InputStreamReader;
import java.io.IOException;
import java.io.PrintWriter;

import java.net.ServerSocket;
import java.net.Socket;

import java.util.ArrayList;
```

```java
import java.util.List;

class ChatServer
{
    private final static int PORT_NO = 8010;
    private ServerSocket listener;
    private List<Connection> clients;
    ChatServer() throws IOException
    {
        listener = new ServerSocket(PORT_NO);
        clients = new ArrayList<>();
        System.out.println("listening on port "+PORT_NO);
    }
    void runServer()
    {
        try
        {
            while (true)
            {
                Socket socket = listener.accept();
                System.out.println("accepted connection");
                Connection con = new Connection(socket);
                synchronized(clients)
                {
                    clients.add(con);
                    con.start();
                    if (clients.size() == 1)
                        con.send("welcome...you're the first user");
                    else
                        con.send("welcome...you're the latest of "+clients.size()+
                                 " users");
                }
            }
        }
        catch (IOException ioe)
        {
            System.err.println("I/O error: "+ioe.getMessage());
            return;
        }
    }
    private class Connection extends Thread
    {
        private volatile BufferedReader br;
        private volatile PrintWriter pw;
        private String clientName;
        Connection(Socket s) throws IOException
        {
            br = new BufferedReader(new InputStreamReader(s.getInputStream()));
            pw = new PrintWriter(s.getOutputStream(), true);
        }
        @Override
        public void run()
```

```java
        {
            String line;
            try
            {
                clientName = br.readLine();
                sendClientsList();
                while ((line = br.readLine()) != null)
                    broadcast(clientName+": "+line);
            }
            catch (IOException ioe)
            {
                System.err.println("I/O error: "+ioe.getMessage());
            }
            finally
            {
                System.out.println(clientName+": "+"finished");
                synchronized(clients)
                {
                    clients.remove(this);
                    broadcast("now "+clients.size()+" users");
                    sendClientsList();
                }
            }
        }
        private void broadcast(String message)
        {
            System.out.println("broadcasting "+message);
            synchronized(clients)
            {
                for (Connection con: clients)
                    con.send(message);
            }
        }
        private void send(String message)
        {
            pw.println(message);
        }
        private void sendClientsList()
        {
            StringBuilder sb = new StringBuilder();
            synchronized(clients)
            {
                for (Connection con: clients)
                {
                    sb.append(con.clientName);
                    sb.append(" ");
                }
                broadcast("!"+sb.toString());
            }
        }
    }
    public static void main(String[] args)
```

```
   {
      try
      {
         System.out.println("ChatServer starting");
         new ChatServer().runServer();
      }
      catch (IOException ioe)
      {
         System.err.println("unable to create server socket");
      }
   }
}
```

Listing 9-2's ChatServer class consists of private constant/nonconstant fields, a constructor, a void runServer() method, a private Connection nested class that subclasses Thread, and a main() method that invokes this constructor followed by runServer() via method call chaining (see Chapter 2).

The constructor attempts to create a server socket; when successful, it creates an array list that stores Connection objects representing incoming connection indications from chat clients.

The runServer() method enters an infinite loop that first invokes accept() to wait for a connection indication and return a Socket instance for communicating with the associated client. It then creates a Connection object that's linked to the Socket instance, adds the Connection object to the clients array, starts the Connection thread, and sends a greeting message to the client associated with the Connection object's socket.

When the Connection thread's run() method starts running, it first obtains the client's name (the name of the user running the client application) via a readLine() method call. It then invokes Connection's void sendClientsList() method to notify all clients about the latest client to join the chat.

sendClientsList() provides this notification by first building an exclamation mark (!)-prefixed string of space-separated client names, and then invoking Connection's void broadcast(String message) method to broadcast this string to all clients participating in the chat.

In turn, broadcast() invokes Connection's void send(message) method on each Connection object stored in the clients array.

The Connection thread's run() method then enters a loop that uses readLine() to read each line from the client, and then broadcasts this line with the client name as a prefix to all clients.

At some point, the client's socket will be closed when its user chooses to quit the chat. This act causes readLine() to return null, which ends the loop and causes the try statement's finally clause to execute. This clause removes the client's Connection object from the clients array and broadcasts messages that identify the number of remaining clients and their names.

Although ChatServer is conceptually simple, its use of volatile and thread synchronization make it appear more difficult.

I declare a variable volatile wherever it can be accessed by multiple threads. The idea is to ensure that ChatServer will work on multicore/multiprocessor machines that contain separated cached copies of the variable.

I use synchronization to ensure that clients have a consistent view of the chat server's state. For example, runServer() executes clients.add(con); through con.send("welcome...you're the latest of "+clients.size()+" users"); in a synchronized block, and also executes clients.remove(this); through sendClientsList(); in another synchronized block that synchronizes on the same clients object, so that a client cannot be removed in between a client being added and a message sent to that client about the current number of clients, and also so that a client cannot be added in between a client being removed and all remaining clients being notified about the current number of clients.

Compile this source code (javac ChatServer.java) and run the application (java ChatServer). It responds by presenting the following output in its command window:

```
ChatServer starting
listening on port 8010
```

Listing 9-3 presents ChatClient's source code.

Listing 9-3. *Accessing the chat server*

```java
import java.awt.BorderLayout;
import java.awt.EventQueue;
import java.awt.GridLayout;

import java.awt.event.ActionEvent;
import java.awt.event.ActionListener;

import java.io.BufferedReader;
import java.io.InputStreamReader;
import java.io.IOException;
import java.io.PrintWriter;

import java.net.Socket;

import javax.swing.BorderFactory;
import javax.swing.JButton;
import javax.swing.JFrame;
import javax.swing.JPanel;
import javax.swing.JScrollPane;
import javax.swing.JTextArea;
import javax.swing.JTextField;

import javax.swing.border.Border;
import javax.swing.border.EtchedBorder;

class ChatClient
{
    final static String SERVER_ADDR = "localhost";
    final static int SERVER_PORT = 8010;
    static Socket socket;
    static volatile BufferedReader br;
    static PrintWriter pw;
    static JButton btnSend;
    static JPanel createGUI()
    {
        JPanel pnlLayout = new JPanel();
        pnlLayout.setBorder(BorderFactory.createEmptyBorder(5, 5, 5, 5));
        pnlLayout.setLayout(new BorderLayout());
        JPanel pnlLeft = new JPanel();
        pnlLeft.setLayout(new BorderLayout());
        final JTextField txtUsername = new JTextField(30);
        pnlLeft.add(txtUsername, BorderLayout.NORTH);
        final JTextArea txtInput = new JTextArea(5, 30);
        txtInput.setEnabled(false);
        pnlLeft.add(new JScrollPane(txtInput), BorderLayout.CENTER);
```

```java
final JTextArea txtOutput = new JTextArea(10, 30);
txtOutput.setFocusable(false);
pnlLeft.add(new JScrollPane(txtOutput), BorderLayout.SOUTH);
pnlLayout.add(pnlLeft, BorderLayout.WEST);
JPanel pnlRight = new JPanel();
pnlRight.setLayout(new BorderLayout());
final JTextArea txtUsers = new JTextArea(10, 10);
txtUsers.setFocusable(false);
Border border = BorderFactory.createEtchedBorder(EtchedBorder.LOWERED);
txtUsers.setBorder(border);
pnlRight.add(txtUsers, BorderLayout.NORTH);
JPanel pnlButtons = new JPanel();
pnlButtons.setLayout(new GridLayout(3, 1));
final JButton btnConnect = new JButton("Connect");
ActionListener al;
al = new ActionListener()
        {
            @Override
            public void actionPerformed(ActionEvent ae)
            {
                txtUsername.setFocusable(false);
                String username = txtUsername.getText().trim();
                try
                {
                    socket = new Socket(SERVER_ADDR, SERVER_PORT);
                    btnConnect.setEnabled(false);
                    InputStreamReader isr;
                    isr = new InputStreamReader(socket.getInputStream());
                    br = new BufferedReader(isr);
                    pw = new PrintWriter(socket.getOutputStream(), true);
                    txtOutput.append(br.readLine()+"\n");
                    pw.println((!username.equals(""))?username:"unknown");
                    txtInput.setEnabled(true);
                    btnSend.setEnabled(true);
                    new Thread(new Runnable()
                            {
                                @Override
                                public void run()
                                {
                                    String line;
                                    try
                                    {
                                        while ((line = br.readLine()) != null)
                                        {
                                            if (line.charAt(0) != '!')
                                            {
                                                txtOutput.append(line+"\n");
                                                continue;
                                            }
                                            txtUsers.setText("");
                                            String[] users;
                                            users = line.substring(1)
```

```
                                          .split(" ");
                                for (String user: users)
                                {
                                    txtUsers.append(user);
                                    txtUsers.append("\n");
                                }
                        }
                    }
                    catch (IOException ioe)
                    {
                        txtOutput.append("lost the link");
                        return;
                    }
                }
            }).start();
        }
        catch (Exception e)
        {
            txtOutput.append("unable to connect to server");
        }
    }
};
btnConnect.addActionListener(al);
pnlButtons.add(btnConnect);
btnSend = new JButton("Send");
btnSend.setEnabled(false);
al = new ActionListener()
    {
        @Override
        public void actionPerformed(ActionEvent ae)
        {
            pw.println(txtInput.getText());
            txtInput.setText("");
        }
    };
btnSend.addActionListener(al);
pnlButtons.add(btnSend);
JButton btnQuit = new JButton("Quit");
al = new ActionListener()
    {
        @Override
        public void actionPerformed(ActionEvent ae)
        {
            try
            {
                if (socket != null)
                    socket.close();
            }
            catch (IOException ioe)
            {
            }
            System.exit(0);
```

```
                  }
              };
      btnQuit.addActionListener(al);
      pnlButtons.add(btnQuit);
      pnlRight.add(pnlButtons, BorderLayout.SOUTH);
      pnlLayout.add(pnlRight, BorderLayout.EAST);
      return pnlLayout;
   }
   public static void main(String[] args)
   {
      Runnable r = new Runnable()
                   {
                       @Override
                       public void run()
                       {
                          JFrame f = new JFrame("ChatClient");
                          f.setDefaultCloseOperation(JFrame.DISPOSE_ON_CLOSE);
                          f.setContentPane(createGUI());
                          f.pack();
                          f.setResizable(false);
                          f.setVisible(true);
                       }
                   };
      EventQueue.invokeLater(r);
   }
}
```

Listing 9-3's ChatClient class consists of constant/nonconstant fields, a JPanel createGUI() class method for creating this application's graphical user interface (GUI), and a main() method for creating the GUI and running the application.

The GUI-creation code presents a couple of items that I didn't discuss in Chapter 7 (for brevity):

- The java.awt.Component class declares a void setFocusable(boolean focusable) method for setting a component's focusable state. In other words, it determines whether or not the user can tab to or click on the component to give that component input focus (e.g., letting the user enter characters in a textfield). Passing false to this method prevents the component from receiving input focus, and I do so on the various textfield/textarea components for this purpose. Although I could have called setEnabled(false) to achieve the same result, I didn't do this because a disabled textfield's/textarea's text appears faint and is hard to read (at least under the default Metal Look and Feel). In contrast, the text is strong and easy to read when the component is not focusable.

- The java.awt.BorderLayout class is used extensively to lay out the GUI. It lets you arrange up to five components in the north, south, east, west, and center areas of its associated container. Components are laid out according to their preferred sizes and the constraints of the container's size. The north and south components may be stretched horizontally; the east and west components may be stretched vertically; the center component may stretch horizontally and vertically to fill any space left over. When adding a component to a container that's managed by a border layout, java.awt.Container's void add(Component comp, Object constraints) method is called with one of BorderLayout's java.lang.String-based constraint constants (e.g., NORTH) as the second argument, to tell the layout manager where to place the component.

The listeners attached to the Connect, Send, and Quit buttons show you how to create a socket that connects to the chat server, communicate with the chat server, and close the socket.

ChatServer and ChatClient communicate over the same port number (8010). Also, ChatClient assumes that ChatServer is running on the same computer by specifying localhost (127.0.0.1). If ChatServer ran on a different computer, you would specify that computer's domain name/IP address instead.

Compile Listing 9-3 (javac ChatClient.java). Assuming that ChatServer is running, start a pair of ChatClient instances by executing java ChatClient in two different command windows.

Figure 9-2 shows users Jack and Jill communicating over their chat clients.

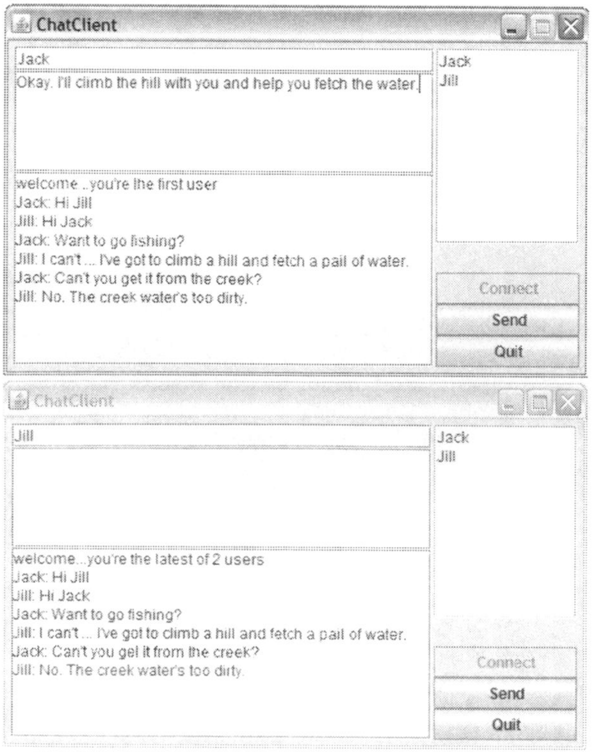

Figure 9-2. Jack is preparing to send a message to Jill.

Enter a name in the top textfield and click the Connect button to connect to the chat server. When no name is specified, the chat client chooses unknown for the username—you cannot change the username after clicking Connect. The textarea to the right of the username textfield displays all users engaged in the chat.

Continue by entering text in the input textarea that appears below the username textfield, and click the Send button to send the entered text to all users. This text appears in the output textarea that appears below the input textarea.

Finally, click the Quit button to terminate the chat.

DatagramSocket and MulticastSocket

The DatagramSocket and MulticastSocket classes let you perform UDP-based communications between a pair of hosts (DatagramSocket) or between multiple hosts (MulticastSocket). With either class, you communicate one-way messages via *datagram packets*, which are arrays of bytes associated with instances of the DatagramPacket class.

⬚ **Note** Although you might think that Socket and ServerSocket are all that you need, DatagramSocket (and its MulticastSocket subclass) have their uses. For example, consider a scenario where a group of machines need to occasionally tell a server that they're alive. It shouldn't matter when the occasional message is lost or even when the message doesn't arrive on time. Another example is a low-priority stock ticker that periodically broadcasts stock prices. When a packet doesn't arrive, odds are that the next packet will arrive and you'll then receive notification of the latest prices. Timely rather than reliable or orderly delivery is more important in realtime applications.

DatagramPacket declares several constructors with DatagramPacket(byte[] buf, int length) being the simplest. This constructor requires you to pass byte array and integer arguments to buf and length, where buf is a data buffer that stores data to be sent or received, and length (which must be less than or equal to buf.length) specifies the number of bytes (starting at buf[0]) to send or receive.

The following example demonstrates this constructor:

```
byte[] buffer = new byte[100];
DatagramPacket dgp = new DatagramPacket(buffer, buffer.length);
```

⬚ **Note** Additional constructors let you specify an offset into buf that identifies the storage location of the first outgoing or incoming byte, and/or let you specify a destination socket address.

DatagramSocket describes a socket for the client or server side of the UDP-communication link. Although this class declares several constructors, I find it convenient in this chapter to use the DatagramSocket() constructor for the client side and the DatagramSocket(int port) constructor for the server side. Either constructor throws java.net.SocketException when it cannot create the datagram socket or bind the datagram socket to a local port.

After an application instantiates DatagramSocket, it calls void send(DatagramPacket dgp) and void receive(DatagramPacket dgp) to send and receive datagram packets.

Listing 9-4 demonstrates DatagramPacket and DatagramSocket in a server context.

Listing 9-4. Receiving datagram packets from and echoing them back to clients

```
import java.io.IOException;

import java.net.DatagramPacket;
import java.net.DatagramSocket;

class DGServer
{
   final static int PORT = 10000;
   public static void main(String[] args) throws IOException
   {
      System.out.println("Server is starting");
      try (DatagramSocket dgs = new DatagramSocket(PORT))
      {
         System.out.println("Send buffer size = "+dgs.getSendBufferSize());
         System.out.println("Receive buffer size = "+
                             dgs.getReceiveBufferSize());
         byte[] data = new byte[100];
         DatagramPacket dgp = new DatagramPacket(data, data.length);
         while (true)
         {
            dgs.receive(dgp);
            System.out.println(new String(data));
            dgs.send(dgp);
         }
      }
      catch (IOException ioe)
      {
         System.err.println("I/O error: "+ioe.getMessage());
      }
   }
}
```

Listing 9-4's main() method first creates a DatagramSocket object and binds the socket to port 10000 on the local host. It then invokes DatagramSocket's int getSendBufferSize() and int getReceiveBufferSize() methods to get the values of the SO_SNDBUF and SO_RCVBUF socket options, which are then output.

■ **Note** Sockets are associated with underlying platform send and receive buffers, and their sizes are accessed by calling getSendBufferSize() and getReceiverBufferSize(). Similarly, their sizes can be set by calling DatagramSocket's void setReceiveBufferSize(int size) and void setSendBufferSize(int size) methods. Although you can adjust these buffer sizes to improve performance, there's a practical limit with regard to UDP. The maximum size of a UDP packet that can be sent or received is 65,507 bytes under IPv4—it's derived from subtracting the 8-byte UDP header and 20-byte IP header values from 65,535. Although you can specify a send/receive buffer with a greater value, doing so is wasteful because the largest packet is restricted to 65,507 bytes. Also, attempting to send/receive a packet greater than 65,507 bytes (regardless of buffer size) results in `IOException`.

---

main() next instantiates DatagramPacket in preparation for receiving a datagram packet from a client and then echoing the packet back to the client. It assumes that packets will be 100 bytes or less in size.

Finally, main() enters an infinite loop that receives a packet, outputs packet content, and sends the packet back to the client—the client's addressing information is stored in DatagramPacket.

Compile Listing 9-4 (javac DGServer.java) and run the application (java DGClient). You should observe output that's the same as or similar to that shown here:

```
Server is starting
Send buffer size = 8192
Receive buffer size = 8192
```

Listing 9-5 demonstrates DatagramPacket and DatagramSocket in a client context.

Listing 9-5. *Sending a datagram packet to and receiving it back from a server*

```java
import java.io.IOException;

import java.net.DatagramPacket;
import java.net.DatagramSocket;
import java.net.InetAddress;

class DGClient
{
   final static int PORT = 10000;
   final static String ADDR = "localhost";
   public static void main(String[] args)
   {
      System.out.println("client is starting");
      DatagramSocket s = null;
      try (DatagramSocket dgs = new DatagramSocket())
      {
         byte[] buffer;
         buffer = "Send me a datagram".getBytes();
         InetAddress ia = InetAddress.getByName(ADDR);
         DatagramPacket dgp = new DatagramPacket(buffer, buffer.length, ia,
                                                 PORT);
         dgs.send(dgp);
         byte[] buffer2 = new byte[100];
         dgp = new DatagramPacket(buffer2, buffer.length, ia, PORT);
         dgs.receive(dgp);
         System.out.println(new String(dgp.getData()));
```

```
        }
        catch (IOException ioe)
        {
            System.err.println("I/O error: "+ioe.getMessage());
        }
    }
}
```

Listing 9-5 is similar to Listing 9-4, but there's one big difference. I use the DatagramPacket(byte[] buf, int length, InetAddress address, int port) constructor to specify the server's destination, which happens to be port 10000 on the local host, in the datagram packet. The send() method call routes the packet to this destination.

Compile Listing 9-5 (javac DGClient.java) and run the application (java DGClient). Assuming that DGServer is also running, you should observe the following output in DGClient's command window (and the last line of this output in DGServer's command window):

```
client is starting
Send me a datagram
```

MulticastSocket describes a socket for the client or server side of a UDP-based multicasting session. Two commonly used constructors are MulticastSocket() (create a multicast socket not bound to a port) and MulticastSocket(int port) (create a multicast socket bound to the specified port).

WHAT IS MULTICASTING?

Previous examples have demonstrated *unicasting*, which occurs when a server sends a message to a single client. However, it's also possible to broadcast the same message to multiple clients (e.g., transmit a "school closed due to bad weather" announcement to all members of a group of parents who have registered with an online program to receive this announcement); this activity is known as *multicasting*.

A server multicasts by sending a sequence of datagram packets to a special IP address, which is known as a *multicast group address*, and a specific port (as specified by a port number). Clients wanting to receive those datagram packets create a multicast socket that uses that port number. They request to join the group through a *join group operation* that specifies the special IP address. At this point, the client can receive datagram packets sent to the group, and can even send datagram packets to other group members. After the client has read all datagram packets that it wants to read, it removes itself from the group by applying a *leave group operation* that specifies the special IP address.

IPv4 addresses 224.0.0.1 to 239.255.255.255 (inclusive) are reserved for use as multicast group addresses.

Listing 9-6 presents a multicasting server.

Listing 9-6. Multicasting datagram packets

```
import java.io.IOException;

import java.net.DatagramPacket;
import java.net.InetAddress;
import java.net.MulticastSocket;
```

```
class MCServer
{
   final static int PORT = 10000;
   public static void main(String[] args)
   {
      try (MulticastSocket mcs = new MulticastSocket())
      {
         InetAddress group = InetAddress.getByName("231.0.0.1");
         byte[] dummy = new byte[0];
         DatagramPacket dgp = new DatagramPacket(dummy, 0, group, PORT);
         int i = 0;
         while (true)
         {
            byte[] buffer = ("line "+i).getBytes();
            dgp.setData(buffer);
            dgp.setLength(buffer.length);
            mcs.send(dgp);
            i++;
         }
      }
      catch (IOException ioe)
      {
         System.err.println("I/O error: "+ioe.getMessage());
      }
   }
}
```

Listing 9-6's main() method first creates a MulticastSocket instance via the MulticastSocket() constructor. The multicast socket doesn't need to bind to a port number because the port number is specified along with the multicast group's IP address (231.0.0.1) as part of the DatagramPacket instance that's subsequently created. (The dummy array is present to prevent a NullPointerException object from being thrown from the DatagramPacket constructor—this array isn't used to store data to be broadcasted.)

At this point, main() enters an infinite loop that first creates an array of bytes from a String instance, and uses the platform's default character encoding (see Chapter 8) to convert from Unicode characters to bytes. (Although extraneous StringBuilder and String objects are created via expression "line "+i in each loop iteration I'm not worried about their impact on garbage collection in this short throwaway application.)

This data buffer is subsequently assigned to the DatagramPacket instance by calling its void setData(byte[] buf) method, and then the datagram packet is broadcast to all members of the group associated with port 10000 and multicast IP address 231.0.0.1.

Compile Listing 9-6 (javac MCServer.java) and run this application (java MCServer). You shouldn't observe any output.

Listing 9-7 presents a multicasting client.

Listing 9-7. Receiving multicasted datagram packets

```
import java.io.IOException;

import java.net.DatagramPacket;
import java.net.InetAddress;
```

```
import java.net.MulticastSocket;

class MCClient
{
    final static int PORT = 10000;
    public static void main(String[] args)
    {
        try (MulticastSocket mcs = new MulticastSocket(PORT))
        {
            InetAddress group = InetAddress.getByName("231.0.0.1");
            mcs.joinGroup(group);
            for (int i = 0; i < 10; i++)
            {
                byte[] buffer = new byte[256];
                DatagramPacket dgp = new DatagramPacket(buffer, buffer.length);
                mcs.receive(dgp);
                byte[] buffer2 = new byte[dgp.getLength()];
                System.arraycopy(dgp.getData(), 0, buffer2, 0, dgp.getLength());
                System.out.println(new String(buffer2));
            }
            mcs.leaveGroup(group);
        }
        catch (IOException ioe)
        {
            System.err.println("I/O error: "+ioe.getMessage());
        }
    }
}
```

Listing 9-7's main() method first creates a MulticastSocket instance bound to port 10000 via the MulticastSocket(int port) constructor.

It then obtains an InetAddress object that contains multicast group IP address 231.0.0.1, and uses this object to join the group at this address by calling MulticastSocket's void joinGroup(InetAddress mcastaddr) method.

main() next receives ten datagram packets, prints their contents, and leaves the group by calling MulticastSocket's void leaveGroup(InetAddress mcastaddr) method with the same multicast IP address as its argument.

Note joinGroup() and leaveGroup() throw IOException when an I/O error occurs while attempting to join or leave the group, or when the IP address is not a multicast IP address.

Because the client doesn't know exactly how long the arrays of bytes will be, it assumes 256 bytes to ensure that the data buffer will hold the entire array. If it tried to print out the returned array, you would see a lot of empty space after the actual data had been printed. To eliminate this space, it invokes DatagramPacket's int getLength() method to obtain the actual length of the array, creates a second byte array (buffer2) with this length, and uses System.arraycopy()—discussed in Chapter 4—to copy this many bytes to buffer2. After converting this byte array to a String object (via the String(byte[] bytes) constructor, which uses the platform's default character set—see Chapter 8 to learn about character sets), it prints the resulting characters to the standard output device.

Compile Listing 9-7 (javac MCClient.java) and run this application (java MCClient). You should observe output similar to the following:

```
line 521103
line 521104
line 521105
line 521106
line 521107
line 521108
line 521109
line 521110
line 521111
line 521112
```

Communicating via URLs

A *Uniform Resource Locator (URL)* is a character string that specifies where a resource (e.g., a web page) is located on a TCP/IP-based network (e.g., the Internet). Also, it provides the means to retrieve that resource. For example, http://tutortutor.ca is a URL that locates my website's main page. The http:// prefix specifies that *HyperText Transfer Protocol (HTTP)*, which is a high-level protocol on top of TCP/IP for locating HTTP resources (e.g., web pages), must be used to retrieve the web page located at tutortutor.ca.

URNS AND URIS

A *Uniform Resource Name (URN)* is a character string that doesn't imply a resource's availability. Even when the resource is available, the URN doesn't provide a way to locate it. For example, urn:isbn:9781430234135 identifies an Apress book named *Android Recipes*, and that's all.

URNs and URLs are examples of *Uniform Resource Identifiers (URIs)*, which are character strings for identifying names (URNs) or resources (URLs). Every URN and URL is also a URI, a fact that I take advantage of in subsequent chapters by specifying URI instead of URL.

The java.net package provides URL and URLConnection classes for accessing URL-based resources. It also provides URLEncoder and URLDecoder classes for encoding and decoding URLs, and the URI class for performing URI-based operations (e.g., relativization) and returning URL instances containing the results.

URL and URLConnection

The URL class represents URLs and provides access to the resources to which they refer. Each URL instance unambiguously identifies an Internet resource.

URL declares several constructors with URL(String s) being the simplest. This constructor creates a URL instance from the String argument passed to s and is demonstrated as follows:

```
try
{
```

```
    URL url = new URL("http://tutortutor.ca");
}
catch (MalformedURLException murle)
{
}
```

This example creates a URL object that uses HTTP to access the web page at http://tutortutor.ca. If I specified an illegal URL (e.g., foo), the constructor would throw java.net.MalformedURLException (an IOException subclass).

Although you'll commonly specify http:// as the protocol prefix, this isn't your only choice. For example, you can also specify file:/// when the resource is located on the local host. Furthermore, you can prepend jar: to either http:// or file:/// when the resource is stored in a JAR file, as demonstrated here:

```
jar:file:///C:./rt.jar!/com/sun/beans/TypeResolver.class
```

The jar: prefix indicates that you want to access a JAR file resource (e.g., a stored classfile). The file:/// prefix identifies the local host's resource location, which happens to be rt.jar (Java 7's runtime JAR file) in the current directory on the Windows C: hard drive in this example.

The path to the JAR file is followed by an exclamation mark (!) to separate the JAR file path from the JAR resource path, which happens to be the /com/sun/beans/TypeResolver.class classfile entry in this JAR file (the leading / character is required).

■ **Note** The URL class in Oracle's Java reference implementation supports additional protocols, including ftp and mailto.

After creating a URL object, you can invoke various URL methods to access portions of the URL. For example, String getProtocol() returns the protocol portion of the URL (e.g., http). You can also retrieve the resource by calling the InputStream openStream() method.

openStream() creates a connection to the resource and returns an InputStream instance for reading resource data from that connection, as demonstrated here:

```
try (InputStream is = url.openStream())
{
   int ch;
   while ((ch = is.read()) != -1)
      System.out.print((char) ch);
}
```

■ **Note** For an HTTP connection, an internal socket is created that connects to HTTP port 80 on the server identified via the URL's domain name/IP address, unless you append a different port number to the domain name/IP address (e.g., http://tutortutor.ca:8080).

I've created an application that demonstrates locating and accessing an arbitrary resource. Listing 9-8 presents its source code.

Listing 9-8. Outputting the contents of the resource identified via a URL command-line argument

```java
import java.io.InputStream;
import java.io.IOException;

import java.net.MalformedURLException;
import java.net.URL;

class GetResource
{
   public static void main(String[] args)
   {
      if (args.length != 1)
      {
         System.err.println("usage: java GetResource url");
         return;
      }
      try
      {
         URL url = new URL(args[0]);
         try (InputStream is = url.openStream())
         {
            int ch;
            while ((ch = is.read()) != -1)
               System.out.print((char) ch);
         }
      }
      catch (MalformedURLException murle)
      {
         System.err.println("invalid URL");
      }
      catch (IOException ioe)
      {
         System.err.println("I/O error: "+ioe.getMessage());
      }
   }
}
```

Compile this source code (javac GetResource.java) and execute java GetResource http://tutortutor.ca. The following output presents a short prefix of the returned web page:

```
<!DOCTYPE html PUBLIC "-//W3C//DTD HTML 4.01//EN"↩
 "http://www.w3.org/TR/html4/strict.dtd">

<html>
  <head>
    <title>
      TutorTutor -- /main
    </title>
```

openStream() is a convenience method for invoking openConnection().getInputStream(). Each of URL's URLConnection openConnection() and URLConnection openConnection(Proxy proxy) methods returns an instance of the java.net.URLConnection class, which represents a communications link between the application and a URL.

URLConnection gives you additional control over client/server communication. For example, you can use this class to output content to various resources that accept content. In contrast, URL only lets you input content via openStream().

URLConnection declares various methods, including the following:

- InputStream getInputStream() returns an input stream that reads from this open connection.

- OutputStream getOutputStream() returns an output stream that writes to this open connection.

- void setDoInput(boolean doinput) specifies that this URLConnection object supports (pass true to doinput) or doesn't support (pass false to doinput) input. Because true is the default, you would only pass true to this method to document your intention to perform input (as I demonstrate in Chapter 11).

- void setDoOutput(boolean dooutput) specifies that this URLConnection object supports (pass true to dooutput) or doesn't support (pass false to dooutput) output. Because false is the default, you must call this method before you can perform output (as demonstrated in Chapter 11).

- void setRequestProperty(String key, String value) sets a request property (e.g., HTTP's accept property). When a key already exists, its value is overwritten with the specified value.

The following example shows you how to obtain a URLConnection object from a URL object referenced by precreated variable url, set its dooutput property, and obtain an output stream for writing to the resource:

```
URLConnection urlc = url.openConnection();
urlc.setDoOutput(true);
OutputStream os = urlc.getOutputStream();
```

URLConnection is subclassed by java.net.HttpURLConnection and java.net.JarURLConnection. These classes declare constants and/or methods that are specific to working with the HTTP protocol or interacting with JAR-based resources.

Note For brevity, I refer you to the JDK documentation on URLConnection, HttpURLConnection, and JarURLConnection; and to Chapter 11's HttpURLConnection examples for more information.

URLEncoder and URLDecoder

HyperText Markup Language (HTML) lets you introduce forms into web pages that solicit information from page visitors. After filling out a form's fields, the visitor clicks the form's Submit button (which often has a different label) and the form content (field names and values) is sent to some server program.

Before sending the form content to the server program, a web browser encodes this data by replacing spaces and other URL-illegal characters, and sets the content's Multipurpose Internet Mail Extensions (MIME) type to application/x-www-form-urlencoded.

Note The data is encoded for HTTP POST and GET operations. Unlike POST, GET requires a *query string* (a ?-prefixed string containing the encoded content) to be appended to the server program's URL.

The java.net package provides URLEncoder and URLDecoder classes to assist you with the tasks of encoding and decoding form content.

URLEncoder applies the following encoding rules:

- Alphanumeric characters "a" through "z", "A" through "Z", and "0" through "9" remain the same.

- Special characters ".", "-", "*", and "_" remain the same.

- The space character " " is converted into a plus sign "+" on Internet Explorer and "%20" on Firefox.

- All other characters are unsafe and are first converted into one or more bytes using some encoding scheme. Each byte is then represented by the three-character string %*xy*, where *xy* is the two-digit hexadecimal representation of that byte. The recommended encoding scheme to use is UTF-8. However, for compatibility reasons, the platform's default encoding is used when an encoding isn't specified.

For example, using UTF-8 as the encoding scheme, the string "The string ü@foo-bar" is converted to "The+string+%C3%BC%40foo-bar". In UTF-8, character ü is encoded as two bytes C3 (hex) and BC (hex), and character @ is encoded as one byte 40 (hex).

URLEncoder declares the following class method for encoding a string:

```
String encode(String s, String enc)
```

This method translates the String argument passed to s into application/x-www-form-urlencoded format using encoding scheme enc. It uses the supplied encoding scheme to obtain the bytes for unsafe characters, and throws java.io.UnsupportedEncodingException when enc's value isn't supported.

URLDecoder applies the following decoding rules:

- Alphanumeric characters "a" through "z", "A" through "Z", and "0" through "9" remain the same.

- Special characters ".", "-", "*", and "_" remain the same.

- The plus sign "+"/"%20" is converted into a space character " ".

- A sequence of the form %*xy* will be treated as representing a byte where *xy* is the two-digit hexadecimal representation of the 8 bits. Then, all substrings containing one or more of these byte sequences consecutively will be replaced by the character(s) whose encoding would result in those consecutive bytes. The encoding scheme used to decode these characters may be specified; when unspecified, the platform's default encoding is used.

URLDecoder declares the following class method for decoding an encoded string:

```
String decode(String s, String enc)
```

This method decodes an application/x-www-form-urlencoded string using the specified encoding scheme. The supplied encoding is used to determine what characters are represented by any consecutive sequences of the form %*xy*. UnsupportedEncodingException is thrown when enc's value isn't supported.

There are two possible ways in which the decoder could deal with illegally encoded strings. It could either leave illegal characters alone or it could throw IllegalArgumentException. Which approach the decoder takes is left to the implementation.

■ **Note** The World Wide Web Consortium Recommendation (http://www.w3.org/TR/html40/appendix/notes.html#non-ascii-chars), which is similar to an RFC, states that UTF-8 should be used as the encoding scheme for encode() and decode(). Not doing so may introduce incompatibilities.

I've created an application that demonstrates URLEncoder and URLDecoder in the context of the previous "The string ü@foo-bar" and "The+string+%C3%BC%40foo-bar" example. Listing 9-9 presents the application's source code.

Listing 9-9. Encoding and decoding an encoded string

```
import java.io.UnsupportedEncodingException;

import java.net.URLDecoder;
import java.net.URLEncoder;

class EncDec
{
   public static void main(String[] args) throws UnsupportedEncodingException
   {
      String encodedData = URLEncoder.encode("The string ü@foo-bar", "UTF-8");
      System.out.println(encodedData);
      System.out.println(URLDecoder.decode(encodedData, "UTF-8"));
   }
}
```

■ **Note** You might want to check out Wikipedia's "Percent-encoding" topic
(http://en.wikipedia.org/wiki/Percent-encoding) to learn more about URL encoding (and the more accurate percent-encoding term).

URI

The URI class represents URIs (e.g., URNs and URLs). It doesn't provide access to a resource when the URI is a URL.

A URI instance stores a character string that conforms to the following syntax at the highest level:

[*scheme*:]*scheme-specific-part*[#*fragment*]

This syntax reveals that every URI optionally begins with a *scheme* followed by a colon character, where a *scheme* can be thought of as an application-level protocol for obtaining an Internet resource. However, this definition is too narrow because it implies that the URI is always a URL. A scheme can have nothing to do with resource location. For example, urn is the scheme for identifying URNs.

A scheme is followed by a *scheme-specific-part* that provides an instance of the scheme. For example, given the http://tutortutor.ca URI, tutortutor.ca is an instance of the http scheme. Scheme-specific-parts conform to the allowable syntax of their schemes and to the overall syntax structure of a URI (including what characters can be specified literally and what characters must be encoded).

A scheme concludes with an optional #-prefixed *fragment*, which is a short string of characters that refers to a resource subordinate to another primary resource. The primary resource is identified by a URI; the fragment points to the subordinate resource. For example, http://tutortutor.ca/document.txt#line=5,10 identifies lines 5 through 10 of a text document named document.txt on my website. (This example is only illustrative; the resource doesn't actually exist.)

URIs can be categorized as absolute or relative. An *absolute URI* begins with a scheme followed by a colon character. The earlier http://tutortutor.ca URI is an example of an absolute URI. Other examples include mailto:jeff@tutortutor.ca and news:comp.lang.java.help. Consider an absolute URI as referring to a resource in a manner independent of the context in which that identifier appears. To use a filesystem analogy, an absolute URI is equivalent to a pathname to a file that starts from the root directory.

A *relative URI* doesn't begin with a scheme (followed by a colon character). An example is tutorials/tutorials.html. Consider a relative URI as referring to a resource in a manner dependent on the context in which that identifier appears. Using the filesystem analogy, the relative URI is like a pathname to a file that starts from the current directory.

URIs also can be categorized as opaque or hierarchical. An *opaque URI* is an absolute URI whose scheme-specific-part doesn't begin with a forward slash (/) character. Examples include http://tutortutor.ca and mailto:jeff@tutortutor.ca. Opaque URIs aren't parsed (beyond identifying their schemes) because scheme-specific-parts don't need to be validated.

A *hierarchical URI* is either an absolute URI whose scheme-specific-part begins with a forward slash character, or is a relative URI.

Unlike an opaque URI, a hierarchical URI's scheme-specific-part must be parsed into the various components identified by the following syntax:

[//*authority*] [*path*] [?*query*] [#*fragment*]

authority identifies the naming authority for the URI's namespace. When present, this component begins with a pair of forward slash characters, is either server-based or registry-based, and terminates with the next forward slash character, question mark character, or no more characters—the end of the URI. Registry-based authority components have scheme-specific syntaxes (and aren't discussed because they're not commonly used), whereas server-based authority components commonly adopt the following syntax:

[*userinfo@*] *host* [*:port*]

This syntax specifies that a server-based authority component optionally begins with user information (e.g., a username) and an "at" (@) character, then continues with the host's name, and optionally concludes with a colon character and a port. For example, jeff@tutortutor.ca is a server-based authority component, in which jeff denotes the user information and tutortutor.ca denotes the host—there's no port.

path identifies the resource's location according to the authority component (when present) or the scheme (when the authority component is absent). A path divides into a sequence of *path segments* (portions of the path), in which forward slash characters are used to separate the segments. The path is absolute when the first path segment begins with a forward slash character; otherwise, the path is relative. For example, /a/b/c constitutes a path with three path segments—a, b, and c. Furthermore, the path is absolute because a forward slash character prefixes the first path segment (a).

query identifies data to be passed to the resource. The resource uses the data to obtain or produce other data that it passes back to the caller. For example, in http://tutortutor.ca/cgi-bin/makepage.cgi?/software/Aquarium, /software/Aquarium represents a query. According to that query, /software/Aquarium is data to be passed to a resource (makepage.cgi), and this data happens to be the absolute path to a directory whose same-named file is merged with boilerplate HTML by a Perl script to generate a resulting web page.

The final component is *fragment*. Although it appears to be part of a URI, it's not. When a URI is used in a retrieval action, the primary resource that performs that action uses the fragment to retrieve the subordinate resource. For example, makepage.cgi is the primary resource and /software/Aquarium is the subordinate resource.

The previous discussion reveals that a complete URI consists of scheme, authority, path, query, and fragment components; or it consists of scheme, user-info, host, port, path, query, and fragment components. To construct a URI instance in the former case, call the URI(String scheme, String authority, String path, String query, String fragment) constructor. In the latter case, call URI(String scheme, String userInfo, String host, int port, String path, String query, String fragment).

Additional constructors are available for creating URI instances. For example, URI(String uri) creates a URI by parsing uri. Regardless of which constructor you call, it throws java.net.URISyntaxException when the resulting URI string has invalid syntax.

Tip The java.io.File class declares a URI toURI() method that you can call to convert a File object's abstract pathname to a URI object. The internal URI's scheme is set to file.

URI declares various getter methods that let you retrieve URI components. For example, String getScheme() lets you retrieve the scheme, and String getFragment() returns a URL-decoded fragment. This class also declares boolean isAbsolute() and boolean isOpaque() methods that return true when a URI is absolute and opaque.

Listing 9-10 presents an application that lets you learn about URI components along with absolute and opaque URIs.

Listing 9-10. *Learning about a URI*

```java
import java.net.URI;
import java.net.URISyntaxException;

class URIComponents
{
   public static void main(String[] args) throws URISyntaxException
   {
      if (args.length != 1)
      {
         System.err.println("usage: java URIComponents uri");
         return;
      }
      URI uri = new URI(args[0]);
      System.out.println("Authority = "+uri.getAuthority());
      System.out.println("Fragment = "+uri.getFragment());
      System.out.println("Host = "+uri.getHost());
      System.out.println("Path = "+uri.getPath());
      System.out.println("Port = "+uri.getPort());
      System.out.println("Query = "+uri.getQuery());
      System.out.println("Scheme = "+uri.getScheme());
      System.out.println("Scheme-specific part = "+uri.getSchemeSpecificPart());
      System.out.println("User Info = "+uri.getUserInfo());
      System.out.println("URI is absolute: "+uri.isAbsolute());
      System.out.println("URI is opaque: "+uri.isOpaque());
   }
}
```

Compile Listing 9-10 (javac URIComponents.java) and run the application as follows: java URIComponents http://tutortutor.ca/cgi-bin/makepage.cgi?/software/Aquarium. You'll observe the following output:

```
Authority = tutortutor.ca
Fragment = null
Host = tutortutor.ca
Path = /cgi-bin/makepage.cgi
Port = -1
Query = /software/Aquarium
Scheme = http
Scheme-specific part = //tutortutor.ca/cgi-bin/makepage.cgi?/software/Aquarium
User Info = null
URI is absolute: true
URI is opaque: false
```

After creating a URI instance, you can perform normalization, resolution, and, relativization operations (discussed shortly) on its contained URI. Although you cannot communicate via this instance, you can convert it to a URL instance for communication purposes (assuming that the URI is actually a URL and not a URN or something else) by invoking its URL toURL() method.

This method throws IllegalArgumentException when the URI doesn't represent an absolute URL, and throws MalformedURLException when a protocol handler for the URL couldn't be found (i.e., the URL doesn't start with a supported protocol such as http or file), or when some other error occurred while constructing the URL instance.

Normalization

Normalization is the process of removing unnecessary "." and ".." path segments from a hierarchical URI's path component. Each "." segment is removed. A ".." segment is removed only when it's preceded by a non-".." segment. Normalization has no effect upon opaque URIs.

URI declares a URI normalize() method for normalizing a URI. This method returns a new URI object that contains the normalized equivalent of its caller's URI.

Listing 9-11 presents an application that lets you experiment with normalize().

***Listing 9-11.** Normalizing URIs*

```
import java.net.URI;
import java.net.URISyntaxException;

class Normalize
{
   public static void main(String[] args) throws URISyntaxException
   {
      if (args.length != 1)
      {
         System.err.println("usage: java Normalize uri");
         return;
      }
      URI uri = new URI(args[0]);
      System.out.println("Normalized URI = "+uri.normalize());
   }
}
```

Compile Listing 9-11 (javac Normalize.java) and run the application as follows: java Normalize a/b/../c/./d. You should observe the following output, which shows that b isn't part of a normalized URI:

```
Normalized URI = a/c/d
```

Resolution

Resolution is the process of resolving one URI against another URI, which is known as the base. The resulting URI is constructed from components of both URIs in the manner specified by RFC 2396 (see http://tools.ietf.org/html/rfc2396), taking components from the *base URI* for those not specified in the *original URI*. For hierarchical URIs, the path of the original is resolved against the path of the base and then normalized.

For example, the result of resolving original URI docs/guide/collections/designfaq.html#28 against base URI http://java.sun.com/j2se/1.3/ is result URI http://java.sun.com/j2se/1.3/docs/guide/collections/designfaq.html#28. As a second example, resolving relative URI ../../../demo/jfc/SwingSet2/src/SwingSet2.java against this result yields http://java.sun.com/j2se/1.3/demo/jfc/SwingSet2/src/SwingSet2.java.

Resolution of both absolute and relative URIs, and of both absolute and relative paths in the case of hierarchical URIs, is supported.

URI declares URI resolve(String str) and URI resolve(URI uri) methods for resolving the original URI argument (passed to str or uri) against the base URI contained in the current URI object (on which this method was called). These methods return either a new URI object containing the original URI or the URI argument when the original URI is already absolute or opaque. Otherwise, they return a new URI object containing the resolved URI. NullPointerException is thrown when str or uri is null. IllegalArgumentException is thrown when str violates RFC 2396 syntax.

Listing 9-12 presents an application that lets you experiment with resolve(String).

Listing 9-12. Resolving URIs

```java
import java.net.URI;
import java.net.URISyntaxException;

class Resolve
{
   public static void main(String[] args) throws URISyntaxException
   {
      if (args.length != 2)
      {
         System.err.println("usage: java Resolve baseuri uri");
         return;
      }
      URI uri = new URI(args[0]);
      System.out.println("Resolved URI = "+uri.resolve(args[1]));
   }
}
```

Compile Listing 9-12 (javac Resolve.java) and run the application as follows: java Resolve http://java.sun.com/j2se/1.3/ docs/guide/collections/designfaq.html#28. You should observe the following output:

```
Resolved URI = http://java.sun.com/j2se/1.3/docs/guide/collections/designfaq.html#28
```

Relativization

Relativization is the inverse of resolution. For any two normalized URIs, relativization undoes the work performed by resolution and resolution undoes the work performed by relativization.

URI declares a URI relativize(URI uri) method for relativizing its uri argument against the URI in the current URI object (on which this method was called)—relativize() throws NullPointerException when uri is null.

▪ **Note** For any two normalized URI instances u and v, u.relativize(u.resolve(v)).equals(v) and u.resolve(u.relativize(v)).equals(v) evaluate to true.

---

relativize() performs relativization of its URI argument's URI against the URI in the URI object on which this method was called as follows:

- If either this URI or the argument URI is opaque, or if the scheme and authority components of the two URIs aren't identical, or if the path of this URI isn't a prefix of the path of the argument URI, the argument URI is returned.

- Otherwise, a new relative hierarchical URI is constructed with query and fragment components taken from the argument URI, and with a path component computed by removing this URI's path from the beginning of the argument URI's path.

Listing 9-13 presents an application that lets you experiment with relativize().

Listing 9-13. Relativizing URIs

```java
import java.net.URI;
import java.net.URISyntaxException;

class Relativize
{
   public static void main(String[] args) throws URISyntaxException
   {
      if (args.length != 2)
      {
         System.err.println("usage: java Relativize uri1 uri2");
         return;
      }
      URI uri1 = new URI(args[0]);
      URI uri2 = new URI(args[1]);
      System.out.println("Relativized URI = "+uri1.relativize(uri2));
   }
}
```

Compile Listing 9-13 (javac Relativize.java) and run the application as follows: java Relativize http://java.sun.com/j2se/1.3/ http://java.sun.com/j2se/1.3/docs/guide/collections/designfaq.html#28. You should observe the following output:

```
Relativized URI = docs/guide/collections/designfaq.html#28
```

Authentication

RFC 1945: Hypertext Transfer Protocol—HTTP/1.0 (http://www.ietf.org/rfc/rfc1945.txt) informs you about HTTP 1.0 providing a simple challenge-response mechanism that a server can use to challenge a client's request to access some resource. Furthermore, the client can use this mechanism to provide *credentials* (typically username and password) that *authenticate* (prove) the client's identity. When the supplied credentials satisfy the server, the user is *authorized* (allowed) to access the resource.

To challenge a client, the originating server issues a "401 Unauthorized" message. This message includes a WWW-Authenticate HTTP header that identifies an *authentication scheme* (the approach taken to achieve authentication) via a case-insensitive *token*. A comma-separated sequence of attribute/value pairs follows the token to supply scheme-specific parameters necessary for performing authentication. The client replies with an Authorization header that provides the credentials.

Note HTTP 1.1 made it possible to authenticate a client with a proxy. To challenge a client, a proxy server issues a "407 Proxy Authentication Required" message, which includes a `Proxy-Authenticate` header. A client replies via a `Proxy-Authorization` header.

Basic Authentication and the Authenticator Class

HTTP 1.0 introduced the *basic authentication scheme* by which a client identifies itself via a username and a password. The basic authentication scheme works as follows:

- The `WWW-Authenticate` header specifies `Basic` as the token and a single `realm="quoted string"` pair that identifies the *realm* (a protected space to which a resource belongs, such as a specific group of web pages) referred to by the browser address.

- In response to this header, the browser displays a dialog box in which a username and password are entered.

- Once entered, the username and password are concatenated into a string (a colon is inserted between the username and password), the string is base64-encoded, and the result is placed in an `Authorization` header that's sent back to the server. (To learn more about base64 encoding, check out Wikipedia's Base64 entry at http://en.wikipedia.org/wiki/Base64.)

- The server base64-decodes these credentials and compares them to values stored in its username/password database. When there's a match, the application is granted access to the resource (and any other resource belonging to the realm).

Greg Stein maintains a testing server at http://test.webdav.org/ that can be used to test basic authentication and more. For example, when you specify http://test.webdav.org/auth-basic/ in your browser, you'll be challenged with a 401 response, as the application in Listing 9-14 demonstrates.

Listing 9-14. Demonstrating the need for basic authentication by outputting the server's various HTTP headers

```java
import java.io.IOException;

import java.net.HttpURLConnection;
import java.net.URL;
import java.net.URLConnection;

import java.util.List;
import java.util.Map;

class BasicAuthNeeded
{
   public static void main(String[] args) throws IOException
   {
      String s = "http://test.webdav.org/auth-basic/";
```

```
            URL url = new URL(s);
            URLConnection urlc = url.openConnection();
            Map<String,List<String>> hf = urlc.getHeaderFields();
            for (String key: hf.keySet())
                System.out.println(key+": "+urlc.getHeaderField(key));
            System.out.println(((HttpURLConnection) urlc).getResponseCode());
        }
}
```

This application connects to the testing address and outputs all server-sent headers and its response code. After compiling the source code (javac BasicAuthNeeded.java), run the application (java BasicAuthNeeded). You should see output that is similar to the following:

```
null: HTTP/1.1 401 Authorization Required
WWW-Authenticate: Basic realm="basic auth area"
Date: Mon, 19 Sep 2011 03:06:06 GMT
Content-Length: 401
Keep-Alive: timeout=15, max=100
Connection: Keep-Alive
Content-Type: text/html; charset=iso-8859-1
Server: Apache/2.0.54 (Debian GNU/Linux) DAV/2 SVN/1.3.2
401
```

The WWW-Authenticate header's realm attribute reveals basic auth area as the realm. Although not shown, any username from user1 through user9 and a password that's the same as the username can be specified to authenticate.

In order to pass this username and password back to the HTTP server, the application must work with the java.net.Authenticator class, as Listing 9-15 demonstrates.

Listing 9-15. Performing basic authentication

```
import java.io.IOException;

import java.net.Authenticator;
import java.net.HttpURLConnection;
import java.net.PasswordAuthentication;
import java.net.URL;
import java.net.URLConnection;

import java.util.List;
import java.util.Map;

class BasicAuthGiven
{
    final static String USERNAME = "user1";
    final static String PASSWORD = "user1";
    static class BasicAuthenticator extends Authenticator
    {
        @Override
        public PasswordAuthentication getPasswordAuthentication()
        {
            System.out.println("Password requested from "+
                               getRequestingHost()+" for authentication "+
```

```
                            "scheme "+getRequestingScheme());
         return new PasswordAuthentication(USERNAME, PASSWORD.toCharArray());
      }
   }
   public static void main(String[] args) throws IOException
   {
      Authenticator.setDefault(new BasicAuthenticator());
      String s = "http://test.webdav.org/auth-basic/";
      URL url = new URL(s);
      URLConnection urlc = url.openConnection();
      Map<String,List<String>> hf = urlc.getHeaderFields();
      for (String key: hf.keySet())
         System.out.println(key+": "+urlc.getHeaderField(key));
      System.out.println(((HttpURLConnection) urlc).getResponseCode());
   }
}
```

Because Authenticator is abstract, it must be subclassed. Its protected PasswordAuthentication getPasswordAuthentication() method must be overridden to return the username and password in a java.net.PasswordAuthentication object. Finally, the void setDefault(Authenticator a) class method must be called to install an instance of the Authenticator subclass for the entire Java Virtual Machine (JVM).

After the authenticator has been installed, the JVM will invoke one of Authenticator's requestPasswordAuthentication() methods, which in turn invokes the overriding getPasswordAuthentication() method, when the HTTP server requires basic authentication. This can be seen in the following output, which proves that the server has granted access to the resource (sort of):

```
Password requested from test.webdav.org for authentication scheme basic
null: HTTP/1.1 404 Not Found
Date: Mon, 19 Sep 2011 03:09:11 GMT
Content-Length: 209
Keep-Alive: timeout=15, max=100
Connection: Keep-Alive
Content-Type: text/html; charset=iso-8859-1
Server: Apache/2.0.54 (Debian GNU/Linux) DAV/2 SVN/1.3.2
404
```

This output shows that authorization has succeeded. However, it also shows that the resource cannot be found. (I guess one can't have everything.)

Digest Authentication

Because the basic authentication scheme assumes a secure and trusted connection between client and server, it transmits credentials in the clear (there's no *encryption* [the process of transforming information, referred to as *plaintext*, via an algorithm known as a *cipher*, into something unreadable except to those possessing special knowledge, usually referred to as a *key*]); base64 can be readily decoded), making it easy for eavesdroppers to access this information. For this reason, HTTP 1.1, which is described in RFC 2616: Hypertext Transfer Protocol—HTTP/1.1 (http://www.ietf.org/rfc/rfc2616.txt), introduced the *digest authentication scheme* to deal with the basic authentication scheme's lack of security. According to this scheme, the WWW-Authenticate header specifies Digest as the token. It also specifies the realm="*quoted string*" attribute pair.

The digest authentication scheme uses *MD5,* which is a one-way cryptographic hashing algorithm, to encrypt the password. It also uses server-generated one-time *nonces* (values that vary with time, such as timestamps and visitor counters) to prevent *replay* (also known as *man-in-the-middle*) attacks. Although the password is secure, the rest of the data is transferred in plain text, accessible to eavesdroppers. Also, there's no way for the client to determine that it's communicating with the appropriate server (there's no way for the server to authenticate itself).

Note For more information about digest authentication, check out Wikipedia's "Digest access authentication" entry (http://en.wikipedia.org/wiki/Digest_access_authentication).

NTLM and Kerberos Authentication

Microsoft developed a proprietary *NTLM authentication scheme,* which is based on its Windows NT Local Area Network (LAN) Manager authentication protocol, to let clients access Internet Information Server (IIS) resources via their Windows credentials. This authentication scheme is often used in corporate environments where single sign-on to intranet sites is desired. The WWW-Authenticate header specifies NTLM as the token; there's no realm="*quoted string*" attribute pair. Unlike the previous two schemes, which are request-oriented, NTLM is connection-oriented.

In the 1980s, MIT developed Kerberos for authenticating users on large, distributed networks. This protocol is more flexible and efficient than NTLM. Furthermore, Kerberos is also considered to be more secure. Some of Kerberos's benefits over NTLM are more efficient authentication to servers, mutual authentication, and delegation of credentials to remote machines.

GSS-API, SPNEGO, and the Negotiate Authentication Scheme

Various security services have been developed to secure networked applications. Services include multiple versions of Kerberos, NTLM, and SESAME (an extension of Kerberos). Because it's difficult to rework an application to remove its dependence on one security service and place its dependence on another security service, the Generic Security Services Application Program Interface (GSS-API) was developed as a standard API for simplifying access to these services. A security service vendor typically provides an implementation of GSS-API as a set of libraries that are installed with the vendor's security software. Underlying a GSS-API implementation sits the actual Kerberos, NTLM, or other *mechanism* for providing credentials.

Note Microsoft provides its own proprietary GSS-API variant, known as Security Service Provider Interface (SSPI), which is highly Windows-specific and somewhat interoperable with the GSS-API.

A pair of networked *peers* (hosts that can be clients or servers) may have multiple installed GSS-API implementations from which to choose. As a result, the Simple and Protected GSS-API Negotiation (SPNEGO) pseudo-mechanism is used by these peers to identify shared GSS-API mechanisms, make an appropriate selection, and establish a security context based on this choice.

Microsoft's *negotiate authentication scheme* (introduced with Windows 2000) uses SPNEGO to select a GSS-API mechanism for HTTP authentication. Initially, this scheme supported only Kerberos and NTLM. Under Integrated Windows authentication (which was formerly known as NTLM authentication, and also known as Windows NT Challenge/Response authentication), when Internet Explorer tries to access a protected resource from IIS, IIS sends two `WWW-Authenticate` headers to this browser. The first header has `Negotiate` as the token; the second header has `NTLM` as the token. Because `Negotiate` is listed first, it has first crack at being recognized by Internet Explorer. When recognized, the browser returns both NTLM and Kerberos information to IIS. IIS uses Kerberos when the following are true:

- The client is Internet Explorer 5.0 or later.

- The server is IIS 5.0 or later.

- The operating system is Windows 2000 or later.

- Both the client and server are members of the same domain or trusted domains.

Otherwise, NTLM is used. If Internet Explorer doesn't recognize `Negotiate`, it returns NTLM information via the NTLM authentication scheme to IIS.

A Java client can provide an `Authenticator` subclass whose `getPasswordAuthentication()` method checks the scheme name returned from the `protected final String getRequestingScheme()` method to determine whether the current scheme is `"negotiate"`. When this is the case, the method can pass the username and password to the HTTP SPNEGO module (assuming that they're needed—no credential cache is available), as illustrated in the following code fragment:

```
class MyAuthenticator extends Authenticator
{
    @Override
    public PasswordAuthentication getPasswordAuthentication()
    {
        if (getRequestingScheme().equalsIgnoreCase("negotiate"))
        {
            String krb5user; // Assume Kerberos 5.
            char[] krb5pass;
            // get krb5user and krb5pass in your own way
            ...
            return (new PasswordAuthentication(krb5user, krb5pass));
        }
        else
        {
            ...
        }
    }
}
```

Note For more information on Java's support for SPNEGO and the other authentication schemes, check out the JDK 7 documentation's "Http Authentication" page at

`http://download.oracle.com/javase/7/docs/technotes/guides/net/http-auth.html`.

Cookie Management

Server applications commonly use *HTTP cookies* (state objects)—*cookies* for short—to persist small amounts of information on clients. For example, the identifiers of currently selected items in a shopping cart can be stored as cookies. It's preferable to store cookies on the client, rather than on the server, because of the potential for millions of cookies (depending on a website's popularity). In that case, not only would a server require a massive amount of storage just for cookies, but also searching for and maintaining cookies would be time consuming.

■ **Note** Check out Wikipedia's "HTTP cookie" entry (http://en.wikipedia.org/wiki/HTTP_cookie) for a quick refresher on cookies.

A server application sends a cookie to a client as part of an HTTP response. A client (e.g., a web browser) sends a cookie to the server as part of an HTTP request. Before Java 5, applications worked with the URLConnection class (and its HttpURLConnection subclass) to get an HTTP response's cookies and to set an HTTP request's cookies. The String getHeaderFieldKey(int n) and String getHeaderField(int n) methods were used to access a response's Set-Cookie headers, and the void setRequestProperty(String key, String value) method was used to create a request's Cookie header.

■ **Note** RFC 2109: HTTP State Management Mechanism (http://www.ietf.org/rfc/rfc2109.txt) describes the Set-Cookie and Cookie headers.

Java 5 introduced the abstract java.net.CookieHandler class as a callback mechanism that connects HTTP state management to an HTTP protocol handler (think concrete HttpURLConnection subclass). An application installs a concrete CookieHandler subclass as the system-wide cookie handler via the CookieHandler class's void setDefault(CookieHandler cHandler) class method. A companion CookieHandler getDefault() class method returns this cookie handler, which is null when a system-wide cookie handler hasn't been installed.

An HTTP protocol handler accesses response and request headers. This handler invokes the system-wide cookie handler's void put(URI uri, Map<String, List<String>> responseHeaders) method to store response cookies in a cookie cache, and invokes the Map<String, List<String>> get(URI uri, Map<String, List<String>> requestHeaders) method to fetch request cookies from this cache. Unlike Java 5, Java 6 introduced a concrete implementation of CookieHandler so that HTTP protocol handlers and applications can work with cookies.

The concrete java.net.CookieManager class extends CookieHandler to manage cookies. A CookieManager object is initialized as follows:

- With a *cookie store* for storing cookies. The cookie store is based on the java.net.CookieStore interface.

- With a *cookie policy* for determining which cookies to accept for storage. The cookie policy is based on the java.net.CookiePolicy interface.

Create a cookie manager by calling either the CookieManager() constructor or the CookieManager(CookieStore store, CookiePolicy policy) constructor. The CookieManager() constructor invokes the latter constructor with null arguments, using the default in-memory cookie store and the default accept-cookies-from-the-original-server-only cookie policy. Unless you plan to create your own CookieStore and CookiePolicy implementations, you'll most likely work with the default constructor. The following example creates and establishes a new CookieManager object as the system-wide cookie handler:

```
CookieHandler.setDefault(new CookieManager());
```

Along with the aforementioned constructors, CookieManager declares the following methods:

- Map<String, List<String>> get(URI uri, Map<String, List<String>> requestHeaders) returns an immutable map of Cookie and Cookie2 request headers for cookies obtained from the cookie store whose path matches uri's path. Although requestHeaders isn't used by the default implementation of this method, it can be used by subclasses. IOException is thrown when an I/O error occurs.

- CookieStore getCookieStore() returns the cookie manager's cookie store.

- void put(URI uri, Map<String, List<String>> responseHeaders) stores all applicable cookies whose Set-Cookie and Set-Cookie2 response headers were retrieved from the specified uri value and placed (with all other response headers) in the immutable responseHeaders map in the cookie store. IOException is thrown when an I/O error occurs.

- void setCookiePolicy(CookiePolicy cookiePolicy) sets the cookie manager's cookie policy to one of CookiePolicy.ACCEPT_ALL (accept all cookies), CookiePolicy.ACCEPT_NONE (accept no cookies), or CookiePolicy.ACCEPT_ORIGINAL_SERVER (accept cookies from original server only—this is the default). Passing null to this method has no effect on the current policy.

In contrast to the get() and put() methods, which are called by HTTP protocol handlers, an application works with the getCookieStore() and setCookiePolicy() methods. Consider Listing 9-16.

Listing 9-16. Listing all cookies for a specific domain

```java
import java.io.IOException;

import java.net.CookieHandler;
import java.net.CookieManager;
import java.net.CookiePolicy;
import java.net.HttpCookie;
import java.net.URL;

import java.util.List;

class ListAllCookies
{
   public static void main(String[] args) throws IOException
   {
      if (args.length != 1)
```

```
    {
        System.err.println("usage: java ListAllCookies url");
        return;
    }

    CookieManager cm = new CookieManager();
    cm.setCookiePolicy(CookiePolicy.ACCEPT_ALL);
    CookieHandler.setDefault(cm);
    new URL(args[0]).openConnection().getContent();
    List<HttpCookie> cookies = cm.getCookieStore().getCookies();
    for (HttpCookie cookie: cookies)
    {
        System.out.println("Name = "+cookie.getName());
        System.out.println("Value = "+cookie.getValue());
        System.out.println("Lifetime (seconds) = "+cookie.getMaxAge());
        System.out.println("Path = "+cookie.getPath());
        System.out.println();
    }
  }
}
```

Listing 9-16 describes a command-line application that obtains and lists all cookies from its single domain-name argument.

After creating a cookie manager and invoking setCookiePolicy() to set the cookie manager's policy to accept all cookies, ListAllCookies installs the cookie manager as the system-wide cookie handler. It next connects to the domain identified by the command-line argument and reads the content (via URL's Object getContent() method).

The cookie store is obtained via getCookieStore() and used to retrieve all nonexpired cookies via its List<HttpCookie> getCookies() method. For each of these java.net.HttpCookies, String getName(), String getValue(), and other HttpCookie methods are invoked to return cookie-specific information.

The following output resulted from invoking java ListAllCookies http://apress.com:

```
Name = frontend
Value = tk95grc7tko42ghghu3qcep5l6
Lifetime (seconds) = 29985
Path = /
```

Note For more information about cookie management, including examples that show you how to create your own CookiePolicy and CookieStore implementations, check out *The Java Tutorial's* "Working With Cookies" lesson (http://java.sun.com/docs/books/tutorial/networking/cookies/index.html).

Interacting with Databases

A *database* (http://en.wikipedia.org/wiki/Database) is an organized collection of data. Although there are many kinds of databases (e.g., hierarchical, object-oriented, and relational), *relational databases*, which organize data into tables that can be related to each other, are common. (Each table row stores a single item, such as an employee, and each column stores a single item attribute, such as an employee's name.)

Except for the most trivial of databases (e.g., Chapter 8's flat file database), databases are created and managed through a *database management system* (DBMS). Relational DBMSes (RDBMSes) support *Structured Query Language* (SQL) for working with tables and more.

■ **Note** For brevity, I assume that you're familiar with SQL. If not, you might want to check out Wikipedia's "SQL" entry (http://en.wikipedia.org/wiki/SQL) for an introduction.

Java supports database creation, access, and more via its relational database-oriented JDBC (Java DataBase Connectivity) API, and this section introduces you to JDBC. Before doing so, it introduces you to Java DB, the RDBMS that I'll use to demonstrate various JDBC features.

Java DB

First introduced by Sun Microsystems as part of JDK 6 (and not included in the JRE) to give developers an RDBMS to test their JDBC code, *Java DB* is a distribution of Apache's open-source Derby product, which is based on IBM's Cloudscape RDBMS code base. This pure-Java RDBMS is also bundled with JDK 7 (and not also in the JRE). It's secure, supports JDBC and SQL (including transactions, stored procedures, and concurrency), and has a small footprint—its core engine and JDBC driver occupy 2MB.

■ **Note** A *JDBC driver* is a classfile plug-in for communicating with a database. I'll have more to say about JDBC drivers when I introduce JDBC later in this chapter.

Java DB is capable of running in an embedded environment or in a client/server environment. In an embedded environment, where an application accesses the database engine via Java DB's *embedded driver*, the database engine runs in the same JVM as the application. Figure 9-3 illustrates the embedded environment architecture, where the database engine is embedded in the application.

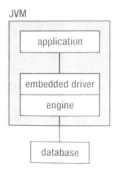

Figure 9-3. *No separate processes are required to start up or shut down an embedded database engine.*

In a client/server environment, client applications and the database engine run in separate JVMs. A client application accesses the network server through Java DB's *client driver*. The network server, which runs in the same JVM as the database engine, accesses the database engine through the embedded driver. Figure 9-4 illustrates this architecture.

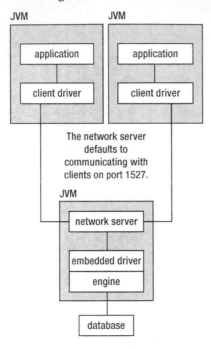

Figure 9-4. Multiple clients communicate with the same database engine through the network server.

Java DB implements the database portion of the architectures shown in Figures 9-3 and 9-4 as a directory with the same name as the database. Within this directory, Java DB creates a log directory to store transaction logs, a seg0 directory to store the data files, and a service.properties file to store configuration parameters.

■ **Note** Java DB doesn't provide an SQL command to drop (destroy) a database. Destroying a database requires that you manually delete its directory structure.

Java DB Installation and Configuration

When you install JDK 7 with the default settings, the bundled Java DB is installed into %JAVA_HOME%\db on Windows platforms, or into the db subdirectory in the equivalent location on Unix/Linux platforms. (For convenience, I adopt the Windows convention when presenting environment variable paths.)

■ **Note** I focus on Java DB 10.8.1.2 in this chapter because it's included with JDK 7 build 1.7.0-b147, which is the Java build on which this book is based.

The db directory contains five files and the following pair of subdirectories:

- The bin directory contains scripts for setting up embedded and client/server environments, running command-line tools, and starting/stopping the network server. You should add this directory to your PATH environment variable so that you can conveniently execute its scripts from anywhere in the filesystem.

- The lib directory contains various JAR files that house the engine library (derby.jar), the command-line tools libraries (derbytools.jar and derbyrun.jar), the network server library (derbynet.jar), the network client library (derbyclient.jar), and various locale libraries. This directory also contains derby.war, which is used to register the network server's servlet at the /derbynet relative path—it's also possible to manage the Java DB network server remotely via the servlet interface (see http://db.apache.org/derby/docs/10.8/adminguide/cadminservlet98430.html).

Additionally, the %JAVA_HOME%\demo\db directory contains various Java DB demos.

Before you can run the tools and demos, and start/stop the network server, you must set the DERBY_HOME environment variable. Set this variable for Windows via set DERBY_HOME=%JAVA_HOME%\db, and for Unix (Korn shell) via export DERBY_HOME=$JAVA_HOME/db.

■ **Note** The embedded and client/server environment setup scripts refer to a DERBY_INSTALL environment variable. According to the "Re: DERBY_INSTALL and DERBY_HOME" mail item (http://www.mail-archive.com/derby-dev@db.apache.org/msg22098.html), DERBY_HOME is equivalent to and replaces DERBY_INSTALL for consistency with other Apache projects.

You must also set the CLASSPATH environment variable. The easiest way to set this environment variable is to run a script file included with Java DB. Windows and Unix/Linux versions of various "set*xxx*CP" script files (which extend the current classpath) are located in the %JAVA_HOME%\db\bin directory. The script file(s) to run will depend on whether you work with the embedded or client/server environment:

- For the embedded environment, invoke setEmbeddedCP to add derby.jar and derbytools.jar to the classpath.

- For the client/server environment, invoke setNetworkServerCP to add derbynet.jar and derbytools.jar to the classpath. In a separate command window, invoke setNetworkClientCP to add derbyclient.jar and derbytools.jar to the classpath.

> ■ **Caution** There's a problem with the Windows setEmbeddedCP.bat, setNetworkClientCP.bat, and setNetworkServerCP.bat files. Each file's @FOR %%X in ("%DERBY_HOME%") DO SET DERBY_HOME=%%~sX line screws up the CLASSPATH environment variable—I think the problem's related to ~sX. I've found that commenting out this line (by prefixing the line with rem and a space) solves the problem.

Java DB Demos

The %JAVA_HOME%\demo\db\programs directory contains HTML documentation that describes the demos included with Java DB; the demo.html file is the entry point into this documentation. These demos include a simple JDBC application for working with Java DB, a network server sample program, and sample programs that are introduced in the *Working with Derby* manual.

> ■ **Note** The *Working with Derby* manual underscores Java DB's Derby heritage. You can download this manual and other Derby manuals from the documentation section (http://db.apache.org/derby/manuals/index.html) of Apache's Derby project site (http://db.apache.org/derby/index.html).

For brevity, I'll focus only on the simple JDBC application that's located in the programs directory's simple subdirectory. This application runs in either the default embedded environment or the client/server environment. It creates and connects to a derbyDB database, introduces a table into this database, performs insert/update/select operations on this table, *drops* (removes) the table, and disconnects from the database.

To run this application in the embedded environment, open a command window and make sure that the DERBY_HOME and CLASSPATH environment variables have been set properly; invoke setEmbeddedCP to set the classpath. Assuming that simple is the current directory, invoke java SimpleApp or java SimpleApp embedded to run this application. You should observe the following output:

```
SimpleApp starting in embedded mode
Loaded the appropriate driver
Connected to and created database derbyDB
Created table location
Inserted 1956 Webster
Inserted 1910 Union
Updated 1956 Webster to 180 Grand
Updated 180 Grand to 300 Lakeshore
Verified the rows
Dropped table location
Committed the transaction
Derby shut down normally
SimpleApp finished
```

This output reveals that an application running in the embedded environment shuts down the database engine before exiting. This is done to perform a checkpoint and release resources. When this shutdown doesn't occur, Java DB notes the absence of the checkpoint, assumes a crash, and causes recovery code to run before the next database connection (which takes longer to complete).

Tip When running `SimpleApp` (or any other Java DB application) in the embedded environment, you can determine where the database directory will be created by setting the `derby.system.home` property. For example, `java -Dderby.system.home=c:\ SimpleApp` causes `derbyDB` to be created in the root directory of the C: drive on a Windows platform.

To run this application in the client/server environment, you need to start the network server and run the application in separate command windows.

In one command window, set `DERBY_HOME`. Start the network server via the `startNetworkServer` script (located in `%JAVA_HOME%\db\bin`), which takes care of setting the classpath. You should see output similar to this:

```
Mon Sep 19 21:23:14 CDT 2011 : Security manager installed using the Basic server⏎ security
policy.
Mon Sep 19 21:23:16 CDT 2011 : Apache Derby Network Server - 10.8.1.2 - (1095077)⏎ started
and ready to accept connections on port 1527
```

In the other command window, set `DERBY_HOME` followed by `CLASSPATH` (via `setNetworkClientCP`). Assuming that `simple` is the current directory, invoke `java SimpleApp derbyClient` to run this application. This time, you should observe the following output:

```
SimpleApp starting in derbyclient mode
Loaded the appropriate driver
Connected to and created database derbyDB
Created table location
Inserted 1956 Webster
Inserted 1910 Union
Updated 1956 Webster to 180 Grand
Updated 180 Grand to 300 Lakeshore
Verified the rows
Dropped table location
Committed the transaction
SimpleApp finished
```

Notice that the database engine is not shut down in the client/server environment. Although not indicated in the output, there's a second difference between running `SimpleApp` in the embedded and client/server environments. In the embedded environment, the `derbyDB` database directory is created in the `simple` directory. In the client/server environment, this database directory is created in the directory that was current when you executed `startNetworkServer`.

When you're finished playing with `SimpleApp` in the client/server environment, you should shut down the network server and database engine. Accomplish this task by invoking the `stopNetworkServer` script (located in `%JAVA_HOME%\db\bin`). You can also shut down (or start and otherwise control) the network server by running the `NetworkServerControl` script (also located in `%JAVA_HOME%\db\bin`). For example, `NetworkServerControl shutdown` shuts down the network server and database engine.

Java DB Command-Line Tools

The %JAVA_HOME%\db\bin directory contains sysinfo, ij, and dblook Windows and Unix/Linux script files for launching command-line tools:

- Run sysinfo to view the Java environment/Java DB configuration.

- Run ij to run scripts that execute ad hoc SQL commands and perform repetitive tasks.

- Run dblook to view all or part of a database's Data Definition Language (DDL).

If you experience trouble with Java DB (e.g., not being able to connect to a database), you can run sysinfo to find out if the problem is configuration-related. This tool reports various settings under the Java Information, Derby Information, and Locale Information headings—I discuss locales in Appendix C. It outputs the following information on my platform:

```
------------------ Java Information ------------------
Java Version:    1.7.0
Java Vendor:     Oracle Corporation
Java home:       C:\Program Files\Java\jdk1.7.0\jre
Java classpath:  C:\Program Files\Java\jdk1.7.0\db\lib\derby.jar;C:\Program↵
Files\Java\jdk1.7.0\db\lib\derbytools.jar;;C:\Program↵
Files\Java\jdk1.7.0\db/lib/derby.jar;C:\Program↵
Files\Java\jdk1.7.0\db/lib/derbynet.jar;C:\Program↵
Files\Java\jdk1.7.0\db/lib/derbyclient.jar;C:\Program↵
Files\Java\jdk1.7.0\db/lib/derbytools.jar
OS name:         Windows XP
OS architecture: x86
OS version:      5.1
Java user name:  Jeff Friesen
Java user home:  C:\Documents and Settings\Jeff Friesen
Java user dir:   C:\PROGRA~1\Java\JDK17~1.0\db\bin
java.specification.name: Java Platform API Specification
java.specification.version: 1.7
java.runtime.version: 1.7.0-b147
--------- Derby Information --------
JRE - JDBC: Java SE 6 - JDBC 4.0
[C:\Program Files\Java\jdk1.7.0\db\lib\derby.jar] 10.8.1.2 - (1095077)
[C:\Program Files\Java\jdk1.7.0\db\lib\derbytools.jar] 10.8.1.2 - (1095077)
[C:\Program Files\Java\jdk1.7.0\db\lib\derbynet.jar] 10.8.1.2 - (1095077)
[C:\Program Files\Java\jdk1.7.0\db\lib\derbyclient.jar] 10.8.1.2 - (1095077)
--------------------------------------------------------
------------------ Locale Information ------------------
Current Locale : [English/United States [en_US]]
Found support for locale: [cs]
        version: 10.8.1.2 - (1095077)
Found support for locale: [de_DE]
        version: 10.8.1.2 - (1095077)
Found support for locale: [es]
        version: 10.8.1.2 - (1095077)
Found support for locale: [fr]
        version: 10.8.1.2 - (1095077)
```

```
Found support for locale: [hu]
        version: 10.8.1.2 - (1095077)
Found support for locale: [it]
        version: 10.8.1.2 - (1095077)
Found support for locale: [ja_JP]
        version: 10.8.1.2 - (1095077)
Found support for locale: [ko_KR]
        version: 10.8.1.2 - (1095077)
Found support for locale: [pl]
        version: 10.8.1.2 - (1095077)
Found support for locale: [pt_BR]
        version: 10.8.1.2 - (1095077)
Found support for locale: [ru]
        version: 10.8.1.2 - (1095077)
Found support for locale: [zh_CN]
        version: 10.8.1.2 - (1095077)
Found support for locale: [zh_TW]
        version: 10.8.1.2 - (1095077)
-------------------------------------------------------
```

The ij script is useful for creating a database and initializing a user's *schema* (a namespace that logically organizes tables and other database objects) by running a script file that specifies appropriate DDL statements. For example, you've created an EMPLOYEES table with its NAME and PHOTO columns, and have created a create_emp_schema.sql script file in the current directory that contains the following line:

```
CREATE TABLE EMPLOYEES(NAME VARCHAR(30), PHOTO BLOB);
```

The following embedded ij script session creates the employees database and EMPLOYEES table:

```
C:\db>ij
ij version 10.8
ij> connect 'jdbc:derby:employees;create=true';
ij> run 'create_emp_schema.sql';
ij> CREATE TABLE EMPLOYEES(NAME VARCHAR(30), PHOTO BLOB);
0 rows inserted/updated/deleted
ij> disconnect;
ij> exit;
C:>\db>
```

The connect command causes the employees database to be created—I'll have more to say about this command's syntax when I introduce JDBC later in this chapter. The run command causes create_emp_schema.sql to execute, and the subsequent pair of lines is generated as a result.

The CREATE TABLE EMPLOYEES(NAME VARCHAR(30), PHOTO BLOB); line is an SQL statement for creating a table named EMPLOYEES with NAME and PHOTO columns. Data items entered into the NAME column are of SQL type VARCHAR (a varying number of characters—a string) with a maximum of 30 characters, and data items entered into the PHOTO column are of SQL type BLOB (a binary large object, such as an image).

■ **Note** I specify SQL statements in uppercase, but you can also specify them in lowercase or mixed case.

After run 'create_emp_schema.sql' finishes, the specified EMPLOYEES table is added to the newly created employees database. To verify the table's existence, run dblook against the employees directory, as the following session demonstrates.

```
C:\db>dblook -d jdbc:derby:employees
-- Timestamp: 2011-09-19 22:17:20.375
-- Source database is: employees
-- Connection URL is: jdbc:derby:employees
-- appendLogs: false


-- ----------------------------------------------
-- DDL Statements for tables
-- ----------------------------------------------

CREATE TABLE "APP"."EMPLOYEES" ("NAME" VARCHAR(30), "PHOTO" BLOB(2147483647));

C:\db>
```

All database objects (e.g., tables and indexes) are assigned to user and system schemas, which logically organize these objects in the same way that packages logically organize classes. When a user creates or accesses a database, Java DB uses the specified username as the namespace name for newly added database objects. In the absence of a username, Java DB chooses APP, as the preceding session output shows.

JDBC

JDBC is an API (associated with the java.sql, javax.sql, javax.sql.rowset, javax.sql.rowset.serial, and javax.sql.rowset.spi packages—I mainly focus on java.sql in this chapter) for communicating with RDBMSes in an RDBMS-independent manner. You can use JDBC to perform various database operations, such as submitting SQL statements that tell the RDBMS to create a relational database or table, and to update or query tabular data.

Note Java 7 supports JDBC 4.1. For a list of JDBC 4.1-specific features, check out

http://download.oracle.com/javase/7/docs/technotes/guides/jdbc/jdbc_41.html.

Data Sources, Drivers, and Connections

Although JDBC is typically used to communicate with RDBMSes, it also can be used to communicate with a flat file database. For this reason, JDBC uses the term *data source* (a data-storage facility ranging from a simple file to a complex relational database managed by an RDBMS) to abstract the source of data.

Because data sources are accessed in different ways (e.g., Chapter 8's flat file database is accessed via methods of the java.io.RandomAccessFile class, whereas Java DB databases are accessed via SQL statements), JDBC uses *drivers* (classfile plug-ins) to abstract over their implementations. This abstraction lets you write an application that can be adapted to an arbitrary data source without having to change a single line of code (in most cases). Drivers are implementations of the java.sql.Driver interface.

JDBC recognizes four types of drivers:

- *Type 1 drivers* implement JDBC as a mapping to another data-access API (e.g., Open Database Connectivity, or ODBC—see http://en.wikipedia.org/wiki/ODBC). The driver converts JDBC method calls into function calls on the other library. The JDBC-ODBC Bridge Driver is an example and is not supported by Oracle. It was commonly used in the early days of JDBC when other kinds of drivers were uncommon.

- *Type 2 drivers* are written partly in Java and partly in native code (see Appendix C). They interact with a data source-specific native client library and are not portable for this reason. Oracle's OCI (Oracle Call Interface) client-side driver is an example.

- *Type 3 drivers* don't depend on native code and communicate with a *middleware server* (a server that sits between the application client and the data source) via an RDBMS-independent protocol. The middleware server then communicates the client's requests to the data source.

- *Type 4 drivers* don't depend on native code and implement the network protocol for a specific data source. The client connects directly to the data source instead of going through a middleware server.

Before you can communicate with a data source, you need to establish a connection. JDBC provides the java.sql.DriverManager class and the javax.sql.DataSource interface for this purpose:

- DriverManager lets an application connect to a data source by specifying a URL. When this class first attempts to establish a connection, it automatically loads any JDBC 4.x drivers located via the classpath. (Pre-JDBC 4.x drivers must be loaded manually.)

- DataSource hides connection details from the application to promote data source portability and is preferred over DriverManager for this reason. Because a discussion of DataSource is somewhat involved (and is typically used in a Java EE context), I focus on DriverManager in this chapter.

Before letting you obtain a data source connection, early JDBC versions required you to explicitly load a suitable driver, by specifying Class.forName() with the name of the class that implements the Driver interface. For example, the JDBC-ODBC Bridge driver was loaded via Class.forName("sun.jdbc.odbc.JdbcOdbcDriver");. Later JDBC versions relaxed this requirement by letting you specify a list of drivers to load via the jdbc.drivers system property. DriverManager would attempt to load all these drivers during its initialization.

Under Java 7, DriverManager first loads all drivers identified by the jdbc.drivers system property. It then uses the java.util.ServiceLoader-based service provider mechanism (discussed in Appendix C) to load all drivers from accessible driver JAR files so that you don't have to explicitly load drivers. This mechanism requires a driver to be packaged into a JAR file that includes META-INF/services/java.sql.Driver. The java.sql.Driver text file must contain a single line that names the driver's implementation of the Driver interface.

Each loaded driver instantiates and registers itself with DriverManager via DriverManager's void registerDriver(Driver driver) class method. When invoked, a getConnection() method walks through registered drivers, returning an implementation of the java.sql.Connection interface from the first driver that recognizes getConnection()'s JDBC URL. (You might want to check out DriverManager's source code to see how this is done.)

■ **Note** To maintain data source-independence, much of JDBC consists of interfaces. Each driver provides implementations of the various interfaces.

To connect to a data source and obtain a Connection instance, call one of DriverManager's Connection getConnection(String url), Connection getConnection(String url, Properties info), or Connection getConnection(String url, String user, String password) methods. With either method, the url argument specifies a string-based URL that starts with the jdbc: prefix and continues with data source-specific syntax.

Consider Java DB. The URL syntax varies depending on the driver. For the embedded driver (when you want to access a local database), this syntax is as follows:

jdbc:derby:*databaseName*;*URLAttributes*

For the client driver (when you want to access a remote database, although you can also access a local database with this driver), this syntax is as follows:

jdbc:derby://*host*:*port*/*databaseName*;*URLAttributes*

With either syntax, *URLAttributes* is an optional sequence of semicolon-delimited *name=value* pairs. For example, create=true tells Java DB to create a new database.

The following example demonstrates the first syntax by telling JDBC to load the Java DB embedded driver and create the database named testdb on the local host:

Connection con = DriverManager.getConnection("jdbc:derby:testdb;create=true");

The following example demonstrates the second syntax by telling JDBC to load the Java DB client driver and create the database named testdb on port 8500 of the xyz host:

Connection con;
con = DriverManager.getConnection("jdbc:derby://xyz:8500/testdb;create=true");

■ **Note** For convenience, this chapter's applications use only the embedded driver connection syntax.

Exceptions

DriverManager's getConnection() methods (and other JDBC methods in the various JDBC interfaces) throw java.sql.SQLException or one of its subclasses when something goes wrong. Along with the methods it inherits from java.lang.Throwable (e.g., String getMessage()), SQLException declares various constructors (not discussed for brevity) and the following methods:

- int getErrorCode() returns a vendor-specific integer error code. Normally this value will be the actual error code returned by the underlying data source.

- SQLException getNextException() returns the SQLException instance chained to this SQLException object (via a call to setNextException(SQLException ex)), or null when there isn't a chained exception.

- String getSQLState() returns a "SQLstate" string that provides an X/Open or SQL:2003 error code identifying the exception.

- Iterator<Throwable> iterator() returns an iterator over the chained SQLExceptions and their causes in proper order. The iterator will be used to iterate over each SQLException and its underlying cause (if any). You would normally not call this method, but would instead use the enhanced for statement (discussed in Chapter 5), which calls iterator(), when you need to iterate over the chain of SQLExceptions.

- void setNextException(SQLException sqlex) appends sqlex to the end of the chain.

One or more SQLExceptions might occur while processing a request, and the code that throws these exceptions can add them to a *chain* of SQLExceptions by invoking setNextException(). Also, an SQLException instance might be thrown as a result of a different exception (e.g., IOException), which is known as that exception's *cause* (see Chapter 3).

SQL state error codes are defined by the ISO/ANSI and Open Group (X/Open) SQL standards. The error code is a 5-character string consisting of a 2-character class value followed by a 3-character subclass value. Class value "00""indicates success, class value "01" indicates a warning, and other class values normally indicate an exception. Examples of SQL state error codes are 00000 (success) and 08001 (unable to connect to the data source).

The following example shows you how you might structure your application to make a connection to a Java DB data source, perform some work, and respond to a thrown SQLException instance:

```
String url = "jdbc:derby:employee;create=true";
try (Connection con = DriverManager.getConnection(url))
{
   // Perform useful work. The following throw statement simulates a
   // JDBC method throwing SQLException.
   throw new SQLException("Unable to access database table",
                          new java.io.IOException("File I/O problem"));
}
catch (SQLException sqlex)
{
   while (sqlex != null)
   {
      System.err.println("SQL error : "+sqlex.getMessage());
      System.err.println("SQL state : "+sqlex.getSQLState());
      System.err.println("Error code: "+sqlex.getErrorCode());
      System.err.println("Cause: "+sqlex.getCause());
      sqlex = sqlex.getNextException();
   }
}
```

Connections must be closed when no longer needed; Connection declares a void close() method for this purpose. Because Connection implements java.lang.AutoCloseable, you can use the try-with-resources statement (see Chapter 3) to have this method automatically called whether or not an exception is thrown.

Assuming that Java DB hasn't been configured (by setting the DERBY_HOME and CLASSPATH environment variables), you should expect the following output:

```
SQL error : No suitable driver found for jdbc:derby:employee;create=true
```

```
SQL state : 08001
Error code: 0
Cause: null
```

If you've configured Java DB, you should observe no output.

SQLException declares several subclasses (e.g., java.sql.BatchUpdateException—an error has occurred during a batch update operation). Many of these subclasses are categorized under java.sql.SQLNonTransientException- and java.sql.SQLTransientException-rooted class hierarchies, where SQLNonTransientException describes failed operations that cannot be retried without changing application source code or some aspect of the data source, and SQLTransientException describes failed operations that can be retried immediately.

Statements

After obtaining a connection to a data source, an application interacts with the data source by issuing SQL statements (e.g., CREATE TABLE, INSERT, SELECT, UPDATE, DELETE, and DROP TABLE). JDBC supports SQL statements via the java.sql.Statement, java.sql.PreparedStatement, and java.sql.CallableStatement interfaces. Furthermore, Connection declares various createStatement(), prepareStatement, and prepareCall() methods that return Statement, PreparedStatement, or CallableStatement implementation instances, respectively.

Statement and ResultSet

Statement is the easiest-to-use interface, and Connection's Statement createStatement() method is the easiest-to-use method for obtaining a Statement instance. After calling this method, you can execute various SQL statements by invoking Statement methods such as the following:

- ResultSet executeQuery(String sql) executes a SELECT statement and (assuming no exception is thrown) provides access to its results via a java.sql.ResultSet instance.

- int executeUpdate(String sql) executes a CREATE TABLE, INSERT, UPDATE, DELETE, or DROP TABLE statement and (assuming no exception is thrown) typically returns the number of table rows affected by this statement.

I've created an EmployeeDB application that demonstrates these methods. Listing 9-17 presents its source code.

Listing 9-17. Creating, inserting values into, querying, and dropping an EMPLOYEES table

```
import java.sql.Connection;
import java.sql.DriverManager;
import java.sql.ResultSet;
import java.sql.SQLException;
import java.sql.Statement;

class EmployeeDB
{
   public static void main(String[] args)
   {
      String url = "jdbc:derby:employee;create=true";
```

```
try (Connection con = DriverManager.getConnection(url))
{
   try (Statement stmt = con.createStatement())
   {
      String sql = "CREATE TABLE EMPLOYEES(ID INTEGER, NAME VARCHAR(30))";
      stmt.executeUpdate(sql);
      sql = "INSERT INTO EMPLOYEES VALUES(1, 'John Doe')";
      stmt.executeUpdate(sql);
      sql = "INSERT INTO EMPLOYEES VALUES(2, 'Sally Smith')";
      stmt.executeUpdate(sql);
      ResultSet rs = stmt.executeQuery("SELECT * FROM EMPLOYEES");
      while (rs.next())
          System.out.println(rs.getInt("ID")+" "+rs.getString("NAME"));
      sql = "DROP TABLE EMPLOYEES";
      stmt.executeUpdate(sql);
   }
}
catch (SQLException sqlex)
{
   while (sqlex != null)
   {
      System.err.println("SQL error : "+sqlex.getMessage());
      System.err.println("SQL state : "+sqlex.getSQLState());
      System.err.println("Error code: "+sqlex.getErrorCode());
      System.err.println("Cause: "+sqlex.getCause());
      sqlex = sqlex.getNextException();
   }
}
}
}
```

After successfully establishing a connection to the employee data source, main() creates a statement and uses it to execute SQL statements for creating, inserting values into, querying, and dropping an EMPLOYEES table.

The executeQuery() method returns a ResultSet object that provides access to a query's tabular results. Each result set is associated with a *cursor* that provides access to a specific row of data. The cursor initially points before the first row; call ResultSet's boolean next() method to advance the cursor to the next row. As long as there's a next row, this method returns true; it returns false when there are no more rows to examine.

ResultSet also declares various methods for returning the current row's column values based on their types. For example, int getInt(String columnLabel) returns the integer value corresponding to the INTEGER-based column identified by columnLabel. Similarly, String getString(String columnLabel) returns the string value corresponding to the VARCHAR-based column identified by columnLabel.

■ **Tip** If you don't have column names but have zero-based column indexes, call ResultSet methods such as int getInt(int columnIndex) and String getString(int columnIndex). However, best practice is to call int getInt(String columnLabel).

Compile Listing 9-17 (javac EmployeeDB.java) and run this application (java EmployeeDB). You should observe the following output:

```
1 John Doe
2 Sally Smith
```

SQL's INTEGER and VARCHAR types map to Java's int and String types. Table 9-1 presents a more complete list of type mappings.

Table 9-1. SQL Type/Java Type Mapping

SQL TYPE	Java Type
ARRAY	java.sql.Array
BIGINT	long
BINARY	byte[]
BIT	boolean
BLOB	java.sql.Blob
BOOLEAN	boolean
CHAR	java.lang.String
CLOB	java.sql.Clob
DATE	java.sql.Date
DECIMAL	java.math.BigDecimal
DOUBLE	double
FLOAT	double
INTEGER	int
LONGVARBINARY	byte[]
LONGVARCHAR	java.lang.String
NUMERIC	java.math.BigDecimal
REAL	float
REF	java.sql.Ref

SMALLINT	short
STRUCT	java.sql.Struct
TIME	java.sql.Time
TIMESTAMP	java.sql.Timestamp
TINYINT	byte
VARBINARY	byte[]
VARCHAR	java.lang.String

PreparedStatement

PreparedStatement is the next easiest-to-use interface, and Connection's PreparedStatement prepareStatement() method is the easiest-to-use method for obtaining a PreparedStatement instance—PreparedStatement is a subinterface of Statement.

Unlike a regular statement, a *prepared statement* represents a precompiled SQL statement. The SQL statement is compiled to improve performance and prevent SQL injection (see http://en.wikipedia.org/wiki/SQL_injection), and the compiled result is stored in a PreparedStatement implementation instance.

You typically obtain this instance when you want to execute the same prepared statement multiple times (e.g., you want to execute an SQL INSERT statement multiple times to populate a database table). Consider the following example:

```
sql = "INSERT INTO EMPLOYEES VALUES(?, ?)";
try (PreparedStatement pstmt = con.prepareStatement(sql))
{
   String[] empNames = {"John Doe", "Sally Smith"};
   for (int i = 0; i < empNames.length; i++)
   {
      pstmt.setInt(1, i+1);
      pstmt.setString(2, empNames[i]);
      pstmt.executeUpdate();
   }
}
```

This example first creates a String object that specifies an SQL INSERT statement. Each "?" character serves as a placeholder for a value that's specified before the statement is executed.

After the PreparedStatement implementation instance has been obtained, this interface's void setInt(int parameterIndex, int x) and void setString(int parameterIndex, String x) methods are called on this instance to provide these values (the first argument passed to each method is a 1-based integer column index into the table associated with the statement—1 corresponds to the leftmost column), and then PreparedStatement's int executeUpdate() method is called to execute this SQL statement. The end result: a pair of rows containing John Doe, Sally Smith, and their respective identifiers are added to the EMPLOYEES table.

CallableStatement

CallableStatement is the most specialized of the statement interfaces; it extends PreparedStatement. You use this interface to execute SQL stored procedures, where a *stored procedure* is a list of SQL statements that perform a specific task (e.g., fire an employee). Java DB differs from other RDBMSes in that a stored procedure's body is implemented as a public static Java method. Furthermore, the class in which this method is declared must be public.

You create a stored procedure by executing an SQL statement that typically begins with CREATE PROCEDURE and then continues with RDBMS-specific syntax. For example, the Java DB syntax for creating a stored procedure, as specified on the web page at http://db.apache.org/derby/docs/dev/ref/rrefcreateprocedurestatement.html, is as follows:

```
CREATE PROCEDURE procedure-name ([ procedure-parameter [, procedure-parameter ] ]*)
[ procedure-element ]*
```

procedure-name is expressed as

```
[ schemaName .] SQL92Identifier
```

procedure-parameter is expressed as

```
[{ IN | OUT | INOUT }] [ parameter-Name ] DataType
```

procedure-element is expressed as

```
{
| [ DYNAMIC ] RESULT SETS INTEGER
| LANGUAGE { JAVA }
| DeterministicCharacteristic
| EXTERNAL NAME string
| PARAMETER STYLE JAVA
| EXTERNAL SECURITY { DEFINER | INVOKER }
| { NO SQL | MODIFIES SQL DATA | CONTAINS SQL | READS SQL DATA }
}
```

Anything between [] is optional, the * to the right of [] indicates that anything between these metacharacters can appear zero or more times, the {} metacharacters surround a list of items, and | separates possible items—only one of these items can be specified.

For example, CREATE PROCEDURE FIRE(IN ID INTEGER) PARAMETER STYLE JAVA LANGUAGE JAVA DYNAMIC RESULT SETS 0 EXTERNAL NAME 'EmployeeDB.fire' creates a stored procedure named FIRE. This procedure specifies an input parameter named ID and is associated with a public static method named fire in a public class named EmployeeDB.

After creating the stored procedure, you need to obtain a CallableStatement implementation instance in order to call that procedure, and you do so by invoking one of Connection's prepareCall() methods; for example, CallableStatement prepareCall(String sql).

The string passed to prepareCall() is an *escape clause* (RDBMS-independent syntax) consisting of an open {, followed by the word call, followed by a space, followed by the name of the stored procedure, followed by a parameter list with "?" placeholder characters for the arguments that will be passed, followed by a closing }.

■ **Note** Escape clauses are JDBC's way of smoothing out some of the differences in how different RDBMS vendors implement SQL. When a JDBC driver detects escape syntax, it converts it into the code that the particular RDBMS understands. This makes escape syntax RDBMS-independent.

Once you have a `CallableStatement` reference, you pass arguments to these parameters in the same way as with `PreparedStatement`. The following example demonstrates:

```
try (CallableStatement cstmt = con.prepareCall("{ call FIRE(?)}"))
{
   cstmt.setInt(1, 2);
   cstmt.execute();
}
```

The `cstmt.setInt(1, 2)` method call assigns 2 to the leftmost stored procedure parameter—parameter index 1 corresponds to the leftmost parameter (or to a single parameter when there's only one). The `cstmt.execute()` method call executes the stored procedure, which results in a callback to the application's `public static void fire(int id)` method.

I've created another version of the `EmployeeDB` application that demonstrates this callable statement. Listing 9-18 presents its source code.

Listing 9-18. Firing an employee via a stored procedure

```
import java.sql.CallableStatement;
import java.sql.Connection;
import java.sql.DriverManager;
import java.sql.ResultSet;
import java.sql.SQLException;
import java.sql.Statement;

public class EmployeeDB
{
   public static void main(String[] args)
   {
      String url = "jdbc:derby:employee;create=true";
      try (Connection con = DriverManager.getConnection(url))
      {
         try (Statement stmt = con.createStatement())
         {
            String sql = "CREATE PROCEDURE FIRE(IN ID INTEGER)"+
                         "    PARAMETER STYLE JAVA"+
                         "    LANGUAGE JAVA"+
                         "    DYNAMIC RESULT SETS 0"+
                         "    EXTERNAL NAME 'EmployeeDB.fire'";
            stmt.executeUpdate(sql);
            sql = "CREATE TABLE EMPLOYEES(ID INTEGER, NAME VARCHAR(30), "+
                                        "FIRED BOOLEAN)";
            stmt.executeUpdate(sql);
            sql = "INSERT INTO EMPLOYEES VALUES(1, 'John Doe', false)";
```

```
            stmt.executeUpdate(sql);
            sql = "INSERT INTO EMPLOYEES VALUES(2, 'Sally Smith', false)";
            stmt.executeUpdate(sql);
            dump(stmt.executeQuery("SELECT * FROM EMPLOYEES"));
            try (CallableStatement cstmt = con.prepareCall("{ call FIRE(?)}"))
            {
                cstmt.setInt(1, 2);
                cstmt.execute();
            }
            dump(stmt.executeQuery("SELECT * FROM EMPLOYEES"));
            sql = "DROP TABLE EMPLOYEES";
            stmt.executeUpdate(sql);
            sql = "DROP PROCEDURE FIRE";
            stmt.executeUpdate(sql);
        }
    }
    catch (SQLException sqlex)
    {
        while (sqlex != null)
        {
            System.err.println("SQL error : "+sqlex.getMessage());
            System.err.println("SQL state : "+sqlex.getSQLState());
            System.err.println("Error code: "+sqlex.getErrorCode());
            System.err.println("Cause: "+sqlex.getCause());
            sqlex = sqlex.getNextException();
        }
    }
}
static void dump(ResultSet rs) throws SQLException
{
    while (rs.next())
        System.out.println(rs.getInt("ID")+" "+rs.getString("NAME")+
                            " "+rs.getBoolean("FIRED"));
    System.out.println();
}
public static void fire(int id) throws SQLException
{
    Connection con = DriverManager.getConnection("jdbc:default:connection");
    String sql = "UPDATE EMPLOYEES SET FIRED=TRUE WHERE ID="+id;
    try (Statement stmt = con.createStatement())
    {
        stmt.executeUpdate(sql);
    }
}
}
```

Much of this listing should be fairly understandable so I'll only discuss the fire() method. As previously stated, this method is invoked as a result of the callable statement invocation.

fire() is called with the integer identifier of the employee to fire. It first accesses the current Connection object by invoking getConnection() with the jdbc.default:connection argument, which is supported by Oracle JVMs through a special internal driver.

After creating an SQL UPDATE statement string to set the FIRED column to true in the EMPLOYEES table row where its ID field equals the value in id, fired() invokes executeUpdate() to update the table appropriately.

Compile Listing 9-18 (javac EmployeeDB.java) and run this application (java EmployeeDB). You should observe the following output:

```
1 John Doe false
2 Sally Smith false

1 John Doe false
2 Sally Smith true
```

Metadata

A data source is typically associated with *metadata* (data about data) that describes the data source. When the data source is an RDBMS, this data is typically stored in a collection of tables.

Metadata includes a list of *catalogs* (RDBMS databases whose tables describe RDBMS objects such as *base tables* [tables that physically exist], *views* [virtual tables], and *indexes* [files that improve the speed of data retrieval operations]), *schemas* (namespaces that partition database objects), and additional information (e.g., version numbers, identifications strings, and limits).

To access a data source's metadata, invoke Connection's DatabaseMetaData getMetaData() method. This method returns an implementation instance of the java.sql.DatabaseMetaData interface.

I've created a MetaData application that demonstrates getMetaData() and various DatabaseMetaData methods. Listing 9-19 presents MetaData's source code.

Listing 9-19. Obtaining metadata from an employee data source

```java
import java.sql.Connection;
import java.sql.DatabaseMetaData;
import java.sql.DriverManager;
import java.sql.ResultSet;
import java.sql.SQLException;
import java.sql.Statement;

class MetaData
{
    public static void main(String[] args)
    {
        String url = "jdbc:derby:employee;create=true";
        try (Connection con = DriverManager.getConnection(url))
        {
            try (Statement stmt = con.createStatement())
            {
                dump(con.getMetaData());
            }
        }
        catch (SQLException sqlex)
        {
            while (sqlex != null)
            {
                System.err.println("SQL error : "+sqlex.getMessage());
```

```
                System.err.println("SQL state : "+sqlex.getSQLState());
                System.err.println("Error code: "+sqlex.getErrorCode());
                System.err.println("Cause: "+sqlex.getCause());
                sqlex = sqlex.getNextException();
            }
        }
    }
    static void dump(DatabaseMetaData dbmd) throws SQLException
    {
        System.out.println("DB Major Version = "+dbmd.getDatabaseMajorVersion());
        System.out.println("DB Minor Version = "+dbmd.getDatabaseMinorVersion());
        System.out.println("DB Product = "+dbmd.getDatabaseProductName());
        System.out.println("Driver Name = "+dbmd.getDriverName());
        System.out.println("Numeric function names for escape clause = "+
                           dbmd.getNumericFunctions());
        System.out.println("String function names for escape clause = "+
                           dbmd.getStringFunctions());
        System.out.println("System function names for escape clause = "+
                           dbmd.getSystemFunctions());
        System.out.println("Time/date function names for escape clause = "+
                           dbmd.getTimeDateFunctions());
        System.out.println("Catalog term: "+dbmd.getCatalogTerm());
        System.out.println("Schema term: "+dbmd.getSchemaTerm());
        System.out.println();
        System.out.println("Catalogs");
        System.out.println("--------");
        ResultSet rsCat = dbmd.getCatalogs();
        while (rsCat.next())
            System.out.println(rsCat.getString("TABLE_CAT"));
        System.out.println();
        System.out.println("Schemas");
        System.out.println("-------");
        ResultSet rsSchem = dbmd.getSchemas();
        while (rsSchem.next())
            System.out.println(rsSchem.getString("TABLE_SCHEM"));
        System.out.println();
        System.out.println("Schema/Table");
        System.out.println("------------");
        rsSchem = dbmd.getSchemas();
        while (rsSchem.next())
        {
            String schem = rsSchem.getString("TABLE_SCHEM");
            ResultSet rsTab = dbmd.getTables(null, schem, "%", null);
            while (rsTab.next())
                System.out.println(schem+" "+rsTab.getString("TABLE_NAME"));
        }
    }
}
```

Listing 9-19's dump() method invokes various methods on its dbmd argument to output assorted metadata.

The int getDatabaseMajorVersion() and int getDatabaseMinorVersion() methods return the major (e.g., 10) and minor (e.g., 8) parts of Java DB's version number. Similarly, String getDatabaseProductName() returns the name of this product (e.g., Apache Derby), and String getDriverName() returns the name of the driver (e.g., Apache Derby Embedded JDBC Driver).

SQL defines various functions that can be invoked as part of SELECT and other statements. For example, you can specify SELECT COUNT(*) AS TOTAL FROM EMPLOYEES to return a one-row-by-one-column result set with the column named TOTAL and the row value containing the number of rows in the EMPLOYEES table.

Because not all RDMSes adopt the same syntax for specifying function calls, JDBC uses a *function escape clause*, consisting of { fn *functionname*(*arguments*) }, to abstract over differences. For example, SELECT {fn UCASE(NAME)} FROM EMPLOYEES selects all NAME column values from EMPLOYEES and uppercases their values in the result set.

The String getNumericFunctions(), String getStringFunctions(), String getSystemFunctions(), and String getTimeDateFunctions() methods return lists of function names that can appear in function escape clauses. For example, getNumericFunctions() returns
ABS,ACOS,ASIN,ATAN,ATAN2,CEILING,COS,COT,DEGREES,EXP,FLOOR,LOG,LOG10,MOD,PI,RADIANS,RAND,SIGN, SIN,SQRT,TAN for Java DB 10.8.

Not all vendors use the same terminology for catalog and schema. For this reason, the String getCatalogTerm() and String getSchemaTerm() methods are present to return the vendor-specific terms, which happen to be CATALOG and SCHEMA for Java DB 10.8.

The ResultSet getCatalogs() method returns a result set of catalog names, which are accessible via the result set's TABLE_CAT column. This result set is empty for Java DB 10.8, which divides a single default catalog into various schemas.

The ResultSet getSchemas() method returns a result set of schema names, which are accessible via the result set's TABLE_SCHEM column. This column contains APP, NULLID, SQLJ, SYS, SYSCAT, SYSCS_DIAG, SYSCS_UTIL, SYSFUN, SYSIBM, SYSPROC, and SYSSTAT values for Java DB 10.8. APP is the default schema in which a user's database objects are stored.

The ResultSet getTables(String catalog, String schemaPattern, String tableNamePattern, String[] types) method returns a result set containing table names (in the TABLE_NAME column) and other table-oriented metadata that match the specified catalog, schemaPattern, tableNamePattern, and types. To obtain a result set of all tables for a specific schema, pass null to catalog and types, the schema name to schemaPattern, and the % wildcard to tableNamePattern.

For example, the SYS schema stores SYSALIASES, SYSCHECKS, SYSCOLPERMS, SYSCOLUMNS, SYSCONGLOMERATES, SYSCONSTRAINTS, SYSDEPENDS, SYSFILES, SYSFOREIGNKEYS, SYSKEYS, SYSPERMS, SYSROLES, SYSROUTINEPERMS, SYSSCHEMAS, SYSSEQUENCES, SYSSTATEMENTS, SYSSTATISTICS, SYSTABLEPERMS, SYSTABLES, SYSTRIGGERS, and SYSVIEWS tables.

Listings 9-17 and 9-18 suffer from an architectural problem. After creating the EMPLOYEES table, suppose that SQLException is thrown before the table is dropped. The next time the EmployeeDB application is run, SQLException is thrown when the application attempts to recreate EMPLOYEES because this table already exists. You have to manually delete the employee directory before you can rerun EmployeeDB.

It would be nice to call some kind of isExist() method before creating EMPLOYEES, but that method doesn't exist. However, we can create this method with help from getTables(), and Listing 9-20 shows you how to accomplish this task.

Listing 9-20. *Determining the existence of EMPLOYEES before creating this table*

```
import java.sql.Connection;
import java.sql.DatabaseMetaData;
import java.sql.DriverManager;
```

```java
import java.sql.ResultSet;
import java.sql.SQLException;
import java.sql.Statement;

class EmployeeDB
{
    public static void main(String[] args)
    {
        String url = "jdbc:derby:employee;create=true";
        try (Connection con = DriverManager.getConnection(url))
        {
            try (Statement stmt = con.createStatement())
            {
                String sql;
                if (!isExist(con, "EMPLOYEES"))
                {
                    System.out.println("EMPLOYEES doesn't exist");
                    sql = "CREATE TABLE EMPLOYEES(ID INTEGER, NAME VARCHAR(30))";
                    stmt.executeUpdate(sql);
                }
                else
                    System.out.println("EMPLOYEES already exists");
                sql = "INSERT INTO EMPLOYEES VALUES(1, 'John Doe')";
                stmt.executeUpdate(sql);
                sql = "INSERT INTO EMPLOYEES VALUES(2, 'Sally Smith')";
                stmt.executeUpdate(sql);
                ResultSet rs = stmt.executeQuery("SELECT * FROM EMPLOYEES");
                while (rs.next())
                    System.out.println(rs.getInt("ID")+" "+rs.getString("NAME"));
                sql = "DROP TABLE EMPLOYEES";
                stmt.executeUpdate(sql);
            }
        }
        catch (SQLException sqlex)
        {
            while (sqlex != null)
            {
                System.err.println("SQL error : "+sqlex.getMessage());
                System.err.println("SQL state : "+sqlex.getSQLState());
                System.err.println("Error code: "+sqlex.getErrorCode());
                System.err.println("Cause: "+sqlex.getCause());
                sqlex = sqlex.getNextException();
            }
        }
    }
    static boolean isExist(Connection con, String tableName) throws SQLException
    {
        DatabaseMetaData dbmd = con.getMetaData();
        ResultSet rs = dbmd.getTables(null, "APP", tableName, null);
        return rs.next();
    }
}
```

Listing 9-20 refactors Listing 9-17 by introducing a boolean isExist(Connection con, String tableName) class method, which returns true when tableName exists, and using this method to determine the existence of EMPLOYEES before creating this table.

When the specified table exists, a ResultSet object containing one row is returned, and ResultSet's next() method returns true. Otherwise, the result set contains no rows and next() returns false.

■ **Caution** isExist() assumes the default APP schema, which might not be the case when usernames are involved (each user's database objects are stored in a schema corresponding to the user's name).

The Planets

Although helpful, the previous JDBC applications fall short in revealing the power of JDBC, especially when combined with Swing. For this reason, I've created a more extensive application named Planets that gives you an opportunity to explore these APIs in a more useful context. Additionally, you'll discover something new about each API.

The Planets application helps its user learn about the solar system's planets by presenting images of the eight planets along with their names and statistics on their diameters (in kilometers), masses (in kilograms), and distances from the Sun (measured in astronomical units, or AUs, where Earth is 1 AU from the Sun).

I've designed Planets to run in two modes. When you execute java Planets initdb, this application creates a planets database, populates its PLANETS table with eight entries (where each entry records a String-based name, a double diameter, a double mass, a double distance, and a javax.swing.ImageIcon object storing the planet's image), and then terminates. When you execute java Planets, this table's content is loaded, and then you see the GUI shown in Figure 9-5.

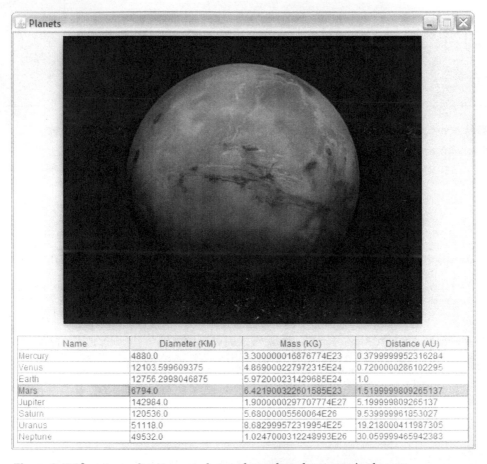

Name	Diameter (KM)	Mass (KG)	Distance (AU)
Mercury	4880.0	3.300000016876774E23	0.3799999952316284
Venus	12103.599609375	4.869000227972315E24	0.7200000286102295
Earth	12756.2998046875	5.972000231429685E24	1.0
Mars	6794.0	6.421900322601585E23	1.5199999809265137
Jupiter	142984.0	1.9000000297707774E27	5.199999809265137
Saturn	120536.0	5.68000005560064E26	9.539999961853027
Uranus	51118.0	8.682999572319954E25	19.218000411987305
Neptune	49532.0	1.0247000312248993E26	30.059999465942383

Figure 9-5. Planets makes it easy to learn about the solar system's planets.

I've organized Planets into Planets and SwingCanvas classes:

- Planets is organized into names, diameters, masses, distances, and iiPhotos static fields that hold planetary information read from the database; a JPanel createGUI() class method that creates the GUI; a void initDB() class method that initializes the database when you execute java Planets initdb; a void loadDB() class method that loads planetary information from the database's PLANETS table (before the GUI is displayed) when you execute java Planets; and the main() entry-point method that launches the application.

- SwingCanvas is organized into iiPhoto and d (dimension) static fields, a SwingCanvas(ImageIcon iiPhoto) constructor that dimensions this component to the size of each image and saves the initial image icon for display, an overriding Dimension getPreferredSize() method that returns the preferred size of this component so that images are fully displayed, an overriding void paint(Graphics g) method that paints the current image icon's image over the component's surface, and a void setPhoto(ImageIcon iiPhoto) method that assigns a new image icon to the canvas component and causes its image to be painted over the component's drawing surface.

The need for brevity restrains me from presenting the entire source code, so I'll present code fragments instead—you'll find the complete source code in this book's accompanying code file (see this book's introduction for more information).

Consider the following initDB() source code:

```
static void initDB()
{
   String[] planets = { "mercury", "venus", "earth", "mars", "jupiter",
                        "saturn", "uranus", "neptune" };
   double[] diameters = { 4880, 12103.6, 12756.3, 6794, 142984, 120536,
                          51118, 49532 };
   double[] masses = { 3.3e23, 4.869e24, 5.972e24, 6.4219e23, 1.9e27,
                       5.68e26, 8.683e25, 1.0247e26 };
   double[] distances = { 0.38, 0.72, 1, 1.52, 5.2, 9.54, 19.218, 30.06 };
   String url = "jdbc:derby:planets;create=true";
   try (Connection con = DriverManager.getConnection(url))
   {
      try (Statement stmt = con.createStatement())
      {
         String sql = "CREATE TABLE PLANETS(NAME VARCHAR(30),"+
                                           "DIAMETER REAL,"+
                                           "MASS REAL,"+
                                           "DISTANCE REAL,"+
                                           "PHOTO BLOB)";
         stmt.executeUpdate(sql);
         sql = "INSERT INTO PLANETS VALUES(?, ?, ?, ?, ?)";
         try (PreparedStatement pstmt = con.prepareStatement(sql))
         {
            for (int i = 0; i < planets.length; i++)
            {
               pstmt.setString(1, planets[i]);
               pstmt.setDouble(2, diameters[i]);
               pstmt.setDouble(3, masses[i]);
               pstmt.setDouble(4, distances[i]);
               Blob blob = con.createBlob();
               try (ObjectOutputStream oos =
                       new ObjectOutputStream(blob.setBinaryStream(1)))
               {
                  ImageIcon photo = new ImageIcon(planets[i]+".jpg");
                  oos.writeObject(photo);
               }
               catch (IOException ioe)
```

```
                   {
                       System.err.println("unable to write "+planets[i]+".jpg");
                   }
                   pstmt.setBlob(5, blob);
                   pstmt.executeUpdate();
                   blob.free(); // Free the blob and release any held resources.
               }
           }
       }
   }
   catch (SQLException sqlex)
   {
       while (sqlex != null)
       {
           System.err.println("SQL error : "+sqlex.getMessage());
           System.err.println("SQL state : "+sqlex.getSQLState());
           System.err.println("Error code: "+sqlex.getErrorCode());
           System.err.println("Cause: "+sqlex.getCause());
           sqlex = sqlex.getNextException();
       }
   }
}
```

This method most importantly demonstrates how to serialize an ImageIcon object to a java.sql.Blob object, and then store the Blob object in a table column of BLOB type.

You first invoke Connection's Blob createBlob() method to create an object that implements the Blob interface. Because the returned object initially contains no data, you need to call Blob's OutputStream setBinaryStream(long pos) method (pos is passed the 1-based starting position within the blob where writing begins) or one of its overloaded setBytes() methods.

If you choose setBinaryStream(), you would then use object serialization (see Chapter 8) to serialize the object to the blob. Don't forget to close the object output stream when you're finished—the try-with-resources statement nicely handles this task for you.

After the Blob object has been created and populated, call one of PreparedStatement's setBlob() methods (e.g., void setBlob(int parameterIndex, Blob x)) to pass the blob to the prepared statement before its execution. Following this execution, the blob must be freed and its resources released.

Consider the following loadDB() source code:

```
static boolean loadDB()
{
    String url = "jdbc:derby:planets;create=false";
    try (Connection con = DriverManager.getConnection(url))
    {
        try (Statement stmt = con.createStatement())
        {
            ResultSet rs = stmt.executeQuery("SELECT COUNT(*) FROM PLANETS");
            rs.next();
            int size = rs.getInt(1);
            names = new String[size];
            diameters = new double[size];
            masses = new double[size];
            distances = new double[size];
            iiPhotos = new ImageIcon[size];
```

```
        rs = stmt.executeQuery("SELECT * FROM PLANETS");
        for (int i = 0; i < size; i++)
        {
            rs.next();
            names[i] = rs.getString(1);
            diameters[i] = rs.getDouble(2);
            masses[i] = rs.getDouble(3);
            distances[i] = rs.getDouble(4);
            Blob blob = rs.getBlob(5);
            try (ObjectInputStream ois =
                    new ObjectInputStream(blob.getBinaryStream()))
            {
                iiPhotos[i] = (ImageIcon) ois.readObject();
            }
            catch (ClassNotFoundException|IOException cnfioe)
            {
                System.err.println("unable to read "+names[i]+".jpg");
            }
            blob.free(); // Free the blob and release any held resources.
        }
        return true;
    }
}
catch (SQLException sqlex)
{
    while (sqlex != null)
    {
        System.err.println("SQL error : "+sqlex.getMessage());
        System.err.println("SQL state : "+sqlex.getSQLState());
        System.err.println("Error code: "+sqlex.getErrorCode());
        System.err.println("Cause: "+sqlex.getCause());
        sqlex = sqlex.getNextException();
    }
    return false;
}
}
```

This method, the inverse of initDB(), shows how to obtain a result set's row count by executing a SQL statement such as SELECT COUNT(*) FROM PLANETS, and how to deserialize a blob's contained object.

The Swing-based GUI consists of a SwingCanvas component (see Chapter 7) and an instance of the javax.swing.JTable class, which is used to display and edit regular two-dimensional tables of cells, and is the perfect component for displaying tabular data.

A complete discussion of JTable and its many supporting types (in the javax.swing and javax.swing.table packages) is beyond the scope of this chapter. Instead, consider the following excerpt from the createGUI() method:

```
TableModel model = new AbstractTableModel()
{
    @Override
    public int getColumnCount()
    {
        return 4;
```

```
        }
        @Override
        public String getColumnName(int column)
        {
            switch (column)
            {
                case 0: return "Name";
                case 1: return "Diameter (KM)";
                case 2: return "Mass (KG)";
                default: return "Distance (AU)";
            }
        }
        @Override
        public int getRowCount()
        {
            return names.length;
        }
        @Override
        public Object getValueAt(int row, int col)
        {
            switch (col)
            {
                case 0: return Character.toUpperCase(names[row].charAt(0))+
                        names[row].substring(1);
                case 1: return diameters[row];
                case 2: return masses[row];
                default: return distances[row];
            }
        }
    };
    final JTable table = new JTable(model);
    table.setSelectionMode(ListSelectionModel.SINGLE_SELECTION);
    table.setRowSelectionInterval(0, 0);
    ListSelectionListener lsl;
    lsl = new ListSelectionListener()
        {
            @Override
            public void valueChanged(ListSelectionEvent lse)
            {
                sc.setPhoto(iiPhotos[table.getSelectedRow()]);
            }
        };
    table.getSelectionModel().addListSelectionListener(lsl);
```

Every JTable instance obtains its data from a table model, which is an instance of a class that implements the javax.swing.table.TableModel interface. I find it convenient to subclass the javax.swing.table.AbstractTableModel class, which implements many of TableModel's methods.

AbstractTableModel doesn't implement int getColumnCount() (the number of columns in the table), int getRowCount() (the number of rows in the table), and Object getValueAt(int row, int col) (the value at the specified row and column), and so it falls to the table model implementation to override these methods to return suitable values.

Although `AbstractTableModel` implements `String getColumnName(int column)`, this implementation only returns default names for the columns using spreadsheet conventions: A, B, C, ... Z, AA, AB, and so on. To return a meaningful name, this method must also be overridden.

The table component will invoke these methods as necessary. When it does, any passed column and/or row values are relative to 0.

After creating the model, it's passed to `JTable`'s `JTable(TableModel dm)` constructor, which creates the table component. Along with the specified table model, the constructor installs a default column model (for use in selecting, adding, removing, and performing other operations on columns) and a default list selection model (for use in selecting one or more rows).

`JTable(TableModel)`'s default list selection model lets the user select one or more rows. Because the user should only be able to select one row at a time (how would the application display multiple planet images simultaneously?), `JTable`'s `void setSelectionMode(int selectionMode)` method is invoked with argument `javax.swing.ListSelectionModel.SINGLE_SELECTION` being passed to `selectionMode`.

When the application starts running, the first table row (Mercury) should be highlighted (to correspond with the displayed Mercury image). This task is accomplished by invoking `JTable`'s `void setRowSelectionInterval(int index0, int index1)` method. Because only row 0 (the first or topmost row) needs to be selected, this value to passed to both `index0` and `index1`. (`setRowSelectionInterval()` lets you select multiple rows, but only when the selection mode isn't `SINGLE_SELECTION`.)

The `SwingCanvas` component initially displays an image of Mercury. When the user selects another table row, that row's planet image must be displayed. This task is accomplished by registering a `javax.swing.event.ListSelectionListener` implementation instance with the table component's `ListSelectionModel` implementation instance, which `JTable`'s `ListSelectionModel getSelectionModel()` method returns.

`ListSelectionListener` declares a `void valueChanged(ListSelectionEvent lse)` method that's called whenever the user selects a row. The selected row is obtained by calling `JTable`'s `int getSelectedRow()` method, which is used to index into `iiPhotos`, whose `ImageIcon` instance is passed to `SwingCanvas`'s `void setPhoto(ImageIcon iiPhoto)` method, which causes the new photo to be displayed.

The architectural style that I chose for the `Planets` application is appropriate for small database tables that can fit entirely in memory. However, you might run into a situation where you need to obtain data from a database table with millions (or more) rows and populate a table component with all this data. Because there isn't enough memory to make this practical, what do you do?

The solution is to read only a small number of rows into a cache (perhaps with help from the Reference API—see Chapter 4) and keep track of the current location. For example, assuming that each row has a unique 1-based integer identifier, you might specify an SQL statement such as `SELECT * FROM EMPLOYEE WHERE ID >= 20 && ID <= 30` to return those rows whose `ID` column contains one of the integer values from 20 through 30. Also, check out "Java: Loading Large Data into JTable or JList" (`http://www.snippetit.com/2009/11/java-loading-large-data-into-jtable-or-jlist/`) to learn how to create an appropriate table model for use in this situation.

Note For more information on JDBC, check out The Java Tutorial's "JDBC: Database Access" trail at `http://download.oracle.com/javase/tutorial/jdbc/TOC.html`.

EXERCISES

The following exercises are designed to test your understanding of network APIs and JDBC:

1. Create a networked version of Blackjack—the version of this game to implement is described after this exercise. Implement a BJDealer application that serves as the dealer and a BJPlayer application that serves as the player. BJDealer waits for a player connection indication and then creates a background thread to service the player—this makes it possible for the dealer to play independent games with multiple players. When BJDealer accepts a socket from a player, it creates java.io.ObjectInputStream and java.io.ObjectOutputStream objects for communicating with the player. Similarly, when BJPlayer creates a socket for communicating with the dealer, it creates ObjectInputStream and ObjectOutputStream objects. Because the ObjectInputStream(InputStream in) constructor blocks until the corresponding ObjectOutputStream instance has written and flushed a serialization stream header, have each of BJDealer and BJPlayer immediately call the flush() method on the created ObjectOutputStream instance. BJDealer serializes Card objects and String-based status messages to BJPlayer; BJPlayer serializes Card objects and String-based commands to BJDealer. BJDealer doesn't present a user interface, whereas BJPlayer presents the user interface shown in Figure 9-6.

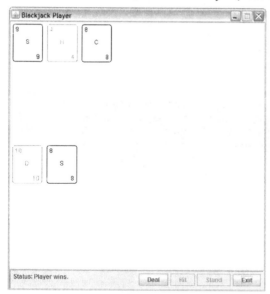

Figure 9-6. BJPlayer's GUI consists of a component to render playing cards (player's cards in top half and dealer's cards in bottom half) and a panel to display status messages and buttons.

The player clicks the Deal button to have the Dealer deal a new hand. This button is subsequently disabled until the player loses or wins. The player clicks the Hit button to request another card from the dealer, and clicks the Stand button when the dealer is standing—these buttons are disabled when Deal is enabled. Finally, the player clicks the Exit button to terminate the game.

To save you some work, Listing 9-21 presents the Card class that each of BJDealer and BJPlayer uses.

Listing 9-21. Describing a playing card in terms of suit and rank

```java
import java.io.Serializable;

import java.util.ArrayList;
import java.util.List;

class Card implements Serializable
{
   enum Suit { CLUBS, DIAMONDS, HEARTS, SPADES }
   enum Rank { ACE, DEUCE, THREE, FOUR, FIVE, SIX, SEVEN, EIGHT, NINE, TEN,
               JACK, QUEEN, KING;
               int getValue()
               {
                   return ordinal()+1;
               }
             }
   private Suit suit;
   private Rank rank;
   private static final List<Card> initialDeck = new ArrayList<Card>();
   Card(Suit suit, Rank rank)
   {
      this.suit = suit;
      this.rank = rank;
   }
   Rank getRank()
   {
      return rank;
   }
   Suit getSuit()
   {
      return suit;
   }
   int getValue()
   {
      return rank.ordinal()+1;
   }
   static
   {
      for (Suit suit: Suit.values())
         for (Rank rank: Rank.values())
            initialDeck.add(new Card(suit, rank));
   }
   static List<Card> newDeck() // Return a new unshuffled deck.
```

```
      {
         // Copy initial deck to new deck.
         List<Card> deck = new ArrayList<Card>(initialDeck);
         return deck;
      }
   }
```

Note *Blackjack* is a card game in which a player competes against the card dealer to see who can come closest to 21 without going over. The first one to reach 21 wins and ends the current round of play. The dealer begins a round by dealing two cards to the player and two cards to herself. The player sees both of her cards and only the first card in the dealer's hand. The dealer checks her hand for a *blackjack* (exactly 21 points). When this is the case, the player loses unless the player also has a blackjack. In this situation, the result is known as a *push* and no one wins or loses. When the dealer's hand is not a blackjack, the player checks her cards for a blackjack and wins when this is the case. Otherwise, since neither the dealer nor the player initially has a blackjack, the game proceeds as follows: A player can request *hits* (additional cards from the dealer—one per hit) until either the sum of a player's cards exceeds 21 (the player loses) or the player decides to *stand* (the player is satisfied with her cards and will wait to see how the dealer's hand progresses). Players typically stand when they believe their hands are good and/or another hit may cause them to exceed 21. After the player stands, the dealer proceeds by showing her second card to the player. The dealer always takes a hit when the sum of her cards is less than 17, and always stands when the sum of her cards is 17 or more. When evaluating the dealer's interim score to see if a hit is required, the ACE always counts for 11, but may count for 1 in the final determination. When the dealer is finished with her hits, her hand is compared with the player's. When it's higher, the dealer wins; when it's lower, the player wins (unless the player exceeded 21); and when they're the same, it's a push and no one wins. Cards deuce (2) through 10 have their face value, JACK is 10, QUEEN is 10, KING is 10, and ACE is 1 or 11 (until the hand is evaluated).

---

2.   Extend the Planets application with new statistics (e.g., number of moons, composition, and internal temperature). Also, provide additional notes (displayed via a label) about the planet. Save all this extra information in the database and retrieve it when the application starts running. You'll find useful information at http://nineplanets.org/.

Summary

A network is a collection of interconnected nodes that can share hardware and software among users. Communication between host nodes occurs via sockets, where a socket is an endpoint in a communications link between two processes. The endpoint consists of an IP address that identifies a host, and a port number that identifies a process running on that network node.

One process writes a message to a socket, which breaks this message into a series of packets and forwards these packets to the other process's socket, which recombines them into the original message for that process's consumption.

TCP is used to create an ongoing conversation between two hosts by sending messages back and forth. Before this conversation can occur, a connection must be established between these hosts. After this connection has been established, TCP enters a pattern of sending a message packet and waiting for a reply that the packet arrived correctly (or for a timeout to expire when the reply doesn't arrive because of a network problem). This send/reply cycle guarantees a reliable connection.

Because it can take time to establish a connection, and because it also takes time to send packets because of the need to receive reply acknowledgments (or timeouts), TCP is fairly slow. In contrast, UDP, which doesn't require connections and packet acknowledgement, is much faster than TCP. However, UDP isn't as reliable (there's no guarantee that a packet will arrive correctly or even arrive) as TCP because there's no acknowledgment. Furthermore, UDP is limited to single-packet one-way conversations.

The java.net package provides Socket and ServerSocket classes for performing TCP-based communications. It also provides DatagramSocket, DatagramPacket, and MulticastSocket classes for performing UDP communications.

A URL is a character string that specifies where a resource (e.g., a web page) is located on a TCP/IP-based network (e.g., the Internet). Also, it provides the means to retrieve that resource.

The java.net package provides URL and URLConnection classes for accessing URL-based resources. It also provides URLEncoder and URLDecoder classes for encoding and decoding URLs, and the URI class for performing URI-based operations (e.g., relativization) and returning URL instances containing the results.

HTTP supports authentication whereby clients (e.g., browser users) must prove their authenticity. Various authentication schemes have been proposed to handle this task; for example, basic and digest. Java provides Authenticator and related types so that networked Java applications can interact with these authentication schemes.

Server applications commonly use *HTTP cookies* (state objects)—*cookies* for short—to persist small amounts of information on clients. Java supports cookie management via CookieManager, CookieHandler, and related types.

A database is an organized collection of data. Although there are many kinds of databases (e.g., hierarchical, object-oriented, and relational), relational databases, which organize data into tables—each row stores a single item, such as an employee, and each column stores a single item attribute, such as an employee's name—that can be related to each other, are common.

Except for the most trivial of databases (e.g., flat file databases), databases are created and managed through a DBMS. RDBMSes support SQL for working with tables and more.

Java supports database creation, access, and more via its relational database-oriented JDBC (Java DataBase Connectivity) API. The JDK also provides Java DB, which is an RDBMS that you can use to test your JDBC-enabled applications.

JDBC provides many features, including drivers for connecting to data sources, connections to data sources, exceptions that store various kinds of information about a data source problem, statements (regular, prepared, and callable) for executing SQL, result sets that store SQL query results, and metadata for learning more about a data source. Prepared statements are precompiled statements and callable statements are used to execute stored procedures.

Chapter 10 introduces you to XML, along with Java's SAX, DOM, StAX, XPath, and XSLT APIs. You even briefly learn about its Validation API.

CHAPTER 10

Parsing, Creating, and Transforming XML Documents

Applications commonly use XML documents to store and exchange data. Java provides extensive support for XML via the SAX, DOM, StAX, XPath, and XSLT APIs. Understanding these APIs is a prerequisite to exploring other Java APIs that depend on XML; for example, web services (discussed in Chapter 11).

Chapter 10 introduces you to SAX, DOM, StAX, XPath, and XSLT. Before delving into these APIs, this chapter provides an introduction to XML for the benefit of those unfamiliar with this technology.

■ **Note** SAX, DOM, StAX, XPath, and XSLT are independent API members of a broader API called Java API for XML Processing (JAXP). JAXP was created to let applications use *XML processors* to parse, create, transform, or perform other operations on XML documents independently of processor implementations, by providing a pluggability layer that lets vendors offer their own implementations without introducing dependencies in application code. Java 7 supports JAXP 1.4.5.

What Is XML?

XML (eXtensible Markup Language) is a *metalanguage* (a language used to describe other languages) for defining *vocabularies* (custom markup languages), which is key to XML's importance and popularity. XML-based vocabularies (e.g., XHTML) let you describe documents in a meaningful way.

XML vocabulary documents are like HTML (see http://en.wikipedia.org/wiki/HTML) documents in that they are text-based and consist of *markup* (encoded descriptions of a document's logical structure) and *content* (document text not interpreted as markup). Markup is evidenced via *tags* (angle bracket-delimited syntactic constructs) and each tag has a name. Furthermore, some tags have *attributes* (name-value pairs).

■ **Note** XML and HTML are descendents of *Standard Generalized Markup Language (SGML)*, which is the original metalanguage for creating vocabularies—XML is essentially a restricted form of SGML, while HTML is an *application* of SGML. The key difference between XML and HTML is that XML invites you to create your own

---

vocabularies with their own tags and rules, whereas HTML gives you a single precreated vocabulary with its own fixed set of tags and rules. XHTML and other XML-based vocabularies are *XML applications*. XHTML was created to be a cleaner implementation of HTML.

If you haven't previously encountered XML, you might be surprised by its simplicity and how closely its vocabularies resemble HTML. You don't need to be a rocket scientist to learn how to create an XML document. To prove this to yourself, check out Listing 10-1.

Listing 10-1. *XML-based recipe for a grilled cheese sandwich*

```
<recipe>
   <title>
      Grilled Cheese Sandwich
   </title>
   <ingredients>
      <ingredient qty="2">
         bread slice
      </ingredient>
      <ingredient>
         cheese slice
      </ingredient>
      <ingredient qty="2">
         margarine pat
      </ingredient>
   </ingredients>
   <instructions>
      Place frying pan on element and select medium heat. For each bread slice, smear
      one pat of margarine on one side of bread slice. Place cheese slice between bread
      slices with margarine-smeared sides away from the cheese. Place sandwich in frying
      pan with one margarine-smeared side in contact with pan. Fry for a couple of
      minutes and flip. Fry other side for a minute and serve.
   </instructions>
</recipe>
```

Listing 10-1 presents an XML document that describes a recipe for making a grilled cheese sandwich. This document is reminiscent of an HTML document in that it consists of tags, attributes, and content. However, that's where the similarity ends. Instead of presenting HTML tags such as <html>, <head>, <img>, and <p>, this informal recipe language presents its own <recipe>, <ingredients>, and other tags.

Note Although Listing 10-1's <title> and </title> tags are also found in HTML, they differ from their HTML counterparts. Web browsers typically display the content between these tags in their titlebars. In contrast, the content between Listing 10-1's <title> and </title> tags might be displayed as a header, spoken aloud, or presented in some other way, depending on the application that parses this document.

XML documents are based on the XML declaration, elements and attributes, character references and CDATA sections, namespaces, and comments and processing instructions. After learning about these fundamentals, you'll learn what it means for an XML document to be well formed, and what it means for an XML document to be valid.

XML Declaration

An XML document will typically begin with the *XML declaration*, special markup that informs an XML parser that the document is XML. The absence of the XML declaration in Listing 10-1 reveals that this special markup isn't mandatory. When the XML declaration is present, nothing can appear before it.

The XML declaration minimally looks like `<?xml version="1.0"?>`, where the nonoptional `version` attribute identifies the version of the XML specification to which the document conforms. The initial version of this specification (1.0) was introduced in 1998 and is widely implemented.

Note The World Wide Web Consortium (W3C), which maintains XML, released version 1.1 in 2004. This version mainly supports the use of line-ending characters used on EBCDIC platforms (see `http://en.wikipedia.org/wiki/EBCDIC`), and the use of scripts and characters that are absent from Unicode 3.2 (see `http://en.wikipedia.org/wiki/Unicode`). Unlike XML 1.0, XML 1.1 is not widely implemented and should be used only by those needing its unique features.

XML supports Unicode, which means that XML documents consist entirely of characters taken from the Unicode character set. The document's characters are encoded into bytes for storage or transmission, and the encoding is specified via the XML declaration's optional encoding attribute. One common encoding is *UTF-8* (see `http://en.wikipedia.org/wiki/UTF-8`), which is a variable-length encoding of the Unicode character set. UTF-8 is a strict superset of ASCII (see `http://en.wikipedia.org/wiki/Ascii`), which means that pure ASCII text files are also UTF-8 documents.

Note In the absence of the XML declaration, or when the XML declaration's encoding attribute is not present, an XML parser typically looks for a special character sequence at the start of a document to determine the document's encoding. This character sequence is known as the *byte-order-mark (BOM)*, and is created by an editor program (such as Microsoft Windows Notepad) when it saves the document according to UTF-8 or some other encoding. For example, the hexadecimal sequence EF BB BF signifies UTF-8 as the encoding. Similarly, FE FF signifies UTF-16 big endian (see `http://en.wikipedia.org/wiki/UTF-16/UCS-2`), FF FE signifies UTF-16 little endian, 00 00 FE FF signifies UTF-32 big endian (see `http://en.wikipedia.org/wiki/UTF-16/UCS-2`), and FF FE 00 00 signifies UTF-32 little endian. UTF-8 is assumed if no BOM is present.

If you'll never use characters apart from the ASCII character set, you can probably forget about the encoding attribute. However, if your native language isn't English, or if you are called upon to create XML documents that include nonASCII characters, you need to properly specify encoding. For example, if your document contains ASCII plus characters from a nonEnglish Western European Language (such as ç, the cedilla used in French, Portuguese, and other languages), you might want to choose ISO-8859-1 as the encoding attribute's value—the document will probably have a smaller size when encoded in this manner than when encoded with UTF-8. Listing 10-2 shows you the resulting XML declaration.

Listing 10-2. An encoded document containing nonASCII characters

```
<?xml version="1.0" encoding="ISO-8859-1"?>
<movie>
    <name>Le Fabuleux Destin d'Amélie Poulain</name>
    <language>français</language>
</movie>
```

The final attribute that can appear in the XML declaration is standalone. This optional attribute determines whether the XML document relies on an external DTD (discussed later in this chapter)—its value is no—or not—its value is yes. The value defaults to no, implying that there is an external DTD. However, because there is no guarantee of a DTD, standalone is rarely used and will not be discussed further.

Elements and Attributes

Following the XML declaration is a *hierarchical* (tree) structure of elements, where an *element* is a portion of the document delimited by a *start tag* (such as <name>) and an *end tag* (such as </name>), or is an *empty-element tag* (a standalone tag whose name ends with a forward slash [/], such as <break/>). Start tags and end tags surround content and possibly other markup whereas empty-element tags do not surround anything. Figure 10-1 reveals Listing 10-1's XML document tree structure.

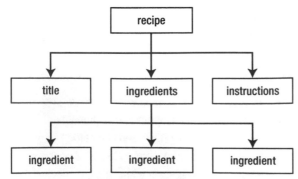

Figure 10-1. Listing 10-1's tree structure is rooted in the recipe element.

As with HTML document structure, the structure of an XML document is anchored in a *root element* (the topmost element). In HTML, the root element is html (the <html> and </html> tag pair). Unlike in HTML, you can choose the root element for your XML documents. Figure 10-1 shows the root element to be recipe.

Unlike the other elements, which have *parent elements*, recipe has no parent. Also, recipe and ingredients have *child elements*: recipe's children are title, ingredients, and instructions; and ingredients' children are three instances of ingredient. The title, instructions, and ingredient elements don't have child elements.

Elements can contain child elements, content, or *mixed content* (a combination of child elements and content). Listing 10-2 reveals that the movie element contains name and language child elements, and also reveals that each of these child elements contains content (language contains français, for example). Listing 10-3 presents another example that demonstrates mixed content along with child elements and content.

Listing 10-3. An abstract element containing mixed content

```
<?xml version="1.0"?>
<article title="The Rebirth of JavaFX" lang="en">
   <abstract>
      JavaFX 2.0 marks a significant milestone in the history of JavaFX. Now that
      Sun Microsystems has passed the torch to Oracle, we have seen the demise of
      JavaFX Script and the emerge of Java APIs (such as
      <code-inline>javafx.application.Application</code-inline>) for interacting
      with this technology. This article introduces you to this new flavor of
      JavaFX, where you learn about JavaFX 2.0 architecture and key APIs.
   </abstract>
   <body>
   </body>
</article>
```

This document's root element is article, which contains abstract and body child elements. The abstract element mixes content with a code-inline element, which contains content. In contrast, the body element is empty.

Note As with Listings 10-1 and 10-2, Listing 10-3 also contains *whitespace* (invisible characters such as spaces, tabs, carriage returns, and line feeds). The XML specification permits whitespace to be added to a document. Whitespace appearing within content (such as spaces between words) is considered part of the content. In contrast, the parser typically ignores whitespace appearing between an end tag and the next start tag. Such whitespace is not considered part of the content.

An XML element's start tag can contain one or more attributes. For example, Listing 10-1's <ingredient> tag has a qty (quantity) attribute, and Listing 10-3's <article> tag has title and lang attributes. Attributes provide additional information about elements. For example, qty identifies the amount of an ingredient that can be added, title identifies an article's title, and lang identifies the language in which the article is written (en for English). Attributes can be optional. For example, if qty is not specified, a default value of 1 is assumed.

Note Element and attribute names may contain any alphanumeric character from English or another language, and may also include the underscore (_), hyphen (-), period (.), and colon (:) punctuation characters. The colon should only be used with namespaces (discussed later in this chapter), and names cannot contain whitespace.

Character References and CDATA Sections

Certain characters cannot appear literally in the content that appears between a start tag and an end tag, or within an attribute value. For example, you cannot place a literal < character between a start tag and an end tag because doing so would confuse an XML parser into thinking that it had encountered another tag.

One solution to this problem is to replace the literal character with a *character reference*, which is a code that represents the character. Character references are classified as numeric character references or character entity references:

- A *numeric character reference* refers to a character via its Unicode code point, and adheres to the format &#nnnn; (not restricted to four positions) or &#xhhhh; (not restricted to four positions), where *nnnn* provides a decimal representation of the code point and *hhhh* provides a hexadecimal representation. For example, Σ and Σ represent the Greek capital letter sigma. Although XML mandates that the x in &#xhhhh; be lowercase, it is flexible in that the leading zero is optional in either format, and in allowing you to specify an uppercase or lowercase letter for each *h*. As a result, Σ, Σ, and Σ are also valid representations of the Greek capital letter sigma.

- A *character entity reference* refers to a character via the name of an *entity* (aliased data) that specifies the desired character as its replacement text. Character entity references are *predefined* by XML and have the format &name;, where *name* is the entity's name. XML predefines five character entity references: < (<), > (>), & (&), ' ('), and " (").

Consider <expression>6 < 4</expression>. You could replace the < with numeric reference <, yielding <expression>6 < 4</expression>, or better yet with <, yielding <expression>6 < 4</expression>. The second choice is clearer and easier to remember.

Suppose you want to embed an HTML or XML document within an element. To make the embedded document acceptable to an XML parser, you would need to replace each literal < (start of tag) and & (start of entity) character with its < and & predefined character entity reference, a tedious and possibly error prone undertaking—you might forget to replace one of these characters. To save you from tedium and potential errors, XML provides an alternative in the form of a CDATA (character data) section.

A *CDATA section* is a section of literal HTML or XML markup and content surrounded by the <![CDATA[prefix and the]]> suffix. You do not need to specify predefined character entity references within a CDATA section, as demonstrated in Listing 10-4.

Listing 10-4. Embedding an XML document in another document's CDATA section

```
<?xml version="1.0"?>
<svg-examples>
   <example>
```

The following Scalable Vector Graphics document describes a blue-filled and
black-stroked rectangle.
```
<![CDATA[<svg width="100%" height="100%" version="1.1"
    xmlns="http://www.w3.org/2000/svg">
  <rect width="300" height="100"
        style="fill:rgb(0,0,255);stroke-width:1; stroke:rgb(0,0,0)"/>
</svg>]]>
  </example>
</svg-examples>
```

Listing 10-4 embeds a Scalable Vector Graphics (SVG) [see http://en.wikipedia.org/wiki/Svg] XML document within the example element of an SVG examples document. The SVG document is placed in a CDATA section, obviating the need to replace all < characters with < predefined character entity references.

Namespaces

It is common to create XML documents that combine features from different XML languages. Namespaces are used to prevent name conflicts when elements and other XML language features appear. Without namespaces, an XML parser could not distinguish between same-named elements or other language features that mean different things, for example, two same-named title elements from two different languages.

Note Namespaces are not part of XML 1.0. They arrived about a year after this specification was released. To ensure backward compatibility with XML 1.0, namespaces take advantage of colon characters, which are legal characters in XML names. Parsers that don't recognize namespaces return names that include colons.

A *namespace* is a Uniform Resource Identifier (URI)-based container that helps differentiate XML vocabularies by providing a unique context for its contained identifiers. The namespace URI is associated with a *namespace prefix* (an alias for the URI) by specifying, typically on an XML document's root element, either the xmlns attribute by itself (which signifies the default namespace) or the xmlns:*prefix* attribute (which signifies the namespace identified as *prefix*), and assigning the URI to this attribute.

Note A namespace's scope starts at the element where it is declared and applies to all of the element's content unless overridden by another namespace declaration with the same prefix name.

When *prefix* is specified, it and a colon character are prepended to the name of each element tag that belongs to that namespace—see Listing 10-5.

***Listing 10-5.** Introducing a pair of namespaces*

```
<?xml version="1.0"?>
<h:html xmlns:h="http://www.w3.org/1999/xhtml"
        xmlns:r="http://www.tutortutor.ca/">
   <h:head>
      <h:title>
         Recipe
      </h:title>
   </h:head>
   <h:body>
   <r:recipe>
      <r:title>
         Grilled Cheese Sandwich
      </r:title>
      <r:ingredients>
         <h:ul>
         <h:li>
         <r:ingredient qty="2">
            bread slice
         </r:ingredient>
         </h:li>
         <h:li>
         <r:ingredient>
            cheese slice
         </r:ingredient>
         </h:li>
         <h:li>
         <r:ingredient qty="2">
            margarine pat
         </r:ingredient>
         </h:li>
         </h:ul>
      </r:ingredients>
      <h:p>
      <r:instructions>
         Place frying pan on element and select medium heat. For each bread slice, smear
         one pat of margarine on one side of bread slice. Place cheese slice between
         bread slices with margarine-smeared sides away from the cheese. Place sandwich
         in frying pan with one margarine-smeared side in contact with pan. Fry for a
         couple of minutes and flip. Fry other side for a minute and serve.
      </r:instructions>
      </h:p>
   </r:recipe>
   </h:body>
</h:html>
```

Listing 10-5 describes a document that combines elements from the XHTML language (see http://en.wikipedia.org/wiki/XHTML) with elements from the recipe language. All element tags that associate with XHTML are prefixed with h:, and all element tags that associate with the recipe language are prefixed with r:.

668

The h: prefix associates with the http://www.w3.org/1999/xhtml URI and the r: prefix associates with the http://www.tutortutor.ca/ URI. XML doesn't mandate that URIs point to document files. It only requires that they be unique in order to guarantee unique namespaces.

This document's separation of the recipe data from the XHTML elements makes it possible to preserve this data's structure while also allowing an XHTML-compliant web browser (e.g., Google Chrome) to present the recipe via a web page (see Figure 10-2).

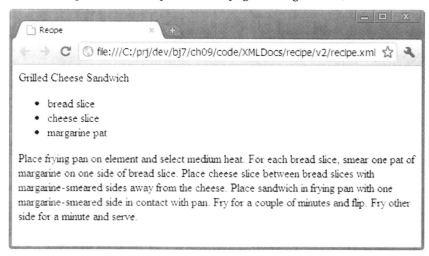

Figure 10-2. Google Chrome presents the recipe data via XHTML tags.

A tag's attributes don't need to be prefixed when those attributes belong to the element. For example, qty is not prefixed in <r:ingredient qty="2">. However, a prefix is required for attributes belonging to other namespaces. For example, suppose you want to add an XHTML style attribute to the document's <r:title> tag, to provide styling for the recipe title when displayed via an application. You can accomplish this task by inserting an XHTML attribute into the title tag, as follows: <r:title h:style="font-family: sans-serif;">. The XHTML style attribute has been prefixed with h: because this attribute belongs to the XHTML language namespace and not to the recipe language namespace.

When multiple namespaces are involved, it can be convenient to specify one of these namespaces as the default namespace, to reduce the tedium in entering namespace prefixes. Consider Listing 10-6.

Listing 10-6. Specifying a default namespace

```
<?xml version="1.0"?>
<html xmlns="http://www.w3.org/1999/xhtml"
      xmlns:r="http://www.tutortutor.ca/">
   <head>
      <title>
          Recipe
      </title>
   </head>
   <body>
   <r:recipe>
      <r:title>
          Grilled Cheese Sandwich
```

```
          </r:title>
          <r:ingredients>
             <ul>
             <li>
             <r:ingredient qty="2">
                bread slice
             </r:ingredient>
             </li>
             <li>
             <r:ingredient>
                cheese slice
             </r:ingredient>
             </li>
             <li>
             <r:ingredient qty="2">
                margarine pat
             </r:ingredient>
             </li>
             </ul>
          </r:ingredients>
          <p>
          <r:instructions>
             Place frying pan on element and select medium heat. For each bread slice, smear
             one pat of margarine on one side of bread slice. Place cheese slice between
             bread slices with margarine-smeared sides away from the cheese. Place sandwich
             in frying pan with one margarine-smeared side in contact with pan. Fry for a
             couple of minutes and flip. Fry other side for a minute and serve.
          </r:instructions>
          </p>
      </r:recipe>
      </body>
</html>
```

Listing 10-6 specifies a default namespace for the XHTML language. No XHTML element tag needs to be prefixed with h:. However, recipe language element tags must still be prefixed with the r: prefix.

Comments and Processing Instructions

XML documents can contain *comments,* which are character sequences beginning with <!-- and ending with -->. For example, you might place <!-- Todo --> in Listing 10-3's body element to remind yourself that you need to finish coding this element.

Comments are used to clarify portions of a document. They can appear anywhere after the XML declaration except within tags, cannot be nested, cannot contain a double hyphen (--) because doing so might confuse an XML parser that the comment has been closed, should not contain a hyphen (-) for the same reason, and are typically ignored during processing. Comments are not content.

XML also permits processing instructions to be present. A *processing instruction* is an instruction that is made available to the application parsing the document. The instruction begins with <? and ends with ?>. The <? prefix is followed by a name known as the *target.* This name typically identifies the application to which the processing instruction is intended. The rest of the processing instruction contains text in a format appropriate to the application. Two examples of processing instructions are <?xml-stylesheet href="modern.xsl" type="text/xml"?> (associate an eXtensible Stylesheet Language

[XSL] style sheet [see http://en.wikipedia.org/wiki/XSL] with an XML document) and <?php /* PHP code */ ?> (pass a PHP code fragment to the application). Although the XML declaration looks like a processing instruction, this is not the case.

Note The XML declaration is not a processing instruction.

Well-Formed Documents

HTML is a sloppy language in which elements can be specified out of order, end tags can be omitted, and so on. The complexity of a web browser's page layout code is partly due to the need to handle these special cases. In contrast, XML is a much stricter language. To make XML documents easier to parse, XML mandates that XML documents follow certain rules:

- *All elements must either have start and end tags or consist of empty-element tags.* For example, unlike the HTML <p> tag that is often specified without a </p> counterpart, </p> must also be present from an XML document perspective.

- *Tags must be nested correctly.* For example, while you'll probably get away with specifying JavaFX in HTML, an XML parser would report an error. In contrast, JavaFX doesn't result in an error.

- *All attribute values must be quoted.* Either single quotes (') or double quotes (") are permissible (although double quotes are the more commonly specified quotes). It is an error to omit these quotes.

- *Empty elements must be properly formatted.* For example, HTML's <br> tag would have to be specified as <br/> in XML. You can specify a space between the tag's name and the / character, although the space is optional.

- *Be careful with case.* XML is a case-sensitive language in which tags differing in case (such as <author> and <Author>) are considered different. It is an error to mix start and end tags of different cases, for example, <author> with </Author>.

XML parsers that are aware of namespaces enforce two additional rules:

- All element and attribute names must not include more than one colon character.

- No entity names, processing instruction targets, or notation names (discussed later) can contain colons.

An XML document that conforms to these rules is *well formed*. The document has a logical and clean appearance, and is much easier to process. XML parsers will only parse well-formed XML documents.

Valid Documents

It is not always enough for an XML document to be well formed; in many cases the document must also be valid. A *valid* document adheres to constraints. For example, a constraint could be placed upon

Listing 10-1's recipe document to ensure that the ingredients element always precedes the instructions element; perhaps an application must first process ingredients.

▨ **Note** XML document validation is similar to a compiler analyzing source code to make sure that the code makes sense in a machine context. For example, each of int, count, =, 1, and ; are valid Java character sequences, but 1 count ; int = is not a valid Java construct (whereas int count = 1; is a valid Java construct).

Some XML parsers perform validation, whereas other parsers do not because validating parsers are harder to write. A parser that performs validation compares an XML document to a grammar document. Any deviation from this document is reported as an error to the application—the document is not valid. The application may choose to fix the error or reject the document. Unlike wellformedness errors, validity errors are not necessarily fatal and the parser can continue to parse the document.

▨ **Note** Validating XML parsers often don't validate by default because validation can be time consuming. They must be instructed to perform validation.

Grammar documents are written in a special language. Two commonly used grammar languages that are supported by JAXP are Document Type Definition and XML Schema.

Document Type Definition

Document Type Definition (DTD) is the oldest grammar language for specifying an XML document's grammar. DTD grammar documents (known as DTDs) are written in accordance to a strict syntax that states what elements may be present and in what parts of a document, and also what is contained within elements (child elements, content, or mixed content) and what attributes may be specified. For example, a DTD may specify that a recipe element must have an ingredients element followed by an instructions element.

Listing 10-7 presents a DTD for the recipe language that was used to construct Listing 10-1's document.

Listing 10-7. The recipe language's DTD

```
<!ELEMENT recipe (title, ingredients, instructions)>
<!ELEMENT title (#PCDATA)>
<!ELEMENT ingredients (ingredient+)>
<!ELEMENT ingredient (#PCDATA)>
<!ELEMENT instructions (#PCDATA)>
<!ATTLIST ingredient qty CDATA "1">
```

This DTD first declares the recipe language's elements. Element declarations take the form `<!ELEMENT name content-specifier>`, where *name* is any legal XML name (it cannot contain whitespace, for example), and *content-specifier* identifies what can appear within the element.

The first element declaration states that exactly one recipe element can appear in the XML document –this declaration does not imply that recipe is the root element. Furthermore, this element must include exactly one each of the title, ingredients, and instructions child elements, and in that order. Child elements must be specified as a comma-separated list. Furthermore, a list is always surrounded by parentheses.

The second element declaration states that the title element contains *parsed character data* (nonmarkup text). The third element declaration states that at least one ingredient element must appear in ingredients. The + character is an example of a regular expression that means one or more. Other expressions that may be used are * (zero or more) and ? (once or not at all). The fourth and fifth element declarations are similar to the second by stating that ingredient and instructions elements contain parsed character data.

■ **Note** Element declarations support three other content specifiers. You can specify `<!ELEMENT name ANY>` to allow any type of element content or `<!ELEMENT name EMPTY>` to disallow any element content. To state that an element contains mixed content, you would specify #PCDATA and a list of element names, separated by vertical bars (|). For example, `<!ELEMENT ingredient (#PCDATA | measure | note)*>` states that the ingredient element can contain a mix of parsed character data, zero or more measure elements, and zero or more note elements. It does not specify the order in which the parsed character data and these elements occur. However, #PCDATA must be the first item specified in the list. When a regular expression is used in this context, it must appear to the right of the closing parenthesis.

Listing 10-7's DTD lastly declares the recipe language's attributes, of which there is only one: qty. Attribute declarations take the form `<!ATTLIST ename aname type default-value>`, where *ename* is the name of the element to which the attribute belongs, *aname* is the name of the attribute, *type* is the attribute's type, and *default-value* is the attribute's default value.

The attribute declaration identifies qty as an attribute of ingredient. It also states that qty's type is CDATA (any string of characters not including the ampersand, less than or greater than signs, or double quotes may appear; these characters may be represented via &, <, >, or ", respectively), and that qty is optional, assuming default value 1 when not present.

MORE ABOUT ATTRIBUTES

DTD lets you specify additional attribute types: ID (create a unique identifier for an attribute that identifies an element), IDREF (an attribute's value is an element located elsewhere in the document), IDREFS (the value consists of multiple IDREFs), ENTITY (you can use external binary data or unparsed entities), ENTITIES (the value consists of multiple entities), NMTOKEN (the value is restricted to any valid XML name), NMTOKENS (the value is composed of multiple XML names), NOTATION (the value is already specified via a

DTD notation declaration), and enumerated (a list of possible values to choose from; values are separated with vertical bars).

Instead of specifying a default value verbatim, you can specify #REQUIRED to mean that the attribute must always be present with some value (`<!ATTLIST ename aname type #REQUIRED>`), #IMPLIED to mean that the attribute is optional and no default value is provided (`<!ATTLIST ename aname type #IMPLIED>`), or #FIXED to mean that the attribute is optional and must always take on the DTD-assigned default value when used (`<!ATTLIST ename aname type #FIXED "value">`).

You can specify a list of attributes in one ATTLIST declaration. For example, `<!ATTLIST ename aname1 type1 default-value1 aname2 type2 default-value2>` declares two attributes identified as *aname1* and *aname2*.

A DTD-based validating XML parser requires that a document include a *document type declaration* identifying the DTD that specifies the document's grammar before it will validate the document.

Note Document Type Definition and document type declaration are two different things. The DTD acronym identifies a Document Type Definition and never identifies a document type declaration.

A document type declaration appears immediately after the XML declaration and is specified in one of the following ways:

- `<!DOCTYPE root-element-name SYSTEM uri>` references an external but private DTD via *uri*. The referenced DTD is not available for public scrutiny. For example, I might store my recipe language's DTD file (recipe.dtd) in a private dtds directory on my www.tutortutor.ca website, and use `<!DOCTYPE recipe SYSTEM "http://www.tutortutor.ca/dtds/recipe.dtd">` to identify this DTD's location via system identifier http://www.tutortutor.ca/dtds/recipe.dtd.

- `<!DOCTYPE root-element-name PUBLIC fpi uri>` references an external but public DTD via *fpi*, a *formal public identifier* (see http://en.wikipedia.org/wiki/Formal_Public_Identifier), and *uri*. If a validating XML parser cannot locate the DTD via public identifier *fpi*, it can use system identifier *uri* to locate the DTD. For example, `<!DOCTYPE html PUBLIC "-//W3C//DTD XHTML 1.0 Transitional//EN" "http://www.w3.org/TR/xhtml1/DTD/xhtml1-transitional.dtd">` references the XHTML 1.0 DTD first via public identifier -//W3C//DTD XHTML 1.0 Transitional//EN, and second via system identifier http://www.w3.org/TR/xhtml1/DTD/xhtml1-transitional.dtd.

- `<!DOCTYPE root-element [ dtd ]>` references an internal DTD, one that is embedded within the XML document. The internal DTD must appear between square brackets.

Listing 10-8 presents Listing 10-1 (minus the child elements between the `<recipe>` and `</recipe>` tags) with an internal DTD.

Listing 10-8. The recipe document with an internal DTD

```
<?xml version="1.0"?>
<!DOCTYPE recipe [
   <!ELEMENT recipe (title, ingredients, instructions)>
   <!ELEMENT title (#PCDATA)>
   <!ELEMENT ingredients (ingredient+)>
   <!ELEMENT ingredient (#PCDATA)>
   <!ELEMENT instructions (#PCDATA)>
   <!ATTLIST ingredient qty CDATA "1">
]>
<recipe>
   <!-- Child elements removed for brevity. -->
</recipe>
```

Note A document can have internal and external DTDs; for example, `<!DOCTYPE recipe SYSTEM "http://www.tutortutor.ca/dtds/recipe.dtd" [ <!ELEMENT ...>]>`. The internal DTD is referred to as the *internal DTD subset* and the external DTD is referred to as the *external DTD subset*. Neither subset can override the element declarations of the other subset.

You can also declare notations, and general and parameter entities within DTDs. A *notation* is an arbitrary piece of data that typically describes the format of unparsed binary data, and typically has the form `<!NOTATION name SYSTEM uri>`, where *name* identifies the notation and *uri* identifies some kind of plugin that can process the data on behalf of the application that is parsing the XML document. For example, `<!NOTATION image SYSTEM "psp.exe">` declares a notation named `image` and identifies Windows executable `psp.exe` as a plugin for processing images.

It is also common to use notations to specify binary data types via Internet media types (see http://en.wikipedia.org/wiki/Internet_media_type). For example, `<!NOTATION image SYSTEM "image/jpeg">` declares an image notation that identifies the image/jpeg Internet media type for Joint Photographic Experts Group images.

General entities are entities referenced from inside an XML document via *general entity references*, syntactic constructs of the form `&name;`. Examples include the predefined `lt`, `gt`, `amp`, `apos`, and `quot` character entities, whose `&lt;`, `&gt;`, `&amp;`, `&apos;`, and `&quot;` character entity references are aliases for characters <, >, &, ', and ", respectively.

General entities are classified as internal or external. An *internal general entity* is a general entity whose value is stored in the DTD, and has the form `<!ENTITY name value>`, where *name* identifies the entity and *value* specifies its value. For example, `<!ENTITY copyright "Copyright &copy; 2011 Jeff Friesen. All rights reserved.">` declares an internal general entity named `copyright`. The value of this entity may include another declared entity, such as `&copy;` (the HTML entity for the copyright symbol), and can be referenced from anywhere in an XML document by specifying `&copyright;`.

An *external general entity* is a general entity whose value is stored outside the DTD. The value might be textual data (such as an XML document), or it might be binary data (such as a JPEG image). External general entities are classified as external parsed general entity and external unparsed entity.

An *external parsed general entity* references an external file that stores the entity's textual data, which is subject to being inserted into a document and parsed by a validating parser when a general entity reference is specified in the document, and which has the form <!ENTITY *name* SYSTEM *uri*>, where *name* identifies the entity and *uri* identifies the external file. For example, <!ENTITY chapter-header SYSTEM "http://www.tutortutor.ca/entities/chapheader.xml"> identifies chapheader.xml as storing the XML content to be inserted into an XML document wherever &chapter-header; appears in the document. The alternative <!ENTITY *name* PUBLIC *fpi uri*> form can be specified.

■ **Caution** Because the contents of an external file may be parsed, this content must be well formed.

An *external unparsed entity* references an external file that stores the entity's binary data, and has the form <!ENTITY *name* SYSTEM *uri* NDATA *nname*>, where *name* identifies the entity, *uri* locates the external file, and NDATA identifies the notation declaration named *nname*. The notation typically identifies a plugin for processing the binary data or the Internet media type of this data. For example, <!ENTITY photo SYSTEM "photo.jpg" NDATA image> associates name photo with external binary file photo.png and notation image. The alternative <!ENTITY *name* PUBLIC *fpi uri* NDATA *nname*> form can be specified.

■ **Note** XML does not allow references to external general entities to appear in attribute values. For example, you cannot specify &chapter-header; in an attribute's value.

Parameter entities are entities referenced from inside a DTD via *parameter entity references*, syntactic constructs of the form %*name*;. They are useful for eliminating repetitive content from element declarations. For example, you are creating a DTD for a large company, and this DTD contains three element declarations: <!ELEMENT salesperson (firstname, lastname)>, <!ELEMENT lawyer (firstname, lastname)>, and <!ELEMENT accountant (firstname, lastname)>. Each element contains repeated child element content. If you need to add another child element (such as middleinitial), you'll need to make sure that all the elements are updated; otherwise, you risk a malformed DTD. Parameter entities can help you solve this problem.

Parameter entities are classified as internal or external. An *internal parameter entity* is a parameter entity whose value is stored in the DTD, and has the form <!ENTITY % *name value*>, where *name* identifies the entity and *value* specifies its value. For example, <!ENTITY % person-name "firstname, lastname"> declares a parameter entity named person-name with value firstname, lastname. Once declared, this entity can be referenced in the three previous element declarations, as follows: <!ELEMENT salesperson (%person-name;)>, <!ELEMENT lawyer (%person-name;)>, and <!ELEMENT accountant (%person-name;)>. Instead of adding middleinitial to each of salesperson, lawyer, and accountant, as was done previously, you would now add this child element to person-name, as in <!ENTITY % person-name "firstname, middleinitial, lastname">, and this change would be applied to these element declarations.

An *external parameter entity* is a parameter entity whose value is stored outside the DTD. It has the form <!ENTITY % *name* SYSTEM *uri*>, where *name* identifies the entity and *uri* locates the external file. For example, <!ENTITY % person-name SYSTEM "http://www.tutortutor.ca/entities/names.dtd"> identifies names.dtd as storing the firstname, lastname text to be inserted into a DTD wherever %person-name; appears in the DTD. The alternative <!ENTITY % *name* PUBLIC *fpi uri*> form can be specified.

> ■ **Note** This discussion sums up the basics of DTD. One additional topic that was not covered (for brevity) is *conditional inclusion*, which lets you specify those portions of a DTD to make available to parsers, and is typically used with parameter entity references.

XML Schema

XML Schema is a grammar language for declaring the structure, content, and *semantics* (meaning) of an XML document. This language's grammar documents are known as *schemas* that are themselves XML documents. Schemas must conform to the XML Schema DTD (see `http://www.w3.org/2001/XMLSchema.dtd`).

XML Schema was introduced by the W3C to overcome limitations with DTD, such as DTD's lack of support for namespaces. Also, XML Schema provides an object-oriented approach to declaring an XML document's grammar. This grammar language provides a much larger set of primitive types than DTD's CDATA and PCDATA types. For example, you'll find integer, floating-point, various date and time, and string types to be part of XML Schema.

> ■ **Note** XML Schema predefines 19 primitive types, which are expressed via the following identifiers: `anyURI`, `base64Binary`, `boolean`, `date`, `dateTime`, `decimal`, `double`, `duration`, `float`, `hexBinary`, `gDay`, `gMonth`, `gMonthDay`, `gYear`, `gYearMonth`, `NOTATION`, `QName`, `string`, and `time`.

XML Schema provides *restriction* (reducing the set of permitted values through constraints), *list* (allowing a sequence of values), and *union* (allowing a choice of values from several types) derivation methods for creating new *simple types* from these primitive types. For example, XML Schema derives 13 integer types from `decimal` through restriction; these types are expressed via the following identifiers: `byte`, `int`, `integer`, `long`, `negativeInteger`, `nonNegativeInteger`, `nonPositiveInteger`, `positiveInteger`, `short`, `unsignedByte`, `unsignedInt`, `unsignedLong`, and `unsignedShort`. It also provides support for creating *complex types* from simple types.

A good way to become familiar with XML Schema is to follow through an example, such as creating a schema for Listing 10-1's recipe language document. The first step in creating this recipe language schema is to identify all its elements and attributes. The elements are `recipe`, `title`, `ingredients`, `instructions`, and `ingredient`; `qty` is the solitary attribute.

The next step is to classify the elements according to XML Schema's *content model*, which specifies the types of child elements and text *nodes* (see `http://en.wikipedia.org/wiki/Node_(computer_science)`) that can be included in an element. An element is considered to be *empty* when the element has no child elements or text nodes, *simple* when only text nodes are accepted, *complex*, when only child elements are accepted, and *mixed* when child elements and text nodes are accepted. None of Listing 10-1's elements have empty or mixed content models. However, the `title`, `ingredient`, and `instructions` elements have simple content models; and the `recipe` and `ingredients` elements have complex content models.

For elements that have a simple content model, we can distinguish between elements having attributes and elements not having attributes. XML Schema classifies elements having a simple content model and no attributes as simple types. Furthermore, it classifies elements having a simple content model and attributes, or elements from other content models as complex types. Furthermore, XML Schema classifies attributes as simple types because they only contain text values—attributes don't have child elements. Listing 10-1's title and instructions elements, and its qty attribute are simple types. Its recipe, ingredients, and ingredient elements are complex types.

At this point, we can begin to declare the schema. The following example presents the introductory schema element:

```
<xs:schema xmlns:xs="http://www.w3.org/2001/XMLSchema">
```

The schema element introduces the grammar. It also assigns the commonly used xs namespace prefix to the standard XML Schema namespace; xs: is subsequently prepended to XML Schema element names.

Next, we use the element element to declare the title and instructions simple type elements, as follows:

```
<xs:element name="title" type="xs:string"/>
<xs:element name="instructions" type="xs:string"/>
```

XML Schema requires that each element have a name and (unlike DTD) be associated with a type, which identifies the kind of data stored in the element. For example, the first element declaration identifies title as the name via its name attribute and string as the type via its type attribute (string or character data appears between the <title> and </title> tags). The xs: prefix in xs:string is required because string is a predefined W3C type.

Continuing, we now use the attribute element to declare the qty simple type attribute, as follows:

```
<xs:attribute name="qty" type="xs:unsignedInt" default="1"/>
```

This attribute element declares an attribute named qty. I've chosen unsignedInt as this attribute's type because quantities are nonnegative values. Furthermore, I've specified 1 as the default value for when qty is not specified—attribute elements default to declaring optional attributes.

Note The order of element and attribute declarations is not significant within a schema.

Now that we've declared the simple types, we can start to declare the complex types. To begin, we'll declare recipe, as follows:

```
<xs:element name="recipe">
   <xs:complexType>
      <xs:sequence>
         <xs:element ref="title"/>
         <xs:element ref="ingredients"/>
         <xs:element ref="instructions"/>
      </xs:sequence>
   </xs:complexType>
</xs:element>
```

This declaration states that recipe is a complex type (via the complexType element) consisting of a sequence (via the sequence element) of one title element followed by one ingredients element followed by one instructions element. Each of these elements is declared by a different element that is referred to by its element's ref attribute.

The next complex type to declare is `ingredients`. The following example provides its declaration:

```
<xs:element name="ingredients">
   <xs:complexType>
      <xs:sequence>
         <xs:element ref="ingredient" maxOccurs="unbounded"/>
      </xs:sequence>
   </xs:complexType>
</xs:element>
```

This declaration states that `ingredients` is a complex type consisting of a sequence of one or more ingredient elements. The "or more" is specified by including `element`'s `maxOccurs` attribute and setting this attribute's value to unbounded.

Note The `maxOccurs` attribute identifies the maximum number of times that an element can occur. A similar `minOccurs` attribute identifies the minimum number of times that an element can occur. Each attribute can be assigned 0 or a positive integer. Furthermore, you can specify `unbounded` for `maxOccurs`, which means that there is no upper limit on occurrences of the element. Each attribute defaults to a value of 1, which means that an element can appear only one time when neither attribute is present.

The final complex type to declare is `ingredient`. Although `ingredient` can contain only text nodes, which implies that it should be a simple type, it is the presence of the `qty` attribute that makes it complex. Check out the following declaration:

```
<xs:element name="ingredient">
   <xs:complexType>
      <xs:simpleContent>
         <xs:extension base="xs:string">
            <xs:attribute ref="qty"/>
         </xs:extension>
      </xs:simpleContent>
   </xs:complexType>
</xs:element>
```

The element named `ingredient` is a complex type (because of its optional qty attribute). The `simpleContent` element indicates that `ingredient` can only contain simple content (text nodes), and the `extension` element indicates that `ingredient` is a new type that extends the predefined `string` type (specified via the base attribute), implying that `ingredient` inherits all of `string`'s attributes and structure. Furthermore, `ingredient` is given an additional qty attribute.

Listing 10-9 combines the previous examples into a complete schema.

Listing 10-9. *The recipe document's schema*

```
<?xml version="1.0"?>
<xs:schema xmlns:xs="http://www.w3.org/2001/XMLSchema">
<xs:element name="title" type="xs:string"/>
<xs:element name="instructions" type="xs:string"/>
```

```
<xs:attribute name="qty" type="xs:unsignedInt" default="1"/>
<xs:element name="recipe">
   <xs:complexType>
      <xs:sequence>
         <xs:element ref="title"/>
         <xs:element ref="ingredients"/>
         <xs:element ref="instructions"/>
      </xs:sequence>
   </xs:complexType>
</xs:element>
<xs:element name="ingredients">
   <xs:complexType>
      <xs:sequence>
         <xs:element ref="ingredient" maxOccurs="unbounded"/>
      </xs:sequence>
   </xs:complexType>
</xs:element>
<xs:element name="ingredient">
   <xs:complexType>
      <xs:simpleContent>
         <xs:extension base="xs:string">
            <xs:attribute ref="qty"/>
         </xs:extension>
      </xs:simpleContent>
   </xs:complexType>
</xs:element>
```

After creating the schema, you'll want to reference it from a recipe document. Accomplish this task by specifying xmlns:xsi and xsi:schemaLocation attributes on the document's root element start tag (<recipe>), as follows:

```
<recipe xmlns="http://www.tutortutor.ca/"
        xmlns:xsi="http://www.w3.org/2001/XMLSchema-instance"
        xsi:schemaLocation="http://www.tutortutor.ca/schemas recipe.xsd">
```

The xmlns attribute identifies http://www.tutortutor.ca/ as the document's default namespace. Unprefixed elements and their unprefixed attributes belong to this namespace.

The xmlns:xsi attribute associates the conventional xsi (XML Schema Instance) prefix with the standard http://www.w3.org/2001/XMLSchema-instance namespace. The only item in the document that's prefixed with xsi: is schemaLocation.

The schemaLocation attribute is used to locate the schema. This attribute's value can be multiple pairs of space-separated values, but is specified as a single pair of such values in this example. The first value (http://www.tutortutor.ca/schemas) identifies the target namespace for the schema, and the second value (recipe.xsd) identifies the location of the schema within this namespace.

■ **Note** Schema files that conform to XML Schema's grammar are commonly assigned the .xsd file extension.

If an XML document declares a namespace (xmlns default or xmlns:*prefix*), that namespace must be made available to the schema so that a validating parser can resolve all references to elements and other schema components for that namespace. We also need to mention which namespace the schema describes, and we do so by including the targetNamespace attribute on the schema element. For example, suppose our recipe document declares a default XML namespace, as follows:

```
<?xml version="1.0"?>
<recipe xmlns="http://www.tutortutor.ca/">
```

At minimum, we would need to modify Listing 10-9's schema element to include targetNameSpace and the recipe document's default namespace as targetNameSpace's value, as follows:

```
<xs:schema targetNamespace="http://www.tutortutor.ca/"
           xmlns:xs="http://www.w3.org/2001/XMLSchema">
```

Perhaps you're wondering why you need to learn about XML Schema when DTD should be good enough for your XML projects. The reason for learning XML Schema is that Chapter 11 introduces you to the XML-based Web Services Description Language (WSDL), and the WSDL example that's presented in that chapter includes an XML Schema-based schema.

Parsing XML Documents with SAX

Simple API for XML (SAX) is an event-based API for parsing an XML document sequentially from start to finish. As a SAX-oriented parser encounters an item from the document's *infoset* (an abstract data model describing an XML document's information—see http://en.wikipedia.org/wiki/XML_Information_Set), it makes this item available to an application as an *event*, by calling one of the methods in one of the application's *handlers* (an object whose methods are called by the parser to make event information available), which the application has previously registered with the parser. The application can then *consume* this event by processing the infoset item in some manner.

■ **Note** According to its official website (http://www.saxproject.org/), SAX originated as an XML parsing API for Java. However, SAX is not exclusive to Java. Microsoft also supports SAX for its .NET framework (see http://saxdotnet.sourceforge.net/).

After taking you on a tour of the SAX API, this section provides a simple demonstration of this API to help you become familiar with its event-based parsing paradigm. It then shows you how to create a custom entity resolver.

Exploring the SAX API

SAX exists in two major versions. Java implements SAX 1 through the javax.xml.parsers package's abstract SAXParser and SAXParserFactory classes, and implements SAX 2 through the org.xml.sax package's XMLReader interface and through the org.xml.sax.helpers package's XMLReaderFactory class. The org.xml.sax, org.xml.sax.ext, and org.xml.sax.helpers packages provide various types that augment both Java implementations.

Note I explore only the SAX 2 implementation because SAX 2 makes available additional infoset items about an XML document (such as comments and CDATA section notifications).

Classes that implement the XMLReader interface describe SAX 2-based parsers. Instances of these classes are obtained by calling the XMLReaderFactory class's createXMLReader() methods. For example, the following example invokes this class's static XMLReader createXMLReader() method to create and return an XMLReader instance:

```
XMLReader xmlr = XMLReaderFactory.createXMLReader();
```

This method call returns an instance of an XMLReader-implementing class and assigns its reference to xmlr.

Note Behind the scenes, createXMLReader() attempts to create an XMLReader instance from system defaults, according to a lookup procedure that first examines the org.xml.sax.driver system property to see if it has a value. If so, this property's value is used as the name of the class that implements XMLReader, and an attempt is made to instantiate this class and return the instance. An instance of the org.xml.sax.SAXException class is thrown when createXMLReader() cannot obtain an appropriate class or instantiate the class.

The returned XMLReader object makes available several methods for configuring the parser and parsing a document's content. These methods are described here:

- ContentHandler getContentHandler() returns the current content handler, which is an instance of a class that implements the org.xml.sax.ContentHandler interface, or the null reference when none has been registered.

- DTDHandler getDTDHandler() returns the current DTD handler, which is an instance of a class that implements the org.xml.sax.DTDHandler interface, or the null reference when none has been registered.

- EntityResolver getEntityResolver() returns the current entity resolver, which is an instance of a class that implements the org.xml.sax.EntityResolver interface, or the null reference when none has been registered.

- ErrorHandler getErrorHandler() returns the current error handler, which is an instance of a class that implements the org.xml.sax.ErrorHandler interface, or the null reference when none has been registered.

- `boolean getFeature(String name)` returns the Boolean value that corresponds to the feature identified by `name`, which must be a fully-qualified URI. This method throws `org.xml.sax.SAXNotRecognizedException` when the name is not recognized as a feature, and throws `org.xml.sax.SAXNotSupportedException` when the name is recognized but the associated value cannot be determined when `getFeature()` is called. `SAXNotRecognizedException` and `SAXNotSupportedException` are subclasses of `SAXException`.

- `Object getProperty(String name)` returns the `java.lang.Object` instance that corresponds to the property identified by `name`, which must be a fully-qualified URI. This method throws `SAXNotRecognizedException` when the name is not recognized as a property, and throws `SAXNotSupportedException` when the name is recognized but the associated value cannot be determined when `getProperty()` is called.

- `void parse(InputSource input)` parses an XML document and does not return until the document has been parsed. The `input` parameter stores a reference to an `org.xml.sax.InputSource` instance, which describes the document's source (such as a `java.io.InputStream` instance, or even a `java.lang.String`-based system identifier URI). This method throws `java.io.IOException` when the source cannot be read, and `SAXException` when parsing fails, probably due to a wellformedness violation.

- `void parse(String systemId)` parses an XML document by executing `parse(new InputSource(systemId));`.

- `void setContentHandler(ContentHandler handler)` registers the content handler identified by `handler` with the parser. The `ContentHandler` interface provides eleven callback methods that are called to report various parsing events (such as the start and end of an element).

- `void setDTDHandler(DTDHandler handler)` registers the DTD handler identified by `handler` with the parser. The `DTDHandler` interface provides a pair of callback methods for reporting on notations and external unparsed entities.

- `void setEntityResolver(EntityResolver resolver)` registers the entity resolver identified by `resolver` with the parser. The `EntityResolver` interface provides a single callback method for resolving entities.

- `void setErrorHandler(ErrorHandler handler)` registers the error handler identified by `handler` with the parser. The `ErrorHandler` interface provides three callback methods that report *fatal errors* (problems that prevent further parsing, such as wellformedness violations), *recoverable errors* (problems that don't prevent further parsing, such as validation failures), and *warnings* (nonerrors that need to be addressed, such as prefixing an element name with the W3C-reserved xml prefix).

- `void setFeature(String name, boolean value)` assigns value to the feature identified by `name`, which must be a fully-qualified URI. This method throws `SAXNotRecognizedException` when the name is not recognized as a feature, and throws `SAXNotSupportedException` when the name is recognized but the associated value cannot be set when `setFeature()` is called.

- void setProperty(String name, Object value) assigns value to the property identified by name, which must be a fully-qualified URI. This method throws SAXNotRecognizedException when the name is not recognized as a property, and throws SAXNotSupportedException when the name is recognized but the associated value cannot be set when setProperty() is called.

If a handler is not installed, all events pertaining to that handler are silently ignored. Not installing an error handler can be problematic because normal processing might not continue, and the application would not be aware that anything had gone wrong. If an entity resolver is not installed, the parser performs its own default resolution. I'll have more to say about entity resolution later in this chapter.

■ **Note** You can install a new content handler, DTD handler, entity resolver, or error handler while the document is being parsed. The parser starts using the handler when the next event occurs.

After obtaining an XMLReader instance, you can configure that instance by setting its features and properties. A *feature* is a name-value pair that describes a parser mode, such as validation. In contrast, a *property* is a name-value pair that describes some other aspect of the parser interface, such as a lexical handler that augments the content handler by providing callback methods for reporting on comments, CDATA delimiters, and a few other syntactic constructs.

Features and properties have names, which must be absolute URIs beginning with the http:// prefix. A feature's value is always a Boolean true/false value. In contrast, a property's value is an arbitrary object. The following example demonstrates setting a feature and a property:

```
xmlr.setFeature("http://xml.org/sax/features/validation", true);
xmlr.setProperty("http://xml.org/sax/properties/lexical-handler",
                 new LexicalHandler() { /* … */ });
```

The setFeature() call enables the validation feature so that the parser will perform validation. Feature names are prefixed with http://xml.org/sax/features/.

■ **Note** Parsers must support the namespaces and namespace-prefixes features. namespaces decides whether URIs and local names are passed to ContentHandler's startElement() and endElement() methods. It defaults to true—these names are passed. The parser can pass empty strings when false. namespace-prefixes decides whether a namespace declaration's xmlns and xmlns:*prefix* attributes are included in the Attributes list passed to startElement(), and also decides whether qualified names are passed as the method's third argument—a *qualified name* is a prefix plus a local name. It defaults to false, meaning that xmlns and xmlns:*prefix* are not included, and that parsers don't have to pass qualified names. No properties are mandatory. The JDK documentation's org.xml.sax package page lists standard SAX 2 features and properties.

The setProperty() call assigns an instance of a class that implements the org.xml.sax.ext.LexicalHandler interface to the lexical-handler property so that interface methods

can be called to report on comments, CDATA sections, and so on. Property names are prefixed with
`http://xml.org/sax/properties/`.

■ **Note** Unlike `ContentHandler`, `DTDHandler`, `EntityResolver`, and `ErrorHandler`, `LexicalHandler` is an extension (it is not part of the core SAX API), which is why `XMLReader` does not declare a `void` `setLexicalHandler(LexicalHandler handler)` method. If you want to install a lexical handler, you must use `XMLReader`'s `setProperty()` method to install the handler as the value of the `http://xml.org/sax/properties/lexical-handler` property.

Features and properties can be read-only or read-write. (In some rare cases, a feature or property might be write-only.) When setting or reading a feature or property, either a `SAXNotSupportedException` or a `SAXNotRecognizedException` instance might be thrown. For example, if you try to modify a read-only feature/property, an instance of the `SAXNotSupportedException` class is thrown. This exception could also be thrown if you call `setFeature()` or `setProperty()` during parsing. Trying to set the validation feature for a parser that doesn't perform validation is a scenario where an instance of the `SAXNotRecognizedException` class is thrown.

The handlers installed by `setContentHandler()`, `setDTDHandler()`, and `setErrorHandler()`, the entity resolver installed by `setEntityResolver()`, and the handler installed by the `lexical-handler` property/`LexicalHandler` interface provide various callback methods that you need to understand before you can codify them to respond effectively to parsing events. `ContentHandler` declares the following content-oriented informational callback methods:

- `void characters(char[] ch, int start, int length)` reports an element's character data via the `ch` array. The arguments that are passed to `start` and `length` identify that portion of the array that's relevant to this method call. Characters are passed via a `char[]` array instead of via a `String` instance as a performance optimization. Parsers commonly store a large amount of the document in an array and repeatedly pass a reference to this array along with updated `start` and `length` values to `characters()`.

- `void endDocument()` reports that the end of the document has been reached. An application might use this method to close an output file or perform some other cleanup.

- `void endElement(String uri, String localName, String qName)` reports that the end of an element has been reached. `uri` identifies the element's namespace URI, or is empty when there is no namespace URI or namespace processing has not been enabled. `localName` identifies the element's local name, which is the name without a prefix (the `html` in `html` or `h:html`, for example). `qName` references the qualified name; for example, `h:html` or `html` when there is no prefix. `endElement()` is invoked when an end tag is detected, or immediately following `startElement()` when an empty-element tag is detected.

- `void endPrefixMapping(String prefix)` reports that the end of a namespace prefix mapping (`xmlns:h`, for example) has been reached, and `prefix` reports this prefix (`h`, for example).

- void ignorableWhitespace(char[] ch, int start, int length) reports *ignorable whitespace* (whitespace located between tags where the DTD doesn't allow mixed content). This whitespace is often used to indent tags. The parameters serve the same purpose as those in the characters() method.

- void processingInstruction(String target, String data) reports a processing instruction, where target identifies the application to which the instruction is directed and data provides the instruction's data (the null reference when there is no data).

- void setDocumentLocator(Locator locator) reports an org.xml.sax.Locator object (an instance of a class implementing the Locator interface) whose int getColumnNumber(), int getLineNumber(), String getPublicId(), and String getSystemId() methods can be called to obtain location information at the end position of any document-related event, even when the parser is not reporting an error. This method is called prior to startDocument(), and is a good place to save the Locator object so that it can be accessed from other callback methods.

- void skippedEntity(String name) reports all skipped entities. Validating parsers resolve all general entity references, but nonvalidating parsers have the option of skipping them because nonvalidating parsers do not read DTDs where these entities are declared. If the nonvalidating parser doesn't read a DTD, it will not know if an entity is properly declared. Instead of attempting to read the DTD and report the entity's replacement text, the nonvalidating parser calls skippedEntity() with the entity's name.

- void startDocument() reports that the start of the document has been reached. An application might use this method to create an output file or perform some other initialization.

- void startElement(String uri, String localName, String qName, Attributes attributes) reports that the start of an element has been reached. uri identifies the element's namespace URI, or is empty when there is no namespace URI or namespace processing has not been enabled. localName identifies the element's local name, qName references its qualified name, and attributes references an array of org.xml.sax.Attribute objects that identify the element's attributes—this array is empty when there are no attributes. startElement() is invoked when a start tag or an empty-element tag is detected.

- void startPrefixMapping(String prefix, String uri) reports that the start of a namespace prefix mapping (xmlns:h="http://www.w3.org/1999/xhtml", for example) has been reached, where prefix reports this prefix (e.g., h) and uri reports the URI to which the prefix is mapped (http://www.w3.org/1999/xhtml, for example).

Each method except for setDocumentLocator() is declared to throw SAXException, which an overriding callback method might choose to throw when it detects a problem.

DTDHandler declares the following DTD-oriented informational callback methods:

- void notationDecl(String name, String publicId, String systemId) reports a notation declaration, where name provides this declaration's name attribute value, publicId provides this declaration's public attribute value (the null reference when this value is not available), and systemId provides this declaration's system attribute value.

- void unparsedEntityDecl(String name, String publicId, String systemId, String notationName) reports an external unparsed entity declaration, where name provides the value of this declaration's name attribute, publicId provides the value of the public attribute (the null reference when this value is not available), systemId provides the value of the system attribute, and notationName provides the NDATA name.

Each method is declared to throw SAXException, which an overriding callback method might choose to throw when it detects a problem.

EntityResolver declares the following callback method:

- InputSource resolveEntity(String publicId, String systemId) is called to let the application resolve an external entity (such as an external DTD subset) by returning a custom InputSource instance that's based on a different URI. This method is declared to throw SAXException when it detects a SAX-oriented problem, and is also declared to throw IOException when it encounters an I/O error, possibly in response to creating an InputStream instance or a java.io.Reader instance for the InputSource being created.

ErrorHandler declares the following error-oriented informational callback methods:

- void error(SAXParseException exception) reports that a recoverable parser error (typically the document is not valid) has occurred; the details are specified via the argument passed to exception. This method is typically overridden to report the error via a command window (see Chapter 1) or to log it to a file or a database.

- void fatalError(SAXParseException exception) reports that an unrecoverable parser error (the document is not well formed) has occurred; the details are specified via the argument passed to exception. This method is typically overridden so that the application can log the error before it stops processing the document (because the document is no longer reliable).

- void warning(SAXParseException e) reports that a nonerror (e.g., an element name begins with the reserved xml character sequence) has occurred; the details are specified via the argument passed to exception. This method is typically overridden to report the warning via a console or to log it to a file or a database.

Each method is declared to throw SAXException, which an overriding callback method might choose to throw when it detects a problem.

LexicalHandler declares the following additional content-oriented informational callback methods:

- void comment(char[] ch, int start, int length) reports a comment via the ch array. The arguments that are passed to start and length identify that portion of the array that's relevant to this method call.

- void endCDATA() reports the end of a CDATA section.

- void endDTD() reports the end of a DTD.

- void endEntity(String name) reports the start of the entity identified by name.

- void startCDATA() reports the start of a CDATA section.

- void startDTD(String name, String publicId, String systemId) reports the start of the DTD identified by name. publicId specifies the declared public identifier for the external DTD subset, or is the null reference when none was declared. Similarly, systemId specifies the declared system identifier for the external DTD subset, or is the null reference when none was declared.

- void startEntity(String name) reports the start of the entity identified by name.

Each method is declared to throw SAXException, which an overriding callback method might choose to throw when it detects a problem.

Because it can be tedious to implement all the methods in each interface, the SAX API conveniently provides the org.xml.sax.helpers.DefaultHandler adapter class to relieve you of this tedium. DefaultHandler implements ContentHandler, DTDHandler, EntityResolver, and ErrorHandler. SAX also provides org.xml.sax.ext.DefaultHandler2, which subclasses DefaultHandler, and which also implements LexicalHandler.

Demonstrating the SAX API

I've created a SAXDemo application to demonstrate the SAX API. The application consists of a SAXDemo entry-point class and a Handler subclass of DefaultHandler2. Listing 10-10 presents the source code to SAXDemo.

Listing 10-10. SAXDemo

```
import java.io.FileReader;
import java.io.IOException;

import org.xml.sax.InputSource;
import org.xml.sax.SAXException;
import org.xml.sax.XMLReader;

import org.xml.sax.helpers.XMLReaderFactory;

class SAXDemo
{
    public static void main(String[] args)
    {
        if (args.length < 1 || args.length > 2)
        {
            System.err.println("usage: java SAXDemo xmlfile [v]");
            return;
        }
        try
        {
            XMLReader xmlr = XMLReaderFactory.createXMLReader();
            if (args.length == 2 && args[1].equals("v"))
                xmlr.setFeature("http://xml.org/sax/features/validation", true);
            xmlr.setFeature("http://xml.org/sax/features/namespace-prefixes",
```

```
                                true);
            Handler handler = new Handler();
            xmlr.setContentHandler(handler);
            xmlr.setDTDHandler(handler);
            xmlr.setEntityResolver(handler);
            xmlr.setErrorHandler(handler);
            xmlr.setProperty("http://xml.org/sax/properties/lexical-handler", handler);
            xmlr.parse(new InputSource(new FileReader(args[0])));
        }
        catch (IOException ioe)
        {
            System.err.println("IOE: "+ioe);
        }
        catch (SAXException saxe)
        {
            System.err.println("SAXE: "+saxe);
        }
    }
}
```

SAXDemo is to be run from the command line. After verifying that one or two command-line arguments (the name of an XML document optionally followed by lowercase letter v, which tells SAXDemo to create a validating parser) have been specified, main() creates an XMLReader instance; conditionally enables the validation feature and enables the namespace-prefixes feature; instantiates the companion Handler class; installs this Handler instance as the parser's content handler, DTD handler, entity resolver, and error handler; installs this Handler instance as the value of the lexical-handler property; creates an input source to read the document from a file; and parses the document.

The Handler class's source code is presented in Listing 10-11.

Listing 10-11. Handler

```
import org.xml.sax.Attributes;
import org.xml.sax.InputSource;
import org.xml.sax.Locator;
import org.xml.sax.SAXParseException;

import org.xml.sax.ext.DefaultHandler2;

class Handler extends DefaultHandler2
{
    private Locator locator;
    @Override
    public void characters(char[] ch, int start, int length)
    {
        System.out.print("characters() [");
        for (int i = start; i < start+length; i++)
            System.out.print(ch[i]);
        System.out.println("]");
    }
    @Override
    public void comment(char[] ch, int start, int length)
```

```java
{
    System.out.print("characters() [");
    for (int i = start; i < start+length; i++)
        System.out.print(ch[i]);
    System.out.println("]");
}
@Override
public void endCDATA()
{
    System.out.println("endCDATA()");
}
@Override
public void endDocument()
{
    System.out.println("endDocument()");
}
@Override
public void endDTD()
{
    System.out.println("endDTD()");
}
@Override
public void endElement(String uri, String localName, String qName)
{
    System.out.print("endElement() ");
    System.out.print("uri=["+uri+"], ");
    System.out.print("localName=["+localName+"], ");
    System.out.println("qName=["+qName+"]");
}
@Override
public void endEntity(String name)
{
    System.out.print("endEntity() ");
    System.out.println("name=["+name+"]");
}
@Override
public void endPrefixMapping(String prefix)
{
    System.out.print("endPrefixMapping() ");
    System.out.println("prefix=["+prefix+"]");
}
@Override
public void error(SAXParseException saxpe)
{
    System.out.println("error() "+saxpe);
}
@Override
public void fatalError(SAXParseException saxpe)
{
    System.out.println("fatalError() "+saxpe);
}
@Override
```

```java
public void ignorableWhitespace(char[] ch, int start, int length)
{
    System.out.print("ignorableWhitespace() [");
    for (int i = start; i < start+length; i++)
        System.out.print(ch[i]);
    System.out.println("]");
}
@Override
public void notationDecl(String name, String publicId, String systemId)
{
    System.out.print("notationDecl() ");
    System.out.print("name=["+name+"]");
    System.out.print("publicId=["+publicId+"]");
    System.out.println("systemId=["+systemId+"]");
}
@Override
public void processingInstruction(String target, String data)
{
    System.out.print("processingInstruction() [");
    System.out.println("target=["+target+"]");
    System.out.println("data=["+data+"]");
}
@Override
public InputSource resolveEntity(String publicId, String systemId)
{
    System.out.print("resolveEntity() ");
    System.out.print("publicId=["+publicId+"]");
    System.out.println("systemId=["+systemId+"]");
    // Do not perform a remapping.
    InputSource is = new InputSource();
    is.setPublicId(publicId);
    is.setSystemId(systemId);
    return is;
}
@Override
public void setDocumentLocator(Locator locator)
{
    System.out.print("setDocumentLocator() ");
    System.out.println("locator=["+locator+"]");
    this.locator = locator;
}
@Override
public void skippedEntity(String name)
{
    System.out.print("skippedEntity() ");
    System.out.println("name=["+name+"]");
}
@Override
public void startCDATA()
{
    System.out.println("startCDATA()");
}
```

```java
@Override
public void startDocument()
{
   System.out.println("startDocument()");
}
@Override
public void startDTD(String name, String publicId, String systemId)
{
   System.out.print("startDTD() ");
   System.out.print("name=["+name+"]");
   System.out.print("publicId=["+publicId+"]");
   System.out.println("systemId=["+systemId+"]");
}
@Override
public void startElement(String uri, String localName, String qName,
                         Attributes attributes)
{
   System.out.print("startElement() ");
   System.out.print("uri=["+uri+"], ");
   System.out.print("localName=["+localName+"], ");
   System.out.println("qName=["+qName+"]");
   for (int i = 0; i < attributes.getLength(); i++)
      System.out.println("  Attribute: "+attributes.getLocalName(i)+", "+
                         attributes.getValue(i));
   System.out.println("Column number=["+locator.getColumnNumber()+"]");
   System.out.println("Line number=["+locator.getLineNumber()+"]");
}
@Override
public void startEntity(String name)
{
   System.out.print("startEntity() ");
   System.out.println("name=["+name+"]");
}
@Override
public void startPrefixMapping(String prefix, String uri)
{
   System.out.print("startPrefixMapping() ");
   System.out.print("prefix=["+prefix+"]");
   System.out.println("uri=["+uri+"]");
}
@Override
public void unparsedEntityDecl(String name, String publicId,
                               String systemId, String notationName)
{
   System.out.print("unparsedEntityDecl() ");
   System.out.print("name=["+name+"]");
   System.out.print("publicId=["+publicId+"]");
   System.out.print("systemId=["+systemId+"]");
   System.out.println("notationName=["+notationName+"]");
}
@Override
public void warning(SAXParseException saxpe)
```

```
    {
        System.out.println("warning() "+saxpe);
    }
}
```

The Handler subclass is pretty straightforward; it outputs every possible piece of information about an XML document, subject to feature and property settings. You will find this class handy for exploring the order in which events occur along with various features and properties.

After compiling Handler's source code, execute java SAXDemo svg-examples.xml (see Listing 10-4). SAXDemo responds by presenting the following output:

```
setDocumentLocator()
locator=[com.sun.org.apache.xerces.internal.parsers.  ➥AbstractSAXParser$LocatorProxy@1f98d58
]
startDocument()
startElement() uri=[], localName=[svg-examples], qName=[svg-examples]
Column number=[15]
Line number=[2]
characters() [
]
startElement() uri=[], localName=[example], qName=[example]
Column number=[13]
Line number=[3]
characters() [
        The following Scalable Vector Graphics document describes a blue-filled and ]
characters() [
        black-stroked rectangle.
        ]
startCDATA()
characters() [<svg width="100%" height="100%" version="1.1"
            xmlns="http://www.w3.org/2000/svg">
        <rect width="300" height="100"
                style="fill:rgb(0,0,255);stroke-width:1; stroke:rgb(0,0,0)"/>
    </svg>]
endCDATA()
characters() [
]
endElement() uri=[], localName=[example], qName=[example]
characters() [
]
endElement() uri=[], localName=[svg-examples], qName=[svg-examples]
endDocument()
```

The first output line (the @1f98d58 value will probably be different) proves that setDocumentLocator() is called first. It also identifies the Locator instance whose getColumnNumber() and getLineNumber() methods are called to output the parser location when startElement() is called—these methods return column and line numbers starting at 1.

Perhaps you're curious about the three instances of the following output:

```
characters() [
]
```

The instance of this output that follows the endCDATA() output is reporting a carriage return/line feed combination that wasn't included in the preceding character() method call, which was passed the contents of the CDATA section minus these line terminator characters. In contrast, the instances of this output that follow the startElement() call for svg-examples and follow the endElement() call for example are somewhat curious. There's no content between <svg-examples> and <example>, and between </example> and </svg-examples>, or is there?

You can satisfy this curiosity by modifying svg-examples.xml to include an internal DTD. Place the following DTD (which indicates that an svg-element contains one or more example elements, and that an example element contains parsed character data) between the XML declaration and the <svg-examples> start tag:

```
<!DOCTYPE svg-examples [
<!ELEMENT svg-examples (example+)>
<!ELEMENT example (#PCDATA)>
]>
```

Continuing, execute java SAXDemo svg-examples.html. This time, you should see the following output:

```
setDocumentLocator()
locator=[com.sun.org.apache.xerces.internal.parsers.   ↩AbstractSAXParser$LocatorProxy@1f98d58
]
startDocument()
startDTD() name=[svg-examples]publicId=[null]systemId=[null]
endDTD()
startElement() uri=[], localName=[svg-examples], qName=[svg-examples]
Column number=[15]
Line number=[6]
ignorableWhitespace() [
    ]
startElement() uri=[], localName=[example], qName=[example]
Column number=[13]
Line number=[7]
characters() [
    The following Scalable Vector Graphics document describes a blue-filled and
    black-stroked rectangle.]
characters() [
    ]
startCDATA()
characters() [<svg width="100%" height="100%" version="1.1"
        xmlns="http://www.w3.org/2000/svg">
      <rect width="300" height="100"
            style="fill:rgb(0,0,255);stroke-width:1; stroke:rgb(0,0,0)"/>
    </svg>]
endCDATA()
characters() [
    ]
endElement() uri=[], localName=[example], qName=[example]
ignorableWhitespace() [
]
endElement() uri=[], localName=[svg-examples], qName=[svg-examples]
endDocument()
```

This output reveals that the ignorableWhitespace() method was called after startElement() for svg-examples and after endElement() for example. The former two calls to characters() that produced the strange output were reporting ignorable whitespace.

Recall that I previously defined *ignorable whitespace* as whitespace located between tags where the DTD doesn't allow mixed content. For example, the DTD indicates that svg-examples shall contain only example elements, not example elements and parsed character data. However, the line terminator following the <svg-examples> tag and the leading whitespace before <example> are parsed character data. The parser now reports these characters by calling ignorableWhitespace().

This time, there are only two occurrences of the following output:

```
characters() [

    ]
```

The first occurrence reports the line terminator separately from the example element's text (before the CDATA section); it did not do so previously, which proves that characters() is called with either all or part of an element's content. Once again, the second occurrence reports the line terminator that follows the CDATA section.

Suppose you want to validate svg-examples.xml without the previously presented internal DTD. If you attempt to do so (by executing java SAXDemo svg-examples.xml v), you will discover among its output a couple of lines that are similar to those shown here:

```
error() org.xml.sax.SAXParseException; lineNumber: 2; columnNumber: 14; Document is↵ invalid:
no grammar found.
error() org.xml.sax.SAXParseException; lineNumber: 2; columnNumber: 14; Document root↵
element "svg-examples", must match DOCTYPE root "null".
```

These lines reveal that a DTD grammar has not been found. Furthermore, the parser reports a mismatch between svg-examples (it considers the first encountered element to be the root element) and null (it considers null to be the name of the root element in the absence of a DTD). Neither violation is considered to be fatal, which is why error() is called instead of fatalError().

Add the internal DTD to svg-examples.xml, and reexecute java SAXDemo svg-examples.xml v. This time, you should see no error()-prefixed lines in the output.

Note SAX 2 validation defaults to validating against a DTD. To validate against an XML Schema-based schema instead, add the schemaLanguage property with the http://www.w3.org/2001/XMLSchema value to the XMLReader instance. Accomplish this task for SAXDemo by specifying

```
xmlr.setProperty("http://java.sun.com/xml/jaxp/properties/schemaLanguage",
"http://www.w3.org/2001/XMLSchema"); before xmlr.parse(new InputSource(new
FileReader(args[0])));.
```

Creating a Custom Entity Resolver

While exploring XML, I introduced you to the concept of *entities*, which are aliased data. I then discussed general entities and parameter entities in terms of their internal and external variants.

Unlike internal entities, whose values are specified in a DTD, the values of external entities are specified outside of a DTD, and are identified via public and/or system identifiers. The system identifier is a URI whereas the public identifier is a formal public identifier.

An XML parser reads an external entity (including the external DTD subset) via an InputSource instance that's connected to the appropriate system identifier. In many cases, you pass a system identifier or InputSource instance to the parser, and let it discover where to find other entities that are referenced from the current document entity.

However, for performance or other reasons, you might want the parser to read the external entity's value from a different system identifier, such as a local DTD copy's system identifier. You can accomplish this task by creating an *entity resolver* that uses the public identifier to choose a different system identifier. Upon encountering an external entity, the parser calls the custom entity resolver to obtain this identifier.

Consider Listing 10-12's formal specification of Listing 10-1's grilled cheese sandwich recipe.

Listing 10-12. XML-based recipe for a grilled cheese sandwich specified in Recipe Markup Language

```xml
<?xml version="1.0" encoding="UTF-8"?>
<!DOCTYPE recipeml PUBLIC "-//FormatData//DTD RecipeML 0.5//EN"
                          "http://www.formatdata.com/recipeml/recipeml.dtd">
<recipeml version="0.5">
   <recipe>
      <head>
         <title>Grilled Cheese Sandwich</title>
      </head>
      <ingredients>
         <ing>
            <amt><qty>2</qty><unit>slice</unit></amt>
            <item>bread</item>
         </ing>
         <ing>
            <amt><qty>1</qty><unit>slice</unit></amt>
            <item>cheese</item>
         </ing>
         <ing>
            <amt><qty>2</qty><unit>pat</unit></amt>
            <item>margarine</item>
         </ing>
      </ingredients>
      <directions>
         <step>Place frying pan on element and select medium heat.</step>
         <step>For each bread slice, smear one pat of margarine on one side of
               bread slice.</step>
         <step>Place cheese slice between bread slices with margarine-smeared
               sides away from the cheese.</step>
         <step>Place sandwich in frying pan with one margarine-smeared size in
               contact with pan.</step>
         <step>Fry for a couple of minutes and flip.</step>
         <step>Fry other side for a minute and serve.</step>
      </directions>
   </recipe>
</recipeml>
```

Listing 10-12 specifies the grilled cheese sandwich recipe in *Recipe Markup Language (RecipeML)*, an XML-based language for marking up recipes. (A company named *FormatData* [see http://www.formatdata.com/] released this format in 2000.)

The document type declaration reports -//FormatData//DTD RecipeML 0.5//EN as the formal public identifier and http://www.formatdata.com/recipeml/recipeml.dtd as the system identifier. Instead of keeping the default mapping, let's map this formal public identifier to recipeml.dtd, a system identifier for a local copy of this DTD file.

To create a custom entity resolver to perform this mapping, we declare a class that implements the EntityResolver interface in terms of its InputSource resolveEntity(String publicId, String systemId) method. We then use the passed publicId value as a key into a map that points to the desired systemId value, and then use this value to create and return a custom InputSource. Listing 10-13 presents the resulting class.

Listing 10-13. LocalRecipeML

```java
import java.util.HashMap;
import java.util.Map;

import org.xml.sax.EntityResolver;
import org.xml.sax.InputSource;
import org.xml.sax.SAXException;

class LocalRecipeML implements EntityResolver
{
    private Map<String, String> mappings = new HashMap<>();
    LocalRecipeML()
    {
        mappings.put("-//FormatData//DTD RecipeML 0.5//EN", "recipeml.dtd");
    }
    @Override
    public InputSource resolveEntity(String publicId, String systemId)
    {
        if (mappings.containsKey(publicId))
        {
            System.out.println("obtaining cached recipeml.dtd");
            systemId = mappings.get(publicId);
            InputSource localSource = new InputSource(systemId);
            return localSource;
        }
        return null;
    }
}
```

Listing 10-13 declares LocalRecipeML. This class's constructor stores the formal public identifier for the RecipeML DTD and the system identifier for a local copy of this DTD's document in a map—notice the use of Java 7's diamond operator (<>) to simplify the hashmap instantiation expression.

Note Although it's unnecessary to use a map in this example (an `if (publicId.equals("-//FormatData//DTD RecipeML 0.5//EN"))` return new `InputSource("recipeml.dtd")` else return `null`; statement would suffice), I've chosen to use a map in case I want to expand the number of mappings in the future. In another scenario, you would probably find a map to be very convenient. For example, it's easier to use a map than to use a series of if statements in a custom entity resolver that maps XHTML's strict, transitional, and frameset formal public identifiers, and also maps its various entity sets to local copies of these document files.

The overriding `resolveEntity()` method uses `publicId`'s argument to locate the corresponding system identifier in the map—the `systemId` parameter value is ignored because it never refers to the local copy of `recipeml.dtd`. When the mapping is found, an `InputSource` object is created and returned. If the mapping could not be found, the null reference would be returned.

To install this custom entity resolver in SAXDemo, specify `xmlr.setEntityResolver(new LocalRecipeML())`; prior to the `parse()` method call. After recompiling the source code, execute java SAXDemo `gcs.xml`, where `gcs.xml` stores Listing 10-12's text. In the resulting output, you should observe the message "`obtaining cached recipeml.dtd`" prior to the call to `startEntity()`.

Tip The SAX API includes an `org.xml.sax.ext.EntityResolver2` interface that provides improved support for resolving entities. If you prefer to implement `EntityResolver2` instead of `EntityResolver`, you must replace the `setEntityResolver()` call to install the entity resolver with a `setFeature()` call whose feature name is `use-entity-resolver2` (don't forget the `http://xml.org/sax/features/` prefix).

Parsing and Creating XML Documents with DOM

Document Object Model (DOM) is an API for parsing an XML document into an in-memory tree of nodes, and for creating an XML document from a tree of nodes. After a DOM parser has created a document tree, an application uses the DOM API to navigate over and extract infoset items from the tree's nodes.

Note DOM originated as an object model for the Netscape Navigator 3 and Microsoft Internet Explorer 3 web browsers. Collectively, these implementations are known as DOM Level 0. Because each vendor's DOM implementation was only slightly compatible with the other, the W3C subsequently took charge of DOM's development to promote standardization, and has so far released DOM Levels 1, 2, and 3. Java 7 supports all three DOM levels through its DOM API.

DOM has two big advantages over SAX. First, DOM permits random access to a document's infoset items whereas SAX only permits serial access. Second, DOM lets you also create XML documents, whereas you can only parse documents with SAX. However, SAX is advantageous over DOM in that it can parse documents of arbitrary size, whereas the size of documents parsed or created by DOM is limited by the amount of available memory for storing the document's node-based tree structure.

This section first introduces you to DOM's tree structure. It then takes you on a tour of the DOM API; you learn how to use this API to parse and create XML documents.

A Tree of Nodes

DOM views an XML document as a tree that's composed of several kinds of nodes. This tree has a single root node, and all nodes except for the root have a parent node. Also, each node has a list of child nodes. If this list is empty, the child node is known as a *leaf node*.

Note DOM permits nodes to exist that are not part of the tree structure. For example, an element node's attribute nodes are not regarded as child nodes of the element node. Also, nodes can be created but not inserted into the tree; they can also be removed from the tree.

Each node has a *node name*, which is the complete name for nodes that have names (such as an element's or an attribute's prefixed name), and *#node-type* for unnamed nodes, where *node-type* is one of cdata-section, comment, document, document-fragment, or text. Nodes also have *local names* (names without prefixes), prefixes, and namespace URIs (although these attributes may be null for certain kinds of nodes, such as comments). Finally, nodes have string values, which happen to be the content of text nodes, comment nodes, and similar text-oriented nodes; normalized values of attributes; and null for everything else.

DOM classifies nodes into twelve types, of which seven types can be considered part of a DOM tree. All these types are described here:

- *Attribute node*: one of an element's attributes. It has a name, a local name, a prefix, a namespace URI, and a normalized string value. The value is *normalized* by resolving any entity references and by converting sequences of whitespace to a single whitespace character. An attribute node has children, which are the text and any entity reference nodes that form its value. Attributes nodes are not regarded as children of their associated element nodes.

- *CDATA section node*: the contents of a CDATA section. Its name is #cdata-section and its value is the CDATA section's text.

- *Comment node*: a document comment. Its name is #comment and its value is the comment text. A comment node has a parent, which is the node that contains the comment.

- *Document fragment node*: an alternative root node. Its name is #document-fragment and it contains anything that an element node can contain (such as other element nodes and even comment nodes). A parser never creates this kind of a node. However, an application can create a document fragment node when it extracts part of a DOM tree to be moved somewhere else. Document fragment nodes let you work with subtrees.

- *Document node*: the root of a DOM tree. Its name is #document, it always has a single element node child, and it will also have a document type child node when the document has a document type declaration. Furthermore, it can have additional child nodes describing comments or processing instructions that appear before or after the root element's start tag. There can be only one document node in the tree.

- *Document type node*: a document type declaration. Its name is the name specified by the document type declaration for the root element. Also, it has a (possibly null) public identifier, a required system identifier, an internal DTD subset (which is possibly null), a parent (the document node that contains the document type node), and lists of DTD-declared notations and general entities. Its value is always set to null.

- *Element node*: a document's element. It has a name, a local name, a (possibly null) prefix, and a namespace URI, which is null when the element doesn't belong to any namespace. An element node contains children, including text nodes, and even comment and processing instruction nodes.

- *Entity node*: the parsed and unparsed entities that are declared in a document's DTD. When a parser reads a DTD, it attaches a map of entity nodes (indexed by entity name) to the document type node. An entity node has a name and a system identifier, and can also have a public identifier if one appears in the DTD. Finally, when the parser reads the entity, the entity node is given a list of read-only child nodes that contain the entity's replacement text.

- *Entity reference node*: a reference to a DTD-declared entity. Each entity reference node has a name, and is included in the tree when the parser does not replace entity references with their values. The parser never includes entity reference nodes for character references (such as & or Σ) because they are replaced by their respective characters and included in a text node.

- *Notation node*: a DTD-declared notation. A parser that reads the DTD attaches a map of notation nodes (indexed by notation name) to the document type node. Each notation node has a name, and a public identifier or a system identifier, whichever identifier was used to declare the notation in the DTD. Notation nodes do not have children.

- *Processing instruction node*: a processing instruction that appears in the document. It has a name (the instruction's target), a string value (the instruction's data), and a parent (its containing node).

- *Text node:* document content. Its name is #text and it represents a portion of an element's content when an intervening node (e.g., a comment) must be created. Characters such as < and & that are represented in the document via character references are replaced by the literal characters that they represent. When these nodes are written to a document, these characters must be escaped.

Although these node types store considerable information about an XML document, there are limitations (such as not exposing whitespace outside of the root element). In contrast, most DTD or schema information, such as element types (<!ELEMENT...>) and attribute types (<xs:attribute...>), cannot be accessed through the DOM.

DOM Level 3 addresses some of the DOM's various limitations. For example, although DOM does not provide a node type for the XML declaration, DOM Level 3 makes it possible to access the XML declaration's version, encoding, and standalone attribute values via attributes of the document node.

■ **Note** Nonroot nodes never exist in isolation. For example, it is never the case for an element node to not belong to a document or to a document fragment. Even when such nodes are disconnected from the main tree, they remain aware of the document or document fragment to which they belong.

Exploring the DOM API

Java implements DOM through the javax.xml.parsers package's abstract DocumentBuilder and DocumentBuilderFactory classes, along with the nonabstract FactoryConfigurationError and ParserConfigurationException classes. The org.w3c.dom, org.w3c.dom.bootstrap, org.w3c.dom.events, and org.w3c.dom.ls packages provide various types that augment this implementation.

The first step in working with DOM is to instantiate DocumentBuilderFactory by calling one its newInstance() methods. For example, the following example invokes DocumentBuilderFactory's static DocumentBuilderFactory newInstance() method:

```
DocumentBuilderFactory dbf = DocumentBuilderFactory.newInstance();
```

Behind the scenes, newInstance() follows an ordered lookup procedure to identify the DocumentBuilderFactory implementation class to load. This procedure first examines the javax.xml.parsers.DocumentBuilderFactory system property, and lastly chooses the Java platform's default DocumentBuilderFactory implementation class when no other class is found. If an implementation class is not available (perhaps the class identified by the javax.xml.parsers.DocumentBuilderFactory system property doesn't exist) or cannot be instantiated, newInstance() throws an instance of the FactoryConfigurationError class. Otherwise, it instantiates the class and returns its instance.

After obtaining a DocumentBuilderFactory instance, you can call various configuration methods to configure the factory. For example, you could call DocumentBuilderFactory's void setNamespaceAware(boolean awareness) method with a true argument to tell the factory that any returned parser (known as a *document builder* to DOM) must provide support for XML namespaces. You can also call void setValidating(boolean validating) with true as the argument to validate documents against their DTDs, or call void setSchema(Schema schema) to validate documents against the javax.xml.validation.Schema instance identified by schema.

VALIDATION API

JAXP includes the Validation API to decouple document parsing from validation, which makes it easier for applications to take advantage of specialized validation libraries that support additional schema languages (e.g., Relax NG—see http://en.wikipedia.org/wiki/RELAX_NG), and which makes it easier to specify the location of a schema.

The Validation API is associated with the javax.xml.validation package, which consists of six classes: Schema, SchemaFactory, SchemaFactoryLoader, TypeInfoProvider, Validator, and ValidatorHandler. Schema is the central class that represents an immutable in-memory representation of a grammar.

The DOM API supports the Validation API via DocumentBuilderFactory's void setSchema(Schema schema) and Schema getSchema() methods. Similarly, SAX 1.0 supports Validation via SAXParserFactory's void setSchema(Schema schema) and Schema getSchema() methods. SAX 2.0 and StAX don't support the Validation API.

The following example provides a demonstration of the Validation API in a DOM context:

```
// Parse an XML document into a DOM tree.
DocumentBuilder parser =

    DocumentBuilderFactory.newInstance().newDocumentBuilder();

Document document = parser.parse(new File("instance.xml"));
// Create a SchemaFactory capable of understanding W3C XML Schema (WXS).
SchemaFactory factory =
    SchemaFactory.newInstance(XMLConstants.W3C_XML_SCHEMA_NS_URI);

// Load a WXS schema, represented by a Schema instance.
Source schemaFile = new StreamSource(new File("mySchema.xsd"));
Schema schema = factory.newSchema(schemaFile);
// Create a Validator instance, which is used to validate an XML document.
Validator validator = schema.newValidator();
// Validate the DOM tree.
try
{
    validator.validate(new DOMSource(document));
}
catch (SAXException saxe)
{
    // XML document is invalid!
}
```

This example refers to XSLT types such as Source. I explore XSLT later in this chapter.

After the factory has been configured, call its DocumentBuilder newDocumentBuilder() method to return a document builder that supports the configuration, as demonstrated here:

```
DocumentBuilder db = dbf.newDocumentBuilder();
```

If a document builder cannot be returned (perhaps the factory cannot create a document builder that supports XML namespaces), this method throws a ParserConfigurationException instance.

Assuming that you've successfully obtained a document builder, what happens next depends on whether you want to parse or create an XML document.

Parsing XML Documents

DocumentBuilder provides several overloaded parse() methods for parsing an XML document into a node tree. These methods differ in how they obtain the document. For example, Document parse(String uri) parses the document that's identified by its string-based URI argument.

Note Each parse() method throws java.lang.IllegalArgumentException when null is passed as the method's first argument, IOException when an input/output problem occurs, and SAXException when the document cannot be parsed. This last exception type implies that DocumentBuilder's parse() methods rely on SAX to take care of the actual parsing work. Because they are more involved in building the node tree, DOM parsers are commonly referred to as *document builders*.

The returned org.w3c.dom.Document object provides access to the parsed document through methods such as DocumentType getDoctype(), which makes the document type declaration available through the org.w3c.dom.DocumentType interface. Conceptually, Document is the root of the document's node tree.

Note Apart from DocumentBuilder, DocumentBuilderFactory, and a few other classes, DOM is based on interfaces, of which Document and DocumentType are examples. Behind the scenes, DOM methods (such as the parse() methods) return objects whose classes implement these interfaces.

Document and all other org.w3c.dom interfaces that describe different kinds of nodes are subinterfaces of the org.w3.dom.Node interface. As such, they inherit Node's constants and methods.

Node declares twelve constants that represent the various kinds of nodes; ATTRIBUTE_NODE and ELEMENT_NODE are examples. When you want to identify the kind of node represented by a given Node object, call Node's short getNodeType() method and compare the returned value to one of these constants.

■ **Note** The rationale for using getNodeType() and these constants, instead of using instanceof and a classname, is that DOM (the object model, not the Java DOM API) was designed to be language independent, and languages such as AppleScript don't have the equivalent of instanceof.

Node declares several methods for getting and setting common node properties. These methods include String getNodeName(), String getLocalName(), String getNamespaceURI(), String getPrefix(), void setPrefix(String prefix), String getNodeValue(), and void setNodeValue(String nodeValue), which let you get and (for some properties) set a node's name (such as #text), local name, namespace URI, prefix, and normalized string value properties.

■ **Note** Various Node methods (e.g., setPrefix() and getNodeValue()) throw an instance of the org.w3c.dom.DOMException class when something goes wrong. For example, setPrefix() throws this exception when the prefix argument contains an illegal character, the node is read-only, or the argument is malformed. Similarly, getNodeValue() throws DOMException when getNodeValue() would return more characters than can fit into a DOMString (a W3C type) variable on the implementation platform. DOMException declares a series of constants (such as DOMSTRING_SIZE_ERR) that classify the reason for the exception.

Node declares several methods for navigating the node tree. Three of its navigation methods are boolean hasChildNodes() (return true when a node has child nodes), Node getFirstChild() (return the node's first child), and Node getLastChild() (return the node's last child). For nodes with multiple children, you'll find the NodeList getChildNodes() method to be handy. This method returns an org.w3c.dom.NodeList instance whose int getLength() method returns the number of nodes in the list, and whose Node item(int index) method returns the node at the indexth position in the list (or null when index's value is not valid—it's less than 0 or greater than or equal to getLength()'s value).

Node declares four methods for modifying the tree by inserting, removing, replacing, and appending child nodes. The Node insertBefore(Node newChild, Node refChild) method inserts newChild before the existing node specified by refChild and returns newChild, Node removeChild(Node oldChild) removes the child node identified by oldChild from the tree and returns oldChild, Node replaceChild(Node newChild, Node oldChild) replaces oldChild with newChild and returns oldChild, and Node appendChild(Node newChild) adds newChild to the end of the current node's child nodes and returns newChild.

Finally, Node declares several utility methods, including Node cloneNode(boolean deep) (create and return a duplicate of the current node, recursively cloning its subtree when true is passed to deep), and void normalize() (descend the tree from the given node and merge all adjacent text nodes, deleting those text nodes that are empty).

■ **Tip** To obtain an element node's attributes, first call Node's NamedNodeMap getAttributes() method. This method returns an org.w3c.dom.NamedNodeMap implementation when the node represents an element; otherwise, it returns null. In addition to declaring methods for accessing these nodes by name (e.g., Node getNamedItem(String name)), NamedNodeMap declares int getLength() and Node item(int index) methods for returning all attribute nodes by index. You would then obtain the Node's name by calling a method such as getNodeName().

As well as inheriting Node's constants and methods, Document declares its own methods. For example, you can call Document's String getXmlEncoding(), boolean getXmlStandalone(), and String getXmlVersion() methods to return the XML declaration's encoding, standalone, and version attribute values, respectively.

Document declares three methods for locating one or more elements: Element getElementById(String elementId), NodeList getElementsByTagName(String tagname), and NodeList getElementsByTagNameNS(String namespaceURI,String localName). The first method returns the element that has an id attribute (as in <img id=...>) matching the value specified by elementId, the second method returns a nodelist of a document's elements (in document order) matching the specified tagName, and the third method is essentially the same as the second method except that only elements matching the given localName and namespaceURI are returned in the nodelist. Pass "*" to namespaceURI to match all namespaces; pass "*" to localName to match all local names.

The returned element node and each element node in the list implement the org.w3c.dom.Element interface. This interface declares methods to return nodelists of descendent elements in the tree, attributes associated with the element, and more. For example, String getAttribute(String name) returns the value of the attribute identified by name, whereas Attr getAttributeNode(String name) returns an attribute node by name. The returned node is an implementation of the org.w3c.dom.Attr interface.

You now have enough information to explore an application for parsing an XML document and outputting the element and attribute information from the resulting DOM tree. Listing 10-14 presents this application's source code.

Listing 10-14. DOMDemo (version 1)

```
import java.io.IOException;

import javax.xml.parsers.DocumentBuilder;
import javax.xml.parsers.DocumentBuilderFactory;
import javax.xml.parsers.FactoryConfigurationError;
import javax.xml.parsers.ParserConfigurationException;

import org.w3c.dom.Attr;
import org.w3c.dom.Document;
import org.w3c.dom.Element;
import org.w3c.dom.NamedNodeMap;
import org.w3c.dom.Node;
import org.w3c.dom.NodeList;

import org.xml.sax.SAXException;
```

```java
class DOMDemo
{
   public static void main(String[] args)
   {
      if (args.length != 1)
      {
         System.err.println("usage: java DOMDemo xmlfile");
         return;
      }
      try
      {
         DocumentBuilderFactory dbf = DocumentBuilderFactory.newInstance();
         dbf.setNamespaceAware(true);
         DocumentBuilder db = dbf.newDocumentBuilder();
         Document doc = db.parse(args[0]);
         System.out.println("Version = "+doc.getXmlVersion());
         System.out.println("Encoding = "+doc.getXmlEncoding());
         System.out.println("Standalone = "+doc.getXmlStandalone());
         System.out.println();
         if (doc.hasChildNodes())
         {
            NodeList nl = doc.getChildNodes();
            for (int i = 0; i < nl.getLength(); i++)
            {
               Node node = nl.item(i);
               if (node.getNodeType() == Node.ELEMENT_NODE)
                  dump((Element) node);
            }
         }
      }
      catch (IOException ioe)
      {
         System.err.println("IOE: "+ioe);
      }
      catch (SAXException saxe)
      {
         System.err.println("SAXE: "+saxe);
      }
      catch (FactoryConfigurationError fce)
      {
         System.err.println("FCE: "+fce);
      }
      catch (ParserConfigurationException pce)
      {
         System.err.println("PCE: "+pce);
      }
   }
   static void dump(Element e)
   {
      System.out.println("Element: "+e.getNodeName()+", "+e.getLocalName()+
                         ", "+e.getPrefix()+", "+e.getNamespaceURI());
```

```
         NamedNodeMap nnm = e.getAttributes();
         if (nnm != null)
            for (int i = 0; i < nnm.getLength(); i++)
            {
               Node node = nnm.item(i);
               Attr attr = e.getAttributeNode(node.getNodeName());
               System.out.printf("  Attribute %s = %s%n", attr.getName(),
                                     attr.getValue());
            }
         NodeList nl = e.getChildNodes();
         for (int i = 0; i < nl.getLength(); i++)
         {
            Node node = nl.item(i);
            if (node instanceof Element)
               dump((Element) node);
         }
      }
   }
}
```

DOMDemo is designed to run at the command line. After verifying that one command-line argument (the name of an XML document) has been specified, main() creates a document builder factory, informs the factory that it wants a namespace-aware document builder, and has the factory return this document builder.

Continuing, main() parses the document into a node tree; outputs the XML declaration's version number, encoding, and standalone attribute values; and recursively dumps all element nodes (starting with the root node) and their attribute values.

Note Regarding the multiple catch blocks, consider it an exercise to replace them with multicatch.

Notice the use of getNodeType() in one part of this listing and instanceof in another part. The getNodeType() method call isn't necessary (it is only present for demonstration) because instanceof can be used instead. However, the cast from Node type to Element type in the dump() method calls is necessary.

Assuming that you've compiled the source code, execute java DOMDemo article.xml to dump Listing 10-3's article XML content. You should observe the following output:

```
Version = 1.0
Encoding = null
Standalone = false

Element: article, article, null, null
  Attribute lang = en
  Attribute title = The Rebirth of JavaFX
Element: abstract, abstract, null, null
Element: code-inline, code-inline, null, null
Element: body, body, null, null
```

Each Element-prefixed line outputs the node name, followed by the local name, followed by the namespace prefix, followed by the namespace URI. The node and local names are identical because namespaces are not being used. For the same reason, the namespace prefix and namespace URI are null.

Continuing, execute java DOMDemo recipe.xml, where recipe.xml contains the content shown in Listing 10-5. This time, you observe the following output, which includes namespace information:

```
Version = 1.0
Encoding = null
Standalone = false

Element: h:html, html, h, http://www.w3.org/1999/xhtml
  Attribute xmlns:h = http://www.w3.org/1999/xhtml
  Attribute xmlns:r = http://www.tutortutor.ca/
Element: h:head, head, h, http://www.w3.org/1999/xhtml
Element: h:title, title, h, http://www.w3.org/1999/xhtml
Element: h:body, body, h, http://www.w3.org/1999/xhtml
Element: r:recipe, recipe, r, http://www.tutortutor.ca/
Element: r:title, title, r, http://www.tutortutor.ca/
Element: r:ingredients, ingredients, r, http://www.tutortutor.ca/
Element: h:ul, ul, h, http://www.w3.org/1999/xhtml
Element: h:li, li, h, http://www.w3.org/1999/xhtml
Element: r:ingredient, ingredient, r, http://www.tutortutor.ca/
  Attribute qty = 2
Element: h:li, li, h, http://www.w3.org/1999/xhtml
Element: r:ingredient, ingredient, r, http://www.tutortutor.ca/
Element: h:li, li, h, http://www.w3.org/1999/xhtml
Element: r:ingredient, ingredient, r, http://www.tutortutor.ca/
  Attribute qty = 2
Element: h:p, p, h, http://www.w3.org/1999/xhtml
Element: r:instructions, instructions, r, http://www.tutortutor.ca/
```

Creating XML Documents

DocumentBuilder declares the abstract Document newDocument() method for creating a document tree. The returned Document object declares various "create" and other methods for creating this tree. For example, Element createElement(String tagName) creates an element named by tagName, returning a new Element object with the specified name, but with its local name, prefix, and namespace URI set to null.

Listing 10-15 presents another version of the DOMDemo application that briefly demonstrates the creation of a document tree.

Listing 10-15. DOMDemo (version 2)

```
import javax.xml.parsers.DocumentBuilder;
import javax.xml.parsers.DocumentBuilderFactory;
import javax.xml.parsers.FactoryConfigurationError;
import javax.xml.parsers.ParserConfigurationException;

import org.w3c.dom.Document;
import org.w3c.dom.Element;
```

```java
import org.w3c.dom.Node;
import org.w3c.dom.NodeList;
import org.w3c.dom.Text;

class DOMDemo
{
   public static void main(String[] args)
   {
      try
      {
         DocumentBuilderFactory dbf = DocumentBuilderFactory.newInstance();
         DocumentBuilder db = dbf.newDocumentBuilder();
         Document doc = db.newDocument();
         // Create the root element.
         Element root = doc.createElement("movie");
         doc.appendChild(root);
         // Create name child element and add it to the root.
         Element name = doc.createElement("name");
         root.appendChild(name);
         // Add a text element to the name element.
         Text text = doc.createTextNode("Le Fabuleux Destin d'Amélie Poulain");
         name.appendChild(text);
         // Create language child element and add it to the root.
         Element language = doc.createElement("language");
         root.appendChild(language);
         // Add a text element to the language element.
         text = doc.createTextNode("français");
         language.appendChild(text);
         System.out.println("Version = "+doc.getXmlVersion());
         System.out.println("Encoding = "+doc.getXmlEncoding());
         System.out.println("Standalone = "+doc.getXmlStandalone());
         System.out.println();
         NodeList nl = doc.getChildNodes();
         for (int i = 0; i < nl.getLength(); i++)
         {
            Node node = nl.item(i);
            if (node.getNodeType() == Node.ELEMENT_NODE)
               dump((Element) node);
         }
      }
      catch (FactoryConfigurationError fce)
      {
         System.err.println("FCE: "+fce);
      }
      catch (ParserConfigurationException pce)
      {
         System.err.println("PCE: "+pce);
      }
   }
   static void dump(Element e)
   {
      System.out.println("Element: "+e.getNodeName()+", "+e.getLocalName()+
```

```
                            ", "+e.getPrefix()+", "+e.getNamespaceURI());
      NodeList nl = e.getChildNodes();
      for (int i = 0; i < nl.getLength(); i++)
      {
         Node node = nl.item(i);
         if (node instanceof Element)
            dump((Element) node);
         else
         if (node instanceof Text)
            System.out.println("Text: "+((Text) node).getWholeText());
      }
   }
}
```

DOMDemo creates Listing 10-2's movie document. It uses Document's createElement() method to create the root movie element and movie's name and language child elements. It also uses Document's Text createTextNode(String data) method to create text nodes that are attached to the name and language nodes. Notice the calls to Node's appendChild() method, to append child nodes (e.g., name) to parent nodes (such as movie).

After creating this tree, DOMDemo outputs the tree's element nodes and other information. This output appears as follows:

```
Version = 1.0
Encoding = null
Standalone = false

Element: movie, null, null, null
Element: name, null, null, null
Text: Le Fabuleux Destin d'Amélie Poulain
Element: language, null, null, null
Text: français
```

The output is pretty much as expected, but there is one problem: the XML declaration's encoding attribute has not been set to ISO-8859-1. It turns out that you cannot accomplish this task via the DOM API. Instead, you need to use the XSLT API for this task. While exploring XSLT, you'll learn how to set the encoding attribute, and you'll also learn how to output this tree to an XML document file.

However, there is one more document-parsing-and-document-creation API to explore (and a tour of the XPath API to accomplish) before we turn our attention to XSLT.

Parsing and Creating XML Documents with StAX

Streaming API for XML (StAX) is an API for parsing an XML document sequentially from start to finish. It is also a document creation API. StAX became a core Java API in the Java 6 release (in late 2006).

STAX VERSUS SAX AND DOM

Because Java already supports SAX and DOM for document parsing and DOM for document creation, you might be wondering why another XML API is needed. The following points justify StAX's presence in core Java:

- StAX (like SAX) can be used to parse documents of arbitrary sizes. In contrast, the maximum size of documents parsed by DOM is limited by the available memory, which makes DOM unsuitable for mobile devices with limited amounts of memory.

- StAX (like DOM) can be used to create documents of arbitrary sizes. In contrast, the maximum size of a document created by DOM is constrained by available memory. SAX cannot be used to create documents.

- StAX (like SAX) makes infoset items available to applications almost immediately. In contrast, these items are not made available by DOM until after it finishes building the tree of nodes.

- StAX (like DOM) adopts the *pull model*, in which the application tells the parser when it is ready to receive the next infoset item. This model is based on the *iterator design pattern* (see `http://sourcemaking.com/design_patterns/iterator`), which results in an application that is easier to write and debug. In contrast, SAX adopts the *push model*, in which the parser passes infoset items via events to the application, whether or not the application is ready to receive them. This model is based on the *observer design pattern* (see `http://sourcemaking.com/design_patterns/observer`), which results in an application that is often harder to write and debug.

Summing up, StAX can parse or create documents of arbitrary size, makes infoset items available to applications almost immediately, and uses the pull model to put the application in charge. Neither SAX nor DOM offers all these advantages.

Java implements StAX through types stored in the `javax.xml.stream`, `javax.xml.stream.events`, and `javax.xml.stream.util` packages. This section introduces you to various types from the first two packages while showing you how to use StAX to parse and create XML documents.

STREAM-BASED VERSUS EVENT-BASED READERS AND WRITERS

StAX parsers are known as *document readers*, and StAX document creators are known as *document writers*. StAX classifies document readers and document writers as stream-based or event-based.

A *stream-based reader* extracts the next infoset item from an input stream via a *cursor* (infoset item pointer). Similarly, a stream-based writer writes the next infoset item to an output stream at the cursor position. The cursor can point to only one item at a time, and always moves forward, typically by one infoset item.

Stream-based readers and writers are appropriate when writing code for memory-constrained environments such as Java ME, because you can use them to create smaller and more efficient code. They also offer better performance for low-level libraries, where performance is important.

An event-based reader extracts the next infoset item from an input stream by obtaining an event. Similarly, an event-based writer writes the next infoset item to the stream by adding an event to the output stream. In contrast to stream-based readers and writers, event-based readers and writers have no concept of a cursor.

Event-based readers and writers are appropriate for creating *XML processing pipelines* (sequences of components that transform the previous component's input and pass the transformed output to the next component in the sequence), for modifying an event sequence, and more.

Parsing XML Documents

Document readers are obtained by calling the various "create" methods that are declared in the `javax.xml.stream.XMLInputFactory` class. These creational methods are organized into two categories: methods for creating stream-based readers and methods for creating event-based readers.

Before you can obtain a stream-based or an event-based reader, you need to obtain an instance of the factory by calling one of the `newFactory()` class methods, such as `XMLInputFactory newFactory()`:

```
XMLInputFactory xmlif = XMLInputFactory.newFactory();
```

■ **Note** You can also call the `XMLInputFactory` `newInstance()` class method but might not wish to do so because its same-named but parameterized companion method has been deprecated to maintain API consistency, and it is probable that `newInstance()` will be deprecated as well.

The `newFactory()` methods follow an ordered lookup procedure to locate the `XMLInputFactory` implementation class. This procedure first examines the `javax.xml.stream.XMLInputFactory` system property, and lastly chooses the name of the Java platform's default `XMLInputFactory` implementation class. If this procedure cannot find a classname, or if the class cannot be loaded (or instantiated), the method throws an instance of the `javax.xml.stream.FactoryConfigurationError` class.

After creating the factory, call `XMLInputFactory`'s void `setProperty(String name, Object value)` method to set various features and properties as necessary. For example, you might execute `xmlif.setProperty(XMLInputFactory.IS_VALIDATING, true);` (true is passed as a Boolean object via autoboxing, discussed in Chapter 5) to request a DTD-validating stream-based reader. However, the default StAX factory implementation throws `IllegalArgumentException` because it doesn't support DTD validation. Similarly, you might execute `xmlif.setProperty(XMLInputFactory.IS_NAMESPACE_AWARE, true);` to request a namespace-aware event-based reader, which is supported.

Parsing Documents with Stream-Based Readers

A stream-based reader is created by calling one of `XMLInputFactory`'s `createXMLStreamReader()` methods, such as `XMLStreamReader createXMLStreamReader(Reader reader)`. These methods throw `javax.xml.stream.XMLStreamException` when the stream-based reader cannot be created.

The following example creates a stream-based reader whose source is a file named `recipe.xml`:

```
Reader reader = new FileReader("recipe.xml");
```

```
XMLStreamReader xmlsr = xmlif.createXMLStreamReader(reader);
```

The low-level XMLStreamReader interface offers the most efficient way to read XML data with StAX. This interface's boolean hasNext() method returns true when there is a next infoset item to obtain; otherwise, it returns false. The int next() method advances the cursor by one infoset item and returns an integer code that identifies this item's type.

Instead of comparing next()'s return value with an integer value, you would compare this value against a javax.xml.stream.XMLStreamConstants infoset constant, such as START_ELEMENT or DTD— XMLStreamReader extends the XMLStreamConstants interface.

Note You can also obtain the type of the infoset item that the cursor is pointing to by calling XMLStreamReader's int getEventType() method. Specifying "Event" in the name of this method is unfortunate because it confuses stream-based readers with event-based readers.

The following example uses the hasNext() and next() methods to codify a parsing loop that detects the start and end of each element:

```
while (xmlsr.hasNext())
{
   switch (xmlsr.next())
   {
      case XMLStreamReader.START_ELEMENT: // Do something at element start.
                                  break;
      case XMLStreamReader.END_ELEMENT   : // Do something at element end.
   }
}
```

XMLStreamReader also declares various methods for extracting infoset information. For example, QName getName() returns the qualified name (as a javax.xml.namespace.QName instance) of the element at the cursor position when next() returns XMLStreamReader.START_ELEMENT or XMLStreamReader.END_ELEMENT.

Note QName describes a qualified name as a combination of namespace URI, local part, and prefix components. After instantiating this immutable class (via a constructor such as QName(String namespaceURI, String localPart, String prefix)), you can return these components by calling QName's String getNamespaceURI(), String getLocalPart(), and String getPrefix() methods.

Listing 10-16 presents the source code to a StAXDemo application that reports an XML document's start and end elements via a stream-based reader.

Listing 10-16. StAXDemo (version 1)

```java
import java.io.FileNotFoundException;
import java.io.FileReader;

import javax.xml.stream.FactoryConfigurationError;
import javax.xml.stream.XMLInputFactory;
import javax.xml.stream.XMLStreamException;
import javax.xml.stream.XMLStreamReader;

class StAXDemo
{
    public static void main(String[] args)
    {
        if (args.length != 1)
        {
            System.err.println("usage: java StAXDemo xmlfile");
            return;
        }
        try
        {
            XMLInputFactory xmlif = XMLInputFactory.newFactory();
            XMLStreamReader xmlsr;
            xmlsr = xmlif.createXMLStreamReader(new FileReader(args[0]));
            while (xmlsr.hasNext())
            {
                switch (xmlsr.next())
                {
                    case XMLStreamReader.START_ELEMENT:
                        System.out.println("START_ELEMENT");
                        System.out.println("  Qname = "+xmlsr.getName());
                        break;
                    case XMLStreamReader.END_ELEMENT:
                        System.out.println("END_ELEMENT");
                        System.out.println("  Qname = "+xmlsr.getName());
                }
            }
        }
        catch (FactoryConfigurationError fce)
        {
            System.err.println("FCE: "+fce);
        }
        catch (FileNotFoundException fnfe)
        {
            System.err.println("FNFE: "+fnfe);
        }
        catch (XMLStreamException xmlse)
        {
            System.err.println("XMLSE: "+xmlse);
        }
    }
}
```

```
}
```

After verifying the number of command-line arguments, Listing 10-16's `main()` method creates a factory, uses the factory to create a stream-based reader that obtains its XML data from the file identified by the solitary command-line argument, and enters a parsing loop. Whenever `next()` returns `XMLStreamReader.START_ELEMENT` or `XMLStreamReader.END_ELEMENT`, `XMLStreamReader`'s `getName()` method is called to return the element's qualified name.

For example, when you execute `StAXDemo` against Listing 10-2's movie document file (`movie.xml`), this application generates the following output:

```
START_ELEMENT
  Qname = movie
START_ELEMENT
  Qname = name
END_ELEMENT
  Qname = name
START_ELEMENT
  Qname = language
END_ELEMENT
  Qname = language
END_ELEMENT
  Qname = movie
```

Note: `XMLStreamReader` declares a `void close()` method that you will want to call to free any resources associated with this stream-based reader when your application is designed to run for an extended period of time. Calling this method doesn't close the underlying input source.

Parsing Documents with Event-Based Readers

An event-based reader is created by calling one of `XMLInputFactory`'s `createXMLEventReader()` methods, such as `XMLEventReader createXMLEventReader(Reader reader)`. These methods throw `XMLStreamException` when the event-based reader cannot be created.

The following example creates an event-based reader whose source is a file named `recipe.xml`:

```
Reader reader = new FileReader("recipe.xml");
XMLEventReader xmler = xmlif.createXMLEventReader(reader);
```

The high-level `XMLEventReader` interface offers a somewhat less efficient but more object-oriented way to read XML data with StAX. This interface's `boolean hasNext()` method returns true when there is a next event to obtain; otherwise, it returns false. The `XMLEvent nextEvent()` method returns the next event as an object whose class implements a subinterface of the `javax.xml.stream.events.XMLEvent` interface.

■ **Note** XMLEvent is the base interface for handling markup events. It declares methods that apply to all subinterfaces; for example, Location getLocation() (return a javax.xml.stream.Location object whose int getCharacterOffset() and other methods return location information about the event) and int getEventType() (return the event type as an XMLStreamConstants infoset constant, such as START_ELEMENT and PROCESSING_INSTRUCTION—XMLEvent extends XMLStreamConstants). XMLEvent is subtyped by other javax.xml.stream.events interfaces that describe different kinds of events (e.g., Attribute) in terms of methods that return infoset item-specific information (such as Attribute's QName getName() and String getValue() methods).

The following example uses the hasNext() and nextEvent() methods to codify a parsing loop that detects the start and end of an element:

```
while (xmler.hasNext())
{
   switch (xmler.nextEvent().getEventType())
   {
      case XMLEvent.START_ELEMENT: // Do something at element start.
                                   break;
      case XMLEvent.END_ELEMENT  : // Do something at element end.
   }
}
```

Listing 10-17 presents the source code to a StAXDemo application that reports an XML document's start and end elements via an event-based reader.

Listing 10-17. StAXDemo (version 2)

```
import java.io.FileNotFoundException;
import java.io.FileReader;

import javax.xml.stream.FactoryConfigurationError;
import javax.xml.stream.XMLEventReader;
import javax.xml.stream.XMLInputFactory;
import javax.xml.stream.XMLStreamException;

import javax.xml.stream.events.EndElement;
import javax.xml.stream.events.StartElement;
import javax.xml.stream.events.XMLEvent;

class StAXDemo
{
   public static void main(String[] args)
   {
      if (args.length != 1)
      {
         System.err.println("usage: java StAXDemo xmlfile");
```

```
            return;
         }
         try
         {
            XMLInputFactory xmlif = XMLInputFactory.newFactory();
            XMLEventReader xmler;
            xmler = xmlif.createXMLEventReader(new FileReader(args[0]));
            while (xmler.hasNext())
            {
               XMLEvent xmle = xmler.nextEvent();
               switch (xmle.getEventType())
               {
                  case XMLEvent.START_ELEMENT:
                     System.out.println("START_ELEMENT");
                     System.out.println("  Qname = "+
                                           ((StartElement) xmle).getName());
                     break;
                  case XMLEvent.END_ELEMENT:
                     System.out.println("END_ELEMENT");
                     System.out.println("  Qname = "+
                                           ((EndElement) xmle).getName());
               }
            }
         }
         catch (FactoryConfigurationError fce)
         {
            System.err.println("FCE: "+fce);
         }
         catch (FileNotFoundException fnfe)
         {
            System.err.println("FNFE: "+fnfe);
         }
         catch (XMLStreamException xmlse)
         {
            System.err.println("XMLSE: "+xmlse);
         }
      }
}
```

After verifying the number of command-line arguments, Listing 10-17's main() method creates a factory, uses the factory to create an event-based reader that obtains its XML data from the file identified by the solitary command-line argument, and enters a parsing loop. Whenever nextEvent() returns XMLEvent.START_ELEMENT or XMLEvent.END_ELEMENT, StartElement's or EndElement's getName() method is called to return the element's qualified name.

For example, when you execute StAXDemo against Listing 10-3's article document file (article.xml), this application generates the following output:

```
START_ELEMENT
  Qname = article
START_ELEMENT
  Qname = abstract
START_ELEMENT
```

```
    Qname = code-inline
END_ELEMENT
    Qname = code-inline
END_ELEMENT
    Qname = abstract
START_ELEMENT
    Qname = body
END_ELEMENT
    Qname = body
END_ELEMENT
    Qname = article
```

Note You can also create a filtered event-based reader to accept or reject various events by calling one of XMLInputFactory's createFilteredReader() methods, such as XMLEventReader createFilteredReader(XMLEventReader reader, EventFilter filter). The javax.stream.xml.EventFilter interface declares a boolean accept(XMLEvent event) method that returns true when the specified event is part of the event sequence; otherwise, it returns false.

Creating XML Documents

Document writers are obtained by calling the various "create" methods that are declared in the javax.xml.stream.XMLOutputFactory class. These creational methods are organized into two categories: methods for creating stream-based writers and methods for creating event-based writers.

Before you can obtain a stream-based or an event-based writer, you need to obtain an instance of the factory by calling one of the newFactory() class methods, such as XMLOutputFactory newFactory():

```
XMLOutputFactory xmlof = XMLOutputFactory.newFactory();
```

Note You can also call the XMLOutputFactory newInstance() class method but might not wish to do so because its same-named but parameterized companion method has been deprecated to maintain API consistency, and it is probable that newInstance() will be deprecated as well.

The newFactory() methods follow an ordered lookup procedure to locate the XMLOutputFactory implementation class. This procedure first examines the javax.xml.stream.XMLOutputFactory system property, and lastly chooses the name of the Java platform's default XMLOutputFactory implementation class. If this procedure cannot find a classname, or if the class cannot be loaded (or instantiated), the method throws an instance of the FactoryConfigurationError class.

After creating the factory, call XMLOutputFactory's void setProperty(String name, Object value) method to set various features and properties as necessary. The only property currently supported by all writers is XMLOutputFactory.IS_REPAIRING_NAMESPACES. When enabled (by passing true or a Boolean object, such as Boolean.TRUE, to value), the document writer takes care of all namespace bindings and declarations, with minimal help from the application. The output is always well formed with respect to namespaces. However enabling this property adds some overhead to the job of writing the XML.

Creating Documents with Stream-Based Writers

A stream-based writer is created by calling one of XMLOutputFactory's createXMLStreamWriter() methods, such as XMLStreamWriter createXMLStreamWriter(Writer writer). These methods throw XMLStreamException when the stream-based writer cannot be created.

The following example creates a stream-based writer whose destination is a file named recipe.xml:

```
Writer writer = new FileWriter("recipe.xml");
XMLStreamWriter xmlsw = xmlof.createXMLStreamWriter(writer);
```

The low-level XMLStreamWriter interface declares several methods for writing infoset items to the destination. The following list describes a few of these methods:

- void close() closes this stream-based writer and frees any associated resources. The underlying writer is not closed.

- void flush() writes any cached data to the underlying writer.

- void setPrefix(String prefix, String uri) identifies the namespace prefix to which the uri value is bound. This prefix is used by variants of the writeStartElement(), writeAttribute(), and writeEmptyElement() methods that take namespace arguments but not prefixes. Also, it remains valid until the writeEndElement() invocation that corresponds to the last writeStartElement() invocation. This method does not create any output.

- void writeAttribute(String localName, String value) writes the attribute identified by localName and having the specified value to the underlying writer. A namespace prefix isn't included. This method escapes &, < and >, and ".

- void writeCharacters(String text) writes text's characters to the underlying writer. This method escapes &, <, and >.

- void writeEndDocument() closes any start tags and writes corresponding end tags to the underlying writer.

- void endElement() writes an end tag to the underlying writer, relying on the internal state of the stream-based writer to determine the tag's prefix and local name.

- void writeNamespace(String prefix, String namespaceURI) writes a namespace to the underlying writer. This method must be called to ensure that the namespace specified by setPrefix() and duplicated in this method call is written; otherwise, the resulting document will not be well formed from a namespace perspective.

- void writeStartDocument() writes the XML declaration to the underlying writer.

- void writeStartElement(String namespaceURI, String localName) writes a start tag with the arguments passed to namespaceURI and localName to the underlying writer.

Listing 10-18 presents the source code to a StAXDemo application that creates a recipe.xml file with many of Listing 10-5's infoset items via a stream-based writer.

Listing 10-18. *StAXDemo (version 3)*

```java
import java.io.FileWriter;
import java.io.IOException;

import javax.xml.stream.FactoryConfigurationError;
import javax.xml.stream.XMLOutputFactory;
import javax.xml.stream.XMLStreamException;
import javax.xml.stream.XMLStreamWriter;

class StAXDemo
{
   public static void main(String[] args)
   {
      try
      {
         XMLOutputFactory xmlof = XMLOutputFactory.newFactory();
         XMLStreamWriter xmlsw;
         xmlsw = xmlof.createXMLStreamWriter(new FileWriter("recipe.xml"));
         xmlsw.writeStartDocument();
         xmlsw.setPrefix("h", "http://www.w3.org/1999/xhtml");
         xmlsw.writeStartElement("http://www.w3.org/1999/xhtml", "html");
         xmlsw.writeNamespace("h", "http://www.w3.org/1999/xhtml");
         xmlsw.writeNamespace("r", "http://www.tutortutor.ca/");
         xmlsw.writeStartElement("http://www.w3.org/1999/xhtml", "head");
         xmlsw.writeStartElement("http://www.w3.org/1999/xhtml", "title");
         xmlsw.writeCharacters("Recipe");
         xmlsw.writeEndElement();
         xmlsw.writeEndElement();
         xmlsw.writeStartElement("http://www.w3.org/1999/xhtml", "body");
         xmlsw.setPrefix("r", "http://www.tutortutor.ca/");
         xmlsw.writeStartElement("http://www.tutortutor.ca/", "recipe");
         xmlsw.writeStartElement("http://www.tutortutor.ca/", "title");
         xmlsw.writeCharacters("Grilled Cheese Sandwich");
         xmlsw.writeEndElement();
         xmlsw.writeStartElement("http://www.tutortutor.ca/", "ingredients");
         xmlsw.setPrefix("h", "http://www.w3.org/1999/xhtml");
         xmlsw.writeStartElement("http://www.w3.org/1999/xhtml", "ul");
         xmlsw.writeStartElement("http://www.w3.org/1999/xhtml", "li");
         xmlsw.setPrefix("r", "http://www.tutortutor.ca/");
         xmlsw.writeStartElement("http://www.tutortutor.ca/", "ingredient");
         xmlsw.writeAttribute("qty", "2");
         xmlsw.writeCharacters("bread slice");
         xmlsw.writeEndElement();
         xmlsw.setPrefix("h", "http://www.w3.org/1999/xhtml");
         xmlsw.writeEndElement();
         xmlsw.writeEndElement();
         xmlsw.setPrefix("r", "http://www.tutortutor.ca/");
         xmlsw.writeEndElement();
```

```
            xmlsw.writeEndDocument();
            xmlsw.flush();
            xmlsw.close();
        }
        catch (FactoryConfigurationError fce)
        {
            System.err.println("FCE: "+fce);
        }
        catch (IOException ioe)
        {
            System.err.println("IOE: "+ioe);
        }
        catch (XMLStreamException xmlse)
        {
            System.err.println("XMLSE: "+xmlse);
        }
    }
}
```

Although Listing 10-18 is fairly easy to follow, you might be somewhat confused by the duplication of namespace URIs in the setPrefix() and writeStartElement() method calls. For example, you might be wondering about the duplicate URIs in xmlsw.setPrefix("h", "http://www.w3.org/1999/xhtml"); and its xmlsw.writeStartElement("http://www.w3.org/1999/xhtml", "html"); successor.

The setPrefix() method call creates a mapping between a namespace prefix (the value) and a URI (the key) without generating any output. The writeStartElement() method call specifies the URI key, which this method uses to access the prefix value, which it then prepends (with a colon character) to the html start tag's name before writing this tag to the underlying writer.

Creating Documents with Event-Based Writers

An event-based writer is created by calling one of XMLOutputFactory's createXMLEventWriter() methods, such as XMLEventWriter createXMLEventWriter(Writer writer). These methods throw XMLStreamException when the event-based writer cannot be created.

The following example creates an event-based writer whose destination is a file named recipe.xml:

```
Writer writer = new FileWriter("recipe.xml");
XMLEventWriter xmlew = xmlof.createXMLEventWriter(writer);
```

The high-level XMLEventWriter interface declares the void add(XMLEvent event) method for adding events that describe infoset items to the output stream implemented by the underlying writer. Each argument passed to event is an instance of a class that implements a subinterface of XMLEvent (such as Attribute and StartElement).

▪ **Tip** XMLEventWriter also declares a void add(XMLEventReader reader) method that you can use to chain an XMLEventReader instance to an XMLEventWriter instance.

To save you the trouble of implementing these interfaces, StAX provides `javax.xml.stream.EventFactory`. This utility class declares various factory methods for creating XMLEvent subinterface implementations. For example, Comment createComment(String text) returns an object whose class implements the javax.xml.stream.events.Comment subinterface of XMLEvent.

Because these factory methods are declared abstract, you must first obtain an instance of the EventFactory class. You can easily accomplish this task by invoking EventFactory's XMLEventFactory newFactory() class method, as follows:

```
XMLEventFactory xmlef = XMLEventFactory.newFactory();
```

You can then obtain an XMLEvent subinterface implementation, as follows:

```
XMLEvent comment = xmlef.createComment("ToDo");
```

Listing 10-19 presents the source code to a StAXDemo application that creates a recipe.xml file with many of Listing 10-5's infoset items via an event-based writer.

Listing 10-19. StAXDemo (version 4)

```
import java.io.FileWriter;
import java.io.IOException;

import java.util.Iterator;

import javax.xml.stream.FactoryConfigurationError;
import javax.xml.stream.XMLEventFactory;
import javax.xml.stream.XMLEventWriter;
import javax.xml.stream.XMLOutputFactory;
import javax.xml.stream.XMLStreamException;

import javax.xml.stream.events.Attribute;
import javax.xml.stream.events.Namespace;
import javax.xml.stream.events.XMLEvent;

class StAXDemo
{
   public static void main(String[] args)
   {
      try
      {
         XMLOutputFactory xmlof = XMLOutputFactory.newFactory();
         XMLEventWriter xmlew;
         xmlew = xmlof.createXMLEventWriter(new FileWriter("recipe.xml"));
         final XMLEventFactory xmlef = XMLEventFactory.newFactory();
         XMLEvent event = xmlef.createStartDocument();
         xmlew.add(event);
         Iterator<Namespace> nsIter;
         nsIter = new Iterator<Namespace>()
         {
            int index = 0;
            Namespace[] ns;
            {
               ns = new Namespace[2];
```

```java
      ns[0] = xmlef.createNamespace("h",
                              "http://www.w3.org/1999/xhtml");
      ns[1] = xmlef.createNamespace("r",
                              "http://www.tutortutor.ca/");
   }
   public boolean hasNext()
   {
      return index != 2;
   }
   public Namespace next()
   {
      return ns[index++];
   }
   public void remove()
   {
      throw new UnsupportedOperationException();
   }
};
event = xmlef.createStartElement("h", "http://www.w3.org/1999/xhtml",
                              "html", null, nsIter);
xmlew.add(event);
event = xmlef.createStartElement("h", "http://www.w3.org/1999/xhtml",
                              "head");
xmlew.add(event);
event = xmlef.createStartElement("h", "http://www.w3.org/1999/xhtml",
                              "title");
xmlew.add(event);
event = xmlef.createCharacters("Recipe");
xmlew.add(event);
event = xmlef.createEndElement("h", "http://www.w3.org/1999/xhtml",
                              "title");
xmlew.add(event);
event = xmlef.createEndElement("h", "http://www.w3.org/1999/xhtml",
                              "head");
xmlew.add(event);
event = xmlef.createStartElement("h", "http://www.w3.org/1999/xhtml",
                              "body");
xmlew.add(event);
event = xmlef.createStartElement("r", "http://www.tutortutor.ca/",
                              "recipe");
xmlew.add(event);
event = xmlef.createStartElement("r", "http://www.tutortutor.ca/",
                              "title");
xmlew.add(event);
event = xmlef.createCharacters("Grilled Cheese Sandwich");
xmlew.add(event);
event = xmlef.createEndElement("r", "http://www.tutortutor.ca/",
                              "title");
xmlew.add(event);
event = xmlef.createStartElement("r", "http://www.tutortutor.ca/",
                              "ingredients");
xmlew.add(event);
```

```java
event = xmlef.createStartElement("h", "http://www.w3.org/1999/xhtml",
                                 "ul");
xmlew.add(event);
event = xmlef.createStartElement("h", "http://www.w3.org/1999/xhtml",
                                 "li");
xmlew.add(event);
Iterator<Attribute> attrIter;
attrIter = new Iterator<Attribute>()
{
   int index = 0;
   Attribute[] attrs;
   {
      attrs = new Attribute[1];
      attrs[0] = xmlef.createAttribute("qty", "2");
   }
   public boolean hasNext()
   {
      return index != 1;
   }
   public Attribute next()
   {
      return attrs[index++];
   }
   public void remove()
   {
      throw new UnsupportedOperationException();
   }
};
event = xmlef.createStartElement("r", "http://www.tutortutor.ca/",
                                 "ingredient", attrIter, null);
xmlew.add(event);
event = xmlef.createCharacters("bread slice");
xmlew.add(event);
event = xmlef.createEndElement("r", "http://www.tutortutor.ca/",
                               "ingredient");
xmlew.add(event);
event = xmlef.createEndElement("h", "http://www.w3.org/1999/xhtml",
                               "li");
xmlew.add(event);
event = xmlef.createEndElement("h", "http://www.w3.org/1999/xhtml",
                               "ul");
xmlew.add(event);
event = xmlef.createEndElement("r", "http://www.tutortutor.ca/",
                               "ingredients");
xmlew.add(event);
event = xmlef.createEndElement("r", "http://www.tutortutor.ca/",
                               "recipe");
xmlew.add(event);
event = xmlef.createEndElement("h", "http://www.w3.org/1999/xhtml",
                               "body");
xmlew.add(event);
event = xmlef.createEndElement("h", "http://www.w3.org/1999/xhtml",
```

```
                                           "html");
          xmlew.add(event);
          xmlew.flush();
          xmlew.close();
       }
       catch (FactoryConfigurationError fce)
       {
           System.err.println("FCE: "+fce);
       }
       catch (IOException ioe)
       {
           System.err.println("IOE: "+ioe);
       }
       catch (XMLStreamException xmlse)
       {
           System.err.println("XMLSE: "+xmlse);
       }
    }
}
```

Listing 10-19 should be fairly easy to follow; it is the event-based equivalent of Listing 10-18. Notice that this listing includes the creation of `java.util.Iterator` instances from anonymous classes that implement this interface. These iterators are created to pass namespaces or attributes to `XMLEventFactory`'s `StartElement createStartElement(String prefix, String namespaceUri, String localName, Iterator attributes, Iterator namespaces)` method. (You can pass null to this parameter when an iterator is not applicable; for example, when the start tag has no attributes.)

Selecting XML Document Nodes with XPath

XPath is a nonXML declarative query language (defined by the W3C) for selecting an XML document's infoset items as one or more nodes. For example, you can use XPath to locate Listing 10-1's third ingredient element and return this element node.

XPath is often used to simplify access to a DOM tree's nodes, and is also used in the context of XSLT (discussed in the next section), typically to select those input document elements (via XPath expressions) that are to be copied to an output document. Java 7 supports XPath 1.0 via JAXP's XPath API, which is assigned package `javax.xml.xpath`.

This section first acquaints you with the XPath 1.0 language. It then demonstrates how XPath simplifies the selection of a DOM tree's nodes. Lastly, the section introduces you to three advanced XPath topics.

XPath Language Primer

XPath views an XML document as a tree of nodes that starts from a root node. XPath recognizes seven kinds of nodes: element, attribute, text, namespace, processing instruction, comment, and document. XPath does not recognize CDATA sections, entity references, or document type declarations.

Note A tree's root node (a DOM Document instance) is not the same as a document's root element. The root node contains the entire document, including the root element, any comments or processing instructions that appear before the root element's start tag, and any comments or processing instructions that appear after the root element's end tag.

XPath provides location path expressions for selecting nodes. A *location path expression* locates nodes via a sequence of *steps* starting from the *context node* (the root node or some other document node that is the current node). The returned set of nodes might be empty, or it might contain one or more nodes.

The simplest location path expression selects the document's root node and consists of a single forward slash character (/). The next simplest location path expression is the name of an element, which selects all child elements of the context node that have that name. For example, ingredient refers to all ingredient child elements of the context node in Listing 10-1's XML document. This XPath expression returns a set of three ingredient nodes when ingredients is the context node. However, if recipe or instructions happened to be the context node, ingredient would not return any nodes (ingredient is a child of ingredients only). When an expression starts with /, the expression represents an absolute path that starts from the root node. For example, /movie selects all movie child elements of the root node in Listing 10-2's XML document.

Attributes are also handled by location path expressions. To select an element's attribute, specify @ followed by the attribute's name. For example, @qty selects the qty attribute node of the context node.

In most cases, you will work with root nodes, element nodes, and attribute nodes. However, you might also need to work with namespace nodes, text nodes, processing-instruction nodes, and comment nodes. Unlike namespace nodes, which are typically handled by XSLT, you'll more likely need to process comments, text, and processing instructions. XPath provides comment(), text(), and processing-instruction() functions for selecting comment, text, and processing-instruction nodes.

The comment() and text() functions don't require arguments because comment and text nodes don't have names. Each comment is a separate comment node, and each text node specifies the longest run of text not interrupted by a tag. The processing-instruction() function may be called with an argument that identifies the target of the processing instruction. If called with no argument, all the context node's processing-instruction child nodes are selected.

XPath supplies three wildcards for selecting unknown nodes. The * wildcard matches any element node regardless of the node's type. It does not match attributes, text nodes, comments, or processing-instruction nodes. When you place a namespace prefix before the *, only elements belonging to that namespace are matched. The node() wildcard is a function that matches all nodes. Finally, the @* wildcard matches all attribute nodes.

Note XPath lets you perform multiple selections by using the vertical bar (|). For example, author/*|publisher/* selects the children of author and the children of publisher, and *|@* matches all elements and attributes, but doesn't match text, comment, or processing-instruction nodes.

XPath lets you combine steps into *compound paths* by using the / character to separate them. For paths beginning with /, the first path step is relative to the root node; otherwise, the first path step is relative to another context node. For example, /movie/name starts with the root node, selects all movie element children of the root node, and selects all name children of the selected movie nodes. If you wanted to return all text nodes of the selected name elements, you would specify /movie/name/text().

Compound paths can include // to select nodes from all descendents of the context node (including the context node). When placed at the start of an expression, // selects nodes from the entire tree. For example, //ingredient selects all ingredient nodes in the tree.

As with filesystems that let you identify the current directory with a single period (.) and its parent directory with a double period (..), you can specify a single period to represent the current node and a double period to represent the parent of the current node. (You would typically use a single period in XSLT to indicate that you want to access the value of the currently matched element.)

It might be necessary to narrow the selection of nodes returned by an XPath expression. For example, /recipe/ingredients/ingredient returns all ingredient nodes, but perhaps you only want to return the first ingredient node. You can narrow the selection by including predicates in the location path.

A *predicate* is a square bracket-delimited Boolean expression that is tested against each selected node. If the expression evaluates to true, that node is included in the set of nodes returned by the XPath expression; otherwise, the node is not included in the set. For example, /recipe/ingredients/ingredient[1] selects the first ingredient element that is a child of the ingredients element.

Predicates can include predefined functions (e.g., last() and position()), operators (e.g., -, <, and =), and other items. For example, /recipe/ingredients/ingredient[last()] selects the last ingredient element that is a child of the ingredients element, /recipe/ingredients/ingredient[last()-1] selects the next-to-last ingredient element that is a child of the ingredients element, /recipe/ingredients/ingredient[position()<3] selects the first two ingredient elements that are children of the ingredients element, //ingredient[@qty] selects all ingredient elements (no matter where they are located) that have qty attributes, and //ingredient[@qty='1'] or //ingredient[@qty="1"] selects all ingredient elements (no matter where they are located) that have qty attributes with value 1.

Although predicates are supposed to be Boolean expressions, the predicate might not evaluate to a Boolean value. For example, it could evaluate to a number or a string—XPath supports Boolean, number (IEEE 754 double precision floating-point values), and string expression types as well as a location path expression's nodeset type. If a predicate evaluates to a number, XPath converts that number to true when it equals the context node's position; otherwise, XPath converts that number to false. If a predicate evaluates to a string, XPath converts that string to true when the string isn't empty; otherwise, XPath converts that string to false. Finally, if a predicate evaluates to a nodeset, XPath converts that nodeset to true when the nodeset is nonempty; otherwise, XPath converts that nodeset to false.

Note The previously presented location path expression examples demonstrate XPath's abbreviated syntax. However, XPath also supports an unabbreviated syntax that is more descriptive of what is happening and is based on an *axis specifier*, which indicates the navigation direction within the XML document's tree representation. For example, where /movie/name selects all movie child elements of the root node followed by all name child elements of the movie elements using the abbreviated syntax, /child::movie/child::name accomplishes the same task with the expanded syntax. Check out Wikipedia's "XPath 1.0" entry (http://en.wikipedia.org/wiki/XPath_1.0) for more information.

Location path expressions (which return nodesets) are one kind of XPath expressions. XPath also supports *general expressions* that evaluate to Boolean (e.g., predicates), number, or string type; for example, position()=2, 6.8, and "Hello". General expressions are often used in XSLT.

XPath Boolean values can be compared via relational operators <, <=, >, >=, =, and !=. Boolean expressions can be combined by using operators and and or. XPath predefines the boolean() function to convert its argument to a string, not() to return true when its Boolean argument is false and vice versa, true() to return true, false() to return false, and lang() to return true or false depending on whether the language of the context node (as specified by xml:lang attributes) is the same as or is a sublanguage of the language specified by the argument string.

XPath provides the +, -, *, div, and mod (remainder) operators for working with numbers—forward slash cannot be used for division because this character is used to separate location steps. All five operators behave like their Java language counterparts. XPath also predefines the number() function to convert its argument to a number, sum() to return the sum of the numeric values represented by the nodes in its nodeset argument, floor() to return the largest (closest to positive infinity) number that is not greater than its number argument and that is an integer, ceiling() to return the smallest (closest to negative infinity) number that is not less than its number argument and that is an integer, and round() to return the number that is closest to the argument and that is an integer. When there are two such numbers, the one closest to positive infinity is returned.

XPath strings are ordered character sequences that are enclosed in single quotes or double quotes. A string literal cannot contain the same kind of quote that is also used to delimit the string. For example, a string that contains a single quote cannot be delimited with single quotes. XPath provides the = and != operators for comparing strings. XPath also predefines the string() function to convert its argument to a string, concat() to return a concatenation of its string arguments, starts-with() to return true when the first argument string starts with the second argument string (and otherwise returns false), contains() to return true when the first argument string contains the second argument string (and otherwise returns false), substring-before() to return the substring of the first argument string that precedes the first occurrence of the second argument string in the first argument string, or the empty string when the first argument string does not contain the second argument string, substring-after() to return the substring of the first argument string that follows the first occurrence of the second argument string in the first argument string, or the empty string when the first argument string does not contain the second argument string, substring() to return the substring of the first (string) argument starting at the position specified in the second (number) argument with length specified in the third (number) argument, string-length() to return the number of characters in its string argument (or the length of the context node when converted to a string in the absence of an argument), normalize-space() to return the argument string with whitespace normalized by stripping leading and trailing whitespace and replacing sequences of whitespace characters by a single space (or performing the same action on the context node when converted to a string in the absence of an argument), and translate() to return the first argument string with occurrences of characters in the second argument string replaced by the character at the corresponding position in the third argument string.

Finally, XPath predefines several functions for use with nodesets: last() returns a number identifying the last node, position() returns a number identifying a node's position, count() returns the number of nodes in its nodeset argument, id() selects elements by their unique IDs and returns a nodeset of these elements, local-name() returns the local part of the qualified name of the first node in its nodeset argument, namespace-uri() returns the namespace part of the qualified name of the first node in its nodeset argument, and name() returns the qualified name of the first node in its nodeset argument.

XPath and DOM

Suppose you need someone in your home to purchase a bag of sugar. You can tell this person to "Please buy me some sugar." Alternatively, you could say the following: "Please open the front door. Walk down to the sidewalk. Turn left. Walk up the sidewalk for three blocks. Turn right. Walk up the sidewalk one block. Enter the store. Go to aisle 7. Walk two meters down the aisle. Pick up a bag of sugar. Walk to a checkout counter. Pay for the sugar. Retrace your steps home." Most people would expect to receive the shorter instruction, and would probably have you committed to an institution if you made a habit out of providing the longer set of instructions.

Traversing a DOM tree of nodes is similar to providing the longer sequence of instructions. In contrast, XPath lets you traverse this tree via a succinct instruction. To see this difference for yourself, consider a scenario where you have an XML-based contacts document that lists your various professional contacts. Listing 10-20 presents a trivial example of such a document.

Listing 10-20. *XML-based contacts database*

```
<?xml version="1.0"?>
<contacts>
    <contact>
        <name>John Doe</name>
        <city>Chicago</city>
        <city>Denver</city>
    </contact>
    <contact>
        <name>Jane Doe</name>
        <city>New York</city>
    </contact>
    <contact>
        <name>Sandra Smith</name>
        <city>Denver</city>
        <city>Miami</city>
    </contact>
    <contact>
        <name>Bob Jones</name>
        <city>Chicago</city>
    </contact>
</contacts>
```

Listing 10-20 reveals a simple XML grammar consisting of a contacts root element that contains a sequence of contact elements. Each contact element contains one name element and one or more city elements (your contact travels frequently and spends a lot of time in each city). (To keep the example simple, I'm not providing a DTD or a schema.)

Suppose you want to locate and output the names of all contacts that live at least part of each year in Chicago. Listing 10-21 presents the source code to a DOMSearch application that accomplishes this task with the DOM API.

Listing 10-21. *Locating Chicago contacts with the DOM API*

```
import java.io.IOException;

import java.util.ArrayList;
import java.util.List;
```

```java
import javax.xml.parsers.DocumentBuilder;
import javax.xml.parsers.DocumentBuilderFactory;
import javax.xml.parsers.FactoryConfigurationError;
import javax.xml.parsers.ParserConfigurationException;

import org.w3c.dom.Document;
import org.w3c.dom.Element;
import org.w3c.dom.Node;
import org.w3c.dom.NodeList;

import org.xml.sax.SAXException;

class DOMSearch
{
    public static void main(String[] args)
    {
        try
        {
            DocumentBuilderFactory dbf = DocumentBuilderFactory.newInstance();
            DocumentBuilder db = dbf.newDocumentBuilder();
            Document doc = db.parse("contacts.xml");
            List<String> contactNames = new ArrayList<String>();
            NodeList contacts = doc.getElementsByTagName("contact");
            for (int i = 0; i < contacts.getLength(); i++)
            {
                Element contact = (Element) contacts.item(i);
                NodeList cities = contact.getElementsByTagName("city");
                boolean chicago = false;
                for (int j = 0; j < cities.getLength(); j++)
                {
                    Element city = (Element) cities.item(j);
                    NodeList children = city.getChildNodes();
                    StringBuilder sb = new StringBuilder();
                    for (int k = 0; k < children.getLength(); k++)
                    {
                        Node child = children.item(k);
                        if (child.getNodeType() == Node.TEXT_NODE)
                            sb.append(child.getNodeValue());
                    }
                    if (sb.toString().equals("Chicago"))
                    {
                        chicago = true;
                        break;
                    }
                }
                if (chicago)
                {
                    NodeList names = contact.getElementsByTagName("name");
                    contactNames.add(names.item(0).getFirstChild().getNodeValue());
                }
            }
```

```
            for (String contactName: contactNames)
               System.out.println(contactName);
         }
         catch (IOException ioe)
         {
            System.err.println("IOE: "+ioe);
         }
         catch (SAXException saxe)
         {
            System.err.println("SAXE: "+saxe);
         }
         catch (FactoryConfigurationError fce)
         {
            System.err.println("FCE: "+fce);
         }
         catch (ParserConfigurationException pce)
         {
            System.err.println("PCE: "+pce);
         }
      }
}
```

After parsing contacts.xml and building the DOM tree, main() uses Document's getElementsByTagName() method to return a NodeList of contact element nodes. For each member of this list, main() extracts the contact element node, and uses this node with getElementsByTagName() to return a NodeList of the contact element node's city element nodes.

For each member of the cities list, main() extracts the city element node, and uses this node with getElementsByTagName() to return a NodeList of the city element node's child nodes—there is only a single child text node in this example, but the presence of a comment or processing instruction would increase the number of child nodes. For example, <city>Chicago<!--The windy city--></city> increases the number of child nodes to 2.

If the child's node type indicates that it is a text node, the child node's value (obtained via getNodeValue()) is stored in a string builder—only one child node is stored in the string builder in this example. If the builder's contents indicate that Chicago has been found, the chicago flag is set to true and execution leaves the cities loop.

If the chicago flag is set when the cities loop exits, the current contact element node's getElementsByTagName() method is called to return a NodeList of the contact element node's name element nodes (of which there should only be one, and which I could enforce through a DTD or schema). It is now a simple matter to extract the first item from this list, call getFirstChild() on this item to return the text node (I assume that only text appears between <name> and </name>), and call getNodeValue() on the text node to obtain its value, which is then added to the contactNames list.

After compiling this source code, run the application. You should observe the following output:

```
John Doe
Bob Jones
```

Traversing the DOM's tree of nodes is a tedious exercise at best and is error-prone at worst. Fortunately, XPath can greatly simplify this situation.

Before writing the XPath equivalent of Listing 10-21, it helps to define a location path expression. For this example, that expression is //contact[city="Chicago"]/name/text(), which uses a predicate to select all contact nodes that contain a Chicago city node, then select all child name nodes from these contact nodes, and finally select all child text nodes from these name nodes.

Listing 10-22 presents the source code to an XPathSearch application that uses this XPath expression and the XPath API to locate Chicago contacts.

Listing 10-22. Locating Chicago contacts with the XPath API

```java
import java.io.IOException;

import javax.xml.parsers.DocumentBuilder;
import javax.xml.parsers.DocumentBuilderFactory;
import javax.xml.parsers.FactoryConfigurationError;
import javax.xml.parsers.ParserConfigurationException;

import javax.xml.xpath.XPath;
import javax.xml.xpath.XPathConstants;
import javax.xml.xpath.XPathException;
import javax.xml.xpath.XPathExpression;
import javax.xml.xpath.XPathFactory;

import org.w3c.dom.Document;
import org.w3c.dom.NodeList;

import org.xml.sax.SAXException;

class XPathSearch
{
   public static void main(String[] args)
   {
      try
      {
         DocumentBuilderFactory dbf = DocumentBuilderFactory.newInstance();
         DocumentBuilder db = dbf.newDocumentBuilder();
         Document doc = db.parse("contacts.xml");
         XPathFactory xpf = XPathFactory.newInstance();
         XPath xp = xpf.newXPath();
         XPathExpression xpe;
         xpe = xp.compile("//contact[city='Chicago']/name/text()");
         Object result = xpe.evaluate(doc, XPathConstants.NODESET);
         NodeList nl = (NodeList) result;
         for (int i = 0; i < nl.getLength(); i++)
            System.out.println(nl.item(i).getNodeValue());
      }
      catch (IOException ioe)
      {
         System.err.println("IOE: "+ioe);
      }
      catch (SAXException saxe)
      {
         System.err.println("SAXE: "+saxe);
      }
      catch (FactoryConfigurationError fce)
      {
         System.err.println("FCE: "+fce);
```

```
      }
      catch (ParserConfigurationException pce)
      {
         System.err.println("PCE: "+pce);
      }
      catch (XPathException xpe)
      {
         System.err.println("XPE: "+xpe);
      }
   }
}
```

After parsing contacts.xml and building the DOM tree, main() instantiates XPathFactory by calling its XPathFactory newInstance() method. The resulting XPathFactory instance can be used to set features (such as secure processing, to process XML documents securely) by calling its void setFeature(String name, boolean value) method, create an XPath object by calling its XPath newXPath() method, and more.

XPath declares an XPathExpression compile(String expression) method for compiling the specified expression (an XPath expression) and returning the compiled expression as an instance of a class that implements the XPathExpression interface. This method throws XPathExpressionException (a subclass of XMLException) when the expression cannot be compiled.

XPath also declares several overloaded evaluate() methods for immediately evaluating an expression and returning the result. Because it can take time to evaluate an expression, you might choose to compile a complex expression first (to boost performance) when you plan to evaluate this expression many times.

After compiling the expression, main() calls XPathExpression's Object evaluate(Object item, QName returnType) method to evaluate the expression. The first argument is the context node for the expression, which happens to be a Document instance in the example. The second argument specifies the kind of object returned by evaluate() and is set to XPathConstants.NODESET, a qualified name for the XPath 1.0 nodeset type, which is implemented via DOM's NodeList interface.

░ **Note** The XPath API maps XPath's Boolean, number, string, and nodeset types to Java's java.lang.Boolean, java.lang.Double, String, and org.w3c.dom.NodeList types, respectively. When calling an evaluate() method, you specify XPath types via XPathConstants constants (BOOLEAN, NUMBER, STRING, and NODESET), and the method takes care of returning an object of the appropriate type. XPathConstants also declares a NODE constant, which doesn't map to a Java type. Instead, it's used to tell evaluate() that you only want the resulting nodeset to contain a single node.

After casting Object to NodeList, main() uses this interface's getLength() and item() methods to traverse the nodelist. For each item in this list, getNodeValue() is called to return the node's value, which is subsequently output. XPathDemo generates the same output as DOMDemo.

Advanced XPath

The XPath API provides three advanced features to overcome limitations with the XPath 1.0 language. These features are namespace contexts, extension functions and function resolvers, and variables and variable resolvers.

Namespace Contexts

When an XML document's elements belong to a namespace (including the default namespace), XPath expressions that query the document must account for this namespace. For nondefault namespaces, the expression doesn't need to use the same namespace prefix; it only needs to use the same URI. However, when a document specifies the default namespace, the expression must use a prefix even though the document doesn't use a prefix.

To appreciate this situation, suppose Listing 10-20's <contacts> tag was declared <contacts xmlns="http://www.tutortutor.ca/"> to introduce a default namespace. Furthermore, suppose that Listing 10-22 included dbf.setNamespaceAware(true); after the line that instantiates DocumentBuilderFactory. If you were to run the revised XPathDemo application against the revised contacts.xml file, you would not see any output.

You can correct this problem by implementing javax.xml.namespace.NamespaceContext to map an arbitrary prefix to the namespace URI, and then registering this namespace context with the XPath instance. Listing 10-23 presents a minimal implementation of the NamespaceContext interface.

Listing 10-23. Minimally implementing NamespaceContext

```
import java.util.Iterator;

import javax.xml.XMLConstants;

import javax.xml.namespace.NamespaceContext;

class NSContext implements NamespaceContext
{
    @Override
    public String getNamespaceURI(String prefix)
    {
        if (prefix == null)
            throw new IllegalArgumentException("prefix is null");
        else
        if (prefix.equals("tt"))
            return "http://www.tutortutor.ca/";
        else
            return null;
    }
    @Override
    public String getPrefix(String uri)
    {
        return null;
    }
    @Override
    public Iterator getPrefixes(String uri)
```

```
    {
        return null;
    }
}
```

The getNamespaceURI() method is passed a prefix argument that must be mapped to a URI. If this argument is null, an IllegalArgumentException object must be thrown (according to the Java documentation). When the argument is the desired prefix value, the namespace URI is returned.

After instantiating the XPath class, you would instantiate NSContext and register this instance with the XPath instance by calling XPath's void setNamespaceContext(NamespaceContext nsContext) method. For example, you would specify xp.setNamespaceContext(new NSContext()); after XPath xp = xpf.newXPath(); to register the NSContext instance with xp.

All that's left to accomplish is to apply the prefix to the XPath expression, which now becomes //tt:contact[tt:city-'Chicago']/tt:name/texl() because the contact, city, and name elements are now part of the default namespace, whose URI is mapped to arbitrary prefix tt in the NSContext instance's getNamespaceURI() method.

Compile and run the revised XPathSearch application and you'll see John Doe followed by Bob Jones on separate lines.

Extension Functions and Function Resolvers

The XPath API lets you define functions (via Java methods) that extend XPath's predefined function repertoire by offering new features not already provided. These Java methods cannot have side effects because XPath functions can be evaluated multiple times and in any order. Furthermore, they cannot override predefined functions; a Java method with the same name as a predefined function is never executed.

Suppose you modify Listing 10-20's XML document to include a birth element that records a contact's date of birth information in YYYY-MM-DD format. Listing 10-24 shows the resulting XML file.

Listing 10-24. *XML-based contacts database with birth information*

```
<?xml version="1.0"?>
<contacts xmlns="http://www.tutortutor.ca/">
    <contact>
        <name>John Doe</name>
        <birth>1953-01-02</birth>
        <city>Chicago</city>
        <city>Denver</city>
    </contact>
    <contact>
        <name>Jane Doe</name>
        <birth>1965-07-12</birth>
        <city>New York</city>
    </contact>
    <contact>
        <name>Sandra Smith</name>
        <birth>1976-11-22</birth>
        <city>Denver</city>
        <city>Miami</city>
    </contact>
    <contact>
```

```
        <name>Bob Jones</name>
        <birth>1958-03-14</birth>
        <city>Chicago</city>
    </contact>
</contacts>
```

Now suppose that you want to select contacts based on birth information. For example, you only want to select contacts whose date of birth is greater than 1960-01-01. Because XPath does not provide this function for you, you decide to declare a date() extension function. Your first step is to declare a Date class that implements the XPathFunction interface—see Listing 10-25.

Listing 10-25. An extension function for returning a date as a milliseconds value

```
import java.text.ParsePosition;
import java.text.SimpleDateFormat;

import java.util.List;

import javax.xml.xpath.XPathFunction;
import javax.xml.xpath.XPathFunctionException;

import org.w3c.dom.Node;
import org.w3c.dom.NodeList;

class Date implements XPathFunction
{
    private final static ParsePosition POS = new ParsePosition(0);
    private SimpleDateFormat sdf = new SimpleDateFormat("yyyy-mm-dd");
    @Override
    public Object evaluate(List args) throws XPathFunctionException
    {
        if (args.size() != 1)
            throw new XPathFunctionException("Invalid number of arguments");
        String value;
        Object o = args.get(0);
        if (o instanceof NodeList)
        {
            NodeList list = (NodeList) o;
            value = list.item(0).getTextContent();
        }
        else
        if (o instanceof String)
            value = (String) o;
        else
            throw new XPathFunctionException("Cannot convert argument type");
        POS.setIndex(0);
        return sdf.parse(value, POS).getTime();
    }
}
```

XPathFunction declares a single Object evaluate(List args) method that XPath calls when it needs to execute the extension function. evaluate() is passed a java.util.List of objects that describe the arguments that were passed to the extension function by the XPath evaluator. Furthermore, this method returns a value of a type appropriate to the extension function (date()'s long integer return type is compatible with XPath's number type).

The date() extension function is intended to be called with a single argument, which is either of type nodeset or of type string. This extension function throws XPathFunctionException when the number of arguments (as indicated by the list's size) is not equal to 1.

When the argument is of type NodeList (a nodeset), the textual content of the first node in the nodeset is obtained; this content is assumed to be a year value in YYYY-MM-DD format (for brevity, I'm overlooking error checking). When the argument is of type String, it is assumed to be a year value in this format. Any other type of argument results in a thrown XPathFunctionException instance.

Date comparison is simplified by converting the date to a milliseconds value. This task is accomplished with the help of the java.text.SimpleDateFormat and java.text.ParsePosition classes. After resetting the ParsePosition object's index (via setIndex(0)), SimpleDateFormat's Date parse(String text, ParsePosition pos) method is called to parse the string according to the pattern established when SimpleDateFormat was instantiated, and starting from the parse position identified by the ParsePosition index. This index is reset prior to the parse() method call because parse() updates this object's index.

The parse() method returns a java.util.Date instance whose long getTime() method is called to return the number of milliseconds represented by the parsed date. (I discuss SimpleDateFormat, ParsePosition, and Date in Appendix C's Internationalization section.)

After implementing the extension function, you need to create a *function resolver*, which is an object whose class implements the XPathFunctionResolver interface, and which tells the XPath evaluator about the extension function (or functions). Listing 10-26 presents the DateResolver class.

Listing 10-26. A function resolver for the date() extension function

```
import javax.xml.namespace.QName;

import javax.xml.xpath.XPathFunction;
import javax.xml.xpath.XPathFunctionResolver;

class DateResolver implements XPathFunctionResolver
{
   private static final QName name = new QName("http://www.tutortutor.ca/",
                                               "date", "tt");
   @Override
   public XPathFunction resolveFunction(QName name, int arity)
   {
      if (name.equals(this.name) && arity == 1)
         return new Date();
      return null;
   }
}
```

XPathFunctionResolver declares a single XPathFunction resolveFunction(QName functionName, int arity) method that XPath calls to identify the name of the extension function and obtain an instance of a Java object whose evaluate() method implements the function.

The functionName parameter identifies the function's qualified name because all extension functions must live in a namespace, and must be referenced via a prefix (which doesn't have to match the prefix in the document). As a result, you must also bind a namespace to the prefix via a namespace context (as demonstrated previously). The arity parameter identifies the number of arguments that the extension function accepts, and is useful when overloading extension functions. If the functionName and arity values are acceptable, the extension function's Java class is instantiated and returned; otherwise, null is returned.

Finally, the function resolver class is instantiated and registered with the XPath instance by calling XPath's void setXPathFunctionResolver(XPathFunctionResolver resolver) method.

The following example demonstrates all these tasks to use date() in XPath expression //tt:contact[tt:date(tt:birth)>tt:date('1960-01-01')]/tt:name/text(), which returns only those contacts whose date of birth is greater than 1960-01-01 (Jane Doe followed by Sandra Smith):

```
DocumentBuilderFactory dbf = DocumentBuilderFactory.newInstance();
dbf.setNamespaceAware(true);
DocumentBuilder db = dbf.newDocumentBuilder();
Document doc = db.parse("contacts.xml");
XPathFactory xpf = XPathFactory.newInstance();
XPath xp = xpf.newXPath();
xp.setNamespaceContext(new NSContext());
xp.setXPathFunctionResolver(new DateResolver());
XPathExpression xpe;
String expr;
expr = "//tt:contact[tt:date(tt:birth)>tt:date('1960-01-01')]"+
       "/tt:name/text()";
xpe = xp.compile(expr);
Object result = xpe.evaluate(doc, XPathConstants.NODESET);
NodeList nl = (NodeList) result;
for (int i = 0; i < nl.getLength(); i++)
   System.out.println(nl.item(i).getNodeValue());
```

Variables and Variable Resolvers

All the previously specified XPath expressions have been based on literal text. XPath also lets you specify variables to parameterize these expressions, in a similar manner to using variables with SQL prepared statements.

A variable appears in an expression by prefixing its name (which may or may not have a namespace prefix) with a $. For example, /a/b[@c=$d]/text() is an XPath expression that selects all a elements of the root node, and all of a's b elements that have c attributes containing the value identified by variable $d, and returns the text of these b elements. This expression corresponds to Listing 10-27's XML document.

Listing 10-27. A simple XML document for demonstrating an XPath variable

```
<?xml version="1.0"?>
<a>
   <b c="x">b1</b>
   <b>b2</b>
   <b c="y">b3</b>
   <b>b4</b>
   <b c="x">b5</b>
</a>
```

To specify variables whose values are obtained during expression evaluation, you must register a variable resolver with your XPath object. A *variable resolver* is an instance of a class that implements the XPathVariableResolver interface in terms of its Object resolveVariable(QName variableName) method, and which tells the evaluator about the variable (or variables).

The variableName parameter contains the qualified name of the variable's name—remember that a variable name may be prefixed with a namespace prefix. This method verifies that the qualified name appropriately names the variable and then returns its value.

After creating the variable resolver, you register it with the XPath instance by calling XPath's void setXPathVariableResolver(XPathVariableResolver resolver) method.

The following example demonstrates all these tasks to specify $d in XPath expression /a/b[@c=$d]/text(), which returns b1 followed by b5. It assumes that Listing 10-27 is stored in a file named example.xml:

```
DocumentBuilderFactory dbf = DocumentBuilderFactory.newInstance();
DocumentBuilder db = dbf.newDocumentBuilder();
Document doc = db.parse("example.xml");
XPathFactory xpf = XPathFactory.newInstance();
XPath xp = xpf.newXPath();
XPathVariableResolver xpvr;
xpvr = new XPathVariableResolver()
      {
          @Override
          public Object resolveVariable(QName varname)
          {
             if (varname.getLocalPart().equals("d"))
                return "x";
             else
                return null;
          }
      };
xp.setXPathVariableResolver(xpvr);
XPathExpression xpe;
xpe = xp.compile("/a/b[@c=$d]/text()");
Object result = xpe.evaluate(doc, XPathConstants.NODESET);
NodeList nl = (NodeList) result;
for (int i = 0; i < nl.getLength(); i++)
   System.out.println(nl.item(i).getNodeValue());
```

■ **Caution** When you qualify a variable name with a namespace prefix (as in $ns:d), you must also register a namespace context to resolve the prefix.

Transforming XML Documents with XSLT

Extensible Stylesheet Language (XSL) is a family of languages for transforming and formatting XML documents. *XSL Transformation (XSLT)* is the XSL language for transforming XML documents to other formats, such as HTML (for presenting an XML document's content via a web browser).

XSLT accomplishes its work by using XSLT processors and stylesheets. An *XSLT processor* is a software component that applies an *XSLT stylesheet* (an XML-based *template* consisting of content and transformation instructions) to an input document (without modifying the document), and copies the transformed result to a *result tree*, which can be output to a file or output stream, or even piped into another XSLT processor for additional transformations. Figure 10-3 illustrates the transformation process.

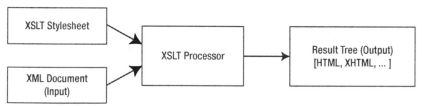

Figure 10-3. *An XSLT processor transforms an XML input document into a result tree.*

The beauty of XSLT is that you don't need to develop custom software applications to perform the transformations. Instead, you simply create an XSLT stylesheet and input it along with the XML document needing to be transformed to an XSLT processor.

This section first introduces you to Java's XSLT API. It then presents two demonstrations of XSLT's usefulness.

Exploring the XSLT API

Java implements XSLT through the types found in the javax.xml.transform, javax.xml.transform.dom, javax.xml.transform.sax, javax.xml.transform.stax, and javax.xml.transform.stream packages. The javax.xml.transform package defines the generic APIs for processing transformation instructions, and for performing a transformation from a *source* (where the XSLT processor's input originates) to a *result* (where the processor's output is sent). The remaining packages define the APIs for obtaining different kinds of sources and results.

The javax.xml.transform.TransformerFactory class is the starting point for working with XSLT. You instantiate TransformerFactory by calling one its newInstance() methods. The following example uses TransformerFactory's static TransformerFactory newInstance() method to create the factory:

TransformerFactory tf = TransformerFactory.newInstance();

Behind the scenes, newInstance() follows an ordered lookup procedure to identify the TransformerFactory implementation class to load. This procedure first examines the javax.xml.transform.TransformerFactory system property, and lastly chooses the Java platform's default TransformerFactory implementation class when no other class is found. If an implementation class is not available (perhaps the class identified by the javax.xml.transform.TransformerFactory system property doesn't exist) or cannot be instantiated, newInstance() throws an instance of the javax.xml.transform.TransformerFactoryConfigurationError class. Otherwise, it instantiates the class and returns its instance.

After obtaining a TransformerFactory instance, you can call various configuration methods to configure the factory. For example, you could call TransformerFactory's void setFeature(String name, boolean value) method to enable a feature (such as secure processing, to transform XML documents securely).

Following the factory's configuration, call one of its newTransformer() methods to create and return instances of the javax.xml.transform.Transformer class. The following example calls Transformer newTransformer() to accomplish this task:

```
Transformer t = tf.newTransformer();
```

The noargument newTransformer() method copies source input to the destination without making any changes. This kind of transformation is known as the *identity transformation*.

To change input, you need to specify a stylesheet, and you accomplish this task by calling the factory's Transformer newTransformer(Source source) method, where the javax.xml.transform.Source interface describes a source for the stylesheet. The following example demonstrates this task:

```
Transformer t = tf.newTransformer(new StreamSource(new FileReader("recipe.xsl")));
```

This example creates a transformer that obtains a stylesheet from a file named recipe.xsl via a javax.xml.transform.stream.StreamSource instance connected to a file reader. It is customary to use the .xsl or .xslt extension to identify XSLT stylesheet files.

The newTransformer() methods throw TransformerConfigurationException when they cannot return a Transformer instance that corresponds to the factory configuration.

After obtaining a Transformer instance, you can call its void setOutputProperty(String name, String value) method to influence a transformation. The javax.xml.transform.OutputKeys class declares constants for frequently used keys. For example, OutputKeys.METHOD is the key for specifying the method for outputting the result tree (as XML, HTML, plain text, or something else).

Tip To set multiple properties in a single method call, create a java.util.Properties object and pass this object as an argument to Transformer's void setOutputProperties(Properties prop) method. Properties set by setOutputProperty() and setOutputProperties() override the stylesheet's xsl:output instruction settings.

Before you can perform a transformation, you need to obtain instances of classes that implement the Source and javax.xml.transform.Result interfaces. You then pass these instances to Transformer's void transform(Source xmlSource, Result outputTarget) method, which throws an instance of the javax.xml.transform.TransformerException class when a problem arises during the transformation.

The following example shows you how to obtain a source and a result, and perform the transformation:

```
Source source = new DOMSource(doc);
Result result = new StreamResult(System.out);
t.transform(source, result);
```

The first line instantiates the javax.xml.transform.dom.DOMSource class, which acts as a holder for a DOM tree rooted in the Document object specified by doc. The second line instantiates the javax.xml.transform.stream.StreamResult class, which acts as a holder for the standard output stream, to which transformed data is sent. The third line reads data from the Source instance and outputs transformed data to the Result instance.

Tip Although Java's default transformers support the various Source and Result implementation classes located in the javax.xml.transform.dom, javax.xml.transform.sax, javax.xml.transform.stax, and javax.xml.transform.stream packages, a nondefault transformer (perhaps specified via the javax.xml.transform.TransformerFactory system property) might be more limited. For this reason, each Source and Result implementation class declares a FEATURE string constant that can be passed to TransformerFactory's boolean getFeature(String name) method. This method returns true when the Source or Result implementation class is supported. For example, tf.getFeature(StreamSource.FEATURE) returns true when stream sources are supported.

The javax.xml.transform.sax.SAXTransformerFactory class provides additional SAX-specific factory methods that you can use, but only when the TransformerFactory instance is also an instance of this class. To help you make the determination, SAXTransformerFactory also declares a FEATURE string constant that you can pass to getFeature(). For example, tf.getFeature(SAXTransformerFactory.FEATURE) returns true when the transformer factory referenced from tf is an instance of SAXTransformerFactory.

Most JAXP interface instances and the factories that return them are not thread-safe. This situation also applies to transformers. Although you can reuse the same transformer multiple times on the same thread, you cannot access the transformer from multiple threads.

This problem can be solved for transformers by using instances of classes that implement the javax.xml.transform.Templates interface. The Java documentation for this interface has this to say: *Templates must be threadsafe for a given instance over multiple threads running concurrently, and may be used multiple times in a given session.* In addition to promoting thread safety, Templates instances can improve performance because they represent compiled XSLT stylesheets.

The following example shows how you might perform a transformation without a Templates object:

```
TransformerFactory tf = TransformerFactory.newInstance();
StreamSource ssStyleSheet = new StreamSource(new FileReader("recipe.xsl"));
Transformer t = tf.newTransformer(ssStyleSheet);
t.transform(new DOMSource(doc), new StreamResult(System.out));
```

You cannot access t's transformer from multiple threads. In contrast, the following example shows you how to construct a transformer from a Templates object so that it can be accessed from multiple threads:

```
TransformerFactory tf = TransformerFactory.newInstance();
StreamSource ssStyleSheet = new StreamSource(new FileReader("recipe.xsl"));
Templates te = tf.newTemplates(ssStylesheet);
```

```
Transformer t = te.newTransformer();
t.transform(new DOMSource(doc), new StreamResult(System.out));
```

The differences are the call to Transformerfactory's Templates newTemplates(Source source) method to create and return objects whose classes implement the Templates interface, and the call to this interface's Transformer newTransformer() method to obtain the Transformer instance.

Demonstrating the XSLT API

Listing 10-15 presents a DOMDemo application that creates a DOM document tree based on Listing 10-2's movie XML document. Unfortunately, it's not possible to use the DOM API to assign ISO-8859-1 to the XML declaration's encoding attribute. Also, it's not possible to use DOM to output this tree to a file or other destination. These problems can be overcome by using XSLT, as demonstrated in the following example:

```
TransformerFactory tf = TransformerFactory.newInstance();
Transformer t = tf.newTransformer();
t.setOutputProperty(OutputKeys.METHOD, "xml");
t.setOutputProperty(OutputKeys.ENCODING, "ISO-8859-1");
t.setOutputProperty(OutputKeys.INDENT, "yes");
t.setOutputProperty("{http://xml.apache.org/xslt}indent-amount", "3");
Source source = new DOMSource(doc);
Result result = new StreamResult(System.out);
t.transform(source, result);
```

After creating a transformer factory and obtaining a transformer from this factory, four output properties are specified to influence the transformation. OutputKeys.METHOD specifies that the result tree will be written out as XML, OutputKeys.ENCODING specifies that ISO-8859-1 will be the value of the XML declaration's encoding attribute, and OutputKeys.INDENT specifies that the transformer can output additional whitespace.

The additional whitespace is used to output the XML across multiple lines instead of on a single line. Because it would be nice to indicate the number of spaces for indenting lines of XML, and because this information cannot be specified via an OutputKeys property, the nonstandard "{http://xml.apache.org/xslt}indent-amount" property (property keys begin with brace-delimited URIs) is used to specify an appropriate value (such as 3 spaces). It's okay to specify this property in this example because Java's default XSLT implementation is based on Apache's XSLT implementation.

After setting properties, a source (the DOM document tree) and a result (the standard output stream) are obtained, and transform() is called to transform the source to the result.

Although this example shows you how to output a DOM tree, and also how to specify an encoding value for the XML declaration of the resulting XML document, the example doesn't really demonstrate the power of XSLT because (apart from setting the encoding attribute value) it performs an identity transformation. A more interesting example would take advantage of a stylesheet.

Consider a scenario where you want to convert Listing 10-1's recipe document to an HTML document for presentation via a web browser. Listing 10-28 presents a stylesheet that a transformer can use to perform the conversion.

Listing 10-28. An XSLT stylesheet for converting a recipe document to an HTML document

```
<?xml version="1.0"?>
<xsl:stylesheet version="1.0"
                xmlns:xsl="http://www.w3.org/1999/XSL/Transform">
<xsl:template match="/recipe">
<html>
   <head>
      <title>Recipes</title>
   </head>

   <body>
      <h2>
         <xsl:value-of select="normalize-space(title)"/>
      </h2>

      <h3>Ingredients</h3>

      <ul>
      <xsl:for-each select="ingredients/ingredient">
        <li>
           <xsl:value-of select="normalize-space(text())"/>
           <xsl:if test="@qty"> (<xsl:value-of select="@qty"/>)</xsl:if>
        </li>
      </xsl:for-each>
      </ul>

      <h3>Instructions</h3>

      <xsl:value-of select="normalize-space(instructions)"/>
   </body>
</html>
</xsl:template>
</xsl:stylesheet>
```

Listing 10-28 reveals that a stylesheet is an XML document. Its root element is stylesheet, which identifies the standard namespace for stylesheets. It's conventional to specify xsl as the namespace prefix for referring to XSLT instruction elements, although any prefix could be specified.

A stylesheet is based on template elements that control how an element and its content are converted. A template focuses on a single element that is identified via the match attribute. This attribute's value is an XPath location path expression, which matches all recipe child nodes of the root element node. Regarding Listing 10-1, only the single recipe root element will be matched and selected.

A template element can contain literal text and stylesheet instructions. For example, the value-of instruction in <xsl:value-of select="normalize-space(title)"/> specifies that the value of the title element (which is a child of the recipe context node) is to be retrieved and copied to the output. Because this text is surrounded by space and newline characters, XPath's normalize-string() function is called to remove this whitespace prior to the title being copied.

XSLT is a powerful declarative language that includes control flow instructions such as for-each and if. In the context of <xsl:for-each select="ingredients/ingredient">, for-each causes all the ingredient child nodes of the ingredients node to be selected and processed one at a time. For each node, <xsl:value-of select="normalize-space(text())"/> is executed to copy the content of the ingredient node, normalized to remove whitespace. Also, the if instruction in `<xsl:if test="@qty">` (`<xsl:value-of select="@qty"/>`) determines whether the ingredient node has a qty attribute, and (if so) copies a space character followed by this attribute's value (surrounded by parentheses) to the output.

■ **Note** There's a lot more to XSLT than can be demonstrated in this short example. To learn more about XSLT, I recommend that you check out *Beginning XSLT 2.0 From Novice to Professional* (http://www.apress.com/9781590593240), an Apress book written by Jeni Tennison. XSLT 2.0 is a superset of XSLT 1.0—Java 7 supports XSLT 1.0.

The following excerpt from an XSLTDemo application that's included with this book's code shows you how to write the Java code to process Listing 10-1 via Listing 10-28's stylesheet:

```
DocumentBuilderFactory dbf = DocumentBuilderFactory.newInstance();
DocumentBuilder db = dbf.newDocumentBuilder();
Document doc = db.parse("recipe.xml");
TransformerFactory tf = TransformerFactory.newInstance();
StreamSource ssStyleSheet;
ssStyleSheet = new StreamSource(new FileReader("recipe.xsl"));
Transformer t = tf.newTransformer(ssStyleSheet);
t.setOutputProperty(OutputKeys.METHOD, "html");
t.setOutputProperty(OutputKeys.INDENT, "yes");
Source source = new DOMSource(doc);
Result result = new StreamResult(System.out);
t.transform(source, result);
```

This excerpt reveals that the output method is set to html, and it also reveals that the resulting HTML should be indented. However, the output is only partly indented, as shown in Listing 10-29.

Listing 10-29. The HTML equivalent of Listing 10-1's recipe document

```
<html>
<head>
<META http-equiv="Content-Type" content="text/html; charset=UTF-8">
<title>Recipes</title>
</head>
<body>
<h2>Grilled Cheese Sandwich</h2>
<h3>Ingredients</h3>
<ul>
<li>bread slice (2)</li>
<li>cheese slice</li>
<li>margarine pat (2)</li>
</ul>
<h3>Instructions</h3>Place frying pan on element and select medium heat. For each bread slice,
smear one pat of margarine on one side of bread slice. Place cheese slice between bread slices
with margarine-smeared sides away from the cheese. Place sandwich in frying pan with one
```

margarine-smeared side in contact with pan. Fry for a couple of minutes and flip. Fry other side for a minute and serve.</body>
</html>

OutputKeys.INDENT and its "yes" value let you output the HTML across multiple lines as opposed to outputting the HTML on a single line. However, the XSLT processor performs no additional indentation, and ignores attempts to specify the number of spaces to indent via code such as t.setOutputProperty("{http://xml.apache.org/xslt}indent-amount", "3");.

Note An XSLT processor outputs a <META> tag when OutputKeys.METHOD is set to "html".

EXERCISES

The following exercises are designed to test your understanding of XML document creation and the SAX, DOM, StAX, XPath, and XSLT APIs:

1. Create a books.xml document file with a books root element. The books element must contain one or more book elements, where a book element must contain one title element, one or more author elements, and one publisher element (and in that order). Furthermore, the book element's <book> tag must contain isbn and pubyear attributes. Record Advanced C++/James Coplien/Addison Wesley/0201548550/1992 in the first book element, Beginning Groovy and Grails/Christopher M. Judd/Joseph Faisal Nusairat/James Shingler/Apress/9781430210450/2008 in the second book element, and Effective Java/Joshua Bloch/Addison Wesley/0201310058/2001 in the third book element.

2. Modify books.xml to include an internal DTD that satisfies Exercise 1's requirements. Use Listing 10-10's SAXDemo application to validate books.xml against its DTD (java SAXDemo books.xml -v).

3. Create a SAXSearch application that searches books.xml for those book elements whose publisher child elements contain text that equals the application's single command-line publisher name argument. Once there is a match, output the title element's text followed by the book element's isbn attribute value. For example, java SAXSearch Apress should output title = Beginning Groovy and Grails, isbn = 9781430210450, whereas java SAXSearch "Addison Wesley" should output title = Advanced C++, isbn = 0201548550 followed by title = Effective Java, isbn = 0201310058 on separate lines. Nothing should output if the command-line publisher name argument does not match a publisher element's text.

4. Create a DOMSearch application that is the equivalent of Exercise 3's SAXSearch application.

5. Create a ParseXMLDoc application that uses a StAX stream-based reader to parse its single command-line argument, an XML document. After creating this reader,

the application should verify that a START_DOCUMENT infoset item has been detected, and then enter a loop that reads the next item and uses a switch statement to output a message corresponding to the item that has been read: ATTRIBUTE, CDATA, CHARACTERS, COMMENT, DTD, END_ELEMENT, ENTITY_DECLARATION, ENTITY_REFERENCE, NAMESPACE, NOTATION_DECLARATION, PROCESSING_INSTRUCTION, SPACE, or START_ELEMENT. When START_ELEMENT is detected, output this element's name and local name, and output the local names and values of all attributes. The loop ends when the END_DOCUMENT infoset item has been detected. Explicitly close the stream reader followed by the file reader upon which it is based. Test this application with Exercise 1's books.xml file.

6. Modify Listing 10-20's contacts document by changing <name>John Doe</name> to <Name>John Doe</Name>. Because you no longer see John Doe in the output when you run Listing 10-22's XPathSearch application (you only see Bob Jones), modify this application's location path expression so that you see John Doe followed by Bob Jones.

7. Create a books.xsl stylesheet file, and a MakeHTML application with a similar structure to the application that processes Listing 10-28's recipe.xsl stylesheet. MakeHTML uses books.xsl to convert Exercise 1's books.xml content to HTML. When viewed in a web browser, the HTML should result in a web page that's similar to the page shown in Figure 10-4.

Advanced C++

ISBN: 0201548550
Publication Year: 1992

James O. Coplien

Beginning Groovy and Grails

ISBN: 9781430210450
Publication Year: 2008

Christopher M. Judd
Joseph Faisal Nusairat
James Shingler

Effective Java

ISBN: 0201310058
Publication Year: 2001

Joshua Bloch

Figure 10-4. Exercise 1's books.xml *content is presented via a web page.*

Summary

Applications often use XML documents to store and exchange data. Before you can understand these documents, you need to understand XML. This understanding requires knowledge of the XML declaration, elements and attributes, character references and CDATA sections, namespaces, and comments and processing instructions. It also involves learning what it means for a document to be well formed, and also what it means for a document to be valid in terms of DTDs and XML Schema-based schemas.

You also need to learn how to process XML documents via JAXP's SAX, DOM, StAX, XPath, and XSLT APIs. SAX is used to parse documents via a callback paradigm, DOM is used to parse and create documents from node trees, StAX is used to parse and create documents in stream-based or event-based contexts, XPath is used to search node trees in a more succinct manner than that offered by the DOM API, and XSLT (with help from XPath) is used to transform XML content to XML, HTML, or another format.

Now that you understand XML and the JAXP APIs for processing XML documents, you'll put this knowledge to good use in Chapter 11, where you learn about Java's support for web services.

Working with Web Services

Web services are popular and widely used, and Java supports their development. This chapter shows you how to use Java's web service development features to create your own web services and/or access web services created by others.

Chapter 11 first introduces you to the topic of web services, emphasizing the SOAP-based and RESTful categories. This chapter then reveals Java's support for web service development in terms of its web service-oriented APIs, annotations, and tools. You also learn about Java's lightweight HTTP server for deploying your web services to a simple web server and testing them in this environment.

Armed with a basic understanding of web services and Java's support for their development, you next learn how to develop SOAP-based and RESTful web services. For each web service category, you learn how to create and access your own web service, and then learn how to access an external web service.

Chapter 11 closes by presenting five advanced web service topics: accessing SOAP-based web services via the SAAJ API, installing a JAX-WS handler to log the flow of SOAP messages, installing a customized lightweight HTTP server to perform authentication, sending attachments to clients from a RESTful web service, and using dispatch clients with providers.

What Are Web Services?

No standard definition for web service has yet been devised because this term means different things to different people. For example, some people define web service as a web application; others define web service in terms of a protocol (e.g., SOAP) that's used by applications to communicate across the Web. Perhaps the best way to define web service is to first define this term's parts:

- *Web*: A huge interconnected network of resources, where a *resource* is a Uniform Resource Identifier (URI)-named data source such as a spreadsheet document, a digitized video, a web page, or even an application. These resources can be accessed via standard Internet protocols (e.g., HTTP or SMTP).

- *Service*: A server-based application or software component that exposes a resource to clients via an exchange of messages according to a *message exchange pattern* (MEP) —see http://en.wikipedia.org/wiki/Message_Exchange_Pattern. The *request-response* MEP is typical.

Given these definitions, we can define *web service* as a server-based application/software component that exposes a Web-based resource to clients via an exchange of messages. These messages may or may not be based on XML, and can be thought of as invoking web service functions and receiving invocation results. Figure 11-1 illustrates this message exchange.

Figure 11-1. *A client exchanges messages with a web service to access a resource.*

■ **Note** Web services are an implementation of *Service-Oriented Architecture (SOA)* —see http://www.xml.com/lpt/a/1292. Think of SOA as a set of design principles or a framework for implementing business logic as reusable services that can be combined in different ways to meet evolving business requirements. SOA is concerned with specification and is not concerned with implementation.

Web services can be classified as simple or complex. Simple web services don't interact with other web services; for example, a standalone server-based application with a single function that returns the current time for a specified timezone. In contrast, complex web services often interact with other web services. For example, a generalized social network web service might interact with Twitter and Facebook web services to obtain and return to its client all Twitter and all Facebook information for a specific individual. Complex web services are also known as *mashups* because they *mash* (combine) data from multiple web services.

THE RATIONALE FOR WEB SERVICES

Companies have historically relied on client/server systems where client applications communicate with server-based backend software through server-based middleware software sandwiched between them. Traditional middleware has been plagued by various problems such as being expensive to obtain and maintain, being unable to communicate with backend software and client applications across the Internet, and being inflexible.

Web services are a new form of middleware based on the Web and (typically) XML. They overcome these and other traditional middleware problems by being based on free and open standards, by their maintainability, by involving the Web, and by being flexible. For example, unlike traditional remote procedure call (RPC)-based middleware (see http://en.wikipedia.org/wiki/Remote_procedure_call for a brief introduction to RPC), which depends upon connections that are tightly coupled (and break easily when an application is modified, hence leading to maintenance headaches), RESTful web services (discussed later) rely on loosely coupled connections, which minimize the effects of application changes. A web service interface (often an XML file) offers an abstraction between client and server software, so that changing one of these components doesn't automatically require that the other component be changed. Maintenance costs are reduced, and reusability increases because the same interface makes it easier to reuse a web service in other applications.

Another benefit of web services is that they preserve a company's significant investment in legacy software. Instead of having to rewrite this software (which was typically written in various languages) from scratch to meet evolving business requirements (which can be a costly undertaking), this software can be exposed to clients via web services, which can be mashed with other web services to achieve these requirements in a cost-effective manner.

SOAP-Based Web Services

A *SOAP-based web service* is a widely used category of web service based on *SOAP*, an XML language for defining *messages* (abstract function invocations or their responses) that can be understood by both ends of a network connection. An exchange of SOAP messages is called an *operation*, which corresponds to a function call and its response, and which is depicted in Figure 11-2.

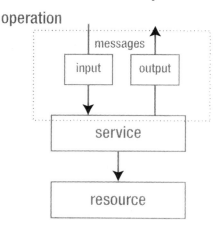

Figure 11-2. *A web service operation consists of input and output messages.*

Related operations are often grouped into an *interface*, which is conceptually similar to a Java interface. A *binding* provides concrete details on how an interface is bound to a messaging protocol (particularly SOAP) to communicate commands, error codes, and other items over the wire.

The combination of a binding and a *network address* (an IP address and a port) URI is known as an *endpoint*, and a collection of endpoints is a web service. Figure 11-3 illustrates this architecture.

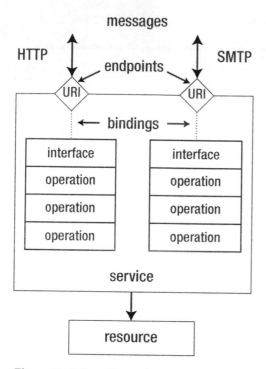

Figure 11-3. Interfaces of operations are accessible via their endpoints.

Although SOAP can be used by itself, as demonstrated later in this chapter's discussion of the SAAJ API, SOAP is typically used with *Web Services Description Language* (WSDL, pronounced whiz-dull), an XML language for defining the operations provided by the service. Unlike WSDL, SOAP, which once stood for Simple Object Access Protocol, is no longer considered to be an acronym. (SOAP is neither simple nor does it relate to objects.)

A *WSDL document* is a formal contract between a SOAP-based web service and its clients, providing all the details needed to interact with the web service. This document lets you group messages into operations and operations into interfaces. It also lets you define a binding for each interface as well as the endpoint address. You will explore WSDL document architecture while learning how to create a SOAP-based web service later in this chapter.

As well as supporting WSDL documents, SOAP-based web services have the following properties:

- *The ability to address complex nonfunctional requirements such as security and transactions*: These requirements are made available via a wide variety of specifications. To promote interoperability among these specifications, an industry consortium known as the *Web Services Interoperability Organization* (WS-I) was formed. WS-I has established a set of profiles, where a *profile* is a set of named web service specifications at specific revision levels, together with a set of implementation and interoperability guidelines recommending how the specifications may be used to develop interoperable web services. For example, the very first profile, WS-I Basic Profile 1.0, consists of the following set of nonproprietary web service specifications: SOAP 1.1, WSDL 1.1, UDDI 2.0, XML 1.0 (Second Edition), XML Schema Part 1: Structures, XML Schema Part 2: Datatypes, RFC2246: The Transport Layer Security Protocol Version 1.0, RFC2459: Internet X.509 Public Key Infrastructure Certificate and CRL Profile, RFC2616: HyperText Transfer Protocol 1.1, RFC2818: HTTP over TLS, RFC2965: HTTP State Management Mechanism, and The Secure Sockets Layer Protocol Version 3.0. Additional profile examples include WS-I Basic Security Profile and Simple SOAP Binding Profile. For more information on these and other profiles, visit the WS-I website at `http://www.ws-i.org/`. Java 7 supports the WS-I Basic Profile.

- *The ability to interact with a web service asynchronously*: Web service clients should be able to interact with a web service in a nonblocking, asynchronous manner. Client-side asynchronous invocation support of web service operations is provided in Java 7.

SOAP-based web services execute in an environment that includes a service requester (the client), a service provider, and a service broker. This environment is shown in Figure 11-4.

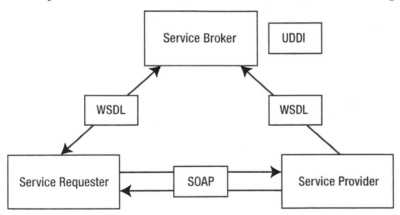

Figure 11-4. *A SOAP-based web service involves a service requester, a service provider, and a service broker (UDDI, for example).*

The service requester, typically a client application (e.g., a web browser), or perhaps another web service, first locates the service provider in some manner. For example, the service requester might send a WSDL document to a service broker, which responds with another WSDL document identifying the service provider's location. The service requester then communicates with the service provider via SOAP messages.

Service providers need to be published so that others can locate and use them. In August 2000, an open industry initiative known as *Universal Description, Discovery, and Integration* (UDDI) was launched to let businesses publish service listings, discover each other, and define how the services or software applications interact over the Internet. However, this platform-independent, XML-based registry was not widely adopted and currently isn't used. Many developers found UDDI to be overly complicated and lacking in functionality, and opted for alternatives such as publishing the information on a website. For example, Google makes its public web services (e.g., Google Maps) available through its http://code.google.com/more/ website.

The SOAP messages that flow between service requesters and service providers are often unseen, being passed as requests and responses between the SOAP libraries of their *web service protocol stacks* (see http://en.wikipedia.org/wiki/Web_services_protocol_stack). However, it's possible to access these messages directly, as you will discover later in this chapter.

Note SOAP-based web services are also known as *big web services* because they are based on many specifications, such as the WS-I profiles mentioned earlier.

RESTful Web Services

SOAP-based web services can be delivered over various protocols such as HTTP, SMTP, FTP, and the more recent Blocks Extensible Exchange Protocol —see http://www.rfc-editor.org/rfc/rfc3080.txt. Delivering SOAP messages over HTTP can be thought of as a special case of a RESTful web service.

Representational State Transfer (REST) is a software architecture style for distributed *hypermedia systems* (systems in which images, text, and other resources are located around networks and are accessible via hyperlinks). The hypermedia system of interest in a web services context is the World Wide Web.

Note Roy Fielding (one of the principal authors of the Hypertext Transfer Protocol [HTTP] specification versions 1.0 and 1.1, and cofounder of the Apache Software Foundation) introduced and defined REST in his doctoral dissertation back in 2000. (Fielding conceived REST as the architectural style of the Web, although he wrote it up long after the Web was a going concern.) REST is widely regarded as the solution to what is considered to be the growing complexity of SOAP-based web services.

The central part of REST is the URI-identifiable resource. REST identifies resources by their Multipurpose Internet Mail Extensions (MIME) types (such as text/xml). Also, resources have states that are captured by their representations. When a client requests a resource from a RESTful web service, the service sends a MIME-typed representation of the resource to the client.

Clients use HTTP's POST, GET, PUT, and DELETE verbs to retrieve representations of resources and to manipulate resources —REST views these verbs as an API and maps them onto the database Create, Read, Update, and Delete (CRUD) operations (see http://en.wikipedia.org/wiki/Create,_read,_update_and_delete for an introduction to CRUD). Table 11-1 reveals this mapping.

Table 11-1. *HTTP Verbs and Their CRUD Counterparts*

HTTP Verb	CRUD Operation
POST	Create new resource based on request data.
GET	Read existing resource without producing side effects (don't modify the resource).
PUT	Update existing resource with request data.
DELETE	Delete existing resource.

Each verb is followed by a URI that identifies the resource. (This immensely simple approach is fundamentally incompatible with SOAP's approach of sending encoded messages to a single resource.) The URI might refer to a collection, such as http://tutortutor.ca/library, or to an element of the collection, such as http://tutortutor.ca/library/9781430234135 —these URIs are only illustrations.

For POST and PUT requests, XML-based resource data is passed as the body of the request. For example, you could interpret POST http://tutortutor.ca/library HTTP/ 1.1 (where HTTP/ 1.1 describes the requester's HTTP version) as a request to insert POST's XML data into the http://tutortutor.ca/library collection resource.

For GET and DELETE requests, the data is typically passed as query strings, where a *query string* is that portion of a URI beginning with a "?" character. For example, where GET http://tutortutor.ca/library might return a list of identifiers for all books in a library resource, GET http://tutortutor.ca/library?isbn=9781430234135 would probably return a representation of the book resource whose query string identifies International Standard Book Number (ISBN) 9781430234135.

Note For a complete description of the mappings between HTTP verbs and their CRUD counterparts, check out the "RESTful Web Service HTTP methods" table in Wikipedia's "Representational State Transfer" entry (http://en.wikipedia.org/wiki/Representational_State_Transfer).

As well as relying on HTTP verbs and MIME types when making requests, REST relies on HTTP's standard response codes, such as 404 (requested resource not found) and 200 (resource operation successful), along with MIME types (when resource representations are being retrieved) for obtaining responses.

■ **Tip** If you are wondering about whether to develop a web service using SOAP or REST, check out "RESTful Web Services vs. "Big" Web Services: Making the Right Architectural Decision" (`http://www.jopera.org/files/www2008-restws-pautasso-zimmermann-leymann.pdf`).

Java and Web Services

Prior to Java 6, Java-based web services were developed exclusively with the Java EE SDK. Although Java EE is the preferred approach for developing web services from a production perspective, because Java EE-based servers provide a very high degree of scalability, a security infrastructure, monitoring facilities, and so on, the repeated deployment of a web service to a Java EE container is time consuming and slows down development.

Java 6 simplified and accelerated web services development by incorporating APIs, annotations, tools, and a lightweight HTTP server (for deploying your web services to a simple web server and testing them in this environment) into its core. Java 7 also supports these components.

ADDING WEB SERVICES SUPPORT TO CORE JAVA CONTROVERSY

Many people have argued that Sun Microsystems should never have added support for web services to Java 6. One criticism is that JAX-WS (the main web services API) encourages a bottom-up approach to building a web service —develop a Java class first and then develop the WSDL contract. In contrast, those who prefer a top-down approach believe that creating the WSDL and schemas first provides the best chance for interoperability (especially when technologies and platforms at both ends of the connection are different), because doing so encourages an interface-based design approach that provides maximum reuse and interoperability.

Davanum Srinivas states two additional criticisms in his "Why bundling JAX-WS in Java6 was a bad idea!" blog post (`http://blogs.cocoondev.org/dims/archives/004717.html`). First, he points out the need to rely on the *Java Endorsed Standards Override Mechanism* (see `http://download.oracle.com/javase/6/docs/technotes/guides/standards/`) to use a subsequent version of JAX-WS (with its new features and/or bug fixes). For example, Java 6 shipped with JAX-WS 2.0. To use its JAX-WS 2.1 successor, you would have to use the Java Endorsed Standards Override Mechanism as described in Vivek Pandey's "Webservices in JDK 6" blog post (`http://weblogs.java.net/blog/vivekp/archive/2006/12/webservices_in.html`). Srinivas's second complaint is that Java 6's web services implementation doesn't support WS-I profiles such as WS-Security.

Arun Gupta, a member of the Sun Microsystems team that integrated web services support into Java 6, counters these criticisms in his "Web services native support in Java6" blog post (`http://blogs.oracle.com/arungupta/entry/web_services_native_support_in`).

Web Service APIs

Java provides several APIs that support web services. In addition to the various JAXP APIs that I discussed in Chapter 10 (and which are also used apart from web services), Java provides the JAX-WS, JAXB, and SAAJ APIs:

- *Java API for XML Web Services (JAX-WS)*: The main API for building web services and clients (in Java) that communicate via XML. JAX-WS replaces the older Java API for Remote Procedure Call Web Services (JAX-RPC) API, and is assigned package javax.xml.ws and various subpackages. Java 7 supports JAX-WS 2.2.4.

- *Java Architecture for XML Binding (JAXB)*: The API for mapping XML Schema-based data types to Java objects and vice versa —see Chapter 10 to learn about XML Schema. JAX-WS delegates data-binding tasks to JAXB. This API is assigned package javax.xml.bind and various subpackages. Java 7 supports JAXB 2.2.4.

- *Soap with Attachments API for Java (SAAJ)*: The API for creating, sending, and receiving SOAP messages with/without attachments. According to Jitendra Kotamraju's "No SAAJ RI dependency in JAX-WS RI" blog post at http://weblogs.java.net/blog/jitu/archive/2007/09/no_saaj_ri_depe_1.html, JAX-WS's dependency on SAAJ for SOAP messages was removed in the reference implementation of JAX-WS 2.1.3 (known as *Metro*, see http://jax-ws.java.net/). This API is assigned the javax.xml.soap package. Java 7 supports SAAJ 1.3.

I will explore JAX-WS and SAAJ in this chapter, but (for brevity) won't be exploring JAXB. If you want a detailed tutorial on this API, I recommend that you check out the extensive JAXB tutorial located at http://jaxb.java.net/tutorial/.

Web Service Annotations

Java 6 introduced several web service annotation types that facilitate web service development, by letting you describe web services declaratively via metadata —see Chapter 3 for an introduction to annotations. You can still develop web services without these annotation types, but you'll soon appreciate their convenience if you decide not to use them.

Most web service annotation types are either part of the Web Services MetaData API (see http://jcp.org/en/jsr/detail?id=181), which is assigned packages javax.jws and javax.jws.soap, or belong to the javax.xml.ws package. The javax.jws package provides the following annotation types:

- HandlerChain associates the web service with an externally defined handler chain. I'll discuss handler chains from the client perspective later in this chapter.

- Oneway indicates that a given @WebMethod annotation has only an input message and no output message.

- WebMethod customizes a method that is exposed as a web service operation.

- WebParam customizes the mapping of an individual parameter to a WSDL message element's part element.

- WebResult customizes the mapping of the return value to a WSDL message element's part element.

- WebService marks a Java class as implementing a web service, or a Java interface as defining a service endpoint interface.

The following annotation types (three of which are deprecated in favor of using the HandlerChain annotation type) belong to the javax.jws.soap package:

- InitParam describes an initialization parameter (a name/value pair passed to the handler during initialization). This annotation type is deprecated.

- SOAPBinding specifies the mapping of the web service onto the SOAP protocol.

- SOAPMessageHandler specifies a single SOAP message handler that runs before and after the web service's business methods. This handler is called in response to SOAP messages targeting the service. This annotation type is deprecated.

- SOAPMessageHandlers specifies a list of SOAP protocol handlers that run before and after the web service's business methods. These handlers are called in response to SOAP messages targeting the service. This annotation type is deprecated.

Finally, javax.xml.ws's most important annotation types from a RESTful webservice perspective are WebServiceProvider and Binding. I will discuss these annotation types later in this chapter.

Web Service Tools

Java provides four command-line-based tools that facilitate web service development. Two of these tools are used to convert between XML Schema-based schemas (see Chapter 10) and Java classes, and the other pair of tools is used in the context of WSDL documents:

- schemagen: WSDL documents use XML Schema data types to describe web service function return and parameter types. This tool generates a schema (often stored in a file with a .xsd extension) from Java classes —one schema file is created for each referenced namespace. After the schema has been created, *XML instance documents* (XML documents that adhere to their schemas) can be converted to and from Java objects via JAXB. The classes contain all the information needed by JAXB to parse the XML for *marshaling* (converting Java objects to XML) and *unmarshaling* (converting XML to Java objects) —the application doesn't perform XML parsing.

- wsgen: This tool reads a compiled web service endpoint interface and generates JAX-WS portable artifacts for web service deployment and invocation. It can alternatively generate a WSDL file and corresponding XML Schema document (when its -wsdl option is specified). This tool isn't required when publishing a web service via Endpoint.publish(), which automatically generates the artifacts and WSDL/schema. You'll learn about Endpoint.publish() later in this chapter.

- wsimport: This tool generates client-support Java classes (artifacts) from a given WSDL document. These classes facilitate writing a client against the service.

- xjc: This tool generates Java classes from a schema. The generated classes contain properties mapped to the XML elements and attributes defined in the schema.

For brevity, I demonstrate only wsimport in this chapter. For demonstrations of schemagen and xjc, check out "Using JAXB schemagen tooling to generate an XML schema file from a Java class" (http://publib.boulder.ibm.com/infocenter/wasinfo/v7r0/index.jsp?topic=/com.ibm.websphere.expr ess.doc/info/exp/ae/twbs_jaxbjava2schema.html) and "Java Architecture for XML Binding (JAXB)" (http://www.oracle.com/technetwork/articles/javase/index-140168.html), respectively.

Lightweight HTTP Server

The Java 7 reference implementation includes a lightweight HTTP server for deploying and testing web services. The server implementation supports the HTTP and HTTPS protocols, and its associated API can be used to create a customized web server to enhance your web service testing or for other purposes.

The server's API is not a formal part of Java, which means that it's not guaranteed to be part of nonreference Java implementations. As a result, the lightweight HTTP server API is stored in the following packages instead of being distributed in packages such as java.net.httpserver and java.net.httpserver.spi:

- com.sun.net.httpserver: This package provides a high-level HTTP server API for building embedded HTTP servers.

- com.sun.net.httpserver.spi: This package provides a pluggable service provider API for installing HTTP server replacement implementations.

The com.sun.net.httpserver package contains an HttpHandler interface, which you must implement to handle HTTP request-response exchanges when creating your own HTTP server. This package also contains seventeen classes; the four most important classes are described in Table 11-2.

Table 11-2. Important Classes in com.sun.net.httpserver

Class	Description
HttpServer	Implements a simple HTTP server bound to an IP address/port number, and listens for incoming TCP connections from clients. One or more associated HttpHandlers process requests and create responses.
HttpsServer	An HttpServer subclass that provides support for HTTPS. It must be associated with an HttpsConfigurator object to configure the HTTPS parameters for each incoming Secure Sockets Layer (SSL) connection.
HttpContext	Describes a mapping between a root URI path and an HttpHandler implementation that is invoked to handle those requests targeting the path.
HttpExchange	Encapsulates an HTTP request and its response. An instance of this class is passed to HttpHandler's void handle(HttpExchange exchange) method to handle the request and generate a response.

Implementing your own lightweight HTTP server consists of three tasks:

1. Create the server. The abstract HttpServer class provides an HttpServer create(InetSocketAddress addr, int backlog) class method for creating a server that handles the HTTP protocol. This method's addr argument specifies a java.net.InetSocketAddress object containing an IP address and port number

for the server's listening socket. The backlog argument specifies the maximum number of TCP connections that can be queued while waiting for acceptance by the server; a value less than or equal to zero causes a system default value to be used. Alternatively, you can pass null to addr or invoke HttpServer's HttpServer create() class method to create a server not bound to an address/port. If you choose this alternative, you will need to invoke HttpServer's void bind(InetSocketAddress addr, int backlog) method before you can use the server.

2. Create a context. After creating the server, you need to create at least one context (an instance of a subclass of the abstract HttpContext class) that maps a root URI path to an implementation of HTTPHandler. Contexts help you organize the applications run by the server (via HTTP handlers). (The HttpServer Java documentation shows how incoming request URIs are mapped to HttpContext paths.) You create a context by invoking HttpServer's HttpContext createContext(String path, HttpHandler handler) method, where path specifies the root URI path, and handler specifies the HttpHandler implementation that handles all requests that target this path. If you prefer, you can invoke HttpContext createContext(String path) without specifying an initial handler. You would later specify the handler by calling HttpContext's void setHandler(HttpHandler h) method.

3. Start the server. After you have created the server and at least one context (including a suitable handler), the final task is to start the server. Accomplish this task by calling HttpServer's void start() method.

I've created a minimal HTTP server application that demonstrates all three tasks. This application's source code appears in Listing 11-1.

Listing 11-1. *A minimal HTTP server application*

```java
import java.io.IOException;
import java.io.OutputStream;

import java.net.InetSocketAddress;

import java.util.List;
import java.util.Map;
import java.util.Set;

import com.sun.net.httpserver.Headers;
import com.sun.net.httpserver.HttpExchange;
import com.sun.net.httpserver.HttpHandler;
import com.sun.net.httpserver.HttpServer;

class MinimalHTTPServer
{
    public static void main(String[] args) throws IOException
    {
        HttpServer server = HttpServer.create(new InetSocketAddress(8000), 0);
        server.createContext("/echo", new Handler());
        server.start();
```

```
   }
}
class Handler implements HttpHandler
{
   @Override
   public void handle(HttpExchange xchg) throws IOException
   {
      Headers headers = xchg.getRequestHeaders();
      Set<Map.Entry<String, List<String>>> entries = headers.entrySet();
      StringBuffer response = new StringBuffer();
      for (Map.Entry<String, List<String>> entry: entries)
         response.append(entry.toString()+"\n");
      xchg.sendResponseHeaders(200, response.length());
      OutputStream os = xchg.getResponseBody();
      os.write(response.toString().getBytes());
      os.close();
   }
}
```

The handler demonstrates the following HttpExchange abstract methods:

- Headers getRequestHeaders() returns an immutable map of an HTTP request's headers.

- void sendResponseHeaders(int rCode, long responseLength) begins to send a response back to the client using the current set of response headers and rCode's numeric code; 200 indicates success.

- OutputStream getResponseBody() returns an output stream to which the response's body is output. This method must be called after calling sendResponseHeaders().

Collectively, these methods are used to echo an incoming request's headers back to the client. Figure 11-5 shows these headers after is sent to the server. Don't forget that placing any path items before echo results in a 404 Not Found page.

Figure 11-5. Echoing an incoming request's headers back to the client.

Before invoking start(), you can specify a java.util.concurrent.Executor instance (see Chapter 6) that handles all HTTP requests. This task is accomplished by calling HttpServer's void setExecutor(Executor executor) method. You can also call Executor getExecutor() to return the current executor (the return value is null when no executor has been set). If you do not call setExecutor() before starting the server, or if you pass null to this method, a default implementation based on the thread created by start() is used.

You can stop a started server by invoking HttpServer's void stop(int delay) method. This method closes the listening socket and prevents any queued exchanges from being processed. It then blocks until all current exchange handlers have finished or delay seconds have elapsed (whichever comes first). An instance of the java.lang.IllegalArgumentException class is thrown when delay is less than zero. Continuing, all open TCP connections are closed, and the thread created by the start() method finishes. A stopped HttpServer cannot be restarted.

Most of this chapter's examples rely on the default lightweight HTTP server that's created whenever you call one of javax.xml.ws.EndPoint class's publish() methods. However, I'll also show you how to create and install a custom lightweight HTTP server to perform authentication later in this chapter.

Working with SOAP-Based Web Services

JAX-WS supports SOAP-based web services. This section first shows you how to create and access your own SOAP-based temperature-conversion web service, publish this web service locally via the default lightweight HTTP server, and access the service via a simple client. It then shows you how to access the Sloan Digital Sky Survey's SOAP-based image cutout web service to obtain astronomy images.

Creating and Accessing a Temperature-Conversion Web Service

The temperature-conversion web service, which I've named TempVerter, consists of a pair of functions for converting degrees Fahrenheit to degrees Celsius and vice versa. Although this example could be architected as a single Java class, I've chosen to follow best practices by architecting it as a Java interface and a Java class. Listing 11-2 presents the web service's TempVerter interface.

Listing 11-2. TempVerter's Service Endpoint Interface

```
package ca.tutortutor.tv;

import javax.jws.WebMethod;
import javax.jws.WebService;

@WebService
public interface TempVerter
{
    @WebMethod double c2f(double degrees);
    @WebMethod double f2c(double degrees);
}
```

TempVerter describes a *Service Endpoint Interface (SEI)*, which is a Java interface that exposes a web service interface's operations in terms of abstract Java methods. Clients communicate with SOAP-based web services via their SEIs.

TempVerter is declared to be an SEI via the @WebService annotation. When a Java interface or class is annotated @WebService, all public methods whose parameters, return values, and declared exceptions follow the rules defined in Section 5 of the JAX-RPC 1.1 specification (http://download.oracle.com/otndocs/jcp/jax_rpc-1_1-mrel-oth-JSpec/) describe web service operations. Because only public methods can be declared in interfaces, the public reserved word isn't necessary when declaring c2f() and f2c(). These methods are implicitly public.

Each of c2f() and f2c() is also annotated @WebMethod. Although @WebMethod is not essential in this example, its presence reinforces the fact that the annotated method exposes a web service operation.

Listing 11-3 presents the web service's TempVerterImpl class.

Listing 11-3. *TempVerter's Service Implementation Bean*

```
package ca.tutortutor.tv;

import javax.jws.WebService;

@WebService(endpointInterface = "ca.tutortutor.tv.TempVerter")
public class TempVerterImpl implements TempVerter
{
   public double c2f(double degrees)
   {
      return degrees*9.0/5.0+32;
   }
   public double f2c(double degrees)
   {
      return (degrees-32)*5.0/9.0;
   }
}
```

TempVerterImpl describes a *Service Implementation Bean (SIB)*, which provides an implementation of the SEI. This class is declared to be a SIB via the @WebService(endpointInterface = "ca.tutortutor.tv.TempVerter") annotation. The endpointInterface element connects this SIB to its SEI, and is necessary to avoid undefined port type errors when running the client application presented later.

The implements TempVerter clause isn't absolutely necessary. If this clause is not present, the TempVerter interface is ignored (and is redundant). However, it's a good idea to keep implements TempVerter so the compiler can verify that the SEI's methods have been implemented in the SIB.

The SIB's method headers aren't annotated @WebMethod because this annotation is typically used in the context of the SEI. However, if you were to add a public method (which conforms to the rules in Section 5 of the JAX-RPC 1.1 specification) to the SIB, and if this method doesn't expose a web service operation, you would annotate the method header @WebMethod(exclude = true). By assigning true to @WebMethod's exclude element, you prevent that method from being associated with an operation.

This web service is ready to be published so that it can be accessed from clients. Listing 11-4 presents a TempVerterPublisher application that accomplishes this task in the context of the default lightweight HTTP server.

Listing 11-4. *Publishing TempVerter*

```
import javax.xml.ws.Endpoint;

import ca.tutortutor.tv.TempVerterImpl;

class TempVerterPublisher
{
   public static void main(String[] args)
```

```
    {
        Endpoint.publish("http://localhost:9901/TempVerter",
                         new TempVerterImpl());
    }
}
```

Publishing the web service involves making a single call to the EndPoint class's Endpoint publish(String address, Object implementor) class method. The address parameter identifies the URI assigned to the web service. I've chosen to publish this web service on the local host by specifying localhost (equivalent to IP address 127.0.0.1) and port number 9901 (which is most likely available). Also, I've arbitrarily choosen /TempVerter as the publication path. The implementor parameter identifies an instance of TempVerter's SIB.

The publish() method creates and publishes an endpoint for the specified implementor object at the given address, and uses the implementor's annotations to create WSDL and XML Schema documents. It causes the necessary server infrastructure to be created and configured by the JAX-WS implementation based on some default configuration. Furthermore, this method causes the application to run indefinitely. (On Windows machines, press the Ctrl and C keys simultaneously to terminate the application.)

Assuming that the current directory contains TempVerterPublisher.java and a ca subdirectory (containing a tutortutor subdirectory, containing a tv subdirectory, containing TempVerter.java and TempVerterImpl.java), execute javac TempVerterPublisher.java to compile this source file along with Listings 11-2 and 11-3.

■ **Tip** The javac compiler tool provides a -d option that you can use to specify the directory where you want to place generated classfiles. That way, you don't mix source files with classfiles.

If the source code compiles successfully, execute java TempVerterPublisher to run this application. You should see no messages and the application should not return to the command prompt.

You can use a web browser to test this web service and access its WSDL document. Start your favorite web browser and enter **http://localhost:9901/TempVerter** in its address bar. Figure 11-6 shows the resulting web page in the Mozilla Firefox web browser.

Figure 11-6. TempVerter's web page provides detailed information on the published web service.

Figure 11-6 presents the web service endpoint's qualified service and port names. (Notice that the package name has been inverted —tv.tutortutor.ca instead of ca.tutortutor.tv). A client uses these names to access the service.

Figure 11-6 also presents the address URI of the web service, the location of the web service's WSDL document (the web service URI suffixed by the ?wsdl query string), and the package-qualified name of the web service implementation class. The WSDL document's location is presented as a link, which you can click to view this document —see Listing 11-5.

Listing 11-5. TempVerter's WSDL document

```
<?xml version="1.0" encoding="UTF-8"?>
<definitions targetNamespace="http://tv.tutortutor.ca/" name="TempVerterImplService">
   <types>
      <xsd:schema>
         <xsd:import namespace="http://tv.tutortutor.ca/"◄
schemaLocation="http://localhost:9901/TempVerter?xsd=1"/>
      </xsd:schema>
   </types>
   <message name="c2f">
      <part name="parameters" element="tns:c2f"/>
   </message>
   <message name="c2fResponse">
      <part name="parameters" element="tns:c2fResponse"/>
   </message>
   <message name="f2c">
      <part name="parameters" element="tns:f2c"/>
   </message>
```

```
    <message name="f2cResponse">
        <part name="parameters" element="tns:f2cResponse"/>
    </message>
    <portType name="TempVerter">
        <operation name="c2f">
            <input wsam:Action="http://tv.tutortutor.ca/TempVerter/c2fRequest"↵
message="tns:c2f"/>
            <output wsam:Action="http://tv.tutortutor.ca/TempVerter/c2fResponse"↵
message="tns:c2fResponse"/>
        </operation>
        <operation name="f2c">
            <input wsam:Action="http://tv.tutortutor.ca/TempVerter/f2cRequest"↵
message="tns:f2c"/>
            <output wsam:Action="http://tv.tutortutor.ca/TempVerter/f2cResponse"↵
message="tns:f2cResponse"/>
        </operation>
    </portType>
    <binding name="TempVerterImplPortBinding" type="tns:TempVerter">
        <soap:binding transport="http://schemas.xmlsoap.org/soap/http" style="document"/>
        <operation name="c2f">
            <soap:operation soapAction=""/>
            <input>
                <soap:body use="literal"/>
            </input>
            <output>
                <soap:body use="literal"/>
            </output>
        </operation>
        <operation name="f2c">
            <soap:operation soapAction=""/>
            <input>
                <soap:body use="literal"/>
            </input>
            <output>
                <soap:body use="literal"/>
            </output>
        </operation>
    </binding>
    <service name="TempVerterImplService">
        <port name="TempVerterImplPort" binding="tns:TempVerterImplPortBinding">
            <soap:address location="http://localhost:9901/TempVerter"/>
        </port>
    </service>
</definitions>
```

A WSDL document is an XML document with a definitions root element, which makes a WSDL document nothing more than a set of definitions. The targetNamespace attribute creates a namespace for all user-defined elements in the WSDL document (such as the c2f element defined via the message element with this name). This namespace is used to distinguish between the user-defined elements of the current WSDL document and user-defined elements of imported WSDL documents, which are identified via WSDL's import element. In a similar fashion, the targetNamespace attribute that appears on an XML Schema-based file's schema element creates a namespace for its user-defined simple type elements, attribute elements, and complex type elements.

The name attribute identifies the web service and is used only to document the service.

■ **Note** The generated `<definitions>` tag is incomplete. A complete tag would include the default namespace, and namespaces for the soap, tns, wsam, and xsd prefixes, as follows: `<definitions name="TempVerterImplService" targetNamespace="http://tv.tutortutor.ca/" xmlns="http://schemas.xmlsoap.org/wsdl/" xmlns:soap="http://schemas.xmlsoap.org/wsdl/soap/" xmlns:tns="http://tv.tutortutor.ca/" xmlns:wsam="http://www.w3.org/2007/05/addressing/metadata" xmlns:xsd="http://www.w3.org/2001/XMLSchema">`. It appears that JAX-WS makes assumptions.

Nested within definitions are types, message, portType, binding, and service elements:

- types presents user-defined data types (used in the context of message elements) under a data type system. Although any type definition language can be used, XML Schema is mandated by the WS-I in Basic Profile 1.0. types can contain zero or more schema elements. This example has a single schema element, which imports an external schema. The types element is optional. It is not present when the service uses only XML Schema builtin simple types, such as strings and integers.

- message defines a one-way request or response message (conceptually a function invocation or an invocation response) that may consist of one or more parts (conceptually equivalent to function parameters or return values). Each part is described by a part element whose name attribute identifies a parameter/return value element. The element attribute identifies another element (defined elsewhere) whose value is passed to this parameter or which provides the response value. Zero or more part elements, and zero or more message elements may be specified.

- portType describes a web service interface via its operations. Each operation element contains input and/or output elements based on the MEP. Listing 11-5 includes both elements. (A fault element for communicating error information can be specified when there is an output element.) The wsam:Action attribute is used with message routing in the context of WS-Addressing —see http://en.wikipedia.org/wiki/WS-Addressing. The message attribute identifies the message element that describes the message via its name attribute (and also provides the part elements describing parameters and return value). operation elements are optional; at least one portType element must be specified.

- binding provides details on how a portType operation (such as c2f or f2c) is transmitted over the wire. This element's type attribute identifies the portType element defined earlier in the document. The nested soap:binding element indicates that a SOAP 1.1 binding is being used. Its transport attribute's URI value identifies HTTP as the transport protocol (SOAP over HTTP), and its style attribute identifies document as the default service style. Each operation element consists of soap:operation, input, and output elements. The soap:operation element is a SOAP extension element that provides extra binding information at the operation level. Servers (such as firewalls) can use the SOAPAction attribute's URI value (when present) to filter SOAP request messages sent via HTTP. The input and output elements contain soap:body elements whose use attributes indicate how message parts appear inside of SOAP's Body element —I present an overview of SOAP later in this chapter. The literal value means that these parts appear literally instead of being encoded. Multiple binding elements can be specified.

- service defines a collection of endpoints in terms of nested port elements that expose bindings —a port element's binding attribute identifies a binding element. Furthermore, the port element identifies the service's address; because we are dealing with a SOAP service, port contains a soap:address element whose location attribute specifies this address.

The types, message, and portType elements are abstract definitions of the web service's interface. They form the interface between the web service and an application. The binding and service elements provide concrete details on how this interface is mapped to messages transmitted over the wire. JAX-WS handles these details on behalf of the application.

STYLE AND USE

The soap:binding element's style attribute affects how a SOAP message's Body element is built by indicating whether the operation is document-oriented (messages contain documents) —the value is document —or RPC-oriented (messages contain parameters and return values) —the value is rpc. I discuss SOAP message architecture later in this chapter.

The soap:body element's use attribute indicates whether the WSDL document's message element's part child elements define the concrete schema of the message —the value is literal —or are encoded via certain encoding rules —the value is encoded.

When use is set to literal, each part element references a concrete schema definition using either the element or type attribute. For element, the referenced element will appear directly under the SOAP message's Body element (for document style bindings) or under an accessor element named after the message part (for rpc style bindings). For type, the referenced type becomes the schema type of the enclosing element (Body for document style or part accessor element for rpc style).

When use is set to encoded, each part element references an abstract type using the type attribute. These abstract types are used to produce a concrete message by applying an encoding specified by the SOAP message's encodingStyle attribute.

For more information on the style and use attributes, check out "Which style of WSDL should I use?" (http://www.ibm.com/developerworks/webservices/library/ws-whichwsdl/).

The types element's schema element identifies the location of the schema where each operation's return and parameter types are stored. The xsd:import tag's schemaLocation attribute identifies this location as http://localhost:9901/TempVerter?xsd=1. When you point your browser to this location, you observe Listing 11-6.

Listing 11-6. The WSDL document's referenced XML Schema document

```
<xs:schema version="1.0" targetNamespace="http://tv.tutortutor.ca/">
    <xs:element name="c2f" type="tns:c2f"/>
    <xs:element name="c2fResponse" type="tns:c2fResponse"/>
    <xs:element name="f2c" type="tns:f2c"/>
    <xs:element name="f2cResponse" type="tns:f2cResponse"/>
    <xs:complexType name="f2c">
        <xs:sequence>
            <xs:element name="arg0" type="xs:double"/>
        </xs:sequence>
    </xs:complexType>
    <xs:complexType name="f2cResponse">
        <xs:sequence>
            <xs:element name="return" type="xs:double"/>
        </xs:sequence>
    </xs:complexType>
    <xs:complexType name="c2f">
        <xs:sequence>
            <xs:element name="arg0" type="xs:double"/>
        </xs:sequence>
    </xs:complexType>
    <xs:complexType name="c2fResponse">
        <xs:sequence>
            <xs:element name="return" type="xs:double"/>
        </xs:sequence>
    </xs:complexType>
</xs:schema>
```

You might want to refer to Chapter 10 for a refresher on how an XML Schema document is formed. When you're finished, check out Listing 11-7's TempVerterClient.java source code, which shows you how a client accesses the TempVerter web service.

Listing 11-7. A client for accessing the TempVerter web service

```
import java.net.URL;

import javax.xml.namespace.QName;

import javax.xml.ws.Service;

import ca.tutortutor.tv.TempVerter;

class TempVerterClient
```

```
{
    public static void main(String[] args) throws Exception
    {
        URL url = new URL("http://localhost:9901/TempVerter?wsdl");
        QName qname = new QName("http://tv.tutortutor.ca/",
                                "TempVerterImplService");
        Service service = Service.create(url, qname);
        qname = new QName("http://tv.tutortutor.ca/", "TempVerterImplPort");
        TempVerter tv = service.getPort(qname, TempVerter.class);
//      TempVerter tv = service.getPort(TempVerter.class);
        System.out.println(tv.c2f(37.0));
        System.out.println(tv.f2c(212.0));
    }
}
```

TempVerterClient first creates a java.net.URL instance that identifies the web service's WSDL file. It then creates a javax.xml.namespace.QName instance that identifies the endpoint's qualified service name (see Figure 11-6). These instances are passed to the javax.xml.ws.Service class's Service create(URL wsdlDocumentLocation, QName serviceName) class method to return a Service instance that provides a client view of a web service.

Service's T getPort(QName portName, Class<T> serviceEndpointInterface) method is then called on the Service instance to return a proxy for communicating with the web service via its endpoint. The qualified name passed to portName identifies the endpoint's qualified port name (see Figure 11-6), which identifies the web service interface whose operations are to be accessed —there is only one interface in this example. The java.lang.Class instance passed to serviceEndpointInterface identifies the TempVerter SEI. This method returns a proxy object whose class implements TempVerter, or throws javax.xml.ws.WebServiceException when something goes wrong (such as when not specifying endpointInterface in the TempVerterImpl SIB's @WebService annotation, and calling Service's T getPort(Class<T> serviceEndpointInterface) method, which uses endpointInterface to access the SEI).

Assuming that getPort() succeeds, the returned object is used to invoke the c2f() and f2c() methods with arguments representing body temperature in degrees Celsius and the boiling point of water in degrees Fahrenheit, respectively.

Compile this class (via javac TempVerterClient.java, which assumes that the current directory contains this source file and a ca subdirectory, containing a tutortutor subdirectory, containing a tv subdirectory, containing Listing 11-2's TempVerter.java source file). If compilation succeeds, execute java TempVerterClient to run this application, which should generate the following output:

```
98.6
100.0
```

Because the WSDL document in Listing 11-5 and the XML Schema document in Listing 11-6 contain enough information to let clients communicate with the web service, you can alternatively use the wsimport tool to generate client-support code from this document, to facilitate creating the client. In the context of TempVerter, you would use this tool as follows:

```
wsimport -keep -p client http://localhost:9901/TempVerter?wsdl
```

wsimport outputs "parsing WSDL...", "Generating code...", and "Compiling code..." messages; and generates the classfiles that a client needs to access this web service. The -keep option causes wsimport to save the source code for these classfiles as well, which helps us learn how clients access the web service, and makes it possible to add client-side handlers for intercepting messages (discussed later in this chapter).

The -p option identifies the package directory in which to store the generated source and/or classfiles. You can specify any meaningful name (such as client) and wsimport will create a package directory with this name, and store the package directory structure underneath.

◾ **Caution** If you don't specify -p and the current directory contains TempVerter's package directory structure, Listing 11-2's TempVerter interface source code (and the classfile) will be overwritten with the contents of a generated TempVerter.java source file (and classfile).

Along with classfiles, wsimport stores TempVerter.java, TempVerterImplService.java, and other source files in the client directory. The former source file's Java interface declares the same methods as Listing 11-2's TempVerter SEI interface, but with c2F and f2C method names replacing c2f and f2c, to adhere to a JAXB naming convention where the first letter of each subsequent word in a method name is capitalized.

The latter file's class, which is presented in Listing 11-8, provides a noargument constructor for instantiating this class, and a getTempVerterImplPort() method that returns an instance of the generated TempVerter interface; the client executes the web service's operations on this instance.

Listing 11-8. A cleaned up service implementation class for accessing the TempVerter web service

```java
package client;

import java.net.MalformedURLException;
import java.net.URL;

import javax.xml.namespace.QName;

import javax.xml.ws.Service;
import javax.xml.ws.WebEndpoint;
import javax.xml.ws.WebServiceClient;
import javax.xml.ws.WebServiceException;
import javax.xml.ws.WebServiceFeature;

/**
 * This class was generated by the JAX-WS RI.
 * JAX-WS RI 2.2.4-b01
 * Generated source version: 2.2
 *
 */
@WebServiceClient(name = "TempVerterImplService",
                  targetNamespace = "http://tv.tutortutor.ca/",
                  wsdlLocation = "http://localhost:9901/TempVerter?wsdl")
public class TempVerterImplService extends Service
{
   private final static URL TEMPVERTERIMPLSERVICE_WSDL_LOCATION;
   private final static WebServiceException TEMPVERTERIMPLSERVICE_EXCEPTION;
   private final static QName TEMPVERTERIMPLSERVICE_QNAME =
      new QName("http://tv.tutortutor.ca/", "TempVerterImplService");
```

```java
static
{
   URL url = null;
   WebServiceException e = null;
   try
   {
      url = new URL("http://localhost:9901/TempVerter?wsdl");
   }
   catch (MalformedURLException ex)
   {
      e = new WebServiceException(ex);
   }
   TEMPVERTERIMPLSERVICE_WSDL_LOCATION = url;
   TEMPVERTERIMPLSERVICE_EXCEPTION = e;
}
public TempVerterImplService()
{
   super(__getWsdlLocation(), TEMPVERTERIMPLSERVICE_QNAME);
}
public TempVerterImplService(WebServiceFeature... features)
{
   super(__getWsdlLocation(), TEMPVERTERIMPLSERVICE_QNAME, features);
}
public TempVerterImplService(URL wsdlLocation)
{
   super(wsdlLocation, TEMPVERTERIMPLSERVICE_QNAME);
}
public TempVerterImplService(URL wsdlLocation, WebServiceFeature... features)
{
   super(wsdlLocation, TEMPVERTERIMPLSERVICE_QNAME, features);
}
public TempVerterImplService(URL wsdlLocation, QName serviceName)
{
   super(wsdlLocation, serviceName);
}
public TempVerterImplService(URL wsdlLocation, QName serviceName,
                             WebServiceFeature... features)
{
   super(wsdlLocation, serviceName, features);
}
/**
 *
 * @return
 *     returns TempVerter
 */
@WebEndpoint(name = "TempVerterImplPort")
public TempVerter getTempVerterImplPort()
{
   return super.getPort(new QName("http://tv.tutortutor.ca/",
                                  "TempVerterImplPort"), TempVerter.class);
}
/**
```

```
 *
 * @param features
 *      A list of {@link javax.xml.ws.WebServiceFeature} to configure on the
 *      proxy. Supported features not in the <code>features</code> parameter
 *      will have their default values.
 * @return
 *      returns TempVerter
 */
@WebEndpoint(name = "TempVerterImplPort")
public TempVerter getTempVerterImplPort(WebServiceFeature... features)
{
    return super.getPort(new QName("http://tv.tutortutor.ca/",
                         "TempVerterImplPort"), TempVerter.class, features);
}
private static URL __getWsdlLocation()
{
    if (TEMPVERTERIMPLSERVICE_EXCEPTION!= null)
    {
        throw TEMPVERTERIMPLSERVICE_EXCEPTION;
    }
    return TEMPVERTERIMPLSERVICE_WSDL_LOCATION;
}
}
```

TempVerterImplService extends the Service class to provide the client view of a web service. There are two items to note:

- The noargument constructor is equivalent to Listing 11-7's Service.create() method call.

- getTempVerterImplPort() is equivalent to Listing 11-7's getPort() method call.

Listing 11-9 presents the source code to a TempVerterClient class that demonstrates how a client can use TempVerter and TempVerterImplService to access the web service.

Listing 11-9. A simplified client for accessing the TempVerter web service

```
import client.TempVerter;
import client.TempVerterImplService;

class TempVerterClient
{
    public static void main(String[] args) throws Exception
    {
        TempVerterImplService tvis = new TempVerterImplService();
        TempVerter tv = tvis.getTempVerterImplPort();
        System.out.println(tv.c2F(37.0));
        System.out.println(tv.f2C(212.0));
    }
}
```

Assuming that the web service is running, and that the current directory contains TempVerterClient.java along with the client subdirectory, execute javac TempVerterClient.java to compile this source code. Then execute java TempVerterClient to run this application. If all goes well, you should observe the following output:

```
98.6
100.0
```

Accessing the Image Cutout Web Service

Although you can create and access your own SOAP-based web services, you might want to access SOAP-based web services created by others. For example, the Sloan Digital Sky Survey (http://www.sdss.org) makes available astronomical images from its image archive via its Image Cutout web service.

Image Cutout's operations are described by its WSDL document at http://casjobs.sdss.org/ImgCutoutDR5/ImgCutout.asmx?wsdl. For example, this WSDL document identifies an operation named GetJpeg for returning a JPEG image of an area of the night sky located in terms of right accension (see http://en.wikipedia.org/wiki/Right_ascension) and declination (see http://en.wikipedia.org/wiki/Declination) degree values.

Before you can write a Java application that lets you access this web service to obtain (and then display) arbitrary images, you need to create artifacts (in the form of Java classes) that let this application interact with the web service. You can generate these artifacts by executing the following wsimport command line:

```
wsimport -keep http://casjobs.sdss.org/ImgCutoutDR5/ImgCutout.asmx?wsdl
```

wsimport creates an org directory within the current directory. org contains an sdss subdirectory, which contains a skyserver subdirectory, which stores the generated classfiles. Furthermore, skyserver stores their source files (thanks to the -keep option).

The generated ImgCutout.java source file reveals a noargument ImgCutout constructor along with an ImgCutoutSoap getImgCutoutSoap() method. Furthermore, ImgCutoutSoap declares a public byte[] getJpeg(double ra, double dec, double scale, int width, int height, String opt) method that corresponds to the GetJpeg operation. Your application interacts with Image Cutout via this constructor and these methods.

The getJpeg() method's parameters are described here:

- ra and dec specify the center coordinates of the image in terms of right ascension and declination values, where each value is expressed in degrees.

- scale specifies a scaling value in terms of arcseconds per pixel. One arcsecond equals 1/1296000 of a circle.

- width and height identify the dimensions of the returned image.

- opt identifies a sequence of character codes for drawing over the image; for example, G (draw a grid over the image), L (label the image), and I (invert the image).

The getJpeg() method returns the image as an array of bytes. It never returns a null reference. When an error occurs, the method returns an image that presents the error message.

Given this information, you next need to figure out how to invoke getJpeg(). The following steps accomplish this task:

1. Import ImgCutout and ImgCutoutSoap from the org.sdss.skyserver package.

2. Instantiate ImgCutout.

3. Invoke getImgCutoutSoap() on the ImgCutout instance.

4. Invoke getJpeg() on the returned ImgCutoutSoap instance.

I've created a SkyView application that demonstrates these tasks. This application presents a Swing-based user interface for entering the values required by getJpeg(), and displays the resulting image. Listing 11-10 presents this application's source code.

Listing 11-10. A client for accessing the Image Cutout web service

```java
import java.awt.BorderLayout;
import java.awt.Dimension;
import java.awt.EventQueue;
import java.awt.FlowLayout;
import java.awt.GridLayout;

import java.awt.event.ActionEvent;
import java.awt.event.ActionListener;

import javax.swing.BorderFactory;
import javax.swing.ImageIcon;
import javax.swing.JButton;
import javax.swing.JFrame;
import javax.swing.JLabel;
import javax.swing.JOptionPane;
import javax.swing.JPanel;
import javax.swing.JTextField;

import org.sdss.skyserver.ImgCutout;
import org.sdss.skyserver.ImgCutoutSoap;

class SkyView extends JFrame
{
   final static int IMAGE_WIDTH = 300;
   final static int IMAGE_HEIGHT = 300;
   static ImgCutoutSoap imgcutoutsoap;
   SkyView()
   {
      super("SkyView");
      setDefaultCloseOperation(EXIT_ON_CLOSE);
      setContentPane(createContentPane());
      pack();
      setResizable(false);
      setVisible(true);
   }
   JPanel createContentPane()
   {
      JPanel pane = new JPanel(new BorderLayout(10, 10));
      pane.setBorder(BorderFactory.createEmptyBorder(10, 10, 10, 10));
      final JLabel lblImage = new JLabel("", JLabel.CENTER);
      lblImage.setPreferredSize(new Dimension(IMAGE_WIDTH+9,
                                              IMAGE_HEIGHT+9));
```

```
lblImage.setBorder(BorderFactory.createEtchedBorder());
pane.add(new JPanel() {{ add(lblImage); }}, BorderLayout.NORTH);
JPanel form = new JPanel(new GridLayout(4, 1));
final JLabel lblRA = new JLabel("Right ascension:");
int width = lblRA.getPreferredSize().width+20;
int height = lblRA.getPreferredSize().height;
lblRA.setPreferredSize(new Dimension(width, height));
lblRA.setDisplayedMnemonic('R');
final JTextField txtRA = new JTextField(15);
lblRA.setLabelFor(txtRA);
form.add(new JPanel()
        {{
            add(lblRA); add(txtRA);
            setLayout(new FlowLayout(FlowLayout.CENTER, 0, 5));
        }});
final JLabel lblDec = new JLabel("Declination:");
lblDec.setPreferredSize(new Dimension(width, height));
lblDec.setDisplayedMnemonic('D');
final JTextField txtDec = new JTextField(15);
lblDec.setLabelFor(txtDec);
form.add(new JPanel()
        {{
            add(lblDec); add(txtDec);
            setLayout(new FlowLayout(FlowLayout.CENTER, 0, 5));
        }});
final JLabel lblScale = new JLabel("Scale:");
lblScale.setPreferredSize(new Dimension(width, height));
lblScale.setDisplayedMnemonic('S');
final JTextField txtScale = new JTextField(15);
lblScale.setLabelFor(txtScale);
form.add(new JPanel()
        {{
            add(lblScale); add(txtScale);
            setLayout(new FlowLayout(FlowLayout.CENTER, 0, 5));
        }});
final JLabel lblDO = new JLabel("Drawing options:");
lblDO.setPreferredSize(new Dimension(width, height));
lblDO.setDisplayedMnemonic('o');
final JTextField txtDO = new JTextField(15);
lblDO.setLabelFor(txtDO);
form.add(new JPanel()
        {{
            add(lblDO); add(txtDO);
            setLayout(new FlowLayout(FlowLayout.CENTER, 0, 5));
        }});

pane.add(form, BorderLayout.CENTER);
final JButton btnGP = new JButton("Get Picture");
ActionListener al;
al = new ActionListener()
    {
        @Override
```

```
            public void actionPerformed(ActionEvent e)
            {
               try
               {
                  double ra = Double.parseDouble(txtRA.getText());
                  double dec = Double.parseDouble(txtDec.getText());
                  double scale = Double.parseDouble(txtScale.getText());
                  String dopt = txtDO.getText().trim();
                  byte[] image = imgcutoutsoap.getJpeg(ra, dec, scale,
                                                       IMAGE_WIDTH,
                                                       IMAGE_HEIGHT,
                                                       dopt);
                  lblImage.setIcon(new ImageIcon(image));
               }
               catch (Exception exc)
               {
                  JOptionPane.showMessageDialog(SkyView.this,
                                                exc.getMessage());
               }
            }
         };
      btnGP.addActionListener(al);
      pane.add(new JPanel() {{ add(btnGP); }}, BorderLayout.SOUTH);
      return pane;
   }
   public static void main(String[] args)
   {
      ImgCutout imgcutout = new ImgCutout();
      imgcutoutsoap = imgcutout.getImgCutoutSoap();
      Runnable r = new Runnable()
                   {
                      @Override
                      public void run()
                      {
                         new SkyView();
                      }
                   };
      EventQueue.invokeLater(r);
   }
}
```

Listing 11-10 is largely concerned with creating SkyView's user interface. (Chapter 7 explains the classes and methods that are used in its construction.) Expressions such as new JPanel () {{ add (lblImage); }} are a convenient shorthand for subclassing javax.swing.JPanel via an anonymous class (see Chapter 3), creating an instance of the subclass panel, (for this example) adding the specified component to the panel via its object initializer, and returning the panel instance.

Assuming that the current directory contains SkyView.java and the org subdirectory, invoke javac SkyView.java to compile this application's source code. Following compilation, invoke java SkyView to run the application. Figure 11-7 shows what you will see when you specify the values that are shown in the figure's text fields.

Figure 11-7. Viewing an image of New Galatic Catalog (NGC) 5792, a spiral galaxy seen nearly edge-on. The bright red star is located in the Milky Way galaxy.

■ **Note** Check out the "Famous Places" page (`http://cas.sdss.org/dr6/en/tools/places/`) at the Sloan Digital Sky Survey/SkyServer website (`http://cas.sdss.org/`) to obtain the right ascension and declination values for various astronomical images.

Working with RESTful Web Services

JAX-WS also supports RESTful web services. This section first shows you how to create and access your own RESTful library web service, publish this web service locally via the default lightweight HTTP server, and access the service via a simple client. It then shows you how to access Google's RESTful Charts web service to obtain chart images corresponding to entered data values.

■ **Note** Java EE provides Java API for RESTful Web Services (JAX-RS) to simplify the creation of RESTful web services via various annotations. For example, @GET is a request method (HTTP verb) designator corresponding to the similarly named HTTP verb. The Java method annotated with this request method designator processes HTTP GET requests. Check out Chapter 19 "Building RESTful Web Services with JAX-RS" in the Java EE 6 Tutorial (see http://download.oracle.com/javaee/6/tutorial/doc/giepu.html) to learn about JAX-RS.

Creating and Accessing a Library Web Service

The library web service, which I've named Library, consists of the four HTTP operations that handle requests to delete a specific book (identified via its ISBN) or all books, get a specific book (identified via its ISBN) or the ISBNs of all books, insert a new book, or update an existing book. Listing 11-11 presents the web service's Library endpoint class.

Listing 11-11. Library's endpoint class

```
import java.beans.XMLDecoder;
import java.beans.XMLEncoder;

import java.io.BufferedInputStream;
import java.io.BufferedOutputStream;
import java.io.FileInputStream;
import java.io.FileOutputStream;
import java.io.IOException;
import java.io.StringReader;

import java.util.ArrayList;
import java.util.HashMap;
import java.util.Iterator;
import java.util.List;
import java.util.Map;
import java.util.Set;

import javax.annotation.Resource;

import javax.xml.transform.Source;
import javax.xml.transform.Transformer;
import javax.xml.transform.TransformerException;
import javax.xml.transform.TransformerFactory;

import javax.xml.transform.dom.DOMResult;

import javax.xml.transform.stream.StreamSource;
```

779

```java
import javax.xml.ws.BindingType;
import javax.xml.ws.Endpoint;
import javax.xml.ws.Provider;
import javax.xml.ws.ServiceMode;
import javax.xml.ws.WebServiceContext;
import javax.xml.ws.WebServiceProvider;

import javax.xml.ws.handler.MessageContext;

import javax.xml.ws.http.HTTPBinding;
import javax.xml.ws.http.HTTPException;

import javax.xml.xpath.XPath;
import javax.xml.xpath.XPathConstants;
import javax.xml.xpath.XPathExpressionException;
import javax.xml.xpath.XPathFactory;

import org.w3c.dom.NodeList;

@WebServiceProvider
@ServiceMode(value = javax.xml.ws.Service.Mode.MESSAGE)
@BindingType(value = HTTPBinding.HTTP_BINDING)
class Library implements Provider<Source>
{
   private final static String LIBFILE = "library.ser";
   @Resource
   private WebServiceContext wsContext;
   private Map<String, Book> library;
   Library()
   {
      try
      {
         library = deserialize();
      }
      catch (IOException ioe)
      {
         library = new HashMap<>();
      }
   }
   @Override
   public Source invoke(Source request)
   {
      if (wsContext == null)
         throw new RuntimeException("dependency injection failed on wsContext");
      MessageContext msgContext = wsContext.getMessageContext();
      switch ((String) msgContext.get(MessageContext.HTTP_REQUEST_METHOD))
      {
         case "DELETE": return doDelete(msgContext);
         case "GET"   : return doGet(msgContext);
         case "POST"  : return doPost(msgContext, request);
         case "PUT"   : return doPut(msgContext, request);
         default      : throw new HTTPException(405);
```

```java
      }
   }
   private Source doDelete(MessageContext msgContext)
   {
      try
      {
         String qs = (String) msgContext.get(MessageContext.QUERY_STRING);
         if (qs == null)
         {
            library.clear();
            serialize();
            StringBuilder xml = new StringBuilder("<?xml version=\"1.0\"?>");
            xml.append("<response>all books deleted</response>");
            return new StreamSource(new StringReader(xml.toString()));
         }
         else
         {
            String[] pair = qs.split("=");
            if (!pair[0].equalsIgnoreCase("isbn"))
               throw new HTTPException(400);
            String isbn = pair[1].trim();
            library.remove(isbn);
            serialize();
            StringBuilder xml = new StringBuilder("<?xml version=\"1.0\"?>");
            xml.append("<response>book deleted</response>");
            return new StreamSource(new StringReader(xml.toString()));
         }
      }
      catch (IOException ioe)
      {
         throw new HTTPException(500);
      }
   }
   private Source doGet(MessageContext msgContext)
   {
      String qs = (String) msgContext.get(MessageContext.QUERY_STRING);
      if (qs == null)
      {
         Set<String> keys = library.keySet();
         Iterator<String> iter = keys.iterator();
         StringBuilder xml = new StringBuilder("<?xml version=\"1.0\"?>");
         xml.append("<isbns>");
         while (iter.hasNext())
            xml.append("<isbn>"+iter.next()+"</isbn>");
         xml.append("</isbns>");
         return new StreamSource(new StringReader(xml.toString()));
      }
      else
      {
         String[] pair = qs.split("=");
         if (!pair[0].equalsIgnoreCase("isbn"))
            throw new HTTPException(400);
```

```java
            String isbn = pair[1].trim();
            Book book = library.get(isbn);
            if (book == null)
               throw new HTTPException(404);
            StringBuilder xml = new StringBuilder("<?xml version=\"1.0\"?>");
            xml.append("<book isbn=\""+book.getISBN()+"\" "+
                       "pubyear=\""+book.getPubYear()+"\">");
            xml.append("<title>"+book.getTitle()+"</title>");
            for (Author author: book.getAuthors())
               xml.append("<author>"+author.getName()+"</author>");
            xml.append("<publisher>"+book.getPublisher()+"</publisher>");
            xml.append("</book>");
            return new StreamSource(new StringReader(xml.toString()));
      }
   }
   private Source doPost(MessageContext msgContext, Source source)
   {
      try
      {
         DOMResult dom = new DOMResult();
         Transformer t = TransformerFactory.newInstance().newTransformer();
         t.transform(source, dom);
         XPathFactory xpf = XPathFactory.newInstance();
         XPath xp = xpf.newXPath();
         NodeList books = (NodeList) xp.evaluate("/book", dom.getNode(),
                                                 XPathConstants.NODESET);
         String isbn = xp.evaluate("@isbn", books.item(0));
         if (library.containsKey(isbn))
            throw new HTTPException(400);
         String pubYear = xp.evaluate("@pubyear", books.item(0));
         String title = xp.evaluate("title", books.item(0)).trim();
         String publisher = xp.evaluate("publisher", books.item(0)).trim();
         NodeList authors = (NodeList) xp.evaluate("author", books.item(0),
                                                   XPathConstants.NODESET);
         List<Author> auths = new ArrayList<>();
         for (int i = 0; i < authors.getLength(); i++)
            auths.add(new Author(authors.item(i).getFirstChild()
                                 .getNodeValue().trim()));
         Book book = new Book(isbn, title, publisher, pubYear, auths);
         library.put(isbn, book);
         serialize();
      }
      catch (IOException | TransformerException e)
      {
         throw new HTTPException(500);
      }
      catch (XPathExpressionException xpee)
      {
         throw new HTTPException(400);
      }
      StringBuilder xml = new StringBuilder("<?xml version=\"1.0\"?>");
      xml.append("<response>book inserted</response>");
```

```java
      return new StreamSource(new StringReader(xml.toString()));
   }
   private Source doPut(MessageContext msgContext, Source source)
   {
      try
      {
         DOMResult dom = new DOMResult();
         Transformer t = TransformerFactory.newInstance().newTransformer();
         t.transform(source, dom);
         XPathFactory xpf = XPathFactory.newInstance();
         XPath xp = xpf.newXPath();
         NodeList books = (NodeList) xp.evaluate("/book", dom.getNode(),
                                            XPathConstants.NODESET);
         String isbn = xp.evaluate("@isbn", books.item(0));
         if (!library.containsKey(isbn))
            throw new HTTPException(400);
         String pubYear = xp.evaluate("@pubyear", books.item(0));
         String title = xp.evaluate("title", books.item(0)).trim();
         String publisher = xp.evaluate("publisher", books.item(0)).trim();
         NodeList authors = (NodeList) xp.evaluate("author", books.item(0),
                                            XPathConstants.NODESET);
         List<Author> auths = new ArrayList<>();
         for (int i = 0; i < authors.getLength(); i++)
            auths.add(new Author(authors.item(i).getFirstChild()
                                 .getNodeValue().trim()));
         Book book = new Book(isbn, title, publisher, pubYear, auths);
         library.put(isbn, book);
         serialize();
      }
      catch (IOException | TransformerException e)
      {
         throw new HTTPException(500);
      }
      catch (XPathExpressionException xpee)
      {
         throw new HTTPException(400);
      }
      StringBuilder xml = new StringBuilder("<?xml version=\"1.0\"?>");
      xml.append("<response>book updated</response>");
      return new StreamSource(new StringReader(xml.toString()));
   }
   private Map<String, Book> deserialize() throws IOException
   {
      try (BufferedInputStream bis
              = new BufferedInputStream(new FileInputStream(LIBFILE));
           XMLDecoder xmld = new XMLDecoder(bis))
      {
         @SuppressWarnings("unchecked")
         Map<String, Book> result = (Map<String, Book>) xmld.readObject();
         return result;
      }
   }
```

```
private void serialize() throws IOException
{
   try (BufferedOutputStream bos
         = new BufferedOutputStream(new FileOutputStream(LIBFILE));
        XMLEncoder xmle = new XMLEncoder(bos))
   {
      xmle.writeObject(library);
   }
}
public static void main(String[] args)
{
   Endpoint.publish("http://localhost:9902/library", new Library());
}
}
```

Following various import statements, Listing 11-11 presents the Library class, which is prefixed with @WebServiceProvider, @ServiceMode, and @Binding annotations.

@WebServiceProvider specifies that Library is a web service endpoint class implementing the javax.xml.ws.Provider<T> interface (an alternative to an SEI for services that need to work at the XML message level) in terms of its T invoke(T request) method. The actual type argument passed to type parameter T identifies the source of request and reponse data, and is one of javax.xml.transform.Source, javax.activation.DataSource, or javax.xml.soap.SOAPMessage. For a RESTful web service provider, you would specify Source or DataSource for T.

■ **Note** Although you can process SOAP messages directly with a web service provider, it is common to ignore these messages by working with @WebService —annotated SEIs and SIBs, as previously discussed. Also, you can work with SOAP messages from an API perspective by using the SAAJ API, which I present later in this chapter.

When a request is made to the RESTful web service, the provider class's invoke() method is called with a source of bytes, such as a POST request's XML document. The invoke() method responds to the request in some appropriate way, returning a source of bytes in XML format that form the service's response. This method throws an instance of the WebServiceException runtime exception class or one of its descendent classes (e.g., javax.xml.ws.http.HTTPException) when something goes wrong.

■ **Note** A class annotated with @WebService exposes a separate method for each web service operation. For example, TempVerter exposes c2f() and f2c() methods for the Celsius-to-Fahrenheit and Fahrenheit-to-Celsius messages. In contrast, @WebServiceProvider exposes a single invoke() method to handle all operations.

@ServiceMode specifies that Library's invoke() method receives entire protocol messages (instead of message payloads) by having its value() element initialized to javax.xml.ws.Service.Mode.MESSAGE. When this annotation isn't present, value() defaults to javax.xml.ws.Service.Mode.PAYLOAD.

■ **Note** @ServiceMode isn't necessary in the context of a RESTful web service, where protocol messages and payloads are identical —I've included this annotation in Listing 11-11 to bring it to your attention. However, @ServiceMode would be necessary when working with SOAP messages (by implementing Provider<SOAPMessage>) and wanting to process the entire message instead of just the payload. You'll learn about SOAP message architecture later in this chapter when I introduce the SAAJ API.

@BindingType specifies that Library's invoke() method receives arbitrary XML messages over HTTP by having its value() element initialized to HTTPBinding.HTTP_BINDING —the default binding is SOAP 1.1 over HTTP. Unlike @ServiceMode, @BindingType must be specified with this initialization; otherwise, you'll receive a runtime exception when a RESTful client sends a nonSOAP request message to this web service provider.

Library first declares a LIBFILE constant that identifies the name of the file that stores information about the books in the library. I could have used JDBC to create and access a library database, but decided to use a file to keep Listing 11-11 from becoming longer.

This string constant is initialized to library.ser, where ser indicates that the file stores serialized data. The stored data is an XML encoding of a map that contains Book and Author instances —I'll present the map, discuss its encoding/decoding, and present these classes shortly.

The LIBFILE constant declaration is followed by a wsContext field declaration, where wsContext is declared to be of type javax.xml.ws.WebServiceContext and is annotated with @Resource. WebServiceContext is an interface that makes it possible for a web service endpoint implementation class to access a request message's context and other information. The @Resource annotation causes an implementation of this interface to be injected into an endpoint implementation class, and causes an instance of this implementation class (a dependency) to be assigned to the variable.

■ **Note** *Dependency injection* refers to the insertion of a class into another class and of objects of the inserted class to be inserted into a class instance. The inserted objects are known as *dependencies* because instances of the class in which these objects were inserted depend upon them. Dependency injection reduces class complexity by offloading developer tasks to a dependency injection framework.

A library field declaration follows the wsContext declaration, where library is declared to be of type Map<String, Book>. This variable stores books in a map, where a book's ISBN serves as a map entry's key, and the book's information is recorded in a Book object that serves as the map entry's value.

Library next declares a noargument constructor whose job is to initialize library. The constructor first attempts to deserialize library.ser's contents to a java.util.HashMap instance by calling the deserialize() method (explained later), and assign the instance's reference to library. If this file does not exist, java.io.IOException is thrown and an empty HashMap instance is created and assigned to library —note the use of Java 7's diamond operator to avoid having to respecify the map's java.lang.String and Book actual type arguments.

The invoke() method is now declared. Its first task is to verify that dependency injection succeeded by testing wsContext to determine if it contains the null reference. If so, dependency injection failed and an instance of the java.lang.RuntimeException class is created with a suitable message and thrown.

Continuing, invoke() calls WebServiceContext's MessageContext getMessageContext() method to return an instance of a class that implements the javax.xml.ws.handler.MessageContext interface. This instance abstracts the message context for the request being served at the time this method is called.

MessageContext extends Map<String, Object>, making MessageContext a special kind of map. This interface declares various constants that are used with the inherited Object get(String key) method to obtain information about the request. For example, get(MessageContext.HTTP_REQUEST_METHOD) returns a String object identifying the HTTP operation that the RESTful client wants performed; for example, POST.

At this point, you might want to convert the string's contents to uppercase and trim off any leading or trailing whitespace. I don't perform these tasks because the client that I present later will not allow an HTTP verb to be specified that isn't entirely uppercase and/or is preceded/followed by whitespace.

Java 7's switch-on-string language feature is used to simplify the logic for invoking the method that corresponds to the HTTP verb. The first argument passed to each of the doDelete(), doGet(), doPost(), and doPut() helper methods is the MessageContext instance (assigned to msgContext). Although not used by doPost() and doPut(), this instance is passed to these methods for consistency —I might want to access the message context from doPost() and doPut() in the future. In contrast, invoke()'s request argument is passed only to doPost() and doPut() so that these methods can access the request's source of bytes, which consist of the XML for the book to be inserted or updated.

If any other HTTP verb (such as HEAD) should be passed as the request method, invoke() responds by throwing an instance of the HTTPException class with a 405 response code (request method not allowed).

The doDelete() method first obtains the query string that identifies the book to delete via its ISBN (as in ?isbn=9781430234135). It does so by calling get(MessageContext.QUERY_STRING) on the msgContext argument passed to this method.

If the null reference returns, there is no query string and doDelete() deletes all entries in the map by executing library.clear(). This method then calls the serialize() method to persist the library map to library.ser, so that the next invocation of this web service will find an empty library.

If a query string was passed, it will be returned in the form *key1* = *value1* & *key2* = *value2* &.... doDelete() assumes that only a single *key* = *value* pair is passed, and splits this pair into an array with two entries.

doDelete() first validates the key as one of isbn, ISBN, or any other uppercase/lowercase mix of these letters. When this key is any other combination of characters, doDelete() throws HTTPException with a 400 response code indicating a bad request. This validation isn't essential where a single key is concerned, but if multiple key/value pairs were passed, you would need to perform validation to differentiate between keys.

After extracting the ISBN value, doDelete() passes this value to library.remove(), which removes the ISBN String object key/Book object value entry from the library map. It then calls serialize() to persist the new map to library.ser, and creates an XML response message that is sent back to the client. The message is returned from invoke() as a String object encapsulated in a java.io.StringReader instance that's encapsulated in a javax.xml.transform.stream.StreamSource object.

If doDelete() encounters a problem, it throws an HTTPException instance with response code 500 indicating an internal error.

The doGet() method is similar to doDelete(). However, it responds to the absence or presence of a query string by returning an XML document containing a list of all ISBNs, or an XML document containing book information for a specific ISBN.

The doPost() and doPut() methods also have similar architectures. Each method first transforms the argument passed to its source parameter (which identifies the XML body of the POST or PUT request) to a javax.xml.transform.dom.DOMResult instance. This instance is then searched via XPath expressions, first for a single book element, then for the <book> tag's isbn and pubyear attributes, and finally for the book element's nested title, author, and publisher elements —multiple author elements might be present. The gathered information is used to construct Author and Book objects, where the Author object(s) is/are stored in the Book object. The resulting Book object is stored in the library map, the map is serialized to library.ser, and a suitable XML message is sent to the client.

As well as providing a slightly different response message, doPost() and doPut() differ in whether or not the book is already recorded (as determined by its ISBN) in the map. If doPost() is called and an entry for the book is in the map, doPost() throws HTTPException with response code 400 (bad request). If doPut() is called and an entry for the book is not in the map, doPut() throws the same exception.

The doPut() method is followed by deserialize() and serialize() methods that are responsible for deserializing a serialized library map from library.ser and serializing this map to library.ser, respectively. These methods accomplish their tasks with the help of the java.beans.XMLDecoder and java.beans.XMLEncoder classes. According to their documentation, XMLEncoder and XMLDecoder are designed to serialize a JavaBean component to an XML-based textual representation and deserialize this representation to a JavaBean component, respectively.

JAVABEANS

JavaBeans is the Java architecture for creating self-contained and reusable components, which are known as *beans*. A bean is instantiated from a class that adheres to at least the following three conventions:

- The class must include a public noargument constructor.

- Each of the class's properties must include an accessor method prefixed by get or is (for a Boolean property) and a mutator method prefixed by set. The name of the property with the first letter uppercased must follow the prefix. For example, a String name; property declaration would include a String getName() accessor method and a void setName(String name) mutator method.

- Instances of the class must be serializable.

The first convention allows applications and frameworks to easily instantiate a bean, the second convention lets them automatically inspect and update bean state, and the third convention allows them to reliably store bean state to and restore bean state from a persistent store (such as a file).

JavaBeans was created so that visual editors could present palettes of Swing components (e.g., JList and JButton) that developers would access to quickly create graphical user interfaces. However, JavaBeans is applicable to any kind of component-oriented editor.

JavaBeans is also useful with *activation frameworks* that determine the type of an arbitrary piece of data, encapsulate access to the data, discover the available operations for the data, and instantiate the appropriate bean to perform those operations.

For example, if a Java-based browser obtained a JPEG image, the JavaBeans Activation Framework would enable the browser to identify that stream of data as a JPEG image. From that type, the browser could locate and instantiate an object for manipulating or viewing that image.

For more information on JavaBeans, check out the "JavaBeans Trail" in Oracle's online Java Tutorial (http://download.oracle.com/javase/tutorial/javabeans/TOC.html).

After creating the necessary output stream to library.ser and instantiating XMLEncoder via Java 7's try-with-resources statement (to ensure proper resource cleanup whether or not an exception is thrown), serialize() invokes XMLEncoder's void writeObject(Object o) method with library as this method's argument so that the entire map will be serialized. The deserialize() method creates the necessary input stream to library.ser, instantiates XMLDecoder, invokes this class's XMLDecoder's Object readObject() method, and returns the deserialized object returned from this method after casting it to Map<String, Book>.

Lastly, Listing 11-11 declares a main() method that publishes this web service on path /library of port 9902 of the local host, by executing Endpoint.publish("http://localhost:9902/library", new Library());.

For completeness, Listing 11-12 presents the Book class, whose beans store information about individual books.

Listing 11-12. Library's Book class

```
import java.util.List;

public class Book implements java.io.Serializable
{
   private String isbn;
   private String title;
   private String publisher;
   private String pubYear;
   private List<Author> authors;
   public Book() {} // Constructor and class must be public for instances to
                    // be treated as beans.
   Book(String isbn, String title, String publisher, String pubYear,
        List<Author> authors)
   {
      setISBN(isbn);
      setTitle(title);
      setPublisher(publisher);
      setPubYear(pubYear);
      setAuthors(authors);
   }
   List<Author> getAuthors() { return authors; }
   String getISBN() { return isbn; }
   String getPublisher() { return publisher; }
   String getPubYear() { return pubYear; }
   String getTitle() { return title; }
   void setAuthors(List<Author> authors) { this.authors = authors; }
   void setISBN(String isbn) { this.isbn = isbn; }
   void setPublisher(String publisher) { this.publisher = publisher; }
   void setPubYear(String pubYear) { this.pubYear = pubYear; }
   void setTitle(String title) { this.title = title; }
}
```

Book depends on an Author class, whose beans store the names of individual authors, and which is presented in Listing 11-13.

Listing 11-13. Library's Author class

```
public class Author implements java.io.Serializable
{
    private String name;
    public Author() {}
    Author(String name) { setName(name); }
    String getName() { return name; }
    void setName(String name) { this.name = name; }
}
```

Now that you understand how the Library web service is implemented, you need a client to try out this web service. Listing 11-14's LibraryClient.java source code demonstrates how a client can access the Library web service via the java.net.HttpURLConnection class.

Listing 11-14. A client for accessing the Library web service

```
import java.io.BufferedReader;
import java.io.InputStreamReader;
import java.io.OutputStream;
import java.io.OutputStreamWriter;

import java.net.HttpURLConnection;
import java.net.URL;

class LibraryClient
{
    final static String LIBURI = "http://localhost:9902/library";
    public static void main(String[] args) throws Exception
    {
        String book1 = "<?xml version=\"1.0\"?>"+
                       "<book isbn=\"0201548550\" pubyear=\"1992\">"+
                       "  <title>"+
                       "    Advanced C+"+
                       "  </title>"+
                       "  <author>"+
                       "    James O. Coplien"+
                       "  </author>"+
                       "  <publisher>"+
                       "    Addison Wesley"+
                       "  </publisher>"+
                       "</book>";
        doPost(book1);
        String book2 = "<?xml version=\"1.0\"?>"+
                       "<book isbn=\"9781430210450\" pubyear=\"2008\">"+
                       "  <title>"+
                       "    Beginning Groovy and Grails"+
                       "  </title>"+
                       "  <author>"+
                       "    Christopher M. Judd"+
                       "  </author>"+
```

```
                        "  <author>"+
                        "    Joseph Faisal Nusairat"+
                        "  </author>"+
                        "  <author>"+
                        "    James Shingler"+
                        "  </author>"+
                        "  <publisher>"+
                        "    Apress"+
                        "  </publisher>"+
                        "</book>";
      doPost(book2);
      doGet(null);
      doGet("0201548550");
      doGet("9781430210450");
      String book1u = "<?xml version=\"1.0\"?>"+
                        "<book isbn=\"0201548550\" pubyear=\"1992\">"+
                        "  <title>"+
                        "    Advanced C++"+
                        "  </title>"+
                        "  <author>"+
                        "    James O. Coplien"+
                        "  </author>"+
                        "  <publisher>"+
                        "    Addison Wesley"+
                        "  </publisher>"+
                        "</book>";
      doPut(book1u);
      doGet("0201548550");
      doDelete("0201548550");
      doGet(null);
   }
   static void doDelete(String isbn) throws Exception
   {
      URL url = new URL(LIBURI+((isbn != null) ? "?isbn="+isbn : ""));
      HttpURLConnection httpurlc = (HttpURLConnection) url.openConnection();
      httpurlc.setRequestMethod("DELETE");
      httpurlc.setDoInput(true);
      InputStreamReader isr;
      isr = new InputStreamReader(httpurlc.getInputStream());
      BufferedReader br = new BufferedReader(isr);
      StringBuilder xml = new StringBuilder();
      String line;
      while ((line = br.readLine()) != null)
         xml.append(line);
      System.out.println(xml);
      System.out.println();
   }
   static void doGet(String isbn) throws Exception
   {
      URL url = new URL(LIBURI+((isbn != null) ? "?isbn="+isbn : ""));
      HttpURLConnection httpurlc = (HttpURLConnection) url.openConnection();
      httpurlc.setRequestMethod("GET");
```

```
      httpurlc.setDoInput(true);
      InputStreamReader isr;
      isr = new InputStreamReader(httpurlc.getInputStream());
      BufferedReader br = new BufferedReader(isr);
      StringBuilder xml = new StringBuilder();
      String line;
      while ((line = br.readLine()) != null)
         xml.append(line);
      System.out.println(xml);
      System.out.println();
   }
   static void doPost(String xml) throws Exception
   {
      URL url = new URL(LIBURI);
      HttpURLConnection httpurlc = (HttpURLConnection) url.openConnection();
      httpurlc.setRequestMethod("POST");
      httpurlc.setDoOutput(true);
      httpurlc.setDoInput(true);
      httpurlc.setRequestProperty("Content-Type", "text/xml");
      OutputStream os = httpurlc.getOutputStream();
      OutputStreamWriter osw = new OutputStreamWriter(os, "UTF-8");
      osw.write(xml);
      osw.close();
      if (httpurlc.getResponseCode() == 200)
      {
         InputStreamReader isr;
         isr = new InputStreamReader(httpurlc.getInputStream());
         BufferedReader br = new BufferedReader(isr);
         StringBuilder sb = new StringBuilder();
         String line;
         while ((line = br.readLine()) != null)
            sb.append(line);
         System.out.println(sb.toString());
      }
      else
         System.err.println("cannot insert book: "+httpurlc.getResponseCode());
      System.out.println();
   }
   static void doPut(String xml) throws Exception
   {
      URL url = new URL(LIBURI);
      HttpURLConnection httpurlc = (HttpURLConnection) url.openConnection();
      httpurlc.setRequestMethod("PUT");
      httpurlc.setDoOutput(true);
      httpurlc.setDoInput(true);
      httpurlc.setRequestProperty("Content-Type", "text/xml");
      OutputStream os = httpurlc.getOutputStream();
      OutputStreamWriter osw = new OutputStreamWriter(os, "UTF-8");
      osw.write(xml);
      osw.close();
      if (httpurlc.getResponseCode() == 200)
      {
```

```
            InputStreamReader isr;
            isr = new InputStreamReader(httpurlc.getInputStream());
            BufferedReader br = new BufferedReader(isr);
            StringBuilder sb = new StringBuilder();
            String line;
            while ((line = br.readLine()) != null)
                sb.append(line);
            System.out.println(sb.toString());
         }
         else
            System.err.println("cannot update book: "+httpurlc.getResponseCode());
         System.out.println();
      }
   }
```

LibraryClient is partitioned into a main() method and four do-prefixed methods for performing DELETE, GET, POST, and PUT operations. main() invokes each "do" method to make a request and output a response.

A "do" method first instantiates the URL class; doDelete() and doGet() attach query strings to their URI arguments when these methods are called with nonnull isbn arguments. The method then invokes URL's URLConnection openConnection() method to return a communications link between the application and URL instance as an instance of a concrete subclass of the abstract java.net.URLConnection class. This concrete subclass is HttpConnection because of the http:// prefix in the argument passed to URL's constructor.

HttpURLConnection's void setRequestMethod(String method) is then called to specify the HTTP verb, which must appear in uppercase with no whitespace. Depending on the "do" method, either void setDoInput(boolean doinput) is called with a true argument, or void setDoInput(boolean doinput) and void setDoOutput(boolean dooutput) are called with true arguments, to signify that an input stream or input and output streams are required to communicate with the web service.

Each of doPost() and doPut() is required to set the Content-Type request header to text/xml, which it accomplishes by passing this header and MIME type to the void setRequestProperty(String key, String value) method. Forgetting to set the content type to text/xml causes the JAX-WS infrastructure to respond with an internal error response code (500).

doDelete() and doGet() read the XML from the connection's input stream and output this XML content to the standard output device. Behind the scenes, the JAX-WS infrastructure makes the string of characters encapsulated in the StringReader instance, which is encapsulated in the StreamSource instance returned from invoke(), available on the input stream.

doPost() and doPut() access the connection's output stream and output their XML content to the stream. Behind the scenes, JAX-WS makes this content available to invoke() as an instance of a class that implements the Source interface. Assuming that the web service responds with a success code (200), each method reads the XML reply from the connection's input stream and outputs this content to the standard output stream.

Compile Library.java (javac Library.java) and LibraryClient.java (javac LibraryClient.java). Run Library in one command window (java Library) and LibraryClient in another command window (java LibraryClient). If all goes well, LibraryClient should generate the following output:

```
<response>book inserted</response>
```

```
<response>book inserted</response>
```

```
<isbns><isbn>9781430210450</isbn><isbn>0201548550</isbn></isbns>
```

```
<book isbn="0201548550" pubyear="1992"><title>Advanced C+</title><author>James O.↩
Coplien</author><publisher>Addison Wesley</publisher></book>

<book isbn="9781430210450" pubyear="2008"><title>Beginning Groovy and↩
Grails</title><author>Christopher M. Judd</author><author>Joseph Faisal↩
Nusairat</author><author>James Shingler</author><publisher>Apress</publisher></book>

<response>book updated</response>

<book isbn="0201548550" pubyear="1992"><title>Advanced C++</title><author>James O.↩
Coplien</author><publisher>Addison Wesley</publisher></book>

<response>book deleted</response>

<isbns><isbn>9781430210450</isbn></isbns>
```

Run LibraryClient a second time and you should observe that the second <response>book inserted</response> message has been replaced with cannot insert book: 400. This message is output because the library map already contains an entry whose key identifies ISBN 9781430210450.

■ **Note** When you rerun LibraryClient and observe the cannot insert book: 400 message, you might also observe strange Library output. Specifically, you might notice a thrown exception whose first line begins with the date and time and continues with com.sun.xml.internal.ws.server.provider.SyncProviderInvokerTube processRequest, whose second line consists of SEVERE: null, and whose third line consists of javax.xml.ws.http.HTTPException. This strange output results from doPost() detecting an attempt to reinsert a book that has already been inserted, and then throwing HTTPException to Library's invoke() method, which is then thrown out of invoke() —it's legal to throw this exception out of invoke(), which is documented to throw WebServiceException (and HTTPException is a descendent of this class). When I first detected this problem, I contacted Oracle (a couple of days before Java 7 was to be released) and was told to submit a bug report. I submitted "Bug ID: 7068897 - Strange error when throwing HTTPException from Provider<Source> invoke() method" and this bug report remained for a couple of days before strangely disappearing. Perhaps I've experienced an anomaly peculiar to running Library on Windows XP Service Pack 3. However, this might be a genuine Java bug.

Accessing Google's Charts Web Service

Accessing someone else's RESTful web service is easier than creating your own because you can forget about JAX-WS and deal only with HttpURLConnection to make a request and retrieve the necessary data. Furthermore, you aren't restricted to retrieving XML data. For example, Google's RESTful Charts web service (http://code.google.com/apis/chart/image/docs/making_charts.html), which is also known as the Chart API, lets you dynamically create and return images of bar, pie, and other kinds of charts.

Google Charts is accessed via the https://chart.googleapis.com/chart URI. You append a query string to this URI that identifies the chart type, size, data, labels, and any other needed information. For example, query string "?cht=p3&chs=450x200&chd=t:60,40&chl=Q1%20(60%)|Q2%20(40%)" describes the following chart type, size, data, and label parameters:

- cht=p3 specifies the chart type as a three-dimensional pie chart.

- chs=450x200 specifies the chart size as 450 pixels wide by 200 pixels high —a chart should be at least two-and-one-half times as wide as it is tall so that all labels are fully visible.

- chd=t:60,40 specifies the chart data in a simple text format —this format consists of a single series of comma-separated values; multiple series are specified by using a vertical bar to separate one series from the next —where the first data item (for the first pie chart slice) is 60 and the second data item (for the second slice) is 40.

- chl=Q1%20(60%)|Q2%20(40%) specifies the chart labels for the pie chart slices as Q1 (60%) and Q2 (40%) —labels are separated by vertical bars and must be URL-encoded (which is why each space character is replaced with %20).

Google Charts defaults to returning the chart as a PNG image. You can return a GIF image instead by including the chof=gif parameter in the query string, or even return a JavaScript Object Notation (JSON)-formatted document (see http://en.wikipedia.org/wiki/JSON) by including the chof=json parameter.

I've created a ViewChart application that passes the aforementioned URI with query string to Google Charts, obtains the generated PNG image of the 3D pie chart, and displays this image. Listing 11-15 presents this application's source code.

Listing 11-15. A client for accessing the Google Charts web service

```
import java.io.InputStream;
import java.io.IOException;

import java.net.HttpURLConnection;
import java.net.URL;

import javax.swing.ImageIcon;
import javax.swing.JFrame;
import javax.swing.JLabel;
import javax.swing.JOptionPane;

class ViewChart
{
   final static String BASEURI = "https://chart.googleapis.com/chart?";
   public static void main(String[] args)
   {
      String qs = "cht=p3&chs=450x200&chd=t:60,40&chl=Q1%20(60%)|Q2%20(40%)";
      ImageIcon ii = doGet(qs);
      if (ii != null)
      {
         JFrame frame = new JFrame("ViewChart");
         frame.setDefaultCloseOperation(JFrame.EXIT_ON_CLOSE);
         frame.setContentPane(new JLabel(ii));
```

```
         frame.pack();
         frame.setResizable(false);
         frame.setVisible(true);
      }
   }
   static ImageIcon doGet(String qs)
   {
      try
      {
         URL url = new URL(BASEURI+qs);
         HttpURLConnection httpurlc;
         httpurlc = (HttpURLConnection) url.openConnection();
         httpurlc.setRequestMethod("GET");
         httpurlc.setDoInput(true);
         if (httpurlc.getResponseCode() == 200)
         {
            InputStream is = httpurlc.getInputStream();
            byte[] bytes = new byte[10000];
            int b, i = 0;
            while ((b = is.read()) != -1)
            {
               bytes[i++] = (byte) b;
               if (i == bytes.length)
               {
                  byte[] bytes2 = new byte[bytes.length*2];
                  System.arraycopy(bytes, 0, bytes2, 0, i);
                  bytes = bytes2;
               }
            }
            byte[] bytes2 = new byte[i];
            System.arraycopy(bytes, 0, bytes2, 0, i);
            return new ImageIcon(bytes2);
         }
         throw new IOException("HTTP Error: "+httpurlc.getResponseCode());
      }
      catch (IOException e)
      {
         JOptionPane.showMessageDialog(null, e.getMessage(), "ViewChart",
                                       JOptionPane.ERROR_MESSAGE);
         return null;
      }
   }
}
```

Listing 11-15 is fairly straightforward. Its main() method invokes doGet() with the query string. If this method returns a javax.swing.ImageIcon object, a Swing-based frame window is created, this window is told to terminate the application when the user clicks the X button on the window's titlebar (for Windows and similar operating systems), a label based on the icon is created and assigned to the frame window as its content pane, the window is *packed* (sized to the preferred size) of the label (which adopts the size of the image icon's image as its preferred size), the window is made nonresizable, and the window is displayed.

The doGet() method creates a URL object, opens an HTTP connection to the URL instance, specifies GET as the request method, tells the connection that it only wants to input content, and proceeds to read the content when the response code is 200 (success).

The content is stored in an array of bytes. If the array is too small to hold all the content, the array is dynamically resized by creating a larger array and copying the original array's content to the new array with help from System.arraycopy(). After all bytes have been read, this array is passed to ImageIcon's ImageIcon(byte[] imageData) constructor to store the PNG image as the basis of the ImageIcon object, which is returned from doGet().

If something goes wrong, an instance of the IOException class or one of its subclasses (such as java.net.MalformedURLException, which signifies that the argument passed to URL's constructor is illegal) is thrown. The catch block handles this exception by invoking javax.swing.JOptionPane's void showMessageDialog(Component parentComponent, Object message, String title, int messageType) to display a suitable error message via a popup dialog box.

Compile Listing 11-15 (javac ViewChart.java) and run the application (java ViewChart). Figure 11-8 shows the resulting chart.

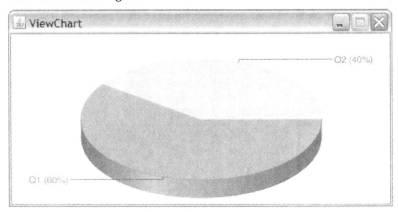

Figure 11-8. A three-dimensional pie chart image is returned from Google's RESTful Charts web service.

■ **Note** Visit http://www.programmableweb.com/apis/directory/ to discover additional examples of RESTful and SOAP-based web services.

Advanced Web Service Topics

Now that the basics of creating and accessing SOAP-based and RESTful web services are out of the way, you're probably ready for more advanced material. This section introduces five advanced web service topics.

You first receive an introduction to the SAAJ API for working with SOAP-based web services at a lower level. You then learn how to create a JAX-WS handler to log the flow of SOAP messages. Next, you learn how to create and install a custom lightweight HTTP server to perform authentication, and also learn how to create a RESTful web service that returns attachments (e.g., a JPEG image) to its clients. Finally, you dig deeper into JAX-WS by exploring the interplay between providers and dispatch clients, and learn how to create a dispatch client that accesses the Source instance returned from a web service provider's invoke() method via a different Source instance in an alternate Library client application.

Working with SAAJ

Soap with Attachments API for Java (SAAJ) is the Java API for creating, sending, and receiving SOAP messages that may or may not have MIME-typed attachments. SAAJ is a lower-level alternative to JAX-WS for sending and receiving SOAP messages.

After presenting an overview of SOAP message architecture, I take you on a tour of SAAJ. When this tour finishes, I present an application that uses this API to access a SOAP-based web service for converting between integer values and Roman numerals. This application reinforces your understanding of SAAJ.

SOAP Message Architecture

A *SOAP message* is an XML document sent from an *initial SOAP sender node* to an *ultimate SOAP receiver node*, mostly likely passing through *intermediate SOAP sender/receiver nodes* along its path. A *SOAP node* is processing logic that operates on a SOAP message.

The SOAP document consists of an Envelope root element that encapsulates an optional Header element and a nonoptional Body element —see Figure 11-9.

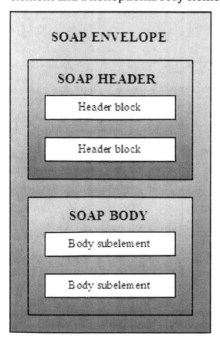

Figure 11-9. A SOAP message's architecture consists of an optional Header element and a mandatory Body element within an Envelope element.

The Header element specifies application-related information (such as authentication details to verify who sent the message) via immediate child elements known as *header blocks*. A header block represents a logical grouping of data that can target an intermediate SOAP node or the ultimate receiver node.

Although header blocks are defined by the application, their start tags may contain the following SOAP-defined attributes to indicate how SOAP nodes should process them:

- encodingStyle identifies the rules used to serialize parts of a SOAP message

- role identifies the SOAP node (via a URI) to which the header block is targeted — this SOAP 1.2-introduced attribute replaces the SOAP 1.1 actor attribute, which performs the same function

- mustUnderstand indicates whether processing of the header block is mandatory (value 1 in SOAP 1.1; true in SOAP 1.2) or optional (value 0 in SOAP 1.1; false in SOAP 1.2)

- relay indicates whether the header block targeted at a SOAP receiver must be relayed to another node if not processed —this attribute was introduced in SOAP 1.2

The Body element contains information that targets the ultimate receiver node. This information is known as the *payload*, and consists of a SOAP-defined Fault child element describing a *fault* (an error being reported by the web service), or child elements that are specific to the web service.

The Fault element contains error and status information that a web service returns to a client. SOAP 1.1 specifies the following child elements of Fault:

- faultcode: This mandatory element provides information about the fault in a form that can be processed by software. SOAP defines a small set of SOAP fault codes that cover basic faults; this set can be extended by applications.

- faultstring: This mandatory element provides information about the fault in a human-readable format.

- faultactor: This element contains the URI of the SOAP node that generated the fault. A SOAP node that is not the ultimate SOAP receiver must include faultactor when creating a fault; an ultimate SOAP receiver doesn't have to include this element, but might choose to do so.

- detail: This element carries application-specific error information related to the Body element. It must be present when Body's contents couldn't be processed successfully. The detail element must not be used to carry error information belonging to header blocks; detailed error information belonging to header blocks is carried within these blocks.

SOAP 1.2 specifies the following child elements of Fault:

- Code: This mandatory element provides information about the fault in a form that can be processed by software. It contains a Value element and an optional Subcode element.

- Reason: This mandatory element provides information about the fault in a human-readable format. Reason contains one or more Text elements, each of which contains information about the fault in a different language.

- Node: This element contains the URI of the SOAP node that generated the fault. A SOAP node that is not the ultimate SOAP receiver must include Node when creating a fault; an ultimate SOAP receiver doesn't have to include this element, but might choose to do so.

- Role: This element contains a URI that identifies the role the node was operating in when the fault occurred.

- Detail: This optional element contains application-specific error information related to the SOAP fault codes describing the fault. Its presence has no significance as to which parts of the faulty SOAP message were processed.

Listing 11-16 presents an example SOAP message.

Listing 11-16. *A SOAP message for calling a SOAP-based library web service's* getTitle() *function to retrieve a book's title when given its ISBN*

```
<SOAP-ENV:Envelope xmlns:SOAP-ENV="http://schemas.xmlsoap.org/soap/envelope/"
                   xmlns:xsd="http://www.w3.org/2001/XMLSchema"
                   xmlns:xsi="http://www.w3.org/2001/XMLSchema-instance">
   <SOAP-ENV:Header />
   <SOAP-ENV:Body>
      <lns:getTitle xmlns:lns="http://tutortutor.ca/library">
         <isbn xsi:type="xsd:string">9781430234135</isbn>
      </lns:getTitle>
   </SOAP-ENV:Body>
</SOAP-ENV:Envelope>
```

This SOAP message describes a request to a library web service to execute its getTitle() function. Furthermore, it describes the type and value of the ISBN argument passed to this function's isbn parameter.

The message begins with the SOAP-ENV-prefixed <Envelope> tag, which describes the SOAP message's envelope. The commonly used SOAP-ENV prefix corresponds to the SOAP 1.1 namespace that provides the schema for SOAP envelopes. The xsd and xsi prefixes correspond to the XML Schema structures and XML Schema Instance namespaces, and are used to denote the XML Schema type that describes the kind of data being passed to getTitle() (a string) via the isbn element.

The empty Header element signifies that there is no SOAP header. In contrast, the Body element identifies a single getTitle operation request.

The getTitle element is namespace-qualified, as recommended by the SOAP 1.1 and 1.2 specifications. In contrast, the isbn child element of getTitle is not namespace-qualified because it inherits getTitle's namespace —the SOAP 1.1 and 1.2 specifications do not mandate that such child elements be namespace-qualified.

SAAJ API Overview

SAAJ is a small API that lets you perform the following tasks:

- Create an endpoint-to-endpoint connection

- Create a SOAP message

- Create an XML fragment

- Add content to the header of a SOAP message

- Add content to the body of a SOAP message

- Create attachment parts and add content to them

- Access/add/modify parts of a SOAP message

- Create/add/modify SOAP fault information

- Extract content from a SOAP message

- Send a SOAP request-response message

SAAJ is associated with the `javax.xml.soap` package, which contains 14 interfaces and 13 classes. Various interfaces and classes extend their counterparts in the `org.w3c.dom` package, implying that part of a SOAP message is organized as a tree of nodes.

The following classes and interfaces are used to specify the structure of a SOAP message:

- `SOAPMessage` represents the entire SOAP message. It contains a single `SOAPPart` instance and zero or more `AttachmentPart` instances.

- `SOAPPart` contains a `SOAPEnvelope` instance, which represents the actual SOAP `Envelope` element.

- `SOAPEnvelope` optionally contains a `SOAPHeader` instance and also contains a mandatory `SOAPBody` instance.

- `SOAPHeader` represents the SOAP message's header block(s).

- `SOAPBody` contains either a `SOAPFault` object or a `SOAPBodyElement` object containing the actual SOAP payload XML content.

- `SOAPFault` stores a SOAP fault message.

Working with SAAJ involves creating a SOAP connection, creating SOAP messages, populating each message with content and optional attachments, sending the messages to an endpoint, and retrieving replies.

You create a connection by working with the `SOAPConnectionFactory` and `SOAPConnection` classes. As its name implies, `SOAPConnectionFactory` is a factory class for retrieving `SOAPConnection` instances (actually, instances of subclasses of the abstract `SOAPConnection` class). A `SOAPConnection` instance represents an endpoint-to-endpoint connection to the web service; the client and web service exchange messages over this connection. The following example shows you how to instantiate the factory and obtain a SOAP connection:

```
SOAPConnectionFactory soapcf = SOAPConnectionFactory.newInstance();
SOAPConnection soapc = soapcf.createConnection();
```

Instantiate the factory by calling `SOAPConnectionFactory`'s `SOAPConnectionFactory newInstance()` method. This method throws `SOAPException` when a `SOAPConnectionFactory` instance cannot be created. If a nonOracle Java implementation doesn't support the SAAJ communication infrastructure, this method throws an instance of the `java.lang.UnsupportedOperationException` class.

After instantiating `SOAPConnectionFactory`, call this instance's `SOAPConnection createConnection()` method to create and return a new `SOAPConnection` object. This method throws `SOAPException` when it's unable to create this object.

Create a SOAP message by working with the MessageFactory and SOAPMessage classes. MessageFactory provides a pair of methods for returning a MessageFactory instance:

- MessageFactory newInstance() creates a MessageFactory object based on the default SOAP 1.1 implementation. This method follows an ordered lookup procedure to locate the MessageFactory implementation class. This procedure first examines the javax.xml.soap.MessageFactory system property, and lastly calls an instance of the SAAJMetaFactory class's MessageFactory newMessageFactory(String protocol) method to return that factory. This method throws SOAPException when it's unable to create the factory.

- MessageFactory newInstance(String protocol) creates a MessageFactory object that is based on the SOAP implementation specified by the protocol argument, which is one of the SOAPConstants interface's DEFAULT_SOAP_PROTOCOL, DYNAMIC_SOAP_PROTOCOL, SOAP_1_1_PROTOCOL, or SOAP_1_2_PROTOCOL constants. This method throws SOAPException when it's unable to create the factory.

After instantiating MessageFactory, call one of the following methods to create a SOAPMessage instance:

- SOAPMessage createMessage() creates and returns a new SOAPMessage object (actually, an instance of a concrete subclass of this abstract class) with default SOAPPart, SOAPEnvelope, SOAPBody (initially empty) and SOAPHeader objects. This method throws SOAPException when a SOAPMessage instance cannot be created, and UnsupportedOperationException when the MessageFactory instance's protocol is DYNAMIC_SOAP_PROTOCOL.

- SOAPMessage createMessage(MimeHeaders headers, InputStream in) internalizes the contents of the given java.io.InputStream object into a new SOAPMessage object and returns this object. The MimeHeaders instance specifies transport-specific headers that describe the various attachments to the SOAP message. This method throws SOAPException when a SOAPMessage instance cannot be created, IOException when there's a problem reading data from the input stream, and IllegalArgumentException when the MessageFactory instance requires one or more MIME headers to be present in the argument passed to headers and these headers are missing.

The following example shows you how to instantiate the factory and create a SOAPMessage object that is ready to be populated:

```
MessageFactory mf = MessageFactory.newInstance();
SOAPMessage soapm = mf.createMessage();
```

SOAPMessage describes a SOAP message optionally followed by MIME-typed attachments. The SOAP message part of this object is defined by an instance of a concrete subclass of the abstract SOAPPart class.

SOAPPart encapsulates an instance of a class that implements the SOAPEnvelope interface, and the SOAPEnvelope instance encapsulates instances of classes that implement the SOAPHeader and SOAPBody interfaces. Call SOAPMessage's SOAPPart getSOAPPart() method to return the SOAPPart instance. You can then call SOAPPart's SOAPEnvelope getEnvelope() method to return the SOAPEnvelope instance, and call SOAPEnvelope's SOAPBody getBody() and SOAPHeader getHeader() methods to return the SOAPEnvelope instance's SOAPBody and SOAPHeader instances.

Tip Because a SOAPEnvelope instance defaults to storing an empty SOAPHeader instance, you can remove this SOAPHeader instance when it's not needed by calling SOAPHeader's inherited (from the javax.xml.soap.Node interface) void detachNode() method.

The following example shows you how to obtain the SOAPPart, SOAPEnvelope, and SOAPBody instances from the SOAPMessage instance, and also how to detach the SOAPHeader instance:

```
SOAPPart soapp = soapm.getSOAPPart();
SOAPEnvelope soape = soapp.getEnvelope();
SOAPBody soapb = soape.getBody();
soape.getHeader().detachNode();
```

Tip SOAPMessage declares SOAPBody getSOAPBody() and SOAPHeader getSOAPHeader() methods that conveniently let you access the SOAPBody and SOAPHeader instances without having to go through getEnvelope(). Calling these methods is equivalent to calling getEnvelope().getBody() and getEnvelope().getHeader(), respectively.

SOAPEnvelope and various other interfaces extend SOAPElement, which provides methods that are applicable to different kinds of element implementation instances. For example, the SOAPElement addNamespaceDeclaration(String prefix, String uri) method is useful for adding a namespace declaration with the specified prefix and uri values to a SOAPEnvelope instance. The following example shows how to add declarations for the xsd and xsi namespaces shown in Listing 11-16 to its Envelope element:

```
soape.addNamespaceDeclaration("xsd", "http://www.w3.org/2001/XMLSchema");
soape.addNamespaceDeclaration("xsi", "http://www.w3.org/2001/XMLSchema-instance");
```

The SOAPBody instance contains either content or a fault. Adding content to the body first requires that you create SOAPBodyElement objects (to store this content) and add these objects to the SOAPBody instance. This task is accomplished by calling either of SOAPBody's two addBodyElement() methods, which create the SOAPBodyElement object, add it to the SOAPBody object, and return a reference to the created object so that you can create method call chains (see Chapter 2 for a discussion of chaining together method calls).

When a new subelement of the SOAP Body element is created, you must specify a fully qualified name in the form of a Name instance or a QName instance. Because the Java documentation for the Name interface states that it may be deprecated in favor of QName, you should get into the habit of using QName instead of Name. As a result, you should use SOAPBody's SOAPBodyElement addBodyElement(QName qname) method instead of using this interface's SOAPBodyElement addBodyElement(Name name) method, as demonstrated here:

```
QName name = new QName("http://tutortutor.ca/library", "getTitle", "lns");
SOAPElement soapel = soapb.addBodyElement(name);
```

SOAPBodyElement instances store subelement instances. You create these subelements and add them to the SOAPBodyElement instance by calling SOAPElement's various addChildElement() methods, such as SOAPElement addChildElement(String localName), which creates a subelement object having the specified localName, adds this subelement object to the SOAPBodyElement object on which this method is called, and returns a reference to the created SOAPElement object for chaining together method calls.

You can then attach a text node to a body element or a subelement by calling SOAPElement's SOAPElement addTextNode(String text) method. You can also call SOAPElement's void setAttribute(String name, String value) method (inherited from SOAPElement's org.w3c.dom.Element ancestor interface) to add attributes to the subelement as appropriate. The following example demonstrates:

```
soapel.addChildElement("isbn").addTextNode("9781430234135").setAttribute("xsi:type",
                                                                         "xsd:string");
```

Attachments are instances of concrete subclasses of the abstract AttachmentPart class. If you need to include an attachment with the SOAP message, call one of SOAPMessage's createAttachmentPart() methods to create and return an AttachmentPart object. After configuring this object, call SOAPMessage's void addAttachmentPart(AttachmentPart attachmentPart) method to add the given attachmentPart-referenced object to this SOAPMessage object.

To send the SOAP message and receive a reply, invoke SOAPConnection's SOAPMessage call(SOAPMessage request, Object to) method. The specified request message is sent to the endpoint identified by to, which may be a String or URL instance. This method throws SOAPException when a SOAP problem occurs, and blocks until it receives a SOAP message, which it returns as a SOAPMessage object. The following example provides a demonstration:

```
String endpoint = "http://tutortutor.ca/library/GetTitle";
// Send the request message identified by soapm to the web service at the specified
// endpoint and return the response message.
SOAPMessage response = soapc.call(soapm, endpoint);
```

Alternatively, you can call SOAPConnection's SOAPMessage get(Object to) method to request a SOAP message. As with call(), get() blocks until there is a reply, and throws SOAPException when a SOAP problem occurs.

After finishing your call() and/or get() invocations, call SOAPConnection's void close() method to close the connection to the endpoint. If this method has already been called, a subsequent attempt to close the connection results in a thrown SOAPException instance.

Roman Numerals and SAAJ

To demonstrate SAAJ in a more practical context, I've created a RomanNumerals application that uses this API to communicate with a SOAP-based Roman Numerals Conversion web service, which converts between Roman numerals and base-10 integer values. This web service's WSDL document is located at http://www.ebob42.com/cgi-bin/Romulan.exe/wsdl/IRoman, and appears in Listing 11-17.

Listing 11-17. WSDL for the Roman numerals/base-10 integer values conversion web service.

```
<definitions name="IRomanservice" targetNamespace="http://eBob42.org/">
   <message name="IntToRomanORequest">
      <part name="Int" type="xs:int"/>
   </message>
   <message name="IntToRomanOResponse">
```

```
            <part name="return" type="xs:string"/>
        </message>
        <message name="RomanToInt1Request">
            <part name="Rom" type="xs:string"/>
        </message>
        <message name="RomanToInt1Response">
            <part name="return" type="xs:int"/>
        </message>
        <portType name="IRoman">
            <operation name="IntToRoman">
                <input message="tns:IntToRoman0Request"/>
                <output message="tns:IntToRoman0Response"/>
            </operation>
            <operation name="RomanToInt">
                <input message="tns:RomanToInt1Request"/>
                <output message="tns:RomanToInt1Response"/>
            </operation>
        </portType>
        <binding name="IRomanbinding" type="tns:IRoman">
            <soap:binding style="rpc" transport="http://schemas.xmlsoap.org/soap/http"/>
            <operation name="IntToRoman">
                <soap:operation soapAction="urn:Roman-IRoman#IntToRoman" style="rpc"/>
                <input message="tns:IntToRoman0Request">
                    <soap:body use="encoded"
                                encodingStyle="http://schemas.xmlsoap.org/soap/encoding/"
                                namespace="urn:Roman-IRoman"/>
                </input>
                <output message="tns:IntToRoman0Response">
                    <soap:body use="encoded"
                                encodingStyle="http://schemas.xmlsoap.org/soap/encoding/"
                                namespace="urn:Roman-IRoman"/>
                </output>
            </operation>
            <operation name="RomanToInt">
                <soap:operation soapAction="urn:Roman-IRoman#RomanToInt" style="rpc"/>
                <input message="tns:RomanToInt1Request">
                    <soap:body use="encoded"
                                encodingStyle="http://schemas.xmlsoap.org/soap/encoding/"
                                namespace="urn:Roman-IRoman"/>
                </input>
                <output message="tns:RomanToInt1Response">
                    <soap:body use="encoded"
                                encodingStyle="http://schemas.xmlsoap.org/soap/encoding/"
                                namespace="urn:Roman-IRoman"/>
                </output>
            </operation>
        </binding>
        <service name="IRomanservice">
            <port name="IRomanPort" binding="tns:IRomanbinding">
                <soap:address
                        location="http://www.ebob42.com/cgi-bin/Romulan.exe/soap/IRoman"/>
            </port>
```

```
    </service>
</definitions>
```

Listing 11-17's WSDL document provides important information for constructing SOAP request and response messages —note the absence of a types element because the service uses only XML Schema builtin simple types; furthermore, the document style is rpc. This information includes the IntToRoman and RomanToInt operation names (which the application calls to perform the conversions) along with parameter and return type information. This listing also presents the service's endpoint address.

Listing 11-18 reveals RomanNumerals.java.

Listing 11-18. Using SAAJ to access the Roman Numerals Conversion web service

```java
import java.awt.BorderLayout;
import java.awt.Color;
import java.awt.EventQueue;
import java.awt.GradientPaint;
import java.awt.Graphics;
import java.awt.Graphics2D;

import java.awt.event.ActionEvent;
import java.awt.event.ActionListener;

import java.io.IOException;

import java.util.Iterator;

import javax.swing.BorderFactory;
import javax.swing.JButton;
import javax.swing.JFrame;
import javax.swing.JLabel;
import javax.swing.JOptionPane;
import javax.swing.JPanel;
import javax.swing.JTextField;

import javax.swing.border.Border;

import javax.xml.namespace.QName;

import javax.xml.soap.MessageFactory;
import javax.xml.soap.SOAPBody;
import javax.xml.soap.SOAPBodyElement;
import javax.xml.soap.SOAPConnection;
import javax.xml.soap.SOAPConnectionFactory;
import javax.xml.soap.SOAPConstants;
import javax.xml.soap.SOAPElement;
import javax.xml.soap.SOAPEnvelope;
import javax.xml.soap.SOAPException;
import javax.xml.soap.SOAPHeader;
import javax.xml.soap.SOAPMessage;

class RomanNumerals extends JFrame
{
```

```
private JTextField txtResult;
RomanNumerals()
{
    super("RomanNumerals");
    setDefaultCloseOperation(EXIT_ON_CLOSE);
    // Create a gradient panel in which to present the GUI.
    GPanel pnl = new GPanel();
    pnl.setLayout(new BorderLayout());
    // Build input panel.
    JPanel pnlInput = new JPanel();
    Border inner = BorderFactory.createEtchedBorder();
    Border outer = BorderFactory.createEmptyBorder(10, 10, 10, 10);
    pnlInput.setBorder(BorderFactory.createCompoundBorder(outer, inner));
    pnlInput.setOpaque(false);
    pnlInput.add(new JLabel("Enter Roman numerals or integer:"));
    final JTextField txtInput = new JTextField(15);
    pnlInput.add(txtInput);
    pnl.add(pnlInput, BorderLayout.NORTH);
    // Build buttons panel.
    JPanel pnlButtons = new JPanel();
    inner = BorderFactory.createEtchedBorder();
    outer = BorderFactory.createEmptyBorder(10, 10, 10, 10);
    pnlButtons.setBorder(BorderFactory.createCompoundBorder(outer, inner));
    pnlButtons.setOpaque(false);
    JButton btnToRoman = new JButton("To Roman");
    ActionListener alToRoman;
    alToRoman = new ActionListener()
                {
                    @Override
                    public void actionPerformed(ActionEvent ae)
                    {
                        try
                        {
                            String roman = toRoman(txtInput.getText());
                            txtResult.setText(roman);
                        }
                        catch (SOAPException se)
                        {
                            JOptionPane.showMessageDialog(RomanNumerals.this,
                                                    se.getMessage());
                        }
                    }
                };
    btnToRoman.addActionListener(alToRoman);
    pnlButtons.add(btnToRoman);
    JButton btnToInteger = new JButton("To Integer");
    ActionListener alToInteger;
    alToInteger = new ActionListener()
                {
                    @Override
                    public void actionPerformed(ActionEvent ae)
                    {
```

```
                    try
                    {
                        String integer = toInteger(txtInput.getText());
                        txtResult.setText(integer);
                    }
                    catch (SOAPException se)
                    {
                        JOptionPane.showMessageDialog(RomanNumerals.this,
                                                      se.getMessage());
                    }
                }
            }
        };
    btnToInteger.addActionListener(alToInteger);
    pnlButtons.add(btnToInteger);
    pnl.add(pnlButtons, BorderLayout.CENTER);
    // Build result panel.
    JPanel pnlResult = new JPanel();
    inner = BorderFactory.createEtchedBorder();
    outer = BorderFactory.createEmptyBorder(10, 10, 10, 10);
    pnlResult.setBorder(BorderFactory.createCompoundBorder(outer, inner));
    pnlResult.setOpaque(false);
    pnlResult.add(new JLabel("Result:"));
    txtResult = new JTextField(35);
    pnlResult.add(txtResult);
    pnl.add(pnlResult, BorderLayout.SOUTH);
    setContentPane(pnl);
    pack();
    setResizable(false);
    setLocationRelativeTo(null); // center on the screen
    setVisible(true);
}
String toInteger(String input) throws SOAPException
{
    // Build a request message. The first step is to create an empty message
    // via a message factory. The default SOAP 1.1 message factory is used.
    MessageFactory mfactory = MessageFactory.newInstance();
    SOAPMessage request = mfactory.createMessage();
    // The request SOAPMessage object contains a SOAPPart object, which
    // contains a SOAPEnvelope object, which contains an empty SOAPHeader
    // object followed by an empty SOAPBody object.
    // Detach the header since a header is not required. This step is
    // optional.
    SOAPHeader header = request.getSOAPHeader();
    header.detachNode();
    // Access the body so that content can be added.
    SOAPBody body = request.getSOAPBody();
    // Add the RomanToInt operation body element to the body.
    QName bodyName = new QName("http://eBob42.org/", "RomanToInt", "tns");
    SOAPBodyElement bodyElement = body.addBodyElement(bodyName);
    // Add the Rom child element to the RomanToInt body element.
    QName name = new QName("Rom");
    SOAPElement element = bodyElement.addChildElement(name);
```

```
element.addTextNode(input).setAttribute("xsi:type", "xs:string");
// Add appropriate namespaces and an encoding style to the envelope.
SOAPEnvelope env = request.getSOAPPart().getEnvelope();
env.addNamespaceDeclaration("env",
                            "http://schemas.xmlsoap.org/soap/envelop/");
env.addNamespaceDeclaration("enc",
                            "http://schemas.xmlsoap.org/soap/encoding/");
env.setEncodingStyle(SOAPConstants.URI_NS_SOAP_ENCODING);
env.addNamespaceDeclaration("xs", "http://www.w3.org/2001/XMLSchema");
env.addNamespaceDeclaration("xsi",
                            "http://www.w3.org/2001/XMLSchema-instance");
// Output the request just built to standard output, to see what the
// SOAP message looks like (which is useful for debugging).
System.out.println("\nSoap request:\n");
try
{
   request.writeTo(System.out);
}
catch (IOException ioe)
{
   JOptionPane.showMessageDialog(RomanNumerals.this,
                                 ioe.getMessage());
}
System.out.println();
// Prepare to send message by obtaining a connection factory and creating
// a connection.
SOAPConnectionFactory factory = SOAPConnectionFactory.newInstance();
SOAPConnection con = factory.createConnection();
// Identify the message's target.
String endpoint = "http://www.ebob42.com/cgi-bin/Romulan.exe/soap/IRoman";
// Call the Web service at the target using the request message. Capture
// the response message and send it to standard output.
SOAPMessage response = con.call(request, endpoint);
System.out.println("\nSoap response:\n");
try
{
   response.writeTo(System.out);
}
catch (IOException ioe)
{
   JOptionPane.showMessageDialog(RomanNumerals.this,
                                 ioe.getMessage());
}
// Close the connection to release resources.
con.close();
// Return a response consisting of the reason for a SOAP Fault or the
// value of the RomanToIntResponse body element's return child element.
if (response.getSOAPBody().hasFault())
   return response.getSOAPBody().getFault().getFaultString();
else
{
   body = response.getSOAPBody();
```

```
        bodyName = new QName("urn:Roman-IRoman", "RomanToIntResponse", "NS1");
        Iterator iter = body.getChildElements(bodyName);
        bodyElement = (SOAPBodyElement) iter.next();
        iter = bodyElement.getChildElements(new QName("return"));
        return ((SOAPElement) iter.next()).getValue();
    }
}
String toRoman(String input) throws SOAPException
{
    // Build a request message. The first step is to create an empty message
    // via a message factory. The default SOAP 1.1 message factory is used.
    MessageFactory mfactory = MessageFactory.newInstance();
    SOAPMessage request = mfactory.createMessage();
    // The request SOAPMessage object contains a SOAPPart object, which
    // contains a SOAPEnvelope object, which contains an empty SOAPHeader
    // object followed by an empty SOAPBody object.
    // Detach the header since a header is not required. This step is
    // optional.
    SOAPHeader header = request.getSOAPHeader();
    header.detachNode();
    // Access the body so that content can be added.
    SOAPBody body = request.getSOAPBody();
    // Add the IntToRoman operation body element to the body.
    QName bodyName = new QName("http://eBob42.org/", "IntToRoman", "tns");
    SOAPBodyElement bodyElement = body.addBodyElement(bodyName);
    // Add the Int child element to the IntToRoman body element.
    QName name = new QName("Int");
    SOAPElement element = bodyElement.addChildElement(name);
    element.addTextNode(input).setAttribute("xsi:type", "xs:int");
    // Add appropriate namespaces and an encoding style to the envelope.
    SOAPEnvelope env = request.getSOAPPart().getEnvelope();
    env.addNamespaceDeclaration("env",
                                "http://schemas.xmlsoap.org/soap/envelop/");
    env.addNamespaceDeclaration("enc",
                                "http://schemas.xmlsoap.org/soap/encoding/");
    env.setEncodingStyle(SOAPConstants.URI_NS_SOAP_ENCODING);
    env.addNamespaceDeclaration("xs", "http://www.w3.org/2001/XMLSchema");
    env.addNamespaceDeclaration("xsi",
                                "http://www.w3.org/2001/XMLSchema-instance");
    // Output the request just built to standard output, to see what the
    // SOAP message looks like (which is useful for debugging).
    System.out.println("\nSoap request:\n");
    try
    {
        request.writeTo(System.out);
    }
    catch (IOException ioe)
    {
        JOptionPane.showMessageDialog(RomanNumerals.this,
                                    ioe.getMessage());
    }
    System.out.println();
```

```java
        // Prepare to send message by obtaining a connection factory and creating
        // a connection.
        SOAPConnectionFactory factory = SOAPConnectionFactory.newInstance();
        SOAPConnection con = factory.createConnection();
        // Identify the message's target.
        String endpoint = "http://www.ebob42.com/cgi-bin/Romulan.exe/soap/IRoman";
        // Call the Web service at the target using the request message. Capture
        // the response message and send it to standard output.
        SOAPMessage response = con.call(request, endpoint);
        System.out.println("\nSoap response:\n");
        try
        {
            response.writeTo(System.out);
        }
        catch (IOException ioe)
        {
            JOptionPane.showMessageDialog(RomanNumerals.this,
                                          ioe.getMessage());
        }
        // Close the connection to release resources.
        con.close();
        // Return a response consisting of the reason for a SOAP Fault or the
        // value of the IntToRomanResponse body element's return child element.
        if (response.getSOAPBody().hasFault())
            return response.getSOAPBody().getFault().getFaultString();
        else
        {
            body = response.getSOAPBody();
            bodyName = new QName("urn:Roman-IRoman", "IntToRomanResponse", "NS1");
            Iterator iter = body.getChildElements(bodyName);
            bodyElement = (SOAPBodyElement) iter.next();
            iter = bodyElement.getChildElements(new QName("return"));
            return ((SOAPElement) iter.next()).getValue();
        }
    }
    public static void main(String[] args)
    {
        Runnable r = new Runnable()
                     {
                         @Override
                         public void run()
                         {
                             new RomanNumerals();
                         }
                     };
        EventQueue.invokeLater(r);
    }
}
class GPanel extends JPanel
{
    private GradientPaint gp;
    @Override
```

```
public void paintComponent(Graphics g)
{
   if (gp == null)
      gp = new GradientPaint(0, 0, Color.pink, 0, getHeight(), Color.orange);
   // Paint a nice gradient background with pink at the top and orange at
   // the bottom.
   ((Graphics2D) g).setPaint(gp);
   g.fillRect(0, 0, getWidth(), getHeight());
}
}
```

Listing 11-18 combines Swing/Abstract Window Toolkit code for creating a user interface with SAAJ code for communicating with the Roman Numerals Conversion web service.

The user interface consists of a pair of textfields and a pair of buttons. One of these textfields is used to enter the Roman numerals or base-10 integer digits of the value to be converted. The other textfield displays the conversion result. Click one of the buttons to convert from Roman numerals to integer digits; click the other button to achieve the opposite conversion. In response to a button click, either the String toInteger(String input) method or the String toRoman(String input) method is called to perform the conversion.

Because I discuss the basics of Java's user interface APIs extensively in Chapter 7, I won't revisit them here. Instead, consider the GPanel (Gradient Panel) class.

I introduced GPanel so that I could generate a colorful background for the application's window. Some user interface designers might disagree with painting a pink-to-orange *gradient* (gradual change in color from an initial color to a final color) as a window background, but I like it. (After all, beauty is in the eye of the beholder.)

GPanel extends JPanel to describe a custom panel whose surface is painted with a gradient whenever its inherited void paintComponent(Graphics g) method is called. This happens when the window is first displayed, and when the window is restored after being minimized (at least on Windows platforms).

GPanel uses the java.awt.GradientPaint class to paint the gradient. (I could have used the Java 6-introduced java.awt.LinearGradientPaint class instead, but flipped a coin and ended up using GradientPaint.) The first two arguments passed to this class's constructor identify the upper-left corner (in user space —see Chapter 7) of the rectangular area over which the gradient is drawn, the third argument specifies the color at the top of the gradient, the fourth and fifth arguments identify the rectangular area's lower-right corner, and the final argument identifies the color at the bottom of the gradient.

Note The instantiation of GradientPaint demonstrates *lazy initialization*, in which an object is not created until the first time it is needed. Check out Wikipedia's "Lazy initialization" entry (http://en.wikipedia.org/wiki/Lazy_initialization) for more information about this pattern.

Ideally, the user interface's components appear over a gradient background, and not over some intermediate background. However, because the user interface is created from panels of components added to the gradient panel, the gradient panel's surface will not show through these "upper" panels unless they are made transparent, by calling their void setOpaque(boolean opaque) method with false as the argument. For example, pnlInput.setOpaque(false); makes the input panel (the panel containing a label and input textfield) transparent so that the gradient background shows through.

Listing 11-18 uses SOAPMessage's void writeTo(OutputStream out) method to output a request or response message to the standard output stream. You'll find this feature helpful for understanding the relationship between SAAJ API calls and the SOAP messages that are constructed, especially if you are having difficulty following the API calls. This feature is also helpful when you've created a SOAP-based web service with a SEI and SIB and are trying to create a SAAJ-based client.

Compile Listing 11-18 (javac RomanNumerals.java) and run this application (java RomanNumerals). Figure 11-10 shows the resulting window with an example conversion from 2011 to MMXI.

Figure 11-10. Converting 2011 to its Roman numerals counterpart.

Additionally RomanNumerals outputs the following request and response SOAP messages:

Soap request:

```
<SOAP-ENV:Envelope xmlns:SOAP-ENV="http://schemas.xmlsoap.org/soap/envelope/"
xmlns:enc="http://schemas.xmlsoap.org/soap/encoding/"
xmlns:env="http://schemas.xmlsoap.org/soap/envelop/"
xmlns:xs="http://www.w3.org/2001/XMLSchema" xmlns:xsi="http://www.w3.org/2001/XMLSchema-
instance" SOAP-ENV:encodingStyle="http://schemas.xmlsoap.org/soap/encoding/"><SOAP-
ENV:Body><tns:IntToRoman xmlns:tns="http://eBob42.org/"><Int
xsi:type="xs:int">2011</Int></tns:IntToRoman></SOAP-ENV:Body></SOAP-ENV:Envelope>
```

Soap response:

```
<?xml version="1.0"?>
<SOAP-ENV:Envelope xmlns:SOAP-ENV="http://schemas.xmlsoap.org/soap/envelope/"
xmlns:xsd="http://www.w3.org/2001/XMLSchema"
xmlns:xsi="http://www.w3.org/2001/XMLSchema-instance" xmlns:SOAP-
ENC="http://schemas.xmlsoap.org/soap/encoding/"><SOAP-ENV:Body SOAP-
ENC:encodingStyle="http://schemas.xmlsoap.org/soap/envelope/"><NS1:IntToRomanResponse
xmlns:NS1="urn:Roman-IRoman"><return
xsi:type="xsd:string">MMXI</return></NS1:IntToRomanResponse></SOAP-ENV:Body></SOAP-
ENV:Envelope>
```

Although the output is tightly packed together and hard to read, you can clearly see the request 2011 and response MMXI values.

Each of Listing 11-18's toInteger() and toRoman() methods extracts the response value by first checking the response message's body to learn if it describes a fault. This task is accomplished by invoking SOAPBody's boolean hasFault() method. If this method returns true, SOAPBody's SOAPFault getFault() method is called to return an object that describes the fault in terms of the SOAPFault interface's methods, and SOAPFault's String getFaultString() method is called to return the string-based fault message.

If hasFault() returns false, the message's body provides the response value that must be extracted. The following excerpt from the toRoman() method handles this extraction task:

```
body = response.getSOAPBody();
bodyName = new QName("urn:Roman-IRoman", "IntToRomanResponse", "NS1");
Iterator iter = body.getChildElements(bodyName);
bodyElement = (SOAPBodyElement) iter.next();
iter = bodyElement.getChildElements(new QName("return"));
return ((SOAPElement) iter.next()).getValue();
```

After calling SOAPMessage's SOAPBody getSOAPBody() convenience method to return the SOAPBody object describing the SOAP message's body, the excerpt creates a QName object that identifies the qualified name for the IntToRomanResponse element. This object is then passed to SOAPBody's inherited Iterator getChildElements(QName qname) method to return a java.util.Iterator instance that will be used to iterate over all IntToRomanResponse child elements of the Body element.

Because there is only one such child element, only a single call to next() is made to return this element, as a SOAPBodyElement instance. This instance is used to invoke getChildElements(), but this time with the qualified name of the return element. The returned iterator's next() method is called to extract the return element as a SOAPElement instance, and getValue() is invoked on this instance to return the value of the return element, which happens to be MMXI.

Logging SOAP Messages with a JAX-WS Handler

The RomanNumerals application used SOAPMessage's void writeTo(OutputStream out) method to dump SOAP messages to the standard output stream. If you want to accomplish this task in the context of Listing 11-7's TempVerterClient application, you need to install a JAX-WS handler.

JAX-WS lets you install a chain of handlers on a web service class, a client class, or both to perform custom processing of request and response messages. For example, you might use a handler to add security information to the message or to log message details.

A *handler* is an instance of a class that ultimately implements the javax.xml.ws.handler.Handler<C extends MessageContext> interface in terms of the following methods:

- void close(MessageContext context) is called at the conclusion of a MEP just before the JAX-WS runtime dispatches a message, fault or exception. This method lets a handler clean up any resources used for processing request-only or request-response message exchanges.

- boolean handleFault(C context) is invoked for fault message processing. This method returns true when the handler wants to continue handling fault messages; otherwise, it returns false. It may throw javax.xml.ws.ProtocolException (a subclass of WebServiceException) or RuntimeException to cause the JAX-WS runtime to cease the handler's fault processing and dispatch the fault.

- `boolean handleMessage(C context)` is invoked for normal processing of inbound and outbound messages. This method returns true when the handler wants to continue handling such messages; otherwise, it returns false. It may throw `ProtocolException` or `RuntimeException` to cause the JAX-WS runtime to cease the handler's normal message processing and generate a fault.

Each method is called with a `MessageContext` or subinterface argument that stores a map of properties for handlers to use to communicate with each other and for other purposes. For example, `MessageContext.MESSAGE_OUTBOUND_PROPERTY` stores a Boolean object that identifies a message's direction. During a request (from client to web service), this property's value is `Boolean.TRUE` from a client handler's perspective and `Boolean.FALSE` from a web service handler's perspective.

JAX-WS supports logical and protocol handlers. A *logical handler* is independent of the message protocol (it only has access to the message payload) and is associated with the `javax.xml.ws.handler.LogicalMessageContext` and `javax.xml.ws.handler.LogicalHandler<C extends LogicalMessageContext>` interfaces. In contrast, a *protocol handler* is tied to a specific protocol; JAX-WS supports SOAP protocol handlers with the `javax.xml.ws.handler.soap.SOAPMessageContext` and `javax.xml.ws.handler.soap.SOAPHandler` interfaces.

To log the flow of SOAP messages, we need to work with `SOAPMessageContext` and `SOAPHandler`. Listing 11-19 presents a `SOAPLoggingHandler` class that implements `SOAPHandler<SOAPMessageContext>` to log the flow of SOAP messages by outputting them to the standard output device.

Listing 11-19. Logging SOAP messages to standard output

```java
import java.io.IOException;
import java.io.PrintStream;

import java.util.Map;
import java.util.Set;

import javax.xml.namespace.QName;

import javax.xml.soap.SOAPException;
import javax.xml.soap.SOAPMessage;

import javax.xml.ws.handler.MessageContext;

import javax.xml.ws.handler.soap.SOAPHandler;
import javax.xml.ws.handler.soap.SOAPMessageContext;

class SOAPLoggingHandler implements SOAPHandler<SOAPMessageContext>
{
    private static PrintStream out = System.out;
    @Override
    public Set<QName> getHeaders()
    {
        return null;
    }
    @Override
    public void close(MessageContext messageContext)
    {
    }
    @Override
```

```java
   public boolean handleFault(SOAPMessageContext soapmc)
   {
      log(soapmc);
      return true;
   }
   @Override
   public boolean handleMessage(SOAPMessageContext soapmc)
   {
      log(soapmc);
      return true;
   }
   private void log(SOAPMessageContext soapmc)
   {
      Boolean outboundProperty = (Boolean)
         soapmc.get(MessageContext.MESSAGE_OUTBOUND_PROPERTY);
      if (outboundProperty.booleanValue())
         out.println("Outbound message:");
      else
         out.println("Inbound message:");
      SOAPMessage soapm = soapmc.getMessage();
      try
      {
         soapm.writeTo(out);
         out.println("\n");
      }
      catch (IOException|SOAPException e)
      {
         out.println("Handler exception: "+e);
      }
   }
}
```

SOAPLoggingHandler first declares a java.io.PrintStream field named out that identifies the destination. Although System.out is assigned to out, you can assign a different output stream to this field for logging SOAP messages to another destination.

SOAPHandler introduces a Set<QName> getHeaders() method for informing the JAX-WS runtime about the SOAP headers that the handler is responsible for processing. This method returns a set of qualified names for those SOAP message header blocks that the handler can process. Although we must implement this method, it returns null because there are no headers to process.

Note Jim White's "Working with Headers in JAX-WS SOAPHandlers" blog post (http://www.intertech.com/Blog/post/Working-with-Headers-in-JAX-WS-SOAPHandlers.aspx) demonstrates the usefulness of getHeaders().

The overriding close() method does nothing because there are no resources that need to be cleaned up. In contrast, handleFault() and handleMessage() invoke the private log() method to log a SOAP message.

The log() method uses its SOAPMessageContext argument to obtain the value of the property identified as MessageContext.MESSAGE_OUTBOUND_PROPERTY. The return value determines whether an Inbound message string or an Outbound message string is logged. log() next uses this argument to invoke the SOAPMessage getMessage() method, which returns a SOAPMessage object whose write(Object o) method is called to write the SOAP message to the stream identified by out.

You need to instantiate this class and add the resulting instance to the client's or the web service's handler chain. Use the @HandlerChain annotation to add this handler to a web service's handler chain. In contrast, Listing 11-20 reveals the programmatic approach to adding a handler to a client's handler chain.

Listing 11-20. Adding a SOAPHandler instance to a client's handler chain

```java
import java.net.URL;

import java.util.List;

import javax.xml.namespace.QName;

import javax.xml.ws.Binding;
import javax.xml.ws.BindingProvider;
import javax.xml.ws.Service;

import javax.xml.ws.handler.Handler;

import ca.tutortutor.tv.TempVerter;

class TempVerterClient
{
   public static void main(String[] args) throws Exception
   {
      URL url = new URL("http://localhost:9901/TempVerter?wsdl");
      QName qname = new QName("http://tv.tutortutor.ca/",
                              "TempVerterImplService");
      Service service = Service.create(url, qname);
      qname = new QName("http://tv.tutortutor.ca/", "TempVerterImplPort");
      TempVerter tv = service.getPort(qname, TempVerter.class);
//      TempVerter tv = service.getPort(TempVerter.class);
      BindingProvider bp = (BindingProvider) tv;
      Binding binding = bp.getBinding();
      List<Handler> hc = binding.getHandlerChain();
      hc.add(new SOAPLoggingHandler());
      binding.setHandlerChain(hc);
      System.out.println(tv.c2f(37.0)+"\n");
      System.out.println(tv.f2c(212.0)+"\n");
   }
}
```

Listing 11-20's main() method accesses the client's handler chain and inserts an instance of SOAPLoggingHandler into this chain by completing the following steps:

1. Cast the proxy instance returned from getPort() to javax.xml.ws.BindingProvider because the proxy instance's class implements

this interface. BindingProvider provides access to the protocol binding and associated context objects for request and response message processing.

2. Call BindingProvider's Binding getBinding() method to return the protocol binding instance, which is an instance of a class that ultimately implements the javax.xml.ws.Binding interface —the class actually implements Binding's javax.xml.ws.soap.SOAPBinding subinterface.

3. Invoke Binding's List<Handler> getHandlerChain() method on this instance to return a copy of the handler chain.

4. Instantiate SOAPLoggingHandler and add this instance to the java.util.List instance of Handler instances.

5. Pass this list of handlers to Binding's void setHandlerChain(List<Handler> chain) method.

Compile the contents of Listing 11-20. Assuming that TempVerterPublisher is running, run TempVerterClient. You should observe the following output:

```
Outbound message:
<S:Envelope xmlns:S="http://schemas.xmlsoap.org/soap/envelope/"><S:Body><ns2:c2f↵
xmlns:ns2="http://tv.tutortutor.ca/"><arg0>37.0</arg0></ns2:c2f></S:Body></S:Envelope>

Inbound message:
<S:Envelope
xmlns:S="http://schemas.xmlsoap.org/soap/envelope/"><S:Header/><S:Body><ns2:c2fResponse
↵xmlns:ns2="http://tv.tutortutor.ca/"><return>98.6</return></ns2:c2fResponse></S:Body><↵/S:E
nvelope>

98.6

Outbound message:
<S:Envelope xmlns:S="http://schemas.xmlsoap.org/soap/envelope/"><S:Body><ns2:f2c↵
xmlns:ns2="http://tv.tutortutor.ca/"><arg0>212.0</arg0></ns2:f2c></S:Body></S:Envelope>

Inbound message:
<S:Envelope↵
xmlns:S="http://schemas.xmlsoap.org/soap/envelope/"><S:Header/><S:Body><ns2:f2cResponse
↵xmlns:ns2="http://tv.tutortutor.ca/"><return>100.0</return></ns2:f2cResponse></S:Body>↵</S:
Envelope>

100.0
```

The S: and ns2: namespace prefixes are generated by JAX-WS.

■ **Note** To learn more about SOAP message handlers (especially on using @HandlerChain), check out Oracle's "Creating and Using SOAP Message Handlers" tutorial (http://download.oracle.com/docs/cd/E12840_01/wls/docs103/webserv_adv/handlers.html).

Authentication and a Customized Lightweight HTTP Server

You can create a customized lightweight HTTP server that offers additional features for testing a web service, and replace the default lightweight HTTP server that is started in response to an Endpoint.publish() invocation with your server. What makes this possible is that Endpoint's void publish(Object serverContext) method can accept as its argument an instance of a class that subclasses the abstract com.sun.net.httpserver.HTTPContext class.

Note You can find JDK 7 documentation on HTTPContext and the rest of the com.sun.net.httpserver package's interface and classes at

http://download.oracle.com/javase/7/docs/jre/api/net/httpserver/spec/com/sun/net/httpserver/package-summary.html.

For example, suppose you want to test basic authentication with your web service —I introduced this topic in Chapter 9. On the client side, you install a default authenticator that supplies a username and password to the web service. Listing 11-21 reveals this authenticator in the context of TempVerterClient.

Listing 11-21. Supporting basic authentication with the TempVerterClient application

```
import java.net.Authenticator;
import java.net.PasswordAuthentication;
import java.net.URL;

import javax.xml.namespace.QName;

import javax.xml.ws.Service;

import ca.tutortutor.tv.TempVerter;

class TempVerterClient
{
   public static void main(String[] args) throws Exception
   {
      Authenticator auth;
      auth = new Authenticator()
      {
         @Override
         protected PasswordAuthentication getPasswordAuthentication()
         {
            return new PasswordAuthentication("x", new char[] { 'y' });
         }
      };
      Authenticator.setDefault(auth);
      URL url = new URL("http://localhost:9901/TempVerter?wsdl");
      QName qname = new QName("http://tv.tutortutor.ca/",
```

```
                                "TempVerterImplService");
        Service service = Service.create(url, qname);
        qname = new QName("http://tv.tutortutor.ca/", "TempVerterImplPort");
        TempVerter tv = service.getPort(qname, TempVerter.class);
//        TempVerter tv = service.getPort(TempVerter.class);
        System.out.println(tv.c2f(37.0));
        System.out.println(tv.f2c(212.0));
    }
}
```

For simplicity, Listing 11-21 embeds x as the username and y as the password in the source code. A more useful and secure application would prompt for this information. At runtime the Java Virtual Machine invokes getPasswordAuthentication() to obtain these credentials and make them available to the HTTP server when requested to do so.

This method will not be called if the HTTP server doesn't make a request, and our current version of TempVerterPublisher will never cause the HTTP server to make this request. However, you can install a customized server that will result in this request, and Listing 11-22 presents an enhanced TempVerterPublisher application that accomplishes this task.

Listing 11-22. *Supporting basic authentication with the TempVerterPublisher application*

```java
import java.io.IOException;

import java.net.InetSocketAddress;

import javax.xml.ws.Endpoint;

import com.sun.net.httpserver.BasicAuthenticator;
import com.sun.net.httpserver.HttpContext;
import com.sun.net.httpserver.HttpServer;

import ca.tutortutor.tv.TempVerterImpl;

class TempVerterPublisher
{
    public static void main(String[] args) throws IOException
    {
        HttpServer server = HttpServer.create(new InetSocketAddress(9901), 0);
        HttpContext context = server.createContext("/TempVerter");
        BasicAuthenticator auth;
        auth = new BasicAuthenticator("myAuth")
        {
            @Override
            public boolean checkCredentials(String username, String password)
            {
                return username.equals("x") && password.equals("y");
            }
        };
        context.setAuthenticator(auth);
        Endpoint endpoint = Endpoint.create(new TempVerterImpl());
        endpoint.publish(context);
        server.start();
```

```
      }
    }
```

The `main()` method first creates an `HTTPServer` instance that describes an HTTP server connected to port 9901 of the local host. This method next creates the `/TempVerter` context, and returns the resulting `HttpContext` subclass object.

Continuing, the abstract `com.sun.net.httpserver.BasicAuthenticator` class is anonymously subclassed to describe a server side implementation of HTTP basic authentication; its `boolean checkCredentials(String username, String password)` method is called to verify the given name and password in the context of the basic authenticator's realm. This method returns true for valid credentials, and false when they are invalid.

After passing the `BasicAuthenticator` instance to `HttpContext`'s `Authenticator setAuthenticator(Authenticator auth)` method, `Endpoint`'s `Endpoint create(Object implementor)` method is called to create an `Endpoint` instance with the specified `TempVerterImpl` instance as implementor's argument. This method's `void publish(Object serverContext)` method is then called with the previous context, and the `HttpServer` instance is started.

If you were to run `TempVerterPublisher` and `TempVerterClient`, you would observe 98.6 followed by 100.0 on two successive lines of output. However, if you modified `TempVerterClient`'s credentials, you would observe a thrown exception in regard to not being able to access the WSDL when `Service service = Service.create(url, qname);` attempts to execute; the WSDL is not accessible because authentication has failed.

■ **Note** Learn more about JAX-WS and basic authentication by checking out Illya Yalovyy's "HTTP basic authentication with JAX-WS (Client)" blog post at http://etfdevlab.blogspot.com/2009/12/http-basic-authentication-with-jax-ws.html.

RESTful Web Services and Attachments

RESTful web services that implement `Provider<Source>` cannot return arbitrary MIME-typed data (e.g., a JPEG image). They can only return XML messages with no attachments. If you want to return an attachment (such as an image file), your web service class must implement the `Provider<DataSource>` interface; the `javax.activation.DataSource` interface provides the JavaBeans Activation Framework with an abstraction of an arbitrary collection of data.

Listing 11-23 presents an Image Publisher RESTful web service that demonstrates how you could use `DataSource` with two other `javax.activation` package types to return a JPEG image to a client.

Listing 11-23. Returning a JPEG image in response to a GET request

```
import javax.activation.DataSource;
import javax.activation.FileDataSource;
import javax.activation.MimetypesFileTypeMap;

import javax.annotation.Resource;

import javax.xml.ws.BindingType;
import javax.xml.ws.Endpoint;
```

```
import javax.xml.ws.Provider;
import javax.xml.ws.ServiceMode;
import javax.xml.ws.WebServiceContext;
import javax.xml.ws.WebServiceProvider;

import javax.xml.ws.handler.MessageContext;

import javax.xml.ws.http.HTTPBinding;
import javax.xml.ws.http.HTTPException;

@WebServiceProvider
@ServiceMode(value = javax.xml.ws.Service.Mode.MESSAGE)
@BindingType(value = HTTPBinding.HTTP_BINDING)
class ImagePublisher implements Provider<DataSource>
{
   @Resource
   private WebServiceContext wsContext;
   @Override
   public DataSource invoke(DataSource request)
   {
      if (wsContext == null)
         throw new RuntimeException("dependency injection failed on wsContext");
      MessageContext msgContext = wsContext.getMessageContext();
      switch ((String) msgContext.get(MessageContext.HTTP_REQUEST_METHOD))
      {
         case "GET"   : return doGet();
         default      : throw new HTTPException(405);
      }
   }
   private DataSource doGet()
   {
      FileDataSource fds = new FileDataSource("balstone.jpg");
      MimetypesFileTypeMap mtftm = new MimetypesFileTypeMap();
      mtftm.addMimeTypes("image/jpeg jpg");
      fds.setFileTypeMap(mtftm);
      System.out.println(fds.getContentType());
      return fds;
   }
   public static void main(String[] args)
   {
      Endpoint.publish("http://localhost:9902/Image", new ImagePublisher());
   }
}
```

Listing 11-23's ImagePublisher class describes a simple RESTful web service whose invoke() method honors only the HTTP GET verb. Its doGet() method responds to a GET request by returning the contents of the balstone.jpg image file to the client.

doGet() first instantiates the javax.activation.FileDataSource class, which implements DataSource, and which encapsulates a file to be returned as an attachment. doGet() passes the name of this file to the FileDataSource(String name) constructor.doGet() next instantiates the javax.activation.MimetypesFileTypeMap class so that it can associate a MIME type with the JPEG file based on its jpg file extension. This mapping is performed by invoking MimetypesFileTypeMap's void addMimeTypes(String mime_types) method, passing "image/jpeg jpg" as the argument (image/jpeg is the MIME type and jpg is the file extension).

Continuing, doGet() invokes FileDataSource's void setFileTypeMap(FileTypeMap map) method to associate the MimetypesFileTypeMap instance with the FileDataSource instance.

After invoking FileDataSource's String getContentType() method to return the MIME type of the file and outputting its return value, doGet() returns the FileDataSource object to invoke(), which returns this object to the JAX-WS runtime.

I've created an ImageClient application to use with ImagePublisher. Because this application's source code is very similar to Listing 11-15's ViewChart source code, I won't present its code here (for brevity) —ImageClient.java is included with this book's source code, however.

Instead, I'll demonstrate ImagePublisher in a web browser context. Compile ImagePublisher.java and execute this application. Once this application is running, launch a web browser and enter **http://localhost:9902/Image** in its address bar. Figure 11-11 shows the result in the Mozilla Firefox web browser —you should also observe image/jpeg in the ImagePublisher application's command window.

Figure 11-11. *Balanced stone at Arches National Park in eastern Utah. (Image courtesy of Public Domain Images,* http://www.public-domain-image.com/nature-landscapes-public-domain-images-

pictures/rock-*formations-public-domain-images-pictures/balanced-stone-at-arches-national-park.jpg.html)*

Modify Listing 11-23, either by removing the `.jpg` extension in `balstone.jpg`, or by commenting out `mtftm.addMimeTypes("image/jpeg jpg");`. After recompiling `ImagePublisher.java`, reexecute this application.

Reload the current web page in the browser. Instead of observing the image being redisplayed, you should (under Firefox) observe a dialog box identifying `application/octet-stream` as the MIME type, and prompting you to save the file or choose a viewer —you will also observe this MIME type in ImagePublisher's command window.

The reason for this change of MIME type has to do with `MimetypesFileTypeMap`'s `String getContentType(String filename)` method. At some point, this method is called to return the content type for the specified filename. When this name is missing an extension, or when a MIME type for the file's extension has not been registered (via a call to `addMimeTypes()`), `getContentType()` returns the default `application/octet-stream` MIME type.

You might want to keep this scenario in mind when customizing `ImagePublisher` (and a client) to work with the HTTP `Accept` request header. (The client specifies an `Accept` header [via `URLConnection`'s `void setRequestProperty(String key, String value)` method] with one or more MIME types that tell the server what kind(s) of data the client wants to receive; the server examines this header and returns this data when the header includes a MIME type that the server can honor.)

■ **Note** If you're wondering why `@ServiceMode(value = javax.xml.ws.Service.Mode.MESSAGE)` is specified in Listing 11-23, the answer is that `Provider<DataSource>` is used for sending attachments, which means that `javax.xml.ws.Service.Mode.PAYLOAD` mode is invalid.

Providers and Dispatch Clients

This chapter presents high-level and low-level approaches to working with JAX-WS. The high-level approach requires you to work with SEIs and SIBs; it simplifies and hides the details of converting between Java method invocations and their corresponding SOAP-based XML messages. The low-level approach lets you work directly with XML messages, and must be followed to implement a RESTful web service.

While discussing how to implement a RESTful web service with JAX-WS, I introduced you to this API's `Provider<T>` interface, whose `invoke()` method is called by a client to receive and process a request, and to return a response. I then demonstrated how a client communicates with a provider by using the `HttpURLConnection` class. Behind the scenes, the JAX-WS runtime takes the information received from the URL connection and creates the proper object to pass to `invoke()`. It also takes the object returned from `invoke()` and makes its contents available to the client via the URL connection's output stream.

JAX-WS also offers the `javax.xml.ws.Dispatch<T>` interface as a client-side companion to `Provider`. A client uses `Dispatch` to construct messages or message payloads as XML, and is known as a *dispatch client*. As with `Provider`, `Dispatch` offers a `T invoke(T)` method. Dispatch clients call this method to send messages synchronously to providers, and to obtain provider responses from this method's return value.

■ **Note** Dispatch offers additional invocation methods, such as Response<T> invokeAsync(T msg) for invoking the Provider's invoke() method asynchronously. This method returns immediately; the result of the Provider's invoke() method is made available in the returned Response<T> object at some point in the future —the javax.xml.ws.Response interface extends the java.util.concurrent.Future<T> interface, which I discuss in Chapter 6.

A dispatch client obtains an object whose class implements Dispatch<T> by invoking one of Service's createDispatch() methods. For example, Dispatch<T> createDispatch(QName portName, Class<T> type, Service.Mode mode) returns a Dispatch instance for communicating with the web service through the port identified by portName, using the specified Source, SOAPMessage, or DataSource counterpart to the actual type argument passed to Provider<T>, and via the service mode (message or payload) passed to mode.

After the Dispatch instance has been obtained, a dispatch client will create an object conforming to the actual type argument passed to T, and pass this instance to the web service provider in a call to Dispatch's invoke() method. To understand the interplay between a dispatch client and a provider, consider a client that invokes Dispatch<Source>'s invoke() method with an XML document made available via the Source argument. The following sequence occurs:

- The provider's JAX-WS runtime dispatches the client request to Provider<Source>'s invoke() method.

- The provider transforms the Source instance into an appropriate javax.xml.transform.Result instance (such as a DOM tree), processes this Result instance in some manner, and returns a Source instance containing XML content to JAX-WS, which transmits the content to Dispatch's invoke() method.

- Dispatch's invoke() method returns another Source instance containing the XML content, which the dispatch client transforms into an appropriate Result instance for processing.

Listing 11-24 demonstrates this interplay by providing an alternate version of the doGet() method that appears in Listing 11-14's LibraryClient application. Instead of working with HttpURLConnection, the alternate doGet() method works with Service and Dispatch.

Listing 11-24. Revised LibraryClient application's doGet() method as a dispatch client

```
static void doGet(String isbn) throws Exception
{
   Service service = Service.create(new QName(""));
   String endpoint = "http://localhost:9902/library";
   service.addPort(new QName(""), HTTPBinding.HTTP_BINDING, endpoint);
   Dispatch<Source> dispatch;
   dispatch = service.createDispatch(new QName(""), Source.class,
                                     Service.Mode.MESSAGE);
   Map<String, Object> reqContext = dispatch.getRequestContext();
   reqContext.put(MessageContext.HTTP_REQUEST_METHOD, "GET");
   if (isbn != null)
```

```java
      reqContext.put(MessageContext.QUERY_STRING, "isbn="+isbn);
Source result;
try
{
   result = dispatch.invoke(null);
}
catch (Exception e)
{
   System.err.println(e);
   return;
}
try
{
   DOMResult dom = new DOMResult();
   Transformer t = TransformerFactory.newInstance().newTransformer();
   t.transform(result, dom);
   XPathFactory xpf = XPathFactory.newInstance();
   XPath xp = xpf.newXPath();
   if (isbn == null)
   {
      NodeList isbns = (NodeList) xp.evaluate("/isbns/isbn/text()",
                                             dom.getNode(),
                                             XPathConstants.NODESET);
      for (int i = 0; i < isbns.getLength(); i++)
         System.out.println(isbns.item(i).getNodeValue());
   }
   else
   {
      NodeList books = (NodeList) xp.evaluate("/book", dom.getNode(),
                                             XPathConstants.NODESET);
      isbn = xp.evaluate("@isbn", books.item(0));
      String pubYear = xp.evaluate("@pubyear", books.item(0));
      String title = xp.evaluate("title", books.item(0)).trim();
      String publisher = xp.evaluate("publisher", books.item(0)).trim();
      NodeList authors = (NodeList) xp.evaluate("author", books.item(0),
                                             XPathConstants.NODESET);
      System.out.println("Title: "+title);
      for (int i = 0; i < authors.getLength(); i++)
         System.out.println("Author: "+authors.item(i).getFirstChild()
                                             .getNodeValue().trim());
      System.out.println("ISBN: "+isbn);
      System.out.println("Publication Year: "+pubYear);
      System.out.println("Publisher: "+publisher);
   }
}
catch (TransformerException e)
{
   System.err.println(e);
}
catch (XPathExpressionException xpee)
{
   System.err.println(xpee);
```

```
    }
    System.out.println();
}
```

This method first invokes Service's `Service create(QName serviceName)` method to create a Service instance that provides a client view of a web service. In contrast to a Service instance created from a WSDL file, where the qualified name of the service implementation class and other information is known to the Service instance, a Service instance created by a dispatch client doesn't need to have knowledge of the service when created; the information will be provided to this instance shortly. As a result, a QName instance with an empty qualified name can be passed to `create()`.

A `Dispatch<T>` instance must be bound to a specific port and endpoint before use. As a result, `doGet()` next invokes Service's `void addPort(QName portName, String bindingId, String endpointAddress)` method to create a new port for the service. (Ports created with this method contain no WSDL port type information and can be used only for creating Dispatch instances.) The QName argument passed to `portName` can contain an empty qualified name. However, an appropriate binding must be specified via a String-based binding identifier. This example specifies `HTTPBinding.HTTP_BINDING` because we are communicating with a RESTful web service via HTTP. Also, the target service's endpoint address must be specified as a URI, which happens to be `http://localhost:9902/library` in this example.

After adding a port to the Service object, `doGet()` invokes `createDispatch()` as explained earlier. Once again, a QName object with an empty qualified name is passed because there is no WSDL to indicate a port name.

The returned `Dispatch<Source>` object's `Map<String,Object> getRequestContext()` method (which Dispatch inherits from its BindingProvider superinterface) is called to obtain the context that is used to initialize the message context for request messages. `doGet()` inserts the request method verb (GET) and query string (isbn=*isbn*) into this map, which will be made available to the provider.

At this point, `doGet()` executes `Source result = dispatch.invoke(null);`, passing null instead of a Source object as an argument because the provider's `doGet()` method expects to receive its data as a query string. If an exception occurs during the invocation, a catch block outputs the exception information and exits `doGet()`. Otherwise, the result object's XML content is transformed into a DOMResult object, which is processed via XPath expressions to obtain result data, which is then output.

If you were to run LibraryClient with Listing 11-24's `doGet()` method, and if you were to use the same book-related data presented earlier in this chapter, you would observe the following output:

```
<response>book inserted</response>

<response>book inserted</response>

9781430210450
0201548550

Title: Advanced C+
Author: James O. Coplien
ISBN: 0201548550
Publication Year: 1992
Publisher: Addison Wesley

Title: Beginning Groovy and Grails
Author: Christopher M. Judd
Author: Joseph Faisal Nusairat
Author: James Shingler
ISBN: 9781430210450
```

Publication Year: 2008
Publisher: Apress

<response>book updated</response>

Title: Advanced C++
Author: James O. Coplien
ISBN: 0201548550
Publication Year: 1992
Publisher: Addison Wesley

<response>book deleted</response>

9781430210450

■ **Note** To simplify this chapter's discussion of web services, I've avoided mention of threads and thread synchronization, until now. According to the JAX-WS 2.2 specification (http://download.oracle.com/otndocs/jcp/jaxws-2.2-mrel3-evalu-oth-JSpec/) client proxy instances (returned from Service's getPort() methods) are not guaranteed to be thread safe. Also, Dispatch instances (returned from Service's createDispatch() methods) are not thread safe. In either case, you must use thread synchronization when these instances will be accessed from multiple threads.

EXERCISES

The following exercises are designed to test your understanding of Java's web services support:

1. Create a SOAP-based Library web service that recognizes two operations, expressed via methods void addBook(String isbn, String title) and String getTitle(String isbn). Create a LibraryClient application that invokes addBook() followed by getTitle() to test this web service.

2. Create a LibraryClientSAAJ application that uses SAAJ to perform the equivalent of LibraryClient's tasks. Use SOAPMessage's writeTo() method to output each of the request and response messages for the addBook and getTitle operations.

3. The RESTful web service described by Listing 11-11's Library class is flawed in that the doDelete() method doesn't notify the client when requested to delete a nonexistent book. How might you modify this method to report this attempt?

Summary

Web services are server-based applications/software components that expose Web resources to clients via exchanges of messages. Companies use web services because they overcome traditional middleware problems by being based on free and open standards, by their maintainability, by involving the Web, and by being flexible. Furthermore, they help companies preserve their significant investments in legacy software.

Web services largely fall into two categories: SOAP-based and RESTful. SOAP-based web services involve the flow of XML messages formatted according to the SOAP XML language protocol between endpoints, which combine network addresses with bindings, where a binding provides concrete details on how an interface of operations (where an operation consists of messages) is bound to the SOAP messaging protocol to communicate commands, error codes, and other items over the wire.

SOAP-based web services typically rely on WSDL documents to identify the operations provided by the service. An XML-based WSDL document serves as a formal contract between a SOAP-based web service and its clients, providing all the details needed to interact with the web service. This document lets you group messages into operations and operations into interfaces. It also lets you define a binding for each interface as well as the endpoint address.

A RESTful web service is based on the REST software architecture style for the World Wide Web. The central part of REST is the URI-identifiable resource. REST identifies resources by their MIME types (e.g., text/xml). Also, resources have states that are captured by their representations. When a client requests a resource from a RESTful web service, the service sends a MIME-typed representation of the resource to the client. Clients use HTTP's POST, GET, PUT, and DELETE verbs to retrieve representations of and manipulate resources —REST views these verbs as an API and maps them onto the database CRUD operations.

Java simplifies and accelerates web services development by incorporating APIs, annotations, tools, and a lightweight HTTP server (for deploying your web services to a simple web server and testing them in this environment) into its core. Key APIs are JAX-WS, JAXB, and SAAJ. Important annotations include WebService, WebMethod, WebServiceProvider, Binding, and ServiceMode. Four tools are also provided to simplify development: schemagen, wsgen, wsimport, and xjc. The lightweight HTTP server is based on a package of types located in the com.sun.net.httpserver package of Oracle's Java reference implementation. Web services published via JAX-WS's Endpoint.publish() method call typically cause the default lightweight HTTP server to be started, although you can create your own HTTP server, make its context available to Endpoint.publish(), and start this server.

After learning how to create and access your own SOAP-based and RESTful web services, and access the SOAP-based and RESTful web services created by others, you'll probably want to learn about advanced web service topics. Chapter 11 partly satisfies this desire by showing you how to access SOAP-based web services via the SAAJ API, install a JAX-WS handler to log the flow of SOAP messages, install a customized lightweight HTTP server to perform authentication, send attachments to clients from a RESTful web service, and use dispatch clients with providers.

And now for something different! Chapter 12 closes the nonappendix portion of this book by introducing you to Android and showing you how to create an Android app.

Java 7 Meets Android

Developing apps for Android devices is popular these days. Perhaps you would like to learn how to develop your own Android apps with Java 7 (although you cannot use APIs and language features newer than Java 5).

Chapter 12 presents a rapid introduction to app development. You first learn about Android architecture and the architecture of an Android app. You then learn how to install the Android SDK and a platform so that you have the tools and an environment to begin app development. Because the SDK provides an emulator to emulate Android devices, you next learn how to create and start an Android Virtual Device (AVD), which you can use to test your apps in lieu of an actual Android device. Finally, you're introduced to a simple app, learn how to create this app via the SDK, and learn how to install and run the app on an AVD.

Note If you want to learn more about Android after reading this chapter, check out *Beginning Android 3* by Mark Murphy (Apress, 2011; ISBN: 978-1-4302-3297-1). You might also want to check out *Android Recipes* by Dave Smith and Jeff Friesen (Apress, 2011; ISBN: 978-1-4302-3413-5). *Android Recipes* teaches you additional Android app architecture fundamentals, shows you how to install the Eclipse IDE and develop an app with that IDE, presents solutions to various app development problems, introduces you to various third-party development tools and the Android NDK, shows you how to create your own libraries and use third-party libraries, and presents app design guidelines.

Exploring Android and Android App Architectures

The *Android Developer's Guide* (http://developer.android.com/guide/index.html) defines *Android* as a *software stack* (a set of software subsystems needed to deliver a fully functional solution) for mobile devices. This stack includes an operating system (a modified version of the Linux kernel), *middleware* (software that connects the low-level operating system to high-level apps), and key apps (written in Java) such as a web browser (known as Browser) and a contact manager (known as Contacts).

Android offers the following features:

- Application framework enabling reuse and replacement of app components
- Bluetooth, EDGE, 3G, and WiFi support (hardware dependent)

- Camera, GPS, compass, and accelerometer support (hardware dependent)

- Dalvik virtual machine optimized for mobile devices

- GSM Telephony support (hardware dependent)

- Integrated browser based on the open source WebKit engine

- Media support for common audio, video, and still image formats (MPEG4, H.264, MP3, AAC, AMR, JPG, PNG, GIF)

- Optimized graphics powered by a custom 2D graphics library; 3D graphics based on the OpenGL ES 1.0 specification (hardware acceleration optional)

- SQLite for structured data storage

Note Although not part of an Android device's software stack, Android's rich development environment (including a device emulator and a plugin for the Eclipse IDE) could also be considered an Android feature.

Android apps are written in Java and can access only the Java APIs described in the API reference at http://developer.android.com/reference/packages.html (as well as Android-oriented third-party APIs). They cannot access Java APIs beyond Java 5. This restriction affects Java 7's try-with-resources statement, which is based on the new java.lang.AutoCloseable interface and API support for suppressed exceptions. You cannot use try-with-resources in your Android source code.

Note Not all Java 5 (and previous version) APIs are supported by Android. For example, Android doesn't support the Abstract Window Toolkit (AWT) or Swing. Instead, it offers a smaller set of user-interface APIs.

Android Architecture

The Android software stack consists of apps at the top, middleware (consisting of an application framework, libraries, and the Android runtime) in the middle, and a Linux kernel with various drivers at the bottom. Figure 12-1 shows this layered architecture.

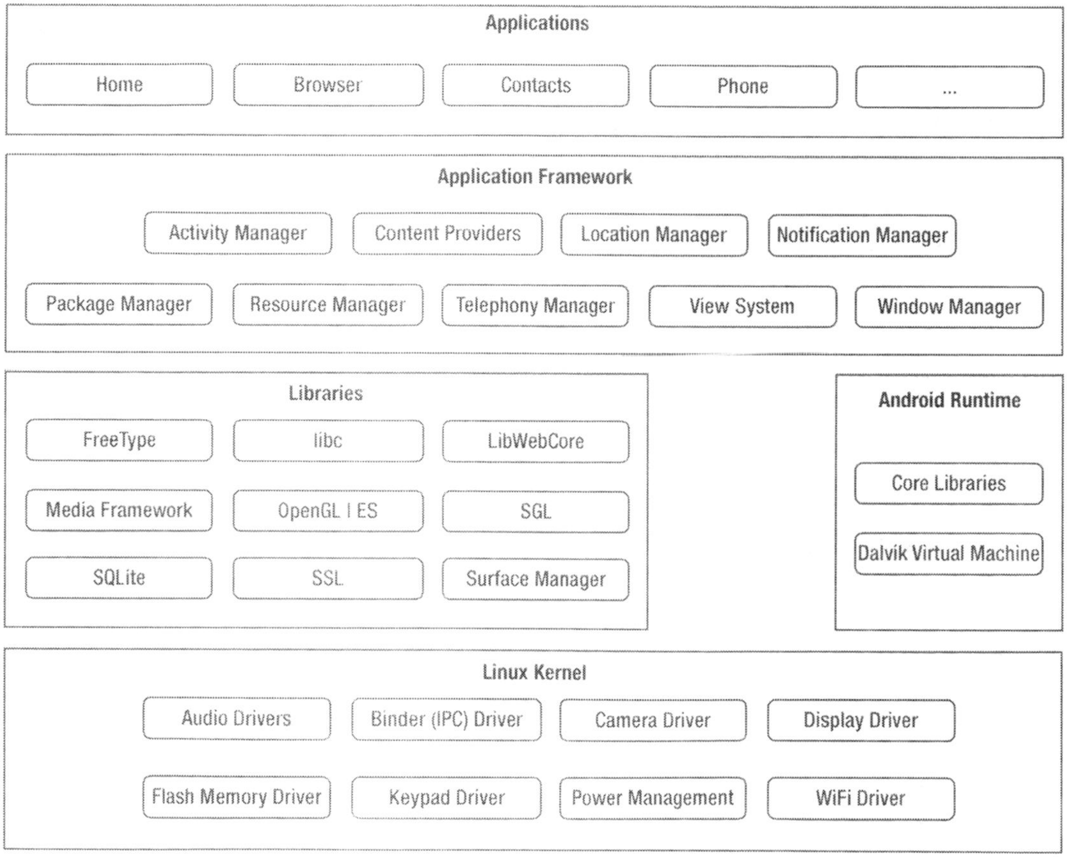

Figure 12-1. *Android's layered architecture consists of several major parts.*

Users care about apps, and Android ships with a variety of useful core apps, which include Browser, Contacts, and Phone. All apps are written in Java . Apps form the top layer of Android's architecture.

Directly beneath the app layer is the *application framework*, a set of high-level building blocks for creating apps. The application framework is preinstalled on Android devices and consists of the following components:

- *Activity Manager.* This component provides an app's *lifecycle* and maintains a shared activity stack for navigating within and among apps. (I discuss both concepts later in this chapter when I present activities.)

- *Content Providers.* These components encapsulate data (e.g., the Browser app's bookmarks) that can be shared among apps.

- *Location Manager.* This component makes it possible for an Android device to be aware of its physical location.

- *Notification Manager*: This component lets an app notify the user of a significant event (e.g., a message's arrival) without interrupting what the user is currently doing.

- *Package Manager*: This component lets an app learn about other app packages that are currently installed on the device. (App packages are discussed later in this chapter.)

- *Resource Manager*: This component lets an app access its application resources, a topic that I discuss later in this chapter.

- *Telephony Manager*: This component lets an app learn about a device's telephony services. It also handles making and receiving phone calls.

- *View System*: This component manages user interface elements and user interface-oriented event generation. (I briefly discuss these topics later in this chapter.)

- *Window Manager*: This component organizes the screen's real estate into windows, allocates drawing surfaces, and performs other window-related jobs.

The components of the application framework rely on a set of C/C++ libraries to perform their jobs. Developers interact with the following libraries by way of framework APIs:

- *FreeType*: This library supports bitmap and vector font rendering.

- *libc*: This library is a BSD-derived implementation of the standard C system library, tuned for embedded Linux-based devices.

- *LibWebCore*: This library offers a modern and fast web browser engine that powers the Android browser and an embeddable web view. It's based on WebKit (http://en.wikipedia.org/wiki/WebKit) and is also used by the Google Chrome and Apple Safari browsers.

- *Media Framework*: These libraries, which are based on PacketVideo's OpenCORE, support the playback and recording of many popular audio and video formats, as well as working with static image files. Supported formats include MPEG4, H.264, MP3, AAC, AMR, JPEG, and PNG.

- *OpenGL | ES*: These 3D graphics libraries provide an OpenGL implementation based on OpenGL ES 1.0 APIs. They use hardware 3D acceleration (where available) or the included (and highly optimized) 3D software rasterizer.

- *SGL*: This library provides the underlying 2D graphics engine.

- *SQLite*: This library provides a powerful and lightweight relational database engine that's available to all apps, and that's also used by Mozilla Firefox and Apple's iPhone for persistent storage.

- *SSL*: This library provides secure sockets layer-based security for network communication.

- *Surface Manager*: This library manages access to the display subsystem, and seamlessly composites 2D and 3D graphic layers from multiple apps.

Android provides a runtime environment that consists of core libraries (implementing a subset of the Apache Harmony Java 5 implementation) and the Dalvik virtual machine (a non-Java virtual machine that's based on processor registers instead of being stack-based).

■ **Note** Google's Dan Bornstein created Dalvik and named this virtual machine after an Icelandic fishing village where some of his ancestors lived.

Each Android app defaults to running in its own Linux process, which hosts an instance of Dalvik. This virtual machine has been designed so that devices can run multiple virtual machines efficiently. This efficiency is largely due to Dalvik executing Dalvik Executable (DEX)-based files—DEX is a format that's optimized for a minimal memory footprint.

■ **Note** Android starts a process when any part of the app needs to execute, and shuts down the process when it's no longer needed and environmental resources are required by other apps.

Perhaps you're wondering how it's possible to have a non-Java virtual machine run Java code. The answer is that Dalvik doesn't run Java code. Instead, Android transforms compiled Java classfiles into the DEX format, and it's this resulting code that gets executed by Dalvik.

Finally, the libraries and Android runtime rely on the Linux kernel (version 2.6.*x*) for underlying core services, such as threading, low-level memory management, a network stack, process management, and a driver model. Furthermore, the kernel acts as an abstraction layer between the hardware and the rest of the software stack.

ANDROID SECURITY MODEL

Android's architecture includes a security model that prevents apps from performing operations considered harmful to other apps, Linux, or users. This security model, which is mostly based on process level enforcement via standard Linux features (such as user and group IDs), places processes in a security sandbox.

By default, the sandbox prevents apps from reading or writing the user's private data (e.g., contacts or emails), reading or writing another app's files, performing network access, keeping the device awake, accessing the camera, and so on. Apps that need to access the network or perform other sensitive operations must first obtain permission to do so.

Android handles permission requests in various ways, typically by automatically allowing or disallowing the request based upon a certificate, or by prompting the user to grant or revoke the permission. Permissions required by an app are declared in the app's manifest file (discussed later in this chapter) so that they are known to Android when the app is installed. These permissions won't subsequently change.

App Architecture

The architecture of an Android app differs from that of an application running on the desktop. App architecture is based upon components that communicate with each other via intents, are described by a manifest, and may use application resources. Collectively, these items are stored in an app package.

Components

An *Android app* is a collection of *components* (activities, broadcast receivers, content providers, and services) that run in a Linux process and that are managed by Android. These components share a set of environmental resources, including databases, preferences, a filesystem, and the Linux process.

Note Not all these components need to be present in an app. For example, one app might consist of activities only, whereas another app might consist of activities and a service.

This component-oriented architecture lets an app reuse the components of other apps, provided that those other apps permit reuse of their components. Component reuse reduces overall memory footprint, which is very important for devices with limited memory.

For example, suppose you're creating a drawing app that lets users choose a color from a palette, and suppose that another app has developed a suitable color chooser and permits this component to be reused. In this scenario, the drawing app can call upon that other app's color chooser to have the user select a color rather than provide its own color chooser. The drawing app doesn't contain the other app's color chooser or even link to this other app. Instead, it starts up the other app's color chooser component when needed.

Android starts a process when any part of the app (e.g., the aforementioned color chooser) is needed, and instantiates the Java objects for that part. This is why Android's apps don't have a single entry point (no C-style main() function, for example). Instead, apps use components that are instantiated and run as needed.

COMMUNICATING VIA INTENTS

Activities, broadcast receivers, and services communicate with each other via *intents*, which are messages that describe operations to perform (e.g., send an email or choose a photo), or (in the case of broadcasts) provide descriptions of external events that have occurred (a device's camera being activated, for example) and are being announced.

Because nearly everything in Android involves intents, there are many opportunities to replace existing components with your own components. For example, Android provides the intent for sending an email. Your app can send that intent to activate the standard mail app, or it can register an activity (discussed shortly) that responds to the "send an email" intent, effectively replacing the standard mail app with its own activity.

These messages are implemented as instances of the `android.content.Intent` class. An `Intent` object describes a message in terms of some combination of the following items:

- *Action*: A string naming the action to be performed or, in the case of broadcast intents, the action that took place and is being reported. Actions are described by `Intent` constants such as `ACTION_CALL` (initiate a phone call), `ACTION_EDIT` (display data for the user to edit), and `ACTION_MAIN` (start up as the initial activity). You can also define your own action strings for activating the components in your app. These strings should include the app package as a prefix (`"com.example.project.SELECT_COLOR"`, for example).

- *Category*: A string that provides additional information about the kind of component that should handle the intent. For example, `CATEGORY_LAUNCHER` means that the calling activity should appear in the device's app launcher as a top-level app. (The app launcher is briefly discussed later in this chapter.)

- *Component name*: A string that specifies the fully qualified name (package plus name) of a component class to use for the intent. The component name is optional. When set, the `Intent` object is delivered to an instance of the designated class. When not set, Android uses other information in the `Intent` object to locate a suitable target.

- *Data*: The uniform resource identifier (URI) of the data on which to operate (e.g., a person record in a contacts database).

- *Extras*: A set of key-value pairs providing additional information that should be delivered to the component handling the intent. For example, given an action for sending an e-mail message, this information could include the message's subject, body, and so on.

- *Flags:* Bit values that instruct Android on how to launch an activity (e.g., which task the activity should belong to—tasks are discussed later in this chapter) and how to treat the activity after launch (e.g., whether the activity can be considered a recent activity). Flags are represented by constants in the `Intent` class; for example, `FLAG_ACTIVITY_NEW_TASK` specifies that this activity will become the start of a new task on this history stack—the history stack is discussed later in this chapter.

- *Type*: The Multipurpose Internet Mail Extensions (MIME) type of the intent data. Normally, Android infers a type from the data. By specifying a type, you disable that inference.

Intents can be classified as explicit or implicit. An *explicit intent* designates the target component by its name (the previously mentioned component name item is assigned a value). Because component names are usually unknown to the developers of other apps, explicit intents are typically used for app-internal messages (e.g., an activity that launches another activity located within the same app). Android delivers an explicit intent to an instance of the designated target class. Only the `Intent` object's component name matters for determining which component should get the intent.

An *implicit intent* doesn't name a target (the component name isn't assigned a value). Implicit intents are often used to start components in other apps. Android searches for the best component (a single activity or service to perform the requested action) or components (a set of broadcast receivers to respond to the broadcast announcement) to handle the implicit intent. During the search, Android compares the contents of the Intent object to *intent filters*, manifest information associated with components that can potentially receive intents.

Filters advertise a component's capabilities and identify only those intents that the component can handle. They open up the component to the possibility of receiving implicit intents of the advertised type. When a component has no intent filters, it can receive only explicit intents. In contrast, a component with filters can receive explicit and implicit intents. Android consults an Intent object's action, category, data, and type when comparing the intent against an intent filter. It doesn't take extras and flags into consideration.

Activities

An *activity* is a component that presents a user interface so that the user can interact with the app. For example, Android's Contacts app includes an activity for entering a new contact, its Phone app includes an activity for dialing a phone number, and its Calculator app includes an activity for performing basic calculations (see Figure 12-2).

Figure 12-2. The main activity of Android's Calculator app lets the user perform basic calculations.

Although an app can include a single activity, it's more typical for apps to include multiple activities. For example, Calculator also includes an "advanced panel" activity that lets the user calculate square roots, perform trigonometry, and carry out other advanced mathematical operations.

■ **Note** Because activities are the most frequently used component, I discuss them in more detail than broadcast receivers, content providers, and services. Check out *Android Recipes* for detailed coverage of these other component categories.

Activities are described by subclasses of the android.app.Activity class, which is an indirect subclass of the abstract android.content.Context class.

░ **Note** Context is an abstract class whose methods let apps access global information about their environments (e.g., their application resources), and allow apps to perform contextual operations, such as launching activities and services, broadcasting intents, and opening private files.

Activity subclasses override various Activity *lifecycle callback methods* that Android calls during the life of an activity. For example, Listing 12-1's SimpleActivity class, which is placed in a package because Android mandates that an app's components are to be stored in a unique package, extends Activity and also overrides the void onCreate(Bundle bundle) and void onDestroy() lifecycle callback methods.

Listing 12-1. A skeletal activity

```
package ca.tutortutor.simpleapp;

import android.app.Activity;

import android.os.Bundle;

public class SimpleActivity extends Activity
{
    @Override
    public void onCreate(Bundle savedInstanceState)
    {
        super.onCreate(savedInstanceState); // Always call superclass method first.
        System.out.println("onCreate(Bundle) called");
    }
    @Override
    public void onDestroy()

    {
        super.onDestroy(); // Always call superclass method first.

        System.out.println("onDestroy() called");

    }
}
```

SimpleActivity's overriding onCreate(Bundle) and onDestroy() methods first invoke their superclass counterparts, a pattern that must be followed when overriding the void onStart(), void onRestart(), void onResume(), void onPause(), and void onStop() lifecycle callback methods.

- onCreate(Bundle) is called when the activity is first created. This method is used to create the activity's user interface, create background threads as needed, and perform other global initialization. onCreate() is passed an android.os.Bundle object containing the activity's previous state, when that state was captured; otherwise, the null reference is passed. Android always calls the onStart() method after calling onCreate(Bundle).

- onStart() is called just before the activity becomes visible to the user. Android calls the onResume() method after calling onStart() when the activity comes to the foreground, and calls the onStop() method after onStart() when the activity becomes hidden.

- onRestart() is called after the activity has been stopped, just prior to it being started again. Android always calls onStart() after calling onRestart().

- onResume() is called just before the activity starts interacting with the user. At this point the activity has the focus and user input is directed to the activity. Android always calls the onPause() method after calling onResume(), but only when the activity must be paused.

- onPause() is called when Android is about to resume another activity. This method is typically used to persist unsaved changes, stop animations that might be consuming processor cycles, and so on. It should perform its job quickly, because the next activity won't be resumed until it returns. Android calls onResume() after calling onPause() when the activity starts interacting with the user, and calls onStop() when the activity becomes invisible to the user.

- onStop() is called when the activity is no longer visible to the user. This may happen because the activity is being destroyed, or because another activity (either an existing one or a new one) has been resumed and is covering the activity. Android calls onRestart() after calling onStop(), when the activity is coming back to interact with the user, and calls the onDestroy() method when the activity is going away.

- onDestroy() is called before the activity is destroyed, unless memory is tight and Android is forced to kill the activity's process. In this scenario, onDestroy() is never called. If onDestroy() is called, it will be the final call that the activity ever receives.

Note Android can kill the process hosting the activity at any time after onPause(), onStop(), or onDestroy() returns. An activity is in a killable state from the time onPause() returns until the time onResume() is called. The activity won't again be killable until onPause() returns.

These seven methods define an activity's entire lifecycle and describe the following three nested loops:

- The *entire lifetime* of an activity is defined as everything from the first call to onCreate(Bundle) through to a single final call to onDestroy(). An activity performs all its initial setup of "global" state in onCreate(Bundle), and releases all remaining environmental resources in onDestroy(). For example, when the activity has a thread running in the background to download data from the network, it might create that thread in onCreate(Bundle) and stop the thread in onDestroy().

- The *visible lifetime* of an activity is defined as everything from a call to onStart() through to a corresponding call to onStop(). During this time, the user can see the activity onscreen, although it might not be in the foreground and interacting with the user. Between these two methods, the activity can maintain resources that are needed to show itself to the user. For example, it can register a broadcast receiver in onStart() to monitor for changes that impact its user interface, and unregister this object in onStop() when the user can no longer see what the activity is displaying. The onStart() and onStop() methods can be called multiple times, as the activity alternates between being visible to and being hidden from the user.

- The *foreground lifetime* of an activity is defined as everything from a call to onResume() through to a corresponding call to onPause(). During this time, the activity is in front of all other activities onscreen and is interacting with the user. An activity can frequently transition between the resumed and paused states; for example, onPause() is called when the device goes to sleep or when a new activity is started, and onResume() is called when an activity result or a new intent is delivered. The code in these two methods should be fairly lightweight.

Note Each lifecycle callback method is a hook that an activity can override to perform appropriate work. All activities must implement onCreate(Bundle) to carry out the initial setup when the activity object is first instantiated. Many activities also implement onPause() to commit data changes and otherwise prepare to stop interacting with the user.

Figure 12-3 illustrates an activity's lifecycle in terms of these seven methods.

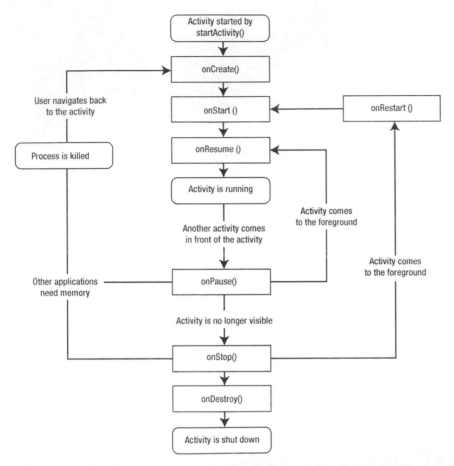

Figure 12-3. The lifecycle of an activity reveals that there's no guarantee of onDestroy() being called.

Because onDestroy() might not be called, you shouldn't count on using this method as a place for saving data. For example, when an activity is editing a content provider's data, those edits should typically be committed in onPause().

In contrast, onDestroy() is usually implemented to free environmental resources (e.g., threads) that are associated with an activity so that a destroyed activity doesn't leave such things around while the rest of its app is still running.

Figure 12-3 reveals that an activity is started by calling startActivity(). More specifically, the activity is started by creating an Intent object describing an explicit or implicit intent, and by passing this object to Context's void startActivity(Intent intent) method (launch a new activity; no result is returned when it finishes).

Alternatively, the activity could be started by calling Activity's void startActivityForResult(Intent intent, int requestCode) method. The specified int result is returned to Activity's void onActivityResult(int requestCode, int resultCode, Intent data) callback method as an argument.

> ■ **Note** The responding activity can look at the initial intent that caused it to be launched by calling Activity's Intent getIntent() method. Android calls the activity's void onNewIntent(Intent intent) method (also located in the Activity class) to pass any subsequent intents to the activity.

Listing 12-1's package statement implies an app named SimpleApp. As well as SimpleActivity serving as its main activity, let's assume that this app includes a SimpleActivity2 class describing an activity for viewing JPEG images. Suppose that you want to start SimpleActivity2 from SimpleActivity's onCreate(Bundle) method. The following example shows you how to accomplish this task:

```
Intent intent = new Intent(SimpleActivity.this, SimpleActivity2.class);
SimpleActivity.this.startActivity(intent);
```

The first line creates an Intent object that describes an explicit intent. It initializes this object by passing the current SimpleActivity instance's reference and SimpleActivity2's java.lang.Class instance to the Intent(Context packageContext, Class<?> clazz) constructor.

The second line passes this Intent object to startActivity(Intent), which is responsible for starting the activity described by SimpleActivity2.class. If startActivity(Intent) was unable to find the specified activity (which shouldn't happen), it would throw an android.content.ActivityNotFoundException instance.

The following example shows you how to start SimpleActivity2 implicitly:

```
Intent intent = new Intent();
intent.setAction(Intent.ACTION_VIEW); // Use Intent constants instead of literal ...
intent.setType("image/jpeg");
intent.addCategory(Intent.CATEGORY_DEFAULT); // ... strings to reduce errors.
SimpleActivity.this.startActivity(intent);
```

The first four lines create an Intent object describing an implicit intent. Values passed to Intent's Intent setAction(String action), Intent setType(String type), and Intent addCategory(String category) methods specify the intent's action, MIME type, and category. They help Android identify SimpleActivity2 as the activity to be started.

ACTIVITIES, TASKS, AND THE ACTIVITY STACK

Android refers to a sequence of related activities as a *task* and provides an *activity stack* (also known as *history stack* or *back stack*) to remember this sequence. The activity starting the task is the initial activity pushed onto the stack and is known as the *root activity*. This activity is typically the activity selected by the user via the device's app launcher. The activity that's currently running is located at the top of the stack.

When the current activity starts another, the new activity is pushed onto the stack and takes focus (becomes the running activity). The previous activity remains on the stack, but is stopped. When an activity stops, the system retains the current state of its user interface.

When the user presses the device's BACK key, the current activity is popped from the stack (the activity is destroyed), and the previous activity resumes operation as the running activity (the previous state of its user interface is restored).

Activities in the stack are never rearranged, only pushed and popped from the stack. Activities are pushed onto the stack when started by the current activity, and popped off the stack when the user leaves them via the BACK key.

Each time the user presses BACK, an activity is popped off the stack to reveal the previous activity. This continues until the user returns to the home screen or to whichever activity was running when the task began. When all activities are removed from the stack, the task no longer exists.

Check out the "Tasks and Back Stack" section in Google's online Android documentation to learn more about activities and tasks: `http://developer.android.com/guide/topics/fundamentals/tasks-and-back-stack.html`.

Broadcast Receivers

A *broadcast receiver* is a component that receives and reacts to broadcasts. Many broadcasts originate in system code; for example, an announcement that the timezone has been changed or the battery power is low.

Apps can also initiate broadcasts. For example, an app may want to let other apps know that some data has finished downloading from the network to the device and is now available for them to use.

Note The abstract `android.content.BroadcastReceiver` class implements broadcast receivers.

Content Providers

A *content provider* is a component that makes a specific set of an app's data available to other apps. The data can be stored in the Android filesystem, in an SQLite database, or in any other manner that makes sense.

Content providers are preferable to directly accessing raw data because they decouple component code from raw data formats. This decoupling prevents code breakage when formats change.

Note The abstract `android.content.ContentProvider` class implements content providers.

Services

A *service* is a component that runs in the background for an indefinite period of time, and which doesn't provide a user interface. As with an activity, a service runs on the process's main thread; it must spawn another thread to perform a time-consuming operation. Services are classified as local or remote:

- A *local service* runs in the same process as the rest of the app. Such services make it easy to implement background tasks.

- A *remote service* runs in a separate process. Such services let you perform interprocess communication.

Note A service is not a separate process, although it can be specified to run in a separate process. Also, a service is not a thread. Instead, a service lets the app tell Android about something it wants to be doing in the background (even when the user is not directly interacting with the app), and lets the app expose some of its functionality to other apps.

Consider a service that plays music in response to a user's music choice via an activity. The user selects the song to play via this activity, and a service is started in response to the selection. The rationale for using a service to play the music is that the user expects the music to keep playing even after the activity that initiated the music leaves the screen.

The service plays the music on another thread to prevent the Application Not Responding dialog box (see Figure 12-4) from appearing.

Figure 12-4. The dreaded Application Not Responding dialog box may result in users uninstalling the app.

Note The abstract android.app.Service class implements services.

Manifest

Android learns about an app's various components (and more) by examining the app's XML-structured manifest file, AndroidManifest.xml. For example, Listing 12-2 shows how this file might declare Listing 12-1's activity component.

Listing 12-2. SimpleApp's manifest file

```
<?xml version="1.0" encoding="utf-8"?>
<manifest xmlns:android="http://schemas.android.com/apk/res/android"
          package="ca.tutortutor.simpleapp">
    <application android:label="@string/app_name" android:icon="@drawable/icon">
        <activity android:name=".SimpleActivity" android:label="@string/app_name">
            <intent-filter>
                <action android:name="android.intent.action.MAIN" />
```

```
            <category android:name="android.intent.category.LAUNCHER" />
        </intent-filter>
    </activity>
    <!-- ... -->
  </application>
</manifest>
```

Listing 12-2 begins with the `<?xml version="1.0" encoding="utf-8"?>` prolog, which identifies this file as an XML version 1.0 file whose content is encoded according to the UTF-8 encoding standard. (Chapter 10 introduces you to XML.)

Listing 12-2 next presents the `manifest` element, which is this XML document's root element: android identifies the Android namespace, and package identifies the app's Java package—each app must have its own Java package, which is `ca.tutortutor.simpleapp` in this example. Additional attributes can be specified. For example, you can specify `versionCode` and `versionName` attributes when you want to identify version information.

Nested within `manifest` is `application`, which is the parent of app component elements. Its `label` and `icon` attributes refer to label and icon application resources that Android devices display to represent the app, and which serve as defaults for individual components whose start tags don't specify these attributes. (I'll discuss application resources shortly.)

■ **Note** Application resources are identified by the @ prefix, followed by a category name (e.g., `string` or `drawable`), /, and the application resource ID (e.g., `app_name` or `icon`).

Nested within `application` is an `activity` element that describes an activity component. The name attribute identifies a class (`SimpleActivity`) that implements the activity. This name begins with a period character to imply that it's relative to `ca.tutortutor.simpleapp`.

■ **Note** The period isn't present when `AndroidManifest.xml` is created at the command line. However, this character is present when this file is created from within Eclipse. Regardless, `SimpleActivity` is relative to `<manifest>`'s package value (`ca.tutortutor.simpleapp`).

The `activity` element can override `application`'s label and icon attributes with its own component-specific label and icon attributes. When either attribute isn't present, `activity` inherits `application`'s label or icon attribute value.

Nested within `activity` is `intent-filter`. This element declares the capabilities of the component described by the enclosing element. For example, it declares the capabilities of the `SimpleActivity` component via its nested action and category elements:

- action identifies the action to perform. For example, this element's name attribute can be assigned `"android.intent.action.MAIN"` to identify the activity as the app's entry point (the first activity to run when the user launches the app).

- category identifies a component category. This tag's name attribute is assigned "android.intent.category.LAUNCHER" to identify the activity as needing to be displayed in the app launcher (discussed later).

■ **Note** Other components are similarly declared: broadcast receivers are declared via receiver elements, content providers are declared via provider elements, and services are declared via service elements. Except for broadcast receivers, which can be created at runtime, components not declared in the manifest are not created by Android.

The <!-- ... --> comment tag indicates that a manifest can define multiple components. For example, I referred to a SimpleActivity2 class while discussing activities. Before you could start this activity (explicitly or implicitly), you would need to introduce an activity element into the manifest.

Consider the following activity element:

```
<activity android:name=".SimpleActivity2" ...>
    <intent-filter>
        <action android:name="android.intent.action.VIEW" />
        <data android:mimeType="image/jpeg" />
        <category android:name="android.intent.category.DEFAULT" />
    </intent-filter>
</activity>
```

SimpleActivity2's intent-filter element helps Android determine that this activity is to be launched when the Intent object's values match the following tag attribute values:

- <action>'s name attribute is assigned "android.intent.action.VIEW".

- <data>'s mimeType attribute is assigned the "image/jpeg" MIME type.

- <category>'s name attribute is assigned "android.intent.category.DEFAULT" to allow the activity to be launched without explicitly specifying its component.

■ **Note** The data element describes the data on which an intent operates. Its mimeType attribute identifies the data's MIME type. Additional attributes can be specified. For example, you could specify path to identify the data's location URI.

AndroidManifest.xml may contain additional information, such as naming any libraries that the app needs to be linked against (besides the default Android library), and identifying all app-enforced permissions (via permission elements) to other apps, such as controlling who can start the app's activities.

Also, the manifest may contain uses-permission elements to identify permissions that the app needs. For example, an app that needs to use the camera would specify the following element: <uses-permission android:name="android.permission.CAMERA" />.

> **Note** uses-permission elements are nested within manifest elements—they appear at the same level as the application element.

At app install time, permissions requested by the app (via uses-permission) are granted to it by Android's package installer, based on checks against the digital signatures of the apps declaring those permissions and/or interaction with the user.

No checks with the user are done while an app is running. It was granted a specific permission when installed and can use that feature as desired, or the permission wasn't granted and any attempt to use the feature will fail without prompting the user.

Application Resources

As well as having a set of *environmental resources* (e.g., databases, preferences, a filesystem, threads, and the Linux process) for its components to share, an app can have its own *application resources*: property animations, tween animations, state lists of colors, drawables, layouts, menus, raw files, simple values (e.g., strings), and arbitrary XML files.

> **Note** Although you can embed application resources such as literal strings in source code, you should separate them into files to facilitate maintenance, localization (discussed in Appendix C), and device adaptability (making your app's user interface look good at different screen sizes, for example).

Android requires that an app store its application resources files in Table 12-1's subdirectories (and their subdirectories, where appropriate) of the app's res directory.

Table 12-1. Application Resource Subdirectories

Directory	Description
anim	Contains XML files that describe tween animations—see http://developer.android.com/guide/topics/graphics/view-animation.html#tween-animation to learn about tween animations.
animator	Contains XML files that describe Android 3.0+ property animations—see http://developer.android.com/guide/topics/graphics/animation.html to learn about property animations.
color	Contains XML files that describe state lists of colors.
drawable	Contains bitmap files (.png, .9.png, .jpg, .gif) or XML files that are compiled into bitmap files, *nine-patches* (resizable bitmaps), state lists,

shapes, animation drawables, and other *drawables.*

layout	Contains XML files that describe user interface layouts.
menu	Contains XML files that describe app menus (e.g., an options menu or a context menu).
raw	Contains arbitrary files in their raw form (e.g., MP3 files). When you need to access the original name of any of these files, you should save that file in res's assets subdirectory instead.
values	Contains XML files that describe simple values, such as strings, integers, and colors.
xml	Contains arbitrary XML files that can be read at runtime.

Starting with Android 1.6, Android first looks for drawables in res's drawable-hdpi, drawable-mdpi, or drawable-ldpi subdirectory, depending on whether the device's screen resolution is high (hdpi), medium (mdpi), or low (ldpi). If it doesn't find the drawable there, it looks in res's drawable subdirectory.

I'll have more to say about application resources when I introduce you to the Java7MeetsAndroid app later in this chapter.

Note To learn more about application resources, check out Google's "Application Resources" guide (http://developer.android.com/guide/topics/resources/index.html).

App Package

Android apps are written in Java. The compiled Java code for an app's components is further transformed into Dalvik's DEX format. The resulting code files along with any other required data and application resources are subsequently bundled into an *App PacKage (APK)*, a file identified by the .apk suffix.

An APK isn't an app, but is used to distribute at least part of the app and install it on a mobile device. It's not an app because its components may reuse another APK's components, and (in this situation) not all the app would reside in a single APK. Also, it may only distribute part of an app. However, it's common to refer to an APK as representing a single app.

An APK must be signed with a certificate (which identifies the app's author) whose private key is held by its developer. The certificate doesn't need to be signed by a certificate authority. Instead, Android allows APKs to be signed with self-signed certificates, which is typical. (*Android Recipes* discusses APK signing.)

APKS, USER IDS, AND SECURITY

Each APK installed on an Android device is given its own unique Linux user ID, and this user ID remains unchanged for as long as the APK resides on that device.

Because security enforcement occurs at the process level, the code contained in any two APKs cannot normally run in the same process, because each APK's code needs to run as a different Linux user. However, you can have the code in both APKs run in the same process by assigning the same name of a user ID to the `<manifest>` tag's `sharedUserId` attribute in each APK's `AndroidManifest.xml` file. When you make these assignments, you tell Android that the two packages are to be treated as being the same app, with the same user ID and file permissions.

In order to retain security, only two APKs signed with the same signature (and requesting the same `sharedUserId` value in their manifests) will be given the same user ID.

Installing the Android SDK and an Android Platform

Now that you have a basic understanding of the Android and Android app architectures, you'll probably want to create an app. However, you cannot do so until you've installed the Android SDK and have also installed an Android platform. This section shows you how to accomplish these tasks.

Accessing System Requirements

Google provides an Android SDK distribution file for each of the Windows, Intel-based Mac OS X, and Linux (i386) operating systems. Before downloading and installing this file, you must be aware of SDK requirements. You cannot use the SDK when your development platform doesn't meet these requirements.

The Android SDK supports the following operating systems:

- Windows XP (32-bit), Vista (32- or 64-bit), or Windows 7 (32- or 64-bit)

- Mac OS X 10.5.8 or later (x86 only)

- Linux (tested on Ubuntu Linux, Lucid Lynx): GNU C Library (glibc) 2.11 or later is required. 64-bit distributions must be able to run 32-bit applications. To learn how to add support for 32-bit applications, see the Ubuntu Linux installation notes at http://developer.android.com/sdk/installing.html#troubleshooting.

You'll quickly discover that the Android SDK is organized into various components: SDK tools, SDK platform tools, different versions of the *Android platform* (also known as the Android software stack), SDK add-ons, USB driver for Windows, samples, and offline documentation. Each component requires a minimum amount of disk storage space; the total required amount of space depends on which components you choose to install:

- *SDK Tools*: The SDK's tools require approximately 35MB of disk storage space and must be installed.

- *SDK Platform Tools*: The SDK's platform tools require approximately 6MB of disk storage space and must be installed.

- *Android platform*: Each Android platform corresponds to a specific version of Android and requires approximately 150MB of disk storage space. At least one Android platform must be installed.

- *SDK Add-on*: Each optional SDK add-on (e.g., Google APIs or a third-party vendor's API libraries) requires approximately 100MB of disk storage space.

- *USB Driver for Windows*: The optional USB driver for the Windows platform requires approximately 10MB of disk storage space. When you're developing on Mac OS X or Linux, you don't need to install the USB driver.

- *Samples*: Each Android platform's optional app examples require approximately 10MB of disk storage space.

- *Offline documentation*: Instead of having to be online to access the Android documentation, you can choose to download the documentation so that you can view it even when not connected to the Internet. The offline documentation requires approximately 250MB of disk storage space.

Finally, you should ensure that the following additional software is installed:

- *JDK 5, JDK 6, or JDK 7*: You need to install one of these Java Development Kits (JDKs) to compile Java code. It's not sufficient to have only a Java Runtime Environment (JRE) installed. Also, you cannot use Java 7 language features that rely on APIs newer than Java 5; the try-with-resources statement is unusable.

- *Apache Ant*: You need to install Ant 1.8 or later so that you can build Android projects.

■ **Note** When a JDK is already installed on your development platform, take a moment to ensure that it meets the previously listed version requirement (5, 6, or 7). Some Linux distributions may include JDK 1.4, which isn't supported for Android development. Also, Gnu Compiler for Java isn't supported.

Installing the Android SDK

Point your browser to http://developer.android.com/sdk/index.html and download the current release of the Android SDK for your platform. For example, you would download one of android-sdk_r12-windows.zip (Windows), android-sdk_r12-mac_x86.zip (Mac OS X [Intel]), and android-sdk_r12-linux_x86.tgz (Linux [i386]) to install Android SDK Release 12. (I focus on Release 12 in this chapter because it's current at time of writing; a new release may be available by the time this book is published.)

■ **Note** Windows developers have the option of downloading and running installer_r12-windows.exe. Google recommends that you use this tool, which automates most of the installation process.

For example, if you run Windows, download android-sdk_r12-windows.zip. After unarchiving this file, move the unarchived android-sdk-windows home directory to a convenient location in your filesystem; for example, you might move the unarchived C:\unzipped\android-sdk_r12-windows\android-sdk-windows home directory to the root directory on your C: drive, resulting in C:\android-sdk-windows.

Note To complete installation, add the tools subdirectory to your PATH environment variable so that you can access the SDK's command-line tools from anywhere in your filesystem.

A subsequent examination of android-sdk-windows shows that this home directory contains the following subdirectories and files:

- *add-ons*: This initially empty directory stores add-ons from Google and other vendors; for example, the Google APIs add-on is stored here.

- *platforms*: This initially empty directory stores Android platforms in separate subdirectories. For example, Android 2.3 would be stored in one platforms subdirectory, whereas Android 2.2 would be stored in another platforms subdirectory.

- *tools*: This directory contains a set of platform-independent development and profiling tools. The tools in this directory may be updated at any time, independent of Android platform releases.

- *SDK Manager.exe*: A special tool that launches the Android SDK and AVD Manager tool, which you use to add components to your SDK.

- *SDK Readme.txt*: This text file welcomes you to the Android SDK and discusses installing an Android platform.

The tools directory contains a variety of useful tools, including the following:

- *android*: Creates and updates Android projects; updates the Android SDK with new platforms, add-ons, and documentation; and creates, deletes, and views *AVDs* (descriptors that describe virtual devices).

- *emulator*: Runs a full Android software stack down to the kernel level, and includes a set of preinstalled apps (e.g., Browser) that you can access. The emulator tool launches an *AVD*.

- *sqlite3*: Manages SQLite databases created by Android apps.

- *zipalign*: Performs archive alignment optimization on APKs.

Installing an Android Platform

Installing the Android SDK is insufficient for developing Android apps; you must also install at least one Android platform. You can accomplish this task via the SDK Manager tool.

Run SDK Manager. This tool presents the Android SDK and AVD Manager dialog box, followed by the Refresh Sources and Choose Packages to Install dialog boxes.

Note You can also use the android tool to display Android SDK and AVD. Accomplish this task by specifying android by itself on the command line.

The Android SDK and AVD Manager dialog box identifies virtual devices, installed packages, and available packages. It also lets you configure proxy server and other settings.

When this dialog box appears for the first time, the Virtual devices entry in the list appearing on the right side of the dialog box is highlighted, and the pane to the right of that list identifies all AVDs that have been created (this list will probably be empty).

After presenting this dialog box, SDK Manager scans Google's servers for available component packages to install. The Refresh Sources dialog box reveals its progress.

After SDK Manager finishes its scan (which may take a few minutes), it presents the Choose Packages to Install dialog box (see Figure 12-5) to let you choose SDK components to install. (If you've installed Android SDK Release 12, and haven't previously installed Android, the only installed component is Android SDK Tools, revision 12.)

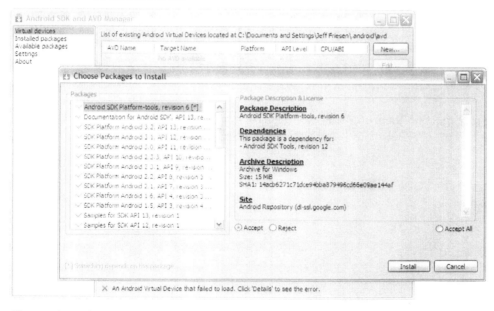

Figure 12-5. *The Packages list identifies those packages that can be installed.*

The Choose Packages to Install dialog box shows a Packages list that identifies those packages that can be installed. It displays checkmarks beside packages that have been accepted for installation, and displays question marks beside those packages that have yet to be accepted.

For the highlighted package, Package Description & License presents a package description, a list of other packages that are dependent on this package being installed, information about the archive that houses the package, and additional information. Also, you can select a radio button to accept or reject the package. If you reject the highlighted package, an X icon will replace the checkmark or question mark icon.

■ **Note** In some cases, an SDK component may require a specific minimum revision of another component or SDK tool. In addition to Package Description & License documenting these dependencies, the development tools will notify you with debug warnings when there's a dependency that you need to address.

Android Platform versions 3.0 and higher refer to tablet-oriented Android. Versions less than 3.0 refer to smartphone-oriented Android. Because this chapter focuses on Android 2.3.3, the only packages that you need to install are Android SDK Platform-tools, revision 6 and SDK Platform Android 2.3.3, API 10, revision 2. All other checked package entries can be unchecked by clicking the Reject option radio button on their respective panes (or by double-clicking list entries).

■ **Note** If you plan to develop apps that will run on devices with older versions of Android, you might want to leave the checkmarks beside those older versions. However, it's not necessary to do so at this point because you can always come back later and add those versions via SDK Manager or android.

After making sure that only these entries are checked, click the Install button to begin installation. Figure 12-6 shows you the resulting Installing Archives dialog box.

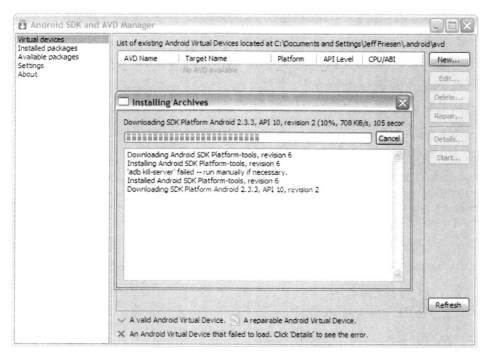

Figure 12-6. *The Installing Archives dialog box reveals the progress of downloading and installing each selected package archive.*

Installing Archives might present an "'adb kill-server' failed—run manually if necessary" message. This message refers to a platform tool named adb, which stands for Android Debug Bridge (ADB).

ADB manages the state of an emulator instance or an Android-powered device. It includes a server that runs as a background process on the development machine. The installer must kill this process before installing platform tools. When this process isn't running, you'll see the aforementioned message.

You'll probably encounter the ADB Restart dialog box, which tells you that a package dependent on Android Debug Bridge (ADB) has been updated, and asking you whether you want to restart ADB now. At this point, it doesn't matter which button you click—you would probably click Yes when the ADB server process had been running before you started to install a package and you want to resume this process following the installation.

Click Close on the Installing Archives dialog box to finish installation.

You should now observe the Android SDK and AVD Manager's Installed packages pane displaying Android SDK Platform-tools, revision 6 and SDK Platform Android 2.3.3, API 10, revision 2 in addition to Android SDK Tools, revision 12. You should also observe the following new subdirectories:

- platform-tools (in android-sdk-windows)

- android-10 (in android-sdk-windows/platforms)

platform-tools contains development tools that may be updated with each platform release. Its tools include aapt (Android Asset Packaging Tool—view, create, and update Zip-compatible archives (.zip, .jar, .apk); and compile resources into binary assets), the aforementioned adb tool, and dx (Dalvik

Executable—generate Dalvik DEX code from Java ".class" files). android-10 stores Android 2.3.3 data and user interface-oriented files.

Tip You might want to add platform-tools to your PATH environment variable so that you can access these tools from anywhere in your filesystem.

Creating and Starting an AVD

After installing the Android SDK and an Android platform, you're ready to start developing Android apps. If you don't have an actual Android device on which to install and run those apps, you can use the emulator tool to emulate a device. This tool works in partnership with an AVD, which is a descriptor that describes various characteristics of the emulated device (e.g., the screen size).

Tip Even when you have an actual Android device, you should also test your apps with the emulator to see how they appear under various screen sizes.

This section first shows you how to create an AVD to describe an emulated device. It then shows you how to start the AVD, and takes you on a tour of its user interface.

Creating an AVD

Launch the Android SDK and AVD Manager dialog box via SDK Manager or android. You'll probably prefer to use android, which prevents the Refresh Sources and Choose Packages to Install dialog boxes from appearing. As shown in Figures 12-5 and 12-6, no AVDs are listed on the Virtual devices pane.

Click the New button. Figure 12-7 shows you the resulting Create new Android Virtual Device (AVD) dialog box.

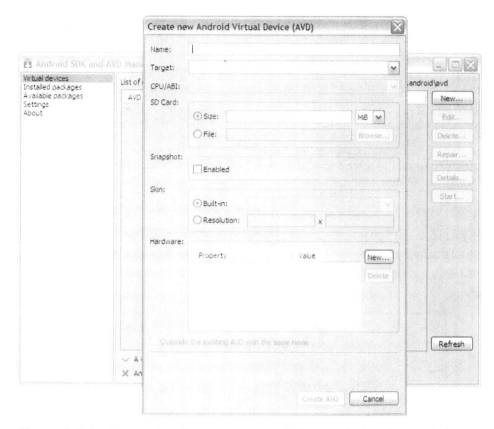

Figure 12-7. *An AVD consists of a name, a target platform, and other characteristics.*

Figure 12-7 reveals that an AVD has a name, targets a specific Android platform, and more. Enter **test_AVD** for the name, select Android 2.3.3 - API Level 10 for the target platform, and enter 100 into the Size field for the SD card.

Selecting Android 2.3.3 - API Level 10 results in Default (WVGA800) being selected for the AVD's skin. Additionally, it presents the following three hardware properties:

- Abstracted LCD density, set to 240 dots per inch

- Max VM application heap size, set to 24MB

- Device ram size, set to 256MB

■ **Tip** To see the entire device screen at a platform screen resolution of 1024x768, you'll need to change the skin from Default (WVGA800) to something lower, such as HVGA. Switching to HVGA also changes Abstracted LCD density to 160.

After keeping the screen defaults and/or making changes, click Create AVD. Then click OK on the resulting Android Virtual Devices Manager dialog box, which summarizes the AVD. The virtual devices pane now includes a test_AVD entry.

Starting the AVD

You must start the AVD, which can take a few minutes to get started, before you can install and run apps on it. Accomplish this task by highlighting the test_AVD entry (on the Virtual devices pane) and clicking the Start button.

A Launch Options dialog box appears, identifying the AVD's skin and screen density. It also provides unchecked checkboxes for scaling the resolution of the emulator's display to match the physical device's screen size, and for wiping user data.

■ **Note** As you update your apps, you'll periodically package and install them on the emulated device, which preserves the apps and their state data across AVD restarts in a user-data disk partition. To ensure that an app runs properly as you update it, you might need to delete the AVD's user-data partition, which is accomplished by checking Wipe user data.

Click the Launch button on the Launch Options dialog box to launch the emulator with the AVD. A Starting Android Emulator dialog box appears, and is followed by command windows (on Windows XP) and the AVD's main window.

The main window is divided into a left pane that displays the Android logo on a black background followed by the home screen, and a right pane that displays phone controls and a keyboard. Figure 12-8 shows these panes for the test_AVD device.

Figure 12-8. *The AVD window presents the home screen on its left, and presents phone controls and a keyboard on its right.*

If you've previously used an Android device, you're probably familiar with the home screen, the phone controls, and the keyboard. If not, there are a few items to keep in mind:

- The *home screen* (see Figure 12-8's left pane) is a special app that serves as a starting point for using an Android device. It displays wallpaper for its background. You can change the wallpaper by clicking the MENU button (in the phone controls), and selecting Wallpaper in the resulting pop-up menu.

- A status bar appears above the home screen (and every app screen). The *status bar* presents the current time, amount of battery power remaining, and other information; and also provides access to notifications.

- The home screen presents a wallpaper background. Click the MENU button in the phone controls followed by Wallpaper in the pop-up menu to change the wallpaper.

- The home screen is capable of displaying *widgets*, which are miniature app views that can be embedded in the home screen and other app screens, and which receive periodic updates. For example, the Google Search widget appears near the top of the home screen in Figure 12-8.

- The *app launcher* appears near the bottom of the home screen. Click its rectangular grid icon to switch to the app launcher screen of app icons, and click any of these icons to launch the respective app. The launcher also presents icons for launching the frequently used Phone and Browser apps.

- The home screen is organized around multiple panes. Click the dots on either side of the app launcher to replace the current pane with the next pane to the left or right. The number of panes that remain to be visited on the left or right is indicated by the number of dots to the left or right of the app launcher.

- The house icon phone control button takes you from wherever you are to the home screen.

- The MENU phone control button presents a context menu with app-specific choices for the currently running app's current screen.

- The curved arrow icon (BACK) phone control button takes you back to the previous activity in the *activity stack*, which is a stack of previously visited screens.

While the AVD is running, you can interact with it by using your mouse to "touch" the touchscreen and your keyboard to "press" the device keys. The following list identifies a few mappings from AVD keys to the development computer's keyboard keys:

- Home maps to Home

- Menu (left softkey) maps to F2 or Page Up

- Star (right softkey) maps to Shift-F2 or Page Down

- Back maps to Esc

- Switch to previous layout orientation (for example, portrait or landscape) maps to KEYPAD_7, Ctrl-F11

- Switch to next layout orientation maps to KEYPAD_9, Ctrl-F12

Tip You must first disable NumLock on your development computer before you can use keypad keys.

Figure 12-8 displays 5554:test_AVD in the titlebar. The 5554 value identifies a console port that you can use to dynamically query and otherwise control the environment of the AVD.

Note Android supports up to 16 concurrently executing AVDs. Each AVD is assigned an even-numbered console port number starting with 5554.

Creating, Installing, and Running an App

Now that you've installed the Android SDK, installed an Android platform, and created and started an AVD, you're ready to create an app, and install and run this app on the AVD. This section introduces you to an app named Java7MeetsAndroid. After presenting and discussing the app's source code and related files, it shows you how to create this app, and install and run it on the previously started AVD.

Introducing Java7MeetsAndroid

Java7MeetsAndroid is a single-activity app that presents an image and a button. The image shows Duke, the Java mascot, over a glowing 7. The button, labeled Wave, starts an animation of Duke waving when clicked.

■ **Note** Check out "Duke, the Java mascot" (http://kenai.com/projects/duke/pages/Home) to learn more about this cool character.

Listing 12-3 presents the Java7MeetsAndroid class.

Listing 12-3. An activity for making Duke wave

```
package ca.tutortutor.j7ma;

import android.app.Activity;

import android.graphics.drawable.AnimationDrawable;

import android.os.Bundle;

import android.view.View;

import android.widget.Button;
import android.widget.ImageView;

public class Java7MeetsAndroid extends Activity
{
    AnimationDrawable dukeAnimation;
    @Override
    public void onCreate(Bundle savedInstanceState)
    {
        super.onCreate(savedInstanceState);
        setContentView(R.layout.main);
        ImageView dukeImage = (ImageView) findViewById(R.id.duke);

        dukeImage.setBackgroundResource(R.drawable.duke_wave);
        dukeAnimation = (AnimationDrawable) dukeImage.getBackground();
        final Button btnWave = (Button) findViewById(R.id.wave);
```

```
            View.OnClickListener ocl;
            ocl = new View.OnClickListener()
            {
               @Override
               public void onClick(View v)
               {
                  dukeAnimation.stop();
                  dukeAnimation.start();
               }
            };
            btnWave.setOnClickListener(ocl);
      }
}
```

Listing 12-3 begins with a package statement that names the package (ca.tutortutor.j7ma) in which its Java7MeetsAndroid class is stored, followed by a series of import statements that import various Android API types. This listing next describes the Java7MeetsAndroid class, which extends Activity.

Java7MeetsAndroid first declares a dukeAnimation instance field of type android.graphics.drawable.AnimationDrawable. Objects of type AnimationDrawable describe frame-by-frame animations, in which the current drawable is replaced with the next drawable in the animation sequence.

 Note AnimationDrawable indirectly extends the abstract android.graphics.drawable.Drawable class, which is a general abstraction for a *drawable*, something that can be drawn (e.g., an image).

All the app's work takes place in Java7MeetsAndroid's overriding onCreate(Bundle) method: no other methods are required, which helps to keep this app simple.

onCreate(Bundle) first invokes its same-named superclass method, a rule that must be followed by all overriding activity methods.

This method then executes setContentView(R.layout.main) to establish the app's user interface. R.layout.main is an identifier (ID) for an application resource, which resides in a separate file. You interpret this ID as follows:

- R is the name of a class that's generated (by the aapt tool) when the app is being built. This class is named R because its content identifies various kinds of application resources (e.g., layouts, images, strings, and colors).

- layout is the name of a class that's nested within R. All application resources whose IDs are stored in this class describe specific layout resources. Each kind of application resource is associated with a nested class that's named in a similar fashion. For example, string identifies string resources.

- main is the name of an int constant declared within layout. This resource ID identifies the main layout resource. Specifically, main refers to a main.xml file that stores the main activity's layout information. main is Java7MeetsAndroid's only layout resource.

R.layout.main is passed to Activity's void setContentView(int layoutResID) method to tell Android to create a user interface screen using the layout information stored in main.xml. Behind the scenes, Android creates the user interface components described in main.xml and positions them on the screen as specified by main.xml's layout data.

The screen is based on *views* (abstractions of user interface components) and *view groups* (views that group related user interface components). Views are instances of classes that subclass the android.view.View class and are analogous to AWT/Swing components. View groups are instances of classes that subclass the abstract android.view.ViewGroup class and are analogous to AWT/Swing containers. Android refers to specific views (e.g., buttons or spinners) as *widgets*.

▪ **Note** Don't confuse widget in this context with widgets shown on the Android home screen. Although the same term is used, user interface widgets and home screen widgets are different.

Continuing, onCreate(Bundle) executes ImageView dukeImage = (ImageView) findViewById(R.id.duke);. This statement first calls View's View findViewById(int id) method to find the android.widget.ImageView element declared in main.xml and identified as duke, and instantiate ImageView and initialize it to its declarative information. The statement then saves this object's reference in local variable dukeImage.

The subsequent dukeImage.setBackgroundResource(R.drawable.duke_wave); statement invokes ImageView's inherited (from View) void setBackgroundResourceMethod(int resID) method to set the view's background to the resource identified by resID. The R.drawable.duke_wave argument identifies an XML file named duke_wave.xml (presented later), which stores information on the animation, and which is stored in res's drawable subdirectory. The setBackgroundResource() call links the dukeImage view to the sequence of images described by duke_wave.xml and that will be drawn on this view; the initial image is drawn as a result of this method call.

ImageView lets an app animate a sequence of drawables by calling AnimationDrawable methods. Before the app can do this, it must obtain ImageView's AnimationDrawable. The dukeAnimation = (AnimationDrawable) dukeImage.getBackground(); assignment statement that follows accomplishes this task by invoking ImageView's inherited (from View) Drawable getBackground() method to return the AnimationDrawable for this ImageView, which is subsequently assigned to the dukeAnimation field. The AnimationDrawable instance is used to start and stop an animation (discussed shortly).

onCreate(Bundle) now turns its attention to creating the Wave button. It invokes findByViewId(int) to obtain the button information from main.xml, and then instantiate the android.widget.Button class.

The View class's nested onClickListener interface is then employed to create a listener object whose void onClick(View v) method is invoked whenever the user clicks the button. The listener is registered with its Button object by calling View's void setOnClickListener(AdapterView.OnClickListener listener) method.

Wave's click listener invokes dukeAnimation.stop(); followed by dukeAnimation.start(); to stop and then start the animation. The stop() method is called before start() to ensure that a subsequent click of the Wave button causes a new animation to begin.

Along with Listing 12-3's Java7MeetsAndroid.java source file, Java7MeetsAndroid relies on three XML resource files and several PNG images. Listing 12-4 presents main.xml, which describes screen layout.

Listing 12-4. The `main.xml` *file storing layout information that includes a pair of widgets*

```xml
<?xml version="1.0" encoding="utf-8"?>
<LinearLayout xmlns:android="http://schemas.android.com/apk/res/android"
              android:orientation="vertical"
              android:layout_width="fill_parent"
              android:layout_height="fill_parent"
              android:gravity="center"
              android:background="#ffffff">
   <ImageView android:id="@+id/duke"
              android:layout_width="wrap_content"
              android:layout_height="wrap_content"
              android:layout_marginBottom="10dip"/>
   <Button android:id="@+id/wave"
              android:layout_width="wrap_content"
              android:layout_height="wrap_content"
              android:text="@string/wave"/>
</LinearLayout>
```

Following the XML declaration, Listing 12-4 declares a `LinearLayout` element that specifies a *layout* (a view group that arranges contained views on an Android device's screen in some manner) for arranging contained widgets (including nested layouts) either horizontally or vertically across the screen.

The `<LinearLayout>` tag specifies several attributes for controlling this linear layout. These attributes include the following:

- `orientation` identifies the linear layout as horizontal or vertical – contained widgets are laid out horizontally or vertically. The default orientation is horizontal. `"horizontal"` and `"vertical"` are the only legal values that can be assigned to this attribute.

- `layout_width` identifies the width of the layout. Legal values include `"fill_parent"` (be as wide as the parent) and `"wrap_content"` (be wide enough to enclose content). `fill_parent` was renamed to `match_parent` in Android 2.2, but is still supported and widely used.

- `layout_height` identifies the height of the layout. Legal values include `"fill_parent"` (be as tall as the parent) and `"wrap_content"` (be tall enough to enclose content).

- `gravity` identifies how the layout is positioned relative to the screen. For example, `"center"` specifies that the layout should be centered horizontally and vertically on the screen.

- `background` identifies a background image, a gradient, or a solid color. For simplicity, I've hardcoded a hexadecimal color identifier to signify a solid white background (#ffffff).

The `LinearLayout` element encapsulates `ImageView` and `Button` elements. Each of these elements specifies an `id` attribute that identifies the element so that it can be referenced from code. The *resource identifier* (special syntax that begins with @) assigned to this attribute begins with the @+id prefix. For example, @+id/duke identifies the ImageView element as duke; this element is referenced from code by specifying R.id.duke.

These elements also specify layout_width and layout_height attributes for determining how their content is laid out. Each attribute is assigned wrap_content so that the element will appear at its natural size.

ImageView specifies a layout_marginBottom attribute to identify a space separator between itself and the button that follows vertically. The space is specified as 10 dips, or *density-independent pixels* (virtual pixels that apps can use to express layout dimensions/positions in a screen density-independent way).

Note A density-independent pixel is equivalent to one physical pixel on a 160-dpi screen, the baseline density assumed by Android. At run time, Android transparently handles any scaling of the required dip units, based on the actual density of the screen in use. Dip units are converted to screen pixels via equation pixels = dips * (density / 160). For example, on a 240-dpi screen, 1 dip equals 1.5 physical pixels. Google recommends using dip units to define your app's user interface to ensure proper display of the UI on different screens.

The Button element's text attribute is assigned @string/wave, which references a string resource named wave. This string resource is stored in an XML file named strings.xml, which is stored in the values subdirectory of res.

Listing 12-5 describes the contents of strings.xml.

Listing 12-5. The strings.xml file storing the app's strings

```xml
<?xml version="1.0" encoding="utf-8"?>
<resources>
    <string name="app_name">Java7MeetsAndroid</string>
    <string name="wave">Wave</string>
</resources>
```

As well as wave, Listing 12-5 reveals a string resource identified as app_name. This resource ID identifies the app's name and is referenced from the app's manifest, typically from the label attribute of the application element start tag (see Listing 12-2).

Listing 12-6 presents duke_wave.xml.

Listing 12-6. The duke_wave.xml file storing the app's animation list of drawable items

```xml
<animation-list xmlns:android="http://schemas.android.com/apk/res/android"
                android:oneshot="true">
    <item android:drawable="@drawable/duke0" android:duration="100" />
    <item android:drawable="@drawable/duke1" android:duration="100" />
    <item android:drawable="@drawable/duke2" android:duration="100" />
    <item android:drawable="@drawable/duke3" android:duration="100" />
    <item android:drawable="@drawable/duke4" android:duration="100" />
    <item android:drawable="@drawable/duke5" android:duration="100" />
    <item android:drawable="@drawable/duke6" android:duration="100" />
    <item android:drawable="@drawable/duke7" android:duration="100" />
    <item android:drawable="@drawable/duke8" android:duration="100" />
    <item android:drawable="@drawable/duke9" android:duration="100" />
```

```
    <item android:drawable="@drawable/duke0" android:duration="100" />
</animation-list>
```

Listing 12-6 presents the animation list of drawables that are connected to dukeImage via the dukeImage.setBackgroundResource(R.drawable.duke_wave); statement.

■ **Note** The animation-list element's oneshot attribute determines whether the animation will cycle in a loop (when this attribute is assigned "false") or occur only once (when it's assigned "true"). When "true" is assigned to oneshot, you must invoke AnimationDrawable()'s stop() method before its start() method to generate another oneshot animation sequence.

Nested inside the animation-list element is a sequence of item elements. Each item element identifies one drawable in the animation sequence via its drawable attribute. The @drawable/dukex resource reference (where *x* ranges from 0 through 9) identifies an image file whose name starts with duke in res's drawable directory. The duration attribute identifies the number of milliseconds that must elapse before the next item element's drawable is displayed.

Listing 12-7 presents Java7MeetsAndroid's AndroidManifest.xml file.

Listing 12-7. Describing the Java7MeetAndroid app

```
<?xml version="1.0" encoding="utf-8"?>
<manifest xmlns:android="http://schemas.android.com/apk/res/android"
          package="ca.tutortutor.j7ma"
          android:versionCode="1"

          android:versionName="1.0">

    <application android:label="@string/app_name" android:icon="@drawable/icon">
        <activity android:name="Java7MeetsAndroid"
                  android:label="@string/app_name">
            <intent-filter>
                <action android:name="android.intent.action.MAIN" />
                <category android:name="android.intent.category.LAUNCHER" />
            </intent-filter>
        </activity>
    </application>
</manifest>
```

Creating Java7MeetsAndroid

Several steps must be followed to create Java7MeetsAndroid. The first step is to use the android tool to create a project. When used in this way, android requires you to adhere to the following syntax (which is spread across multiple lines for readability):

```
android create project --target target_ID
                       --name your_project_name
                       --path /path/to/your/project/project_name
                       --activity your_activity_name
```

```
--package your_package_namespace
```
Except for --name (or -n), which specifies the project's name (when provided, this name will be used for the resulting .apk filename when you build your app), all the following options are required:

- The --target (or -t) option specifies the app's build target. The *target_ID* value is an integer value that identifies an Android platform. You can obtain this value by invoking android list targets. If you've only installed the Android 2.3.3 platform, this command should output a single Android 2.3.3 platform target identified as integer ID 1.

- The --path (or -p) option specifies the project directory's location. The directory is created if it doesn't exist.

- The --activity (or -a) option specifies the name for the default activity class. The resulting classfile is created inside */path/to/your/project/project_name/src/your_package_namespace/*, and is used as the .apk filename if --name (or -n) isn't specified.

- The --package (or -k) option specifies the project's package namespace, which must follow the rules for packages that are specified in the Java language.

Assuming a Windows XP platform, and assuming a C:\prj\dev hierarchy where the Java7MeetsAndroid project is to be stored in C:\prj\dev\Java7MeetsAndroid, invoke the following command from anywhere in the filesystem to create Java7MeetsAndroid:

```
android create project -t 1 -p C:\prj\dev\Java7MeetsAndroid -a Java7MeetsAndroid -k↵
ca.tutortutor.j7ma
```

This command creates various directories and adds files to some of these directories. It specifically creates the following file and directory structure within C:\prj\dev\Java7MeetsAndroid:

- AndroidManifest.xml is the manifest file for the app being built. This file is synchronized to the Activity subclass previously specified via the --activity or -a option.

- bin is the output directory for the Apache Ant build script.

- build.properties is a customizable properties file for the build system. You can edit this file to override default build settings used by Apache Ant, and provide a pointer to your keystore and key alias so that the build tools can sign your app when built in release mode (discussed in *Android Recipes*).

- build.xml is the Apache Ant build script for this project.

- default.properties is the default properties file for the build system. Don't modify this file.

- libs contains private libraries (when required).

- local.properties contains the location of the Android SDK home directory.

- proguard.cfg contains configuration data for *ProGuard*, an SDK tool that lets developers obfuscate their code (making it very difficult to reverse engineer the code) as an integrated part of a release build.

- res contains the project's application resources.

- src contains the project's source code.

res contains the following directories:

- drawable-hdpi contains drawable resources (such as icons) for high-density screens.

- drawable-ldpi contains drawable resources for low-density screens.

- drawable-mdpi contains drawable resources for medium-density screens.

- layout contains layout files.

- values contains value files.

Also, src contains the ca\tutortutor\j7ma directory structure, and the final j7ma subdirectory contains a skeletal Java7MeetsAndroid.java source file.

Before you can create this app, you need to perform the following tasks:

- Replace the skeletal Java7MeetsAndroid.java source file with Listing 12-3.

- Replace the layout subdirectory's skeletal main.xml file with Listing 12-4.

- Replace the values subdirectory's skeletal strings.xml file with Listing 12-5.

- Create a drawable directory underneath res. Copy the duke0.png through duke9.png images located in this book's code file along with Listing 12-6's duke_wave.xml file to drawable.

The generated AndroidManifest.xml file should be fine, although you can replace it with Listing 12-7 if desired.

Assuming that C:\prj\dev\Java7MeetsAndroid is current, build this app with the help of Apache's ant tool, which defaults to processing this directory's build.xml file. At the command line, specify ant followed by debug or release to indicate the build mode:

- *Debug mode*: Build the app for testing and debugging. The build tools sign the resulting APK with a debug key and optimize the APK with zipalign. Specify ant debug.

- *Release mode*: Build the app for release to users. You must sign the resulting APK with your private key, and then optimize the APK with zipalign. (I discuss these tasks in *Android Recipes*.) Specify ant release.

Build Java7MeetsAndroid in debug mode by invoking ant debug from the C:\prj\dev\Java7MeetsAndroid directory. This command creates a gen subdirectory containing the ant-generated R.java file (in a ca\tutortutor\j7ma directory hierarchy), and stores the created Java7MeetsAndroid-debug.apk file in the bin subdirectory.

Installing and Running Java7MeetsAndroid

If you successfully created Java7MeetsAndroid-debug.apk, you can install this APK on the previously started AVD. You can accomplish this task by using the adb tool, as follows:

adb install C:\prj\dev\Java7MeetsAndroid\bin\Java7MeetsAndroid-debug.apk

After a few moments, you should see several messages similar to those shown here:

```
325 KB/s (223895 bytes in 0.671s)
        pkg: /data/local/tmp/Java7MeetsAndroid-debug.apk
Success
```

You might have to repeat the aforementioned command line a few times should you encounter a
"device offline" error message.

Select the app launcher (grid) icon at the bottom of the home screen. Figure 12-9 shows you the
highlighted Java7MeetsAndroid entry.

*Figure 12-9. The highlighted Java7MeetsAndroid app entry displays the standard icon and a label that
automatically scrolls horizontally when the icon and label are highlighted.*

Note Each of the res directory's drawable-hdpi, drawable-mdpi, and drawable-ldpi subdirectories contains
an icon.png file that presents a different size of the default icon shown in Figure 12-9. You can replace all three
versions of the icon with your own icon, if desired.

Click the highlighted icon and you should see the screen shown in Figure 12-10—I've clicked the
Wave button so this screen is showing one frame of the animation.

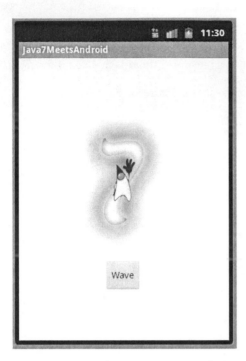

Figure 12-10. *Duke waves at you each time you click Wave.*

When you're tired of playing with this app, click the BACK (curved arrow) button in the phone controls or press the Esc key to revert to the previous screen, which should be the app launcher with its app icons.

You can uninstall this app by clicking the MENU button (on the app launcher screen), selecting Manage apps from the pop-up menu, highlighting Java7MeetsAndroid in the apps list, clicking this entry, and clicking the Uninstall button.

■ **Tip** During development, you'll find it easier and faster to use the adb tool to uninstall an app. For example, specify adb uninstall ca.tutortutor.j7ma to uninstall Java7MeetsAndroid. You must specify the app's package name to uninstall it.

EXERCISES

The following exercises are designed to test your understanding of Android app development:

1. Create SimpleApp using Listing 12-1 as the source code for this app's SimpleActivity.java source file. You should end up with a SimpleApp-debug.apk file in the bin subdirectory. (Hint: you'll need to use the android

tool's -n command-line option.) Install this APK on the running test_AVD emulated device.

2. When you view this app's icon and label on the app launcher screen, you'll notice that the label says SimpleActivity instead of SimpleApp. Why?

3. How would you uninstall SimpleApp from test_AVD?

4. Expand SimpleApp by including a SimpleActivity2.java source file whose onCreate(Bundle) method is similar to SimpleActivity.java's onCreate(Bundle) method but consists of super.onCreate(savedInstanceState); followed by Toast.makeText(this, getIntent().toString(), Toast.LENGTH_LONG).show();. (The android.widget.Toast class is useful for briefly displaying short debugging messages in lieu of using System.out.println(), whose output can be viewed only after invoking adb logcat. Because so many messages are output to this log, it can be difficult to locate System.out.println() content, which is why you'll probably find Toast to be more useful.) Refactor SimpleActivity's onCreate(Bundle) method to start SimpleActivity2 via an implicit intent, as demonstrated earlier in this chapter.

5. Continuing from Exercise 4, create SimpleApp (make sure to refactor AndroidManifest.xml to account for SimpleActivity2). After installing the refactored SimpleApp, click its app launcher StartActivity icon. What happens?

Summary

The Android Developer's Guide defines Android as a software stack (a set of software subsystems needed to deliver a fully functional solution) for mobile devices. This stack includes an operating system (a modified version of the Linux kernel), middleware (software that connects the low-level operating system to high-level apps), and key apps (written in Java) such as a web browser (known as Browser) and a contact manager (known as Contacts).

Android presents a layered architecture that includes an application framework (Activity Manager, Content Providers, Location Manager, Notification Manager, Package Manager, Resource Manager, Telephony Manager, View System, and Window Manager), libraries (FreeType, libc, LibWebCore, Media Framework, OpenGL I ES, SGL, SQLite, SSL, and Surface Manager), the Android runtime (Core Libraries and Dalvik Virtual Machine), and a Linux kernel.

The architecture of an Android app differs from that of an application running on the desktop. App architecture is based upon components (activities, broadcast receivers, content providers, and services) that communicate with each other via intents, are described by a manifest, and may use application resources. Collectively, these items are stored in an app package, also known as an APK.

Before you can create an app, you need to install the Android SDK and an Android platform. You then need to create an AVD and start the AVD before you can install and run your app.

Java7MeetsAndroid describes a single-activity app that presents an image and a button. The image shows Duke, the Java mascot, over a glowing 7. The button, labeled Wave, starts an animation of Duke waving when clicked. In addition to its Java7MeetsAndroid.java source file, this app consists of main.xml, strings.xml, duke_wave.xml, and duke0.png through duke9.png application resource files. It also has its own AndroidManifest.xml manifest.

Index

■ A

ABD (Android Debug Bridge), 853
abs( ) method, 230
absolute pathname, 513–515
abstract classes, 109–110, 396
abstract methods, 109–110
abstract pathnames, 513, 581
abstract types, 123
Abstract Window Toolkit. *See* AWT
AbstractButton class, 508
AbstractCollection class, 320, 400
AbstractList class, 320, 396, 400
AbstractMap class, 320, 400
AbstractQueue class, 320, 395, 400
AbstractSequentialList class, 320, 400
AbstractSet class, 320, 400
AbstractTableModel class, 656
accept( ) method, 520–521, 593–594
AccessibleObject class, 271
accessing data, 585–661
    databases, 628–659
        Java DB, 629–636
        JDBC API, 636–659
    networks, 585–628
        authentication, 620–625
        cookies, 626–628
        sockets, 585–609
        URLs, 609–620
ActionEvent object, 442–443
actionPerformed( ) method, 578
activeCount( ) method, 289
activities, component of Android app, 836–841
Activity class, 836, 841
activity lifecycle, 838
activity stack, 831, 841, 858
add( ) method, 138, 197, 322, 329, 331, 335, 342, 355, 360, 578
addAll( ) method, 323, 325, 329
addAppt( ) method, 101–103

addAppts( ) method, 101–102
addEmployee( ) method, 140
addFirst( ) method, 360
addition operator, 25
additive operators, 30
addLast( ) method, 360
addNotify( ) method, 439
addresses, socket, 587–588
addSuppressed( ) method, 158
addxListener( ) method, 442
advanced language features, 131–225
    annotations, 184–194
        discovering, 185–188
        processing, 192–194
    assertions, 175–184
        avoiding, 183
        control-flow invariants, 178–179
        declaring, 176–177
        enabling and disabling, 183–184
        internal invariants, 177–178
    enumerated type, 212–225
    exceptions, 155–175
        defined, 155
        throwing exceptions, 161–163
    generics, 194–212
        arrays and, 208–210
        collections and need for type safety, 195–197
        generic methods, 206–208
        varargs and, 211–212
    nested types, 131–143
        anonymous classes, 138–140
        interfaces within classes, 143
        local classes, 140–143
        nonstatic member classes, 135–138
        static member classes, 131–135
    packages, 144–153
        defined, 144–145
        import statement, 146–147
        and JAR files, 153
        package statement, 145–146

advanced language features, packages (*cont.*)
    playing with, 148–152
    uniqueness of package names, 145
  static imports, 153–154
AffineTransform class, 488
ages array, 36
agile software development, 122
algorithm, 181
allOf( ) method, 343–344
American National Institute of Standards &
  Technology (NIST), 590
American Standard Code for Information
  Interchange (ASCII), 566
AND operator, 342
Android apps, 829–869
  architecture of, 829–847
    Android software stack, 830–833
    APK file, 847
    application resources, 846–847
    components, 834–843
    manifest file, 843–846
  AVD, 854–858
  creating, installing, and running, 859–868
  installing SDK and platform for, 848–854
Android Debug Bridge (ABD), 853
android-sdk-windows, 850, 853
Android software stack, 830–833
Android Virtual Devices (AVDs), 829, 854–858
AndroidManifest.xml file, 848, 866
Animals class, 128
animation-list element, 864
annotations, 184–194
  discovering annotations, 185–188
  processing annotations, 192–194
  type declarations, meta-annotations in,
    190–192
  web service, 759–760
anonymous classes, 138–140
Apache Ant, 849, 865
APIs (Application Programming Interfaces)
  JDBC, 647
  legacy, 391–395
  web service, 759
APK (App Package) files, 847
app launcher, 835, 841, 845, 858, 867–869
App Package (APK) files, 847
append( ) method, 278, 533, 535, 568
appendable interface, 568
appendChild( ) method, 712
application element, 846, 863
Application Not Responding dialog box, 843

Application Programming Interfaces. *See* APIs
application resources, 846–847
apps, Java7MeetsAndroid. *See*
  Java7MeetsAndroid app
Appt object, 102
ApptCalendar class, 101–103
Area class, 497
area( ) method, 145
Area object, 497–498
arguments, passing to methods, 69
ArithmeticException object, 34, 163
Array class, 259, 271
array index operator, 25, 30–31
array initializers, 22
array types, 19, 198
ArrayBlockingQueue, 413–414, 416
arraycopy( ) method, 281, 318
ArrayDeque class, 363–364
ArrayDeque( ) method, 363
ArrayIndexOutOfBoundsException class, 232
ArrayList class, 122–123, 333–334
ArrayList( ) method, 320, 331, 333–334, 390–391,
  396, 400
arrays and generics, 208–210
Arrays class, 181, 212, 320, 388–389, 395, 400,
  432
arrays, creating with new operator, 57–59
ArrayStoreException class, 209, 224
ASCII (American Standard Code for
  Information Interchange), 566
AssertionError class, 158, 176–178, 183
assertions, 175–184
  avoiding assertions, 183
  control-flow invariants, 178–179
  declaring assertions, 176–177
  enabling and disabling assertions, 183–184
  internal invariants, 177–178
assignment operators, 25, 31
assignment statements, 36
associativity, 35
Atomic class, variables of, 419
AttachmentPart class, 805
AttachmentPart object, 805
attachments, RESTful web services and, 822–
  825
Attr interface, 707
Attribute node, 701
ATTRIBUTE_NODE, 705
authentication
  and customized lightweight HTTP server,
    820–822

overview, 620–625
Authenticator class, 622
Author class, 789–791
autoboxing, and unboxing, 327–329
AutoCloseable interface, 175, 830
automatic resource management, 174–175
available( ) method, 568
AVDs (Android Virtual Devices), 829, 854–858
avoiding assertions, 183
await( ) method, 411–413
awaitTermination( ) method, 403–404
AWT (Abstract Window Toolkit) API, 435–463
    component classes
        demonstrating, 443–456
        overview of, 437–440
    containers
        demonstrating, 443–456
        overview of, 440–441
    data transfer, 461–463
    events
        demonstrating, 443–456
        overview of, 442–443
    images, 456–461
    layout managers
        demonstrating, 443–456
        overview of, 441–442
    toolkits, 436
AWTEvent class, 442

■ B

BACK key, 841–842
back stack, 841
BandCombineOp class, 501
BasicAuthenticator class, 822
Because class, 68, 84, 130
BigDecimal class, 306–311, 318
BigInteger class, 312–318
binary search, 388–389
Binding interface, 819
Birds class, 391
bitset, 342–343, 392–394
BitSet class, 394
BitSet( ) method, 391–395, 397, 399–400
Bitwise AND operator, 25
Bitwise complement operator, 25
Bitwise exclusive OR operator, 25
Bitwise inclusive OR operator, 25
bitwise operators, 31
blank final, 63

Blob interface, 654
Blob object, 654
BLOB type, 654
BlockingQueue, 413–416, 418
Book class, 787–790
boolean canExecute( ) method, 517
boolean canRead( ) method, 517
boolean canWrite( ) method, 517
Boolean class, 240–242
boolean createNewFile( ) method, 521
boolean delete( ) method, 522
boolean exists( ) method, 517
Boolean expression, 32, 36–37, 41–45, 47–48
boolean isAbsolute( ) method, 515
boolean isDirectory( ) method, 517
boolean isFile( ) method, 517
boolean isHidden( ) method, 518
Boolean literal, 21
boolean markSupported( ) method, 540
boolean mkdir( ) method, 522
Boolean object, 240–242, 714, 720, 816
Boolean property, 789
boolean setReadOnly( ) method, 523
Boolean type, 26–27, 373
boolean valid( ) method, 529
booleanValue( ) method, 241
Border interface, 467
BorderFactory class, 467
BorderLayout class, 602
boxing, autoboxing and unboxing, 327–329
BoxLayout class, 578
Bridge driver, 637
broadcast receivers, component of Android
    app, 842
BroadcastReceiver class, 842
BrokenBarrierException class, 410
buffered images
    architecture of, 500
    processing, 501–507
        convolving images, 502–506
        lookup tables, 506–507
BufferedImage class
    buffered images
        architecture of, 500
        processing, 501–507
    overview, 498–500
BufferedImageOp interface, 501
BufferedInputStream class, 538, 550–551, 567–
    568, 580–581
BufferedOutputStream class, 538, 550–551,
    567–568, 580

BufferedReader, 567–568, 572–574, 576, 580–581
BufferedWriter, 567–568
bugs, 156, 175
Bundle object, 837
Button class, 861
Button element, 862
Button object, 861
ButtonModel interface, 468
ButtonUI class, 468
Byte class, 247–249
bytecode verifier, 3

C

CAG (Constructive Area Geometry), 497–498
Calculator app, 836
Calendar class, 186
call( ) method, 405, 409
Callable interface, 401
CallableStatement interface, 644–647
callback framework, 104
canonical, 515–517, 570
Canvas class, 453, 476
Car class, 60, 62–63, 65, 87, 89, 100
Car object, 60, 62–63, 87
Card class, 659
case-sensitive language, 16
cast operator, 26, 31–32
CDATA (Character Data) sections, 668–669, 701
ceiling( ) method, 730
Cell class, 398
Census class, 128
changing forms. *See* polymorphism
char readChar( ) method, 527
Character class, 135, 242–243, 399
Character Data (CDATA) sections, 668–669, 701
character encoding, 564, 566, 568–570
character literal, 21
character( ) method, 696
Character object, 242, 418
character references, and CDATA sections, 668–669
character sets, 566
characters( ) method, 688
ChatClient class, 601
ChatServer class, 597
checkError( ) method, 565
Circle class, 48, 105–106, 108, 119, 145–147, 154, 202

Circle type, 144
class browser, 257
Class class, 257
class field initializers, 78–79, 81
class fields
    declaring and accessing, 62–63
    declaring read-only instance and, 63–64
class initializers, 78–79
class invariants, 182–183
class methods, 65, 68, 270
Class object, 91, 219, 257, 259–260, 265, 267, 271–272, 378
ClassCastException class, 111, 194, 210, 325, 369, 381–382, 384–386
classes and objects
    creating arrays with new operator, 57–59
    creating objects with new operator and constructor, 52–53
    declaring classes, 52
    formalizing class interfaces, 115–124
        declaring interfaces, 115–116
        extending interfaces, 120–122
        implementing interfaces, 117–120
        use of, 122–124
    garbage collectors, 124
    inheriting state and behaviors, 84–104
        composition, 100
        extending classes, 85–91
        trouble with implementation inheritance, 100–104
    initializing, 78–84
        class initializers, 78–79
        initialization order, 81–84
        instance initializers, 80–81
    polymorphism, 104–115
        abstract classes and abstract methods, 109–110
        covariant return types, 113–115
        downcasting and runtime type identification, 111–113
        upcasting and late binding, 105–109
    specifying constructor parameters and local variables, 53–57
classes, extending, 85–91
classfiles, 2
classloader, 3
ClassName assertions, 184
ClassNotFoundException class, 263
cleanup, performing, 170–175
client code, 76
clients, dispatch, 825–828

clinit( ) method, 84
Clipboard object, 461
clipping shape attribute, 491
clone( ) method, 91–93, 95, 104, 116, 189, 218–220
Cloneable interface, 93, 184, 189
CloneNotSupportedException, 92–94
Close file, 529
close( ) method, 172, 175, 536, 546, 550, 572, 593, 639, 805, 817
Closeable interface, 532
closed interval, 347
closed range, 347
code point, 17
Coin class, 220
col.iterator( ) method, 326, 328
Collection interface, Iterable interface and, 322–329
    autoboxing and unboxing, 327–329
    Iterator interface and enhanced for statement, 325–327
collections, 319–400
    Collections Framework API, 319–391
        architecture of, 319–322
        Deque interface, 359–364
        Iterable and Collection interfaces, 322–329
        List interface, 329–335
        Map interface, 364–380
        NavigableMap interface, 383–387
        NavigableSet interface, 351–354
        Queue interface, 355–359
        Set interface, 335–344
        SortedMap interface, 380–383
        SortedSet interface, 344–351
        utility classes, 388–391
    concurrent, 413–415
    custom, 395–400
    legacy APIs, 391–395
    and need for type safety, 195–197
Collections class, 207, 319, 327, 344, 388, 390, 392, 396, 399, 432
Collections Framework API, 319–391
    architecture of, 319–322
    Deque interface, 359–364
    Iterable and Collection interfaces, 322–329
        autoboxing and unboxing, 327–329
        Iterator interface and enhanced for statement, 325–327
    List interface, 329–335
        ArrayList class, 333–334

LinkedList class, 334–335
Map interface, 364–380
    EnumMap class, 379–380
    HashMap class, 370–376
    IdentityHashMap class, 376–378
    TreeMap class, 369–370
    WeakHashMap class, 378–379
NavigableMap interface, 383–387
NavigableSet interface, 351–354
Queue interface, 355–359
Set interface, 335–344
    EnumSet class, 341–344
    HashSet class, 337–341
    TreeSet class, 336–337
SortedMap interface, 380–383
SortedSet interface, 344–351
utility classes, 388–391
collisions, 371
ColoredPoint[] type, 109
ColorModel class, 500
Colors interface, 121
ColorSpace class, 500
Command-line interface, 5
command-line tools, Java DB database, 634–636
comment feature, 12
comment node, 701
comments
    Javadoc, 13–15
    multiline, 12–13
    overview, 12
    and processing instructions, 672–673
    single-line, 12
Comparable interface, 202–204, 320–322, 336, 369, 389, 524
Comparator interface, 320–322
comparator( ) method, 347
compare( ) method, 427
compareTo( ) method, 202–203, 220, 320, 349–351, 383, 388, 524
compatible class change, 557
compile-time constant, 64
compile-time search, 147–148
Component class, 437, 451, 601
component classes
    AWT API, overview of, 437–440
    demonstrating, 443–456
components, lightweight, 466–467
ComponentUI class, 468
Composite interface, 489
composite rule attribute, 489–490

compositing, rasterizing and, 483–484
composition, 100
Compound assignment operator, 26
compound expressions, 24–35
    additive operators, 30
    array index operator, 30–31
    assignment operators, 31
    bitwise operators, 31
    cast operator, 31–32
    conditional operators, 32–33
    equality operators, 33
    logical operators, 33
    member access operator, 33
    method call operator, 33
    multiplicative operators, 33–34
    object creation operator, 34
    precedence and associativity, 35
    relational operators, 34
    shift operators, 34
    unary minus/plus operators, 35
compound paths, 729
compound statements, 36, 39, 43, 45–46
compute( ) method, 424–426
concat( ) method, 730
concurrency utilities, 401–426
    Atomic class variables, 419
    concurrent collections, 413–415
    executors, 401–410
    Fork/Join framework, 420–426
    locks package, 416–418
    synchronizers, 410–413
    ThreadLocalRandom class, 420
ConcurrentHashMap class, 413
ConcurrentSkipListMap class, 413–414
Conditional AND operator, 26
conditional operators, 26, 32–33
Conditional OR operator, 26
connect( ) method, 156, 222
Connection interface, 637
Connection object, 597, 646
connections, data sources, 636–638
Console class, 149
Constructive Area Geometry (CAG), 497–498
constructor parameters, specifying, 53–57
Container class, 440, 465
containers
    demonstrating, 443–456
    heavyweight, 464–466
    lightweight, components and, 466–467
    overview of, 440–441
contains( ) method, 493–494, 496

containsKey( ) method, 365, 378
content providers, component of Android app,
    842
ContentHandler interface, 684–685
ContentProvider class, 842
Context class, 836
continue statements, 47–49
control-flow invariants, 177–179, 223
Conversions class, 68
convert( ) method, 161–162, 164–166
convolving, images, 502–506
CookieHandler class, 626
CookieManager class, 626–627
CookiePolicy interface, 626
cookies, 626–628
CookieStore interface, 626
copy( ) method, 173–175
CopyOnWriteArrayList, 414
Countable interface, 128
countdown latch, 410–413
countDown( ) method, 411–412
countdown( ) method, 413
CountDownLatch class, 410–411
counter variable, 22
CountingThreads, 284, 286, 317
covariant return types, 113–115
Create object, 476
Create, Read, Update, and Delete (CRUD), 756
createBlob( ) method, 654
createConnection( ) method, 802
Created table, 632–633
createDispatch( ) method, 826, 828–829
createElement( ) method, 712
createGraphics( ) method, 499
createGUI( ) method, 459, 655
createReturnType( ) method, 114
createStatement( ) method, 640
createTempFile( ) method, 522–524
createXMLReader( ) method, 684, 690
CRUD (Create, Read, Update, and Delete), 756
cstmt.execute( ) method, 645
curFile( ) method, 459
current( ) method, 420
currentThread( ) method, 285
currentTimeMillis( ) method, 279–281
custom exception classes, 159–160
cyclic barrier, 410
CyclicBarrier class, 410–411, 413

■ D

Dalvik Executable (DEX), 833, 854
data access. *See* accessing data
Data Definition Language (DDL), 634
data sources, drivers, 636–638
data transfer, 461–463
database management system (DBMS), 629
DatabaseMetaData interface, 647
databases, 628–659
    Java DB, 629–636
        command-line tools, 634–636
        demos, 632–633
        installation and configuration of, 630–
           631
    JDBC API, 636–659
        data sources, drivers, and connections,
           636–638
        exceptions, 638–640
        metadata, 647–651
        Planets application, 651–659
        statements, 640–647
DataBuffer class, 500
DatagramSocket class, and MulticastSocket
    class, 603–609
DataInput interface, 528, 552
DataInputStream class, DataOutputStream
    class and, 551–552
DataOutput interface, 528, 552, 555, 561–562
DataOutputStream class, and DataInputStream
    class, 551–552
DataOutputStream method, 552–553
DataSource interface, 637, 822
Date class, 94, 186, 281, 580, 738
DateResolver class, 739
Daylight Saving Time (DST), 592
DBMS (database management system), 629
DDL (Data Definition Language), 634
deadlock, 301, 303
debug mode, 866
decision statements, 36–40
    if-else statement, 37–39
    if statement, 36–37
    switch statement, 40
Deck class, 188, 191, 194, 222
declaring
    annotating source code, 188–192
    annotation types, 188–192
    assertions, 176–177

    classes, 52
    interfaces, 115–116
    using own generic types, 198–200
deep cloning, 93
deep copying, 93
deepEquals( ) method, 427, 433
defaultReadObject( ) method, 561
defaultWriteObject( ) method, 561
delegates, UI, 467–468
deleteOnExit( ) method, 523
denomValue( ) method, 215
Deque interface, 359–364
describe( ) method, 88–91
deserialize( ) method, 787, 790
Design-by-Contract, 179–183
    class invariants, 182–183
    postconditions, 181–182
    preconditions, 180–181
detachNode( ) method, 804
DEX (Dalvik Executable), 833, 854
diamond operator, 197, 334, 699
Dimension class, 441, 453, 461
dimensions, 19
discovering annotations, 185–188
dispatch clients, providers and, 825–828
dispose( ) method, 445
divide( ) method, 71, 410
Division operator, 26
do-while statement, 44–45
document fragment node, 702
document node, 702
Document object, 705, 710, 744
Document Object Model. *See* DOM
document readers, 713
Document Type Definition (DTD), 674–678
documentation comment, 13
DocumentBuilder class, 703–705, 708, 710–711,
    734, 740–741, 747
DocumentBuilderFactory class, 703–704, 707–
    708, 711, 732, 736, 740–741, 747
DocumentType interface, 705
doDelete( ) method, 788, 829
doGet( ) method, 788, 798, 823, 826, 828
doLayout( ) method, 459
DOM (Document Object Model), 700–712
    API, 703–712
    tree of nodes, 701–703
    XPath language and, 731–735
DOMException class, 706
DOMResult object, 828
DOMSource class, 744

doPut( ) method, 788–789
Double class, Float class and, 243–247
Double object, 243–244
downcasting, 111–113
DragRectPane class, 496
draw( ) method, 104–106, 108–109, 116, 118, 122, 130, 486
drawable attribute, 864
Drawable class, 860
Drawable interface, 115, 117–119, 122
Driver class, 316
Driver driver, 637
Driver interface, 636–637
DriverDemo class, 316
DriverManager class, 637
drivers, data sources, 636–638
Dropped table, 632–633
DST (Daylight Saving Time), 592
DTD (Document Type Definition), 674–678
DTD file, 676, 699
DTDHandler interface, 684–685
dump( ) method, 221, 334, 648, 709
dumpBitset( ) method, 393–394
DumpFileInHex class, 542–543
DumpFileInHex.class file, 543
DumpFileInHex.class.hex file, 543

▨ E

early binding, 108
eat( ) method, 127
EchoArgs class, 48
EDT (event-dispatch thread), 577
Element interface, 707
element node, 702
Element object, 710
Element type, 709
ELEMENT_NODE, 705, 708, 711
elements array, 125
elements( ) method, 391
Employee class, 64, 74, 92, 146, 187, 350, 374, 556–557, 562
Employee( ) method, 562–564
Employee object, 69, 92, 94, 124, 183, 196–197, 349, 554, 556
Employee type, 197
employee.dat file, 556, 559
EMPLOYEES table, 635–636, 640–641, 647, 649
empty abstract pathname, 513–514
empty statements, 45–47, 56

EMPTY_LIST class, 391
emptyList( ) method, 391
enabling and disabling assertions, 183–184
encapsulating state and behaviors, 59–77
    hiding information, 74–77
    representing behaviors via methods, 65–73
        chaining together instance method calls, 67
        declaring and invoking class methods, 68
        declaring and invoking instance methods, 65–66
        invoking methods recursively, 71–72
        overloading methods, 72–73
        passing arguments to methods, 69
        returning from method via return statement, 69–71
        reviewing method-invocation rules, 73
    representing state via fields, 60–64
        declaring and accessing class fields, 62–63
        declaring and accessing instance fields, 60–62
        declaring read-only instance and class fields, 63–64
        reviewing field-access rules, 64
EndPoint class, 764, 766
Endpoint.publish( ) method, 830
Enterprise Edition (Java EE) SDK, 4
entire lifetime, 838
entity node, 702
entity reference node, 702
entity resolvers, custom, 697–700
EntityResolver interface, 684–685, 699
entrySet( ) method, 365, 367–370, 381, 399
Enum class
    extending, 220–225
    overview, 218–225
enumerated type, 212–214, 224
Enumeration interface, 391, 395, 400
EnumMap class, 379–380
enums
    enhancing, 215–218
    overview, 214–218
    trouble with traditional enumerated types, 213–214
EnumSet class, 341–344
equality operators, 26, 33
equals( ) method, 95, 218, 245, 321, 329, 340, 351, 374, 426, 433
EqualsDemo class, 433

equalsIgnoreCase( ) method, 275
equals(Object) method, 99
equalTo( ) method, 77
error codes versus objects, 155–156
ErrorHandler interface, 684–685
escape sequences, 20–21
EtchedBorder class, 467
evaluate( ) method, 735, 739
even( ) method, 37–38
event-based readers, parsing documents with, 717–719
event-based writers, creating documents with, 723–727
event-dispatch thread (EDT), 577
EventFactory class, 724
EventFilter interface, 720
EventQueue class, 445
events
    demonstrating, 443–456
    overview of, 442–443
example element, 669, 696–697
exceptions, 155–175, 638–640
    defined, 155
    throwing exceptions, 161–163
exchange( ) method, 410
Exchanger class, 410
EXE file, 265
execute( ) method, 413
executeQuery( ) method, 641
executeUpdate( ) method, 643
execution environment, 3
ExecutionException, 403–404, 406, 408–410
Executor interface, 401
executors, 401–410
ExecutorService, 402–403, 406–408, 412, 414, 416, 421, 434
explicit intent, 835, 841
expressions
    overview, 20
    simple, 20–24
extending
    classes, 85–91
    functions, and function resolvers, 737–740
    interfaces, 120–122
Extensible Markup Language documents. *See* XML
Extensible Stylesheet Language Transformation (XSLT), 742–748
external general entity, 677
external parameter entity, 678
external parsed general entity, 677

external unparsed entity, 677–678, 689
externalization, 562–564

F

factorial( ) method, 72, 313–315
FactoryConfigurationError class, 703, 714, 720
FailedInitialization class, 263
fatal errors, 685
field-access rules, 64
fields, representing state via, 60–64
    declaring and accessing class fields, 62–63
    declaring and accessing instance fields, 60–62
    declaring read-only instance and class fields, 63–64
    reviewing field-access rules, 64
FIFO (First-in, first-out), 355
File class, 56, 150, 238, 511–524, 570, 581, 616
File file, 512, 514, 516, 518, 520, 525, 573, 576
File getAbsoluteFile( ) method, 514
File getCanonicalFile( ) method, 515
File getParentFile( ) method, 515
File object, 511, 514–515, 518–519, 521–522, 524–525, 616
FileDataSource class, 823–824
FileDescriptor class, 526, 528–529
FileDescriptor getFD( ) method, 526
FileFilter interface, 521
FileInputStream class, 171, 173, 541–543
filename parameter, 53–56, 58, 127
FilenameFilter interface, 520
FileNotFoundException class, 162, 164–167, 170–173
FileOutputStream class, 541–543, 580
FileOutputStream object, 171
FileReader class, 568, 570–579
filesystem, 511
filesystems, 511–581
    File class, 511–524
    RandomAccessFile class, 525–536
    streams, 536–565
        classes of, 536–552, 564–565
        object serialization and deserialization, 553–564
    writer and reader classes, 565–579
        FileWriter and FileReader, 570–579
        OutputStreamWriter and InputStreamReader, 568–570
        overview of, 566–568

filesystems, writer and reader classes (*cont.*)
    Writer and Reader, 568
FileWriter class, and FileReader class, 570–579
fill( ) method, 119
Fillable interface, 119
fillables, 119
fillInStackTrace( ) method, 157–158
filter( ) method, 501, 503
FilterInputStream class, 544–550, 555, 567–568
FilterOutputStream class, 544–550, 555, 568
FilterReader, 567–568
FilterWriter, 567–568
final rethrow feature, 167
finalize( ) method, 91–92, 97–98, 218–219, 249, 255
find( ) method, 574
FindAll class, 573, 577
findAll( ) method, 573–574, 577–578
fire( ) method, 646
FIRED column, 647
First-in, first-out (FIFO), 355
firstName variable, 19, 22
FLAG_ACTIVITY_NEW_TASK, 835
Flat file, 536
flat file database, 529–530, 533, 536
Float class, and Double class, 243–247
Float object, 244
floating-point literal, 22, 551
flush( ) method, 539, 565, 592, 658
font attribute, 488
Font object, 452, 488
FontMetrics class, 453
foo( ) method, 120
for statement
    enhanced, Iterator interface and, 325–327
    overview, 41–42
foreground lifetime, 839
Fork/Join framework, 420–426
ForkJoinPool, 421, 424–425
ForkJoinTask, 421, 425
formal type parameter list, 197–198, 203–204, 220, 224
format( ) method, 307
Formatter class, 543, 568
forms, changing. *See* polymorphism
forName( ) method, 193, 260, 271
forwarding, 103
fos.close( ) method, 175
Frame class, 445, 450
fromInclusive, 352, 386
fromIndex, 331, 333, 395

function resolvers, extension functions and, 737–740
Future interface, 405
Future object, 407

■ G

garbage collectors, 124
general entities, 677
general entity references, 677, 688
generic methods, 206–208, 224
generic types, 197–205
    declaring and using your own generic types, 198–200
    need for wildcards, 204–205
    type parameter bounds, 201–203
    type parameter scope, 203–204
generics, 194–212
    arrays and generics, 208–210
    collections and need for type safety, 195–197
    generic methods, 206–208
    varargs and generics, 211–212
get( ) method, 99, 251, 253, 255–256, 268, 306, 404, 407, 409
getAge( ) method, 554, 556–557, 563
getAndIncrement( ) method, 419
getAnnotation( ) method, 193
getAttributes( ) method, 707
getAvailableFontFamilyNames( ) method, 477
getBackground( ) method, 452, 861
getBinding( ) method, 819
getBounds( ) method, 480, 493
getCanonicalFile( ) method, 515, 524
getCapabilities( ) method, 316
getCapabilitiesEx( ) method, 316
getCatalogs( ) method, 649
getCause( ) method, 158
getChildNodes( ) method, 706
getClass( ) method, 219, 271
getColor( ) method, 452
getConfigurations( ) method, 479
getConnection( ) method, 637–638
getContent( ) method, 628
getContentHandler( ) method, 684
getContentPane( ) method, 465
getContentType( ) method, 824
getCookies( ) method, 628
getDeclaringClass( ) method, 219
getDefaultConfiguration( ) method, 479

getDefaultScreenDevice( ) method, 478
getDirectory( ) method, 459
getDTDHandler( ) method, 684
getElementsByTagName( ) method, 733
getEncoding( ) method, 570
getEntityResolver( ) method, 684
getEnvelope( ) method, 803
getErrorHandler( ) method, 684
getEventType( ) method, 715
getFault( ) method, 815
getFaultString( ) method, 815
getFD( ) method, 528
getFeature( ) method, 685, 744
getFont( ) method, 452
getFontMetrics( ) method, 453
getHandlerChain( ) method, 819
getHeaders( ) method, 817
getID( ) method, 128
getImage( ) method, 456, 459
getImgCutoutSoap( ) method, 776
getIntent( ) method, 841
getJpeg( ) method, 776
getLastChild( ) method, 706
getLength( ) method, 608, 706
getLocalName( ) method, 694, 706, 708, 711
getMessage( ) method, 818
getMessageContext( ) method, 788
getMetaData( ) method, 647
getMethods( ) method, 193
getName( ) method, 196, 285, 515–516, 521, 554,
    556, 563, 717, 719
getNamespaceURI( ) method, 706, 708, 712,
    715, 736–737
getNextID( ) method, 294–295, 419
getNodeName( ) method, 706–709, 711
getNodeType( ) method, 705–706, 708–709, 711,
    732
getNodeValue( ) method, 706, 732–735, 740–741
getPasswordAuthentication( ) method, 623, 625
getPath( ) method, 514, 516–517, 573, 576
getPort( ) method, 775, 829
getPreferredSize( ) method, 653
getPrefix( ) method, 706, 708, 712, 715, 736
getPriority( ) method, 286
getProperty( ) method, 279–281, 328, 392, 513
getRadius( ) method, 106, 111
getRaster( ) method, 503
getRequestContext( ) method, 828
getRequestingScheme( ) method, 625
getSchemas( ) method, 649
getScreenDevices( ) method, 478

getSelectedRow( ) method, 657
getSelectedText( ) method, 463
getSelectionModel( ) method, 657
getSharedChar( ) method, 299–301
getSize( ) method, 127
getSOAPPart( ) method, 803
getStackTrace( ) method, 158
getSuppressed( ) method, 175
getSystemClipboard( ) method, 461
getTempVerterImplPort( ) method, 773
getText( ) method, 446
getThreadGroup( ) method, 288
getTime( ) method, 580, 739
getType( ) method, 478
getXmlEncoding( ) method, 707–708, 711
Google Charts web service, 795–798
GOTO statement, 51
gradeLetters variable, 19, 22
GradientPaint class, 813
Graph class, 232
graphical user interfaces. See GUIs
Graphics class, 80, 107, 109, 451, 453, 457, 485
Graphics2D class, 481–492
    rendering attributes, 484–492
        clipping shape, 491
        composite rule, 489–490
        font, 488
        paint, 485
        rendering hints, 492
        stroke, 486–487
        transformation, 488–489
    rendering pipeline, 481–484
GraphicsConfiguration method,
    GraphicsEnvironment class, GraphicsDevice
    method and, 477–481
GraphicsDevice method, GraphicsEnvironment
    class, GraphicsConfiguration method and,
    477–481
GraphicsEnvironment class, 477–481
GUIs (graphical user interfaces), 435–509
    AWT API, 435–463
        component classes, 440–443
        containers, 441–443
        data transfer, 461–463
        events, 442–443, 456
        images, 456–461
        layout managers, 441–443, 456
        toolkits, 436
    Java 2D extensions, 477–507
        BufferedImage class, 498–507
        Graphics2D class, 481–492

GUIs, Java 2D extensions (*cont.*)
GraphicsEnvironment class, GraphicsDevice method, and GraphicsConfiguration method, 477–481
Shape interface, 493–498
Swing API, 463–477
extended architecture, 464–470
sampling components of, 470–477

H

handle, 529
Handler class, 691
handlers, JAX-WS. *See* JAX-WS handler
handling exceptions, 163–170
handling multiple exception types, 164–166
rethrowing exceptions, 166–170
hasChildNodes( ) method, 706, 708
hasFault( ) method, 815
Hash table, 337
hashCode( ) method, 97, 99, 219, 323, 336, 340, 351, 373, 375, 396
HashCodeBuilder class, 374
HashMap class, 138, 370–376
HashMap( ) method, 320, 337, 370, 372, 374–375, 377–378, 389, 400
HashMapDemo, 372–373, 376
HashSet class, 337–341
HashSet( ) method, 320, 337–341, 389, 400
Hashtable class, 392
hasMoreElements( ) method, 391
hasNext( ) method, 195, 326, 334, 353, 368, 396, 715, 717, 719, 726
hasPrevious( ) method, 331, 335
headSet( ) method, 345–347, 352, 354
heap pollution, 211–212, 224
heavyweight containers, 464–466
HelloWorld class, 6–11, 14–15, 55
helper methods, 74
hiding information, 74–77
history stack, 835, 841
home screen, 842, 856–858, 861, 867
homogenous, 196
HTTP (Hypertext Transfer Protocol), 761–764, 820–822
HttpContext class, 762
HTTPContext class, 820
HTTPException class, 788
HttpHandler interface, 761

HttpsConfigurator object, 761
HttpServer class, 761
HttpURLConnection class, 791, 825
Hypertext Transfer Protocol (HTTP), 761–764, 820–822

I

I/O activity, 568
ID column, 657
ID (identifier), 860
identifiers, 16
identity check, 95
IdentityHashMap class, 320, 376–378, 400
if-else statement, 37–39
if statement, 36–37
ignorableWhitespace( ) method, 697
IIS (Internet Information Server), 624
IllegalAccessException class, 269
IllegalArgumentException class, 162, 424, 522–523, 525, 531, 544, 547, 737, 764
IllegalMonitorStateException class, 298
IllegalStateException, 322–323, 326, 332, 355–356, 359, 361, 368
Image class, 52–54, 74, 91, 127, 253
Image Cutout web service, 776–779
Image object, 52, 54–55, 58–59, 126, 253–254, 456, 460
ImageCache class, 253
ImageCanvas class, 457, 459
ImageIcon class, 499, 651, 654, 797–798
ImageObserver interface, 457
ImagePublisher class, 823
images
convolving, 502–506
overview, 456–461
imageType parameter, 53–56, 127
ImageView element, 859, 861–863
immutable class, 88
implementation inheritance, 100–104
implementing interfaces, 117–120
implicit intent, 836, 840–841, 869
import statement, 146–147
incompatible class change, 557
index.html file, 5, 15
IndexOutOfBoundsException, 329–331, 393
Inequality operator, 26
InetAddress class, 587–588, 608
InetSocketAddress class, 588, 761
infinite loop, 45–46

infix operator, 25
information hiding, 60–61, 74, 76, 87, 115
ingredient element, 664, 672, 674, 677, 680, 682, 722, 727, 746–747
InheritableThreadLocal class, 282, 305–306, 318
inheriting state and behaviors, 84–104
    composition, 100
    extending classes, 85–91
    object class, 91–100
        cloning, 92–94
        equality, 95–97
        finalization, 97–98
        hash codes, 98–99
        string representation, 100
    trouble with implementation inheritance, 100–104
init( ) method, 80, 84
initCause( ) method, 157
InitDemo class, 82–83
initialCapacity, 333, 337–338, 357, 359, 372
initialization order, 81–84
initialize section, 41
initializers
    class, 78–79
    instance, 80–81
initializing classes and objects, 78–84
    class initializers, 78–79
    initialization order, 81–84
    instance initializers, 80–81
Input class, 49
input stream, 536, 540, 544, 546, 548, 551, 556, 567, 570, 581
InputSource object, 700
InputStream class, 536, 538–541, 551–552, 555, 568–569
InputStream object, 803
InputStreamReader class, 568–570, 572, 580–581
INSERT statement, 643
Insets class, 467
installing
    JDK 7, 4–5
    NetBeans 7, 8–9
instance field initializers, 78, 80–81
instance fields, 60–62, 74, 78, 83–84, 92–94
instance initializers, 80–81
instance methods, 270
    chaining together, 67
    declaring and invoking, 65–66
instanceMethod1( ) method, 302–303
instanceMethod2( ) method, 302–303

instanceof operator, 96–97, 111–112
InstantiationException class, 267
instructions elements, 675, 679–680
int available( ) method, 539
int hashCode( ) method, 525
int length( ) method, 393
int read( ) method, 527, 540, 546–548
int readInt( ) method, 527
int size( ) method, 324, 366, 393
INTEGER-based column, 641
Integer class, 247–249
integer literal, 21–24
Integer object, 247, 305–306, 327–329
integer type, 2, 16, 25, 27, 29–30
integer values, 551
Integer.MAX_VALUE, 324, 366
Intent class, 835
Intent object, 835–836, 840–841, 845
intents, 834–837, 841, 869
interface inheritance, 84, 118, 120, 130
interfaces, 115–124
    within classes, 143
    declaring interfaces, 115–116
    extending interfaces, 120–122
    implementing interfaces, 117–120
    why use interfaces?, 122–124
intern( ) method, 275
internal general entity, 677
internal invariants, 177–178
International Organization for Standardization (ISO), 566
International Standard Book Number (ISBN), 757
Internet Information Server (IIS), 624
Internet Protocol (IP), 585–586, 588
interpreter, 3
interrupt( ) method, 283–284
InterruptedException class, 403–404, 406, 409, 412, 414–415, 417
intValue( ) method, 327
InvalidClassException class, 559
InvalidMediaFormatException class, 160–162, 164–166
invariant, 177–179, 182, 222–223
InvocationTargetException class, 267
InvoiceCalc, 306–307, 310–311
invoke( ) method, 269–271, 786–787, 795, 799, 823, 825–826
invokeAll( ) method, 426
invokeLater( ) method, 578
invoke(T) method, 825

IOException class, 174, 525, 565, ?570, 571–574, 577, 798
IP addresses, 586–587
IP (Internet Protocol), 585–586, 588
isAlive( ) method, 287
isAnnotationPresent( ) method, 193
isBlank( ) method, 47
ISBN (International Standard Book Number), 757
isDone( ) method, 409, 426
isExist( ) method, 649
isFull( ) method, 222
isInfinite( ) method, 244
isLetter( ) method, 399
isLightweight( ) method, 439
isNaN( ) method, 244
isNegative( ) method, 242
ISO (International Organization for Standardization), 566
isSorted( ) method, 182
isStopped( ) method, 296–297
Iter class, 141
Iterable interface, and Collection interface, 322–329
    autoboxing and unboxing, 327–329
    Iterator interface and enhanced for statement, 325–327
Iterable method, 323
iterations, 41–42, 47
Iterator interface, 141–142, 325–327, 395, 400
iterator( ) method, 141, 322–330
Iterator object, 143

■ J

JAR files, 144, 147, 153, 235, 239, 265, 610, 631, 637
jar tool, 5
Java
    JDK 7, 4–7
        installing, 4–5
        working with, 5–7
    as language, 1–3
    NetBeans 7, 7–12
        installing, 8–9
        working with, 9–12
    as platform, 3–4
Java 2D extensions, 477–507
    BufferedImage class, 498–507
    Graphics2D class, 481–492

rendering attributes, 484–492
    rendering pipeline, 481–484
GraphicsEnvironment class, GraphicsDevice method, and GraphicsConfiguration method, 477–481
Shape interface, 493–498
Java API for XML Processing (JAXP), 663, 744
Java API for XML Web Services (JAX-WS) handler, 815–819
Java Architecture for XML Binding (JAXB), 759, 761
Java class, 634, 740, 758, 760, 764, 776, 833
Java Database Connectivity. See JDBC
Java DB database, 629–636
    command-line tools, 634–636
    demos, 632–633
    installation and configuration of, 630–631
Java EE (Enterprise Edition) SDK, 4
Java Foundation Classes (JFC), 435
Java interface, 753, 760, 764, 773
Java language, and web services, 758–764
    annotations, 759–760
    APIs, 759
    lightweight HTTP server, 761–764
    tools, 760–761
Java ME (Mobile Edition) SDK, 4
Java method, 79, 81, 644, 737, 764, 781, 825
Java Native Interface (JNI), 3
Java object, 57, 739, 759–760, 834
Java Runtime Environment (JRE), 5, 849
Java Server Pages (JSP), 4
java tool, 5
Java type, 735
Java Virtual Machine (JVM), 3, 51, 139, 254, 511, 623
Java7MeetsAndroid app, 859–868
javac tool, 5, 7, 48
Javadoc comments, 13–15
javadoc tool, 5, 14
java.io.FileNotFoundException, 516
java.io.SyncFailedException, 529
java.io.UnsupportedEncodingException, 569
java.lang.ArithmeticException, 159
java.lang.ArrayIndexOutOfBoundsException, 159
java.lang.InterruptedException, 403
java.math.BigDecimal local variable, 410
JavaQuiz class, 399
JavaScript Object Notation (JSON), 796
java.util.concurrent package, 282

JAX-WS (Java API for XML Web Services)
handler, 815–819
JAXB (Java Architecture for XML Binding), 759,
761
JAXP (Java API for XML Processing), 663, 744
JButton class, 468
JComponent class, 466
JDBC (Java Database Connectivity) API, 636–
659
data sources, drivers, and connections, 636–
638
exceptions, 638–640
metadata, 647–651
Planets application, 651–659
statements, 640–647
CallableStatement interface, 644–647
PreparedStatement interface, 643
Statement interface and ResultSet
object, 640–642
JDBC method, 637–639
JDBCFilterDriver class, 79
JDK 7, 4–7
installing, 4–5
working with, 5–7
JFC (Java Foundation Classes), 435
JFrame class, 466
JIT (Just-In-Time) compiler, 3
JLayer class, 474
JLayeredPane class, 464
JNI (Java Native Interface), 3
join( ) method, 287
JPEG file, 823
jre directory, 5
JRE (Java Runtime Environment), 5, 849
JRootPane class, 464
JScrollPane class, 578
JSON (JavaScript Object Notation), 796
JSP (Java Server Pages), 4
JTable class, 655
JTable table, 656
Just-In-Time (JIT) compiler, 3
JVM (Java Virtual Machine), 3, 51, 139, 254, 511,
623

▦ K

Kernel class, 502
KeyEvent class, 508
keypad keys, 858
keywords, 16

▦ L

label attribute, 46, 863
Label class, 473
labeled continue statements, 47–49
LAN (Local Area Network), 624
language APIs, 227–318
BigDecimal class, 306–311
BigInteger class, 312–318
Math and StrictMath classes, 227–235
Package class, 235–240
primitive type wrapper classes, 240–249
Boolean, 240–242
Character, 242–243
Float and Double, 243–247
Integer, Long, Short, and Byte, 247–249
Number, 249
Reference, 249–256
basic terminology of, 250–251
PhantomReference class, 255–256
and ReferenceQueue class, 251–252
SoftReference class, 252–254
WeakReference class, 254–255
Reflection, 257–271
String class, 272–275
StringBuffer and StringBuilder classes, 276–
278
System class, 279–281
Threading, 282–306
Runnable and Thread interfaces, 282–
291
thread synchronization, 291–306
language features of Java, 12–49
array types, 19
assignment statements, 36
comments, 12
compound expressions, 24–35
additive operators, 30
array index operator, 30–31
assignment operators, 31
bitwise operators, 31
cast operator, 31–32
conditional operators, 32–33
equality operators, 33
logical operators, 33
member access operator, 33
method call operator, 33
multiplicative operators, 33–34
object creation operator, 34
precedence and associativity, 35

language features of Java, compound expressions (*cont.*)
    relational operators, 34
    shift operators, 34
    unary minus/plus operators, 35
  decision statements, 36–40
    if-else statement, 37–39
    if statement, 36–37
    switch statement, 40
  expressions, 20
  identifiers, 16
  Javadoc comments, 13–15
  loop statements, 41–49
    continue and labeled continue statements, 47–49
    do-while statement, 44–45
    looping over empty statement, 45–47
    for statement, 41–42
    while statement, 42–43
  multiline comments, 12–13
  overview, 1–3
  primitive types, 17–18
  simple expressions, 20–24
  single-line comments, 12
  statements, 36
  types, 16
  user-defined types, 18
  variables, 19–20
LargeObject class, 256
LargeObject object, 256, 379
last-in, first-out (LIFO), 355, 421
late binding, 105–109
Launch Options dialog box, 856
LayerUI class, 474
layout managers
  demonstrating, 443–456
  overview of, 441–442
LayoutManager interface, 441
lazy initialization, 430
Left shift operator, 27
legacy APIs, 391–395
length( ) method, 33
LexicalHandler interface, 686–687
Library class, 786, 829
library web service, 781–795
lifecycle callback methods, 837
LIFO (last-in, first-out), 355, 421
lightweight components, and containers, 466–467
lightweight HTTP server, 820–822
linear congruential generator, 430, 434

linear search, 388
LinearGradientPaint class, 813
LinearLayout element, 862
LinkedBlockingDeque class, 413
LinkedList class, 298, 334–335, 399–400
LinkedList( ) method, 320, 331, 334–335, 356, 396, 399–400
LinkedTransferQueue class, 414
List interface, 329–335
  ArrayList class, 333–334
  LinkedList class, 334–335
List.hashCode( ) method, 396
ListIterator interface, 331
listIterator( ) method, 330–331
literals, 16, 20
Local Area Network (LAN), 624
local classes, 140–143
local service, 842
local variables, 53–57, 64, 67, 93, 124
Location object, 718
location path expression, 728–729, 733, 746, 749
Locator interface, 688
Locator object, 688
lock( ) method, 294, 417–418
lockInterruptibly( ) method, 416
locks package, 416–418
log( ) method, 572, 817–818
Logger class, 102
Logger interface, 148–149, 155
logging SOAP messages, with JAX-WS handler, 815–819
LoggingApptCalendar class, 101–104
Logical AND operator, 27
Logical complement operator, 27
Logical exclusive OR operator, 27
Logical inclusive OR operator, 27
logical operators, 33
Long class, 247–249
long getFilePointer( ) method, 527
long lastModified( ) method, 518
long length( ) method, 518, 527
Long object, 247
LookAndFeel class, 469
lookup tables, 506–507
LookupTable class, 506
LookupTable table, 507
loop-control variables, 41
loop statements, 41–49
  continue and labeled continue statements, 47–49
  do-while statement, 44–45

looping over empty statement, 45–47
for statement, 41–42
while statement, 42–43
looping over empty statement, 45–47

M

m( ) method, 111, 141
magnitude bits, 18
main( ) method, 6–7, 122, 127, 256, 269, 543, 546, 790
makeMap( ) method, 547, 550
manifest files, 843–846
Map interface, 364–380
EnumMap class, 379–380
HashMap class, 370–376
IdentityHashMap class, 376–378
TreeMap class, 369–370
WeakHashMap class, 378–379
Map.Entry interface, 368
mark( ) method, 540–541
marker annotations, 188–189
marker interface, 116
Math class, and StrictMath class, 227–235
Math.random( ) method, 58, 127, 412, 420, 431
MatMult class, 423, 425
Matrix class, 421
matrix variables, 22
matrix.length, 31, 42
matrix[row].length, 42
mayInterruptIfRunning, 405
Media class, 160–161
MediaTracker class, 460
member access operator, 27, 33
MENU button, 857, 868
MenuComponent class, 438
MEP (message exchange pattern), 751
merge( ) method, 212
message exchange pattern (MEP), 751
MessageContext interface, 788
MessageFactory object, 803
meta-annotations, 190–192, 223
metadata, 184–185, 189, 193, 223, 526, 647–651
metalanguage, 663
method call operator, 33
method-call stack, 67
method-invocation rules, 73
method-invocation stack, 67
Method method, 270
Method object, 193, 259, 269–270

MethodInvocationDemo, 270
methods
invoking recursively, 71–72
overloading, 72–73
passing arguments to, 69
representing behaviors via, 65–73
chaining together instance method calls, 67
declaring and invoking class methods, 68
declaring and invoking instance methods, 65–66
invoking methods recursively, 71–72
overloading methods, 72–73
passing arguments to methods, 69
returning from method via return statement, 69–71
reviewing method-invocation rules, 73
returning from via return statements, 69–71
MIME (Multipurpose Internet Mail Extensions), 613, 756, 835
MIME type, 757, 794, 823–825, 830, 841, 845
mimeType attribute, 845
MimetypesFileTypeMap class, 823
Mixing class, 79
Mobile Edition (Java ME) SDK, 4
Model-View-Controller (MVC), 467
Modifier class, 269
monitor, 294
move( ) method, 127–128
movie elements, 729
MulticastSocket class, DatagramSocket class and, 603–609
multicatch language feature, 166
multiline comments, 12–13
multiple exception types, handling, 164–166
multiple inheritance, 84, 130
MultipleGradientPaint class, 485
multiplicative operators, 28, 33–34
multiply( ) method, 423
Multipurpose Internet Mail Extensions (MIME), 613, 756, 835
mutable keys, 376
mutual exclusion, 294, 297–298
MVC (Model-View-Controller), 467

N

name attribute, 844–845
NAME column, 635, 649

Name interface, 804
name( ) method, 217
namespace contexts, 736–737
namespace prefix, 669, 710, 736, 746
NamespaceContext interface, 736
namespaces, 669–672
NavigableMap interface, 319, 383–387, 400
NavigableSet interface, 351–354, 414
negotiate authentication scheme, 625
nested loops, 46, 48
nested types, 131–143
    anonymous classes, 138–140
    interfaces within classes, 143
    local classes, 140–143
    nonstatic member classes, 135–138
    static member classes, 131–135
NetBeans 7, 7–12
    installing, 8–9
    working with, 9–12
network endpoints, 536
Network Interface Card (NIC), 586
networks, 585–628
    authentication, 620–625
    cookies, 626–628
    sockets, 585–609
        addresses, 587–588
        DatagramSocket and MulticastSocket
            classes, 603–609
        Socket and ServerSocket classes, 589–
            603
        socket options, 588–589
    URLs, 609–620
        URI class, 615–620
        URL and URLConnection classes, 609–
            612
        URLEncoder and URLDecoder classes,
            612–614
newDocument( ) method, 710
newDocumentBuilder( ) method, 704
newFactory( ) method, 714, 716, 719–720, 722,
    724
newFixedThreadPool( ) method, 409
newInstance( ) method, 267, 703, 708, 714, 732,
    735, 741, 743, 745, 802
newTransformer( ) method, 743, 745
newXPath( ) method, 735
next( ) method, 195, 197, 326, 399, 431, 641, 651,
    715, 815
nextDouble( ) method, 431
nextElement( ) method, 391
nextEvent( ) method, 717–718

nextIndex( ) method, 332
NIC (Network Interface Card), 586
NIST (American National Institute of Standards
    & Technology), 590
No argument assertions, 184
Node class, 397–398, 705
Node interface, 705, 804
node name, 701, 710
Node type, 709
NodeList interface, 735
nodes
    tree of, 701–703
    XML document, selecting with XPath
        language, 727–741
Nodes class, 397
nonstatic member classes, 135–138
nonterminating decimal expansion, 410
normalize( ) method, 618
normalize-space( ) method, 730, 746
NoSuchElementException, 326, 331, 344–345,
    356, 360–361, 381–382, 389
notation node, 673, 676–678, 689, 702
notifyAll( ) method, 264, 298
NotSerializableException class, 554
NullPointerException class, 126, 426, 429, 514,
    522, 527, 539–540, 544, 547
NullPointerExceptions, 390, 428
Number class, 249
number( ) method, 730
NumberFormat class, 307
NumberFormatException object, 246
numElements, 364
numeric type, 18, 25–26, 28–29
NumLock, 858
numRecs( ) method, 533

O

object class, 91–100
    cloning, 92–94
    equality, 95–97
    finalization, 97–98
    hash codes, 98–99
    string representation, 100
object creation operator, 28, 34
object deserialization, serialization and, 553–
    564
    custom, 558–561
    default, 553–557
    externalization, 562–564

object graph, 554
Object object, 267–268, 273
object serialization, deserialization and, 553–
    564
        custom, 558–561
        default, 553–557
        externalization, 562–564
ObjectInputStream class, 555
ObjectOutputStream class, 538, 554–556, 558–
    559, 561–564
Objects class, 92, 161, 400, 426–430, 434
Objects.requireNonNull( ) method, 429
odd( ) method, 37–38
offer( ) method, 356, 418
onClickListener interface, 861
onDestroy( ) method, 837–838, 840
onPause( ) method, 837–840
onRestart( ) method, 837–838
onResume( ) method, 837–839
onStart( ) method, 837–839
onStop( ) method, 837–839
openConnection( ) method, 794
openStream( ) method, 610
operand expression, 24
operator and constructor, creating objects with
    new, 52–53
OR operator, 342
OutOfMemoryError class, 254
output stream, 536–537, 539, 545, 547, 550, 559,
    564, 567, 581
OutputInputStream class, 554
OutputKeys class, 743
OutputKeys property, 745
outputList( ) method, 205
OutputReversedInt class, 49
OutputStream class, 536, 538–541, 550, 555,
    569–570, 581
OutputStreamWriter class, 568–570
overloading methods, 72–73

P

pack( ) method, 440, 459, 474
Package class, 235–240, 318
package helloworld statement, 11
Package object, 236, 238, 260
package statement, 145–146
PackageName assertions, 184
packages, 144–153
        defined, 144–145

import statement, 146–147
package statement, 145–146
packages and JAR files, 153
playing with packages, 148–152
uniqueness of package names, 145
paint attribute, 485
Paint interface, 485
paint( ) method, 455, 460, 476–477, 481, 488,
    508
Panel object, 449
parallelism, 420
parameter entities, 678
parameterized type, 196–198, 203, 211, 224
parent pathname, 514–516
parse( ) method, 700, 705, 739
parsed character data, 675, 696–697
parseDouble( ) method, 246
ParsePosition object, 739
ParserConfigurationException, 703, 705, 707–
    708, 710–711, 732–735
parsing
    documents
        with event-based readers, 717–719
        with stream-based readers, 714–717
    XML documents
        with DOM, 700–712
        with SAX, 683–700
        with StAX, 712–727
Parsing command, 246
Part object, 533
partition, 519
PartsDB class, 530, 532
PasswordAuthentication object, 623
PATH variable, 850, 854
pathname strings, 513
PC (producer-consumer application), 414
peek( ) method, 356, 360–361, 363–364
peekFirst( ) method, 363
PhantomReference class, 249, 255–256
PhantomReference object, 250–251, 255–256
Phaser class, 411
PHOTO column, 635
PLAFs (Pluggable Look And Feels), 468–470
Planet class, 338–340
Planets application, 651–659
PLANETS table, 651–652
platforms
        Android, installing, 848–854
        Java as, 3–4
playing with packages, 148–152
Pluggable Look And Feels (PLAFs), 468–470

PNG (Portable Network Graphics), 55, 265
Point class, 96–97, 99–100, 105, 109, 374
pointers, 3
poll( ) method, 356, 418
pollFirst( ) method, 352, 354, 361–363
Polygon class, 491
polymorphism, 104–115
    abstract classes and abstract methods, 109–110
    covariant return types, 113–115
    downcasting and runtime type identification, 111–113
    upcasting and late binding, 105–109
Pool class, 433
pop( ) method, 125–126, 363, 391
Portable Network Graphics (PNG), 55, 265
postconditions, 181–182
Postdecrement operator, 28
postfix operator, 25
Postincrement operator, 28
precedence, 35
preconditions, 180–181
predecessor( ) method, 348, 398
Predecrement operator, 28
prefix operator, 25
Preincrement operator, 28
PreparedStatement interface, 643
prepareStatement( ) method, 643
pressure simulation, 167
previous( ) method, 331–332, 335
previousIndex( ) method, 332
prime number, 316
primitive type wrapper classes, 240–249
    Boolean, 240–242
    Character, 242–243
    Float and Double, 243–247
    Integer, Long, Short, and Byte, 247–249
    Number, 249
primitive types, 17–18
print( ) method, 564–565
printBalance( ) method, 67
printDetails( ) method, 65–66, 71, 73
println( ) method, 73, 87, 552, 556, 558, 564–565, 572, 592
printReport( ) method, 69
printStackTrace( ) method, 162, 290
PrintStream class, 564–565
PrintWriter class, 564, 592
Priority queue, 355
PriorityQueue class, 356–359
PriorityQueue( ) method, 320, 356–359, 400

private command-line option, 14
PrivateAccess class, 77
PROCEDURE procedure, 644
processing annotations, 192–194
processing-instruction( ) method, 728
processing instruction node, 672–673, 688, 702, 727–728, 733
processing instructions, comments and, 672–673
processing pipelines, 714
processLine( ) method, 47–48
producer-consumer application (PC), 414
profiling, 123
Properties object, 392, 743
provider elements, 845
providers, and dispatch clients, 825–828
Proxy class, 590
public method, 6, 93
publish( ) method, 764, 766
pull model, 713
push( ) method, 125
put( ) method, 99

Q

QName object, 815, 828
Queue class, 222
Queue interface, 355–359, 363, 414

R

random access, 525–526, 529, 581
Random class, 434
Random( ) method, 430–434
random number generators, 430, 434
Random object, 547
RandomAccess interface, 396
RandomAccessFile class, 525–536
Raster class, 500
rasterizing, and compositing, 483–484
RasterOp interface, 501
raw type, 198, 205, 210, 224
RDBMSes (Relational DBMSes), 629
Read file, 56
read( ) method, 533, 539, 546–548, 550–551, 568–570
read-only instance, declaring class fields and, 63–64
Reader class, Writer class and, 568
readers

classes of, 565–579
　FileWriter and FileReader, 570–579
　OutputStreamWriter and
　　InputStreamReader, 568–570
　overview of, 566–568
　Writer and Reader, 568
parsing documents with
　event-based readers, 717–719
　stream-based readers, 714–717
readExternal( ) method, 562–564
readLine( ) method, 45, 592, 597
readObject( ) method, 554–559, 561, 563, 790
ready( ) method, 568
receiver elements, 845
RecipeML (Recipe Markup Language), 698–699
recoverable errors, 685
Rectangle class, 109, 132–133, 146, 494
recursion, 71
recursive type bound, 203
RecursiveAction, 421, 424–425
ReentrantLock, 416
refactoring, 47–48
Reference API, 249–256
　basic terminology of, 250–251
　PhantomReference class, 255–256
　and ReferenceQueue class, 251–252
　SoftReference class, 252–254
　WeakReference class, 254–255
Reference object, 250–252, 254–255
reference types, 18
reference variables, 19
referenced object, 113, 124
ReferenceQueue class, Reference API and, 251–252
ReferenceQueue object, 251–252, 254–256
Reflection API, 257–271
reification, 209, 224
Reject option radio button, 852
RejectedExecutionException, 402–405
Relational DBMSes (RDBMSes), 629
Relational greater than operator, 28
Relational greater than or equal to operator, 28
Relational less than operator, 28
Relational less than or equal to operator, 28
relational operators, 34
Relational type, 29
relative pathname, 513–514
release mode, 866
Remainder operator, 29
remote procedure call (RPC), 158, 752
remote service, 843

remove( ) method, 324–325, 329, 331–332, 356, 361, 366, 384–385
removeFirst( ) method, 361–363
rendering attributes, 484–492
　clipping shape, 491
　composite rule, 489–490
　font, 488
　paint, 485
　rendering hints, 492
　stroke, 486–487
　transformation, 488–489
rendering hints attribute, 492
rendering pipeline, 481–484
RenderingHints class, 492
repaint( ) method, 455–457
Representational State Transfer. See REST
requestPasswordAuthentication( ) method, 623
requireNonNull( ) method, 428–429
reserved words, 1–2, 16
reset( ) method, 540–541
resolveEntity( ) method, 700
resolvers
　entity, custom, 697–700
　function, extension functions and, 737–740
　variable, variables and, 740–741
resource management, automatic, 174–175
Response interface, 826
REST (Representational State Transfer) web
　services, 756–757, 780–798
　and attachments, 822–825
　Google Charts, 795–798
　library, 781–795
ResultSet object, 640–642, 651
rethrowing exceptions, 166–170
return statement, returning from method via, 69–71
RGB type, 498
RI class, 615
R.java file, 866
RL class, 609
rnd( ) method, 231
Roman numerals, and SAAJ API, 805–815
root directory, 511–513
RootPaneContainer interface, 465
round( ) method, 306, 730
RPC (remote procedure call), 158, 752
RTTI (runtime type identification), 257
run( ) method, 282–283, 285, 289, 402, 405, 412, 445, 578, 597
Runnable interface, and Thread interface, 282–291

RunnableTask( ) method, 401–402
runServer( ) method, 597
runtime exception, 159
runtime search, 148
runtime type identification, 105, 111–113
runtime type identification (RTTI), 257
RuntimeException class, 787

■ S

SAAJ (Soap with Attachments API for Java),
    799–815
    overview of, 801–805
    Roman numerals and, 805–815
    SOAP messages, architecture of, 799–801
SAAJMetaFactory class, 803
safety, need for type, 195–197
SampleModel class, 500
SavingsAccount class, 67, 306
SAX (Streaming API for XML)
    API
        demonstrating, 690–697
        overview, 683–690
    custom entity resolver, 697–700
SAXException class, 684
SAXNotRecognizedException class, 687
SAXNotSupportedException class, 685–687
SAXTransformerFactory class, 744
Scalable Vector Graphics (SVG), 669, 695–696
ScheduledExecutorService interface, 407, 434
Schema-based file, 769
Schema type, 801
ScrambledInputStream class, 548
ScrambledOutputStream class, 545
ScrollPane class, 459, 578
SDK Manager, 850–852, 854
SDKs (Software Development Kits), Android,
    848–854
searching for packages and types
    compile-time search, 147–148
    runtime search, 148
Secure Sockets Layer (SSL), 755, 761
security model, 833
Security Service Provider Interface (SSPI), 624
SEI interface, 773
select( ) method, 533
SELECT statement, 640
selector expression, 40, 42
Semaphore class, 411, 433
SemaphoreDemo class, 433

send( ) method, 606
sendClientsList( ) method, 597
separator character, 512–514
separatorChar class, 513
SerEmployee class, 558–561
Serializable interface, 553–554
SerializationDemo class, 556, 558–560, 563
serialize( ) method, 788–789
ServerSocket class, Socket class and, 589–603
Service class, 772, 775, 828, 843
service elements, 845
Service.create( ) method, 775
services, component of Android app, 842–843
Set interface, 335–344
    EnumSet class, 341–344
    HashSet class, 337–341
    TreeSet class, 336–337
set( ) method, 186, 316, 332
setAge( ) method, 377
setColor( ) method, 485
setDefaultCloseOperation( ) method, 474
setDocumentLocator( ) method, 688, 693, 695–
    696
setEntityResolver( ) method, 685, 687, 691, 700
setFeature( ) method, 685–687, 690, 700, 735,
    743
setImage( ) method, 459–461
setLastModified( ) method, 580
setName( ) method, 70, 76, 377
setPrefix( ) method, 723
setPriority( ) method, 286
setProperty( ) method, 686–687, 691, 697, 714,
    720
setRoundRect( ) method, 494, 496
setScale( ) method, 311
setSharedChar( ) method, 299–301
setStackTrace( ) method, 158
setUI( ) method, 469
setVisible( ) method, 451
Shape class, 104, 109–110, 122–123, 130, 201
Shape interface, 482, 491, 493–498
Shape object, 497
Shared object, 300–301
shift operators, 34
short-circuiting, 26–27, 32
Short class, 247–249, 328
shuffle( ) method, 188, 432
shutdown( ) method, 403–404
shutdownNow( ) method, 404, 409, 412, 415,
    418
Signed right shift operator, 29

Simple and Protected GSS-API Negotiation (SPNEGO), 624
simple expressions, 20–24
Simple Mail Transfer Protocol (SMTP), 586
Simple Object Access Protocol. *See* SOAP
simple statements, 36
SimpleActivity class, 837
SimpleApp-debug.apk file, 868
single inheritance, 84, 130
single-line comments, 12
size( ) method, 316
skippedEntity( ) method, 688, 693
SMTP (Simple Mail Transfer Protocol), 586
SOAP (Simple Object Access Protocol)-based web services, 753–756, 764–779
    Image Cutout, 776–779
    temperature-conversion, 764–776
SOAP (Simple Object Access Protocol) messages
    architecture of, 799–801
    logging with JAX-WS handler, 815–819
Soap with Attachments API for Java. *See* SAAJ
SOAPBody object, 804, 809, 811, 815
SOAPBodyElement object, 802, 804–805
SOAPConnection class, 802
SOAPConstants interface, 803
SOAPElement object, 805
SOAPEnvelope interface, 803
SOAPEnvelope object, 809, 811
SOAPFault interface, 815
SOAPFault object, 802
SOAPLoggingHandler class, 816
SOAPMessage object, 803, 805, 809, 811, 818
SOAPPart class, 803
SOAPPart object, 809, 811
Socket class, and ServerSocket class, 589–603
SocketAddress class, 588
sockets, 585–609
    addresses, 587–588
    DatagramSocket and MulticastSocket classes, 603–609
    Socket and ServerSocket classes, 589–603
    socket options, 588–589
SoftReference class, 250, 252–254
Software Development Kits (SDKs), Android, 848–854
software stacks, Android, 830–833
sort( ) method, 181, 202–203
SortedMap interface, 380–383
SortedSet interface, 319, 336, 344–351, 357, 381, 400

SortedShapesList class, 203
source code, representing exceptions in, 155–160
    custom exception classes, 159–160
    error codes versus objects, 155–156
    throwable class hierarchy, 156–159
Source database, 636
Source interface, 743, 794
Source object, 828
speak( ) method, 139
Speaker class, 140
SplashCanvas class, 454–455, 509
split( ) method, 193
SPNEGO (Simple and Protected GSS-API Negotiation), 624
SQL command, 630, 634
SQL statement, 635–636, 640–641, 643–644, 655, 657
SQL (Structured Query Language), 629, 635
SQLException object, 638
SQLite database, 842, 850
SQLTransientException-rooted class, 640
srchText variable, 573, 575–578
SSL (Secure Sockets Layer), 755, 761
SSPI (Security Service Provider Interface), 624
ST (Standard Time), 592
Stack class, 125–126, 391
Standard Time (ST), 592
start( ) method, 283, 285–286, 762, 764, 864
startActivity( ) method, 840
startDir variable, 575, 578
startElement( ) method, 686–688, 694–697
startSignal, 411–413
Statement interface, and ResultSet object, 640–642
statements, 640–647
    assignment, 36
    CallableStatement interface, 644–647
    overview, 36
    PreparedStatement interface, 643
    Statement interface and ResultSet object, 640–642
static imports, 153–154
static member classes, 131–135
status bar, 857
StAX (Streaming API for XML), creating documents, 712–727
    with event-based writers, 723–727
    with stream-based writers, 721–723
StAX (Streaming API for XML), parsing documents

StAX (Streaming API for XML), parsing documents (*cont.*)
    with event-based readers, 717–719
    with stream-based readers, 714–717
stop( ) method, 295–296, 861, 864
stopThread( ) method, 295–297
stream-based readers, parsing documents with, 714–717
stream-based writers, creating documents with, 721–723
stream unique identifier (SUID), 557
Streaming API for XML. *See* SAX
StreamResult class, 744
streams, classes of, 536–565
    BufferedOutputStream and BufferedInputStream, 550–551
    DataOutputStream and DataInputStream, 551–552
    FileOutputStream and FileInputStream, 541–543
    FilterOutputStream and FilterInputStream, 544–550
    OutputStream and InputStream, 538–541
    overview of, 536–538
    PrintStream, 564–565
StreamSource object, 788
StrictMath class, Math class and, 227–235
String[] args, 6
String class, 18, 76, 147, 272–275, 318, 374, 554
String concatenation operator, 29
String getAbsolutePath( ) method, 514
String getCanonicalPath( ) method, 515
String getName( ) method, 515, 554, 563
String getParent( ) method, 515
String getPath( ) method, 515
string-length( ) method, 730
string literal, 20–21, 26
String( ) method, 578, 730, 746, 794
String object, 33, 42, 274–275, 347, 373, 455, 553, 643, 788
String parameter, 54
String toString( ) method, 516, 558, 560
String type, 29, 565, 642, 841
StringBuffer class, 95, 276–278
StringBuffer/StringBuilder object, 278
StringBuilder class, StringBuffer class and, 276–278
StringBuilder object, 278
StringSelection object, 463
StringTokenizer class, 395
stroke attribute, 486–487

Stroke interface, 486
Structured Query Language (SQL), 629, 635
Stub class, 193
Stub type, 192
StubFinder, 257, 275
subList( ) method, 331–333, 345
submit( ) method, 407
SubReturnType class, 113–115
subSet( ) method, 345–348, 352, 354
substring-after( ) method, 730
substring-before( ) method, 730
substring( ) method, 730
Subtraction operator, 29
successor( ) method, 348
SUID (stream unique identifier), 557
sum( ) method, 69, 730
super( ) method, 87
SuppressWarnings type, 190
SVG (Scalable Vector Graphics), 669, 695–696
Swing API, 463–477
    extended architecture, 464–470
        heavyweight containers, 464–466
        lightweight components and containers, 466–467
        PLAFs, 468–470
        UI delegates, 467–468
    sampling components of, 470–477
        SwingCanvas class, 476–477
        TempVerter application, 471–476
Swing class, 473
SwingCanvas class, 476–477
SwingUtilities class, 469
SwingWorker class, 578
switch statement, 40
sync( ) method, 529
synchronizedSet( ) method, 389–390
synchronizers, 410–413
synchronizing, threads, 291–306
System class, 73, 279–281, 318, 328, 446, 513, 538
system requirements, Android SDK, 848–849
System.gc( ) method, 379
System.in.read( ) method, 43–46
System.out.println( ) method, 43, 54, 59, 73, 82, 86, 99, 107, 127, 301
System.out.println(msg), 102

T

TABLE statement, 640
TABLE_CAT column, 649
TableModel interface, 656
TABLE_NAME column, 649
tables, lookup, 506–507
TABLE_SCHEM column, 649
tagging interface, 116
tags, 663–664, 666, 671–673, 676, 688, 697, 721
tailSet( ) method, 345–347, 353–354
target, 672
targetNamespace attribute, 683
TCP (Transmission Control Protocol), 585
TempConversion, 217–219
temperature-conversion web service, 764–776
temperature variable, 19, 22
Templates interface, 744–745
Templates object, 744
TempVerter application, 471–476
TempVerter class, 445, 450
TempVerter interface, 764–765, 773
TempVerterClient class, 775
TempVerterImpl class, 765
ternary operator, 24–25
test section, 41–42
text node, 703
TextArea class, 462
Thread class, 594
thread communication, 297–298
Thread interface, Runnable interface and, 282–291
thread-local variable, 304
Thread object, 282–289, 296, 594
ThreadGroup class, 282, 288–290, 318
Threading API, 282–306
    Runnable and Thread interfaces, 282–291
    thread synchronization, 291–306
Thread.interrupt( ) method, 404
ThreadLocal class, 282, 304–305, 318
ThreadLocalRandom class, 419–420, 434
threads, synchronizing, 291–306
Thread.sleep( ) method, 293
Throwable class, 166
throwable class hierarchy
    checked exceptions versus runtime
        exceptions, 159
    overview, 156–159
throwing exceptions, 161–163

throws clause, 161–165, 168, 189, 223
title elements, 669, 675, 680, 746, 748
toAlignedBinaryString( ) method, 248, 278
toArray( ) method, 324–325, 344, 381
Toast class, 869
toBoolean( ) method, 265
toDenomination( ) method, 215
ToDo class, 136, 142
ToDoList class, 137, 141–142
toHexStr( ) method, 542–543
toInclusive, 352, 386
toIndex, 331, 333
tokens, 217
Toolkit class, 436, 456
Toolkit method, 436
toolkits, 436
tools, web service, 760–761
toRoman( ) method, 815
toString( ) method, 92, 127, 202, 214, 219, 277, 311, 381, 391, 559
toUpperCase( ) method, 428–429
toURI( ) method, 616
toURL( ) method, 617
traditional enumerated types, trouble with, 213–214
TrafficFlow class, 154
Transferable interface, 461–462
transferring data, 461–463
transformation attribute, 488–489
Transformer class, 743
TransformerException class, 743
TransformerFactory class, 742
TransformerFactoryConfigurationError class, 743
translate( ) method, 730
Transmission Control Protocol (TCP), 585
tree of nodes, 701–703
TreeMap class, 369–370
TreeMap( ) method, 320, 348–349, 370, 381–382, 386–387, 395, 400
TreeSet class, 336–337
TreeSet( ) method, 320, 336, 338, 342, 346, 348, 350–351, 395, 400
Triangle class, 49, 146
Truck class, 85, 87, 91, 95
tryLock( ) method, 416
twos-complement, 18
Tx method, 488
Type parameter, 197–198, 200–201, 203–206
type parameter bounds, 201–203
type parameter scope, 203–204

type safety, need for, 195–197
types
    array, 19
    overview, 16
    primitive, 17–18
    user-defined, 18

■ U

UDDI (Universal Description, Discovery, and
    Integration), 756
UDP (User Datagram Protocol), 585
UIManager class, 469
UIs (User Interfaces), delegates, 467–468
unary minus operator, 29, 35
unary operator, 24–25
unary plus operator, 29, 35
unboxing, autoboxing and, 327–329
UNC (Universal Naming Convention), 513
uncaughtException( ) method, 290
unchecked exception, 159, 161–163
unicode escape sequences, 21
Unicode Transformation Format (UTF), 566
uniform resource identifier (URI), 669, 751, 835
Uniform Resource Locators. See URLs
uniqueness of package names, 145
Universal Character Set, 17
Universal Description, Discovery, and
    Integration (UDDI), 756
Universal Naming Convention (UNC), 513
Unix-oriented file, 395
unlimited serialization, 554
unlock( ) method, 417–418
unreferenced object, 124
Unsigned right shift operator, 30
UnsupportedOperationException class, 322–
    324, 326, 329, 331–332, 365, 368, 389
upcasting, 105–109
update( ) method, 533
update section, 41–42
UPDATE statement, 647
updateUI( ) method, 469
upper bound, 201, 203–204, 206, 224
URI class, 609, 615–620, 661
URI object, 616, 618–620
URI (uniform resource identifier), 669, 751, 835
URL class, 609–612, 794
URL command, 611
URL object, 610, 612, 798
URLConnection class, 609–612, 626, 661, 794

URLConnection object, 612
URLDecoder class, 612–614
URLEncoder class, 612–614
URLs (Uniform Resource Locators), 609–620
    URI class, 615–620
    URL and URLConnection classes, 609–612
    URLEncoder and URLDecoder classes, 612–
        614
USB driver, 848–849
UseCompass class, 222
UseEmployee class, 186–187
User Datagram Protocol (UDP), 585
user-defined types, 18
User Interfaces (UIs), delegates, 467–468
uses-permission element, 845–846
UTF (Unicode Transformation Format), 566
UTFDataFormatException class, 553
utility APIs, 401–434
    concurrency utilities, 401–426
        Atomic class variables, 419
        concurrent collections, 413–415
        executors, 401–410
        Fork/Join framework, 420–426
        locks package, 416–418
        synchronizers, 410–413
        ThreadLocalRandom class, 420
    Objects class, 426–430
    random method, 430–434
utility classes, 68, 388–391

■ V

valid documents, 673–683
    DTD, 674–678
    XML Schema language, 679–683
validate( ) method, 439
Validation API, 704
value( ) method, 193
value1, statement1, 40
valueOf( ) method, 328–329, 395
values( ) method, 219, 367
varargs and generics, 211–212
varargs methods/constructors, 69
VARCHAR-based column, 641
variables, 19–20, 740–741
Vehicle class, 85, 87, 110
versionCode attribute, 844, 864
versionName attribute, 844, 864
View class, 861
view( ) method, 265–266

Viewer class, 267
ViewGroup class, 861
ViewPNG class, 266
visible lifetime, 839
vocabularies, 663–664, 669
void clear( ) method, 323, 365, 392
void close( ) method, 526, 531, 538, 540, 717, 721
void deleteOnExit( ) method, 522
void endElement( ) method, 721
void flush( ) method, 538
void method, 20
void sync( ) method, 529
void writeEndDocument( ) method, 721
void writeStartDocument( ) method, 721

▨ W

wait( ) method, 264, 298–301
WC (word-counting application), 399
WeakHashMap class, 255, 378–379
WeakReference class, 254–255
WeakReference object, 250, 254
web services, 751–830
    authentication and customized lightweight
        HTTP server, 820–822
    description of, 751–757
        RESTful web services, 756–757
        SOAP-based web services, 753–756
    Java language and, 758–764
        lightweight HTTP server, 761–764
        web service annotations, 759–760
        web service APIs, 759
        web service tools, 760–761
    JAX-WS handler, SOAP messages, 815–819
    providers and dispatch clients, 825–828
    RESTful, 780–798
        and attachments, 822–825
        Google Charts web service, 795–798
        library web service, 781–795
    SAAJ API, 799–815
        overview of, 801–805
        Roman numerals and, 805–815
        SOAP messages, 799–801
    SOAP-based, 764–779
        Image Cutout web service, 776–779
        temperature-conversion web service, 764–776
Web Services Description Language (WSDL), 683

while statement, 42–43
while(true) loop, 46
widgets, 857, 861–862
wildcards, need for, 204–205
WindowAdapter class, 443
windowClosing( ) method, 459, 466
WindowConstants interface, 466
WindowListener object, 466
Windows command, 152, 239, 565
word-counting application (WC), 399
work stealing, 421
wrapper classes, primitive type, 240–249
    Boolean class, 240–242
    Character class, 242–243
    Float and Double classes, 243–247
    Integer, Long, Short, and Byte classes, 247–249
    Number class, 249
write( ) method, 174, 533, 544–545, 550–551, 568–569
writeEmptyElement( ) method, 721
writeEndElement( ) method, 721–722
writeExternal( ) method, 562
writeObject( ) method, 555, 561, 563
Writer class, and Reader class, 568
writers
    classes of, 565–579
        FileWriter and FileReader, 570–579
        OutputStreamWriter and InputStreamReader, 568–570
        overview of, 566–568
        Writer and Reader, 568
    event-based, creating documents with, 723–727
    stream-based, creating documents with, 721–723
writeStartElement( ) method, 721–723
writeStr( ) method, 542–543
writeTo( ) method, 829
WSDL file, 760, 772, 828
WSDL (Web Services Description Language), 683

▨ X

XML declaration, 665–666
XML (Extensible Markup Language)
    documents, 663–750
        character references and CDATA sections, 668–669

comments and processing instructions, 672–673

elements and attributes, 666–667

namespaces, 669–672

XML (Extensible Markup Language) (*Cont.*)

parsing

with DOM, 700–712

with SAX, 683–700

with StAX, 712–727

rules for, 673

Schema language, 679–683

selecting nodes of with XPath language, 727–741

advanced, 736–741

and DOM, 731–735

primer on, 727–730

transforming with XSLT, 742–748

valid, 673–683

DTD, 674–678

XML Schema language, 679–683

XML declaration, 665–666

XML file, 468, 737, 752, 846–847, 861, 863

XML parsers, 673–674

XML processing pipelines, 714

XMLEvent interface, 717

XMLEventReader interface, 717

XMLEventWriter interface, 723

XMLInputFactory class, 714

xmlns attribute, 669, 682

XMLOutputFactory class, 720

XMLReader-implementing class, 684

XMLReader interface, 683–684

XMLReader object, 684

XMLReaderFactory class, 683–684

XMLStreamConstants interface, 715

XMLStreamReader interface, 715

XMLStreamWriter interface, 721

XPath class, 737

XPath language

advanced, 736–741

extension functions and function resolvers, 737–740

namespace contexts, 736–737

variables and variable resolvers, 740–741

and DOM, 731–735

primer on, 727–730

selecting XML document nodes with, 727–741

XPath object, 735, 741

XPathExpression interface, 735

XPathFunction interface, 738

XPathFunctionResolver interface, 739

XPathVariableResolver interface, 741

XSLT (Extensible Stylesheet Language Transformation), 742–748

xValue( ) method, 249

Y, Z

yield( ) method, 291

CPSIA information can be obtained at www.ICGtesting.com
Printed in the USA
LVOW110207201212

312533LV00027B/354/P